KU-713-453

ALL GLORY TO ŚRĪ GURU AND GAURĀṄGA

ŚRĪMAD BHĀGAVATAM

of

KṚṢṆA-DVAIPĀYANA VYĀSA

एष साक्षाद्धरेरंशो जातो लोकरिरक्षया ।
इयं च तत्परा हि श्रीरनुजज्ञेऽनपायिनी ॥ ६ ॥

eṣa sākṣād dharer aṁśo
jāto loka-rirakṣayā
iyaṁ ca tat-parā hi śrīr
anujajñe 'napāyinī

(p. 697)

BOOKS by
His Divine Grace
A. C. Bhaktivedanta Swami Prabhupāda

Bhagavad-gītā As It Is
Śrīmad-Bhāgavatam, cantos 1–10 (12 vols.)
Śrī Caitanya-caritāmṛta (17 vols.)
Teachings of Lord Caitanya
The Nectar of Devotion
The Nectar of Instruction
Śrī Īśopaniṣad
Easy Journey to Other Planets
Kṛṣṇa Consciousness: The Topmost Yoga System
Kṛṣṇa, The Supreme Personality of Godhead (3 vols.)
Perfect Questions, Perfect Answers
Teachings of Lord Kapila, the Son of Devahūti
Transcendental Teachings of Prahlāda Mahārāja
Dialectic Spiritualism—A Vedic View of Western Philosophy
Teachings of Queen Kuntī
Kṛṣṇa, the Reservoir of Pleasure
The Science of Self-Realization
The Path of Perfection
Search for Liberation
Life Comes from Life
The Perfection of Yoga
Beyond Birth and Death
On the Way to Kṛṣṇa
Geetār-gan (Bengali)
Vairāgya-vidyā (Bengali)
Buddhi-yoga (Bengali)
Bhakti-ratna-bolī (Bengali)
Rāja-vidyā: The King of Knowledge
Elevation to Kṛṣṇa Consciousness
Kṛṣṇa Consciousness: The Matchless Gift
Back to Godhead magazine (founder)

A complete catalog is available upon request.

Bhaktivedanta Book Trust
3764 Watseka Avenue
Los Angeles, California 90034

Bhaktivedanta Book Trust
P.O. Box 262
Botany
N. S. W. 2019, Australia

ŚRĪMAD BHĀGAVATAM

Fourth Canto

"The Creation of the Fourth Order"

(Part One—Chapters 1-19)

With the Original Sanskrit Text,
Its Roman Transliteration, Synonyms,
Translation and Elaborate Purports

by

His Divine Grace
A.C. Bhaktivedanta Swami Prabhupāda
Founder-*Ācārya* of the International Society for Krishna Consciousness

THE BHAKTIVEDANTA BOOK TRUST
Los Angeles · London · Stockholm · Bombay · Sydney

Readers interested in the subject matter of this book
are invited by the International Society for Krishna Consciousness
to correspond with its Secretary at either of the following addresses:

International Society for Krishna Consciousness
P. O. Box 262
Botany
N. S. W. 2019
Australia

International Society for Krishna Consciousness
3764 Watseka Avenue
Los Angeles, California 90034

KING ALFRED'S COLLEGE
WINCHESTER
294.5
SRI
01378678

First Printing, 1987: 5,000 copies

© 1987 Bhaktivedanta Book Trust
All Rights Reserved
Printed in Singapore

Library of Congress Cataloging in Publication Data (Revised)

Purāṇas. Bhāgavatapurāṇa. English and Sanskrit.
Śrīmad-Bhāgavatam: with the original Sanskrit text, its roman transliteration, synonyms, translation and elaborate purports.

In English and Sanskrit.
Translation of: Bhāgavatapurāṇa
Includes index.
Contents: 1st canto. Creation—2nd canto. The cosmic manifestation—3rd canto. The status quo (2 v)—4th canto. The creation of the fourth order (2 v)—5th canto. The creative impetus—6th canto. Prescribed duties for mankind—7th canto. The science of God—8th canto. Withdrawal of the cosmic creations—9th canto. Liberation—10th canto. The summum bonum (4 v)—11th canto. General history (2 v)—12th canto. The age of deterioration.
Cantos 10 (v 2-4), 11 and 12 by Hridayananda dāsa Goswami, completing the great work of His Divine Grace A. C. Bhaktivedanta Swami Prabhupāda; Sanskrit editing by Gopīparāṇadhana dāsa Adhikārī.
1. Purāṇas. Bhāgavatapurāṇa—Criticism, interpretation, etc. I. Bhaktivedanta Swami, A. C., 1896-1977. II. Title.
BL1140.4.B432E5 1987 294.5'925 87-25585
ISBN 0-89213-254x (v. 5)

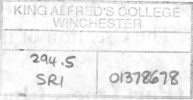

Table of Contents

Preface *xv*
Introduction *xix*

CHAPTER ONE
Genealogical Table of the Daughters of Manu **1**
Three Daughters of Svāyambhuva Manu 1
Yajña Born of Ākūti 5
Twelve Boys Born of Yajña and Dakṣiṇā 9
Pūrṇimā's Descendants Described 13
The Severe Austerities of Atri Muni and Anasūyā 17
Brahmā, Viṣṇu and Śiva Visit Atri Muni 21
Atri Muni Benedicted by the Three Deities 27
Birth of the Great Mystic Dattātreya 30
Seven Spotless Sages Born of Vasiṣṭha 34
The Universe Populated by Descendants of Kardama 38
The Joyful Appearance of Nara-Nārāyaṇa 41
Forty-nine Fire-gods Generated 47

CHAPTER TWO
Dakṣa Curses Lord Śiva **53**
Lord Śiva, Spiritual Master of the World 54
Dakṣa Offended by Lord Śiva 59
Dakṣa Speaks Against Lord Śiva 60
Lord Śiva Cursed by Dakṣa 66
Dakṣa Cursed by Nandīśvara 70

The Followers of Lord Śiva Cursed by Bhṛgu 76
Lord Śiva Leaves the Arena of Sacrifice 85
The Demigods Depart for Their Abodes 87

CHAPTER THREE
Talks Between Lord Śiva and Satī **89**
Tension Between Dakṣa and Lord Śiva 89
The Great Sacrifice Planned by Dakṣa 91
Satī's Desire to Attend the Sacrifice 95
Women Hanker for Material Affection 99
Śiva Remembers the Malicious Speeches of Dakṣa 103
Dakṣa Proud of Material Assets 106
Dakṣa Intolerant of Śiva's High Position 110
Śiva Worships Vāsudeva in Pure Consciousness 113
Śiva's Advice to Satī 117

CHAPTER FOUR
Satī Quits Her Body **119**
Satī's Mind Unsettled 119
Satī Leaves Her Husband 123
Satī Dissatisfied by Dakṣa's Silence 127
Satī Condemns Her Father 129
Śiva's Order Never Neglected 135
Inauspicious Qualities of Śiva 138
Satī Condemns Her Body 142
Opulences of Self-realized Souls 146
Satī Absorbs Herself in Mystic *Yoga* 150
Satī Quits Her Body in Blazing Fire 155
Dakṣa Unworthy to Be a *Brāhmaṇa* 159
Bhṛgu Muni Creates the Ṛbhu Demigods 162

CHAPTER FIVE

Frustration of the Sacrifice of Dakṣa **165**

Śiva Becomes Angry 165

The Fearful Black Demon Created 167

Śiva's Soldiers Follow the Fierce Personality 170

Lord Śiva's Dance of Dissolution 174

The Destruction of the Sacrificial Arena 177

Dakṣa Beheaded by Vīrabhadra 184

CHAPTER SIX

Brahmā Satisfies Lord Śiva **187**

Priests and Demigods Approach Lord Brahmā 188

Lord Śiva Easily Pleased 190

The Abode of Kailāsa 193

The Lake in Which Satī Bathed 200

Celestial Damsels Enjoy in Sanctified Rivers 203

The Airplanes of the Heavenly Denizens 205

Śiva Surrounded by Saintly Persons 211

Lord Śiva, Chief of All Thinkers 217

Lord Brahmā Speaks to Śiva 219

Miscreants Destined to Ghastly Hells 223

Envious Persons Already Killed by Providence 226

Vaiṣṇavas Never Bewildered by *Māyā* 229

The Recommended Sacrifice for This Age 233

CHAPTER SEVEN

The Sacrifice Performed by Dakṣa **235**

Śiva Pacified by the Words of Lord Brahmā 235

Dakṣa Given a Goat's Head 242

Dakṣa's Heart Cleansed 244

Dakṣa's Prayers to Lord Śiva 246
The *Brāhmaṇas* Arrange to Offer Oblations 251
The Appearance of Lord Nārāyaṇa 254
Lord Viṣṇu Worshipable by Everyone 257
Dakṣa Offers Respectful Prayers to the Lord 260
The Formidable Fort of Conditional Existence 263
The Insurmountable Spell of Illusory Energy 266
Viṣṇu's Form Pleasing to the Mind and Eyes 270
The Mind Compared to an Elephant 274
Viṣṇu, the Shelter of the Quality of Goodness 282
Demigods Depend on Viṣṇu for Protection 285
The Value of the Human Form of Life 289
Lord Viṣṇu Is Everything 291
Chanting the Lord's Holy Name 294
Supersoul, the Self-sufficient Witness 297
One Who Knows Brahman 301
Dakṣa Situated on the Religious Path 304

CHAPTER EIGHT
Dhruva Mahārāja Leaves Home for the Forest **309**
The *Brahmacārī* Sons of Brahmā 309
Irreligion Also Brahmā's Son 311
The Descendants of Svāyambhuva Manu 314
Dhruva Mahārāja Insulted 318
Dhruva Leaves the Palace 321
The Advice of Dhruva's Mother 324
Taking Shelter of the Lord's Lotus Feet 328
The Great Sage Nārada Struck With Wonder 332
Living Entities Controlled by Previous Actions 335

Crossing Over the Darkness of Nescience 340
Dhruva Lacking Brahminical Humility 343
The Expert Advice of Nārada Muni 348
The Virtuous Forest Named Madhuvana 351
The Goal of Meditation Is the Personality of Godhead 354
The Lord Is a Person 358
Perfect Human Beings Flying in the Sky 363
Tulasī Leaves Very Dear to Kṛṣṇa 367
Prescribed Paraphernalia for Worship of the Lord 372
Dhruva Mahārāja Enters Madhuvana Forest 376
Nārada Muni Advises the King 380
Following the Orders of the Spiritual Master 383
Dhruva Mahārāja Captures the Supreme Lord 389
The Lord Reassures the Demigods 396

CHAPTER NINE
Dhruva Mahārāja Returns Home 397
The Lord Appears Before Dhruva 399
Dhruva Offers Conclusive Prayers 400
The Lord Is Like a Desire Tree 410
The Different Varieties of Living Entities 417
Lord Viṣṇu Enjoys the Results of Sacrifices 421
The Lord Congratulates Dhruva 427
Dhruva Is Awarded the Polestar 429
Lord Viṣṇu Returns to His Abode 436
Dhruva Ashamed of His Material Demands 439
The Shelter of the Lotus Feet of the Lord 444
King Uttānapāda Considers Himself Wretched 454
Dhruva's Reunion With His Father 458
Sunīti Was the Mother of a Great Hero 463

Description of the Capital City 466
Dhruva Enthroned as Emperor 476

CHAPTER TEN
Dhruva Mahārāja's Fight With the Yakṣas 479
Dhruva's Brother Killed by a Yakṣa 481
The Yakṣas Valiantly Exhibit Their Prowess 486
Dhruva Shoots Incessant Arrows 490
The Mystic Tricks of the Demons 494

CHAPTER ELEVEN
Svāyambhuva Manu Advises Dhruva Mahārāja to Stop Fighting 501
Dhruva's Arrows Dismay the Enemy Soldiers 504
Svāyambhuva Manu Gives Good Instruction 507
Creation of the Material World 515
The Lord in His Feature of Eternal Time 523
Birth and Death Caused by the Supreme 530
Anger Is the Enemy of Spiritual Realization 538

CHAPTER TWELVE
Dhruva Mahārāja Goes Back to Godhead 543
Kuvera Speaks to Dhruva Mahārāja 543
Kuvera Offers a Benediction to Dhruva 550
Dhruva Performs Many Ceremonial Sacrifices 554
Dhruva as Direct Father of the Citizens 558
Dhruva Mahārāja Retires to the Forest 564
Associates of Viṣṇu Come Before Dhruva 569

Nanda and Sunanda Address Dhruva 573
Dhruva Prepares to Board the Transcendental Plane 579
Dhruva Remembers His Poor Mother 583
Nārada Chants the Glories of Dhruva 594
Devotees Like to Hear About Dhruva 599
The Narration of Dhruva Mahārāja Is Sublime Knowledge 606

CHAPTER THIRTEEN
Description of the Descendants of Dhruva Mahārāja **611**
Vidura Inquires About the Pracetās 613
Dhruva's Son Utkala Does Not Desire the Throne 616
Vatsara Elevated to the Royal Throne 622
King Vena Cursed by the Sages 626
Sacrifice Performed by King Aṅga 631
King Aṅga Offers Oblations to Viṣṇu 638
Vena as Grandson of Death Personified 642
King Aṅga Gives Up His Home 648

CHAPTER FOURTEEN
The Story of King Vena **651**
Vena Installed on the Throne 652
King Vena Stops Religious Rituals 655
The Great Sages Speak to King Vena 662
Qualifications of a Pious King 667
King Vena Replies to the *Brāhmaṇas* 673
King Vena Condemned by the Sages 678
Sunīthā Preserves the Dead Body of Vena 682
Bāhuka Born From the Thighs of Vena 690

CHAPTER FIFTEEN
King Pṛthu's Appearance and Coronation **693**
Male and Female Born of the Arms of Vena 694
The Goddess of Fortune Incarnated as Arci 697
King Pṛthu Is Placed on the Throne 702
King Pṛthu Speaks 708

CHAPTER SIXTEEN
Praise of King Pṛthu by the Professional Reciters **713**
The Reciters Continue to Praise the King 713
King Pṛthu as a Chastiser to the Irreligious 718
King Pṛthu as a Protector of the World 722
King Pṛthu to Remain Just Like Fire 726
The King Will Respect All Women 730
The King Will Perform One Hundred Sacrifices 739

CHAPTER SEVENTEEN
Mahārāja Pṛthu Becomes Angry at the Earth **743**
The Citizens Suffer Starvation 750
The Earth Flees From King Pṛthu 754
The Cow-shaped Earth Appeals to the King 757
King Pṛthu Replies to the Earthly Planet 760
Pṛthu Mahārāja Becomes Like Yamarāja 766
The Planet Earth Speaks 767
The Lord in the Form of the Original Boar 775

CHAPTER EIGHTEEN
Pṛthu Mahārāja Milks the Earth Planet 779
The Planet Earth Tries to Convince the King 779
Grains Being Used by Nondevotees 784
Earth Fulfills the King's Desire 789
The Demigods Milk Nectar From the Earth 794
The Demons Milk Blood From the Earth 801
Earth Supplies Everyone His Food 804

CHAPTER NINETEEN
King Pṛthu's One Hundred Horse Sacrifices 811
Viṣṇu Present at the Sacrifices of King Pṛthu 813
King Pṛthu Presented With Various Gifts 819
Indra Takes the Sacrificial Horse 822
Indra Abandons His False Dress 827
Indra Adopts Several Orders of *Sannyāsa* 833
Lord Brahmā Stops the Sacrifice 837
Unwanted Desires Even Amongst the Demigods 842
King Pṛthu Concludes a Peace With Indra 848

Appendixes
The Author 855
References 859
Genealogical Tables 860
Glossary 863
Sanskrit Pronunciation Guide 876
Index of Sanskrit Verses 879
Index of Verses Quoted 901
General Index 905

Preface

We must know the present need of human society. And what is that need? Human society is no longer bounded by geographical limits to particular countries or communities. Human society is broader than in the Middle Ages, and the world tendency is toward one state or one human society. The ideals of spiritual communism, according to *Śrīmad-Bhāgavatam,* are based more or less on the oneness of the entire human society, nay, of the entire energy of living beings. The need is felt by great thinkers to make this a successful ideology. *Śrīmad-Bhāgavatam* will fill this need in human society. It begins, therefore, with an aphorism of Vedānta philosophy, *janmādy asya yataḥ,* to establish the ideal of a common cause.

Human society, at the present moment, is not in the darkness of oblivion. It has made rapid progress in the fields of material comforts, education and economic development throughout the entire world. But there is a pinprick somewhere in the social body at large, and therefore there are large-scale quarrels, even over less important issues. There is need of a clue as to how humanity can become one in peace, friendship and prosperity with a common cause. *Śrīmad-Bhāgavatam* will fill this need, for it is a cultural presentation for the respiritualization of the entire human society.

Śrīmad-Bhāgavatam should be introduced also in the schools and colleges, for it is recommended by the great student-devotee Prahlāda Mahārāja in order to change the demoniac face of society.

kaumāra ācaret prājño
dharmān bhāgavatān iha
durlabhaṁ mānuṣaṁ janma
tad apy adhruvam artha-dam
(*Bhāg.* 7.6.1)

Disparity in human society is due to lack of principles in a godless civilization. There is God, or the Almighty One, from whom everything emanates, by whom everything is maintained and in whom everything is merged to rest. Material science has tried to find the ultimate source of creation very insufficiently, but it is a fact that there is one ultimate source of everything that be. This ultimate source is explained rationally and authoritatively in the beautiful *Bhāgavatam,* or *Śrīmad-Bhāgavatam.*

Śrīmad-Bhāgavatam is the transcendental science not only for knowing the ultimate source of everything but also for knowing our relation with Him and our duty toward perfection of the human society on the basis of this perfect knowledge. It is powerful reading matter in the Sanskrit language, and it is now rendered into English elaborately so that simply by a careful reading one will know God perfectly well, so much so that the reader will be sufficiently educated to defend himself from the onslaught of atheists. Over and above this, the reader will be able to convert others to accepting God as a concrete principle.

Śrīmad-Bhāgavatam begins with the definition of the ultimate source. It is a bona fide commentary on the *Vedānta-sūtra* by the same author, Śrīla Vyāsadeva, and gradually it develops into nine cantos up to the highest state of God realization. The only qualification one needs to study this great book of transcendental knowledge is to proceed step by step cautiously and not jump forward haphazardly as with an ordinary book. It should be gone through chapter by chapter, one after another. The reading matter is so arranged with the original Sanskrit text, its English transliteration, synonyms, translation and purports so that one is sure to become a God-realized soul at the end of finishing the first nine cantos.

The Tenth Canto is distinct from the first nine cantos because it deals directly with the transcendental activities of the Personality of Godhead, Śrī Kṛṣṇa. One will be unable to capture the effects of the Tenth Canto without going through the first nine cantos. The book is complete in twelve cantos, each independent, but it is good for all to read them in small installments one after another.

I must admit my frailties in presenting *Śrīmad-Bhāgavatam,* but still I am hopeful of its good reception by the thinkers and leaders of society on the strength of the following statement of *Śrīmad-Bhāgavatam* (1.5.11):

tad-vāg-visargo janatāgha-viplavo
yasmin prati-ślokam abaddhavaty api

nāmāny anantasya yaśo 'ṅkitāni yac
chṛṇvanti gāyanti gṛṇanti sādhavaḥ

"On the other hand, that literature which is full of descriptions of the transcendental glories of the name, fame, form and pastimes of the unlimited Supreme Lord is a transcendental creation meant for bringing about a revolution in the impious life of a misdirected civilization. Such transcendental literature, even though irregularly composed, is heard, sung and accepted by purified men who are thoroughly honest."

Oṁ tat sat

A. C. Bhaktivedanta Swami

Introduction

"This *Bhāgavata Purāṇa* is as brilliant as the sun, and it has arisen just after the departure of Lord Kṛṣṇa to His own abode, accompanied by religion, knowledge, etc. Persons who have lost their vision due to the dense darkness of ignorance in the age of Kali shall get light from this *Purāṇa*." (*Śrīmad-Bhāgavatam* 1.3.43)

The timeless wisdom of India is expressed in the *Vedas,* ancient Sanskrit texts that touch upon all fields of human knowledge. Originally preserved through oral tradition, the *Vedas* were first put into writing five thousand years ago by Śrīla Vyāsadeva, the "literary incarnation of God." After compiling the *Vedas,* Vyāsadeva set forth their essence in the aphorisms known as *Vedānta-sūtras. Śrīmad-Bhāgavatam* (*Bhāgavata Purāṇa*) is Vyāsadeva's commentary on his own *Vedānta-sūtras.* It was written in the maturity of his spiritual life under the direction of Nārada Muni, his spiritual master. Referred to as "the ripened fruit of the tree of Vedic literature," *Śrīmad-Bhāgavatam* is the most complete and authoritative exposition of Vedic knowledge.

After compiling the *Bhāgavatam,* Vyāsa imparted the synopsis of it to his son, the sage Śukadeva Gosvāmī. Śukadeva Gosvāmī subsequently recited the entire *Bhāgavatam* to Mahārāja Parīkṣit in an assembly of learned saints on the bank of the Ganges at Hastināpura (now Delhi). Mahārāja Parīkṣit was the emperor of the world and was a great *rājarṣi* (saintly king). Having received a warning that he would die within a week, he renounced his entire kingdom and retired to the bank of the Ganges to fast until death and receive spiritual enlightenment. The *Bhāgavatam* begins with Emperor Parīkṣit's sober inquiry to Śukadeva Gosvāmī: "You are the spiritual master of great saints and devotees. I am therefore begging you to show the way of perfection for all persons, and especially for one who is about to die. Please let me know what a man should hear, chant, remember and worship, and also what he should not do. Please explain all this to me."

Śukadeva Gosvāmī's answer to this question, and numerous other questions posed by Mahārāja Parīkṣit, concerning everything from the nature of the self to the origin of the universe, held the assembled sages in rapt attention continuously for the seven days leading up to the king's death. The sage Sūta Gosvāmī, who was present in that assembly when Śukadeva Gosvāmī first recited *Śrīmad-Bhāgavatam,* later repeated the *Bhāgavatam* before a gathering of sages in the forest of Naimiṣāraṇya. Those sages, concerned about the spiritual welfare of the people in general, had gathered to perform a long, continuous chain of sacrifices to counteract the degrading influence of the incipient age of Kali. In response to the sages' request that he speak the essence of Vedic wisdom, Sūta Gosvāmī repeated from memory the entire eighteen thousand verses of *Śrīmad-Bhāgavatam,* as spoken by Śukadeva Gosvāmī to Mahārāja Parīkṣit.

The reader of *Śrīmad-Bhāgavatam* hears Sūta Gosvāmī relate the questions of Mahārāja Parīkṣit and the answers of Śukadeva Gosvāmī. Also, Sūta Gosvāmī sometimes responds directly to questions put by Śaunaka Ṛṣi, the spokesman for the sages gathered at Naimiṣāraṇya. One therefore simultaneously hears two dialogues: one between Mahārāja Parīkṣit and Śukadeva Gosvāmī on the bank of the Ganges, and another at Naimiṣāraṇya between Sūta Gosvāmī and the sages at Naimiṣāraṇya forest, headed by Śaunaka Ṛṣi. Furthermore, while instructing King Parīkṣit, Śukadeva Gosvāmī often relates historical episodes and gives accounts of lengthy philosophical discussions between such great souls as Nārada Muni and Vasudeva. With this understanding of the history of the *Bhāgavatam,* the reader will easily be able to follow its intermingling of dialogues and events from various sources. Since philosophical wisdom, not chronological order, is most important in the text, one need only be attentive to the subject matter of *Śrīmad-Bhāgavatam* to appreciate fully its profound message.

The translators of this edition compare the *Bhāgavatam* to sugar candy—wherever you taste it, you will find it equally sweet and relishable. Therefore, to taste the sweetness of the *Bhāgavatam,* one may begin by reading any of its volumes. After such an introductory taste, however, the serious reader is best advised to go back to the First Canto and then proceed through the *Bhāgavatam,* canto after canto, in its natural order.

This edition of the *Bhāgavatam* is the first complete English translation of this important text with an elaborate commentary, and it is the first widely available to the English-speaking public. The first twelve volumes (Canto One through Canto Ten, Part One) are the product of the scholarly and devotional effort of His Divine Grace A. C. Bhaktivedanta Swami Prabhupāda, the founder-*ācārya* of the International

Society for Krishna Consciousness and the world's most distinguished teacher of Indian religious and philosophical thought. His consummate Sanskrit scholarship and intimate familiarity with Vedic culture and thought as well as the modern way of life combine to reveal to the West a magnificent exposition of this important classic. After the departure of Śrīla Prabhupāda from this world in 1977, his monumental work of translating and annotating *Śrīmad-Bhāgavatam* has been continued by his disciples Hridayananda dāsa Goswami and Gopīparāṇadhana dāsa.

Readers will find this work of value for many reasons. For those interested in the classical roots of Indian civilization, it serves as a vast reservoir of detailed information on virtually every one of its aspects. For students of comparative philosophy and religion, the *Bhāgavatam* offers a penetrating view into the meaning of India's profound spiritual heritage. To sociologists and anthropologists, the *Bhāgavatam* reveals the practical workings of a peaceful and scientifically organized Vedic culture, whose institutions were integrated on the basis of a highly developed spiritual world view. Students of literature will discover the *Bhāgavatam* to be a masterpiece of majestic poetry. For students of psychology, the text provides important perspectives on the nature of consciousness, human behavior and the philosophical study of identity. Finally, to those seeking spiritual insight, the *Bhāgavatam* offers simple and practical guidance for attainment of the highest self-knowledge and realization of the Absolute Truth. The entire multivolume text, presented by the Bhaktivedanta Book Trust, promises to occupy a significant place in the intellectual, cultural and spiritual life of modern man for a long time to come.

—The Publishers

CHAPTER ONE

Genealogical Table of the Daughters of Manu

TEXT 1

मैत्रेय उवाच
मनोस्तु शतरूपायां तिस्रः कन्याश्च जज्ञिरे ।
आकूतिर्देवहूतिश्च प्रसूतिरिति विश्रुताः ॥ १ ॥

maitreya uvāca
manos tu śatarūpāyāṁ
tisraḥ kanyāś ca jajñire
ākūtir devahūtiś ca
prasūtir iti viśrutāḥ

maitreyaḥ uvāca—the great sage Maitreya said; *manoḥ tu*—of Svāyambhuva Manu; *śatarūpāyām*—in his wife Śatarūpā; *tisraḥ*—three; *kanyāḥ ca*—daughters also; *jajñire*—gave birth; *ākūtiḥ*—named Ākūti; *devahūtiḥ*—named Devahūti; *ca*—also; *prasūtiḥ*—named Prasūti; *iti*—thus; *viśrutāḥ*—well known.

TRANSLATION

Śrī Maitreya said: Svāyambhuva Manu begot three daughters in his wife Śatarūpā, and their names were Ākūti, Devahūti and Prasūti.

PURPORT

First of all let us offer our respectful obeisances unto our spiritual master, Oṁ Viṣṇupāda Śrī Śrīmad Bhaktisiddhānta Sarasvatī Gosvāmī Prabhupāda, by whose order I am engaged in this herculean task of writing commentary on the *Śrīmad-Bhāgavatam* as the Bhaktivedanta purports. By his grace we have finished three cantos already, and we are just trying to begin the Fourth Canto. By his divine grace let us offer our respectful obeisances unto Lord Caitanya, who began this Kṛṣṇa consciousness movement of *Bhāgavata-dharma* five hundred years ago, and through His grace let us offer our obeisances to the six Gosvāmīs, and then let us offer our obeisances to Rādhā and Kṛṣṇa, the spiritual couple who enjoy eternally in Vṛndāvana with Their cowherd boys and damsels in Vrajabhūmi. Let us also offer our respectful obeisances to all the devotees and eternal servitors of the Supreme Lord.

In this Fourth Canto of *Śrīmad-Bhāgavatam* there are thirty-one chapters, and all these chapters describe the secondary creation by Brahmā and the Manus. The Supreme Lord Himself does the real creation by agitating His material energy, and then, by His order, Brahmā, the first living creature in the universe, attempts to create the different planetary systems and their inhabitants, expanding the population through his progeny, like Manu and other progenitors of living entities, who work perpetually under the order of the Supreme Lord. In the First Chapter of this Fourth Canto there are descriptions of the three daughters of Svāyambhuva Manu and their descendants. The next six chapters describe the sacrifice performed by King Dakṣa and how it was spoiled. Thereafter the activities of Mahārāja Dhruva are described in five chapters. Then, in eleven chapters, the activities of King Pṛthu are described, and the next eight chapters are devoted to the activities of the Pracetā kings.

As described in the first verse of this chapter, Svāyambhuva Manu had three daughters, named Ākūti, Devahūti and Prasūti. Of these three daughters, one daughter, Devahūti, has already been described, along with her husband, Kardama Muni, and her son, Kapila Muni. In this chapter the descendants of the first daughter, Ākūti, will specifically be described. Svāyambhuva Manu was the son of Brahmā. Brahmā had many other sons, but Manu's name is specifically mentioned first because he was a great devotee of the Lord. In this verse there is also the word *ca*, indicating that besides the three daughters mentioned, Svāyambhuva Manu also had two sons.

TEXT 2

आकूतिं रुचये प्रादादपि भ्रातृमतीं नृपः ।
पुत्रिकाधर्ममाश्रित्य शतरूपानुमोदितः ॥ २ ॥

ākūtiṁ rucaye prādād
api bhrātṛmatīṁ nṛpaḥ
putrikā-dharmam āśritya
śatarūpānumoditaḥ

ākūtim—Ākūti; *rucaye*—unto the great sage Ruci; *prādāt*—handed over; *api*—although; *bhrātṛ-matīm*—daughter having a brother; *nṛpaḥ*—the King; *putrikā*—get the resultant son; *dharmam*—religious rites; *āśritya*—taking shelter; *śatarūpā*—by the wife of Svāyambhuva Manu; *anumoditaḥ*—being sanctioned.

TRANSLATION

Ākūti had two brothers, but in spite of her brothers, King Svāyambhuva Manu handed her over to Prajāpati Ruci on the condition that the son born of her be returned to Manu as his son. This he did in consultation with his wife, Śatarūpā.

PURPORT

Sometimes a sonless person offers his daughter to a husband on the condition that his grandson be returned to him to be adopted as his son and inherit his property. This is called *putrikā-dharma*, which means that by execution of religious rituals one gets a son, although one is sonless by one's own wife. But here we see extraordinary behavior in Manu, for in spite of his having two sons, he handed over his first daughter to Prajāpati Ruci on the condition that the son born of his daughter be returned to him as his son. Śrīla Viśvanātha Cakravartī Ṭhākura comments in this connection that King Manu knew that the Supreme Personality of Godhead would take birth in the womb of Ākūti; therefore, in spite of having two sons, he wanted the particular son born of Ākūti because he was ambitious to have the Supreme Personality of Godhead appear as his son and grandson. Manu is the lawgiver of mankind, and since he personally executed the *putrikā-dharma*, we may accept that such a system may be adopted by mankind also. Thus, even though one has a son, if one wants to have a particular son from one's daughter, one may give one's daughter in charity on that condition. That is the opinion of Śrīla Jīva Gosvāmī.

TEXT 3

प्रजापतिः स भगवान् रुचिस्तस्यामजीजनत् ।
मिथुनं ब्रह्मवर्चस्वी परमेण समाधिना ॥ ३ ॥

prajāpatiḥ sa bhagavān
rucis tasyām ajījanat
mithunaṁ brahma-varcasvī
parameṇa samādhinā

prajāpatiḥ—one who is entrusted with begetting children; *saḥ*—he; *bhagavān*—the most opulent; *ruciḥ*—the great sage Ruci; *tasyām*—in her; *ajījanat*—gave birth; *mithunam*—couple; *brahma-varcasvī*—spiritually very much powerful; *parameṇa*—with great strength; *samādhinā*—in trance.

TRANSLATION

Ruci, who was very powerful in his brahminical qualifications and was appointed one of the progenitors of the living entities, begot one son and one daughter by his wife, Ākūti.

PURPORT

The word *brahma-varcasvī* is very significant. Ruci was a *brāhmaṇa*, and he executed the brahminical duties very rigidly. As stated in *Bhagavad-gītā*, the brahminical qualifications are control of the senses, control of the mind, cleanliness within and without, development of spiritual and material knowledge, simplicity, truthfulness, faith in the Supreme Personality of Godhead, etc. There are many qualities which indicate a brahminical personality, and it is understood that Ruci followed all the brahminical principles rigidly. Therefore he is specifically mentioned as *brahma-varcasvī*. One who is born of a *brāhmaṇa* father but does not act as a *brāhmaṇa* is called, in Vedic language, a *brahma-bandhu*, and is calculated to be on the level of *śūdras* and women. Thus in the *Bhāgavatam* we find that *Mahābhārata* was specifically compiled by Vyāsadeva for *strī-śūdra-brahma-bandhu*. *Strī* means women, *śūdra* means the lower class of civilized human society, and *brahma-bandhu* means persons who are born in the families of *brāhmaṇas* but do not follow the rules and regulations carefully. All of these three classes are called less intelligent; they have no access to the study of the *Vedas*, which are specifically meant for persons who have acquired the brahminical qualifications. This restriction is based not upon any sectarian distinction but upon qualification. The Vedic literatures cannot be understood unless one has developed the brahminical qualifications. It is regrettable, therefore, that persons who have no brahminical qualifications and have never been trained under a bona fide spiritual master nevertheless comment on Vedic literatures like the *Śrīmad-Bhāgavatam* and other *Purāṇas*, for such persons cannot deliver their real message. Ruci was considered a first-class *brāhmaṇa;* therefore he is mentioned here as *brahma-varcasvī*, one who had full prowess in brahminical strength.

TEXT 4

यस्तयोः पुरुषः साक्षाद्विष्णुर्यज्ञस्वरूपधृक् ।
या स्त्री सा दक्षिणा भूतेरंशभूतानपायिनी ॥ ४ ॥

yas tayoḥ puruṣaḥ sākṣād
viṣṇur yajña-svarūpa-dhṛk
yā strī sā dakṣiṇā bhūter
aṁśa-bhūtānapāyinī

yaḥ—one who; *tayoḥ*—out of them; *puruṣaḥ*—male; *sākṣāt*—directly; *viṣṇuḥ*—the Supreme Lord; *yajña*—Yajña; *svarūpa-dhṛk*—accepting the form; *yā*—the other; *strī*—female; *sā*—she; *dakṣiṇā*—Dakṣiṇā; *bhūteḥ*—of the goddess of fortune; *aṁśa-bhūtā*—being a plenary expansion; *anapāyinī*—never to be separated.

TRANSLATION

Of the two children born of Ākūti, the male child was directly an incarnation of the Supreme Personality of Godhead, and His name was Yajña, which is another name of Lord Viṣṇu. The female child was a partial incarnation of Lakṣmī, the goddess of fortune, the eternal consort of Lord Viṣṇu.

PURPORT

Lakṣmī, the goddess of fortune, is the eternal consort of Lord Viṣṇu. Here it is stated that both the Lord and Lakṣmī, who are eternal consorts, appeared from Ākūti simultaneously. Both the Lord and His consort are beyond this material creation, as confirmed by many authorities (*nārāyaṇaḥ paro 'vyaktāt*); therefore their eternal relationship cannot be changed, and Yajña, the boy born of Ākūti, later married the goddess of fortune.

TEXT 5

आनिन्ये स्वगृहं पुत्र्याः पुत्रं विततरोचिषम् ।
स्वायम्भुवो मुदा युक्तो रुचिर्जग्राह दक्षिणाम् ॥ ५ ॥

āninye sva-gṛhaṁ putryāḥ
putraṁ vitata-rociṣam
svāyambhuvo mudā yukto
rucir jagrāha dakṣiṇām

āninye—brought to; *sva-gṛham*—home; *putryāḥ*—born of the daughter; *putram*—the son; *vitata-rociṣam*—very powerful; *svāyambhuvaḥ*—the Manu named Svāyambhuva; *mudā*—being very pleased; *yuktaḥ*—with; *ruciḥ*—the great sage Ruci; *jagrāha*—kept; *dakṣiṇām*—the daughter named Dakṣiṇā.

TRANSLATION

Svāyambhuva Manu very gladly brought home the beautiful boy named Yajña, and Ruci, his son-in-law, kept with him the daughter, Dakṣiṇā.

PURPORT

Svāyambhuva Manu was very glad to see that his daughter Ākūti had given birth to both a boy and girl. He was afraid that he would take one son and that because of this his son-in-law Ruci might be sorry. Thus when he heard that a daughter was born along with the boy, he was very glad. Ruci, according to his promise, returned his male child to

Svāyambhuva Manu and decided to keep the daughter, whose name was Dakṣiṇā. One of Lord Viṣṇu's names is Yajña because He is the master of the *Vedas.* The name Yajña comes from *yajuṣāṁ patiḥ,* which means "Lord of all sacrifices." In the *Yajur Veda* there are different ritualistic prescriptions for performing *yajñas,* and the beneficiary of all such *yajñas* is the Supreme Lord, Viṣṇu. Therefore it is stated in *Bhagavad-gītā* (3.9), *yajñārthāt karmaṇaḥ:* one should act, but one should perform one's prescribed duties only for the sake of Yajña, or Viṣṇu. If one does not act for the satisfaction of the Supreme Personality of Godhead, or if one does not perform devotional service, then there will be reactions to all one's activities. It does not matter if the reaction is good or bad; if our activities are not dovetailed with the desire of the Supreme Lord, or if we do not act in Kṛṣṇa consciousness, then we shall be responsible for the results of all our activities. There is always a reaction to every kind of action, but if actions are performed for Yajña, there is no reaction. Thus if one acts for Yajña, or the Supreme Personality of Godhead, one is not entangled in the material condition, for it is mentioned in the *Vedas* and also in *Bhagavad-gītā* that the *Vedas* and the Vedic rituals are all meant for understanding the Supreme Personality of Godhead, Kṛṣṇa. From the very beginning one should try to act in Kṛṣṇa consciousness; that will free one from the reactions of material activities.

TEXT 6

तां कामयानां भगवानुवाह यजुषां पतिः ।
तुष्टायां तोषमापन्नोऽजनयद् द्वादशात्मजान् ॥ ६ ॥

tāṁ kāmayānāṁ bhagavān
uvāha yajuṣāṁ patiḥ
tuṣṭāyāṁ toṣam āpanno
'janayad dvādaśātmajān

tām—her; *kāmayānām*—desiring; *bhagavān*—the Lord; *uvāha*—married; *yajuṣām*—of all sacrifices; *patiḥ*—master; *tuṣṭāyām*—in His wife, who was very much pleased; *toṣam*—great pleasure; *āpannaḥ*—having obtained; *ajanayat*—gave birth; *dvādaśa*—twelve; *ātmajān*—sons.

TRANSLATION

The Lord of the ritualistic performance of yajña later married Dakṣiṇā, who was anxious to have the Personality of Godhead as her husband, and in this wife the Lord was also very much pleased to beget twelve children.

PURPORT

An ideal husband and wife are generally called Lakṣmī-Nārāyaṇa to compare them to the Lord and the goddess of fortune, for it is significant that Lakṣmī-Nārāyaṇa are forever happy as husband and wife. A wife should always remain satisfied with her husband, and a husband should always remain satisfied with his wife. In the *Cāṇakya-śloka*, the moral instructions of Cāṇakya Paṇḍita, it is said that if a husband and wife are always satisfied with one another, then the goddess of fortune automatically comes. In other words, where there is no disagreement between husband and wife, all material opulence is present, and good children are born. Generally, according to Vedic civilization, the wife is trained to be satisfied in all conditions, and the husband, according to Vedic instruction, is required to please the wife with sufficient food, ornaments and clothing. Then, if they are satisfied with their mutual dealings, good children are born. In this way the entire world can become peaceful, but unfortunately in this age of Kali there are no ideal husbands and wives; therefore unwanted children are produced, and there is no peace and prosperity in the present-day world.

TEXT 7

तोषः प्रतोषः संतोषो भद्रः शान्तिरिडस्पतिः ।
इध्मः कविर्विभुः स्वह्नः सुदेवो रोचनो द्विषट् ॥ ७ ॥

toṣaḥ pratoṣaḥ santoṣo
bhadraḥ śāntir iḍaspatiḥ
idhmaḥ kavir vibhuḥ svahnaḥ
sudevo rocano dvi-ṣaṭ

toṣaḥ—Toṣa; *pratoṣaḥ*—Pratoṣa; *santoṣaḥ*—Santoṣa; *bhadraḥ*—Bhadra; *śāntiḥ*—Śānti; *iḍaspatiḥ*—Iḍaspati; *idhmaḥ*—Idhma; *kaviḥ*—

Kavi; *vibhuḥ*—Vibhu; *svahnaḥ*—Svahna; *sudevaḥ*—Sudeva; *rocanaḥ*—Rocana; *dvi-ṣaṭ*—twelve.

TRANSLATION

The twelve boys born of Yajña and Dakṣiṇā were named Toṣa, Pratoṣa, Santoṣa, Bhadra, Śānti, Iḍaspati, Idhma, Kavi, Vibhu, Svahna, Sudeva and Rocana.

TEXT 8

तुषिता नाम ते देवा आसन् स्वायम्भुवान्तरे ।
मरीचिमिश्रा ऋषयो यज्ञः सुरगणेश्वरः ॥ ८ ॥

tuṣitā nāma te devā
āsan svāyambhuvāntare
marīci-miśrā ṛṣayo
yajñaḥ sura-gaṇeśvaraḥ

tuṣitāḥ—the category of the Tuṣitas; *nāma*—of the name; *te*—all of them; *devāḥ*—demigods; *āsan*—became; *svāyambhuva*—the name of the Manu; *antare*—at that period; *marīci-miśrāḥ*—headed by Marīci; *ṛṣayaḥ*—great sages; *yajñaḥ*—the incarnation of Lord Viṣṇu; *sura-gaṇa-īśvaraḥ*—the king of the demigods.

TRANSLATION

During the time of Svāyambhuva Manu, these sons all became the demigods collectively named the Tuṣitas. Marīci became the head of the seven ṛṣis, and Yajña became the king of the demigods, Indra.

PURPORT

During the life of Svāyambhuva Manu, six kinds of living entities were generated from the demigods known as the Tuṣitas, from the sages headed by Marīci, and from descendants of Yajña, king of the demigods, and all of them expanded their progeny to observe the order of the Lord to fill the universe with living entities. These six kinds of living entities are known as *manus, devas, manu-putras, aṁśāvatāras, sureśvaras* and *ṛṣis.* Yajña, being the incarnation of the Supreme Personality of Godhead, became the leader of the demigods, Indra.

TEXT 9

प्रियव्रतोत्तानपादौ मनुपुत्रौ महौजसौ ।
तत्पुत्रपौत्रनप्तृणामनुवृत्तं तदन्तरम् ॥ ९ ॥

priyavratottānapādau
manu-putrau mahaujasau
tat-putra-pautra-naptṛṇām
anuvṛttaṁ tad-antaram

priyavrata—Priyavrata; *uttānapādau*—Uttānapāda; *manu-putrau*—sons of Manu; *mahā-ojasau*—very great, powerful; *tat*—their; *putra*—sons; *pautra*—grandsons; *naptṛṇām*—grandsons from the daughter; *anuvṛttam*—following; *tat-antaram*—in that Manu's period.

TRANSLATION

Svāyambhuva Manu's two sons, Priyavrata and Uttānapāda, became very powerful kings, and their sons and grandsons spread all over the three worlds during that period.

TEXT 10

देवहूतिमदात्तात कर्दमायात्मजां मनुः ।
तत्सम्बन्धि श्रुतप्रायं भवता गदतो मम ॥१०॥

devahūtim adāt tāta
kardamāyātmajāṁ manuḥ
tat-sambandhi śruta-prāyaṁ
bhavatā gadato mama

devahūtim—Devahūti; *adāt*—handed over; *tāta*—my dear son; *kardamāya*—unto the great sage Kardama; *atmajam*—daughter; *manuḥ*—Lord Svāyambhuva Manu; *tat-sambandhi*—in that connection; *śruta-*

His Divine Grace
A. C. Bhaktivedanta Swami Prabhupāda
Founder-Ācārya of the International Society for Krishna Consciousness

PLATE ONE: As soon as he saw Lord Brahmā, Lord Viṣṇu and Lord Śiva, Atri Muni became extremely pleased, and he approached them on one leg despite great difficulty. (*p. 22*)

PLATE TWO: When Śrī Nara-Nārāyaṇa Ṛṣi appeared, bands in the heavenly planets began to play, the Gandharvas and Kinnaras sang, beautiful damsels danced, and many demigods showered flowers upon the scene below. (*p. 42*)

PLATE THREE: One day, hearing of a great, festive sacrifice to be held at her father's house, Satī asked Śiva to let her attend, though she had not been invited. (*p. 95*)

PLATE FOUR: Satī sat down on the floor and absorbed herself in mystic *yoga*. Then, meditating on the fiery elements and Lord Śiva's lotus feet, she caused her body to ignite and burn to ashes. (*pp. 150-55*)

PLATE FIVE: Lord Brahmā and the other demigods and sages saw Lord Śiva sitting in meditation under a huge banyan tree on Kailāsa Hill. Surrounded by exalted persons like Kuvera and the four Kumāras, Lord Śiva looked as grave as eternal time. (*p. 210*)

PLATE SIX: As soon as Dakṣa had offered clarified butter and chanted *mantras* from the *Yajur Veda*, Lord Viṣṇu appeared in the sacrificial arena, riding upon the back of Garuḍa. (*p. 253*)

PLATE SEVEN: When Dhruva tried to join his brother on his father's lap, Dhruva's stepmother forbade him. Enraged, the boy began to breathe heavily, like a snake struck by a stick. (*p. 318*)

PLATE EIGHT: Nārada Muni instructed Dhruva on the process of mystic devotional meditation and then thought it wise to go visit King Uttānapāda. Nārada wished to encourage him, knowing that the King was deeply worried about his son's safety. (*p. 376*)

PLATE NINE: Dhruva was greatly agitated by transcendental ecstasy when he saw his Lord. Falling flat before Him like a rod, Dhruva became absorbed in love of Godhead. (*p. 400*)

PLATE TEN: Dhruva prayed as follows: "My dear Lord, by Your unbroken glance You are the supreme witness of all stages of intellectual activities. You are the original Personality of Godhead, full with the six opulences of strength, wealth, fame, beauty, knowledge and renunciation." (*p. 420*)

PLATE ELEVEN: The Lord stands above the material modes (goodness, passion and ignorance), which in turn tightly control the activities of all unenlightened souls. Under illusion, these souls think themselves the exploiters or the exploited, but in reality they must all remain servants of the modes of nature until they surrender to the Lord. (*p. 421*)

PLATE TWELVE: Dhruva heard threatening thunder and saw flashing lightning and severe rainfall. He also saw many lions, tigers and mad elephants, as well as enormous serpents vomiting forth fire and coming to devour him. (*p. 496*)

PLATE THIRTEEN: After boarding a transcendental airplane for the journey to Vaikuṇṭha, Dhruva Mahārāja thought, "How shall I go alone to Vaikuṇṭha and leave behind my poor mother?" Nanda and Sunanda could understand his mind, and thus they showed him that

mother, Sunīti, was traveling in another plane. Then the planes ›nded and started for the spiritual world. While Dhruva passed ›ugh space, he saw all the planets of the solar system, and the ›igods in their airplanes showered flowers upon him like rain. (*p. 586*)

PLATE FOURTEEN: As a partial representation of the Supreme Lord, King Pṛth embodied His monarchical power. Thus at King Pṛthu's coronation the various dem gods offered him wonderful gifts. (*p. 703*)

prāyam—heard almost in full; *bhavatā*—by you; *gadataḥ*—spoken; *mama*—by me.

TRANSLATION

My dear son, Svāyambhuva Manu handed over his very dear daughter Devahūti to Kardama Muni. I have already spoken to you about them, and you have heard about them almost in full.

TEXT 11

दक्षाय ब्रह्मपुत्राय प्रसूतिं भगवान्मनुः ।
प्रायच्छद्यत्कृतः सर्गस्त्रिलोक्यां विततो महान् ॥११॥

dakṣāya brahma-putrāya
prasūtiṁ bhagavān manuḥ
prāyacchad yat-kṛtaḥ sargas
tri-lokyāṁ vitato mahān

dakṣāya—unto Prajāpati Dakṣa; *brahma-putrāya*—the son of Lord Brahmā; *prasūtim*—Prasūti; *bhagavān*—the great personality; *manuḥ*—Svāyambhuva Manu; *prāyacchat*—handed over; *yat-kṛtaḥ*—done by whom; *sargaḥ*—creation; *tri-lokyām*—in the three worlds; *vitataḥ*—expanded; *mahān*—greatly.

TRANSLATION

Svāyambhuva Manu handed over his daughter Prasūti to the son of Brahmā named Dakṣa, who was also one of the progenitors of the living entities. The descendants of Dakṣa are spread throughout the three worlds.

TEXT 12

याः कर्दमसुताः प्रोक्ता नव ब्रह्मर्षिपत्नयः ।
तासां प्रसूतिप्रसवं प्रोच्यमानं निबोध मे ॥१२॥

yāḥ kardama-sutāḥ proktā
nava brahmarṣi-patnayaḥ

tāsāṁ prasūti-prasavaṁ
procyamānaṁ nibodha me

yāḥ—those who; *kardama-sutāḥ*—the daughters of Kardama; *proktāḥ*—were mentioned; *nava*—nine; *brahma-ṛṣi*—great sages of spiritual knowledge; *patnayaḥ*—wives; *tāsām*—their; *prasūti-prasavam*—generations of sons and grandsons; *procyamānam*—describing; *nibodha*—try to understand; *me*—from me.

TRANSLATION

You have already been informed about the nine daughters of Kardama Muni, who were handed over to nine different sages. I shall now describe the descendants of those nine daughters. Please hear from me.

PURPORT

The Third Canto has already described how Kardama Muni begot nine daughters in Devahūti and how all the daughters were later handed over to great sages like Marīci, Atri and Vasiṣṭha.

TEXT 13

पत्नी मरीचेस्तु कला सुषुवे कर्दमात्मजा ।
कश्यपं पूर्णिमानं च ययोरापूरितं जगत् ॥१३॥

patnī marīces tu kalā
suṣuve kardamātmajā
kaśyapaṁ pūrṇimānaṁ ca
yayor āpūritaṁ jagat

patnī—wife; *marīceḥ*—of the sage named Marīci; *tu*—also; *kalā*—named Kalā; *suṣuve*—gave birth; *kardama-ātmajā*—daughter of Kardama Muni; *kaśyapam*—of the name Kaśyapa; *pūrṇimānam ca*—and of the name Pūrṇimā; *yayoḥ*—by whom; *āpūritam*—spread all over; *jagat*—the world.

TRANSLATION

Kardama Muni's daughter Kalā, who was married to Marīci, gave birth to two children, whose names were Kaśyapa and Pūrṇimā. Their descendants are spread all over the world.

TEXT 14

पूर्णिमासूत विरजं विश्वगं च परंतप ।
देवकुल्यां हरेः पादशौचाद्याभूत्सरिद्दिवः ॥१४॥

pūrṇimāsūta virajaṁ
viśvagaṁ ca parantapa
devakulyāṁ hareḥ pāda-
śaucād yābhūt sarid divaḥ

pūrṇimā—Pūrṇimā; *asūta*—begot; *virajam*—a son named Viraja; *viśvagam ca*—and named Viśvaga; *param-tapa*—O annihilator of enemies; *devakulyām*—a daughter named Devakulyā; *hareḥ*—of the Supreme Personality of Godhead; *pāda-śaucāt*—by the water which washed His lotus feet; *yā*—she; *abhūt*—became; *sarit divaḥ*—the transcendental water within the banks of the Ganges.

TRANSLATION

My dear Vidura, of the two sons, Kaśyapa and Pūrṇimā, Pūrṇimā begot three children, namely Viraja, Viśvaga and Devakulyā. Of these three, Devakulyā was the water which washed the lotus feet of the Personality of Godhead and which later on transformed into the Ganges of the heavenly planets.

PURPORT

Of the two sons Kaśyapa and Pūrṇimā, herein Pūrṇimā's descendants are described. An elaborate description of these descendants will be given in the Sixth Canto. It is also understood herein that Devakulyā is the presiding deity of the River Ganges, which comes down from the heavenly planets to this planet and is accepted to be sanctified because it touched the lotus feet of the Supreme Personality of Godhead, Hari.

TEXT 15

अत्रेः पत्न्यनसूया त्रीञ्जज्ञे सुयशसः सुतान् ।
दत्तं दुर्वाससं सोममात्मेशब्रह्मसम्भवान् ॥१५॥

atreḥ patny anasūyā trīñ
jajñe suyaśasaḥ sutān
dattaṁ durvāsasaṁ somam
ātmeśa-brahma-sambhavān

atreḥ—of Atri Muni; *patnī*—wife; *anasūyā*—named Anasūyā; *trīn*—three; *jajñe*—bore; *su-yaśasaḥ*—very famous; *sutān*—sons; *dattam*—Dattātreya; *durvāsasam*—Durvāsā; *somam*—Soma (the moon-god); *ātma*—the Supersoul; *īśa*—Lord Śiva; *brahma*—Lord Brahmā; *sambhavān*—incarnations of.

TRANSLATION

Anasūyā, the wife of Atri Muni, gave birth to three very famous sons—Soma, Dattātreya and Durvāsā—who were partial representations of Lord Viṣṇu, Lord Śiva and Lord Brahmā. Soma was a partial representation of Lord Brahmā, Dattātreya was a partial representation of Lord Viṣṇu, and Durvāsā was a partial representation of Lord Śiva.

PURPORT

In this verse we find the words *ātma-īśa-brahma-sambhavān. Ātma* means the Supersoul, or Viṣṇu, *īśa* means Lord Śiva, and *brahma* means the four-headed Lord Brahmā. The three sons born of Anasūyā—Dattātreya, Durvāsā and Soma—were born as partial representations of these three demigods. *Ātma* is not in the category of the demigods or living entities because He is Viṣṇu; therefore He is described as *vibhinnāṁśa-bhūtānām*. The Supersoul, Viṣṇu, is the seed-giving father of all living entities, including Brahmā and Lord Śiva. Another meaning of the word *ātma* may be accepted in this way: the principle who is the Supersoul in every *ātmā*, or, one may say, the soul of everyone, became manifested as Dattātreya, because the word *aṁśa*, part and parcel, is used here.

In *Bhagavad-gītā* the individual souls are also described as parts of the Supreme Personality of Godhead, or Supersoul, so why not accept that Dattātreya was one of those parts? Lord Śiva and Lord Brahmā are also described here as parts, so why not accept all of them as ordinary individual souls? The answer is that the manifestations of Viṣṇu and those of the ordinary living entities are certainly all parts and parcels of the Supreme Lord, and no one is equal to Him, but among the parts and parcels there are different categories. In the *Varāha Purāṇa* it is nicely explained that some of the parts are *svāṁśa* and some are *vibhinnāṁśa. Vibhinnāṁśa* parts are called *jīvas*, and *svāṁśa* parts are in the Viṣṇu category. In the *jīva* category, the *vibhinnāṁśa* parts and parcels, there are also gradations. That is explained in the *Viṣṇu Purāṇa*, where it is clearly stated that the individual parts and parcels of the Supreme Lord are subject to being covered by the external energy, called illusion, or *māyā*. Such individual parts and parcels, who can travel to any part of the Lord's creation, are called *sarva-gata* and are suffering the pangs of material existence. They are proportionately freed from the coverings of ignorance under material existence according to different levels of work and under different influences of the modes of material nature. For example, the sufferings of *jīvas* situated in the mode of goodness are less than those of *jīvas* situated in the mode of ignorance. Pure Kṛṣṇa consciousness, however, is the birthright of all living entities because every living entity is part and parcel of the Supreme Lord. The consciousness of the Lord is also in the part and parcel, and according to the proportion to which that consciousness is cleared of material dirt, the living entities are differently situated. In the *Vedānta-sūtra*, the living entities of different gradations are compared to candles or lamps with different candle power. For example, some electric bulbs have the power of one thousand candles, some have the power of five hundred candles, some the power of one hundred candles, some fifty candles, etc., but all electric bulbs have light. Light is present in every bulb, but the gradations of light are different. Similarly, there are gradations of Brahman. The Viṣṇu *svāṁśa* expansions of the Supreme Lord in different Viṣṇu forms are like lamps, Lord Śiva is also like a lamp, and the supreme candle power, or the one-hundred-percent light, is Kṛṣṇa. The *viṣṇu-tattva* has ninety-four percent, the *śiva-tattva* has eighty-four percent, Lord Brahmā has seventy-eight percent, and the living entities are also like Brahmā, but in the conditioned state their power is still more dim. There are gradations of Brahman, and no one can deny this fact. Therefore the words *ātmeśa-brahma-sambhavān* indicate that Dattātreya was directly part and parcel of Viṣṇu, whereas Durvāsā and Soma were parts and parcels of Lord Śiva and Lord Brahmā.

TEXT 16

विदुर उवाच
अत्रेर्गृहे सुरश्रेष्ठाः स्थित्युत्पत्त्यन्तहेतवः ।
किञ्चिच्चिकीर्षवो जाता एतदाख्याहि मे गुरो ॥१६॥

vidura uvāca
atrer gṛhe sura-śreṣṭhāḥ
sthity-utpatty-anta-hetavaḥ
kiñcic cikīrṣavo jātā
etad ākhyāhi me guro

viduraḥ uvāca—Śrī Vidura said; *atreḥ gṛhe*—in the house of Atri; *sura-śreṣṭhāḥ*—chief demigods; *sthiti*—maintenance; *utpatti*—creation; *anta*—destruction; *hetavaḥ*—causes; *kiñcit*—something; *cikīrṣavaḥ*—desiring to do; *jātāḥ*—appeared; *etat*—this; *ākhyāhi*—tell; *me*—to me; *guro*—my dear spiritual master.

TRANSLATION

After hearing this, Vidura inquired from Maitreya: My dear master, how is it that the three deities Brahmā, Viṣṇu and Śiva, who are the creator, maintainer and destroyer of the whole creation, became the offspring of the wife of Atri Muni?

PURPORT

The inquisitiveness of Vidura was quite fitting, for he understood that when the Supersoul, Lord Brahmā and Lord Śiva all appeared through the person of Anasūyā, the wife of Atri Muni, there must have been some great purpose. Otherwise why should they have appeared in such a way?

TEXT 17

मैत्रेय उवाच

ब्रह्मणा चोदितः सृष्टावत्रिर्ब्रह्मविदां वरः ।
सह पत्न्या ययावृक्षं कुलाद्रिं तपसि स्थितः ॥१७॥

maitreya uvāca
brahmaṇā coditaḥ sṛṣṭāv
atrir brahma-vidāṁ varaḥ
saha patnyā yayāv ṛkṣaṁ
kulādriṁ tapasi sthitaḥ

maitreyaḥ uvāca—Śrī Maitreya Ṛṣi said; *brahmaṇā*—by Lord Brahmā; *coditaḥ*—being inspired; *sṛṣṭau*—for creation; *atriḥ*—Atri; *brahma-vidām*—of the persons learned in spiritual knowledge; *varaḥ*—the chief; *saha*—with; *patnyā*—wife; *yayau*—went; *ṛkṣam*—to the mountain named Ṛkṣa; *kula-adrim*—great mountain; *tapasi*—for austerities; *sthitaḥ*—remained.

TRANSLATION

Maitreya said: When Lord Brahmā ordered Atri Muni to create generations after marrying Anasūyā, Atri Muni and his wife went to perform severe austerities in the valley of the mountain known as Ṛkṣa.

TEXT 18

तस्मिन् प्रसूनस्तबकपलाशाशोककानने ।
वार्भिःस्रवद्भिरुद्घुष्टे निर्विन्ध्यायाः समन्ततः ॥१८॥

tasmin prasūna-stabaka-
palāśāśoka-kānane
vārbhiḥ sravadbhir udghuṣṭe
nirvindhyāyāḥ samantataḥ

tasmin—in that; *prasūna-stabaka*—bunches of flowers; *palāśa*—*palāśa* trees; *aśoka*—*aśoka* trees; *kānane*—in the forest garden;

vārbhiḥ—by the waters; *sravadbhiḥ*—flowing; *udghuṣṭe*—in sound; *nirvindhyāyāḥ*—of the River Nirvindhyā; *samantataḥ*—everywhere.

TRANSLATION

In that mountain valley flows a river named Nirvindhyā. On the bank of the river are many aśoka trees and other plants full of palāśa flowers, and there is always the sweet sound of water flowing from a waterfall. The husband and wife reached that beautiful place.

TEXT 19

प्राणायामेन संयम्य मनो वर्षशतं मुनिः ।
अतिष्ठदेकपादेन निर्द्वन्द्वोऽनिलभोजनः ॥१९॥

prāṇāyāmena saṁyamya
mano varṣa-śataṁ muniḥ
atiṣṭhad eka-pādena
nirdvandvo 'nila-bhojanaḥ

prāṇāyāmena—by practice of the breathing exercise; *saṁyamya*—controlling; *manaḥ*—mind; *varṣa-śatam*—one hundred years; *muniḥ*—the great sage; *atiṣṭhat*—remained there; *eka-pādena*—standing on one leg; *nirdvandvaḥ*—without duality; *anila*—air; *bhojanaḥ*—eating.

TRANSLATION

There the great sage concentrated his mind by the yogic breathing exercises, and thereby controlling all attachment, he remained standing on one leg only, eating nothing but air, and stood there on one leg for one hundred years.

TEXT 20

शरणं तं प्रपद्येऽहं य एव जगदीश्वरः ।
प्रजामात्मसमां मह्यं प्रयच्छत्विति चिन्तयन् ॥२०॥

śaraṇaṁ taṁ prapadye 'haṁ
ya eva jagad-īśvaraḥ

prajām ātma-samāṁ mahyaṁ
prayacchatv iti cintayan

śaraṇam—taking shelter; *tam*—unto Him; *prapadye*—surrender; *aham*—I; *yaḥ*—one who; *eva*—certainly; *jagat-īśvaraḥ*—master of the universe; *prajām*—son; *ātma-samām*—like Himself; *mahyam*—unto me; *prayacchatu*—let Him give; *iti*—thus; *cintayan*—thinking.

TRANSLATION

He was thinking: May the Lord of the universe, of whom I have taken shelter, kindly be pleased to offer me a son exactly like Him.

PURPORT

It appears that the great sage Atri Muni had no specific idea of the Supreme Personality of Godhead. Of course, he must have been conversant with the Vedic information that there is a Supreme Personality of Godhead who is the creator of the universe, from whom everything emanated, who maintains this created manifestation, and in whom the entire manifestation is conserved after dissolution. *Yato vā imāni bhūtāni* (*Taittirīya Upaniṣad* 3.1.1). The Vedic *mantras* give us information of the Supreme Personality of Godhead, so Atri Muni concentrated his mind upon that Supreme Personality of Godhead, even without knowing His name, just to beg from Him a child exactly on His level. This kind of devotional service, in which knowledge of God's name is lacking, is also described in *Bhagavad-gītā* where the Lord says that four kinds of men with backgrounds of pious activities come to Him asking for what they need. Atri Muni wanted a son exactly like the Lord, and therefore he is not supposed to have been a pure devotee, because he had a desire to be fulfilled, and that desire was material. Although he wanted a son exactly like the Supreme Personality of Godhead, this desire was material because he did not want the Personality of Godhead Himself, but only a child exactly like Him. If he had desired the Supreme Personality of Godhead as his child, he would have been completely free of material desires because he would have wanted the Supreme Absolute Truth, but because he wanted a similar child, his desire was material. Thus Atri Muni cannot be counted among the pure devotees.

TEXT 21

तप्यमानं त्रिभुवनं प्राणायामैधसाग्निना ।
निर्गतेन मुनेर्मूर्ध्नः समीक्ष्य प्रभवस्त्रयः ॥२१॥

tapyamānaṁ tri-bhuvanaṁ
prāṇāyāmaidhasāgninā
nirgatena muner mūrdhnaḥ
samīkṣya prabhavas trayaḥ

tapyamānam—while practicing austerities; *tri-bhuvanam*—the three worlds; *prāṇāyāma*—practice by breathing exercise; *edhasā*—fuel; *agninā*—by the fire; *nirgatena*—issuing out; *muneḥ*—of the great sage; *mūrdhnaḥ*—the top of the head; *samīkṣya*—looking over; *prabhavaḥ trayaḥ*—the three great gods (Brahmā, Viṣṇu and Maheśvara).

TRANSLATION

While Atri Muni was engaged in these severe austerities, a blazing fire came out of his head by virtue of his breathing exercise, and that fire was seen by the three principal deities of the three worlds.

PURPORT

According to Śrīla Jīva Gosvāmī, the fire of *prāṇāyāma* is mental satisfaction. That fire was perceived by the Supersoul, Viṣṇu, and thereby Lord Brahmā and Śiva also perceived it. Atri Muni, by his breathing exercise, concentrated on the Supersoul, or the Lord of the universe. As confirmed in *Bhagavad-gītā*, the Lord of the universe is Vāsudeva (*vāsudevaḥ sarvam iti*), and, by the direction of Vāsudeva, Lord Brahmā and Lord Śiva work. Therefore, on the direction of Vāsudeva, both Lord Brahmā and Lord Śiva perceived the severe penance adopted by Atri Muni, and thus they were pleased to come down, as stated in the next verse.

TEXT 22

अप्सरोमुनिगन्धर्वसिद्धविद्याधरोरगैः ।
वितायमानयशसस्तदाश्रमपदं ययुः ॥२२॥

apsaro-muni-gandharva-
siddha-vidyādharoragaiḥ
vitāyamāna-yaśasas
tad-āśrama-padaṁ yayuḥ

apsaraḥ—heavenly society women; *muni*—great sages; *gandharva*—inhabitants of the Gandharva planet; *siddha*—of Siddhaloka; *vidyā-dhara*—other demigods; *uragaiḥ*—the inhabitants of Nāgaloka; *vitāyamāna*—being spread; *yaśasaḥ*—fame, reputation; *tat*—his; *āśrama-padam*—hermitage; *yayuḥ*—went.

TRANSLATION

At that time, the three deities approached the hermitage of Atri Muni, accompanied by the denizens of the heavenly planets, such as the celestial beauties, the Gandharvas, the Siddhas, the Vidyādharas and the Nāgas. Thus they entered the āśrama of the great sage, who had become famous by his austerities.

PURPORT

It is advised in the Vedic literatures that one should take shelter of the Supreme Personality of Godhead, who is the Lord of the universe and the master of creation, maintenance and dissolution. He is known as the Supersoul, and when one worships the Supersoul, all other deities, such as Brahmā and Śiva, appear with Lord Viṣṇu because they are directed by the Supersoul.

TEXT 23

तत्प्रादुर्भावसंयोगविद्योतितमना मुनिः ।
उत्तिष्ठन्नेकपादेन ददर्श विबुधर्षभान् ॥२३॥

tat-prādurbhāva-saṁyoga-
vidyotita-manā muniḥ
uttiṣṭhann eka-pādena
dadarśa vibudharṣabhān

tat—their; *prādurbhāva*—appearance; *saṁyoga*—simultaneously; *vidyotita*—enlightened; *manāḥ*—in the mind; *muniḥ*—the great sage;

uttiṣṭhan—being awakened; *eka-pādena*—even on one leg; *dadarśa*—saw; *vibudha*—demigods; *ṛṣabhān*—the great personalities.

TRANSLATION

The sage was standing on one leg, but as soon as he saw that the three deities had appeared before him, he was so pleased to see them all together that despite great difficulty he approached them on one leg.

TEXT 24

प्रणम्य दण्डवद्भूमावुपतस्थेऽर्हणाञ्जलिः ।
वृषहंससुपर्णस्थान् स्वैः स्वैश्चिह्नैश्च चिह्नितान् ॥२४॥

praṇamya daṇḍavad bhūmāv
upatasthe 'rhaṇāñjaliḥ
vṛṣa-haṁsa-suparṇa-sthān
svaiḥ svaiś cihnaiś ca cihnitān

praṇamya—offering obeisances; *daṇḍa-vat*—like a rod; *bhūmau*—ground; *upatasthe*—fell down; *arhaṇa*—all paraphernalia for worship; *añjaliḥ*—folded hands; *vṛṣa*—bull; *haṁsa*—swan; *suparṇa*—the Garuḍa bird; *sthān*—situated; *svaiḥ*—own; *svaiḥ*—own; *cihnaiḥ*—by symbols; *ca*—and; *cihnitān*—being recognized.

TRANSLATION

Thereafter he began to offer prayers to the three deities, who were seated on different carriers—a bull, a swan and Garuḍa—and who held in their hands a drum, kuśa grass and a discus. The sage offered them his respects by falling down like a stick.

PURPORT

Daṇḍa means "a long rod," and *vat* means "like." Before a superior, one has to fall down on the ground just like a stick, and this sort of offering of respect is called *daṇḍavat.* Atri Ṛṣi offered his respect to the three deities in that way. They were identified by their different carriers and different symbolic representations. In that connection it is stated here that Lord Viṣṇu was sitting on Garuḍa, a big aquiline bird, and was carrying in His hand a disc, Brahmā was sitting on a swan and had in his hand *kuśa* grass, and Lord Śiva was sitting on a bull and carrying in his hand a small drum called a *ḍamaru.* Atri Ṛṣi recognized them by their symbolic representations and different carriers, and thus he offered them prayers and respects.

TEXT 25

कृपावलोकेन हसद्वदनेनोपलम्भितान् ।
तद्रोचिषा प्रतिहते निमील्य मुनिरक्षिणी ॥२५॥

kṛpāvalokena hasad-
vadanenopalambhitān
tad-rociṣā pratihate
nimīlya munir akṣiṇī

kṛpā-avalokena—glancing with mercy; *hasat*—smiling; *vadanena*—with faces; *upalambhitān*—appearing very much satisfied; *tat*—their; *rociṣā*—by the glaring effulgence; *pratihate*—being dazzled; *nimīlya*—closing; *muniḥ*—the sage; *akṣiṇī*—his eyes.

TRANSLATION

Atri Muni was greatly pleased to see that the three devas were gracious towards him. His eyes were dazzled by the effulgence of their bodies, and therefore he closed his eyes for the time being.

PURPORT

Since the deities were smiling, he could understand that they were pleased with him. Their glaring bodily effulgence was intolerable to his eyes, so he closed them for the time being.

TEXTS 26–27

चेतस्तत्प्रवणं युञ्जन्नस्तावीत्संहताञ्जलिः ।
श्लक्ष्णया सूक्तया वाचा सर्वलोकगरीयसः ॥२६॥

अत्रिरुवाच
विश्वोद्भवस्थितिलयेषु विभज्यमानै-
र्मायागुणैरनुयुगं विगृहीतदेहाः ।
ते ब्रह्मविष्णुगिरिशाः प्रणतोऽस्म्यहं व-
स्तेभ्यः क एव भवतां म इहोपहूतः ॥२७॥

cetas tat-pravaṇaṁ yuñjann
astāvīt saṁhatāñjaliḥ
ślakṣṇayā sūktayā vācā
sarva-loka-garīyasaḥ

atrir uvāca
viśvodbhava-sthiti-layeṣu vibhajyamānair
māyā-guṇair anuyugaṁ vigṛhīta-dehāḥ
te brahma-viṣṇu-giriśāḥ praṇato 'smy ahaṁ vas
tebhyaḥ ka eva bhavatāṁ ma ihopahūtaḥ

cetaḥ—heart; *tat-pravaṇam*—fixing on them; *yuñjan*—making; *astāvīt*—offered prayers; *saṁhata-añjaliḥ*—with folded hands; *ślakṣṇayā*—ecstatic; *sūktayā*—prayers; *vācā*—words; *sarva-loka*—all over the world; *garīyasaḥ*—honorable; *atriḥ uvāca*—Atri said; *viśva*—the universe; *udbhava*—creation; *sthiti*—maintenance; *layeṣu*—in destruction; *vibhajyamānaiḥ*—being divided; *māyā-guṇaiḥ*—by the external modes of nature; *anuyugam*—according to different millenniums; *vigṛhīta*—accepted; *dehāḥ*—bodies; *te*—they; *brahma*—Lord Brahmā; *viṣṇu*—Lord Viṣṇu; *giriśāḥ*—Lord Śiva; *praṇataḥ*—bowed; *asmi*—am; *aham*—I; *vaḥ*—unto you; *tebhyaḥ*—from them; *kaḥ*—who; *eva*—certainly; *bhavatām*—of you; *me*—by me; *iha*—here; *upahūtaḥ*—called for.

TRANSLATION

But since his heart was already attracted by the deities, somehow or other he gathered his senses, and with folded hands and sweet words he began to offer prayers to the predominating deities of the universe. The great sage Atri said: O Lord Brahmā, Lord Viṣṇu and Lord Śiva, you have divided yourself into three bodies by ac-

cepting the three modes of material nature, as you do in every millennium for the creation, maintenance and dissolution of the cosmic manifestation. I offer my respectful obeisances unto all of you and beg to inquire whom of you three I have called by my prayer.

PURPORT

Atri Ṛṣi called for the Supreme Personality of Godhead, *jagad-īśvara*, the Lord of the universe. The Lord must exist before the creation, otherwise how could He be its Lord? If someone constructs a big building, this indicates that he must have existed before the building was constructed. Therefore the Supreme Lord, the creator of the universe, must be transcendental to the material modes of nature. But it is known that Viṣṇu takes charge of the mode of goodness, Brahmā takes charge of the mode of passion, and Lord Śiva takes charge of the mode of ignorance. Therefore Atri Muni said, "That *jagad-īśvara*, the Lord of the universe, must be one of you, but since three of you have appeared, I cannot recognize whom I have called. You are all so kind. Please let me know who is actually *jagad-īśvara*, the Lord of the universe." In fact, Atri Ṛṣi was doubtful about the constitutional position of the Supreme Lord, Viṣṇu, but he was quite certain that the Lord of the universe cannot be one of the creatures created by *māyā*. His very inquiry about whom he had called indicates that he was in doubt about the constitutional position of the Lord. Therefore he prayed to all three, "Kindly let me know who is the transcendental Lord of the universe." He was certain, of course, that not all of them could be the Lord, but the Lord of the universe was one of the three.

TEXT 28

एको मयेह भगवान् विविधप्रधानै-
श्चित्तीकृतः प्रजननाय कथं नु यूयम् ।
अत्रागतास्तनुभृतां मनसोऽपि दूराद्
ब्रूत प्रसीदत महानिह विस्मयो मे ॥२८॥

eko mayeha bhagavān vividha-pradhānaiś
cittī-kṛtaḥ prajananāya kathaṁ nu yūyam

atrāgatās tanu-bhṛtāṁ manaso 'pi dūrād
brūta prasīdata mahān iha vismayo me

ekaḥ—one; *mayā*—by me; *iha*—here; *bhagavān*—great personality; *vividha*—various; *pradhānaiḥ*—by paraphernalia; *cittī-kṛtaḥ*—fixed in mind; *prajananāya*—for begetting a child; *katham*—why; *nu*—however; *yūyam*—all of you; *atra*—here; *āgatāḥ*—appeared; *tanu-bhṛtām*—of the embodied; *manasaḥ*—the minds; *api*—although; *dūrāt*—from far beyond; *brūta*—kindly explain; *prasīdata*—being merciful to me; *mahān*—very great; *iha*—this; *vismayaḥ*—doubt; *me*—of mine.

TRANSLATION

I called for the Supreme Personality of Godhead, desiring a son like Him, and I thought of Him only. But although He is far beyond the mental speculation of man, all three of you have come here. Kindly let me know how you have come, for I am greatly bewildered about this.

PURPORT

Atri Muni was confidently aware that the Supreme Personality of Godhead is the Lord of the universe, so he prayed for the one Supreme Lord. He was surprised, therefore, that three of them appeared.

TEXT 29

मैत्रेय उवाच
इति तस्य वचः श्रुत्वा त्रयस्ते विबुधर्षभाः ।
प्रत्याहुः श्लक्ष्णया वाचा प्रहस्य तमृषिं प्रभो ॥२९॥

maitreya uvāca
iti tasya vacaḥ śrutvā
trayas te vibudharṣabhāḥ
pratyāhuḥ ślakṣṇayā vācā
prahasya tam ṛṣiṁ prabho

maitreyaḥ uvāca—the sage Maitreya said; *iti*—thus; *tasya*—his; *vacaḥ*—words; *śrutvā*—after hearing; *trayaḥ te*—all three; *vibudha*—demigods; *ṛṣabhāḥ*—chiefs; *pratyāhuḥ*—replied; *ślakṣṇayā*—gentle; *vācā*—voices; *prahasya*—smiling; *tam*—unto him; *ṛṣim*—the great sage; *prabho*—O mighty one.

TRANSLATION

The great sage Maitreya continued: Upon hearing Atri Muni speak in that way, the three great deities smiled, and they replied in the following sweet words.

TEXT 30

देवा ऊचुः

यथा कृतस्ते सङ्कल्पो भाव्यं तेनैव नान्यथा ।
सत्सङ्कल्पस्य ते ब्रह्मन् यद्वै ध्यायति ते वयम् ॥३०॥

devā ūcuḥ
yathā kṛtas te saṅkalpo
bhāvyaṁ tenaiva nānyathā
sat-saṅkalpasya te brahman
yad vai dhyāyati te vayam

devāḥ ūcuḥ—the demigods replied; *yathā*—as; *kṛtaḥ*—done; *te*—by you; *saṅkalpaḥ*—determination; *bhāvyam*—to be done; *tena eva*—by that; *na anyathā*—not otherwise; *sat-saṅkalpasya*—one whose determination is never lost; *te*—of you; *brahman*—O dear *brāhmaṇa; yat*—that which; *vai*—certainly; *dhyāyati*—meditating; *te*—all of them; *vayam*—we are.

TRANSLATION

The three deities told Atri Muni: Dear brāhmaṇa, you are perfect in your determination, and therefore as you have decided, so it will happen; it will not happen otherwise. We are all the same person upon whom you were meditating, and therefore we have all come to you.

PURPORT

Atri Muni unspecifically thought of the Personality of Godhead, the Lord of the universe, although he had no clear idea of the Lord of the universe nor of His specific form. Mahā-Viṣṇu, from whose breathing millions of universes emanate and into whom they are again withdrawn, may be accepted as the Lord of the universe. Garbhodakaśāyī Viṣṇu, from whose abdomen sprouted the lotus flower which is the birthplace of Brahmā, may also be considered the Lord of the universe. Similarly, Kṣīrodakaśāyī Viṣṇu, who is the Supersoul of all living entities, may also be considered the Lord of the universe. Then, under the order of Kṣīrodakaśāyī Viṣṇu, the Viṣṇu form within this universe, Lord Brahmā and Lord Śiva may also be accepted as the Lords of the universe.

Viṣṇu is the Lord of the universe because He is its maintainer. Similarly, Brahmā creates the different planetary systems and the population, so he also may be considered the Lord of the universe. Or Lord Śiva, who is ultimately the destroyer of the universe, also may be considered its Lord. Therefore, since Atri Muni did not specifically mention whom he wanted, all three—Brahmā, Viṣṇu and Lord Śiva—came before him. They said, "Since you were thinking of having a son exactly like the Supreme Personality of Godhead, the Lord of the universe, your determination will be fulfilled." In other words, one's determination is fulfilled according to the strength of one's devotion. As stated in *Bhagavad-gītā* (9.25): *yānti deva-vratā devān pitṝn yānti pitṛ-vratāḥ*. If one is attached to a particular demigod, one is promoted to the abode of that demigod; if one is attached to the Pitās, or forefathers, one is promoted to their planet; and similarly if one is attached to the Supreme Personality of Godhead, Kṛṣṇa, one is promoted to the abode of Lord Kṛṣṇa. Atri Muni had no clear conception of the Lord of the universe; therefore the three presiding deities who are actually the lords of the universe in the three departments of the modes of nature all came before him. Now, according to the strength of his determination for a son, his desire would be fulfilled by the grace of the Lord.

TEXT 31

अथास्मदंशभूतास्ते आत्मजा लोकविश्रुताः ।
भवितारोऽङ्ग भद्रं ते विस्रप्स्यन्ति च ते यशः ॥३१॥

athāsmad-aṁśa-bhūtās te
ātmajā loka-viśrutāḥ
bhavitāro 'ṅga bhadraṁ te
visrapsyanti ca te yaśaḥ

atha—therefore; *asmat*—our; *aṁśa-bhūtāḥ*—plenary expansions; *te*—your; *ātmajāḥ*—sons; *loka-viśrutāḥ*—very famous in the world; *bhavitāraḥ*—in the future will be born; *aṅga*—dear great sage; *bhadram*—all good fortune; *te*—unto you; *visrapsyanti*—will spread; *ca*—also; *te*—your; *yaśaḥ*—reputation.

TRANSLATION

You will have sons who will represent a partial manifestation of our potency, and because we desire all good fortune for you, those sons will glorify your reputation throughout the world.

TEXT 32

एवं कामवरं दत्त्वा प्रतिजग्मुः सुरेश्वराः ।
सभाजितास्तयोः सम्यग्दम्पत्योर्मिषतोस्ततः ॥३२॥

evaṁ kāma-varaṁ dattvā
pratijagmuḥ sureśvarāḥ
sabhājitās tayoḥ samyag
dampatyor miṣatos tataḥ

evam—thus; *kāma-varam*—desired benediction; *dattvā*—offering; *pratijagmuḥ*—returned; *sura-īśvarāḥ*—the chief demigods; *sabhājitāḥ*—being worshiped; *tayoḥ*—while they; *samyak*—perfectly; *dampatyoḥ*—the husband and wife; *miṣatoḥ*—were looking on; *tataḥ*—from there.

TRANSLATION

Thus, while the couple looked on, the three deities Brahmā, Viṣṇu and Maheśvara disappeared from that place after bestowing upon Atri Muni the benediction.

TEXT 33

सोमोऽभूद्ब्रह्मणोंऽशेन दत्तो विष्णोस्तु योगवित् ।
दुर्वासाः शंकरस्यांशो निबोधाङ्गिरसः प्रजाः ॥३३॥

somo 'bhūd brahmaṇo 'ṁśena
datto viṣṇos tu yogavit
durvāsāḥ śaṅkarasyāṁśo
nibodhāṅgirasaḥ prajāḥ

somaḥ—the king of the moon planet; *abhūt*—appeared; *brahmaṇaḥ*—of Lord Brahmā; *aṁśena*—partial expansion; *dattaḥ*—Dattātreya; *viṣṇoḥ*—of Viṣṇu; *tu*—but; *yoga-vit*—very powerful *yogī; durvāsāḥ*—Durvāsā; *śaṅkarasya aṁśaḥ*—partial expansion of Lord Śiva; *nibodha*—just try to understand; *aṅgirasaḥ*—of the great sage Aṅgirā; *prajāḥ*—generations.

TRANSLATION

Thereafter, from the partial representation of Brahmā, the moon-god was born of them; from the partial representation of Viṣṇu, the great mystic Dattātreya was born; and from the partial representation of Śaṅkara [Lord Śiva], Durvāsā was born. Now you may hear from me of the many sons of Aṅgirā.

TEXT 34

श्रद्धा त्वङ्गिरसः पत्नी चतस्रोऽसूत कन्यकाः ।
सिनीवाली कुहू राका चतुर्थ्यनुमतिस्तथा ॥३४॥

śraddhā tv aṅgirasaḥ patnī
catasro 'sūta kanyakāḥ
sinīvālī kuhū rākā
caturthy anumatis tathā

śraddhā—Śraddhā; *tu*—but; *aṅgirasaḥ*—of Aṅgirā Ṛṣi; *patnī*—wife; *catasraḥ*—four; *asūta*—gave birth; *kanyakāḥ*—daughters; *sinīvālī*—Sinīvālī; *kuhūḥ*—Kuhū; *rākā*—Rākā; *caturthī*—the fourth one; *anumatiḥ*—Anumati; *tathā*—also.

TRANSLATION

Aṅgirā's wife, Śraddhā, gave birth to four daughters, named Sinīvālī, Kuhū, Rākā and Anumati.

TEXT 35

तत्पुत्रावपरावास्तां ख्यातौ स्वारोचिषेऽन्तरे ।
उतथ्यो भगवान् साक्षाद्ब्रह्मिष्ठश्च बृहस्पतिः ॥३५॥

tat-putrāv aparāv āstāṁ
khyātau svārociṣe 'ntare
utathyo bhagavān sākṣād
brahmiṣṭhaś ca bṛhaspatiḥ

tat—his; *putrau*—sons; *aparau*—others; *āstām*—were born; *khyātau*—very famous; *svārociṣe*—in the Svārociṣa millennium; *antare*—of the Manu; *utathyaḥ*—Utathya; *bhagavān*—very mighty; *sākṣāt*—directly; *brahmiṣṭhaḥ ca*—fully spiritually advanced; *bṛhaspatiḥ*—Bṛhaspati.

TRANSLATION

Besides these four daughters, she also had another two sons. One of them was known as Utathya, and the other was the learned scholar Bṛhaspati.

TEXT 36

पुलस्त्योऽजनयत्पत्न्यामगस्त्यं च हविर्भुवि ।
सोऽन्यजन्मनि दह्राग्निर्विश्रवाश्च महातपाः ॥३६॥

pulastyo 'janayat patnyām
agastyaṁ ca havirbhuvi
so 'nya-janmani dahrāgnir
viśravāś ca mahā-tapāḥ

pulastyaḥ—the sage Pulastya; *ajanayat*—begot; *patnyām*—in his wife; *agastyam*—the great sage Agastya; *ca*—also; *havirbhuvi*—in Havirbhū; *saḥ*—he (Agastya); *anya-janmani*—in the next birth;

dahra-agniḥ—the digesting fire; *viśravāḥ*—Viśravā; *ca*—and; *mahā-tapāḥ*—greatly powerful because of austerity.

TRANSLATION

Pulastya begot in his wife, Havirbhū, one son of the name Agastya, who in his next birth became Dahrāgni. Besides him, Pulastya begot another very great and saintly son, whose name was Viśravā.

TEXT 37

तस्य यक्षपतिर्देवः कुबेरस्त्विडविडासुतः ।
रावणः कुम्भकर्णश्च तथान्यस्यां विभीषणः ॥३७॥

tasya yakṣa-patir devaḥ
kuberas tv iḍaviḍā-sutaḥ
rāvaṇaḥ kumbhakarṇaś ca
tathānyasyāṁ vibhīṣaṇaḥ

tasya—his; *yakṣa-patiḥ*—the king of the Yakṣas; *devaḥ*—demigod; *kuberaḥ*—Kuvera; *tu*—and; *iḍaviḍā*—of Iḍaviḍā; *sutaḥ*—son; *rāvaṇaḥ*—Rāvaṇa; *kumbhakarṇaḥ*—Kumbhakarṇa; *ca*—also; *tathā*—so; *anyasyām*—in the other; *vibhīṣaṇaḥ*—Vibhīṣaṇa.

TRANSLATION

Viśravā had two wives. The first wife was Iḍaviḍā, from whom Kuvera, the master of all Yakṣas, was born, and the next wife was named Keśinī, from whom three sons were born—Rāvaṇa, Kumbhakarṇa and Vibhīṣaṇa.

TEXT 38

पुलहस्य गतिर्भार्या त्रीनसूत सती सुतान् ।
कर्मश्रेष्ठं वरीयांसं सहिष्णुं च महामते ॥३८॥

pulahasya gatir bhāryā
trīn asūta satī sutān

karmaśreṣṭhaṁ varīyāṁsaṁ
sahiṣṇuṁ ca mahā-mate

pulahasya—of Pulaha; *gatiḥ*—Gati; *bhāryā*—wife; *trīn*—three; *asūta*—gave birth; *satī*—chaste; *sutān*—sons; *karma-śreṣṭham*—very expert in fruitive activities; *varīyāṁsam*—very respectable; *sahiṣṇum*—very tolerant; *ca*—also; *mahā-mate*—O great Vidura.

TRANSLATION

Gati, the wife of the sage Pulaha, gave birth to three sons, named Karmaśreṣṭha, Varīyān and Sahiṣṇu, and all of them were great sages.

PURPORT

Gati, the wife of Pulaha, was the fifth daughter of Kardama Muni. She was very faithful to her husband, and all her sons were as good as he.

TEXT 39

क्रतोरपि क्रिया भार्या वालखिल्यानसूयत ।
ऋषीन्षष्टिसहस्राणि ज्वलतो ब्रह्मतेजसा ॥३९॥

krator api kriyā bhāryā
vālakhilyān asūyata
ṛṣīn ṣaṣṭi-sahasrāṇi
jvalato brahma-tejasā

kratoḥ—of the great sage Kratu; *api*—also; *kriyā*—Kriyā; *bhāryā*—wife; *vālakhilyān*—just like Vālakhilya; *asūyata*—begot; *ṛṣīn*—sages; *ṣaṣṭi*—sixty; *sahasrāṇi*—thousand; *jvalataḥ*—very brilliant; *brahma-tejasā*—by dint of the Brahman effulgence.

TRANSLATION

Kratu's wife, Kriyā, gave birth to sixty thousand great sages, named the Vālakhilyas. All these sages were greatly advanced in spiritual knowledge, and their bodies were illuminated by such knowledge.

PURPORT

Kriyā was the sixth daughter of Kardama Muni, and she produced sixty thousand sages, who were known as the Vālakhilyas because they all retired from family life as *vānaprasthas.*

TEXT 40

ऊर्जायां जज्ञिरे पुत्रा वसिष्ठस्य परन्तप ।
चित्रकेतुप्रधानास्ते सप्त ब्रह्मर्षयोऽमलाः ॥४०॥

ūrjāyāṁ jajñire putrā
vasiṣṭhasya parantapa
citraketu-pradhānās te
sapta brahmarṣayo 'malāḥ

ūrjāyām—in Ūrjā; *jajñire*—took birth; *putrāḥ*—sons; *vasiṣṭhasya*—of the great sage Vasiṣṭha; *parantapa*—O great one; *citraketu*—Citraketu; *pradhānāḥ*—headed by; *te*—all the sons; *sapta*—seven; *brahma-ṛṣayaḥ*—great sages with spiritual knowledge; *amalāḥ*—without contamination.

TRANSLATION

The great sage Vasiṣṭha begot in his wife, Ūrjā, sometimes called Arundhatī, seven spotlessly great sages, headed by the sage named Citraketu.

TEXT 41

चित्रकेतुः सुरोचिश्च विरजा मित्र एव च ।
उल्बणो वसुभृद्यानो द्युमान् शक्त्यादयोऽपरे ॥४१॥

citraketuḥ surociś ca
virajā mitra eva ca
ulbaṇo vasubhṛdyāno
dyumān śakty-ādayo 'pare

citraketuḥ—Citraketu; *surociḥ ca*—and Suroci; *virajāḥ*—Virajā; *mitraḥ*—Mitra; *eva*—also; *ca*—and; *ulbaṇaḥ*—Ulbaṇa; *vasubhṛdyā-*

naḥ—Vasubhṛdyāna; *dyumān*—Dyumān; *śakti-ādayaḥ*—sons headed by Śakti; *apare*—from his other wife.

TRANSLATION

The names of these seven sages are as follows: Citraketu, Suroci, Virajā, Mitra, Ulbaṇa, Vasubhṛdyāna and Dyumān. Some other very competent sons were born from Vasiṣṭha's other wife.

PURPORT

Ūrjā, who is sometimes known as Arundhatī and was the wife of Vasiṣṭha, was the ninth daughter of Kardama Muni.

TEXT 42

चित्तिस्त्वथर्वणः पत्नी लेभे पुत्रं धृतव्रतम् ।
दध्यञ्चमश्वशिरसं भृगोर्वंशं निबोध मे ॥४२॥

cittis tv atharvaṇaḥ patnī
lebhe putraṁ dhṛta-vratam
dadhyañcam aśvaśirasaṁ
bhṛgor vaṁśaṁ nibodha me

cittiḥ—Citti; *tu*—also; *atharvaṇaḥ*—of Atharvā; *patnī*—wife; *lebhe*—got; *putram*—son; *dhṛta-vratam*—completely dedicated to a vow; *dadhyañcam*—Dadhyañca; *aśvaśirasam*—Aśvaśirā; *bhṛgoḥ vaṁśam*—generations of Bhṛgu; *nibodha*—try to understand; *me*—from me.

TRANSLATION

Citti, wife of the sage Atharvā, gave birth to a son named Aśvaśirā by accepting a great vow called Dadhyañca. Now you may hear from me about the descendants of the sage Bhṛgu.

PURPORT

The wife of Atharvā known as Citti is also known as Śānti. She was the eighth daughter of Kardama Muni.

TEXT 43

भृगुः ख्यात्यां महाभागः पत्न्यां पुत्रानजीजनत् ।
धातारं च विधातारं श्रियं च भगवत्पराम् ॥४३॥

bhṛguḥ khyātyāṁ mahā-bhāgaḥ
patnyāṁ putrān ajījanat
dhātāraṁ ca vidhātāraṁ
śriyaṁ ca bhagavat-parām

bhṛguḥ—the great sage Bhṛgu; *khyātyām*—in his wife, Khyāti; *mahā-bhāgaḥ*—greatly fortunate; *patnyām*—unto the wife; *putrān*—sons; *ajījanat*—gave birth; *dhātāram*—Dhātā; *ca*—also; *vidhātāram*—Vidhātā; *śriyam*—a daughter named Śrī; *ca bhagavat-parām*—and a great devotee of the Lord.

TRANSLATION

The sage Bhṛgu was highly fortunate. In his wife, known as Khyāti, he begot two sons, named Dhātā and Vidhātā, and one daughter, named Śrī, who was very much devoted to the Supreme Personality of Godhead.

TEXT 44

आयतिं नियतिं चैव सुते मेरुस्तयोरदात् ।
ताभ्यां तयोरभवतां मृकण्डः प्राण एव च ॥४४॥

āyatiṁ niyatiṁ caiva
sute merus tayor adāt
tābhyāṁ tayor abhavatāṁ
mṛkaṇḍaḥ prāṇa eva ca

āyatim—Āyati; *niyatim*—Niyati; *ca eva*—also; *sute*—daughters; *meruḥ*—the sage Meru; *tayoḥ*—unto those two; *adāt*—gave in marriage; *tābhyām*—out of them; *tayoḥ*—both of them; *abhavatām*—appeared; *mṛkaṇḍaḥ*—Mṛkaṇḍa; *prāṇaḥ*—Prāṇa; *eva*—certainly; *ca*—and.

TRANSLATION

The sage Meru had two daughters, named Āyati and Niyati, whom he gave in charity to Dhātā and Vidhātā. Āyati and Niyati gave birth to two sons, Mṛkaṇḍa and Prāṇa.

TEXT 45

मार्कण्डेयो मृकण्डस्य प्राणाद्वेदशिरा मुनिः ।
कविश्च भार्गवो यस्य भगवानुशना सुतः ॥४५॥

mārkaṇḍeyo mṛkaṇḍasya
prāṇād vedaśirā muniḥ
kaviś ca bhārgavo yasya
bhagavān uśanā sutaḥ

mārkaṇḍeyaḥ—Mārkaṇḍeya; *mṛkaṇḍasya*—of Mṛkaṇḍa; *prāṇāt*—from Prāṇa; *vedaśirāḥ*—Vedaśirā; *muniḥ*—great sage; *kaviḥ ca*—of the name Kavi; *bhārgavaḥ*—of the name Bhārgava; *yasya*—whose; *bhagavān*—greatly powerful; *uśanā*—Śukrācārya; *sutaḥ*—son.

TRANSLATION

From Mṛkaṇḍa, Mārkaṇḍeya Muni was born, and from Prāṇa the sage Vedaśirā, whose son was Uśanā [Śukrācārya], also known as Kavi. Thus Kavi also belonged to the descendants of the Bhṛgu dynasty.

TEXTS 46–47

त एते मुनयः क्षत्तर्लोकान् सर्गैरभावयन् ।
एष कर्दमदौहित्रसंतानः कथितस्तव ॥४६॥
शृण्वतः श्रद्दधानस्य सद्यः पापहरः परः ।
प्रसूतिं मानवीं दक्ष उपयेमे ह्यजात्मजः ॥४७॥

ta ete munayaḥ kṣattar
lokān sargair abhāvayan
eṣa kardama-dauhitra-
santānaḥ kathitas tava

śṛṇvataḥ śraddadhānasya
sadyaḥ pāpa-haraḥ paraḥ
prasūtiṁ mānavīṁ dakṣa
upayeme hy ajātmajaḥ

te—they; *ete*—all; *munayaḥ*—great sages; *kṣattaḥ*—O Vidura; *lokān*—the three worlds; *sargaiḥ*—with their descendants; *abhāvayan*—filled; *eṣaḥ*—this; *kardama*—of the sage Kardama; *dauhitra*—grandsons; *santānaḥ*—offspring; *kathitaḥ*—already spoken; *tava*—unto you; *śṛṇvataḥ*—hearing; *śraddadhānasya*—of the faithful; *sadyaḥ*—immediately; *pāpa-haraḥ*—reducing all sinful activities; *paraḥ*—great; *prasūtim*—Prasūti; *mānavīm*—daughter of Manu; *dakṣaḥ*—King Dakṣa; *upayeme*—married; *hi*—certainly; *aja-ātmajaḥ*—son of Brahmā.

TRANSLATION

My dear Vidura, the population of the universe was thus increased by the descendants of these sages and the daughters of Kardama. Anyone who hears the descriptions of this dynasty with faith will be relieved from all sinful reactions. Another of Manu's daughters, known as Prasūti, married the son of Brahmā named Dakṣa.

TEXT 48

तस्यां ससर्ज दुहितॄः षोडशामललोचनाः ।
त्रयोदशादाद्धर्माय तथैकामग्नये विभुः ॥४८॥

tasyāṁ sasarja duhitṝḥ
ṣoḍaśāmala-locanāḥ
trayodaśādād dharmāya
tathaikām agnaye vibhuḥ

tasyām—unto her; *sasarja*—created; *duhitṝḥ*—daughters; *ṣoḍaśa*—sixteen; *amala-locanāḥ*—with lotuslike eyes; *trayodaśa*—thirteen; *adāt*—gave; *dharmāya*—to Dharma; *tathā*—so; *ekām*—one daughter; *agnaye*—to Agni; *vibhuḥ*—Dakṣa.

TRANSLATION

Dakṣa begot sixteen very beautiful daughters with lotuslike eyes in his wife Prasūti. Of these sixteen daughters, thirteen were given in marriage to Dharma, and one daughter was given to Agni.

TEXTS 49–52

पितृभ्य एकां युक्तेभ्यो भवायैकां भवच्छिदे ।
श्रद्धा मैत्री दया शान्तिस्तुष्टिः पुष्टिः क्रियोन्नतिः॥४९॥
बुद्धिर्मेधा तितिक्षा ह्रीर्मूर्तिर्धर्मस्य पत्नयः ।
श्रद्धासूत शुभं मैत्री प्रसादमभयं दया ॥५०॥
शान्तिः सुखं मुदं तुष्टिः स्मयं पुष्टिरसूयत ।
योगं क्रियोन्नतिर्दर्पमर्थं बुद्धिरसूयत ॥५१॥
मेधा स्मृतिं तितिक्षा तु क्षेमं ह्रीः प्रश्रयं सुतम् ।
मूर्तिः सर्वगुणोत्पत्तिर्नरनारायणावृषी ॥५२॥

pitṛbhya ekāṁ yuktebhyo
bhavāyaikāṁ bhava-cchide
śraddhā maitrī dayā śāntis
tuṣṭiḥ puṣṭiḥ kriyonnatiḥ

buddhir medhā titikṣā hrīr
mūrtir dharmasya patnayaḥ
śraddhāsūta śubhaṁ maitrī
prasādam abhayaṁ dayā

śāntiḥ sukhaṁ mudaṁ tuṣṭiḥ
smayaṁ puṣṭir asūyata
yogaṁ kriyonnatir darpam
arthaṁ buddhir asūyata

medhā smṛtiṁ titikṣā tu
kṣemaṁ hrīḥ praśrayaṁ sutam
mūrtiḥ sarva-guṇotpattir
nara-nārāyaṇāv ṛṣī

pitṛbhyaḥ—to the Pitās; *ekām*—one daughter; *yuktebhyaḥ*—the assembled; *bhavāya*—to Lord Śiva; *ekām*—one daughter; *bhava-chide*—who delivers from the material entanglement; *śraddhā, maitrī, dayā, śāntiḥ, tuṣṭiḥ, puṣṭiḥ, kriyā, unnatiḥ, buddhiḥ, medhā, titikṣā, hrīḥ, mūrtiḥ*—names of thirteen daughters of Dakṣa; *dharmasya*—of Dharma; *patnayaḥ*—the wives; *śraddhā*—Śraddhā; *asūta*—gave birth to; *śubham*—Śubha; *maitrī*—Maitrī; *prasādam*—Prasāda; *abhayam*—Abhaya; *dayā*—Dayā; *śāntiḥ*—Śānti; *sukham*—Sukha; *mudam*—Muda; *tuṣṭiḥ*—Tuṣṭi; *smayam*—Smaya; *puṣṭiḥ*—Puṣṭi; *asūyata*—gave birth to; *yogam*—Yoga; *kriyā*—Kriyā; *unnatiḥ*—Unnati; *darpam*—Darpa; *artham*—Artha; *buddhiḥ*—Buddhi; *asūyata*—begot; *medhā*—Medhā; *smṛtim*—Smṛti; *titikṣā*—Titikṣā; *tu*—also; *kṣemam*—Kṣema; *hrīḥ*—Hrī; *praśrayam*—Praśraya; *sutam*—son; *mūrtiḥ*—Mūrti; *sarva-guṇa*—of all respectable qualities; *utpattiḥ*—the reservoir; *nara-nārāyaṇau*—both Nara and Nārāyaṇa; *ṛṣī*—the two sages.

TRANSLATION

One of the remaining two daughters was given in charity to the Pitṛloka, where she resides very amicably, and the other was given to Lord Śiva, who is the deliverer of sinful persons from material entanglement. The names of the thirteen daughters of Dakṣa who were given to Dharma are Śraddhā, Maitrī, Dayā, Śānti, Tuṣṭi, Puṣṭi, Kriyā, Unnati, Buddhi, Medhā, Titikṣā, Hrī and Mūrti. These thirteen daughters produced the following sons: Śraddhā gave birth to Śubha, Maitrī produced Prasāda, Dayā gave birth to Abhaya, Śānti gave birth to Sukha, Tuṣṭi gave birth to Muda, Puṣṭi gave birth to Smaya, Kriyā gave birth to Yoga, Unnati gave birth to Darpa, Buddhi gave birth to Artha, Medhā gave birth to Smṛti, Titikṣā gave birth to Kṣema, and Hrī gave birth to Praśraya. Mūrti, a reservoir of all respectable qualities, gave birth to Śrī Nara-Nārāyaṇa, the Supreme Personality of Godhead.

TEXT 53

ययोर्जन्मन्यदो विश्वमभ्यनन्दत्सुनिर्वृतम् ।
मनांसि ककुभो वाताः प्रसेदुः सरितोऽद्रयः ॥५३॥

yayor janmany ado viśvam
abhyanandat sunirvṛtam
manāṁsi kakubho vātāḥ
praseduḥ sarito 'drayaḥ

yayoḥ—both of whom (Nara and Nārāyaṇa); *janmani*—on the appearance; *adaḥ*—that; *viśvam*—universe; *abhyanandat*—became glad; *su-nirvṛtam*—full of joy; *manāṁsi*—everyone's mind; *kakubhaḥ*—the directions; *vātāḥ*—the air; *praseduḥ*—became pleasant; *saritaḥ*—the rivers; *adrayaḥ*—the mountains.

TRANSLATION

On the occasion of the appearance of Nara-Nārāyaṇa, the entire world was full of joy. Everyone's mind became tranquil, and thus in all directions the air, the rivers and the mountains became pleasant.

TEXTS 54–55

दिव्यवाद्यन्त तूर्याणि पेतुः कुसुमवृष्टयः ।
मुनयस्तुष्टुवुस्तुष्टा जगुर्गन्धर्वकिन्नराः ॥५४॥
नृत्यन्ति स्म स्त्रियो देव्य आसीत्परममङ्गलम् ।
देवा ब्रह्मादयः सर्वे उपतस्थुरभिष्टवैः ॥५५॥

divy avādyanta tūryāṇi
petuḥ kusuma-vṛṣṭayaḥ
munayas tuṣṭuvus tuṣṭā
jagur gandharva-kinnarāḥ

nṛtyanti sma striyo devya
āsīt parama-maṅgalam
devā brahmādayaḥ sarve
upatasthur abhiṣṭavaiḥ

divi—in the heavenly planets; *avādyanta*—vibrated; *tūryāṇi*—a band of instruments; *petuḥ*—they showered; *kusuma*—of flowers; *vṛṣṭayaḥ*—showers; *munayaḥ*—the sages; *tuṣṭuvuḥ*—chanted Vedic prayers; *tuṣṭāḥ*—pacified; *jaguḥ*—began to sing; *gandharva*—the Gandharvas; *kinnarāḥ*—the Kinnaras; *nṛtyanti sma*—danced; *striyaḥ*—the beautiful damsels; *devyaḥ*—of the heavenly planets; *āsīt*—were visible; *parama-maṅgalam*—the highest good fortune; *devāḥ*—the demigods; *brahma-ādayaḥ*—Brahmā and others; *sarve*—all; *upatasthuḥ*—worshiped; *abhiṣṭavaiḥ*—with respectful prayers.

TRANSLATION

In the heavenly planets, bands began to play, and they showered flowers from the sky. The pacified sages chanted Vedic prayers, the denizens of heaven known as the Gandharvas and Kinnaras sang, the beautiful damsels of the heavenly planets danced, and in this way, at the time of the appearance of Nara-Nārāyaṇa, all signs of good fortune were visible. Just at that time, great demigods like Brahmā also offered their respectful prayers.

TEXT 56

देवा ऊचुः

यो मायया विरचितं निजयात्मनीदं
खे रूपभेदमिव तत्प्रतिचक्षणाय ।
एतेन धर्मसदने ऋषिमूर्तिनाद्य
प्रादुश्चकार पुरुषाय नमः परस्मै ॥५६॥

devā ūcuḥ
yo māyayā viracitaṁ nijayātmanīdaṁ
khe rūpa-bhedam iva tat-praticakṣaṇāya
etena dharma-sadane ṛṣi-mūrtinādya
prāduścakāra puruṣāya namaḥ parasmai

devāḥ—the demigods; *ūcuḥ*—said; *yaḥ*—who; *māyayā*—by the external energy; *viracitam*—was created; *nijayā*—by His own; *ātmani*—being situated in Him; *idam*—this; *khe*—in the sky; *rūpa-bhedam*—bunches of clouds; *iva*—as if; *tat*—of Himself; *praticakṣaṇāya*—for manifesting; *etena*—with this; *dharma-sadane*—in the house of Dharma; *ṛṣi-mūrtinā*—with the form of a sage; *adya*—today; *prā-*

duścakāra—appeared; *puruṣāya*—unto the Personality of Godhead; *namaḥ*—respectful obeisances; *parasmai*—the Supreme.

TRANSLATION

The demigods said: Let us offer our respectful obeisances unto the transcendental Personality of Godhead, who created as His external energy this cosmic manifestation, which is situated in Him as the air and clouds are situated in space, and who has now appeared in the form of Nara-Nārāyaṇa Ṛṣi in the house of Dharma.

PURPORT

The universal form of the Lord is the cosmic manifestation, which is an exhibition of the external energy of the Supreme Personality of Godhead. In space there are innumerable varieties of planets and also the air, and in the air there are variously colored clouds, and sometimes we see airplanes running from one place to another. Thus the entire cosmic manifestation is full of variety, but actually that variety is a manifestation of the external energy of the Supreme Lord, and that energy is situated in Him. Now the Lord Himself, after manifesting His energy, appeared within the creation of His energy, which is simultaneously one with and different from Himself, and therefore the demigods offered their respects to the Supreme Personality of Godhead, who manifests Himself in such varieties. There are some philosophers, called nondualists, who because of their impersonal conception think that varieties are false. In this verse it is specifically stated, *yo māyayā viracitam.* This indicates that the varieties are a manifestation of the energy of the Supreme Personality of Godhead. Thus because the energy is nondifferent from the Godhead, the varieties are also factual. The material varieties may be temporary, but they are not false. They are a reflection of the spiritual varieties. Here the word *praticakṣaṇāya,* "there are varieties," announces the glories of the Supreme Personality of Godhead, who appeared as Nara-Nārāyaṇa Ṛṣi and who is the origin of all varieties of material nature.

TEXT 57

सोऽयं स्थितिव्यतिकरोपशमाय सृष्टान्
सत्त्वेन नः सुरगणाननुमेयतत्त्वः ।

दृश्याददभ्रकरुणेन विलोकनेन
यच्छ्रीनिकेतममलं क्षिपतारविन्दम् ॥५७॥

so 'yaṁ sthiti-vyatikaropaśamāya sṛṣṭān
sattvena naḥ sura-gaṇān anumeya-tattvaḥ
dṛśyād adabhra-karuṇena vilokanena
yac chrī-niketam amalaṁ kṣipatāravindam

saḥ—that; *ayam*—He; *sthiti*—of the created world; *vyatikara*—calamities; *upaśamāya*—for destroying; *sṛṣṭān*—created; *sattvena*—by the mode of goodness; *naḥ*—us; *sura-gaṇān*—the demigods; *anumeya-tattvaḥ*—understood by the *Vedas; dṛśyāt*—glance over; *adabhra-karuṇena*—merciful; *vilokanena*—glance; *yat*—which; *śrī-niketam*—the home of the goddess of fortune; *amalam*—spotless; *kṣipata*—supersedes; *aravindam*—lotus.

TRANSLATION

Let that Supreme Personality of Godhead, who is understood by truly authorized Vedic literature and who has created peace and prosperity to destroy all calamities of the created world, be kind enough to bestow His glance upon the demigods. His merciful glance can supersede the beauty of the spotless lotus flower which is the home of the goddess of fortune.

PURPORT

The Supreme Personality of Godhead, who is the origin of the cosmic manifestation, is covered by the wonderful activities of material nature, just as outer space or the illumination of the sun and moon is sometimes covered by clouds or dust. It is very difficult to find the origin of the cosmic manifestation; therefore material scientists conclude that nature is the ultimate cause of all manifestations. But from *śāstra*, or authentic literature like *Bhagavad-gītā* and other Vedic scriptures, we understand that behind this wonderful cosmic manifestation is the Supreme Personality of Godhead, and in order to maintain the regular procedures of the cosmic manifestation and to be visible to the eyes of persons who are in the mode of goodness, the Lord appears. He is the cause of the creation and dissolution of the cosmic manifestation. The demigods therefore prayed for His merciful glance upon them in order to be blessed.

TEXT 58

एवं सुरगणैस्तात भगवन्तावभिष्टुतौ ।
लब्धावलोकैर्ययतुरर्चितौ गन्धमादनम् ॥५८॥

evaṁ sura-gaṇais tāta
bhagavantāv abhiṣṭutau
labdhāvalokair yayatur
arcitau gandhamādanam

evam—thus; *sura-gaṇaiḥ*—by the demigods; *tāta*—O Vidura; *bhagavantau*—the Supreme Personality of Godhead; *abhiṣṭutau*—having been praised; *labdha*—having obtained; *avalokaiḥ*—the glance (of mercy); *yayatuḥ*—departed; *arcitau*—having been worshiped; *gandha-mādanam*—to the Gandhamādana Hill.

TRANSLATION

[Maitreya said:] O Vidura, thus the demigods worshiped with prayers the Supreme Personality of Godhead appearing as the sage Nara-Nārāyaṇa. The Lord glanced upon them with mercy and then departed for Gandhamādana Hill.

TEXT 59

ताविमौ वै भगवतो हरेरंशाविहागतौ ।
भारव्ययाय च भुवः कृष्णौ यदुकुरूद्वहौ ॥५९॥

tāv imau vai bhagavato
harer aṁśāv ihāgatau
bhāra-vyayāya ca bhuvaḥ
kṛṣṇau yadu-kurūdvahau

tau—both; *imau*—these; *vai*—certainly; *bhagavataḥ*—of the Supreme Personality of Godhead; *hareḥ*—of Hari; *aṁśau*—part and parcel expansion; *iha*—here (in this universe); *āgatau*—has appeared; *bhāra-vyayāya*—for mitigation of the burden; *ca*—and; *bhuvaḥ*—of the world; *kṛṣṇau*—the two Kṛṣṇas (Kṛṣṇa and Arjuna); *yadu-kuru-udvahau*—who are the best of the Yadu and Kuru dynasties respectively.

TRANSLATION

That Nara-Nārāyaṇa Ṛṣi, who is a partial expansion of Kṛṣṇa, has now appeared in the dynasties of Yadu and Kuru, in the forms of Kṛṣṇa and Arjuna respectively, to mitigate the burden of the world.

PURPORT

Nārāyaṇa is the Supreme Personality of Godhead, and Nara is a part of the Supreme Personality of Godhead, Nārāyaṇa. Thus the energy and the energetic together are the Supreme Personality of Godhead. Maitreya informed Vidura that Nara, the portion of Nārāyaṇa, had appeared in the family of the Kurus and that Nārāyaṇa, the plenary expansion of Kṛṣṇa, had come as Kṛṣṇa, the Supreme Personality of Godhead, with the purpose of delivering suffering humanity from the pangs of material burdens. In other words, Nārāyaṇa Ṛṣi was now present in the world in the forms of Kṛṣṇa and Arjuna.

TEXT 60

स्वाहाभिमानिनश्चाग्नेरात्मजांस्त्रीनजीजनत् ।
पावकं पवमानं च शुचिं च हुतभोजनम् ॥६०॥

svāhābhimāninaś cāgner
ātmajāṁs trīn ajījanat
pāvakaṁ pavamānaṁ ca
śuciṁ ca huta-bhojanam

svāhā—Svāhā, the wife of Agni; *abhimāninaḥ*—the presiding deity of fire; *ca*—and; *agneḥ*—from Agni; *ātmajān*—sons; *trīn*—three; *ajījanat*—produced; *pāvakam*—Pāvaka; *pavamānam ca*—and Pavamāna; *śucim ca*—and Śuci; *huta-bhojanam*—eating the oblations of sacrifice.

TRANSLATION

The predominating deity of fire begot in his wife, Svāhā, three children, named Pāvaka, Pavamāna and Śuci, who exist by eating the oblations offered to the fire of sacrifice.

PURPORT

After describing the descendants of the thirteen wives of Dharma, who were all daughters of Dakṣa, Maitreya now describes the fourteenth daughter of Dakṣa, Svāhā, and her three sons. Oblations offered in the sacrificial fire are meant for the demigods, and on behalf of the demigods the three sons of Agni and Svāhā, namely Pāvaka, Pavamāna and Śuci, accept the oblations.

TEXT 61

तेभ्योऽग्नयः समभवन् चत्वारिंशच्च पञ्च च ।
त एवैकोनपञ्चाशत्साकं पितृपितामहैः ॥६१॥

tebhyo 'gnayaḥ samabhavan
catvārimśac ca pañca ca
ta evaikonapañcāśat
sākaṁ pitṛ-pitāmahaiḥ

tebhyaḥ—from them; *agnayaḥ*—fire-gods; *samabhavan*—were produced; *catvārimśat*—forty; *ca*—and; *pañca*—five; *ca*—and; *te*—they; *eva*—certainly; *ekona-pañcāśat*—forty-nine; *sākam*—along with; *pitṛ-pitāmahaiḥ*—with the fathers and grandfather.

TRANSLATION

From those three sons another forty-five descendants were generated, who are also fire-gods. The total number of fire-gods is therefore forty-nine, including the fathers and the grandfather.

PURPORT

The grandfather is Agni, and the sons are Pāvaka, Pavamāna and Śuci. Counting these four, plus forty-five grandsons, there are altogether forty-nine different fire-gods.

TEXT 62

वैतानिके कर्मणि यन्नामभिर्ब्रह्मवादिभिः ।
आग्नेय्य इष्टयो यज्ञे निरूप्यन्तेऽग्नयस्तु ते ॥६२॥

vaitānike karmaṇi yan-
nāmabhir brahma-vādibhiḥ
āgneyya iṣṭayo yajñe
nirūpyante 'gnayas tu te

vaitānike—offering of oblations; *karmaṇi*—the activity; *yat*—of the fire-gods; *nāmabhiḥ*—by the names; *brahma-vādibhiḥ*—by impersonalist *brāhmaṇas; āgneyyaḥ*—for Agni; *iṣṭayaḥ*—sacrifices; *yajñe*—in the sacrifice; *nirūpyante*—are the objective; *agnayaḥ*—the forty-nine fire-gods; *tu*—but; *te*—those.

TRANSLATION

These forty-nine fire-gods are the beneficiaries of the oblations offered in the Vedic sacrificial fire by impersonalist brāhmaṇas.

PURPORT

Impersonalists who perform Vedic fruitive sacrifices are attracted to the various fire-gods and offer oblations in their name. The forty-nine fire-gods are described herewith.

TEXT 63

अग्निष्वात्ता बर्हिषदः सोम्याः पितर आज्यपाः ।
साग्नयोऽनग्नयस्तेषां पत्नी दाक्षायणी स्वधा ॥६३॥

agniṣvāttā barhiṣadaḥ
saumyāḥ pitara ājyapāḥ
sāgnayo 'nagnayas teṣāṁ
patnī dākṣāyaṇī svadhā

agniṣvāttāḥ—the Agniṣvāttas; *barhiṣadaḥ*—the Barhiṣadas; *saumyāḥ*—the Saumyas; *pitaraḥ*—the forefathers; *ājyapāḥ*—the Ājyapas; *sa-agnayaḥ*—those whose means is by fire; *anagnayaḥ*—those whose means is without fire; *teṣām*—of them; *patnī*—the wife; *dākṣāyaṇī*—the daughter of Dakṣa; *svadhā*—Svadhā.

TRANSLATION

The Agniṣvāttas, the Barhiṣadas, the Saumyas and the Ājyapas are the Pitās. They are either sāgnika or niragnika. The wife of all these Pitās is Svadhā, who is the daughter of King Dakṣa.

TEXT 64

तेभ्यो दधार कन्ये द्वे वयुनां धारिणीं स्वधा ।
उभे ते ब्रह्मवादिन्यौ ज्ञानविज्ञानपारगे ॥६४॥

tebhyo dadhāra kanye dve
vayunāṁ dhāriṇīṁ svadhā
ubhe te brahma-vādinyau
jñāna-vijñāna-pārage

tebhyaḥ—from them; *dadhāra*—produced; *kanye*—daughters; *dve*—two; *vayunām*—Vayunā; *dhāriṇīm*—Dhāriṇī; *svadhā*—Svadhā; *ubhe*—both of them; *te*—they; *brahma-vādinyau*—impersonalists; *jñāna-vijñāna-pāra-ge*—expert in both transcendental and Vedic knowledge.

TRANSLATION

Svadhā, who was offered to the Pitās, begot two daughters named Vayunā and Dhāriṇī, both of whom were impersonalists and were expert in transcendental and Vedic knowledge.

TEXT 65

भवस्य पत्नी तु सती भवं देवमनुव्रता ।
आत्मनः सदृशं पुत्रं न लेभे गुणशीलतः ॥६५॥

bhavasya patnī tu satī
bhavaṁ devam anuvratā
ātmanaḥ sadṛśaṁ putraṁ
na lebhe guṇa-śīlataḥ

bhavasya—of Bhava (Lord Śiva); *patnī*—the wife; *tu*—but; *satī*—named Satī; *bhavam*—to Bhava; *devam*—a demigod; *anuvratā*—faithfully engaged in service; *ātmanaḥ*—of herself; *sadṛśam*—similar; *putram*—a son; *na lebhe*—did not obtain; *guṇa-śīlataḥ*—by good qualities and by character.

TRANSLATION

The sixteenth daughter, whose name was Satī, was the wife of Lord Śiva. She could not produce a child, although she always faithfully engaged in the service of her husband.

TEXT 66

पितर्यप्रतिरूपे स्वे भवायानागसे रुषा ।
अप्रौढैवात्मनात्मानमजहाद्योगसंयुता ॥६६॥

pitary apratirūpe sve
bhavāyānāgase ruṣā
apraudhaivātmanātmānam
ajahād yoga-saṁyutā

pitari—as a father; *apratirūpe*—unfavorable; *sve*—her own; *bhavāya*—unto Lord Śiva; *anāgase*—faultless; *ruṣā*—with anger; *apraudhā*—before attaining maturity; *eva*—even; *ātmanā*—by herself; *ātmānam*—the body; *ajahāt*—gave up; *yoga-saṁyutā*—by mystic *yoga.*

TRANSLATION

The reason is that Satī's father, Dakṣa, used to rebuke Lord Śiva in spite of Śiva's faultlessness. Consequently, before attaining a mature age, Satī gave up her body by dint of yogic mystic power.

PURPORT

Lord Śiva, being the head of all mystic *yogīs,* never even constructed a home for his residence. Satī was the daughter of a great king, Dakṣa, and because his youngest daughter, Satī, selected as her husband Lord Śiva, King Dakṣa was not very much satisfied with her. Therefore whenever she met her father, he unnecessarily criticized her husband, although

Lord Śiva was faultless. Because of this, before attaining a mature age Satī gave up the body given by her father, Dakṣa, and therefore she could not produce a child.

Thus end the Bhaktivedanta purports of the Fourth Canto, First Chapter, of the Śrīmad-Bhāgavatam, *entitled "Genealogical Table of the Daughters of Manu."*

CHAPTER TWO

Dakṣa Curses Lord Śiva

TEXT 1

विदुर उवाच
भवे शीलवतां श्रेष्ठे दक्षो दुहितृवत्सलः ।
विद्वेषमकरोत्कस्मादनादृत्यात्मजां सतीम् ॥ १ ॥

vidura uvāca
bhave śīlavatāṁ śreṣṭhe
dakṣo duhitṛ-vatsalaḥ
vidveṣam akarot kasmād
anādṛtyātmajāṁ satīm

viduraḥ uvāca—Vidura said; *bhave*—towards Lord Śiva; *śīla-vatām*—among the gentle; *śreṣṭhe*—the best; *dakṣaḥ*—Dakṣa; *duhitṛ-vatsalaḥ*—being affectionate towards his daughter; *vidveṣam*—enmity; *akarot*—did exhibit; *kasmāt*—why; *anādṛtya*—neglecting; *ātmajām*—his own daughter; *satīm*—Satī.

TRANSLATION

Vidura inquired: Why was Dakṣa, who was so affectionate towards his daughter, envious of Lord Śiva, who is the best among the gentle? Why did he neglect his daughter Satī?

PURPORT

In the Second Chapter of the Fourth Canto, the cause of the dissension between Lord Śiva and Dakṣa, which was due to a great sacrifice arranged by Dakṣa for the pacification of the entire universe, is explained. Lord Śiva is described here as the best of the gentle because he is not envious of anyone, he is equal to all living entities, and all other good qualities are present in his personality. The word *śiva* means "all-auspicious." No one can be an enemy of Lord Śiva's, for he is so peaceful and renounced that he does not even construct a house for his residence, but lives underneath a tree, always detached from all worldly things. The personality of Lord Śiva symbolizes the best of gentleness. Why, then, was Dakṣa, who offered his beloved daughter to such a gentle personality, inimical towards Lord Śiva so intensely that Satī, the daughter of Dakṣa and wife of Lord Śiva, gave up her body?

TEXT 2

कस्तं चराचरगुरुं निर्वैरं शान्तविग्रहम् ।
आत्मारामं कथं द्वेष्टि जगतो दैवतं महत् ॥ २ ॥

kas taṁ carācara-guruṁ
nirvairaṁ śānta-vigraham
ātmārāmaṁ kathaṁ dveṣṭi
jagato daivataṁ mahat

kaḥ—who (Dakṣa); *tam*—him (Lord Śiva); *cara-acara*—of the whole world (both animate and inanimate); *gurum*—the spiritual master; *nirvairam*—without enmity; *śānta-vigraham*—having a peaceful personality; *ātma-ārāmam*—satisfied in himself; *katham*—how; *dveṣṭi*—hates; *jagataḥ*—of the universe; *daivatam*—demigod; *mahat*—the great.

TRANSLATION

Lord Śiva, the spiritual master of the entire world, is free from enmity, is a peaceful personality, and is always satisfied in himself. He is the greatest among the demigods. How is it possible that Dakṣa could be inimical towards such an auspicious personality?

PURPORT

Lord Śiva is described here as *carācara-guru,* the spiritual master of all animate and inanimate objects. He is sometimes known as Bhūtanātha, which means "the worshipable deity of the dull-headed." *Bhūta* is also sometimes taken to indicate the ghosts. Lord Śiva takes charge of reforming persons who are ghosts and demons, not to speak of others, who are godly; therefore he is the spiritual master of everyone, both the dull and demoniac and the highly learned Vaiṣṇavas. It is also stated, *vaiṣṇavānāṁ yathā śambhuḥ:* Śambhu, Lord Śiva, is the greatest of all Vaiṣṇavas. On one hand he is the worshipable object of the dull demons, and on the other he is the best of all Vaiṣṇavas, or devotees, and he has a *sampradāya* called the Rudra-sampradāya. Even if he is an enemy or is sometimes angry, such a personality cannot be the object of envy, so Vidura, in astonishment, asked why he was taken as such, especially by Dakṣa. Dakṣa is also not an ordinary person. He is a Prajāpati, in charge of fathering population, and all his daughters are highly elevated, especially Satī. The word *satī* means "the most chaste." Whenever there is consideration of chastity, Satī, this wife of Lord Śiva and daughter of Dakṣa, is considered first. Vidura, therefore, was astonished. "Dakṣa is such a great man," he thought, "and is the father of Satī. And Lord Śiva is the spiritual master of everyone. How then could there possibly be so much enmity between them that Satī, the most chaste goddess, could give up her body because of their quarrel?"

TEXT 3

एतदाख्याहि मे ब्रह्मन् जामातुः श्वशुरस्य च ।
विद्वेषस्तु यतः प्राणांस्तत्यजे दुस्त्यजान्सती ॥ ३ ॥

etad ākhyāhi me brahman
jāmātuḥ śvaśurasya ca
vidveṣas tu yataḥ prāṇāṁs
tatyaje dustyajān satī

etat—thus; *ākhyāhi*—please tell; *me*—to me; *brahman*—O *brāhmaṇa; jāmātuḥ*—of the son-in-law (Lord Śiva); *śvaśurasya*—of the father-in-law (Dakṣa); *ca*—and; *vidveṣaḥ*—quarrel; *tu*—as to; *yataḥ*—from what cause; *prāṇān*—her life; *tatyaje*—gave up; *dustyajān*—which is impossible to give up; *satī*—Satī.

TRANSLATION

My dear Maitreya, to part with one's life is very difficult. Would you kindly explain to me how such a son-in-law and father-in-law

could quarrel so bitterly that the great goddess Satī could give up her life?

TEXT 4

मैत्रेय उवाच
पुरा विश्वसृजां सत्रे समेताः परमर्षयः ।
तथामरगणाः सर्वे सानुगा मुनयोऽग्नयः ॥ ४ ॥

maitreya uvāca
purā viśva-sṛjāṁ satre
sametāḥ paramarṣayaḥ
tathāmara-gaṇāḥ sarve
sānugā munayo 'gnayaḥ

maitreyaḥ uvāca—the sage Maitreya said; *purā*—formerly (at the time of Svāyambhuva Manu); *viśva-sṛjām*—of the creators of the universe; *satre*—at a sacrifice; *sametāḥ*—were assembled; *paramarṣayaḥ*—the great sages; *tathā*—and also; *amara-gaṇāḥ*—the demigods; *sarve*—all; *sa-anugāḥ*—along with their followers; *munayaḥ*—the philosophers; *agnayaḥ*—the fire-gods.

TRANSLATION

The sage Maitreya said: In a former time, the leaders of the universal creation performed a great sacrifice in which all the great sages, philosophers, demigods and fire-gods assembled with their followers.

PURPORT

Upon being asked by Vidura, the sage Maitreya began to explain the cause of the misunderstanding between Lord Śiva and Dakṣa, because of which the goddess Satī gave up her body. Thus begins the history of a great sacrifice performed by the leaders of the universal creation, namely Marīci, Dakṣa and Vasiṣṭha. These great personalities arranged for a great sacrifice, for which demigods like Indra and the fire-gods assembled with their followers. Lord Brahmā and Lord Śiva were also present.

TEXT 5

तत्र प्रविष्टमृषयो दृष्ट्वार्कमिव रोचिषा ।
भ्राजमानं वितिमिरं कुर्वन्तं तन्महत्सदः ॥ ५ ॥

tatra praviṣṭam ṛṣayo
dṛṣṭvārkam iva rociṣā
bhrājamānaṁ vitimiraṁ
kurvantaṁ tan mahat sadaḥ

tatra—there; *praviṣṭam*—having entered; *ṛṣayaḥ*—the sages; *dṛṣṭvā*—seeing; *arkam*—the sun; *iva*—just like; *rociṣā*—with luster; *bhrājamānam*—shining; *vitimiram*—free from darkness; *kurvantam*—making; *tat*—that; *mahat*—great; *sadaḥ*—assembly.

TRANSLATION

When Dakṣa, the leader of the Prajāpatis, entered that assembly, his personal bodily luster as bright as the effulgence of the sun, the entire assembly was illuminated, and all the assembled personalities became insignificant in his presence.

TEXT 6

उदतिष्ठन् सदस्यास्ते स्वधिष्ण्येभ्यः सहाग्नयः ।
ऋते विरिञ्चां शर्वं च तद्भासाक्षिप्तचेतसः ॥ ६ ॥

udatiṣṭhan sadasyās te
sva-dhiṣṇyebhyaḥ sahāgnayaḥ
ṛte viriñcāṁ śarvaṁ ca
tad-bhāsākṣipta-cetasaḥ

udatiṣṭhan—stood up; *sadasyāḥ*—the members of the assembly; *te*—they; *sva-dhiṣṇyebhyaḥ*—from their own seats; *saha-agnayaḥ*—along with the fire-gods; *ṛte*—except for; *viriñcām*—Brahmā; *śarvam*—Śiva; *ca*—and; *tat*—his (Dakṣa's); *bhāsa*—by the luster; *ākṣipta*—are influenced; *cetasaḥ*—those whose minds.

TRANSLATION

Influenced by his personal bodily luster, all the fire-gods and other participants in that great assembly, with the exceptions of Lord Brahmā and Lord Śiva, gave up their own sitting places and stood in respect for Dakṣa.

TEXT 7

सदसस्पतिभिर्दक्षो भगवान् साधु सत्कृतः ।
अजं लोकगुरुं नत्वा निषसाद तदाज्ञया ॥ ७ ॥

sadasas-patibhir dakṣo
bhagavān sādhu sat-kṛtaḥ
ajaṁ loka-guruṁ natvā
niṣasāda tad-ājñayā

sadasaḥ—of the assembly; *patibhiḥ*—by the leaders; *dakṣaḥ*—Dakṣa; *bhagavān*—the possessor of all opulences; *sādhu*—properly; *sat-kṛtaḥ*—was welcomed; *ajam*—to the unborn (Brahmā); *loka-gurum*—to the teacher of the universe; *natvā*—making obeisances; *niṣasāda*—sat down; *tat-ājñayā*—by his (Brahmā's) order.

TRANSLATION

Dakṣa was adequately welcomed by the president of the great assembly, Lord Brahmā. After offering Lord Brahmā respect, Dakṣa, by the order of Brahmā, properly took his seat.

TEXT 8

प्राङ्निषण्णं मृडं दृष्ट्वा नामृष्यत्तदनादृतः ।
उवाच वामं चक्षुर्भ्यामभिवीक्ष्य दहन्निव ॥ ८ ॥

prāṅ-niṣaṇṇaṁ mṛḍaṁ dṛṣṭvā
nāmṛṣyat tad-anādṛtaḥ
uvāca vāmaṁ cakṣurbhyām
abhivīkṣya dahann iva

prāk—before; *niṣaṇṇam*—being seated; *mṛḍam*—Lord Śiva; *dṛṣṭvā*—seeing; *na amṛṣyat*—did not tolerate; *tat*—by him (Śiva); *anādṛtaḥ*—not being respected; *uvāca*—said; *vāmam*—dishonest; *cakṣurbhyām*—with both eyes; *abhivīkṣya*—looking at; *dahan*—burning; *iva*—as if.

TRANSLATION

Before taking his seat, however, Dakṣa was very much offended to see Lord Śiva sitting and not showing him any respect. At that time, Dakṣa became greatly angry, and, his eyes glowing, he began to speak very strongly against Lord Śiva.

PURPORT

Lord Śiva, being the son-in-law of Dakṣa, was expected to show his father-in-law respect by standing with the others, but because Lord Brahmā and Lord Śiva are the principal demigods, their positions are greater than Dakṣa's. Dakṣa, however, could not tolerate this, and he took it as an insult by his son-in-law. Previously, also, he was not very much satisfied with Lord Śiva, for Śiva looked very poor and was niggardly in dress.

TEXT 9

श्रूयतां ब्रह्मर्षयो मे सहदेवाः सहाग्नयः ।
साधूनां ब्रुवतो वृत्तं नाज्ञानान्न च मत्सरात् ॥ ९ ॥

śrūyatāṁ brahmarṣayo me
saha-devāḥ sahāgnayaḥ
sādhūnāṁ bruvato vṛttaṁ
nājñānān na ca matsarāt

śrūyatām—hear; *brahma-ṛṣayaḥ*—O sages among the *brāhmaṇas;* *me*—unto me; *saha-devāḥ*—O demigods; *saha-agnayaḥ*—O fire-gods; *sādhūnām*—of the gentle; *bruvataḥ*—speaking; *vṛttam*—the manners; *na*—not; *ajñānāt*—from ignorance; *na ca*—and not; *matsarāt*—from envy.

TRANSLATION

All sages, brāhmaṇas and fire-gods present, please hear me with attention, for I speak about the manners of gentle persons. I do not speak out of ignorance or envy.

PURPORT

In speaking against Lord Śiva, Dakṣa tried to pacify the assembly by presenting in a very tactful way that he was going to speak about the manners of gentle persons, although naturally this might affect some unmannerly upstarts and the assembly might be unhappy because they did not want even unmannerly persons to be offended. In other words, he was in complete knowledge that he was speaking against Lord Śiva in spite of Śiva's spotless character. As far as envy is concerned, from the very beginning he was envious of Lord Śiva; therefore he could not distinguish his own particular envy. Although he spoke like a man in ignorance, he wanted to cover his statements by saying that he was not speaking for impudent and envious reasons.

TEXT 10

अयं तु लोकपालानां यशोघ्नो निरपत्रपः ।
सद्भिराचरितः पन्था येन स्तब्धेन दूषितः ॥१०॥

ayaṁ tu loka-pālānāṁ
yaśo-ghno nirapatrapaḥ
sadbhir ācaritaḥ panthā
yena stabdhena dūṣitaḥ

ayam—he (Śiva); *tu*—but; *loka-pālānām*—of the governors of the universe; *yaśaḥ-ghnaḥ*—spoiling the fame; *nirapatrapaḥ*—shameless; *sadbhiḥ*—by those of gentle manner; *ācaritaḥ*—followed; *panthāḥ*—the path; *yena*—by whom (Śiva); *stabdhena*—being devoid of proper actions; *dūṣitaḥ*—is polluted.

TRANSLATION

Śiva has spoiled the name and fame of the governors of the universe and has polluted the path of gentle manners. Because he is shameless, he does not know how to act.

PURPORT

Dakṣa wanted to impress upon the minds of all the great sages assembled in that meeting that Śiva, being one of the demigods, had ruined the good reputations of all the demigods by his unmannerly behavior. The words used against Lord Śiva by Dakṣa can also be understood in a different way, in a good sense. For example, he stated that Śiva is *yaśo-ghna*, which means "one who spoils name and fame." So this can also be interpreted to mean that he was so famous that his fame killed all other fame. Again, Dakṣa used the word *nirapatrapa*, which also can be used in two senses. One sense is "one who is stunted," and another sense is "one who is the maintainer of persons who have no other shelter." Generally Lord Śiva is known as the lord of the *bhūtas*, or lower grade of living creatures. They take shelter of Lord Śiva because he is very kind to everyone and is very quickly satisfied. Therefore he is called Āśutoṣa. To such men, who cannot approach other demigods or Viṣṇu, Lord Śiva gives shelter. Therefore the word *nirapatrapa* can be used in that sense.

TEXT 11

एष मे शिष्यतां प्राप्तो यन्मे दुहितुरग्रहीत् ।
पाणिं विप्राग्निमुखतः सावित्र्या इव साधुवत् ॥११॥

eṣa me śiṣyatāṁ prāpto
yan me duhitur agrahīt
pāṇiṁ viprāgni-mukhataḥ
sāvitryā iva sādhuvat

eṣaḥ—he (Śiva); *me*—my; *śiṣyatām*—subordinate position; *prāptaḥ*—accepted; *yat*—because; *me duhituḥ*—of my daughter; *agrahīt*—he took; *pāṇim*—the hand; *vipra-agni*—of *brāhmaṇas* and fire; *mukhataḥ*—in the presence; *sāvitryāḥ*—Gāyatrī; *iva*—like; *sādhuvat*—like an honest person.

TRANSLATION

He has already accepted himself as my subordinate by marrying my daughter in the presence of fire and brāhmaṇas. He has married my daughter, who is equal to Gāyatrī, and has pretended to be just like an honest person.

PURPORT

Dakṣa's statement that Lord Śiva pretended to be an honest person means that Śiva was dishonest because in spite of accepting the position of Dakṣa's son-in-law, he was not respectful to Dakṣa.

TEXT 12

गृहीत्वा मृगशावाक्ष्याः पाणिं मर्कटलोचनः ।
प्रत्युत्थानाभिवादार्हे वाचाप्यकृत नोचितम् ॥१२॥

gṛhītvā mṛga-śāvākṣyāḥ
pāṇiṁ markaṭa-locanaḥ
pratyutthānābhivādārhe
vācāpy akṛta nocitam

gṛhītvā—taking; *mṛga-śāva*—like a deer cub; *akṣyāḥ*—of her who has eyes; *pāṇim*—the hand; *markaṭa*—of a monkey; *locanaḥ*—he who has the eyes; *pratyutthāna*—of rising from one's seat; *abhivāda*—the honor; *arhe*—to me, who deserves; *vācā*—with sweet words; *api*—even; *akṛta na*—he did not do; *ucitam*—honor.

TRANSLATION

He has eyes like a monkey's, yet he has married my daughter, whose eyes are just like those of a deer cub. Nevertheless he did not stand up to receive me, nor did he think it fit to welcome me with sweet words.

TEXT 13

लुप्तक्रियायाशुचये मानिने भिन्नसेतवे ।
अनिच्छन्नप्यदां बालां शूद्रायेवोशतीं गिरम् ॥१३॥

lupta-kriyāyāśucaye
mānine bhinna-setave
anicchann apy adāṁ bālāṁ
śūdrāyevośatīṁ giram

lupta-kriyāya—not observing rules and regulations; *aśucaye*—impure; *mānine*—proud; *bhinna-setave*—having broken all rules of civility; *anicchan*—not desiring; *api*—although; *adām*—handed over; *bālām*—my daughter; *śūdrāya*—unto a *śūdra; iva*—as; *uśatīm giram*—the message of the *Vedas.*

TRANSLATION

I had no desire to give my daughter to this person, who has broken all rules of civility. Because of not observing the required rules and regulations, he is impure, but I was obliged to hand over my daughter to him just as one teaches the messages of the Vedas to a śūdra.

PURPORT

A *śūdra* is forbidden to take lessons from the *Vedas* because a *śūdra*, due to his unclean habits, is not worthy to hear such instructions. This restriction, that unless one has acquired the brahminical qualifications one should not read the Vedic literatures, is like the restriction that a law student should not enter a law college unless he has been graduated from all lower grades. According to the estimation of Dakṣa, Śiva was unclean in habits and not worthy to have the hand of his daughter, Satī, who was so enlightened, beautiful and chaste. The word used in this connection is *bhinna-setave*, which refers to one who has broken all the regulations for good behavior by not following the Vedic principles. In other words, according to Dakṣa the entire transaction of the marriage of his daughter with Śiva was not in order.

TEXTS 14–15

प्रेतावासेषु घोरेषु प्रेतैर्भूतगणैर्वृतः ।
अटत्युन्मत्तवन्नग्नो व्युप्तकेशो हसन् रुदन् ॥१४॥
चिताभस्मकृतस्नानः प्रेतस्रङ्न्रस्थिभूषणः ।
शिवापदेशो ह्यशिवो मत्तो मत्तजनप्रियः ।
पतिः प्रमथनाथानां तमोमात्रात्मकात्मनाम् ॥१५॥

pretāvāseṣu ghoreṣu
pretair bhūta-gaṇair vṛtaḥ

aṭaty unmattavan nagno
vyupta-keśo hasan rudan

citā-bhasma-kṛta-snānaḥ
preta-sraṅ-nrasthi-bhūṣaṇaḥ
śivāpadeśo hy aśivo
matto matta-jana-priyaḥ
patiḥ pramatha-nāthānāṁ
tamo-mātrātmakātmanām

preta-āvāseṣu—at the burning places of dead bodies; *ghoreṣu*—horrible; *pretaiḥ*—by the Pretas; *bhūta-gaṇaiḥ*—by the Bhūtas; *vṛtaḥ*—accompanied by; *aṭati*—he wanders; *unmatta-vat*—like a madman; *nagnaḥ*—naked; *vyupta-keśaḥ*—having scattered hair; *hasan*—laughing; *rudan*—crying; *citā*—of the funeral pyre; *bhasma*—with the ashes; *kṛta-snānaḥ*—taking bath; *preta*—of the skulls of dead bodies; *srak*—having a garland; *nṛ-asthi-bhūṣaṇaḥ*—ornamented with dead men's bones; *śiva-apadeśaḥ*—who is *śiva*, or auspicious, only in name; *hi*—for; *aśivaḥ*—inauspicious; *mattaḥ*—crazy; *matta-jana-priyaḥ*—very dear to the crazy beings; *patiḥ*—the leader; *pramatha-nāthānām*—of the lords of the Pramathas; *tamaḥ-mātra-ātmaka-ātmanām*—of those grossly in the mode of ignorance.

TRANSLATION

He lives in filthy places like crematoriums, and his companions are the ghosts and demons. Naked like a madman, sometimes laughing and sometimes crying, he smears crematorium ashes all over his body. He does not bathe regularly, and he ornaments his body with a garland of skulls and bones. Therefore only in name is he Śiva, or auspicious; actually, he is the most mad and inauspicious creature. Thus he is very dear to crazy beings in the gross mode of ignorance, and he is their leader.

PURPORT

Those who do not regularly bathe are supposed to be in association with ghosts and crazy creatures. Lord Śiva appeared to be like that, but his name, Śiva, is actually fitting, for he is very kind to persons who are in the darkness of the mode of ignorance, such as unclean drunkards who do not regularly bathe. Lord Śiva is so kind that he gives shelter to such creatures and gradually elevates them to spiritual consciousness. Although it is very difficult to raise such creatures to spiritual understanding, Lord Śiva takes charge of them, and therefore, as stated in the *Vedas*, Lord Śiva is all-auspicious. Thus by his association even such fallen souls can be elevated. Sometimes it is seen that great personalities meet with fallen souls, not for any personal interest but for the benefit of those souls. In the creation of the Lord there are different kinds of living creatures. Some of them are in the mode of goodness, some are in the mode of passion, and some are in the mode of ignorance. Lord Viṣṇu takes charge of persons who are advanced Kṛṣṇa conscious Vaiṣṇavas, and Lord Brahmā takes charge of persons who are very much attached to material activities, but Lord Śiva is so kind that he takes charge of persons who are in gross ignorance and whose behavior is lower than that of the animals. Therefore Lord Śiva is especially called auspicious.

TEXT 16

तस्मा उन्मादनाथाय नष्टशौचाय दुर्हृदे ।
दत्ता बत मया साध्वी चोदिते परमेष्ठिना ॥१६॥

tasmā unmāda-nāthāya
naṣṭa-śaucāya durhṛde
dattā bata mayā sādhvī
codite parameṣṭhinā

tasmai—to him; *unmāda-nāthāya*—to the lord of ghosts; *naṣṭa-śaucāya*—being devoid of all cleanliness; *durhṛde*—heart filled with nasty things; *dattā*—was given; *bata*—alas; *mayā*—by me; *sādhvī*—Satī; *codite*—being requested; *parameṣṭhinā*—by the supreme teacher (Brahmā).

TRANSLATION

On the request of Lord Brahmā I handed over my chaste daughter to him, although he is devoid of all cleanliness and his heart is filled with nasty things.

PURPORT

It is the duty of parents to hand over their daughters to suitable persons just befitting their family tradition in cleanliness, gentle behavior, wealth, social position, etc. Dakṣa was repentant that on the request of Brahmā, who was his father, he had handed over his daughter to a person who, according to his calculation, was nasty. He was so angry that he did not acknowledge that the request was from his father. Instead, he referred to Brahmā as *parameṣṭhī*, the supreme teacher in the universe; because of his temperament of gross anger, he was not even prepared to accept Brahmā as his father. In other words, he accused even Brahmā of being less intelligent because he had advised Dakṣa to hand over his beautiful daughter to such a nasty fellow. In anger one forgets everything, and thus Dakṣa, in anger, not only accused the great Lord Śiva, but criticized his own father, Lord Brahmā, for his not very astute advice that Dakṣa hand over his daughter to Lord Śiva.

TEXT 17

मैत्रेय उवाच
विनिन्द्यैवं स गिरिशमप्रतीपमवस्थितम् ।
दक्षोऽथाप उपस्पृश्य क्रुद्धः शप्तुं प्रचक्रमे ॥१७॥

maitreya uvāca
vinindyaivaṁ sa giriśam
apratīpam avasthitam
dakṣo 'thāpa upaspṛśya
kruddhaḥ śaptuṁ pracakrame

maitreyaḥ uvāca—Maitreya said; *vinindya*—abusing; *evam*—thus; *saḥ*—he (Dakṣa); *giriśam*—Śiva; *apratīpam*—without any hostility; *avasthitam*—remaining; *dakṣaḥ*—Dakṣa; *atha*—now; *apaḥ*—water; *upaspṛśya*—washing hands and mouth; *kruddhaḥ*—angry; *śaptum*—to curse; *pracakrame*—began to.

TRANSLATION

The sage Maitreya continued: Thus Dakṣa, seeing Lord Śiva sitting as if against him, washed his hands and mouth and cursed him in the following words.

TEXT 18

अयं तु देवयजन इन्द्रोपेन्द्रादिभिर्भवः ।
सह भागं न लभतां देवैर्देवगणाधमः ॥१८॥

ayaṁ tu deva-yajana
indropendrādibhir bhavaḥ
saha bhāgaṁ na labhatāṁ
devair deva-gaṇādhamaḥ

ayam—that; *tu*—but; *deva-yajane*—in the sacrifice of the demigods; *indra-upendra-ādibhiḥ*—with Indra, Upendra and the others; *bhavaḥ*—Śiva; *saha*—along with; *bhāgam*—a portion; *na*—not; *labhatām*—should obtain; *devaiḥ*—with the demigods; *deva-gaṇa-adhamaḥ*—the lowest of all the demigods.

TRANSLATION

The demigods are eligible to share in the oblations of sacrifice, but Lord Śiva, who is the lowest of all the demigods, should not have a share.

PURPORT

Because of this curse, Śiva was deprived of his share in the oblations of Vedic sacrifices. It was due to the curse of Dakṣa, Śrī Viśvanātha Cakravartī comments in this connection, that Lord Śiva was saved from the calamity of taking part with other demigods, who were all materialistic. Lord Śiva is the greatest devotee of the Supreme Personality of Godhead, and it is not fitting for him to eat or sit with materialistic persons like the demigods. Thus the curse of Dakṣa was indirectly a blessing, for Śiva would not have to eat or sit with other demigods, who were too materialistic. There is a practical example set for us by Gaurakiśora dāsa Bābājī Mahārāja, who used to sit on the side of a latrine to chant Hare Kṛṣṇa. Many materialistic persons used to come and bother him and disturb his daily routine of chanting, so to avoid their company he used to sit by the side of a latrine, where materialistic persons would not go because of the filth and the obnoxious smell. However, Gaurakiśora dāsa Bābājī Mahārāja was so great that he was accepted as the spiritual master of such a great personality as His Divine Grace Oṁ Viṣṇupāda Śrī Śrīmad

Bhaktisiddhānta Sarasvatī Gosvāmī Mahārāja. The conclusion is that Lord Śiva behaved in his own way to avoid materialistic persons who might disturb him in his prosecution of devotional service.

TEXT 19

निषिध्यमानः स सदस्यमुख्यै-
र्दक्षो गिरित्राय विसृज्य शापम् ।
तस्माद्विनिष्क्रम्य विवृद्धमन्यु-
र्जगाम कौरव्य निजं निकेतनम् ॥१९॥

niṣidhyamānaḥ sa sadasya-mukhyair
dakṣo giritrāya visṛjya śāpam
tasmād viniṣkramya vivṛddha-manyur
jagāma kauravya nijaṁ niketanam

niṣidhyamānaḥ—being requested not to; *saḥ*—he (Dakṣa); *sadasya-mukhyaiḥ*—by the members of the sacrifice; *dakṣaḥ*—Dakṣa; *giri-trāya*—to Śiva; *visṛjya*—giving; *śāpam*—a curse; *tasmāt*—from that place; *viniṣkramya*—going out; *vivṛddha-manyuḥ*—being exceedingly angry; *jagāma*—went; *kauravya*—O Vidura; *nijam*—to his own; *niketanam*—home.

TRANSLATION

Maitreya continued: My dear Vidura, in spite of the requests of all the members of the sacrificial assembly, Dakṣa, in great anger, cursed Lord Śiva and then left the assembly and went back to his home.

PURPORT

Anger is so detrimental that even a great personality like Dakṣa, out of anger, left the arena where Brahmā was presiding and all the great sages and pious and saintly persons were assembled. All of them requested him not to leave, but, infuriated, he left, thinking that the auspicious place was not fit for him. Puffed up by his exalted position, he thought that no one was greater than he in argument. It appears that all the members of the assembly, including Lord Brahmā, requested him not to be angry and leave their company, but in spite of all these requests, he left. That is the effect of cruel anger. In *Bhagavad-gītā*, therefore, it is advised that one who desires to make tangible advancement in spiritual consciousness must avoid three things—lust, anger and the mode of passion. Actually we can see that lust, anger and passion make a man crazy, even though he be as great as Dakṣa. The very name Dakṣa suggests that he was expert in all material activities, but still, because of his aversion towards such a saintly personality as Śiva, he was attacked by these three enemies—anger, lust and passion. Lord Caitanya, therefore, advised that one be very careful not to offend Vaiṣṇavas. He compared offenses toward a Vaiṣṇava to a mad elephant. As a mad elephant can do anything horrible, so when a person offends a Vaiṣṇava he can perform any abominable action.

TEXT 20

विज्ञाय शापं गिरिशानुगाग्रणी-
नन्दीश्वरो रोषकषायदूषितः ।
दक्षाय शापं विससर्ज दारुणं
ये चान्वमोदंस्तदवाच्यतां द्विजाः ॥२०॥

vijñāya śāpaṁ giriśānugāgraṇīr
nandīśvaro roṣa-kaṣāya-dūṣitaḥ
dakṣāya śāpaṁ visasarja dāruṇaṁ
ye cānvamodaṁs tad-avācyatāṁ dvijāḥ

vijñāya—understanding; *śāpam*—the curse; *giriśa*—of Śiva; *anuga-agraṇīḥ*—one of the principal associates; *nandīśvaraḥ*—Nandīśvara; *roṣa*—anger; *kaṣāya*—red; *dūṣitaḥ*—blinded; *dakṣāya*—to Dakṣa; *śāpam*—a curse; *visasarja*—gave; *dāruṇam*—harsh; *ye*—who; *ca*—and; *anvamodan*—tolerated; *tat-avācyatām*—the cursing of Śiva; *dvijāḥ*—*brāhmaṇas*.

TRANSLATION

Upon understanding that Lord Śiva had been cursed, Nandīśvara, one of Lord Śiva's principal associates, became greatly angry. His eyes became red, and he prepared to curse Dakṣa and all the brāhmaṇas present there who had tolerated Dakṣa's cursing Śiva in harsh words.

PURPORT

There is a long-standing dissension among some of the neophyte Vaiṣṇavas and Śaivites; they are always at loggerheads. When Dakṣa cursed Lord Śiva in harsh words, some of the *brāhmaṇas* present might have enjoyed it because some *brāhmaṇas* do not very much admire Lord Śiva. This is due to their ignorance of Lord Śiva's position. Nandīśvara was affected by the cursing, but he did not follow the example of Lord Śiva, who was also present there. Although Lord Śiva could also have cursed Dakṣa in a similar way, he was silent and tolerant; but Nandīśvara, his follower, was not tolerant. Of course, as a follower it was right for him not to tolerate an insult to his master, but he should not have cursed the *brāhmaṇas* who were present. The entire issue was so complicated that those who were not strong enough forgot their positions, and thus cursing and countercursing went on in that great assembly. In other words, the material field is so unsteady that even personalities like Nandīśvara, Dakṣa and many of the *brāhmaṇas* present were infected by the atmosphere of anger.

TEXT 21

य एतन्मर्त्यमुद्दिश्य भगवत्यप्रतिद्रुहि ।
द्रुह्यत्यज्ञः पृथग्दृष्टिस्तत्त्वतो विमुखो भवेत् ॥२१॥

ya etan martyam uddiśya
bhagavaty apratidruhi
druhyaty ajñaḥ pṛthag-dṛṣṭis
tattvato vimukho bhavet

yaḥ—who (Dakṣa); *etat martyam*—this body; *uddiśya*—with reference to; *bhagavati*—to Śiva; *apratidruhi*—who is not envious;

druhyati—bears envy; *ajñaḥ*—less intelligent persons; *pṛthak-dṛṣṭiḥ*—the vision of duality; *tattvataḥ*—from transcendental knowledge; *vimukhaḥ*—bereft; *bhavet*—may become.

TRANSLATION

Anyone who has accepted Dakṣa as the most important personality and neglected Lord Śiva because of envy is less intelligent and, because of visualizing in duality, will be bereft of transcendental knowledge.

PURPORT

The first curse by Nandīśvara was that anyone supporting Dakṣa was foolishly identifying himself with the body, and therefore, because Dakṣa had no transcendental knowledge, supporting him would deprive one of transcendental knowledge. Dakṣa, Nandīśvara said, identified himself with the body like other materialistic persons and was trying to derive all kinds of facilities in relationship with the body. He had excessive attachment for the body and, in relation to the body, with wife, children, home and other such things, which are different from the soul. Therefore Nandīśvara's curse was that anyone who supported Dakṣa would be bereft of transcendental knowledge of the soul and thus also be deprived of knowledge of the Supreme Personality of Godhead.

TEXT 22

गृहेषु कूटधर्मेषु सक्तो ग्राम्यसुखेच्छया ।
कर्मतन्त्रं वितनुते वेदवादविपन्नधीः ॥२२॥

gṛheṣu kūṭa-dharmeṣu
sakto grāmya-sukhecchayā
karma-tantraṁ vitanute
veda-vāda-vipanna-dhīḥ

gṛheṣu—in householder life; *kūṭa-dharmeṣu*—of pretentious religiosity; *saktaḥ*—being attracted; *grāmya-sukha-icchayā*—by desire for material happiness; *karma-tantram*—fruitive activities; *vitanute*—he performs; *veda-vāda*—by the explanations of the *Vedas; vipanna-dhīḥ*—intelligence being lost.

TRANSLATION

Pretentiously religious householder life, in which one is attracted to material happiness and thus also attracted to the superficial explanation of the Vedas, robs one of all intelligence and attaches one to fruitive activities as all in all.

PURPORT

Persons who identify with bodily existence are attached to the fruitive activities described in the Vedic literature. For example, in the *Vedas* it is said that one who observes the *cāturmāsya* vow will attain eternal happiness in the heavenly kingdom. In *Bhagavad-gītā*, it is said that this flowery language of the *Vedas* mostly attracts persons who identify with the body. To them such happiness as that of the heavenly kingdom is everything; they do not know that beyond that is the spiritual kingdom, or kingdom of God, and they have no knowledge that one can go there. Thus they are bereft of transcendental knowledge. Such persons are very careful in observing the rules and regulations of household life in order to be promoted in the next life to the moon or other heavenly planets. It is stated here that such persons are attached to *grāmya-sukha*, which means "material happiness," without knowledge of eternal, blissful spiritual life.

TEXT 23

बुद्‌ध्या पराभिध्यायिन्या विस्मृतात्मगतिः पशुः ।
स्त्रीकामः सोऽस्त्वतितरां दक्षो बस्तमुखोऽचिरात् ॥२३॥

buddhyā parābhidhyāyinyā
vismṛtātma-gatiḥ paśuḥ
strī-kāmaḥ so 'stv atitarāṁ
dakṣo basta-mukho 'cirāt

buddhyā—by intelligence; *para-abhidhyāyinyā*—by accepting the body as the self; *vismṛta-ātma-gatiḥ*—having forgotten the knowledge of Viṣṇu; *paśuḥ*—an animal; *strī-kāmaḥ*—attached to sex life; *saḥ*—he (Dakṣa); *astu*—let; *atitarām*—excessive; *dakṣaḥ*—Dakṣa; *basta-mukhaḥ*—the face of a goat; *acirāt*—in a very short time.

TRANSLATION

Dakṣa has accepted the body as all in all. Therefore, since he has forgotten the viṣṇu-pāda, or viṣṇu-gati, and is attached to sex life only, within a short time he will have the face of a goat.

TEXT 24

विद्याबुद्धिरविद्यायां कर्ममय्यामसौ जडः ।
संसरन्त्विह ये चामुमनु शर्वावमानिनम् ॥२४॥

vidyā-buddhir avidyāyāṁ
karmamayyām asau jaḍaḥ
saṁsarantv iha ye cāmum
anu śarvāvamāninam

vidyā-buddhiḥ—materialistic education and intelligence; *avidyā-yām*—in nescience; *karma-mayyām*—formed of fruitive activities; *asau*—he (Dakṣa); *jaḍaḥ*—dull; *saṁsarantu*—let them take birth again and again; *iha*—here in this world; *ye*—who; *ca*—and; *amum*—Dakṣa; *anu*—following; *śarva*—Śiva; *avamāninam*—insulting.

TRANSLATION

Those who have become as dull as matter by cultivating materialistic education and intelligence are nesciently involved in fruitive activities. Such men have purposely insulted Lord Śiva. May they continue in the cycle of repeated birth and death.

PURPORT

The three curses mentioned above are sufficient to make one as dull as stone, void of spiritual knowledge and preoccupied with materialistic education, which is nescience. After uttering these curses, Nandīśvara then cursed the *brāhmaṇas* to continue in the cycle of birth and death because of their supporting Dakṣa in blaspheming Lord Śiva.

TEXT 25

गिरः श्रुतायाः पुष्पिण्या मधुगन्धेन भूरिणा ।
मथ्ना चोन्मथितात्मानः सम्मुह्यन्तु हरद्विषः ॥२५॥

giraḥ śrutāyāḥ puṣpiṇyā
madhu-gandhena bhūriṇā
mathnā conmathitātmānaḥ
sammuhyantu hara-dviṣaḥ

giraḥ—words; *śrutāyāḥ*—of the *Vedas; puṣpiṇyāḥ*—flowery; *madhu-gandhena*—with the scent of honey; *bhūriṇā*—profuse; *mathnā*—enchanting; *ca*—and; *unmathita-ātmānaḥ*—whose minds have become dull; *sammuhyantu*—let them remain attached; *hara-dviṣaḥ*—envious of Lord Śiva.

TRANSLATION

May those who are envious of Lord Śiva, being attracted by the flowery language of the enchanting Vedic promises, and who have thus become dull, always remain attached to fruitive activities.

PURPORT

The Vedic promises of elevation to higher planets for a better standard of materialistic life are compared to flowery language because in a flower there is certainly an aroma but that aroma does not last for a very long time. In a flower there is honey, but that honey is not eternal.

TEXT 26

सर्वभक्षा द्विजा वृत्त्यै धृतविद्यातपोव्रताः ।
वित्तदेहेन्द्रियारामा याचका विचरन्त्विह ॥२६॥

sarva-bhakṣā dvijā vṛttyai
dhṛta-vidyā-tapo-vratāḥ

vitta-dehendriyārāmā
yācakā vicarantv iha

sarva-bhakṣāḥ—eating everything; *dvijāḥ*—the *brāhmaṇas; vṛttyai*—for maintaining the body; *dhṛta-vidyā*—having taken to education; *tapaḥ*—austerity; *vratāḥ*—and vows; *vitta*—money; *deha*—the body; *indriya*—the senses; *ārāmāḥ*—the satisfaction; *yācakāḥ*—as beggars; *vicarantu*—let them wander; *iha*—here.

TRANSLATION

These brāhmaṇas take to education, austerity and vows only for the purpose of maintaining the body. They shall be devoid of discrimination between what to eat and what not to eat. They will acquire money, begging from door to door, simply for the satisfaction of the body.

PURPORT

The third curse inflicted by Nandīśvara on the *brāhmaṇas* who supported Dakṣa is completely functioning in the age of Kali. The so-called *brāhmaṇas* are no longer interested in understanding the nature of the Supreme Brahman, although a *brāhmaṇa* means one who has attained knowledge about Brahman. In the *Vedānta-sūtra* also it is stated, *athāto brahma-jijñāsā:* this human form of life is meant for realization of the Supreme Brahman, the Absolute Truth, or, in other words, human life is meant for one's elevation to the post of a *brāhmaṇa.* Unfortunately the modern *brāhmaṇas,* or so-called *brāhmaṇas* who come in originally brahminical families, have left their own occupational duties, but they do not allow others to occupy the posts of *brāhmaṇas.* The qualifications for *brāhmaṇas* are described in the scriptures, in *Śrīmad-Bhāgavatam, Bhagavad-gītā* and all other Vedic literatures. *Brāhmaṇa* is not a hereditary title or position. If someone from a non-*brāhmaṇa* family (for example, one born in a family of *śūdras)* tries to become a *brāhmaṇa* by being properly qualified under the instruction of a bona fide spiritual master, these so-called *brāhmaṇas* will object. Such *brāhmaṇas,* having been cursed by Nandīśvara, are actually in a position where they have no discrimination between eatables and noneatables and simply live to maintain the perishable material body and its family. Such fallen conditioned souls are not worthy to be called *brāhmaṇas*, but in Kali-yuga they claim to be *brāhmaṇas*, and if a person actually tries to attain the brahminical qualifications, they try to hinder his progress. This is the situation in the present age. Caitanya Mahāprabhu condemned this principle very strongly. During His conversation with Rāmānanda Rāya, He said that regardless of whether a person is born in a *brāhmaṇa* family or *śūdra* family, regardless of whether he is a householder or a *sannyāsī*, if he knows the science of Kṛṣṇa he must be a spiritual master. Caitanya Mahāprabhu had many so-called *śūdra* disciples like Haridāsa Ṭhākura and Rāmānanda Rāya. Even the Gosvāmīs, who were principal students of Lord Caitanya, were also ostracized from *brāhmaṇa* society, but Caitanya Mahāprabhu, by His grace, made them first-class Vaiṣṇavas.

TEXT 27

तस्यैवं वदतः शापं श्रुत्वा द्विजकुलाय वै ।
भृगुः प्रत्यसृजच्छापं ब्रह्मदण्डं दुरत्ययम् ॥२७॥

tasyaivaṁ vadataḥ śāpaṁ
śrutvā dvija-kulāya vai
bhṛguḥ pratyasṛjac chāpaṁ
brahma-daṇḍam duratyayam

tasya—his (Nandīśvara's); *evam*—thus; *vadataḥ*—words; *śāpam*—the curse; *śrutvā*—hearing; *dvija-kulāya*—unto the *brāhmaṇas; vai*—indeed; *bhṛguḥ*—Bhṛgu; *pratyasṛjat*—made; *śāpam*—a curse; *brahma-daṇḍam*—the punishment of a *brāhmaṇa; duratyayam*—insurmountable.

TRANSLATION

When all the hereditary brāhmaṇas were thus cursed by Nandīśvara, the sage Bhṛgu, as a reaction, condemned the followers of Lord Śiva with this very strong brahminical curse.

PURPORT

The word *duratyaya* is particularly used in reference to a *brahma-daṇḍa*, or curse by a *brāhmaṇa*. A curse by a *brāhmaṇa* is very strong; therefore it is called *duratyaya*, or insurmountable. As the Lord states in

Bhagavad-gītā, the stringent laws of nature are insurmountable; similarly, if a curse is uttered by a *brāhmaṇa*, that curse is also insurmountable. But *Bhagavad-gītā* also says that the curses or benedictions of the material world are, after all, material creations. The *Caitanya-caritāmṛta* confirms that that which is accepted in this material world to be a benediction and that which is taken to be a curse are both on the same platform because they are material. To get out of this material contamination, one should take shelter of the Supreme Personality of Godhead, as recommended in *Bhagavad-gītā* (7.14): *mām eva ye prapadyante māyām etāṁ taranti te.* The best path is to transcend all material curses and benedictions and take shelter of the Supreme Lord, Kṛṣṇa, and remain in a transcendental position. Persons who have taken shelter of Kṛṣṇa are always peaceful; they are never cursed by anyone, nor do they attempt to curse anyone. That is a transcendental position.

TEXT 28

भवव्रतधरा ये च ये च तान् समनुव्रताः ।
पाषण्डिनस्ते भवन्तु सच्छास्त्रपरिपन्थिनः ॥२८॥

bhava-vrata-dharā ye ca
ye ca tān samanuvratāḥ
pāṣaṇḍinas te bhavantu
sac-chāstra-paripanthinaḥ

bhava-vrata-dharāḥ—taking a vow to satisfy Lord Śiva; *ye*—who; *ca*—and; *ye*—who; *ca*—and; *tān*—such principles; *samanuvratāḥ*—following; *pāṣaṇḍinaḥ*—atheists; *te*—they; *bhavantu*—let them become; *sat-śāstra-paripanthinaḥ*—diverted from transcendental scriptural injunctions.

TRANSLATION

One who takes a vow to satisfy Lord Śiva or who follows such principles will certainly become an atheist and be diverted from transcendental scriptural injunctions.

PURPORT

It is sometimes seen that devotees of Lord Śiva imitate the characteristics of Lord Śiva. For example, Lord Śiva drank an ocean of poison, so some of the followers of Lord Śiva imitate him and try to take intoxicants like *gāñjā* (marijuana). Here the curse is that if someone follows such principles he must become an infidel and turn against the principles of Vedic regulation. It is said that such devotees of Lord Śiva will be *sac-chāstra-paripanthinaḥ*, which means "opposed to the conclusion of *śāstra*, or scripture." This is confirmed in the *Padma Purāṇa* also. Lord Śiva was ordered by the Supreme Personality of Godhead to preach the impersonal, or Māyāvāda, philosophy for a particular purpose, just as Lord Buddha preached the philosophy of voidness for particular purposes mentioned in the *śāstras*.

Sometimes it is necessary to preach a philosophical doctrine which is against the Vedic conclusion. In the *Śiva Purāṇa* it is stated that Lord Śiva said to Pārvatī that in the Kali-yuga, in the body of a *brāhmaṇa*, he would preach the Māyāvāda philosophy. Thus it is generally found that the worshipers of Lord Śiva are Māyāvādī followers. Lord Śiva himself says, *māyāvādam asac-chāstram. Asat-śāstra*, as explained here, means the doctrine of Māyāvāda impersonalism, or becoming one with the Supreme. Bhṛgu Muni cursed that persons who worshiped Lord Śiva would become followers of this Māyāvāda *asat-śāstra*, which attempts to establish that the Supreme Personality of Godhead is impersonal. Besides that, among the worshipers of Lord Śiva there is a section who live a devilish life. *Śrīmad-Bhāgavatam* and *Nārada-pañcarātra* are authorized scriptures that are considered *sat-śāstra*, or scriptures which lead one to the path of God realization. *Asat-śāstras* are just the opposite.

TEXT 29

नष्टशौचा मूढधियो जटाभस्मास्थिधारिणः ।
विशन्तु शिवदीक्षायां यत्र दैवं सुरासवम् ॥२९॥

naṣṭa-śaucā mūḍha-dhiyo
jaṭā-bhasmāsthi-dhāriṇaḥ
viśantu śiva-dīkṣāyāṁ
yatra daivaṁ surāsavam

naṣṭa-śaucāḥ—cleanliness being abandoned; *mūḍha-dhiyaḥ*—foolish; *jaṭā-bhasma-asthi-dhāriṇaḥ*—wearing long hair, ashes and bones;

viśantu—may enter; *śiva-dīkṣāyām*—into initiation of worship of Śiva; *yatra*—where; *daivam*—are spiritual; *sura-āsavam*—wine and liquor.

TRANSLATION

Those who vow to worship Lord Śiva are so foolish that they imitate him by keeping long hair on their heads. When initiated into worship of Lord Śiva, they prefer to live on wine, flesh and other such things.

PURPORT

Indulging in wine and meat, keeping long hair on one's head, not bathing daily, and smoking *gāñjā* (marijuana) are some of the habits which are accepted by foolish creatures who do not have regulated lives. By such behavior one becomes devoid of transcendental knowledge. In the initiation into the Śiva *mantra* there are *mudrikāṣṭaka*, in which it is sometimes recommended that one make his sitting place on the vagina and thus desire *nirvāṇa*, or dissolution of existence. In that process of worship, wine is needed, or sometimes, in place of wine, palm tree juice which is converted into an intoxicant. This is also offered according to *Śiva-āgama*, a scripture on the method of worshiping Lord Śiva.

TEXT 30

ब्रह्म च ब्राह्मणांश्चैव यद्यूयं परिनिन्दथ ।
सेतुं विधारणं पुंसामतः पाषण्डमाश्रिताः ॥३०॥

brahma ca brāhmaṇāṁś caiva
yad yūyaṁ parinindatha
setuṁ vidhāraṇaṁ puṁsām
ataḥ pāṣaṇḍam āśritāḥ

brahma—the *Vedas; ca*—and; *brāhmaṇān*—the *brāhmaṇas; ca*—and; *eva*—certainly; *yat*—because; *yūyam*—you; *parinindatha*—blaspheme; *setum*—Vedic principles; *vidhāraṇam*—holding; *puṁsām*—of mankind; *ataḥ*—therefore; *pāṣaṇḍam*—atheism; *āśritāḥ*—have taken shelter.

TRANSLATION

Bhṛgu Muni continued: Since you blaspheme the Vedas and the brāhmaṇas, who are followers of the Vedic principles, it is understood that you have already taken shelter of the doctrine of atheism.

PURPORT

Bhṛgu Muni, in cursing Nandīśvara, said that not only would they be degraded as atheists because of this curse, but they had already fallen to the standard of atheism because they had blasphemed the *Vedas*, which are the source of human civilization. Human civilization is based on the qualitative divisions of social order, namely the intelligent class, the martial class, the productive class and the laborer class. The *Vedas* provide the right direction for advancing in spiritual cultivation and economic development and regulating the principle of sense gratification, so that ultimately one may be liberated from material contamination to his real state of spiritual identification (*ahaṁ brahmāsmi*). As long as one is in the contamination of material existence, one changes bodies from the aquatics up to the position of Brahmā, but the human form of life is the highest perfectional life in the material world. The *Vedas* give directions by which to elevate oneself in the next life. The *Vedas* are the mother for such instructions, and the *brāhmaṇas*, or persons who are in knowledge of the *Vedas*, are the father. Thus if one blasphemes the *Vedas* and *brāhmaṇas*, naturally one goes down to the status of atheism. The exact word used in Sanskrit is *nāstika*, which refers to one who does not believe in the *Vedas* but manufactures some concocted system of religion. Śrī Caitanya Mahāprabhu has said that the followers of the Buddhist system of religion are *nāstikas*. In order to establish his doctrine of nonviolence, Lord Buddha flatly refused to believe in the *Vedas*, and thus, later on, Śaṅkarācārya stopped this system of religion in India and forced it to go outside India. Here it is stated, *brahma ca brāhmaṇān*. *Brahma* means the *Vedas*. *Ahaṁ brahmāsmi* means "I am in full knowledge." The Vedic assertion is that one should think that he is Brahman, for actually he is Brahman. If *brahma*, or the Vedic spiritual science, is condemned, and the masters of the spiritual science, the *brāhmaṇas*, are condemned, then where does human civilization stand? Bhṛgu Muni said, "It is not due to my cursing that you shall become atheists; you are already situated in the principle of atheism. Therefore you are condemned."

TEXT 31

एष एव हि लोकानां शिवः पन्थाः सनातनः ।
यं पूर्वे चानुसंतस्थुर्यत्प्रमाणं जनार्दनः ॥३१॥

eṣa eva hi lokānāṁ
śivaḥ panthāḥ sanātanaḥ
yaṁ pūrve cānusantasthur
yat-pramāṇaṁ janārdanaḥ

eṣaḥ—the *Vedas; eva*—certainly; *hi*—for; *lokānām*—of all people; *śivaḥ*—auspicious; *panthāḥ*—path; *sanātanaḥ*—eternal; *yam*—which (Vedic path); *pūrve*—in the past; *ca*—and; *anusantasthuḥ*—was rigidly followed; *yat*—in which; *pramāṇam*—the evidence; *janārdanaḥ*—Janārdana.

TRANSLATION

The Vedas give the eternal regulative principles for auspicious advancement in human civilization which have been rigidly followed in the past. The strong evidence of this principle is the Supreme Personality of Godhead, who is called Janārdana, the well-wisher of all living entities.

PURPORT

In the *Bhagavad-gītā* the Supreme Personality of Godhead, Kṛṣṇa, has claimed that He is the father of all living entities, regardless of form. There are 8,400,000 different species of life forms, and Lord Kṛṣṇa claims that He is the father of all. Because the living entities are parts and parcels of the Supreme Personality of Godhead, they are all sons of the Lord, and for their benefit, because they are hovering under the impression that they can lord it over material nature, the *Vedas* are given to them for their guidance. Therefore the *Vedas* are called *apauruṣeya*, for they are not written by any man or demigod, including the first living creature, Brahmā. Brahmā is not the creator or author of the *Vedas.* He is also one of the living beings in this material world; therefore he does not have the power to write or speak the *Vedas* independently. Every living entity within this material world is subject to four deficiencies: he commits mistakes, he accepts one thing for another, he cheats, and he has imperfect senses. The *Vedas*, however, are not written by any living creature within this material world. Therefore they are said to be *apauruṣeya*. No one can trace out the history of the *Vedas*. Of course, modern human civilization has no chronological history of the world or the universe, and it cannot present actual historical facts older than three thousand years. But no one has traced out when the *Vedas* were written, because they were never written by any living being within this material world. All other systems of knowledge are defective because they have been written or spoken by men or demigods who are products of this material creation, but *Bhagavad-gītā* is *apauruṣeya*, for it was not spoken by any human being or any demigod of this material creation; it was spoken by Lord Kṛṣṇa, who is beyond the material creation. That is accepted by such stalwart scholars as Śaṅkarācārya, not to speak of other *ācāryas* such as Rāmānujācārya and Madhvācārya. Śaṅkarācārya has accepted that Nārāyaṇa and Kṛṣṇa are transcendental, and in *Bhagavad-gītā* also Lord Kṛṣṇa has established, *ahaṁ sarvasya prabhavo mattaḥ sarvaṁ pravartate:* "I am the origin of everything; everything emanates from Me." This material creation, including Brahmā and Śiva and all the demigods, has been created by Him, for everything has emanated from Him. He also says that the purpose of all the *Vedas* is to understand Him (*vedaiś ca sarvair aham eva vedyaḥ*). He is the original *veda-vit*, or knower of the *Vedas*, and *vedānta-kṛt*, or compiler of *Vedānta*. Brahmā is not the compiler of the *Vedas*.

In the beginning of *Śrīmad-Bhāgavatam* it is established, *tene brahma hṛdā:* the Supreme Absolute Truth, the Personality of Godhead, instructed Brahmā in the Vedic knowledge through his heart. Therefore the evidence that Vedic knowledge is free from the defects of mistakes, illusions, cheating and imperfection is that it is spoken by the Supreme Personality of Godhead, Janārdana, and has thus been followed from time immemorial, beginning from Brahmā. The Vedic religion or the principles of the *Vedas* have been followed by the highly cultured population of India since time immemorial; no one can trace out the history of Vedic religion. Therefore it is *sanātana*, and any blasphemy against the *Vedas* is calculated to be atheism. The *Vedas* are described as *setu,* which means "a bridge." If one wants to attain his spiritual existence, one has to cross an ocean of nescience. The *Vedas* are the bridge by which to cross such a great ocean.

The *Vedas* describe how to divide the human race into four divisions according to quality and working capacity. This is a very scientific system, and it is also *sanātana,* for no one can trace out its history and it has no dissolution. No one can stop the system of *varṇa* and *āśrama,* or the castes and divisions. For example, whether or not one accepts the name *brāhmaṇa,* there is a class in society which is known as the intelligent class and which is interested in spiritual understanding and philosophy. Similarly, there is a class of men who are interested in administration and in ruling others. In the Vedic system these martially spirited men are called *kṣatriyas.* Similarly, everywhere there is a class of men who are interested in economic development, business, industry and moneymaking; they are called *vaiśyas.* And there is another class who are neither intelligent nor martially spirited nor endowed with the capacity for economic development but who simply can serve others. They are called *śūdras,* or the laborer class. This system is *sanātana*—it comes from time immemorial, and it will continue in the same way. There is no power in the world which can stop it. Therefore, since this *sanātana-dharma* system is eternal, one can elevate himself to the highest standard of spiritual life by following the Vedic principles.

It is stated that formerly the sages followed this system; therefore to follow the Vedic system is to follow the standard etiquette of society. But the followers of Lord Śiva, who are drunkards, who are addicted to intoxicants and sex life, who do not bathe and who smoke *gāñjā,* are against all human etiquette. The conclusion is that persons who rebel against the Vedic principles are themselves the evidence that the *Vedas* are authoritative, because by not following the Vedic principles they become like animals. Such animalistic persons are themselves evidence of the supremacy of the Vedic regulations.

TEXT 32

तद्ब्रह्म परमं शुद्धं सतां वर्त्म सनातनम् ।
विगर्ह्य यात पाषण्डं दैवं वो यत्र भूतराट् ॥३२॥

tad brahma paramaṁ śuddhaṁ
satāṁ vartma sanātanam
vigarhya yāta pāṣaṇḍaṁ
daivaṁ vo yatra bhūta-rāṭ

tat—that; *brahma*—*Veda;* *paramam*—supreme; *śuddham*—pure; *satām*—of the saintly persons; *vartma*—path; *sanātanam*—eternal; *vigarhya*—blaspheming; *yāta*—should go; *pāṣaṇḍam*—to atheism; *daivam*—deity; *vaḥ*—your; *yatra*—where; *bhūta-rāṭ*—the lord of the *bhūtas.*

TRANSLATION

By blaspheming the principles of the Vedas, which are the pure and supreme path of the saintly persons, certainly you followers of Bhūtapati, Lord Śiva, will descend to the standard of atheism without a doubt.

PURPORT

Lord Śiva is described here as *bhūta-rāṭ.* The ghosts and those who are situated in the material mode of ignorance are called *bhūtas,* so *bhūta-rāṭ* refers to the leader of the creatures who are in the lowest standard of the material modes of nature. Another meaning of *bhūta* is anyone who has taken birth or anything which is produced, so in that sense Lord Śiva may be accepted as the father of this material world. Here, of course, Bhṛgu Muni takes Lord Śiva as the leader of the lowest creatures. The characteristics of the lowest class of men have already been described—they do not bathe, they have long hair on their heads, and they are addicted to intoxicants. In comparison with the path followed by the followers of Bhūtarāṭ, the Vedic system is certainly excellent, for it promotes people to spiritual life as the highest eternal principle of human civilization. If one decries or blasphemes the Vedic principles, then he falls to the standard of atheism.

TEXT 33

मैत्रेय उवाच
तस्यैवं वदतः शापं भृगोः स भगवान् भवः ।
निश्चक्राम ततः किञ्चिद्विमना इव सानुगः ॥३३॥

maitreya uvāca
tasyaivaṁ vadataḥ śāpaṁ
bhṛgoḥ sa bhagavān bhavaḥ
niścakrāma tataḥ kiñcid
vimanā iva sānugaḥ

maitreyaḥ uvāca—Maitreya said; *tasya*—of him; *evam*—thus; *vadataḥ*—being spoken; *śāpam*—curse; *bhṛgoḥ*—of Bhṛgu; *saḥ*—he; *bhagavān*—the possessor of all opulences; *bhavaḥ*—Lord Śiva; *niścakrāma*—went; *tataḥ*—from there; *kiñcit*—somewhat; *vimanāḥ*—morose; *iva*—as; *sa-anugaḥ*—followed by his disciples.

TRANSLATION

The sage Maitreya said: When such cursing and countercursing was going on between Lord Śiva's followers and the parties of Dakṣa and Bhṛgu, Lord Śiva became very morose. Not saying anything, he left the arena of the sacrifice, followed by his disciples.

PURPORT

Here Lord Śiva's excellent character is described. In spite of the cursing and countercursing between the parties of Dakṣa and Śiva, because he is the greatest Vaiṣṇava he was so sober that he did not say anything. A Vaiṣṇava is always tolerant, and Lord Śiva is considered the topmost Vaiṣṇava, so his character, as shown in this scene, is excellent. He became morose because he knew that these people, both his men and Dakṣa's, were unnecessarily cursing and countercursing one another, without any interest in spiritual life. From his point of view, he did not see anyone as lower or higher, because he is a Vaiṣṇava. As stated in *Bhagavad-gītā* (5.18), *paṇḍitāḥ sama-darśinaḥ:* one who is perfectly learned does not see anyone as lesser or greater, because he sees everyone from the spiritual platform. Thus the only alternative left to Lord Śiva was to leave in order to stop his follower, Nandīśvara, as well as Bhṛgu Muni, from cursing and countercursing in that way.

TEXT 34

तेऽपि विश्वसृजः सत्रं सहस्रपरिवत्सरान् ।
संविधाय महेष्वास यत्रेज्य ऋषभो हरिः ॥३४॥

te 'pi viśva-sṛjaḥ satraṁ
sahasra-parivatsarān
saṁvidhāya maheṣvāsa
yatrejya ṛṣabho hariḥ

te—those; *api*—even; *viśva-sṛjaḥ*—progenitors of the universal population; *satram*—the sacrifice; *sahasra*—one thousand; *parivat-sarān*—years; *saṁvidhāya*—performing; *maheṣvāsa*—O Vidura; *yatra*—in which; *ijyaḥ*—to be worshiped; *ṛṣabhaḥ*—the presiding Deity of all demigods; *hariḥ*—Hari.

TRANSLATION

The sage Maitreya continued: O Vidura, all the progenitors of the universal population thus executed a sacrifice for thousands of years, for sacrifice is the best way to worship the Supreme Lord, Hari, the Personality of Godhead.

PURPORT

It is clearly stated here that the stalwart personalities who generate the entire population of the world are interested in satisfying the Supreme Personality of Godhead by offering sacrifices. The Lord also says in *Bhagavad-gītā* (5.29), *bhoktāraṁ yajña-tapasām.* One may engage in performing sacrifices and severe austerities for perfection, but they are all meant to satisfy the Supreme Lord. If such activities are performed for personal satisfaction, one is involved in *pāṣaṇḍa,* or atheism; but when they are performed for the satisfaction of the Supreme Lord, one is following the Vedic principle. All the assembled sages performed sacrifices for one thousand years.

TEXT 35

आप्लुत्यावभृथं यत्र गङ्गा यमुनयान्विता ।
विरजेनात्मना सर्वे स्वं स्वं धाम ययुस्ततः ॥३५॥

āplutyāvabhṛthaṁ yatra
gaṅgā yamunayānvitā
virajenātmanā sarve
svaṁ svaṁ dhāma yayus tataḥ

āplutya—taking a bath; *avabhṛtham*—the bath which is taken after performing sacrifices; *yatra*—where; *gaṅgā*—the River Ganges; *yamunayā*—by the River Yamunā; *anvitā*—mixed; *virajena*—without infection; *ātmanā*—by the mind; *sarve*—all; *svam svam*—their respective; *dhāma*—abodes; *yayuḥ*—went; *tataḥ*—from there.

TRANSLATION

My dear Vidura, carrier of bows and arrows, all the demigods who were performing the sacrifice took their bath at the confluence of the Ganges and the Yamunā after completing the yajña performance. Such a bath is called avabhṛtha-snāna. After thus becoming purified in heart, they departed for their respective abodes.

PURPORT

After Lord Śiva and, previously, Dakṣa, left the arena of sacrifice, the sacrifice was not stopped; the sages went on for many years in order to satisfy the Supreme Lord. The sacrifice was not destroyed for want of Śiva and Dakṣa, and the sages went on with their activities. In other words, it may be assumed that if one does not worship the demigods, even up to Lord Śiva and Brahmā, one can nevertheless satisfy the Supreme Personality of Godhead. This is also confirmed in *Bhagavad-gītā* (7.20). *Kāmais tais tair hṛta-jñānāḥ prapadyante 'nya-devatāḥ.* Persons who are impelled by lust and desire go to the demigods to derive some material benefit. *Bhagavad-gītā* uses the very specific words *nāsti buddhiḥ*, meaning "persons who have lost their sense or intelligence." Only such persons care for demigods and want to derive material benefit from them. Of course, this does not mean that one should not show respect to the demigods; but there is no need to worship them. One who is honest may be faithful to the government, but he does not need to bribe the government servants. Bribery is illegal; one does not bribe a government servant, but that does not mean that one does not show him respect. Similarly, one who engages in the transcendental loving service of the Supreme Lord does not need to worship any demigod, nor does he have any tendency to show disrespect to the demigods. Elsewhere in *Bhagavad-gītā* (9.23) it is stated, *ye 'py anya-devatā-bhaktā yajante śraddhayānvitāḥ.* The Lord says that anyone who worships the demigods is also worshiping Him, but he is worshiping *avidhi-pūrvakam*, which means "without following the regulative principles." The regulative principle is to worship the Supreme Personality of Godhead. Worship of demigods may indirectly be worship of the Personality of Godhead, but it is not regulated. By worshiping the Supreme Lord, one automatically serves all the demigods because they are parts and parcels of the whole. If one supplies water to the root of a tree, all the parts of the tree, such as the leaves and branches, are automatically satisfied, and if one supplies food to the stomach, all the limbs of the body—the hands, legs, fingers, etc.—are nourished. Thus by worshiping the Supreme Personality of Godhead one can satisfy all the demigods, but by worshiping all the demigods one does not completely worship the Supreme Lord. Therefore worship of the demigods is irregular, and it is disrespectful to the scriptural injunctions.

In this age of Kali it is practically impossible to perform the *deva-yajña*, or sacrifices to the demigods. As such, in this age *Śrīmad-Bhāgavatam* recommends *saṅkīrtana-yajña. Yajñaiḥ saṅkīrtana-prāyair yajanti hi sumedhasaḥ* (*Bhāg.* 11.5.32). "In this age the intelligent person completes the performances of all kinds of *yajñas* simply by chanting Hare Kṛṣṇa, Hare Kṛṣṇa, Kṛṣṇa Kṛṣṇa, Hare Hare/ Hare Rāma, Hare Rāma, Rāma Rāma, Hare Hare." *Tasmin tuṣṭe jagat tuṣṭaḥ:* "When Lord Viṣṇu is satisfied, all the demigods, who are parts and parcels of the Supreme Lord, are satisfied."

Thus end the Bhaktivedanta purports of the Fourth Canto, Second Chapter, of the Śrīmad-Bhāgavatam, *entitled "Dakṣa Curses Lord Śiva."*

CHAPTER THREE

Talks Between Lord Śiva and Satī

TEXT 1

मैत्रेय उवाच
सदा विद्विषतोरेवं कालो वै ध्रियमाणयोः ।
जामातुः श्वशुरस्यापि सुमहानतिचक्रमे ॥ १ ॥

maitreya uvāca
sadā vidviṣator evaṁ
kālo vai dhriyamāṇayoḥ
jāmātuḥ śvaśurasyāpi
sumahān aticakrame

maitreyaḥ uvāca—Maitreya said; *sadā*—constantly; *vidviṣatoḥ*—the tension; *evam*—in this manner; *kālaḥ*—time; *vai*—certainly; *dhriyamāṇayoḥ*—continued to bear; *jāmātuḥ*—of the son-in-law; *śvaśurasya*—of the father-in-law; *api*—even; *su-mahān*—a very great; *aticakrame*—passed.

TRANSLATION

Maitreya continued: In this manner the tension between the father-in-law and son-in-law, Dakṣa and Lord Śiva, continued for a considerably long period.

PURPORT

The previous chapter has already explained that Vidura questioned the sage Maitreya as to the cause of the misunderstanding between Lord Śiva and Dakṣa. Another question is why the strife between Dakṣa and his son-in-law caused Satī to destroy her body. The chief reason for Satī's giving up her body was that her father, Dakṣa, began another sacrificial performance, to which Lord Śiva was not invited at all. Generally, when any sacrifice is performed, although each and every sacrifice is intended to pacify the Supreme Personality of Godhead, Viṣṇu, all the demigods, especially Lord Brahmā and Lord Śiva and the other principal demigods, such as Indra and Candra, are invited, and they take part. It is said that unless all the demigods are present, no sacrifice is complete. But in the tension between the father-in-law and son-in-law, Dakṣa began another *yajña* performance, to which Lord Śiva was not invited. Dakṣa was the chief progenitor employed by Lord Brahmā, and he was a son of Brahmā, so he had a high position and was also very proud.

TEXT 2

यदाभिषिक्तो दक्षस्तु ब्रह्मणा परमेष्ठिना ।
प्रजापतीनां सर्वेषामाधिपत्ये स्मयोऽभवत् ॥ २ ॥

yadābhiṣikto dakṣas tu
brahmaṇā parameṣṭhinā
prajāpatīnāṁ sarveṣām
ādhipatye smayo 'bhavat

yadā—when; *abhiṣiktaḥ*—appointed; *dakṣaḥ*—Dakṣa; *tu*—but; *brahmaṇā*—by Brahmā; *parameṣṭhinā*—the supreme teacher; *prajāpatīnām*—of the Prajāpatis; *sarveṣām*—of all; *ādhipatye*—as the chief; *smayaḥ*—puffed up; *abhavat*—he became.

TRANSLATION

When Lord Brahmā appointed Dakṣa the chief of all the Prajāpatis, the progenitors of population, Dakṣa became very much puffed up.

PURPORT

Although he was envious and was inimical towards Lord Śiva, Dakṣa was appointed the chief of all Prajāpatis. That was the cause of his excessive pride. When a man becomes too proud of his material possessions, he can perform any disastrous act, and therefore Dakṣa acted out of false prestige. That is described in this chapter.

TEXT 3

इष्ट्वा स वाजपेयेन ब्रह्मिष्ठानभिभूय च ।
बृहस्पतिसवं नाम समारेभे क्रतूत्तमम् ॥ ३ ॥

iṣṭvā sa vājapeyena
brahmiṣṭhān abhibhūya ca
bṛhaspati-savaṁ nāma
samārebhe kratūttamam

iṣṭvā—after performing; *saḥ*—he (Dakṣa); *vājapeyena*—with a *vājapeya* sacrifice; *brahmiṣṭhān*—Śiva and his followers; *abhibhūya*—neglecting; *ca*—and; *bṛhaspati-savam*—the *bṛhaspati-sava; nāma*—called; *samārebhe*—began; *kratu-uttamam*—the best of sacrifices.

TRANSLATION

Dakṣa began a sacrifice named vājapeya, and he became excessively confident of his support by Lord Brahmā. He then performed another great sacrifice, named bṛhaspati-sava.

PURPORT

In the *Vedas* it is prescribed that before performing a *bṛhaspati-sava* sacrifice, one should perform the sacrifice named *vājapeya.* While performing these sacrifices, however, Dakṣa neglected great devotees like Lord Śiva. According to Vedic scriptures, the demigods are eligible to participate in *yajñas* and share the oblations, but Dakṣa wanted to avoid them. All sacrifices are intended to pacify Lord Viṣṇu, but Lord Viṣṇu includes all His devotees. Brahmā, Lord Śiva and the other demigods are all obedient servants of Lord Viṣṇu; therefore Lord Viṣṇu is never satisfied without them. But Dakṣa, being puffed up with his power, wanted to deprive Lord Brahmā and Lord Śiva of participation in the sacrifice, understanding that if one satisfies Viṣṇu, it is not necessary to satisfy His followers. But that is not the process. Viṣṇu wants His followers to be satisfied first. Lord Kṛṣṇa says, *mad-bhakta-pūjābhyadhikā:* "The worship of My devotees is better than worship of Me." Similarly, in the *Śiva Purāṇa,* it is stated that the best mode of worship is to offer oblations to Viṣṇu, but better than that is to worship the devotees of Kṛṣṇa. Thus Dakṣa's determination to neglect Lord Śiva in the sacrifices was not fitting.

TEXT 4

तस्मिन् ब्रह्मर्षयः सर्वे देवर्षिपितृदेवताः ।
आसन् कृतस्वस्त्ययनास्तत्पत्न्यश्च सभर्तृकाः ॥ ४ ॥

tasmin brahmarṣayaḥ sarve
devarṣi-pitṛ-devatāḥ
āsan kṛta-svastyayanās
tat-patnyaś ca sa-bhartṛkāḥ

tasmin—in that (sacrifice); *brahma-ṛṣayaḥ*—the *brahmarṣis; sarve*—all; *devarṣi*—the *devarṣis; pitṛ*—ancestors; *devatāḥ*—demigods; *āsan*—were; *kṛta-svasti-ayanāḥ*—were very nicely decorated with ornaments; *tat-patnyaḥ*—their wives; *ca*—and; *sa-bhartṛkāḥ*—along with their husbands.

TRANSLATION

While the sacrifice was being performed, many brahmarṣis, great sages, ancestral demigods and other demigods, their wives all very nicely decorated with ornaments, attended from different parts of the universe.

PURPORT

In any auspicious ceremony, such as a marriage ceremony, sacrificial ceremony or *pūjā* ceremony, it is auspicious for married women to decorate themselves very nicely with ornaments, fine clothing and cosmetics. These are auspicious signs. Many heavenly women assembled with their husbands, the *devarṣis*, demigods and *rājarṣis*, in that great sacrifice named *bṛhaspati-sava.* It is specifically mentioned in this verse that they approached with their husbands, for when a woman is decorated nicely, her husband becomes more cheerful. The nice decorations, ornaments and dress of the wives of the demigods and sages and the cheerfulness of the demigods and sages themselves were all auspicious signs for the ceremony.

TEXTS 5–7

तदुपश्रुत्य नभसि खेचराणां प्रजल्पताम् ।
सती दाक्षायणी देवी पितृयज्ञमहोत्सवम् ॥ ५ ॥
व्रजन्तीः सर्वतो दिग्भ्य उपदेववरस्त्रियः ।
विमानयानाः सप्रेष्ठा निष्ककण्ठीः सुवाससः॥ ६ ॥
दृष्ट्वा स्वनिलयाभ्याशे लोलाक्षीर्मृष्टकुण्डलाः ।
पतिं भूतपतिं देवमौत्सुक्यादभ्यभाषत ॥ ७ ॥

tad upaśrutya nabhasi
khe-carāṇāṁ prajalpatām
satī dākṣāyaṇī devī
pitṛ-yajña-mahotsavam

vrajantīḥ sarvato digbhya
upadeva-vara-striyaḥ
vimāna-yānāḥ sa-preṣṭhā
niṣka-kaṇṭhīḥ suvāsasaḥ

dṛṣṭvā sva-nilayābhyāśe
lolākṣīr mṛṣṭa-kuṇḍalāḥ
patiṁ bhūta-patiṁ devam
autsukyād abhyabhāṣata

tat—then; *upaśrutya*—hearing; *nabhasi*—in the sky; *khe-carāṇām*—of those who were flying in the air (the Gandharvas); *prajalpatām*—the conversation; *satī*—Satī; *dākṣāyaṇī*—the daughter of Dakṣa; *devī*—the wife of Śiva; *pitṛ-yajña-mahā-utsavam*—the great festival of sacrifice performed by her father; *vrajantīḥ*—were going; *sarvataḥ*—from all; *digbhyaḥ*—directions; *upadeva-vara-striyaḥ*—the beautiful wives of the demigods; *vimāna-yānāḥ*—flying in their airplanes; *sa-preṣṭhāḥ*—along with their husbands; *niṣka-kaṇṭhīḥ*—having nice necklaces with lockets; *su-vāsasaḥ*—dressed in fine clothing; *dṛṣṭvā*—seeing; *sva-nilaya-abhyāśe*—near her residence; *lola-akṣīḥ*—having beautiful glittering eyes; *mṛṣṭa-kuṇḍalāḥ*—nice earrings; *patim*—her husband; *bhūta-patim*—the master of the *bhūtas;*

devam—the demigod; *autsukyāt*—from great anxiety; *abhyabhāṣata*—she spoke.

TRANSLATION

The chaste lady Satī, the daughter of Dakṣa, heard the heavenly denizens flying in the sky conversing about the great sacrifice being performed by her father. When she saw that from all directions the beautiful wives of the heavenly denizens, their eyes very beautifully glittering, were near her residence and were going to the sacrifice dressed in fine clothing and ornamented with earrings and necklaces with lockets, she approached her husband, the master of the bhūtas, in great anxiety, and spoke as follows.

PURPORT

It appears that the residence of Lord Śiva was not on this planet but somewhere in outer space, otherwise how could Satī have seen the airplanes coming from different directions towards this planet and heard the passengers talking about the great sacrifice being performed by Dakṣa? Satī is described here as Dākṣāyaṇī because she was the daughter of Dakṣa. The mention of *upadeva-vara* refers to inferior demigods like the Gandharvas, Kinnaras and Uragas, who are not exactly demigods but between the demigods and human beings. They were also coming in planes. The word *sva-nilayābhyāśe* indicates that they were passing right near her residential quarters. The dresses and bodily features of the wives of the heavenly denizens are very nicely described here. Their eyes moved, their earrings and other ornaments glittered and glared, their dresses were the nicest possible, and all of them had special lockets on their necklaces. Each woman was accompanied by her husband. Thus they looked so beautiful that Satī, Dākṣāyaṇī, was impelled to dress similarly and go to the sacrifice with her husband. That is the natural inclination of a woman.

TEXT 8

सत्युवाच

प्रजापतेस्ते श्वशुरस्य साम्प्रतं
निर्यापितो यज्ञमहोत्सवः किल ।

वयं च तत्राभिसराम वाम ते
यद्यर्थितामी विबुधा व्रजन्ति हि ॥ ८ ॥

saty uvāca
prajāpates te śvaśurasya sāmpratam
niryāpito yajña-mahotsavaḥ kila
vayaṁ ca tatrābhisarāma vāma te
yady arthitāmī vibudhā vrajanti hi

satī uvāca—Satī said; *prajāpateḥ*—of Dakṣa; *te*—your; *śvaśurasya*—of your father-in-law; *sāmpratam*—nowadays; *niryāpitaḥ*—has been started; *yajña-mahā-utsavaḥ*—a great sacrifice; *kila*—certainly; *vayam*—we; *ca*—and; *tatra*—there; *abhisarāma*—may go; *vāma*—O my dear Lord Śiva; *te*—your; *yadi*—if; *arthitā*—desire; *amī*—these; *vibudhāḥ*—demigods; *vrajanti*—are going; *hi*—because.

TRANSLATION

Satī said: My dear Lord Śiva, your father-in-law is now executing great sacrifices, and all the demigods, having been invited by him, are going there. If you desire, we may also go.

PURPORT

Satī knew of the tension between her father and her husband, but still she expressed to her husband, Lord Śiva, that since such sacrifices were going on at her father's house and so many demigods were going, she also desired to go. But she could not express her willingness directly, and so she told her husband that if he desired to go, then she could also accompany him. In other words, she submitted her desire very politely to her husband.

TEXT 9

तस्मिन् भगिन्यो मम भर्तृभिः स्वकै-
र्ध्रुवं गमिष्यन्ति सुहृद्दिदृक्षवः ।
अहं च तस्मिन् भवताभिकामये
सहोपनीतं परिबर्हमर्हितुम् ॥ ९ ॥

tasmin bhaginyo mama bhartṛbhiḥ svakair
dhruvaṁ gamiṣyanti suhṛd-didṛkṣavaḥ
ahaṁ ca tasmin bhavatābhikāmaye
sahopanītaṁ paribarham arhitum

tasmin—in that sacrifice; *bhaginyaḥ*—sisters; *mama*—my; *bhartṛbhiḥ*—with their husbands; *svakaiḥ*—their own; *dhruvam*—surely; *gamiṣyanti*—will go; *suhṛt-didṛkṣavaḥ*—desiring to meet the relatives; *aham*—I; *ca*—and; *tasmin*—in that assembly; *bhavatā*—with you (Lord Śiva); *abhikāmaye*—I desire; *saha*—with; *upanītam*—given; *paribarham*—ornaments of decoration; *arhitum*—to accept.

TRANSLATION

I think that all my sisters must have gone to this great sacrificial ceremony with their husbands just to see their relatives. I also desire to decorate myself with the ornaments given to me by my father and go there with you to participate in that assembly.

PURPORT

It is a woman's nature to want to decorate herself with ornaments and nice dresses and accompany her husband to social functions, meet friends and relatives, and enjoy life in that way. This propensity is not unusual, for woman is the basic principle of material enjoyment. Therefore in Sanskrit the word for woman is *strī*, which means "one who expands the field of material enjoyment." In the material world there is an attraction between woman and man. This is the arrangement of conditional life. A woman attracts a man, and in that way the scope of material activities, involving house, wealth, children and friendship, increases, and thus instead of decreasing one's material demands, one becomes entangled in material enjoyment. Lord Śiva, however, is different; therefore his name is Śiva. He is not at all attracted by material enjoyment, although his wife, Satī, was the daughter of a very great leader and was given to him by the request of Brahmā. Lord Śiva was reluctant, but Satī, as a woman, the daughter of a king, wanted enjoyment. She wanted to go to her father's house, just as her other sisters might have done, and meet them and enjoy social life. Here, she specifically indicated that she would decorate herself with the ornaments given by her father. She did not say that she would decorate herself with the ornaments given by her husband because her husband was callous about all such matters. He did not know how to decorate his wife and take part in social life because he was always in ecstasy with thoughts of the Supreme Personality of Godhead. According to the Vedic system, a daughter is given a sufficient dowry at the time of her marriage, and therefore Satī was also given a dowry by her father, and ornaments were included. It is also the custom that the husband gives some ornaments, but here it is particularly mentioned that her husband, being materially almost nothing, could not do so; therefore she wanted to decorate herself with the ornaments given by her father. It was fortunate for Satī that Lord Śiva did not take the ornaments from his wife and spend them for *gāñjā*, because those who imitate Lord Śiva in smoking *gāñjā* exploit everything from household affairs; they take all of their wives' property and spend on smoking, intoxication and similar other activities.

TEXT 10

तत्र स्वसॄर्मे ननु भर्तृसम्मिता
मातृष्वसॄः क्लिन्नधियं च मातरम् ।
द्रक्ष्ये चिरोत्कण्ठमना महर्षिभि-
रुन्नीयमानं च मृडाध्वरध्वजम् ॥१०॥

tatra svasṝr me nanu bhartṛ-sammitā
mātṛ-ṣvasṝḥ klinna-dhiyaṁ ca mātaram
drakṣye cirotkaṇṭha-manā maharṣibhir
unnīyamānaṁ ca mṛḍādhvara-dhvajam

tatra—there; *svasṝḥ*—own sisters; *me*—my; *nanu*—surely; *bhartṛ-sammitāḥ*—along with their husbands; *mātṛ-svasṝḥ*—the sisters of my mother; *klinna-dhiyam*—affectionate; *ca*—and; *mātaram*—mother; *drakṣye*—I shall see; *cira-utkaṇṭha-manāḥ*—being very anxious for a long time; *mahā-ṛṣibhiḥ*—by great sages; *unnīyamānam*—being raised; *ca*—and; *mṛḍa*—O Śiva; *adhvara*—sacrifice; *dhvajam*—flags.

TRANSLATION

My sisters, my mother's sisters and their husbands, and other affectionate relatives must be assembled there, so if I go I shall be

able to see them, and I shall be able to see the flapping flags and the performance of the sacrifice by the great sages. For these reasons, my dear husband, I am very much anxious to go.

PURPORT

As stated before, the tension between the father-in-law and son-in-law persisted for a considerable time. Satī, therefore, had not gone to her father's house for a long while. Thus she was very anxious to go to her father's house, particularly because on that occasion her sisters and their husbands and her mother's sisters would be there. As is natural for a woman, she wanted to dress equally to her other sisters and also be accompanied by her husband. She did not, of course, want to go alone.

TEXT 11

त्वय्येतदाश्चर्यमजात्ममायया
विनिर्मितं भाति गुणत्रयात्मकम् ।
तथाप्यहं योषिदतत्त्वविच्च ते
दीना दिदृक्षे भव मे भवक्षितिम् ॥११॥

tvayy etad āścaryam ajātma-māyayā
vinirmitaṁ bhāti guṇa-trayātmakam
tathāpy ahaṁ yoṣid atattva-vic ca te
dīnā didṛkṣe bhava me bhava-kṣitim

tvayi—in you; *etat*—this; *āścaryam*—wonderful; *aja*—O Lord Śiva; *ātma-māyayā*—by the external energy of the Supreme Lord; *vinirmitam*—created; *bhāti*—appears; *guṇa-traya-ātmakam*—being an interaction of the three modes of material nature; *tathā api*—even so; *aham*—I; *yoṣit*—woman; *atattva-vit*—not conversant with the truth; *ca*—and; *te*—your; *dīnā*—poor; *didṛkṣe*—I wish to see; *bhava*—O Lord Śiva; *me*—my; *bhava-kṣitim*—place of birth.

TRANSLATION

This manifested cosmos is a wonderful creation of the interaction of the three material modes, or the external energy of the

Supreme Lord. This truth is fully known to you. Yet I am but a poor woman, and, as you know, I am not conversant with the truth. Therefore I wish to see my birthplace once more.

PURPORT

Dākṣāyaṇī, Satī, knew very well that her husband, Lord Śiva, was not very much interested in the glaring manifestation of the material world, which is caused by the interaction of the three modes of nature. Therefore she addressed her husband as *aja*, which refers to one who has transcended the bondage of birth and death, or one who has realized his eternal position. She stated, "The illusion of accepting the perverted reflection, the material or cosmic manifestation, to be real is not present in you, because you are self-realized. For you the attraction of social life and the consideration that someone is father, someone is mother and someone is sister, which are illusory relationships, is already over; but because I am a poor woman, I am not so advanced in transcendental realization. Therefore naturally these appear to me as real." Only less intelligent persons accept this perverted reflection of the spiritual world to be real. Those who are under the spell of the external energy accept this manifestation to be fact, whereas those who are advanced in spiritual realization know that it is illusion. Actual reality is elsewhere, in the spiritual world. "But as far as I am concerned," Satī said, "I do not have much knowledge about self-realization. I am poor because I do not know the actual facts. I am attracted by my birthplace, and I want to see it." One who has attraction for his birthplace, for his body, and for other such items mentioned in the *Bhāgavatam* is considered to be like an ass or a cow. Satī might have heard all this many times from her husband, Lord Śiva, but because she was a woman, *yoṣit*, she still hankered after the same material objects of affection. The word *yoṣit* means "one who is enjoyed." Therefore woman is called *yoṣit*. In spiritual advancement, association with *yoṣit* is always restricted because if one is like a play doll in the hands of *yoṣit*, then all his spiritual advancement is at once stopped. It is said, "Those who are just like playthings in the hands of a woman (*yoṣit-krīḍā-mṛgeṣu*) cannot make any advancement in spiritual realization."

TEXT 12

पश्य प्रयान्तीरभवान्ययोषितो
ऽप्यलंकृताः कान्तसखा वरूथशः ।
यासां व्रजद्भिः शितिकण्ठ मण्डितं
नभो विमानैः कलहंसपाण्डुभिः ॥१२॥

paśya prayāntīr abhavānya-yoṣito
'py alaṅkṛtāḥ kānta-sakhā varūthaśaḥ
yāsāṁ vrajadbhiḥ śiti-kaṇṭha maṇḍitaṁ
nabho vimānaiḥ kala-haṁsa-pāṇḍubhiḥ

paśya—just see; *prayāntīḥ*—going; *abhava*—O never-born; *anya-yoṣitaḥ*—other women; *api*—certainly; *alaṅkṛtāḥ*—ornamented; *kānta-sakhāḥ*—with their husbands and friends; *varūthaśaḥ*—in large numbers; *yāsām*—of them; *vrajadbhiḥ*—flying; *śiti-kaṇṭha*—O blue-throated one; *maṇḍitam*—decorated; *nabhaḥ*—the sky; *vimānaiḥ*—with airplanes; *kala-haṁsa*—swans; *pāṇḍubhiḥ*—white.

TRANSLATION

O never-born, O blue-throated one, not only my relatives but also other women, dressed in nice clothes and decorated with ornaments, are going there with their husbands and friends. Just see how their flocks of white airplanes have made the entire sky very beautiful.

PURPORT

Here Lord Śiva is addressed as *abhava,* which means "one who is never born," although generally he is known as *bhava,* "one who is born." Rudra, Lord Śiva, is actually born from between the eyes of Brahmā, who is called Svayambhū because he is not born of any human being or material creature but is born directly from the lotus flower which grows from the abdomen of Viṣṇu. When Lord Śiva is addressed here as *abhava,* this may be taken to mean "one who has never felt material miseries." Satī wanted to impress upon her husband that even those who were not related to her father were also going, to say nothing of herself, who was intimately related with him. Lord Śiva is addressed here as blue throated. Lord Śiva drank an ocean of poison and kept it in his throat, not swallowing it or allowing it to go down to his stomach, and thus his throat became blue. Since then he has been known as *nīlakaṇṭha*, or blue throated. The reason that Lord Śiva drank an ocean of poison was for others' benefit. When the ocean was churned by the demigods and the demons, the churning at first produced poison, so because the poisonous ocean might have affected others who were not so advanced, Lord Śiva drank all the ocean water. In other words, he could drink such a great amount of poison for others' benefit, and now, since his wife was personally requesting him to go to her father's house, even if he did not wish to give that permission, he should do so out of his great kindness.

TEXT 13

कथं सुतायाः पितृगेहकौतुकं
निशम्य देहः सुरवर्य नेङ्गते ।
अनाहुता अप्यभियन्ति सौहृदं
भर्तुर्गुरोर्देहकृतश्च केतनम् ॥१३॥

kathaṁ sutāyāḥ pitṛ-geha-kautukaṁ
niśamya dehaḥ sura-varya neṅgate
anāhutā apy abhiyanti sauhṛdaṁ
bhartur guror deha-kṛtaś ca ketanam

katham—how; *sutāyāḥ*—of a daughter; *pitṛ-geha-kautukam*—the festival in the house of her father; *niśamya*—hearing; *dehaḥ*—the body; *sura-varya*—O best of the demigods; *na*—not; *iṅgate*—disturbed; *anāhutāḥ*—without being called; *api*—even; *abhiyanti*—goes; *sauhṛdam*—a friend; *bhartuḥ*—of the husband; *guroḥ*—of the spiritual master; *deha-kṛtaḥ*—of the father; *ca*—and; *ketanam*—the house.

TRANSLATION

O best of the demigods, how can the body of a daughter remain undisturbed when she hears that some festive event is taking place in her father's house? Even though you may be considering that I

have not been invited, there is no harm if one goes to the house of one's friend, husband, spiritual master or father without invitation.

TEXT 14

तन्मे प्रसीदेदममर्त्य वाञ्छितं
कर्तुं भवान्कारुणिको बतार्हति ।
त्वयात्मनोऽर्धेऽहमदभ्रचक्षुषा
निरूपिता मानुगृहाण याचितः ॥१४॥

tan me prasīdedam amartya vāñchitaṁ
kartuṁ bhavān kāruṇiko batārhati
tvayātmano 'rdhe 'ham adabhra-cakṣuṣā
nirūpitā mānugṛhāṇa yācitaḥ

tat—therefore; *me*—unto me; *prasīda*—please be kind; *idam*—this; *amartya*—O immortal lord; *vāñchitam*—desire; *kartum*—to do; *bhavān*—Your Honor; *kāruṇikaḥ*—kind; *bata*—O lord; *arhati*—is able; *tvayā*—by you; *ātmanaḥ*—of your own body; *ardhe*—in the half; *aham*—I; *adabhra-cakṣuṣā*—having all knowledge; *nirūpitā*—am situated; *mā*—to me; *anugṛhāṇa*—please show kindness; *yācitaḥ*—requested.

TRANSLATION

O immortal Śiva, please be kind towards me and fulfill my desire. You have accepted me as half of your body; therefore please show kindness towards me and accept my request.

TEXT 15

ऋषिरुवाच
एवं गिरित्रः प्रिययाभिभाषितः
प्रत्यभ्यधत्त प्रहसन् सुहृत्प्रियः ।
संस्मारितो मर्मभिदः कुवागिषून्
यानाह को विश्वसृजां समक्षतः ॥१५॥

ṛṣir uvāca
evaṁ giritraḥ priyayābhibhāṣitaḥ
pratyabhyadhatta prahasan suhṛt-priyaḥ
saṁsmārito marma-bhidaḥ kuvāg-iṣūn
yān āha ko viśva-sṛjāṁ samakṣataḥ

ṛṣiḥ uvāca—the great sage Maitreya said; *evam*—thus; *giritraḥ*—Lord Śiva; *priyayā*—by his dear wife; *abhibhāṣitaḥ*—being spoken to; *pratyabhyadhatta*—replied; *prahasan*—while smiling; *suhṛt-priyaḥ*—dear to the relatives; *saṁsmāritaḥ*—remembering; *marma-bhidaḥ*—heart piercing; *kuvāk-iṣūn*—malicious words; *yān*—which (words); *āha*—said; *kaḥ*—who (Dakṣa); *viśva-sṛjām*—of the creators of the universal manifestation; *samakṣataḥ*—in the presence.

TRANSLATION

The great sage Maitreya said: Lord Śiva, the deliverer of the hill Kailāsa, having thus been addressed by his dear wife, replied smilingly, although at the same time he remembered the malicious, heart-piercing speeches delivered by Dakṣa before the guardians of the universal affairs.

PURPORT

When Lord Śiva heard from his wife about Dakṣa, the psychological effect was that he immediately remembered the strong words spoken against him in the assembly of the guardians of the universe, and, remembering those words, he was sorry at heart, although to please his wife he smiled. In *Bhagavad-gītā* it is said that a liberated person is always in mental equilibrium in both the distress and the happiness of this material world. Therefore the question may now be raised why a liberated personality like Lord Śiva was so unhappy because of the words of Dakṣa. The answer is given by Śrīla Viśvanātha Cakravartī Ṭhākura. Lord Śiva is *ātmārāma*, or situated in complete self-realization, but because he is the incarnation in charge of the material mode of ignorance, *tamo-guṇa*, he is sometimes affected by the pleasure and pain of the material world. The difference between the pleasure and pain of this material world and that of the spiritual world is that in the spiritual world the effect is qualitatively absolute. Therefore one may feel sorry in the absolute world, but the manifestation of so-called pain is always full of bliss. For instance, once Lord Kṛṣṇa, in His childhood, was chastised by His mother, Yaśodā, and Lord Kṛṣṇa cried. But although He shed tears from His eyes, this is not to be considered a reaction of the mode of ignorance, for the incident was full of transcendental pleasure. When Kṛṣṇa was playing in so many ways, sometimes it appeared that He caused distress to the *gopīs*, but actually such dealings were full of transcendental bliss. That is the difference between the material and spiritual worlds. The spiritual world, where everything is pure, is pervertedly reflected in this material world. Since everything in the spiritual world is absolute, in the spiritual varieties of apparent pleasure and pain there is no perception other than eternal bliss, whereas in the material world, because everything is contaminated by the modes of material nature, there are feelings of pleasure and pain. Therefore because Lord Śiva, although a fully self-realized person, was in charge of the material mode of ignorance, he felt sorrow.

TEXT 16

श्रीभगवानुवाच
त्वयोदितं शोभनमेव शोभने
अनाहुता अप्यभियन्ति बन्धुषु ।
ते यद्यनुत्पादितदोषदृष्टयो
बलीयसानात्म्यमदेन मन्युना ॥१६॥

śrī-bhagavān uvāca
tvayoditaṁ śobhanam eva śobhane
anāhutā apy abhiyanti bandhuṣu
te yady anutpādita-doṣa-dṛṣṭayo
balīyasānātmya-madena manyunā

śrī-bhagavān uvāca—the great lord replied; *tvayā*—by you; *uditam*—said; *śobhanam*—is true; *eva*—certainly; *śobhane*—my dear beautiful wife; *anāhutāḥ*—without being invited; *api*—even; *abhiyanti*—go; *bandhuṣu*—among friends; *te*—those (friends); *yadi*—if; *anutpādita-doṣa-dṛṣṭayaḥ*—not finding fault; *balīyasā*—more important; *anātmya-madena*—by pride caused by identification with the body; *manyunā*—by anger.

TRANSLATION

The great lord replied: My dear beautiful wife, you have said that one may go to a friend's house without being invited, and this is true, provided such a friend does not find fault with the guest because of bodily identification and thereby become angry towards him.

PURPORT

Lord Śiva could foresee that as soon as Satī reached her father's house, her father, Dakṣa, being too puffed up because of bodily identification, would be angry at her presence, and although she was innocent and faultless, he would be mercilessly angry towards her. Lord Śiva warned that since her father was too puffed up by his material possessions, he would be angry, and this would be intolerable for her. Therefore it was better that she not go. This fact was already experienced by Lord Śiva because although Lord Śiva was faultless, Dakṣa had cursed him in so many harsh words.

TEXT 17

विद्यातपोवित्तवपुर्वयःकुलैः
सतां गुणैः षड्भिरसत्तमेतरैः ।
स्मृतौ हतायां भृतमानदुर्दृशः
स्तब्धा न पश्यन्ति हि धाम भूयसाम् ॥१७॥

vidyā-tapo-vitta-vapur-vayaḥ-kulaiḥ
satāṁ guṇaiḥ ṣaḍbhir asattametaraiḥ
smṛtau hatāyāṁ bhṛta-māna-durdṛśaḥ
stabdhā na paśyanti hi dhāma bhūyasām

vidyā—education; *tapaḥ*—austerity; *vitta*—wealth; *vapuḥ*—beauty of body, etc.; *vayaḥ*—youth; *kulaiḥ*—with heritage; *satām*—of the pious; *guṇaiḥ*—by such qualities; *ṣaḍbhiḥ*—six; *asattama-itaraiḥ*—having the opposite result to those who are not great souls; *smṛtau*—

good sense; *hatāyām*—being lost; *bhṛta-māna-durdṛśaḥ*—blind due to pride; *stabdhāḥ*—being proud; *na*—not; *paśyanti*—see; *hi*—for; *dhāma*—the glories; *bhūyasām*—of the great souls.

TRANSLATION

Although the six qualities education, austerity, wealth, beauty, youth and heritage are for the highly elevated, one who is proud of possessing them becomes blind, and thus he loses his good sense and cannot appreciate the glories of great personalities.

PURPORT

It may be argued that since Dakṣa was very learned, wealthy and austere and had descended from a very exalted heritage, how could he be unnecessarily angry towards another? The answer is that when the qualities of good education, good parentage, beauty and sufficient wealth are misplaced in a person who is puffed up by all these possessions, they produce a very bad result. Milk is a very nice food, but when milk is touched by an envious serpent it becomes poisonous. Similarly, material assets such as education, wealth, beauty and good parentage are undoubtedly nice, but when they decorate persons of a malicious nature, then they act adversely. Another example, given by Cāṇakya Paṇḍita, is that a serpent that has a jewel on its head is still fearful because it is a serpent. A serpent, by nature, is envious of other living entities, even though they be faultless. When a serpent bites another creature, it is not necessarily because the other creature is at fault; it is the habit of the serpent to bite innocent creatures. Similarly, although Dakṣa was qualified by many material assets, because he was proud of his possessions and because he was envious, all those qualities were polluted. It is sometimes, therefore, detrimental for a person advancing in spiritual consciousness, or Kṛṣṇa consciousness, to possess such material assets. Kuntīdevī, while offering prayers to Kṛṣṇa, addressed Him as *akiñcana-gocara*, one who is easily approached by those who are bereft of all material acquisitions. Material exhaustion is an advantage for advancement in Kṛṣṇa consciousness, although if one is conscious of his eternal relationship with the Supreme Personality of Godhead, one can utilize one's material assets, such as great learning and beauty and exalted ancestry, for the service of the Lord; then such assets become glorious. In other words, unless one is Kṛṣṇa conscious, all his material possessions are zero, but when this zero is by the side of the Supreme One, it at once increases in value to ten. Unless situated by the side of the Supreme One, zero is always zero; one may add one hundred zeros, but the value will still remain zero. Unless one's material assets are used in Kṛṣṇa consciousness, they may play havoc and degrade the possessor.

TEXT 18

नैतादृशानां स्वजनव्यपेक्षया
गृहान् प्रतीयादनवस्थितात्मनाम् ।
येऽभ्यागतान् वक्रधियाभिचक्षते
आरोपितभ्रूभिरमर्षणाक्षिभिः ॥१८॥

naitādṛśānāṁ sva-jana-vyapekṣayā
gṛhān pratīyād anavasthitātmanām
ye 'bhyāgatān vakra-dhiyābhicakṣate
āropita-bhrūbhir amarṣaṇākṣibhiḥ

na—not; *etādṛśānām*—like this; *sva-jana*—kinsmen; *vyapekṣayā*—depending on that; *gṛhān*—in the house of; *pratīyāt*—one should go; *anavasthita*—disturbed; *ātmanām*—mind; *ye*—those; *abhyāgatān*—guests; *vakra-dhiyā*—with a cold reception; *abhicakṣate*—looking at; *āropita-bhrūbhiḥ*—with raised eyebrows; *amarṣaṇa*—angry; *akṣibhiḥ*—with the eyes.

TRANSLATION

One should not go to anyone's house, even on the consideration of his being a relative or a friend, when the man is disturbed in his mind and looks upon the guest with raised eyebrows and angry eyes.

PURPORT

However low a person may be, he is never unkind to his children, wife and nearest kin; even a tiger is kind to its cubs, for within the animal kingdom the cubs are treated very nicely. Since Satī was the daughter of Dakṣa, however cruel and contaminated he might be, naturally it was expected that he would receive her very nicely. But here it is indicated by the word *anavasthita* that such a person cannot be trusted. Tigers are very kind to their cubs, but it is also known that sometimes they eat them. Malicious persons should not be trusted, because they are always unsteady. Thus Satī was advised not to go to her father's house because to accept such a father as a relative and to go to his house without being properly invited was not suitable.

TEXT 19

तथारिभिर्न व्यथते शिलीमुखैः
शेतेऽर्दिताङ्गो हृदयेन दूयता ।
स्वानां यथा वक्रधियां दुरुक्तिभि-
र्दिवानिशं तप्यति मर्मताडितः ॥१९॥

tathāribhir na vyathate śilīmukhaiḥ
śete 'rditāṅgo hṛdayena dūyatā
svānāṁ yathā vakra-dhiyāṁ duruktibhir
divā-niśaṁ tapyati marma-tāḍitaḥ

tathā—so; *aribhiḥ*—enemy; *na*—not; *vyathate*—is hurt; *śilīmukhaiḥ*—by the arrows; *śete*—rests; *ardita*—aggrieved; *aṅgaḥ*—a part; *hṛdayena*—by the heart; *dūyatā*—grieving; *svānām*—of relatives; *yathā*—as; *vakra-dhiyām*—deceitful; *duruktibhiḥ*—by harsh words; *divā-niśam*—day and night; *tapyati*—suffers; *marma-tāḍitaḥ*—one whose feelings are hurt.

TRANSLATION

Lord Śiva continued: If one is hurt by the arrows of an enemy, one is not as aggrieved as when cut by the unkind words of a relative, for such grief continues to rend one's heart day and night.

PURPORT

Satī might have concluded that she would take the risk of going to her father's house, and even if her father spoke unkindly against her she would be tolerant, as a son sometimes tolerates the reproaches of his parents. But Lord Śiva reminded her that she would not be able to tolerate such unkind words because natural psychology dictates that although one can suffer harm from an enemy and not mind so much because pain inflicted by an enemy is natural, when one is hurt by the strong words of a relative, one suffers the effects continually, day and night, and sometimes the injury becomes so intolerable that one commits suicide.

TEXT 20

व्यक्तं त्वमुत्कृष्टगतेः प्रजापतेः
प्रियात्मजानामसि सुभ्रु मे मता ।
तथापि मानं न पितुः प्रपत्स्यसे
मदाश्रयात्कः परितप्यते यतः ॥२०॥

vyaktaṁ tvam utkṛṣṭa-gateḥ prajāpateḥ
priyātmajānām asi subhru me matā
tathāpi mānaṁ na pituḥ prapatsyase
mad-āśrayāt kaḥ paritapyate yataḥ

vyaktam—it is clear; *tvam*—you; *utkṛṣṭa-gateḥ*—having the best behavior; *prajāpateḥ*—of Prajāpati Dakṣa; *priyā*—the pet; *ātmajānām*—of the daughters; *asi*—you are; *subhru*—O you with the beautiful eyebrows; *me*—my; *matā*—considered; *tathā api*—yet; *mānam*—honor; *na*—not; *pituḥ*—from your father; *prapatsyase*—you will meet with; *mat-āśrayāt*—from connection with me; *kaḥ*—Dakṣa; *paritapyate*—is feeling pain; *yataḥ*—from whom.

TRANSLATION

My dear white-complexioned wife, it is clear that of the many daughters of Dakṣa you are the pet, yet you will not be honored at his house because of your being my wife. Rather, you will be sorry that you are connected with me.

PURPORT

Lord Śiva put forward the argument that even if Satī proposed to go alone, without her husband, still she would not be received well because she was his wife. There was every chance of a catastrophe, even if she wanted to go alone. Therefore Lord Śiva indirectly requested her not to go to her father's house.

TEXT 21

पापच्यमानेन हृदातुरेन्द्रियः
समृद्धिभिः पूरुषबुद्धिसाक्षिणाम् ।
अकल्प एषामधिरोढुमञ्जसा
परं पदं द्वेष्टि यथासुरा हरिम् ॥२१॥

pāpacyamānena hṛdāturendriyaḥ
samṛddhibhiḥ pūruṣa-buddhi-sākṣiṇām
akalpa eṣām adhiroḍhum añjasā
paraṁ padaṁ dveṣṭi yathāsurā harim

pāpacyamānena—burning; *hṛdā*—with a heart; *ātura-indriyaḥ*—who is distressed; *samṛddhibhiḥ*—by the pious reputation, etc.; *pūruṣa-buddhi-sākṣiṇām*—of those who are always absorbed in thought of the Supreme Lord; *akalpaḥ*—being unable; *eṣām*—of those persons; *adhiroḍhum*—to rise; *añjasā*—quickly; *param*—merely; *padam*—to the standard; *dveṣṭi*—envy; *yathā*—as much as; *asurāḥ*—the demons; *harim*—the Supreme Personality of Godhead.

TRANSLATION

One who is conducted by false ego and thus always distressed, both mentally and sensually, cannot tolerate the opulence of self-realized persons. Being unable to rise to the standard of self-realization, he envies such persons as much as demons envy the Supreme Personality of Godhead.

PURPORT

The real reason for the enmity between Lord Śiva and Dakṣa is explained here. Dakṣa was envious of Lord Śiva because of Śiva's high position as an incarnation of a quality of the Supreme Personality of Godhead and because Śiva was directly in contact with the Supersoul and was therefore honored and given a better sitting place than he. There were many other reasons also. Dakṣa, being materially puffed up, could not tolerate the high position of Lord Śiva, so his anger at Lord Śiva's not standing up in his presence was only the final manifestation of his envy. Lord Śiva is always in meditation and always perceives the Supersoul, as expressed here by the words *pūruṣa-buddhi-sākṣiṇām.* The position of one whose intelligence is always absorbed in meditation upon the Supreme Personality of Godhead is very great and cannot be imitated by anyone, especially an ordinary person. When Dakṣa entered the arena of *yajña,* Lord Śiva was in meditation and might not have seen Dakṣa enter, but Dakṣa took the opportunity to curse him because Dakṣa had maintained an envious attitude towards Lord Śiva for a long time. Those who are actually self-realized see every individual body as a temple of the Supreme Personality of Godhead because the Supreme Personality of Godhead, in His Paramātmā feature, is residing in everyone's body.

When one offers respect to the body, it is not to the material body but to the presence of the Supreme Lord. Thus one who is always in meditation upon the Supreme Lord is always offering Him obeisances. But since Dakṣa was not very elevated, he thought that obeisances were offered to the material body, and because Lord Śiva did not offer respect to his material body, Dakṣa became envious. Such persons, being unable to rise to the standard of self-realized souls like Lord Śiva, are always envious. The example given here is very suitable. *Asuras,* demons or atheists, are always envious of the Supreme Personality of Godhead; they simply want to kill Him. Even in this age we find some so-called scholars commenting on *Bhagavad-gītā* who are envious of Kṛṣṇa. When Kṛṣṇa says, *man-manā bhava mad-bhaktaḥ* (Bg. 18.65)—"Always think of Me, become My devotee, and surrender unto Me"—the so-called scholars comment that it is not to Kṛṣṇa that we have to surrender. That is envy. The *asuras* or atheists, the demons, without reason or cause, are envious of the Supreme Personality of Godhead. Similarly, instead of offering respect to self-realized persons, foolish men who cannot approach the highest standard of self-realization are always envious, although there is no reason.

TEXT 22

प्रत्युद्गमप्रश्रयणाभिवादनं
विधीयते साधु मिथः सुमध्यमे ।

प्राज्ञैः परस्मै पुरुषाय चेतसा
गुहाशयायैव न देहमानिने ॥२२॥

pratyudgama-praśrayaṇābhivādanaṁ
vidhīyate sādhu mithaḥ sumadhyame
prājñaiḥ parasmai puruṣāya cetasā
guhā-śayāyaiva na deha-mānine

pratyudgama—standing up from one's seat; *praśrayaṇa*—welcoming; *abhivādanam*—obeisances; *vidhīyate*—are intended; *sādhu*—proper; *mithaḥ*—mutually; *su-madhyame*—my dear young wife; *prājñaiḥ*—by the wise; *parasmai*—unto the Supreme; *puruṣāya*—unto the Supersoul; *cetasā*—with the intelligence; *guhā-śayāya*—sitting within the body; *eva*—certainly; *na*—not; *deha-mānine*—to the person identifying with the body.

TRANSLATION

My dear young wife, certainly friends and relatives offer mutual greetings by standing up, welcoming one another and offering obeisances. But those who are elevated to the transcendental platform, being intelligent, offer such respects to the Supersoul, who is sitting within the body, not to the person who identifies with the body.

PURPORT

It may be argued that since Dakṣa was the father-in-law of Lord Śiva, it was certainly the duty of Lord Śiva to offer him respect. In answer to that argument it is explained here that when a learned person stands up or offers obeisances in welcome, he offers respect to the Supersoul, who is sitting within everyone's heart. It is seen, therefore, among Vaiṣṇavas, that even when a disciple offers obeisances to his spiritual master, the spiritual master immediately returns the obeisances because they are mutually offered not to the body but to the Supersoul. Therefore the spiritual master also offers respect to the Supersoul situated in the body of the disciple. The Lord says in *Śrīmad-Bhāgavatam* that offering respect to His devotee is more valuable than offering respect to Him. Devotees do not identify with the body, so offering respect to a Vaiṣṇava means offering respect to Viṣṇu. It is stated also that as a matter of etiquette as soon as one sees a Vaiṣṇava one must immediately offer him respect, indicating the Supersoul sitting within. A Vaiṣṇava sees the body as a temple of Viṣṇu. Since Lord Śiva had already offered respect to the Supersoul in Kṛṣṇa consciousness, offering respect to Dakṣa, who identified with his body, was already performed. There was no need to offer respect to his body, for that is not directed by any Vedic injunction.

TEXT 23

सत्त्वं विशुद्धं वसुदेवशब्दितं
यदीयते तत्र पुमानपावृतः ।
सत्त्वे च तस्मिन् भगवान् वासुदेवो
ह्यधोक्षजो मे नमसा विधीयते ॥२३॥

sattvaṁ viśuddhaṁ vasudeva-śabditaṁ
yad īyate tatra pumān apāvṛtaḥ
sattve ca tasmin bhagavān vāsudevo
hy adhokṣajo me namasā vidhīyate

sattvam—consciousness; *viśuddham*—pure; *vasudeva*—Vasudeva; *śabditam*—known as; *yat*—because; *īyate*—is revealed; *tatra*—there; *pumān*—the Supreme Person; *apāvṛtaḥ*—without any covering; *sattve*—in consciousness; *ca*—and; *tasmin*—in that; *bhagavān*—the Supreme Personality of Godhead; *vāsudevaḥ*—Vāsudeva; *hi*—because; *adhokṣajaḥ*—transcendental; *me*—by me; *namasā*—with obeisances; *vidhīyate*—worshiped.

TRANSLATION

I am always engaged in offering obeisances to Lord Vāsudeva in pure Kṛṣṇa consciousness. Kṛṣṇa consciousness is always pure consciousness, in which the Supreme Personality of Godhead, known as Vāsudeva, is revealed without any covering.

PURPORT

The living entity is constitutionally pure. *Asaṅgo hy ayaṁ puruṣaḥ.* In the Vedic literature it is said that the soul is always pure and uncontaminated by material attachment. The identification of the body with the soul is due to misunderstanding. As soon as one is fully Kṛṣṇa conscious it is to be understood that one is in his pure, original constitutional position. This state of existence is called *śuddha-sattva*, which means that it is transcendental to the material qualities. Since this *śuddha-sattva* existence is under the direct action of the internal potency, in this state the activities of material consciousness stop. For example, when iron is put into a fire, it becomes warm, and when red-hot, although it is iron, it acts like fire. Similarly, when copper is surcharged with electricity, its action as copper stops; it acts as electricity. *Bhagavad-gītā* (14.26) also confirms that anyone who engages in unadulterated devotional service to the Lord is at once elevated to the position of pure Brahman:

māṁ ca yo 'vyabhicāreṇa
bhakti-yogena sevate
sa guṇān samatītyaitān
brahma-bhūyāya kalpate

Therefore *śuddha-sattva*, as described in this verse, is the transcendental position, which is technically called *vasudeva*. Vasudeva is also the name of the person from whom Kṛṣṇa appears. This verse explains that the pure state is called *vasudeva* because in that state Vāsudeva, the Supreme Personality of Godhead, is revealed without any covering. To execute unadulterated devotional service, therefore, one must follow the rules and regulations of devotional service without desire to gain material profit by fruitive activities or mental speculation.

In pure devotional service one simply serves the Supreme Personality of Godhead as a matter of duty, without reason and without being impeded by material conditions. That is called *śuddha-sattva*, or *vasudeva*, because in that stage the Supreme Person, Kṛṣṇa, is revealed in the heart of the devotee. Śrīla Jīva Gosvāmī has very nicely described this *vasudeva*, or *śuddha-sattva*, in his *Bhagavat-sandarbha*. He explains that *aṣṭottara-śata* (108) is added to the name of the spiritual master to indicate one who is situated in *śuddha-sattva*, or in the transcendental state of *vasudeva*. The word *vasudeva* is also used for other purposes. For example, *vasudeva* also means one who is everywhere, or all-pervading.

The sun is also called *vasudeva-śabditam*. The word *vasudeva* may be utilized for different purposes, but whatever purpose we adopt, Vāsudeva means the all-pervading or localized Supreme Personality of Godhead. In *Bhagavad-gītā* (7.19) it is also stated, *vāsudevaḥ sarvam iti.* Factual realization is to understand Vāsudeva, the Supreme Personality of Godhead, and surrender unto Him. *Vasudeva* is the ground wherein Vāsudeva, the Supreme Personality of Godhead, is revealed. When one is free from the contamination of material nature and is situated in pure Kṛṣṇa consciousness, or in the *vasudeva* state, Vāsudeva, the Supreme Person, is revealed. This state is also called *kaivalya*, which means "pure consciousness." *Jñānaṁ sāttvikaṁ kaivalyam.* When one is situated in pure, transcendental knowledge, one is situated in *kaivalya.* Therefore *vasudeva* also means *kaivalya*, a word which is generally used by impersonalists. Impersonal *kaivalya* is not the last stage of realization, but in Kṛṣṇa consciousness *kaivalya*, when one understands the Supreme Personality of Godhead, then one is successful. In that pure state, by hearing, chanting, remembering, etc., because of the development of knowledge of the science of Kṛṣṇa, one can understand the Supreme Personality of Godhead. All these activities are under the guidance of the internal energy of the Supreme Lord.

The action of the internal potency is also described in this verse as *apāvṛtaḥ*, free from any covering. Because the Supreme Personality of Godhead, His name, His form, His quality, His paraphernalia, etc., being transcendental, are beyond material nature, it is not possible to understand any one of them with the materialistic senses. When the senses are purified by the discharge of pure devotional service (*hṛṣīkeṇa hṛṣīkeśa-sevanaṁ bhaktir ucyate*), the pure senses can see Kṛṣṇa without covering. Now one may inquire that since factually the devotee has the same material existential body, how is it possible that the same materialistic eyes become purified by devotional service? The example, as stated by Lord Caitanya, is that devotional service cleanses the mirror of the mind. In a clean mirror one can see one's face very distinctly. Similarly, simply by cleansing the mirror of the mind one can have a clear conception of the Supreme Personality of Godhead. It is stated in *Bhagavad-gītā* (8.8), *abhyāsa-yoga-yuktena.* By executing one's prescribed duties in devotional service, *cetasā nānya-gāminā*, or simply by hearing about God and chanting about Him, if one's mind is always engaged in chanting and hearing and is not allowed to go elsewhere, one can realize the Supreme Personality of Godhead. As confirmed by Lord Caitanya, by the *bhakti-yoga* process, beginning from hearing and chanting, one can cleanse the heart and mind, and thus one can clearly see the face of the Supreme Personality of Godhead.

Lord Śiva said that since his heart was always filled with the conception of Vāsudeva, the Supreme Personality of Godhead, because of the Supreme Lord's presence within his mind and heart, he was always offering obeisances unto that Supreme Godhead. In other words, Lord Śiva is always in trance, *samādhi.* This *samādhi* is not under the control of the devotee; it is under the control of Vāsudeva, for the entire internal energy of the Supreme Personality of Godhead acts under His order. Of course, the material energy also acts by His order, but His direct will is specifically executed through the spiritual energy. Thus by His spiritual energy He reveals Himself. It is stated in *Bhagavad-gītā* (4.6), *sambhavāmy ātma-māyayā. Ātma-māyayā* means "internal potency." By His sweet will He reveals Himself by His internal potency, being satisfied by the transcendental loving service of the devotee. The devotee never commands, "My dear Lord, please come here so that I can see You." It is not the position of the devotee to command the Supreme Personality of Godhead to come before him or to dance before him. There are many so-called devotees who command the Lord to come before them dancing. The Lord, however, is not subject to anyone's command, but if He is satisfied by one's pure devotional activities, He reveals Himself. Therefore a meaningful word in this verse is *adhokṣaja,* for it indicates that the activities of our material senses will fail to realize the Supreme Personality of Godhead. One cannot realize the Supreme Personality of Godhead simply by the attempt of one's speculative mind, but if one desires he can subdue all the material activities of his senses, and the Lord, by manifesting His spiritual energy, can reveal Himself to the pure devotee. When the Supreme Personality of Godhead reveals Himself to the pure devotee, the devotee has no other duty than to offer Him respectful obeisances. The Absolute Truth reveals Himself to the devotee in His form. He is not formless. Vāsudeva is not formless, for it is stated in this verse that as soon as the Lord reveals Himself, the devotee offers his obeisances. Obeisances are offered to a person, not to anything impersonal. One should not accept the Māyāvāda interpretation that Vāsudeva is impersonal. As stated in *Bhagavad-gītā*, *prapadyate*, one surrenders. One surrenders to a person, not to impersonal nonduality. Whenever there is a question of surrendering or offering obeisances, there must be an object of surrender or obeisances.

TEXT 24

तत्ते निरीक्ष्यो न पितापि देहकृद्
दक्षो मम द्विट् तदनुव्रताश्च ये ।
यो विश्वसृग्यज्ञगतं वरोरु मा-
मनागसं दुर्वचसाकरोत्तिरः ॥२४॥

tat te nirīkṣyo na pitāpi deha-kṛd
dakṣo mama dviṭ tad-anuvratāś ca ye
yo viśvasṛg-yajña-gataṁ varoru mām
anāgasaṁ durvacasākarot tiraḥ

tat—therefore; *te*—your; *nirīkṣyaḥ*—to be seen; *na*—not; *pitā*—your father; *api*—although; *deha-kṛt*—the giver of your body; *dakṣaḥ*—Dakṣa; *mama*—my; *dviṭ*—envious; *tat-anuvratāḥ*—his (Dakṣa's) followers; *ca*—also; *ye*—who; *yaḥ*—who (Dakṣa); *viśva-sṛk*—of the Viśvasṛks; *yajña-gatam*—being present at the sacrifice; *vara-ūru*—O Satī; *mām*—me; *anāgasam*—being innocent; *durvacasā*—with cruel words; *akarot tiraḥ*—has insulted.

TRANSLATION

Therefore you should not see your father, although he is the giver of your body, because he and his followers are envious of me. Because of his envy, O most worshipful one, he has insulted me with cruel words although I am innocent.

PURPORT

For a woman, both the husband and the father are equally worshipable. The husband is the protector of a woman during her youthful life, whereas the father is her protector during her childhood. Thus both are worshipable, but especially the father because he is the giver of the body.

Lord Śiva reminded Satī, "Your father is undoubtedly worshipable, even more than I am, but take care, for although he is the giver of your body, he may also be the taker of your body because when you see your father, because of your association with me, he may insult you. An insult from a relative is worse than death, especially when one is well situated."

TEXT 25

यदि व्रजिष्यस्यतिहाय मद्वचो
भद्रं भवत्या न ततो भविष्यति ।
सम्भावितस्य स्वजनात्पराभवो
यदा स सद्यो मरणाय कल्पते ॥२५॥

yadi vrajiṣyasy atihāya mad-vaco
bhadraṁ bhavatyā na tato bhaviṣyati
sambhāvitasya sva-janāt parābhavo
yadā sa sadyo maraṇāya kalpate

yadi—if; *vrajiṣyasi*—you will go; *atihāya*—neglecting; *mat-vacaḥ*—my words; *bhadram*—good; *bhavatyāḥ*—your; *na*—not; *tataḥ*—then; *bhaviṣyati*—will become; *sambhāvitasya*—most respectable; *sva-janāt*—by your own relative; *parābhavaḥ*—are insulted; *yadā*—when; *saḥ*—that insult; *sadyaḥ*—immediately; *maraṇāya*—to death; *kalpate*—is equal.

TRANSLATION

If in spite of this instruction you decide to go, neglecting my words, the future will not be good for you. You are most respectable, and when you are insulted by your relative, this insult will immediately be equal to death.

Thus end the Bhaktivedanta purports of the Fourth Canto, Third Chapter, of the Śrīmad-Bhāgavatam, *entitled "Talks Between Lord Śiva and Satī."*

CHAPTER FOUR

Satī Quits Her Body

TEXT 1

मैत्रेय उवाच
एतावदुक्त्वा विरराम शंकरः
पत्न्यङ्गनाशं ह्युभयत्र चिन्तयन् ।
सुहृद्दिदृक्षुः परिशङ्किता भवा-
न्निष्क्रामती निर्विशती द्विधास सा ॥१॥

maitreya uvāca
etāvad uktvā virarāma śaṅkaraḥ
patny-aṅga-nāśaṁ hy ubhayatra cintayan
suhṛd-didṛkṣuḥ pariśaṅkitā bhavān
niṣkrāmatī nirviśatī dvidhāsa sā

maitreyaḥ uvāca—Maitreya said; *etāvat*—so much; *uktvā*—after speaking; *virarāma*—was silent; *śaṅkaraḥ*—Lord Śiva; *patnī-aṅga-nāśam*—the destruction of the body of his wife; *hi*—since; *ubhayatra*—in both cases; *cintayan*—understanding; *suhṛt-didṛkṣuḥ*—being anxious to see her relatives; *pariśaṅkitā*—being afraid; *bhavāt*—of Śiva; *niṣkrāmatī*—moving out; *nirviśatī*—moving in; *dvidhā*—divided; *āsa*—was; *sā*—she (Satī).

TRANSLATION

The sage Maitreya said: Lord Śiva was silent after speaking to Satī, seeing her between decisions. Satī was very much anxious to see her relatives at her father's house, but at the same time she was afraid of Lord Śiva's warning. Her mind unsettled, she moved in and out of the room as a swing moves this way and that.

PURPORT

Satī's mind was divided about whether to go to her father's house or obey the orders of Lord Śiva. The struggle between the two decisions was so strong that she was pushed from one side of the room to another, and she began to move just like the pendulum of a clock.

TEXT 2

सुहृद्दिदृक्षाप्रतिघातदुर्मनाः
स्नेहाद्रुदत्यश्रुकलातिविह्वला ।
भवं भवान्यप्रतिपूरुषं रुषा
प्रधक्ष्यतीवैक्षत जातवेपथुः ॥ २ ॥

suhṛd-didṛkṣā-pratighāta-durmanāḥ
snehād rudaty aśru-kalātivihvalā
bhavaṁ bhavāny apratipūruṣaṁ ruṣā
pradhakṣyatīvaikṣata jāta-vepathuḥ

suhṛt-didṛkṣā—of the desire to see her relatives; *pratighāta*—the prevention; *durmanāḥ*—feeling sorry; *snehāt*—from affection; *rudatī*—crying; *aśru-kalā*—by drops of tears; *ativihvalā*—very much afflicted; *bhavam*—Lord Śiva; *bhavānī*—Satī; *aprati-pūruṣam*—without an equal or rival; *ruṣā*—with anger; *pradhakṣyatī*—to blast; *iva*—as if; *aikṣata*—looked at; *jāta-vepathuḥ*—shaking.

TRANSLATION

Satī felt very sorry at being forbidden to go see her relatives at her father's house, and due to affection for them, tears fell from her eyes. Shaking and very much afflicted, she looked at her uncommon husband, Lord Śiva, as if she were going to blast him with her vision.

PURPORT

The word *apratipūruṣam*, used in this verse, means "one who has no equal." Lord Śiva has no equal in the material world in regard to equality towards everyone. His wife, Satī, knew that her husband was equal towards everyone, so why in this case was he so unkind to his wife that he did not allow her to go to her father's house? This distressed her more than she could tolerate, and she looked at her husband as if she were ready to blast him with her vision. In other words, since Lord Śiva is the *ātmā* (*śiva* also means *ātmā*), it is indicated here that Satī was prepared to commit suicide. Another meaning of the word *apratipūruṣa* is "the personality who has no rival." Since Lord Śiva could not be persuaded to give her permission, Satī took shelter of a woman's last weapon, weeping, which forces a husband to agree to the proposal of his wife.

TEXT 3

ततो विनिःश्वस्य सती विहाय तं
शोकेन रोषेण च दूयता हृदा ।
पित्रोरगात्स्त्रैणविमूढधीर्गृहान्
प्रेम्णात्मनो योऽर्धमदात्सतां प्रियः ॥३॥

tato viniḥśvasya satī vihāya taṁ
śokena roṣeṇa ca dūyatā hṛdā
pitror agāt straiṇa-vimūḍha-dhīr gṛhān
premṇātmano yo 'rdham adāt satāṁ priyaḥ

tataḥ—then; *viniḥśvasya*—breathing very heavily; *satī*—Satī; *vihāya*—leaving; *tam*—him (Lord Śiva); *śokena*—by bereavement; *roṣeṇa*—by anger; *ca*—and; *dūyatā*—afflicted; *hṛdā*—with the heart; *pitroḥ*—of her father; *agāt*—she went; *straiṇa*—by her womanly nature; *vimūḍha*—deluded; *dhīḥ*—intelligence; *gṛhān*—to the house; *premṇā*—due to affection; *ātmanaḥ*—of his body; *yaḥ*—who; *ardham*—half; *adāt*—gave; *satām*—to the saintly; *priyaḥ*—dear.

TRANSLATION

Thereafter Satī left her husband, Lord Śiva, who had given her half his body due to affection. Breathing very heavily because of anger and bereavement, she went to the house of her father. This less intelligent act was due to her being a weak woman.

PURPORT

According to the Vedic conception of family life, the husband gives half his body to his wife, and the wife gives half of her body to her husband. In other words, a husband without a wife or a wife without a husband is incomplete. Vedic marital relationship existed between Lord Śiva and Satī, but sometimes, due to weakness, a woman becomes very much attracted by the members of her father's house, and this happened to Satī. In this verse it is specifically mentioned that she wanted to leave such a great husband as Śiva because of her womanly weakness. In other words, womanly weakness exists even in the relationship between husband and wife. Generally, separation between husband and wife is due to womanly behavior; divorce takes place due to womanly weakness. The best course for a woman is to abide by the orders of her husband. That makes family life very peaceful. Sometimes there may be misunderstandings between husband and wife, as found even in such an elevated family relationship as that of Satī and Lord Śiva, but a wife should not leave her husband's protection because of such a misunderstanding. If she does so, it is understood to be due to her womanly weakness.

TEXT 4

तामन्वगच्छन् द्रुतविक्रमां सती-
मेकां त्रिनेत्रानुचराः सहस्रशः ।
सपार्षदयक्षा मणिमन्मदादयः
पुरोवृषेन्द्रास्तरसा गतव्यथाः ॥ ४ ॥

tām anvagacchan druta-vikramāṁ satīm
ekāṁ tri-netrānucarāḥ sahasraśaḥ
sa-pārṣada-yakṣā maṇiman-madādayaḥ
puro-vṛṣendrās tarasā gata-vyathāḥ

tām—her (Satī); *anvagacchan*—followed; *druta-vikramām*—leaving rapidly; *satīm*—Satī; *ekām*—alone; *tri-netra*—of Lord Śiva (who has three eyes); *anucarāḥ*—the followers; *sahasraśaḥ*—by thousands; *sa-pārṣada-yakṣāḥ*—accompanied by his personal associates and the

Yakṣas; *maṇimat-mada-ādayaḥ*—Maṇimān, Mada, etc.; *puraḥ-vṛṣa-indrāḥ*—having the Nandī bull in front; *tarasā*—swiftly; *gata-vyathāḥ*—without fear.

TRANSLATION

When they saw Satī leaving alone very rapidly, thousands of Lord Śiva's disciples, headed by Maṇimān and Mada, quickly followed her with his bull Nandī in front and accompanied by the Yakṣas.

PURPORT

Satī was going very fast so that she might not be checked by her husband, but she was immediately followed by the many thousands of disciples of Lord Śiva, headed by the Yakṣas, Maṇimān and Mada. The word *gata-vyathāḥ*, used in this connection, means "without fear." Satī did not care that she was going alone; therefore she was almost fearless. The word *anucarāḥ* is also significant, for it indicates that Lord Śiva's disciples were always ready to sacrifice anything for Lord Śiva. All of them could understand the desire of Śiva, who did not want Satī to go alone. *Anucarāḥ* means "those who can immediately understand the purpose of their master."

TEXT 5

तां सारिकाकन्दुकदर्पणाम्बुज-
श्वेतातपत्रव्यजनस्रगादिभिः ।
गीतायनैर्दुन्दुभिशङ्खवेणुभि-
र्वृषेन्द्रमारोप्य विटङ्किता ययुः ॥ ५ ॥

tāṁ sārikā-kanduka-darpaṇāmbuja-
śvetātapatra-vyajana-srag-ādibhiḥ
gītāyanair dundubhi-śaṅkha-veṇubhir
vṛṣendram āropya viṭaṅkitā yayuḥ

tām—her (Satī); *sārikā*—pet bird; *kanduka*—ball; *darpaṇa*—mirror; *ambuja*—lotus flower; *śveta-ātapatra*—white umbrella; *vyajana*—chowrie; *srak*—garland; *ādibhiḥ*—and others; *gītā-ayanaiḥ*—accompanied with music; *dundubhi*—drums; *śaṅkha*—conchshells;

veṇubhiḥ—with flutes; *vṛṣa-indram*—on the bull; *āropya*—placing; *viṭaṅkitāḥ*—decorated; *yayuḥ*—they went.

TRANSLATION

The disciples of Lord Śiva arranged for Satī to be seated on the back of a bull and gave her the bird which was her pet. They bore a lotus flower, a mirror and all such paraphernalia for her enjoyment and covered her with a great canopy. Followed by a singing party with drums, conchshells and bugles, the entire procession was as pompous as a royal parade.

TEXT 6

आब्रह्मघोषोर्जितयज्ञवैशसं
विप्रर्षिजुष्टं विबुधैश्च सर्वशः ।
मृद्दार्वयःकाञ्चनदर्भचर्मभि-
निसृष्टभाण्डं यजनं समाविशत् ॥ ६ ॥

ābrahma-ghoṣorjita-yajña-vaiśasaṁ
viprarṣi-juṣṭaṁ vibudhaiś ca sarvaśaḥ
mṛd-dārv-ayaḥ-kāñcana-darbha-carmabhir
nisṛṣṭa-bhāṇḍaṁ yajanaṁ samāviśat

ā—from all sides; *brahma-ghoṣa*—with the sounds of the Vedic hymns; *ūrjita*—decorated; *yajña*—sacrifice; *vaiśasam*—destruction of animals; *viprarṣi-juṣṭam*—attended by the great sages; *vibudhaiḥ*—with demigods; *ca*—and; *sarvaśaḥ*—on all sides; *mṛt*—clay; *dāru*—wood; *ayaḥ*—iron; *kāñcana*—gold; *darbha*—*kuśa* grass; *carmabhiḥ*—skins; *nisṛṣṭa*—made of; *bhāṇḍam*—sacrificial animals and pots; *yajanam*—sacrifice; *samāviśat*—entered.

TRANSLATION

She then reached her father's house, where the sacrifice was being performed, and entered the arena where everyone was chanting the Vedic hymns. The great sages, brāhmaṇas and demigods were all assembled there, and there were many sacrificial

animals, as well as pots made of clay, stone, gold, grass and skin, which were all requisite for the sacrifice.

PURPORT

When learned sages and *brāhmaṇas* assemble to chant Vedic *mantras*, some of them also engage in arguing about the conclusion of the scriptures. Thus some of the sages and *brāhmaṇas* were arguing, and some of them were chanting the Vedic *mantras*, so the entire atmosphere was surcharged with transcendental sound vibration. This transcendental sound vibration has been simplified in the transcendental vibration Hare Kṛṣṇa, Hare Kṛṣṇa, Kṛṣṇa Kṛṣṇa, Hare Hare/ Hare Rāma, Hare Rāma, Rāma Rāma, Hare Hare. In this age, no one is expected to be highly educated in the Vedic ways of understanding because people are very slow, lazy and unfortunate. Therefore Lord Caitanya has recommended the sound vibration Hare Kṛṣṇa, and in the *Śrīmad-Bhāgavatam* (11.5.32) it is also recommended: *yajñaiḥ saṅkīrtana-prāyair yajanti hi sumedhasaḥ.* At the present moment it is impossible to gather sacrificial necessities because of the poverty of the population and their lack of knowledge in Vedic *mantras.* Therefore for this age it is recommended that people gather together and chant the Hare Kṛṣṇa *mantra* to satisfy the Supreme Personality of Godhead, who is accompanied by His associates. Indirectly this indicates Lord Caitanya, who is accompanied by His associates Nityānanda, Advaita and others. That is the process of performing *yajña* in this age.

Another significant point in this verse is that there were animals for sacrifice. That these animals were meant for sacrifice does not mean that they were meant to be killed. The great sages and realized souls assembled were performing *yajñas*, and their realization was tested by animal sacrifice, just as, in modern science, tests are made on animals to determine the effectiveness of a particular medicine. The *brāhmaṇas* entrusted with the performance of *yajña* were very realized souls, and to test their realization an old animal was offered in the fire and rejuvenated. That was the test of a Vedic *mantra.* The animals gathered were not meant to be killed and eaten. The real purpose of a sacrifice was not to replace a slaughterhouse but to test a Vedic *mantra* by giving an animal new life. Animals were used to test the power of Vedic *mantras*, not for meat.

TEXT 7

तामागतां तत्र न कश्चनाद्रियद्
विमानितां यज्ञकृतो भयाज्जनः ।
ऋते स्वसॄर्वै जननीं च सादराः
प्रेमाश्रुकण्ठ्यः परिषस्वजुर्मुदा ॥ ७ ॥

tām āgatāṁ tatra na kaścanādriyad
vimānitāṁ yajña-kṛto bhayāj janaḥ
ṛte svasṝr vai jananīṁ ca sādarāḥ
premāśru-kaṇṭhyaḥ pariṣasvajur mudā

tām—her (Satī); *āgatām*—having arrived; *tatra*—there; *na*—not; *kaścana*—anyone; *ādriyat*—received; *vimānitām*—not receiving respect; *yajña-kṛtaḥ*—of the performer of the sacrifice (Dakṣa); *bhayāt*—from fear; *janaḥ*—person; *ṛte*—except; *svasṝḥ*—her own sisters; *vai*—indeed; *jananīm*—mother; *ca*—and; *sa-ādarāḥ*—with respect; *prema-aśru-kaṇṭhyaḥ*—whose throats were filled with tears of affection; *pariṣasvajuḥ*—embraced; *mudā*—with glad faces.

TRANSLATION

When Satī, with her followers, reached the arena, because all the people assembled were afraid of Dakṣa, none of them received her well. No one welcomed her but her mother and sisters, who, with tears in their eyes and with glad faces, welcomed her and talked with her very pleasingly.

PURPORT

The mother and sisters of Satī could not follow the others, who did not receive Satī very well. Due to natural affection, they immediately embraced her with tears in their eyes and with loving feelings. This shows that women as a class are very softhearted; their natural affection and love cannot be checked by artificial means. Although the men present were very learned *brāhmaṇas* and demigods, they were afraid of their superior, Dakṣa, and because they knew that their welcoming Satī would displease him, although in their minds they wanted to receive her, they could not do so. Women are naturally softhearted, but men are sometimes very hardhearted.

TEXT 8

सौदर्यसम्प्रश्नसमर्थवार्तया
मात्रा च मातृष्वसृभिश्च सादरम् ।
दत्तां सपर्यां वरमासनं च सा
नादत्त पित्राप्रतिनन्दिता सती ॥ ८ ॥

saudarya-sampraśna-samartha-vārtayā
mātrā ca mātṛ-ṣvasṛbhiś ca sādaram
dattāṁ saparyāṁ varam āsanaṁ ca sā
nādatta pitrāpratinanditā satī

saudarya—of her sisters; *sampraśna*—with the greetings; *samartha*—proper; *vārtayā*—tidings; *mātrā*—by her mother; *ca*—and; *mātṛ-svasṛbhiḥ*—by her aunts; *ca*—and; *sa-ādaram*—along with respect; *dattām*—which was offered; *saparyām*—worship, adoration; *varam*—presents; *āsanam*—a seat; *ca*—and; *sā*—she (Satī); *na ādatta*—did not accept; *pitrā*—by her father; *apratinanditā*—not being welcomed; *satī*—Satī.

TRANSLATION

Although she was received by her sisters and mother, she did not reply to their words of reception, and although she was offered a seat and presents, she did not accept anything, for her father neither talked with her nor welcomed her by asking about her welfare.

PURPORT

Satī did not accept the greetings offered by her sisters and mother, for she was not at all satisfied by her father's silence. Satī was the youngest child of Dakṣa, and she knew that she was his pet. But now, because of her association with Lord Śiva, Dakṣa forgot all his affection for his daughter, and this very much aggrieved her. The material bodily conception is so polluted that even upon slight provocation all our relationships of love and affection are nullified. Bodily relationships are so transient that even though one is affectionate towards someone in a bodily relationship, a slight provocation terminates this intimacy.

TEXT 9

अरुद्रभागं तमवेक्ष्य चाध्वरं
पित्रा च देवे कृतहेलनं विभौ ।
अनादृता यज्ञसदस्यधीश्वरी
चुकोप लोकानिव धक्ष्यती रुषा ॥ ९ ॥

arudra-bhāgaṁ tam avekṣya cādhvaraṁ
pitrā ca deve kṛta-helanaṁ vibhau
anādṛtā yajña-sadasy adhīśvarī
cukopa lokān iva dhakṣyatī ruṣā

arudra-bhāgam—having no oblations for Lord Śiva; *tam*—that; *avekṣya*—seeing; *ca*—and; *adhvaram*—place of sacrifice; *pitrā*—by her father; *ca*—and; *deve*—to Lord Śiva; *kṛta-helanam*—contempt having been shown; *vibhau*—to the lord; *anādṛtā*—not being received; *yajña-sadasi*—in the assembly of the sacrifice; *adhīśvarī*—Satī; *cukopa*—became greatly angry; *lokān*—the fourteen worlds; *iva*—as if; *dhakṣyatī*—burning; *ruṣā*—with anger.

TRANSLATION

Present in the arena of sacrifice, Satī saw that there were no oblations for her husband, Lord Śiva. Next she realized that not only had her father failed to invite Lord Śiva, but when he saw Lord Śiva's exalted wife, Dakṣa did not receive her either. Thus she became greatly angry, so much so that she looked at her father as if she were going to burn him with her eyes.

PURPORT

By offering oblations in the fire while chanting the Vedic *mantra svāhā*, one offers respect to all the demigods, great sages and Pitās, including Lord Brahmā, Lord Śiva and Lord Viṣṇu. It is customary that Śiva is one of those who are offered respects, but Satī, while personally present in the arena, saw that the *brāhmaṇas* did not utter the *mantra* offering oblations to Lord Śiva, *namaḥ śivāya svāhā.* She was not sorry for herself, for she was ready to come to her father's house without being invited, but she wanted to see whether or not her husband was being respected. To see her relatives, her sisters and mother, was not so important; even when she was received by her mother and sisters she did not care, for she was most concerned that her husband was being insulted in the sacrifice. When she marked the insult, she became greatly angry, and she looked at her father so angrily that Dakṣa appeared to burn in her vision.

TEXT 10

जगर्ह सामर्षविपन्नया गिरा
शिवद्विषं धूमपथश्रमस्मयम् ।
स्वतेजसा भूतगणान् समुत्थितान्
निगृह्य देवी जगतोऽभिश‍ृण्वतः ॥१०॥

jagarha sāmarṣa-vipannayā girā
śiva-dviṣaṁ dhūma-patha-śrama-smayam
sva-tejasā bhūta-gaṇān samutthitān
nigṛhya devī jagato 'bhiśṛṇvataḥ

jagarha—began to condemn; *sā*—she; *amarṣa-vipannayā*—indistinct through anger; *girā*—with words; *śiva-dviṣam*—the enemy of Lord Śiva; *dhūma-patha*—in sacrifices; *śrama*—by troubles; *smayam*—very proud; *sva-tejasā*—by her order; *bhūta-gaṇān*—the ghosts; *samutthitān*—ready (to injure Dakṣa); *nigṛhya*—stopped; *devī*—Satī; *jagataḥ*—in the presence of all; *abhiśṛṇvataḥ*—being heard.

TRANSLATION

The followers of Lord Śiva, the ghosts, were ready to injure or kill Dakṣa, but Satī stopped them by her order. She was very angry and sorrowful, and in that mood she began to condemn the process of sacrificial fruitive activities and persons who are very proud of such unnecessary and troublesome sacrifices. She especially condemned her father, speaking against him in the presence of all.

PURPORT

The process of offering sacrifices is especially meant to satisfy Viṣṇu, who is called Yajñeśa because He is the enjoyer of the fruits of all sacrifice. *Bhagavad-gītā* (5.29) also confirms this fact. The Lord says, *bhoktāraṁ yajña-tapasām.* He is the actual beneficiary of all sacrifices. Not knowing this fact, less intelligent men offer sacrifices for some material benefit. To derive personal material benefits for sense gratification is the reason persons like Dakṣa and his followers perform sacrifices. Such sacrifices are condemned here as a labor of love without actual profit. This is confirmed in *Śrīmad-Bhāgavatam.* One may prosecute the Vedic injunctions of offering sacrifices and other fruitive activities, but if by such activities one does not develop attraction for Viṣṇu, they are useless labors. One who has developed love for Viṣṇu must develop love and respect for Viṣṇu's devotees. Lord Śiva is considered the foremost personality amongst the Vaiṣṇavas. *Vaiṣṇavānāṁ yathā śambhuḥ.* Thus when Satī saw that her father was performing great sacrifices but had no respect for the greatest devotee, Lord Śiva, she was very angry. This is fitting; when Viṣṇu or a Vaiṣṇava is insulted, one should be angry. Lord Caitanya, who always preached nonviolence, meekness and humility, also became angry when Nityānanda was offended by Jagāi and Mādhāi, and He wanted to kill them. When Viṣṇu or a Vaiṣṇava is blasphemed or dishonored, one should be very angry. Narottama dāsa Ṭhākura said, *krodha bhakta-dveṣi jane.* We have anger, and that anger can be a great quality when directed against a person who is envious of the Supreme Personality of Godhead or His devotee. One should not be tolerant when a person is offensive towards Viṣṇu or a Vaiṣṇava. The anger of Satī towards her father was not objectionable, for although he was her father, he was trying to insult the greatest Vaiṣṇava. Thus Satī's anger against her father was quite applaudable.

TEXT 11

देव्युवाच

न यस्य लोकेऽस्त्यतिशायनः प्रिय-
स्तथाप्रियो देहभृतां प्रियात्मनः ।
तस्मिन् समस्तात्मनि मुक्तवैरके
ऋते भवन्तं कतमः प्रतीपयेत् ॥११॥

devy uvāca
na yasya loke 'sty atiśāyanaḥ priyas
tathāpriyo deha-bhṛtāṁ priyātmanaḥ
tasmin samastātmani mukta-vairake
ṛte bhavantaṁ katamaḥ pratīpayet

devī uvāca—the blessed goddess said; *na*—not; *yasya*—of whom; *loke*—in the material world; *asti*—is; *atiśāyanaḥ*—having no rival; *priyaḥ*—dear; *tathā*—so; *apriyaḥ*—enemy; *deha-bhṛtām*—bearing material bodies; *priya-ātmanaḥ*—who is the most beloved; *tasmin*—towards Lord Śiva; *samasta-ātmani*—the universal being; *mukta-vairake*—who is free from all enmity; *ṛte*—except; *bhavantam*—for you; *katamaḥ*—who; *pratīpayet*—would be envious.

TRANSLATION

The blessed goddess said: Lord Śiva is the most beloved of all living entities. He has no rival. No one is very dear to him, and no one is his enemy. No one but you could be envious of such a universal being, who is free from all enmity.

PURPORT

In *Bhagavad-gītā* (9.29) the Lord says, *samo 'haṁ sarva-bhūteṣu:* "I am equal to all living entities." Similarly, Lord Śiva is a qualitative incarnation of the Supreme Personality of Godhead, so he has almost the same qualities as the Supreme Lord. Therefore he is equal to everyone; no one is his enemy, and no one is his friend, but one who is envious by nature can become the enemy of Lord Śiva. Therefore Satī accused her father, "No one but you could be envious of Lord Śiva or be his enemy." Other sages and learned *brāhmaṇas* were present, but they were not envious of Lord Śiva, although they were all dependent on Dakṣa. Therefore no one but Dakṣa could be envious of Lord Śiva. That was the accusation of Satī.

TEXT 12

दोषान् परेषां हि गुणेषु साधवो
गृह्णन्ति केचिन्न भवादृशो द्विज ।

गुणांश्च फल्गून् बहुलीकरिष्णवो
महत्तमास्तेष्वविदद्भवानघम् ॥१२॥

doṣān pareṣāṁ hi guṇeṣu sādhavo
gṛhṇanti kecin na bhavādṛśo dvija
guṇāṁś ca phalgūn bahulī-kariṣṇavo
mahattamās teṣv avidad bhavān agham

doṣān—faults; *pareṣām*—of others; *hi*—for; *guṇeṣu*—in the qualities; *sādhavaḥ*—*sādhus;* *gṛhṇanti*—find; *kecit*—some; *na*—not; *bhavādṛśaḥ*—like you; *dvija*—O twice-born; *guṇān*—qualities; *ca*—and; *phalgūn*—small; *bahulī-kariṣṇavaḥ*—greatly magnifies; *mahattamāḥ*—the greatest persons; *teṣu*—among them; *avidat*—find; *bhavān*—you; *agham*—the fault.

TRANSLATION

Twice-born Dakṣa, a man like you can simply find fault in the qualities of others. Lord Śiva, however, not only finds no faults with others' qualities, but if someone has a little good quality, he magnifies it greatly. Unfortunately, you have found fault with such a great soul.

PURPORT

King Dakṣa is addressed here by his daughter Satī as *dvija*, twice-born. Twice-born refers to the higher classes of men, namely the *brāhmaṇas*, *kṣatriyas* and *vaiśyas.* In other words, a *dvija* is not an ordinary man but one who has studied the Vedic literature from a spiritual master and can discriminate between good and bad. Therefore it is supposed that he understands logic and philosophy. Satī, Dakṣa's daughter, put before him sound arguments. There are some highly qualified persons who accept only the good qualities of others. Just as a bee is always interested in the honey in the flower and does not consider the thorns and colors, highly qualified persons, who are uncommon, accept only the good qualities of others, not considering their bad qualities, whereas the common man can judge what are good qualities and what are bad qualities.

Among the uncommonly good souls there are still gradations, and the best good soul is one who accepts an insignificant asset of a person and magnifies that good quality. Lord Śiva is also called Āśutoṣa, which refers to one who is satisfied very easily and who offers to any person the highest level of benediction. For example, once a devotee of Lord Śiva wanted the benediction that whenever he touched someone on the head, that person's head would at once be separated from his trunk. Lord Śiva agreed. Although the benediction asked was not very commendable because the devotee wanted to kill his enemy, Lord Śiva considered the devotee's good quality in worshiping and satisfying him and granted the benediction. Thus Lord Śiva accepted his bad qualities as magnificently good qualities. But Satī accused her father, "You are just the opposite. Although Lord Śiva has so many good qualities and no bad qualities at all, you have accepted him as bad and found fault with him. Because of your accepting his good qualities to be bad, instead of your becoming the most exalted soul you have become the most fallen. A man becomes the greatest soul by accepting the goodness of others' qualities, but by unnecessarily considering others' good qualities to be bad, you have become the lowest of the fallen souls."

TEXT 13

नाश्चर्यमेतद्यदसत्सु सर्वदा
महद्विनिन्दा कुणपात्मवादिषु ।
सेर्ष्यं महापूरुषपादपांसुभि-
र्निरस्ततेजःसु तदेव शोभनम् ॥१३॥

nāścaryam etad yad asatsu sarvadā
mahad-vinindā kuṇapātma-vādiṣu
serṣyaṁ mahāpūruṣa-pāda-pāṁsubhir
nirasta-tejaḥsu tad eva śobhanam

na—not; *āścaryam*—wonderful; *etat*—this; *yat*—which; *asatsu*—evil; *sarvadā*—always; *mahat-vinindā*—the deriding of great souls; *kuṇapa-ātma-vādiṣu*—among those who have accepted the dead body as the self; *sa-īrṣyam*—envy; *mahā-pūruṣa*—of great personalities; *pāda-pāṁsubhiḥ*—by the dust of the feet; *nirasta-tejaḥsu*—whose glory is diminished; *tat*—that; *eva*—certainly; *śobhanam*—very good.

TRANSLATION

It is not wonderful for persons who have accepted the transient material body as the self to engage always in deriding great souls. Such envy on the part of materialistic persons is very good because that is the way they fall down. They are diminished by the dust of the feet of great personalities.

PURPORT

Everything depends on the strength of the recipient. For example, due to the scorching sunshine many vegetables and flowers dry up, and many grow luxuriantly. Thus it is the recipient that causes growth and dwindling. Similarly, *mahīyasāṁ pāda-rajo-'bhiṣekam:* the dust of the lotus feet of great personalities offers all good to the recipient, but the same dust can also do harm. Those who are offenders at the lotus feet of a great personality dry up; their godly qualities diminish. A great soul may forgive offenses, but Kṛṣṇa does not excuse offenses to the dust of that great soul's feet, just as one can tolerate the scorching sunshine on one's head but cannot tolerate the scorching sunshine on one's feet. An offender glides down more and more; therefore he naturally continues to commit offenses at the feet of the great soul. Offenses are generally committed by persons who falsely identify with the impermanent body. King Dakṣa was deeply engrossed in a misconception because he identified the body with the soul. He offended the lotus feet of Lord Śiva because he thought that his body, being the father of the body of Satī, was superior to Lord Śiva's. Generally, less intelligent men misidentify in that way, and they act in the bodily concept of life. Thus they are subject to commit more and more offenses at the lotus feet of great souls. One who has such a concept of life is considered to be in the class of animals like cows and asses.

TEXT 14

यद् द्वयक्षरं नाम गिरेरितं नृणां
सकृत्प्रसङ्गादघमाशु हन्ति तत् ।
पवित्रकीर्तिं तमलङ्घ्यशासनं
भवानहो द्वेष्टि शिवं शिवेतरः ॥१४॥

yad dvy-akṣaraṁ nāma gireritaṁ nṛṇāṁ
sakṛt prasaṅgād agham āśu hanti tat
pavitra-kīrtiṁ tam alaṅghya-śāsanaṁ
bhavān aho dveṣṭi śivaṁ śivetaraḥ

yat—which; *dvi-akṣaram*—consisting of two letters; *nāma*—named; *girā īritam*—merely being pronounced by the tongue; *nṛṇām*—persons; *sakṛt*—once; *prasaṅgāt*—from the heart; *agham*—sinful activities; *āśu*—immediately; *hanti*—destroys; *tat*—that; *pavitra-kīrtim*—whose fame is pure; *tam*—him; *alaṅghya-śāsanam*—whose order is never neglected; *bhavān*—you; *aho*—oh; *dveṣṭi*—envy; *śivam*—Lord Śiva; *śiva-itaraḥ*—who are inauspicious.

TRANSLATION

Satī continued: My dear father, you are committing the greatest offense by envying Lord Śiva, whose very name, consisting of two syllables, śi and va, purifies one of all sinful activities. His order is never neglected. Lord Śiva is always pure, and no one but you envies him.

PURPORT

Since Lord Śiva is the greatest soul among the living entities within this material world, his name, Śiva, is very auspicious for persons who identify the body with the soul. If such persons take shelter of Lord Śiva, gradually they will understand that they are not the material body but are spirit soul. *Śiva* means *maṅgala*, or auspicious. Within the body the soul is auspicious. *Ahaṁ brahmāsmi:* "I am Brahman." This realization is auspicious. As long as one does not realize his identity as the soul, whatever he does is inauspicious. *Śiva* means "auspicious," and devotees of Lord Śiva gradually come to the platform of spiritual identification, but that is not all. Auspicious life begins from the point of spiritual identification. But there are still more duties—one has to understand one's relationship with the Supreme Soul. If one is actually a devotee of Lord Śiva, he comes to the platform of spiritual realization, but if he is not intelligent enough, then he stops at that point, only realizing that he is spirit soul (*ahaṁ brahmāsmi*). If he is intelligent enough, however, he should continue to act in the way of Lord Śiva, for Lord Śiva is always absorbed in the thought of Vāsudeva. As previously explained, *sattvaṁ viśuddhaṁ vasudeva-śabditam:* Lord Śiva is always in meditation on the lotus feet of Vāsudeva, Śrī Kṛṣṇa. Thus the auspicious position of Lord Śiva is realized if one takes to the worship of Viṣṇu, because Lord Śiva says in the *Śiva Purāṇa* that the topmost worship is worship of Lord Viṣṇu. Lord Śiva is worshiped because he is the greatest devotee of Lord Viṣṇu. One should not, however, make the mistake of considering Lord Śiva and Lord Viṣṇu to be on the same level. That is also an atheistic idea. It is also enjoined in the *Vaiṣṇavīya Purāṇa* that Viṣṇu, or Nārāyaṇa, is the exalted Supreme Personality of Godhead, and no one should be compared to Him as equal, even Lord Śiva or Lord Brahmā, not to speak of other demigods.

TEXT 15

यत्पादपद्मं महतां मनोऽलिभि-
र्निषेवितं ब्रह्मरसासवार्थिभिः ।
लोकस्य यद्वर्षति चाशिषोऽर्थिन-
स्तस्मै भवान् द्रुह्यति विश्वबन्धवे ॥१५॥

yat-pāda-padmaṁ mahatāṁ mano-'libhir
niṣevitaṁ brahma-rasāsavārthibhiḥ
lokasya yad varṣati cāśiṣo 'rthinas
tasmai bhavān druhyati viśva-bandhave

yat-pāda-padmam—the lotus feet of whom; *mahatām*—of the higher personalities; *manaḥ-alibhiḥ*—by the bees of the mind; *niṣevitam*—being engaged at; *brahma-rasa*—of transcendental bliss (*brahmānanda*); *āsava-arthibhiḥ*—seeking the nectar; *lokasya*—of the common man; *yat*—which; *varṣati*—he fulfills; *ca*—and; *āśiṣaḥ*—desires; *arthinaḥ*—seeking; *tasmai*—towards him (Lord Śiva); *bhavān*—you; *druhyati*—are envious; *viśva-bandhave*—unto the friend of all living entities within the three worlds.

TRANSLATION

You are envious of Lord Śiva, who is the friend of all living entities within the three worlds. For the common man he fulfills all

desires, and because of their engagement in thinking of his lotus feet, he also blesses higher personalities who are seeking after brahmānanda [transcendental bliss].

PURPORT

Ordinarily there are two classes of men. One class, who are grossly materialistic, want material prosperity, and their desires are fulfilled if they worship Lord Śiva. Lord Śiva, being very quickly satisfied, satisfies the material desires of the common man very quickly; therefore it is seen that ordinary men are very much apt to worship him. Next, those who are disgusted or frustrated with the materialistic way of life worship Lord Śiva to attain salvation, which entails freedom from material identification. One who understands that he is not the material body but is spirit soul is liberated from ignorance. Lord Śiva also offers that facility. People generally practice religion for economic development, to get some money, for by getting money they can satisfy their senses. But when they are frustrated they want spiritual *brahmānanda*, or merging into the Supreme. These four principles of material life—religion, economic development, sense gratification and liberation—exist, and Lord Śiva is the friend of both the ordinary man and the man who is elevated in spiritual knowledge. Thus it was not good for Dakṣa to create enmity towards him. Even Vaiṣṇavas, who are above both the ordinary and the elevated men in this world, also worship Lord Śiva as the greatest Vaiṣṇava. Thus he is the friend of everyone—the common men, the elevated men and the devotees of the Lord—so no one should disrespect or create enmity towards Lord Śiva.

TEXT 16

किं वा शिवाख्यमशिवं न विदुस्त्वदन्ये
ब्रह्मादयस्तमवकीर्य जटाः श्मशाने ।
तन्माल्यभस्मनृकपाल्यवसत्पिशाचै-
र्ये मूर्धभिर्दधति तच्चरणावसृष्टम् ॥१६॥

kiṁ vā śivākhyam aśivaṁ na vidus tvad anye
brahmādayas tam avakīrya jaṭāḥ śmaśāne

tan-mālya-bhasma-nṛkapāly avasat piśācair
ye mūrdhabhir dadhati tac-caraṇāvasṛṣṭam

kim vā—whether; *śiva-ākhyam*—named Śiva; *aśivam*—inauspicious; *na viduḥ*—do not know; *tvat anye*—other than you; *brahma-ādayaḥ*—Brahmā and others; *tam*—him (Lord Śiva); *avakīrya*—scattered; *jaṭāḥ*—having twisted hair; *śmaśāne*—in the crematorium; *tat-mālya-bhasma-nṛ-kapālī*—who is garlanded with human skulls and smeared with ashes; *avasat*—associated; *piśācaiḥ*—with demons; *ye*—who; *mūrdhabhiḥ*—with the head; *dadhati*—place; *tat-caraṇa-avasṛṣṭam*—fallen from his lotus feet.

TRANSLATION

Do you think that greater, more respectable personalities than you, such as Lord Brahmā, do not know this inauspicious person who goes under the name Lord Śiva? He associates with the demons in the crematorium, his locks of hair are scattered all over his body, he is garlanded with human skulls and smeared with ashes from the crematorium, but in spite of all these inauspicious qualities, great personalities like Brahmā honor him by accepting the flowers offered to his lotus feet and placing them with great respect on their heads.

PURPORT

It is useless to condemn a great personality like Lord Śiva, and this is being stated by his wife, Satī, to establish the supremacy of her husband. First she said, "You call Lord Śiva inauspicious because he associates with demons in crematoriums, covers his body with the ashes of the dead, and garlands himself with the skulls of human beings. You have shown so many defects, but you do not know that his position is always transcendental. Although he appears inauspicious, why do personalities like Brahmā respect the dust of his lotus feet and place on their heads with great respect those very garlands which are condemned by you?" Since Satī was a chaste woman and the wife of Lord Śiva, it was her duty to establish the elevated position of Lord Śiva, not only by sentiment but by facts. Lord Śiva is not an ordinary living entity. This is the conclusion of Vedic scripture. He is neither on the level of the Supreme Personality of Godhead nor on the level of the ordinary living entities. Brahmā is in almost all cases an ordinary living entity. Sometimes, when there is no ordinary living entity available, the post of Brahmā is occupied by an expansion of Lord Viṣṇu, but generally this post is occupied by a greatly pious living entity within this universe. Thus Lord Śiva's position is constitutionally higher than that of Lord Brahmā, although Lord Śiva appeared as the son of Brahmā. Here it is mentioned that even personalities like Brahmā accept the so-called inauspicious flowers and the dust of the lotus feet of Lord Śiva. Great sages like Marīci, Atri, Bhṛgu and the others among the nine great sages who are descendants of Brahmā also respect Lord Śiva in such a way because they all know that Lord Śiva is not an ordinary living entity.

In many *Purāṇas* it is sometimes asserted that a demigod is elevated to such a high position that he is almost on an equal level with the Supreme Personality of Godhead, but the conclusion that Lord Viṣṇu is the Supreme Personality of Godhead is confirmed in every scripture. Lord Śiva is described in the *Brahma-saṁhitā* to be like curd or yogurt. Curd is not different from milk. Since milk is transformed into curd, in one sense curd is also milk. Similarly, Lord Śiva is in one sense the Supreme Personality of Godhead, but in another sense he is not, just as curd is milk although we have to distinguish between the two. These descriptions are in the Vedic literature. Whenever we find that a demigod occupies a position apparently more elevated than that of the Supreme Personality of Godhead, it is just to draw the devotee's attention to that particular demigod. It is also stated in the *Bhagavad-gītā* (9.25) that if one wants to worship a particular demigod, the Supreme Personality of Godhead, who is sitting in everyone's heart, gives one greater and greater attachment for that demigod so that one may be elevated to the demigod's abode. *Yānti deva-vratā devān.* By worshiping demigods one can elevate himself to the abodes of the demigods; similarly, by worshiping the Supreme Personality of Godhead one can be elevated to the spiritual kingdom. This is stated in different places in Vedic literature. Here Lord Śiva is praised by Satī, partially due to her personal respect for Lord Śiva, since he is her husband, and partially due to his exalted position, which exceeds that of ordinary living entities, even Lord Brahmā.

The position of Lord Śiva is accepted by Lord Brahmā, so Dakṣa, Satī's father, should also recognize him. That was the point of Satī's statement.

She did not actually come to her father's house to participate in the function, although before coming she pleaded with her husband that she wanted to see her sisters and her mother. That was a plea only, for actually at heart she maintained the idea that she would convince her father, Dakṣa, that it was useless to continue being envious of Lord Śiva. That was her main purpose. When she was unable to convince her father, she gave up the body he had given her, as will be seen in the following verses.

TEXT 17

कर्णौ पिधाय निरयाद्यदकल्प ईशे
धर्मावितर्यसृणिभिर्नृभिरस्यमाने ।
छिन्द्यात्प्रसह्य रुशतीमसतीं प्रभुश्चे-
ज्जिह्वामसूनपि ततो विसृजेत्स धर्मः ॥१७॥

karṇau pidhāya nirayād yad akalpa īśe
dharmāvitary asṛṇibhir nṛbhir asyamāne
chindyāt prasahya ruśatīm asatīṁ prabhuś cej
jihvām asūn api tato visṛjet sa dharmaḥ

karṇau—both ears; *pidhāya*—blocking; *nirayāt*—one should go away; *yat*—if; *akalpaḥ*—unable; *īśe*—the master; *dharma-avitari*—the controller of religion; *asṛṇibhiḥ*—by irresponsible; *nṛbhiḥ*—persons; *asyamāne*—being blasphemed; *chindyāt*—he should cut; *prasahya*—by force; *ruśatīm*—vilifying; *asatīm*—of the blasphemer; *prabhuḥ*—one is able; *cet*—if; *jihvām*—tongue; *asūn*—(his own) life; *api*—certainly; *tataḥ*—then; *visṛjet*—should give up; *saḥ*—that; *dharmaḥ*—is the process.

TRANSLATION

Satī continued: If one hears an irresponsible person blaspheme the master and controller of religion, one should block his ears and go away if unable to punish him. But if one is able to kill, then one should by force cut out the blasphemer's tongue and kill the offender, and after that one should give up his own life.

PURPORT

The argument offered by Satī is that a person who vilifies a great personality is the lowest of all creatures. But, by the same argument, Dakṣa could also defend himself by saying that since he was a Prajāpati, the master of many living creatures and one of the great officers of the great universal affairs, his position was so exalted that Satī should accept his good qualities instead of vilifying him. The answer to that argument is that Satī was not vilifying but defending. If possible she should have cut out Dakṣa's tongue because he blasphemed Lord Śiva. In other words, since Lord Śiva is the protector of religion, a person who vilifies him should be killed at once, and after killing such a person, one should give up one's life. That is the process, but because Dakṣa happened to be the father of Satī, she decided not to kill him but to give up her own life in order to compensate for the great sin she had committed by hearing blasphemy of Lord Śiva. The instruction set forth here in *Śrīmad-Bhāgavatam* is that one should not tolerate at any cost the activities of a person who vilifies or blasphemes an authority. If one is a *brāhmaṇa* he should not give up his body because by doing so he would be responsible for killing a *brāhmaṇa;* therefore a *brāhmaṇa* should leave the place or block his ears so that he will not hear the blasphemy. If one happens to be a *kṣatriya* he has the power to punish any man; therefore a *kṣatriya* should at once cut out the tongue of the vilifier and kill him. But as far as the *vaiśyas* and *śūdras* are concerned, they should immediately give up their bodies. Satī decided to give up her body because she thought herself to be among the *śūdras* and *vaiśyas.* As stated in *Bhagavad-gītā* (9.32), *striyo vaiśyās tathā śūdrāḥ.* Women, laborers and the mercantile class are on the same level. Thus since it is recommended that *vaiśyas* and *śūdras* should immediately give up their bodies upon hearing blasphemy of an exalted person like Lord Śiva, she decided to give up her life.

TEXT 18

अतस्तवोत्पन्नमिदं कलेवरं
न धारयिष्ये शितिकण्ठगर्हिणः ।
जग्धस्य मोहाद्धि विशुद्धिमन्धसो
जुगुप्सितस्योद्धरणं प्रचक्षते ॥१८॥

atas tavotpannam idaṁ kalevaraṁ
na dhārayiṣye śiti-kaṇṭha-garhiṇaḥ
jagdhasya mohād dhi viśuddhim andhaso
jugupsitasyoddharaṇaṁ pracakṣate

ataḥ—therefore; *tava*—from you; *utpannam*—received; *idam*—this; *kalevaram*—body; *na dhārayiṣye*—I shall not bear; *śiti-kaṇṭha-garhiṇaḥ*—who have blasphemed Lord Śiva; *jagdhasya*—which has been eaten; *mohāt*—by mistake; *hi*—because; *viśuddhim*—the purification; *andhasaḥ*—of food; *jugupsitasya*—poisonous; *uddharaṇam*—vomiting; *pracakṣate*—declare.

TRANSLATION

Therefore I shall no longer bear this unworthy body, which has been received from you, who have blasphemed Lord Śiva. If someone has taken food which is poisonous, the best treatment is to vomit.

PURPORT

Since Satī was the representation of the external potency of the Lord, it was in her power to vanquish many universes, including many Dakṣas, but in order to save her husband from the charge that he employed his wife, Satī, to kill Dakṣa because he could not do so due to his inferior position, she decided to give up her body.

TEXT 19

न वेदवादाननुवर्तते मतिः
स्व एव लोके रमतो महामुनेः ।
यथा गतिर्देवमनुष्ययोः पृथक्
स्व एव धर्मे न परं क्षिपेत्स्थितः ॥१९॥

na veda-vādān anuvartate matiḥ
sva eva loke ramato mahā-muneḥ
yathā gatir deva-manuṣyayoḥ pṛthak
sva eva dharme na paraṁ kṣipet sthitaḥ

na—not; *veda-vādān*—rules and regulations of the *Vedas; anuvartate*—follow; *matiḥ*—the mind; *sve*—in his own; *eva*—certainly; *loke*—in the self; *ramataḥ*—enjoying; *mahā-muneḥ*—of elevated transcendentalists; *yathā*—as; *gatiḥ*—the way; *deva-manuṣyayoḥ*—of the men and the demigods; *pṛthak*—separately; *sve*—in your own; *eva*—alone; *dharme*—occupational duty; *na*—not; *param*—another; *kṣipet*—should criticize; *sthitaḥ*—being situated.

TRANSLATION

It is better to execute one's own occupational duty than to criticize others'. Elevated transcendentalists may sometimes forgo the rules and regulations of the Vedas, since they do not need to follow them, just as the demigods travel in space whereas ordinary men travel on the surface of the earth.

PURPORT

The behavior of the most elevated transcendentalist and that of the most fallen conditioned soul appears to be the same. The elevated transcendentalist can surpass all the regulations of the *Vedas*, just as the demigods traveling in space surpass all the jungles and rocks on the surface of the globe, although a common man, who has no such ability to travel in space, has to face all those impediments. Although the most dear Lord Śiva appears not to observe all the rules and regulations of the *Vedas*, he is not affected by such disobedience, but a common man who wants to imitate Lord Śiva is mistaken. A common man must observe all the rules and regulations of the *Vedas* which a person who is in the transcendental position does not need to observe. Dakṣa found fault with Lord Śiva for not observing all the strict rules and regulations of the *Vedas*, but Satī asserted that he had no need to observe such rules. It is said that for one who is powerful like the sun or the fire, there is no consideration of purity or impurity. The sunshine can sterilize an impure place, whereas if someone else were to pass such a place he would be affected. One should not try to imitate Lord Śiva; rather, one should strictly follow one's prescribed occupational duties. One should never vilify a great personality like Lord Śiva.

TEXT 20

कर्म प्रवृत्तं च निवृत्तमप्यृतं
वेदे विविच्योभयलिङ्गमाश्रितम् ।
विरोधि तद्यौगपदैककर्तरि
द्वयं तथा ब्रह्मणि कर्म नर्च्छति ॥२०॥

karma pravṛttaṁ ca nivṛttam apy ṛtaṁ
vede vivicyobhaya-liṅgam āśritam
virodhi tad yaugapadaika-kartari
dvayaṁ tathā brahmaṇi karma narcchati

karma—activities; *pravṛttam*—attached to material enjoyment; *ca*—and; *nivṛttam*—materially detached; *api*—certainly; *ṛtam*—true; *vede*—in the *Vedas;* *vivicya*—distinguished; *ubhaya-liṅgam*—symptoms of both; *āśritam*—directed; *virodhi*—contradictory; *tat*—that; *yaugapada-eka-kartari*—both activities in one person; *dvayam*—two; *tathā*—so; *brahmaṇi*—in one who is transcendentally situated; *karma*—activities; *na ṛcchati*—are neglected.

TRANSLATION

In the Vedas there are directions for two kinds of activities—activities for those who are attached to material enjoyment and activities for those who are materially detached. In consideration of these two kinds of activities, there are two kinds of people, who have different symptoms. If one wants to see two kinds of activities in one person, that is contradictory. But both kinds of activities may be neglected by a person who is transcendentally situated.

PURPORT

The Vedic activities are so designed that the conditioned soul who has come to enjoy the material world may do so under direction so that at the end he becomes detached from such material enjoyment and is eligible to enter into the transcendental position. The four different social orders—*brahmacarya*, *gṛhastha*, *vānaprastha* and *sannyāsa*—gradually train a person to come to the platform of transcendental life. The activities and dress of a *gṛhastha*, or householder, are different from those of a *sannyāsī*, one in the renounced order of life. It is impossible for one person to adopt both orders. A *sannyāsī* cannot act like a householder, nor can a householder act like a *sannyāsī*, but above these two kinds of persons, one who engages in material activities and one who has renounced material activities, there is the person who is transcendental to both. Lord Śiva is in the transcendental position because, as stated before, he is always absorbed in the thought of Lord Vāsudeva within himself. Therefore neither the activities of the *gṛhastha* nor those of the *sannyāsī* in the renounced order can be applicable for him. He is in the *paramahaṁsa* stage, the highest perfectional stage of life. The transcendental position of Lord Śiva is also explained in *Bhagavad-gītā* (2.52–53). It is stated there that when one fully engages in the transcendental service of the Lord by performing activities without fruitive results, one is elevated to the transcendental position. At that time he has no obligation to follow the Vedic injunctions or the different rules and regulations of the *Vedas*. When one is above the directions of the Vedic ritualistic injunctions for attaining different allurements and is fully absorbed in transcendental thought, which means thought of the Supreme Personality of Godhead in devotional service, one is in the position called *buddhi-yoga*, or *samādhi*, ecstasy. For a person who has attained this stage, neither the Vedic activities for realizing material enjoyment nor those for renunciation are applicable.

TEXT 21

मा वः पदव्यः पितरस्मदास्थिता
या यज्ञशालासु न धूमवर्त्मभिः ।
तदन्नतृप्तैरसुभृद्भिरीडिता
अव्यक्तलिङ्गा अवधूतसेविताः ॥२१॥

mā vaḥ padavyaḥ pitar asmad-āsthitā
yā yajña-śālāsu na dhūma-vartmabhiḥ
tad-anna-tṛptair asu-bhṛdbhir īḍitā
avyakta-liṅgā avadhūta-sevitāḥ

mā—are not; *vaḥ*—yours; *padavyaḥ*—opulences; *pitaḥ*—O father; *asmat-āsthitāḥ*—possessed by us; *yāḥ*—which (opulences); *yajña-śālāsu*—in the sacrificial fire; *na*—not; *dhūma-vartmabhiḥ*—by the path of sacrifices; *tat-anna-tṛptaiḥ*—satisfied by the foodstuff of the sacrifice; *asu-bhṛdbhiḥ*—satisfying bodily necessities; *īḍitāḥ*—praised; *avyakta-liṅgāḥ*—whose cause is unmanifested; *avadhūta-sevitāḥ*—achieved by the self-realized souls.

TRANSLATION

My dear father, the opulence we possess is impossible for either you or your flatterers to imagine, for persons who engage in fruitive activities by performing great sacrifices are concerned with satisfying their bodily necessities by eating foodstuff offered as a sacrifice. We can exhibit our opulences simply by desiring to do so. This can be achieved only by great personalities who are renounced, self-realized souls.

PURPORT

Satī's father was under the impression that he was exalted in both prestige and opulence and that he had offered his daughter to a person who was not only poor but devoid of all culture. Her father might have been thinking that although she was a chaste woman, greatly adherent to her husband, her husband was in a deplorable condition. To counteract such thoughts, Satī said that the opulence possessed by her husband could not be understood by materialistic persons like Dakṣa and his followers, who were flatterers and were engaged in fruitive activities. Her husband's position was different. He possessed all opulences, but he did not like to exhibit them. Therefore such opulences are called *avyakta,* or unmanifested. But if required, simply by willing, Lord Śiva can show his wonderful opulences, and such an event is predicted here, for it would soon occur. The opulence Lord Śiva possesses is enjoyable in renunciation and love of God, not in material exhibition of sense gratificatory methods. Such opulences are possessed by personalities like the Kumāras, Nārada and Lord Śiva, not by others.

In this verse the performers of the Vedic rituals are condemned. They have been described here as *dhūma-vartmabhiḥ,* those who maintain themselves on the remnants of sacrificial foodstuff. There are two kinds of foodstuff offered in sacrifice. One kind is food offered in fruitive ritualistic sacrifices, and the other, the best, is food offered to Viṣṇu. Although in all cases Viṣṇu is the chief Deity on the sacrificial altar, the performers of fruitive rituals aim to satisfy various demigods to achieve in return some material prosperity. Real sacrifice, however, is to satisfy Lord Viṣṇu, and the remnants of such sacrifices are beneficial for advancement in devotional service. The process of elevation by performing sacrifices other than those aimed at Viṣṇu is very slow, and therefore it has been condemned in this verse. Viśvanātha Cakravartī has described the ritualistic performers to be like crows because crows delight in eating the remnants of food which has been thrown into the dustbin. All the *brāhmaṇas* who were present for the sacrifice were also condemned by Satī.

Whether or not King Dakṣa and his flatterers could understand the position of Lord Śiva, Satī wanted to impress upon her father that he should not think her husband to be without opulence. Satī, being the devoted wife of Lord Śiva, offers all kinds of material opulences to the worshipers of Lord Śiva. This fact is explained in the *Śrīmad-Bhāgavatam*, in the Tenth Canto. Lord Śiva's worshipers sometimes appear more opulent than the worshipers of Lord Viṣṇu because Durgā, or Satī, being the superintendent in charge of material affairs, can offer all material opulences to the worshipers of Lord Śiva in order to glorify her husband, whereas the worshipers of Viṣṇu are meant for spiritual elevation, and therefore their material opulence is sometimes found to decrease. These points are very nicely discussed in the Tenth Canto.

TEXT 22

नैतेन देहेन हरे कृतागसो
देहोद्भवेनालमलं कुजन्मना ।
व्रीडा ममाभूत्कुजनप्रसङ्गत-
स्तज्जन्म धिग् यो महतामवद्यकृत् ॥२२॥

naitena dehena hare kṛtāgaso
dehodbhavenālam alaṁ kujanmanā
vrīḍā mamābhūt kujana-prasaṅgatas
taj janma dhig yo mahatām avadya-kṛt

na—not; *etena*—by this; *dehena*—by the body; *hare*—to Lord Śiva; *kṛta-āgasaḥ*—having committed offenses; *deha-udbhavena*—produced from your body; *alam alam*—enough, enough; *ku-janmanā*—with a contemptible birth; *vrīḍā*—shame; *mama*—my; *abhūt*—was; *ku-jana-prasaṅgataḥ*—from a relationship with a bad person; *tat janma*—that birth; *dhik*—shameful; *yaḥ*—who; *mahatām*—of the great personalities; *avadya-kṛt*—an offender.

TRANSLATION

You are an offender at the lotus feet of Lord Śiva, and unfortunately I have a body produced from yours. I am very much ashamed of our bodily relationship, and I condemn myself because my body is contaminated by a relationship with a person who is an offender at the lotus feet of the greatest personality.

PURPORT

Lord Śiva is the greatest of all devotees of Lord Viṣṇu. It is stated, *vaiṣṇavānāṁ yathā śambhuḥ.* Śambhu, Lord Śiva, is the greatest of all devotees of Lord Viṣṇu. In the previous verses, Satī has described that Lord Śiva is always in a transcendental position because he is situated in pure *vasudeva. Vasudeva* is that state from which Kṛṣṇa, Vāsudeva, is born, so Lord Śiva is the greatest devotee of Lord Kṛṣṇa, and Satī's behavior is exemplary because no one should tolerate blasphemy against Lord Viṣṇu or His devotee. Satī is aggrieved not for her personal association with Lord Śiva but because her body is related with that of Dakṣa, who is an offender at Lord Śiva's lotus feet. She feels herself to be condemned because of the body given by her father, Dakṣa.

TEXT 23

गोत्रं त्वदीयं भगवान् वृषध्वजो
दाक्षायणीत्याह यदा सुदुर्मनाः ।
व्यपेतनर्मस्मितमाशु तदाऽहं
व्युत्स्रक्ष्य एतत्कुणपं त्वदङ्गजम् ॥२३॥

gotraṁ tvadīyaṁ bhagavān vṛṣadhvajo
dākṣāyaṇīty āha yadā sudurmanāḥ

vyapeta-narma-smitam āśu tadā 'haṁ
vyutsrakṣya etat kuṇapaṁ tvad-aṅgajam

gotram—family relationship; *tvadīyam*—your; *bhagavān*—the possessor of all opulences; *vṛṣadhvajaḥ*—Lord Śiva; *dākṣāyaṇī*—Dākṣāyaṇī (the daughter of Dakṣa); *iti*—thus; *āha*—calls; *yadā*—when; *su-durmanāḥ*—very morose; *vyapeta*—disappear; *narma-smitam*—my jolliness and smile; *āśu*—immediately; *tadā*—then; *aham*—I; *vyutsrak-ṣye*—I shall give up; *etat*—this (body); *kuṇapam*—dead body; *tvat-aṅga-jam*—produced from your body.

TRANSLATION

Because of our family relationship, when Lord Śiva addresses me as Dākṣāyaṇī I at once become morose, and my jolliness and my smile at once disappear. I feel very much sorry that my body, which is just like a bag, has been produced by you. I shall therefore give it up.

PURPORT

The word *dākṣāyaṇī* means "the daughter of King Dakṣa." Sometimes, when there was relaxed conversation between husband and wife, Lord Śiva used to call Satī "the daughter of King Dakṣa," and because this very word reminded her about her family relationship with King Dakṣa, she at once became ashamed because Dakṣa was an incarnation of all offenses. Dakṣa was the embodiment of envy, for he unnecessarily blasphemed a great personality, Lord Śiva. Simply upon hearing the word *dākṣāyaṇī*, she felt afflicted because of reference to the context because her body was the symbol of all the offensiveness with which Dakṣa was endowed. Since her body was constantly a source of unhappiness, she decided to give it up.

TEXT 24

मैत्रेय उवाच

इत्यध्वरे दक्षमनूद्य शत्रुहन्
क्षितावुदीचीं निषसाद शान्तवाक् ।
स्पृष्ट्वा जलं पीतदुकूलसंवृता
निमील्य दृग्योगपथं समाविशत् ॥२४॥

maitreya uvāca
ity adhvare dakṣam anūdya śatru-han
kṣitāv udīcīṁ niṣasāda śānta-vāk
spṛṣṭvā jalaṁ pīta-dukūla-saṁvṛtā
nimīlya dṛg yoga-pathaṁ samāviśat

maitreyaḥ uvāca—Maitreya said; *iti*—thus; *adhvare*—in the arena of sacrifice; *dakṣam*—to Dakṣa; *anūdya*—speaking; *śatru-han*—O annihilator of enemies; *kṣitau*—on the ground; *udīcīm*—facing north; *niṣasāda*—sat down; *śānta-vāk*—in silence; *spṛṣṭvā*—after touching; *jalam*—water; *pīta-dukūla-saṁvṛtā*—dressed in yellow garments; *nimīlya*—closing; *dṛk*—the vision; *yoga-patham*—the mystic *yoga* process; *samāviśat*—became absorbed.

TRANSLATION

Maitreya the sage told Vidura: O annihilator of enemies, while thus speaking to her father in the arena of sacrifice, Satī sat down on the ground and faced north. Dressed in saffron garments, she sanctified herself with water and closed her eyes to absorb herself in the process of mystic yoga.

PURPORT

It is said that when a man desires to quit his body he dresses in saffron garments. Therefore it appears that Satī changed her dress, indicating that she was going to quit the body given her by Dakṣa. Dakṣa was Satī's father, so instead of killing Dakṣa she decided that it would be better to destroy the part of his body which was hers. Thus she decided to give up the body of Dakṣa by the yogic process. Satī was the wife of Lord Śiva, who is known as Yogeśvara, the best among all *yogīs*, because he knows all the mystic processes of *yoga*, so it appeared that Satī also knew them. Either she learned *yoga* from her husband or she was enlightened because she was the daughter of such a great king as Dakṣa. The perfection of *yoga* is that one can give up one's body or release oneself from the embodiment of material elements according to one's desire. *Yogīs* who have attained perfection are not subject to death by natural laws; such perfect *yogīs* can leave the body whenever they desire. Generally the *yogī* first of all becomes mature in controlling the air passing within the body, thus bringing the soul to the top of the brain. Then when the body bursts into flames, the *yogī* can go anywhere he likes. This *yoga* system recognizes the soul, and thus it is distinct from the so-called *yoga* process for controlling the cells of the body, which has been discovered in the modern age. The real *yoga* process accepts the transmigration of the soul from one planet to another or one body to another; and it appears from this incident that Satī wanted to transfer her soul to another body or sphere.

TEXT 25

कृत्वा समानावनिलौ जितासना
सोदानमुत्थाप्य च नाभिचक्रतः ।
शनैर्हृदि स्थाप्य धियोरसि स्थितं
कण्ठाद् भ्रुवोर्मध्यमनिन्दितानयत् ॥२५॥

kṛtvā samānāv anilau jitāsanā
sodānam utthāpya ca nābhi-cakrataḥ
śanair hṛdi sthāpya dhiyorasi sthitaṁ
kaṇṭhād bhruvor madhyam aninditānayat

kṛtvā—after placing; *samānau*—in equilibrium; *anilau*—the *prāṇa* and *apāna* airs; *jita-āsanā*—having controlled the sitting posture; *sā*—Satī; *udānam*—the life air; *utthāpya*—raising; *ca*—and; *nābhi-cakrataḥ*—at the circle in the navel; *śanaiḥ*—gradually; *hṛdi*—in the heart; *sthāpya*—placing; *dhiyā*—with the intelligence; *urasi*—towards the pulmonary passage; *sthitam*—having been placed; *kaṇṭhāt*—through the throat; *bhruvoḥ*—of the eyebrows; *madhyam*—to the middle; *aninditā*—the blameless (Satī); *ānayat*—raised.

TRANSLATION

First of all she sat in the required sitting posture, and then she carried the life air upwards and placed it in the position of equilibrium near the navel. Then she raised her life air, mixed

with intelligence, to the heart and then gradually towards the pulmonary passage and from there to between her eyebrows.

PURPORT

The yogic process is to control the air passing within the body in different places called *ṣaṭ-cakra*, the six circles of air circulation. The air is raised from the abdomen to the navel, from the navel to the heart, from the heart to the throat, from the throat to between the eyebrows and from between the eyebrows to the top of the cerebrum. That is the sum and substance of practicing *yoga*. Before practicing the real *yoga* system, one has to practice the sitting postures because this helps in the breathing exercises which control the airs going upwards and downwards. This is a great technique which one has to practice to attain the highest perfectional stage of *yoga*, but such practice is not meant for this age. No one in this age can attain the perfectional stage of such *yoga*, but people indulge in practicing sitting postures, which is more or less a gymnastic process. By such bodily gymnastics one may develop good circulation and may therefore keep one's body fit, but if one simply restricts oneself to that gymnastic process one cannot attain the highest perfectional stage. The *yoga* process, as described in the *Keśava-śruti*, prescribes how one can control his living force according to his desire and transmigrate from one body to another or from one place to another. In other words, *yoga* practice is not meant to keep the body fit. Any transcendental process of spiritual realization automatically helps one to keep the body fit, for it is the spirit soul that keeps the body always fresh. As soon as the spirit soul is out of the body, the material body immediately begins to decompose. Any spiritual process keeps the body fit without separate endeavor, but if one takes it that the ultimate aim of *yoga* is to maintain the body, then he is mistaken. The real perfection of *yoga* is elevation of the soul to a higher position or the liberation of the soul from material entanglement. Some *yogīs* try to elevate the soul to higher planetary systems, where the standard of life is different from that of this planet and where the material comforts, life-span and other facilities for self-realization are greater, and some *yogīs* endeavor to elevate the soul to the spiritual world, the spiritual Vaikuṇṭha planets. The *bhakti-yoga* process directly elevates the soul to the spiritual planets, where life is eternally blissful and full of knowledge; therefore *bhakti-yoga* is considered to be the greatest of all *yoga* systems.

TEXT 26

एवं स्वदेहं महतां महीयसा
मुहुः समारोपितमङ्कमादरात् ।
जिहासती दक्षरुषा मनस्विनी
दधार गात्रेष्वनिलाग्निधारणाम् ॥२६॥

evaṁ sva-dehaṁ mahatāṁ mahīyasā
muhuḥ samāropitam aṅkam ādarāt
jihāsatī dakṣa-ruṣā manasvinī
dadhāra gātreṣv anilāgni-dhāraṇām

evam—thus; *sva-deham*—her own body; *mahatām*—of the great saints; *mahīyasā*—most worshipful; *muhuḥ*—again and again; *samāropitam*—seated; *aṅkam*—on the lap; *ādarāt*—respectfully; *jihāsatī*—wishing to give up; *dakṣa-ruṣā*—due to anger towards Dakṣa; *manasvinī*—voluntarily; *dadhāra*—placed; *gātreṣu*—on the limbs of the body; *anila-agni-dhāraṇām*—meditation on the fire and air.

TRANSLATION

Thus, in order to give up her body, which had been so respectfully and affectionately seated on the lap of Lord Śiva, who is worshiped by great sages and saints, Satī, due to anger towards her father, began to meditate on the fiery air within the body.

PURPORT

Lord Śiva is described herein as the best of all great souls. Although Satī's body was born of Dakṣa, Lord Śiva used to adore her by sitting her on his lap. This is considered a great token of respect. Thus Satī's body was not ordinary, but still she decided to give it up because it was the source of unhappiness because of its connection with Dakṣa. This severe example set by Satī is to be followed. One should be extremely careful about associating with persons who are not respectful to the higher authorities. It is instructed, therefore, in the Vedic literature that one should always be free from the association of atheists and nondevotees and should try to associate with devotees, for by the association of a devotee one can be elevated to the platform of self-realization. This injunction is stressed in many places in *Śrīmad-Bhāgavatam;* if one wants to be liberated from the clutches of material existence, then one has to associate with great souls, and if one wants to continue one's material existential life, then one may associate with persons who are materialistic. The materialistic way of life is based on sex life. Thus both becoming addicted to sex life and associating with persons who are addicted to sex life are condemned in the Vedic literature because such association will simply interfere with one's spiritual progress. However, association with great personalities, devotees who are great souls, will elevate one to the spiritual platform. Satīdevī decided to quit the body she had obtained from Dakṣa's body, and she wanted to transfer herself to another body so that she might have completely uncontaminated association with Lord Śiva. Of course, it is understood that in her next life she would take birth as the daughter of the Himalayas, Pārvatī, and then she would again accept Lord Śiva as her husband. Satī and Lord Śiva are eternally related; even after she changes her body, their relationship is never broken.

TEXT 27

ततः स्वभर्तुश्चरणाम्बुजासवं
जगद्गुरोश्चिन्तयती न चापरम् ।
ददर्श देहो हतकल्मषः सती
सद्यः प्रजज्वाल समाधिजाग्निना ॥२७॥

tataḥ sva-bhartuś caraṇāmbujāsavaṁ
jagad-guroś cintayatī na cāparam
dadarśa deho hata-kalmaṣaḥ satī
sadyaḥ prajajvāla samādhijāgninā

tataḥ—there; *sva-bhartuḥ*—of her husband; *caraṇa-ambuja-āsavam*—on the nectar of the lotus feet; *jagat-guroḥ*—of the supreme spiritual teacher of the universe; *cintayatī*—meditating; *na*—not; *ca*—and;

aparam—not other (than her husband); *dadarśa*—saw; *dehaḥ*—her body; *hata-kalmaṣaḥ*—taints of sin being destroyed; *satī*—Satī; *sadyaḥ*—soon; *prajajvāla*—burned; *samādhi-ja-agninā*—by fire produced by meditation.

TRANSLATION

Satī concentrated all her meditation on the holy lotus feet of her husband, Lord Śiva, who is the supreme spiritual master of all the world. Thus she became completely cleansed of all taints of sin and quit her body in a blazing fire by meditation on the fiery elements.

PURPORT

Satī at once thought of the lotus feet of her husband, Lord Śiva, who is one of the three great personalities of Godhead in charge of the management of the material world, and simply by meditating on his lotus feet she derived such great pleasure that she forgot everything in relationship with her body. This pleasure was certainly material because she gave up her body for another body that was also material, but by this example we can appreciate the devotee's pleasure in concentrating his mind and attention on the lotus feet of the Supreme Lord, Viṣṇu, or Kṛṣṇa. There is such transcendental bliss in simply meditating on the lotus feet of the Lord that one can forget everything but the Lord's transcendental form. This is the perfection of yogic *samādhi*, or ecstasy. In this verse it is stated that by such meditation she became free from all contamination. What was that contamination? The contamination was her concept of the body derived from Dakṣa, but she forgot that bodily relationship in trance. The purport is that when one becomes free from all bodily relationships within this material world and simply places himself in the position of an eternal servant of the Supreme Lord, it is to be understood that all the contamination of his material attachment has been burned by the blazing fires of transcendental ecstasy. It is not necessary for one to manifest a blazing fire externally, for if one forgets all his bodily relationships within this material world and becomes situated in his spiritual identity, it is said that one has been freed from all material contamination by the blazing fire of yogic *samādhi*, or ecstasy. That is the topmost perfection of *yoga*. If one keeps his bodily relationships within this material world and poses himself as a great *yogī*, he is not a bona fide *yogī*. In *Śrīmad-Bhāgavatam* (2.4.15) it is stated, *yat-kīrtanaṁ yat-smaraṇaṁ*. Simply by chanting the holy name of the Supreme Personality of Godhead, simply by remembering the lotus feet of Kṛṣṇa, simply by offering prayers to the Supreme Personality of Godhead, one is immediately freed from material contamination, the material bodily concept, by the blazing fire of ecstasy. This effect takes place immediately, without a second's delay.

According to Śrī Jīva Gosvāmī, that Satī quit her body means that she gave up within her heart her relationship with Dakṣa. Śrī Viśvanātha Cakravartī Ṭhākura also comments that since Satī is the superintendent deity of the external potency, when she quit her body she did not get a spiritual body but simply transferred from the body she had received from Dakṣa. Other commentators also say that she immediately transferred herself into the womb of Menakā, her future mother. She gave up the body she had received from Dakṣa and immediately transferred herself to another, better body, but this does not mean that she got a spiritual body.

TEXT 28

तत्पश्यतां खे भुवि चाद्भुतं महद्
हाहेति वादः सुमहानजायत ।
हन्त प्रिया दैवतमस्य देवी
जहावसून् केन सती प्रकोपिता ॥२८॥

tat paśyatāṁ khe bhuvi cādbhutaṁ mahad
hā heti vādaḥ sumahān ajāyata
hanta priyā daivatamasya devī
jahāv asūn kena satī prakopitā

tat—that; *paśyatām*—of those who had seen; *khe*—in the sky; *bhuvi*—on the earth; *ca*—and; *adbhutam*—wonderful; *mahat*—great; *hā hā*—oh, oh; *iti*—thus; *vādaḥ*—roar; *su-mahān*—tumultuous; *ajāyata*—occurred; *hanta*—alas; *priyā*—the beloved; *daiva-tamasya*—of the most respectable demigod (Lord Śiva); *devī*—Satī; *jahau*—quit; *asūn*—her life; *kena*—by Dakṣa; *satī*—Satī; *prakopitā*—angered.

TRANSLATION

When Satī annihilated her body in anger, there was a tumultuous roar all over the universe. Why had Satī, the wife of the most respectable demigod, Lord Śiva, quit her body in such a manner?

PURPORT

There was a tumultuous roaring all over the universe in the societies of the demigods of different planets because Satī was the daughter of Dakṣa, the greatest of all kings, and the wife of Lord Śiva, the greatest of all demigods. Why did she become so angry that she gave up her body? Since she was the daughter of a great personality and wife of a great personality, she had nothing to desire, but still she gave up her body in dissatisfaction. Certainly this was astonishing. One cannot attain complete satisfaction even if one is situated in the greatest material opulence. There was nothing Satī could not achieve either from her relationship with her father or from her relationship with the greatest of the demigods, but still, for some reason, she was dissatisfied. Therefore, *Śrīmad-Bhāgavatam* (1.2.6) explains that one has to achieve real satisfaction (*yayātmā suprasīdati*), but *ātmā*—the body, mind and soul—all become completely satisfied only if one develops devotional service to the Absolute Truth. *Sa vai puṁsāṁ paro dharmo yato bhaktir adhokṣaje. Adhokṣaja* means the Absolute Truth. If one can develop his unflinching love for the transcendental Supreme Personality of Godhead, that can give complete satisfaction, otherwise there is no possibility of satisfaction in the material world or anywhere else.

TEXT 29

अहो अनात्म्यं महदस्य पश्यत
प्रजापतेर्यस्य चराचरं प्रजाः ।
जहावसन्न् यद्विमतात्मजा सती
मनस्विनी मानमभीक्ष्णमर्हति ॥२९॥

aho anātmyaṁ mahad asya paśyata
prajāpater yasya carācaraṁ prajāḥ

jahāv asūn yad-vimatātmajā satī
manasvinī mānam abhīkṣṇam arhati

aho—oh; *anātmyam*—neglect; *mahat*—great; *asya*—of Dakṣa; *paśyata*—just see; *prajāpateḥ*—of the Prajāpati; *yasya*—of whom; *cara-acaram*—all living entities; *prajāḥ*—offspring; *jahau*—gave up; *asūn*—her body; *yat*—by whom; *vimatā*—disrespected; *ātma-jā*—his own daughter; *satī*—Satī; *manasvinī*—voluntarily; *mānam*—respect; *abhīkṣṇam*—repeatedly; *arhati*—deserved.

TRANSLATION

It was astonishing that Dakṣa, who was Prajāpati, the maintainer of all living entities, was so disrespectful to his own daughter, Satī, who was not only chaste but was also a great soul, that she gave up her body because of his neglect.

PURPORT

The word *anātmya* is significant. *Ātmya* means "the life of the soul," so this word indicates that although Dakṣa appeared to be living, actually he was a dead body, otherwise how could he neglect Satī, who was his own daughter? It was the duty of Dakṣa to look after the maintenance and comforts of all living entities because he was situated as Prajāpati, the governor of all living entities. Therefore how is it that he neglected his own daughter, who was the most exalted and chaste woman, a great soul, and who therefore deserved the most respectful treatment from her father? The death of Satī because of her being neglected by Dakṣa, her father, was most astonishing to all the great demigods of the universe.

TEXT 30

सोऽयं दुर्मर्षहृदयो ब्रह्मध्रुक् च
लोकेऽपकीर्तिं महतीमवाप्स्यति ।
यदङ्गजां स्वां पुरुषद्विड्युद्यतां
न प्रत्यषेधन्मृतयेऽपराधतः ॥३०॥

so 'yaṁ durmarṣa-hṛdayo brahma-dhruk ca
loke 'pakīrtiṁ mahatīm avāpsyati

yad-aṅgajāṁ svāṁ puruṣa-dviḍ udyatāṁ
na pratyaṣedhan mṛtaye 'parādhataḥ

saḥ—he; *ayam*—that; *durmarṣa-hṛdayaḥ*—hardhearted; *brahma-dhruk*—unworthy to be a *brāhmaṇa; ca*—and; *loke*—in the world; *apakīrtim*—ill fame; *mahatīm*—extensive; *avāpsyati*—will gain; *yat-aṅga-jām*—the daughter of whom; *svām*—own; *puruṣa-dviṭ*—the enemy of Lord Śiva; *udyatām*—who was preparing; *na pratyaṣedhat*—did not prevent; *mṛtaye*—for death; *aparādhataḥ*—because of his offenses.

TRANSLATION

Dakṣa, who is so hardhearted that he is unworthy to be a brāhmaṇa, will gain extensive ill fame because of his offenses to his daughter, because of not having prevented her death, and because of his great envy of the Supreme Personality of Godhead.

PURPORT

Dakṣa is described here as most hardhearted and therefore unqualified to be a *brāhmaṇa. Brahma-dhruk* is described by some commentators to mean *brahma-bandhu,* or friend of the *brāhmaṇas.* A person who is born in a *brāhmaṇa* family but has no brahminical qualifications is called a *brahma-bandhu. Brāhmaṇas* are generally very softhearted and forbearing because they have the power to control the senses and the mind. Dakṣa, however, was not forbearing. For the simple reason that his son-in-law, Lord Śiva, did not stand up to show him the formality of respect, he became so angry and hardhearted that he tolerated even the death of his dearest daughter. Satī tried her best to mitigate the misunderstanding between the son-in-law and the father-in-law by coming to her father's house, even without an invitation, and at that time Dakṣa should have received her, forgetting all past misunderstandings. But he was so hardhearted that he was unworthy to be called an Āryan or *brāhmaṇa.* Thus his ill fame still continues. *Dakṣa* means "expert," and he was given this name because of his ability to beget many hundreds and thousands of children. Persons who are too sexually inclined and materialistic become so hardhearted because of a slight loss of prestige that they can tolerate even the death of their children.

TEXT 31

वदत्येवं जने सत्या दृष्ट्वासुत्यागमद्भुतम् ।
दक्षं तत्पार्षदा हन्तुमुदतिष्ठन्नुदायुधाः ॥३१॥

vadaty evaṁ jane satyā
dṛṣṭvāsu-tyāgam adbhutam
dakṣaṁ tat-pārṣadā hantum
udatiṣṭhann udāyudhāḥ

vadati—were talking; *evam*—thus; *jane*—while the people; *satyāḥ*—of Satī; *dṛṣṭvā*—after seeing; *asu-tyāgam*—the death; *adbhutam*—wonderful; *dakṣam*—Dakṣa; *tat-pārṣadāḥ*—the attendants of Lord Śiva; *hantum*—to kill; *udatiṣṭhan*—stood up; *udāyudhāḥ*—with uplifted weapons.

TRANSLATION

While people were talking among themselves about the wonderful voluntary death of Satī, the attendants who had come with her readied themselves to kill Dakṣa with their weapons.

PURPORT

The attendants who came with Satī were meant to protect her from calamities, but since they were unable to protect their master's wife, they decided to die for her, and before dying they wanted to kill Dakṣa. It is the duty of attendants to give protection to their master, and in case of failure it is their duty to die.

TEXT 32

तेषामापततां वेगं निशाम्य भगवान् भृगुः ।
यज्ञघ्नघ्नेन यजुषा दक्षिणाग्नौ जुहाव ह ॥३२॥

teṣām āpatatāṁ vegaṁ
niśāmya bhagavān bhṛguḥ
yajña-ghna-ghnena yajuṣā
dakṣiṇāgnau juhāva ha

teṣām—of them; *āpatatām*—who were approaching; *vegam*—the impulse; *niśāmya*—after seeing; *bhagavān*—the possessor of all opulences; *bhṛguḥ*—Bhṛgu Muni; *yajña-ghna-ghnena*—for killing the destroyers of the *yajña; yajuṣā*—with hymns of the *Yajur Veda; dakṣiṇa-agnau*—in the southern side of the sacrificial fire; *juhāva*—offered oblations; *ha*—certainly.

TRANSLATION

They came forward forcibly, but Bhṛgu Muni saw the danger and, offering oblations into the southern side of the sacrificial fire, immediately uttered mantric hymns from the Yajur Veda by which the destroyers of yajñic performances could be killed immediately.

PURPORT

Here is one example of powerful hymns in the *Vedas* which, when chanted, could perform wonderful acts. In the present age of Kali it is not possible to find expert *mantra* chanters; therefore all the sacrifices recommended in the *Vedas* are forbidden in this age. The only sacrifice recommended in this age is the chanting of the Hare Kṛṣṇa *mantra* because in this age it is not possible to accumulate the needed funds for performing sacrifices, not to speak of finding expert *brāhmaṇas* who can chant the *mantras* perfectly.

TEXT 33

अध्वर्युणा ह्रूयमाने देवा उत्पेतुरोजसा ।
ऋभवो नाम तपसा सोमं प्राप्ताः सहस्रशः ॥३३॥

adhvaryuṇā hūyamāne
devā utpetur ojasā
ṛbhavo nāma tapasā
somaṁ prāptāḥ sahasraśaḥ

adhvaryuṇā—by the priest, Bhṛgu; *hūyamāne*—oblations being offered; *devāḥ*—demigods; *utpetuḥ*—became manifested; *ojasā*—with great strength; *ṛbhavaḥ*—the Ṛbhus; *nāma*—named; *tapasā*—by penance; *somam*—Soma; *prāptāḥ*—having achieved; *sahasraśaḥ*—by the thousands.

TRANSLATION

When Bhṛgu Muni offered oblations in the fire, immediately many thousands of demigods named Ṛbhus became manifested. All of them were powerful, having achieved strength from Soma, the moon.

PURPORT

It is stated here that many thousands of demigods named Ṛbhus became manifested because of the oblations offered in the fire and the chanting of the hymns from the *Yajur Veda*. *Brāhmaṇas* like Bhṛgu Muni were so powerful that they could create such powerful demigods simply by chanting the Vedic *mantras*. Vedic *mantras* are still available, but the chanters are not. By chanting Vedic *mantras* or chanting the Gāyatrī or *ṛg-mantra* one can attain the results one desires. In the present age of Kali it is recommended by Lord Caitanya that simply by chanting Hare Kṛṣṇa one can attain all perfection.

TEXT 34

तैरलातायुधैः सर्वे प्रमथाः सहगुह्यकाः
हन्यमाना दिशो भेजुरुशद्भिर्ब्रह्मतेजसा ॥३४॥

tair alātāyudhaiḥ sarve
pramathāḥ saha-guhyakāḥ
hanyamānā diśo bhejur
uśadbhir brahma-tejasā

taiḥ—by them; *alāta-āyudhaiḥ*—with weapons of firebrands; *sarve*—all; *pramathāḥ*—the ghosts; *saha-guhyakāḥ*—along with the Guhyakas; *hanyamānāḥ*—being attacked; *diśaḥ*—in different directions; *bhejuḥ*—fled; *uśadbhiḥ*—glowing; *brahma-tejasā*—by brahminical power.

TRANSLATION

When the Ṛbhu demigods attacked the ghosts and Guhyakas with half-burned fuel from the yajña fire, all these attendants of

Satī fled in different directions and disappeared. This was possible simply because of brahma-tejas, brahminical power.

PURPORT

The word *brahma-tejasā*, used in this verse, is significant. In those days, *brāhmaṇas* were so powerful that simply by desiring and by chanting a Vedic *mantra*, they could accomplish very wonderful effects. But in the present age of degradation there are no such *brāhmaṇas*. According to the *Pāñcarātrika* system, in this age the entire population is supposed to consist of *śūdras* because the brahminical culture has been lost. But if anyone displays the signs of understanding Kṛṣṇa consciousness, he should be accepted, according to Vaiṣṇava *smṛti* regulations, as a prospective *brāhmaṇa* and should be given all facilities to achieve the highest perfection. The most magnanimous gift of Lord Caitanya's is that the highest perfection of life is available in this fallen age if one simply adopts the process of chanting Hare Kṛṣṇa, which is able to bring about the fulfillment of all activities in self-realization.

Thus end the Bhaktivedanta purports of the Fourth Canto, Fourth Chapter, of the Śrīmad-Bhāgavatam, *entitled "Satī Quits Her Body."*

CHAPTER FIVE

Frustration of the Sacrifice of Dakṣa

TEXT 1

मैत्रेय उवाच
भवो भवान्या निधनं प्रजापते-
रसत्कृताया अवगम्य नारदात् ।
स्वपार्षदसैन्यं च तदध्वरर्भुभि-
र्विद्रावितं क्रोधमपारमादधे ॥ १ ॥

maitreya uvāca
bhavo bhavānyā nidhanaṁ prajāpater
asat-kṛtāyā avagamya nāradāt
sva-pārṣada-sainyaṁ ca tad-adhvararbhubhir
vidrāvitaṁ krodham apāram ādadhe

maitreyaḥ uvāca—Maitreya said; *bhavaḥ*—Lord Śiva; *bhavānyāḥ*—of Satī; *nidhanam*—the death; *prajāpateḥ*—because of Prajāpati Dakṣa; *asat-kṛtāyāḥ*—having been insulted; *avagamya*—hearing about; *nāradāt*—from Nārada; *sva-pārṣada-sainyam*—the soldiers of his own associates; *ca*—and; *tat-adhvara*—(produced from) his (Dakṣa's) sacrifice; *ṛbhubhiḥ*—by the Ṛbhus; *vidrāvitam*—were driven away; *krodham*—anger; *apāram*—unbounded; *ādadhe*—showed.

TRANSLATION

Maitreya said: When Lord Śiva heard from Nārada that Satī, his wife, was now dead because of Prajāpati Dakṣa's insult to her and that his soldiers had been driven away by the Ṛbhu demigods, he became greatly angry.

PURPORT

Lord Śiva understood that Satī, being the youngest daughter of Dakṣa, could present the case of Lord Śiva's purity of purpose and would thus be able to mitigate the misunderstanding between Dakṣa and himself. But such a compromise was not attained, and Satī was deliberately insulted by her father by not being received properly when she visited his house without being invited. Satī herself could have killed her father, Dakṣa, because she is the personified material energy and has immense power to kill and create within this material universe. In the *Brahma-saṁhitā* her strength is described: she is capable of creating and dissolving many universes. But although she is so powerful, she acts under the direction of the Supreme Personality of Godhead, Kṛṣṇa, as His shadow. It would not have been difficult for Satī to punish her father, but she thought that since she was his daughter, it was not proper for her to kill him. Thus she decided to give up her own body, which she had obtained from his, and Dakṣa did not even check her.

When Satī passed away, giving up her body, the news was conveyed by Nārada to Lord Śiva. Nārada always carries the news of such events because he knows their import. When Lord Śiva heard that his chaste wife, Satī, was dead, he naturally became exceedingly angry. He also understood that Bhṛgu Muni had created the Ṛbhudeva demigods by uttering the *mantras* of the *Yajur Veda* and that these demigods had driven away all of his soldiers who were present in the arena of sacrifice. Therefore, he wanted to reply to this insult, and thus he decided to kill Dakṣa because he was the cause of the death of Satī.

TEXT 2

क्रुद्धः सुदष्टौष्ठपुटः स धूर्जटि-
जटां तडिद्वह्निसटोग्ररोचिषम् ।
उत्कृत्य रुद्रः सहसोत्थितो हसन्
गम्भीरनादो विससर्ज तां भुवि ॥ २ ॥

kruddhaḥ sudaṣṭauṣṭha-puṭaḥ sa dhūr-jaṭir
jaṭāṁ taḍid-vahni-saṭogra-rociṣam
utkṛtya rudraḥ sahasotthito hasan
gambhīra-nādo visasarja tāṁ bhuvi

kruddhaḥ—very angry; *su-daṣṭa-oṣṭha-puṭaḥ*—pressing his lips with his teeth; *saḥ*—he (Lord Śiva); *dhūḥ-jaṭiḥ*—having a cluster of hair on his head; *jaṭām*—one hair; *taḍit*—of electricity; *vahni*—of fire; *saṭā*—a flame; *ugra*—terrible; *rociṣam*—blazing; *utkṛtya*—snatching; *rudraḥ*—Lord Śiva; *sahasā*—at once; *utthitaḥ*—stood up; *hasan*—laughing; *gambhīra*—deep; *nādaḥ*—sound; *visasarja*—dashed; *tām*—that (hair); *bhuvi*—on the ground.

TRANSLATION

Thus Lord Śiva, being extremely angry, pressed his lips with his teeth and immediately snatched from his head a strand of hair which blazed like electricity or fire. He stood up at once, laughing like a madman, and dashed the hair to the ground.

TEXT 3

ततोऽतिकायस्तनुवा स्पृशन्दिवं
सहस्रबाहुर्घनरुक् त्रिसूर्यदृक् ।
करालदंष्ट्रो ज्वलदग्निमूर्धजः
कपालमाली विविधोद्यतायुधः ॥ ३ ॥

tato 'tikāyas tanuvā spṛśan divaṁ
sahasra-bāhur ghana-ruk tri-sūrya-dṛk
karāla-daṁṣṭro jvalad-agni-mūrdhajaḥ
kapāla-mālī vividhodyatāyudhaḥ

tataḥ—at this time; *atikāyaḥ*—a great personality (Vīrabhadra); *tanuvā*—with his body; *spṛśan*—touching; *divam*—the sky; *sahasra*—a thousand; *bāhuḥ*—arms; *ghana-ruk*—of black color; *tri-sūrya-dṛk*—as bright as three suns combined; *karāla-daṁṣṭraḥ*—having very fearful teeth; *jvalat-agni*—(like) burning fire; *mūrdhajaḥ*—having hair on his head; *kapāla-mālī*—garlanded with men's heads; *vividha*—various kinds; *udyata*—upraised; *āyudhaḥ*—equipped with weapons.

TRANSLATION

A fearful black demon as high as the sky and as bright as three suns combined was thereby created, his teeth very fearful and the hairs on his head like burning fire. He had thousands of arms,

equipped with various weapons, and he was garlanded with the heads of men.

TEXT 4

तं किं करोमीति गृणन्तमाह
बद्धाञ्जलिं भगवान् भूतनाथः ।
दक्षं सयज्ञं जहि मद्भटानां
त्वमग्रणी रुद्र भटांशको मे ॥ ४ ॥

taṁ kiṁ karomīti gṛṇantam āha
baddhāñjaliṁ bhagavān bhūta-nāthaḥ
dakṣaṁ sa-yajñaṁ jahi mad-bhaṭānāṁ
tvam agraṇī rudra bhaṭāṁśako me

tam—to him (Vīrabhadra); *kim*—what; *karomi*—shall I do; *iti*—thus; *gṛṇantam*—asking; *āha*—ordered; *baddha-añjalim*—with folded hands; *bhagavān*—the possessor of all opulences (Lord Śiva); *bhūta-nāthaḥ*—the lord of the ghosts; *dakṣam*—Dakṣa; *sa-yajñam*—along with his sacrifice; *jahi*—kill; *mat-bhaṭānām*—of all my associates; *tvam*—you; *agraṇīḥ*—the chief; *rudra*—O Rudra; *bhaṭa*—O expert in battle; *aṁśakaḥ*—born of my body; *me*—my.

TRANSLATION

When that gigantic demon asked with folded hands, "What shall I do, my lord?" Lord Śiva, who is known as Bhūtanātha, directly ordered, "Because you are born from my body, you are the chief of all my associates. Therefore, kill Dakṣa and his soldiers at the sacrifice."

PURPORT

Here is the beginning of competition between *brahma-tejas* and *śiva-tejas.* By *brahma-tejas,* brahminical strength, Bhṛgu Muni had created the Ṛbhu demigods, who had driven away the soldiers of Lord Śiva stationed in the arena. When Lord Śiva heard that his soldiers had been driven away, he created the tall black demon Vīrabhadra to retaliate. There is sometimes a competition between the mode of goodness and the mode of ignorance. That is the way of material existence. Even when one is situated in the mode of goodness, there is every possibility that his position will be mixed with or attacked by the mode of passion or ignorance. That is the law of material nature. Although pure goodness, or *śuddha-sattva*, is the basic principle in the spiritual world, pure manifestation of goodness is not possible in this material world. Thus, the struggle for existence between different material qualities is always present. This quarrel between Lord Śiva and Bhṛgu Muni, centering around Prajāpati Dakṣa, is the practical example of such competition between the different qualitative modes of material nature.

TEXT 5

आज्ञप्त एवं कुपितेन मन्युना
स देवदेवं परिचक्रमे विभुम् ।
मेने तदात्मानमसङ्गरंहसा
महीयसां तात सहः सहिष्णुम् ॥ ५ ॥

ājñapta evaṁ kupitena manyunā
sa deva-devaṁ paricakrame vibhum
mene tadātmānam asaṅga-raṁhasā
mahīyasāṁ tāta sahaḥ sahiṣṇum

ājñaptaḥ—being ordered; *evam*—in this manner; *kupitena*—angry; *manyunā*—by Lord Śiva (who is anger personified); *saḥ*—he (Vīrabhadra); *deva-devam*—he who is worshiped by the demigods; *paricakrame*—circumambulated; *vibhum*—Lord Śiva; *mene*—considered; *tadā*—at that time; *ātmānam*—himself; *asaṅga-raṁhasā*—with the power of Lord Śiva that cannot be opposed; *mahīyasām*—of the most powerful; *tāta*—my dear Vidura; *sahaḥ*—strength; *sahiṣṇum*—capable of coping with.

TRANSLATION

Maitreya continued: My dear Vidura, that black person was the personified anger of the Supreme Personality of Godhead, and he was prepared to execute the orders of Lord Śiva. Thus, considering himself capable of coping with any power offered against him, he circumambulated Lord Śiva.

TEXT 6

अन्वीयमानः स तु रुद्रपार्षदै-
भृशं नदद्भिर्व्यनदत्सुभैरवम् ।
उद्यम्य शूलं जगदन्तकान्तकं
सम्प्राद्रवद् घोषणभूषणाङ्घ्रिः ॥ ६ ॥

anvīyamānaḥ sa tu rudra-pārṣadair
bhṛśaṁ nadadbhir vyanadat subhairavam
udyamya śūlaṁ jagad-antakāntakaṁ
samprādravad ghoṣaṇa-bhūṣaṇāṅghriḥ

anvīyamānaḥ—being followed; *saḥ*—he (Vīrabhadra); *tu*—but; *rudra-pārṣadaiḥ*—by the soldiers of Lord Śiva; *bhṛśam*—tumultuously; *nadadbhiḥ*—roaring; *vyanadat*—sounded; *su-bhairavam*—very fearful; *udyamya*—carrying; *śūlam*—a trident; *jagat-antaka*—death; *antakam*—killing; *samprādravat*—hurried towards (the sacrifice of Dakṣa); *ghoṣaṇa*—roaring; *bhūṣaṇa-aṅghriḥ*—with bangles on his legs.

TRANSLATION

Many other soldiers of Lord Śiva followed the fierce personality in a tumultuous uproar. He carried a great trident, fearful enough to kill even death, and on his legs he wore bangles which seemed to roar.

TEXT 7

अथर्त्विजो यजमानः सदस्याः
ककुभ्युदीच्यां प्रसमीक्ष्य रेणुम् ।
तमः किमेतत्कुत एतद्रजोऽभू-
दिति द्विजा द्विजपत्न्यश्च दध्युः ॥ ७ ॥

athartvijo yajamānaḥ sadasyāḥ
kakubhy udīcyāṁ prasamīkṣya reṇum
tamaḥ kim etat kuta etad rajo 'bhūd
iti dvijā dvija-patnyaś ca dadhyuḥ

atha—at that time; *ṛtvijaḥ*—the priests; *yajamānaḥ*—the chief person performing the sacrifice (Dakṣa); *sadasyāḥ*—all the persons assembled in the sacrificial arena; *kakubhi udīcyām*—in the northern direction; *prasamīkṣya*—seeing; *reṇum*—the dust storm; *tamaḥ*—darkness; *kim*—what; *etat*—this; *kutaḥ*—from where; *etat*—this; *rajaḥ*—dust; *abhūt*—has come; *iti*—thus; *dvijāḥ*—the *brāhmaṇas; dvija-patnyaḥ*—the wives of the *brāhmaṇas; ca*—and; *dadhyuḥ*—began to speculate.

TRANSLATION

At that time, all the persons assembled in the sacrificial arena—the priests, the chief of the sacrificial performance, and the brāhmaṇas and their wives—wondered where the darkness was coming from. Later they could understand that it was a dust storm, and all of them were full of anxiety.

TEXT 8

वाता न वान्ति न हि सन्ति दस्यवः
प्राचीनबर्हिर्जीवति होग्रदण्डः ।
गावो न काल्यन्त इदं कुतो रजो
लोकोऽधुना किं प्रलयाय कल्पते ॥ ८ ॥

vātā na vānti na hi santi dasyavaḥ
prācīna-barhir jīvati hogra-daṇḍaḥ
gāvo na kālyanta idaṁ kuto rajo
loko 'dhunā kiṁ pralayāya kalpate

vātāḥ—the winds; *na vānti*—are not blowing; *na*—not; *hi*—because; *santi*—are possible; *dasyavaḥ*—plunderers; *prācīna-barhiḥ*—old King Barhi; *jīvati*—is living; *ha*—still; *ugra-daṇdaḥ*—who would sternly punish; *gāvaḥ*—the cows; *na kālyante*—are not being driven; *idam*—this; *kutaḥ*—from where; *rajaḥ*—dust; *lokaḥ*—the planet; *adhunā*—now; *kim*—is it; *pralayāya*—for dissolution; *kalpate*—to be considered ready.

TRANSLATION

Conjecturing on the origin of the storm, they said: There is no wind blowing, and no cows are passing, nor is it possible that this dust storm could be raised by plunderers, for there is still the strong King Barhi, who would punish them. Where is this dust storm blowing from? Is the dissolution of the planet now to occur?

PURPORT

Specifically significant in this verse is *prācīna-barhir jīvati.* The king of that part of the land was known as Barhi, and although he was old, he was still living, and he was a very strong ruler. Thus there was no possibility of an invasion by thieves and plunderers. Indirectly it is stated here that thieves, plunderers, rogues and unwanted population can exist only in a state or kingdom where there is no strong ruler. When, in the name of justice, thieves are allowed liberty, the state and kingdom are disturbed by such plunderers and unwanted population. The dust storm created by the soldiers and assistants of Lord Śiva resembled the situation at the time of the dissolution of this world. When there is a need for the dissolution of the material creation, this function is conducted by Lord Śiva. Therefore the situation now created by him resembled the dissolution of the cosmic manifestation.

TEXT 9

प्रसूतिमिश्राः स्त्रिय उद्विग्नचित्ता
ऊचुर्विपाको वृजिनस्यैव तस्य ।
यत्पश्यन्तीनां दुहितॄणां प्रजेशः
सुतां सतीमवदध्यावनागाम् ॥ ९ ॥

prasūti-miśrāḥ striya udvigna-cittā
ūcur vipāko vṛjinasyaiva tasya
yat paśyantīnām duhitṝṇām prajeśaḥ
sutām satīm avadadhyāv anāgām

prasūti-miśrāḥ—headed by Prasūti; *striyaḥ*—the women; *udvigna-cittāḥ*—being very anxious; *ūcuḥ*—said; *vipākaḥ*—the resultant danger; *vṛjinasya*—of the sinful activity; *eva*—indeed; *tasya*—his (Dakṣa's); *yat*—because; *paśyantīnām*—who were looking on; *duhitṝṇām*—of her sisters; *prajeśaḥ*—the lord of the created beings (Dakṣa); *sutām*—his daughter; *satīm*—Satī; *avadadhyau*—insulted; *anāgām*—completely innocent.

TRANSLATION

Prasūti, the wife of Dakṣa, along with the other women assembled, became very anxious and said: This danger has been created by Dakṣa because of the death of Satī, who, even though completely innocent, quit her body as her sisters looked on.

PURPORT

Prasūti, being a softhearted woman, could immediately understand that the imminent danger approaching was due to the impious activity of hardhearted Prajāpati Dakṣa. He was so cruel that he would not save her youngest daughter, Satī, from the act of committing suicide in the presence of her sisters. Satī's mother could understand how much Satī had been pained by the insult of her father. Satī had been present along with the other daughters, and Dakṣa had purposely received all of them but her because she happened to be the wife of Lord Śiva. This consideration convinced the wife of Dakṣa of the danger which was now ahead, and thus she knew that Dakṣa must be prepared to die for his heinous act.

TEXT 10

यस्त्वन्तकाले व्युप्तजटाकलापः
स्वशूलसूच्यर्पितदिग्गजेन्द्रः ।
वितत्य नृत्यत्युदितास्त्रदोर्ध्वजा-
नुच्चाट्टहासस्तनयित्नुभिन्नदिक् ॥१०॥

yas tv anta-kāle vyupta-jaṭā-kalāpaḥ
sva-śūla-sūcy-arpita-dig-gajendraḥ
vitatya nṛtyaty uditāstra-dor-dhvajān
uccāṭṭa-hāsa-stanayitnu-bhinna-dik

yaḥ—who (Lord Śiva); *tu*—but; *anta-kāle*—at the time of dissolution; *vyupta*—having scattered; *jaṭā-kalāpaḥ*—his bunch of hair; *sva-śūla*—his own trident; *sūci*—on the points; *arpita*—pierced; *dik-gajendraḥ*—the rulers of the different directions; *vitatya*—scattering; *nṛtyati*—dances; *udita*—upraised; *astra*—weapons; *doḥ*—hands; *dhvajān*—flags; *ucca*—loud; *aṭṭa-hāsa*—laughing; *stanayitnu*—by the thundering sound; *bhinna*—divided; *dik*—the directions.

TRANSLATION

At the time of dissolution, Lord Śiva's hair is scattered, and he pierces the rulers of the different directions with his trident. He laughs and dances proudly, scattering their hands like flags, as thunder scatters the clouds all over the world.

PURPORT

Prasūti, who appreciated the power and strength of her son-in-law, Lord Śiva, is describing what he does at the time of dissolution. This description indicates that the strength of Lord Śiva is so great that Dakṣa's power could not be set in comparison to it. At the time of dissolution, Lord Śiva, with his trident in hand, dances over the rulers of the different planets, and his hair is scattered, just as the clouds are scattered over all directions in order to plunge the different planets into incessant torrents of rain. In the last phase of dissolution, all the planets become inundated with water, and that inundation is caused by the dancing of Lord Śiva. This dance is called the *pralaya* dance, or dance of dissolution. Prasūti could understand that the dangers ahead resulted not only from Dakṣa's having neglected her daughter, but also because of his neglecting the prestige and honor of Lord Śiva.

TEXT 11

अमर्षयित्वा तमसह्यतेजसं
मन्युप्लुतं दुर्निरीक्ष्यं भ्रुकुट्या ।
करालदंष्ट्राभिरुदस्तभागणं
स्यात्स्वस्ति किं कोपयतो विधातुः ॥११॥

amarṣayitvā tam asahya-tejasaṁ
manyu-plutaṁ durnirīkṣyaṁ bhru-kuṭyā
karāla-daṁṣṭrābhir udasta-bhāgaṇaṁ
syāt svasti kiṁ kopayato vidhātuḥ

amarṣayitvā—after causing to become angry; *tam*—him (Lord Śiva); *asahya-tejasam*—with an unbearable effulgence; *manyu-plutam*—filled with anger; *durnirīkṣyam*—not able to be looked at; *bhru-kuṭyā*—by the movement of his brows; *karāla-daṁṣṭrābhiḥ*—by his fearful teeth; *udasta-bhāgaṇam*—having scattered the luminaries; *syāt*—there should be; *svasti*—good fortune; *kim*—how; *kopayataḥ*—causing (Lord Śiva) to be angry; *vidhātuḥ*—of Brahmā.

TRANSLATION

The gigantic black man bared his fearful teeth. By the movements of his brows he scattered the luminaries all over the sky, and he covered them with his strong, piercing effulgence. Because of the misbehavior of Dakṣa, even Lord Brahmā, Dakṣa's father, could not have been saved from the great exhibition of anger.

TEXT 12

बह्वेवमुद्विग्नदृशोच्यमाने
जनेन दक्षस्य मुहुर्महात्मनः ।
उत्पेतुरुत्पाततमाः सहस्रशो
भयावहा दिवि भूमौ च पर्यक् ॥१२॥

bahv evam udvigna-dṛśocyamāne
janena dakṣasya muhur mahātmanaḥ
utpetur utpātatamāḥ sahasraśo
bhayāvahā divi bhūmau ca paryak

bahu—much; *evam*—in this manner; *udvigna-dṛśā*—with nervous glances; *ucyamāne*—while this was being said; *janena*—by the persons (assembled at the sacrifice); *dakṣasya*—of Dakṣa; *muhuḥ*—again and again; *mahā-ātmanaḥ*—stronghearted; *utpetuḥ*—appeared; *utpāta-tamāḥ*—very powerful symptoms; *sahasraśaḥ*—by the thousands;

bhaya-āvahāḥ—producing fear; *divi*—in the sky; *bhūmau*—on the earth; *ca*—and; *paryak*—from all sides.

TRANSLATION

While all the people talked amongst themselves, Dakṣa saw dangerous omens from all sides, from the earth and from the sky.

PURPORT

In this verse Dakṣa has been described as *mahātmā.* The word *mahātmā* has been commented upon by different commentators in various manners. Vīrarāghava Ācārya has indicated that this word *mahātmā* means "steady in heart." That is to say that Dakṣa was so stronghearted that even when his beloved daughter was prepared to lay down her life, he was steady and unshaken. But in spite of his being so stronghearted, he was perturbed when he saw the various disturbances created by the gigantic black demon. Viśvanātha Cakravartī Ṭhākura remarks in this connection that even if one is called *mahātmā*, a great soul, unless he exhibits the symptoms of a *mahātmā*, he should be considered a *durātmā*, or a degraded soul. In *Bhagavad-gītā* (9.13) the word *mahātmā* describes the pure devotee of the Lord: *mahātmānas tu māṁ pārtha daivīṁ prakṛtim āśritāḥ.* A *mahātmā* is always under the guidance of the internal energy of the Supreme Personality of Godhead, and thus how could such a misbehaved person as Dakṣa be a *mahātmā*? A *mahātmā* is supposed to have all the good qualities of the demigods, and thus Dakṣa, lacking those qualities, could not be called a *mahātmā;* he should instead be called *durātmā*, a degraded soul. The word *mahātmā* to describe the qualifications of Dakṣa is used sarcastically.

TEXT 13

तावत्स रुद्रानुचरैर्महामखो
नानायुधैर्वामनकैरुदायुधैः ।
पिङ्गैः पिशङ्गैर्मकरोदराननैः
पर्याद्रवद्भिर्विदुरान्वरुध्यत ॥१३॥

tāvat sa rudrānucarair mahā-makho
nānāyudhair vāmanakair udāyudhaiḥ

piṅgaiḥ piśaṅgair makarodarānanaiḥ
paryādravadbhir vidurānvarudhyata

tāvat—very quickly; *saḥ*—that; *rudra-anucaraiḥ*—by the followers of Lord Śiva; *mahā-makhaḥ*—the arena of the great sacrifice; *nānā*—various kinds; *āyudhaiḥ*—with weapons; *vāmanakaiḥ*—of short stature; *udāyudhaiḥ*—upraised; *piṅgaiḥ*—blackish; *piśaṅgaiḥ*—yellowish; *makara-udara-ānanaiḥ*—with bellies and faces like sharks'; *paryādravadbhiḥ*—running all around; *vidura*—O Vidura; *anvarudhyata*—was surrounded.

TRANSLATION

My dear Vidura, all the followers of Lord Śiva surrounded the arena of sacrifice. They were of short stature and were equipped with various kinds of weapons; their bodies appeared to be like those of sharks, blackish and yellowish. They ran all around the sacrificial arena and thus began to create disturbances.

TEXT 14

केचिद्बभञ्जुः प्राग्वंशं पत्नीशालां तथापरे ।
सद आग्नीध्रशालां च तद्विहारं महानसम् ॥१४॥

kecid babhañjuḥ prāg-vaṁśaṁ
patnī-śālāṁ tathāpare
sada āgnīdhra-śālāṁ ca
tad-vihāraṁ mahānasam

kecit—some; *babhañjuḥ*—pulled down; *prāk-vaṁśam*—the pillars of the sacrificial pandal; *patnī-śālām*—the female quarters; *tathā*—also; *apare*—others; *sadaḥ*—the sacrificial arena; *āgnīdhra-śālām*—the house of the priests; *ca*—and; *tat-vihāram*—the house of the chief of the sacrifice; *mahā-anasam*—the house of the kitchen department.

TRANSLATION

Some of the soldiers pulled down the pillars which were supporting the pandal of sacrifice, some of them entered the female

quarters, some began destroying the sacrificial arena, and some entered the kitchen and the residential quarters.

TEXT 15

रुरुजुर्यज्ञपात्राणि तथैकेऽग्नीननाशयन् ।
कुण्डेष्वमूत्रयन् केचिद्बिभिदुर्वेदिमेखलाः ॥१५॥

rurujur yajña-pātrāṇi
tathaike 'gnīn anāśayan
kuṇḍeṣv amūtrayan kecid
bibhidur vedi-mekhalāḥ

rurujuḥ—broke; *yajña-pātrāṇi*—the pots used in the sacrifice; *tathā*—so; *eke*—some; *agnīn*—the sacrificial fires; *anāśayan*—extinguished; *kuṇḍeṣu*—on the sacrificial arenas; *amūtrayan*—passed urine; *kecit*—some; *bibhiduḥ*—tore down; *vedi-mekhalāḥ*—the boundary lines of the sacrificial arena.

TRANSLATION

They broke all the pots made for use in the sacrifice, and some of them began to extinguish the sacrificial fire. Some tore down the boundary line of the sacrificial arena, and some passed urine on the arena.

TEXT 16

अबाधन्त मुनीनन्ये एके पत्नीरतर्जयन् ।
अपरे जगृहुर्देवान् प्रत्यासन्नान् पलायितान् ॥१६॥

abādhanta munīn anye
eke patnīr atarjayan
apare jagṛhur devān
pratyāsannān palāyitān

abādhanta—blocked the way; *munīn*—the sages; *anye*—others; *eke*—some; *patnīḥ*—the women; *atarjayan*—threatened; *apare*—others; *jagṛhuḥ*—arrested; *devān*—the demigods; *pratyāsannān*—near at hand; *palāyitān*—who were fleeing.

TRANSLATION

Some blocked the way of the fleeing sages, some threatened the women assembled there, and some arrested the demigods who were fleeing the pandal.

TEXT 17

भृगुं बबन्ध मणिमान् वीरभद्रः प्रजापतिम् ।
चण्डेशः पूषणं देवं भगं नन्दीश्वरोऽग्रहीत् ॥१७॥

bhṛguṁ babandha maṇimān
vīrabhadraḥ prajāpatim
caṇḍeśaḥ pūṣaṇaṁ devaṁ
bhagaṁ nandīśvaro 'grahīt

bhṛgum—Bhṛgu Muni; *babandha*—arrested; *maṇimān*—Maṇimān; *vīrabhadraḥ*—Vīrabhadra; *prajāpatim*—Prajāpati Dakṣa; *caṇḍeśaḥ*—Caṇḍeśa; *pūṣaṇam*—Pūṣā; *devam*—the demigod; *bhagam*—Bhaga; *nandīśvaraḥ*—Nandīśvara; *agrahīt*—arrested.

TRANSLATION

Maṇimān, one of the followers of Lord Śiva, arrested Bhṛgu Muni, and Vīrabhadra, the black demon, arrested Prajāpati Dakṣa. Another follower, who was named Caṇḍeśa, arrested Pūṣā. Nandīśvara arrested the demigod Bhaga.

TEXT 18

सर्व एवर्त्विजो दृष्ट्वा सदस्याः सदिवौकसः ।
तैरर्द्यमानाः सुभृशं ग्रावभिर्नैकधाद्रवन् ॥१८॥

sarva evartvijo dṛṣṭvā
sadasyāḥ sa-divaukasaḥ
tair ardyamānāḥ subhṛśaṁ
grāvabhir naikadhā 'dravan

sarve—all; *eva*—certainly; *ṛtvijaḥ*—the priests; *dṛṣṭvā*—after seeing; *sadasyāḥ*—all the members assembled in the sacrifice; *sa-divaukasaḥ*—

along with the demigods; *taiḥ*—by those (stones); *ardyamānāḥ*—being disturbed; *su-bhṛśam*—very greatly; *grāvabhiḥ*—by stones; *na ekadhā*—in different directions; *adravan*—began to disperse.

TRANSLATION

There was a continuous shower of stones, and all the priests and other members assembled at the sacrifice were put into immense misery. For fear of their lives, they dispersed in different directions.

TEXT 19

जुह्वतः स्रुवहस्तस्य श्मश्रूणि भगवान् भवः ।
भृगोर्लुलुञ्चे सदसि योऽहसच्छ्मश्रु दर्शयन् ॥१९॥

juhvataḥ sruva-hastasya
śmaśrūṇi bhagavān bhavaḥ
bhṛgor luluñce sadasi
yo 'hasac chmaśru darśayan

juhvataḥ—offering sacrificial oblations; *sruva-hastasya*—with the sacrificial ladle in his hand; *śmaśrūṇi*—the mustache; *bhagavān*—the possessor of all opulences; *bhavaḥ*—Vīrabhadra; *bhṛgoḥ*—of Bhṛgu Muni; *luluñce*—tore out; *sadasi*—in the midst of the assembly; *yaḥ*—who (Bhṛgu Muni); *ahasat*—had smiled; *śmaśru*—his mustache; *darśayan*—showing.

TRANSLATION

Vīrabhadra tore off the mustache of Bhṛgu, who was offering the sacrificial oblations with his hands in the fire.

TEXT 20

भगस्य नेत्रे भगवान् पातितस्य रुषा भुवि ।
उज्जहार सदस्थोऽक्ष्णा यः शपन्तमसूसुचत् ॥२०॥

bhagasya netre bhagavān
pātitasya ruṣā bhuvi

ujjahāra sada-stho 'kṣṇā
yaḥ śapantam asūsucat

bhagasya—of Bhaga; *netre*—both eyes; *bhagavān*—Vīrabhadra; *pātitasya*—having been thrust; *ruṣā*—with great anger; *bhuvi*—on the ground; *ujjahāra*—plucked out; *sada-sthaḥ*—while situated in the assembly of the Viśvasṛks; *akṣṇā*—by the movement of his eyebrows; *yaḥ*—who (Bhaga); *śapantam*—(Dakṣa) who was cursing (Lord Śiva); *asūsucat*—encouraged.

TRANSLATION

Vīrabhadra immediately caught Bhaga, who had been moving his eyebrows during Bhṛgu's cursing of Lord Śiva, and out of great anger thrust him to the ground and forcibly put out his eyes.

TEXT 21

पूष्णो ह्यपातयद्दन्तान् कालिङ्गस्य यथा बलः ।
शप्यमाने गरिमणि योऽहसद्दर्शयन्दतः ॥२१॥

pūṣṇo hy apātayad dantān
kāliṅgasya yathā balaḥ
śapyamāne garimaṇi
yo 'hasad darśayan dataḥ

pūṣṇaḥ—of Pūṣā; *hi*—since; *apātayat*—extracted; *dantān*—the teeth; *kāliṅgasya*—of the King of Kaliṅga; *yathā*—as; *balaḥ*—Baladeva; *śapyamāne*—while being cursed; *garimaṇi*—Lord Śiva; *yaḥ*—who (Pūṣā); *ahasat*—smiled; *darśayan*—showing; *dataḥ*—his teeth.

TRANSLATION

Just as Baladeva knocked out the teeth of Dantavakra, the King of Kaliṅga, during the gambling match at the marriage ceremony of Aniruddha, Vīrabhadra knocked out the teeth of both Dakṣa, who had shown them while cursing Lord Śiva, and Pūṣā, who by smiling sympathetically had also shown his teeth.

PURPORT

Here a reference is made to the marriage of Aniruddha, a grandson of Lord Kṛṣṇa's. He kidnapped the daughter of Dantavakra, and thereafter he was arrested. Just as he was to be punished for the kidnapping, the soldiers from Dvārakā arrived, headed by Balarāma, and a fight ensued amongst the *kṣatriyas.* This sort of fight was very common, especially during marriage ceremonies, when everyone was in a challenging spirit. In that challenging spirit, a fight was sure to occur, and in such fights there was commonly killing and misfortune. After finishing such fighting, the parties would come to a compromise, and everything would be settled. This Dakṣa *yajña* was similar to such events. Now all of them—Dakṣa and the demigods Bhaga and Pūṣā and Bhṛgu Muni—were punished by the soldiers of Lord Śiva, but later everything would come to a peaceful end. So this spirit of fighting between one another was not exactly inimical. Because everyone was so powerful and wanted to show his strength by Vedic *mantra* or mystic power, all these fighting skills were very elaborately exhibited by the different parties at the Dakṣa *yajña.*

TEXT 22

आक्रम्योरसि दक्षस्य शितधारेण हेतिना ।
छिन्दन्नपि तदुद्धर्तुं नाशक्नोत् त्र्यम्बकस्तदा ॥२२॥

ākramyorasi dakṣasya
śita-dhāreṇa hetinā
chindann api tad uddhartuṁ
nāśaknot tryambakas tadā

ākramya—having sat; *urasi*—on the chest; *dakṣasya*—of Dakṣa; *śita-dhāreṇa*—having a sharp blade; *hetinā*—with a weapon; *chindan*—cutting; *api*—even though; *tat*—that (head); *uddhartum*—to separate; *na aśaknot*—was not able; *tri-ambakaḥ*—Vīrabhadra (who had three eyes); *tadā*—after this.

TRANSLATION

Then Vīrabhadra, the giantlike personality, sat on the chest of Dakṣa and tried to separate his head from his body with sharp weapons, but was unsuccessful.

TEXT 23

शस्त्रैरस्त्रान्वितैरेवमनिर्भिन्नत्वचं हरः ।
विस्मयं परममापन्नो दध्यौ पशुपतिश्चिरम् ॥२३॥

śastrair astrānvitair evam
anirbhinna-tvacaṁ haraḥ
vismayaṁ param āpanno
dadhyau paśupatiś ciram

śastraiḥ—with weapons; *astra-anvitaiḥ*—with hymns (*mantras*); *evam*—thus; *anirbhinna*—not being cut; *tvacam*—the skin; *haraḥ*—Vīrabhadra; *vismayam*—bewilderment; *param*—greatest; *āpannaḥ*—was struck with; *dadhyau*—thought; *paśupatiḥ*—Vīrabhadra; *ciram*—for a long time.

TRANSLATION

He tried to cut the head of Dakṣa with hymns as well as weapons, but still it was hard to cut even the surface of the skin of Dakṣa's head. Thus Vīrabhadra was exceedingly bewildered.

TEXT 24

दृष्ट्वा संज्ञपनं योगं पशूनां स पतिर्मखे ।
यजमानपशोः कस्य कायात्तेनाहरच्छिरः ॥२४॥

dṛṣṭvā saṁjñapanaṁ yogaṁ
paśūnāṁ sa patir makhe
yajamāna-paśoḥ kasya
kāyāt tenāharac chiraḥ

dṛṣṭvā—having seen; *saṁjñapanam*—for the killing of the animals in the sacrifice; *yogam*—the device; *paśūnām*—of the animals; *saḥ*—he (Vīrabhadra); *patiḥ*—the lord; *makhe*—in the sacrifice; *yajamāna-paśoḥ*—who was an animal in the form of the chief of the sacrifice; *kasya*—of Dakṣa; *kāyāt*—from the body; *tena*—by that (device); *aharat*—severed; *śiraḥ*—his head.

TRANSLATION

Then Vīrabhadra saw the wooden device in the sacrificial arena by which the animals were to have been killed. He took the opportunity of this facility to behead Dakṣa.

PURPORT

In this connection it is to be noted that the device used for killing animals in the sacrifice was not designed to facilitate eating their flesh. The killing was specifically intended to give a new life to the sacrificed animal by the power of Vedic *mantra.* The animals were sacrificed to test the strength of Vedic *mantras; yajñas* were performed as a test of the *mantra.* Even in the modern age, tests are executed on animal bodies in the physiology laboratory. Similarly, whether or not the *brāhmaṇas* were uttering the Vedic hymns correctly was tested by sacrifice in the arena. On the whole, the animals thus sacrificed were not at all the losers. Some old animals would be sacrificed, but in exchange for their old bodies they received other, new bodies. That was the test of Vedic *mantras.* Vīrabhadra, instead of sacrificing animals with the wooden device, immediately beheaded Dakṣa, to the astonishment of everyone.

TEXT 25

साधुवादस्तदा तेषां कर्म तत्तस्य पश्यताम् ।
भूतप्रेतपिशाचानामन्येषां तद्विपर्ययः ॥२५॥

sādhu-vādas tadā teṣāṁ
karma tat tasya paśyatām
bhūta-preta-piśācānāṁ
anyeṣāṁ tad-viparyayaḥ

sādhu-vādaḥ—joyful exclamation; *tadā*—at that time; *teṣām*—of those (followers of Lord Śiva); *karma*—action; *tat*—that; *tasya*—of him (Vīrabhadra); *paśyatām*—seeing; *bhūta-preta-piśācānām*—of the *bhūtas* (ghosts), *pretas* and *piśācas; anyeṣām*—of the others (in the party of Dakṣa); *tat-viparyayaḥ*—the opposite of that (an exclamation of grief).

TRANSLATION

Upon seeing the action of Vīrabhadra, the party of Lord Śiva was pleased and cried out joyfully, and all the bhūtas, ghosts and demons that had come made a tumultuous sound. On the other hand, the brāhmaṇas in charge of the sacrifice cried out in grief at the death of Dakṣa.

TEXT 26

जुहावैतच्छिरस्तस्मिन्दक्षिणाग्नावमर्षितः ।
तद्देवयजनं दग्ध्वा प्रातिष्ठद् गुह्यकालयम् ॥२६॥

juhāvaitac chiras tasmin
dakṣiṇāgnāv amarṣitaḥ
tad-deva-yajanaṁ dagdhvā
prātiṣṭhad guhyakālayam

juhāva—sacrificed as an oblation; *etat*—that; *śiraḥ*—head; *tasmin*—in that; *dakṣiṇa-agnau*—in the sacrificial fire on the southern side; *amarṣitaḥ*—Vīrabhadra, being greatly angry; *tat*—of Dakṣa; *deva-yajanam*—the arrangements for the sacrifice to the demigods; *dagdhvā*—having set fire; *prātiṣṭhat*—departed; *guhyaka-ālayam*—to the abode of the Guhyakas (Kailāsa).

TRANSLATION

Vīrabhadra then took the head and with great anger threw it into the southern side of the sacrificial fire, offering it as an oblation. In this way the followers of Lord Śiva devastated all the arrangements for sacrifice. After setting fire to the whole arena, they departed for their master's abode, Kailāsa.

Thus end the Bhaktivedanta purports of the Fourth Canto, Fifth Chapter, of the Śrīmad-Bhāgavatam, *entitled "Frustration of the Sacrifice of Dakṣa."*

CHAPTER SIX

Brahmā Satisfies Lord Śiva

TEXTS 1–2

मैत्रेय उवाच
अथ देवगणाः सर्वे रुद्रानीकैः पराजिताः ।
शूलपट्टिशनिस्त्रिंशगदापरिघमुद्गरैः ॥ १ ॥
संछिन्नभिन्नसर्वाङ्गाः सर्त्विक्सभ्या भयाकुलाः ।
स्वयम्भुवे नमस्कृत्य कार्त्स्न्येनैतन्न्यवेदयन् ॥ २ ॥

maitreya uvāca
atha deva-gaṇāḥ sarve
rudrānīkaiḥ parājitāḥ
śūla-paṭṭiśa-nistriṁśa-
gadā-parigha-mudgaraiḥ

sañchinna-bhinna-sarvāṅgāḥ
sartvik-sabhyā bhayākulāḥ
svayambhuve namaskṛtya
kārtsnyenaitan nyavedayan

maitreyaḥ uvāca—Maitreya said; *atha*—after this; *deva-gaṇāḥ*—the demigods; *sarve*—all; *rudra-anīkaiḥ*—by the soldiers of Lord Śiva; *parājitāḥ*—having been defeated; *śūla*—trident; *paṭṭiśa*—a sharp-edged spear; *nistriṁśa*—a sword; *gadā*—mace; *parigha*—an iron bludgeon; *mudgaraiḥ*—a hammerlike weapon; *sañchinna-bhinna-sarva-aṅgāḥ*—all the limbs wounded; *sa-ṛtvik-sabhyāḥ*—with all the priests and members of the sacrificial assembly; *bhaya-ākulāḥ*—with great fear; *svayambhuve*—unto Lord Brahmā; *namaskṛtya*—after offering obeisances; *kārtsnyena*—in detail; *etat*—the events of Dakṣa's sacrifice; *nyavedayan*—reported.

TRANSLATION

All the priests and other members of the sacrificial assembly and all the demigods, having been defeated by the soldiers of Lord Śiva and injured by weapons like tridents and swords, approached Lord Brahmā with great fear. After offering him obeisances, they began to speak in detail of all the events which had taken place.

TEXT 3

उपलभ्य पुरैवैतद्भगवानब्जसम्भवः ।
नारायणश्च विश्वात्मा न कस्याध्वरमीयतुः ॥ ३ ॥

upalabhya puraivaitad
bhagavān abja-sambhavaḥ
nārāyaṇaś ca viśvātmā
na kasyādhvaram īyatuḥ

upalabhya—knowing; *purā*—beforehand; *eva*—certainly; *etat*—all these events of Dakṣa's sacrifice; *bhagavān*—the possessor of all opulences; *abja-sambhavaḥ*—born from a lotus flower (Lord Brahmā); *nārāyaṇaḥ*—Nārāyaṇa; *ca*—and; *viśva-ātmā*—the Supersoul of the entire universe; *na*—not; *kasya*—of Dakṣa; *adhvaram*—to the sacrifice; *īyatuḥ*—did go.

TRANSLATION

Both Lord Brahmā and Viṣṇu had already known that such events would occur in the sacrificial arena of Dakṣa, and knowing beforehand, they did not go to the sacrifice.

PURPORT

As stated in *Bhagavad-gītā* (7.26), *vedāhaṁ samatītāni vartamānāni cārjuna.* The Lord says, "I know everything that has happened in the past and is going to happen in the future." Lord Viṣṇu is omniscient, and He therefore knew what would happen at Dakṣa's sacrificial arena. For this reason neither Nārāyaṇa nor Lord Brahmā attended the great sacrifice performed by Dakṣa.

TEXT 4

तदाकर्ण्य विभुः प्राह तेजीयसि कृतागसि ।
क्षेमाय तत्र सा भूयान्न प्रायेण बुभूषताम् ॥ ४ ॥

tad ākarṇya vibhuḥ prāha
tejīyasi kṛtāgasi
kṣemāya tatra sā bhūyān
na prāyeṇa bubhūṣatām

tat—the events related by the demigods and the others; *ākarṇya*—after hearing; *vibhuḥ*—Lord Brahmā; *prāha*—replied; *tejīyasi*—a great personality; *kṛta-āgasi*—has been offended; *kṣemāya*—for your happiness; *tatra*—in that way; *sā*—that; *bhūyāt na*—is not conducive; *prāyeṇa*—generally; *bubhūṣatām*—desire to exist.

TRANSLATION

When Lord Brahmā heard everything from the demigods and the members who had attended the sacrifice, he replied: You cannot be happy in executing a sacrifice if you blaspheme a great personality and thereby offend his lotus feet. You cannot have happiness in that way.

PURPORT

Lord Brahmā explained to the demigods that although Dakṣa wanted to enjoy the results of fruitive sacrificial activities, it is not possible to enjoy when one offends a great personality like Lord Śiva. It was good for Dakṣa to have died in the fight because if he had lived he would have committed such offenses at the lotus feet of great personalities again and again. According to Manu's law, when a person commits murder, punishment is beneficial for him because if he is not killed he might commit more and more murders and therefore be entangled in his future lives for having killed so many persons. Therefore the king's punishment of a murderer is appropriate. If those who are extremely offensive are killed by the grace of the Lord, that is good for them. In other words, Lord Brahmā explained to the demigods that it was good for Dakṣa to have been killed.

TEXT 5

अथापि यूयं कृतकिल्बिषा भवं
ये बर्हिषो भागभाजं परादुः ।
प्रसादयध्वं परिशुद्धचेतसा
क्षिप्रप्रसादं प्रगृहीताङ्घ्रिपद्मम् ॥ ५ ॥

athāpi yūyaṁ kṛta-kilbiṣā bhavaṁ
ye barhiṣo bhāga-bhājaṁ parāduḥ
prasādayadhvaṁ pariśuddha-cetasā
kṣipra-prasādaṁ pragṛhītāṅghri-padmam

atha api—still; *yūyam*—all of you; *kṛta-kilbiṣāḥ*—having committed offenses; *bhavam*—Lord Śiva; *ye*—all of you; *barhiṣaḥ*—of the sacrifice; *bhāga-bhājam*—entitled to a share; *parāduḥ*—have excluded; *prasādayadhvam*—all of you should satisfy; *pariśuddha-cetasā*—without mental reservations; *kṣipra-prasādam*—quick mercy; *pragṛhīta-aṅghri-padmam*—his lotus feet having been taken shelter of.

TRANSLATION

You have excluded Lord Śiva from taking part in the sacrificial results, and therefore you are all offenders at his lotus feet. Still, if you go without mental reservations and surrender unto him and fall down at his lotus feet, he will be very pleased.

PURPORT

Lord Śiva is also called Āśutoṣa. *Āśu* means "very soon," and *toṣa* means "to become satisfied." The demigods were advised to go to Lord Śiva and beg his pardon, and because he is very easily pleased, it was certain that their purpose would be served. Lord Brahmā knew the mind of Lord Śiva very well, and he was confident that the demigods, who were offenders at his lotus feet, could mitigate their offenses by going to him and surrendering without reservation.

TEXT 6

आशासाना जीवितमध्वरस्य
लोकः सपालः कुपिते न यस्मिन् ।

तमाशु देवं प्रियया विहीनं
क्षमापयध्वं हृदि विद्धं दुरुक्तैः ॥ ६ ॥

āśāsānā jīvitam adhvarasya
lokaḥ sa-pālaḥ kupite na yasmin
tam āśu devaṁ priyayā vihīnaṁ
kṣamāpayadhvaṁ hṛdi viddhaṁ duruktaiḥ

āśāsānāḥ—wishing to ask; *jīvitam*—for the duration; *adhvarasya*—of the sacrifice; *lokaḥ*—all the planets; *sa-pālaḥ*—with their controllers; *kupite*—when angered; *na*—not; *yasmin*—whom; *tam*—that; *āśu*—at once; *devam*—Lord Śiva; *priyayā*—of his dear wife; *vihīnam*—having been deprived; *kṣamāpayadhvam*—beg his pardon; *hṛdi*—in his heart; *viddham*—very much afflicted; *duruktaiḥ*—by unkind words.

TRANSLATION

Lord Brahmā also advised them that Lord Śiva is so powerful that by his anger all the planets and their chief controllers can be destroyed immediately. Also, he said that Lord Śiva was especially sorry because he had recently lost his dear wife and was also very much afflicted by the unkind words of Dakṣa. Under the circumstances, Lord Brahmā suggested, it would behoove them to go at once and beg his pardon.

TEXT 7

नाहं न यज्ञो न च यूयमन्ये
ये देहभाजो मुनयश्च तत्त्वम् ।
विदुः प्रमाणं बलवीर्ययोर्वा
यस्यात्मतन्त्रस्य क उपायं विधित्सेत् ॥ ७ ॥

nāhaṁ na yajño na ca yūyam anye
ye deha-bhājo munayaś ca tattvam
viduḥ pramāṇaṁ bala-vīryayor vā
yasyātma-tantrasya ka upāyaṁ vidhitset

na—not; *aham*—I; *na*—nor; *yajñaḥ*—Indra; *na*—nor; *ca*—and; *yūyam*—all of you; *anye*—others; *ye*—who; *deha-bhājaḥ*—of those who bear material bodies; *munayaḥ*—the sages; *ca*—and; *tattvam*—the truth; *viduḥ*—know; *pramāṇam*—the extent; *bala-vīryayoḥ*—of the strength and power; *vā*—or; *yasya*—of Lord Śiva; *ātma-tantrasya*—of Lord Śiva, who is self-dependent; *kaḥ*—what; *upāyam*—means; *vidhitset*—should wish to devise.

TRANSLATION

Lord Brahmā said that no one, not even himself, Indra, all the members assembled in the sacrificial arena, or all the sages, could know how powerful Lord Śiva is. Under the circumstances, who would dare to commit an offense at his lotus feet?

PURPORT

After Lord Brahmā advised the demigods to go to Lord Śiva and beg his pardon, it was suggested how he should be satisfied and how the matter should be placed before him. Brahmā also asserted that none of the conditioned souls, including himself and all the demigods, could know how to satisfy Lord Śiva. But he said, "It is known that he is very easily satisfied, so let us try to satisfy him by falling at his lotus feet."

Actually the position of the subordinate is always to surrender to the Supreme. That is the instruction of *Bhagavad-gītā*. The Lord asks everyone to give up all kinds of concocted occupations and simply surrender unto Him. That will protect the conditioned souls from all sinful reactions. Similarly, in this case Brahmā also suggested that they go and surrender unto the lotus feet of Lord Śiva, for since he is very kind and easily satisfied, this action would prove effective.

TEXT 8

स इत्थमादिश्य सुरानजस्तु तैः
समन्वितः पितृभिः सप्रजेशैः ।
ययौ स्वधिष्ण्यान्निलयं पुरद्विषः
कैलासमद्रिप्रवरं प्रियं प्रभोः ॥ ८ ॥

sa ittham ādiśya surān ajas tu taiḥ
samanvitaḥ pitṛbhiḥ sa-prajeśaiḥ
yayau sva-dhiṣṇyān nilayaṁ pura-dviṣaḥ
kailāsam adri-pravaraṁ priyaṁ prabhoḥ

saḥ—he (Brahmā); *ittham*—thus; *ādiśya*—after instructing; *surān*—the demigods; *ajaḥ*—Lord Brahmā; *tu*—then; *taiḥ*—those; *samanvitaḥ*—followed; *pitṛbhiḥ*—by the Pitās; *sa-prajeśaiḥ*—along with the lords of the living entities; *yayau*—went; *sva-dhiṣṇyāt*—from his own place; *nilayam*—the abode; *pura-dviṣaḥ*—of Lord Śiva; *kailāsam*—Kailāsa; *adri-pravaram*—the best among mountains; *priyam*—dear; *prabhoḥ*—of the lord (Śiva).

TRANSLATION

After thus instructing all the demigods, the Pitās and the lords of the living entities, Lord Brahmā took them with him and left for the abode of Lord Śiva, known as the Kailāsa Hill.

PURPORT

The abode of Lord Śiva, which is known as Kailāsa, is described in the fourteen verses which follow.

TEXT 9

जन्मौषधितपोमन्त्रयोगसिद्धैर्नरेतरैः ।
जुष्टं किंनरगन्धर्वैरप्सरोभिर्वृतं सदा ॥ ९ ॥

janmauṣadhi-tapo-mantra-
yoga-siddhair naretaraiḥ
juṣṭaṁ kinnara-gandharvair
apsarobhir vṛtaṁ sadā

janma—birth; *auṣadhi*—herbs; *tapaḥ*—austerity; *mantra*—Vedic hymns; *yoga*—mystic *yoga* practices; *siddhaiḥ*—with perfected beings; *nara-itaraiḥ*—by demigods; *juṣṭam*—enjoyed; *kinnara-gandharvaiḥ*—by Kinnaras and Gandharvas; *apsarobhiḥ*—by Apsarās; *vṛtam*—full of; *sadā*—always.

TRANSLATION

The abode known as Kailāsa is full of different herbs and vegetables, and it is sanctified by Vedic hymns and mystic yoga practice. Thus the residents of that abode are demigods by birth and have all mystic powers. Besides them there are other human beings,

who are known as Kinnaras and Gandharvas and are accompanied by their beautiful wives, who are known as Apsarās, or angels.

TEXT 10

नानामणिमयैः शृङ्गैर्नानाधातुविचित्रितैः ।
नानाद्रुमलतागुल्मैर्नानामृगगणावृतैः ॥१०॥

nānā-maṇimayaiḥ śṛṅgair
nānā-dhātu-vicitritaiḥ
nānā-druma-latā-gulmair
nānā-mṛga-gaṇāvṛtaiḥ

nānā—different kinds; *maṇi*—jewels; *mayaiḥ*—made of; *śṛṅgaiḥ*—with the peaks; *nānā-dhātu-vicitritaiḥ*—decorated with various minerals; *nānā*—various; *druma*—trees; *latā*—creepers; *gulmaiḥ*—plants; *nānā*—various; *mṛga-gaṇa*—by groups of deer; *āvṛtaiḥ*—inhabited by.

TRANSLATION

Kailāsa is full of mountains filled with all kinds of valuable jewels and minerals and surrounded by all varieties of valuable trees and plants. The top of the hill is nicely decorated by various types of deer.

TEXT 11

नानामलप्रस्रवणैर्नानाकन्दरसानुभिः ।
रमणं विहरन्तीनां रमणैः सिद्धयोषिताम् ॥११॥

nānāmala-prasravaṇair
nānā-kandara-sānubhiḥ
ramaṇaṁ viharantīnāṁ
ramaṇaiḥ siddha-yoṣitām

nānā—various; *amala*—transparent; *prasravaṇaiḥ*—with waterfalls; *nānā*—various; *kandara*—caves; *sānubhiḥ*—with summits; *ramaṇam*—giving pleasure; *viharantīnām*—sporting; *ramaṇaiḥ*—with their lovers; *siddha-yoṣitām*—of the damsels of the mystics.

TRANSLATION

There are many waterfalls, and in the mountains there are many beautiful caves in which the very beautiful wives of the mystics are found.

TEXT 12

मयूरकेकाभिरुतं मदान्धालिविमूर्च्छितम् ।
प्लावितै रक्तकण्ठानां कूजितैश्च पतत्त्रिणाम् ॥१२॥

mayūra-kekābhirutaṁ
madāndhāli-vimūrcchitam
plāvitai rakta-kaṇṭhānāṁ
kūjitaiś ca patattriṇām

mayūra—peacocks; *kekā*—with the cries; *abhirutam*—resounding; *mada*—by intoxication; *andha*—blinded; *ali*—by the bees; *vimūrcchitam*—resounded; *plāvitaiḥ*—with the singing; *rakta-kaṇṭhānām*—of the cuckoos; *kūjitaiḥ*—with the whispering; *ca*—and; *patattriṇām*—of other birds.

TRANSLATION

On Kailāsa Hill there is always the rhythmical sound of the peacocks' sweet vibrations and the bees' humming. Cuckoos are always singing, and other birds whisper amongst themselves.

TEXT 13

आह्वयन्तमिवोद्धस्तैर्द्विजान् कामदुघैर्द्रुमैः ।
व्रजन्तमिव मातङ्गैर्गृणन्तमिव निर्झरैः ॥१३॥

āhvayantam ivoddhastair
dvijān kāma-dughair drumaiḥ
vrajantam iva mātaṅgair
gṛṇantam iva nirjharaiḥ

āhvayantam—calling; *iva*—as if; *ut-hastaiḥ*—with upraised hands (branches); *dvijān*—the birds; *kāma-dughaiḥ*—yielding desires; *drumaiḥ*—with trees; *vrajantam*—moving; *iva*—as if; *mātaṅgaiḥ*—by elephants; *gṛṇantam*—resounding; *iva*—as if; *nirjharaiḥ*—by the waterfalls.

TRANSLATION

There are tall trees with straight branches that appear to call the sweet birds, and when herds of elephants pass through the hills, it appears that the Kailāsa Hill moves with them. When the waterfalls resound, it appears that Kailāsa Hill does also.

TEXTS 14–15

मन्दारैः पारिजातैश्च सरलैश्चोपशोभितम् ।
तमालैः शालतालैश्च कोविदारासनार्जुनैः ॥१४॥
चूतैः कदम्बैर्नीपैश्च नागपुन्नागचम्पकैः ।
पाटलाशोकबकुलैः कुन्दैः कुरबकैरपि ॥१५॥

mandāraiḥ pārijātaiś ca
saralaiś copaśobhitam
tamālaiḥ śāla-tālaiś ca
kovidārāsanārjunaiḥ

cūtaiḥ kadambair nīpaiś ca
nāga-punnāga-campakaiḥ
pāṭalāśoka-bakulaiḥ
kundaiḥ kurabakair api

mandāraiḥ—with *mandāras; pārijātaiḥ*—with *pārijātas; ca*—and; *saralaiḥ*—with *saralas; ca*—and; *upaśobhitam*—decorated; *tamālaiḥ*—with *tamāla* trees; *śāla-tālaiḥ*—with *śālas* and *tālas; ca*—and; *kovidāra-āsana-arjunaiḥ*—*kovidāras*, *āsanas* (*vijaya-sāras*) and *arjuna* trees (*kāñcanārakas*); *cūtaiḥ*—with *cūtas* (a species of mango); *kadambaiḥ*—with *kadambas; nīpaiḥ*—with *nīpas* (*dhūli-kadambas*); *ca*—and; *nāga-punnāga-campakaiḥ*—with *nāgas*, *punnāgas* and *campakas; pāṭala-aśoka-bakulaiḥ*—with *pāṭalas*, *aśokas* and *bakulas; kundaiḥ*—with *kundas; kurabakaiḥ*—with *kurabakas; api*—also.

TRANSLATION

The whole of Kailāsa Hill is decorated with various kinds of trees, of which the following names may be mentioned: mandāra, pārijāta, sarala, tamāla, tāla, kovidāra, āsana, arjuna, āmra-jāti (mango), kadamba, dhūli-kadamba, nāga, punnāga, campaka, pāṭala, aśoka, bakula, kunda and kurabaka. The entire hill is decorated with such trees, which produce flowers with fragrant aromas.

TEXT 16

स्वर्णार्णशतपत्रैश्च वररेणुकजातिभिः ।
कुब्जकैर्मल्लिकाभिश्च माधवीभिश्च मण्डितम् ॥१६॥

svarṇārṇa-śata-patraiś ca
vara-reṇuka-jātibhiḥ
kubjakair mallikābhiś ca
mādhavībhiś ca maṇḍitam

svarṇārṇa—golden colored; *śata-patraiḥ*—with lotuses; *ca*—and; *vara-reṇuka-jātibhiḥ*—with *varas, reṇukas* and *mālatīs; kubjakaiḥ*—with *kubjakas; mallikābhiḥ*—with *mallikās; ca*—and; *mādhavībhiḥ*—with *mādhavīs; ca*—and; *maṇḍitam*—decorated.

TRANSLATION

There are other trees also which decorate the hill, such as the golden lotus flower, the cinnamon tree, mālatī, kubja, mallikā and mādhavī.

TEXT 17

पनसोदुम्बराश्वत्थप्लक्षन्यग्रोधहिङ्गुभिः ।
भूर्जैरोषधिभिः पूगै राजपूगैश्च जम्बुभिः ॥१७॥

panasodumbarāśvattha-
plakṣa-nyagrodha-hiṅgubhiḥ
bhūrjair oṣadhibhiḥ pūgai
rājapūgaiś ca jambubhiḥ

panasa-udumbara-aśvattha-plakṣa-nyagrodha-hiṅgubhiḥ—with *panasas* (jackfruit trees), *udumbaras, aśvatthas, plakṣas, nyagrodhas* and trees producing asafetida; *bhūrjaiḥ*—with *bhūrjas; oṣadhibhiḥ*—with betel nut trees; *pūgaiḥ*—with *pūgas; rājapūgaiḥ*—with *rājapūgas; ca*—and; *jambubhiḥ*—with *jambus.*

TRANSLATION

Kailāsa Hill is also decorated with such trees as kata, jackfruit, julara, banyan trees, plakṣas, nyagrodhas and trees producing asafetida. Also there are trees of betel nuts and bhūrja-patra, as well as rājapūga, blackberries and similar other trees.

TEXT 18

खर्जूराम्रातकाम्राद्यैः प्रियालमधुकेङ्गुदैः ।
द्रुमजातिभिरन्यैश्च राजितं वेणुकीचकैः ॥१८॥

kharjūrāmrātakāmrādyaiḥ
priyāla-madhukeṅgudaiḥ
druma-jātibhir anyaiś ca
rājitaṁ veṇu-kīcakaiḥ

kharjūra-āmrātaka-āmra-ādyaiḥ—with *kharjūras, āmrātakas, āmras* and others; *priyāla-madhuka-iṅgudaiḥ*—with *priyālas, madhukas* and *iṅgudas; druma-jātibhiḥ*—with varieties of trees; *anyaiḥ*—other; *ca*—and; *rājitam*—decorated; *veṇu-kīcakaiḥ*—with *veṇus* (bamboos) and *kīcakas* (hollow bamboos).

TRANSLATION

There are mango trees, priyāla, madhuka and iṅguda. Besides these there are other trees, like thin bamboos, kīcaka and varieties of other bamboo trees, all decorating the tract of Kailāsa Hill.

TEXTS 19–20

कुमुदोत्पलकह्लारशतपत्रवनर्द्धिभिः ।
नलिनीषु कलं कूजत्खगवृन्दोपशोभितम् ॥१९॥

मृगैः शाखामृगैः क्रोडैर्मृगेन्द्रैर्ऋक्षशल्यकैः ।
गवयैः शरभैर्व्याघ्रै रुरुभिर्महिषादिभिः ॥२०॥

kumudotpala-kahlāra-
śatapatra-vanarddhibhiḥ
nalinīṣu kalaṁ kūjat-
khaga-vṛndopaśobhitam

mṛgaiḥ śākhāmṛgaiḥ kroḍair
mṛgendrair ṛkṣa-śalyakaiḥ
gavayaiḥ śarabhair vyāghrai
rurubhir mahiṣādibhiḥ

kumuda—kumuda; *utpala*—utpala; *kahlāra*—kahlāra; *śatapatra*—lotuses; *vana*—forest; *ṛddhibhiḥ*—being covered with; *nalinīṣu*—in the lakes; *kalam*—very sweetly; *kūjat*—whispering; *khaga*—of birds; *vṛnda*—groups; *upaśobhitam*—decorated with; *mṛgaiḥ*—with deer; *śākhā-mṛgaiḥ*—with monkeys; *kroḍaiḥ*—with boars; *mṛga-indraiḥ*—with lions; *ṛkṣa-śalyakaiḥ*—with *ṛkṣas* and *śalyakas; gavayaiḥ*—with forest cows; *śarabhaiḥ*—with forest asses; *vyāghraiḥ*—with tigers; *rurubhiḥ*—with small deer; *mahiṣa-ādibhiḥ*—with buffalo, etc.

TRANSLATION

There are different kinds of lotus flowers, such as kumuda, utpala and śatapatra. The forest appears to be a decorated garden, and the small lakes are full of various kinds of birds who whisper very sweetly. There are many kinds of other animals also, like deer, monkeys, boars, lions, ṛkṣas, śalyakas, forest cows, forest asses, tigers, small deer, buffalo and many other animals, who are fully enjoying their lives.

TEXT 21

कर्णान्त्रैकपदाश्वास्यैर्निर्जुष्टं वृकनाभिभिः ।
कदलीखण्डसंरुद्धनलिनीपुलिनश्रियम् ॥२१॥

karṇāntraikapadāśvāsyair
nirjuṣṭaṁ vṛka-nābhibhiḥ

kadalī-khaṇḍa-saṁruddha-
nalinī-pulina-śriyam

karṇāntra—by the *karṇāntra; ekapada*—the *ekapada; aśvāsyaiḥ*—by the *aśvāsya; nirjuṣṭam*—fully enjoyed; *vṛka-nābhibhiḥ*—by the *vṛka* and *nābhi,* or *kastūrī* deer; *kadalī*—of banana trees; *khaṇḍa*—with groups; *saṁruddha*—covered; *nalinī*—of small lakes filled with lotus flowers; *pulina*—with the sandy banks; *śriyam*—very beautiful.

TRANSLATION

There are varieties of deer, such as karṇāntra, ekapada, aśvāsya, vṛka and kastūrī, the deer which bears musk. Besides the deer there are many banana trees which decorate the small hillside lakes very nicely.

TEXT 22

पर्यस्तं नन्दया सत्याः स्नानपुण्यतरोदया ।
विलोक्य भूतेशगिरिं विबुधा विस्मयं ययुः ॥२२॥

paryastaṁ nandayā satyāḥ
snāna-puṇyatarodayā
vilokya bhūteśa-giriṁ
vibudhā vismayaṁ yayuḥ

paryastam—surrounded; *nandayā*—by the Nandā; *satyāḥ*—of Satī; *snāna*—by the bathing; *puṇya-tara*—especially flavored; *udayā*—with water; *vilokya*—after seeing; *bhūta-īśa*—of Bhūteśa (the lord of the ghosts, Lord Śiva); *girim*—the mountain; *vibudhāḥ*—the demigods; *vismayam*—wonder; *yayuḥ*—obtained.

TRANSLATION

There is a small lake named Alakanandā in which Satī used to take her bath, and that lake is especially auspicious. All the demigods, after seeing the specific beauty of Kailāsa Hill, were struck with wonder at the great opulence to be found there.

PURPORT

According to the commentary called *Śrī-Bhāgavata-candra-candrikā*, the water in which Satī used to bathe was Ganges water. In other words, the Ganges flowed through the Kailāsa-parvata. There is every possibility of accepting such a statement because Ganges water also flows from the hair of Lord Śiva. Since Ganges water rests on the head of Lord Śiva and then flows to the other parts of the universe, it is quite possible that the water in which Satī bathed, which was certainly very nicely scented, was Ganges water.

TEXT 23

ददृशुस्तत्र ते रम्यामलकां नाम वै पुरीम् ।
वनं सौगन्धिकं चापि यत्र तन्नाम पङ्कजम् ॥२३॥

dadṛśus tatra te ramyām
alakāṁ nāma vai purīm
vanaṁ saugandhikaṁ cāpi
yatra tan-nāma paṅkajam

dadṛśuḥ—saw; *tatra*—there (in Kailāsa); *te*—they (the demigods); *ramyām*—very attractive; *alakām*—Alakā; *nāma*—known as; *vai*—indeed; *purīm*—abode; *vanam*—forest; *saugandhikam*—Saugandhika; *ca*—and; *api*—even; *yatra*—in which place; *tat-nāma*—known by that name; *paṅkajam*—species of lotus flowers.

TRANSLATION

Thus the demigods saw the wonderfully beautiful region known as Alakā in the forest known as Saugandhika, which means "full of fragrance." The forest is known as Saugandhika because of its abundance of lotus flowers.

PURPORT

Sometimes Alakā is known as Alakā-purī, which is also the name of the abode of Kuvera. Kuvera's abode, however, cannot be seen from Kailāsa. Therefore the region of Alakā referred to here is different from the Alakā-purī of Kuvera. According to Vīrarāghava Ācārya, *alakā* means "uncommonly beautiful." In the region of Alakā the demigods saw, there is a type of lotus flower known as Saugandhika that distributes an especially fragrant scent.

TEXT 24

नन्दा चालकनन्दा च सरितौ बाह्यतः पुरः ।
तीर्थपादपदाम्भोजरजसातीव पावने ॥२४॥

nandā cālakanandā ca
saritau bāhyataḥ puraḥ
tīrthapāda-padāmbhoja-
rajasātīva pāvane

nandā—the Nandā; *ca*—and; *alakanandā*—the Alakanandā; *ca*—and; *saritau*—two rivers; *bāhyataḥ*—outside; *puraḥ*—from the city; *tīrtha-pāda*—of the Supreme Personality of Godhead; *pada-ambhoja*—of the lotus feet; *rajasā*—by the dust; *atīva*—exceedingly; *pāvane*—sanctified.

TRANSLATION

They also saw the two rivers named Nandā and Alakanandā. These two rivers are sanctified by the dust of the lotus feet of the Supreme Personality of Godhead, Govinda.

TEXT 25

ययोः सुरस्त्रियः क्षत्तरवरुह्य स्वधिष्ण्यतः ।
क्रीडन्ति पुंसः सिञ्चन्त्यो विगाह्य रतिकर्शिताः ॥२५॥

yayoḥ sura-striyaḥ kṣattar
avaruhya sva-dhiṣṇyataḥ
krīḍanti puṁsaḥ siñcantyo
vigāhya rati-karśitāḥ

yayoḥ—in both of which (rivers); *sura-striyaḥ*—the celestial damsels along with their husbands; *kṣattaḥ*—O Vidura; *avaruhya*—descending; *sva-dhiṣṇyataḥ*—from their own airplanes; *krīḍanti*—they play; *puṁ-*

saḥ—their husbands; *siñcantyaḥ*—sprinkling with water; *vigāhya*—after entering (the water); *rati-karśitāḥ*—whose enjoyment has become diminished.

TRANSLATION

My dear Kṣattā, Vidura, the celestial damsels come down to those rivers in their airplanes with their husbands, and after sexual enjoyment, they enter the water and enjoy sprinkling their husbands with water.

PURPORT

It is understood that even the damsels of the heavenly planets are polluted by thoughts of sex enjoyment, and therefore they come in airplanes to bathe in the rivers Nandā and Alakanandā. It is significant that these rivers, Nandā and Alakanandā, are sanctified by the dust of the lotus feet of the Supreme Personality of Godhead. In other words, just as the Ganges is sacred because its water emanates from the toes of the Supreme Personality of Godhead, Nārāyaṇa, so whenever water or anything is in touch with devotional service to the Supreme Personality of Godhead, it is purified and spiritualized. The rules and regulations of devotional service are based on this principle: anything in touch with the lotus feet of the Lord is immediately freed from all material contamination.

The damsels of the heavenly planets, polluted by thoughts of sex life, come down to bathe in the sanctified rivers and enjoy sprinkling water on their husbands. Two words are very significant in this connection. *Rati-karśitāḥ* means that the damsels become morose after sex enjoyment. Although they accept sex enjoyment as a bodily demand, afterwards they are not happy.

Another significant point is that Lord Govinda, the Supreme Personality of Godhead, is described here as Tīrthapāda. *Tīrtha* means "sanctified place," and *pāda* means "the lotus feet of the Lord." People go to a sanctified place to free themselves from all sinful reactions. In other words, those who are devoted to the lotus feet of the Supreme Personality of Godhead, Kṛṣṇa, automatically become sanctified. The Lord's lotus feet are called *tīrtha-pāda* because under their protection there are hundreds and thousands of saintly persons who sanctify the sacred places of pilgrimage. Śrīla Narottama dāsa Ṭhākura, a great *ācārya* of the

Gauḍīya Vaiṣṇava-sampradāya, advises us not to travel to different places of pilgrimage. Undoubtedly it is troublesome to go from one place to another, but one who is intelligent can take shelter of the lotus feet of Govinda and thereby be automatically sanctified as the result of his pilgrimage. Anyone who is fixed in the service of the lotus feet of Govinda is called *tīrtha-pāda;* he does not need to travel on various pilgrimages, for he can enjoy all the benefits of such travel simply by engaging in the service of the lotus feet of the Lord. Such a pure devotee, who has implicit faith in the lotus feet of the Lord, can create sacred places in any part of the world where he decides to remain. *Tīrthī-kurvanti tīrthāni* (*Bhāg.* 1.13.10). The places are sanctified due to the presence of pure devotees; any place automatically becomes a place of pilgrimage if either the Lord or His pure devotee remains or resides there. In other words, such a pure devotee, who is engaged one hundred percent in the service of the Lord, can remain anywhere in the universe, and that part of the universe immediately becomes a sacred place where he can peacefully render service to the Lord as the Lord desires.

TEXT 26

ययोस्तत्स्नानविभ्रष्टनवकुङ्कुमपिञ्जरम् ।
वितृषोऽपि पिबन्त्यम्भः पाययन्तो गजा गजीः ॥२६॥

yayos tat-snāna-vibhraṣṭa-
nava-kuṅkuma-piñjaram
vitṛṣo 'pi pibanty ambhaḥ
pāyayanto gajā gajīḥ

yayoḥ—in both of which rivers; *tat-snāna*—by the bathing of them (the damsels of the heavenly planets); *vibhraṣṭa*—fallen off; *nava*—fresh; *kuṅkuma*—with *kuṅkuma* powder; *piñjaram*—yellow; *vitṛṣaḥ*—not being thirsty; *api*—even; *pibanti*—drink; *ambhaḥ*—the water; *pāyayantaḥ*—causing to drink; *gajāḥ*—the elephants; *gajīḥ*—the female elephants.

TRANSLATION

After the damsels of the heavenly planets bathe in the water, it becomes yellowish and fragrant due to the kuṅkuma from their

bodies. Thus the elephants come to bathe there with their wives, the she-elephants, and they also drink the water, although they are not thirsty.

TEXT 27

तारहेममहारत्नविमानशतसंकुलाम् ।
जुष्टां पुण्यजनस्त्रीभिर्यथा खं सतडिद्घनम् ॥२७॥

tāra-hema-mahāratna-
vimāna-śata-saṅkulām
juṣṭāṁ puṇyajana-strībhir
yathā khaṁ sataḍid-ghanam

tāra-hema—of pearls and gold; *mahā-ratna*—valuable jewels; *vimāna*—of airplanes; *śata*—with hundreds; *saṅkulām*—crowded; *juṣṭām*—occupied, enjoyed; *puṇyajana-strībhiḥ*—by the wives of the Yakṣas; *yathā*—as; *kham*—the sky; *sa-taḍit-ghanam*—with the lightning and the clouds.

TRANSLATION

The airplanes of the heavenly denizens are bedecked with pearls, gold and many valuable jewels. The heavenly denizens are compared to clouds in the sky decorated with occasional flashes of electric lightning.

PURPORT

The airplanes described in this verse are different from the airplanes of which we have experience. In the *Śrīmad-Bhāgavatam* and all the Vedic literatures, there are many descriptions of *vimāna*, which means "airplanes." On different planets there are different kinds of airplanes. On this gross planet earth, there are airplanes run by machine, but on other planets the airplanes are run not by machine but by mantric hymns. They are also used especially for enjoyment by the denizens of the heavenly planets so that they can go from one planet to another. On other planets which are called Siddhalokas, the denizens can travel from one planet to another without airplanes. The beautiful airplanes from the heavenly planets are compared here to the sky because they fly in the sky; the passengers are compared to the clouds. The beautiful damsels, the wives of the denizens of the heavenly planets, are compared to lightning. In summation, the airplanes with their passengers which came from higher planets to Kailāsa were very pleasant to look at.

TEXT 28

हित्वा यक्षेश्वरपुरीं वनं सौगन्धिकं च तत् ।
द्रुमैः कामदुघैर्हृद्यं चित्रमाल्यफलच्छदैः ॥२८॥

hitvā yakṣeśvara-purīṁ
vanaṁ saugandhikaṁ ca tat
drumaiḥ kāma-dughair hṛdyaṁ
citra-mālya-phala-cchadaiḥ

hitvā—passing over; *yakṣa-īśvara*—the lord of the Yakṣas (Kuvera); *purīm*—the abode; *vanam*—the forest; *saugandhikam*—named Saugandhika; *ca*—and; *tat*—that; *drumaiḥ*—with trees; *kāma-dughaiḥ*—yielding desires; *hṛdyam*—attractive; *citra*—variegated; *mālya*—flowers; *phala*—fruits; *chadaiḥ*—leaves.

TRANSLATION

While traveling, the demigods passed over the forest known as Saugandhika, which is full of varieties of flowers, fruits and desire trees. While passing over the forest, they also saw the regions of Yakṣeśvara.

PURPORT

Yakṣeśvara is also known as Kuvera, and he is the treasurer of the demigods. In the descriptions of him in Vedic literature, it is stated that he is fabulously rich. It appears from these verses that Kailāsa is situated near the residential quarters of Kuvera. It is also stated here that the forest was full of desire trees. In *Brahma-saṁhitā* we learn about the desire tree which is found in the spiritual world, especially in Kṛṣṇaloka, the abode of Lord Kṛṣṇa. We learn here that such desire trees are also found in Kailāsa, the residence of Lord Śiva, by the grace of Kṛṣṇa. It thus appears that Kailāsa has a special significance; it is almost like the residence of Lord Kṛṣṇa.

TEXT 29

रक्तकण्ठखगानीकस्वरमण्डितषट्पदम् ।
कलहंसकुलप्रेष्ठं खरदण्डजलाशयम् ॥२९॥

rakta-kaṇṭha-khagānīka-
svara-maṇḍita-ṣaṭpadam
kalahaṁsa-kula-preṣṭhaṁ
kharadaṇḍa-jalāśayam

rakta—reddish; *kaṇṭha*—necks; *khaga-anīka*—of many birds; *svara*—with the sweet sounds; *maṇḍita*—decorated; *ṣaṭ-padam*—bees; *kalahaṁsa-kula*—of groups of swans; *preṣṭham*—very dear; *khara-daṇḍa*—lotus flowers; *jala-āśayam*—lakes.

TRANSLATION

In that celestial forest there were many birds whose necks were colored reddish and whose sweet sounds mixed with the humming of the bees. The lakes were abundantly decorated with crying swans as well as strong-stemmed lotus flowers.

PURPORT

The beauty of the forest was intensified by the presence of various lakes. It is described herein that the lakes were decorated with lotus flowers and with swans who played and sang with the birds and the humming bees. Considering all these attributes, one can imagine how beautiful this spot was and how much the demigods passing through enjoyed the atmosphere. There are many paths and beautiful spots created by man on this planet earth, but none of them can surpass those of Kailāsa, as they are described in these verses.

TEXT 30

वनकुञ्जरसंघृष्टहरिचन्दनवायुना ।
अधि पुण्यजनस्त्रीणां मुहुरुन्मथयन्मनः ॥३०॥

vana-kuñjara-saṅghṛṣṭa-
haricandana-vāyunā
adhi puṇyajana-strīṇāṁ
muhur unmathayan manaḥ

vana-kuñjara—by wild elephants; *saṅghṛṣṭa*—rubbed against; *hari-candana*—the sandalwood trees; *vāyunā*—by the breeze; *adhi*—further; *puṇyajana-strīṇām*—of the wives of the Yakṣas; *muhuḥ*—again and again; *unmathayat*—agitating; *manaḥ*—the minds.

TRANSLATION

All these atmospheric influences unsettled the forest elephants who flocked together in the sandalwood forest, and the blowing wind agitated the minds of the damsels there for further sexual enjoyment.

PURPORT

Whenever there is a nice atmosphere in the material world, immediately there is an awakening of the sexual appetite in the minds of materialistic persons. This tendency is present everywhere within this material world, not only on this earth but in higher planetary systems as well. In complete contrast with the influence of this atmosphere on the minds of the living entities within the material world is the description of the spiritual world. The women there are hundreds and thousands of times more beautiful than the women here in this material world, and the spiritual atmosphere is also many times better. Yet despite the pleasant atmosphere, the minds of the denizens do not become agitated because in the spiritual world, the Vaikuṇṭha planets, the spiritualistic minds of the inhabitants are so much absorbed in the spiritual vibration of chanting the glories of the Lord that such enjoyment could not be surpassed by any other enjoyment, even sex, which is the culmination of all pleasure in the material world. In other words, in the Vaikuṇṭha world, in spite of its better atmosphere and facilities, there is no impetus for sex life. As stated in *Bhagavad-gītā* (2.59), *paraṁ dṛṣṭvā nivartate:* the inhabitants are so spiritually enlightened that in the presence of such spirituality, sex life is insignificant.

TEXT 31

वैदूर्यकृतसोपाना वाप्य उत्पलमालिनीः ।
प्राप्तं किम्पुरुषैर्दृष्ट्वा त आराद्ददृशुर्वटम् ॥३१॥

vaidūrya-kṛta-sopānā
vāpya utpala-mālinīḥ
prāptaṁ kimpuruṣair dṛṣṭvā
ta ārād dadṛśur vaṭam

vaidūrya-kṛta—made of *vaidūrya; sopānāḥ*—staircases; *vāpyaḥ*—lakes; *utpala*—of lotus flowers; *mālinīḥ*—containing rows; *prāptam*—inhabited; *kimpuruṣaiḥ*—by the Kimpuruṣas; *dṛṣṭvā*—after seeing; *te*—those demigods; *ārāt*—not far away; *dadṛśuḥ*—saw; *vaṭam*—a banyan tree.

TRANSLATION

They also saw that the bathing ghāṭas and their staircases were made of vaidūrya-maṇi. The water was full of lotus flowers. Passing by such lakes, the demigods reached a place where there was a great banyan tree.

TEXT 32

स योजनशतोत्सेधः पादोनविटपायतः ।
पर्यक्कृताचलच्छायो निर्नीडस्तापवर्जितः ॥३२॥

sa yojana-śatotsedhaḥ
pādona-viṭapāyataḥ
paryak-kṛtācala-cchāyo
nirnīḍas tāpa-varjitaḥ

saḥ—that banyan tree; *yojana-śata*—one hundred *yojanas* (eight hundred miles); *utsedhaḥ*—height; *pāda-ūna*—less by a quarter (six hundred miles); *viṭapa*—by the branches; *āyataḥ*—spread out; *paryak*—all around; *kṛta*—made; *acala*—unshaken; *chāyaḥ*—the shadow; *nirnīḍaḥ*—without bird nests; *tāpa-varjitaḥ*—without heat.

TRANSLATION

That banyan tree was eight hundred miles high, and its branches spread over six hundred miles around. The tree cast a fine shade which permanently cooled the temperature, yet there was no noise of birds.

PURPORT

Generally, in every tree there are bird nests, and the birds congregate in the evening and create noise. But it appears that this banyan tree was devoid of nests, and therefore it was calm, quiet and peaceful. There were no disturbances from noise or heat, and therefore this place was just suitable for meditation.

TEXT 33

तस्मिन्महायोगमये मुमुक्षुशरणे सुराः ।
ददृशुः शिवमासीनं त्यक्तामर्षमिवान्तकम् ॥३३॥

tasmin mahā-yogamaye
mumukṣu-śaraṇe surāḥ
dadṛśuḥ śivam āsīnaṁ
tyaktāmarṣam ivāntakam

tasmin—under that tree; *mahā-yoga-maye*—having many sages engaged in meditation on the Supreme; *mumukṣu*—of those who desire liberation; *śaraṇe*—the shelter; *surāḥ*—the demigods; *dadṛśuḥ*—saw; *śivam*—Lord Śiva; *āsīnam*—seated; *tyakta-amarṣam*—having given up anger; *iva*—as; *antakam*—eternal time.

TRANSLATION

The demigods saw Lord Śiva sitting under that tree, which was competent to give perfection to mystic yogīs and deliver all people. As grave as time eternal, he appeared to have given up all anger.

PURPORT

In this verse the word *mahā-yogamaye* is very significant. *Yoga* means meditation on the Supreme Personality of Godhead, and *mahā-yoga* means those who engage in the devotional service of Viṣṇu. Meditation means remembering, *smaraṇam.* There are nine different kinds of devotional service, of which *smaraṇam* is one process; the *yogī* remembers the form of Viṣṇu within his heart. Thus there were many devotees engaged in meditation on Lord Viṣṇu under the big banyan tree.

The Sanskrit word *mahā* is derived from the affix *mahat.* This affix is used when there is a great number or quantity, so *mahā-yoga* indicates that there were many great *yogīs* and devotees meditating on the form of Lord Viṣṇu. Generally such meditators are desirous of liberation from material bondage, and they are promoted to the spiritual world, to one of the Vaikuṇṭhas. Liberation means freedom from material bondage or nescience. In the material world we are suffering life after life because of our bodily identification, and liberation is freedom from that miserable condition of life.

TEXT 34

सनन्दनाद्यैर्महासिद्धैः शान्तैः संशान्तविग्रहम् ।
उपास्यमानं सख्या च भर्त्रा गुह्यकरक्षसाम् ॥३४॥

sanandanādyair mahā-siddhaiḥ
śāntaiḥ saṁśānta-vigraham
upāsyamānaṁ sakhyā ca
bhartrā guhyaka-rakṣasām

sanandana-ādyaiḥ—the four Kumāras, headed by Sanandana; *mahā-siddhaiḥ*—liberated souls; *śāntaiḥ*—saintly; *saṁśānta-vigraham*—the grave and saintly Lord Śiva; *upāsyamānam*—was being praised; *sakhyā*—by Kuvera; *ca*—and; *bhartrā*—by the master; *guhyaka-rakṣasām*—of the Guhyakas and the Rākṣasas.

TRANSLATION

Lord Śiva sat there, surrounded by saintly persons like Kuvera, the master of the Guhyakas, and the four Kumāras, who were already liberated souls. Lord Śiva was grave and saintly.

PURPORT

The personalities sitting with Lord Śiva are significant because the four Kumāras were liberated from birth. It may be remembered that after their birth these Kumāras were requested by their father to get married and beget children in order to increase the population of the newly created universe. But they refused, and at that time Lord Brahmā was angry. In that angry mood, Rudra, or Lord Śiva, was born. Thus they were intimately related. Kuvera, the treasurer of the demigods, is fabulously rich. Thus Lord Śiva's association with the Kumāras and Kuvera indicates that he has all transcendental and material opulences. Actually, he is the qualitative incarnation of the Supreme Lord; therefore his position is very exalted.

TEXT 35

विद्यातपोयोगपथमास्थितं तमधीश्वरम् ।
चरन्तं विश्वसुहृदं वात्सल्याल्लोकमङ्गलम् ॥३५॥

vidyā-tapo-yoga-patham
āsthitaṁ tam adhīśvaram
carantaṁ viśva-suhṛdaṁ
vātsalyāl loka-maṅgalam

vidyā—knowledge; *tapaḥ*—austerity; *yoga-patham*—the path of devotional service; *āsthitam*—situated; *tam*—him (Lord Śiva); *adhīśvaram*—the master of the senses; *carantam*—performing (austerity, etc.); *viśva-suhṛdam*—the friend of the whole world; *vātsalyāt*—out of full affection; *loka-maṅgalam*—auspicious for everyone.

TRANSLATION

The demigods saw Lord Śiva situated in his perfection as the master of the senses, knowledge, fruitive activities and the path of achieving perfection. He was the friend of the entire world, and by virtue of his full affection for everyone, he was very auspicious.

PURPORT

Lord Śiva is full of wisdom and *tapasya*, austerity. One who knows the modes of work is understood to be situated on the path of devotional service to the Supreme Personality of Godhead. One cannot serve the Supreme Personality of Godhead unless one has achieved full perfectional knowledge in the ways and means of performing devotional service.

Lord Śiva is described here as *adhīśvara. Īśvara* means "controller," and *adhīśvara* means particularly "controller of the senses." Generally our materially contaminated senses are apt to engage in sense gratificatory activities, but when a person is elevated by wisdom and austerity, the senses then become purified, and they become engaged in the service of the Supreme Personality of Godhead. Lord Śiva is the emblem of such perfection, and therefore in the scriptures it is said, *vaiṣṇavānāṁ yathā śambhuḥ:* Lord Śiva is a Vaiṣṇava. Lord Śiva, by his actions within this material world, teaches all conditioned souls how to engage in devotional service twenty-four hours a day. Therefore he is described here as *loka-maṅgala,* good fortune personified for all conditioned souls.

TEXT 36

लिङ्गं च तापसाभीष्टं भस्मदण्डजटाजिनम् ।
अङ्गेन संध्याभ्ररुचा चन्द्रलेखां च बिभ्रतम् ॥३६॥

liṅgaṁ ca tāpasābhīṣṭaṁ
bhasma-daṇḍa-jaṭājinam
aṅgena sandhyābhra-rucā
candra-lekhāṁ ca bibhratam

liṅgam—symptom; *ca*—and; *tāpasa-abhīṣṭam*—desired by Śaivite ascetics; *bhasma*—ashes; *daṇḍa*—staff; *jaṭā*—matted hair; *ajinam*—antelope skin; *aṅgena*—with his body; *sandhyā-ābhra*—reddish; *rucā*—colored; *candra-lekhām*—the crest of a half-moon; *ca*—and; *bibhratam*—bearing.

TRANSLATION

He was seated on a deerskin and was practicing all forms of austerity. Because his body was smeared with ashes, he looked like an evening cloud. On his hair was the sign of a half-moon, a symbolic representation.

PURPORT

Lord Śiva's symptoms of austerity are not exactly those of a Vaiṣṇava. Lord Śiva is certainly the number one Vaiṣṇava, but he exhibits a feature for a particular class of men who cannot follow the Vaiṣṇava principles. The Śaivites, the devotees of Lord Śiva, generally dress like Lord Śiva, and sometimes they indulge in smoking and taking intoxicants. Such practices are never accepted by the followers of Vaiṣṇava rituals.

TEXT 37

उपविष्टं दर्भमय्यां बृस्यां ब्रह्म सनातनम् ।
नारदाय प्रवोचन्तं पृच्छते शृण्वतां सताम् ॥३७॥

upaviṣṭaṁ darbhamayyāṁ
bṛsyāṁ brahma sanātanam
nāradāya pravocantaṁ
pṛcchate śṛṇvatāṁ satām

upaviṣṭam—seated; *darbha-mayyām*—made of *darbha*, straw; *bṛsyām*—on a mattress; *brahma*—the Absolute Truth; *sanātanam*—the eternal; *nāradāya*—unto Nārada; *pravocantam*—speaking; *pṛcchate*—asking; *śṛṇvatām*—listening; *satām*—of the great sages.

TRANSLATION

He was seated on a straw mattress and speaking to all present, including the great sage Nārada, to whom he specifically spoke about the Absolute Truth.

PURPORT

The lord was sitting on a mattress of straw because such a sitting place is accepted by persons who are practicing austerities to gain understanding of the Absolute Truth. In this verse it is specifically mentioned that he was speaking to the great sage Nārada, a celebrated devotee. Nārada was asking Lord Śiva about devotional service, and Śiva, being the topmost Vaiṣṇava, was instructing him. In other words, Lord Śiva and Nārada were discussing the knowledge of the *Veda*, but it is to be understood that the subject matter was devotional service. Another point in this connection is that Lord Śiva is the supreme instructor and the great sage Nārada is the supreme audience. Therefore, the supreme subject matter of Vedic knowledge is *bhakti*, or devotional service.

TEXT 38

कृत्वोरौ दक्षिणे सव्यं पादपद्मं च जानुनि ।
बाहुं प्रकोष्ठेऽक्षमालामासीनं तर्कमुद्रया ॥३८॥

kṛtvorau dakṣiṇe savyaṁ
pāda-padmaṁ ca jānuni
bāhuṁ prakoṣṭhe 'kṣa-mālām
āsīnaṁ tarka-mudrayā

kṛtvā—having placed; *ūrau*—thigh; *dakṣiṇe*—at the right; *savyam*—the left; *pāda-padmam*—lotus feet; *ca*—and; *jānuni*—on his knee; *bāhum*—hand; *prakoṣṭhe*—in the end of the right hand; *akṣa-mālām*—*rudrākṣa* beads; *āsīnam*—sitting; *tarka-mudrayā*—with the *mudrā* of argument.

TRANSLATION

His left leg was placed on his right thigh, and his left hand was placed on his left thigh. In his right hand he held rudrākṣa beads. This sitting posture is called vīrāsana. He sat in the vīrāsana posture, and his finger was in the mode of argument.

PURPORT

The sitting posture described herein is called *vīrāsana* according to the system of *aṣṭāṅga-yoga* performances. In the performance of *yoga* there are eight divisions, such as *yama* and *niyama*—controlling, following the rules and regulations, then practicing the sitting postures, etc. Besides *vīrāsana* there are other sitting postures, such as *padmāsana* and *siddhāsana*. Practice of these *āsanas* without elevating oneself to the position of realizing the Supersoul, Viṣṇu, is not the perfectional stage of *yoga*. Lord Śiva is called *yogīśvara*, the master of all *yogīs*, and Kṛṣṇa is also called *yogeśvara*. *Yogīśvara* indicates that no one can surpass the *yoga* practice of Lord Śiva, and *yogeśvara* indicates that no one can surpass the yogic perfection of Kṛṣṇa. Another significant word is *tarka-mudrā*. This indicates that the fingers are opened and the second finger is raised, along with the arm, to impress the audience with some subject matter. This is actually a symbolic representation.

TEXT 39

तं ब्रह्मनिर्वाणसमाधिमाश्रितं
व्युपाश्रितं गिरिशं योगकक्षाम् ।
सलोकपाला मुनयो मनूना-
माद्यं मनुं प्राञ्जलयः प्रणेमुः ॥३९॥

taṁ brahma-nirvāṇa-samādhim āśritaṁ
vyupāśritaṁ giriśaṁ yoga-kakṣām
sa-loka-pālā munayo manūnām
ādyaṁ manuṁ prāñjalayaḥ praṇemuḥ

tam—him (Lord Śiva); *brahma-nirvāṇa*—in *brahmānanda; samādhim*—in trance; *āśritam*—absorbed; *vyupāśritam*—leaning on; *giriśam*—Lord Śiva; *yoga-kakṣām*—having his left knee firmly fixed with a knotted cloth; *sa-loka-pālāḥ*—along with the demigods (headed by Indra); *munayaḥ*—the sages; *manūnām*—of all thinkers; *ādyam*—the chief; *manum*—thinker; *prāñjalayaḥ*—with folded palms; *praṇemuḥ*—offered respectful obeisances.

TRANSLATION

All the sages and demigods, headed by Indra, offered their respectful obeisances unto Lord Śiva with folded hands. Lord Śiva was dressed in saffron garments and absorbed in trance, thus appearing to be the foremost of all sages.

PURPORT

In this verse the word *brahmānanda* is significant. This *brahmānanda*, or *brahma-nirvāṇa*, is explained by Prahlāda Mahārāja. When one is completely absorbed in the *adhokṣaja*, the Supreme Personality of Godhead, who is beyond the sense perception of materialistic persons, one is situated in *brahmānanda.*

It is impossible to conceive of the existence, name, form, quality and pastimes of the Supreme Personality of Godhead because He is transcendentally situated beyond the conception of materialistic persons. Because materialists cannot imagine or conceive of the Supreme Personality of

Godhead, they may think that God is dead, but factually He is always existing in His *sac-cid-ānanda-vigraha,* His eternal form. Constant meditation concentrated on the form of the Lord is called *samādhi,* ecstasy or trance. *Samādhi* means particularly concentrated attention, so one who has achieved the qualification of always meditating on the Personality of Godhead is to be understood to be always in trance and enjoying *brahma-nirvāṇa,* or *brahmānanda.* Lord Śiva exhibited those symptoms, and therefore it is stated that he was absorbed in *brahmānanda.*

Another significant word is *yoga-kakṣām. Yoga-kakṣā* is the sitting posture in which the left thigh is fixed under one's tightly knotted saffron-colored garment. Also the words *manūnām ādyam* are significant here because they mean a philosopher, or one who is thoughtful and can think very nicely. Such a man is called *manu.* Lord Śiva is described in this verse as the chief of all thinkers. Lord Śiva, of course, does not engage in useless mental speculation, but as stated in the previous verse, he is always thoughtful regarding how to deliver the demons from their fallen condition of life. It is said that during the advent of Lord Caitanya, Sadāśiva appeared as Advaita Prabhu, and Advaita Prabhu's chief concern was to elevate the fallen conditioned souls to the platform of devotional service to Lord Kṛṣṇa. Since people were engaged in useless occupations which would continue their material existence, Lord Śiva, in the form of Lord Advaita, appealed to the Supreme Lord to appear as Lord Caitanya to deliver these illusioned souls. Actually Lord Caitanya appeared on the request of Lord Advaita. Similarly, Lord Śiva has a *sampradāya,* the Rudra-sampradāya. He is always thinking about the deliverance of the fallen souls, as exhibited by Lord Advaita Prabhu.

TEXT 40

स तूपलभ्यागतमात्मयोनिं
सुरासुरेशैरभिवन्दिताङ्घ्रिः ।
उत्थाय चक्रे शिरसाभिवन्दन-
मर्हत्तमः कस्य यथैव विष्णुः ॥४०॥

sa tūpalabhyāgatam ātma-yoniṁ
surāsureśair abhivanditāṅghriḥ

utthāya cakre śirasābhivandanam
arhattamaḥ kasya yathaiva viṣṇuḥ

saḥ—Lord Śiva; *tu*—but; *upalabhya*—seeing; *āgatam*—had arrived; *ātma-yonim*—Lord Brahmā; *sura-asura-īśaiḥ*—by the best of the demigods and demons; *abhivandita-aṅghriḥ*—whose feet are worshiped; *utthāya*—standing up; *cakre*—made; *śirasā*—with his head; *abhivandanam*—respectful; *arhattamaḥ*—Vāmanadeva; *kasya*—of Kaśyapa; *yathā eva*—just as; *viṣṇuḥ*—Viṣṇu.

TRANSLATION

Lord Śiva's lotus feet were worshiped by both the demigods and demons, but still, in spite of his exalted position, as soon as he saw that Lord Brahmā was there among all the other demigods, he immediately stood up and offered him respect by bowing down and touching his lotus feet, just as Vāmanadeva offered His respectful obeisances to Kaśyapa Muni.

PURPORT

Kaśyapa Muni was in the category of the living entities, but he had a transcendental son, Vāmanadeva, who was an incarnation of Viṣṇu. Thus although Lord Viṣṇu is the Supreme Personality of Godhead, He offered His respects to Kaśyapa Muni. Similarly, when Lord Kṛṣṇa was a child He used to offer His respectful obeisances to His mother and father, Nanda and Yaśodā. Also, at the Battle of Kurukṣetra, Lord Kṛṣṇa touched the feet of Mahārāja Yudhiṣṭhira because the King was His elder. It appears, then, that the Personality of Godhead, Lord Śiva and other devotees, in spite of their being situated in exalted positions, instructed by practical example how to offer obeisances to their superiors. Lord Śiva offered his respectful obeisances to Brahmā because Brahmā was his father, just as Kaśyapa Muni was the father of Vāmana.

TEXT 41

तथापरे सिद्धगणा महर्षिभि-
र्ये वै समन्तादनु नीललोहितम् ।

नमस्कृतः प्राह शशाङ्कशेखरं
कृतप्रणामं प्रहसन्निवात्मभूः ॥४१॥

tathāpare siddha-gaṇā maharṣibhir
ye vai samantād anu nīlalohitam
namaskṛtaḥ prāha śaśāṅka-śekharaṁ
kṛta-praṇāmaṁ prahasann ivātmabhūḥ

tathā—so; *apare*—the others; *siddha-gaṇāḥ*—the Siddhas; *mahā-ṛṣibhiḥ*—along with the great sages; *ye*—who; *vai*—indeed; *samantāt*—from all sides; *anu*—after; *nīlalohitam*—Lord Śiva; *namaskṛtaḥ*—making obeisances; *prāha*—said; *śaśāṅka-śekharam*—to Lord Śiva; *kṛta-praṇāmam*—having made obeisances; *prahasan*—smiling; *iva*—as; *ātmabhūḥ*—Lord Brahmā.

TRANSLATION

All the sages who were sitting with Lord Śiva, such as Nārada and others, also offered their respectful obeisances to Lord Brahmā. After being so worshiped, Lord Brahmā, smiling, began to speak to Lord Śiva.

PURPORT

Lord Brahmā was smiling because he knew that Lord Śiva is not only easily satisfied but easily irritated as well. He was afraid that Lord Śiva might be in an angry mood because he had lost his wife and had been insulted by Dakṣa. In order to conceal this fear, he smiled and addressed Lord Śiva as follows.

TEXT 42

ब्रह्मोवाच
जाने त्वामीशं विश्वस्य जगतो योनिबीजयोः ।
शक्तेः शिवस्य च परं यत्तद्ब्रह्म निरन्तरम् ॥४२॥

brahmovāca
jāne tvām īśaṁ viśvasya
jagato yoni-bījayoḥ
śakteḥ śivasya ca paraṁ
yat tad brahma nirantaram

brahmā uvāca—Lord Brahmā said; *jāne*—I know; *tvām*—you (Lord Śiva); *īśam*—the controller; *viśvasya*—of the entire material manifestation; *jagataḥ*—of the cosmic manifestation; *yoni-bījayoḥ*—of both the mother and father; *śakteḥ*—of potency; *śivasya*—of Śiva; *ca*—and; *param*—the Supreme; *yat*—which; *tat*—that; *brahma*—without change; *nirantaram*—with no material qualities.

TRANSLATION

Lord Brahmā said: My dear Lord Śiva, I know that you are the controller of the entire material manifestation, the combination father and mother of the cosmic manifestation, and the Supreme Brahman beyond the cosmic manifestation as well. I know you in that way.

PURPORT

Although Lord Brahmā had received very respectful obeisances from Lord Śiva, he knew that Lord Śiva was in a more exalted position than himself. Lord Śiva's position is described in *Brahma-saṁhitā:* there is no difference between Lord Viṣṇu and Lord Śiva in their original positions, but still Lord Śiva is different from Lord Viṣṇu. The example is given that the milk in yogurt is not different from the original milk from which it was made.

TEXT 43

त्वमेव भगवन्नेतच्छिवशक्त्योः स्वरूपयोः ।
विश्वं सृजसि पास्यत्सि क्रीडन्नूर्णपटो यथा ॥४३॥

tvam eva bhagavann etac
chiva-śaktyoḥ svarūpayoḥ
viśvaṁ sṛjasi pāsy atsi
krīḍann ūrṇā-paṭo yathā

tvam—you; *eva*—certainly; *bhagavan*—O my lord; *etat*—this; *śiva-śaktyoḥ*—being situated in your auspicious energy; *svarūpayoḥ*—by your personal expansion; *viśvam*—this universe; *sṛjasi*—create; *pāsi*—maintain; *atsi*—annihilate; *krīḍan*—working; *ūrṇa-paṭaḥ*—spider's web; *yathā*—just like.

TRANSLATION

My dear lord, you create this cosmic manifestation, maintain it, and annihilate it by expansion of your personality, exactly as a spider creates, maintains and winds up its web.

PURPORT

In this verse the word *śiva-śakti* is significant. *Śiva* means "auspicious," and *śakti* means "energy." There are many types of energies of the Supreme Lord, and all of them are auspicious. Brahmā, Viṣṇu and Maheśvara are called *guṇa-avatāras*, or incarnations of material qualities. In the material world we compare these different incarnations from different angles of vision, but since all of them are expansions of the supreme auspicious, all of them are auspicious, although sometimes we consider one quality of nature to be higher or lower than another. The mode of ignorance, or *tamo-guṇa*, is considered very much lower than the others, but in the higher sense it is also auspicious. The example may be given herein that the government has both an educational department and criminal department. An outsider may consider the criminal department inauspicious, but from the government's point of view it is as important as the education department, and therefore the government finances both departments equally, without discrimination.

TEXT 44

त्वमेव धर्मार्थदुघाभिपत्तये
दक्षेण सूत्रेण ससर्जिथाध्वरम् ।
त्वयैव लोकेऽवसिताश्च सेतवो
यान्ब्राह्मणाः श्रद्दधते धृतव्रताः ॥४४॥

tvam eva dharmārtha-dughābhipattaye
dakṣeṇa sūtreṇa sasarjithādhvaram
tvayaiva loke 'vasitāś ca setavo
yān brāhmaṇāḥ śraddadhate dhṛta-vratāḥ

tvam—Your Lordship; *eva*—certainly; *dharma-artha-dugha*—benefit derived from religion and economic development; *abhipattaye*—for their protection; *dakṣeṇa*—by Dakṣa; *sūtreṇa*—making him the cause; *sasarjitha*—created; *adhvaram*—sacrifices; *tvayā*—by you; *eva*—certainly; *loke*—in this world; *avasitāḥ*—regulated; *ca*—and; *setavaḥ*—respect for the *varṇāśrama* institution; *yān*—which; *brāhmaṇāḥ*—the *brāhmaṇas; śraddadhate*—respect very much; *dhṛta-vratāḥ*—taking it as a vow.

TRANSLATION

My dear lord, Your Lordship has introduced the system of sacrifices through the agency of Dakṣa, and thus one may derive the benefits of religious activities and economic development. Under your regulative principles, the institution of the four varṇās and āśramas is respected. The brāhmaṇas therefore vow to follow this system strictly.

PURPORT

The Vedic system of *varṇa* and *āśrama* is never to be neglected, for these divisions are created by the Supreme Lord Himself for the upkeep of social and religious order in human society. The *brāhmaṇas*, as the intelligent class of men in society, must vow to steadily respect this regulative principle. The tendency in this age of Kali to make a classless society and not observe the principles of *varṇa* and *āśrama* is a manifestation of an impossible dream. Destruction of the social and spiritual orders will not bring fulfillment of the idea of a classless society. One should strictly observe the principles of *varṇa* and *āśrama* for the satisfaction of the creator, for it is stated in the *Bhagavad-gītā* by Lord Kṛṣṇa that the four orders of the social system—*brāhmaṇas, kṣatriyas, vaiśyas* and *śūdras*—are His creation. They should act according to the regulative principles of this institution and satisfy the Lord, just as different parts of the body all engage in the service of the whole. The whole is the Supreme Personality of Godhead in His *virāṭ-rūpa*, or universal form. The *brāhmaṇas, kṣatriyas, vaiśyas* and *śūdras* are respectively the mouth, arms, abdomen and legs of the universal form of the Lord. As long as they are engaged in the service of the complete whole, their position is secure, otherwise they fall down from their respective positions and become degraded.

TEXT 45

त्वं कर्मणां मङ्गल मङ्गलानां
कर्तुः स्वलोकं तनुषे स्वः परं वा ।
अमङ्गलानां च तमिस्रमुल्बणं
विपर्ययः केन तदेव कस्यचित् ॥४५॥

tvaṁ karmaṇāṁ maṅgala maṅgalānāṁ
kartuḥ sva-lokaṁ tanuṣe svaḥ paraṁ vā
amaṅgalānāṁ ca tamisram ulbaṇaṁ
viparyayaḥ kena tad eva kasyacit

tvam—Your Lordship; *karmaṇām*—of the prescribed duties; *maṅgala*—O most auspicious; *maṅgalānām*—of the auspicious; *kartuḥ*—of the performer; *sva-lokam*—respective higher planetary systems; *tanuṣe*—expand; *svaḥ*—heavenly planets; *param*—transcendental world; *vā*—or; *amaṅgalānām*—of the inauspicious; *ca*—and; *tamisram*—the name of a particular hell; *ulbaṇam*—ghastly; *viparyayaḥ*—the opposite; *kena*—why; *tat eva*—certainly that; *kasyacit*—for someone.

TRANSLATION

O most auspicious lord, you have ordained the heavenly planets, the spiritual Vaikuṇṭha planets and the impersonal Brahman sphere as the respective destinations of the performers of auspicious activities. Similarly, for others, who are miscreants, you have destined different kinds of hells which are horrible and ghastly. Yet sometimes it is found that their destinations are just the opposite. It is very difficult to ascertain the cause of this.

PURPORT

The Supreme Personality of Godhead is called the supreme will. It is by the supreme will that everything is happening. It is said, therefore, that not a blade of grass moves without the supreme will. Generally it is prescribed that performers of pious activities are promoted to the higher planetary systems, devotees are promoted to the Vaikuṇṭhas, or spiritual worlds, and impersonal speculators are promoted to the impersonal Brahman effulgence; but it sometimes so happens that a miscreant like Ajāmila is immediately promoted to the Vaikuṇṭhaloka simply by chanting the name of Nārāyaṇa. Although when Ajāmila uttered this vibration he intended to call his son Nārāyaṇa, Lord Nārāyaṇa took it seriously and immediately gave him promotion to Vaikuṇṭhaloka, despite his background, which was full of sinful activities. Similarly King Dakṣa was always engaged in the pious activities of performing sacrifices, yet simply because of creating a little misunderstanding with Lord Śiva, he was severely taken to task. The conclusion is, therefore, that the supreme will is the ultimate judgment; no one can argue upon this. A pure devotee therefore submits in all circumstances to the supreme will of the Lord, accepting it as all-auspicious.

tat te 'nukampāṁ susamīkṣamāṇo
bhuñjāna evātma-kṛtaṁ vipākam
hṛd-vāg-vapurbhir vidadhan namas te
jīveta yo mukti-pade sa dāya-bhāk
(*Bhāg.* 10.14.8)

The purport of this verse is that when a devotee is in a calamitous condition he takes it as a benediction of the Supreme Lord and takes responsibility himself for his past misdeeds. In such a condition, he offers still more devotional service and is not disturbed. One who lives in such a disposition of mind, engaged in devotional service, is the most eligible candidate for promotion to the spiritual world. In other words, such a devotee's claim for promotion to the spiritual world is assured in all circumstances.

TEXT 46

न वै सतां त्वच्चरणार्पितात्मनां
भूतेषु सर्वेष्वभिपश्यतां तव ।
भूतानि चात्मन्यपृथग्दिदृक्षतां
प्रायेण रोषोऽभिभवेद्यथा पशुम् ॥४६॥

na vai satāṁ tvac-caraṇārpitātmanāṁ
bhūteṣu sarveṣv abhipaśyatāṁ tava

bhūtāni cātmany apṛthag-didṛkṣatāṁ
prāyeṇa roṣo 'bhibhaved yathā paśum

na—not; *vai*—but; *satām*—of the devotees; *tvat-caraṇa-arpita-ātmanām*—of those who are completely surrendered at your lotus feet; *bhūteṣu*—among living entities; *sarveṣu*—all varieties; *abhipaśyatām*—perfectly seeing; *tava*—your; *bhūtāni*—living entities; *ca*—and; *ātmani*—in the Supreme; *apṛthak*—nondifferent; *didṛkṣatām*—those who see like that; *prāyeṇa*—almost always; *roṣaḥ*—anger; *abhibhavet*—takes place; *yathā*—exactly like; *paśum*—the animals.

TRANSLATION

My dear Lord, devotees who have fully dedicated their lives unto your lotus feet certainly observe your presence as Paramātmā in each and every being, and as such they do not differentiate between one living being and another. Such persons treat all living entities equally. They never become overwhelmed by anger like animals, who can see nothing without differentiation.

PURPORT

When the Supreme Personality of Godhead becomes angry or kills a demon, materially this may appear unfavorable, but spiritually it is a blissful blessing upon him. Therefore pure devotees do not make any distinction between the Lord's anger and His blessings. They see both with reference to the Lord's behavior with others and themselves. A devotee does not find fault with the behavior of the Lord in any circumstances.

TEXT 47

पृथग्धियः कर्मदृशो दुराशयाः
परोदयेनार्पितहृद्रुजोऽनिशम् ।
परान् दुरुक्तैर्वितुदन्त्यरुन्तुदा-
स्तान्मावधीद्दैववधान् भवद्विधः ॥४७॥

pṛthag-dhiyaḥ karma-dṛśo durāśayāḥ
parodayenārpita-hṛd-rujo 'niśam

parān duruktair vitudanty aruntudās
tān māvadhīd daiva-vadhān bhavad-vidhaḥ

pṛthak—differently; *dhiyaḥ*—those who are thinking; *karma*—fruitive activities; *dṛśaḥ*—observer; *durāśayāḥ*—mean minded; *para-udayena*—by others' flourishing condition; *arpita*—given up; *hṛt*—heart; *rujaḥ*—anger; *aniśam*—always; *parān*—others; *duruktaiḥ*—harsh words; *vitudanti*—gives pain; *aruntudāḥ*—by piercing words; *tān*—unto them; *mā*—not; *avadhīt*—kill; *daiva*—by providence; *vadhān*—already killed; *bhavat*—you; *vidhaḥ*—like.

TRANSLATION

Persons who observe everything with differentiation, who are simply attached to fruitive activities, who are mean minded, who are always pained to see the flourishing condition of others and who thus give distress to them by uttering harsh and piercing words have already been killed by providence. Thus there is no need for them to be killed again by an exalted personality like you.

PURPORT

Persons who are materialistic and always engaged in fruitive activities for material profit cannot endure seeing the flourishing life of others. Except for a few persons in Kṛṣṇa consciousness, the entire world is full of such envious persons, who are perpetually full of anxieties because they are attached to the material body and are without self-realization. Since their hearts are always filled with anxiety, it is understood that they have already been killed by providence. Thus Lord Śiva, as a self-realized Vaiṣṇava, was advised not to kill Dakṣa. A Vaiṣṇava is described as *para-duḥkha-duḥkhī* because although he is never distressed in any condition of life, he is distressed to see others in a distressed condition. Vaiṣṇavas, therefore, should not try to kill by any action of the body or mind, but should try to revive the Kṛṣṇa consciousness of others out of compassion for them. The Kṛṣṇa consciousness movement has been started to deliver the envious persons of the world from the clutches of *māyā*, and even though devotees are sometimes put into trouble, they push on the Kṛṣṇa consciousness movement in all tolerance. Lord Caitanya advises:

tṛṇād api sunīcena
taror api sahiṣṇunā
amāninā mānadena
kīrtanīyaḥ sadā hariḥ

"One can chant the holy name of the Lord in a humble state of mind, thinking himself lower than the straw in the street. One should be more tolerant than the tree, devoid of all sense of false prestige and ready to offer all respects to others. In such a state of mind one can chant the holy name of the Lord constantly." (*Śikṣāṣṭaka* 3)

A Vaiṣṇava should follow the examples of such Vaiṣṇavas as Haridāsa Ṭhākura, Nityānanda Prabhu and also Lord Jesus Christ. There is no need to kill anyone who has already been killed. But it should be noted herewith that a Vaiṣṇava should not tolerate the blaspheming of Viṣṇu or Vaiṣṇavas, although he should tolerate personal insults to himself.

TEXT 48

यस्मिन् यदा पुष्करनाभमायया
दुरन्तया स्पृष्टधियः पृथग्दृशः ।
कुर्वन्ति तत्र ह्यनुकम्पया कृपां
न साधवो दैवबलात्कृते क्रमम् ॥४८॥

yasmin yadā puṣkara-nābha-māyayā
durantayā spṛṣṭa-dhiyaḥ pṛthag-dṛśaḥ
kurvanti tatra hy anukampayā kṛpāṁ
na sādhavo daiva-balāt kṛte kramam

yasmin—in some place; *yadā*—when; *puṣkara-nābha-māyayā*—by the illusory energy of Puṣkaranābha, the Supreme Personality of Godhead; *durantayā*—insurmountable; *spṛṣṭa-dhiyaḥ*—bewildered; *pṛthak-dṛśaḥ*—the same persons who see differently; *kurvanti*—do; *tatra*—there; *hi*—certainly; *anukampayā*—out of compassion; *kṛpām*—mercy; *na*—never; *sādhavaḥ*—saintly persons; *daiva-balāt*—by providence; *kṛte*—being done; *kramam*—prowess.

TRANSLATION

My dear lord, if in some places materialists, who are already bewildered by the insurmountable illusory energy of the Supreme Godhead, sometimes commit offenses, a saintly person, with compassion, does not take this seriously. Knowing that they commit offenses because they are overpowered by the illusory energy, he does not show his prowess to counteract them.

PURPORT

It is said that the beauty of a *tapasvī*, or saintly person, is forgiveness. There are many instances in the spiritual history of the world in which many saintly persons, although unnecessarily harassed, did not take action, although they could have done so. Parīkṣit Mahārāja, for example, was unnecessarily cursed by a *brāhmaṇa* boy, and this was very much regretted by the boy's father, but Parīkṣit Mahārāja accepted the curse and agreed to die within a week as the *brāhmaṇa* boy desired. Parīkṣit Mahārāja was the emperor and was full in power both spiritually and materially, but out of compassion and out of respect for the *brāhmaṇa* community, he did not counteract the action of the *brāhmaṇa* boy but agreed to die within seven days. Because it was desired by Kṛṣṇa that Parīkṣit Mahārāja agree to the punishment so that the instruction of *Śrīmad-Bhāgavatam* would thus be revealed to the world, Parīkṣit Mahārāja was advised not to take action. A Vaiṣṇava is personally tolerant for the benefit of others. When he does not show his prowess, this does not mean that he is lacking in strength; rather, it indicates that he is tolerant for the welfare of the entire human society.

TEXT 49

भवांस्तु पुंसः परमस्य मायया
दुरन्तयास्पृष्टमतिः समस्तदृक् ।
तया हतात्मस्वनुकर्मचेतः-
स्वनुग्रहं कर्तुमिहार्हसि प्रभो ॥४९॥

bhavāṁs tu puṁsaḥ paramasya māyayā
durantayāspṛṣṭa-matiḥ samasta-dṛk

tayā hatātmasv anukarma-cetaḥsv
anugrahaṁ kartum ihārhasi prabho

bhavān—Your Lordship; *tu*—but; *puṁsaḥ*—of the person; *paramasya*—the supreme; *māyayā*—by the material energy; *durantayā*—of great potency; *aspṛṣṭa*—unaffected; *matiḥ*—intelligence; *samasta-dṛk*—seer or knower of everything; *tayā*—by the same illusory energy; *hata-ātmasu*—bewildered at heart; *anukarma-cetaḥsu*—whose hearts are attracted by fruitive activities; *anugraham*—mercy; *kartum*—to do; *iha*—in this case; *arhasi*—desire; *prabho*—O lord.

TRANSLATION

My dear lord, you are never bewildered by the formidable influence of the illusory energy of the Supreme Personality of Godhead. Therefore you are omniscient and should be merciful and compassionate toward those who are bewildered by the same illusory energy and are very much attached to fruitive activities.

PURPORT

A Vaiṣṇava is never bewildered by the influence of the external energy because he is engaged in the transcendental loving service of the Lord. The Lord states in *Bhagavad-gītā* (7.14):

daivī hy eṣā guṇamayī
mama māyā duratyayā
mām eva ye prapadyante
māyām etāṁ taranti te

"My divine energy consisting of the three modes of material nature is difficult to overcome. But those who have surrendered unto Me can easily cross beyond it." A Vaiṣṇava should take care of those who are bewildered by this *māyā* instead of becoming angry with them, because without a Vaiṣṇava's mercy they have no way to get out of the clutches of *māyā.* Those who have been condemned by *māyā* are rescued by the mercy of devotees.

vāñchā-kalpatarubhyaś ca
kṛpā-sindhubhya eva ca
patitānāṁ pāvanebhyo
vaiṣṇavebhyo namo namaḥ

"I offer my respectful obeisances unto all the Vaiṣṇava devotees of the Lord. They are just like desire trees who can fulfill the desires of everyone, and they are full of compassion for the fallen conditioned souls." Those who are under the influence of the illusory energy are attracted to fruitive activities, but a Vaiṣṇava preacher attracts their hearts to the Supreme Personality of Godhead, Śrī Kṛṣṇa.

TEXT 50

कुर्वध्वरस्योद्धरणं हतस्य भोः
त्वयासमाप्तस्य मनो प्रजापतेः ।
न यत्र भागं तव भागिनो ददुः
कुयाजिनो येन मखो निनीयते ॥५०॥

kurv adhvarasyoddharaṇaṁ hatasya bhoḥ
tvayāsamāptasya mano prajāpateḥ
na yatra bhāgaṁ tava bhāgino daduḥ
kuyājino yena makho ninīyate

kuru—just execute; *adhvarasya*—of the sacrifice; *uddharaṇam*—complete regularly; *hatasya*—killed; *bhoḥ*—O; *tvayā*—by you; *asamāptasya*—of the unfinished sacrifice; *mano*—O Lord Śiva; *prajāpateḥ*—of Mahārāja Dakṣa; *na*—not; *yatra*—where; *bhāgam*—share; *tava*—your; *bhāginaḥ*—deserving to take the share; *daduḥ*—did not give; *ku-yājinaḥ*—bad priests; *yena*—by the bestower; *makhaḥ*—sacrifice; *ninīyate*—gets the result.

TRANSLATION

My dear Lord Śiva, you are a shareholder of a portion of the sacrifice, and you are the giver of the result. The bad priests did not deliver your share, and therefore you destroyed everything,

and the sacrifice remains unfinished. Now you can do the needful and take your rightful share.

TEXT 51

जीवताद्यजमानोऽयं प्रपद्येताक्षिणी भगः ।
भृगोः श्मश्रूणि रोहन्तु पूष्णो दन्ताश्च पूर्ववत् ॥५१॥

jīvatād yajamāno 'yaṁ
prapadyetākṣiṇī bhagaḥ
bhṛgoḥ śmaśrūṇi rohantu
pūṣṇo dantāś ca pūrvavat

jīvatāt—let him be alive; *yajamānaḥ*—the performer of the sacrifice (Dakṣa); *ayam*—this; *prapadyeta*—let him get back; *akṣiṇī*—by the eyes; *bhagaḥ*—Bhagadeva; *bhṛgoḥ*—of the sage Bhṛgu; *śmaśrūṇi*—mustache; *rohantu*—may grow again; *pūṣṇaḥ*—of Pūṣādeva; *dantāḥ*—the chain of teeth; *ca*—and; *pūrva-vat*—like before.

TRANSLATION

My dear lord, by your mercy the performer of the sacrifice (King Dakṣa) may get back his life, Bhaga may get back his eyes, Bhṛgu his mustache, and Pūṣā his teeth.

TEXT 52

देवानां भग्नगात्राणामृत्विजां चायुधाश्मभिः ।
भवतानुगृहीतानामाशु मन्योऽस्त्वनातुरम् ॥५२॥

devānāṁ bhagna-gātrāṇām
ṛtvijāṁ cāyudhāśmabhiḥ
bhavatānugṛhītānām
āśu manyo 'stv anāturam

devānām—of the demigods; *bhagna-gātrāṇām*—whose limbs are badly broken; *ṛtvijām*—of the priests; *ca*—and; *āyudha-aśmabhiḥ*—by weapons and by stones; *bhavatā*—by you; *anugṛhītānām*—being favored; *āśu*—at once; *manyo*—O Lord Śiva (in an angry mood); *astu*—let there be; *anāturam*—recovery from injuries.

TRANSLATION

O Lord Śiva, may the demigods and the priests whose limbs have been broken by your soldiers recover from the injuries by your grace.

TEXT 53

एष ते रुद्र भागोऽस्तु यदुच्छिष्टोऽध्वरस्य वै ।
यज्ञस्ते रुद्रभागेन कल्पतामद्य यज्ञहन् ॥५३॥

eṣa te rudra bhāgo 'stu
yad-ucchiṣṭo 'dhvarasya vai
yajñas te rudra bhāgena
kalpatām adya yajña-han

eṣaḥ—this; *te*—your; *rudra*—O Lord Śiva; *bhāgaḥ*—portion; *astu*—let it be; *yat*—whatever; *ucchiṣṭaḥ*—is the remainder; *adhvarasya*—of the sacrifice; *vai*—indeed; *yajñaḥ*—the sacrifice; *te*—your; *rudra*—O Rudra; *bhāgena*—by the portion; *kalpatām*—may be completed; *adya*—today; *yajña-han*—O destroyer of the sacrifice.

TRANSLATION

O destroyer of the sacrifice, please take your portion of the sacrifice and let the sacrifice be completed by your grace.

PURPORT

A sacrifice is a ceremony performed to please the Supreme Personality of Godhead. In the *Śrīmad-Bhāgavatam*, First Canto, Second Chapter, it is stated that everyone should try to understand whether the Supreme Personality of Godhead is satisfied by his activity. In other words, the aim of our activities should be to satisfy the Supreme Personality of Godhead. Just as in an office it is the duty of the worker to see that the proprietor or the master is satisfied, so everyone's duty is to see whether the Supreme Personality of Godhead is satisfied by one's activity. Activities to satisfy the Supreme Godhead are prescribed in the Vedic literature, and execution of such activities is called *yajña.* In other words, acting on behalf of the Supreme Lord is called *yajña.* One should know very well that any activity besides *yajña* is the cause of material bondage. That is explained in *Bhagavad-gītā* (3.9): *yajñārthāt karmaṇo 'nyatra loko 'yaṁ karma-bandhanaḥ. Karma-bandhanaḥ* means that if we do not work for the satisfaction of the Supreme Lord, Viṣṇu, then the reaction of our work will bind us. One should not work for his own sense gratification. Everyone should work for the satisfaction of God. That is called *yajña.*

After the *yajña* was performed by Dakṣa, all the demigods expected *prasāda,* the remnants of foodstuffs offered to Viṣṇu. Lord Śiva is one of the demigods, so naturally he also expected his share of the *prasāda* from the *yajña.* But Dakṣa, out of his envy of Lord Śiva, neither invited Śiva to participate in the *yajña* nor gave him his share after the offering. But after the destruction of the *yajña* arena by the followers of Lord Śiva, Lord Brahmā pacified him and assured him that he would get his share of *prasāda.* Thus he was requested to rectify whatever destruction was caused by his followers.

In *Bhagavad-gītā* (3.11) it is said that all the demigods are satisfied when one performs *yajña.* Because the demigods expect *prasāda* from *yajñas, yajña* must be performed. Those who engage in sense gratificatory, materialistic activities must perform *yajña,* otherwise they will be implicated. Thus Dakṣa, being the father of mankind, was performing *yajña,* and Lord Śiva expected his share. But since Śiva was not invited, there was trouble. By the mediation of Lord Brahmā, however, everything was settled satisfactorily.

The performance of *yajña* is a very difficult task because all the demigods must be invited to participate in the *yajña.* In this Kali-yuga it is not possible to perform such costly sacrifices, nor is it possible to invite the demigods to participate. Therefore in this age it is recommended, *yajñaiḥ saṅkīrtana-prāyair yajanti hi sumedhasaḥ* (*Bhāg.* 11.5.32). Those who are intelligent should know that in the Kali-yuga there is no possibility of performing the Vedic sacrifices. But unless one pleases the demigods, there will be no regulated seasonal activities or rainfall. Everything is controlled by the demigods. Under the circumstances, in this age, in order to keep the balance of social peace and prosperity, all intelligent men should execute the performance of *saṅkīrtana-yajña* by chanting the holy names Hare Kṛṣṇa, Hare Kṛṣṇa, Kṛṣṇa Kṛṣṇa, Hare Hare/ Hare Rāma, Hare Rāma, Rāma Rāma, Hare Hare. One should invite people, chant Hare Kṛṣṇa, and then distribute *prasāda*. This *yajña* will satisfy all the demigods, and thus there will be peace and prosperity in the world. Another difficulty in performing the Vedic rituals is that if one fails to satisfy even one demigod out of the many hundreds of thousands of demigods, just as Dakṣa failed to satisfy Lord Śiva, there will be disaster. But in this age the performance of sacrifice has been simplified. One can chant Hare Kṛṣṇa, and by pleasing Kṛṣṇa one can satisfy all the demigods automatically.

Thus end the Bhaktivedanta purports of the Fourth Canto, Sixth Chapter, of the Śrīmad-Bhāgavatam, *entitled "Brahmā Satisfies Lord Śiva."*

CHAPTER SEVEN

The Sacrifice Performed by Dakṣa

TEXT 1

मैत्रेय उवाच
इत्यजेनानुनीतेन भवेन परितुष्यता ।
अभ्यधायि महाबाहो प्रहस्य श्रूयतामिति ॥ १ ॥

maitreya uvāca
ity ajenānunītena
bhavena paritusyatā
abhyadhāyi mahā-bāho
prahasya śrūyatām iti

maitreyaḥ—Maitreya; *uvāca*—said; *iti*—thus; *ajena*—by Lord Brahmā; *anunītena*—pacified; *bhavena*—by Lord Śiva; *paritusyatā*—fully satisfied; *abhyadhāyi*—said; *mahā-bāho*—O Vidura; *prahasya*—smiling; *śrūyatām*—listen; *iti*—thus.

TRANSLATION

The sage Maitreya said: O mighty-armed Vidura, Lord Śiva, being thus pacified by the words of Lord Brahmā, spoke as follows in answer to Lord Brahmā's request.

TEXT 2

महादेव उवाच
नाघं प्रजेश बालानां वर्णये नानुचिन्तये ।
देवमायाभिभूतानां दण्डस्तत्र धृतो मया ॥ २ ॥

mahādeva uvāca
nāghaṁ prajeśa bālānāṁ
varṇaye nānucintaye
deva-māyābhibhūtānāṁ
daṇḍas tatra dhṛto mayā

mahādevaḥ—Lord Śiva; *uvāca*—said; *na*—not; *agham*—offense; *prajā-īśa*—O lord of created beings; *bālānām*—of the children; *varṇaye*—I regard; *na*—not; *anucintaye*—I consider; *deva-māyā*—the external energy of the Lord; *abhibhūtānām*—of those deluded by; *daṇḍaḥ*—rod; *tatra*—there; *dhṛtaḥ*—used; *mayā*—by me.

TRANSLATION

Lord Śiva said: My dear father, Brahmā, I do not mind the offenses created by the demigods. Because these demigods are childish and less intelligent, I do not take a serious view of their offenses, and I have punished them only in order to right them.

PURPORT

There are two types of punishment. One is that which a conqueror imposes on an enemy, and the other is like that a father imposes on his son. There is a gulf of difference between these two kinds of punishment. Lord Śiva is by nature a Vaiṣṇava, a great devotee, and his name in this connection is Āśutoṣa. He is always satisfied, and therefore he did not become angry as if he were an enemy. He is not inimical to any living entity; rather, he always wishes the welfare of all. Whenever he chastises a person, it is just like a father's punishment of his son. Lord Śiva is like a father because he never takes seriously any offense by any living entities, especially the demigods.

TEXT 3

प्रजापतेर्दग्धशीर्ष्णो भवत्वजमुखं शिरः ।
मित्रस्य चक्षुषेक्षेत भागं स्वं बर्हिषो भगः ॥ ३ ॥

prajāpater dagdha-śīrṣṇo
bhavatv aja-mukhaṁ śiraḥ

mitrasya cakṣuṣekṣeta
bhāgaṁ svaṁ barhiṣo bhagaḥ

prajāpateḥ—of Prajāpati Dakṣa; *dagdha-śīrṣṇaḥ*—whose head has been burned to ashes; *bhavatu*—let there be; *aja-mukham*—with the face of a goat; *śiraḥ*—a head; *mitrasya*—of Mitra; *cakṣuṣā*—through the eyes; *īkṣeta*—may see; *bhāgam*—share; *svam*—his own; *barhiṣaḥ*—of the sacrifice; *bhagaḥ*—Bhaga.

TRANSLATION

Lord Śiva continued: Since the head of Dakṣa has already been burned to ashes, he will have the head of a goat. The demigod known as Bhaga will be able to see his share of sacrifice through the eyes of Mitra.

TEXT 4

पूषा तु यजमानस्य दद्भिर्जक्षतु पिष्टभुक् ।
देवाः प्रकृतसर्वाङ्गा ये म उच्छेषणं ददुः ॥ ४ ॥

pūṣā tu yajamānasya
dadbhir jakṣatu piṣṭa-bhuk
devāḥ prakṛta-sarvāṅgā
ye ma uccheṣaṇaṁ daduḥ

pūṣā—Pūṣā; *tu*—but; *yajamānasya*—of the performer of the sacrifice; *dadbhiḥ*—with the teeth; *jakṣatu*—chew; *piṣṭa-bhuk*—eating flour; *devāḥ*—the demigods; *prakṛta*—made; *sarva-aṅgāḥ*—complete; *ye*—who; *me*—unto me; *uccheṣaṇam*—a share of the sacrifice; *daduḥ*—gave.

TRANSLATION

The demigod Pūṣā will be able to chew only through the teeth of his disciples, and if alone, he will have to satisfy himself by eating dough made from chickpea flour. But the demigods who have agreed to give me my share of the sacrifice will recover from all their injuries.

PURPORT

The demigod Pūṣā became dependent on his disciples for chewing. Otherwise he was allowed to swallow only dough made of chickpea flour. Thus his punishment continued. He could not use his teeth for eating, since he had laughed at Lord Śiva, deriding him by showing his teeth. In other words, it was not appropriate for him to have teeth, for he had used them against Lord Śiva.

TEXT 5

बाहुभ्यामश्विनोः पूष्णो हस्ताभ्यां कृतबाहवः ।
भवन्त्वध्वर्यवश्चान्ये बस्तश्मश्रुर्भृगुर्भवेत् ॥ ५ ॥

bāhubhyām aśvinoḥ pūṣṇo
hastābhyāṁ kṛta-bāhavaḥ
bhavantv adhvaryavaś cānye
basta-śmaśrur bhṛgur bhavet

bāhubhyām—with two arms; *aśvinoḥ*—of Aśvinī-kumāra; *pūṣṇaḥ*—of Pūṣā; *hastābhyām*—with two hands; *kṛta-bāhavaḥ*—those in need of arms; *bhavantu*—they will have to; *adhvaryavaḥ*—the priests; *ca*—and; *anye*—others; *basta-śmaśruḥ*—the beard of the goat; *bhṛguḥ*—Bhṛgu; *bhavet*—he may have.

TRANSLATION

Those who have had their arms cut off will have to work with the arms of Aśvinī-kumāra, and those whose hands were cut off will have to do their work with the hands of Pūṣā. The priests will also have to act in that manner. As for Bhṛgu, he will have the beard from the goat's head.

PURPORT

Bhṛgu Muni, a great supporter of Dakṣa, was awarded the beard of the goat's head which was substituted for the head of Dakṣa. It appears from the exchange of Dakṣa's head that the modern scientific theory that the brain substance is the cause of all intelligent work is not valid. The brain substance of Dakṣa and that of a goat are different, but Dakṣa still acted like himself, even though his head was replaced by that of a goat. The conclusion is that it is the particular consciousness of an individual soul which acts. The brain substance is only an instrument which has nothing to do with real intelligence. The real intelligence, mind and consciousness are part of the particular individual soul. It will be found in the verses ahead that after Dakṣa's head was replaced by the goat's head, he was as intelligent as he had previously been. He prayed very nicely to satisfy Lord Śiva and Lord Viṣṇu, which is not possible for a goat to do. Therefore it is definitely concluded that the brain substance is not the center of intelligence; it is the consciousness of a particular soul that works intelligently. The whole movement of Kṛṣṇa consciousness is to purify the consciousness. It doesn't matter what kind of brain one has because if he simply transfers his consciousness from matter to Kṛṣṇa, his life becomes successful. It is confirmed by the Lord Himself in *Bhagavad-gītā* that anyone who takes up Kṛṣṇa consciousness achieves the highest perfection of life, regardless of whatever abominable condition of life he may have fallen into. Specifically, anyone in Kṛṣṇa consciousness goes back to Godhead, back to home, on leaving his present material body.

TEXT 6

मैत्रेय उवाच
तदा सर्वाणि भूतानि श्रुत्वा मीढुष्टमोदितम् ।
परितुष्टात्मभिस्तात साधु साध्वित्यथाब्रुवन् ॥ ६ ॥

maitreya uvāca
tadā sarvāṇi bhūtāni
śrutvā mīḍhuṣṭamoditam
parituṣṭātmabhis tāta
sādhu sādhv ity athābruvan

maitreyaḥ—the sage Maitreya; *uvāca*—said; *tadā*—at that time; *sarvāṇi*—all; *bhūtāni*—personalities; *śrutvā*—after hearing; *mīḍhuḥ-ṭama*—the best of the benedictors (Lord Śiva); *uditam*—spoken by; *parituṣṭa*—being satisfied; *ātmabhiḥ*—by heart and soul; *tāta*—my dear Vidura; *sādhu sādhu*—well done, well done; *iti*—thus; *atha abruvan*—as we have said.

TRANSLATION

The great sage Maitreya said: My dear Vidura, all the personalities present were very much satisfied in heart and soul upon hearing the words of Lord Śiva, who is the best among the benedictors.

PURPORT

In this verse Lord Śiva is described as *mīḍhuṣṭama*, the best of the benedictors. He is also known as Āśutoṣa, which indicates that he is very quickly satisfied and very quickly angered. It is said in *Bhagavad-gītā* that less intelligent persons go to the demigods for material benedictions. In this connection, people generally go to Lord Śiva, and because he is always quickly satisfied and gives benedictions to his devotees without consideration, he is called *mīḍhuṣṭama*, or the best of the benedictors. Materialistic persons are always anxious to get material profit, but they are not serious about spiritual profit.

Sometimes, of course, it so happens that Lord Śiva becomes the best benedictor in spiritual life. It is said that once a poor *brāhmaṇa* worshiped Lord Śiva for a benediction, and Lord Śiva advised the devotee to go to see Sanātana Gosvāmī. The devotee went to Sanātana Gosvāmī and informed him that Lord Śiva had advised him to seek out the best benediction from him (Sanātana). Sanātana had a touchstone with him, which he kept with the garbage. On the request of the poor *brāhmaṇa*, Sanātana Gosvāmī gave him the touchstone, and the *brāhmaṇa* was very happy to have it. He now could get as much gold as he desired simply by touching the touchstone to iron. But after he left Sanātana, he thought, "If a touchstone is the best benediction, why has Sanātana Gosvāmī kept it with the garbage?" He therefore returned and asked Sanātana Gosvāmī, "Sir, if this is the best benediction, why did you keep it with the garbage?" Sanātana Gosvāmī then informed him, "Actually, this is not the best benediction. But are you prepared to take the best benediction from me?" The *brāhmaṇa* said, "Yes, sir. Lord Śiva has sent me to you for the best benediction." Then Sanātana Gosvāmī asked him to throw the touchstone in the water nearby and then come back. The poor *brāhmaṇa* did so, and when he returned, Sanātana Gosvāmī initiated him with the Hare Kṛṣṇa *mantra*. Thus by the benediction of Lord Śiva the *brāhmaṇa* got the association of the best devotee of Lord Kṛṣṇa and was thus initiated in the *mahā-mantra*, Hare Kṛṣṇa, Hare Kṛṣṇa, Kṛṣṇa Kṛṣṇa, Hare Hare/ Hare Rāma, Hare Rāma, Rāma Rāma, Hare Hare.

TEXT 7

ततो मीढ्वांसमामन्त्र्य शुनासीराः सहर्षिभिः ।
भूयस्तद्देवयजनं समीढ्वद्वेधसो ययुः ॥ ७ ॥

tato mīḍhvāṁsam āmantrya
śunāsīrāḥ saharṣibhiḥ
bhūyas tad deva-yajanaṁ
sa-mīḍhvad-vedhaso yayuḥ

tataḥ—thereafter; *mīḍhvāṁsam*—Lord Śiva; *āmantrya*—inviting; *śunāsīrāḥ*—the demigods headed by King Indra; *saha ṛṣibhiḥ*—with all the great sages, headed by Bhṛgu; *bhūyaḥ*—again; *tat*—that; *deva-yajanam*—place where the demigods are worshiped; *sa-mīḍhvat*—with Lord Śiva; *vedhasaḥ*—with Lord Brahmā; *yayuḥ*—went.

TRANSLATION

Thereafter, Bhṛgu, the chief of the great sages, invited Lord Śiva to come to the sacrificial arena. Thus the demigods, accompanied by the sages, Lord Śiva, and Lord Brahmā, all went to the place where the great sacrifice was being performed.

PURPORT

The whole sacrifice arranged by King Dakṣa had been disturbed by Lord Śiva. Therefore all the demigods present there, along with Lord Brahmā and the great sages, specifically requested Lord Śiva to come and revive the sacrificial fire. There is a common phrase, *śiva-hīna-yajña:* "Any sacrifice without the presence of Lord Śiva is baffled." Lord Viṣṇu is Yajñeśvara, the Supreme Personality in the matter of sacrifice, yet in each *yajña* it is necessary for all the demigods, headed by Lord Brahmā and Lord Śiva, to be present.

TEXT 8

विधाय कार्त्स्न्येन च तद्यदाह भगवान् भवः ।
संदधुः कस्य कायेन सवनीयपशोः शिरः ॥ ८ ॥

vidhāya kārtsnyena ca tad
yad āha bhagavān bhavaḥ
sandadhuḥ kasya kāyena
savanīya-paśoḥ śiraḥ

vidhāya—executing; *kārtsnyena*—all in all; *ca*—also; *tat*—that; *yat*—which; *āha*—was said; *bhagavān*—the Lord; *bhavaḥ*—Śiva; *sandadhuḥ*—executed; *kasya*—of the living (Dakṣa); *kāyena*—with the body; *savanīya*—meant for sacrifice; *paśoḥ*—of the animal; *śiraḥ*—head.

TRANSLATION

After everything was executed exactly as directed by Lord Śiva, Dakṣa's body was joined to the head of the animal meant to be killed in the sacrifice.

PURPORT

This time, all the demigods and great sages were very careful not to irritate Lord Śiva. Therefore whatever he asked was done. It is specifically said here that Dakṣa's body was joined to the head of an animal (a goat).

TEXT 9

संधीयमाने शिरसि दक्षो रुद्राभिवीक्षितः ।
सद्यः सुप्त इवोत्तस्थौ ददृशे चाग्रतो मृडम् ॥ ९ ॥

sandhīyamāne śirasi
dakṣo rudrābhivīkṣitaḥ
sadyaḥ supta ivottasthau
dadṛśe cāgrato mṛḍam

sandhīyamāne—being executed; *śirasi*—by the head; *dakṣaḥ*—King Dakṣa; *rudra-abhivīkṣitaḥ*—having been seen by Rudra (Lord Śiva);

sadyaḥ—immediately; *supte*—sleeping; *iva*—like; *uttasthau*—awakened; *dadṛśe*—saw; *ca*—also; *agrataḥ*—in front; *mṛḍam*—Lord Śiva.

TRANSLATION

When the animal's head was fixed on the body of King Dakṣa, Dakṣa was immediately brought to consciousness, and as he awakened from sleep, the King saw Lord Śiva standing before him.

PURPORT

The example given here is that Dakṣa got up as if he were awakened from deep sleep. In Sanskrit this is called *supta ivottasthau.* The meaning is that after a man awakens from sleep, he immediately remembers all the duties which he must execute. Dakṣa was killed, and his head was taken away and burned to ashes. His body was lying dead, but by the grace of Lord Śiva, as soon as the head of a goat was joined to the body, Dakṣa came back to consciousness again. This indicates that consciousness is also individual. Dakṣa actually took another body when he took on the head of a goat, but because consciousness is individual, his consciousness remained the same although his bodily condition changed. Thus bodily construction has nothing to do with the development of consciousness. Consciousness is carried with the transmigration of the soul. There are many instances of this in Vedic history, such as the case of Mahārāja Bharata. After quitting his body as a king, Mahārāja Bharata was transferred to the body of a deer, but he retained the same consciousness. He knew that although formerly he was King Bharata, he had been transferred to the body of a deer because of his absorption in thinking of a deer at the time of his death. In spite of his having the body of a deer, however, his consciousness was as good as it was in the body of King Bharata. The arrangement by the Lord is so nice that if a person's consciousness is turned into Kṛṣṇa consciousness, there is no doubt that in his next life he will be a great devotee of Kṛṣṇa, even if he is offered a different type of body.

TEXT 10

तदा वृषध्वजद्वेषकलिलात्मा प्रजापतिः ।
शिवावलोकादभवच्छरद्ध्रद इवामलः ॥१०॥

tadā vṛṣadhvaja-dveṣa-
kalilātmā prajāpatiḥ
śivāvalokād abhavac
charad-dhrada ivāmalaḥ

tadā—at that time; *vṛṣa-dhvaja*—Lord Śiva, who rides on a bull; *dveṣa*—envy; *kalila-ātmā*—polluted heart; *prajāpatiḥ*—King Dakṣa; *śiva*—Lord Śiva; *avalokāt*—by seeing him; *abhavat*—became; *śarat*—in the autumn; *hradaḥ*—lake; *iva*—like; *amalaḥ*—cleansed.

TRANSLATION

At that time, when Dakṣa saw Lord Śiva, who rides upon a bull, his heart, which was polluted by envy of Lord Śiva, was immediately cleansed, just as the water in a lake is cleansed by autumn rains.

PURPORT

Here is an example of why Lord Śiva is called auspicious. If anyone sees Lord Śiva with devotion and reverence, his heart is immediately cleansed. King Dakṣa was polluted by envy of Lord Śiva, and yet by seeing him with a little love and devotion, his heart immediately became cleansed. In the rainy season, the reservoirs of water become dirty and muddy, but as soon as the autumn rain comes, all the water immediately becomes clear and transparent. Similarly, although Dakṣa's heart was impure because of his having slandered Lord Śiva, for which he was severely punished, Dakṣa now came to consciousness, and just by seeing Lord Śiva with veneration and respect, he became immediately purified.

TEXT 11

भवस्तवाय कृतधीर्नाशक्नोदनुरागतः ।
औत्कण्ठ्याद्बाष्पकलया सम्परेतां सुतां स्मरन् ॥११॥

bhava-stavāya kṛta-dhīr
nāśaknod anurāgataḥ
autkaṇṭhyād bāṣpa-kalayā
samparetāṁ sutāṁ smaran

bhava-stavāya—for praying to Lord Śiva; *kṛta-dhīḥ*—although decided; *na*—never; *aśaknot*—was able; *anurāgataḥ*—by feeling; *autkaṇṭhyāt*—because of eagerness; *bāṣpa-kalayā*—with tears in the eyes; *samparetām*—dead; *sutām*—daughter; *smaran*—remembering.

TRANSLATION

King Dakṣa wanted to offer prayers to Lord Śiva, but as he remembered the ill-fated death of his daughter Satī, his eyes filled with tears, and in bereavement his voice choked up, and he could not say anything.

TEXT 12

कृच्छ्रात्संस्तभ्य च मनः प्रेमविह्वलितः सुधीः ।
शशंस निर्व्यलीकेन भावेनेशं प्रजापतिः ॥१२॥

kṛcchrāt saṁstabhya ca manaḥ
prema-vihvalitaḥ sudhīḥ
śaśaṁsa nirvyalīkena
bhāveneśaṁ prajāpatiḥ

kṛcchrāt—with great endeavor; *saṁstabhya*—pacifying; *ca*—also; *manaḥ*—mind; *prema-vihvalitaḥ*—bewildered by love and affection; *su-dhīḥ*—one who has come to his real senses; *śaśaṁsa*—praised; *nir-vyalīkena*—without duplicity, or with great love; *bhāvena*—in feeling; *īśam*—to Lord Śiva; *prajāpatiḥ*—King Dakṣa.

TRANSLATION

At this time, King Dakṣa, afflicted by love and affection, was very much awakened to his real senses. With great endeavor, he pacified his mind, checked his feelings, and with pure consciousness began to offer prayers to Lord Śiva.

TEXT 13

दक्ष उवाच
भूयाननुग्रह अहो भवता कृतो मे
दण्डस्त्वया मयि भृतो यदपि प्रलब्धः।

न ब्रह्मबन्धुषु च वां भगवन्नवज्ञा
तुभ्यं हरेश्च कुत एव धृतव्रतेषु ॥१३॥

dakṣa uvāca
bhūyān anugraha aho bhavatā kṛto me
daṇḍas tvayā mayi bhṛto yad api pralabdhaḥ
na brahma-bandhuṣu ca vāṁ bhagavann avajñā
tubhyaṁ hareś ca kuta eva dhṛta-vrateṣu

dakṣaḥ—King Dakṣa; *uvāca*—said; *bhūyān*—very great; *anugrahaḥ*—favor; *aho*—alas; *bhavatā*—by you; *kṛtaḥ*—done; *me*—upon me; *daṇḍaḥ*—punishment; *tvayā*—by you; *mayi*—unto me; *bhṛtaḥ*—done; *yat api*—although; *pralabdhaḥ*—defeated; *na*—neither; *brahma-bandhuṣu*—unto an unqualified *brāhmaṇa; ca*—also; *vām*—both of you; *bhagavan*—my lord; *avajñā*—negligence; *tubhyam*—of you; *hareḥ ca*—of Lord Viṣṇu; *kutaḥ*—where; *eva*—certainly; *dhṛta-vrateṣu*—one who is engaged in the performance of sacrifice.

TRANSLATION

King Dakṣa said: My dear Lord Śiva, I committed a great offense against you, but you are so kind that instead of withdrawing your mercy, you have done me a great favor by punishing me. You and Lord Viṣṇu never neglect even useless, unqualified brāhmaṇas. Why, then, should you neglect me, who am engaged in performing sacrifices?

PURPORT

Although Dakṣa felt defeated, he knew that his punishment was simply the great mercy of Lord Śiva. He remembered that Lord Śiva and Lord Viṣṇu are never neglectful of the *brāhmaṇas*, even though the *brāhmaṇas* are sometimes unqualified. According to Vedic civilization, a descendant of a *brāhmaṇa* family should never be heavily punished. This was exemplified in Arjuna's treatment of Aśvatthāmā. Aśvatthāmā was the son of a great *brāhmaṇa*, Droṇācārya, and in spite of his having committed the great offense of killing all the sleeping sons of the Pāṇḍavas, for which he was condemned even by Lord Kṛṣṇa, Arjuna excused him by not killing him because he happened to be the son of a *brāhmaṇa.* The word *brahma-bandhuṣu* used here is significant. *Brahma-bandhu* means a person who is born of a *brāhmaṇa* father but whose activities are not up to the standard of the *brāhmaṇas.* Such a person is not a *brāhmaṇa* but a *brahma-bandhu.* Dakṣa proved himself to be a *brahma-bandhu.* He was born of a great *brāhmaṇa* father, Lord Brahmā, but his treatment of Lord Śiva was not exactly brahminical; therefore he admitted that he was not a perfect *brāhmaṇa.* Lord Śiva and Lord Viṣṇu, however, are affectionate even to an imperfect *brāhmaṇa.* Lord Śiva punished Dakṣa not as one does his enemy; rather, he punished Dakṣa just to bring him to his senses, so that he would know that he had done wrong. Dakṣa could understand this, and he acknowledged the great mercy of Lord Kṛṣṇa and Lord Śiva towards the fallen *brāhmaṇas,* including even himself. Although he was fallen, his vow was to execute the sacrifice, as is the duty of *brāhmaṇas,* and thus he began his prayers to Lord Śiva.

TEXT 14

विद्यातपोव्रतधरान् मुखतः स्म विप्रान्
ब्रह्मात्मतत्त्वमवितुं प्रथमं त्वमस्राक् ।
तद्ब्राह्मणान् परम सर्वविपत्सु पासि
पालः पशूनिव विभो प्रगृहीतदण्डः ॥१४॥

vidyā-tapo-vrata-dharān mukhataḥ sma viprān
brahmātma-tattvam avituṁ prathamaṁ tvam asrāk
tad brāhmaṇān parama sarva-vipatsu pāsi
pālaḥ paśūn iva vibho pragṛhīta-daṇḍaḥ

vidyā—learning; *tapaḥ*—austerities; *vrata*—vows; *dharān*—the followers; *mukhataḥ*—from the mouth; *sma*—was; *viprān*—the *brāhmaṇas; brahmā*—Lord Brahmā; *ātma-tattvam*—self-realization; *avitum*—to disseminate; *prathamam*—first; *tvam*—you; *asrāk*—created; *tat*—therefore; *brāhmaṇān*—the *brāhmaṇas; parama*—O great one; *sarva*—all; *vipatsu*—in dangers; *pāsi*—you protect; *pālaḥ*—like the protector; *paśūn*—the animals; *iva*—like; *vibho*—O great one; *pragṛhīta*—taking in hand; *daṇḍaḥ*—a stick.

TRANSLATION

My dear great and powerful Lord Śiva, you were created first from the mouth of Lord Brahmā in order to protect the brāhmaṇas in pursuing education, austerities, vows and self-realization. As protector of the brāhmaṇas, you always protect the regulative principles they follow, just as a cowherd boy keeps a stick in his hand to give protection to the cows.

PURPORT

The specific function of a human being in society, irrespective of his social status, is to practice control of the mind and senses by observing the regulative principles enjoined in the Vedic *śāstras.* Lord Śiva is called *paśupati* because he protects the living entities in their developed consciousness so that they may follow the Vedic system of *varṇa* and *āśrama.* The word *paśu* refers to the animal as well as to the human entity. It is stated here that Lord Śiva is always interested in protecting the animals and the animalistic living entities, who are not very advanced in the spiritual sense. It is also stated that the *brāhmaṇas* are produced from the mouth of the Supreme Lord. We should always remember that Lord Śiva is being addressed as the representative of the Supreme Lord, Viṣṇu. In the Vedic literature it is described that the *brāhmaṇas* are born from the mouth of the universal form of Viṣṇu, the *kṣatriyas* are born from His arms, the *vaiśyas* from His abdomen or waist, and the *śūdras* from His legs. In the formation of a body, the head is the principal factor. The *brāhmaṇas* are born from the mouth of the Supreme Personality of Godhead in order to accept charity for worship of Viṣṇu and to spread Vedic knowledge. Lord Śiva is known as *paśupati,* the protector of the *brāhmaṇas* and other living entities. He protects them from the attacks of non-*brāhmaṇas,* or uncultured persons who are against the self-realization process.

Another feature of this word is that persons who are simply attached to the ritualistic portion of the *Vedas* and do not understand the situation of the Supreme Personality of Godhead are not any more advanced than animals. In the beginning of *Śrīmad-Bhāgavatam* it is confirmed that even though one performs the rituals of the *Vedas,* if he does not develop a sense of Kṛṣṇa consciousness, then all his labor in performing Vedic rituals is considered to be simply a waste of time. Lord Śiva's aim in destroying the Dakṣa *yajña* was to punish Dakṣa because by neglecting him (Lord Śiva), Dakṣa was committing a great offense. Lord Śiva's punishment was just like that of a cowherd boy, who keeps a stick to frighten his animals. It is commonly said that to give protection to animals, a stick is needed because animals cannot reason and argue. Their reasoning and argument is *argumentum ad baculum;* unless there is a rod, they do not obey. Force is required for the animalistic class of men, whereas those who are advanced are convinced by reasons, arguments and scriptural authority. Persons who are simply attached to Vedic rituals, without further advancement of devotional service, or Kṛṣṇa consciousness, are almost like animals, and Lord Śiva is in charge of giving them protection and sometimes punishing them, as he punished Dakṣa.

TEXT 15

योऽसौ मयाविदिततत्त्वदृशा सभायां
क्षिप्तो दुरुक्तिविशिखैर्विगणय्य तन्माम् ।
अर्वाक् पतन्तमर्हत्तमनिन्दयापाद्
दृष्ट्यार्द्रया स भगवान् स्वकृतेन तुष्येत् ॥१५॥

yo 'sau mayāvidita-tattva-dṛśā sabhāyāṁ
kṣipto durukti-viśikhair vigaṇayya tan mām
arvāk patantam arhattama-nindayāpād
dṛṣṭyārdrayā sa bhagavān sva-kṛtena tuṣyet

yaḥ—who; *asau*—that; *mayā*—by me; *avidita-tattva*—without knowing the actual fact; *dṛśā*—by experience; *sabhāyām*—in the assembly; *kṣiptaḥ*—was abused; *durukti*—unkind words; *viśikhaiḥ*—by the arrows of; *vigaṇayya*—taking no notice of; *tat*—that; *mām*—me; *arvāk*—downwards; *patantam*—gliding down to hell; *arhat-tama*—the most respectable; *nindayā*—by defamation; *apāt*—saved; *dṛṣṭyā*—seeing; *ārdrayā*—out of compassion; *saḥ*—that; *bhagavān*—Your Lordship; *sva-kṛtena*—by your own mercy; *tuṣyet*—be satisfied.

TRANSLATION

I did not know your full glories. For this reason, I threw arrows of sharp words at you in the open assembly, although you did not

take them into account. I was going down to hell because of my disobedience to you, who are the most respectable personality, but you took compassion upon me and saved me by awarding punishment. I request that you be pleased by your own mercy, since I cannot satisfy you by my words.

PURPORT

As usual, a devotee in an adverse condition of life accepts such a condition to be the mercy of the Lord. Factually, the insulting words used by Dakṣa against Lord Śiva were enough to have him thrown perpetually into a hellish life. But Lord Śiva, being kind toward him, awarded him punishment to neutralize the offense. King Dakṣa realized this and, feeling obliged for Lord Śiva's magnanimous behavior, wanted to show his gratitude. Sometimes a father punishes his child, and when the child is grown up and comes to his senses, he understands that the father's punishment was not actually punishment but mercy. Similarly, Dakṣa appreciated that the punishment offered to him by Lord Śiva was a manifestation of Lord Śiva's mercy. That is the symptom of a person making progress on the path of Kṛṣṇa consciousness. It is said that a devotee in Kṛṣṇa consciousness never takes any miserable condition of life to be condemnation by the Supreme Personality of Godhead. He accepts the miserable condition to be the grace of the Lord. He thinks, "I would have been punished or put into a more dangerous condition of life due to my past misdeeds, but the Lord has protected me. Thus I have received only a little punishment as token execution of the law of *karma.*" Thinking of His grace in that way, a devotee always surrenders to the Supreme Personality of Godhead more and more seriously and is not disturbed by such so-called punishment.

TEXT 16

मैत्रेय उवाच

क्षमाप्यैवं स मीढ्वांसं ब्रह्मणा चानुमन्त्रितः ।
कर्म सन्तानयामास सोपाध्यायर्त्विगादिभिः ॥१६॥

maitreya uvāca
kṣamāpyaivaṁ sa mīḍhvāṁsaṁ

brahmaṇā cānumantritaḥ
karma santānayām āsa
sopādhyāyartvig-ādibhiḥ

maitreyaḥ—the sage Maitreya; *uvāca*—said; *kṣamā*—forgiveness; *āpya*—receiving; *evam*—thus; *saḥ*—King Dakṣa; *mīḍhvāṁsam*—unto Lord Śiva; *brahmaṇā*—along with Lord Brahmā; *ca*—also; *anumantritaḥ*—being permitted; *karma*—the sacrifice; *santānayām āsa*—began again; *sa*—along with; *upādhyāya*—learned sages; *ṛtvik*—the priests; *ādibhiḥ*—and others.

TRANSLATION

The great sage Maitreya said: Thus being pardoned by Lord Śiva, King Dakṣa, with the permission of Lord Brahmā, again began the performance of the yajña, along with the great learned sages, the priests and others.

TEXT 17

वैष्णवं यज्ञसन्तत्यै त्रिकपालं द्विजोत्तमाः ।
पुरोडाशं निरवपन् वीरसंसर्गशुद्धये ॥१७॥

vaiṣṇavaṁ yajña-santatyai
tri-kapālaṁ dvijottamāḥ
puroḍāśaṁ niravapan
vīra-saṁsarga-śuddhaye

vaiṣṇavam—meant for Lord Viṣṇu or His devotees; *yajña*—sacrifice; *santatyai*—for performances; *tri-kapālam*—three kinds of offerings; *dvija-uttamāḥ*—the best of the *brāhmaṇas; puroḍāśam*—the oblation called *puroḍāśa; niravapan*—offered; *vīra*—Vīrabhadra and other followers of Lord Śiva; *saṁsarga*—contamination (*doṣa*) due to his touching; *śuddhaye*—for purification.

TRANSLATION

Thereafter, in order to resume the activities of sacrifice, the brāhmaṇas first arranged to purify the sacrificial arena of the contamination caused by the touch of Vīrabhadra and the other

ghostly followers of Lord Śiva. Then they arranged to offer into the fire the oblations known as puroḍāśa.

PURPORT

Lord Śiva's followers and devotees, headed by Vīrabhadra, are known as *vīras*, and they are ghostly demons. Not only did they pollute the entire sacrificial arena by their very presence, but they disturbed the whole situation by passing stool and urine. Therefore, the infection they had created was to be first purified by the method of offering *puroḍāśa* oblations. A *viṣṇu-yajña*, or an offering to Lord Viṣṇu, cannot be performed uncleanly. To offer anything in an unclean state is called a *sevāparādha.* The worship of the Viṣṇu Deity in the temple is also *viṣṇu-yajña.* In all Viṣṇu temples, therefore, the priest who takes care of the *arcanā-vidhi* must be very clean. Everything should be always kept neat and clean, and the foodstuffs should be prepared in a neat and clean manner. All these regulative principles are described in *The Nectar of Devotion.* There are thirty-two kinds of offenses in discharging *arcanā* service. It is required, therefore, that one be extremely careful not to be unclean. Generally, whenever any ritualistic ceremony is begun, the holy name of Lord Viṣṇu is first chanted in order to purify the situation. Whether one is in a pure or impure condition, internally or externally, if one chants or even remembers the holy name of the Supreme Personality of Godhead Viṣṇu, one immediately becomes purified. The *yajña* arena was desecrated by the presence of Lord Śiva's followers, headed by Vīrabhadra, and therefore the entire arena had to be sanctified. Although Lord Śiva was present and he is all-auspicious, it was still necessary to sanctify the place because his followers had broken into the arena and committed so many obnoxious acts. That sanctification was possible only by chanting the holy name of Viṣṇu, Trikapāla, which can sanctify the three worlds. In other words, it is admitted herein that the followers of Lord Śiva are generally unclean. They are not even very hygienic; they do not take baths regularly, they wear long hair, and they smoke *gāñjā.* Persons of such irregular habits are counted amongst the ghosts. Since they were present in the sacrificial arena, the atmosphere became polluted, and it had to be sanctified by *trikapāla* oblations, which indicated the invocation of Viṣṇu's favor.

TEXT 18

अध्वर्युणात्तहविषा यजमानो विशाम्पते ।
धिया विशुद्धया दध्यौ तथा प्रादुरभूद्धरिः ॥१८॥

adhvaryuṇātta-haviṣā
yajamāno viśāmpate
dhiyā viśuddhayā dadhyau
tathā prādurabhūd dhariḥ

adhvaryuṇā—with the *Yajur Veda; ātta*—taking; *haviṣā*—with clarified butter; *yajamānaḥ*—King Dakṣa; *viśām-pate*—O Vidura; *dhiyā*—in meditation; *viśuddhayā*—sanctified; *dadhyau*—offered; *tathā*—immediately; *prāduḥ*—manifest; *abhūt*—became; *hariḥ*—Hari, the Lord.

TRANSLATION

The great sage Maitreya said to Vidura: My dear Vidura, as soon as King Dakṣa offered the clarified butter with Yajur Veda mantras in sanctified meditation, Lord Viṣṇu appeared there in His original form as Nārāyaṇa.

PURPORT

Lord Viṣṇu is all-pervading. Any devotee who, in sanctified meditation, following the regulative principles, chants the required *mantras* in service and in a devotional mood can see Viṣṇu. It is said in the *Brahma-saṁhitā* that a devotee whose eyes are anointed with the ointment of love of Godhead can see the Supreme Personality of Godhead always within his heart. Lord Śyāmasundara is so kind to His devotee.

TEXT 19

तदा स्वप्रभया तेषां द्योतयन्त्या दिशो दश ।
मुष्णंस्तेज उपानीतस्तार्क्ष्येण स्तोत्रवाजिना ॥१९॥

tadā sva-prabhayā teṣāṁ
dyotayantyā diśo daśa

muṣṇaṁs teja upānītas
tārkṣyeṇa stotra-vājinā

tadā—at that time; *sva-prabhayā*—by His own effulgence; *teṣām*—all of them; *dyotayantyā*—by brightness; *diśaḥ*—directions; *daśa*—ten; *muṣṇan*—diminishing; *tejaḥ*—effulgence; *upānītaḥ*—brought; *tārkṣyeṇa*—by Garuḍa; *stotra-vājinā*—whose wings are called Bṛhat and Rathantara.

TRANSLATION

Lord Nārāyaṇa was seated on the shoulder of Stotra, or Garuḍa, who had big wings. As soon as the Lord appeared, all directions were illuminated, diminishing the luster of Brahmā and the others present.

PURPORT

A description of Nārāyaṇa is given in the following two *ślokas.*

TEXT 20

श्यामो हिरण्यरशनोऽर्ककिरीटजुष्टो
नीलालकभ्रमरमण्डितकुण्डलास्यः ।
शङ्खाब्जचक्रशरचापगदासिचर्म-
व्यग्रैर्हिरण्मयभुजैरिव कर्णिकारः ॥२०॥

śyāmo hiraṇya-raśano 'rka-kirīṭa-juṣṭo
nīlālaka-bhramara-maṇḍita-kuṇḍalāsyaḥ
śaṅkhābja-cakra-śara-cāpa-gadāsi-carma-
vyagrair hiraṇmaya-bhujair iva karṇikāraḥ

śyāmaḥ—blackish; *hiraṇya-raśanaḥ*—a garment like gold; *arka-kirīṭa-juṣṭaḥ*—with a helmet as dazzling as the sun; *nīla-alaka*—bluish curls; *bhramara*—big black bees; *maṇḍita-kuṇḍala-āsyaḥ*—having a face decorated with earrings; *śaṅkha*—conchshell; *abja*—lotus flower; *cakra*—wheel; *śara*—arrows; *cāpa*—bow; *gadā*—club; *asi*—sword; *carma*—shield; *vyagraiḥ*—filled with; *hiraṇmaya*—golden (bracelets and bangles); *bhujaiḥ*—with hands; *iva*—as; *karṇikāraḥ*—flower tree.

TRANSLATION

His complexion was blackish, His garment yellow like gold, and His helmet as dazzling as the sun. His hair was bluish, the color of black bees, and His face was decorated with earrings. His eight hands held a conchshell, wheel, club, lotus flower, arrow, bow, shield and sword, and they were decorated with golden ornaments such as bangles and bracelets. His whole body resembled a blossoming tree beautifully decorated with various kinds of flowers.

PURPORT

The face of Lord Viṣṇu as described in this verse appears like a lotus flower with bees humming over it. All of the ornaments on the body of Lord Viṣṇu resemble molten gold of the reddish-gold color of the morning sunrise. The Lord appears, just as the morning sun rises, to protect the whole universal creation. His arms display different weapons, and His eight hands are compared to the eight petals of a lotus flower. All the weapons mentioned are for the protection of His devotees.

Generally in the four hands of Viṣṇu there are a wheel, club, conchshell and lotus flower. These four symbols are seen in the four hands of Viṣṇu in different arrangements. The club and the wheel are the Lord's symbols of punishment for the demons and miscreants, and the lotus flower and conchshell are used to bless the devotees. There are always two classes of men, the devotees and the demons. As confirmed in *Bhagavad-gītā* (*paritrāṇāya sādhūnām*), the Lord is always ready for the protection of the devotees and annihilation of the demons. There are demons and devotees in this material world, but in the spiritual world there is no such distinction. In other words, Lord Viṣṇu is the proprietor of both the material and spiritual worlds. In the material world almost everyone is of the demoniac nature, but there are also devotees, who appear to be in the material world although they are always situated in the spiritual world. A devotee's position is always transcendental, and he is always protected by Lord Viṣṇu.

TEXT 21

वक्षस्यधिश्रितवधूर्वनमाल्युदार-
हासावलोककलया रमयंश्च विश्वम् ।

पार्श्वभ्रमद्‌व्यजनचामरराजहंसः
श्वेतातपत्रशशिनोपरि रज्यमानः ॥२१॥

vakṣasy adhiśrita-vadhūr vana-māly udāra-
hāsāvaloka-kalayā ramayaṁś ca viśvam
pārśva-bhramad-vyajana-cāmara-rāja-haṁsaḥ
śvetātapatra-śaśinopari rajyamānaḥ

vakṣasi—on the chest; *adhiśrita*—situated; *vadhūḥ*—a woman (the goddess of fortune, Lakṣmī); *vana-mālī*—garlanded with forest flowers; *udāra*—beautiful; *hāsa*—smiling; *avaloka*—glance; *kalayā*—with a small part; *ramayan*—pleasing; *ca*—and; *viśvam*—the whole world; *pārśva*—side; *bhramat*—moving back and forth; *vyajana-cāmara*—white yak-tail hair for fanning; *rāja-haṁsaḥ*—swan; *śveta-ātapatra-śaśinā*—with a white canopy like the moon; *upari*—above; *rajya-mānaḥ*—looking beautiful.

TRANSLATION

Lord Viṣṇu looked extraordinarily beautiful because the goddess of fortune and a garland were situated on His chest. His face was beautifully decorated with a smiling attitude which can captivate the entire world, especially the devotees. Fans of white hair appeared on both sides of the Lord like white swans, and the white canopy overhead looked like the moon.

PURPORT

The smiling face of Lord Viṣṇu is pleasing to the whole world. Not only devotees but even nondevotees are attracted by such a smile. This verse nicely describes how the sun, moon, eight-petaled lotus flower and humming black bees were represented by the fans of hair, the overhead canopy, the moving earrings on both sides of His face, and His blackish hair. All together, accompanied by the conchshell, wheel, club, lotus flower, bow, arrows, shield and sword in His hands, these presented a grand and beautiful audience for Lord Viṣṇu which captivated all the demigods there, including Dakṣa and Lord Brahmā.

TEXT 22

तमुपागतमालक्ष्य सर्वे सुरगणादयः ।
प्रणेमुः सहसोत्थाय ब्रह्मेन्द्रत्र्यक्षनायकाः ॥२२॥

tam upāgatam ālakṣya
sarve sura-gaṇādayaḥ
praṇemuḥ sahasotthāya
brahmendra-tryakṣa-nāyakāḥ

tam—Him; *upāgatam*—arrived; *ālakṣya*—after seeing; *sarve*—all; *sura-gaṇa-ādayaḥ*—the demigods and others; *praṇemuḥ*—obeisances; *sahasā*—immediately; *utthāya*—after standing up; *brahma*—Lord Brahmā; *indra*—Lord Indra; *tri-akṣa*—Lord Śiva (who has three eyes); *nāyakāḥ*—led by.

TRANSLATION

As soon as Lord Viṣṇu was visible, all the demigods—Lord Brahmā and Lord Śiva, the Gandharvas and all present there—immediately offered their respectful obeisances by falling down straight before Him.

PURPORT

It appears that Lord Viṣṇu is the Supreme Lord even of Lord Śiva and Lord Brahmā, what to speak of the demigods, Gandharvas and ordinary living entities. It is stated in a prayer, *yaṁ brahmā varuṇendra-rudra-marutāḥ:* all the demigods worship Lord Viṣṇu. Similarly, *dhyānāvasthita-tad-gatena manasā paśyanti yaṁ yoginaḥ: yogīs* concentrate their minds on the form of Lord Viṣṇu. Thus Lord Viṣṇu is worshipable by all demigods, all Gandharvas and even Lord Śiva and Lord Brahmā. *Tad viṣṇoḥ paramaṁ padaṁ sadā paśyanti sūrayaḥ:* Viṣṇu is therefore the Supreme Personality of Godhead. Even though Lord Śiva was previously referred to in prayers by Lord Brahmā as the Supreme, when Lord Viṣṇu appeared, Śiva also fell prostrated before Him to offer respectful obeisances.

TEXT 23

तत्तेजसा हतरुचः सन्नजिह्वाः ससाध्वसाः ।
मूर्ध्ना धृताञ्जलिपुटा उपतस्थुरधोक्षजम् ॥२३॥

tat-tejasā hata-rucaḥ
sanna-jihvāḥ sa-sādhvasāḥ
mūrdhnā dhṛtāñjali-puṭā
upatasthur adhokṣajam

tat-tejasā—by the glaring effulgence of His body; *hata-rucaḥ*—having faded lusters; *sanna-jihvāḥ*—having silent tongues; *sa-sādhvasāḥ*—having fear of Him; *mūrdhnā*—with the head; *dhṛta-añjali-puṭāḥ*—with hands touched to the head; *upatasthuḥ*—prayed; *adhokṣajam*—to Adhokṣaja, the Supreme Personality of Godhead.

TRANSLATION

In the presence of the glaring effulgence of the bodily luster of Nārāyaṇa, everyone else's luster faded away, and everyone stopped speaking. Fearful with awe and veneration, all present touched their hands to their heads and prepared to offer their prayers to the Supreme Personality of Godhead, Adhokṣaja.

TEXT 24

अप्यर्वाग्वृत्तयो यस्य महि त्वात्मभुवादयः ।
यथामति गृणन्ति स्म कृतानुग्रहविग्रहम् ॥२४॥

apy arvāg-vṛttayo yasya
mahi tv ātmabhuv-ādayaḥ
yathā-mati gṛṇanti sma
kṛtānugraha-vigraham

api—still; *arvāk-vṛttayah*—beyond the mental activities; *yasya*—whose; *mahi*—glory; *tu*—but; *ātmabhū-ādayaḥ*—Brahmā, etc.; *yatha-mati*—according to their different capacities; *gṛṇanti sma*—offered prayers; *kṛta-anugraha*—manifested by His grace; *vigraham*—transcendental form.

TRANSLATION

Although the mental scope of even demigods like Brahmā was unable to comprehend the unlimited glories of the Supreme Lord, they were all able to perceive the transcendental form of the Supreme Personality of Godhead by His grace. Only by such grace could they offer their respectful prayers according to their different capacities.

PURPORT

The Supreme Lord, the Personality of Godhead, is always unlimited, and His glories cannot be completely enumerated by anyone, even by a personality like Lord Brahmā. It is said that Ananta, a direct incarnation of the Lord, has unlimited mouths, and with each mouth He has been trying to describe the glories of the Lord for an unlimited span of time, yet the glories of the Lord remain unlimited, and He therefore never finishes. It is not possible for any ordinary living entity to understand or to glorify the unlimited Personality of Godhead, but one can offer prayers or service to the Lord according to one's particular capacity. This capacity is increased by the service spirit. *Sevonmukhe hi jihvādau* means that the service of the Lord begins with the tongue. This refers to chanting. By chanting Hare Kṛṣṇa, one begins the service of the Lord. Another function of the tongue is to taste and accept the Lord's *prasāda*. We have to begin our service to the Unlimited with the tongue and become perfect in chanting, and accepting the Lord's *prasāda*. To accept the Lord's *prasāda* means to control the entire set of senses. The tongue is considered to be the most uncontrollable sense because it hankers for so many unwholesome eatables, thereby forcing the living entity into the dungeon of material conditional life. As the living entity transmigrates from one form of life to another, he has to eat so many abominable foodstuffs that finally there is no limit. The tongue should be engaged in chanting and in eating the Lord's *prasāda* so that the other senses will be controlled. Chanting is the medicine, and *prasāda* is the diet. With these processes one can begin his service, and as the service increases, the Lord reveals more and more to the devotee. But there is no limit to His glories, and there is no limit to engaging oneself in the service of the Lord.

TEXT 25

दक्षो गृहीतार्हणसादनोत्तमं
यज्ञेश्वरं विश्वसृजां परं गुरुम् ।
सुनन्दनन्दाद्यनुगैर्वृतं मुदा
गृणन् प्रपेदे प्रयतः कृताञ्जलिः॥२५॥

dakṣo gṛhītārhaṇa-sādanottamaṁ
yajñeśvaraṁ viśva-sṛjāṁ paraṁ gurum
sunanda-nandādy-anugair vṛtaṁ mudā
gṛṇan prapede prayataḥ kṛtāñjaliḥ

dakṣaḥ—Dakṣa; *gṛhīta*—accepted; *arhaṇa*—rightful; *sādana-uttamam*—sacrificial vessel; *yajña-īśvaram*—unto the master of all sacrifices; *viśva-sṛjām*—of all the Prajāpatis; *param*—the supreme; *gurum*—preceptor; *sunanda-nanda-ādi-anugaiḥ*—by associates like Sunanda and Nanda; *vṛtam*—surrounded; *mudā*—with great pleasure; *gṛṇan*—offering respectful prayers; *prapede*—took shelter; *prayataḥ*—having a subdued mind; *kṛta-añjaliḥ*—with folded hands.

TRANSLATION

When Lord Viṣṇu accepted the oblations offered in the sacrifice, Dakṣa, the Prajāpati, began with great pleasure to offer respectful prayers unto Him. The Supreme Personality of Godhead is actually the master of all sacrifices and preceptor of all the Prajāpatis, and He is served even by such personalities as Nanda and Sunanda.

TEXT 26

दक्ष उवाच
शुद्धं स्वधाम्न्युपरताखिलबुद्ध्यवस्थं
चिन्मात्रमेकमभयं प्रतिषिध्य मायाम् ।

तिष्ठंस्तयैव पुरुषत्वमुपेत्य तस्या-
मास्ते भवानपरिशुद्ध इवात्मतन्त्रः ॥२६॥

dakṣa uvāca
śuddhaṁ sva-dhāmny uparatākhila-buddhy-avasthaṁ
cin-mātram ekam abhayaṁ pratiṣidhya māyām
tiṣṭhaṁs tayaiva puruṣatvam upetya tasyām
āste bhavān apariśuddha ivātma-tantraḥ

dakṣaḥ—Dakṣa; *uvāca*—said; *śuddham*—pure; *sva-dhāmni*—in Your own abode; *uparata-akhila*—completely turned back; *buddhi-avastham*—position of mental speculation; *cit-mātram*—completely spiritual; *ekam*—one without a second; *abhayam*—fearless; *pratiṣidhya*—controlling; *māyām*—material energy; *tiṣṭhan*—being situated; *tayā*—with her (Māyā); *eva*—certainly; *puruṣatvam*—overseer; *upetya*—entering into; *tasyām*—in her; *āste*—is present; *bhavān*—Your Lordship; *apariśuddhaḥ*—impure; *iva*—as if; *ātma-tantraḥ*—self-sufficient.

TRANSLATION

Dakṣa addressed the Supreme Personality of Godhead: My dear Lord, You are transcendental to all speculative positions. You are completely spiritual, devoid of all fear, and You are always in control of the material energy. Even though You appear in the material energy, You are situated transcendentally. You are always free from material contamination because You are completely self-sufficient.

TEXT 27

ऋत्विज ऊचुः
तत्त्वं न ते वयमनञ्जन रुद्रशापात्
कर्मण्यवग्रहधियो भगवन्विदामः ।
धर्मोपलक्षणमिदं त्रिवृदध्वराख्यं
ज्ञातं यदर्थमधिदैवमदोव्यवस्थाः ॥२७॥

ṛtvija ūcuḥ
tattvaṁ na te vayam anañjana rudra-śāpāt
karmaṇy avagraha-dhiyo bhagavan vidāmaḥ

dharmopalakṣaṇam idaṁ trivṛd adhvarākhyaṁ
jñātaṁ yad-artham adhidaivam ado vyavasthāḥ

ṛtvijaḥ—the priests; *ūcuḥ*—began to say; *tattvam*—truth; *na*—not; *te*—of Your Lordship; *vayam*—all of us; *anañjana*—without material contamination; *rudra*—Lord Śiva; *śāpāt*—by his curse; *karmaṇi*—in fruitive activities; *avagraha*—being too much attached; *dhiyaḥ*—of such intelligence; *bhagavan*—O Lord; *vidāmaḥ*—know; *dharma*—religion; *upalakṣaṇam*—symbolized; *idam*—this; *tri-vṛt*—the three departments of knowledge of the *Vedas; adhvara*—sacrifice; *ākhyam*—of the name; *jñātam*—known to us; *yat*—that; *artham*—for the matter of; *adhidaivam*—for worshiping the demigods; *adaḥ*—this; *vyavasthāḥ*—arrangement.

TRANSLATION

The priests addressed the Lord, saying: O Lord, transcendental to material contamination, by the curse offered by Lord Śiva's men we have become attached to fruitive activities, and thus we are now fallen and therefore do not know anything about You. On the contrary, we are now involved in the injunctions of the three departments of the Vedic knowledge under the plea of executing rituals in the name of yajña. We know that You have made arrangements for distributing the respective shares of the demigods.

PURPORT

The *Vedas* are known as *traiguṇya-viṣayā vedāḥ* (Bg. 2.45). Those who are serious students of the *Vedas* are very much attached to the ritualistic ceremonies mentioned in the *Vedas*, and therefore these *veda-vādīs* cannot understand that the ultimate goal of the *Vedas* is to understand Lord Kṛṣṇa, or Viṣṇu. Those who have transcended the qualitative Vedic attractions, however, can understand Kṛṣṇa, who is never contaminated by the material qualities. Therefore Lord Viṣṇu is addressed here as *anañjana* (free from material contamination). In *Bhagavad-gītā* (2.42) the crude Vedic scholars have been deprecated by Kṛṣṇa as follows:

yām imāṁ puṣpitāṁ vācaṁ
pravadanty avipaścitaḥ

veda-vāda-ratāḥ pārtha
nānyad astīti vādinaḥ

"Men of small knowledge are very much attached to the flowery words of the *Vedas*, and they say that there is nothing more than this."

TEXT 28

सदस्या ऊचुः
उत्पत्त्यध्वन्यशरण उरुक्लेशदुर्गेऽन्तकोग्र-
व्यालान्विष्टे विषयमृगतृष्यात्मगेहोरुभारः ।
द्वन्द्वश्वभ्रे खलमृगभये शोकदावेऽज्ञसार्थः
पादौकस्ते शरणद कदा याति कामोपसृष्टः ॥२८॥

sadasyā ūcuḥ
utpatty-adhvany aśaraṇa uru-kleśa-durge 'ntakogra-
vyālānviṣṭe viṣaya-mṛga-tṛṣy ātma-gehoru-bhāraḥ
dvandva-śvabhre khala-mṛga-bhaye śoka-dāve 'jña-sārthaḥ
pādaukas te śaraṇada kadā yāti kāmopasṛṣṭaḥ

sadasyāḥ—the members of the assembly; *ūcuḥ*—said; *utpatti*—repeated birth and death; *adhvani*—on the path of; *aśaraṇe*—not having a place to take shelter; *uru*—great; *kleśa*—troublesome; *durge*—in the formidable fort; *antaka*—termination; *ugra*—ferocious; *vyāla*—snakes; *anviṣṭe*—being infested with; *viṣaya*—material happiness; *mṛga-tṛṣi*—mirage; *ātma*—body; *geha*—home; *uru*—heavy; *bhāraḥ*—burden; *dvandva*—dual; *śvabhre*—holes, ditches of so-called happiness and distress; *khala*—ferocious; *mṛga*—animals; *bhaye*—being afraid of; *śoka-dāve*—the forest fire of lamentation; *ajña-sa-arthaḥ*—for the interest of the rascals; *pāda-okaḥ*—shelter of Your lotus feet; *te*—unto You; *śaraṇa-da*—giving shelter; *kadā*—when; *yāti*—went; *kāma-upasṛṣṭaḥ*—being afflicted by all sorts of desires.

TRANSLATION

The members of the assembly addressed the Lord: O exclusive shelter for all who are situated in troubled life, in this formidable

fort of conditional existence the time element, like a snake, is always looking for an opportunity to strike. This world is full of ditches of so-called distress and happiness, and there are many ferocious animals always ready to attack. The fire of lamentation is always blazing, and the mirage of false happiness is always alluring, but one has no shelter from them. Thus foolish persons live in the cycle of birth and death, always overburdened in discharging their so-called duties, and we do not know when they will accept the shelter of Your lotus feet.

PURPORT

Persons who are not in Kṛṣṇa consciousness are living a very precarious life, as described in this verse, but all these circumstantial conditions are due to forgetfulness of Kṛṣṇa. The Kṛṣṇa consciousness movement is meant to give relief to all these bewildered and distressed persons; therefore it is the greatest relief work for all human society, and the workers thereof are the greatest well-wishers, for they follow in the footsteps of Lord Caitanya, who is the greatest friend to all living entities.

TEXT 29

रुद्र उवाच
तव वरद वराङ्घ्रावाशिषेहाखिलार्थे
ह्यपि मुनिभिरसक्तैरादरेणार्हणीये ।
यदि रचितधियं माविद्यलोकोऽपविद्धं
जपति न गणये तत्त्वत्परानुग्रहेण ॥२९॥

rudra uvāca
tava varada varāṅghrāv āśiṣehākhilārthe
hy api munibhir asaktair ādareṇārhaṇīye
yadi racita-dhiyaṁ māvidya-loko 'paviddhaṁ
japati na gaṇaye tat tvat-parānugraheṇa

rudraḥ uvāca—Lord Śiva said; *tava*—Your; *vara-da*—O supreme benefactor; *vara-aṅghrau*—precious lotus feet; *āśiṣā*—by desire; *iha*—in the material world; *akhila-arthe*—for fulfillment; *hi api*—certainly;

munibhiḥ—by the sages; *asaktaiḥ*—liberated; *ādareṇa*—with care; *arhaṇīye*—worshipable; *yadi*—if; *racita-dhiyam*—mind fixed; *mā*—me; *avidya-lokaḥ*—the ignorant persons; *apaviddham*—unpurified activity; *japati*—utters; *na gaṇaye*—do not value; *tat*—it; *tvat-para-anugraheṇa*—by compassion like Yours.

TRANSLATION

Lord Śiva said: My dear Lord, my mind and consciousness are always fixed on Your lotus feet, which, as the source of all benediction and the fulfillment of all desires, are worshiped by all liberated great sages because Your lotus feet are worthy of worship. With my mind fixed on Your lotus feet, I am no longer disturbed by persons who blaspheme me, claiming that my activities are not purified. I do not mind their accusations, and I excuse them out of compassion, just as You exhibit compassion toward all living entities.

PURPORT

Lord Śiva expresses herein his regret at having been angry and having disturbed the sacrificial activities of Dakṣa. King Dakṣa had insulted him in many ways, and thus he had become angry and had frustrated the entire sacrificial ceremony. Later, when he was pleased, the *yajña* performances were reinstituted, and therefore he regretted his activities. Now he says that because his mind is fixed on the lotus feet of the Supreme Lord, Viṣṇu, he is no longer disturbed by the ordinary critics of his way of life. From this statement by Lord Śiva it is understood that as long as one is on the material platform one is affected by the three modes of material nature. As soon as one is in Kṛṣṇa consciousness, however, one is no longer affected by such material activities. One should therefore always be fixed in Kṛṣṇa consciousness, busy in the transcendental loving service of the Lord. It is guaranteed that such a devotee will never be affected by the actions and reactions of the three modes of material nature. This fact is also corroborated in *Bhagavad-gītā:* anyone who is fixed in the transcendental service of the Lord has surpassed all the material qualities and is situated in the status of Brahman realization, in which one is not afflicted by hankering for material objects. The recommendation of the *Śrīmad-Bhāgavatam* is that one should always be

Kṛṣṇa conscious and should never forget his transcendental relationship with the Lord. This program has to be followed strictly by everyone. From the statement of Lord Śiva it is understood that he was always in Kṛṣṇa consciousness, and thus he remained free from material affliction. The only remedy, therefore, is to continue Kṛṣṇa consciousness rigidly, in order to get out of the contamination of the material modes.

TEXT 30

भृगुरुवाच

यन्मायया गहनयापहृतात्मबोधा
ब्रह्मादयस्तनुभृतस्तमसि स्वपन्तः ।
नात्मन् श्रितं तव विदन्त्यधुनापि तत्त्वं
सोऽयं प्रसीदतु भवान् प्रणतात्मबन्धुः ॥३०॥

bhṛgur uvāca
yan māyayā gahanayāpahṛtātma-bodhā
brahmādayas tanu-bhṛtas tamasi svapantaḥ
nātman-śritaṁ tava vidanty adhunāpi tattvaṁ
so 'yaṁ prasīdatu bhavān praṇatātma-bandhuḥ

bhṛguḥ uvāca—Śrī Bhṛgu said; *yat*—who; *māyayā*—by illusory energy; *gahanayā*—insurmountable; *apahṛta*—stolen; *ātma-bodhāḥ*—knowledge of the constitutional position; *brahma-ādayaḥ*—Lord Brahmā, etc.; *tanu-bhṛtaḥ*—embodied living entities; *tamasi*—in the darkness of illusion; *svapantaḥ*—lying down; *na*—not; *ātman*—in the living entity; *śritam*—situated in; *tava*—Your; *vidanti*—understand; *adhunā*—now; *api*—certainly; *tattvam*—absolute position; *saḥ*—You; *ayam*—this; *prasīdatu*—be kind; *bhavān*—Your Lordship; *praṇata-ātma*—surrendered soul; *bandhuḥ*—friend.

TRANSLATION

Śrī Bhṛgu said: My dear Lord, all living entities, beginning from the highest, namely Lord Brahmā, down to the ordinary ant, are under the influence of the insurmountable spell of illusory energy, and thus they are ignorant of their constitutional position.

Everyone believes in the concept of the body, and all are thus submerged in the darkness of illusion. They are actually unable to understand how You live in every living entity as the Supersoul, nor can they understand Your absolute position. But You are the eternal friend and protector of all surrendered souls. Therefore, please be kind toward us and forgive all our offenses.

PURPORT

Bhṛgu Muni was conscious of the scandalous behavior exhibited by each and every one of them, including Brahmā and Lord Śiva, in the sacrificial ceremony of Dakṣa. By mentioning Brahmā, the chief of all living entities within this material world, he wanted to state that everyone, including also Brahmā and Lord Śiva, is under the concept of the body and under the spell of material energy—all but Viṣṇu. That is the version of Bhṛgu. As long as one is under the concept of the body as self, it is very difficult to understand the Supersoul or the Supreme Personality of Godhead. Conscious that he was not greater than Brahmā, Bhṛgu included himself in the list of offenders. Ignorant personalities, or conditioned souls, have no choice but to accept their precarious condition under material nature. The only remedy is to surrender to Viṣṇu and always pray to be excused. One should depend only on the causeless mercy of the Lord for deliverance and not even slightly on one's own strength. That is the perfect position of a Kṛṣṇa conscious person. The Lord is everyone's friend, but He is especially friendly to the surrendered soul. The simple process, therefore, is that a conditioned soul should remain surrendered to the Lord, and the Lord will give him all protection to keep him out of the clutches of material contamination.

TEXT 31

ब्रह्मोवाच

नैतत्स्वरूपं भवतोऽसौ पदार्थ-
भेदग्रहैः पुरुषो यावदीक्षेत् ।
ज्ञानस्य चार्थस्य गुणस्य चाश्रयो
मायामयाद् व्यतिरिक्तो मतस्त्वम् ॥३१॥

brahmovāca
naitat svarūpaṁ bhavato 'sau padārtha-
bheda-grahaiḥ puruṣo yāvad īkṣet
jñānasya cārthasya guṇasya cāśrayo
māyāmayād vyatirikto matas tvam

brahmā uvāca—Lord Brahmā said; *na*—not; *etat*—this; *svarūpam*—eternal form; *bhavataḥ*—Your; *asau*—that other; *pada-artha*—knowledge; *bheda*—different; *grahaiḥ*—by the acquiring; *puruṣaḥ*—person; *yāvat*—as long as; *īkṣet*—wants to see; *jñānasya*—of knowledge; *ca*—also; *arthasya*—of the objective; *guṇasya*—of the instruments of knowledge; *ca*—also; *āśrayaḥ*—the basis; *māyā-mayāt*—from being made of material energy; *vyatiriktaḥ*—distinct; *mataḥ*—regarded; *tvam*—You.

TRANSLATION

Lord Brahmā said: My dear Lord, Your personality and eternal form cannot be understood by any person who is trying to know You through the different processes of acquiring knowledge. Your position is always transcendental to the material creation, whereas the empiric attempt to understand You is material, as are its objectives and instruments.

PURPORT

It is said that the transcendental name, qualities, activities, paraphernalia, etc., of the Supreme Personality of Godhead cannot be understood with our material senses. The attempt of the empiric philosophers to understand the Absolute Truth by speculation is always futile because their process of understanding, their objective and the instruments by which they try to understand the Absolute Truth are all material. The Lord is *aprākṛta*, beyond the creation of the material world. This fact is also accepted by the great impersonalist Śaṅkarācārya: *nārāyaṇaḥ paro 'vyaktād aṇḍam avyakta-sambhavam. Avyakta*, or the original material cause, is beyond this material manifestation and is the cause of the material world. Because Nārāyaṇa, the Supreme Personality of Godhead, is beyond the material world, one cannot speculate upon Him by any material method. One has to understand the Supreme Personality of Godhead simply by the transcendental method of Kṛṣṇa consciousness. This is confirmed in *Bhagavad-gītā* (18.55). *Bhaktyā mām abhijānāti:* only by devotional service can one understand the transcendental form of the Lord. The difference between the impersonalists and the personalists is that the impersonalists, limited by their speculative processes, cannot even approach the Supreme Personality of Godhead, whereas the devotees please the Supreme Personality of Godhead through His transcendental loving service. *Sevonmukhe hi:* due to the service attitude of the devotee, the Lord is revealed to him. The Supreme Lord cannot be understood by materialistic persons even though He is present before them. In *Bhagavad-gītā*, Lord Kṛṣṇa therefore condemns such materialists as *mūḍhas. Mūḍha* means "rascal." It is said in the *Gītā*, "Only rascals think of Lord Kṛṣṇa as an ordinary person. They do not know what Lord Kṛṣṇa's position is or what His transcendental potencies are." Unaware of His transcendental potencies, the impersonalists deride the person of Lord Kṛṣṇa, whereas the devotees, by dint of their service attitude, can understand Him as the Personality of Godhead. In the Tenth Chapter of *Bhagavad-gītā*, Arjuna also confirmed that it is very difficult to understand the personality of the Lord.

TEXT 32

इन्द्र उवाच
इदमप्यच्युत विश्वभावनं
वपुरानन्दकरं मनोदृशाम् ।
सुरविद्विट्क्षपणैरुदायुधै-
र्भुजदण्डैरुपपन्नमष्टभिः ॥३२॥

indra uvāca
idam apy acyuta viśva-bhāvanaṁ
vapur ānanda-karaṁ mano-dṛśām
sura-vidviṭ-kṣapaṇair udāyudhair
bhuja-daṇḍair upapannam aṣṭabhiḥ

indraḥ uvāca—King Indra said; *idam*—this; *api*—certainly; *acyuta*—O infallible one; *viśva-bhāvanam*—for the welfare of the universe; *vapuḥ*—transcendental form; *ānanda-karam*—a cause of pleasure; *manaḥ-dṛśām*—to the mind and the eye; *sura-vidviṭ*—envious of Your devotees; *kṣapaṇaiḥ*—by punishment; *ud-āyudhaiḥ*—with uplifted weapons; *bhuja-daṇḍaiḥ*—with arms; *upapannam*—possessed of; *aṣṭabhiḥ*—with eight.

TRANSLATION

King Indra said: My dear Lord, Your transcendental form with eight hands and weapons in each of them appears for the welfare of the entire universe, and it is very pleasing to the mind and eyes. In such a form, Your Lordship is always prepared to punish the demons, who are envious of Your devotees.

PURPORT

It is generally understood from revealed scriptures that Lord Viṣṇu appears with four hands, but in this particular sacrificial arena Lord Viṣṇu arrived with eight hands. King Indra said, "Even though we are accustomed to see Your four-handed Viṣṇu form, this appearance with eight hands is as real as the four-handed form." As Lord Brahmā had said, to realize the transcendental form of the Lord is beyond the power of the senses. In reply to that statement by Brahmā, King Indra said that even though the transcendental form of the Lord is not perceivable by the material senses, His activities and His transcendental form can be understood. The Lord's uncommon features, uncommon activities and uncommon beauty can be perceived even by an ordinary man. For example, when Lord Kṛṣṇa appeared just like a six- or seven-year-old boy in Vṛndāvana, He was approached by the residents there. There were torrents of rain, and the Lord saved the residents of Vṛndāvana by lifting Govardhana Hill and resting it on the little finger of His left hand for seven days. This uncommon feature of the Lord should convince even materialistic persons who want to speculate to the limit of their material senses. The activities of the Lord are pleasing to experimental vision also, but impersonalists will not believe in His identity because they study the personality of the Lord by comparing their personality to His. Because men in this material world cannot lift a hill, they do not believe that the Lord can lift one. They accept the statements of *Śrīmad-Bhāgavatam* to be allegorical, and they try to interpret them in their own way. But factually the Lord lifted the hill in the presence of all the inhabitants of

Vṛndāvana, as corroborated by great *ācāryas* and authors like Vyāsadeva and Nārada. Everything about the Lord—His activities, pastimes and uncommon features—should be accepted as is, and in this way, even in our present condition, we can understand the Lord. In the instance herein, King Indra confirmed: "Your presence with eight hands is as good as Your presence with four hands." There is no doubt about it.

TEXT 33

पत्न्य ऊचुः
यज्ञोऽयं तव यजनाय केन सृष्टो
विध्वस्तः पशुपतिनाद्य दक्षकोपात् ।
तं नस्त्वं शवशयनाभशान्तमेधं
यज्ञात्मन्नलिनरुचा दृशा पुनीहि ॥३३॥

patnya ūcuḥ
yajño 'yaṁ tava yajanāya kena sṛṣṭo
vidhvastaḥ paśupatinādya dakṣa-kopāt
taṁ nas tvaṁ śava-śayanābha-śānta-medhaṁ
yajñātman nalina-rucā dṛśā punīhi

patnyaḥ ūcuḥ—the wives of the executors of the sacrifice said; *yajñaḥ*—the sacrifice; *ayam*—this; *tava*—Your; *yajanāya*—worshiping; *kena*—by Brahmā; *sṛṣṭaḥ*—arranged; *vidhvastaḥ*—devastated; *paśupatinā*—by Lord Śiva; *adya*—today; *dakṣa-kopāt*—from anger at Dakṣa; *tam*—it; *naḥ*—our; *tvam*—You; *śava-śayana*—dead bodies; *ābha*—like; *śānta-medham*—the still sacrificial animals; *yajña-ātman*—O Lord of sacrifice; *nalina*—lotus; *rucā*—beautiful; *dṛśā*—by the vision of Your eyes; *punīhi*—sanctify.

TRANSLATION

The wives of the performers of the sacrifice said: My dear Lord, this sacrifice was arranged under the instruction of Brahmā, but unfortunately Lord Śiva, being angry at Dakṣa, devastated the entire scene, and because of his anger the animals meant for sacrifice are lying dead. Therefore the preparations of the yajña have been

lost. Now, by the glance of Your lotus eyes, the sanctity of this sacrificial arena may be again invoked.

PURPORT

Animals were offered in sacrifice in order to give them renewed life; that was the purpose of having animals there. Offering an animal in sacrifice and giving him renewed life was the evidence of the strength of chanting *mantras*. Unfortunately, when Dakṣa's sacrifice was devastated by Lord Śiva, some of the animals were killed. (One was killed just to replace the head of Dakṣa.) Their bodies were lying about, and the sacrificial arena was turned into a crematorium. Thus the real purpose of *yajña* was lost.

Lord Viṣṇu, being the ultimate objective of such sacrificial ceremonies, was requested by the wives of the priests to glance over the *yajña* arena with His causeless mercy so that the routine work of the *yajña* might be continued. The purport here is that animals should not be unnecessarily killed. They were used to prove the strength of the *mantras* and were to have been rejuvenated by the use of the *mantras*. They should not have been killed, as they were by Lord Śiva to replace the head of Dakṣa with an animal's head. It was pleasing to see an animal sacrificed and rejuvenated, and that pleasing atmosphere had been lost. The wives of the priests requested that the animals be brought back to life by the glance of Lord Viṣṇu to make a pleasing *yajña*.

TEXT 34

ऋषय ऊचुः
अनन्वितं ते भगवन् विचेष्टितं
यदात्मना चरसि हि कर्म नाज्यसे ।
विभूतये यत उपसेदुरीश्वरीं
न मन्यते स्वयमनुवर्ततीं भवान् ॥३४॥

ṛṣaya ūcuḥ
ananvitaṁ te bhagavan viceṣṭitaṁ
yad ātmanā carasi hi karma nājyase

vibhūtaye yata upasedur īśvarīṁ
na manyate svayam anuvartatīṁ bhavān

ṛṣayaḥ—the sages; *ūcuḥ*—prayed; *ananvitam*—wonderful; *te*—Your; *bhagavan*—O possessor of all opulences; *viceṣṭitam*—activities; *yat*—which; *ātmanā*—by Your potencies; *carasi*—You execute; *hi*—certainly; *karma*—to such activities; *na ajyase*—You are not attached; *vibhūtaye*—for her mercy; *yataḥ*—from whom; *upaseduḥ*—worshiped; *īśvarīm*—Lakṣmī, the goddess of fortune; *na manyate*—are not attached; *svayam*—Yourself; *anuvartatīm*—to Your obedient servant (Lakṣmī); *bhavān*—Your Lordship.

TRANSLATION

The sages prayed: Dear Lord, Your activities are most wonderful, and although You do everything by Your different potencies, You are not at all attached to such activities. You are not even attached to the goddess of fortune, who is worshiped by the great demigods like Brahmā, who pray to achieve her mercy.

PURPORT

In *Bhagavad-gītā* it is said that the Lord has no desire to achieve any result from His wonderful activities, nor has He any need to perform them. But still, in order to give an example to people in general, He sometimes acts, and those activities are very wonderful. He is not attached to anything. *Na māṁ karmāṇi limpanti:* although He acts very wonderfully, He is not at all attached to anything (Bg. 4.14). He is self-sufficient. The example is given here that the goddess of fortune, Lakṣmī, is always engaged in the service of the Lord, but still He is not attached to her. Even great demigods like Brahmā worship the goddess of fortune in order to win her favor, but although the Lord is worshiped by many hundreds and thousands of goddesses of fortune, He is not at all attached to any one of them. This distinction concerning the exalted transcendental position of the Lord is specifically mentioned by the great sages; He is not like the ordinary living entity, who is attached to the results of pious activities.

TEXT 35

सिद्धा ऊचुः

अयं त्वत्कथामृष्टपीयूषनद्यां
मनोवारणः क्लेशदावाग्निदग्धः ।
तृषार्तोऽवगाढो न सस्मार दावं
न निष्क्रामति ब्रह्मसम्पन्नवन्नः ॥३५॥

siddhā ūcuḥ
ayaṁ tvat-kathā-mṛṣṭa-pīyūṣa-nadyāṁ
mano-vāraṇaḥ kleśa-dāvāgni-dagdhaḥ
tṛṣārto 'vagāḍho na sasmāra dāvaṁ
na niṣkrāmati brahma-sampannavan naḥ

siddhāḥ—the Siddhas; *ūcuḥ*—prayed; *ayam*—this; *tvat-kathā*—Your pastimes; *mṛṣṭa*—pure; *pīyūṣa*—of nectar; *nadyām*—in the river; *manaḥ*—of the mind; *vāraṇaḥ*—the elephant; *kleśa*—sufferings; *dāva-agni*—by the forest fire; *dagdhaḥ*—burned; *tṛṣā*—thirst; *ārtaḥ*—afflicted; *avagāḍhaḥ*—being immersed; *na sasmāra*—does not remember; *dāvam*—the forest fire or the miseries; *na niṣkrāmati*—not come out; *brahma*—the Absolute; *sampanna-vat*—like having merged; *naḥ*—our.

TRANSLATION

The Siddhas prayed: Like an elephant that has suffered in a forest fire but can forget all its troubles by entering a river, our minds, O Lord, always merge in the nectarean river of Your transcendental pastimes, and they desire never to leave such transcendental bliss, which is as good as the pleasure of merging in the Absolute.

PURPORT

This statement is from the Siddhas, the inhabitants of Siddhaloka, where the eight kinds of material perfection are complete. The residents of Siddhaloka have full control in thc cight kinds of yogic perfection, but from their statement it appears that they are pure devotees. They always merge in the nectarean river of hearing of the pastimes of the Lord. Hearing of the pastimes of the Lord is called *kṛṣṇa-kathā*. Similarly, there is a statement by Prahlāda Mahārāja that those who are always merged in the ocean of the nectar of describing the Lord's pastimes are liberated and have no fear of the material condition of life. The Siddhas say that the mind of an ordinary person is full of anxieties. The example is given of the elephant who has suffered in a forest fire and who enters into a river for relief. If persons who are suffering in the forest fire of this material existence will only enter into the nectarean river of the description of the pastimes of the Lord, they will forget all the troubles of the miserable material existence. The Siddhas do not care for fruitive activities, such as performing sacrifices and achieving the good results. They simply merge in the transcendental discussions of the pastimes of the Lord. That makes them completely happy, without care for pious or impious activities. For those who are always in Kṛṣṇa consciousness there is no need to perform any kind of pious or impious sacrifices or activities. Kṛṣṇa consciousness is itself complete, for it includes all the processes praised in the Vedic scriptures.

TEXT 36

यजमान्युवाच
स्वागतं ते प्रसीदेश तुभ्यं नमः
श्रीनिवास श्रिया कान्तया त्राहि नः ।
त्वामृतेऽधीश नाङ्गैर्मखः शोभते
शीर्षहीनः कबन्धो यथा पुरुषः ॥३६॥

yajamāny uvāca
svāgataṁ te prasīdeśa tubhyaṁ namaḥ
śrīnivāsa śriyā kāntayā trāhi naḥ
tvām ṛte 'dhīśa nāṅgair makhaḥ śobhate
śīrṣa-hīnaḥ ka-bandho yathā puruṣaḥ

yajamānī—the wife of Dakṣa; *uvāca*—prayed; *su-āgatam*—auspicious appearance; *te*—Your; *prasīda*—become pleased; *īśa*—my dear Lord; *tubhyam*—unto You; *namaḥ*—respectful obeisances; *śrīnivāsa*—O abode of the goddess of fortune; *śriyā*—with Lakṣmī; *kāntayā*—Your wife; *trāhi*—protect; *naḥ*—us; *tvām*—You; *ṛte*—without; *adhīśa*—O supreme controller; *na*—not; *aṅgaiḥ*—with bodily limbs;

makhaḥ—the sacrificial arena; *śobhate*—is beautiful; *śīrṣa-hīnaḥ*—without the head; *ka-bandhaḥ*—possessed of only a body; *yathā*—as; *puruṣaḥ*—a person.

TRANSLATION

The wife of Dakṣa prayed as follows: My dear Lord, it is very fortunate that You have appeared in this arena of sacrifice. I offer my respectful obeisances unto You, and I request that You be pleased on this occasion. The sacrificial arena is not beautiful without You, just as a body is not beautiful without the head.

PURPORT

Another name of Lord Viṣṇu is Yajñeśvara. In *Bhagavad-gītā* it is said that all activities should be performed as *viṣṇu-yajña*, for the pleasure of Lord Viṣṇu. Unless we please Him, whatever we do is the cause of our bondage in the material world. This is confirmed herein by the wife of Dakṣa: "Without Your presence, the grandeur of this sacrificial ceremony is useless, just as a body without the head, however decorated it may be, is useless." The comparison is equally applicable to the social body. Material civilization is very proud of being advanced, but it is actually the useless trunk of a body without a head. Without Kṛṣṇa consciousness, without an understanding of Viṣṇu, the Supreme Personality of Godhead, any advancement in a civilization, no matter how sophisticated, is of no value. There is a statement in the *Hari-bhakti-sudhodaya* (3.11):

bhagavad-bhakti-hīnasya
jātiḥ śāstraṁ japas tapaḥ
aprāṇasyaiva dehasya
maṇḍanaṁ loka-rañjanam

The purport is that sometimes when a friend or relative dies, especially among lower class men, the dead body is decorated. Dressed and ornamented, the body is taken in procession. That sort of decoration of the dead body has no actual value because the life force is already gone. Similarly, any aristocracy, any social prestige or any advancement of material civilization without Kṛṣṇa consciousness is as good as the decoration of a dead body. The name of the wife of Dakṣa was Prasūti, and she was the daughter of Svāyambhuva Manu. Her sister, Devahūti, was married to Kardama Muni, and Kapiladeva, the Personality of Godhead, became her son. Prasūti, then, was the aunt of Lord Viṣṇu. She was asking the favor of Lord Viṣṇu in an affectionate mode; since she was His aunt, she sought some special favor. Also significant in this verse is that the Lord is praised with the goddess of fortune. Wherever Lord Viṣṇu is worshiped, naturally there is the favor of the goddess of fortune. Lord Viṣṇu is addressed as *amṛta*, transcendental. The demigods, including Brahmā and Lord Śiva, were produced after the creation, but Lord Viṣṇu existed before the creation. He is addressed, therefore, as *amṛta.* Lord Viṣṇu is worshiped with His internal energy by the Vaiṣṇavas. Prasūti, the wife of Dakṣa, implored the Lord to turn the priests into Vaiṣṇavas instead of simply fruitive workers performing sacrifices for some material benefits.

TEXT 37

लोकपाला ऊचुः
दृष्टः किं नो दृग्भिरसद्ग्रहैस्त्वं
प्रत्यग्द्रष्टा दृश्यते येन विश्वम् ।
माया ह्येषा भवदीया हि भूमन्
यस्त्वं षष्ठः पञ्चभिर्भासि भूतैः ॥३७॥

lokapālā ūcuḥ
dṛṣṭaḥ kiṁ no dṛgbhir asad-grahais tvaṁ
pratyag-draṣṭā dṛśyate yena viśvam
māyā hy eṣā bhavadīyā hi bhūman
yas tvaṁ ṣaṣṭhaḥ pañcabhir bhāsi bhūtaiḥ

loka-pālāḥ—the governors of the different planets; *ūcuḥ*—said; *dṛṣṭaḥ*—seen; *kim*—whether; *naḥ*—by us; *dṛgbhiḥ*—by the material senses; *asat-grahaiḥ*—revealing the cosmic manifestation; *tvam*—You; *pratyak-draṣṭā*—inner witness; *dṛśyate*—is seen; *yena*—by whom; *viśvam*—the universe; *māyā*—material world; *hi*—because; *eṣā*—this; *bhavadīyā*—Your; *hi*—certainly; *bhūman*—O possessor of the universe; *yaḥ*—because; *tvam*—You; *ṣaṣṭhaḥ*—the sixth; *pañcabhiḥ*—with the five; *bhāsi*—appear; *bhūtaiḥ*—with the elements.

TRANSLATION

The governors of various planets spoke as follows: Dear Lord, we believe only in our direct perception, but under the circumstances we do not know whether we have actually seen You with our material senses. By our material senses we can simply perceive the cosmic manifestation, but You are beyond the five elements. You are the sixth. We see You, therefore, as a creation of the material world.

PURPORT

The governors of the various planets are certainly materially opulent and very puffed up. Such persons are unable to understand the transcendental, eternal form of the Lord. In the *Brahma-saṁhitā* it is stated that only persons who have anointed their eyes with love of Godhead can see the Personality of Godhead in every step of their activities. Also, in the prayers of Kuntī (*Bhāg.* 1.8.26) it is stated that only those who are *akiñcana-gocaram*, who are not materially puffed up, can see the Supreme Personality of Godhead; others are bewildered and cannot even think of the Absolute Truth.

TEXT 38

योगेश्वरा ऊचुः

प्रेयान्न तेऽन्योऽस्त्यमुतस्त्वयि प्रभो
विश्वात्मनीक्षेन्न पृथग्य आत्मनः ।
अथापि भक्त्येशतयोपधावता-
मनन्यवृत्त्यानुगृहाण वत्सल ॥३८॥

yogeśvarā ūcuḥ
preyān na te 'nyo 'sty amutas tvayi prabho
viśvātmanīkṣen na pṛthag ya ātmanaḥ
athāpi bhaktyeśa tayopadhāvatām
ananya-vṛttyānugṛhāṇa vatsala

yoga-īśvarāḥ—the great mystics; *ūcuḥ*—said; *preyān*—very dear; *na*—not; *te*—of You; *anyaḥ*—another; *asti*—there is; *amutaḥ*—from that; *tvayi*—in You; *prabho*—dear Lord; *viśva-ātmani*—in the Supersoul of all living entities; *īkṣet*—see; *na*—not; *pṛthak*—different; *yaḥ*—who; *ātmanaḥ*—the living entities; *atha api*—so much more; *bhaktyā*—with devotion; *īśa*—O Lord; *tayā*—with it; *upadhāvatām*—of those who worship; *ananya-vṛttyā*—unfailing; *anugṛhāṇa*—favor; *vatsala*—O favorable Lord.

TRANSLATION

The great mystics said: Dear Lord, persons who see You as nondifferent from themselves, knowing that You are the Supersoul of all living entities, are certainly very, very dear to You. You are very favorable toward those who engage in devotional service, accepting You as the Lord and themselves as the servants. By Your mercy, You are always inclined in their favor.

PURPORT

It is indicated in this verse that the monists and the great mystics know the Supreme Personality of Godhead as one. This oneness is not the misunderstanding that a living entity is equal in every respect to the Supreme Personality of Godhead. This monism is based on pure knowledge as described and confirmed in *Bhagavad-gītā* (7.17): *priyo hi jñānino 'tyartham ahaṁ sa ca mama priyaḥ.* The Lord says that those who are advanced in transcendental knowledge and know the science of Kṛṣṇa consciousness are very dear to Him, and He also is very dear to them. Those who are actually in perfect knowledge of the science of God know that the living entities are superior energy of the Supreme Lord. This is stated in *Bhagavad-gītā*, Seventh Chapter: the material energy is inferior, and the living entities are superior energy. Energy and the energetic are nondifferent; therefore, energies possess the same quality as the energetic. Persons who are in full knowledge of the Personality of Godhead, analyzing His different energies and knowing their own constitutional position, are certainly very, very dear to the Lord. Persons, however, who may not even be conversant with knowledge of the Supreme Personality but who always think of the Lord with love and faith, feeling that He is great and that they are His parts and parcels, ever His servitors, are even more favored by Him. The particular significance of this verse is that the Lord is addressed as *vatsala. Vatsala* means "always favorably disposed." The Lord's name is *bhakta-vatsala.* The Lord is famous as *bhakta-vatsala*, which means that He is always favorably inclined to the devotees, whereas He is never addressed anywhere in the Vedic literature as *jñāni-vatsala.*

TEXT 39

जगदुद्भवस्थितिलयेषु दैवतो
बहुभिद्यमानगुणयात्ममायया ।
रचितात्मभेदमतये स्वसंस्थया
विनिवर्तितभ्रमगुणात्मने नमः ॥३९॥

jagad-udbhava-sthiti-layeṣu daivato
bahu-bhidyamāna-guṇayātma-māyayā
racitātma-bheda-mataye sva-saṁsthayā
vinivartita-bhrama-guṇātmane namaḥ

jagat—the material world; *udbhava*—creation; *sthiti*—maintenance; *layeṣu*—in annihilation; *daivataḥ*—destiny; *bahu*—many; *bhidyamāna*—being variegated; *guṇayā*—by material qualities; *ātma-māyayā*—by His material energy; *racita*—produced; *ātma*—in the living entities; *bheda-mataye*—who produced different inclinations; *sva-saṁsthayā*—by His internal potency; *vinivartita*—caused to stop; *bhrama*—interaction; *guṇa*—of material modes; *ātmane*—unto Him in His personal form; *namaḥ*—obeisances.

TRANSLATION

We offer our respectful obeisances unto the Supreme, who has created varieties of manifestations and put them under the spell of the three qualities of the material world in order to create, maintain and annihilate them. He Himself is not under the control of the external energy; in His personal feature He is completely devoid of the variegated manifestation of material qualities, and He is under no illusion of false identification.

PURPORT

Two situations are described in this verse. One is the creation, maintenance and annihilation of the material world, and the other is the Lord's own establishment. There is also quality in the Lord's own establishment, the kingdom of God. It is stated here that Goloka is His personal situation. There is also quality in Goloka, but that quality is not divided into creation, maintenance and annihilation. In the external energy, the interaction of the three qualities makes it possible for things to be created, maintained and annihilated. But in the spiritual world, or the kingdom of God, there is no such exhibition, since everything is eternal, sentient and blissful. There is a class of philosophers who misunderstand the appearance of the Personality of Godhead within this material world. They are under the impression that when the Supreme Personality of Godhead appears, He is under the spell of the three qualities, like all the other living entities who appear within this material world. That is their misunderstanding; as it is clearly stated here (*sva-saṁsthayā*), by His internal potency He is transcendental to all these material qualities. Similarly, in *Bhagavad-gītā* the Lord says, "I appear by My internal potency." Both the internal and external potencies are under the control of the Supreme, so He does not come under the control of either of these potencies. Rather, everything is under His control. In order to manifest His transcendental name, form, quality, pastimes and paraphernalia, He brings into action His internal energy. On account of the variegatedness of the external potency, there are manifestations of many qualitative demigods, beginning with Brahmā and Lord Śiva, and people are attracted to these demigods according to their own material quality. But when one is transcendental or surpasses the material qualities, he is simply fixed in the worship of the Supreme Personality. This fact is explained in *Bhagavad-gītā:* anyone engaged in the service of the Lord is already transcendental to the variegatedness and interaction of the three material qualities. The summary is that the conditioned souls are being pulled by the action and reaction of the material qualities, which create a differentiation of energies. But in the spiritual world the worshipable one is the Supreme Lord and no one else.

TEXT 40

ब्रह्मोवाच

नमस्ते श्रितसत्त्वाय धर्मादीनां च सूतये ।
निर्गुणाय च यत्काष्ठां नाहं वेदापरेऽपि च ॥४०॥

brahmovāca
namas te śrita-sattvāya
dharmādīnāṁ ca sūtaye
nirguṇāya ca yat-kāṣṭhāṁ
nāhaṁ vedāpare 'pi ca

brahma—the personified *Vedas; uvāca*—said; *namaḥ*—respectful obeisances; *te*—unto You; *śrita-sattvāya*—the shelter of the quality of goodness; *dharma-ādīnām*—of all religion, austerity and penance; *ca*—and; *sūtaye*—the source; *nirguṇāya*—transcendental to material qualities; *ca*—and; *yat*—of whom (of the Supreme Lord); *kāṣṭhām*—the situation; *na*—not; *aham*—I; *veda*—know; *apare*—others; *api*—certainly; *ca*—and.

TRANSLATION

The personified Vedas said: We offer our respectful obeisances unto You, the Lord, the shelter of the quality of goodness and therefore the source of all religion, austerity and penance, for You are transcendental to all material qualities and no one knows You or Your actual situation.

PURPORT

In the material world there is the trinity of the three material qualities. Lord Viṣṇu has accepted the superintendence of the quality of goodness, which is the source of religion, knowledge, austerity, renunciation, opulence, etc. Because of this, actual peace, prosperity, knowledge and religion can be attained when the living entities are under the control of the quality of goodness in the material world. As soon as they are subjected to the control of the other two qualities, namely passion and ignorance, their precarious conditional life becomes intolerable. But Lord Viṣṇu, in His original position, is always *nirguṇa*, which means transcendental to these material qualities. *Guṇa* means "quality," and *nir* means "negation." This does not indicate, however, that He has no qualities; He has transcendental qualities by which He appears and manifests His pastimes. The positive transcendental qualitative manifestation is unknown to the students of the *Vedas* as well as to the great stalwart demigods like Brahmā and Śiva. Actually, the transcendental qualities are manifested only to the devotees. As confirmed in *Bhagavad-gītā*, simply by discharging devotional service one can understand the transcendental position of the Supreme Lord. Those who are in the mode of goodness can partially enter into the transcendental understanding, but it is advised in *Bhagavad-gītā* that one has to surpass this. The Vedic principles are based on the three qualities of the material modes. One has to transcend the three qualities, and then one can be situated in pure and simple spiritual life.

TEXT 41

अग्निरुवाच
यत्तेजसाहं सुसमिद्धतेजा
हव्यं वहे स्वध्वर आज्यसिक्तम् ।
तं यज्ञियं पञ्चविधं च पञ्चभिः
स्विष्टं यजुर्भिः प्रणतोऽस्मि यज्ञम् ॥४१॥

agnir uvāca
yat-tejasāhaṁ susamiddha-tejā
havyaṁ vahe svadhvara ājya-siktam
taṁ yajñiyaṁ pañca-vidhaṁ ca pañcabhiḥ
sviṣṭaṁ yajurbhiḥ praṇato 'smi yajñam

agniḥ—the fire-god; *uvāca*—said; *yat-tejasā*—by whose effulgence; *aham*—I; *su-samiddha-tejāḥ*—as luminous as blazing fire; *havyam*—offerings; *vahe*—I am accepting; *su-adhvare*—in the sacrifice; *ājya-siktam*—mixed with butter; *tam*—that; *yajñiyam*—the protector of the sacrifice; *pañca-vidham*—five; *ca*—and; *pañcabhiḥ*—by five; *su-iṣṭam*—worshiped; *yajurbhiḥ*—Vedic hymns; *praṇataḥ*—offer respectful obeisances; *asmi*—I; *yajñam*—to Yajña (Viṣṇu).

TRANSLATION

The fire-god said: My dear Lord, I offer my respectful obeisances unto You because by Your favor I am as luminous as blazing fire and I accept the offerings mixed with butter and offered in sacrifice. The five kinds of offerings according to the Yajur Veda are all Your different energies, and You are worshiped by five

kinds of Vedic hymns. Sacrifice means Your Supreme Personality of Godhead.

PURPORT

In *Bhagavad-gītā* it is clearly said that *yajña* should be performed for Lord Viṣṇu. Lord Viṣṇu has one thousand popular, transcendental names, out of which one name is Yajña. It is clearly said that everything should be done for the satisfaction of Yajña, or Viṣṇu. All other actions a person may take are only causes for his bondage. Everyone has to perform *yajña* according to the Vedic hymns. As stated in the *Upaniṣads*, fire, the altar, the auspicious full moon, the period of four months called *cāturmāsya*, the sacrificial animal, and the beverage called *soma* are necessary requisites, as are the specific hymns mentioned in the *Vedas* and composed of four letters. One hymn is as follows: *āśrāvayeti catur-akṣaraṁ astu śrauṣaḍ iti catur-akṣaraṁ yajeti dvābhyāṁ ye yajāmahaḥ.* These *mantras*, chanted according to the *śruti* and *smṛti* literatures, are only to please Lord Viṣṇu. For the deliverance of those who are materially conditioned and attached to material enjoyment, performing *yajña* and following the rules and regulations of the four divisions of society and of spiritual life are recommended. It is said in the *Viṣṇu Purāṇa* that by offering sacrifice to Viṣṇu one can gradually be liberated. The whole target of life, therefore, is to please Lord Viṣṇu. That is *yajña.* Any person who is in Kṛṣṇa consciousness has dedicated his life for the satisfaction of Kṛṣṇa, the origin of all Viṣṇu forms, and by offering worship and *prasāda* daily, he becomes the best performer of *yajña.* In the *Śrīmad-Bhāgavatam* it is clearly stated that in this age of Kali the only successful performance of *yajña*, or sacrifice, is *yajñaiḥ saṅkīrtana-prāyaiḥ:* the best type of sacrifice is simply to chant Hare Kṛṣṇa, Hare Kṛṣṇa, Kṛṣṇa Kṛṣṇa, Hare Hare/ Hare Rāma, Hare Rāma, Rāma Rāma, Hare Hare. This *yajña* is offered before the form of Lord Caitanya, as other *yajñas* are offered before the form of Lord Viṣṇu. These recommendations are found in the Eleventh Canto of the *Śrīmad-Bhāgavatam.* Moreover, this *yajña* performance confirms that Lord Caitanya Mahāprabhu is Viṣṇu Himself. As Lord Viṣṇu appeared at the Dakṣa *yajña* long, long ago, Lord Caitanya has appeared in this age to accept our *saṅkīrtana-yajña.*

TEXT 42

देवा ऊचुः
पुरा कल्पापाये स्वकृतमुदरीकृत्य विकृतं
त्वमेवाद्यस्तस्मिन् सलिल उरगेन्द्राधिशयने ।
पुमान् शेषे सिद्धैर्हृदि विमृशिताध्यात्मपदविः
स एवाद्याक्ष्णोर्यः पथि चरसि भृत्यानवसि नः॥४२॥

devā ūcuḥ
purā kalpāpāye sva-kṛtam udarī-kṛtya vikṛtaṁ
tvam evādyas tasmin salila uragendrādhiśayane
pumān śeṣe siddhair hṛdi vimṛśitādhyātma-padaviḥ
sa evādyākṣṇor yaḥ pathi carasi bhṛtyān avasi naḥ

devāḥ—the demigods; *ūcuḥ*—said; *purā*—formerly; *kalpa-apāye*—at the devastation of the *kalpa; sva-kṛtam*—self-produced; *udarī-kṛtya*—having drawn within Your abdomen; *vikṛtam*—effect; *tvam*—You; *eva*—certainly; *ādyaḥ*—original; *tasmin*—in that; *salile*—water; *uraga-indra*—on Śeṣa; *adhiśayane*—on the bed; *pumān*—personality; *śeṣe*—taking rest; *siddhaiḥ*—by the liberated souls (like Sanaka, etc.); *hṛdi*—in the heart; *vimṛśita*—meditated on; *adhyātma-padaviḥ*—the path of philosophical speculation; *saḥ*—He; *eva*—certainly; *adya*—now; *akṣṇoḥ*—of both eyes; *yaḥ*—who; *pathi*—on the path; *carasi*—You move; *bhṛtyān*—servants; *avasi*—protect; *naḥ*—us.

TRANSLATION

The demigods said: Dear Lord, formerly, when there was a devastation, You conserved all the different energies of material manifestation. At that time, all the inhabitants of the higher planets, represented by such liberated souls as Sanaka, were meditating on You by philosophical speculation. You are therefore the original person, and You rest in the water of devastation on the bed of the Śeṣa snake. Now, today, You are visible to us, who are all Your servants. Please give us protection.

PURPORT

The devastation indicated in this verse is the partial devastation of the lower planets within the universe when Lord Brahmā goes to sleep. The higher planetary systems, beginning with Maharloka, Janaloka and Tapoloka, are not inundated at the time of this devastation. The Lord is the creator, as indicated in this verse, because the energies of creation are manifested through His body, and after annihilation, He conserves all the energy within His abdomen.

Another significant point in this verse is that the demigods said, "We are all Your servants (*bhṛtyān*). Give us Your protection." The demigods depend on the protection of Viṣṇu; they are not independent. *Bhagavad-gītā*, therefore, condemns the worship of demigods because there is no need of it and clearly states that only those who have lost their sense go asking favors of the demigods. Generally, if anyone has material desires to be fulfilled, he can ask Viṣṇu instead of going to the demigods. Those who worship demigods are not very intelligent. Besides that, the demigods say, "We are Your eternal servants." So those who are servants, or devotees of the Lord, are not very much concerned with fruitive activities, the performance of the prescribed *yajñas*, or mental speculation. They simply serve the Supreme Personality of Godhead sincerely, with love and faith, performing everything with that loving service, and the Lord gives such devotees direct protection. In *Bhagavad-gītā* Lord Kṛṣṇa says, "Simply surrender unto Me, and I will give you protection from all the reactions of sinful activities." This material world is so created that one has to act sinfully, knowingly or unknowingly, and unless his life is dedicated to Viṣṇu, he has to suffer all the reactions of sinful activities. But one who surrenders and dedicates his life for the service of the Lord has direct protection from the Lord. He has no fear of suffering from sinful activities, nor does he desire, willingly or unwillingly, to do anything which is sinful.

TEXT 43

गन्धर्वा ऊचुः

अंशांशास्ते देव मरीच्यादय एते

ब्रह्मेन्द्राद्या देवगणा रुद्रपुरोगाः ।

क्रीडाभाण्डं विश्वमिदं यस्य विभूमन्
तस्मै नित्यं नाथ नमस्ते करवाम ॥४३॥

gandharvā ūcuḥ
aṁśāṁśās te deva marīcy-ādaya ete
brahmendrādyā deva-gaṇā rudra-purogāḥ
krīḍā-bhāṇḍaṁ viśvam idaṁ yasya vibhūman
tasmai nityaṁ nātha namas te karavāma

gandharvāḥ—the Gandharvas; *ūcuḥ*—said; *aṁśa-aṁśāḥ*—parts and parcels of Your body; *te*—Your; *deva*—dear Lord; *marīci-ādayaḥ*—Marīci and the great sages; *ete*—these; *brahma-indra-ādyāḥ*—headed by Brahmā and Indra; *deva-gaṇāḥ*—the demigods; *rudra-purogāḥ*—having Lord Śiva as the chief; *krīḍā-bhāṇḍam*—a plaything; *viśvam*—the whole creation; *idam*—this; *yasya*—of whom; *vibhūman*—the Supreme Almighty Great; *tasmai*—unto Him; *nityam*—always; *nātha*—O Lord; *namaḥ*—respectful obeisances; *te*—unto You; *karavāma*—we offer.

TRANSLATION

The Gandharvas said: Dear Lord, all the demigods, including Lord Śiva, Lord Brahmā, Indra and Marīci and the great sages, are all only differentiated parts and parcels of Your body. You are the Supreme Almighty Great; the whole creation is just like a plaything for You. We always accept You as the Supreme Personality of Godhead, and we offer our respectful obeisances unto You.

PURPORT

In the *Brahma-saṁhitā* it is said that Kṛṣṇa is the Supreme Personality of Godhead. There may be many gods, from Brahmā, Lord Śiva, Indra and Candra down to the rulers of the lower planetary systems, the presidents, ministers, chairmen and kings. In fact, anyone can think that he is God. That is the false, puffed-up conviction of material life. Actually Viṣṇu is the Supreme Lord, but there is even one above Viṣṇu, for Viṣṇu is also the plenary portion of a part of Kṛṣṇa. In this verse this is referred to by the word *aṁśāṁśāḥ*, which refers to part and parcel of a part and parcel. There are similar verses in the *Caitanya-caritāmṛta* which indicate that the Supreme Lord's parts and parcels again expand into other parts and parcels. As described in *Śrīmad-Bhāgavatam*, there are many manifestations of Viṣṇu and many manifestations of living entities. Viṣṇu manifestations are called *svāṁśa*, partial manifestations, and the living entities are called *vibhinnāṁśa*. The demigods like Brahmā and Indra have been promoted to such exalted positions by pious activities and austerities, but actually Viṣṇu, or Kṛṣṇa, is the master of everyone. In the *Caitanya-caritāmṛta* it is said, *ekale īśvara kṛṣṇa, āra saba bhṛtya*. This means that Kṛṣṇa alone is the Supreme Personality of Godhead, and all others, even the *viṣṇu-tattva* and certainly the living entities, are His servitors. Baladeva is the immediate expansion of Kṛṣṇa. He also engages in the service of Kṛṣṇa, and certainly the ordinary living entities are serving. Everyone is created, constitutionally, for serving Kṛṣṇa. Here the Gandharvas acknowledge that although the demigods may represent themselves as the Supreme, actually they are not supreme. Real supremacy belongs to Kṛṣṇa. *Kṛṣṇas tu bhagavān svayam* is the statement of *Śrīmad-Bhāgavatam:* "Kṛṣṇa is the only Supreme Lord." Worship of Kṛṣṇa alone, therefore, includes worship of all the parts and parcels, just as watering the root of a tree also waters all the branches, twigs, leaves and flowers.

TEXT 44

विद्याधरा ऊचुः

त्वन्माययार्थमभिपद्य कलेवरेऽस्मिन्
कृत्वा ममाहमिति दुर्मतिरुत्पथैः स्वैः ।
क्षिप्तोऽप्यसद्विषयलालस आत्ममोहं
युष्मत्कथामृतनिषेवक उद्व्युदस्येत् ॥४४॥

vidyādharā ūcuḥ
tvan-māyayārtham abhipadya kalevare 'smin
kṛtvā mamāham iti durmatir utpathaiḥ svaiḥ
kṣipto 'py asad-viṣaya-lālasa ātma-mohaṁ
yuṣmat-kathāmṛta-niṣevaka udvyudasyet

vidyādharāḥ—the Vidyādharas; *ūcuḥ*—said; *tvat-māyayā*—by Your external potency; *artham*—the human body; *abhipadya*—after obtaining; *kalevare*—in the body; *asmin*—in this; *kṛtvā*—having misidentified; *mama*—mine; *aham*—I; *iti*—thus; *durmatiḥ*—the ignorant person; *utpathaiḥ*—by wrong roads; *svaiḥ*—by one's own belongings; *kṣiptaḥ*—distracted; *api*—even; *asat*—temporary; *viṣaya-lālasaḥ*—having his happiness in sense objects; *ātma-moham*—the illusion of the body as the self; *yuṣmat*—Your; *kathā*—topics; *amṛta*—nectar; *niṣevakaḥ*—relishing; *ut*—from a long distance; *vyudasyet*—can be delivered.

TRANSLATION

The Vidyādharas said: Dear Lord, this human form of body is meant for attaining the highest perfectional objective, but, impelled by Your external energy, the living entity misidentifies himself with his body and with the material energy, and therefore, influenced by māyā, he wants to become happy by material enjoyment. He is misled and always attracted by temporary, illusory happiness. But Your transcendental activities are so powerful that if one engages in the hearing and chanting of such topics, he can be delivered from illusion.

PURPORT

The human form of life is called *arthada* because the body can very nicely help the embodied soul to achieve the highest perfection. Prahlāda Mahārāja said that even though temporary, the body can give us the highest perfectional achievement. In the process of evolution from the lower to the higher grade of living, the human form of life is a great boon. But *māyā* is so strong that in spite of achieving this great boon of the human form of life, we are influenced by temporary material happiness, and we forget our goal of life. We are attracted by things which will cease to exist. The beginning of such attraction is the temporary body. In this horrible condition of life there is only one way of liberation—to engage in the activities of transcendental chanting and hearing of the holy name of the Supreme Lord: Hare Kṛṣṇa, Hare Kṛṣṇa, Kṛṣṇa Kṛṣṇa, Hare Hare/ Hare Rāma, Hare Rāma, Rāma Rāma, Hare Hare. The words *yuṣmat-kathāmṛta-niṣevakah* mean "those who engage in relishing the nectar of the topics of Your Lordship." There are two narrative books which especially concern the words and activities of Kṛṣṇa. *Bhagavad-gītā* is the instruction given by Kṛṣṇa, and *Śrīmad-Bhāgavatam* is the book containing topics exclusively about Kṛṣṇa and His devotees. These two books are the special nectar of the words of Kṛṣṇa. For those who engage in the preaching of these two Vedic literatures it is very easy to get out of the illusory conditional life imposed upon us by *māyā.* The illusion is that the conditioned soul does not try to understand his spiritual identity. He is more interested in his external body, which is only a flash and which will be finished as soon as the time is designated. The whole atmosphere will change when the living entity has to transmigrate from one body to another. Under the spell of *māyā,* he will again be satisfied in a different atmosphere. This spell of *māyā* is called *āvaraṇātmikā śakti* because it is so strong that the living entity is satisfied in any abominable condition. Even if he is born as a worm living within the intestine or abdomen in the midst of urine and stool, still he is satisfied. This is the covering influence of *māyā.* But the human form of life is a chance to understand, and if one misses this opportunity, he is most unfortunate. The way to get out of illusory *māyā* is to engage in the topics of Kṛṣṇa. Lord Caitanya advocated a process whereby everyone may remain in his present position without change but simply hear from the proper authoritative sources about Kṛṣṇa. Lord Caitanya advised everyone to spread the word of Kṛṣṇa. He advised, "All of you become spiritual masters. Your duty is simply to talk to whomever you meet of Kṛṣṇa or of the instructions given by Kṛṣṇa." The International Society for Krishna Consciousness is operating for this purpose. We do not ask anyone to first change his position and then come to us. Instead, we invite everyone to come with us and simply chant Hare Kṛṣṇa, Hare Kṛṣṇa, Kṛṣṇa Kṛṣṇa, Hare Hare/ Hare Rāma, Hare Rāma, Rāma Rāma, Hare Hare, because we know that if one simply chants and hears the topics of Kṛṣṇa, one's life will change; he will see a new light, and his life will be successful.

TEXT 45

ब्राह्मणा ऊचुः

त्वं क्रतुस्त्वं हविस्त्वं हुताशः स्वयं
त्वं हि मन्त्रः समिद्दर्भपात्राणि च ।
त्वं सदस्यर्त्विजो दम्पती देवता
अग्निहोत्रं स्वधा सोम आज्यं पशुः ॥४५॥

brāhmaṇā ūcuḥ
tvaṁ kratus tvaṁ havis tvaṁ hutāśaḥ svayaṁ
tvaṁ hi mantraḥ samid-darbha-pātrāṇi ca
tvaṁ sadasyartvijo dampatī dcvatā
agnihotraṁ svadhā soma ājyaṁ paśuḥ

brāhmaṇāḥ—the *brāhmaṇas; ūcuḥ*—said; *tvam*—You; *kratuḥ*—sacrifice; *tvam*—You; *haviḥ*—offering of clarified butter; *tvam*—You; *huta-āśaḥ*—fire; *svayam*—personified; *tvam*—You; *hi*—for; *mantraḥ*—the Vedic hymns; *samit-darbha-pātrāṇi*—the fuel, the *kuśa* grass and the sacrificial pots; *ca*—and; *tvam*—You; *sadasya*—the members of the assembly; *ṛtvijaḥ*—the priests; *dampatī*—the chief person of the sacrifice and his wife; *devatā*—demigods; *agni-hotram*—the sacred fire ceremony; *svadhā*—the offering to the forefathers; *somaḥ*—the *soma* plant; *ājyam*—the clarified butter; *paśuḥ*—the sacrificial animal.

TRANSLATION

The brāhmaṇas said: Dear Lord, You are sacrifice personified. You are the offering of clarified butter, You are the fire, You are the chanting of Vedic hymns by which the sacrifice is conducted, You are the fuel, You are the flame, You are the kuśa grass, and You are the sacrificial pots. You are the priests who perform the yajña, You are the demigods headed by Indra, and You are the sacrificial animal. Everything that is sacrificed is You or Your energy.

PURPORT

In this statement Lord Viṣṇu's all-pervasiveness is partially explained. It is said in the *Viṣṇu Purāṇa* that as a fire situated in one place emanates its heat and illumination everywhere, so whatever we see within the material or spiritual worlds is nothing but a manifestation of different energies emanating from the Supreme Personality of Godhead. The *brāhmaṇas'* statement is that Lord Viṣṇu is everything—the fire, the offering, the clarified butter, the utensils, the place of sacrifice and the *kuśa.* He is everything. It is confirmed herein that the performance of *saṅkīrtana-yajña* in this age is as good as all other *yajñas* in all other ages. If one performs *saṅkīrtana-yajña* by chanting Hare Kṛṣṇa, Hare Kṛṣṇa, Kṛṣṇa Kṛṣṇa, Hare Hare/ Hare Rāma, Hare Rāma, Rāma Rāma,

Hare Hare, there is no need to arrange elaborate paraphernalia for the prescribed sacrificial ceremonies recommended in the *Vedas.* In the chant of the holy names, Hare and Kṛṣṇa, *Hare* means the energy of Kṛṣṇa, and *Kṛṣṇa* is the *viṣṇu-tattva.* Combined together they are everything. In this age, persons are harassed by the influence of Kali-yuga and cannot arrange for all the requisite paraphernalia for performing sacrifice as recommended in the *Vedas.* But if one simply chants Hare Kṛṣṇa, it is to be understood that he is performing all kinds of *yajña* because there is nothing within our vision except Hare (the energy of Kṛṣṇa) and Kṛṣṇa. There is no difference between Kṛṣṇa and His energies. Thus since everything is a manifestation of His energy, it is to be understood that everything is Kṛṣṇa. One simply has to accept everything in Kṛṣṇa consciousness, and he is a liberated person. One should not misunderstand that because everything is Kṛṣṇa, Kṛṣṇa has no personal identity. Kṛṣṇa is so full that in spite of keeping Himself separate from everything by His energy, He is everything. This is confirmed in *Bhagavad-gītā,* Ninth Chapter. He is spread throughout the creation as everything, but still He is not everything. The philosophy recommended by Lord Caitanya is that He is simultaneously one and different.

TEXT 46

त्वं पुरा गां रसाया महासूकरो
दंष्ट्रया पद्मिनीं वारणेन्द्रो यथा ।
स्तूयमानो नदल्लीलया योगिभि-
र्व्युज्जहर्थ त्रयीगात्र यज्ञक्रतुः ॥४६॥

tvaṁ purā gāṁ rasāyā mahā-sūkaro
daṁṣṭrayā padminīṁ vāraṇendro yathā
stūyamāno nadal līlayā yogibhir
vyujjahartha trayī-gātra yajña-kratuḥ

tvam—You; *purā*—in the past; *gām*—the earth; *rasāyāḥ*—from within the water; *mahā sūkaraḥ*—the great boar incarnation; *daṁṣṭrayā*—with Your tusk; *padminīm*—a lotus; *vāraṇa-indraḥ*—an elephant; *yathā*—as; *stūyamānaḥ*—being offered prayers; *nadan*—

vibrating; *līlayā*—very easily; *yogibhiḥ*—by great sages like Sanaka, etc.; *vyujjahartha*—picked up; *trayī-gātra*—O personified Vedic knowledge; *yajña-kratuḥ*—having the form of sacrifice.

TRANSLATION

Dear Lord, O personified Vedic knowledge, in the past millennium, long, long ago, when You appeared as the great boar incarnation, You picked up the world from the water, as an elephant picks up a lotus flower from a lake. When You vibrated transcendental sound in that gigantic form of a boar, the sound was accepted as a sacrificial hymn, and great sages like Sanaka meditated upon it and offered prayers for Your glorification.

PURPORT

A significant word used in this verse is *trayī-gātra*, which means that the transcendental form of the Lord is the *Vedas*. Anyone who engages in the worship of the Deity, or the form of the Lord in the temple, is understood to be studying all the *Vedas* twenty-four hours a day. Simply by decorating the Deities of the Lord, Rādhā and Kṛṣṇa, in the temple, one very minutely studies the injunctions of the *Vedas*. Even a neophyte devotee who simply engages in the worship of the Deity is understood to be in direct touch with the purport of Vedic knowledge. As confirmed in *Bhagavad-gītā* (15.15), *vedaiś ca sarvair aham eva vedyaḥ:* the purport of the *Vedas* is to understand Him, Kṛṣṇa. One who worships and serves Kṛṣṇa directly has understood the truths of the *Vedas*.

TEXT 47

स प्रसीद त्वमस्माकमाकाङ्क्षतां
दर्शनं ते परिभ्रष्टसत्कर्मणाम् ।
कीर्त्यमाने नृभिर्नाम्नि यज्ञेश ते
यज्ञविघ्नाः क्षयं यान्ति तस्मै नमः ॥४७॥

sa prasīda tvam asmākam ākāṅkṣatāṁ
darśanaṁ te paribhraṣṭa-sat-karmaṇām

kīrtyamāne nṛbhir nāmni yajñeśa te
yajña-vighnāḥ kṣayaṁ yānti tasmai namaḥ

saḥ—that same person; *prasīda*—be pleased; *tvam*—You; *asmākam*—upon us; *ākāṅkṣatām*—awaiting; *darśanam*—audience; *te*—Your; *paribhraṣṭa*—fallen down; *sat-karmaṇām*—of whom the performance of sacrifice; *kīrtyamāne*—being chanted; *nṛbhiḥ*—by persons; *nāmni*—Your holy name; *yajña-īśa*—O Lord of sacrifice; *te*—Your; *yajña-vighnāḥ*—obstacles; *kṣayam*—destruction; *yānti*—attain; *tasmai*—unto You; *namaḥ*—respectful obeisances.

TRANSLATION

Dear Lord, we were awaiting Your audience because we have been unable to perform the yajñas according to the Vedic rituals. We pray unto You, therefore, to be pleased with us. Simply by chanting Your holy name, one can surpass all obstacles. We offer our respectful obeisances unto You in Your presence.

PURPORT

The *brāhmaṇa* priests were very hopeful that their sacrifice would be carried out without obstacles now that Lord Viṣṇu was present. It is significant in this verse that the *brāhmaṇas* say, "Simply by chanting Your holy name we can surpass the obstacles, but now You are personally present." The performance of *yajña* by Dakṣa was obstructed by the disciples and followers of Lord Śiva. The *brāhmaṇas* indirectly criticized the followers of Lord Śiva, but because the *brāhmaṇas* were always protected by Lord Viṣṇu, Śiva's followers could not do any harm to their prosecution of the sacrificial process. There is a saying that when Kṛṣṇa protects someone, no one can do him harm, and when Kṛṣṇa wants to kill someone, no one can protect him. The vivid example was Rāvaṇa. Rāvaṇa was a great devotee of Lord Śiva, but when Lord Rāmacandra wanted to kill him, Lord Śiva could not protect him. If some demigod, even Lord Śiva or Lord Brahmā, wants to do harm to a devotee, Kṛṣṇa protects the devotee. But when Kṛṣṇa wants to kill someone, such as Rāvaṇa or Hiraṇyakaśipu, no demigod can protect him.

TEXT 48

मैत्रेय उवाच

इति दक्षः कविर्यज्ञं भद्र रुद्राभिमर्शितम् ।
कीर्त्यमाने हृषीकेशे संनिन्ये यज्ञभावने ॥४८॥

maitreya uvāca
iti dakṣaḥ kavir yajñaṁ
bhadra rudrābhimarśitam
kīrtyamāne hṛṣīkeśe
sanninye yajña-bhāvane

maitreyaḥ—Maitreya; *uvāca*—said; *iti*—thus; *dakṣaḥ*—Dakṣa; *kaviḥ*—being purified in consciousness; *yajñam*—the sacrifice; *bhadra*—O Vidura; *rudra-abhimarśitam*—devastated by Vīrabhadra; *kīrtyamāne*—being glorified; *hṛṣīkeśe*—Hṛṣīkeśa (Lord Viṣṇu); *sanninye*—arranged for restarting; *yajña-bhāvane*—the protector of sacrifice.

TRANSLATION

Śrī Maitreya said: After Lord Viṣṇu was glorified by all present, Dakṣa, his consciousness purified, arranged to begin again the yajña which had been devastated by the followers of Lord Śiva.

TEXT 49

भगवान् स्वेन भागेन सर्वात्मा सर्वभागभुक् ।
दक्षं बभाष आभाष्य प्रीयमाण इवानघ ॥४९॥

bhagavān svena bhāgena
sarvātmā sarva-bhāga-bhuk
dakṣaṁ babhāṣa ābhāṣya
prīyamāṇa ivānagha

bhagavān—Lord Viṣṇu; *svena*—with His own; *bhāgena*—with the share; *sarva-ātmā*—the Supersoul of all living entities; *sarva-bhāga-bhuk*—the enjoyer of the results of all sacrifices; *dakṣam*—Dakṣa;

babhāṣe—said; *ābhāṣya*—addressing; *prīyamāṇaḥ*—being satisfied; *iva*—as; *anagha*—O sinless Vidura.

TRANSLATION

Maitreya continued: My dear sinless Vidura, Lord Viṣṇu is actually the enjoyer of the results of all sacrifices. Yet because of His being the Supersoul of all living entities, He was satisfied simply with His share of the sacrificial offerings. He therefore addressed Dakṣa in a pleasing attitude.

PURPORT

In *Bhagavad-gītā* (5.29) it is said, *bhoktāraṁ yajña-tapasām:* Lord Viṣṇu, or Kṛṣṇa, is the supreme enjoyer of all the results of sacrifices, austerities and penances; in whatever one may engage, the ultimate goal is Viṣṇu. If a person does not know that, he is misled. As the Supreme Personality of Godhead, Viṣṇu has nothing to demand from anyone. He is self-satisfied, self-sufficient, but He accepts the offerings of *yajña* because of His friendly attitude toward all living entities. When His share of the sacrificial results was offered to Him, He appeared very pleased. It is said in *Bhagavad-gītā* (9.26), *patraṁ puṣpaṁ phalaṁ toyaṁ yo me bhaktyā prayacchati:* if any devotee offers Him even a small leaf, or a flower or water, if it is offered with love and affection, the Lord accepts it and is pleased. Although He is self-sufficient and does not need anything from anyone, He accepts such offerings because, as Supersoul, He has such a friendly attitude toward all living entities. Another point here is that He does not encroach upon another's share. In the *yajña* there is a share for the demigods, Lord Śiva, and Lord Brahmā, and a share for Lord Viṣṇu. He is satisfied with His own share and does not encroach upon others'. Indirectly, He indicated that He was not satisfied with Dakṣa's trying to deny Lord Śiva his share. Maitreya addressed Vidura as sinless because Vidura was a pure Vaiṣṇava and never committed any offense to any demigod. Although Vaiṣṇavas accept Lord Viṣṇu as the Supreme, they are not prone to offend demigods. They give the demigods proper respect. Vaiṣṇavas accept Lord Śiva as the best Vaiṣṇava. For a Vaiṣṇava there is no possibility of offending any demigods, and the demigods are also pleased with the Vaiṣṇava because they are faultless devotees of Lord Viṣṇu.

TEXT 50

श्रीभगवानुवाच
अहं ब्रह्मा च शर्वश्च जगतः कारणं परम् ।
आत्मेश्वर उपद्रष्टा स्वयंदृगविशेषणः ॥५०॥

śrī-bhagavān uvāca
ahaṁ brahmā ca śarvaś ca
jagataḥ kāraṇaṁ param
ātmeśvara upadraṣṭā
svayan-dṛg aviśeṣaṇaḥ

śrī-bhagavān—Lord Viṣṇu; *uvāca*—said; *aham*—I; *brahmā*—Brahmā; *ca*—and; *śarvaḥ*—Lord Śiva; *ca*—and; *jagataḥ*—of the material manifestation; *kāraṇam*—cause; *param*—supreme; *ātma-īśvaraḥ*—the Supersoul; *upadraṣṭā*—the witness; *svayam-dṛk*—self-sufficient; *aviśeṣaṇaḥ*—there is no difference.

TRANSLATION

Lord Viṣṇu replied: Brahmā, Lord Śiva and I are the supreme cause of the material manifestation. I am the Supersoul, the self-sufficient witness. But impersonally there is no difference between Brahmā, Lord Śiva and Me.

PURPORT

Lord Brahmā was born out of the transcendental body of Lord Viṣṇu, and Lord Śiva was born out of the body of Brahmā. Lord Viṣṇu, therefore, is the supreme cause. In the *Vedas* also it is stated that in the beginning there was only Viṣṇu, Nārāyaṇa; there was no Brahmā or Śiva. Similarly, Śaṅkarācārya confirmed this: *nārāyaṇaḥ paraḥ.* Nārāyaṇa, or Lord Viṣṇu, is the origin, and Brahmā and Śiva are manifested after creation. Lord Viṣṇu is also *ātmeśvara*, the Supersoul in everyone. Under His direction, everything is prompted from within. For example, in the beginning of the *Śrīmad-Bhāgavatam* it is stated, *tene brahma hṛdā:* He first educated Lord Brahmā from within.

In *Bhagavad-gītā* (10.2) Lord Kṛṣṇa states, *aham ādir hi devānām:* Lord Viṣṇu, or Kṛṣṇa, is the origin of all demigods, including Lord

Brahmā and Lord Śiva. In another place in *Bhagavad-gītā* (10.8) Kṛṣṇa states, *ahaṁ sarvasya prabhavaḥ:* "Everything is generated from Me." This includes all the demigods. Similarly, in the *Vedānta-sūtra: janmādy asya yataḥ*. And in the *Upaniṣads* is the statement *yato vā imāni bhūtāni jāyante*. Everything is generated from Lord Viṣṇu, everything is maintained by Him, and everything is annihilated by His energy. Therefore, by their actions and reactions, the energies which come from Him create the cosmic manifestations and also dissolve the whole creation. Thus the Lord is the cause and also the effect. Whatever effect we see is the interaction of His energy, and because the energy is generated from Him, He is both cause and effect. Simultaneously, everything is different and the same. It is said that everything is Brahman: *sarvaṁ khalv idaṁ brahma*. In the highest vision, nothing is beyond Brahman, and therefore Lord Brahmā and Lord Śiva are certainly nondifferent from Him.

TEXT 51

आत्ममायां समाविश्य सोऽहं गुणमयीं द्विज ।
सृजन् रक्षन् हरन् विश्वं दध्रे संज्ञां क्रियोचिताम् ॥५१॥

ātma-māyāṁ samāviśya
so 'haṁ guṇamayīṁ dvija
sṛjan rakṣan haran viśvaṁ
dadhre saṁjñāṁ kriyocitām

ātma-māyām—My energy; *samāviśya*—having entered; *saḥ*—Myself; *aham*—I; *guṇa-mayīm*—composed of the modes of material nature; *dvi-ja*—O twice-born Dakṣa; *sṛjan*—creating; *rakṣan*—maintaining; *haran*—annihilating; *viśvam*—the cosmic manifestation; *dadhre*—I cause to be born; *saṁjñām*—a name; *kriyā-ucitām*—according to the activity.

TRANSLATION

The Lord continued: My dear Dakṣa Dvija, I am the original Personality of Godhead, but in order to create, maintain and annihilate this cosmic manifestation, I act through My material energy, and according to the different grades of activity, My representations are differently named.

PURPORT

As explained in *Bhagavad-gītā* (7.5), *jīva-bhūtāṁ mahā-bāho:* the whole world is energy released from the supreme source, the Personality of Godhead, who, it is further stated in *Bhagavad-gītā*, acts in superior energies and inferior energies. The superior energy is the living entity, who is part and parcel of the Supreme Lord. As parts and parcels, the living entities are not different from the Supreme Lord; the energy emanated from Him is not different from Him. But in the actual activity of this material world, the living entity is under the different qualities of material energy and in different forms. There are 8,400,000 life forms. The same living entity acts under the influence of the different qualities of material nature. The entities have different bodies, but originally, in the beginning of creation, Lord Viṣṇu is alone. For the purpose of creation, Brahmā is manifested, and for annihilation there is Lord Śiva. As far as the spiritual entrance into the material world is concerned, all beings are part and parcel of the Supreme Lord, but under the covering of different material qualities they have different names. Lord Brahmā and Lord Śiva are qualitative incarnations of Viṣṇu, as *guṇa-avatāras*, and Viṣṇu with them accepts control of the quality of goodness; therefore He is also a qualitative incarnation like Lord Śiva and Lord Brahmā. Actually the different names exist for different directions, otherwise the origin is one only.

TEXT 52

तस्मिन् ब्रह्मण्यद्वितीये केवले परमात्मनि ।
ब्रह्मरुद्रौ च भूतानि भेदेनाज्ञोऽनुपश्यति ॥५२॥

tasmin brahmaṇy advitīye
kevale paramātmani
brahma-rudrau ca bhūtāni
bhedenājño 'nupaśyati

tasmin—Him; *brahmaṇi*—the Supreme Brahman; *advitīye*—without a second; *kevale*—being one; *parama-ātmani*—the Supersoul; *brahma-rudrau*—both Brahmā and Śiva; *ca*—and; *bhūtāni*—the living entities; *bhedena*—with separation; *ajñaḥ*—one who is not properly conversant; *anupaśyati*—thinks.

TRANSLATION

The Lord continued: One who is not in proper knowledge thinks that demigods like Brahmā and Śiva are independent, or he even thinks that the living entities are independent.

PURPORT

The living entities, including Brahmā, are not independently separated, but are counted within the marginal potency of the Supreme Lord. The Supreme Lord, being the Supersoul in every living entity, including Lord Brahmā and Lord Śiva, is directing everyone in the activities of the material modes of nature. No one can act independently of the sanction of the Lord, and therefore, indirectly, no one is different from the Supreme Person—certainly not Brahmā and Rudra, who are incarnations of the material nature's modes of passion and ignorance.

TEXT 53

यथा पुमान्न स्वाङ्गेषु शिरःपाण्यादिषु क्वचित् ।
पारक्यबुद्धिं कुरुते एवं भूतेषु मत्परः ॥५३॥

yathā pumān na svāṅgeṣu
śiraḥ-pāṇy-ādiṣu kvacit
pārakya-buddhiṁ kurute
evaṁ bhūteṣu mat-paraḥ

yathā—as; *pumān*—a person; *na*—not; *sva-aṅgeṣu*—in his own body; *śiraḥ-pāṇi-ādiṣu*—between the head and the hands and other parts of the body; *kvacit*—sometimes; *pārakya-buddhim*—differentiation; *kurute*—make; *evam*—thus; *bhūteṣu*—among living entities; *mat-paraḥ*—My devotee.

TRANSLATION

A person with average intelligence does not think the head and other parts of the body to be separate. Similarly, My devotee does not differentiate Viṣṇu, the all-pervading Personality of Godhead, from any thing or any living entity.

PURPORT

Whenever there is disease in any part of the body, the whole body takes care of the ailing part. Similarly, a devotee's oneness is manifested in His compassion for all conditioned souls. *Bhagavad-gītā* (5.18) says, *paṇḍitāḥ sama-darśinaḥ:* those who are learned see everyone's conditional life equally. Devotees are compassionate to every conditioned soul, and therefore they are known as *apārakya-buddhi.* Because devotees are learned and know that every living entity is part and parcel of the Supreme Lord, they preach Kṛṣṇa consciousness to everyone so that everyone may be happy. If a particular part of the body is diseased, the whole attention of the body goes to that part. Similarly, devotees care for any person who is forgetful of Kṛṣṇa and therefore in material consciousness. The equal vision of the devotee is that he works to get all living entities back home, back to Godhead.

TEXT 54

त्रयाणामेकभावानां यो न पश्यति वै भिदाम् ।
सर्वभूतात्मनां ब्रह्मन् स शान्तिमधिगच्छति ॥५४॥

trayāṇām eka-bhāvānāṁ
yo na paśyati vai bhidām
sarva-bhūtātmanāṁ brahman
sa śāntim adhigacchati

trayāṇām—of the three; *eka-bhāvānām*—having one nature; *yaḥ*—who; *na paśyati*—does not see; *vai*—certainly; *bhidām*—separateness; *sarva-bhūta-ātmanām*—of the Supersoul of all living entities; *brahman*—O Dakṣa; *saḥ*—he; *śāntim*—peace; *adhigacchati*—realizes.

TRANSLATION

The Lord continued: One who does not consider Brahmā, Viṣṇu, Śiva or the living entities in general to be separate from the Supreme, and who knows Brahman, actually realizes peace; others do not.

PURPORT

Two words are very significant in this verse. *Trayāṇām* indicates "three," namely Lord Brahmā, Lord Śiva and Lord Viṣṇu. *Bhidām* means "different." They are three, and therefore they are separate, but at the same time they are one. This is the philosophy of simultaneous oneness and difference, which is called *acintya-bhedābheda-tattva*. The example given in the *Brahma-saṁhitā* is that milk and yogurt are simultaneously one and different; both are milk, but the yogurt has become changed. In order to achieve real peace, one should see everything and every living entity, including Lord Brahmā and Lord Śiva, as non-different from the Supreme Personality of Godhead. No one is independent. Every one of us is an expansion of the Supreme Personality of Godhead. This accounts for unity in diversity. There are diverse manifestations, but, at the same time, they are one in Viṣṇu. Everything is an expansion of Viṣṇu's energy.

TEXT 55

मैत्रेय उवाच
एवं भगवतादिष्टः प्रजापतिपतिर्हरिम् ।
अर्चित्वा क्रतुना स्वेन देवानुभयतोऽयजत् ॥५५॥

maitreya uvāca
evaṁ bhagavatādiṣṭaḥ
prajāpati-patir harim
arcitvā kratunā svena
devān ubhayato 'yajat

maitreyaḥ—Maitreya; *uvāca*—said; *evam*—thus; *bhagavatā*—by the Supreme Personality of Godhead; *ādiṣṭaḥ*—having been instructed; *prajāpati-patiḥ*—the head of all the Prajāpatis; *harim*—Hari; *arcitvā*—after worshiping; *kratunā*—with the sacrificial ceremonies; *svena*—his own; *devān*—the demigods; *ubhayataḥ*—separately; *ayajat*—worshiped.

TRANSLATION

The sage Maitreya said: Thus Dakṣa, the head of all Prajāpatis, having been nicely instructed by the Supreme Personality of God-

head, worshiped Lord Viṣṇu. After worshiping Him by performing the prescribed sacrificial ceremonies, Dakṣa separately worshiped Lord Brahmā and Lord Śiva.

PURPORT

Lord Viṣṇu should be offered everything, and His *prasāda* should be distributed to all the demigods. This practice is still followed in the temple of Jagannātha at Purī. There are many temples of demigods around the main temple of Jagannātha, and the *prasāda* which is offered first to Jagannātha is distributed to all the demigods. The deity of Bhagālin is worshiped with the *prasāda* of Viṣṇu, and also, in the famous Lord Śiva temple of Bhuvaneśvara, the *prasāda* of Lord Viṣṇu or Lord Jagannātha is offered to the deity of Lord Śiva. This is the Vaiṣṇava principle. The Vaiṣṇava does not deride even ordinary living entities, including the small ant; everyone is offered proper respect according to his position. The offering, however, is in relation to the center, the Supreme Personality of Godhead, Kṛṣṇa, or Viṣṇu. The devotee who is highly elevated sees the relationship to Kṛṣṇa in everything; he does not see anything as being independent of Kṛṣṇa. That is his vision of oneness.

TEXT 56

रुद्रं च स्वेन भागेन ह्युपाधावत्समाहितः ।
कर्मणोदवसानेन सोमपानितरानपि ।
उदवस्य सहर्त्विग्भिः सस्नाववभृथं ततः ॥५६॥

rudraṁ ca svena bhāgena
hy upādhāvat samāhitaḥ
karmaṇodavasānena
somapān itarān api
udavasya sahartvigbhiḥ
sasnāv avabhṛthaṁ tataḥ

rudram—Lord Śiva; *ca*—and; *svena*—with his own; *bhāgena*—share; *hi*—since; *upādhāvat*—he worshiped; *samāhitaḥ*—with concentrated mind; *karmaṇā*—by the performance; *udavasānena*—by the act of finishing; *soma-pān*—demigods; *itarān*—other; *api*—even;

udavasya—after finishing; *saha*—along with; *ṛtvigbhiḥ*—with the priests; *sasnau*—bathed; *avabhṛtham*—the *avabhṛtha* bath; *tataḥ*—then.

TRANSLATION

With all respect, Dakṣa worshiped Lord Śiva with his share of the remnants of the yajña. After finishing the ritualistic sacrificial activities, he satisfied all the other demigods and the other people assembled there. Then, after finishing all these duties with the priests, he took a bath and was fully satisfied.

PURPORT

Lord Rudra, Śiva, was properly worshiped with his share of the remnants of the *yajña.* Yajña is Viṣṇu, and whatever *prasāda* is offered to Viṣṇu is offered to everyone, even to Lord Śiva. Śrīdhara Svāmī also comments in this connection, *svena bhāgena:* the remnants of the *yajña* are offered to all the demigods and others.

TEXT 57

तस्मा अप्यनुभावेन स्वेनैवावाप्तराधसे ।
धर्म एव मतिं दत्त्वा त्रिदशास्ते दिवं ययुः ॥५७॥

tasmā apy anubhāvena
svenaivāvāpta-rādhase
dharma eva matiṁ dattvā
tridaśās te divaṁ yayuḥ

tasmai—unto him (Dakṣa); *api*—even; *anubhāvena*—by worshiping the Supreme Lord; *svena*—by his own; *eva*—certainly; *avāpta-rādhase*—having attained perfection; *dharme*—in religion; *eva*—certainly; *matim*—intelligence; *dattvā*—having given; *tridaśāḥ*—demigods; *te*—those; *divam*—to the heavenly planets; *yayuḥ*—went.

TRANSLATION

Thus worshiping the Supreme Lord Viṣṇu by the ritualistic performance of sacrifice, Dakṣa was completely situated on the

religious path. Moreover, all the demigods who had assembled at the sacrifice blessed him that he might increase his piety, and then they left.

PURPORT

Although Dakṣa was considerably advanced in religious principles, he awaited the blessings of the demigods. Thus the great sacrifice conducted by Dakṣa ended in harmony and peace.

TEXT 58

एवं दाक्षायणी हित्वा सती पूर्वकलेवरम् ।
जज्ञे हिमवतः क्षेत्रे मेनायामिति शुश्रुम ॥५८॥

evaṁ dākṣāyaṇī hitvā
satī pūrva-kalevaram
jajñe himavataḥ kṣetre
menāyām iti śuśruma

evam—thus; *dākṣāyaṇī*—the daughter of Dakṣa; *hitvā*—after giving up; *satī*—Satī; *pūrva-kalevaram*—her former body; *jajñe*—was born; *himavataḥ*—of the Himalayas; *kṣetre*—in the wife; *menāyām*—in Menā; *iti*—thus; *śuśruma*—I have heard.

TRANSLATION

Maitreya said: I have heard that after giving up the body she had received from Dakṣa, Dākṣāyaṇī (his daughter) took her birth in the kingdom of the Himalayas. She was born as the daughter of Menā. I heard this from authoritative sources.

PURPORT

Menā is also known as Menakā and is the wife of the king of the Himalayas.

TEXT 59

तमेव दयितं भूय आवृङ्क्ते पतिमम्बिका ।
अनन्यभावैकगतिं शक्तिः सुप्तेव पूरुषम् ॥५९॥

tam eva dayitaṁ bhūya
āvṛṅkte patim ambikā
ananya-bhāvaika-gatiṁ
śaktiḥ supteva pūruṣam

tam—him (Lord Śiva); *eva*—certainly; *dayitam*—beloved; *bhūyaḥ*—again; *āvṛṅkte*—accepted; *patim*—as her husband; *ambikā*—Ambikā, or Satī; *ananya-bhāvā*—without attachment for others; *eka-gatim*—the one goal; *śaktiḥ*—the feminine (marginal and external) energies; *suptā*—lying dormant; *iva*—as; *pūruṣam*—the masculine (Lord Śiva, as representative of the Supreme Lord).

TRANSLATION

Ambikā [goddess Durgā], who was known as Dākṣāyiṇī [Satī], again accepted Lord Śiva as her husband, just as different energies of the Supreme Personality of Godhead act during the course of a new creation.

PURPORT

According to a verse of the Vedic *mantras, parāsya śaktir vividhaiva śrūyate:* the Supreme Personality of Godhead has different varieties of energies. *Śakti* is feminine, and the Lord is *puruṣa*, masculine. It is the duty of the female to serve under the supreme *puruṣa.* As stated in *Bhagavad-gītā*, all living entities are marginal energies of the Supreme Lord. Therefore it is the duty of all living entities to serve this Supreme Person. Durgā is the representation in the material world of both the marginal and external energies, and Lord Śiva is the representation of the Supreme Person. The connection of Lord Śiva and Ambikā, or Durgā, is eternal. Satī could not accept any husband but Lord Śiva. How Lord Śiva remarried Durgā as Himavatī, the daughter of the Himalayas, and how Kārttikeya was born, is a great story in itself.

TEXT 60

एतद्भगवतः शम्भोः कर्म दक्षाध्वरद्रुहः ।
श्रुतं भागवताच्छिष्यादुद्धवान्मे बृहस्पतेः ॥६०॥

etad bhagavataḥ śambhoḥ
karma dakṣādhvara-druhaḥ
śrutaṁ bhāgavatāc chiṣyād
uddhavān me bṛhaspateḥ

etat—this; *bhagavataḥ*—of the possessor of all opulences; *śambhoḥ*—of Śambhu (Lord Śiva); *karma*—story; *dakṣa-adhvara-druhaḥ*—who devastated the sacrifice of Dakṣa; *śrutam*—was heard; *bhāgavatāt*—from a great devotee; *śiṣyāt*—from the disciple; *uddhavāt*—from Uddhava; *me*—by me; *bṛhaspateḥ*—of Bṛhaspati.

TRANSLATION

Maitreya said: My dear Vidura, I heard this story of the Dakṣa yajña, which was devastated by Lord Śiva, from Uddhava, a great devotee and a disciple of Bṛhaspati.

TEXT 61

इदं पवित्रं परमीशचेष्टितं
यशस्यमायुष्यमघौघमर्षणम् ।
यो नित्यदाकर्ण्य नरोऽनुकीर्तयेद्
धुनोत्यघं कौरव भक्तिभावतः ॥६१॥

idaṁ pavitraṁ param īśa-ceṣṭitaṁ
yaśasyam āyuṣyam aghaugha-marṣaṇam
yo nityadākarṇya naro 'nukīrtayed
dhunoty aghaṁ kaurava bhakti-bhāvataḥ

idam—this; *pavitram*—pure; *param*—supreme; *īśa-ceṣṭitam*—pastime of the Supreme Lord; *yaśasyam*—fame; *āyuṣyam*—long duration of life; *agha-ogha-marṣaṇam*—destroying sins; *yaḥ*—who; *nityadā*—always; *ākarṇya*—after hearing; *naraḥ*—a person; *anukīrtayet*—should narrate; *dhunoti*—clears off; *agham*—material contamination; *kaurava*—O descendant of Kuru; *bhakti-bhāvataḥ*—with faith and devotion.

TRANSLATION

The great sage Maitreya concluded: If one hears and again narrates, with faith and devotion, this story of the Dakṣa yajña as it was conducted by the Supreme Personality of Godhead, Viṣṇu, then certainly one is cleared of all contamination of material existence, O son of Kuru.

Thus end the Bhaktivedanta purports of the Fourth Canto, Seventh Chapter, of the Śrīmad-Bhāgavatam, *entitled "The Sacrifice Performed by Dakṣa."*

CHAPTER EIGHT

Dhruva Mahārāja Leaves Home for the Forest

TEXT 1

मैत्रेय उवाच
सनकाद्या नारदश्च ऋभुर्हंसोऽरुणिर्यतिः ।
नैते गृहान् ब्रह्मसुता ह्यावसन्नूर्ध्वरेतसः ॥ १ ॥

maitreya uvāca
sanakādyā nāradaś ca
ṛbhur haṁso 'ruṇir yatiḥ
naite gṛhān brahma-sutā
hy āvasann ūrdhva-retasaḥ

maitreyaḥ uvāca—Maitreya said; *sanaka-ādyāḥ*—those headed by Sanaka; *nāradaḥ*—Nārada; *ca*—and; *ṛbhuḥ*—Ṛbhu; *haṁsaḥ*—Haṁsa; *aruṇiḥ*—Aruṇi; *yatiḥ*—Yati; *na*—not; *ete*—all these; *gṛhān*—at home; *brahma-sutāḥ*—sons of Brahmā; *hi*—certainly; *āvasan*—did live; *ūrdhva-retasaḥ*—unadulterated celibates.

TRANSLATION

The great sage Maitreya said: The four great Kumāra sages headed by Sanaka, as well as Nārada, Ṛbhu, Haṁsa, Aruṇi and Yati, all sons of Brahmā, did not live at home, but became ūrdhva-retā, or naiṣṭhika-brahmacārīs, unadulterated celibates.

PURPORT

The system of *brahmacarya* has been current since the birth of Brahmā. A section of the population, especially male, did not marry at all. Instead of allowing their semen to be driven downwards, they used to lift the semen up to the brain. They are called *ūrdhva-retasaḥ*, those who lift up. Semen is so important that if, by the yogic process, one can lift the semen up to the brain, he can perform wonderful work—one's memory is enabled to act very swiftly, and the duration of life is increased. *Yogīs* can thus perform all kinds of austerity with steadiness and be elevated to the highest perfectional stage, even to the spiritual world. Vivid examples of *brahmacārīs* who accepted this principle of life are the four sages Sanaka, Sanandana, Sanātana and Sanat-kumāra, as well as Nārada and others.

Another significant phrase here is *naite gṛhān hy āvasan*, "they did not live at home." *Gṛha* means "home" as well as "wife." In fact, "home" means wife; "home" does not mean a room or a house. One who lives with a wife lives at home, otherwise a *sannyāsī* or *brahmacārī*, even though he may live in a room or in a house, does not live at home. That they did not live at home means that they did not accept a wife, and so there was no question of their discharging semen. Semen is meant to be discharged when one has a home, a wife and the intention to beget children, otherwise there is no injunction for discharging semen. These principles were followed from the beginning of creation, and such *brahmacārīs* never created progeny. This narration has dealt with the descendants of Lord Brahmā from Manu's daughter Prasūti. Prasūti's daughter was Dākṣāyaṇī, or Satī, in relation to whom the story of the Dakṣa *yajña* was narrated. Maitreya is now explaining about the progeny of the sons of Brahmā. Out of the many sons of Brahmā, the *brahmacārī* sons headed by Sanaka and Nārada did not marry at all, and therefore there is no question of narrating the history of their descendants.

TEXT 2

मृषाधर्मस्य भार्यासीद्दम्भं मायां च शत्रुहन् ।
असूत मिथुनं तत्तु निर्ऋतिर्जगृहेऽप्रजः ॥ २ ॥

mṛṣādharmasya bhāryāsīd
dambhaṁ māyāṁ ca śatru-han
asūta mithunaṁ tat tu
nirṛtir jagṛhe 'prajaḥ

mṛṣā—Mṛṣā; *adharmasya*—of Irreligion; *bhāryā*—wife; *āsīt*—was; *dambham*—Bluffing; *māyām*—Cheating; *ca*—and; *śatru-han*—O slayer of enemies; *asūta*—produced; *mithunam*—combination; *tat*—that; *tu*—but; *nirṛtiḥ*—Nirṛti; *jagṛhe*—took; *aprajaḥ*—being childless.

TRANSLATION

Another son of Lord Brahmā was Irreligion, whose wife's name was Falsity. From their combination were born two demons named Dambha, or Bluffing, and Māyā, or Cheating. These two demons were taken by a demon named Nirṛti, who had no children.

PURPORT

It is understood herein that Adharma, Irreligion, was also a son of Brahmā, and he married his sister Mṛṣā. This is the beginning of sex life between brother and sister. This unnatural combination of sex life can be possible in human society only where there is Adharma, or Irreligion. It is understood that in the beginning of creation Brahmā created not only saintly sons like Sanaka, Sanātana and Nārada but also demonic offspring like Nirṛti, Adharma, Dambha and Falsity. Everything was created by Brahmā in the beginning. Regarding Nārada, it is understood that because his previous life was very pious and his association very good, he was born as Nārada. Others were also born in their own capacities, according to their backgrounds. The law of *karma* continues birth after birth, and when there is a new creation, the same *karma* comes back with the living entities. They are born in different capacities according to *karma* even though their father is originally Brahmā, who is the exalted qualitative incarnation of the Supreme Personality of Godhead.

TEXT 3

तयोः समभवल्लोभो निकृतिश्च महामते ।
ताभ्यां क्रोधश्च हिंसा च यद्दुरुक्तिः स्वसा कलिः ॥३॥

tayoḥ samabhaval lobho
nikṛtiś ca mahā-mate
tābhyāṁ krodhaś ca hiṁsā ca
yad duruktiḥ svasā kaliḥ

tayoḥ—those two; *samabhavat*—were born; *lobhaḥ*—Greed; *nikṛtiḥ*—Cunning; *ca*—and; *mahā-mate*—O great soul; *tābhyām*—from both of them; *krodhaḥ*—Anger; *ca*—and; *hiṁsā*—Envy; *ca*—and; *yat*—from both of whom; *duruktiḥ*—Harsh Speech; *svasā*—sister; *kaliḥ*—Kali.

TRANSLATION

Maitreya told Vidura: O great soul, from Dambha and Māyā were born Greed and Nikṛti, or Cunning. From their combination came children named Krodha (Anger) and Hiṁsā (Envy), and from their combination were born Kali and his sister Durukti (Harsh Speech).

TEXT 4

दुरुक्तौ कलिराधत्त भयं मृत्युं च सत्तम ।
तयोश्च मिथुनं जज्ञे यातना निरयस्तथा ॥ ४ ॥

duruktau kalir ādhatta
bhayaṁ mṛtyuṁ ca sattama
tayoś ca mithunaṁ jajñe
yātanā nirayas tathā

duruktau—in Durukti; *kaliḥ*—Kali; *ādhatta*—produced; *bhayam*—Fearfulness; *mṛtyum*—Death; *ca*—and; *sat-tama*—O greatest of all good men; *tayoḥ*—of those two; *ca*—and; *mithunam*—by combination; *jajñe*—were produced; *yātanā*—Excessive Pain; *nirayaḥ*—Hell; *tathā*—as well.

TRANSLATION

O greatest of all good men, by the combination of Kali and Harsh Speech were born children named Mṛtyu (Death) and Bhīti (Fear). From the combination of Mṛtyu and Bhīti came children named Yātanā (Excessive Pain) and Niraya (Hell).

TEXT 5

संग्रहेण मयाख्यातः प्रतिसर्गस्तवानघ ।
त्रिःश्रुत्वैतत्पुमान् पुण्यं विधुनोत्यात्मनो मलम् ॥५॥

saṅgraheṇa mayākhyātaḥ
pratisargas tavānagha
triḥ śrutvaitat pumān puṇyaṁ
vidhunoty ātmano malam

saṅgraheṇa—in summary; *mayā*—by me; *ākhyātaḥ*—is explained; *pratisargaḥ*—cause of devastation; *tava*—your; *anagha*—O pure one; *triḥ*—three times; *śrutvā*—having heard; *etat*—this description; *pumān*—one who; *puṇyam*—piety; *vidhunoti*—washes off; *ātmanaḥ*—of the soul; *malam*—contamination.

TRANSLATION

My dear Vidura, I have summarily explained the causes of devastation. One who hears this description three times attains piety and washes the sinful contamination from his soul.

PURPORT

The creation takes place on the basis of goodness, but devastation takes place because of irreligion. That is the way of material creation and devastation. Here it is stated that the cause of devastation is Adharma, or Irreligion. The descendants of Irreligion and Falsity, born one after another, are Bluffing, Cheating, Greed, Cunning, Anger, Envy, Quarrel, Harsh Speech, Death, Fear, Severe Pain and Hell. All these descendants are described as signs of devastation. If a person is pious and hears about these causes of devastation, he will feel hatred for all these, and that will cause his advancement in a life of piety. Piety refers to the process of cleansing the heart. As recommended by Lord Caitanya, one has to cleanse the dust from the mirror of the mind, and then advancement on the path of liberation begins. Here also the same process is recommended. *Malam* means "contamination." We should learn to despise all the causes of devastation, beginning from irreligion and cheating, and then we shall be able to make advancement in a life of piety. The possibility of our attaining Kṛṣṇa consciousness will be easier, and we shall not be subjected to repeated devastation. The present life is repeated birth and death, but if we seek the path of liberation, we may be saved from repeated suffering.

TEXT 6

अथातः कीर्तये वंशं पुण्यकीर्तेः कुरूद्वह ।
स्वायम्भुवस्यापि मनोर्हरेरंशांशजन्मनः ॥ ६ ॥

athātaḥ kīrtaye vaṁśaṁ
puṇya-kīrteḥ kurūdvaha
svāyambhuvasyāpi manor
harer aṁśāṁśa-janmanaḥ

atha—now; *ataḥ*—hereafter; *kīrtaye*—I shall describe; *vaṁśam*—dynasty; *puṇya-kīrteḥ*—celebrated for virtuous activities; *kuru-udvaha*—O best of the Kurus; *svāyambhuvasya*—of Svāyambhuva; *api*—even; *manoḥ*—of the Manu; *hareḥ*—of the Personality of Godhead; *aṁśa*—plenary expansion; *aṁśa*—part of; *janmanaḥ*—born of.

TRANSLATION

Maitreya continued: O best of the Kuru dynasty, I shall now describe before you the descendants of Svāyambhuva Manu, who was born of a part of a plenary expansion of the Supreme Personality of Godhead.

PURPORT

Lord Brahmā is a powerful expansion of the Supreme Personality of Godhead. Although Brahmā is *jīva-tattva,* he is empowered by the Lord, and therefore he is considered a plenary expansion of the Supreme Godhead. Sometimes it happens that when there is no suitable living being to be empowered to act as Brahmā, the Supreme Lord Himself appears as Brahmā. Brahmā is the plenary expansion of the Supreme Personality of Godhead, and Svāyambhuva Manu was the direct son of Brahmā. The great sage Maitreya is now going to explain about the descendants of this Manu, all of whom are widely celebrated for their pious activities. Before speaking of these pious descendants, Maitreya has already described the descendants of impious activities, representing anger, envy, unpalatable speech, quarrel, fear and death. Purposely, therefore, he is next relating the history of the life of Dhruva Mahārāja, the most pious king within this universe.

TEXT 7

प्रियव्रतोत्तानपादौ शतरूपापतेः सुतौ ।
वासुदेवस्य कलया रक्षायां जगतः स्थितौ ॥ ७ ॥

priyavratottānapādau
śatarūpā-pateḥ sutau
vāsudevasya kalayā
rakṣāyāṁ jagataḥ sthitau

priyavrata—Priyavrata; *uttānapādau*—Uttānapāda; *śatarūpā-pateḥ*—of Queen Śatarūpā and her husband, Manu; *sutau*—the two sons; *vāsudevasya*—of the Supreme Personality of Godhead; *kalayā*—by plenary expansion; *rakṣāyām*—for the protection; *jagataḥ*—of the world; *sthitau*—for the maintenance.

TRANSLATION

Svāyambhuva Manu had two sons by his wife, Śatarūpā, and the names of the sons were Uttānapāda and Priyavrata. Because both of them were descendants of a plenary expansion of Vāsudeva, the Supreme Personality of Godhead, they were very competent to rule the universe to maintain and protect the citizens.

PURPORT

It is said that these two kings, Uttānapāda and Priyavrata, were specifically empowered by the Supreme Personality of Godhead, unlike the great King Ṛṣabha, who was the Supreme Personality of Godhead Himself.

TEXT 8

जाये उत्तानपादस्य सुनीतिः सुरुचिस्तयोः ।
सुरुचिः प्रेयसी पत्युर्नेतरा यत्सुतो ध्रुवः ॥ ८ ॥

jāye uttānapādasya
sunītiḥ surucis tayoḥ
suruciḥ preyasī patyur
netarā yat-suto dhruvaḥ

jāye—of the two wives; *uttānapādasya*—of King Uttānapāda; *sunītiḥ*—Sunīti; *suruciḥ*—Suruci; *tayoḥ*—of both of them; *suruciḥ*—Suruci; *preyasī*—very dear; *patyuḥ*—of the husband; *na itarā*—not the other; *yat*—whose; *sutaḥ*—son; *dhruvaḥ*—Dhruva.

TRANSLATION

King Uttānapāda had two queens, named Sunīti and Suruci. Suruci was much more dear to the King; Sunīti, who had a son named Dhruva, was not his favorite.

PURPORT

The great sage Maitreya wanted to describe the pious activities of the kings. Priyavrata was the first son of Svāyambhuva Manu, and Uttānapāda was the second, but the great sage Maitreya immediately began to speak of Dhruva Mahārāja, the son of Uttānapāda, because Maitreya was very eager to describe pious activities. The incidents in the life of Dhruva Mahārāja are very attractive for devotees. From his pious actions, one can learn how one can detach himself from material possessions and how one can enhance one's devotional service by severe austerities and penances. By hearing the activities of pious Dhruva, one can enhance one's faith in God and can directly connect with the Supreme Personality of Godhead, and thus one can very soon be elevated to the transcendental platform of devotional service. The example of Dhruva Mahārāja's austerities can immediately generate a feeling of devotional service in the hearts of the hearers.

TEXT 9

एकदा सुरुचेः पुत्रमङ्कमारोप्य लालयन् ।
उत्तमं नारुरुक्षन्तं ध्रुवं राजाभ्यनन्दत ॥ ९ ॥

ekadā suruceḥ putram
aṅkam āropya lālayan
uttamaṁ nārurukṣantaṁ
dhruvaṁ rājābhyanandata

ekadā—once upon a time; *suruceḥ*—of Queen Suruci; *putram*—the son; *aṅkam*—on the lap; *āropya*—placing; *lālayan*—while patting; *ut-*

tamam—Uttama; *na*—did not; *āruruksantam*—trying to get on; *dhruvam*—Dhruva; *rājā*—the King; *abhyanandata*—welcome.

TRANSLATION

Once upon a time, King Uttānapāda was patting the son of Suruci, Uttama, placing him on his lap. Dhruva Mahārāja was also trying to get on the King's lap, but the King did not very much welcome him.

TEXT 10

तथा चिकीर्षमाणं तं सपत्न्यास्तनयं ध्रुवम् ।
सुरुचिः शृण्वतो राज्ञः सेर्ष्यमाहातिगर्विता ॥१०॥

tathā cikīrṣamāṇaṁ taṁ
sapatnyās tanayaṁ dhruvam
suruciḥ śṛṇvato rājñaḥ
serṣyam āhātigarvitā

tathā—thus; *cikīrṣamāṇam*—the child Dhruva, who was trying to get up; *tam*—unto him; *sa-patnyāḥ*—of her co-wife (Sunīti); *tanayam*—son; *dhruvam*—Dhruva; *suruciḥ*—Queen Suruci; *śṛṇvataḥ*—while hearing; *rājñaḥ*—of the King; *sa-īrṣyam*—with envy; *āha*—said; *ati-garvitā*—being too proud.

TRANSLATION

While the child, Dhruva Mahārāja, was trying to get on the lap of his father, Suruci, his stepmother, became very envious of the child, and with great pride she began to speak so as to be heard by the King himself.

PURPORT

The King, of course, was equally affectionate toward both his sons, Uttama and Dhruva, so he had a natural inclination to take Dhruva, as well as Uttama, on his lap. But because of his favoritism towards his queen Suruci, he could not welcome Dhruva Mahārāja, despite his feelings. King Uttānapāda's feeling was understood by Suruci, and therefore with great pride she began to speak about the King's affection for her. This is the nature of woman. If a woman understands that her husband regards her as a favorite and is especially affectionate to her, she takes undue advantage. These symptoms are visible even in such an elevated society as the family of Svāyambhuva Manu. Therefore it is concluded that the feminine nature of woman is present everywhere.

TEXT 11

न वत्स नृपतेर्धिष्ण्यं भवानारोढुमर्हति ।
न गृहीतो मया यत्त्वं कुक्षावपि नृपात्मजः ॥११॥

na vatsa nṛpater dhiṣṇyaṁ
bhavān āroḍhum arhati
na gṛhīto mayā yat tvaṁ
kukṣāv api nṛpātmajaḥ

na—not; *vatsa*—my dear child; *nṛpateḥ*—of the King; *dhiṣṇyam*—seat; *bhavān*—yourself; *āroḍhum*—to get on; *arhati*—deserve; *na*—not; *gṛhītaḥ*—taken; *mayā*—by me; *yat*—because; *tvam*—you; *kukṣau*—in the womb; *api*—although; *nṛpa-ātmajaḥ*—son of the King.

TRANSLATION

Queen Suruci told Dhruva Mahārāja: My dear child, you do not deserve to sit on the throne or on the lap of the King. Surely you are also the son of the King, but because you did not take your birth from my womb, you are not qualified to sit on your father's lap.

PURPORT

Queen Suruci very proudly informed Dhruva Mahārāja that to be the King's son was not the qualification for sitting on the lap or throne of the King. Rather, this privilege was dependent on one's having taken birth from her womb. In other words, she indirectly informed Dhruva Mahārāja that although he happened to be born of the King, he was considered an illegitimate son because of his birth from the womb of the other queen.

TEXT 12

बालोऽसि बत नात्मानमन्यस्त्रीगर्भसम्भृतम् ।
नूनं वेद भवान् यस्य दुर्लभेऽर्थे मनोरथः ॥१२॥

bālo 'si bata nātmānam
anya-strī-garbha-sambhṛtam
nūnaṁ veda bhavān yasya
durlabhe 'rthe manorathaḥ

bālaḥ—child; *asi*—you are; *bata*—however; *na*—not; *ātmānam*—my own; *anya*—other; *strī*—woman; *garbha*—womb; *sambhṛtam*—born by; *nūnam*—however; *veda*—just try to know; *bhavān*—yourself; *yasya*—of which; *durlabhe*—unapproachable; *arthe*—matter; *manaḥ-rathaḥ*—desirous.

TRANSLATION

My dear child, you are unaware that you were born not of my womb but of another woman. Therefore you should know that your attempt is doomed to failure. You are trying to fulfill a desire which is impossible to fulfill.

PURPORT

The small child, Dhruva Mahārāja, was naturally affectionate toward his father, and he did not know that there was a distinction between his two mothers. This distinction was pointed out by Queen Suruci, who informed him that since he was a child he did not understand the distinction between the two queens. This is another statement of Queen Suruci's pride.

TEXT 13

तपसाराध्य पुरुषं तस्यैवानुग्रहेण मे ।
गर्भे त्वं साधयात्मानं यदीच्छसि नृपासनम् ॥१३॥

tapasārādhya puruṣaṁ
tasyaivānugraheṇa me

garbhe tvaṁ sādhayātmānaṁ
yadīcchasi nṛpāsanam

tapasā—by austerities; *ārādhya*—having satisfied; *puruṣam*—the Supreme Personality of Godhead; *tasya*—by His; *eva*—only; *anugraheṇa*—by the mercy of; *me*—my; *garbhe*—in the womb; *tvam*—you; *sādhaya*—place; *ātmānam*—yourself; *yadi*—if; *icchasi*—you desire; *nṛpa-āsanam*—on the throne of the King.

TRANSLATION

If you at all desire to rise to the throne of the King, then you have to undergo severe austerities. First of all you must satisfy the Supreme Personality of Godhead, Nārāyaṇa, and then, when you are favored by Him because of such worship, you shall have to take your next birth from my womb.

PURPORT

Suruci was so envious of Dhruva Mahārāja that she indirectly asked him to change his body. According to her, first of all he had to die, then take his next body in her womb, and only then would it be possible for Dhruva Mahārāja to ascend the throne of his father.

TEXT 14

मैत्रेय उवाच
मातुः सपत्न्याः स दुरुक्तिविद्धः
श्वसन् रुषा दण्डहतो यथाहिः ।
हित्वा मिषन्तं पितरं सन्नवाचं
जगाम मातुः प्ररुदन् सकाशम् ॥१४॥

maitreya uvāca
mātuḥ sapatnyāḥ sa durukti-viddhaḥ
śvasan ruṣā daṇḍa-hato yathāhiḥ
hitvā miṣantaṁ pitaraṁ sanna-vācaṁ
jagāma mātuḥ prarudan sakāśam

maitreyaḥ uvāca—the great sage Maitreya said; *mātuḥ*—of his mother; *sa-patnyāḥ*—of the co-wife; *saḥ*—he; *durukti*—harsh words; *viddhaḥ*—being pierced by; *śvasan*—breathing very heavily; *ruṣā*—out of anger; *daṇḍa-hataḥ*—struck by a stick; *yathā*—as much as; *ahiḥ*—a snake; *hitvā*—giving up; *miṣantam*—simply looking over; *pitaram*—his father; *sanna-vācam*—silently; *jagāma*—went; *mātuḥ*—to his mother; *prarudan*—weeping; *sakāśam*—near.

TRANSLATION

The sage Maitreya continued: My dear Vidura, as a snake, when struck by a stick, breathes very heavily, Dhruva Mahārāja, having been struck by the strong words of his stepmother, began to breathe very heavily because of great anger. When he saw that his father was silent and did not protest, he immediately left the palace and went to his mother.

TEXT 15

तं निःश्वसन्तं स्फुरिताधरोष्ठं
सुनीतिरुत्सङ्ग उदूह्य बालम् ।
निशम्य तत्पौरमुखान्नितान्तं
सा विव्यथे यद्गदितं सपत्न्या ॥१५॥

taṁ niḥśvasantaṁ sphuritādharoṣṭhaṁ
sunītir utsaṅga udūhya bālam
niśamya tat-paura-mukhān nitāntaṁ
sā vivyathe yad gaditaṁ sapatnyā

tam—him; *niḥśvasantam*—heavily breathing; *sphurita*—trembling; *adhara-oṣṭham*—upper and lower lips; *sunītiḥ*—Queen Sunīti; *utsaṅge*—on her lap; *udūhya*—lifting; *bālam*—her son; *niśamya*—after hearing; *tat-paura-mukhāt*—from the mouths of other inhabitants; *nitāntam*—all descriptions; *sā*—she; *vivyathe*—became aggrieved; *yat*—that which; *gaditam*—spoken; *sa-patnyā*—by her co-wife.

TRANSLATION

When Dhruva Mahārāja reached his mother, his lips were trembling in anger, and he was crying very grievously. Queen Sunīti

immediately lifted her son onto her lap, while the palace residents who had heard all the harsh words of Suruci related everything in detail. Thus Sunīti also became greatly aggrieved.

TEXT 16

सोत्सृज्य धैर्यं विललाप शोक-
दावाग्निना दावलतेव बाला ।
वाक्यं सपत्न्याः स्मरती सरोज-
श्रिया दृशा बाष्पकलामुवाह ॥१६॥

sotsṛjya dhairyaṁ vilalāpa śoka-
dāvāgninā dāva-lateva bālā
vākyaṁ sapatnyāḥ smaratī saroja-
śriyā dṛśā bāṣpa-kalām uvāha

sā—she; *utsṛjya*—giving up; *dhairyam*—patience; *vilalāpa*—lamented; *śoka-dāva-agninā*—by the fire of grief; *dāva-latā iva*—like burnt leaves; *bālā*—the woman; *vākyam*—words; *sa-patnyāḥ*—spoken by her co-wife; *smaratī*—remember; *saroja-śriyā*—a face as beautiful as a lotus; *dṛśā*—by looking; *bāṣpa-kalām*—weeping; *uvāha*—said.

TRANSLATION

This incident was unbearable to Sunīti's patience. She began to burn as if in a forest fire, and in her grief she became just like a burnt leaf and so lamented. As she remembered the words of her co-wife, her bright, lotuslike face filled with tears, and thus she spoke.

PURPORT

When a man is aggrieved, he feels exactly like a burnt leaf in a forest fire. Sunīti's position was like that. Although her face was as beautiful as a lotus flower, it dried up because of the burning fire caused by the harsh words of her co-wife.

TEXT 17

दीर्घं श्वसन्ती वृजिनस्य पार-
मपश्यती बालकमाह बाला ।

मामङ्गलं तात परेषु मंस्था
भुङ्क्ते जनो यत्परदुःखदस्तत् ॥१७॥

dīrghaṁ śvasantī vṛjinasya pāram
apaśyatī bālakam āha bālā
māmaṅgalaṁ tāta pareṣu maṁsthā
bhuṅkte jano yat para-duḥkhadas tat

dīrgham—heavy; *śvasantī*—breathing; *vṛjinasya*—of the danger; *pāram*—limitation; *apaśyatī*—without finding; *bālakam*—to her son; *āha*—said; *bālā*—the lady; *mā*—let there not be; *amaṅgalam*—ill fortune; *tāta*—my dear son; *pareṣu*—unto others; *maṁsthāḥ*—desire; *bhuṅkte*—suffered; *janaḥ*—person; *yat*—that which; *para-duḥkha-daḥ*—who is apt to inflict pains upon others; *tat*—that.

TRANSLATION

She also was breathing very heavily, and she did not know the factual remedy for the painful situation. Not finding any remedy, she said to her son: My dear son, don't wish for anything inauspicious for others. Anyone who inflicts pains upon others suffers himself from that pain.

TEXT 18

सत्यं सुरुच्याभिहितं भवान्मे
यद् दुर्भगाया उदरे गृहीतः ।
स्तन्येन वृद्धश्च विलज्जते यां
भार्येति वा वोढुमिडस्पतिर्माम् ॥१८॥

satyaṁ surucyābhihitaṁ bhavān me
yad durbhagāyā udare gṛhītaḥ
stanyena vṛddhaś ca vilajjate yāṁ
bhāryeti vā voḍhum iḍaspatir mām

satyam—truth; *surucyā*—by Queen Suruci; *abhihitam*—narrated; *bhavān*—unto you; *me*—of me; *yat*—because; *durbhagāyāḥ*—of the unfortunate; *udare*—in the womb; *gṛhītaḥ*—taken birth; *stanyena*—

fed by the breast milk; *vṛddhaḥ ca*—grown up; *vilajjate*—becomes ashamed; *yām*—unto one; *bhāryā*—wife; *iti*—thus; *vā*—or; *voḍhum*—to accept; *iḍaḥ-patiḥ*—the King; *mām*—me.

TRANSLATION

Sunīti said: My dear boy, whatever has been spoken by Suruci is so, because the King, your father, does not consider me his wife or even his maidservant. He feels ashamed to accept me. Therefore it is a fact that you have taken birth from the womb of an unfortunate woman, and by being fed from her breast you have grown up.

TEXT 19

आतिष्ठ तत्तात विमत्सरस्त्व-
मुक्तं समात्रापि यदव्यलीकम् ।
आराधयाधोक्षजपादपद्मं
यदीच्छसेऽध्यासनमुत्तमो यथा ॥१९॥

ātiṣṭha tat tāta vimatsaras tvam
uktaṁ samātrāpi yad avyalīkam
ārādhayādhokṣaja-pāda-padmaṁ
yadīcchase 'dhyāsanam uttamo yathā

ātiṣṭha—just execute; *tat*—that; *tāta*—my dear son; *vimatsaraḥ*—without being envious; *tvam*—unto you; *uktam*—said; *samātrā api*—by your stepmother; *yat*—whatever; *avyalīkam*—they are all factual; *ārādhaya*—just begin worshiping; *adhokṣaja*—the Transcendence; *pāda-padmam*—lotus feet; *yadi*—if; *icchase*—desire; *adhyāsanam*—to be seated along with; *uttamaḥ*—your stepbrother; *yathā*—as much as.

TRANSLATION

My dear boy, whatever has been spoken by Suruci, your stepmother, although very harsh to hear, is factual. Therefore, if you desire at all to sit on the same throne as your stepbrother, Uttama, then give up your envious attitude and immediately try to execute the instructions of your stepmother. Without further delay, you

must engage yourself in worshiping the lotus feet of the Supreme Personality of Godhead.

PURPORT

The harsh words used by Suruci to her stepson were true because unless one is favored by the Supreme Personality of Godhead one cannot achieve any success in life. Man proposes, God disposes. Sunīti, the mother of Dhruva Mahārāja, agreed with her co-wife's advice that Dhruva engage himself in the worship of the Supreme Personality of Godhead. Indirectly, the words of Suruci were a benediction for Dhruva Mahārāja, for because of the influence of his stepmother's words, he became a great devotee.

TEXT 20

यस्याङ्घ्रिपद्मं परिचर्य विश्व-
विभावनायात्तगुणाभिपत्तेः ।
अजोऽध्यतिष्ठत्खलु पारमेष्ठ्यं
पदं जितात्मश्वसनाभिवन्द्यम् ॥२०॥

yasyāṅghri-padmaṁ paricarya viśva-
vibhāvanāyātta-guṇābhipatteḥ
ajo 'dhyatiṣṭhat khalu pārameṣṭhyaṁ
padaṁ jitātma-śvasanābhivandyam

yasya—whose; *aṅghri*—leg; *padmam*—lotus feet; *paricarya*—worshiping; *viśva*—universe; *vibhāvanāya*—for creating; *ātta*—received; *guṇa-abhipatteḥ*—for acquiring the required qualifications; *ajaḥ*—the unborn (Lord Brahmā); *adhyatiṣṭhat*—became situated; *khalu*—undoubtedly; *pārameṣṭhyam*—the supreme position within the universe; *padam*—position; *jita-ātma*—one who has conquered his mind; *śvasana*—by controlling the life air; *abhivandyam*—worshipable.

TRANSLATION

Sunīti continued: The Supreme Personality of Godhead is so great that simply by worshiping His lotus feet, your great-grandfather, Lord Brahmā, acquired the necessary qualifications

to create this universe. Although he is unborn and is the chief of all living creatures, he is situated in that exalted post because of the mercy of the Supreme Personality of Godhead, whom even great yogīs worship by controlling the mind and regulating the life air [prāṇa].

PURPORT

Sunīti cited the example of Lord Brahmā, who was Dhruva Mahārāja's great-grandfather. Although Lord Brahmā is also a living being, by his penance and austerity he acquired the exalted position of creator of this universe by the mercy of the Supreme Lord. To become successful in any attempt, one not only has to undergo severe penances and austerities, but also must be dependent on the mercy of the Supreme Personality of Godhead. This indication had been given to Dhruva Mahārāja by his stepmother and was now confirmed by his own mother, Sunīti.

TEXT 21

तथा मनुर्वो भगवान् पितामहो
यमेकमत्या पुरुदक्षिणैर्मखैः ।
इष्ट्वाभिपेदे दुरवापमन्यतो
भौमं सुखं दिव्यमथापवर्ग्यम् ॥२१॥

tathā manur vo bhagavān pitāmaho
yam eka-matyā puru-dakṣiṇair makhaiḥ
iṣṭvābhipede duravāpam anyato
bhaumaṁ sukhaṁ divyam athāpavargyam

tathā—similarly; *manuḥ*—Svāyambhuva Manu; *vaḥ*—your; *bhagavān*—worshipable; *pitāmahaḥ*—grandfather; *yam*—unto whom; *eka-matyā*—with unflinching devotion; *puru*—great; *dakṣiṇaiḥ*—charity; *makhaiḥ*—by executing sacrifices; *iṣṭvā*—worshiping; *abhipede*—achieved; *duravāpam*—difficult to achieve; *anyataḥ*—by any other means; *bhaumam*—material; *sukham*—happiness; *divyam*—celestial; *atha*—thereafter; *āpavargyam*—liberation.

TRANSLATION

Sunīti informed her son: Your grandfather Svāyambhuva Manu executed great sacrifices with distribution of charity, and thereby, with unflinching faith and devotion, he worshiped and satisfied the Supreme Personality of Godhead. By acting in that way, he achieved the greatest success in material happiness and afterwards achieved liberation, which is impossible to obtain by worshiping the demigods.

PURPORT

The success of one's life is measured by one's material happiness in this life and liberation in the next. Such success can be achieved only by the grace of the Supreme Personality of Godhead. The words *eka-matyā* mean concentrating one's mind on the Lord without deviation. This process of undeviating worship of the Supreme Lord is also expressed in *Bhagavad-gītā* as *ananya-bhāk.* "That which is impossible to obtain from any other source" is also mentioned here. "Other source" refers to worship of the demigods. It is especially stressed here that the opulence of Manu was due to his undeviating faithfulness in the transcendental service of the Lord. One who diverts his mind to worshiping many demigods to obtain material happiness is considered bereft of intelligence. If anyone wants even material happiness, he can worship the Supreme Lord without deviation, and persons who are desirous of liberation can also worship the Supreme Lord and achieve their goal of life.

TEXT 22

तमेव वत्साश्रय भृत्यवत्सलं
मुमुक्षुभिर्मृग्यपदाब्जपद्धतिम् ।
अनन्यभावे निजधर्मभाविते
मनस्यवस्थाप्य भजस्व पूरुषम् ॥२२॥

tam eva vatsāśraya bhṛtya-vatsalaṁ
mumukṣubhir mṛgya-padābja-paddhatim
ananya-bhāve nija-dharma-bhāvite
manasy avasthāpya bhajasva pūruṣam

tam—Him; *eva*—also; *vatsa*—my dear boy; *āśraya*—take shelter; *bhṛtya-vatsalam*—of the Supreme Personality of Godhead, who is very kind to His devotees; *mumukṣubhiḥ*—also by persons desiring liberation; *mṛgya*—to be sought; *pada-abja*—lotus feet; *paddhatim*—system; *ananya-bhāve*—in an unflinching situation; *nija-dharma-bhāvite*—being situated in one's original constitutional position; *manasi*—unto the mind; *avasthāpya*—placing; *bhajasva*—go on executing devotional service; *pūruṣam*—the Supreme Person.

TRANSLATION

My dear boy, you also should take shelter of the Supreme Personality of Godhead, who is very kind to His devotees. Persons seeking liberation from the cycle of birth and death always take shelter of the lotus feet of the Lord in devotional service. Becoming purified by executing your allotted occupation, just situate the Supreme Personality of Godhead in your heart, and without deviating for a moment, engage always in His service.

PURPORT

The system of *bhakti-yoga* described by Queen Sunīti to her son is the standard way of God realization. Everyone can continue in his constitutional occupational duties and at the same time keep the Supreme Personality of Godhead within his heart. This was also instructed by the Lord Himself to Arjuna in *Bhagavad-gītā:* "Go on fighting, but keep Me within your mind." That should be the motto of every honest person seeking perfection in Kṛṣṇa consciousness. In this connection, Queen Sunīti advised her son that the Supreme Personality of Godhead is known as *bhṛtya-vatsala,* which indicates that He is very kind to His devotees. She said, "You came to me crying, having been insulted by your stepmother, but I am unable to do any good for you. But Kṛṣṇa is so kind to His devotees that if you go to Him, then the combined kindness of millions of mothers like me will be surpassed by His affectionate and tender dealings. When everyone else fails to mitigate one's misery, Kṛṣṇa is able to help the devotee." Queen Sunīti also stressed that the process of approaching the Supreme Personality of Godhead is not easy, but is sought after by great sages who are very advanced in spiritual realization. Queen Sunīti also indicated by her instruction that Dhruva Mahārāja was only a small child, five years old, and it was not possible for him to purify himself by the way of *karma-kāṇḍa.* But by the process of *bhakti-yoga,* even a child less than five years old, or anyone of any age, can be purified. That is the special significance of *bhakti-yoga.* Therefore she advised him not to accept worship of the demigods or any other process, but simply to take to the Supreme Personality of Godhead, and the result would be all perfection. As soon as one places the Supreme Personality of Godhead within one's heart, everything becomes easy and successful.

TEXT 23

नान्यं ततः पद्मपलाशलोचनाद्
दुःखच्छिदं ते मृगयामि कंचन ।
यो मृग्यते हस्तगृहीतपद्मया
श्रियेतरैरङ्ग विमृग्यमाणया ॥२३॥

nānyaṁ tataḥ padma-palāśa-locanād
duḥkha-cchidaṁ te mṛgayāmi kañcana
yo mṛgyate hasta-gṛhīta-padmayā
śriyetarair aṅga vimṛgyamāṇayā

na anyam—no others; *tataḥ*—therefore; *padma-palāśa-locanāt*—from the lotus-eyed Supreme Personality of Godhead; *duḥkha-chidam*—one who can mitigate others' difficulties; *te*—your; *mṛgayāmi*—I am searching after; *kañcana*—anyone else; *yaḥ*—who; *mṛgyate*—searches; *hasta-gṛhīta-padmayā*—taking a lotus flower in the hand; *śriyā*—the goddess of fortune; *itaraiḥ*—by others; *aṅga*—my dear boy; *vimṛgyamāṇayā*—one who is worshiped.

TRANSLATION

My dear Dhruva, as far as I am concerned, I do not find anyone who can mitigate your distress but the Supreme Personality of Godhead, whose eyes are like lotus petals. Many demigods such as Lord Brahmā seek the pleasure of the goddess of fortune, but the goddess of fortune herself, with a lotus flower in her hand, is always ready to render service to the Supreme Lord.

PURPORT

Sunīti pointed out herewith that the benediction received from the Supreme Personality of Godhead and that received from the demigods are not on an equal level. Foolish persons say that no matter whom one worships one will get the same result, but actually that is not a fact. In *Bhagavad-gītā* it is also said that benedictions received from the demigods are all temporary and are meant for the less intelligent. In other words, because the demigods are all materialistically conditioned souls, although they are situated in very exalted positions, their benedictions cannot be permanent. Permanent benediction is spiritual benediction, since a spirit soul is eternal. It is also said in *Bhagavad-gītā* that only persons who have lost their intelligence go to worship the demigods. Therefore Sunīti told her son that he should not seek the mercy of the demigods, but should directly approach the Supreme Personality of Godhead to mitigate his misery.

Material opulences are controlled by the Supreme Personality of Godhead through His different potencies and specifically the goddess of fortune. Therefore, those who are after material opulences seek the pleasure or mercy of the goddess of fortune. Even the highly placed demigods worship the goddess of fortune, but the goddess of fortune, Mahā-Lakṣmī herself, is always seeking the pleasure of the Supreme Personality of Godhead. Anyone, therefore, who takes to the worship of the Supreme Lord automatically receives the blessings of the goddess of fortune. At this stage of his life, Dhruva Mahārāja was seeking material opulences, and his mother advised rightly that even for material opulences it is better to worship not the demigods but the Supreme Lord.

Although a pure devotee does not seek benedictions from the Supreme Lord for material advancement, it is stated in *Bhagavad-gītā* that pious persons go to the Lord even for material benedictions. A person who goes to the Supreme Personality of Godhead for material gain is gradually purified in association with the Supreme Lord. Thus he becomes free from all material desires and is elevated to the platform of spiritual life. Unless one is raised to the spiritual platform, it is not possible for him to completely transcend all material contamination.

Sunīti, the mother of Dhruva, was a farseeing woman, and therefore she advised her son to worship the Supreme Lord and no one else. The

Lord is described herein as lotus eyed (*padma-palāśa-locanāt*). When a person is fatigued, if he sees a lotus flower all his fatigue can be immediately reduced to nil. Similarly, when an aggrieved person sees the lotus face of the Supreme Personality of Godhead, immediately all his grief is reduced. A lotus flower is also an insignia in the hand of Lord Viṣṇu as well as in the hand of the goddess of fortune. The worshipers of the goddess of fortune and Lord Viṣṇu together are certainly very opulent in all respects, even in material life. The Lord is sometimes described as *śiva-viriñci-nutam*, which means that Lord Śiva and Lord Brahmā also offer their respectful obeisances unto the lotus feet of the Supreme Personality of Godhead, Nārāyaṇa.

TEXT 24

मैत्रेय उवाच

एवं संजल्पितं मातुराकर्ण्यार्थागमं वचः ।
संनियम्यात्मनात्मानं निश्चक्राम पितुः पुरात् ॥२४॥

maitreya uvāca
evaṁ sañjalpitaṁ mātur
ākarṇyārthāgamaṁ vacaḥ
sanniyamyātmanātmānaṁ
niścakrāma pituḥ purāt

maitreyaḥ uvāca—the great sage Maitreya said; *evam*—thus; *sañjalpitam*—spoken together; *mātuḥ*—from the mother; *ākarṇya*—hearing; *artha-āgamam*—purposeful; *vacaḥ*—words; *sanniyamya*—controlling; *ātmanā*—by the mind; *ātmānam*—own self; *niścakrāma*—got out; *pituḥ*—of the father; *purāt*—from the house.

TRANSLATION

The great sage Maitreya continued: The instruction of Dhruva Mahārāja's mother, Sunīti, was actually meant for fulfilling his desired objective. Therefore, after deliberate consideration and with intelligence and fixed determination, he left his father's house.

PURPORT

Both the mother and the son were lamenting Dhruva Mahārāja's having been insulted by his stepmother and his father's not having taken any step on this issue. But mere lamentation is useless—one should find out the means to mitigate one's lamentation. Thus both mother and son decided to take shelter of the lotus feet of the Lord because that is the only solution to all material problems. It is indicated in this connection that Dhruva Mahārāja left his father's capital city to go to a secluded place to search out the Supreme Personality of Godhead. It is the instruction of Prahlāda Mahārāja also that if one is seeking peace of mind he should free himself from all contamination of family life and take shelter of the Supreme Godhead by going to the forest. To the Gauḍīya Vaiṣṇava this forest is the forest of Vṛndā, or Vṛndāvana. If one takes shelter of Vṛndāvana under Vṛndāvaneśvarī, Śrīmatī Rādhārāṇī, certainly all the problems of his life are solved very easily.

TEXT 25

नारदस्तदुपाकर्ण्य ज्ञात्वा तस्य चिकीर्षितम् ।
स्पृष्ट्वा मूर्धन्यघघ्नेन पाणिना प्राह विस्मितः ॥२५॥

nāradas tad upākarṇya
jñātvā tasya cikīrṣitam
spṛṣṭvā mūrdhany agha-ghnena
pāṇinā prāha vismitaḥ

nāradaḥ—the great sage Nārada; *tat*—that; *upākarṇya*—overhearing; *jñātvā*—and knowing; *tasya*—his (Dhruva Mahārāja's); *cikīrṣitam*—activities; *spṛṣṭvā*—by touching; *mūrdhani*—on the head; *agha-ghnena*—which can drive away all sinful activities; *pāṇinā*—by the hand; *prāha*—said; *vismitaḥ*—being surprised.

TRANSLATION

The great sage Nārada overheard this news, and understanding all the activities of Dhruva Mahārāja, he was struck with wonder. He approached Dhruva, and touching the boy's head with his all-virtuous hand, he spoke as follows.

PURPORT

When Dhruva Mahārāja was talking with his mother, Sunīti, of all the incidents that had taken place in the palace, Nārada was not present. Thus the question may be raised how Nārada overheard all these topics. The answer is that Nārada is *trikāla-jña;* he is so powerful that he can understand the past, future and present of everyone's heart, just like the Supersoul, the Supreme Personality of Godhead. Therefore, after understanding the strong determination of Dhruva Mahārāja, Nārada came to help him. It may be explained in this way: The Supreme Personality of Godhead is present in everyone's heart, and as soon as He understands that a living entity is serious about entering devotional service, He sends His representative. In this way Nārada was sent to Dhruva Mahārāja. This is explained in the *Caitanya-caritāmṛta. Guru-kṛṣṇa-prasāde pāya bhakti-latā-bīja:* by the grace of the spiritual master and Kṛṣṇa, one can enter into devotional service. Because of Dhruva Mahārāja's determination, Kṛṣṇa, the Supersoul, immediately sent His representative, Nārada, to initiate him.

TEXT 26

अहो तेजः क्षत्रियाणां मानभङ्गममृष्यताम् ।
बालोऽप्ययं हृदा धत्ते यत्समातुरसद्वचः ॥२६॥

aho tejaḥ kṣatriyāṇāṁ
māna-bhaṅgam amṛṣyatām
bālo 'py ayaṁ hṛdā dhatte
yat samātur asad-vacaḥ

aho—how surprising it is; *tejaḥ*—power; *kṣatriyāṇām*—of the *kṣatriyas; māna-bhaṅgam*—hurting the prestige; *amṛṣyatām*—unable to tolerate; *bālaḥ*—only a child; *api*—although; *ayam*—this; *hṛdā*—at heart; *dhatte*—has taken; *yat*—that which; *sa-mātuḥ*—of the stepmother; *asat*—unpalatable; *vacaḥ*—words.

TRANSLATION

How wonderful are the powerful kṣatriyas. They cannot tolerate even a slight infringement upon their prestige. Just imagine! This

boy is only a small child, yet harsh words from his stepmother proved unbearable to him.

PURPORT

The qualifications of the *kṣatriyas* are described in *Bhagavad-gītā.* Two important qualifications are to have a sense of prestige and not to flee from battle. It appears that the *kṣatriya* blood within the body of Dhruva Mahārāja was naturally very active. If the brahminical, *kṣatriya* or *vaiśya* culture is maintained in a family, naturally the sons and grandsons inherit the spirit of the particular class. Therefore, according to the Vedic system, the *saṁskāra,* or the reformatory system, is maintained very rigidly. If one fails to observe the reformatory measures current in the family, one is immediately degraded to a lower standard of life.

TEXT 27

नारद उवाच

नाधुनाप्यवमानं ते सम्मानं वापि पुत्रक ।
लक्षयामः कुमारस्य सक्तस्य क्रीडनादिषु ॥२७॥

nārada uvāca
nādhunāpy avamānaṁ te
sammānaṁ vāpi putraka
lakṣayāmaḥ kumārasya
saktasya krīḍanādiṣu

nāradaḥ uvāca—the great sage Nārada said; *na*—not; *adhunā*—just now; *api*—although; *avamānam*—insult; *te*—unto you; *sammānam*—offering respects; *vā*—or; *api*—certainly; *putraka*—my dear boy; *lakṣayāmaḥ*—I can see; *kumārasya*—of boys like you; *saktasya*—being attached; *krīḍana-ādiṣu*—to sports and frivolities.

TRANSLATION

The great sage Nārada told Dhruva: My dear boy, you are only a little boy whose attachment is to sports and other frivolities. Why are you so affected by words insulting your honor?

PURPORT

Ordinarily if a child is rebuked as a rascal or fool, he smiles and does not take such insulting words very seriously. Similarly, if words of honor are offered, he does not appreciate them. But in the case of Dhruva Mahārāja, the *kṣatriya* spirit was so strong that he could not tolerate a slight insult from his stepmother which injured his *kṣatriya* prestige.

TEXT 28

विकल्पे विद्यमानेऽपि न ह्यसंतोषहेतवः ।
पुंसो मोहमृते भिन्ना यल्लोके निजकर्मभिः ॥२८॥

vikalpe vidyamāne 'pi
na hy asantoṣa-hetavaḥ
puṁso moham ṛte bhinnā
yal loke nija-karmabhiḥ

vikalpe—alternation; *vidyamāne api*—although there is; *na*—not; *hi*—certainly; *asantoṣa*—dissatisfaction; *hetavaḥ*—causes; *puṁsaḥ*—of the persons; *moham ṛte*—without being illusioned; *bhinnāḥ*—separated; *yat loke*—within this world; *nija-karmabhiḥ*—by his own work.

TRANSLATION

My dear Dhruva, if you feel that your sense of honor has been insulted, you still have no cause for dissatisfaction. This kind of dissatisfaction is another feature of the illusory energy; every living entity is controlled by his previous actions, and therefore there are different varieties of life for enjoying or suffering.

PURPORT

In the *Vedas* it is said that the living entity is always uncontaminated and unaffected by material association. The living entity gets different types of material bodies because of his previous fruitive actions. If, however, one understands the philosophy that as a living spirit soul he has an affinity for neither suffering nor enjoyment, then he is considered to be a liberated person. It is confirmed in *Bhagavad-gītā* (18.54), *brahma-bhūtaḥ prasannātmā:* when one is actually situated on the transcendental platform, he has nothing for which to lament and nothing for which to hanker. Nārada Ṛṣi first of all wanted to impress upon Dhruva Mahārāja that he was only a child; he should not have been affected by words of insult or honor. And if he were so developed as to understand honor and insult, then this understanding should have been applied in his own life; he should have known that honor and dishonor are both destined only by one's previous actions; therefore one should not be sorry or happy under any circumstances.

TEXT 29

परितुष्येत्ततस्तात तावन्मात्रेण पूरुषः ।
दैवोपसादितं यावद्वीक्ष्येश्वरगतिं बुधः ॥२९॥

paritușyet tatas tāta
tāvan-mātreṇa pūruṣaḥ
daivopasāditaṁ yāvad
vīkṣyeśvara-gatiṁ budhaḥ

paritușyet—one should be satisfied; *tataḥ*—therefore; *tāta*—my dear boy; *tāvat*—up to such; *mātreṇa*—quality; *pūruṣaḥ*—a person; *daiva*—destiny; *upasāditam*—offered by; *yāvat*—as; *vīkṣya*—seeing; *īśvara-gatim*—the process of the Supreme; *budhaḥ*—one who is intelligent.

TRANSLATION

The process of the Supreme Personality of Godhead is very wonderful. One who is intelligent should accept that process and be satisfied with whatever comes, favorable or unfavorable, by His supreme will.

PURPORT

The great sage Nārada instructed Dhruva Mahārāja that one should be satisfied in all circumstances. Everyone who is intelligent should know that because of our concept of bodily existence, we are subjected to suffering and enjoyment. One who is in the transcendental position, beyond the concept of bodily life, is considered to be intelligent. One who is a devotee especially accepts all reverses as gifts of the Supreme Lord.

When a devotee is put into distress, he accepts this as God's mercy and offers Him repeated obeisances with his body, mind and intellect. An intelligent person, therefore, should be always satisfied, depending on the mercy of the Lord.

TEXT 30

अथ मात्रोपदिष्टेन योगेनावरुरुत्ससि ।
यत्प्रसादं स वै पुंसां दुराराध्यो मतो मम ॥३०॥

atha mātropadiṣṭena
yogenāvarurutsasi
yat-prasādaṁ sa vai puṁsāṁ
durārādhyo mato mama

atha—therefore; *mātrā*—by your mother; *upadiṣṭena*—being instructed; *yogena*—by mystic meditation; *avarurutsasi*—want to elevate yourself; *yat-prasādam*—whose mercy; *saḥ*—that; *vai*—certainly; *puṁsām*—of the living entities; *durārādhyaḥ*—very difficult to perform; *mataḥ*—opinion; *mama*—my.

TRANSLATION

Now you have decided to undertake the mystic process of meditation under the instruction of your mother, just to achieve the mercy of the Lord, but in my opinion such austerities are not possible for any ordinary man. It is very difficult to satisfy the Supreme Personality of Godhead.

PURPORT

The process of *bhakti-yoga* is simultaneously very difficult and very easy to perform. Śrī Nārada Muni, the supreme spiritual master, is testing Dhruva Mahārāja to see how determined he is to prosecute devotional service. This is the process of accepting a disciple. The great sage Nārada has come to Dhruva under the direction of the Supreme Personality of Godhead just to initiate him, yet he is testing Dhruva's determination to execute the process. It is a fact, however, that for a sincere person devotional service is very easy. But for one who is not determined and sincere, this process is very difficult.

TEXT 31

मुनयः पदवीं यस्य निःसङ्गेनोरुजन्मभिः ।
न विदुर्मृगयन्तोऽपि तीव्रयोगसमाधिना ॥३१॥

munayaḥ padavīṁ yasya
niḥsaṅgenoru-janmabhiḥ
na vidur mṛgayanto 'pi
tīvra-yoga-samādhinā

munayaḥ—great sages; *padavīm*—path; *yasya*—whose; *niḥsaṅ-gena*—by detachment; *uru-janmabhiḥ*—after many births; *na*—never; *viduḥ*—understood; *mṛgayantaḥ*—searching for; *api*—certainly; *tīvra-yoga*—severe austerities; *samādhinā*—by trance.

TRANSLATION

Nārada Muni continued: After trying this process for many, many births and remaining unattached to material contamination, placing themselves continually in trance and executing many types of austerities, many mystic yogīs were unable to find the end of the path of God realization.

TEXT 32

अतो निवर्ततामेष निर्बन्धस्तव निष्फलः ।
यतिष्यति भवान् काले श्रेयसां समुपस्थिते ॥३२॥

ato nivartatām eṣa
nirbandhas tava niṣphalaḥ
yatiṣyati bhavān kāle
śreyasāṁ samupasthite

ataḥ—hereafter; *nivartatām*—just stop yourself; *eṣaḥ*—this; *nir-bandhaḥ*—determination; *tava*—your; *niṣphalaḥ*—without any result; *yatiṣyati*—in the future you should try; *bhavān*—yourself; *kāle*—in due course of time; *śreyasām*—opportunities; *samupasthite*—being present.

TRANSLATION

For this reason, my dear boy, you should not endeavor for this; it will not be successful. It is better that you go home. When you are grown up, by the mercy of the Lord you will get a chance for these mystic performances. At that time you may execute this function.

PURPORT

Generally, a thoroughly trained person takes to spiritual perfection at the end of his life. According to the Vedic system, therefore, life is divided into four stages. In the beginning, one becomes a *brahmacārī*, a student who studies Vedic knowledge under the authoritative guidance of a spiritual master. He then becomes a householder and executes household duties according to the Vedic process. Then the householder becomes a *vānaprastha*, and gradually, when he is mature, he renounces household life and *vānaprastha* life also and takes to *sannyāsa*, completely devoting himself to devotional service.

Generally, people think that childhood is meant for enjoying life by engaging oneself in sports and play, youth is meant for enjoying the company of young girls, and when one becomes old, at the time of death, then he may try to execute devotional service or a mystic *yoga* process. But this conclusion is not for devotees who are actually serious. The great sage Nārada is instructing Dhruva Mahārāja just to test him. Actually, the direct order is that from any point of life one should begin rendering devotional service. But it is the duty of the spiritual master to test the disciple to see how seriously he desires to execute devotional service. Then he may be initiated.

TEXT 33

यस्य यद् दैवविहितं स तेन सुखदुःखयोः ।
आत्मानं तोषयन्देही तमसः पारमृच्छति ॥३३॥

yasya yad daiva-vihitaṁ
sa tena sukha-duḥkhayoḥ
ātmānaṁ toṣayan dehī
tamasaḥ pāram ṛcchati

yasya—anyone; *yat*—that which; *daiva*—by destiny; *vihitam*—destined; *saḥ*—such a person; *tena*—by that; *sukha-duḥkhayoḥ*—happiness or distress; *ātmānam*—one's self; *toṣayan*—being satisfied; *dehī*—an embodied soul; *tamasaḥ*—of the darkness; *pāram*—to the other side; *ṛcchati*—crosses.

TRANSLATION

One should try to keep himself satisfied in any condition of life—whether distress or happiness—which is offered by the supreme will. A person who endures in this way is able to cross over the darkness of nescience very easily.

PURPORT

Material existence consists of pious and impious fruitive activities. As long as one is engaged in any kind of activity other than devotional service, it will result in the happiness and distress of this material world. When we enjoy life in so-called material happiness, it is to be understood that we are diminishing the resultant actions of our pious activities. And when we are put into suffering, it is to be understood that we are diminishing the resultant actions of our impious activities. Instead of being attached to the circumstantial happiness and distress resulting from pious or impious activities, if we want to get out of the clutches of this nescience, then whatever position we are put in by the will of the Lord we should accept. Thus if we simply surrender unto the Supreme Personality of Godhead, we shall get out of the clutches of this material existence.

TEXT 34

गुणाधिकान्मुदं लिप्सेदनुक्रोशं गुणाधमात् ।
मैत्रीं समानादन्विच्छेन्न तापैरभिभूयते ॥३४॥

guṇādhikān mudaṁ lipsed
anukrośaṁ guṇādhamāt
maitrīṁ samānād anvicchen
na tāpair abhibhūyate

guṇa-adhikāt—one who is more qualified; *mudam*—pleasure; *lipset*—one should feel; *anukrośam*—compassion; *guṇa-adhamāt*—one who is less qualified; *maitrīm*—friendship; *samānāt*—with an equal; *anvicchet*—one should desire; *na*—not; *tāpaiḥ*—by tribulation; *abhibhūyate*—becomes affected.

TRANSLATION

Every man should act like this: when he meets a person more qualified than himself, he should be very pleased; when he meets someone less qualified than himself, he should be compassionate toward him; and when he meets someone equal to himself, he should make friendship with him. In this way one is never affected by the threefold miseries of this material world.

PURPORT

Generally when we find someone more qualified than ourselves, we become envious of him; when we find someone less qualified, we deride him; and when we find someone equal we become very proud of our activities. These are the causes of all material tribulations. The great sage Nārada therefore advised that a devotee should act perfectly. Instead of being envious of a more qualified man, one should be jolly to receive him. Instead of being oppressive to a less qualified man, one should be compassionate toward him just to raise him to the proper standard. And when one meets an equal, instead of being proud of one's own activities before him, one should treat him as a friend. One should also have compassion for the people in general, who are suffering due to forgetfulness of Kṛṣṇa. These important functions will make one happy within this material world.

TEXT 35

ध्रुव उवाच
सोऽयं शमो भगवता सुखदुःखहतात्मनाम् ।
दर्शितः कृपया पुंसां दुर्दर्शोऽस्मद्विधैस्तु यः ॥३५॥

dhruva uvāca
so 'yaṁ śamo bhagavatā
sukha-duḥkha-hatātmanām

darśitaḥ kṛpayā puṁsāṁ
durdarśo 'smad-vidhais tu yaḥ

dhruvaḥ uvāca—Dhruva Mahārāja said; *saḥ*—that; *ayam*—this; *śamaḥ*—equilibrium of mind; *bhagavatā*—by Your Lordship; *sukha-duḥkha*—happiness and miseries; *hata-ātmanām*—those who are affected; *darśitaḥ*—shown; *kṛpayā*—by mercy; *puṁsām*—of the people; *durdarśaḥ*—very difficult to perceive; *asmat-vidhaiḥ*—by persons like us; *tu*—but; *yaḥ*—whatever you have said.

TRANSLATION

Dhruva Mahārāja said: My dear Lord Nāradajī, for a person whose heart is disturbed by the material conditions of happiness and distress, whatever you have so kindly explained for attainment of peace of mind is certainly a very good instruction. But as far as I am concerned, I am covered by ignorance, and this kind of philosophy does not touch my heart.

PURPORT

There are various classes of men. One class is called *akāmīs*, referring to those who have no material desire. Desire must exist, either material or spiritual. Material desire arises when one wants to satisfy one's personal senses. One who is ready to sacrifice anything to satisfy the Supreme Personality of Godhead can be said to have spiritual desire. Dhruva did not accept the instruction given by the great saint Nārada because he thought himself unfit for such instruction, which prohibited all material desires. It is not a fact, however, that those who have material desires are prohibited from worshiping the Supreme Personality of Godhead. This is the essential instruction from the life of Dhruva. He frankly admitted that his heart was full of material desires. He was very much affected by the cruel words of his stepmother, whereas those who are spiritually advanced do not care about anyone's condemnation or adoration.

In *Bhagavad-gītā* it is said that persons who are actually advanced in spiritual life do not care for the dual behavior of this material world. But Dhruva Mahārāja frankly admitted that he was not beyond the affliction of material distress and happiness. He was confident that the instruction given by Nārada was valuable, yet he could not accept it. The question raised here is whether or not a person afflicted by material desires is fit to worship the Supreme Personality of Godhead. The answer is that everyone is fit to worship Him. Even if one has many material desires to fulfill, he should take to Kṛṣṇa consciousness and worship the Supreme Lord Kṛṣṇa, who is so merciful that He fulfills everyone's desires. Through this narration it will become very clear that no one is barred from worshiping the Supreme Personality of Godhead, even if one has many material desires.

TEXT 36

अथापि मेऽविनीतस्य क्षात्त्रं घोरमुपेयुषः ।
सुरुच्या दुर्वचोबाणैर्न भिन्ने श्रयते हृदि ॥३६॥

athāpi me 'vinītasya
kṣāttraṁ ghoram upeyuṣaḥ
surucyā durvaco-bāṇair
na bhinne śrayate hṛdi

atha api—therefore; *me*—my; *avinītasya*—not very submissive; *kṣāttram*—the spirit of a *kṣatriya; ghoram*—intolerant; *upeyuṣaḥ*—achieved; *surucyāḥ*—of Queen Suruci; *durvacaḥ*—harsh words; *bāṇaiḥ*—by the arrows; *na*—not; *bhinne*—being pierced; *śrayate*—remain in; *hṛdi*—the heart.

TRANSLATION

My dear lord, I am very impudent for not accepting your instructions, but this is not my fault. It is due to my having been born in a kṣatriya family. My stepmother, Suruci, has pierced my heart with her harsh words. Therefore your valuable instruction does not stand in my heart.

PURPORT

It is said that the heart or mind is just like an earthen pot; once broken, it cannot be repaired by any means. Dhruva Mahārāja gave this example to Nārada Muni. He said that his heart, having been pierced by the arrows of his stepmother's harsh words, felt so broken that nothing seemed valuable but his desire to counteract her insult. His stepmother had said that because he was born from the womb of Sunīti, a neglected queen of Mahārāja Uttānapāda, Dhruva Mahārāja was not fit to sit either on the throne or on his father's lap. In other words, according to his stepmother, he could not be declared king. Dhruva Mahārāja's determination, therefore, was to become king of a planet exalted even beyond that possessed by Lord Brahmā, the greatest of all the demigods.

Dhruva Mahārāja indirectly informed the great sage Nārada that there are four kinds of human spirit—the brahminical spirit, the *kṣatriya* spirit, the *vaiśya* spirit and the *śūdra* spirit. The spirit of one caste is not applicable to the members of another. The philosophical spirit enunciated by Nārada Muni might have been suitable for a *brāhmaṇa* spirit, but it was not suitable for a *kṣatriya.* Dhruva frankly admitted that he was lacking in brahminical humility and was therefore unable to accept the philosophy of Nārada Muni.

The statements of Dhruva Mahārāja indicate that unless a child is trained according to his tendency, there is no possibility of his developing his particular spirit. It was the duty of the spiritual master or teacher to observe the psychological movement of a particular boy and thus train him in a particular occupational duty. Dhruva Mahārāja, having already been trained in the *kṣatriya* spirit, would not accept the brahminical philosophy. In America we have practical experience of this incompatibility of the brahminical and *kṣatriya* temperaments. The American boys, who have simply been trained as *śūdras,* are not at all fit to fight in battle. Therefore, when they are called to join the military, they refuse because they do not have *kṣatriya* spirit. This is a cause of great dissatisfaction in society.

That the boys do not have the *kṣatriya* spirit does not mean that they are trained in brahminical qualities; they are trained as *śūdras,* and thus in frustration they are becoming hippies. However, as soon as they enter the Kṛṣṇa consciousness movement being started in America, they are trained to meet the brahminical qualifications, even though they have fallen to the lowest conditions as *śūdras.* In other words, since the Kṛṣṇa consciousness movement is open for everyone, people in general can attain the brahminical qualifications. This is the greatest need at the present moment, for now there are actually no *brāhmaṇas* or *kṣatriyas* but only some *vaiśyas* and, for the most part, *śūdras.* The classification of society into *brāhmaṇas*, *kṣatriyas*, *vaiśyas* and *śūdras* is very scientific. In the human social body, the *brāhmaṇas* are considered the head, the *kṣatriyas* are the arms, the *vaiśyas* are the belly, and the *śūdras* are the legs. At the present moment the body has legs and a belly, but there are no arms or head, and therefore society is topsy-turvy. It is necessary to reestablish the brahminical qualifications in order to raise the fallen human society to the highest standard of spiritual consciousness.

TEXT 37

पदं त्रिभुवनोत्कृष्टं जिगीषोः साधु वर्त्म मे ।
ब्रूह्यस्मत्पितृभिर्ब्रह्मन्नन्यैरप्यनधिष्ठितम् ॥३७॥

padaṁ tri-bhuvanotkṛṣṭaṁ
jigīṣoḥ sādhu vartma me
brūhy asmat-pitṛbhir brahmann
anyair apy anadhiṣṭhitam

padam—position; *tri-bhuvana*—the three worlds; *utkṛṣṭam*—the best; *jigīṣoḥ*—desirous; *sādhu*—honest; *vartma*—way; *me*—unto me; *brūhi*—please tell; *asmat*—our; *pitṛbhiḥ*—by the forefathers, the father and grandfather; *brahman*—O great *brāhmaṇa; anyaiḥ*—by others; *api*—even; *anadhiṣṭhitam*—not acquired.

TRANSLATION

O learned brāhmaṇa, I want to occupy a position more exalted than any yet achieved within the three worlds by anyone, even by my fathers and grandfathers. If you will oblige, kindly advise me of an honest path to follow by which I can achieve the goal of my life.

PURPORT

When Dhruva Mahārāja refused to accept the brahminical instruction of Nārada Muni, naturally the next question would be what sort of instruction he wanted. So even before Nārada Muni asked, Dhruva Mahārāja expressed his heartfelt desire. His father, of course, was the emperor of the entire world, and his grandfather, Lord Brahmā, was the creator of the universe. Dhruva Mahārāja expressed his desire to possess a kingdom better than those of his father and grandfather. He frankly stated that he wanted a kingdom which had no competitor within the three worlds, namely the higher, middle and lower planetary systems. The greatest personality within this universe is Lord Brahmā, and Dhruva Mahārāja wanted a position even greater than his. He wanted to take advantage of Nārada Muni's presence because he knew very well that if Nārada Muni, the greatest devotee of Lord Kṛṣṇa, could bless him or show him the path, then certainly he would be able to occupy a more exalted position than any person within the three worlds. Thus he wanted help from Nāradajī to achieve that position. Dhruva Mahārāja wanted a position greater than that of Brahmā. This was practically an impossible proposition, but by pleasing the Supreme Personality of Godhead a devotee can achieve even the impossible.

One particular point mentioned here is that Dhruva Mahārāja wanted to occupy an exalted position not by hook or by crook, but by honest means. This indicates that if Kṛṣṇa offered him such a position, then he would accept it. That is the nature of a devotee. He may desire material gain, but he accepts it only if Kṛṣṇa offers it. Dhruva Mahārāja was sorry to refuse the instruction of Nārada Muni; therefore he requested him to be merciful to him by showing a path by which he could fulfill his mind's desires.

TEXT 38

नूनं भवान् भगवतो योऽङ्गजः परमेष्ठिनः ।
वितुदन्नटते वीणां हिताय जगतोऽर्कवत् ॥३८॥

nūnaṁ bhavān bhagavato
yo 'ṅgajaḥ parameṣṭhinaḥ
vitudann aṭate vīṇāṁ
hitāya jagato 'rkavat

nūnam—certainly; *bhavān*—Your Honor; *bhagavataḥ*—of the Lord; *yaḥ*—that which; *aṅga-jaḥ*—born from the body; *parameṣṭhinaḥ*—Lord Brahmā; *vitudan*—by playing on; *aṭate*—travel all over; *vīṇām*—a musical instrument; *hitāya*—for the welfare; *jagataḥ*—of the world; *arka-vat*—like the sun.

TRANSLATION

My dear lord, you are a worthy son of Lord Brahmā, and you travel, playing on your musical instrument, the vīṇā, for the welfare of the entire universe. You are like the sun, which rotates in the universe for the benefit of all living beings.

PURPORT

Dhruva Mahārāja, although a young child, expressed his hope that he might be offered the benediction of a kingdom which would exceed in opulence those of his father and grandfather. He also expressed his gladness that he had met such an exalted person as Nārada, whose only concern was to illuminate the world, like the sun, which rotates all over the universe only for the purpose of benefiting the inhabitants of all planets. Nārada Muni travels all over the universe for the sole purpose of performing the best welfare activity for the entire universe by teaching everyone how to become a devotee of the Supreme Personality of Godhead. Thus Dhruva Mahārāja felt fully assured that Nārada Muni could fulfill his desire, even though the desire was very extraordinary.

The example of the sun is very significant. The sun is so kind that he distributes his sunshine everywhere, without consideration. Dhruva Mahārāja requested Nārada Muni to be merciful to him. He pointed out that Nārada travels all over the universe just for the purpose of doing good to all conditioned souls. He requested that Nārada Muni show his mercy by awarding him the benefit of his particular desire. Dhruva Mahārāja was strongly determined to fulfill his desire, and it was for that purpose that he had left his home and palace.

TEXT 39

मैत्रेय उवाच

इत्युदाहृतमाकर्ण्य भगवान्नारदस्तदा ।
प्रीतः प्रत्याह तं बालं सद्वाक्यमनुकम्पया ॥३९॥

maitreya uvāca
ity udāhṛtam ākarṇya
bhagavān nāradas tadā

prītaḥ pratyāha taṁ bālaṁ
sad-vākyam anukampayā

maitreyaḥ uvāca—the sage Maitreya continued; *iti*—thus; *udāhṛtam*—being spoken; *ākarṇya*—hearing; *bhagavān nāradaḥ*—the great personality Nārada; *tadā*—thereupon; *prītaḥ*—being pleased; *pratyāha*—replied; *tam*—him; *bālam*—the boy; *sat-vākyam*—good advice; *anukampayā*—being compassionate.

TRANSLATION

The sage Maitreya continued: The great personality Nārada Muni, upon hearing the words of Dhruva Mahārāja, became very compassionate toward him, and in order to show him his causeless mercy, he gave him the following expert advice.

PURPORT

Since the great sage Nārada is the foremost spiritual master, naturally his only activity is to bestow the greatest benefit upon whomever he meets. Dhruva Mahārāja, however, was a child, and so his demand was also that of a playful child. Still, the great sage became compassionate toward him, and for his welfare he spoke the following verses.

TEXT 40

नारद उवाच
जनन्याभिहितः पन्थाः स वै निःश्रेयसस्य ते ।
भगवान् वासुदेवस्तं भज तं प्रवणात्मना ॥४०॥

nārada uvāca
jananyābhihitaḥ panthāḥ
sa vai niḥśreyasasya te
bhagavān vāsudevas taṁ
bhaja taṁ pravaṇātmanā

nāradaḥ uvāca—the great sage Nārada said; *jananyā*—by your mother; *abhihitaḥ*—stated; *panthāḥ*—the path; *saḥ*—that; *vai*—certainly; *niḥśreyasasya*—the ultimate goal of life; *te*—for you; *bhagavān*—the Supreme Personality of Godhead; *vāsudevaḥ*—Kṛṣṇa;

tam—unto Him; *bhaja*—render your service; *tam*—by Him; *pravaṇa-ātmanā*—fully absorbing your mind.

TRANSLATION

The great sage Nārada told Dhruva Mahārāja: The instruction given by your mother, Sunīti, to follow the path of devotional service to the Supreme Personality of Godhead, is just suitable for you. You should therefore completely absorb yourself in the devotional service of the Lord.

PURPORT

Dhruva Mahārāja's demand was to achieve an abode even greater than Lord Brahmā's. Within this universe, Lord Brahmā is supposed to be in the most exalted position, for he is the chief of all demigods, but Dhruva Mahārāja wanted a realm beyond his. Therefore his desire was not to be fulfilled by worshiping any demigod. As described in *Bhagavad-gītā*, the benedictions offered by the demigods are all temporary. Therefore Nārada Muni asked Dhruva Mahārāja to follow the path recommended by his mother—to worship Kṛṣṇa, Vāsudeva. When Kṛṣṇa offers anything, it is beyond the expectation of the devotee. Both Sunīti and Nārada Muni knew that the demand of Dhruva Mahārāja was impossible for any demigod to fulfill, and therefore both of them recommended following the process of devotional service to Lord Kṛṣṇa.

Nārada Muni is referred to here as *bhagavān* because he can bless any person just as the Supreme Personality of Godhead can. He was very pleased with Dhruva Mahārāja, and he could have at once personally given whatever he wanted, but that is not the duty of the spiritual master. His duty is to engage the disciple in proper devotional service as prescribed in the *śāstras.* Kṛṣṇa was similarly present before Arjuna, and even though He could have given him all facilities for victory over the opposing party without a fight, He did not do so; instead He asked Arjuna to fight. In the same way, Nārada Muni asked Dhruva Mahārāja to undergo devotional discipline in order to achieve the desired result.

TEXT 41

धर्मार्थकाममोक्षाख्यं य इच्छेच्छ्रेय आत्मनः ।
एकं ह्येव हरेस्तत्र कारणं पादसेवनम् ॥४१॥

dharmārtha-kāma-mokṣākhyaṁ
ya icchec chreya ātmanaḥ
ekaṁ hy eva hares tatra
kāraṇaṁ pāda-sevanam

dharma-artha-kāma-mokṣa—the four principles religiosity, economic development, sense gratification and liberation; *ākhyam*—by the name; *yaḥ*—who; *icchet*—may desire; *śreyaḥ*—the goal of life; *ātmanaḥ*—of the self; *ekam hi eva*—only the one; *hareḥ*—of the Supreme Personality of Godhead; *tatra*—in that; *kāraṇam*—the cause; *pāda-sevanam*—worshiping the lotus feet.

TRANSLATION

Any person who desires the fruits of the four principles religiosity, economic development, sense gratification and, at the end, liberation, should engage himself in the devotional service of the Supreme Personality of Godhead, for worship of His lotus feet yields the fulfillment of all of these.

PURPORT

In *Bhagavad-gītā* it is said that only with the sanction of the Supreme Personality of Godhead can the demigods offer benedictions. Therefore, whenever any sacrifice is offered to a demigod, the Supreme Lord in the form of *nārāyaṇa-śilā*, or *śālagrāma-śilā*, is put forward to observe the sacrifice. Actually, the demigods cannot give any benediction without the sanction of the Supreme Lord. Nārada Muni, therefore, advised that even for religiosity, economic development, sense gratification or liberation, one should approach the Supreme Personality of Godhead, offer prayers and ask for the fulfillment of one's desire at the lotus feet of the Lord. That is real intelligence. An intelligent person never goes to demigods to pray for anything. He goes directly to the Supreme Personality of Godhead, who is the cause of all benediction.

As Lord Śrī Kṛṣṇa has said in *Bhagavad-gītā*, performance of ritualistic ceremonies is not actually religion. The real path of religion is to surrender at the lotus feet of the Lord. For one who is actually surrendered to the lotus feet of the Lord, there is no question of any separate endeavor for economic development. A devotee engaged in service to the

Lord is not disappointed in the satisfaction of his senses. If he wants to satisfy his senses, Kṛṣṇa fulfills that desire. As far as liberation is concerned, any devotee fully engaged in the service of the Lord is already liberated; therefore there is no separate necessity for his liberation.

Nārada Muni therefore advised Dhruva Mahārāja to take shelter of Vāsudeva, Lord Kṛṣṇa, and engage himself in the way that his mother had advised, for that would help him fulfill his desire. In this verse Nārada Muni has especially stressed the devotional service of the Lord as the only way. In other words, even if one is full of material desires, he can continue his devotional service to the Lord, and all his desires will be fulfilled.

TEXT 42

तत्तात गच्छ भद्रं ते यमुनायास्तटं शुचि ।
पुण्यं मधुवनं यत्र सांनिध्यं नित्यदा हरेः ॥४२॥

tat tāta gaccha bhadraṁ te
yamunāyās taṭaṁ śuci
puṇyaṁ madhuvanaṁ yatra
sānnidhyaṁ nityadā hareḥ

tat—that; *tāta*—my dear son; *gaccha*—go; *bhadram*—good fortune; *te*—for you; *yamunāyāḥ*—of the Yamunā; *taṭam*—bank; *śuci*—being purified; *puṇyam*—the holy; *madhu-vanam*—of the name Madhuvana; *yatra*—where; *sānnidhyam*—being nearer; *nityadā*—always; *hareḥ*—of the Supreme Personality of Godhead.

TRANSLATION

My dear boy, I therefore wish all good fortune for you. You should go to the bank of the Yamunā, where there is a virtuous forest named Madhuvana, and there be purified. Just by going there, one draws nearer to the Supreme Personality of Godhead, who always lives there.

PURPORT

Both Nārada Muni and Sunīti, the mother of Dhruva Mahārāja, advised Dhruva Mahārāja to worship the Supreme Personality of Godhead. Now, Nārada Muni is especially giving him directions how this worship of the Supreme Person can very quickly fructify. He recommends that Dhruva Mahārāja go to the bank of the Yamunā, where there is a forest of the name Madhuvana, and begin his meditation and worship there.

Places of pilgrimage yield a special advantage for a devotee in quickly advancing his spiritual life. Lord Kṛṣṇa lives everywhere, but still it is very easy to approach Him in holy places of pilgrimage because these places are inhabited by great sages. Lord Śrī Kṛṣṇa says that He lives wherever His devotees are chanting the glories of His transcendental activities. There are many places of pilgrimage in India, and especially prominent are Badarī-nārāyaṇa, Dvārakā, Rāmeśvara and Jagannātha Purī. These sacred places are called the four *dhāmas. Dhāma* refers to a place where one can immediately contact the Supreme Lord. To go to Badarī-nārāyaṇa one has to pass through Hardwar on the path to the Supreme Personality of Godhead. Similarly, there are other holy places of pilgrimage, such as Prayāga (Allahabad) and Mathurā, and the topmost of them all is Vṛndāvana. Unless one is very advanced in spiritual life, it is recommended that he live in such holy places and execute devotional service there. But an advanced devotee like Nārada Muni who is engaged in preaching work can serve the Supreme Lord anywhere. Sometimes he even goes to the hellish planets. Hellish conditions do not affect Nārada Muni because he is engaged in greatly responsible activities in devotional service. According to the statement of Nārada Muni, Madhuvana, which is still existing in the Vṛndāvana area, in the district of Mathurā, is a most sacred place. Many saintly persons still live there and engage in the devotional service of the Lord.

There are twelve forests in the area of Vṛndāvana, and Madhuvana is one of them. Pilgrims from all parts of India assemble together and visit all twelve of these forests. There are five forests on the eastern bank of the Yamunā: Bhadravana, Bilvavana, Lauhavana, Bhāṇḍīravana and Mahāvana. On the western side of the bank there are seven: Madhuvana, Tālavana, Kumudavana, Bahulāvana, Kāmyavana, Khadiravana and Vṛndāvana. In those twelve forests there are different *ghāṭas*, or bathing places. They are listed as follows: (1) Avimukta, (2) Adhirūḍha, (3) Guhya-tīrtha, (4) Prayāga-tīrtha, (5) Kanakhala, (6) Tinduka-tīrtha, (7) Sūrya-tīrtha, (8) Vaṭasvāmī, (9) Dhruva-ghāṭa (Dhruva-ghāṭa, where there are many nice trees of fruits and flowers, is famous because Dhruva Mahārāja meditated and underwent severe penances and austerities there in an elevated spot), (10) Ṛṣi-tīrtha, (11) Mokṣa-tīrtha, (12) Budha-tīrtha, (13) Gokarṇa, (14) Kṛṣṇagaṅgā, (15) Vaikuṇṭha, (16) Asi-kuṇḍa, (17) Catuḥ-sāmudrika-kūpa, (18) Akrūra-tīrtha (when Kṛṣṇa and Balarāma were going to Mathurā in the chariot driven by Akrūra, all of them took baths in this *ghāṭa*), (19) Yājñika-vipra-sthāna, (20) Kubjā-kūpa, (21) Raṅga-sthāla, (22) Mañcha-sthala, (23) Mallayuddha-sthāna, and (24) Daśāśvamedha.

TEXT 43

स्नात्वानुसवनं तस्मिन् कालिन्द्याः सलिले शिवे ।
कृत्वोचितानि निवसन्नात्मनः कल्पितासनः ॥४३॥

snātvānusavanaṁ tasmin
kālindyāḥ salile śive
kṛtvocitāni nivasann
ātmanaḥ kalpitāsanaḥ

snātvā—after taking bath; *anusavanam*—three times; *tasmin*—in that; *kālindyāḥ*—in the River Kālindī (the Yamunā); *salile*—in the water; *śive*—which is very auspicious; *kṛtvā*—performing; *ucitāni*—suitable; *nivasan*—sitting; *ātmanaḥ*—of the self; *kalpita-āsanaḥ*—having prepared a sitting place.

TRANSLATION

Nārada Muni instructed: My dear boy, in the waters of the Yamunā River, which is known as Kālindī, you should take three baths daily because the water is very auspicious, sacred and clear. After bathing, you should perform the necessary regulative principles for aṣṭāṅga-yoga and then sit down on your āsana [sitting place] in a calm and quiet position.

PURPORT

It appears from this statement that Dhruva Mahārāja had already been instructed how to practice the eightfold *yoga* system, which is known as *aṣṭāṅga-yoga.* This system is explained in our *Bhagavad-gītā As It Is,* in the chapter entitled, "*Sāṅkhya-yoga,*" pages 319–322. It is understood that in *aṣṭāṅga-yoga* one practices settling the mind and then concentrating it on the form of Lord Viṣṇu, as will be described in the following verses. It is clearly stated here that *aṣṭāṅga-yoga* is not a bodily gymnastic exercise, but a practice to concentrate the mind on the form of Viṣṇu. Before sitting on his *āsana*, which is also described in *Bhagavad-gītā*, one has to cleanse himself very nicely in clear or sacred water thrice daily. The water of the Yamunā is naturally very clear and pure, and thus if anyone bathes there three times, undoubtedly he will be very greatly purified externally. Nārada Muni, therefore, instructed Dhruva Mahārāja to go to the bank of the Yamunā and thus become externally purified. This is part of the gradual process of practicing mystic *yoga*.

TEXT 44

प्राणायामेन त्रिवृता प्राणेन्द्रियमनोमलम् ।
शनैर्व्युदस्याभिध्यायेन्मनसा गुरुणा गुरुम् ॥४४॥

prāṇāyāmena tri-vṛtā
prāṇendriya-mano-malam
śanair vyudasyābhidhyāyen
manasā guruṇā gurum

prāṇāyāmena—by breathing exercises; *tri-vṛtā*—by the three recommended ways; *prāṇa-indriya*—the life air and the senses; *manaḥ*—mind; *malam*—impurity; *śanaiḥ*—gradually; *vyudasya*—giving up; *abhidhyāyet*—meditate upon; *manasā*—by the mind; *guruṇā*—undisturbed; *gurum*—the supreme spiritual master, Kṛṣṇa.

TRANSLATION

After sitting on your seat, practice the three kinds of breathing exercises, and thus gradually control the life air, the mind and the senses. Completely free yourself from all material contamination, and with great patience begin to meditate on the Supreme Personality of Godhead.

PURPORT

In this verse the entire *yoga* system is described in summary, and special stress is given to the breathing exercises for stopping the disturbing mind. The mind, by nature, is always oscillating, for it is very fickle, but the breathing exercise is meant to control it. This process of controlling the mind might have been very possible in those days millions of years ago when Dhruva Mahārāja took to it, but at the present moment the mind has to be fixed directly on the lotus feet of the Lord by the chanting process. By chanting the Hare Kṛṣṇa *mantra* one immediately concentrates on the sound vibration and thinks of the lotus feet of the Lord, and very quickly one is elevated to the position of *samādhi*, or trance. If one goes on chanting the holy names of the Lord, which are not different from the Supreme Personality of Godhead, naturally his mind becomes absorbed in thought of the Lord.

It is here recommended to Dhruva Mahārāja that he meditate on the supreme *guru*, or supreme spiritual master. The supreme spiritual master is Kṛṣṇa, who is therefore known as *caitya-guru*. This refers to the Supersoul, who is sitting in everyone's heart. He helps from within as stated in *Bhagavad-gītā*, and He sends the spiritual master, who helps from without. The spiritual master is the external manifestation of the *caitya-guru*, or the spiritual master sitting in everyone's heart.

The process by which we give up our thoughts of material things is called *pratyāhāra*, which entails being freed from all material thoughts and engagements. The word *abhidhyāyet*, which is used in this verse, indicates that unless one's mind is fixed, one cannot meditate. The conclusion, therefore, is that meditation means thinking of the Lord within. Whether one comes to that stage by the *aṣṭāṅga-yoga* system or by the method recommended in the *śāstras* especially for this present age—to constantly chant the holy name of the Lord—the goal is to meditate on the Supreme Personality of Godhead.

TEXT 45

प्रसादाभिमुखं शश्वत्प्रसन्नवदनेक्षणम् ।
सुनासं सुभ्रुवं चारुकपोलं सुरसुन्दरम् ॥४५॥

prasādābhimukhaṁ śaśvat
prasanna-vadanekṣaṇam
sunāsaṁ subhruvaṁ cāru-
kapolaṁ sura-sundaram

prasāda-abhimukham—always prepared to offer causeless mercy; *śaśvat*—always; *prasanna*—pleasing; *vadana*—mouth; *īkṣaṇam*—vision; *su-nāsam*—very nicely constructed nose; *su-bhruvam*—very nicely decorated eyebrows; *cāru*—beautiful; *kapolam*—forehead; *sura*—the demigods; *sundaram*—good looking.

TRANSLATION

[The form of the Lord is described herein.] The Lord's face is perpetually very beautiful and pleasing in attitude. To the devotees who see Him, He appears never to be displeased, and He is always prepared to award benedictions to them. His eyes, His nicely decorated eyebrows, His raised nose and His broad forehead are all very beautiful. He is more beautiful than all the demigods.

PURPORT

This verse clearly explains how one has to meditate on the form of the Lord. Impersonal meditation is a bogus invention of modern days. In none of the Vedic literatures is impersonal meditation recommended. In *Bhagavad-gītā*, when meditation is recommended, the word *mat-paraḥ*, which means "pertaining to Me," is used. Any Viṣṇu form pertains to Lord Kṛṣṇa because Lord Kṛṣṇa is the original Viṣṇu form. Sometimes someone tries to meditate upon the impersonal Brahman, which is described in *Bhagavad-gītā* as *avyakta*, meaning "unmanifested" or "impersonal." But it is remarked by the Lord Himself that those who are attached to this impersonal feature of the Lord suffer a very troublesome task because no one can concentrate on the impersonal feature. One has to concentrate on the form of the Lord, which is described here in connection with Dhruva Mahārāja's meditation. As will be apparent from later descriptions, Dhruva Mahārāja perfected this kind of meditation, and his *yoga* was successful.

TEXT 46

तरुणं रमणीयाङ्गमरुणोष्ठेक्षणाधरम् ।
प्रणताश्रयणं नृम्णं शरण्यं करुणार्णवम् ॥४६॥

taruṇaṁ ramaṇīyāṅgam
aruṇoṣṭhekṣaṇādharam

praṇatāśrayaṇaṁ nṛmṇaṁ
śaraṇyaṁ karuṇārṇavam

taruṇam—youthful; *ramaṇīya*—attractive; *aṅgam*—all parts of the body; *aruṇa-oṣṭha*—lips pinkish like the rising sun; *īkṣaṇa-adharam*—eyes of the same nature; *praṇata*—one who is surrendered; *āśrayaṇam*—shelter of the surrendered; *nṛmṇam*—transcendentally pleasing in all respects; *śaraṇyam*—the person unto whom it is just worthy to surrender; *karuṇā*—merciful like; *arṇavam*—the ocean.

TRANSLATION

Nārada Muni continued: The Lord's form is always youthful. Every limb and every part of His body is properly formed, free from defect. His eyes and lips are pinkish like the rising sun. He is always prepared to give shelter to the surrendered soul, and anyone so fortunate as to look upon Him feels all satisfaction. The Lord is always worthy to be the master of the surrendered soul, for He is the ocean of mercy.

PURPORT

Everyone has to surrender to someone superior. That is always the nature of our living condition. At the present moment we are trying to surrender to someone—either to society or to our nation, family, state or government. The surrendering process already exists, but it is never perfect because the person or institution unto whom we surrender is imperfect, and our surrender, having so many ulterior motives, is also imperfect. As such, in the material world no one is worthy to accept anyone's surrender, nor does anyone fully surrender to anyone else unless obliged to do so. But here the surrendering process is voluntary, and the Lord is worthy to accept the surrender. This surrender by the living entity occurs automatically as soon as he sees the beautiful youthful nature of the Lord.

The description given by Nārada Muni is not imaginary. The form of the Lord is understood by the *paramparā* system. Māyāvādī philosophers say that we have to imagine the form of the Lord, but here Nārada Muni does not say that. Rather, he gives the description of the Lord from authoritative sources. He is himself an authority, and he is able to go to

Vaikuṇṭhaloka and see the Lord personally; therefore his description of the bodily features of the Lord is not imagination. Sometimes we give instructions to our students about the bodily features of the Lord, and they paint Him. Their paintings are not imaginary. The description is given through disciplic succession, just like that given by Nārada Muni, who sees the Lord and describes His bodily features. Therefore, such descriptions should be accepted, and if they are painted, that is not imaginative painting.

TEXT 47

श्रीवत्साङ्कं घनश्यामं पुरुषं वनमालिनम् ।
शङ्खचक्रगदापद्मैरभिव्यक्तचतुर्भुजम् ॥४७॥

śrīvatsāṅkaṁ ghana-śyāmaṁ
puruṣaṁ vana-mālinam
śaṅkha-cakra-gadā-padmair
abhivyakta-caturbhujam

śrīvatsa-aṅkam—the mark of Śrīvatsa on the chest of the Lord; *ghana-śyāmam*—deeply bluish; *puruṣam*—the Supreme Person; *vana-mālinam*—with a garland of flowers; *śaṅkha*—conchshell; *cakra*—wheel; *gadā*—club; *padmaiḥ*—lotus flower; *abhivyakta*—manifested; *catuḥ-bhujam*—four handed.

TRANSLATION

The Lord is further described as having the mark of Śrīvatsa, or the sitting place of the goddess of fortune, and His bodily hue is deep bluish. The Lord is a person, He wears a garland of flowers, and He is eternally manifest with four hands, which hold [beginning from the lower left hand] a conchshell, wheel, club and lotus flower.

PURPORT

Here in this verse the word *puruṣam* is very significant. The Lord is never female. He is always malc (*puruṣa*). Therefore the impersonalist who imagines the Lord's form as that of a woman is mistaken. The Lord appears in female form if necessary, but His perpetual form is *puruṣa* because He is originally male. The feminine feature of the Lord is displayed by goddesses of fortune—Lakṣmī, Rādhārāṇī, Sītā, etc. All these goddesses of fortune are servitors of the Lord; they are not the Supreme, as falsely imagined by the impersonalist. Lord Kṛṣṇa in His Nārāyaṇa feature is always four handed. On the Battlefield of Kurukṣetra, when Arjuna wanted to see His universal form, He showed this feature of four-handed Nārāyaṇa. Some devotees are of the opinion that Kṛṣṇa is an incarnation of Nārāyaṇa, but the *Bhāgavata* school says that Nārāyaṇa is a manifestation of Kṛṣṇa.

TEXT 48

किरीटिनं कुण्डलिनं केयूरवलयान्वितम् ।
कौस्तुभाभरणग्रीवं पीतकौशेयवाससम् ॥४८॥

kirīṭinaṁ kuṇḍalinaṁ
keyūra-valayānvitam
kaustubhābharaṇa-grīvaṁ
pīta-kauśeya-vāsasam

kirīṭinam—the Lord is decorated with a jeweled helmet; *kuṇḍalinam*—with pearl earrings; *keyūra*—jeweled necklace; *valaya-anvitam*—with jeweled bracelets; *kaustubha-ābharaṇa-grīvam*—His neck is decorated by the Kaustubha jewel; *pīta-kauśeya-vāsasam*—and He is dressed with yellow silk garments.

TRANSLATION

The entire body of the Supreme Personality of Godhead, Vāsudeva, is decorated. He wears a valuable jeweled helmet, necklaces and bracelets, His neck is adorned with the Kaustubha jewel, and He is dressed in yellow silk garments.

TEXT 49

काञ्चीकलापपर्यस्तं लसत्काञ्चननूपुरम् ।
दर्शनीयतमं शान्तं मनोनयनवर्धनम् ॥४९॥

kāñcī-kalāpa-paryastaṁ
lasat-kāñcana-nūpuram

darśanīyatamaṁ śāntaṁ
mano-nayana-vardhanam

kāñcī-kalāpa—small bells; *paryastam*—surrounding the waist; *lasat-kāñcana-nūpuram*—His legs are decorated with golden ankle bells; *darśanīya-tamam*—the superexcellent feature; *śāntam*—peaceful, calm and quiet; *manaḥ-nayana-vardhanam*—very pleasing to the eyes and the mind.

TRANSLATION

The Lord is decorated with small golden bells around His waist, and His lotus feet are decorated with golden ankle bells. All His bodily features are very attractive and pleasing to the eyes. He is always peaceful, calm and quiet and very pleasing to the eyes and the mind.

TEXT 50

पद्भ्यां नखमणिश्रेण्या विलसद्भ्यां समर्चताम् ।
हृत्पद्मकर्णिकाधिष्ण्यमाक्रम्यात्मन्यवस्थितम् ॥५०॥

padbhyāṁ nakha-maṇi-śreṇyā
vilasadbhyāṁ samarcatām
hṛt-padma-karṇikā-dhiṣṇyam
ākramyātmany avasthitam

padbhyām—by His lotus feet; *nakha-maṇi-śreṇyā*—by the light of the jewellike nails on the toes; *vilasadbhyām*—glittering lotus feet; *samarcatām*—persons who are engaged in worshiping them; *hṛt-padma-karṇikā*—the whorl of the lotus flower of the heart; *dhiṣṇyam*—situated; *ākramya*—seizing; *ātmani*—in the heart; *avasthitam*—situated.

TRANSLATION

Real yogīs meditate upon the transcendental form of the Lord as He stands on the whorl of the lotus of their hearts, the jewellike nails of His lotus feet glittering.

TEXT 51

स्मयमानमभिध्यायेत्सानुरागावलोकनम् ।
नियतेनैकभूतेन मनसा वरदर्षभम् ॥ ५१॥

smayamānam abhidhyāyet
sānurāgāvalokanam
niyatenaika-bhūtena
manasā varadarṣabham

smayamānam—the Lord's smiling; *abhidhyāyet*—one should meditate upon Him; *sa-anurāga-avalokanam*—one who is looking toward the devotees with great affection; *niyatena*—in this way, regularly; *eka-bhūtena*—with great attention; *manasā*—with the mind; *vara-darṣabham*—one should meditate upon the greatest bestower of benedictions.

TRANSLATION

The Lord is always smiling, and the devotee should constantly see the Lord in this form, as He looks very mercifully toward the devotee. In this way the meditator should look toward the Supreme Personality of Godhead, the bestower of all benedictions.

PURPORT

The word *niyatena* is very significant in this connection, for it indicates that one should execute the meditation practice as stated above. One should not manufacture a way of meditation on the Supreme Personality of Godhead, but should follow the authorized *śāstras* and personalities. By this prescribed method one can practice concentration upon the Lord until one is so fixed that he remains in trance, thinking always of the form of the Lord. The word used here is *eka-bhūtena,* which means "with great attention and concentration." If one concentrates on the descriptions of the bodily features of the Lord, one will never fall down.

TEXT 52

एवं भगवतो रूपं सुभद्रं ध्यायतो मनः ।
निर्वृत्या परया तूर्णं सम्पन्नं न निवर्तते ॥५२॥

evaṁ bhagavato rūpaṁ
subhadraṁ dhyāyato manaḥ
nirvṛtyā parayā tūrṇaṁ
sampannaṁ na nivartate

evam—thus; *bhagavataḥ*—of the Supreme Personality of Godhead; *rūpam*—form; *su-bhadram*—very auspicious; *dhyāyataḥ*—meditating; *manaḥ*—the mind; *nirvṛtyā*—being freed from all material contamination; *parayā*—transcendental; *tūrṇam*—very soon; *sampannam*—being enriched; *na*—never; *nivartate*—come down.

TRANSLATION

One who meditates in this way, concentrating his mind upon the always auspicious form of the Lord, is very soon freed from all material contamination, and he does not come down from meditation upon the Lord.

PURPORT

This fixed meditation is called *samādhi*, or trance. A person constantly engaged in the transcendental loving service of the Lord cannot be deviated from meditating on the form of the Lord, as described herein. The *arcana-mārga*, or the devotional path prescribed in the *Pāñcarātra* system of devotional service for worshiping the Deity in the temple, makes the devotee think constantly of the Lord; that is *samādhi*, or trance. One who practices in this way cannot deviate from the service of the Lord, and that makes him perfect in the mission of human life.

TEXT 53

जपश्च परमो गुह्यः श्रूयतां मे नृपात्मज ।
यं सप्तरात्रं प्रपठन् पुमान् पश्यति खेचरान् ॥५३॥

japaś ca paramo guhyaḥ
śrūyatāṁ me nṛpātmaja
yaṁ sapta-rātraṁ prapaṭhan
pumān paśyati khecarān

japaḥ ca—the chanting *mantra* in this connection; *paramaḥ*—very, very; *guhyaḥ*—confidential; *śrūyatām*—please hear; *me*—from me; *nṛpa-ātmaja*—O son of the King; *yam*—which; *sapta-rātram*—seven nights; *prapaṭhan*—chanting; *pumān*—a person; *paśyati*—can see; *khe-carān*—human beings who travel in space.

TRANSLATION

O son of the King, now I shall speak unto you the mantra which is to be chanted with this process of meditation. One who carefully chants this mantra for seven nights can see the perfect human beings flying in the sky.

PURPORT

Within this universe there is a planet called Siddhaloka. The inhabitants of Siddhaloka are by nature perfect in the *yoga* achievements, which are of eight varieties: one can become smaller than the smallest, lighter than the lightest, or bigger than the biggest; one can immediately get whatever he likes, one can even create a planet, etc. These are some of the yogic perfections. By virtue of the *laghimā-siddhi*, or purificatory process to become lighter than the lightest, the inhabitants of Siddhaloka can fly in the sky without airplanes or airships. It is hinted herein by Nārada Muni to Dhruva Mahārāja that by meditating upon the transcendental form of the Lord and at the same time chanting the *mantra* one becomes so perfect within seven days that he can see the human beings who fly in the sky. Nārada Muni uses the word *japaḥ*, which indicates that the *mantra* to be chanted is very confidential. One may ask, "If it is confidential, why is it mentioned in the writing of *Śrīmad-Bhāgavatam*?" It is confidential in this sense: one may receive a published *mantra* anywhere, but unless it is accepted through the chain of disciplic succession, the *mantra* does not act. It is said by authoritative sources that any *mantra* chanted without having been received from the disciplic succession has no efficacy.

Another point established in this verse is that meditation should be carried on with the chanting of a *mantra*. Chanting of the Hare Kṛṣṇa *mantra* is the easiest process of meditation in this age. As soon as one chants the Hare Kṛṣṇa *mantra*, he sees the forms of Kṛṣṇa, Rāma and

Their energies, and that is the perfect stage of trance. One should not artificially try to see the form of the Lord while chanting Hare Kṛṣṇa, but when the chanting is performed offenselessly the Lord will automatically reveal Himself to the view of the chanter. The chanter, therefore, has to concentrate on hearing the vibration, and without extra endeavor on his part, the Lord will automatically appear.

TEXT 54

ॐ नमो भगवते वासुदेवाय ।
मन्त्रेणानेन देवस्य कुर्याद् द्रव्यमयीं बुधः ।
सपर्यां विविधैर्द्रव्यैर्देशकालविभागवित् ॥५४॥

oṁ namo bhagavate vāsudevāya
mantreṇānena devasya
kuryād dravyamayīṁ budhaḥ
saparyāṁ vividhair dravyair
deśa-kāla-vibhāgavit

oṁ—O my Lord; *namaḥ*—I offer my respectful obeisances; *bhagavate*—unto the Supreme Personality of Godhead; *vāsudevāya*—unto the Supreme Lord, Vāsudeva; *mantreṇa*—by this hymn, or *mantra; anena*—this; *devasya*—of the Lord; *kuryāt*—one should do; *dravyamayīm*—physical; *budhaḥ*—one who is learned; *saparyām*—worship by the prescribed method; *vividhaiḥ*—with varieties; *dravyaiḥ*—paraphernalia; *deśa*—according to country; *kāla*—time; *vibhāga-vit*—one who knows the divisions.

TRANSLATION

Oṁ namo bhagavate vāsudevāya. This is the twelve-syllable mantra for worshiping Lord Kṛṣṇa. One should install the physical forms of the Lord, and with the chanting of the mantra one should offer flowers and fruits and other varieties of foodstuffs exactly according to the rules and regulations prescribed by authorities. But this should be done in consideration of place, time, and attendant conveniences and inconveniences.

PURPORT

Oṁ namo bhagavate vāsudevāya is known as the *dvādaśākṣara-mantra.* This *mantra* is chanted by Vaiṣṇava devotees, and it begins with *praṇava,* or *oṁkāra.* There is an injunction that those who are not *brāhmaṇas* cannot pronounce the *praṇava mantra.* But Dhruva Mahārāja was born a *kṣatriya.* He at once admitted before Nārada Muni that as a *kṣatriya* he was unable to accept Nārada's instruction of renunciation and mental equilibrium, which are the concern of a *brāhmaṇa.* Still, although not a *brāhmaṇa* but a *kṣatriya,* Dhruva was allowed, on the authority of Nārada, to pronounce the *praṇava oṁkāra.* This is very significant. Especially in India, the caste *brāhmaṇas* object greatly when persons from other castes, who are not born in *brāhmaṇa* families, recite this *praṇava mantra.* But here is tacit proof that if a person accepts the Vaiṣṇava *mantra* or Vaiṣṇava way of worshiping the Deity, he is allowed to chant the *praṇava mantra.* In *Bhagavad-gītā* the Lord personally accepts that anyone, even one of a low species, can be elevated to the highest position and go back home, back to Godhead, simply if he worships properly.

The prescribed rules, as stated here by Nārada Muni, are that one should accept the *mantra* through a bona fide spiritual master and hear the *mantra* in the right ear. Not only should one chant or murmur the *mantra,* but in front of him he must have the Deity, or physical form of the Lord. Of course, when the Lord appears it is no longer a physical form. For example, when an iron rod is made red-hot in a fire, it is no longer iron; it is fire. Similarly, when we make a form of the Lord—whether of wood or stone or metal or jewels or paint, or even a form within the mind—it is a bona fide, spiritual, transcendental form of the Lord. Not only must one receive the *mantra* from the bona fide spiritual master like Nārada Muni or his representative in the disciplic succession, but one must chant the *mantra.* And not only must one chant, but he should also offer whatever foodstuff is available in his part of the world, according to time and convenience.

The method of worship—chanting the *mantra* and preparing the forms of the Lord—is not stereotyped, nor is it exactly the same everywhere. It is specifically mentioned in this verse that one should take consideration of the time, place and available conveniences. Our Kṛṣṇa consciousness movement is going on throughout the entire world, and we also install Deities in different centers. Sometimes our Indian friends, puffed up with concocted notions, criticize, "This has not been done. That has not been done." But they forget this instruction of Nārada Muni to one of the greatest Vaiṣṇavas, Dhruva Mahārāja. One has to consider the particular time, country and conveniences. What is convenient in India may not be convenient in the Western countries. Those who are not actually in the line of *ācāryas*, or who personally have no knowledge of how to act in the role of *ācārya*, unnecessarily criticize the activities of the ISKCON movement in countries outside of India. The fact is that such critics cannot do anything personally to spread Kṛṣṇa consciousness. If someone does go and preach, taking all risks and allowing all considerations for time and place, it might be that there are changes in the manner of worship, but that is not at all faulty according to *śāstra.* Śrīmad Vīrarāghava Ācārya, an *ācārya* in the disciplic succession of the Rāmānuja-sampradāya, has remarked in his commentary that *caṇḍālas*, or conditioned souls who are born in lower than *śūdra* families, can also be initiated according to circumstances. The formalities may be slightly changed here and there to make them Vaiṣṇavas.

Lord Caitanya Mahāprabhu recommends that His name should be heard in every nook and corner of the world. How is this possible unless one preaches everywhere? The cult of Lord Caitanya Mahāprabhu is *bhāgavata-dharma*, and He especially recommends *kṛṣṇa-kathā*, or the cult of *Bhagavad-gītā* and *Śrīmad-Bhāgavatam.* He recommends that every Indian, considering this task to be *para-upakāra*, or welfare activity, take the Lord's message to other residents of the world. "Other residents of the world" does not refer only to those who are exactly like the Indian *brāhmaṇas* and *kṣatriyas*, or like the caste *brāhmaṇas*, who claim to be *brāhmaṇas* because they were born in the families of *brāhmaṇas.* The principle that only Indians and Hindus should be brought into the Vaiṣṇava cult is a mistaken idea. There should be propaganda to bring everyone to the Vaiṣṇava cult. The Kṛṣṇa consciousness movement is meant for this purpose. There is no bar to propagating the Kṛṣṇa consciousness movement even among people who are born in *caṇḍāla, mleccha* or *yavana* families. Even in India, this point has been enunciated by Śrīla Sanātana Gosvāmī in his book *Hari-bhakti-vilāsa*, which is *smṛti* and is the authorized Vedic guide for Vaiṣṇavas in their daily behavior. Sanātana Gosvāmī says that as bell metal can turn to gold when mixed with mercury in a chemical process, so, by the bona fide *dīkṣā*, or initiation method, anyone can become a Vaiṣṇava. One should take initiation from a bona fide spiritual master coming in the disciplic succession, who is authorized by his predecessor spiritual master. This is called *dīkṣā-vidhāna.* Lord Kṛṣṇa states in *Bhagavad-gītā*, *vyapāśritya:* one should accept a spiritual master. By this process the entire world can be converted to Kṛṣṇa consciousness.

TEXT 55

सलिलैः शुचिभिर्माल्यैर्वन्यैर्मूलफलादिभिः ।
शस्ताङ्कुरांशुकैश्चार्चेत्तुलस्या प्रियया प्रभुम् ॥५५॥

salilaiḥ śucibhir mālyair
vanyair mūla-phalādibhiḥ
śastāṅkurāṁśukaiś cārcet
tulasyā priyayā prabhum

salilaiḥ—by use of water; *śucibhiḥ*—being purified; *mālyaiḥ*—by garlands; *vanyaiḥ*—of forest flowers; *mūla*—roots; *phala-ādibhiḥ*—by different kinds of vegetables and fruits; *śasta*—the newly grown grass; *aṅkura*—buds; *aṁśukaiḥ*—by the skin of trees, such as the *bhūrja;* *ca*—and; *arcet*—should worship; *tulasyā*—by the *tulasī* leaves; *priyayā*—which are very dear to the Lord; *prabhum*—the Lord.

TRANSLATION

One should worship the Lord by offering pure water, pure flower garlands, fruits, flowers and vegetables, which are available in the forest, or by collecting newly grown grasses, small buds of flowers or even the skins of trees, and if possible, by offering tulasī leaves, which are very dear to the Supreme Personality of Godhead.

PURPORT

It is specifically mentioned herein that *tulasī* leaves are very dear to the Supreme Personality of Godhead, and devotees should take particular care to have *tulasī* leaves in every temple and center of worship. In the Western countries, while engaged in propagating the Kṛṣṇa consciousness movement, we were brought great unhappiness because we could not find *tulasī* leaves. We are very much obliged, therefore, to our disciple Śrīmatī Govinda dāsī because she has taken much care to grow *tulasī* plants from seeds, and she has been successful by the grace of Kṛṣṇa. Now *tulasī* plants are growing in almost every center of our movement.

Tulasī leaves are very important in the method of worshiping the Supreme Personality of Godhead. In this verse the word *salilaiḥ* means "by the water." Of course, Dhruva Mahārāja was worshiping on the bank of the Yamunā. The Yamunā and the Ganges are sacred, and sometimes devotees in India insist that the Deity must be worshiped with water of the Ganges or Yamunā. But here we understand *deśa-kāla* to mean "according to time and country." In the Western countries there is no River Yamunā or Ganges—water from such sacred rivers is not available. Does this mean that the *arcā* worship should for that reason be stopped? No. *Salilaiḥ* refers to any water—whatever is available—but it must be very clear and collected purely. That water can be used. The other paraphernalia, such as flower garlands, fruits and vegetables, should be collected according to the country and according to their availability. *Tulasī* leaves are very important for satisfying the Lord, so as far as possible an arrangement should be made for growing *tulasī* leaves. Dhruva Mahārāja was advised to worship the Lord with the fruits and flowers available in the forest. In the *Bhagavad-gītā* Kṛṣṇa frankly says that He accepts vegetables, fruits, flowers, etc. One should not offer Lord Vāsudeva anything other than what is prescribed herein by the great authority Nārada Muni. One cannot offer to the Deity according to one's whims; since these fruits and vegetables are available anywhere in the universe, we should observe this small point very attentively.

TEXT 56

लब्ध्वा द्रव्यमयीमर्चां क्षित्यम्ब्वादिषु वार्चयेत् ।
आभृतात्मा मुनिः शान्तो यतवाङ्मितवन्यभुक् ॥५६॥

labdhvā dravyamayīm arcāṁ
kṣity-ambv-ādiṣu vārcayet

ābhṛtātmā muniḥ śānto
yata-vāṅ mita-vanya-bhuk

labdhvā—by getting; *dravya-mayīm*—made of physical elements; *arcām*—worshipable Deity; *kṣiti*—earth; *ambu*—water; *ādiṣu*—beginning with; *vā*—or; *arcayet*—worship; *ābhṛta-ātmā*—one who is fully self-controlled; *muniḥ*—a great personality; *śāntaḥ*—peacefully; *yata-vāk*—controlling the force of talking; *mita*—frugal; *vanya-bhuk*—eating whatever is available in the forest.

TRANSLATION

It is possible to worship a form of the Lord made of physical elements such as earth, water, pulp, wood and metal. In the forest one can make a form with no more than earth and water and worship Him according to the above principles. A devotee who has full control over his self should be very sober and peaceful and must be satisfied simply with eating whatever fruits and vegetables are available in the forest.

PURPORT

It is essential for a devotee to worship the form of the Lord and not only meditate upon the form of the Lord within his mind with the chanting of the *mantra* given by the spiritual master. The worship of the form must be present. The impersonalist takes unnecessary trouble to meditate upon or worship something impersonal, and the path is very precarious. We are not advised to follow the impersonalist way of meditating on or worshiping the Lord. Dhruva Mahārāja was advised to worship a form made of earth and water because in the jungle, if it is not possible to have a form made of metal, wood or stone, the best process is to take earth mixed with water and make a form of the Lord and worship Him. The devotee should not be anxious about cooking food; whatever is available in the forest or in the city among the fruit and vegetable groups should be offered to the Deity, and the devotee should be satisfied eating that. He should not be anxious to have very palatable dishes. Of course, wherever it is possible, one should offer the Deities the best foodstuffs, prepared within the category of fruits and vegetables, cooked or uncooked. The important factor is that the devotee should be regulated (*mita-bhuk*); that is one of the good qualifications of a devotee. He should not hanker to satisfy the tongue with a particular kind of foodstuff. He should be satisfied to eat whatever *prasāda* is available by the grace of the Lord.

TEXT 57

स्वेच्छावतारचरितैरचिन्त्यनिजमायया ।
करिष्यत्युत्तमश्लोकस्तद् ध्यायेद्धृदयङ्गमम् ॥५७॥

svecchāvatāra-caritair
acintya-nija-māyayā
kariṣyaty uttamaślokas
tad dhyāyed dhṛdayaṅ-gamam

sva-icchā—by His own supreme will; *avatāra*—incarnation; *caritaiḥ*—activities; *acintya*—inconceivable; *nija-māyayā*—by His own potency; *kariṣyati*—performs; *uttama-ślokaḥ*—the Supreme Personality of Godhead; *tat*—that; *dhyāyet*—one should meditate; *hṛdayam-gamam*—very attractive.

TRANSLATION

My dear Dhruva, besides worshiping the Deity and chanting the mantra three times a day, you should meditate upon the transcendental activities of the Supreme Personality of Godhead in His different incarnations, as exhibited by His supreme will and personal potencies.

PURPORT

Devotional service comprises nine prescribed practices—hearing, chanting, remembering, worshiping, serving, offering everything to the Deity, etc. Here Dhruva Mahārāja is advised not only to meditate on the form of the Lord, but to think of His transcendental pastimes in His different incarnations. Māyāvādī philosophers take the incarnation of the Lord to be in the same category as the ordinary living entity. This is a great mistake. The incarnation of the Supreme Personality of Godhead is not forced to act by the material laws of nature. The word *svecchā* is used here to indicate that He appears out of His supreme will. The conditioned soul is forced to accept a particular type of body according to his *karma* given by the laws of material nature under the direction of the Supreme Lord. But when the Lord appears, He is not forced by the dictation of material nature; He appears as He likes by His own internal potency. That is the difference. The conditioned soul accepts a particular type of body, such as the body of a hog, by his work and by the superior authority of material nature. But when Lord Kṛṣṇa appears in the incarnation of a boar, He is not the same kind of hog as an ordinary animal. Kṛṣṇa appears as Varāha-avatāra in an expansive feature which cannot be compared to an ordinary hog's. His appearance and disappearance are inconceivable to us. In the *Bhagavad-gītā* it is clearly said that He appears by His own internal potency for the protection of the devotees and the annihilation of the nondevotees. A devotee should always consider that Kṛṣṇa does not appear as an ordinary human being or ordinary beast; His appearance as Varāha-mūrti or a horse or tortoise is an exhibition of His internal potency. In the *Brahma-saṁhitā* it is said, *ānanda-cinmaya-rasa-pratibhāvitābhiḥ:* one should not mistake the appearance of the Lord as a human being or a beast to be the same as the birth of an ordinary conditioned soul, who is forced to appear by the laws of nature, whether as an animal, as a human being or as a demigod. This kind of thinking is offensive. Lord Caitanya Mahāprabhu has condemned the Māyāvādīs as offensive to the Supreme Personality of Godhead because of their thinking that the Lord and the conditioned living entities are one and the same.

Nārada advises Dhruva to meditate on the pastimes of the Lord, which is as good as the meditation of concentrating one's mind on the form of the Lord. As meditation on any form of the Lord is valuable, so is chanting of different names of the Lord, such as Hari, Govinda and Nārāyaṇa. But in this age we are especially advised to chant the Hare Kṛṣṇa *mantra* as enunciated in the *śāstra:* Hare Kṛṣṇa, Hare Kṛṣṇa, Kṛṣṇa Kṛṣṇa, Hare Hare/ Hare Rāma, Hare Rāma, Rāma Rāma, Hare Hare.

TEXT 58

परिचर्या भगवतो यावत्यः पूर्वसेविताः ।
ता मन्त्रहृदयेनैव प्रयुञ्ज्यान्मन्त्रमूर्तये ॥५८॥

paricaryā bhagavato
yāvatyaḥ pūrva-sevitāḥ
tā mantra-hṛdayenaiva
prayuñjyān mantra-mūrtaye

paricaryāḥ—service; *bhagavataḥ*—of the Personality of Godhead; *yāvatyaḥ*—as they are prescribed (as above mentioned); *pūrva-sevitāḥ*—recommended or done by previous *ācāryas; tāḥ*—that; *mantra*—hymns; *hṛdayena*—within the heart; *eva*—certainly; *prayuñjyāt*—one should worship; *mantra-mūrtaye*—who is nondifferent from the *mantra.*

TRANSLATION

One should follow in the footsteps of previous devotees regarding how to worship the Supreme Lord with the prescribed paraphernalia, or one should offer worship within the heart by reciting the mantra to the Personality of Godhead, who is nondifferent from the mantra.

PURPORT

It is recommended here that even if one cannot arrange to worship the forms of the Lord with all recommended paraphernalia, one can simply think about the form of the Lord and mentally offer everything recommended in the *śāstras,* including flowers, *candana* pulp, conchshell, umbrella, fan and *cāmara.* One can meditate upon offering and chant the twelve-syllable *mantra, oṁ namo bhagavate vāsudevāya.* Since the *mantra* and the Supreme Personality of Godhead are nondifferent, one can worship the form of the Lord with the *mantra* in the absence of physical paraphernalia. The story of the *brāhmaṇa* who worshiped the Lord within his mind, as related in *Bhakti-rasāmṛta-sindhu,* or *The Nectar of Devotion,* should be consulted in this connection. If paraphernalia is not present physically, one can think of the items and offer them to the Deity by chanting the *mantra.* Such are the liberal and potent facilities in the process of devotional service.

TEXTS 59–60

एवं कायेन मनसा वचसा च मनोगतम् ।
परिचर्यमाणो भगवान् भक्तिमत्परिचर्यया ॥५९॥

पुंसाममायिनां सम्यग्भजतां भाववर्धनः ।
श्रेयो दिशत्यभिमतं यद्धर्मादिषु देहिनाम् ॥६०॥

evaṁ kāyena manasā
vacasā ca mano-gatam
paricaryamāṇo bhagavān
bhaktimat-paricaryayā

puṁsām amāyināṁ samyag
bhajatāṁ bhāva-vardhanaḥ
śreyo diśaty abhimataṁ
yad dharmādiṣu dehinām

evam—thus; *kāyena*—by the body; *manasā*—by the mind; *vacasā*—by the words; *ca*—also; *manaḥ-gatam*—simply by thinking of the Lord; *paricaryamāṇaḥ*—engaged in the devotional service; *bhagavān*—the Supreme Personality of Godhead; *bhakti-mat*—according to the regulative principles of devotional service; *paricaryayā*—by worshiping the Lord; *puṁsām*—of the devotee; *amāyinām*—who is sincere and serious; *samyak*—perfectly; *bhajatām*—engaged in devotional service; *bhāva-vardhanaḥ*—the Lord, who increases the ecstasy of the devotee; *śreyaḥ*—ultimate goal; *diśati*—bestows; *abhimatam*—desire; *yat*—as they are; *dharma-ādiṣu*—regarding spiritual life and economic development; *dehinām*—of the conditioned souls.

TRANSLATION

Anyone who thus engages in the devotional service of the Lord, seriously and sincerely, with his mind, words and body, and who is fixed in the activities of the prescribed devotional methods, is blessed by the Lord according to his desire. If a devotee desires material religiosity, economic development, sense gratification or liberation from the material world, he is awarded these results.

PURPORT

Devotional service is so potent that one who renders devotional service can receive whatever he likes as a benediction from the Supreme Personality of Godhead. The conditioned souls are very much attached to the material world, and thus by performing religious rites they want the material benefits known as *dharma* and *artha*.

TEXT 61

विरक्तश्चेन्द्रियरतौ भक्तियोगेन भूयसा ।
तं निरन्तरभावेन भजेताद्धा विमुक्तये ॥६१॥

viraktaś cendriya-ratau
bhakti-yogena bhūyasā
taṁ nirantara-bhāvena
bhajetāddhā vimuktaye

viraktaḥ ca—completely renounced order of life; *indriya-ratau*—in the matter of sense gratification; *bhakti-yogena*—by the process of devotional service; *bhūyasā*—with great seriousness; *tam*—unto Him (the Supreme); *nirantara*—constantly, twenty-four hours daily; *bhāvena*—in the topmost stage of ecstasy; *bhajeta*—must worship; *addhā*—directly; *vimuktaye*—for liberation.

TRANSLATION

If one is very serious about liberation, he must stick to the process of transcendental loving service, engaging twenty-four hours a day in the highest stage of ecstasy, and he must certainly be aloof from all activities of sense gratification.

PURPORT

There are different stages of perfection according to different persons' objectives. Generally people are *karmīs*, for they engage in activities of sense gratification. Above the *karmīs* are the *jñānīs*, who are trying to become liberated from material entanglement. *Yogīs* are still more advanced because they meditate on the lotus feet of the Supreme Personality of Godhead. And above all these are the devotees, who simply engage in the transcendental loving service of the Lord; they are situated seriously on the topmost platform of ecstasy.

Here Dhruva Mahārāja is advised that if he has no desire for sense gratification, then he should directly engage himself in the transcendental loving service of the Lord. The path of *apavarga*, or liberation, begins from the stage called *mokṣa.* In this verse the word *vimuktaye,* "for liberation," is especially mentioned. If one wants to be happy within this material world, he may aspire to go to the different material planetary systems where there is a higher standard of sense gratification, but real *mokṣa,* or liberation, is performed without any such desire. This is explained in the *Bhakti-rasāmṛta-sindhu* by the term *anyābhilāṣitā-śūnyam,* "without desire for material sense gratification." For persons who are still inclined to enjoy material life in different stages or on different planets, the stage of liberation in *bhakti-yoga* is not recommended. Only persons who are completely free from the contamination of sense gratification can execute *bhakti-yoga,* or the process of devotional service, very purely. The activities on the path of *apavarga* up to the stages of *dharma, artha* and *kāma* are meant for sense gratification, but when one comes to the stage of *mokṣa,* the impersonalist liberation, the practitioner wants to merge into the existence of the Supreme. But that is also sense gratification. When one goes above the stage of liberation, however, he at once becomes one of the associates of the Lord to render transcendental loving service. That is technically called *vimukti.* For this specific *vimukti* liberation, Nārada Muni recommends that one directly engage himself in devotional service.

TEXT 62

इत्युक्तस्तं परिक्रम्य प्रणम्य च नृपार्भकः ।
ययौ मधुवनं पुण्यं हरेश्चरणचर्चितम् ॥६२॥

ity uktas taṁ parikramya
praṇamya ca nṛpārbhakaḥ
yayau madhuvanaṁ puṇyaṁ
hareś caraṇa-carcitam

iti—thus; *uktaḥ*—being spoken; *tam*—him (Nārada Muni); *parikramya*—by circumambulating; *praṇamya*—by offering obeisances; *ca*—also; *nṛpa-arbhakaḥ*—the boy of the King; *yayau*—went to; *madhuvanam*—a forest in Vṛndāvana known as Madhuvana; *puṇyam*—which is auspicious and pious; *hareḥ*—of the Lord; *caraṇa-carcitam*—imprinted by the lotus feet of Lord Kṛṣṇa.

TRANSLATION

When Dhruva Mahārāja, the son of the King, was thus advised by the great sage Nārada, he circumambulated Nārada, his spiritual master, and offered him respectful obeisances. Then he started for Madhuvana, which is always imprinted with the lotus footprints of Lord Kṛṣṇa and which is therefore especially auspicious.

TEXT 63

तपोवनं गते तस्मिन्प्रविष्टोऽन्तःपुरं मुनिः ।
अर्हितार्हणको राज्ञा सुखासीन उवाच तम् ॥६३॥

tapo-vanaṁ gate tasmin
praviṣṭo 'ntaḥ-puraṁ muniḥ
arhitārhaṇako rājñā
sukhāsīna uvāca tam

tapaḥ-vanam—the forest path where Dhruva Mahārāja executed his austerity; *gate*—having thus approached; *tasmin*—there; *praviṣṭaḥ*—having entered; *antaḥ-puram*—within the private house; *muniḥ*—the great sage Nārada; *arhita*—being worshiped; *arhaṇakaḥ*—by respectful behavior; *rājñā*—by the King; *sukha-āsinaḥ*—when he comfortably sat on his seat; *uvāca*—said; *tam*—unto him (the King).

TRANSLATION

After Dhruva entered Madhuvana Forest to execute devotional service, the great sage Nārada thought it wise to go to the King to see how he was faring within the palace. When Nārada Muni approached, the King received him properly, offering him due obeisances. After being seated comfortably, Nārada began to speak.

TEXT 64

नारद उवाच

राजन् किं ध्यायसे दीर्घं मुखेन परिशुष्यता ।
किं वा न रिष्यते कामो धर्मो वार्थेन संयुतः ॥६४॥

nārada uvāca
rājan kiṁ dhyāyase dīrghaṁ
mukhena pariśuṣyatā
kiṁ vā na riṣyate kāmo
dharmo vārthena saṁyutaḥ

nāradaḥ uvāca—the great sage Nārada Muni said; *rājan*—my dear King; *kim*—what; *dhyāyase*—thinking of; *dīrgham*—very deeply; *mukhena*—with your face; *pariśuṣyatā*—as if drying up; *kim vā*—whether; *na*—not; *riṣyate*—been lost; *kāmaḥ*—sense gratification; *dharmaḥ*—religious rituals; *vā*—or; *arthena*—with economic development; *saṁyutaḥ*—along with.

TRANSLATION

The great sage Nārada inquired: My dear King, your face appears to be withering up, and you look like you have been thinking of something for a very long time. Why is that? Have you been hampered in following your path of religious rites, economic development and sense gratification?

PURPORT

The four stages of advancement of human civilization are religiosity, economic development, sense gratification and, for some, the stage of liberation. Nārada Muni did not inquire from the King about his liberation, but only regarding the state management, which is meant for advancement of the three principles religiosity, economic development and sense gratification. Since those who engage in such activities are not interested in liberation, Nārada did not inquire from the King about this. Liberation is meant for persons who have lost all interest in religious ritualistic ceremonies, economic development and sense gratification.

TEXT 65

राजोवाच
सुतो मे बालको ब्रह्मन् स्त्रैणेनाकरुणात्मना ।
निर्वासितः पञ्चवर्षः सह मात्रा महान्कविः ॥६५॥

rājovāca
suto me bālako brahman
straiṇenākaruṇātmanā
nirvāsitaḥ pañca-varṣaḥ
saha mātrā mahān kaviḥ

rājā uvāca—the King replied; *sutaḥ*—son; *me*—my; *bālakaḥ*—tender boy; *brahman*—my dear *brāhmaṇa; straiṇena*—one who is too addicted to his wife; *akaruṇā-ātmanā*—one who is very hard of heart and without mercy; *nirvāsitaḥ*—is banished; *pañca-varṣaḥ*—although the boy is five years old; *saha*—with; *mātrā*—mother; *mahān*—great personality; *kaviḥ*—devotee.

TRANSLATION

The King replied: O best of the brāhmaṇas, I am very much addicted to my wife, and I am so fallen that I have abandoned all merciful behavior, even to my son, who is only five years old. I have banished him and his mother, even though he is a great soul and a great devotee.

PURPORT

In this verse there are some specific words which are to be understood very carefully. The King said that since he was very much addicted to his wife, he had lost all his mercy. That is the result of becoming too affectionate toward women. The King had two wives; the first wife was Sunīti, and the second was Suruci. He was too attached to the second wife, however, so he could not behave well with Dhruva Mahārāja. That was the cause of Dhruva's leaving home to perform austerities. Although as a father the King was affectionate toward his son, he minimized his affection for Dhruva Mahārāja because he was too much addicted to the second wife. Now he was repenting that both Dhruva Mahārāja and his mother, Sunīti, were practically banished. Dhruva Mahārāja went to the forest, and since his mother was being neglected by the King, she was therefore almost banished also. The King repented having banished his boy, for Dhruva was only five years old and a father should not banish his wife and children or neglect their maintenance. Repentant over his neglect of both Sunīti and her son, he was morose, and his face appeared withered. According to *Manu-smṛti*, one should never desert his wife and children. In a case where the wife and children are disobedient and do not follow the principles of home life, they are sometimes given up. But in the case of Dhruva Mahārāja this was not applicable because Dhruva was very mannerly and obedient. Moreover, he was a great devotee. Such a person is never to be neglected, yet the King was obliged to banish him. Now he was very sorry.

TEXT 66

अप्यनाथं वने ब्रह्मन्मास्मादन्त्यर्भकं वृकाः ।
श्रान्तं शयानं क्षुधितं परिम्लानमुखाम्बुजम् ॥६६॥

apy anāthaṁ vane brahman
mā smādanty arbhakaṁ vṛkāḥ
śrāntaṁ śayānaṁ kṣudhitaṁ
parimlāna-mukhāmbujam

api—certainly; *anātham*—without being protected by anyone; *vane*—in the forest; *brahman*—my dear *brāhmaṇa; mā*—whether or not; *sma*—did not; *adanti*—devour; *arbhakam*—the helpless boy; *vṛkāḥ*—wolves; *śrāntam*—being fatigued; *śayānam*—lying down; *kṣudhitam*—being hungry; *parimlāna*—emaciated; *mukha-ambujam*—his face, which is just like a lotus flower.

TRANSLATION

My dear brāhmaṇa, the face of my son was just like a lotus flower. I am thinking of his precarious condition. He is unprotected, and he might be very hungry. He might have lain down somewhere in the forest, and the wolves might have attacked him to eat his body.

TEXT 67

अहो मे बत दौरात्म्यं स्त्रीजितस्योपधारय ।
योऽङ्कं प्रेम्णारुरुक्षन्तं नाभ्यनन्दमसत्तमः ॥६७॥

aho me bata daurātmyaṁ
strī-jitasyopadhāraya

yo 'ṅkaṁ premṇāruruksantaṁ
nābhyanandam asattamaḥ

aho—alas; *me*—my; *bata*—certainly; *daurātmyam*—cruelty; *strī-jitasya*—conquered by a woman; *upadhāraya*—just think of me in this regard; *yaḥ*—who; *aṅkam*—lap; *premṇā*—out of love; *āruruksan-tam*—trying to rise onto it; *na*—not; *abhyanandam*—received properly; *asat-tamaḥ*—the most cruel.

TRANSLATION

Alas, just see how I was conquered by my wife! Just imagine my cruelty! Out of love and affection the boy was trying to get up on my lap, but I did not receive him, nor did I even pat him for a moment. Just imagine how hardhearted I am.

TEXT 68

नारद उवाच
मा मा शुचः स्वतनयं देवगुप्तं विशाम्पते ।
तत्प्रभावमविज्ञाय प्रावृङ्क्ते यद्यशो जगत् ॥६८॥

nārada uvāca
mā mā śucaḥ sva-tanayaṁ
deva-guptaṁ viśāmpate
tat-prabhāvam avijñāya
prāvṛṅkte yad-yaśo jagat

nāradaḥ uvāca—the great sage Nārada said; *mā*—do not; *mā*—do not; *śucaḥ*—be aggrieved; *sva-tanayam*—of your own son; *deva-guptam*—he is well protected by the Lord; *viśām-pate*—O master of human society; *tat*—his; *prabhāvam*—influence; *avijñāya*—without knowing; *prāvṛṅkte*—widespread; *yat*—whose; *yaśaḥ*—reputation; *jagat*—all over the world.

TRANSLATION

The great sage Nārada replied: My dear King, please do not be aggrieved about your son. He is well protected by the Supreme

Personality of Godhead. Although you have no actual information of his influence, his reputation is already spread all over the world.

PURPORT

Sometimes when we hear that great sages and devotees go to the forest and engage themselves in devotional service or meditation, we become surprised: how can one live in the forest and not be taken care of by anyone? But the answer, given by a great authority, Nārada Muni, is that such persons are well protected by the Supreme Personality of Godhead. *Śaraṇāgati*, or surrender, means acceptance or firm belief that wherever the surrendered soul lives he is always protected by the Supreme Personality of Godhead; he is never alone or unprotected. Dhruva Mahārāja's affectionate father thought his young boy, only five years old, to be in a very precarious position in the jungle, but Nārada Muni assured him, "You do not have sufficient information about the influence of your son." Anyone who engages in devotional service, anywhere within this universe, is never unprotected.

TEXT 69

सुदुष्करं कर्म कृत्वा लोकपालैरपि प्रभुः ।
ऐष्यत्यचिरतो राजन् यशो विपुलयंस्तव ॥६९॥

suduṣkaraṁ karma kṛtvā
loka-pālair api prabhuḥ
aiṣyaty acirato rājan
yaśo vipulayaṁs tava

su-duṣkaram—impossible to perform; *karma*—work; *kṛtvā*—after performing; *loka-pālaiḥ*—by great personalities; *api*—even; *prabhuḥ*—quite competent; *aiṣyati*—will come back; *aciratah*—without delay; *rājan*—my dear King; *yaśaḥ*—reputation; *vipulayan*—causing to become great; *tava*—your.

TRANSLATION

My dear King, your son is very competent. He will perform activities which would be impossible even for great kings and sages.

Very soon he will complete his task and come back home. You should know that he will also spread your reputation all over the world.

PURPORT

Here in this verse Nārada Muni has described Dhruva Mahārāja as *prabhu.* This word is applicable to the Supreme Personality of Godhead. Sometimes the spiritual master is addressed as Prabhupāda. *Prabhu* means "the Supreme Personality of Godhead," and *pāda* means "post." According to Vaiṣṇava philosophy, the spiritual master occupies the post of the Supreme Personality of Godhead, or in other words he is the bona fide representative of the Supreme Lord. Dhruva Mahārāja is also described here as *prabhu* because he is an *ācārya* of the Vaiṣṇava school. Another meaning of *prabhu* is "master of the senses," just like the word *svāmī.* Another significant word is *suduṣkaram,* "very difficult to perform." What was the task that Dhruva Mahārāja undertook? The most difficult task in life is to satisfy the Supreme Personality of Godhead, and Dhruva Mahārāja would be able to do that. We must remember that Dhruva Mahārāja was not fickle; he was determined to execute his service and then come back. Every devotee, therefore, should be determined that in this life he will be able to satisfy the Supreme Personality of Godhead and by that process go back home, back to Godhead. That is the perfection of the highest mission of life.

TEXT 70

मैत्रेय उवाच
इति देवर्षिणा प्रोक्तं विश्रुत्य जगतीपतिः ।
राजलक्ष्मीमनादृत्य पुत्रमेवान्वचिन्तयत् ॥७०॥

maitreya uvāca
iti devarṣiṇā proktaṁ
viśrutya jagatī-patiḥ
rāja-lakṣmīm anādṛtya
putram evānvacintayat

maitreyaḥ uvāca—the great sage Maitreya said; *iti*—thus; *devarṣiṇā*—by the great sage Nārada; *proktam*—spoken; *viśrutya*—hearing; *jagatī-patiḥ*—the King; *rāja-lakṣmīm*—the opulence of his big kingdom; *anādṛtya*—without taking care of; *putram*—his son; *eva*—certainly; *anvacintayat*—began to think of him.

TRANSLATION

The great Maitreya continued: The King, Uttānapāda, after being advised by Nārada Muni, practically gave up all duties in relation with his kingdom, which was very vast and wide, opulent like the goddess of fortune, and he simply began to think of his son Dhruva.

TEXT 71

तत्राभिषिक्तः प्रयतस्तामुपोष्य विभावरीम् ।
समाहितः पर्यचरदृष्यादेशेन पूरुषम् ॥७१॥

tatrābhiṣiktaḥ prayatas
tām upoṣya vibhāvarīm
samāhitaḥ paryacarad
ṛṣy-ādeśena pūruṣam

tatra—thereupon; *abhiṣiktaḥ*—after taking a bath; *prayataḥ*—with great attention; *tām*—that; *upoṣya*—fasting; *vibhāvarīm*—night; *samāhitaḥ*—perfect attention; *paryacarat*—worshiped; *ṛṣi*—by the great sage Nārada; *ādeśena*—as advised; *pūruṣam*—the Supreme Personality of Godhead.

TRANSLATION

Elsewhere, Dhruva Mahārāja, having arrived at Madhuvana, took his bath in the River Yamunā and observed fasting in the night with great care and attention. After that, as advised by the great sage Nārada, he engaged himself in worshiping the Supreme Personality of Godhead.

PURPORT

The significance of this particular verse is that Dhruva Mahārāja acted exactly according to the advice of his spiritual master, the great sage Nārada. Śrīla Viśvanātha Cakravartī also advises that if we want to be successful in our attempt to go back to Godhead, we must very seriously act according to the instruction of the spiritual master. That is the way of perfection. There need be no anxiety over attaining perfection because if one follows the instruction given by the spiritual master he is sure to attain perfection. Our only concern should be how to execute the order of the spiritual master. A spiritual master is expert in giving special instructions to each of his disciples, and if the disciple executes the order of the spiritual master, that is the way of his perfection.

TEXT 72

त्रिरात्रान्ते त्रिरात्रान्ते कपित्थबदराशनः ।
आत्मवृत्त्यनुसारेण मासं निन्येऽर्चयन्हरिम् ॥७२॥

tri-rātrānte tri-rātrānte
kapittha-badarāśanaḥ
ātma-vṛtty-anusāreṇa
māsaṁ ninye 'rcayan harim

tri—three; *rātra-ante*—at the end of night; *tri*—three; *rātra-ante*—at the end of night; *kapittha-badara*—fruits and berries; *aśanaḥ*—eating; *ātma-vṛtti*—just to preserve the body; *anusāreṇa*—as it was necessary, minimum; *māsam*—one month; *ninye*—passed away; *arcayan*—worshiping; *harim*—the Supreme Personality of Godhead.

TRANSLATION

For the first month Dhruva Mahārāja ate only fruits and berries on every third day, only to keep his body and soul together, and in this way he progressed in his worship of the Supreme Personality of Godhead.

PURPORT

Kapittha is a flower which is known in Indian vernacular as *kayeta.* We do not find an English equivalent for the name of this flower, but its fruit is generally not accepted by human beings; it is eaten by monkeys in the forest. Dhruva Mahārāja, however, accepted such fruits, not for luxurious feasting but just to keep his body and soul together. The body needs food, but a devotee should not accept foodstuff to satisfy the tongue in sense gratification. It is recommended in *Bhagavad-gītā* that one should accept as much food as necessary to keep the body fit, but one should not eat for luxury. Dhruva Mahārāja is an *ācārya*, and by undergoing severe austerities and penances he teaches us how one should execute devotional service. We must carefully know the process of Dhruva Mahārāja's service; how severely he passed his days will be shown in later verses. We should always remember that to become a bona fide devotee of the Lord is not an easy task, but in this age, by the mercy of Lord Caitanya, it has been made very easy. But if we do not follow even the liberal instructions of Lord Caitanya, how can we expect to discharge our regular duties in devotional service? It is not possible in this age to follow Dhruva Mahārāja in his austerity, but the principles must be followed; we should not disregard the regulative principles given by our spiritual master, for they make it easier for the conditioned soul. As far as our ISKCON movement is concerned, we simply ask that one observe the four prohibitive rules, chant sixteen rounds and, instead of indulging in luxurious eating for the tongue, simply accept *prasāda* offered to the Lord. This does not mean that with our fasting the Lord should also fast. The Lord should be given foodstuff which is as nice as possible. But we should not make it a point to satisfy our own tongues. As far as possible we should accept simple foodstuff, just to keep the body and soul together to execute devotional service.

It is our duty to remember always that in comparison to Dhruva Mahārāja we are insignificant. We cannot do anything like what Dhruva Mahārāja did for self-realization because we are absolutely incompetent to execute such service. But by Lord Caitanya's mercy we have been given all concessions possible for this age, so at least we should always remember that neglect of our prescribed duties in devotional service will not make us successful in the mission we have undertaken. It is our duty to follow in the footsteps of Dhruva Mahārāja, for he was very determined. We should also be determined to finish our duties in executing devotional service in this life; we should not wait for another life to finish our job.

TEXT 73

द्वितीयं च तथा मासं षष्ठे षष्ठेऽर्भको दिने ।
तृणपर्णादिभिः शीर्णैः कृतान्नोऽभ्यर्चयन्विभुम् ॥७३॥

dvitīyaṁ ca tathā māsaṁ
ṣaṣṭhe ṣaṣṭhe 'rbhako dine
tṛṇa-parṇādibhiḥ śīrṇaiḥ
kṛtānno 'bhyarcayan vibhum

dvitīyam—the next month; *ca*—also; *tathā*—as mentioned above; *māsam*—month; *ṣaṣṭhe ṣaṣṭhe*—every sixth day; *arbhakaḥ*—the innocent boy; *dine*—on days; *tṛṇa-parṇa-ādibhiḥ*—by grasses and leaves; *śīrṇaiḥ*—which were dry; *kṛta-annaḥ*—made for his food; *abhyarcayan*—and thus continued his method of worship; *vibhum*—for the Supreme Personality of Godhead.

TRANSLATION

In the second month Dhruva Mahārāja ate only every six days, and for his eatables he took dry grass and leaves. Thus he continued his worship.

TEXT 74

तृतीयं चानयन्मासं नवमे नवमेऽहनि ।
अब्भक्ष उत्तमश्लोकमुपाधावत्समाधिना ॥७४॥

tṛtīyaṁ cānayan māsaṁ
navame navame 'hani
ab-bhakṣa uttamaślokam
upādhāvat samādhinā

tṛtīyam—the third month; *ca*—also; *ānayan*—passing; *māsam*—one month; *navame navame*—on each ninth; *ahani*—on the day; *ap-bhakṣaḥ*—drinking water only; *uttama-ślokam*—the Supreme Personality of Godhead, who is worshiped by selected verses; *upādhāvat*—worshiped; *samādhinā*—in trance.

TRANSLATION

In the third month he drank water only every nine days. Thus he remained completely in trance and worshiped the Supreme Personality of Godhead, who is adored by selected verses.

TEXT 75

चतुर्थमपि वै मासं द्वादशे द्वादशेऽहनि ।
वायुभक्षो जितश्वासो ध्यायन्देवमधारयत् ॥७५॥

caturtham api vai māsaṁ
dvādaśe dvādaśe 'hani
vāyu-bhakṣo jita-śvāso
dhyāyan devam adhārayat

caturtham—fourth; *api*—also; *vai*—in that way; *māsam*—the month; *dvādaśe dvādaśe*—on the twelfth; *ahani*—day; *vāyu*—air; *bhakṣaḥ*—eating; *jita-śvāsaḥ*—controlling the breathing process; *dhyāyan*—meditating; *devam*—the Supreme Lord; *adhārayat*—worshiped.

TRANSLATION

In the fourth month Dhruva Mahārāja became a complete master of the breathing exercise, and thus he inhaled air only every twelfth day. In this way he became completely fixed in his position and worshiped the Supreme Personality of Godhead.

TEXT 76

पञ्चमे मास्यनुप्राप्ते जितश्वासो नृपात्मजः ।
ध्यायन् ब्रह्म पदैकेन तस्थौ स्थाणुरिवाचलः ॥७६॥

pañcame māsy anuprāpte
jita-śvāso nṛpātmajaḥ
dhyāyan brahma padaikena
tasthau sthāṇur ivācalaḥ

pañcame—in the fifth; *māsi*—in the month; *anuprāpte*—being situated; *jita-śvāsaḥ*—and still controlling the breathing; *nṛpa-ātmajaḥ*—the son of the King; *dhyāyan*—meditating; *brahma*—the Supreme Personality of Godhead; *padā ekena*—with one leg; *tasthau*—stood; *sthāṇuḥ*—just like a column; *iva*—like; *acalaḥ*—without movement.

TRANSLATION

By the fifth month, Mahārāja Dhruva, the son of the King, had controlled his breathing so perfectly that he was able to stand on only one leg, just as a column stands, without motion, and concentrate his mind fully on the Parabrahman.

TEXT 77

सर्वतो मन आकृष्य हृदि भूतेन्द्रियाशयम् ।
ध्यायन्भगवतो रूपं नाद्राक्षीत्किंचनापरम् ॥७७॥

sarvato mana ākṛṣya
hṛdi bhūtendriyāśayam
dhyāyan bhagavato rūpaṁ
nādrākṣīt kiñcanāparam

sarvataḥ—in all respects; *manaḥ*—mind; *ākṛṣya*—concentrating; *hṛdi*—in the heart; *bhūta-indriya-āśayam*—resting place of the senses and the objects of the senses; *dhyāyan*—meditating; *bhagavataḥ*—of the Supreme Personality of Godhead; *rūpam*—form; *na adrākṣīt*—did not see; *kiñcana*—anything; *aparam*—else.

TRANSLATION

He completely controlled his senses and their objects, and in this way he fixed his mind, without diversion to anything else, upon the form of the Supreme Personality of Godhead.

PURPORT

The yogic principles of meditation are clearly explained here. One has to fix one's mind upon the form of the Supreme Personality of Godhead without diversion to any other objective. It is not that one can meditate or concentrate on an impersonal objective. To try to do so is simply a waste of time, for it is unnecessarily troublesome, as explained in *Bhagavad-gītā*.

TEXT 78

आधारं महदादीनां प्रधानपुरुषेश्वरम् ।
ब्रह्म धारयमाणस्य त्रयो लोकाश्चकम्पिरे ॥७८॥

ādhāraṁ mahad-ādīnāṁ
pradhāna-puruṣeśvaram
brahma dhārayamāṇasya
trayo lokāś cakampire

ādhāram—repose; *mahat-ādīnām*—of the material sum total known as the *mahat-tattva; pradhāna*—the chief; *puruṣa-īśvaram*—master of all living entities; *brahma*—the Supreme Brahman, the Personality of Godhead; *dhārayamāṇasya*—having taken into the heart; *trayaḥ*—the three planetary systems; *lokāḥ*—all the planets; *cakampire*—began to tremble.

TRANSLATION

When Dhruva Mahārāja thus captured the Supreme Personality of Godhead, who is the refuge of the total material creation and who is the master of all living entities, the three worlds began to tremble.

PURPORT

In this verse the particular word *brahma* is very significant. *Brahman* refers to one who not only is the greatest, but has the potency to expand to an unlimited extent. How was it possible for Dhruva Mahārāja to capture Brahman within his heart? This question has been very nicely answered by Jīva Gosvāmī. He says that the Supreme Personality of Godhead is the origin of Brahman, for since He comprises everything material and spiritual, there cannot be anything greater than He. In the *Bhagavad-gītā* also the Supreme Godhead says, "I am the resting place of Brahman." Many persons, especially the Māyāvādī philosophers, consider Brahman the biggest, all-expanding substance, but according to this verse and other Vedic literatures, such as *Bhagavad-gītā*, the resting place of Brahman is the Supreme Personality of Godhead, just as the resting place of the sunshine is the sun globe. Śrīla Jīva Gosvāmī, therefore, says that since the transcendental form of the Lord is the seed of all greatness, He is the Supreme Brahman. Since the Supreme Brahman was situated in the heart of Dhruva Mahārāja, he became heavier than the heaviest, and therefore everything trembled in all three worlds and in the spiritual world.

The *mahat-tattva*, or the sum total of the material creation, is to be understood to be the ultimate end of all universes, including all the living entities therein. Brahman is the resort of the *mahat-tattva*, which includes all material and spiritual entities. It is described in this connection that the Supreme Brahman, the Personality of Godhead, is the master of both *pradhāna* and *puruṣa. Pradhāna* means subtle matter, such as ether. *Puruṣa* means the spiritual spark living entities who are entangled in that subtle material existence. These may also be described as *parā prakṛti* and *aparā prakṛti*, as stated in *Bhagavad-gītā.* Kṛṣṇa, being the controller of both the *prakṛtis*, is thus the master of *pradhāna* and *puruṣa.* In the Vedic hymns also the Supreme Brahman is described as *antaḥ-praviṣṭaḥ śāstā.* This indicates that the Supreme Personality of Godhead is controlling everything and entering into everything. The *Brahma-saṁhitā* (5.35) further confirms this. *Aṇḍāntara-stha-paramāṇu-cayāntara-stham:* He has entered not only the universes, but even the atom. In *Bhagavad-gītā* (10.42) Kṛṣṇa also says, *viṣṭabhyāham idaṁ kṛtsnam.* The Supreme Personality of Godhead controls everything by entering into everything. By associating constantly with the Supreme Personality in his heart, Dhruva Mahārāja naturally became equal to the greatest, Brahman, by His association, and thus became the heaviest, and the entire universe trembled. In conclusion, a person who always concentrates on the transcendental form of Kṛṣṇa within his heart can very easily strike the whole world with wonder at his activities. This is the perfection of *yoga* performance, as confirmed in *Bhagavad-gītā* (6.47). *Yoginām api sarveṣām:* of all *yogīs*, the *bhakti-yogī*, who thinks of Kṛṣṇa always within his heart and engages in His loving transcendental service, is the topmost. Ordinary *yogīs* can exhibit wonderful material activities, known as *aṣṭa-siddhi*, eight kinds of yogic perfection, but a pure devotee of the Lord can surpass these perfections by performing activities which can make the whole universe tremble.

TEXT 79

यदैकपादेन स पार्थिवार्भक-
स्तस्थौ तदङ्गुष्ठनिपीडिता मही ।
ननाम तत्रार्धमिभेन्द्रधिष्ठिता
तरीव सव्येतरतः पदे पदे ॥७९॥

yadaika-pādena sa pārthivārbhakas
tasthau tad-aṅguṣṭha-nipīḍitā mahī
nanāma tatrārdham ibhendra-dhiṣṭhitā
tarīva savyetarataḥ pade pade

yadā—when; *eka*—with one; *pādena*—leg; *saḥ*—Dhruva Mahārāja; *pārthiva*—the King's; *arbhakaḥ*—child; *tasthau*—remained standing; *tat-aṅguṣṭha*—his big toe; *nipīḍitā*—being pressed; *mahī*—the earth; *nanāma*—bent down; *tatra*—then; *ardham*—half; *ibha-indra*—the king of elephants; *dhiṣṭhitā*—being situated; *tarī iva*—like a boat; *savya-itarataḥ*—right and left; *pade pade*—in every step.

TRANSLATION

As Dhruva Mahārāja, the King's son, kept himself steadily standing on one leg, the pressure of his big toe pushed down half the earth, just as an elephant being carried on a boat rocks the boat left and right with his every step.

PURPORT

The most significant expression in this verse is *pārthivārbhakaḥ*, son of the King. When Dhruva Mahārāja was at home, although he was a king's son, he was prevented from getting on the lap of his father. But when he became advanced in self-realization, or devotional service, by the pressure of his toe he could push down the whole earth. That is the difference between ordinary consciousness and Kṛṣṇa consciousness. In ordinary consciousness a king's son may be refused something even by his father, but when the same person becomes fully Kṛṣṇa conscious within his heart, he can push down the earth with the pressure of his toe.

One cannot argue, "How is it that Dhruva Mahārāja, who was prevented from getting up on the lap of his father, could press down the whole earth?" This argument is not very much appreciated by the learned, for it is an example of *nagna-mātṛkā* logic. By this logic one would think that because his mother in her childhood was naked, she should remain naked even when she is grown up. The stepmother of Dhruva Mahārāja might have been thinking in a similar way: since she had refused to allow him to get up on the lap of his father, how could Dhruva perform such wonderful activities as pressing down the whole earth? She must have been very surprised when she learned that Dhruva Mahārāja, by concentrating constantly on the Supreme Personality of Godhead within his heart, could press down the entire earth, like an elephant who presses down the boat on which it is loaded.

TEXT 80

तस्मिन्नभिध्यायति विश्वमात्मनो
द्वारं निरुध्यासुमनन्यया धिया ।
लोका निरुच्छ्वासनिपीडिता भृशं
सलोकपालाः शरणं ययुर्हरिम् ॥८०॥

tasminn abhidhyāyati viśvam ātmano
dvāraṁ nirudhyāsum ananyayā dhiyā
lokā nirucchvāsa-nipīḍitā bhṛśaṁ
sa-loka-pālāḥ śaraṇaṁ yayur harim

tasmin—Dhruva Mahārāja; *abhidhyāyati*—when meditating with full concentration; *viśvam ātmanaḥ*—the total body of the universe; *dvāram*—the holes; *nirudhya*—closed; *asum*—the life air; *ananyayā*—without being diverted; *dhiyā*—meditation; *lokāḥ*—all the planets; *nirucchvāsa*—having stopped breathing; *nipīḍitāḥ*—thus being suffocated; *bhṛśam*—very soon; *sa-loka-pālāḥ*—all the great demigods from different planets; *śaraṇam*—shelter; *yayuḥ*—took; *harim*—of the Supreme Personality of Godhead.

TRANSLATION

When Dhruva Mahārāja became practically one in heaviness with Lord Viṣṇu, the total consciousness, due to his fully concentrating, and closing all the holes of his body, the total universal breathing became choked up, and all the great demigods in all the planetary systems felt suffocated and thus took shelter of the Supreme Personality of Godhead.

PURPORT

When hundreds of persons are sitting in an airplane, although they remain individual units, they each share in the total force of the airplane, which runs at thousands of miles per hour; similarly, when unit energy is identified with the service of the total energy, the unit energy becomes as powerful as the total energy. As explained in the previous verse, Dhruva Mahārāja, because of his spiritual advancement, became almost the total heaviness, and thus he pressed down the whole earth. Moreover, by such spiritual power his unit body became the total body of the universe. Thus when he closed the holes of his unit body to firmly concentrate his mind on the Supreme Personality of Godhead, all the units of the universe—namely all the living entities, including the big demigods—felt the pressure of suffocation, as if their breathing were being choked. Therefore they all took shelter of the Supreme Personality of Godhead because they were perplexed as to what had happened.

This example of Dhruva Mahārāja's closing the holes of his personal body and thereby closing the breathing holes of the total universe clearly indicates that a devotee, by his personal devotional service, can influence all the people of the whole world to become devotees of the Lord. If there is only one pure devotee in pure Kṛṣṇa consciousness, he can change the total consciousness of the world into Kṛṣṇa consciousness. This is not very difficult to understand if we study the behavior of Dhruva Mahārāja.

TEXT 81

देवा ऊचुः

नैवं विदामो भगवन् प्राणरोधं

चराचरस्याखिलसत्त्वधाम्नः ।

विधेहि तन्नो वृजिनाद्विमोक्षं
प्राप्ता वयं त्वां शरणं शरण्यम् ॥८१॥

devā ūcuḥ
naivaṁ vidāmo bhagavan prāṇa-rodhaṁ
carācarasyākhila-sattva-dhāmnaḥ
vidhehi tan no vṛjinād vimokṣaṁ
prāptā vayaṁ tvāṁ śaraṇaṁ śaraṇyam

devāḥ ūcuḥ—all the demigods said; *na*—not; *evam*—thus; *vidāmaḥ*—we can understand; *bhagavan*—O Personality of Godhead; *prāṇa-rodham*—how we feel our breathing choked; *cara*—moving; *acarasya*—not moving; *akhila*—universal; *sattva*—existence; *dhāmnaḥ*—the reservoir of; *vidhehi*—kindly do the needful; *tat*—therefore; *naḥ*—our; *vṛjināt*—from the danger; *vimokṣam*—liberation; *prāptāḥ*—approaching; *vayam*—all of us; *tvām*—unto You; *śaraṇam*—shelter; *śaraṇyam*—worthy to be taken shelter of.

TRANSLATION

The demigods said: Dear Lord, You are the refuge of all moving and nonmoving living entities. We feel all living entities to be suffocating, their breathing processes choked up. We have never experienced such a thing. Since You are the ultimate shelter of all surrendered souls, we have therefore approached You; kindly save us from this danger.

PURPORT

Dhruva Mahārāja's influence, attained by executing devotional service unto the Lord, was felt even by the demigods, who had never before experienced such a situation. Because of Dhruva Mahārāja's controlling his breathing, the entire universal breathing process was choked. It is by the will of the Supreme Personality of Godhead that material entities cannot breathe whereas spiritual entities are able to breathe; material entities are products of the Lord's external energy, whereas spiritual entities are products of the Lord's internal energy. The demigods approached the Supreme Personality of Godhead, who is the controller of both kinds of entities, in order to know why their breathing was choked. The Supreme Lord is the ultimate goal for the solution to all problems within this material world. In the spiritual world there are no problems, but the material world is always problematic. Since the Supreme Personality of Godhead is the master of both the material and spiritual worlds, it is better to approach Him in all problematic situations. Those who are devotees, therefore, have no problems in this material world. *Viśvaṁ pūrṇa-sukhāyate* (*Caitanya-candrāmṛta*): devotees are free from all problems because they are fully surrendered unto the Supreme Personality of Godhead. For a devotee, everything in the world is very pleasing because he knows how to use everything in the transcendental loving service of the Lord.

TEXT 82

श्रीभगवानुवाच

मा भैष्ट बालं तपसो दुरत्यया-
न्निवर्तयिष्ये प्रतियात स्वधाम ।
यतो हि वः प्राणनिरोध आसी-
दौत्तानपादिर्मयि संगतात्मा ॥८२॥

śrī-bhagavān uvāca
mā bhaiṣṭa bālaṁ tapaso duratyayān
nivartayiṣye pratiyāta sva-dhāma
yato hi vaḥ prāṇa-nirodha āsīd
auttānapādir mayi saṅgatātmā

śrī-bhagavān uvāca—the Supreme Personality of Godhead replied; *mā bhaiṣṭa*—do not be afraid; *bālam*—the boy Dhruva; *tapasaḥ*—by his severe austerity; *duratyayāt*—strongly determined; *nivartayiṣye*—I shall ask him to stop this; *pratiyāta*—you can return; *sva-dhāma*—your own respective homes; *yataḥ*—from whom; *hi*—certainly; *vaḥ*—your; *prāṇa-nirodhaḥ*—choking the life air; *āsīt*—happened; *auttānapādiḥ*—on account of the son of King Uttānapāda; *mayi*—unto Me; *saṅgata-ātmā*—fully absorbed in thought of Me.

TRANSLATION

The Supreme Personality of Godhead replied: My dear demigods, do not be perturbed by this. It is due to the severe austerity and full determination of the son of King Uttānapāda, who is now fully absorbed in thought of Me. He has obstructed the universal breathing process. You can safely return to your respective homes. I shall stop this boy in his severe acts of austerities, and you will be saved from this situation.

PURPORT

Here one word, *saṅgatātmā*, is misinterpreted by the Māyāvādī philosophers, who say that the self of Dhruva Mahārāja became one with the Supreme Self, the Personality of Godhead. The Māyāvādī philosophers want to prove by this word that the Supersoul and the individual soul become united in this way and that after such unification the individual soul has no separate existence. But here it is clearly said by the Supreme Lord that Dhruva Mahārāja was so absorbed in meditation on the thought of the Supreme Personality of Godhead that He Himself, the universal consciousness, was attracted to Dhruva. In order to please the demigods, He wanted to go Himself to Dhruva Mahārāja to stop him from this severe austerity. The Māyāvādī philosophers' conclusion that the Supersoul and the individual soul become united is not supported by this statement. Rather, the Supersoul, the Personality of Godhead, wanted to stop Dhruva Mahārāja from this severe austerity.

By pleasing the Supreme Personality of Godhead, one pleases everyone, just as by watering the root of a tree one satisfies every branch, twig and leaf of the tree. If one can attract the Supreme Personality of Godhead, one naturally attracts the whole universe because Kṛṣṇa is the supreme cause of the universe. All the demigods were afraid of being totally vanquished by suffocation, but the Personality of Godhead assured them that Dhruva Mahārāja was a great devotee of the Lord and was not about to annihilate everyone in the universe. A devotee is never envious of other living entities.

Thus end the Bhaktivedanta purports of the Fourth Canto, Eighth Chapter, of the Śrīmad-Bhāgavatam, *entitled "Dhruva Mahārāja Leaves Home for the Forest."*

CHAPTER NINE

Dhruva Mahārāja Returns Home

TEXT 1

मैत्रेय उवाच
त एवमुत्सन्नभया उरुक्रमे
कृतावनामाः प्रययुस्त्रिविष्टपम् ।
सहस्रशीर्षापि ततो गरुत्मता
मधोर्वनं भृत्यदिदृक्षया गतः ॥ १ ॥

maitreya uvāca
ta evam utsanna-bhayā urukrame
kṛtāvanāmāḥ prayayus tri-viṣṭapam
sahasraśīrṣāpi tato garutmatā
madhor vanaṁ bhṛtya-didṛkṣayā gataḥ

maitreyaḥ uvāca—the great sage Maitreya continued; *te*—the demigods; *evam*—thus; *utsanna-bhayāḥ*—being freed from all fears; *urukrame*—unto the Supreme Personality of Godhead, whose actions are uncommon; *kṛta-avanāmāḥ*—they offered their obeisances; *prayayuḥ*—they returned; *tri-viṣṭapam*—to their respective heavenly planets; *sahasra-śīrṣā api*—also the Personality of Godhead known as Sahasraśīrṣā; *tataḥ*—from there; *garutmatā*—getting up on the back of Garuḍa; *madhoḥ vanam*—the forest known as Madhuvana; *bhṛtya*—servant; *didṛkṣayā*—wishing to see him; *gataḥ*—went.

TRANSLATION

The great sage Maitreya told Vidura: When the demigods were thus reassured by the Personality of Godhead, they were freed from all fears, and after offering their obeisances, they returned to

their heavenly planets. Then the Lord, who is nondifferent from the Sahasraśīrṣā incarnation, got on the back of Garuḍa, who carried Him to the Madhuvana Forest to see His servant Dhruva.

PURPORT

The word *sahasraśīrṣā* refers to the Personality of Godhead known as Garbhodakaśāyī Viṣṇu. Although the Lord appeared as Kṣīrodakaśāyī Viṣṇu, He has been described here as Sahasraśīrṣā Viṣṇu because He is nondifferent from Garbhodakaśāyī Viṣṇu. According to Śrīla Sanātana Gosvāmī in his *Bhāgavatāmṛta*, the Sahasraśīrṣā Personality of Godhead who appeared at that time was the incarnation known as Pṛśnigarbha. He created the planet known as Dhruvaloka for the habitation of Dhruva Mahārāja.

TEXT 2

स वै धिया योगविपाकतीव्रया
हृत्पद्मकोशे स्फुरितं तडित्प्रभम् ।
तिरोहितं सहसैवोपलक्ष्य
बहिःस्थितं तदवस्थं ददर्श ॥ २ ॥

sa vai dhiyā yoga-vipāka-tīvrayā
hṛt-padma-kośe sphuritaṁ taḍit-prabham
tirohitaṁ sahasaivopalakṣya
bahiḥ-sthitaṁ tad-avasthaṁ dadarśa

saḥ—Dhruva Mahārāja; *vai*—also; *dhiyā*—by meditation; *yoga-vipāka-tīvrayā*—on account of mature realization of the yogic process; *hṛt*—the heart; *padma-kośe*—on the lotus of; *sphuritam*—manifested; *taḍit-prabham*—brilliant like lightning; *tirohitam*—having disappeared; *sahasā*—all of a sudden; *eva*—also; *upalakṣya*—by observing; *bahiḥ-sthitam*—externally situated; *tat-avastham*—in the same posture; *dadarśa*—was able to see.

TRANSLATION

The form of the Lord, which was brilliant like lightning and in which Dhruva Mahārāja, in his mature yogic process, was fully ab-

sorbed in meditation, all of a sudden disappeared. Thus Dhruva was perturbed, and his meditation broke. But as soon as he opened his eyes he saw the Supreme Personality of Godhead personally present, just as he had been seeing the Lord in his heart.

PURPORT

Because of his mature position in yogic meditation, Dhruva Mahārāja was constantly observing the form of the Personality of Godhead within his heart, but all of a sudden, when the Supreme Personality disappeared from his heart, he thought that he had lost Him. Dhruva Mahārāja was perturbed, but upon opening his eyes and breaking his meditation he saw the same form of the Lord before him. In the *Brahma-saṁhitā* (5.38) it is said, *premāñjana-cchurita-bhakti-vilocanena:* a saintly person who has developed love of Godhead by devotional service always sees the Lord's transcendental form of Śyāmasundara. This Śyāmasundara form of the Lord within the heart of a devotee is not imaginary. When a devotee becomes mature in his prosecution of devotional service, he sees face to face the same Śyāmasundara he has thought of during the entire course of his devotional service. Since the Supreme Lord is absolute, the form within the heart of a devotee, the form in the temple and the original form in Vaikuṇṭha, Vṛndāvana-dhāma, are all the same; they are nondifferent from one another.

TEXT 3

तद्दर्शनेनागतसाध्वसः क्षिता-
वबन्दताङ्गं विनमय्य दण्डवत् ।
दृग्भ्यां प्रपश्यन् प्रपिबन्निवार्भक-
श्चुम्बन्निवास्येन भुजैरिवाश्लिषन् ॥ ३ ॥

tad-darśanenāgata-sādhvasaḥ kṣitāv
avandatāṅgaṁ vinamayya daṇḍavat
dṛgbhyāṁ prapaśyan prapibann ivārbhakaś
cumbann ivāsyena bhujair ivāśliṣan

tat-darśanena—after seeing the Lord; *āgata-sādhvasaḥ*—Dhruva Mahārāja, being greatly confused; *kṣitau*—on the ground; *avandata*—offered obeisances; *aṅgam*—his body; *vinamayya*—prostrating; *daṇḍa-vat*—just like a rod; *dṛgbhyām*—with his eyes; *prapaśyan*—looking upon; *prapiban*—drinking; *iva*—like; *arbhakaḥ*—the boy; *cumban*—kissing; *iva*—like; *āsyena*—with his mouth; *bhujaiḥ*—with his arms; *iva*—like; *āśliṣan*—embracing.

TRANSLATION

When Dhruva Mahārāja saw his Lord just in front of him, he was greatly agitated and offered Him obeisances and respect. He fell flat before Him like a rod and became absorbed in love of Godhead. Dhruva Mahārāja, in ecstasy, looked upon the Lord as if he were drinking the Lord with his eyes, kissing the lotus feet of the Lord with his mouth, and embracing the Lord with his arms.

PURPORT

Naturally, when Dhruva Mahārāja personally saw the Supreme Personality of Godhead face to face, he was very much agitated in awe and respect, and it appeared as if he were drinking the entire body of the Lord with his eyes. The devotee's love for the Supreme Personality of Godhead is so intense that he wants to kiss the lotus feet of the Lord constantly, and he wants to touch the tips of the toes of the Lord and constantly embrace His lotus feet. All these features of Dhruva Mahārāja's bodily expression indicate that upon seeing the Lord face to face he developed the eight kinds of transcendental ecstasy in his body.

TEXT 4

स तं विवक्षन्तमतद्विदं हरि-
ज्ञात्वास्य सर्वस्य च हृद्यवस्थितः ।
कृताञ्जलिं ब्रह्ममयेन कम्बुना
पस्पर्श बालं कृपया कपोले ॥ ४ ॥

sa taṁ vivakṣantam atad-vidaṁ harir
jñātvāsya sarvasya ca hṛdy avasthitaḥ

kṛtāñjaliṁ brahmamayena kambunā
pasparśa bālaṁ kṛpayā kapole

saḥ—the Supreme Personality of Godhead; *tam*—Dhruva Mahārāja; *vivakṣantam*—wanting to offer prayers describing His qualities; *a-tat-vidam*—not experienced at that; *hariḥ*—the Personality of Godhead; *jñātvā*—having understood; *asya*—of Dhruva Mahārāja; *sarvasya*—of everyone; *ca*—and; *hṛdi*—in the heart; *avasthitaḥ*—being situated; *kṛta-añjalim*—situated with folded hands; *brahma-mayena*—just consistent with the words of the Vedic hymns; *kambunā*—with His conchshell; *pasparśa*—touched; *bālam*—the boy; *kṛpayā*—out of causeless mercy; *kapole*—on the forehead.

TRANSLATION

Although Dhruva Mahārāja was a small boy, he wanted to offer prayers to the Supreme Personality of Godhead in suitable language. But because he was inexperienced, he could not adjust himself immediately. The Supreme Personality of Godhead, being situated in everyone's heart, could understand Dhruva Mahārāja's awkward position. Out of His causeless mercy He touched His conchshell to the forehead of Dhruva Mahārāja, who stood before Him with folded hands.

PURPORT

Every devotee wants to chant the transcendental qualities of the Lord. Devotees are always interested in hearing about the Lord's transcendental qualities, and they are always eager to glorify these qualities, but sometimes they feel inconvenienced by humbleness. The Personality of Godhead, being situated in everyone's heart, specifically gives a devotee intelligence to describe Him. It is therefore understood that when a devotee writes or speaks about the Supreme Personality of Godhead, his words are dictated by the Lord from within. This is confirmed in *Bhagavad-gītā*, Tenth Chapter: to those who constantly engage in the transcendental loving service of the Lord, the Lord, from within, dictates what to do next in order to serve Him. When Dhruva Mahārāja felt hesitant, not knowing how to describe the Lord for want of sufficient experience, the Lord, out of His causeless mercy, touched His conchshell to Dhruva's forehead, and he was transcendentally inspired. This transcendental inspiration is called *brahma-maya* because when one is thus inspired, the sound he produces exactly corresponds to the sound vibration of the *Vedas.* This is not the ordinary sound vibration of this material world. Therefore the sound vibration of the Hare Kṛṣṇa *mantra,* although presented in the ordinary alphabet, should not be taken as mundane or material.

TEXT 5

स वै तदैव प्रतिपादितां गिरं
दैवीं परिज्ञातपरात्मनिर्णयः ।
तं भक्तिभावोऽभ्यगृणादसत्वरं
परिश्रुतोरुश्रवसं ध्रुवक्षितिः ॥ ५ ॥

sa vai tadaiva pratipāditāṁ giraṁ
daivīṁ parijñāta-parātma-nirṇayaḥ
taṁ bhakti-bhāvo 'bhyagṛṇād asatvaraṁ
pariśrutoru-śravasaṁ dhruva-kṣitiḥ

saḥ—Dhruva Mahārāja; *vai*—certainly; *tadā*—at that time; *eva*—just; *pratipāditām*—having attained; *giram*—speech; *daivīm*—transcendental; *parijñāta*—understood; *para-ātma*—of the Supreme Soul; *nirṇayaḥ*—the conclusion; *tam*—to the Lord; *bhakti-bhāvaḥ*—situated in devotional service; *abhyagṛṇāt*—offered prayers; *asatvaram*—without any hasty conclusion; *pariśruta*—widely known; *uru-śravasam*—whose fame; *dhruva-kṣitiḥ*—Dhruva, whose planet would not be annihilated.

TRANSLATION

At that time Dhruva Mahārāja became perfectly aware of the Vedic conclusion and understood the Absolute Truth and His relationship with all living entities. In accordance with the line of devotional service to the Supreme Lord, whose fame is widespread, Dhruva, who in the future would receive a planet which would

never be annihilated, even during the time of dissolution, offered his deliberate and conclusive prayers.

PURPORT

There are many important items to be considered in this verse. First of all, the relationship between the Absolute Truth and the relative material and spiritual energies is here understood by a student who has complete knowledge of the Vedic literature. Dhruva Mahārāja never went to any school or academic teacher to learn the Vedic conclusion, but because of his devotional service to the Lord, as soon as the Lord appeared and touched his forehead with His conchshell, automatically the entire Vedic conclusion was revealed to him. That is the process of understanding Vedic literature. One cannot understand it simply by academic learning. The *Vedas* indicate that only to one who has unflinching faith in the Supreme Lord as well as in the spiritual master is the Vedic conclusion revealed.

The example of Dhruva Mahārāja is that he engaged himself in devotional service to the Lord according to the order of his spiritual master, Nārada Muni. As a result of his rendering such devotional service with great determination and austerity, the Personality of Godhead personally manifested Himself before him. Dhruva was only a child. He wanted to offer nice prayers to the Lord, but because he lacked sufficient knowledge, he hesitated; but by the mercy of the Lord, as soon as the Lord's conchshell touched his forehead, he became completely aware of the Vedic conclusion. That conclusion is based on proper understanding of the difference between *jīva* and Paramātmā, the individual soul and the Supersoul. The individual soul is forever a servant of the Supersoul, and therefore his relationship with the Supersoul is to offer service. That is called *bhakti-yoga*, or *bhakti-bhāva*. Dhruva Mahārāja offered his prayers to the Lord not in the way of the impersonalist philosophers, but as a devotee. Therefore, it is clearly said here, *bhakti-bhāva*. The only prayers worth offering are those offered to the Supreme Personality of Godhead, whose reputation is spread far and wide. Dhruva Mahārāja wanted to have the kingdom of his father, but his father refused even to allow him to get on his lap. In order to fulfill his desire, the Lord had already created a planet known as the polestar, Dhruvaloka, which was never to be annihilated even at the time of the dissolution of the universe. Dhruva Mahārāja attained this perfection not by acting hastily, but by patiently executing the order of his spiritual master, and therefore he became so successful that he saw the Lord face to face. Now he was further enabled, by the causeless mercy of the Lord, to offer fitting prayers to the Lord. To glorify or offer prayers unto the Supreme, one needs the Lord's mercy. One cannot write to glorify the Lord unless one is endowed with His causeless mercy.

TEXT 6

ध्रुव उवाच
योऽन्तः प्रविश्य मम वाचमिमां प्रसुप्तां
संजीवयत्यखिलशक्तिधरः स्वधाम्ना ।
अन्यांश्च हस्तचरणश्रवणत्वगादीन्
प्राणान्नमो भगवते पुरुषाय तुभ्यम् ॥ ६ ॥

dhruva uvāca
yo 'ntaḥ praviśya mama vācam imāṁ prasuptāṁ
sañjīvayaty akhila-śakti-dharaḥ sva-dhāmnā
anyāṁś ca hasta-caraṇa-śravaṇa-tvag-ādīn
prāṇān namo bhagavate puruṣāya tubhyam

dhruvaḥ uvāca—Dhruva Mahārāja said; *yaḥ*—the Supreme Lord who; *antaḥ*—within; *praviśya*—entering; *mama*—my; *vācam*—words; *imām*—all these; *prasuptām*—which are all inactive or dead; *sañjīvayati*—rejuvenates; *akhila*—universal; *śakti*—energy; *dharaḥ*—possessing; *sva-dhāmnā*—by His internal potency; *anyān ca*—other limbs also; *hasta*—like hands; *caraṇa*—legs; *śravaṇa*—ears; *tvak*—skin; *ādīn*—and so on; *prāṇān*—life force; *namaḥ*—let me offer my obeisances; *bhagavate*—unto the Supreme Personality of Godhead; *puruṣāya*—the Supreme Person; *tubhyam*—unto You.

TRANSLATION

Dhruva Mahārāja said: My dear Lord, You are all-powerful. After entering within me, You have enlivened all my sleeping

senses—my hands, legs, ears, touch sensation, life force and especially my power of speech. Let me offer my respectful obeisances unto You.

PURPORT

Dhruva Mahārāja could understand very easily the difference between his condition before and after attaining spiritual realization and seeing the Supreme Personality of Godhead face to face. He could understand that his life force and activities had been sleeping. Unless one comes to the spiritual platform, his bodily limbs, mind and other facilities within the body are understood to be sleeping. Unless one is spiritually situated, all his activities are taken as a dead man's activities or ghostly activities. Śrīla Bhaktivinoda Ṭhākura has composed a song in which he addresses himself: "O living entity, get up! How long shall you sleep on the lap of *māyā*? Now you have the opportunity of possessing a human form of body; now try to get up and realize yourself." The *Vedas* also declare, "Get up! Get up! You have the opportunity, the boon of the human form of life—now realize yourself." These are the Vedic injunctions.

Dhruva Mahārāja actually experienced that upon enlightenment of his senses on the spiritual platform he could understand the essence of Vedic instruction—that the Supreme Godhead is the Supreme Person; He is not impersonal. Dhruva Mahārāja could immediately understand this fact. He was aware that for a very long time he was practically sleeping, and he felt the impetus to glorify the Lord according to the Vedic conclusion. A mundane person cannot offer any prayer or glorify the Supreme Personality of Godhead, because he has no realization of the Vedic conclusion.

When Dhruva Mahārāja, therefore, found this difference within himself, he could immediately understand that it was because of the causeless mercy of the Lord. He offered obeisances to the Lord with great respect and reverence, completely understanding that the Lord's favor was upon him. This spiritual enlivenment of Dhruva Mahārāja's senses and mind was due to the action of the internal potency of the Lord. In this verse, therefore, the word *sva-dhāmnā* means "by spiritual energy." Spiritual enlightenment is possible by the mercy of the spiritual energy of the Lord. The chanting of the Hare Kṛṣṇa *mantra* is first addressed to the spiritual energy of the Lord, Hare. This spiritual energy acts when a living entity fully surrenders and accepts his position as an eternal servitor. When a person places himself at the disposal or order of the Supreme Lord, that is called *sevonmukha;* at that time the spiritual energy gradually reveals the Lord to him.

Without revelation by the spiritual energy, one is unable to offer prayers glorifying the Lord. Any amount of philosophical speculation or poetic expression by mundane persons is still considered to be the action and reaction of the material energy. When one is actually enlivened by the spiritual energy, all his senses become purified, and he engages only in the service of the Lord. At that time his hands, legs, ears, tongue, mind, genitals—everything—engage in the service of the Lord. Such an enlightened devotee no longer has any material activities, nor has he any interest in being materially engaged. This process of purifying the senses and engaging them in the service of the Lord is known as *bhakti,* or devotional service. In the beginning, the senses are engaged by the direction of the spiritual master and *śāstra,* and after realization, when the same senses are purified, the engagement continues. The difference is that in the beginning the senses are engaged in a mechanical way, but after realization they are engaged in spiritual understanding.

TEXT 7

एकस्त्वमेव भगवन्निदमात्मशक्त्या
मायाख्ययोरुगुणया महदाद्यशेषम् ।
सृष्ट्वानुविश्य पुरुषस्तदसद्गुणेषु
नानेव दारुषु विभावसुवद्विभासि ॥ ७ ॥

ekas tvam eva bhagavann idam ātma-śaktyā
māyākhyayoru-guṇayā mahad-ādy-aśeṣam
sṛṣṭvānuviśya puruṣas tad-asad-guṇeṣu
nāneva dāruṣu vibhāvasuvad vibhāsi

ekaḥ—one; *tvam*—you; *eva*—certainly; *bhagavan*—O my Lord; *idam*—this material world; *ātma-śaktyā*—by Your own potency; *māyā-ākhyayā*—of the name *māyā; uru*—greatly powerful; *guṇayā*—consisting of the modes of nature; *mahat-ādi*—the *mahat-tattva*, etc.; *aśeṣam*—unlimited; *sṛṣṭvā*—after creating; *anuviśya*—then after entering; *puruṣaḥ*—the Supersoul; *tat*—of *māyā; asat-guṇeṣu*—into the temporarily manifested qualities; *nānā*—variously; *iva*—as if; *dāruṣu*—into pieces of wood; *vibhāvasu-vat*—just like fire; *vibhāsi*—You appear.

TRANSLATION

My Lord, You are the supreme one, but by Your different energies You appear differently in the spiritual and material worlds. You create the total energy of the material world by Your external potency, and after creation You enter within the material world as the Supersoul. You are the Supreme Person, and through the temporary modes of material nature You create varieties of manifestation, just as fire, entering into wood of different shapes, burns brilliantly in different varieties.

PURPORT

Dhruva Mahārāja realized that the Supreme Absolute Truth, the Personality of Godhead, acts through His different energies, not that He becomes void or impersonal and thus becomes all-pervading. The Māyāvādī philosopher thinks that the Absolute Truth, being spread throughout the cosmic manifestation, has no personal form. But here Dhruva Mahārāja, upon realization of the Vedic conclusion, says, "You are spread all over the cosmic manifestation by Your energy." This energy is basically spiritual, but because it acts in the material world temporarily, it is called *māyā*, or illusory energy. In other words, for everyone but the devotees the Lord's energy acts as external energy. Dhruva Mahārāja could understand this fact very nicely, and he could understand also that the energy and the energetic are one and the same. The energy cannot be separated from the energetic.

The identity of the Supreme Personality of Godhead in the feature of Paramātmā, or Supersoul, is admitted herein. His original, spiritual energy enlivens the material energy, and thus the dead body appears to have life force. Voidist philosophers think that under certain material conditions the symptoms of life occur in the material body, but the fact is that the material body cannot act on its own. Even a machine needs separate energy (electricity, steam, etc.). It is stated in this verse that the material energy acts in varieties of material bodies, just as fire burns differently in different wood according to the size and quality of the wood. In the case of devotees the same energy is transformed into spiritual energy; this is possible because the energy is originally spiritual, not material. As it is said, *viṣṇu-śaktiḥ parā proktā*. The original energy inspires a devotee, and thus he engages all his bodily limbs in the service of the Lord. The same energy, as external potency, engages the ordinary nondevotees in material activities for sense enjoyment. We should mark the difference between *māyā* and *sva-dhāma*—for devotees the *sva-dhāma* acts, whereas in the case of nondevotees the *māyā* energy acts.

TEXT 8

त्वद्दत्तया वयुनयेदमचष्ट विश्वं
सुप्तप्रबुद्ध इव नाथ भवत्प्रपन्नः ।
तस्यापवर्ग्यशरणं तव पादमूलं
विस्मर्यते कृतविदा कथमार्तबन्धो ॥ ८ ॥

tvad-dattayā vayunayedam acaṣṭa viśvaṁ
supta-prabuddha iva nātha bhavat-prapannaḥ
tasyāpavargya-śaraṇaṁ tava pāda-mūlaṁ
vismaryate kṛta-vidā katham ārta-bandho

tvat-dattayā—given by You; *vayunayā*—by knowledge; *idam*—this; *acaṣṭa*—could see; *viśvam*—whole universe; *supta-prabuddhaḥ*—a man rising from sleep; *iva*—like; *nātha*—O my Lord; *bhavat-prapannaḥ*—Lord Brahmā, who is surrendered unto You; *tasya*—his; *āpavargya*—of persons desiring liberation; *śaraṇam*—the shelter; *tava*—Your; *pāda-mūlam*—lotus feet; *vismaryate*—can be forgotten; *kṛta-vidā*—by a learned person; *katham*—how; *ārta-bandho*—O friend of the distressed.

TRANSLATION

O my master, Lord Brahmā is fully surrendered unto You. In the beginning You gave him knowledge, and thus he could see and

understand the entire universe, just as a person awakens from sleep and visualizes his immediate duties. You are the only shelter of all persons who desire liberation, and You are the friend of all who are distressed. How, therefore, can a learned person who has perfect knowledge ever forget You?

PURPORT

The Supreme Personality of Godhead cannot be forgotten even for a moment by His surrendered devotees. The devotee understands that the Lord's causeless mercy is beyond his estimation; he cannot know how much he is benefited by the grace of the Lord. The more a devotee engages himself in the devotional service of the Lord, the more encouragement is supplied by the energy of the Lord. In the *Bhagavad-gītā* the Lord says that to those who are constantly engaged in devotional service with love and affection, the Supreme Personality of Godhead gives intelligence from within, and thus they may make further progress. Being so encouraged, the devotee can never forget, at any moment, the Personality of Godhead. He always feels obliged to Him for having achieved increased power in devotional service by His grace. Saintly persons like Sanaka, Sanātana and Lord Brahmā were able to see the entire universe, by the mercy of the Lord, through knowledge of the Lord. The example is given that a person may apparently abstain from sleep all day, but as long as he is not spiritually enlightened he is actually sleeping. He may sleep at night and perform his duties in the daytime, but as long as he does not come to the platform of working in spiritual enlightenment he is considered to be always sleeping. A devotee, therefore, never forgets the benefit derived from the Lord.

The Lord is addressed here as *ārta-bandhu*, which means "friend of the distressed." As stated in *Bhagavad-gītā*, after many, many births of executing severe austerities in search of knowledge, one comes to the point of real knowledge and becomes wise when one surrenders unto the Supreme Personality of Godhead. The Māyāvādī philosopher, who does not surrender unto the Supreme Person, is understood to be lacking in real knowledge. The devotee in perfect knowledge cannot forget his obligation to the Lord at any moment.

TEXT 9

नूनं विमुष्टमतयस्तव मायया ते
ये त्वां भवाप्ययविमोक्षणमन्यहेतोः ।
अर्चन्ति कल्पकतरुं कुणपोपभोग्य-
मिच्छन्ति यत्स्पर्शजं निरयेऽपि नृणाम् ॥९॥

nūnaṁ vimuṣṭa-matayas tava māyayā te
ye tvāṁ bhavāpyaya-vimokṣaṇam anya-hetoḥ
arcanti kalpaka-taruṁ kuṇapopabhogyam
icchanti yat sparśajaṁ niraye 'pi nṝṇām

nūnam—certainly; *vimuṣṭa-matayaḥ*—those who have lost their right intelligence; *tava*—Your; *māyayā*—by the influence of the illusory energy; *te*—they; *ye*—who; *tvām*—You; *bhava*—from birth; *apyaya*—and death; *vimokṣaṇam*—the cause of liberation; *anya-hetoḥ*—for other purposes; *arcanti*—worship; *kalpaka-tarum*—who are like the desire tree; *kuṇapa*—of this dead body; *upabhogyam*—sense gratification; *icchanti*—they desire; *yat*—that which; *sparśa-jam*—derived by touch sensation; *niraye*—in hell; *api*—even; *nṝṇām*—for persons.

TRANSLATION

Persons who worship You simply for the sense gratification of this bag of skin are certainly influenced by Your illusory energy. In spite of having You, who are like a desire tree and are the cause of liberation from birth and death, foolish persons, such as me, desire benedictions from You for sense gratification, which is available even for those who live in hellish conditions.

PURPORT

Dhruva Mahārāja repented because he had come to the Lord to render devotional service for material profit. He here condemns his attitude. Only due to gross lack of knowledge does one worship the Lord for material profit or for sense gratification. The Lord is like a desire tree. Anyone can have whatever he desires from the Lord, but people in general do not know what kind of benediction they should ask from Him. Happiness derived from the touch of skin, or sensuous happiness, is present in the life of hogs and dogs. Such happiness is very insignificant. If a devotee worships the Lord for such insignificant happiness, he must be considered devoid of all knowledge.

TEXT 10

या निर्वृतिस्तनुभृतां तव पादपद्म-
ध्यानाद्भवज्जनकथाश्रवणेन वा स्यात् ।
सा ब्रह्मणि स्वमहिमन्यपि नाथ मा भूत्
किं त्वन्तकासिलुलितात्पततां विमानात् ॥१०॥

yā nirvṛtis tanu-bhṛtāṁ tava pāda-padma-
dhyānād bhavaj-jana-kathā-śravaṇena vā syāt
sā brahmaṇi sva-mahimany api nātha mā bhūt
kiṁ tv antakāsi-lulitāt patatāṁ vimānāt

yā—that which; *nirvṛtiḥ*—bliss; *tanu-bhṛtām*—of the embodied; *tava*—Your; *pāda-padma*—lotus feet; *dhyānāt*—from meditating upon; *bhavat-jana*—from Your intimate devotees; *kathā*—topics; *śravaṇena*—by hearing; *vā*—or; *syāt*—comes into being; *sā*—that bliss; *brahmaṇi*—in the impersonal Brahman; *sva-mahimani*—Your own magnificence; *api*—even; *nātha*—O Lord; *mā*—never; *bhūt*—exists; *kim*—what to speak of; *tu*—then; *antaka-asi*—by the sword of death; *lulitāt*—being destroyed; *patatām*—of those who fall down; *vimānāt*—from their airplanes.

TRANSLATION

My Lord, the transcendental bliss derived from meditating upon Your lotus feet or hearing about Your glories from pure devotees is so unlimited that it is far beyond the stage of brahmānanda, wherein one thinks himself merged in the impersonal Brahman as one with the Supreme. Since brahmānanda is also defeated by the transcendental bliss derived from devotional service, then what to

speak of the temporary blissfulness of elevating oneself to the heavenly planets, which is ended by the separating sword of time? Although one may be elevated to the heavenly planets, he falls down in due course of time.

PURPORT

The transcendental bliss derived from devotional service, primarily from *śravaṇaṁ kīrtanam,* hearing and chanting, cannot be compared to the happiness derived by *karmīs* by elevating themselves to the heavenly planets or by *jñānīs* or *yogīs,* who enjoy oneness with the supreme impersonal Brahman. *Yogīs* generally meditate upon the transcendental form of Viṣṇu, but devotees not only meditate upon Him but actually engage in the direct service of the Lord. In the previous verse we find the phrase *bhavāpyaya,* which refers to birth and death. The Lord can give relief from the chain of birth and death. It is a misunderstanding to think, as do the monists, that when one gets relief from the process of birth and death he merges into the Supreme Brahman. Here it is clearly said that the transcendental bliss derived from *śravaṇaṁ kīrtanam* by pure devotees cannot be compared to *brahmānanda,* or the impersonal conception of transcendental bliss derived by merging into the Absolute.

The position of *karmīs* is still more degraded. Their aim is to elevate themselves to the higher planetary systems. It is said, *yānti deva-vratā devān:* persons who worship the demigods are elevated to the heavenly planets (Bg. 9.25). But elsewhere in *Bhagavad-gītā* (9.21) we find, *kṣīṇe puṇye martya-lokaṁ viśanti:* those who are elevated to the higher planetary systems must come down again as soon as the results of their pious activities are exhausted. They are like the modern astronauts who go to the moon; as soon as their fuel is used up, they are obliged to come back down to this earth. As the modern astronauts who go to the moon or other heavenly planets by force of jet propulsion have to come down again after exhausting their fuel, so also do those who are elevated to the heavenly planets by force of *yajñas* and pious activities. *Antakāsi-lulitāt:* by the sword of time one is cut from his exalted position within this material world, and he comes down again. Dhruva Mahārāja appreciated that the results of devotional service are far more valuable than merging into the Absolute or being elevated to the heavenly planets. The words *patatāṁ vimānāt* are very significant. *Vimāna* means "airplane." Those who are elevated to the heavenly planets are like airplanes, which drop when they run out of fuel.

TEXT 11

भक्तिं मुहुः प्रवहतां त्वयि मे प्रसङ्गो
भूयादनन्त महताममलाशयानाम् ।
येनाञ्जसोल्बणमुरुव्यसनं भवाब्धिं
नेष्ये भवद्गुणकथामृतपानमत्तः ॥११॥

bhaktiṁ muhuḥ pravahatāṁ tvayi me prasaṅgo
bhūyād ananta mahatām amalāśayānām
yenāñjasolbaṇam uru-vyasanaṁ bhavābdhiṁ
neṣye bhavad-guṇa-kathāmṛta-pāna-mattaḥ

bhaktim—devotional service; *muhuḥ*—constantly; *pravahatām*—of those who perform; *tvayi*—unto You; *me*—my; *prasaṅgaḥ*—intimate association; *bhūyāt*—may it become; *ananta*—O unlimited; *mahatām*—of the great devotees; *amala-āśayānām*—whose hearts are freed from material contamination; *yena*—by which; *añjasā*—easily; *ulbaṇam*—terrible; *uru*—great; *vyasanam*—full of dangers; *bhava-abdhim*—the ocean of material existence; *neṣye*—I shall cross; *bhavat*—Your; *guṇa*—transcendental qualities; *kathā*—pastimes; *amṛta*—nectar, eternal; *pāna*—by drinking; *mattaḥ*—mad.

TRANSLATION

Dhruva Mahārāja continued: O unlimited Lord, kindly bless me so that I may associate with great devotees who engage in Your transcendental loving service constantly, as the waves of a river constantly flow. Such transcendental devotees are completely situated in an uncontaminated state of life. By the process of devotional service I shall surely be able to cross the nescient ocean of material existence, which is filled with the waves of blazing, firelike dangers. It will be very easy for me, for I am becoming mad to

hear about Your transcendental qualities and pastimes, which are eternally existent.

PURPORT

The significant point in Dhruva Mahārāja's statement is that he wanted the association of pure devotees. Transcendental devotional service cannot be complete and cannot be relishable without the association of devotees. We have therefore established the International Society for Krishna Consciousness. Anyone who is trying to be aloof from this Krishna Consciousness Society and yet engage in Kṛṣṇa consciousness is living in a great hallucination, for this is not possible. From this statement by Dhruva Mahārāja it is clear that unless one is associated with devotees, his devotional service does not mature; it does not become distinct from material activities. The Lord says, *satāṁ prasaṅgān mama vīrya-saṁvido bhavanti hṛt-karṇa-rasāyanāḥ* (*Bhāg.* 3.25.25). Only in the association of pure devotees can the words of Lord Kṛṣṇa be fully potent and relishable to the heart and ear. Dhruva Mahārāja explicitly wanted the association of devotees. That association in devotional activities is just like the waves of an incessantly flowing river. In our Krishna Consciousness Society we have full engagement twenty-four hours a day. Every moment of our time is always busily engaged in the service of the Lord. This is called the incessant flow of devotional service.

A Māyāvādī philosopher may question us, "You may be very happy in the association of devotees, but what is your plan for crossing the ocean of material existence?" Dhruva Mahārāja's answer is that it is not very difficult. He clearly says that this ocean can be crossed very easily if one simply becomes mad to hear the glories of the Lord. *Bhavad-guṇa-kathā:* for anyone who persistently engages in hearing the topics of the Lord from *Śrīmad Bhagavad-gītā, Śrīmad-Bhāgavatam* and *Caitanya-caritāmṛta* and who is actually addicted to this process, just as one becomes addicted to intoxicants, it is very easy to cross the nescience of material existence. The ocean of material nescience is compared to a blazing fire, but to a devotee this blazing fire is insignificant because he is completely absorbed in devotional service. Although the material world is blazing fire, to a devotee it appears full of pleasure (*viśvaṁ pūrṇa-sukhāyate*).

The purport of this statement by Dhruva Mahārāja is that devotional service in the association of devotees is the cause of the development of further devotional service. By devotional service only is one elevated to the transcendental planet Goloka Vṛndāvana, and there also there is only devotional service, for the activities of devotional service both in this world and in the spiritual world are one and the same. Devotional service does not change. The example of a mango can be given here. If one gets an unripe mango, it is still a mango, and when it is ripe it remains the same mango, but it has become more tasteful and relishable. Similarly, there is devotional service performed according to the direction of the spiritual master and the injunctions and regulative principles of *śāstra*, and there is devotional service in the spiritual world, rendered directly in association with the Supreme Personality of Godhead. But they are both the same. There is no change. The difference is that one stage is unripe and the other is ripe and more relishable. It is possible to mature in devotional service only in the association of devotees.

TEXT 12

ते न स्मरन्त्यतितरां प्रियमीश मर्त्यं
ये चान्वदः सुतसुहृद्गृहवित्तदाराः ।
ये त्वब्जनाभ भवदीयपदारविन्द-
सौगन्ध्यलुब्धहृदयेषु कृतप्रसङ्गाः ॥१२॥

te na smaranty atitarāṁ priyam īśa martyaṁ
ye cānv adaḥ suta-suhṛd-gṛha-vitta-dārāḥ
ye tv abja-nābha bhavadīya-padāravinda-
saugandhya-lubdha-hṛdayeṣu kṛta-prasaṅgāḥ

te—they; *na*—never; *smaranti*—remember; *atitarām*—highly; *priyam*—dear; *īśa*—O Lord; *martyam*—material body; *ye*—they who; *ca*—also; *anu*—in relationship with; *adaḥ*—that; *suta*—sons; *suhṛt*—friends; *gṛha*—home; *vitta*—wealth; *dārāḥ*—and wife; *ye*—those who; *tu*—then; *abja-nābha*—O Lord who have a lotus navel; *bhavadīya*—of Your; *pada-aravinda*—lotus feet; *saugandhya*—the fragrance; *lubdha*—have achieved; *hṛdayeṣu*—with devotees whose hearts; *kṛta-prasaṅgāḥ*—have association.

TRANSLATION

O Lord who have a lotus navel, if a person happens to associate with a devotee whose heart always hankers after Your lotus feet, seeking always their fragrance, he is never attached to the material body or, in a bodily relationship, to offspring, friends, home, wealth and wife, which are very, very dear to materialistic persons. Indeed, he does not care for them.

PURPORT

A special advantage in devotional service is that devotees not only enjoy the transcendental pastimes of the Lord by hearing and chanting and glorifying them, but also are not very much attached to their bodies, unlike the *yogīs*, who are too attached to the body and who think that by performing bodily gymnastic exercises they will advance in spiritual consciousness. *Yogīs* are generally not very much interested in devotional service; they want to regulate the breathing process. This is simply a bodily concern. Here Dhruva Mahārāja plainly says that a devotee has no more bodily interest. He knows that he is not the body. From the very beginning, therefore, without wasting time in bodily exercises, a devotee searches out a pure devotee and simply by his association becomes more advanced in spiritual consciousness than any *yogī*. Because a devotee knows that he is not the body, he is never affected by bodily happiness or distress. He is not interested in bodily relationships with wife, children, home, bank balance, etc., or in the distress and happiness which come from these things. This is the special advantage of being a devotee. This status of life is possible only when a person is interested in associating with a pure devotee, who always enjoys the fragrance of the lotus feet of the Lord.

TEXT 13

तिर्यङ्नगद्विजसरीसृपदेवदैत्य-
मर्त्यादिभिः परिचितं सदसद्विशेषम् ।
रूपं स्थविष्ठमज ते महदाद्यनेकं
नातः परं परम वेद्मि न यत्र वादः ॥१३॥

tiryaṅ-naga-dvija-sarīsṛpa-deva-daitya-
martyādibhiḥ paricitaṁ sad-asad-viśeṣam
rūpaṁ sthaviṣṭham aja te mahad-ādy-anekaṁ
nātaḥ paraṁ parama vedmi na yatra vādaḥ

tiryak—by animals; *naga*—trees; *dvija*—birds; *sarīsṛpa*—reptiles; *deva*—demigods; *daitya*—demons; *martya-ādibhiḥ*—by men, etc.; *paricitam*—pervaded; *sat-asat-viśeṣam*—with varieties manifest and unmanifest; *rūpam*—form; *sthaviṣṭham*—gross universal; *aja*—O Unborn; *te*—Your; *mahat-ādi*—caused by the total material energy, etc.; *anekam*—various causes; *na*—not; *ataḥ*—from this; *param*—transcendental; *parama*—O Supreme; *vedmi*—I know; *na*—not; *yatra*—where; *vādaḥ*—various arguments.

TRANSLATION

My dear Lord, O Supreme Unborn, I know that the different varieties of living entities, such as animals, trees, birds, reptiles, demigods and human beings, are spread throughout the universe, which is caused by the total material energy, and I know that they are sometimes manifest and sometimes unmanifest; but I have never experienced the supreme form I behold as I see You now. Now all kinds of methods of theorizing have come to an end.

PURPORT

In the *Bhagavad-gītā* the Lord says that He has spread Himself throughout the universe, but although everything is resting upon Him, He is aloof. The same concept is expressed here by Dhruva Mahārāja. He states that before seeing the transcendental form of the Lord, he had experienced only the varieties of material forms, which are counted at 8,400,000 species of aquatics, birds, beasts, etc. The fact is that unless one engages in the devotional service of the Lord, it is impossible to understand the ultimate form of the Lord. This is also confirmed in the *Bhagavad-gītā* (18.55). *Bhaktyā mām abhijānāti:* factual understanding of the Absolute Truth, who is the Supreme Person, cannot be obtained by any process other than devotional service.

Dhruva Mahārāja here compares his previous state of understanding with the perfection of understanding in the presence of the Supreme Lord. The position of a living entity is to render service; unless he comes to the stage of appreciating the Supreme Personality of Godhead, he engages in the service of the various forms of trees, reptiles, animals, men, demigods, etc. One can experience that one man engages in the service of a dog, another serves plants and creepers, another the demigods, and another humanity, or his boss in the office—but no one is engaged in the service of Kṛṣṇa. Aside from common men, even men who are elevated in terms of spiritual understanding are at the utmost engaged in the service of the *virāṭ-rūpa*, or, unable to understand the ultimate form of the Lord, they worship voidism by meditation. Dhruva Mahārāja, however, had been blessed by the Supreme Lord. When the Lord touched His conchshell to Dhruva's forehead, real knowledge was revealed from within, and Dhruva could understand the Lord's transcendental form. Dhruva Mahārāja here admits that not only was he ignorant, but by years he was only a child. It would not have been possible for an ignorant child to appreciate the supreme form of the Lord had he not been blessed by the Lord, who had touched His conchshell to Dhruva's forehead.

TEXT 14

कल्पान्त एतदखिलं जठरेण गृह्णन्
शेते पुमान् स्वदृगनन्तसखस्तदङ्के ।
यन्नाभिसिन्धुरुहकाञ्चनलोकपद्म-
गर्भे द्युमान् भगवते प्रणतोऽस्मि तस्मै ॥१४॥

kalpānta etad akhilaṁ jaṭhareṇa gṛhṇan
śete pumān sva-dṛg ananta-sakhas tad-aṅke
yan-nābhi-sindhu-ruha-kāñcana-loka-padma-
garbhe dyumān bhagavate praṇato 'smi tasmai

kalpa-ante—at the end of the millennium; *etat*—this universe; *akhilam*—all; *jaṭhareṇa*—within the belly; *gṛhṇan*—withdrawing; *śete*—lies down; *pumān*—the Supreme Person; *sva-dṛk*—looking upon Himself; *ananta*—the unlimited being Śeṣa; *sakhaḥ*—accompanied by; *tat-aṅke*—on His lap; *yat*—from whose; *nābhi*—navel; *sindhu*—ocean;

ruha—sprouted; *kāñcana*—golden; *loka*—planet; *padma*—of the lotus; *garbhe*—on the whorl; *dyumān*—Lord Brahmā; *bhagavate*—unto the Supreme Personality of Godhead; *praṇataḥ*—offering obeisances; *asmi*—I am; *tasmai*—unto Him.

TRANSLATION

My dear Lord, at the end of each millennium the Supreme Personality of Godhead Garbhodakaśāyī Viṣṇu dissolves everything manifested within the universe into His belly. He lies down on the lap of Śeṣa Nāga, from His navel sprouts a golden lotus flower on a stem, and on that lotus Lord Brahmā is created. I can understand that You are the same Supreme Godhead. I therefore offer my respectful obeisances unto You.

PURPORT

Dhruva Mahārāja's understanding of the Supreme Personality of Godhead is complete. In the *Vedas* it is said, *yasmin vijñāte sarvam evaṁ vijñātaṁ bhavati:* knowledge received through the transcendental, causeless mercy of the Lord is so perfect that by that knowledge the devotee becomes acquainted with all the different manifestations of the Lord. Lord Kṣīrodakaśāyī Viṣṇu was present before Dhruva Mahārāja, who could also understand the Lord's two other forms, namely Garbhodakaśāyī Viṣṇu and Kāraṇodakaśāyī (Mahā) Viṣṇu. Regarding Mahā-Viṣṇu, it is stated in the *Brahma-saṁhitā* (5.48):

yasyaika-niśvasita-kālam athāvalambya
jīvanti loma-vilajā jagad-aṇḍa-nāthāḥ
viṣṇur mahān sa iha yasya kalā-viśeṣo
govindam ādi-puruṣaṁ tam ahaṁ bhajāmi

At the end of each and every millennium, when all the material worlds are dissolved, everything enters the body of Garbhodakaśāyī Viṣṇu, who is lying on the lap of Śeṣa Nāga, another form of the Lord.

Those who are not devotees cannot understand the different forms of Viṣṇu and their positions in regard to the creation. Sometimes the atheists argue, "How can a flower stem sprout from the navel of

Garbhodakaśāyī Viṣṇu?" They consider all the statements of the *śāstras* to be stories. As a result of their inexperience in the Absolute Truth and their reluctance to accept authority, they become more and more atheistic; they cannot understand the Supreme Personality of Godhead. But a devotee like Dhruva Mahārāja, by the grace of the Lord, knows all the manifestations of the Lord and their different positions. It is said that anyone who has even a little of the Lord's grace can understand His glories; others may go on speculating on the Absolute Truth, but they will always be unable to understand the Lord. In other words, unless one comes in contact with a devotee it is not possible to understand the transcendental form or the spiritual world and its transcendental activities.

TEXT 15

त्वं नित्यमुक्तपरिशुद्धविबुद्ध आत्मा
कूटस्थ आदिपुरुषो भगवांस्त्र्यधीशः ।
यद्बुद्ध्यवस्थितिमखण्डितया स्वदृष्ट्या
द्रष्टा स्थितावधिमखो व्यतिरिक्त आस्से ॥ १५ ॥

tvaṁ nitya-mukta-pariśuddha-vibuddha ātmā
kūṭa-stha ādi-puruṣo bhagavāṁs try-adhīśaḥ
yad-buddhy-avasthitim akhaṇḍitayā sva-dṛṣṭyā
draṣṭā sthitāv adhimakho vyatirikta āsse

tvam—You; *nitya*—eternally; *mukta*—liberated; *pariśuddha*—uncontaminated; *vibuddhaḥ*—full of knowledge; *ātmā*—the Supreme Soul; *kūṭa-sthaḥ*—changeless; *ādi*—original; *puruṣaḥ*—person; *bhagavān*—the Lord, full with six opulences; *tri-adhīśaḥ*—master of the three modes; *yat*—whence; *buddhi*—of intellectual activities; *avasthitim*—all stages; *akhaṇḍitayā*—unbroken; *sva-dṛṣṭyā*—by transcendental vision; *draṣṭā*—You witness; *sthitau*—for maintaining (the universe); *adhimakhaḥ*—enjoyer of the results of all sacrifices; *vyatiriktaḥ*—differently; *āsse*—You are situated.

TRANSLATION

My Lord, by Your unbroken transcendental glance You are the supreme witness of all stages of intellectual activities. You are eter-

nally liberated, Your existence is situated in pure goodness, and You are existent in the Supersoul without change. You are the original Personality of Godhead, full with six opulences, and You are eternally the master of the three modes of material nature. Thus, You are always different from the ordinary living entities. As Lord Viṣṇu, You maintain all the affairs of the entire universe, and yet You stand aloof and are the enjoyer of the results of all sacrifices.

PURPORT

An atheistic argument against the supremacy of the Supreme Personality of Godhead states that if God, the Supreme Person, appears and disappears and sleeps and awakens, then what is the difference between God and the living entity? Dhruva Mahārāja is carefully distinguishing the existence of the Supreme Personality of Godhead from that of the living entities. He points out the following differences. The Lord is eternally liberated. Whenever He appears, even within this material world, He is never entangled by the three modes of material nature. He is known, therefore, as *try-adhīśa,* the master of the three modes of material nature. In *Bhagavad-gītā* (7.14) it is said, *daivī hy eṣā guṇamayī mama māyā duratyayā:* the living entities are all entangled in the three modes of material nature. The external energy of the Lord is very strong, but the Lord, as the master of the three modes of material nature, is ever liberated from the action and reaction of those modes. He, therefore, is uncontaminated, as stated in the *Īśopaniṣad.* The contamination of the material world does not affect the Supreme Godhead. Kṛṣṇa therefore says in the *Bhagavad-gītā* that those who are rascals and fools think of Him as an ordinary human being, not knowing His *paraṁ bhāvam. Paraṁ bhāvam* refers to His being always transcendentally situated. Material contamination cannot affect Him.

Another difference between the Lord and the living entity is that a living entity is always in darkness. Even though he may be situated in the mode of goodness, there are still so many things which are unknown to him. But it is not the same for the Supreme Personality of Godhead. He knows past, present and future and everything that is happening in everyone's heart. *Bhagavad-gītā* confirms this (*vedāhaṁ samatītāni*). The Lord is not part of the soul—He is the unchangeable Supreme Soul, and the living entities are His parts and parcels. The living entity is forced to appear in this material world under the direction of *daiva-māyā*, but when the Lord appears, He comes by His own internal potency, *ātma-māyā*. Besides that, a living entity is within the time of past, present and future. His life has a beginning, a birth, and in the conditioned state his life ends with death. But the Lord is *ādi-puruṣa*, the original person. In the *Brahma-saṁhitā* Lord Brahmā offers his respect to the *ādi-puruṣa*, Govinda, the original person, who has no beginning, whereas the creation of this material world has a beginning. The *Vedānta* says, *janmādy asya yataḥ:* everything is born from the Supreme, but the Supreme has no birth. He has all the six opulences in full and beyond comparison, He is the master of material nature, His intelligence is not broken under any circumstances, and He stands aloof, although He is the maintainer of the whole creation. As stated in the *Vedas* (*Kaṭha Upaniṣad* 2.2.13), *nityo nityānāṁ cetanaś cetanānām.* The Lord is the supreme maintainer. Living entities are meant to serve Him by offering sacrifices, for He is the rightful enjoyer of the results of all sacrifices. Everyone, therefore, should engage himself in the devotional service of the Lord with his life, his riches, his intelligence and his words. This is the original, constitutional position of the living entities. One should never compare the sleeping of an ordinary living entity to the sleeping of the Supreme Personality of Godhead in the Causal Ocean. There is no stage at which the living entity can compare to the Supreme Person. The Māyāvādī philosophers, being unable to adjust to all this, come to the conclusion of impersonalism or voidism.

TEXT 16

यस्मिन् विरुद्धगतयो ह्यनिशं पतन्ति
विद्यादयो विविधशक्तय आनुपूर्व्यात् ।
तद्ब्रह्म विश्वभवमेकमनन्तमाद्य-
मानन्दमात्रमविकारमहं प्रपद्ये ॥१६॥

yasmin viruddha-gatayo hy aniśaṁ patanti
vidyādayo vividha-śaktaya ānupūrvyāt

tad brahma viśva-bhavam ekam anantam ādyam
ānanda-mātram avikāram ahaṁ prapadye

yasmin—in whom; *viruddha-gatayaḥ*—of opposite character; *hi*—certainly; *aniśam*—always; *patanti*—are manifest; *vidyā-ādayaḥ*—knowledge and ignorance, etc.; *vividha*—various; *śaktayaḥ*—energies; *ānupūrvyāt*—continually; *tat*—that; *brahma*—Brahman; *viśva-bhavam*—the cause of material creation; *ekam*—one; *anantam*—unlimited; *ādyam*—original; *ānanda-mātram*—simply blissful; *avikāram*—changeless; *aham*—I; *prapadye*—offer my obeisances.

TRANSLATION

My dear Lord, in Your impersonal manifestation of Brahman there are always two opposing elements—knowledge and ignorance. Your multienergies are continually manifest, but the impersonal Brahman, which is undivided, original, changeless, unlimited and blissful, is the cause of the material manifestation. Because You are the same impersonal Brahman, I offer my respectful obeisances unto You.

PURPORT

In the *Brahma-saṁhitā* it is said that the unlimited impersonal Brahman is the effulgence of the transcendental body of Govinda. In that unlimited effulgent aura of the Supreme Personality of Godhead there are innumerable universes with innumerable planets of different categories. Although the Supreme Person is the original cause of all causes, His impersonal effulgence, known as Brahman, is the immediate cause of the material manifestation. Dhruva Mahārāja, therefore, offered his respectful obeisances unto the impersonal feature of the Lord. One who realizes this impersonal feature can enjoy the unchangeable *brahmānanda*, described here as spiritual bliss.

Śrīla Viśvanātha Cakravartī Ṭhākura describes that this impersonal feature, or Brahman manifestation, of the Supreme Lord is meant for persons who are essentially very advanced but still not able to understand the personal features or variegatedness of the spiritual world. Such devotees are known as *jñāna-miśra-bhaktas*, or devotees whose devotional service is mixed with empiric knowledge. Because the impersonal Brahman realization is a partial understanding of the Absolute Truth, Dhruva Mahārāja offers his respectful obeisances.

It is said that this impersonal Brahman is the distant realization of the Absolute Truth. Although apparently Brahman seems to be devoid of energy, factually it has different energies working under the headings of knowledge and ignorance. On account of these different energies, there is continually a manifestation of *vidyā* and *avidyā. Vidyā* and *avidyā* are very nicely described in *Īśopaniṣad.* It is said there that sometimes, due to *avidyā,* or a poor fund of knowledge, one accepts the Absolute Truth as ultimately impersonal. But in fact the impersonal and personal realizations develop in proportion to the development of devotional service. The more we develop our devotional service, the more closely we approach the Absolute Truth, which, in the beginning, when we realize the Absolute Truth from a distant place, is manifest as impersonal.

People in general, who are under the influence of *avidyā-śakti,* or *māyā,* have neither knowledge nor devotion. But when a person who is a little advanced and is therefore called a *jñānī* advances even more, he is in the category of a *jñāna-miśra-bhakta,* or a devotee whose love is mixed with empiric knowledge. When he is still further advanced, he can realize that the Absolute Truth is a person with multienergies. An advanced devotee can understand the Lord and His creative energy. As soon as one accepts the creative energy of the Absolute Truth, the six opulences of the Supreme Personality of Godhead are also understood. Devotees who are still further advanced, in full knowledge, can understand the transcendental pastimes of the Lord. Only on that platform can one fully enjoy transcendental bliss. An example is given in this connection by Viśvanātha Cakravartī Ṭhākura of a person proceeding towards a destination. As he approaches, he sees the destination from a distant place, just as we see a city from a distance. At that time he simply understands that the city is situated at a distance. When, however, he comes still nearer, he sees the domes and flags. But as soon as he enters the city, he sees various paths, gardens, lakes, and marketplaces with shops, and persons buying. He sees varieties of cinema houses, and he sees dancing and jubilation. When a person actually enters the city and personally sees the activities of the city, he becomes satisfied.

TEXT 17

सत्याशिषो हि भगवंस्तव पादपद्म-
माशीस्तथानुभजतः पुरुषार्थमूर्तेः ।
अप्येवमर्य भगवान् परिपाति दीनान्
वाश्रेव वत्सकमनुग्रहकातरोऽस्मान् ॥१७॥

satyāśiṣo hi bhagavaṁs tava pāda-padmam
āśīs tathānubhajataḥ puruṣārtha-mūrteḥ
apy evam arya bhagavān paripāti dīnān
vāśreva vatsakam anugraha-kātaro 'smān

satya—real; *āśiṣaḥ*—compared with other benedictions; *hi*—certainly; *bhagavan*—my Lord; *tava*—Your; *pāda-padmam*—lotus feet; *āśīḥ*—benediction; *tathā*—in that way; *anubhajataḥ*—for the devotees; *puruṣa-artha*—of the real goal of life; *mūrteḥ*—the personification; *api*—although; *evam*—thus; *arya*—O Lord; *bhagavān*—the Personality of Godhead; *paripāti*—maintains; *dīnān*—the poor in heart; *vāśrā*—a cow; *iva*—like; *vatsakam*—unto the calf; *anugraha*—to bestow mercy; *kātaraḥ*—eager; *asmān*—upon me.

TRANSLATION

My Lord, O Supreme Lord, You are the supreme personified form of all benediction. Therefore, for one who abides in Your devotional service with no other desire, worshiping Your lotus feet is better than becoming king and lording it over a kingdom. That is the benediction of worshiping Your lotus feet. To ignorant devotees like me, You are the causelessly merciful maintainer, just like a cow, who takes care of the newly born calf by supplying milk and giving it protection from attack.

PURPORT

Dhruva Mahārāja was cognizant of the defective nature of his own devotional service. Pure devotional service is without material form and is not covered by mental speculation or fruitive activities. Pure devotional service is therefore called *ahaitukī*, unmotivated. Dhruva Mahārāja knew that he had come to worship the Lord in devotional service with a motive—to get the kingdom of his father. Such an adulterated devotee can never see the Supreme Personality of Godhead face to face. He therefore felt very grateful for the causeless mercy of the Lord. The Lord is so merciful that not only does He fulfill the desires of a devotee who is driven by ignorance and desires for material benefit, but He also gives such a devotee all protection, just as a cow gives milk to a newly born calf. In the *Bhagavad-gītā* it is said that the Lord gives intelligence to the constantly engaged devotee so that he may gradually approach the Lord without difficulty. A devotee must be very sincere in his devotional service; then, although there may be many things wrong on the devotee's part, Kṛṣṇa will guide him and gradually elevate him to the highest position of devotional service.

The Lord is addressed herein by Dhruva Mahārāja as *puruṣārtha-mūrti*, the ultimate goal of life. Generally *puruṣārtha* is taken to mean execution of a type of religious principle or worship of God in order to get material benediction. Prayers for material benediction are intended for satisfying the senses. And when one is frustrated and cannot fully satisfy the senses in spite of all endeavor, he desires liberation, or freedom from material existence. These activities are generally called *puruṣārtha.* But actually the ultimate goal is to understand the Supreme Personality of Godhead. This is called *pañcama-puruṣārtha*, the ultimate goal of life. Lord Caitanya therefore taught us not to ask from the Supreme Personality any benediction such as material wealth, popularity or a good wife. One should simply pray to the Lord to be constantly engaged in His transcendental loving service. Dhruva Mahārāja, being cognizant of his desire for material benefit, wanted protection from the Lord so that he might not be misled or deviated from the path of devotional service by material desires.

TEXT 18

मैत्रेय उवाच

अथाभिष्टुत एवं वै सत्संकल्पेन धीमता ।
भृत्यानुरक्तो भगवान् प्रतिनन्द्येदमब्रवीत् ॥१८॥

maitreya uvāca
athābhiṣṭuta evaṁ vai
sat-saṅkalpena dhīmatā
bhṛtyānurakto bhagavān
pratinandyedam abravīt

maitreyaḥ uvāca—Maitreya said; *atha*—then; *abhiṣṭutaḥ*—being worshiped; *evam*—thus; *vai*—certainly; *sat-saṅkalpena*—by Dhruva Mahārāja, who had only good desires in his heart; *dhī-matā*—because he was very intelligent; *bhṛtya-anuraktaḥ*—very favorably disposed towards devotees; *bhagavān*—the Supreme Personality of Godhead; *pratinandya*—having congratulated him; *idam*—this; *abravīt*—said.

TRANSLATION

The great sage Maitreya continued: My dear Vidura, when Dhruva Mahārāja, who had good intentions in his heart, finished his prayer, the Supreme Lord, the Personality of Godhead, who is very kind to His devotees and servants, congratulated him, speaking as follows.

TEXT 19

श्रीभगवानुवाच
वेदाहं ते व्यवसितं हृदि राजन्यबालक ।
तत्प्रयच्छामि भद्रं ते दुरापमपि सुव्रत ॥१९॥

śrī-bhagavān uvāca
vedāhaṁ te vyavasitaṁ
hṛdi rājanya-bālaka
tat prayacchāmi bhadraṁ te
durāpam api suvrata

śrī-bhagavān uvāca—the Personality of Godhead said; *veda*—know; *aham*—I; *te*—your; *vyavasitam*—determination; *hṛdi*—within the heart; *rājanya-bālaka*—O son of the King; *tat*—that; *prayacchāmi*—I shall give you; *bhadram*—all good fortune; *te*—unto you; *durāpam*—although it is very difficult to obtain; *api*—in spite of; *su-vrata*—one who has taken a pious vow.

TRANSLATION

The Personality of Godhead said: My dear Dhruva, son of the King, you have executed pious vows, and I also know the desire within your heart. Although your desire is very ambitious and very difficult to fulfill, I shall favor you with its fulfillment. All good fortune unto you.

PURPORT

The Lord is so merciful to His devotee that He immediately said to Dhruva Mahārāja, "Let there be all good fortune for you." The fact is that Dhruva Mahārāja was very much afraid in his mind, for he had aspired after material benefit in discharging his devotional service and this was hampering him from reaching the stage of love of God. In the *Bhagavad-gītā* (2.44) it is said, *bhogaiśvarya-prasaktānām:* those who are addicted to material pleasure cannot be attracted to devotional service. It was true that at heart Dhruva Mahārāja wanted a kingdom that would be far better than Brahmaloka. This was a natural desire for a *kṣatriya.* He was also only five years old, and in his childish way he desired to have a kingdom far greater than his father's, grandfather's or great-grandfather's. His father, Uttānapāda, was the son of Manu, and Manu was the son of Lord Brahmā. Dhruva wanted to excel all these great family members. The Lord knew Dhruva Mahārāja's childish ambition, but how was it possible to offer Dhruva a position more exalted than Lord Brahmā's?

The Lord assured Dhruva Mahārāja that Dhruva would not be bereft of the Lord's love. He encouraged Dhruva not to be worried that he childishly had material desires and at the same time had the pure aspiration to be a great devotee. Generally, the Lord does not award a pure devotee material opulence, even though he may desire it. But Dhruva Mahārāja's case was different. The Lord knew that he was such a great devotee that in spite of having material opulence he would never be deviated from love of God. This example illustrates that a highly qualified devotee can have the facility of material enjoyment and at the same time execute love of God. This, however, was a special case for Dhruva Mahārāja.

TEXTS 20–21

नान्यैरधिष्ठितं भद्र यद्भ्राजिष्णु ध्रुवक्षिति ।
यत्र ग्रहर्क्षताराणां ज्योतिषां चक्रमाहितम् ॥२०॥
मेढ्यां गोचक्रवत्स्थास्नु परस्तात्कल्पवासिनाम् ।
धर्मोऽग्निः कश्यपः शुक्रो मुनयो ये वनौकसः ।
चरन्ति दक्षिणीकृत्य भ्रमन्तो यत्सतारकाः ॥२१॥

nānyair adhiṣṭhitaṁ bhadra
yad bhrājiṣṇu dhruva-kṣiti
yatra graharkṣa-tārāṇāṁ
jyotiṣāṁ cakram āhitam

meḍhyāṁ go-cakravat sthāsnu
parastāt kalpa-vāsinām
dharmo 'gniḥ kaśyapaḥ śukro
munayo ye vanaukasaḥ
caranti dakṣiṇī-kṛtya
bhramanto yat satārakāḥ

na—never; *anyaiḥ*—by others; *adhiṣṭhitam*—was ruled; *bhadra*—My good boy; *yat*—which; *bhrājiṣṇu*—brightly glowing; *dhruva-kṣiti*—the land known as Dhruvaloka; *yatra*—where; *graha*—planets; *ṛkṣa*—constellations; *tārāṇām*—and stars; *jyotiṣām*—by luminaries; *cakram*—encirclement; *āhitam*—is done; *meḍhyām*—around a central pole; *go*—of bulls; *cakra*—a multitude; *vat*—like; *sthāsnu*—stationary; *parastāt*—beyond; *kalpa*—a day of Brahmā (millennium); *vāsinām*—those who live; *dharmaḥ*—Dharma; *agniḥ*—Agni; *kaśyapaḥ*—Kaśyapa; *śukraḥ*—Śukra; *munayaḥ*—great sages; *ye*—all of them who; *vana-okasaḥ*—living in the forest; *caranti*—move; *dakṣiṇī-kṛtya*—keeping it to their right; *bhramantaḥ*—circumambulating; *yat*—which planet; *satārakāḥ*—with all the stars.

TRANSLATION

The Supreme Personality of Godhead continued: My dear Dhruva, I shall award you the glowing planet known as the

polestar, which will continue to exist even after the dissolution at the end of the millennium. No one has ever ruled this planet, which is surrounded by all the solar systems, planets and stars. All the luminaries in the sky circumambulate this planet, just as bulls tread around a central pole for the purpose of crushing grains. Keeping the polestar to their right, all the stars inhabited by the great sages like Dharma, Agni, Kaśyapa and Śukra circumambulate this planet, which continues to exist even after the dissolution of all others.

PURPORT

Although the polestar existed before its occupation by Dhruva Mahārāja, it had no predominating deity. Dhruvaloka, our polestar, is the center for all other stars and solar systems, for all of them circle around Dhruvaloka just as a bull crushes grains by walking around and around a central pole. Dhruva wanted the best of all planets, and although it was a childish prayer, the Lord satisfied his demand. A small child may demand something from his father which his father has never given to anyone else, yet out of affection the father offers it to the child; similarly, this unique planet, Dhruvaloka, was offered to Mahārāja Dhruva. The specific significance of this planet is that until the entire universe is annihilated this planet will remain, even during the devastation which takes place during the night of Lord Brahmā. There are two kinds of dissolutions, one during the night of Lord Brahmā and one at the end of Lord Brahmā's life. At the end of Brahmā's life, selected personalities go back home, back to Godhead. Dhruva Mahārāja is one of them. The Lord assured Dhruva that he would exist beyond the partial dissolution of this universe. Thus at the end of the complete dissolution, Dhruva Mahārāja would go directly to Vaikuṇṭhaloka, to a spiritual planet in the spiritual sky. Śrīla Viśvanātha Cakravartī Ṭhākura comments in this connection that Dhruvaloka is one of the *lokas* like Śvetadvīpa, Mathurā and Dvārakā. They are all eternal places in the kingdom of Godhead, which is described in the *Bhagavad-gītā* (*tad dhāma paramam*) and in the *Vedas* (*oṁ tad viṣṇoḥ paramaṁ padaṁ sadā paśyanti sūrayaḥ*). The words *parastāt kalpa-vāsinām*, "transcendental to the planets inhabited after the dissolution," refer to the

Vaikuṇṭha planets. In other words, Dhruva Mahārāja's promotion to the Vaikuṇṭhalokas was guaranteed by the Supreme Personality of Godhead.

TEXT 22

प्रस्थिते तु वनं पित्रा दत्त्वा गां धर्मसंश्रयः ।
षट्त्रिंशद्वर्षसाहस्रं रक्षिताव्याहतेन्द्रियः ॥२२॥

prasthite tu vanaṁ pitrā
dattvā gāṁ dharma-saṁśrayaḥ
ṣaṭ-triṁśad-varṣa-sāhasraṁ
rakṣitāvyāhatendriyaḥ

prasthite—after departure; *tu*—but; *vanam*—to the forest; *pitrā*—by your father; *dattvā*—awarding; *gām*—the whole world; *dharma-saṁśrayaḥ*—under the protection of piety; *ṣaṭ-triṁśat*—thirty-six; *varṣa*—years; *sāhasram*—one thousand; *rakṣitā*—you will rule; *avyāhata*—without decay; *indriyaḥ*—the power of the senses.

TRANSLATION

After your father goes to the forest and awards you the rule of his kingdom, you will rule continuously the entire world for thirty-six thousand years, and all your senses will continue to be as strong as they are now. You will never become old.

PURPORT

In the Satya-yuga people generally lived for one hundred thousand years. Dhruva Mahārāja's ruling the world for thirty-six thousand years was quite possible in those days.

TEXT 23

त्वद्भ्रातर्युत्तमे नष्टे मृगयायां तु तन्मनाः ।
अन्वेषन्ती वनं माता दावाग्निं सा प्रवेक्ष्यति ॥२३॥

tvad-bhrātary uttame naṣṭe
mṛgayāyāṁ tu tan-manāḥ
anveṣantī vanaṁ mātā
dāvāgniṁ sā pravekṣyati

tvat—your; *bhrātari*—brother; *uttame*—Uttama; *naṣṭe*—being killed; *mṛgayāyām*—in hunting; *tu*—then; *tat-manāḥ*—being too afflicted; *anveṣantī*—while searching out; *vanam*—in the forest; *mātā*—the mother; *dāva-agnim*—in the forest fire; *sā*—she; *pravekṣyati*—will enter.

TRANSLATION

The Lord continued: Sometime in the future your brother, Uttama, will go hunting in the forest, and while absorbed in hunting, he will be killed. Your stepmother, Suruci, being maddened upon the death of her son, will go to search him out in the forest, but she will be devoured by a forest fire.

PURPORT

Dhruva Mahārāja came to the forest to search out the Supreme Personality of Godhead with a revenging spirit against his stepmother. His stepmother had insulted Dhruva, who was not an ordinary person, but a great Vaiṣṇava. An offense at the lotus feet of a Vaiṣṇava is the greatest offense in this world. Because of having insulted Dhruva Mahārāja, Suruci would become mad upon the death of her son and would enter a forest fire, and thus her life would be ended. This was specifically mentioned by the Lord to Dhruva because he was determined for revenge against her. From this we should take the lesson that we should never try to insult a Vaiṣṇava. Not only should we not insult a Vaiṣṇava, but we should not insult anyone unnecessarily. When Suruci insulted Dhruva Mahārāja, he was just a child. She of course did not know that Dhruva was a great recognized Vaiṣṇava, and so her offense was committed unknowingly. When one serves a Vaiṣṇava unknowingly, one still gets the good result, and if one unknowingly insults a Vaiṣṇava, one suffers the bad result. A Vaiṣṇava is especially favored by the Supreme Personality of Godhead. Pleasing him or displeasing him directly affects the pleasure and displeasure of the Supreme Lord. Śrīla Viśvanātha Cakravartī Ṭhākura, in his eight stanzas of prayer to the spiritual master, has sung, *yasya prasādād bhagavat-prasādaḥ:* by pleasing the spiritual master, who is a pure Vaiṣṇava, one pleases the Personality of Godhead, but if one displeases the spiritual master one does not know where he is going.

TEXT 24

इष्ट्वा मां यज्ञहृदयं यज्ञैः पुष्कलदक्षिणैः ।
भुक्त्वा चेहाशिषः सत्या अन्ते मां संस्मरिष्यसि ॥ २४॥

iṣṭvā māṁ yajña-hṛdayaṁ
yajñaiḥ puṣkala-dakṣiṇaiḥ
bhuktvā cehāśiṣaḥ satyā
ante māṁ saṁsmariṣyasi

iṣṭvā—after worshiping; *mām*—Me; *yajña-hṛdayam*—the heart of all sacrifices; *yajñaiḥ*—by great sacrifices; *puṣkala-dakṣiṇaiḥ*—comprehending distribution of great charities; *bhuktvā*—after enjoying; *ca*—also; *iha*—within this world; *āśiṣaḥ*—blessings; *satyāḥ*—true; *ante*—at the end; *mām*—Me; *saṁsmariṣyasi*—you will be able to remember.

TRANSLATION

The Lord continued: I am the heart of all sacrifices. You will be able to perform many great sacrifices and also give great charities. In this way you will be able to enjoy the blessings of material happiness in this life, and at the time of your death you will be able to remember Me.

PURPORT

The most important factor in this verse is the Lord's instructions regarding how to remember the Supreme Personality of Godhead at the end of life. *Ante nārāyaṇa-smṛtiḥ:* the result of whatever we do in executing spiritual activities is successful if we can remember Nārāyaṇa, the Supreme Personality of Godhead. This program of constant remembrance can be disturbed by many things, but Dhruva Mahārāja's life would be so pure, as assured by the Lord Himself, that Dhruva would never forget Him. Thus at the time of his death he would remember the Supreme Lord, and before his death he would enjoy this material world, not by sense gratification, but by performing great sacrifices. As stated in the *Vedas*, when one performs great sacrifices he must give charity, not only to the *brāhmaṇas*, but also to the *kṣatriyas, vaiśyas* and *śūdras*. It is assured here that Dhruva Mahārāja would be able to perform such activities. In this age of Kali, however, the great sacrifice is the performance of *saṅkīrtana-yajña*. Our Kṛṣṇa consciousness movement is designed to teach people (and to learn ourselves) the exact instruction of the Personality of Godhead. In this way we shall continuously perform the *saṅkīrtana-yajña* and continuously chant the Hare Kṛṣṇa *mantra*. Then at the end of our lives we shall certainly be able to remember Kṛṣṇa, and our program of life will be successful. In this age, distribution of *prasāda* has replaced distribution of money. No one has sufficient money to distribute, but if we distribute *kṛṣṇa-prasāda* as far as possible, this is more valuable than the distribution of money.

TEXT 25

ततो गन्तासि मत्स्थानं सर्वलोकनमस्कृतम् ।
उपरिष्टादृषिभ्यस्त्वं यतो नावर्तते गतः ॥२५॥

tato gantāsi mat-sthānaṁ
sarva-loka-namaskṛtam
upariṣṭād ṛṣibhyas tvaṁ
yato nāvartate gataḥ

tataḥ—thereafter; *gantā asi*—you will go; *mat-sthānam*—to My abode; *sarva-loka*—by all planetary systems; *namaḥ-kṛtam*—offered obeisances; *upariṣṭāt*—situated higher; *ṛṣibhyaḥ*—than the planetary systems of the *ṛṣis; tvam*—you; *yataḥ*—wherefrom; *na*—never; *āvartate*—will come back; *gataḥ*—having gone there.

TRANSLATION

The Personality of Godhead continued: My dear Dhruva, after your material life in this body, you will go to My planet, which is

always offered obeisances by the residents of all other planetary systems. It is situated above the planets of the seven ṛṣis, and having gone there you will never have to come back again to this material world.

PURPORT

In this verse the word *nāvartate* is very significant. The Lord says, "You will not come back to this material world, for you will reach *mat-sthānam*, My abode." Therefore Dhruvaloka, or the polestar, is the abode of Lord Viṣṇu within this material world. Upon it there is an ocean of milk, and within that ocean there is an island known as Śvetadvīpa. It is clearly indicated that this planet is situated above the seven planetary systems of the *ṛṣis*, and because this planet is Viṣṇuloka, it is worshiped by all other planetary systems. It may be questioned here what will happen to the planet known as Dhruvaloka at the time of the dissolution of this universe. The answer is simple: Dhruvaloka remains, like other Vaikuṇṭhalokas beyond this universe. Śrīla Viśvanātha Cakravartī Ṭhākura has commented in this connection that the very word *nāvartate* indicates that this planet is eternal.

TEXT 26

मैत्रेय उवाच

इत्यर्चितः स भगवानतिदिश्यात्मनः पदम् ।
बालस्य पश्यतो धाम स्वमगाद्गरुडध्वजः ॥२६॥

maitreya uvāca
ity arcitaḥ sa bhagavān
atidiśyātmanaḥ padam
bālasya paśyato dhāma
svam agād garuḍa-dhvajaḥ

maitreyaḥ uvāca—the great sage Maitreya continued to speak; *iti*—thus; *arcitaḥ*—being honored and worshiped; *saḥ*—the Supreme Lord; *bhagavān*—the Personality of Godhead; *atidiśya*—after offering; *ātmanaḥ*—His personal; *padam*—residence; *bālasya*—while the boy;

paśyataḥ—was looking on; *dhāma*—to His abode; *svam*—own; *agāt*—He returned; *garuḍa-dhvajaḥ*—Lord Viṣṇu, whose flag bears the emblem of Garuḍa.

TRANSLATION

The great sage Maitreya said: After being worshiped and honored by the boy, Dhruva Mahārāja, and after offering him His abode, Lord Viṣṇu, on the back of Garuḍa, returned to His abode, as Dhruva Mahārāja looked on.

PURPORT

From this verse it appears that Lord Viṣṇu awarded Dhruva Mahārāja the same abode in which He resides. His abode is described in the *Bhagavad-gītā* (15.6): *yad gatvā na nivartante tad dhāma paramaṁ mama.*

TEXT 27

सोऽपि संकल्पजं विष्णोः पादसेवोपसादितम् ।
प्राप्य संकल्पनिर्वाणं नातिप्रीतोऽभ्यगात्पुरम्॥२७॥

so 'pi saṅkalpajaṁ viṣṇoḥ
pāda-sevopasāditam
prāpya saṅkalpa-nirvāṇaṁ
nātiprīto 'bhyagāt puram

saḥ—he (Dhruva Mahārāja); *api*—although; *saṅkalpa-jam*—the desired result; *viṣṇoḥ*—of Lord Viṣṇu; *pāda-sevā*—by serving the lotus feet; *upasāditam*—obtained; *prāpya*—having achieved; *saṅkalpa*—of his determination; *nirvāṇam*—the satisfaction; *na*—not; *atiprītaḥ*—very much pleased; *abhyagāt*—he returned; *puram*—to his home.

TRANSLATION

Despite having achieved the desired result of his determination by worshiping the lotus feet of the Lord, Dhruva Mahārāja was not very pleased. Thus he returned to his home.

PURPORT

By worshiping the lotus feet of the Lord in devotional service as instructed by Nārada Muni, Dhruva Mahārāja achieved the desired result. His desire was to get a very exalted position, excelling that of his father, grandfather and great-grandfather, and although it was a somewhat childish determination because Dhruva Mahārāja was nothing but a small child, Lord Viṣṇu, the Supreme Personality of Godhead, is so kind and merciful that He fulfilled Dhruva's desire. Dhruva Mahārāja wanted a residence more exalted than any ever occupied by anyone else in his family. Therefore he was offered the planet in which the Lord personally resides, and his determination was completely satisfied. Still, when Dhruva Mahārāja returned home he was not very much pleased, for although in pure devotional service there is no demand from the Lord, because of his childish nature he had demanded something. Thus although the Lord also fulfilled his desire, he was not very pleased. Rather, he was ashamed that he had demanded something from the Lord, for he should not have done this.

TEXT 28

विदुर उवाच
सुदुर्लभं यत्परमं पदं हरे-
र्मायाविनस्तच्चरणार्चनार्जितम् ।
लब्ध्वाप्यसिद्धार्थमिवैकजन्मना
कथं स्वमात्मानममन्यतार्थवित् ॥२८॥

vidura uvāca
sudurlabhaṁ yat paramaṁ padaṁ harer
māyāvinas tac-caraṇārcanārjitam
labdhvāpy asiddhārtham ivaika-janmanā
kathaṁ svam ātmānam amanyatārtha-vit

viduraḥ uvāca—Vidura continued to inquire; *sudurlabham*—very rare; *yat*—that which; *paramam*—is the supreme; *padam*—situation; *hareḥ*—of the Supreme Personality of Godhead; *māyā-vinaḥ*—very affectionate; *tat*—His; *caraṇa*—lotus feet; *arcana*—by worshiping; *ar-jitam*—achieved; *labdhvā*—having attained; *api*—although; *asiddha-artham*—not fulfilled; *iva*—as if; *eka-janmanā*—in the duration of one life; *katham*—why; *svam*—own; *ātmānam*—heart; *amanyata*—he felt; *artha-vit*—being very wise.

TRANSLATION

Śrī Vidura inquired: My dear brāhmaṇa, the abode of the Lord is very difficult to attain. It can be attained only by pure devotional service, which alone pleases the most affectionate, merciful Lord. Dhruva Mahārāja achieved this position even in one life, and he was very wise and conscientious. Why, then, was he not very pleased?

PURPORT

Saint Vidura's inquiry is very relevant. The word *artha-vit*, which refers to one who knows how to discriminate between reality and unreality, is very significant in this connection. An *artha-vit* is also called *paramahaṁsa.* A *paramahaṁsa* accepts only the active principle of everything; just as a swan accepts only the milk from a mixture of water and milk, a *paramahaṁsa* accepts only the Supreme Personality of Godhead as his life and soul, neglecting all external, material things. Dhruva Mahārāja was in this category, and due to his determination he achieved the result he desired, but still when he returned home he was not very pleased.

TEXT 29

मैत्रेय उवाच

मातुः सपत्न्या वाग्बाणैर्हृदि विद्धस्तु तान् स्मरन् ।
नैच्छन्मुक्तिपतेर्मुक्तिं तस्मात्तापमुपेयिवान् ॥२९॥

maitreya uvāca
mātuḥ sapatnyā vāg-bāṇair
hṛdi viddhas tu tān smaran

naicchan mukti-pater muktiṁ
tasmāt tāpam upeyivān

maitreyaḥ uvāca—the great sage Maitreya replied; *mātuḥ*—of his mother; *sa-patnyāḥ*—of the co-wife; *vāk-bāṇaiḥ*—by the arrows of harsh words; *hṛdi*—in the heart; *viddhaḥ*—pierced; *tu*—then; *tān*—all of them; *smaran*—remembering; *na*—not; *aicchat*—desired; *mukti-pateḥ*—from the Lord, whose lotus feet give liberation; *muktim*—salvation; *tasmāt*—therefore; *tāpam*—grief; *upeyivān*—he suffered.

TRANSLATION

Maitreya answered: Dhruva Mahārāja's heart, which was pierced by the arrows of the harsh words of his stepmother, was greatly aggrieved, and thus when he fixed upon his goal of life he did not forget her misbehavior. He did not demand actual liberation from this material world, but at the end of his devotional service, when the Supreme Personality of Godhead appeared before him, he was simply ashamed of the material demands he had in his mind.

PURPORT

This important verse has been discussed by many stalwart commentators. Why was Dhruva Mahārāja not very pleased, even after achieving the goal of life he desired? A pure devotee is always free from any kind of material desires. In the material world, one's material desires are all most demonic; one thinks of others as one's enemies, one thinks of revenge against one's enemies, one aspires to become the topmost leader or topmost person in this material world, and thus one competes with all others. This has been described in the *Bhagavad-gītā*, Sixteenth Chapter, as asuric. A pure devotee has no demand from the Lord. His only concern is to serve the Lord sincerely and seriously, and he is not at all concerned about what will happen in the future. In the *Mukunda-mālā-stotra*, King Kulaśekhara, author of the book, states in his prayer: "My dear Lord, I don't want any position of sense gratification within this material world. I simply want to engage in Your service perpetually." Similarly, Lord Caitanya, in His *Sikṣāṣṭaka*, also prayed, "My Lord, I do not want any amount of material wealth, I do not want any number of materialistic followers, nor do I want any attractive wife to enjoy. The only thing I want is that I may engage life after life in Your service." Lord Caitanya did not pray even for *mukti*, or liberation.

In this verse Maitreya replied to Vidura that Dhruva Mahārāja, influenced by a revengeful attitude towards his insulting stepmother, did not think of *mukti*, nor did he know what *mukti* was. Therefore he failed to aim for *mukti* as his goal in life. But a pure devotee also does not want liberation. He is a soul completely surrendered to the Supreme Lord, and he does not demand anything from the Lord. This position was realized by Dhruva Mahārāja when he saw the Supreme Personality of Godhead present personally before him because he was elevated to the *vasudeva* platform. The *vasudeva* platform refers to the stage at which material contamination is conspicuous by absence only, or in other words where there is no question of the material modes of nature—goodness, passion and ignorance—and one can therefore see the Supreme Personality of Godhead. Because on the *vasudeva* platform one can see God face to face, the Lord is also called Vāsudeva.

Dhruva Mahārāja's demand was for a position so exalted that it was never enjoyed even by Lord Brahmā, his great-grandfather. Kṛṣṇa, the Supreme Personality of Godhead, is so affectionate and kind towards His devotee, especially to a devotee like Dhruva Mahārāja, who went to render devotional service in the forest alone at the age of only five years, that although the motive might be impure, the Lord does not consider the motive; He is concerned with the service. But if a devotee has a particular motive, the Lord directly or indirectly knows it, and therefore He does not leave the devotee's material desires unfulfilled. These are some of the special favors by the Lord to a devotee.

Dhruva Mahārāja was offered Dhruvaloka, a planet that was never resided upon by any conditioned soul. Even Brahmā, although the topmost living creature within this universe, was not allowed to enter the Dhruvaloka. Whenever there is a crisis within this universe, the demigods go to see the Supreme Personality of Godhead Kṣīrodakaśāyī Viṣṇu, and they stand on the beach of the Milk Ocean. So the fulfillment of Dhruva Mahārāja's demand—a position more exalted than that of even his great-grandfather, Brahmā—was offered to him.

Here in this verse the Lord is described as *mukti-pati*, which means "one under whose lotus feet there are all kinds of *mukti*." There are five kinds of *mukti—sāyujya, sārūpya, sālokya, sāmīpya* and *sārṣṭi*. Out of these five *muktis*, which can be achieved by any person engaged in devotional service to the Lord, the one which is known as *sāyujya* is generally demanded by Māyāvādī philosophers; they demand to become one with the impersonal Brahman effulgence of the Lord. In the opinion of many scholars, this *sāyujya-mukti*, although counted among the five kinds of *mukti*, is not actually *mukti* because from *sāyujya-mukti* one may again fall down to this material world. This information we have from *Śrīmad-Bhāgavatam* (10.2.32), wherein it is said, *patanty adhaḥ*, which means "they again fall down." The monist philosopher, after executing severe austerity, merges into the impersonal effulgence of the Lord, but the living entity always wants reciprocation in loving affairs. Therefore, although the monist philosopher is elevated to the status of being one with the effulgence of the Lord, because there is no facility for associating with the Lord and rendering service unto Him, he again falls into this material world, and his service propensity is satisfied by materialistic welfare activities like humanitarianism, altruism and philanthropy. There are many instances of such falldowns, even for great *sannyāsīs* in the Māyāvāda school.

Therefore Vaiṣṇava philosophers do not accept *sāyujya-mukti* to be within the category of *mukti*. According to them, *mukti* means transferal to the loving service of the Lord from one's position of serving *māyā*. Lord Caitanya also says in this connection that the constitutional position of a living entity is to render service to the Lord. That is real *mukti*. When one is situated in his original position, giving up artificial positions, he is called *mukta*, or liberated. In the *Bhagavad-gītā* this is confirmed: anyone who engages in rendering transcendental loving service to the Lord is considered to be *mukta*, or *brahma-bhūta*. It is said in *Bhagavad-gītā* that a devotee is considered to be on the *brahma-bhūta* platform when he has no material contamination. In the *Padma Purāṇa* this is also confirmed: *mukti* means engagement in the service of the Lord.

The great sage Maitreya explained that Dhruva Mahārāja did not desire in the beginning to engage in the service of the Lord, but he wanted an exalted position better than his great-grandfather's. This is more or less not service to the Lord but service to the senses. Even if one gets the position of Brahmā, the most exalted position in this material world, he is a conditioned soul. Śrīla Prabodhānanda Sarasvatī says that if one is elevated to real, pure devotional service, he considers even great demigods like Brahmā and Indra to be on an equal level with an insignificant insect. The reason is that an insignificant insect has a desire for sense gratification and even a great personality like Lord Brahmā also wants to dominate this material nature.

Sense gratification means domination over material nature. The whole competition between conditioned souls is based upon domination of this material nature. Modern scientists are proud of their knowledge because they are discovering new methods to dominate the laws of material nature. They think that this is the advancement of human civilization—the more they can dominate the material laws, the more advanced they think they are. Dhruva Mahārāja's propensity in the beginning was like that. He wanted to dominate this material world in a greater position than Lord Brahmā. Therefore elsewhere it is described that after the appearance of the Lord, when Dhruva Mahārāja thought and compared his determination to his final reward, he realized that he had wanted a few particles of broken glass but instead had received many diamonds. As soon as he saw the Supreme Personality of Godhead face to face, he immediately became conscious of the unimportance of his demand from the Lord to have an exalted position better than Lord Brahmā's.

When Dhruva Mahārāja became situated on the *vasudeva* platform due to seeing the Lord face to face, all his material contamination was cleared. Thus he became ashamed of what his demands were and what he had achieved. He was very much ashamed to think that although he had gone to Madhuvana, giving up the kingdom of his father, and he had gotten a spiritual master like Nārada Muni, he was still thinking of revenge against his stepmother and wanted to occupy an exalted post within this material world. These were the causes for his moroseness even after he received all the desired benedictions from the Lord.

When Dhruva Mahārāja factually saw the Supreme Personality of Godhead, there was no question of a revengeful attitude towards his stepmother nor any aspiration to lord it over the material world, but the Supreme Personality is so kind that He knew that Dhruva Mahārāja wanted these. Speaking before Dhruva Mahārāja, He used the word *vedāham* because when Dhruva Mahārāja demanded material benefits, the Lord was present within his heart and so knew everything. The Lord always knows everything a man is thinking. This is confirmed in *Bhagavad-gītā* also: *vedāhaṁ samatītāni.*

The Lord fulfilled all Dhruva Mahārāja's desires. His revengeful attitude towards his stepmother and stepbrother was satisfied, his desire for a more exalted position than that of his great-grandfather was also fulfilled, and at the same time, his eternal position in Dhruvaloka was fixed. Although Dhruva Mahārāja's achievement of an eternal planet was not conceived of by him, Kṛṣṇa thought, "What will Dhruva do with an exalted position within this material world?" Therefore He gave Dhruva the opportunity to rule this material world for thirty-six thousand years with unchangeable senses and the chance to perform many great sacrifices and thus become the most reputed king within this material world. And, after finishing with all this material enjoyment, Dhruva would be promoted to the spiritual world, which includes the Dhruvaloka.

TEXT 30

ध्रुव उवाच
समाधिना नैकभवेन यत्पदं
विदुः सनन्दादय ऊर्ध्वरेतसः ।
मासैरहं षड्भिरमुष्य पादयो-
श्छायामुपेत्यापगतः पृथङ्मतिः ॥३०॥

dhruva uvāca
samādhinā naika-bhavena yat padaṁ
viduḥ sanandādaya ūrdhva-retasaḥ
māsair ahaṁ ṣaḍbhir amuṣya pādayoś
chāyām upetyāpagataḥ pṛthaṅ-matiḥ

dhruvaḥ uvāca—Dhruva Mahārāja said; *samādhinā*—by practicing *yoga* in trance; *na*—never; *eka-bhavena*—by one birth; *yat*—which; *padam*—position; *viduḥ*—understood; *sananda-ādayaḥ*—the four *brahmacārīs* headed by Sanandana; *ūrdhva-retasaḥ*—infallible celibates; *māsaiḥ*—within months; *aham*—I; *ṣaḍbhiḥ*—six; *amuṣya*—of Him; *pādayoḥ*—of the lotus feet; *chāyām*—shelter; *upetya*—

achieving; *apagataḥ*—fell down; *pṛthak-matiḥ*—my mind fixed on things other than the Lord.

TRANSLATION

Dhruva Mahārāja thought to himself: To endeavor to be situated in the shade of the lotus feet of the Lord is not an ordinary task because even the great brahmacārīs headed by Sanandana, who practiced aṣṭāṅga-yoga in trance, attained the shelter of the Lord's lotus feet only after many, many births. Within six months I achieved the same result, yet due to my thinking differently from the Lord, I fell down from my position.

PURPORT

In this verse Dhruva Mahārāja himself explains the cause of his moroseness. First he laments that to see the Supreme Personality of Godhead directly is not easy. Even great saintly persons like the four celebrated *brahmacārīs* headed by Sanandana—Sanandana, Sanaka, Sanātana and Sanat-kumāra—practiced the *yoga* system for many, many births and remained in trance before getting the opportunity to see the Supreme Lord face to face. As far as Dhruva Mahārāja was concerned, he saw the Supreme Lord personally after only six months of practice in devotional service. He expected, therefore, that as soon as he met the Supreme Lord, the Lord would take him to His abode immediately, without waiting. Dhruva Mahārāja could understand very clearly that the Lord had offered him the rule of the world for thirty-six thousand years because in the beginning he was under the spell of the material energy and wanted to take revenge against his stepmother and rule over his father's kingdom. Dhruva Mahārāja greatly lamented his propensity for ruling the material world and his revengeful attitude towards other living entities.

TEXT 31

अहो बत ममानात्म्यं मन्दभाग्यस्य पश्यत ।
भवच्छिदः पादमूलं गत्वायाचे यदन्तवत् ॥३१॥

aho bata mamānātmyaṁ
manda-bhāgyasya paśyata
bhava-cchidaḥ pāda-mūlaṁ
gatvā yāce yad antavat

aho—oh; *bata*—alas; *mama*—my; *anātmyam*—bodily consciousness; *manda-bhāgyasya*—of the unfortunate; *paśyata*—just see; *bhava*—material existence; *chidaḥ*—of the Lord, who can cut off; *pāda-mūlam*—the lotus feet; *gatvā*—having approached; *yāce*—I prayed for; *yat*—that which; *anta-vat*—perishable.

TRANSLATION

Alas, just look at me! I am so unfortunate. I approached the lotus feet of the Supreme Personality of Godhead, who can immediately cut the chain of the repetition of birth and death, but still, out of my foolishness, I prayed for things which are perishable.

PURPORT

The word *anātmyam* is very significant in this verse. *Ātmā* means "the soul," and *anātmya* means "without any conception of the soul." Śrīla Ṛṣabhadeva instructed his sons that unless a human being comes to the point of understanding the *ātmā*, or spiritual position, whatever he does is ignorance, and this brings only defeat in his life. Dhruva Mahārāja regrets his unfortunate position, for although he approached the Supreme Personality of Godhead, who is always able to give His devotee the highest benediction of cessation of the repetition of birth and death, which is impossible for any demigod to offer, he foolishly wanted something perishable. When Hiraṇyakaśipu asked immortality from Lord Brahmā, Lord Brahmā expressed his inability to offer such a benediction because he himself is not immortal; therefore immortality, or complete cessation of the chain of repeated birth and death, can be offered by the Supreme Lord, the Personality of Godhead Himself, not by others. *Hariṁ vinā na sṛtiṁ taranti.* It is said that without the blessings of Hari, the Supreme Personality of Godhead, no one can stop the continuous chain of birth and death within this material world.

Therefore the Supreme Lord is also called *bhava-cchit.* The Vaiṣṇava philosophy in the process of Kṛṣṇa consciousness prohibits the devotee from all kinds of material aspirations. A Vaiṣṇava devotee should always be *anyābhilāṣitā-śūnya*, free from all material aspirations for the results of fruitive activities or empiric philosophical speculation. Dhruva Mahārāja was actually initiated by Nārada Muni, the greatest Vaiṣṇava, in the chanting of *oṁ namo bhagavate vāsudevāya.* This *mantra* is a *viṣṇu-mantra,* for by practicing the chanting of this *mantra* one is elevated to the Viṣṇuloka. Dhruva Mahārāja regrets that although he was initiated in the *viṣṇu-mantra* by a Vaiṣṇava, he still aspired for material benefits. That was another cause for lamentation. Although he got the result of the *viṣṇu-mantra* by the causeless mercy of the Lord, he lamented how foolish he was to have strived for material benefits while practicing devotional service. In other words, every one of us who is engaged in devotional service in Kṛṣṇa consciousness should be completely free from all material aspirations. Otherwise we will have to lament like Dhruva Mahārāja.

TEXT 32

मतिर्विदूषिता देवैः पतद्भिरसहिष्णुभिः ।
यो नारदवचस्तथ्यं नाग्राहिषमसत्तमः ॥३२॥

matir vidūṣitā devaiḥ
patadbhir asahiṣṇubhiḥ
yo nārada-vacas tathyaṁ
nāgrāhiṣam asattamaḥ

matiḥ—intelligence; *vidūṣitā*—contaminated; *devaiḥ*—by the demigods; *patadbhiḥ*—who will fall down; *asahiṣṇubhiḥ*—intolerant; *yaḥ*—I who; *nārada*—of the great sage Nārada; *vacaḥ*—of the instructions; *tathyam*—the truth; *na*—not; *agrāhiṣam*—could accept; *asat-tamaḥ*—the most wretched.

TRANSLATION

Since all the demigods who are situated in the higher planetary system will have to come down again, they are all envious of my being elevated to Vaikuṇṭhaloka by devotional service. These in-

tolerant demigods have dissipated my intelligence, and only for this reason could I not accept the genuine benediction of the instructions of Sage Nārada.

PURPORT

As shown by many instances in the Vedic literature, when a person undergoes severe austerities, the demigods become very much perturbed because they are always afraid of losing their posts as the predominating deities of the heavenly planets. It is known to them that their position in the higher planetary system is impermanent, as it is stated in the *Bhagavad-gītā*, Ninth Chapter (*kṣīṇe puṇye martya-lokaṁ viśanti*). It is said in the *Gītā* that after exhausting the results of their pious activities, all the demigods, who are inhabitants of the higher planetary system, have to come back again to this earth.

It is a fact that the demigods control the different activities of the limbs of our bodies. Factually we are not free even in moving our eyelids. Everything is controlled by them. Dhruva Mahārāja's conclusion is that these demigods, being envious of his superior position in devotional service, conspired against him to pollute his intelligence, and thus although he was the disciple of a great Vaiṣṇava, Nārada Muni, he could not accept Nārada's valid instructions. Now Dhruva Mahārāja regretted very much that he had neglected these instructions. Nārada Muni had asked him, "Why should you bother about insult or adoration from your stepmother?" He of course said to Dhruva Mahārāja that since Dhruva was only a child, what did he have to do with such insult or adoration? But Dhruva Mahārāja was determined to achieve the benediction of the Supreme Personality of Godhead, and therefore Nārada advised him to go back home for the time being, and in mature time he could try to practice devotional service. Dhruva Mahārāja regretted that he had rejected the advice of Nārada Muni and was adamant in asking him for something perishable, namely revenge against his stepmother for her insult, and possession of the kingdom of his father.

Dhruva Mahārāja regretted very much that he could not take seriously the instruction of his spiritual master and that his consciousness was therefore contaminated. Still, the Lord is so merciful that due to Dhruva's execution of devotional service He offered Dhruva the ultimate Vaiṣṇava goal.

TEXT 33

दैवीं मायामुपाश्रित्य प्रसुप्त इव भिन्नदृक् ।
तप्ये द्वितीयेऽप्यसति भ्रातृभ्रातृव्यहृद्रुजा ॥३३॥

daivīṁ māyām upāśritya
prasupta iva bhinna-dṛk
tapye dvitīye 'py asati
bhrātṛ-bhrātṛvya-hṛd-rujā

daivīm—of the Personality of Godhead; *māyām*—the illusory energy; *upāśritya*—taking shelter of; *prasuptaḥ*—dreaming while asleep; *iva*—like; *bhinna-dṛk*—having separated vision; *tapye*—I lamented; *dvitīye*—in the illusory energy; *api*—although; *asati*—temporary; *bhrātṛ*—brother; *bhrātṛvya*—enemy; *hṛt*—within the heart; *rujā*—by lamentation.

TRANSLATION

Dhruva Mahārāja lamented: I was under the influence of the illusory energy; being ignorant of the actual facts, I was sleeping on her lap. Under a vision of duality, I saw my brother as my enemy, and falsely I lamented within my heart, thinking, "They are my enemies."

PURPORT

Real knowledge is revealed to a devotee only when he comes to the right conclusion about life by the grace of the Lord. Our creation of friends and enemies within this material world is something like dreaming at night. In dreams we create so many things out of various impressions in the subconscious mind, but all such creations are simply temporary and unreal. In the same way, although apparently we are awake in material life, because we have no information of the soul and the Supersoul, we create many friends and enemies simply out of imagination. Śrīla Kṛṣṇadāsa Kavirāja Gosvāmī says that within this material world or material consciousness, good and bad are the same. The distinction between good and bad is simply a mental concoction. The actual fact is that all living entities are sons of God, or by-products of His marginal energy. Because of our being contaminated by the modes of material nature, we distinguish one spiritual spark from another. That is also another kind of dreaming. It is stated in the *Bhagavad-gītā* that those who are actually learned do not make any distinction between a learned scholar, a *brāhmaṇa*, an elephant, a dog and a *caṇḍāla*. They do not see in terms of the external body; rather, they see the person as spirit soul. By higher understanding one can know that the material body is nothing but a combination of the five material elements. In that sense also the bodily construction of a human being and that of a demigod are one and the same. From the spiritual point of view we are all spiritual sparks, parts and parcels of the Supreme Spirit, God. Either materially or spiritually we are basically one, but we make friends and enemies as dictated by the illusory energy. Dhruva Mahārāja therefore said, *daivīṁ māyām upāśritya:* the cause of his bewilderment was his association with the illusory, material energy.

TEXT 34

मयैतत्प्रार्थितं व्यर्थं चिकित्सेव गतायुषि ।
प्रसाद्य जगदात्मानं तपसा दुष्प्रसादनम् ।
भवच्छिदमयाचेऽहं भवं भाग्यविवर्जितः ॥३४॥

mayaitat prārthitaṁ vyarthaṁ
cikitseva gatāyuṣi
prasādya jagad-ātmānaṁ
tapasā duṣprasādanam
bhava-cchidam ayāce 'haṁ
bhavaṁ bhāgya-vivarjitaḥ

mayā—by me; *etat*—this; *prārthitam*—prayed for; *vyartham*—uselessly; *cikitsā*—treatment; *iva*—like; *gata*—has ended; *āyuṣi*—for one whose life; *prasādya*—after satisfying; *jagat-ātmānam*—the soul of the universe; *tapasā*—by austerity; *duṣprasādanam*—who is very difficult to satisfy; *bhava-chidam*—the Personality of Godhead, who can cut the chain of birth and death; *ayāce*—prayed for; *aham*—I; *bhavam*—repetition of birth and death; *bhāgya*—fortune; *vivarjitaḥ*—being without.

TRANSLATION

It is very difficult to satisfy the Supreme Personality of Godhead, but in my case, although I have satisfied the Supersoul of the whole universe, I have prayed only for useless things. My activities were exactly like treatment given to a person who is already dead. Just see how unfortunate I am, for in spite of meeting the Supreme Lord, who can cut one's link with birth and death, I have prayed for the same conditions again.

PURPORT

Sometimes it so happens that a devotee engaged in the loving service of the Lord desires some material benefit in exchange for this service. This is not the proper way to discharge devotional service. Out of ignorance, of course, sometimes a devotee does so, but Dhruva Mahārāja regrets his personal behavior in this connection.

TEXT 35

स्वाराज्यं यच्छतो मौढ्यान्मानो मे भिक्षितो बत ।
ईश्वरात्क्षीणपुण्येन फलीकारानिवाधनः ॥३५॥

svārājyaṁ yacchato mauḍhyān
māno me bhikṣito bata
īśvarāt kṣīṇa-puṇyena
phalī-kārān ivādhanaḥ

svārājyam—His devotional service; *yacchataḥ*—from the Lord, who was willing to offer; *mauḍhyāt*—by foolishness; *mānaḥ*—material prosperity; *me*—by me; *bhikṣitaḥ*—was asked for; *bata*—alas; *īśvarāt*—from a great emperor; *kṣīṇa*—reduced; *puṇyena*—whose pious activities; *phalī-kārān*—broken particles of husked rice; *iva*—like; *adhanaḥ*—a poor man.

TRANSLATION

Because of my state of complete foolishness and paucity of pious activities, although the Lord offered me His personal service, I

wanted material name, fame and prosperity. My case is just like that of the poor man who, when he satisfied a great emperor who wanted to give him anything he might ask, out of ignorance asked only a few broken grains of husked rice.

PURPORT

In this verse the word *svārājyam,* which means "complete independence," is very significant. A conditioned soul does not know what complete independence is. Complete independence means situation in one's own constitutional position. The real independence of a living entity, who is part and parcel of the Supreme Personality of Godhead, is to remain always dependent on the Supreme Lord, just like a child who plays in complete independence, guided by his parents, who watch over him. The independence of the conditioned soul does not mean to fight with the obstacles offered by *māyā,* but to surrender to Kṛṣṇa. In the material world, everyone is trying to become completely independent simply by fighting against the obstacles offered by *māyā.* This is called the struggle for existence. Real independence is to be reinstated in the service of the Lord. Anyone who goes to the Vaikuṇṭha planets or Goloka Vṛndāvana planet is freely offering his service to the Lord. That is complete independence. Just contrary to this is material overlordship, which we wrongly take to be independence. Many great political leaders have tried to establish independence, but due to such so-called independence the people's dependence has only increased. The living entity cannot be happy trying to be independent in the material world. One has to surrender, therefore, unto the lotus feet of the Lord and engage in his original, eternal service.

Dhruva Mahārāja regrets that he wanted material opulence and greater prosperity than that of his great-grandfather, Lord Brahmā. His begging from the Lord was like a poor man's asking a great emperor for a few grains of broken rice. The conclusion is that anyone who is engaged in the loving service of the Lord should never ask for material prosperity from the Lord. The awarding of material prosperity simply depends on the stringent rules and regulations of the external energy. Pure devotees ask the Lord only for the privilege of serving Him. This is our real independence. If we want anything else, it is a sign of our misfortune.

TEXT 36

मैत्रेय उवाच
न वै मुकुन्दस्य पदारविन्दयो
रजोजुषस्तात भवादृशा जनाः ।
वाञ्छन्ति तद्दास्यमृतेऽर्थमात्मनो
यदृच्छया लब्धमनःसमृद्धयः ॥३६॥

maitreya uvāca
na vai mukundasya padāravindayo
rajo-juṣas tāta bhavādṛśā janāḥ
vāñchanti tad-dāsyam ṛte 'rtham ātmano
yadṛcchayā labdha-manaḥ-samṛddhayaḥ

maitreyaḥ uvāca—the great sage Maitreya continued; *na*—never; *vai*—certainly; *mukundasya*—of the Lord, who can give liberation; *pada-aravindayoḥ*—of the lotus feet; *rajaḥ-juṣaḥ*—persons who are eager to taste the dust; *tāta*—my dear Vidura; *bhavādṛśāḥ*—like yourself; *janāḥ*—persons; *vāñchanti*—desire; *tat*—His; *dāsyam*—servitorship; *ṛte*—without; *artham*—interest; *ātmanaḥ*—for themselves; *yadṛcchayā*—automatically; *labdha*—by what is achieved; *manaḥ-samṛddhayaḥ*—considering themselves very rich.

TRANSLATION

The great sage Maitreya continued: My dear Vidura, persons like you, who are pure devotees of the lotus feet of Mukunda [the Supreme Personality of Godhead, who can offer liberation] and who are always attached to the honey of His lotus feet, are always satisfied in serving at the lotus feet of the Lord. In any condition of life, such persons remain satisfied, and thus they never ask the Lord for material prosperity.

PURPORT

In the *Bhagavad-gītā* the Lord says that He is the supreme enjoyer, the supreme proprietor of everything and anything within this creation, and the supreme friend of everyone. When one knows these things perfectly, he is always satisfied. The pure devotee never hankers after any kind of material prosperity. The *karmīs*, however, or *jñānīs* or *yogīs* endeavor always for their own personal happiness. *Karmīs* work day and night to improve their economic condition, *jñānīs* undergo severe austerities in order to get liberation, and *yogīs* also undergo severe austerities by practicing the *yoga* system for attainment of wonderful mystic powers. A devotee, however, is not interested in such activities; he does not want mystic powers or liberation or material prosperity. He is satisfied in any condition of life, as long as he is constantly engaged in the service of the Lord. The Lord's feet are compared to the lotus, wherein there is saffron dust. A devotee is always engaged in drinking the honey from the lotus feet of the Lord. Unless one is freed from all material desires, he cannot actually taste the honey from the Lord's lotus feet. One has to discharge his devotional duties without being disturbed by the coming and going of material circumstances. This desirelessness for material prosperity is called *niṣkāma.* One should not mistakenly think that *niṣkāma* means giving up all desires. That is impossible. A living entity is eternally existent, and he cannot give up desires. A living entity must have desires; that is the symptom of life. When there is a recommendation to become desireless, it is to be understood that this means that we should not desire anything for our sense gratification. For a devotee this state of mind, *nihspṛha,* is the right position. Actually every one of us already has an arrangement for our standard of material comforts. A devotee should always remain satisfied with the standard of comforts offered by the Lord, as stated in the *Īśopaniṣad* (*tena tyaktena bhuñjīthāḥ*). This saves time for executing Kṛṣṇa consciousness.

TEXT 37

आकर्ण्यात्मजमायान्तं सम्परेत्य यथागतम् ।
राजा न श्रद्दधे भद्रमभद्रस्य कुतो मम ॥३७॥

ākarṇyātma-jam āyāntam
samparetya yathāgatam
rājā na śraddadhe bhadram
abhadrasya kuto mama

ākarṇya—having heard; *ātma-jam*—his son; *āyāntam*—coming back; *samparetya*—after dying; *yathā*—as if; *āgatam*—coming back; *rājā*—King Uttānapāda; *na*—did not; *śraddadhe*—have any confidence; *bhadram*—good fortune; *abhadrasya*—of the impious; *kutaḥ*—whence; *mama*—my.

TRANSLATION

When King Uttānapāda heard that his son Dhruva was coming back home, as if coming back to life after death, he could not put his faith in this message, for he was doubtful of how it could happen. He considered himself the most wretched, and therefore he thought that it was not possible for him to attain such good fortune.

PURPORT

Dhruva Mahārāja, a five-year-old boy, went to the forest for penance and austerity, and the King could not at all believe that a small boy of such a tender age could live in the forest. He was certain that Dhruva was dead. He therefore could not fix his faith in the message that Dhruva Mahārāja was coming back home again. For him this message said that a dead man was coming back home, and so he could not believe it. After Dhruva Mahārāja's departure from home, King Uttānapāda thought that he was the cause of Dhruva's leaving, and thus he considered himself the most wretched. Therefore, even though it was possible that his lost son was coming back from the kingdom of death, he thought that since he was most sinful it was not possible for him to be so fortunate as to get back his lost son.

TEXT 38

श्रद्धाय वाक्यं देवर्षेर्हर्षवेगेन धर्षितः ।
वार्ताहर्तुरतिप्रीतो हारं प्रादान्महाधनम् ॥३८॥

śraddhāya vākyaṁ devarṣer
harṣa-vegena dharṣitaḥ
vārtā-hartur atiprīto
hāraṁ prādān mahā-dhanam

śraddhāya—keeping faith; *vākyam*—in the words; *devarṣeḥ*—of the great sage Nārada; *harṣa-vegena*—by great satisfaction; *dharṣitaḥ*—overwhelmed; *vārtā-hartuḥ*—with the messenger who brought the news; *atiprītaḥ*—being very satisfied; *hāram*—a pearl necklace; *prādāt*—offered; *mahā-dhanam*—very valuable.

TRANSLATION

Although he could not believe the words of the messenger, he had full faith in the word of the great sage Nārada. Thus he was greatly overwhelmed by the news, and he immediately offered the messenger a highly valuable necklace in great satisfaction.

TEXTS 39–40

सदश्वं रथमारुह्य कार्तस्वरपरिष्कृतम् ।
ब्राह्मणैः कुलवृद्धैश्च पर्यस्तोऽमात्यबन्धुभिः ॥३९॥
शङ्खदुन्दुभिनादेन ब्रह्मघोषेण वेणुभिः ।
निश्चक्राम पुरात्तूर्णमात्मजाभीक्षणोत्सुकः ॥४०॥

sad-aśvaṁ ratham āruhya
kārtasvara-pariṣkṛtam
brāhmaṇaiḥ kula-vṛddhaiś ca
paryasto 'mātya-bandhubhiḥ

śaṅkha-dundubhi-nādena
brahma-ghoṣeṇa veṇubhiḥ
niścakrāma purāt tūrṇam
ātmajābhīkṣaṇotsukaḥ

sat-aśvam—drawn by very fine horses; *ratham*—chariot; *āruhya*—getting on; *kārtasvara-pariṣkṛtam*—bedecked with golden filigree; *brāhmaṇaiḥ*—with *brāhmaṇas; kula-vṛddhaiḥ*—along with elderly personalities of the family; *ca*—also; *paryastaḥ*—being surrounded; *amātya*—by officers and ministers; *bandhubhiḥ*—and friends; *śaṅkha*—of conchshells; *dundubhi*—and kettledrums; *nādena*—with the sound; *brahma-ghoṣeṇa*—by the chanting of Vedic *mantras;*

veṇubhiḥ—by flutes; *niścakrāma*—he came out; *purāt*—from the city; *tūrṇam*—with great haste; *ātma-ja*—son; *abhīkṣaṇa*—to see; *utsukaḥ*—very eager.

TRANSLATION

Then King Uttānapāda, being very eager to see the face of his lost son, mounted a chariot drawn by excellent horses and bedecked with golden filigree. Taking with him many learned brāhmaṇas, all the elderly personalities of his family, his officers, his ministers and his immediate friends, he immediately left the city. As he proceeded in this parade, there were auspicious sounds of conchshells, kettledrums, flutes, and the chanting of Vedic mantras to indicate all good fortune.

TEXT 41

सुनीतिः सुरुचिश्चास्य महिष्यौ रुक्मभूषिते ।
आरुह्य शिबिकां सार्धमुत्तमेनाभिजग्मतुः ॥४१॥

sunītiḥ suruciś cāsya
mahiṣyau rukma-bhūṣite
āruhya śibikāṁ sārdham
uttamenābhijagmatuḥ

sunītiḥ—Queen Sunīti; *suruciḥ*—Queen Suruci; *ca*—also; *asya*—of the King; *mahiṣyau*—queens; *rukma-bhūṣite*—being decorated with golden ornaments; *āruhya*—getting on; *śibikām*—a palanquin; *sārdham*—along with; *uttamena*—the King's other son, Uttama; *abhijagmatuḥ*—all proceeded along.

TRANSLATION

Both the queens of King Uttānapāda, namely Sunīti and Suruci, along with his other son, Uttama, appeared in the procession. The queens were seated on a palanquin.

PURPORT

After the departure of Dhruva Mahārāja from the palace, the King was very afflicted, but by the kind words of Saint Nārada he was partially satisfied. He could understand the great fortune of his wife Sunīti and the great misfortune of Queen Suruci, for these facts were certainly very open in the palace. But still when the news reached the palace that Dhruva Mahārāja was returning, his mother, Sunīti, out of her great compassion and due to being the mother of a great Vaiṣṇava, did not hesitate to take the other wife, Suruci, and her son, Uttama, on the same palanquin. That was the greatness of Queen Sunīti, the mother of the great Vaiṣṇava Dhruva Mahārāja.

TEXTS 42–43

तं दृष्ट्वोपवनाभ्याश आयान्तं तरसा रथात् ।
अवरुह्य नृपस्तूर्णमासाद्य प्रेमविह्वलः ॥४२॥
परिरेभेऽङ्गजं दोर्भ्यां दीर्घोत्कण्ठमनाः श्वसन् ।
विष्वक्सेनाङ्घ्रिसंस्पर्शहताशेषाघबन्धनम् ॥४३॥

taṁ dṛṣṭvopavanābhyāśa
āyāntaṁ tarasā rathāt
avaruhya nṛpas tūrṇam
āsādya prema-vihvalaḥ

parirebhe 'ṅgajaṁ dorbhyāṁ
dīrghotkaṇṭha-manāḥ śvasan
viṣvaksenāṅghri-saṁsparśa-
hatāśeṣāgha-bandhanam

tam—him (Dhruva Mahārāja); *dṛṣṭvā*—having seen; *upavana*—the small forest; *abhyāśe*—near; *āyāntam*—returning; *tarasā*—with great haste; *rathāt*—from the chariot; *avaruhya*—got down; *nṛpaḥ*—the King; *tūrṇam*—immediately; *āsādya*—coming near; *prema*—with love; *vihvalaḥ*—overwhelmed; *parirebhe*—he embraced; *aṅga-jam*—his son; *dorbhyām*—with his arms; *dīrgha*—for a long time; *utkaṇṭha*—anxious; *manāḥ*—the King, whose mind; *śvasan*—breathing heavily; *viṣvaksena*—of the Lord; *aṅghri*—by the lotus feet; *saṁsparśa*—being touched; *hata*—were destroyed; *aśeṣa*—unlimited; *agha*—material contamination; *bandhanam*—whose bondage.

TRANSLATION

Upon seeing Dhruva Mahārāja approaching the neighboring small forest, King Uttānapāda with great haste got down from his chariot. He had been very anxious for a long time to see his son Dhruva, and therefore with great love and affection he went forward to embrace his long-lost boy. Breathing very heavily, the King embraced him with both arms. But Dhruva Mahārāja was not the same as before; he was completely sanctified by spiritual advancement due to having been touched by the lotus feet of the Supreme Personality of Godhead.

TEXT 44

अथाजिघ्रन्मुहुर्मूर्ध्नि शीतैर्नयनवारिभिः ।
स्नापयामास तनयं जातोद्दाममनोरथः ॥४४॥

athājighran muhur mūrdhni
śītair nayana-vāribhiḥ
snāpayām āsa tanayaṁ
jātoddāma-manorathaḥ

atha—thereupon; *ājighran*—smelling; *muhuḥ*—again and again; *mūrdhni*—on the head; *śītaiḥ*—cold; *nayana*—of his eyes; *vāribhiḥ*—with the water; *snāpayām āsa*—he bathed; *tanayam*—son; *jāta*—fulfilled; *uddāma*—great; *manaḥ-rathaḥ*—his desire.

TRANSLATION

Reunion with Dhruva Mahārāja fulfilled King Uttānapāda's long-cherished desire, and for this reason he smelled Dhruva's head again and again and bathed him with torrents of very cold tears.

PURPORT

By nature's way, when a man cries, there may be two causes. When one cries in great happiness upon the fulfillment of some desire, the tears coming forth from the eyes are very cold and pleasing, whereas tears in times of distress are very hot.

TEXT 45

अभिवन्द्य पितुः पादावाशीर्भिश्चाभिमन्त्रितः ।
ननाम मातरौ शीर्ष्णा सत्कृतः सज्जनाग्रणीः ॥४५॥

abhivandya pituḥ pādāv
āśīrbhiś cābhimantritaḥ
nanāma mātarau śīrṣṇā
sat-kṛtaḥ saj-janāgraṇīḥ

abhivandya—worshiping; *pituḥ*—of his father; *pādau*—the feet; *āśīrbhiḥ*—with benedictions; *ca*—and; *abhimantritaḥ*—was addressed; *nanāma*—he bowed; *mātarau*—to his two mothers; *śīrṣṇā*—with his head; *sat-kṛtaḥ*—was honored; *sat-jana*—of the nobles; *agraṇīḥ*—the foremost.

TRANSLATION

Then Dhruva Mahārāja, the foremost of all nobles, first of all offered his obeisances at the feet of his father and was honored by his father with various questions. He then bowed his head at the feet of his two mothers.

PURPORT

It may be questioned why Dhruva Mahārāja offered his respect not only to his mother but also to his stepmother, due to whose insults he had to leave home. The answer is that after achieving perfection by self-realization and seeing the Supreme Personality of Godhead face to face, Dhruva Mahārāja was completely freed from all contamination of material desire. Feelings of insult or honor in this material world are never perceived by a devotee. Lord Caitanya therefore says that one has to be humbler than the grass and, He recommends, more tolerant than the tree to execute devotional service. Dhruva Mahārāja, therefore, has in this verse been described as *saj-janāgraṇīḥ*, the foremost of noble men. The pure devotee is the noblest of all, and he has no feelings of animosity towards anyone. Duality due to animosity is a creation of this material world. There is no such thing in the spiritual world, which is the absolute reality.

TEXT 46

सुरुचिस्तं समुत्थाप्य पादावनतमर्भकम् ।
परिष्वज्याह जीवेति बाष्पगद्गदया गिरा ॥४६॥

surucis taṁ samutthāpya
pādāvanatam arbhakam
pariṣvajyāha jīveti
bāṣpa-gadgadayā girā

suruciḥ—Queen Suruci; *tam*—him; *samutthāpya*—having picked up; *pāda-avanatam*—fallen at her feet; *arbhakam*—the innocent boy; *pariṣvajya*—embracing; *āha*—she said; *jīva*—may you live long; *iti*—thus; *bāṣpa*—with tears; *gadgadayā*—choked up; *girā*—with words.

TRANSLATION

Suruci, the younger mother of Dhruva Mahārāja, seeing that the innocent boy had fallen at her feet, immediately picked him up, embracing him with her hands, and with tears of feeling she blessed him with the words, "My dear boy, long may you live!"

TEXT 47

यस्य प्रसन्नो भगवान् गुणैर्मैत्र्यादिभिर्हरिः ।
तस्मै नमन्ति भूतानि निम्नमाप इव स्वयम् ॥४७॥

yasya prasanno bhagavān
guṇair maitry-ādibhir hariḥ
tasmai namanti bhūtāni
nimnam āpa iva svayam

yasya—anyone with whom; *prasannaḥ*—is pleased; *bhagavān*—the Personality of Godhead; *guṇaiḥ*—by qualities; *maitrī-ādibhiḥ*—by friendship, etc.; *hariḥ*—Lord Hari; *tasmai*—unto him; *namanti*—offer respect; *bhūtāni*—all living entities; *nimnam*—to low ground; *āpaḥ*—water; *iva*—just as; *svayam*—automatically.

TRANSLATION

Unto one who has transcendental qualities due to friendly behavior with the Supreme Personality of Godhead, all living entities offer honor, just as water automatically flows down by nature.

PURPORT

The question may be raised in this connection why Suruci, who was not at all favorably disposed towards Dhruva, blessed him, "Long may you live," which means that she also desired good fortune for him. The answer is given in this verse. Since Dhruva Mahārāja was blessed by the Lord, due to his transcendental qualities everyone was bound to offer him all respects and benediction, just as water, by its nature, flows downward. A devotee of the Lord does not demand respect from anyone, but wherever he goes he is honored by everyone throughout the whole world with all respect. Śrīnivāsa Ācārya said that the six Gosvāmīs of Vṛndāvana are respected throughout the entire universe because a devotee, having pleased the Supreme Personality of Godhead, the source of all emanations, automatically pleases everyone, and thus everyone offers him respect.

TEXT 48

उत्तमश्च ध्रुवश्चोभावन्योन्यं प्रेमविह्वलौ ।
अङ्गसङ्गादुत्पुलकावस्रौघं मुहुरूहतुः ॥४८॥

uttamaś ca dhruvaś cobhāv
anyonyaṁ prema-vihvalau
aṅga-saṅgād utpulakāv
asraughaṁ muhur ūhatuḥ

uttamaḥ ca—also Uttama; *dhruvaḥ ca*—Dhruva also; *ubhau*—both; *anyonyam*—one another; *prema-vihvalau*—being overwhelmed with affection; *aṅga-saṅgāt*—by embracing; *utpulakau*—their hair stood up; *asra*—of tears; *ogham*—torrents; *muhuḥ*—again and again; *ūhatuḥ*—they exchanged.

TRANSLATION

The two brothers Uttama and Dhruva Mahārāja also exchanged their tears. They were overwhelmed by the ecstasy of love and affection, and when they embraced one another, the hair on their bodies stood up.

TEXT 49

सुनीतिरस्य जननी प्राणेभ्योऽपि प्रियं सुतम् ।
उपगुह्य जहावाधिं तदङ्गस्पर्शनिर्वृता ॥४९॥

sunītir asya jananī
prāṇebhyo 'pi priyaṁ sutam
upaguhya jahāv ādhiṁ
tad-aṅga-sparśa-nirvṛtā

sunītiḥ—Sunīti, the real mother of Dhruva Mahārāja; *asya*—his; *jananī*—mother; *prāṇebhyaḥ*—more than life air; *api*—even; *priyam*—dear; *sutam*—son; *upaguhya*—embracing; *jahau*—gave up; *ādhim*—all grief; *tat-aṅga*—his body; *sparśa*—touching; *nirvṛtā*—being satisfied.

TRANSLATION

Sunīti, the real mother of Dhruva Mahārāja, embraced the tender body of her son, who was dearer to her than her own life, and thus forgot all material grief, for she was very pleased.

TEXT 50

पयःस्तनाभ्यां सुस्राव नेत्रजैः सलिलैः शिवैः ।
तदाभिषिच्यमानाभ्यां वीर वीरसुवो मुहुः ॥५०॥

payaḥ stanābhyāṁ susrāva
netra-jaiḥ salilaiḥ śivaiḥ
tadābhiṣicyamānābhyāṁ
vīra vīra-suvo muhuḥ

payaḥ—milk; *stanābhyām*—from both breasts; *susrāva*—began to flow down; *netra-jaiḥ*—from the eyes; *salilaiḥ*—by tears; *śivaiḥ*—

auspicious; *tadā*—at that time; *abhiṣicyamānābhyām*—being wetted; *vīra*—my dear Vidura; *vīra-suvaḥ*—of the mother who gave birth to a hero; *muhuḥ*—constantly.

TRANSLATION

My dear Vidura, Sunīti was the mother of a great hero. Her tears, together with the milk flowing from her breasts, wet the whole body of Dhruva Mahārāja. This was a great, auspicious sign.

PURPORT

When Deities are installed, They are washed with milk, yogurt and water, and this ceremony is called *abhiṣeka.* In this verse it has been especially mentioned that the tears which flowed down from the eyes of Sunīti were all-auspicious. This auspiciousness of the *abhiṣeka* ceremony performed by his beloved mother was an indication that in the very near future Dhruva Mahārāja would be installed on the throne of his father. The history of Dhruva Mahārāja's leaving home was that his father refused to give him a place on his lap, and Dhruva Mahārāja determined that unless he got the throne of his father he would not come back. Now this *abhiṣeka* ceremony performed by his beloved mother was an indication that he would occupy the throne of Mahārāja Uttānapāda.

It is also significant in this verse that Sunīti, mother of Dhruva Mahārāja, is described as *vīra-sū,* a mother who produced a great hero. There are many heroes in the world, but there is no comparison to Dhruva Mahārāja, who was not only a heroic emperor of this planet, but also a great devotee. A devotee is also a great hero because he conquers the influence of *māyā.* When Lord Caitanya inquired from Rāmānanda Rāya about the most famous man in this world, the latter replied that anyone who is known as a great devotee of the Lord is to be accepted as the most famous.

TEXT 51

तां शशंसुर्जना राज्ञीं दिष्टया ते पुत्र आर्तिहा ।
प्रतिलब्धश्चिरं नष्टो रक्षिता मण्डलं भुवः ॥५१॥

tāṁ śaśaṁsur janā rājñīṁ
diṣṭyā te putra ārti-hā

pratilabdhaś ciraṁ naṣṭo
rakṣitā maṇḍalaṁ bhuvaḥ

tām—unto Queen Sunīti; *śaśaṁsuḥ*—offered praise; *janāḥ*—the people in general; *rājñīm*—unto the Queen; *diṣṭyā*—by fortune; *te*—your; *putraḥ*—son; *ārti-hā*—will vanquish all your pains; *pratilabdhaḥ*—now returned; *ciram*—since a long time; *naṣṭaḥ*—lost; *rakṣitā*—will protect; *maṇḍalam*—the globe; *bhuvaḥ*—earthly.

TRANSLATION

The residents of the palace praised the Queen: Dear Queen, your beloved son was lost a long time ago, and it is your great fortune that he now has come back. It appears, therefore, that your son will be able to protect you for a very long time and will put an end to all your material pangs.

TEXT 52

अभ्यर्चितस्त्वया नूनं भगवान् प्रणतार्तिहा ।
यदनुध्यायिनो धीरा मृत्युं जिग्युः सुदुर्जयम् ॥५२॥

abhyarcitas tvayā nūnaṁ
bhagavān praṇatārti-hā
yad-anudhyāyino dhīrā
mṛtyuṁ jigyuḥ sudurjayam

abhyarcitaḥ—worshiped; *tvayā*—by you; *nūnam*—however; *bhagavān*—the Supreme Personality of Godhead; *praṇata-ārti-hā*—who can deliver His devotees from the greatest danger; *yat*—whom; *anudhyāyinaḥ*—constantly meditating upon; *dhīrāḥ*—great saintly persons; *mṛtyum*—death; *jigyuḥ*—conquered; *sudurjayam*—which is very, very difficult to overcome.

TRANSLATION

Dear Queen, you must have worshiped the Supreme Personality of Godhead, who delivers His devotees from the greatest danger. Persons who constantly meditate upon Him surpass the course of birth and death. This perfection is very difficult to achieve.

PURPORT

Dhruva Mahārāja was the lost child of Queen Sunīti, but during his absence she always meditated upon the Supreme Personality of Godhead, who is able to rescue His devotee from all dangers. While Dhruva Mahārāja was absent from his home, not only did he undergo severe austerities in the forest of Madhuvana, but at home also his mother prayed to the Supreme Lord for his safety and good fortune. In other words, the Lord was worshiped by both the mother and the son, and both were able to achieve the supreme benediction from the Supreme Lord. The word *sudurjayam*, an adjective which indicates that no one can conquer death, is very significant. When Dhruva Mahārāja was away from his home, his father thought that he was dead. Ordinarily a king's son only five years old and away from home in the forest would certainly be supposed dead, but by the mercy of the Supreme Personality of Godhead, not only was he saved, but he was blessed with the highest perfection.

TEXT 53

लाल्यमानं जनैरेवं ध्रुवं सभ्रातरं नृपः ।
आरोप्य करिणीं हृष्टः स्तूयमानोऽविशत्पुरम् ॥५३॥

lālyamānaṁ janair evaṁ
dhruvaṁ sabhrātaraṁ nṛpaḥ
āropya kariṇīṁ hṛṣṭaḥ
stūyamāno 'viśat puram

lālyamānam—being thus praised; *janaiḥ*—by the people in general; *evam*—thus; *dhruvam*—Mahārāja Dhruva; *sa-bhrātaram*—with his brother; *nṛpaḥ*—the King; *āropya*—placing; *kariṇīm*—on the back of a she-elephant; *hṛṣṭaḥ*—being so pleased; *stūyamānaḥ*—and being so praised; *aviśat*—returned; *puram*—to his capital.

TRANSLATION

The sage Maitreya continued: My dear Vidura, when everyone was thus praising Dhruva Mahārāja, the King was very happy, and he had Dhruva and his brother seated on the back of a

she-elephant. Thus he returned to his capital, where he was praised by all classes of men.

TEXT 54

तत्र तत्रोपसंक्लृप्तैर्लसन्मकरतोरणैः ।
सवृन्दैः कदलीस्तम्भैः पूगपोतैश्च तद्विधैः ॥५४॥

tatra tatropasaṅklptair
lasan-makara-toraṇaiḥ
savṛndaiḥ kadalī-stambhaiḥ
pūga-potaiś ca tad-vidhaiḥ

tatra tatra—here and there; *upasaṅklptaiḥ*—set up; *lasat*—brilliant; *makara*—shark-shaped; *toraṇaiḥ*—with arched gateways; *sa-vṛndaiḥ*—with bunches of fruits and flowers; *kadalī*—of banana trees; *stambhaiḥ*—with columns; *pūga-potaiḥ*—with young betel nut trees; *ca*—also; *tat-vidhaiḥ*—of that kind.

TRANSLATION

The whole city was decorated with columns of banana trees containing bunches of fruits and flowers, and betel nut trees with leaves and branches were seen here and there. There were also many gates set up which were structured to give the appearance of sharks.

PURPORT

Auspicious ceremonies with decorations of the green leaves of palms, coconut trees, betel nut trees and banana trees, and fruits, flowers and leaves are an age-old custom in India. To receive his great son Dhruva Mahārāja, King Uttānapāda arranged a good reception, and all the citizens very enthusiastically took part with great jubilation.

TEXT 55

चूतपल्लववासःस्रङ्मुक्तादामविलम्बिभिः ।
उपस्कृतं प्रतिद्वारमपां कुम्भैः सदीपकैः ॥५५॥

cūta-pallava-vāsaḥ-sraṅ-
muktā-dāma-vilambibhiḥ
upaskṛtaṁ prati-dvāram
apāṁ kumbhaiḥ sadīpakaiḥ

cūta-pallava—with mango leaves; *vāsaḥ*—cloth; *srak*—flower garlands; *muktā-dāma*—strings of pearls; *vilambibhiḥ*—hanging; *upaskṛtam*—decorated; *prati-dvāram*—at every gate; *apām*—full of water; *kumbhaiḥ*—with waterpots; *sa-dīpakaiḥ*—with burning lamps.

TRANSLATION

At each and every gate there were burning lamps and big waterpots decorated with differently colored cloth, strings of pearls, flower garlands and hanging mango leaves.

TEXT 56

प्राकारैर्गोपुरागारैः शातकुम्भपरिच्छदैः ।
सर्वतोऽलंकृतं श्रीमद्विमानशिखरद्युभिः ॥५६॥

prākārair gopurāgāraiḥ
śātakumbha-paricchadaiḥ
sarvato 'laṅkṛtaṁ śrīmad-
vimāna-śikhara-dyubhiḥ

prākāraiḥ—with surrounding walls; *gopura*—city gates; *āgāraiḥ*—with houses; *śātakumbha*—golden; *paricchadaiḥ*—with ornamental work; *sarvataḥ*—on all sides; *alaṅkṛtam*—decorated; *śrīmat*—valuable, beautiful; *vimāna*—airplanes; *śikhara*—domes; *dyubhiḥ*—glittering.

TRANSLATION

In the capital city there were many palaces, city gates and surrounding walls, which were already very, very beautiful, and on this occasion all of them were decorated with golden ornaments. The domes of the city palaces glittered, as did the domes of the beautiful airplanes which hovered over the city.

PURPORT

Regarding the mention of airplanes here, it is suggested by Śrīmad Vijayadhvaja Tīrtha that on this occasion the demigods from higher planetary systems also came in their airplanes to bestow their blessings on Dhruva Mahārāja on his arrival at the capital of his father. It also appears that all the domes of the city palaces as well as the pinnacles of the airplanes were decorated with ornamental work in gold, and, being reflected by the sunshine, they were all glittering. We can observe a specific distinction between Dhruva Mahārāja's time and modern days, for the airplanes in those days were made of gold, whereas at the present moment airplanes are made of base aluminum. This just gives a hint of the opulence of Dhruva Mahārāja's days and the poverty of modern times.

TEXT 57

मृष्टचत्वररथ्याट्टमार्गं चन्दनचर्चितम् ।
लाजाक्षतैः पुष्पफलैस्तण्डुलैर्बलिभिर्युतम् ।।५७।।

mṛṣṭa-catvara-rathyāṭṭa-
mārgaṁ candana-carcitam
lājākṣataiḥ puṣpa-phalais
taṇḍulair balibhir yutam

mṛṣṭa—fully cleansed; *catvara*—quadrangles; *rathyā*—highways; *aṭṭa*—raised sitting places; *mārgam*—lanes; *candana*—with sandalwood; *carcitam*—sprinkled; *lāja*—with fried rice; *akṣataiḥ*—and barley; *puṣpa*—with flowers; *phalaiḥ*—and fruits; *taṇḍulaiḥ*—with rice; *balibhiḥ*—auspicious presentations; *yutam*—provided with.

TRANSLATION

All the quadrangles, lanes and streets in the city, and the raised sitting places at the crossings, were thoroughly cleansed and sprinkled with sandalwood water; and auspicious grains such as rice and barley, and flowers, fruits and many other auspicious presentations were scattered all over the city.

TEXTS 58-59

ध्रुवाय पथि दृष्टाय तत्र तत्र पुरस्त्रियः ।
सिद्धार्थाक्षतदध्यम्बुदूर्वापुष्पफलानि च ॥५८॥
उपजह्रुः प्रयुञ्जाना वात्सल्यादाशिषः सतीः ।
शृण्वंस्तद्वल्गुगीतानि प्राविशद्भवनं पितुः ॥५९॥

dhruvāya pathi dṛṣṭāya
tatra tatra pura-striyaḥ
siddhārthākṣata-dadhy-ambu-
dūrvā-puṣpa-phalāni ca

upajahruḥ prayuñjānā
vātsalyād āśiṣaḥ satīḥ
śṛṇvaṁs tad-valgu-gītāni
prāviśad bhavanaṁ pituḥ

dhruvāya—on Dhruva; *pathi*—on the road; *dṛṣṭāya*—seen; *tatra tatra*—here and there; *pura-striyaḥ*—household ladies; *siddhārtha*—white mustard seed; *akṣata*—barley; *dadhi*—curd; *ambu*—water; *dūrvā*—newly grown grass; *puṣpa*—flowers; *phalāni*—fruits; *ca*—also; *upajahruḥ*—they showered; *prayuñjānāḥ*—uttering; *vātsalyāt*—out of affection; *āśiṣaḥ*—blessings; *satīḥ*—gentle ladies; *śṛṇvan*—hearing; *tat*—their; *valgu*—very pleasing; *gītāni*—songs; *prāviśat*—he entered; *bhavanam*—the palace; *pituḥ*—of his father.

TRANSLATION

Thus as Dhruva Mahārāja passed on the road, from every place in the neighborhood all the gentle household ladies assembled to see him, and out of maternal affection they offered their blessings, showering him with white mustard seed, barley, curd, water, newly grown grass, fruits and flowers. In this way Dhruva Mahārāja, while hearing the pleasing songs sung by the ladies, entered the palace of his father.

TEXT 60

महामणिव्रातमये स तस्मिन् भवनोत्तमे ।
लालितो नितरां पित्रा न्यवसद्दिवि देववत् ॥६०॥

mahāmaṇi-vrātamaye
sa tasmin bhavanottame
lālito nitarāṁ pitrā
nyavasad divi devavat

mahā-maṇi—greatly valuable jewels; *vrāta*—groups of; *maye*—bedecked with; *saḥ*—he (Dhruva Mahārāja); *tasmin*—in that; *bhavana-uttame*—brilliant house; *lālitaḥ*—being raised; *nitarām*—always; *pitrā*—by the father; *nyavasat*—lived there; *divi*—in the higher planetary systems; *deva-vat*—like the demigods.

TRANSLATION

Dhruva Mahārāja thereafter lived in his father's palace, which had walls bedecked with highly valuable jewels. His affectionate father took particular care of him, and he dwelled in that house just as the demigods live in their palaces in the higher planetary systems.

TEXT 61

पयःफेननिभाः शय्या दान्ता रुक्मपरिच्छदाः।
आसनानि महार्हाणि यत्र रौक्मा उपस्कराः ॥६१॥

payaḥ-phena-nibhāḥ śayyā
dāntā rukma-paricchadāḥ
āsanāni mahārhāṇi
yatra raukmā upaskarāḥ

payaḥ—milk; *phena*—foam; *nibhāḥ*—like; *śayyāḥ*—bedding; *dāntāḥ*—made of ivory; *rukma*—golden; *paricchadāḥ*—with embellishments; *āsanāni*—sitting places; *mahā-arhāṇi*—very valuable; *yatra*—where; *raukmāḥ*—golden; *upaskarāḥ*—furniture.

TRANSLATION

The bedding in the palace was as white as the foam of milk and was very soft. The bedsteads were made of ivory with embellishments of gold, and the chairs, benches and other sitting places and furniture were made of gold.

TEXT 62

यत्र स्फटिककुड्येषु महामारकतेषु च ।
मणिप्रदीपा आभान्ति ललनारत्नसंयुताः ॥६२॥

yatra sphaṭika-kuḍyeṣu
mahā-mārakateṣu ca
maṇi-pradīpā ābhānti
lalanā-ratna-saṁyutāḥ

yatra—where; *sphaṭika*—made of marble; *kuḍyeṣu*—on walls; *mahā-mārakateṣu*—bedecked with valuable jewels like sapphires; *ca*—also; *maṇi-pradīpāḥ*—lamps made of jewels; *ābhānti*—shone; *lalanā*—female figures; *ratna*—made of jewels; *saṁyutāḥ*—held by.

TRANSLATION

The palace of the King was surrounded by walls made of marble with many engravings made of valuable jewels like sapphires, which depicted beautiful women with shining jewel lamps in their hands.

PURPORT

The description of King Uttānapāda's palace depicts the state of affairs many hundreds and thousands of years ago, long before *Śrīmad-Bhāgavatam* was compiled. Since it is described that Mahārāja Dhruva ruled for thirty-six thousand years, he must have lived in the Satya-yuga, when people lived for one hundred thousand years. The life durations in the four *yugas* are also mentioned in the Vedic literature. In the Satya-yuga people used to live for one hundred thousand years, in the Tretā-yuga people lived for ten thousand years, in Dvāpara-yuga they lived for one thousand years, and in this age, Kali-yuga, people may live up to one hundred years. With the progressive advance of each new *yuga*, the duration of human life is reduced by ninety percent—from one hundred thousand to ten thousand, from ten thousand to one thousand, and from one thousand to one hundred.

It is said that Dhruva Mahārāja was the great-grandson of Lord Brahmā. This indicates that Dhruva Mahārāja's time was in the Satya-yuga in the beginning of creation. During one day of Lord Brahmā, as stated in the *Bhagavad-gītā*, there are many Satya-yugas. According to the Vedic calculation, at the present moment the twenty-eighth millennium is current. It can be calculated that Dhruva Mahārāja lived many millions of years ago, but the description of the palace of Dhruva's father is so glorious that we cannot accept that advanced human civilization did not exist even forty or fifty thousand years ago. There were walls like those in the palace of Mahārāja Uttānapāda even very recently, during the Mogul period. Anyone who has seen the Red Fort in Delhi must have marked that the walls are made of marble and were once decorated with jewels. During the British period all these jewels were taken away and dispatched to the British Museum.

The conception of worldly opulence was formerly based mainly on natural resources such as jewels, marble, silk, ivory, gold and silver. The advancement of economic development was not based on big motorcars. Advancement of human civilization depends not on industrial enterprises, but on possession of natural wealth and natural food, which is all supplied by the Supreme Personality of Godhead so that we may save time for self-realization and success in the human form of body.

Another aspect of this verse is that Dhruva Mahārāja's father, Uttānapāda, would very soon give up attachment for his palaces and would go to the forest for self-realization. From the description of *Śrīmad-Bhāgavatam*, therefore, we can make a very thorough comparative study of modern civilization and the civilization of mankind in the other millenniums, Satya-yuga, Tretā-yuga and Dvāpara-yuga.

TEXT 63

उद्यानानि च रम्याणि विचित्रैरमरद्रुमैः ।
कूजद्विहङ्गमिथुनैर्गायन्मत्तमधुव्रतैः ॥६३॥

udyānāni ca ramyāṇi
vicitrair amara-drumaiḥ
kūja-dvihaṅga-mithunair
gāyan-matta-madhuvrataiḥ

udyānāni—gardens; *ca*—also; *ramyāṇi*—very beautiful; *vicitraiḥ*—various; *amara-drumaiḥ*—with trees brought from the heavenly planets; *kūja*—singing; *dvihaṅga*—of birds; *mithunaiḥ*—with pairs; *gāyat*—humming; *matta*—mad; *madhu-vrataiḥ*—with bumblebees.

TRANSLATION

The King's residence was surrounded by gardens wherein there were varieties of trees brought from the heavenly planets. In those trees there were pairs of sweetly singing birds and almost-mad bumblebees, which made a very relishable buzzing sound.

PURPORT

In this verse the word *amara-drumaiḥ*, "with trees brought from the heavenly planets," is very significant. The heavenly planets are known as Amaraloka, the planets where death is very much delayed, because the people there live for ten thousand years according to the calculations of the demigods, in which our six months are equal to one day. The demigods live in the heavenly planets for months, years and ten-thousands of years according to demigod time, and then again, after the results of their pious activities are exhausted, they fall down to this earth. These are the statements that can be collected from Vedic literature. As the people there live for ten thousand years, so also do the trees. Of course, here on this earth there are many trees which live for ten thousand years, so what to speak of the trees on the heavenly planets? They must live for more than many ten-thousands of years, and sometimes, as practiced even now, some valuable trees are taken from one place to another.

It is elsewhere stated that when Lord Kṛṣṇa went to the heavenly planets with His wife Satyabhāmā He took a *pārijāta* flower tree from heaven and brought it to the earth. There was a fight between Kṛṣṇa and the demigods due to the *pārijāta* tree's being taken from heaven to this planet. The *pārijāta* was planted in the palace of Lord Kṛṣṇa which was occupied by Queen Satyabhāmā. The flower and fruit trees in the heavenly planets are superior, for they are very pleasant and tasteful, and it appears that in the palace of Mahārāja Uttānapāda there were many varieties of such trees.

TEXT 64

वाप्यो वैदूर्यसोपानाः पद्मोत्पलकुमुद्वतीः ।
हंसकारण्डवकुलैर्जुष्टाश्चक्राह्वसारसैः ॥६४॥

vāpyo vaidūrya-sopānāḥ
padmotpala-kumud-vatīḥ
haṁsa-kāraṇḍava-kulair
juṣṭāś cakrāhva-sārasaiḥ

vāpyaḥ—lakes; *vaidūrya*—emerald; *sopānāḥ*—with staircases; *padma*—lotuses; *utpala*—blue lotuses; *kumut-vatīḥ*—full of lilies; *haṁsa*—swans; *kāraṇḍava*—and ducks; *kulaiḥ*—by flocks of; *juṣṭāḥ*—inhabited; *cakrāhva*—by *cakravākas* (geese); *sārasaiḥ*—and by cranes.

TRANSLATION

There were emerald staircases which led to lakes full of variously colored lotus flowers and lilies, and swans, kāraṇḍavas, cakravākas, cranes and similar other valuable birds were visible in those lakes.

PURPORT

It appears that not only was the palace surrounded by compounds and gardens with varieties of trees, but there were small man-made lakes also, where the water was full of many-colored lotus flowers and lilies, and to get down to the lakes there were staircases made of valuable jewels such as emeralds. By the beautifully positioned garden houses there were many luxuriant birds, such as swans, *cakravākas*, *kāraṇḍavas* and cranes. These birds generally do not live in filthy places like crows do. The atmosphere of the city was very healthy and beautiful; it can simply be imagined from its description.

TEXT 65

उत्तानपादो राजर्षिः प्रभावं तनयस्य तम् ।
श्रुत्वा दृष्ट्वाद्भुततमं प्रपेदे विस्मयं परम् ॥६५॥

uttānapādo rājarṣiḥ
prabhāvaṁ tanayasya tam
śrutvā dṛṣṭvādbhutatamaṁ
prapede vismayaṁ param

uttānapādaḥ—King Uttānapāda; *rāja-ṛṣiḥ*—great saintly king; *prabhāvam*—influence; *tanayasya*—of his son; *tam*—that; *śrutvā*—hearing; *dṛṣṭvā*—seeing; *adbhuta*—wonderful; *tamam*—in the superlative degree; *prapede*—happily felt; *vismayam*—wonder; *param*—supreme.

TRANSLATION

The saintly King Uttānapāda, hearing of the glorious deeds of Dhruva Mahārāja and personally seeing also how influential and great he was, felt very satisfied, for Dhruva's activities were wonderful to the supreme degree.

PURPORT

When Dhruva Mahārāja was in the forest executing his austerities, his father, Uttānapāda, heard everything about his very wonderful activities. Although Dhruva Mahārāja was the son of a king and was only five years old, he went to the forest and executed devotional service under strict austerity. Therefore his acts were all wonderful, and when he came back home, naturally, because of his spiritual qualifications, he became very popular amongst the citizens. He must have performed many wonderful activities by the grace of the Lord. No one is more satisfied than the father of a person who is credited with glorious activities. Mahārāja Uttānapāda was not an ordinary king; he was a *rājarṣi*, a saintly king. Formerly this earth was ruled by one saintly king only. Kings were trained to become saintly; therefore they had no other concern than the welfare of the citizens. These saintly kings were properly trained, and as mentioned in *Bhagavad-gītā* also, the science of God, or the *yoga* system of devotional service known as *Bhagavad-gītā*, was spoken to the saintly king of the sun planet, and gradually it descended through the *kṣatriya* kings who were generated from the sun and the moon. If the head of the government is saintly, certainly the citizens become saintly, and they are very happy because both their spiritual and physical needs and hankerings are satisfied.

TEXT 66

वीक्ष्योढवयसं तं च प्रकृतीनां च सम्मतम् ।
अनुरक्तप्रजं राजा ध्रुवं चक्रे भुवः पतिम् ॥६६॥

vīkṣyoḍha-vayasaṁ taṁ ca
prakṛtīnāṁ ca sammatam
anurakta-prajaṁ rājā
dhruvaṁ cakre bhuvaḥ patim

vīkṣya—after seeing; *ūḍha-vayasam*—mature in age; *tam*—Dhruva; *ca*—and; *prakṛtīnām*—by the ministers; *ca*—also; *sammatam*—approved of; *anurakta*—beloved; *prajam*—by his subjects; *rājā*—the King; *dhruvam*—Dhruva Mahārāja; *cakre*—made; *bhuvaḥ*—of the earth; *patim*—master.

TRANSLATION

When, after concentration, King Uttānapāda saw that Dhruva Mahārāja was suitably mature to take charge of the kingdom and that his ministers were agreeable and the citizens were also very fond of him, he enthroned Dhruva as emperor of this planet.

PURPORT

Although it is misconceived that formerly the monarchial government was autocratic, from the description of this verse it appears that not only was King Uttānapāda a *rājarṣi*, but before installing his beloved son Dhruva on the throne of the empire of the world, he consulted his ministerial officers, considered the opinion of the public, and also personally examined Dhruva's character. Then the King installed him on the throne to take charge of the affairs of the world.

When a Vaiṣṇava king like Dhruva Mahārāja is the head of the government of the entire world, the world is so happy that it is not possible to imagine or describe. Even now, if people would all become Kṛṣṇa conscious, the democratic government of the present day would be exactly like the kingdom of heaven. If all people became Kṛṣṇa conscious they would vote for persons of the category of Dhruva Mahārāja. If the post of chief executive were occupied by such a Vaiṣṇava, all the problems of satanic government would be solved. The youthful generation of the present day is very enthusiastic in trying to overthrow the government in different parts of the world. But unless people are Kṛṣṇa conscious like Dhruva Mahārāja, there will be no appreciable changes in government because people who hanker to attain political position by hook or by crook cannot think of the welfare of the people. They are only busy to keep their position of prestige and monetary gain. They have very little time to think of the welfare of the citizens.

TEXT 67

आत्मानं च प्रवयसमाकलय्य विशाम्पतिः ।
वनं विरक्तः प्रातिष्ठद्विमृशन्नात्मनो गतिम् ॥६७॥

ātmānaṁ ca pravayasam
ākalayya viśāmpatiḥ
vanaṁ viraktaḥ prātiṣṭhad
vimṛśann ātmano gatim

ātmānam—himself; *ca*—also; *pravayasam*—advanced in age; *ākalayya*—considering; *viśāmpatiḥ*—King Uttānapāda; *vanam*—to the forest; *viraktaḥ*—detached; *prātiṣṭhat*—departed; *vimṛśan*—deliberating on; *ātmanaḥ*—of the self; *gatim*—salvation.

TRANSLATION

After considering his advanced age and deliberating on the welfare of his spiritual self, King Uttānapāda detached himself from worldly affairs and entered the forest.

PURPORT

This is the sign of a *rājarṣi.* King Uttānapāda was very opulent and was emperor of the world, and these attachments were certainly very great. Modern politicians are not as great as kings like Mahārāja Uttānapāda, but because they get some political power for some days, they become so much attached to their positions that they never retire unless they are removed from their posts by cruel death or killed by some opposing political party. It is within our experience that the politicians in India do not quit their positions until death. This was not the practice in olden days, as it is evident from the behavior of King Uttānapāda. Immediately after installing his worthy son Dhruva Mahārāja on the throne, he left his home and palace. There are hundreds and thousands of instances like this in which kings, in their mature age, would give up their kingdoms and go to the forest to practice austerity. Practice of austerity is the main business of human life. As Mahārāja Dhruva practiced austerity in his early age, his father, Mahārāja Uttānapāda, in his old age also practiced austerity in the forest. In modern days however, it is not possible to give up one's home and go to the forest to practice austerity, but if people of all ages would take shelter of the Kṛṣṇa consciousness movement and practice the simple austerities of no illicit sex, no intoxication, no gambling and no meat-eating, and chant the Hare Kṛṣṇa *mantra* regularly (sixteen rounds), by this practical method it would be a very easy task to get salvation from this material world.

Thus end the Bhaktivedanta purports of the Fourth Canto, Ninth Chapter, of the Śrīmad-Bhāgavatam, *entitled "Dhruva Mahārāja Returns Home."*

CHAPTER TEN

Dhruva Mahārāja's Fight With the Yakṣas

TEXT 1

मैत्रेय उवाच
प्रजापतेर्दुहितरं शिशुमारस्य वै ध्रुवः ।
उपयेमे भ्रमिं नाम तत्सुतौ कल्पवत्सरौ ॥ १ ॥

maitreya uvāca
prajāpater duhitaraṁ
śiśumārasya vai dhruvaḥ
upayeme bhramiṁ nāma
tat-sutau kalpa-vatsarau

maitreyaḥ uvāca—the great sage Maitreya continued; *prajāpateḥ*—of the Prajāpati; *duhitaram*—daughter; *śiśumārasya*—of Śiśumāra; *vai*—certainly; *dhruvaḥ*—Dhruva Mahārāja; *upayeme*—married; *bhramim*—Bhrami; *nāma*—named; *tat-sutau*—her sons; *kalpa*—Kalpa; *vatsarau*—Vatsara.

TRANSLATION

The great sage Maitreya said: My dear Vidura, thereafter Dhruva Mahārāja married the daughter of Prajāpati Śiśumāra, whose name was Bhrami, and two sons named Kalpa and Vatsara were born of her.

PURPORT

It appears that Dhruva Mahārāja married after being installed on the throne of his father and after the departure of his father to the forest for self-realization. It is very important to note in this connection that since

Mahārāja Uttānapāda was greatly affectionate towards his son, and since it is the duty of a father to get his sons and daughters married as quickly as possible, why did he not get his son married before he left home? The answer is that Mahārāja Uttānapāda was a *rājarṣi,* saintly king. Although he was busy in his political affairs and duties of government management, he was very anxious for self-realization. Therefore as soon as his son Dhruva Mahārāja was quite worthy to take charge of the government, he took this opportunity to leave home, just like his son, who, without fear, left home for self-realization, even at the age of five years. These are rare instances from which we can see that the importance of spiritual realization is above all other important work. Mahārāja Uttānapāda knew very well that to get his son Dhruva Mahārāja married was not so important that it should take preference to his going away to the forest for self-realization.

TEXT 2

इलायामपि भार्यायां वायोः पुत्र्यां महाबलः ।
पुत्रमुत्कलनामानं योषिद्रत्नमजीजनत् ॥ २ ॥

ilāyām api bhāryāyāṁ
vāyoḥ putryāṁ mahā-balaḥ
putram utkala-nāmānaṁ
yoṣid-ratnam ajījanat

ilāyām—unto his wife named Ilā; *api*—also; *bhāryāyām*—unto his wife; *vāyoḥ*—of the demigod Vāyu (controller of air); *putryām*—unto the daughter; *mahā-balaḥ*—the greatly powerful Dhruva Mahārāja; *putram*—son; *utkala*—Utkala; *nāmānam*—of the name; *yoṣit*—female; *ratnam*—jewel; *ajījanat*—he begot.

TRANSLATION

The greatly powerful Dhruva Mahārāja had another wife, named Ilā, who was the daughter of the demigod Vāyu. By her he begot a son named Utkala and a very beautiful daughter.

TEXT 3

उत्तमस्त्वकृतोद्वाहो मृगयायां बलीयसा ।
हतः पुण्यजनेनाद्रौ तन्मातास्य गतिं गता ॥ ३ ॥

uttamas tv akṛtodvāho
mṛgayāyāṁ balīyasā
hataḥ puṇya-janenādrau
tan-mātāsya gatiṁ gatā

uttamaḥ—Uttama; *tu*—but; *akṛta*—without; *udvāhaḥ*—marriage; *mṛgayāyām*—on a hunting excursion; *balīyasā*—very powerful; *hataḥ*—was killed; *puṇya-janena*—by a Yakṣa; *adrau*—on the Himalaya Mountains; *tat*—his; *mātā*—mother (Suruci); *asya*—of her son; *gatim*—way; *gatā*—followed.

TRANSLATION

Dhruva Mahārāja's younger brother Uttama, who was still unmarried, once went on a hunting excursion and was killed by a powerful Yakṣa in the Himalaya Mountains. Along with him, his mother, Suruci, also followed the path of her son [she died].

TEXT 4

ध्रुवो भ्रातृवधं श्रुत्वा कोपामर्षशुचार्पितः ।
जैत्रं स्यन्दनमास्थाय गतः पुण्यजनालयम् ॥ ४ ॥

dhruvo bhrātṛ-vadhaṁ śrutvā
kopāmarṣa-śucārpitaḥ
jaitraṁ syandanam āsthāya
gataḥ puṇya-janālayam

dhruvaḥ—Dhruva Mahārāja; *bhrātṛ-vadham*—the killing of his brother; *śrutvā*—hearing this news; *kopa*—anger; *amarṣa*—vengeance; *śucā*—lamentation; *arpitaḥ*—being filled with; *jaitram*—victorious;

syandanam—chariot; *āsthāya*—getting on; *gataḥ*—went; *puṇya-jana-ālayam*—to the city of the Yakṣas.

TRANSLATION

When Dhruva Mahārāja heard of the killing of his brother Uttama by the Yakṣas in the Himalaya Mountains, being overwhelmed with lamentation and anger, he got on his chariot and went out for victory over the city of the Yakṣas, Alakāpurī.

PURPORT

Dhruva Mahārāja's becoming angry, overwhelmed with grief, and envious of the enemies was not incompatible with his position as a great devotee. It is a misunderstanding that a devotee should not be angry, envious or overwhelmed by lamentation. Dhruva Mahārāja was the king, and when his brother was unceremoniously killed, it was his duty to take revenge against the Yakṣas from the Himalayas.

TEXT 5

गत्वोदीचीं दिशं राजा रुद्रानुचरसेविताम् ।
ददर्श हिमवद्द्रोण्यां पुरीं गुह्यकसंकुलाम् ॥ ५ ॥

gatvodīcīṁ diśaṁ rājā
rudrānucara-sevitām
dadarśa himavad-droṇyāṁ
purīṁ guhyaka-saṅkulām

gatvā—going; *udīcīm*—northern; *diśam*—direction; *rājā*—King Dhruva; *rudra-anucara*—by followers of Rudra, Lord Śiva; *sevitām*—inhabited; *dadarśa*—saw; *himavat*—Himalayan; *droṇyām*—in a valley; *purīm*—a city; *guhyaka*—ghostly persons; *saṅkulām*—full of.

TRANSLATION

Dhruva Mahārāja went to the northern direction of the Himalayan range. In a valley he saw a city full of ghostly persons who were followers of Lord Śiva.

PURPORT

In this verse it is stated that the Yakṣas are more or less devotees of Lord Śiva. By this indication the Yakṣas may be taken to be the Himalayan tribes like the Tibetans.

TEXT 6

दध्मौ शङ्खं बृहद्बाहुः खं दिशश्चानुनादयन् ।
येनोद्विग्नदृशः क्षत्तरुपदेव्योऽत्रसन्भृशम् ॥ ६ ॥

dadhmau śaṅkhaṁ bṛhad-bāhuḥ
khaṁ diśaś cānunādayan
yenodvigna-dṛśaḥ kṣattar
upadevyo 'trasan bhṛśam

dadhmau—blew; *śaṅkham*—conchshell; *bṛhat-bāhuḥ*—the mighty-armed; *kham*—the sky; *diśaḥ ca*—and all directions; *anunādayan*—causing to resound; *yena*—by which; *udvigna-dṛśaḥ*—appeared very anxious; *kṣattaḥ*—my dear Vidura; *upadevyaḥ*—the wives of the Yakṣas; *atrasan*—became frightened; *bhṛśam*—greatly.

TRANSLATION

Maitreya continued: My dear Vidura, as soon as Dhruva Mahārāja reached Alakāpurī, he immediately blew his conchshell, and the sound reverberated throughout the entire sky and in every direction. The wives of the Yakṣas became very much frightened. From their eyes it was apparent that they were full of anxiety.

TEXT 7

ततो निष्क्रम्य बलिन उपदेवमहाभटाः ।
असहन्तस्तन्निनादमभिपेतुरुदायुधाः ॥ ७ ॥

tato niṣkramya balina
upadeva-mahā-bhaṭāḥ
asahantas tan-ninādam
abhipetur udāyudhāḥ

tataḥ—thereafter; *niṣkramya*—coming out; *balinaḥ*—very powerful; *upadeva*—of Kuvera; *mahā-bhaṭāḥ*—great soldiers; *asahantaḥ*—unable to tolerate; *tat*—of the conchshell; *ninādam*—sound; *abhipetuḥ*—attacked; *udāyudhāḥ*—equipped with various weapons.

TRANSLATION

O hero Vidura, the greatly powerful heroes of the Yakṣas, unable to tolerate the resounding vibration of the conchshell of Dhruva Mahārāja, came forth from their city with weapons and attacked Dhruva.

TEXT 8

स तानापततो वीर उग्रधन्वा महारथः ।
एकैकं युगपत्सर्वानहन् बाणैस्त्रिभिस्त्रिभिः ॥ ८ ॥

sa tān āpatato vīra
ugra-dhanvā mahā-rathaḥ
ekaikaṁ yugapat sarvān
ahan bāṇais tribhis tribhiḥ

saḥ—Dhruva Mahārāja; *tān*—all of them; *āpatataḥ*—falling upon him; *vīraḥ*—hero; *ugra-dhanvā*—powerful bowman; *mahā-rathaḥ*—who could fight with many chariots; *eka-ekam*—one after another; *yugapat*—simultaneously; *sarvān*—all of them; *ahan*—killed; *bāṇaiḥ*—by arrows; *tribhiḥ tribhiḥ*—by threes.

TRANSLATION

Dhruva Mahārāja, who was a great charioteer and certainly a great bowman also, immediately began to kill them by simultaneously discharging arrows three at a time.

TEXT 9

ते वै ललाटलग्नैस्तैरिषुभिः सर्व एव हि ।
मत्वा निरस्तमात्मानमाशंसन् कर्म तस्य तत् ॥ ९ ॥

te vai lalāṭa-lagnais tair
iṣubhiḥ sarva eva hi
matvā nirastam ātmānam
āśaṁsan karma tasya tat

te—they; *vai*—certainly; *lalāṭa-lagnaiḥ*—intent upon their heads; *taiḥ*—by those; *iṣubhiḥ*—arrows; *sarve*—all of them; *eva*—certainly; *hi*—without fail; *matvā*—thinking; *nirastam*—defeated; *ātmānam*—themselves; *āśaṁsan*—praised; *karma*—action; *tasya*—of him; *tat*—that.

TRANSLATION

When the heroes of the Yakṣas saw that all their heads were being thus threatened by Dhruva Mahārāja, they could very easily understand their awkward position, and they concluded that they would certainly be defeated. But, as heroes, they lauded the action of Dhruva.

PURPORT

This spirit of fighting in a sporting attitude is very significant in this verse. The Yakṣas were severely attacked. Dhruva Mahārāja was their enemy, but still, upon witnessing the wonderful, heroic acts of Mahārāja Dhruva, they were very pleased with him. This straightforward appreciation of an enemy's prowess is a characteristic of real *kṣatriya* spirit.

TEXT 10

तेऽपि चामुममृष्यन्तः पादस्पर्शमिवोरगाः ।
शरैरविध्यन् युगपद् द्विगुणं प्रचिकीर्षवः ॥१०॥

te 'pi cāmum amṛṣyantaḥ
pāda-sparśam ivoragāḥ
śarair avidhyan yugapad
dvi-guṇaṁ pracikīrṣavaḥ

te—the Yakṣas; *api*—also; *ca*—and; *amum*—at Dhruva; *amṛṣyantaḥ*—being intolerant of; *pāda-sparśam*—being touched by the feet; *iva*—like; *uragāḥ*—serpents; *śaraiḥ*—with arrows; *avidhyan*—struck; *yugapat*—simultaneously; *dvi-guṇam*—twice as much; *pracikīrṣavaḥ*—trying to retaliate.

TRANSLATION

Just like serpents, who cannot tolerate being trampled upon by anyone's feet, the Yakṣas, being intolerant of the wonderful prowess of Dhruva Mahārāja, threw twice as many arrows—six from each of their soldiers—and thus they very valiantly exhibited their prowess.

TEXTS 11–12

ततः परिघनिस्त्रिंशैः प्रासशूलपरश्वधैः ।
शक्त्यृष्टिभिर्भुशुण्डीभिश्चित्रवाजैः शरैरपि ॥११॥
अभ्यवर्षन् प्रकुपिताः सरथं सहसारथिम् ।
इच्छन्तस्तत्प्रतीकर्तुमयुतानां त्रयोदश ॥१२॥

tataḥ parigha-nistriṁśaiḥ
prāsaśūla-paraśvadhaiḥ
śakty-ṛṣṭibhir bhuśuṇḍībhiś
citra-vājaiḥ śarair api

abhyavarṣan prakupitāḥ
sarathaṁ saha-sārathim
icchantas tat pratīkartum
ayutānāṁ trayodaśa

tataḥ—thereupon; *parigha*—with iron bludgeons; *nistriṁśaiḥ*—and swords; *prāsa-śūla*—with tridents; *paraśvadhaiḥ*—and lances; *śakti*—with pikes; *ṛṣṭibhiḥ*—and spears; *bhuśuṇḍībhiḥ*—with *bhuśuṇḍī* weapons; *citra-vājaiḥ*—having various feathers; *śaraiḥ*—with arrows; *api*—also; *abhyavarṣan*—they showered Dhruva; *prakupitāḥ*—being angry; *sa-ratham*—along with his chariot; *saha-sārathim*—along with his charioteer; *icchantaḥ*—desiring; *tat*—Dhruva's activities; *pratī-kartum*—to counteract; *ayutānām*—of ten-thousands; *trayodaśa*—thirteen.

TRANSLATION

The Yakṣa soldiers were 130,000 strong, all greatly angry and all desiring to defeat the wonderful activities of Dhruva Mahārāja.

With full strength they showered upon Mahārāja Dhruva, along with his chariot and charioteer, various types of feathered arrows, parighas [iron bludgeons], nistriṁśas [swords], prāsaśūlas [tridents], paraśvadhas [lances], śaktis [pikes], ṛṣṭis [spears] and bhuśuṇḍī weapons.

TEXT 13

औत्तानपादिः स तदा शस्त्रवर्षेण भूरिणा ।
न एवादृश्यताच्छन्न आसारेण यथा गिरिः ॥१३॥

auttānapādiḥ sa tadā
śastra-varṣeṇa bhūriṇā
na evādṛśyatācchanna
āsāreṇa yathā giriḥ

auttānapādiḥ—Dhruva Mahārāja; *saḥ*—he; *tadā*—at that time; *śastra-varṣeṇa*—by a shower of weapons; *bhūriṇā*—incessant; *na*—not; *eva*—certainly; *adṛśyata*—was visible; *ācchannaḥ*—being covered; *āsāreṇa*—by constant rainfall; *yathā*—as; *giriḥ*—a mountain.

TRANSLATION

Dhruva Mahārāja was completely covered by an incessant shower of weapons, just as a mountain is covered by incessant rainfall.

PURPORT

Śrīla Viśvanātha Cakravartī Ṭhākura points out in this connection that although Dhruva Mahārāja was covered by the incessant arrows of the enemy, this does not mean that he succumbed in the battle. The example of a mountain peak's being covered by incessant rain is just suitable, for when a mountain is covered by incessant rain, all dirty things are washed from the body of the mountain. Similarly, the incessant shower of arrows from the enemy gave Dhruva Mahārāja new vigor to defeat them. In other words, whatever incompetency he might have had was washed away.

TEXT 14

हाहाकारस्तदैवासीत्सिद्धानां दिवि पश्यताम् ।
हतोऽयं मानवः सूर्यो मग्नः पुण्यजनार्णवे ॥१४॥

hāhā-kāras tadaivāsīt
siddhānāṁ divi paśyatām
hato 'yaṁ mānavaḥ sūryo
magnaḥ puṇya-janārṇave

hāhā-kāraḥ—tumult of disappointment; *tadā*—at that time; *eva*—certainly; *āsīt*—became manifest; *siddhānām*—of all the residents of Siddhaloka; *divi*—in the sky; *paśyatām*—who were observing the fight; *hataḥ*—killed; *ayam*—this; *mānavaḥ*—grandson of Manu; *sūryaḥ*—sun; *magnaḥ*—set; *puṇya-jana*—of the Yakṣas; *arṇave*—in the ocean.

TRANSLATION

All the Siddhas from the higher planetary systems were observing the fight from the sky, and when they saw that Dhruva Mahārāja had been covered by the incessant arrows of the enemy, they roared tumultuously, "The grandson of Manu, Dhruva, is now lost!" They cried that Dhruva Mahārāja was just like the sun and that now he had set within the ocean of the Yakṣas.

PURPORT

In this verse the word *mānava* is very significant. Generally this word is used to mean "human being." Dhruva Mahārāja is also described here as *mānava*. Not only is Dhruva Mahārāja a descendant of Manu, but all human society descends from Manu. According to Vedic civilization, Manu is the lawgiver. Even today Hindus in India follow the laws given by Manu. Everyone, therefore, in human society is a *mānava*, or descendant from Manu, but Dhruva Mahārāja is a distinguished *mānava* because he is a great devotee.

The denizens of the planet Siddhaloka, where the residents can fly in the sky without airplanes, were anxious over Dhruva Mahārāja's welfare in the battlefield. Śrīla Rūpa Gosvāmī says, therefore, that not only is a devotee well protected by the Supreme Lord, but all the demigods, and even ordinary men, are anxious for his security and safety. The comparison given here that Dhruva Mahārāja appeared to merge in the ocean of the Yakṣas is also significant. When the sun sets on the horizon, it appears that the sun drowns in the ocean, but factually the sun has no difficulty. Similarly, although Dhruva appeared to drown in the ocean of the Yakṣas, he had no difficulty. As the sun rises again in due course at the end of night, so Dhruva Mahārāja, although he might have been in difficulty (because, after all, it was a fight, and in any fighting activities there are reverses), that did not mean that he was defeated.

TEXT 15

नदत्सु यातुधानेषु जयकाशिष्वथो मृधे ।
उदतिष्ठद्रथस्तस्य नीहारादिव भास्करः ॥१५॥

nadatsu yātudhāneṣu
jaya-kāśiṣv atho mṛdhe
udatiṣṭhad rathas tasya
nīhārād iva bhāskaraḥ

nadatsu—while exclaiming; *yātudhāneṣu*—the ghostly Yakṣas; *jaya-kāśiṣu*—proclaiming victory; *atho*—then; *mṛdhe*—in the fighting; *udatiṣṭhat*—appeared; *rathaḥ*—the chariot; *tasya*—of Dhruva Mahārāja; *nīhārāt*—from the mist; *iva*—like; *bhāskaraḥ*—the sun.

TRANSLATION

The Yakṣas, being temporarily victorious, exclaimed that they had conquered Dhruva Mahārāja. But in the meantime Dhruva's chariot suddenly appeared, just as the sun suddenly appears from within foggy mist.

PURPORT

Here Dhruva Mahārāja is compared to the sun and the great assembly of the Yakṣas to foggy mist. Fog is insignificant in comparison with the sun. Although the sun is sometimes seen to be covered by fog, in fact the sun cannot be covered by anything. Our eyes may be covered by a cloud, but the sun is never covered. By this comparison to the sun, the greatness of Dhruva Mahārāja in all circumstances is affirmed.

TEXT 16

धनुर्विस्फूर्जयन्दिव्यं द्विषतां खेदमुद्वहन् ।
अस्त्रौघं व्यधमद्बाणैर्घनानीकमिवानिलः ॥१६॥

dhanur visphūrjayan divyaṁ
dviṣatāṁ khedam udvahan
astraughaṁ vyadhamad bāṇair
ghanānīkam ivānilaḥ

dhanuḥ—his bow; *visphūrjayan*—twanging; *divyam*—wonderful; *dviṣatām*—of the enemies; *khedam*—lamentation; *udvahan*—creating; *astra-ogham*—different types of weapons; *vyadhamat*—he scattered; *bāṇaiḥ*—with his arrows; *ghana*—of clouds; *anīkam*—an army; *iva*—like; *anilaḥ*—the wind.

TRANSLATION

Dhruva Mahārāja's bow and arrows twanged and hissed, causing lamentation in the hearts of his enemies. He began to shoot incessant arrows, shattering all their different weapons, just as the blasting wind scatters the assembled clouds in the sky.

TEXT 17

तस्य ते चापनिर्मुक्ता भित्त्वा वर्माणि रक्षसाम् ।
कायानाविविशुस्तिग्मा गिरीनशनयो यथा ॥१७॥

tasya te cāpa-nirmuktā
bhittvā varmāṇi rakṣasām
kāyān āviviśus tigmā
girīn aśanayo yathā

tasya—of Dhruva; *te*—those arrows; *cāpa*—from the bow; *nirmuktāḥ*—released; *bhittvā*—having pierced; *varmāṇi*—shields; *rakṣasām*—of the demons; *kāyān*—bodies; *āviviśuḥ*—entered; *tigmāḥ*—sharp; *girīn*—mountains; *aśanayaḥ*—thunderbolts; *yathā*—just like.

TRANSLATION

The sharp arrows released from the bow of Dhruva Mahārāja pierced the shields and bodies of the enemy, like the thunderbolts released by the King of heaven, which dismantle the bodies of the mountains.

TEXTS 18–19

भल्लैः संछिद्यमानानां शिरोभिश्चारुकुण्डलैः ।
ऊरुभिर्हेमतालाभैर्दोर्भिर्वलयवल्गुभिः ॥१८॥
हारकेयूरमुकुटैरुष्णीषैश्च महाधनैः ।
आस्तृतास्ता रणभुवो रेजुर्वीरमनोहराः ॥१९॥

bhallaiḥ sañchidyamānānāṁ
śirobhiś cāru-kuṇḍalaiḥ
ūrubhir hema-tālābhair
dorbhir valaya-valgubhiḥ

hāra-keyūra-mukuṭair
uṣṇīṣaiś ca mahā-dhanaiḥ
āstṛtās tā raṇa-bhuvo
rejur vīra-mano-harāḥ

bhallaiḥ—by his arrows; *sañchidyamānānām*—of the Yakṣas who were cut to pieces; *śirobhiḥ*—with heads; *cāru*—beautiful; *kuṇḍalaiḥ*—with earrings; *ūrubhiḥ*—with thighs; *hema-tālābhaiḥ*—like golden palm trees; *dorbhiḥ*—with arms; *valaya-valgubhiḥ*—with beautiful bracelets; *hāra*—with garlands; *keyūra*—armlets; *mukuṭaiḥ*—and helmets; *uṣṇīṣaiḥ*—with turbans; *ca*—also; *mahā-dhanaiḥ*—very valuable; *āstṛtāḥ*—covered; *tāḥ*—those; *raṇa-bhuvaḥ*—battlefield; *rejuḥ*—began to glimmer; *vīra*—of the heroes; *manaḥ-harāḥ*—bewildering the minds.

TRANSLATION

The great sage Maitreya continued: My dear Vidura, the heads of those who were cut to pieces by the arrows of Dhruva Mahārāja were decorated very beautifully with earrings and turbans. The

legs of their bodies were as beautiful as golden palm trees, their arms were decorated with golden bracelets and armlets, and on their heads there were very valuable helmets bedecked with gold. All these ornaments lying on that battlefield were very attractive and could bewilder the mind of a hero.

PURPORT

It appears that in those days soldiers used to go to the battlefield highly decorated with golden ornaments and with helmets and turbans, and when they were dead the booty was taken by the enemy party. Their falling dead in battle with their many golden ornamental dresses was certainly a lucrative opportunity for the heroes on the battlefield.

TEXT 20

हतावशिष्टा इतरे रणाजिराद्
रक्षोगणाः क्षत्रियवर्यसायकैः ।
प्रायो विवृक्णावयवा विदुद्रुवु-
मृगेन्द्रविक्रीडितयूथपा इव ॥२०॥

hatāvaśiṣṭā itare raṇājirād
rakṣo-gaṇāḥ kṣatriya-varya-sāyakaiḥ
prāyo vivṛknāvayavā vidudruvur
mṛgendra-vikrīḍita-yūthapā iva

hata-avaśiṣṭāḥ—the remaining soldiers who were not killed; *itare*—others; *raṇa-ajirāt*—from the battlefield; *rakṣaḥ-gaṇāḥ*—the Yakṣas; *kṣatriya-varya*—of the greatest of the *kṣatriyas*, or warriors; *sāyakaiḥ*—by the arrows; *prāyaḥ*—mostly; *vivṛkṇa*—cut to pieces; *avayavāḥ*—their bodily limbs; *vidudruvuḥ*—fled; *mṛgendra*—by a lion; *vikrīḍita*—being defeated; *yūthapāḥ*—elephants; *iva*—like.

TRANSLATION

The remaining Yakṣas who somehow or other were not killed had their limbs cut to pieces by the arrows of the great warrior Dhruva Mahārāja. Thus they began to flee, just as elephants flee when defeated by a lion.

TEXT 21

अपश्यमानः स तदाततायिनं
महामृधे कंचन मानवोत्तमः ।
पुरीं दिदृक्षन्नपि नाविशद् द्विषां
न मायिनां वेद चिकीर्षितं जनः ॥२१॥

apaśyamānaḥ sa tadātatāyinaṁ
mahā-mṛdhe kañcana mānavottamaḥ
purīṁ didṛkṣann api nāviśad dviṣāṁ
na māyināṁ veda cikīrṣitaṁ janaḥ

apaśyamānaḥ—while not observing; *saḥ*—Dhruva; *tadā*—at that time; *ātatāyinam*—armed opposing soldiers; *mahā-mṛdhe*—in that great battlefield; *kañcana*—any; *mānava-uttamaḥ*—the best of the human beings; *purīm*—the city; *didṛkṣan*—wishing to see; *api*—although; *na āviśat*—did not enter; *dviṣām*—of the enemies; *na*—not; *māyinām*—of the mystics; *veda*—knows; *cikīrṣitam*—the plans; *janaḥ*—anyone.

TRANSLATION

Dhruva Mahārāja, the best of human beings, observed that in that great battlefield not one of the opposing soldiers was left standing with proper weapons. He then desired to see the city of Alakāpurī, but he thought to himself, "No one knows the plans of the mystic Yakṣas."

TEXT 22

इति ब्रुवंश्चित्ररथः स्वसारथिं
यत्तः परेषां प्रतियोगशङ्कितः ।
शुश्राव शब्दं जलधेरिवेरितं
नभस्वतो दिक्षु रजोऽन्वदृश्यत ॥२२॥

iti bruvaṁś citra-rathaḥ sva-sārathiṁ
yattaḥ pareṣāṁ pratiyoga-śaṅkitaḥ
śuśrāva śabdaṁ jaladher iveritaṁ
nabhasvato dikṣu rajo 'nvadṛśyata

iti—thus; *bruvan*—talking; *citra-rathaḥ*—Dhruva Mahārāja, whose chariot was very beautiful; *sva-sārathim*—to his charioteer; *yattaḥ*—being on guard; *pareṣām*—from his enemies; *pratiyoga*—counterattack; *śaṅkitaḥ*—being apprehensive; *śuśrāva*—heard; *śabdam*—sound; *jala-dheḥ*—from the ocean; *iva*—as if; *īritam*—resounded; *nabhasvataḥ*—because of wind; *dikṣu*—in all directions; *rajaḥ*—dust; *anu*—then; *adṛśyata*—was perceived.

TRANSLATION

In the meantime, while Dhruva Mahārāja, doubtful of his mystic enemies, was talking with his charioteer, they heard a tremendous sound, as if the whole ocean were there, and they found that from the sky a great dust storm was coming over them from all directions.

TEXT 23

क्षणेनाच्छादितं व्योम घनानीकेन सर्वतः ।
विस्फुरत्तडिता दिक्षु त्रासयत्स्तनयित्नुना ॥२३॥

kṣaṇenācchāditaṁ vyoma
ghanānīkena sarvataḥ
visphurat-taḍitā dikṣu
trāsayat-stanayitnunā

kṣaṇena—within a moment; *ācchāditam*—was covered; *vyoma*—the sky; *ghana*—of dense clouds; *anīkena*—with a mass; *sarvataḥ*—everywhere; *visphurat*—dazzling; *taḍitā*—with lightning; *dikṣu*—in all directions; *trāsayat*—threatening; *stanayitnunā*—with thundering.

TRANSLATION

Within a moment the whole sky was overcast with dense clouds, and severe thundering was heard. There was glittering electric lightning and severe rainfall.

TEXT 24

ववृषू रुधिरौघासृक्पूयविण्मूत्रमेदसः ।
निपेतुर्गगनादस्य कबन्धान्यग्रतोऽनघ ॥२४॥

vavṛṣū rudhiraughāsṛk-
pūya-viṇ-mūtra-medasaḥ
nipetur gaganād asya
kabandhāny agrato 'nagha

vavṛṣuḥ—showered; *rudhira*—of blood; *ogha*—an inundation; *asṛk*—mucus; *pūya*—pus; *viṭ*—stool; *mūtra*—urine; *medasaḥ*—and marrow; *nipetuḥ*—began to fall; *gaganāt*—from the sky; *asya*—of Dhruva; *kabandhāni*—trunks of bodies; *agrataḥ*—in front; *anagha*—O faultless Vidura.

TRANSLATION

My dear faultless Vidura, in that rainfall there was blood, mucus, pus, stool, urine and marrow falling heavily before Dhruva Mahārāja, and there were trunks of bodies falling from the sky.

TEXT 25

ततः खेऽदृश्यत गिरिर्निपेतुः सर्वतोदिशम् ।
गदापरिघनिस्त्रिंशमुसलाः साश्मवर्षिणः ॥२५॥

tataḥ khe 'dṛśyata girir
nipetuḥ sarvato-diśam
gadā-parigha-nistriṁśa-
musalāḥ sāśma-varṣiṇaḥ

tataḥ—thereafter; *khe*—in the sky; *adṛśyata*—was visible; *giriḥ*—a mountain; *nipetuḥ*—fell down; *sarvataḥ-diśam*—from all directions; *gadā*—clubs; *parigha*—iron bludgeons; *nistriṁśa*—swords; *musalāḥ*—maces; *sa-aśma*—great pieces of stone; *varṣiṇaḥ*—with a shower of.

TRANSLATION

Next, a great mountain was visible in the sky, and from all directions hailstones fell, along with lances, clubs, swords, iron bludgeons and great pieces of stone.

TEXT 26

अहयोऽशनिनिःश्वासा वमन्तोऽग्निं रुषाक्षिभिः ।
अभ्यधावन् गजा मत्ताः सिंहव्याघ्राश्च यूथशः ॥२६॥

ahayo 'śani-niḥśvāsā
vamanto 'gniṁ ruṣākṣibhiḥ
abhyadhāvan gajā mattāḥ
siṁha-vyāghrāś ca yūthaśaḥ

ahayaḥ—serpents; *aśani*—thunderbolts; *niḥśvāsāḥ*—breathing; *vamantaḥ*—vomiting; *agnim*—fire; *ruṣā-akṣibhiḥ*—with angry eyes; *abhyadhāvan*—came forward; *gajāḥ*—elephants; *mattāḥ*—mad; *siṁha*—lions; *vyāghrāḥ*—tigers; *ca*—also; *yūthaśaḥ*—in groups.

TRANSLATION

Dhruva Mahārāja also saw many big serpents with angry eyes, vomiting forth fire and coming to devour him, along with groups of mad elephants, lions and tigers.

TEXT 27

समुद्र ऊर्मिभिर्भीमः प्लावयन् सर्वतो भुवम् ।
आससाद महाह्रादः कल्पान्त इव भीषणः ॥२७॥

samudra ūrmibhir bhīmaḥ
plāvayan sarvato bhuvam
āsasāda mahā-hrādaḥ
kalpānta iva bhīṣaṇaḥ

samudraḥ—the sea; *ūrmibhiḥ*—with waves; *bhīmaḥ*—fierce; *plāvayan*—inundating; *sarvataḥ*—in all directions; *bhuvam*—the earth; *āsasāda*—came forward; *mahā-hrādaḥ*—making great sounds; *kalpa-ante*—(the dissolution) at the end of a *kalpa; iva*—like; *bhīṣaṇaḥ*—fearful.

TRANSLATION

Then, as if it were the time of the dissolution of the whole world, the fierce sea with foaming waves and great roaring sounds came forward before him.

TEXT 28

एवंविधान्यनेकानि त्रासनान्यमनस्विनाम् ।
ससृजुस्तिग्मगतय आसुर्या माययासुराः ॥२८॥

evaṁ-vidhāny anekāni
trāsanāny amanasvinām
sasṛjus tigma-gataya
āsuryā māyayāsurāḥ

evam-vidhāni—(phenomena) like this; *anekāni*—many varieties of; *trāsanāni*—fearful; *amanasvinām*—to the less intelligent men; *sasṛjuḥ*—they created; *tigma-gatayaḥ*—of heinous nature; *āsuryā*—demoniac; *māyayā*—by illusion; *asurāḥ*—the demons.

TRANSLATION

The demon Yakṣas are by nature very heinous, and by their demoniac power of illusion they can create many strange phenomena to frighten one who is less intelligent.

TEXT 29

ध्रुवे प्रयुक्तामसुरैस्तां मायामतिदुस्तराम् ।
निशम्य तस्य मुनयः शमाशंसन् समागताः ॥२९॥

dhruve prayuktām asurais
tāṁ māyām atidustarām
niśamya tasya munayaḥ
śam āśaṁsan samāgatāḥ

dhruve—against Dhruva; *prayuktām*—inflicted; *asuraiḥ*—by the demons; *tām*—that; *māyām*—mystic power; *ati-dustarām*—very dangerous; *niśamya*—after hearing; *tasya*—his; *munayaḥ*—the great sages; *śam*—good fortune; *āśaṁsan*—giving encouragement for; *samāgatāḥ*—assembled.

TRANSLATION

When the great sages heard that Dhruva Mahārāja was overpowered by the illusory mystic tricks of the demons, they immediately assembled to offer him auspicious encouragement.

TEXT 30

मुनय ऊचुः
औत्तानपाद भगवांस्तव शार्ङ्गधन्वा
देवः क्षिणोत्ववनतार्तिहरो विपक्षान् ।
यन्नामधेयमभिधाय निशम्य चाद्धा
लोकोऽञ्जसा तरति दुस्तरमङ्ग मृत्युम् ॥३०॥

munaya ūcuḥ
auttānapāda bhagavāṁs tava śārṅgadhanvā
devaḥ kṣiṇotv avanatārti-haro vipakṣān
yan-nāmadheyam abhidhāya niśamya cāddhā
loko 'ñjasā tarati dustaram aṅga mṛtyum

munayaḥ ūcuḥ—the sages said; *auttānapāda*—O son of King Uttānapāda; *bhagavān*—the Supreme Personality of Godhead; *tava*—your; *śārṅga-dhanvā*—one who bears the bow called Śārṅga; *devaḥ*—the Lord; *kṣiṇotu*—may He kill; *avanata*—of the surrendered soul; *ārti*—the distresses; *haraḥ*—who removes; *vipakṣān*—enemies; *yat*—whose; *nāmadheyam*—holy name; *abhidhāya*—uttering; *niśamya*—hearing; *ca*—also; *addhā*—immediately; *lokaḥ*—persons; *añjasā*—fully; *tarati*—overcome; *dustaram*—insurmountable; *aṅga*—O Dhruva; *mṛtyum*—death.

TRANSLATION

All the sages said: Dear Dhruva, O son of King Uttānapāda, may the Supreme Personality of Godhead known as Śārṅgadhanvā, who relieves the distresses of His devotees, kill all your threatening

enemies. The holy name of the Lord is as powerful as the Lord Himself. Therefore, simply by chanting and hearing the holy name of the Lord, many men can be fully protected from fierce death without difficulty. Thus a devotee is saved.

PURPORT

The great *ṛṣis* approached Dhruva Mahārāja at a time when his mind was very perplexed due to the magical feats exhibited by the Yakṣas. A devotee is always protected by the Supreme Personality of Godhead. By His inspiration only, the sages came to encourage Dhruva Mahārāja and assure him that there was no danger because he was a soul fully surrendered to the Supreme Lord. By the grace of the Lord, if a devotee, at the time of death, can simply chant His holy name—Hare Kṛṣṇa, Hare Kṛṣṇa, Kṛṣṇa Kṛṣṇa, Hare Hare/ Hare Rāma, Hare Rāma, Rāma Rāma, Hare Hare—simply by chanting this *mahā-mantra,* he immediately surpasses the great ocean of the material sky and enters the spiritual sky. He never has to come back for repetition of birth and death. Simply by chanting the holy name of the Lord, one can surpass the ocean of death, so Dhruva Mahārāja was certainly able to surpass the illusory magical feats of the Yakṣas, which for the time being disturbed his mind.

Thus end the Bhaktivedanta purports of the Fourth Canto, Tenth Chapter, of the Śrīmad-Bhāgavatam, *entitled "Dhruva Mahārāja's Fight With the Yakṣas."*

CHAPTER ELEVEN

Svāyambhuva Manu Advises Dhruva Mahārāja to Stop Fighting

TEXT 1

मैत्रेय उवाच

निशम्य गदतामेवमृषीणां धनुषि ध्रुवः ।
संदधेऽस्त्रमुपस्पृश्य यन्नारायणनिर्मितम् ॥ १ ॥

maitreya uvāca
niśamya gadatām evam
ṛṣīṇāṁ dhanuṣi dhruvaḥ
sandadhe 'stram upaspṛśya
yan nārāyaṇa-nirmitam

maitreyaḥ uvāca—the sage Maitreya continued to speak; *niśamya*—having heard; *gadatām*—the words; *evam*—thus; *ṛṣīṇām*—of the sages; *dhanuṣi*—upon his bow; *dhruvaḥ*—Dhruva Mahārāja; *sandadhe*—fixed; *astram*—an arrow; *upaspṛśya*—after touching water; *yat*—that which; *nārāyaṇa*—by Nārāyaṇa; *nirmitam*—was made.

TRANSLATION

Śrī Maitreya said: My dear Vidura, when Dhruva Mahārāja heard the encouraging words of the great sages, he performed the ācamana by touching water and then took up his arrow made by Lord Nārāyaṇa and fixed it upon his bow.

PURPORT

Dhruva Mahārāja was given a specific arrow made by Lord Nārāyaṇa Himself, and he now fixed it upon his bow to finish the illusory atmosphere created by the Yakṣas. As it is stated in the *Bhagavad-gītā*

(7.14), *mām eva ye prapadyante māyām etāṁ taranti te.* Without Nārāyaṇa, the Supreme Personality of Godhead, no one is able to overcome the action of the illusory energy. Śrī Caitanya Mahāprabhu has also given us a nice weapon for this age, as stated in the *Bhāgavatam: sāṅgopāṅgāstra*—in this age, the *nārāyaṇāstra*, or weapon to drive away *māyā*, is the chanting of the Hare Kṛṣṇa *mantra* in pursuance of the associates of Lord Caitanya, such as Advaita Prabhu, Nityānanda, Gadādhara and Śrīvāsa.

TEXT 2

संधीयमान एतस्मिन्माया गुह्यकनिर्मिताः ।
क्षिप्रं विनेशुर्विदुर क्लेशा ज्ञानोदये यथा ॥ २ ॥

sandhīyamāna etasmin
māyā guhyaka-nirmitāḥ
kṣipraṁ vineśur vidura
kleśā jñānodaye yathā

sandhīyamāne—while joining to his bow; *etasmin*—this *nārāyaṇāstra; māyāḥ*—the illusions; *guhyaka-nirmitāḥ*—created by the Yakṣas; *kṣipram*—very soon; *vineśuḥ*—were destroyed; *vidura*—O Vidura; *kleśāḥ*—illusory pains and pleasures; *jñāna-udaye*—upon the arising of knowledge; *yathā*—just as.

TRANSLATION

As soon as Dhruva Mahārāja joined the nārāyaṇāstra arrow to his bow, the illusion created by the Yakṣas was immediately vanquished, just as all material pains and pleasures are vanquished when one becomes fully cognizant of the self.

PURPORT

Kṛṣṇa is like the sun, and *māyā*, or the illusory energy of Kṛṣṇa, is like darkness. Darkness means absence of light; similarly, *māyā* means absence of Kṛṣṇa consciousness. Kṛṣṇa consciousness and *māyā* are always there, side by side. As soon as there is awakening of Kṛṣṇa consciousness, all the illusory pains and pleasures of material existence are vanquished. *Māyām etāṁ taranti te:* constant chanting of the *mahā-mantra* will keep us always aloof from the illusory energy of *māyā.*

TEXT 3

तस्यार्षास्त्रं धनुषि प्रयुञ्जतः
सुवर्णपुङ्खाः कलहंसवाससः ।
विनिःसृता आविविशुर्द्विषद्बलं
यथा वनं भीमरवाः शिखण्डिनः ॥ ३ ॥

tasyārṣāstraṁ dhanuṣi prayuñjataḥ
suvarṇa-puṅkhāḥ kalahaṁsa-vāsasaḥ
viniḥsṛtā āviviśur dviṣad-balaṁ
yathā vanaṁ bhīma-ravāḥ śikhaṇḍinaḥ

tasya—while Dhruva; *ārṣa-astram*—the weapon given by Nārāyaṇa Ṛṣi; *dhanuṣi*—on his bow; *prayuñjataḥ*—fixed; *suvarṇa-puṅkhāḥ*—(arrows) with golden shafts; *kalahaṁsa-vāsasaḥ*—with feathers like the wings of a swan; *viniḥsṛtāḥ*—sprang out; *āviviśuḥ*—entered; *dviṣat-balam*—the soldiers of the enemy; *yathā*—just as; *vanam*—into a forest; *bhīma-ravāḥ*—making a tumultuous sound; *śikhaṇḍinaḥ*—peacocks.

TRANSLATION

Even as Dhruva Mahārāja fixed the weapon made by Nārāyaṇa Ṛṣi onto his bow, arrows with golden shafts and feathers like the wings of a swan flew out from it. They entered the enemy soldiers with a great hissing sound, just as peacocks enter a forest with tumultuous crowing.

TEXT 4

तैस्तिग्मधारैः प्रधने शिलीमुखै-
रितस्ततः पुण्यजना उपद्रुताः ।
तमभ्यधावन् कुपिता उदायुधाः
सुपर्णमुन्नद्धफणा इवाहयः ॥ ४ ॥

tais tigma-dhāraiḥ pradhane śilī-mukhair
itas tataḥ puṇya-janā upadrutāḥ
tam abhyadhāvan kupitā udāyudhāḥ
suparṇam unnaddha-phaṇā ivāhayaḥ

taiḥ—by those; *tigma-dhāraiḥ*—which had a sharp point; *pradhane*—on the battlefield; *śilī-mukhaiḥ*—arrows; *itaḥ tataḥ*—here and there; *puṇya-janāḥ*—the Yakṣas; *upadrutāḥ*—being greatly agitated; *tam*—towards Dhruva Mahārāja; *abhyadhāvan*—rushed; *kupitāḥ*—being angry; *udāyudhāḥ*—with upraised weapons; *suparṇam*—towards Garuḍa; *unnaddha-phaṇāḥ*—with upraised hoods; *iva*—like; *ahayaḥ*—serpents.

TRANSLATION

Those sharp arrows dismayed the enemy soldiers, who became almost unconscious, but various Yakṣas on the battlefield, in a rage against Dhruva Mahārāja, somehow or other collected their weapons and attacked. Just as serpents agitated by Garuḍa rush towards Garuḍa with upraised hoods, all the Yakṣa soldiers prepared to overcome Dhruva Mahārāja with their upraised weapons.

TEXT 5

स तान् पृषत्कैरभिधावतो मृधे
निकृत्तबाहूरुशिरोधरोदरान् ।
निनाय लोकं परमर्कमण्डलं
व्रजन्ति निर्भिद्य यमूर्ध्वरेतसः ॥ ५ ॥

sa tān pṛṣatkair abhidhāvato mṛdhe
nikṛtta-bāhūru-śirodharodarān
ināya lokaṁ param arka-maṇḍalaṁ
vrajanti nirbhidya yam ūrdhva-retasaḥ

saḥ—he (Dhruva Mahārāja); *tān*—all the Yakṣas; *pṛṣatkaiḥ*—by his arrows; *abhidhāvataḥ*—coming forward; *mṛdhe*—in the battlefield; *nikṛtta*—being separated; *bāhu*—arms; *ūru*—thighs; *śiraḥ-dhara*—necks; *udarān*—and bellies; *ināya*—delivered; *lokam*—to the planet;

param—supreme; *arka-maṇḍalam*—the sun globe; *vrajanti*—go; *nirbhidya*—piercing; *yam*—to which; *ūrdhva-retasaḥ*—those who do not discharge semen at any time.

TRANSLATION

When Dhruva Mahārāja saw the Yakṣas coming forward, he immediately took his arrows and cut the enemies to pieces. Separating their arms, legs, heads and bellies from their bodies, he delivered the Yakṣas to the planetary system which is situated above the sun globe and which is attainable only by first-class brahmacārīs, who have never discharged their semen.

PURPORT

To be killed by the Lord or by His devotees is auspicious for nondevotees. The Yakṣas were killed indiscriminately by Dhruva Mahārāja, but they attained the planetary system attainable only for *brahmacārīs* who never discharged their semen. As the impersonalist *jñānīs* or the demons killed by the Lord attain Brahmaloka, or Satyaloka, persons killed by a devotee of the Lord also attain Satyaloka. To reach the Satyaloka planetary system described here, one has to be elevated above the sun globe. Killing, therefore, is not always bad. If the killing is done by the Supreme Personality of Godhead or His devotee or in great sacrifices, it is for the benefit of the entity killed in that way. Material so-called nonviolence is very insignificant in comparison to killing done by the Supreme Personality of Godhead or His devotees. Even when a king or the state government kills a person who is a murderer, that killing is for the benefit of the murderer, for thus he may become cleared of all sinful reactions.

An important word in this verse is *ūrdhva-retasaḥ*, which means *brahmacārīs* who have never discharged semen. Celibacy is so important that even though one does not undergo any austerities, penances or ritualistic ceremonies prescribed in the *Vedas*, if one simply keeps himself a pure *brahmacārī*, not discharging his semen, the result is that after death he goes to the Satyaloka. Generally, sex life is the cause of all miseries in the material world. In the Vedic civilization sex life is restricted in various ways. Out of the whole population of the social structure, only the *gṛhasthas* are allowed restricted sex life. All others refrain from sex.

The people of this age especially do not know the value of not discharging semen. As such, they are variously entangled with material qualities and suffer an existence of struggle only. The word *ūrdhva-retasaḥ* especially indicates the Māyāvādī *sannyāsīs*, who undergo strict principles of austerity. But in the *Bhagavad-gītā* (8.16) the Lord says that even if one goes up to Brahmaloka, he again comes back (*ābrahma-bhuvanāl lokāḥ punar āvartino 'rjuna*). Therefore, actual *mukti*, or liberation, can be attained only by devotional service, because by devotional service one can go above Brahmaloka, or to the spiritual world, wherefrom he never comes back. Māyāvādī *sannyāsīs* are very proud of becoming liberated, but actual liberation is not possible unless one is in touch with the Supreme Lord in devotional service. It is said, *hariṁ vinā na sṛtiṁ taranti:* without Kṛṣṇa's mercy, no one can have liberation.

TEXT 6

तान् हन्यमानानभिवीक्ष्य गुह्यका-
ननागसश्चित्ररथेन भूरिशः ।
औत्तानपादिं कृपया पितामहो
मनुर्जगादोपगतः सहर्षिभिः ॥ ६ ॥

tān hanyamānān abhivīkṣya guhyakān
anāgasaś citra-rathena bhūriśaḥ
auttānapādiṁ kṛpayā pitāmaho
manur jagādopagataḥ saharṣibhiḥ

tān—those Yakṣas; *hanyamānān*—being killed; *abhivīkṣya*—seeing; *guhyakān*—the Yakṣas; *anāgasaḥ*—offenseless; *citra-rathena*—by Dhruva Mahārāja, who had a beautiful chariot; *bhūriśaḥ*—greatly; *auttānapādim*—unto the son of Uttānapāda; *kṛpayā*—out of mercy; *pitāmahaḥ*—the grandfather; *manuḥ*—Svāyambhuva Manu; *jagāda*—gave instructions; *upagataḥ*—approached; *saha-ṛṣibhiḥ*—with great sages.

TRANSLATION

When Svāyambhuva Manu saw that his grandson Dhruva Mahārāja was killing so many of the Yakṣas who were not actually

offenders, out of his great compassion he approached Dhruva with great sages to give him good instruction.

PURPORT

Dhruva Mahārāja attacked Alakāpurī, the city of the Yakṣas, because his brother was killed by one of them. Actually only one of the citizens, not all of them, was guilty of killing his brother, Uttama. Dhruva Mahārāja, of course, took a very serious step when his brother was killed by the Yakṣas. War was declared, and the fighting was going on. This sometimes happens in present days also—for one man's fault a whole state is sometimes attacked. This kind of wholesale attack is not approved by Manu, the father and lawgiver of the human race. He therefore wanted to stop his grandson Dhruva from continuing to kill the Yakṣa citizens who were not offenders.

TEXT 7

मनुरुवाच
अलं वत्सातिरोषेण तमोद्वारेण पाप्मना ।
येन पुण्यजनानेतानवधीस्त्वमनागसः ॥ ७ ॥

manur uvāca
alaṁ vatsātiroṣeṇa
tamo-dvāreṇa pāpmanā
yena puṇya-janān etān
avadhīs tvam anāgasaḥ

manuḥ uvāca—Manu said; *alam*—enough; *vatsa*—my dear boy; *ati-roṣeṇa*—with excessive anger; *tamaḥ-dvāreṇa*—the path of ignorance; *pāpmanā*—sinful; *yena*—by which; *puṇya-janān*—the Yakṣas; *etān*—all these; *avadhīḥ*—you have killed; *tvam*—you; *anāgasaḥ*—offenseless.

TRANSLATION

Lord Manu said: My dear son, please stop. It is not good to become unnecessarily angry—it is the path to hellish life. Now you are going beyond the limit by killing Yakṣas who are actually not offenders.

PURPORT

In this verse the word *atiroṣeṇa* means "with unnecessary anger." When Dhruva Mahārāja went beyond the limits of necessary anger, his grandfather, Svāyambhuva Manu, immediately came to protect him from further sinful action. From this we can understand that killing is not bad, but when killing is done unnecessarily or when an offenseless person is killed, such killing opens the path to hell. Dhruva Mahārāja was saved from such sinful action because he was a great devotee.

A *kṣatriya* is allowed to kill only for maintenance of the law and order of the state; he is not allowed to kill or commit violence without reason. Violence is certainly a path leading to a hellish condition of life, but it is also required for maintenance of the law and order of the state. Here Lord Manu prohibited Dhruva Mahārāja from killing the Yakṣas because only one of them was punishable for killing his brother, Uttama; not all of the Yakṣa citizens were punishable. We find in modern warfare, however, that attacks are made upon innocent citizens who are without fault. According to the law of Manu, such warfare is a most sinful activity. Furthermore, at the present moment civilized nations are unnecessarily maintaining many slaughterhouses for killing innocent animals. When a nation is attacked by its enemies, the wholesale slaughter of the citizens should be taken as a reaction to their own sinful activities. That is nature's law.

TEXT 8

नास्मत्कुलोचितं तात कर्मैतत्सद्विगर्हितम् ।
वधो यदुपदेवानामारब्धस्तेऽकृतैनसाम् ॥ ८ ॥

nāsmat-kulocitaṁ tāta
karmaitat sad-vigarhitam
vadho yad upadevānām
ārabdhas te 'kṛtainasām

na—not; *asmat-kula*—our family; *ucitam*—befitting; *tāta*—my dear son; *karma*—action; *etat*—this; *sat*—by authorities on religion; *vigarhitam*—forbidden; *vadhaḥ*—the killing; *yat*—which; *upadevānām*—of the Yakṣas; *ārabdhaḥ*—was undertaken; *te*—by you; *akṛta-enasām*—of those who are sinless.

TRANSLATION

My dear son, the killing of the sinless Yakṣas which you have undertaken is not at all approved by authorities, and it does not befit our family, which is supposed to know the laws of religion and irreligion.

TEXT 9

नन्वेकस्यापराधेन प्रसङ्गाद् बहवो हताः ।
भ्रातुर्वधाभितप्तेन त्वयाङ्ग भ्रातृवत्सल ॥ ९ ॥

nanv ekasyāparādhena
prasaṅgād bahavo hatāḥ
bhrātur vadhābhitaptena
tvayāṅga bhrātṛ-vatsala

nanu—certainly; *ekasya*—of one (Yakṣa); *aparādhena*—with the offense; *prasaṅgāt*—because of their association; *bahavaḥ*—many; *hatāḥ*—have been killed; *bhrātuḥ*—of your brother; *vadha*—by the death; *abhitaptena*—being aggrieved; *tvayā*—by you; *aṅga*—my dear son; *bhrātṛ-vatsala*—affectionate to your brother.

TRANSLATION

My dear son, it has been proved that you are very much affectionate towards your brother and are greatly aggrieved at his being killed by the Yakṣas, but just consider—for one Yakṣa's offense, you have killed many others, who are innocent.

TEXT 10

नायं मार्गो हि साधूनां हृषीकेशानुवर्तिनाम् ।
यदात्मानं पराग्गृह्य पशुवद्भूतवैशसम् ॥१०॥

nāyaṁ mārgo hi sādhūnāṁ
hṛṣīkeśānuvartinām
yad ātmānaṁ parāg gṛhya
paśuvad bhūta-vaiśasam

na—never; *ayam*—this; *mārgaḥ*—path; *hi*—certainly; *sādhūnām*—of honest persons; *hṛṣīkeśa*—of the Supreme Personality of Godhead; *anuvartinām*—following the path; *yat*—which; *ātmānam*—self; *parāk*—the body; *gṛhya*—thinking to be; *paśu-vat*—like animals; *bhūta*—of living entities; *vaiśasam*—killing.

TRANSLATION

One should not accept the body as the self and thus, like the animals, kill the bodies of others. This is especially forbidden by saintly persons, who follow the path of devotional service to the Supreme Personality of Godhead.

PURPORT

The words *sādhūnāṁ hṛṣīkeśānuvartinām* are very significant. *Sādhu* means "a saintly person." But who is a saintly person? A saintly person is he who follows the path of rendering service unto the Supreme Personality of Godhead, Hṛṣīkeśa. In the *Nārada-pañcarātra* it is said, *hṛṣīkeṇa hṛṣīkeśa-sevanaṁ bhaktir ucyate:* the process of rendering favorable service to the Supreme Personality of Godhead with one's senses is called *bhakti,* or devotional service. Therefore, why should a person who is already engaged in the service of the Lord engage himself in personal sense gratification? Dhruva Mahārāja is advised here by Lord Manu that he is a pure servitor of the Lord. Why should he unnecessarily engage, like the animals, in the bodily concept of life? An animal thinks that the body of another animal is his food; therefore, in the bodily concept of life, one animal attacks another. A human being, especially one who is a devotee of the Lord, should not act like this. A *sādhu,* a saintly devotee, is not supposed to kill animals unnecessarily.

TEXT 11

सर्वभूतात्मभावेन भूतावासं हरिं भवान् ।
आराध्याप दुराराध्यं विष्णोस्तत्परमं पदम् ॥११॥

sarva-bhūtātma-bhāvena
bhūtāvāsaṁ hariṁ bhavān

ārādhyāpa durārādhyaṁ
viṣṇos tat paramaṁ padam

sarva-bhūta—in all living entities; *ātma*—upon the Supersoul; *bhāvena*—with meditation; *bhūta*—of all existence; *āvāsam*—the abode; *harim*—Lord Hari; *bhavān*—you; *ārādhya*—by worshiping; *āpa*—have achieved; *durārādhyam*—very difficult to propitiate; *viṣṇoḥ*—of Lord Viṣṇu; *tat*—that; *paramam*—supreme; *padam*—situation.

TRANSLATION

It is very difficult to achieve the spiritual abode of Hari, in the Vaikuṇṭha planets, but you are so fortunate that you are already destined to go to that abode by worshiping Him as the supreme abode of all living entities.

PURPORT

The material bodies of all living entities cannot exist unless sheltered by the spirit soul and the Supersoul. The spirit soul is dependent on the Supersoul, who is present even within the atom. Therefore, since anything, material or spiritual, is completely dependent on the Supreme Lord, the Supreme Lord is referred to here as *bhūtāvāsa.* Dhruva Mahārāja, as a *kṣatriya*, could have argued with his grandfather, Manu, when Manu requested him to stop fighting. But even though Dhruva could have argued that as a *kṣatriya* it was his duty to fight with the enemy, he was informed that since every living entity is a residence of the Supreme Lord and can be considered a temple of the Lord, the unnecessary killing of any living entity is not permitted.

TEXT 12

स त्वं हरेरनुध्यातस्तत्पुंसामपि सम्मतः ।
कथं त्ववद्यं कृतवाननुशिक्षन् सतां व्रतम् ॥१२॥

sa tvaṁ harer anudhyātas
tat-puṁsām api sammataḥ
kathaṁ tv avadyaṁ kṛtavān
anuśikṣan satāṁ vratam

saḥ—that person; *tvam*—you; *hareḥ*—by the Supreme Lord; *anudhyātaḥ*—being always remembered; *tat*—His; *puṁsām*—by the devotees; *api*—also; *sammataḥ*—esteemed; *katham*—why; *tu*—then; *avadyam*—abominable (act); *kṛtavān*—you have undertaken; *anuśikṣan*—setting the example; *satām*—of saintly persons; *vratam*—a vow.

TRANSLATION

Because you are a pure devotee of the Lord, the Lord is always thinking of you, and you are also recognized by all His confidential devotees. Your life is meant for exemplary behavior. I am therefore surprised—why have you undertaken such an abominable task?

PURPORT

Dhruva Mahārāja was a pure devotee and was accustomed to always thinking of the Lord. Reciprocally, the Lord always thinks of those pure devotees who think of Him only, twenty-four hours a day. As a pure devotee does not know anything beyond the Lord, so the Lord does not know anything beyond His pure devotee. Svāyambhuva Manu pointed out this fact to Dhruva Mahārāja: "Not only are you a pure devotee, but you are recognized by all pure devotees of the Lord. You should always act in such an exemplary way that others may learn from you. Under the circumstances, it is surprising that you have killed so many faultless Yakṣas."

TEXT 13

तितिक्षया करुणया मैत्र्या चाखिलजन्तुषु ।
समत्वेन च सर्वात्मा भगवान् सम्प्रसीदति ॥१३॥

titikṣayā karuṇayā
maitryā cākhila-jantuṣu
samatvena ca sarvātmā
bhagavān samprasīdati

titikṣayā—by tolerance; *karuṇayā*—by mercy; *maitryā*—by friendship; *ca*—also; *akhila*—universal; *jantuṣu*—unto the living entities;

samatvena—by equilibrium; *ca*—also; *sarva-ātmā*—the Supersoul; *bhagavān*—the Personality of Godhead; *samprasīdati*—becomes very satisfied.

TRANSLATION

The Lord is very satisfied with His devotee when the devotee greets other people with tolerance, mercy, friendship and equality.

PURPORT

It is the duty of an advanced devotee in the second stage of devotional perfection to act in accordance with this verse. There are three stages of devotional life. In the lowest stage, a devotee is simply concerned with the Deity in the temple, and he worships the Lord with great devotion, according to rules and regulations. In the second stage the devotee is cognizant of his relationship with the Lord, his relationship with fellow devotees, his relationship with persons who are innocent and his relationship with persons who are envious. Sometimes devotees are ill-treated by envious persons. It is advised that an advanced devotee should be tolerant; he should show complete mercy to persons who are ignorant or innocent. A preacher-devotee is meant to show mercy to innocent persons, whom he can elevate to devotional service. Everyone, by constitutional position, is an eternal servant of God. Therefore, a devotee's business is to awaken everyone's Kṛṣṇa consciousness. That is his mercy. As for a devotee's treatment of other devotees who are his equals, he should maintain friendship with them. His general view should be to see every living entity as part of the Supreme Lord. Different living entities appear in different forms of dress, but according to the instruction of the *Bhagavad-gītā*, a learned person sees all living entities equally. Such treatment by the devotee is very much appreciated by the Supreme Lord. It is said, therefore, that a saintly person is always tolerant and merciful, he is a friend to everyone, never an enemy to anyone, and he is peaceful. These are some of the good qualities of a devotee.

TEXT 14

सम्प्रसन्ने भगवति पुरुषः प्राकृतैर्गुणैः ।
विमुक्तो जीवनिर्मुक्तो ब्रह्म निर्वाणमृच्छति ॥१४॥

samprasanne bhagavati
puruṣaḥ prākṛtair guṇaiḥ
vimukto jīva-nirmukto
brahma nirvāṇam ṛcchati

samprasanne—upon satisfaction; *bhagavati*—of the Supreme Personality of Godhead; *puruṣaḥ*—a person; *prākṛtaiḥ*—from the material; *guṇaiḥ*—modes of nature; *vimuktaḥ*—being liberated; *jīva-nirmuktaḥ*—freed from the subtle body also; *brahma*—unlimited; *nirvāṇam*—spiritual bliss; *ṛcchati*—achieves.

TRANSLATION

One who actually satisfies the Supreme Personality of Godhead during one's lifetime becomes liberated from the gross and subtle material conditions. Thus being freed from all material modes of nature, he achieves unlimited spiritual bliss.

PURPORT

In the previous verse it has been explained that one should treat all living entities with tolerance, mercy, friendship and equality. By such behavior one satisfies the Supreme Personality of Godhead, and upon His satisfaction the devotee immediately becomes free from all material conditions. The Lord also confirms this in the *Bhagavad-gītā:* "Anyone who sincerely and seriously engages in My service immediately becomes situated in the transcendental stage wherein he can enjoy unlimited spiritual bliss." Everyone in this material world is struggling hard in order to achieve blissful life. Unfortunately, people do not know how to achieve it. Atheists do not believe in God, and certainly they do not please Him. Here it is clearly said that upon pleasing the Supreme Personality of Godhead one immediately attains to the spiritual platform and enjoys unlimited blissful life. To become free from material existence means to become free from the influence of material nature.

The word *samprasanne*, which is used in this verse, means "being satisfied." A person should act in such a way that the Lord is satisfied by the activity; it is not that he himself is to be satisfied. Of course, when the Lord is satisfied, the devotee automatically becomes satisfied. This is the secret of the process of *bhakti-yoga.* Outside of *bhakti-yoga*, everyone is trying to satisfy himself. No one is trying to satisfy the Lord. *Karmīs* grossly try to satisfy their senses, but even those who are elevated to the platform of knowledge also try to satisfy themselves, in a subtle form. *Karmīs* try to satisfy themselves by sense gratification, and *jñānīs* try to satisfy themselves by subtle activities or mental speculation and thinking themselves to be God. *Yogīs* also try to satisfy themselves, by thinking that they can achieve different mystic perfections. But only devotees try to satisfy the Supreme Personality of Godhead. The devotees' process of self-realization is completely different from the processes of the *karmīs, jñānīs* and *yogīs.* Everyone else is trying to satisfy himself, whereas the devotee tries only to satisfy the Lord. The devotional process is completely different from the others; by working to please the Lord by engaging his senses in the Lord's loving service, the devotee is immediately situated on the transcendental platform, and he enjoys unlimited blissful life.

TEXT 15

भूतैः पञ्चभिरारब्धैर्योषित्पुरुष एव हि ।
तयोर्व्यवायात्सम्भूतिर्योषित्पुरुषयोरिह ॥१५॥

bhūtaiḥ pañcabhir ārabdhair
yoṣit puruṣa eva hi
tayor vyavāyāt sambhūtir
yoṣit-puruṣayor iha

bhūtaiḥ—by the material elements; *pañcabhiḥ*—five; *ārabdhaiḥ*—developed; *yoṣit*—woman; *puruṣaḥ*—man; *eva*—just so; *hi*—certainly; *tayoḥ*—of them; *vyavāyāt*—by sexual life; *sambhūtiḥ*—the further creation; *yoṣit*—of women; *puruṣayoḥ*—and of men; *iha*—in this material world.

TRANSLATION

The creation of the material world begins with the five elements, and thus everything, including the body of a man or a woman, is created of these elements. By the sexual life of man and woman, the number of men and women in this material world is further increased.

PURPORT

When Svāyambhuva Manu saw that Dhruva Mahārāja understood the philosophy of Vaiṣṇavism and yet was still dissatisfied because of his brother's death, he gave him an explanation of how this material body is created by the five elements of material nature. In the *Bhagavad-gītā* it is also confirmed, *prakṛteḥ kriyamāṇāni:* everything is created, maintained and annihilated by the material modes of nature. In the background, of course, there is the direction of the Supreme Personality of Godhead. This is also confirmed in the *Bhagavad-gītā* (*mayādhyakṣeṇa*). In the Ninth Chapter, Kṛṣṇa says, "Under My superintendence material nature is acting." Svāyambhuva Manu wanted to impress on Dhruva Mahārāja that the death of the material body of his brother was not actually the Yakṣas' fault; it was an act of the material nature. The Supreme Personality of Godhead has immense varieties of potencies, and they act in different gross and subtle ways.

It is by such powerful potencies that the universe is created, although grossly it appears to be no more than the five elements—earth, water, fire, air and ether. Similarly, the bodies of all species of living entities, whether human beings or demigods, animals or birds, are also created by the same five elements, and by sexual union they expand into more and more living entities. That is the way of creation, maintenance and annihilation. One should not be disturbed by the waves of material nature in this process. Dhruva Mahārāja was indirectly advised not to be afflicted by the death of his brother because our relationship with the body is completely material. The real self, spirit soul, is never annihilated or killed by anyone.

TEXT 16

एवं प्रवर्तते सर्गः स्थितिः संयम एव च ।
गुणव्यतिकराद्राजन् मायया परमात्मनः ॥१६॥

evaṁ pravartate sargaḥ
sthitiḥ saṁyama eva ca
guṇa-vyatikarād rājan
māyayā paramātmanaḥ

evam—thus; *pravartate*—occurs; *sargaḥ*—creation; *sthitiḥ*—maintenance; *saṁyamaḥ*—annihilation; *eva*—certainly; *ca*—and; *guṇa*—of the modes; *vyatikarāt*—by interaction; *rājan*—O King; *māyayā*—by the illusory energy; *parama-ātmanaḥ*—of the Supreme Personality of Godhead.

TRANSLATION

Manu continued: My dear King Dhruva, it is simply by the illusory, material energy of the Supreme Personality of Godhead and by the interaction of the three modes of material nature that creation, maintenance and annihilation take place.

PURPORT

First, creation takes place with the ingredients of the five elements of material nature. Then, by the interaction of the modes of material nature, maintenance also takes place. When a child is born, the parents immediately see to its maintenance. This tendency for maintenance of offspring is present not only in human society, but in animal society as well. Even tigers care for their cubs, although their propensity is to eat other animals. By the interaction of the material modes of nature, creation, maintenance and also annihilation take place inevitably. But at the same time we should know that all is conducted under the superintendence of the Supreme Personality of Godhead. Everything is going on under that process. Creation is the action of the *rajo-guṇa*, the mode of passion; maintenance is the action of *sattva-guṇa*, the mode of goodness; and annihilation is the action of *tamo-guṇa*, the mode of ignorance. We can see that those who are situated in the mode of goodness live longer than those who are situated in the *tamo-guṇa* or *rajo-guṇa*. In other words, if one is elevated to the mode of goodness, he is elevated to a higher planetary system, where the duration of life is very great. *Ūrdhvaṁ gacchanti sattva-sthāḥ:* great *ṛṣis*, sages and *sannyāsīs* who maintain themselves in *sattva-guṇa*, or the mode of material goodness, are elevated to a higher planetary system. Those who are transcendental even to the material modes of nature are situated in the mode of pure goodness; they attain eternal life in the spiritual world.

TEXT 17

निमित्तमात्रं तत्रासीन्निर्गुणः पुरुषर्षभः ।
व्यक्ताव्यक्तमिदं विश्वं यत्र भ्रमति लोहवत् ॥१७॥

nimitta-mātraṁ tatrāsīn
nirguṇaḥ puruṣarṣabhaḥ
vyaktāvyaktam idaṁ viśvaṁ
yatra bhramati lohavat

nimitta-mātram—remote cause; *tatra*—then; *āsīt*—was; *nirguṇaḥ*—uncontaminated; *puruṣa-ṛṣabhaḥ*—the Supreme Person; *vyakta*—manifested; *avyaktam*—unmanifested; *idam*—this; *viśvam*—world; *yatra*—where; *bhramati*—moves; *loha-vat*—like iron.

TRANSLATION

My dear Dhruva, the Supreme Personality of Godhead is uncontaminated by the material modes of nature. He is the remote cause of the creation of this material cosmic manifestation. When He gives the impetus, many other causes and effects are produced, and thus the whole universe moves, just as iron moves by the integrated force of a magnet.

PURPORT

How the external energy of the Supreme Personality of Godhead works within this material world is explained in this verse. Everything is happening by the energy of the Supreme Lord. The atheistic philosophers, who do not agree to accept the Supreme Personality of Godhead as the original cause of creation, think that the material world moves by the action and reaction of different material elements. A simple example of the interaction of elements occurs when we mix soda and acid and the movement of effervescence is produced. But one cannot produce life by such interaction of chemicals. There are 8,400,000 different species of life, with different wishes and different actions. How the material force is working cannot be explained just on the basis of chemical reaction. A suitable example in this connection is that of the potter and the potter's wheel. The potter's wheel rotates, and several varieties of earthen pots come out. There are many causes for the earthen pots, but the original cause is the potter, who sets a force on the wheel. That force comes by his superintendence. The same idea is explained in *Bhagavad-gītā*—behind all material action and reaction there is Kṛṣṇa, the Supreme Personality of Godhead. Kṛṣṇa says that everything depends on His energy, and yet He is not everywhere. The pot is produced under certain conditions of action and reaction of material energy, but the potter is not in the pot. In a similar way, the material creation is set up by the Lord, but He remains aloof. As stated in the *Vedas*, He simply glanced over it, and the agitation of matter immediately began.

In *Bhagavad-gītā* it is also said that the Lord impregnates the material energy with the part-and-parcel *jīvas*, and thus the different forms and different activities immediately ensue. Because of the different desires and karmic activities of the *jīva* soul, different types of bodies in different species are produced. In Darwin's theory there is no acceptance of the living entity as spirit soul, and therefore his explanation of evolution is incomplete. Varieties of phenomena occur within this universe on account of the actions and reactions of the three material modes, but the original creator, or the cause, is the Supreme Personality of Godhead, who is mentioned here as *nimitta-mātram*, the remote cause. He simply pushes the wheel with His energy. According to the Māyāvādī philosophers, the Supreme Brahman has transformed Himself into many varieties of forms, but that is not the fact. He is always transcendental to the actions and reactions of the material *guṇas*, although He is the cause of all causes. Lord Brahmā says, therefore, in the *Brahma-saṁhitā* (5.1):

īśvaraḥ paramaḥ kṛṣṇaḥ
sac-cid-ānanda-vigrahaḥ
anādir ādir govindaḥ
sarva-kāraṇa-kāraṇam

There are many causes and effects, but the original cause is Śrī Kṛṣṇa.

TEXT 18

स खल्विदं भगवान् कालशक्त्या
गुणप्रवाहेण विभक्तवीर्यः ।

करोत्यकर्तैव निहन्त्यहन्ता
चेष्टा विभूम्नः खलु दुर्विभाव्या ॥१८॥

sa khalv idaṁ bhagavān kāla-śaktyā
guṇa-pravāheṇa vibhakta-vīryaḥ
karoty akartaiva nihanty ahantā
ceṣṭā vibhūmnaḥ khalu durvibhāvyā

saḥ—the; *khalu*—however; *idam*—this (universe); *bhagavān*—the Personality of Godhead; *kāla*—of time; *śaktyā*—by the force; *guṇa-pravāheṇa*—by the interaction of the modes of nature; *vibhakta*—divided; *vīryaḥ*—(whose) potencies; *karoti*—acts upon; *akartā*—the nondoer; *eva*—although; *nihanti*—kills; *ahantā*—nonkiller; *ceṣṭā*—the energy; *vibhūmnaḥ*—of the Lord; *khalu*—certainly; *durvibhāvyā*—inconceivable.

TRANSLATION

The Supreme Personality of Godhead, by His inconceivable supreme energy, time, causes the interaction of the three modes of material nature, and thus varieties of energy become manifest. It appears that He is acting, but He is not the actor. He is killing, but He is not the killer. Thus it is understood that only by His inconceivable power is everything happening.

PURPORT

The word *durvibhāvyā* means "inconceivable by our tiny brain," and *vibhakta-vīryaḥ* means "divided in varieties of potencies." This is the right explanation of the display of creative energies in the material world. We can better understand the mercy of God by an example: a government state is always supposed to be merciful, but sometimes, in order to keep law and order, the government employs its police force, and thus punishment is meted out to the rebellious citizens. Similarly, the Supreme Personality of Godhead is always merciful and full of transcendental qualities, but certain individual souls have forgotten their relationship with Kṛṣṇa and have endeavored to lord it over material nature. As a result of their endeavor, they are involved in varieties of material interaction. It is incorrect to argue, however, that because energy issues from the Supreme Personality of Godhead, He is the actor. In the previous verse, the word *nimitta-mātram* indicates that the Supreme Lord is completely aloof from the action and reaction of this material world. How is everything being done? The word "inconceivable" has been used. It is not within the power of one's small brain to comprehend; unless one accepts the inconceivable power and energy of the Lord, one cannot make any progress. The forces which act are certainly set up by the Supreme Personality of Godhead, but He is always aloof from their action and reaction. The varieties of energies produced by the interaction of material nature produce the varieties of species of life and their resultant happiness and unhappiness.

How the Lord acts is nicely explained in the *Viṣṇu Purāṇa:* fire is situated in one place, while the heat and light produced by the fire act in many different ways. Another example given is that the electric powerhouse is situated in one place, but by its energies many different types of machinery move. The production is never identical with the original source of the energy, but the original source of energy, being the prime factor, is simultaneously one with and different from the product. Therefore, Lord Caitanya's philosophy, *acintya-bhedābheda-tattva*, is the perfect way of understanding. In this material world, the Lord incarnates in three forms—as Brahmā, Viṣṇu and Śiva—by which He takes charge of the three modes of material nature. By His incarnation of Brahmā He creates, as the incarnation of Viṣṇu He maintains, and by His incarnation of Śiva, He also annihilates. But the original source of Brahmā, Viṣṇu and Śiva—Garbhodakaśāyī Viṣṇu—is always apart from these actions and reactions of material nature.

TEXT 19

सोऽनन्तोऽन्तकरः कालोऽनादिरादिकृदव्ययः।
जनं जनेन जनयन्मारयन्मृत्युनान्तकम् ॥१९॥

so 'nanto 'nta-karaḥ kālo
'nādir ādi-kṛd avyayaḥ
janaṁ janena janayan
mārayan mṛtyunāntakam

saḥ—He; *anantaḥ*—infinite; *anta-karaḥ*—annihilator; *kālaḥ*—time; *anādiḥ*—without beginning; *ādi-kṛt*—beginning of everything; *avyayaḥ*—without decrease; *janam*—living entities; *janena*—by living entities; *janayan*—causing to be born; *mārayan*—killing; *mṛtyunā*—by death; *antakam*—killers.

TRANSLATION

My dear Dhruva, the Supreme Personality of Godhead is ever existing, but in the form of time, He is the killer of everything. He has no beginning, although He is the beginning of everything, nor is He ever exhaustible, although everything is exhausted in due course of time. The living entities are created through the agency of the father and killed through the agency of death, but He is perpetually free of birth and death.

PURPORT

The supreme authority and inconceivable power of the Supreme Personality of Godhead can be minutely studied from this verse. He is always unlimited. That means that He has no creation or end. He is, however, death (in the form of time), as described in *Bhagavad-gītā*. Kṛṣṇa says, "I am death. I take away everything at the end of life." Eternal time is also without beginning, but it is the creator of all creatures. The example is given of touchstone, which creates many valuable stones and jewels but does not decrease in power. Similarly, creation occurs many times, everything is maintained, and, after a time, everything is annihilated—but the original creator, the Supreme Lord, remains untouched and undiminished in power. The secondary creation is made by Brahmā, but Brahmā is created by the Supreme Godhead. Lord Śiva annihilates the whole creation, but at the end he is also annihilated by Viṣṇu. Lord Viṣṇu remains. In the Vedic hymns it is stated that in the beginning there is only Viṣṇu and that He alone remains at the end.

An example can help us to understand the inconceivable potency of the Supreme Lord. In the recent history of warfare the Supreme Personality of Godhead created a Hitler and, before that, a Napoleon Bonaparte, and they each killed many living entities in war. But in the end Bonaparte and Hitler were also killed. People are still very much interested in writing and reading books about Hitler and Bonaparte and how they killed so many people in war. Year after year many books are published for public reading regarding Hitler's killing thousands of Jews in confinement. But no one is researching who killed Hitler and who created such a gigantic killer of human beings. The devotees of the Lord are not much interested in the study of the flickering history of the world. They are interested only in Him who is the original creator, maintainer and annihilator. That is the purpose of the Kṛṣṇa consciousness movement.

TEXT 20

न वै स्वपक्षोऽस्य विपक्ष एव वा
परस्य मृत्योर्विशतः समं प्रजाः ।
तं धावमानमनुधावन्त्यनीशा
यथा रजांस्यनिलं भूतसङ्घाः ॥२०॥

na vai sva-pakṣo 'sya vipakṣa eva vā
parasya mṛtyor viśataḥ samaṁ prajāḥ
taṁ dhāvamānam anudhāvanty anīśā
yathā rajāṁsy anilaṁ bhūta-saṅghāḥ

na—not; *vai*—however; *sva-pakṣaḥ*—ally; *asya*—of the Supreme Personality of Godhead; *vipakṣaḥ*—enemy; *eva*—certainly; *vā*—or; *parasya*—of the Supreme; *mṛtyoḥ*—in the form of time; *viśataḥ*—entering; *samam*—equally; *prajāḥ*—living entities; *tam*—Him; *dhāvamānam*—moving; *anudhāvanti*—follow behind; *anīśāḥ*—dependent living entities; *yathā*—as; *rajāṁsi*—particles of dust; *anilam*—the wind; *bhūta-saṅghāḥ*—other material elements.

TRANSLATION

The Supreme Personality of Godhead, in His feature of eternal time, is present in the material world and is neutral towards everyone. No one is His ally, and no one is His enemy. Within the

jurisdiction of the time element, everyone enjoys or suffers the result of his own karma, or fruitive activities. As, when the wind blows, small particles of dust fly in the air, so, according to one's particular karma, one suffers or enjoys material life.

PURPORT

Although the Supreme Personality of Godhead is the original cause of all causes, He is not responsible for anyone's material sufferings or enjoyment. There is no such partiality on the part of the Supreme Lord. The less intelligent accuse the Supreme Lord of being partial and claim that this is why one enjoys in this material world and another suffers. But this verse specifically says that there is no such partiality on the part of the Supreme Lord. Living entities, however, are never independent. As soon as they declare their independence of the supreme controller, they are immediately put into this material world to try their luck freely, as far as possible. When the material world is created for such misguided living entities, they create their own *karma*, fruitive activities, and take advantage of the time element, and thereby they create their own fortune or misfortune. Everyone is created, everyone is maintained, and everyone is ultimately killed. As far as these three things are concerned, the Lord is equal to everyone; it is according to one's *karma* that one suffers and enjoys. The living entity's higher or lower position, his suffering and enjoying, are due to his own *karma*. The exact word used in this connection is *anīśāḥ*, which means "dependent on their own *karma*." The example is given that the government gives everyone the facilities for governmental action and management, but by one's own choice one creates a situation which obliges him to exist under different types of consciousness. The example given in this verse is that when the wind blows, particles of dust float in the air. Gradually lightning occurs, and then torrents of rain follow, and thus the rainy season creates a situation of varieties in the forest. God is very kind—He gives everyone an equal chance—but by the resultant actions of one's own *karma* one suffers or enjoys this material world.

TEXT 21

आयुषोऽपचयं जन्तोस्तथैवोपचयं विभुः ।
उभाभ्यां रहितः स्वस्थो दुःस्थस्य विदधात्यसौ ॥२१॥

āyuṣo 'pacayaṁ jantos
tathaivopacayaṁ vibhuḥ
ubhābhyāṁ rahitaḥ sva-stho
duḥsthasya vidadhāty asau

āyuṣaḥ—of duration of life; *apacayam*—diminution; *jantoḥ*—of the living entities; *tathā*—similarly; *eva*—also; *upacayam*—increase; *vibhuḥ*—the Supreme Personality of Godhead; *ubhābhyām*—from both of them; *rahitaḥ*—free; *sva-sthaḥ*—always situated in His transcendental position; *duḥsthasya*—of the living entities under the laws of *karma; vidadhāti*—awards; *asau*—He.

TRANSLATION

The Supreme Personality of Godhead, Viṣṇu, is all-powerful, and He awards the results of one's fruitive activities. Thus, although one living entity's duration of life is very small whereas that of another is very great, He is always in His transcendental position, and there is no question of lessening or increasing His duration of life.

PURPORT

Both the mosquito and Lord Brahmā are living entities in the material world; both are minute sparks and are part of the Supreme Lord. The very short duration of the life of the mosquito and the very long lifetime of Lord Brahmā are both awarded by the Supreme Personality of Godhead according to the results of their *karma.* But in the *Brahma-saṁhitā* we find it said, *karmāṇi nirdahati:* the Lord diminishes or vanquishes the reactions of devotees. The same fact is explained in *Bhagavad-gītā. Yajñārthāt karmaṇo 'nyatra:* one should perform *karma* only for the purpose of satisfying the Supreme Lord, otherwise one is bound by the action and reaction of *karma.* Under the laws of *karma* a living entity wanders within the universe under the rule of eternal time, and sometimes he becomes a mosquito and sometimes Lord Brahmā. To a sane man this business is not very fruitful. *Bhagavad-gītā* (9.25) gives a warning to the living entities: *yānti deva-vratā devān*—those who are addicted to the worship of the demigods go to the planets of the demigods, and those who are addicted to worship of the Pitās, forefathers, go to the Pitās. Those who are inclined to material activities remain in the material sphere. But persons who engage in devotional service reach the abode of the Supreme Personality of Godhead, where there is neither birth nor death nor different varieties of life under the influence of the law of *karma.* The best interest of the living entity is to engage himself in devotional service and go back home, back to Godhead. Śrīla Bhaktivinoda Ṭhākura advised: "My friend, you are being washed away in material nature's waves of time. Please try to understand that you are the eternal servant of the Lord. Then everything will stop, and you will be eternally happy."

TEXT 22

केचित्कर्म वदन्त्येनं स्वभावमपरे नृप ।
एके कालं परे दैवं पुंसः काममुतापरे ॥२२॥

kecit karma vadanty enaṁ
svabhāvam apare nṛpa
eke kālaṁ pare daivaṁ
puṁsaḥ kāmam utāpare

kecit—some; *karma*—fruitive activities; *vadanti*—explain; *enam*—that; *svabhāvam*—nature; *apare*—others; *nṛpa*—my dear King Dhruva; *eke*—some; *kālam*—time; *pare*—others; *daivam*—fate; *puṁsaḥ*—of the living entity; *kāmam*—desire; *uta*—also; *apare*—others.

TRANSLATION

The differentiation among varieties of life and their suffering and enjoyment is explained by some to be the result of karma. Others say it is due to nature, others due to time, others due to fate, and still others say that it is due to desire.

PURPORT

There arc different types of philosophers—*mīmāṁsakas,* atheists, astronomers, sexualists and so many other classifications of mental speculators. The real conclusion is that it is our work only that binds us within this material world in different varieties of life. How these varieties have sprung up is explained in the *Vedas:* it is due to the desire of the living entity. The living entity is not a dead stone; he has different varieties of desire, or *kāma.* The *Vedas* say, *kāmo 'karṣīt.* The living entities are originally parts of the Lord, like sparks of a fire, but they have dropped to this material world, attracted by a desire to lord it over nature. That is a fact. Every living entity is trying to lord it over the material resources to the best of his ability.

This *kāma,* or desire, cannot be annihilated. There are some philosophers who say that if one gives up his desires, he again becomes liberated. But it is not at all possible to give up desire, for desire is a symptom of the living entity. If there were no desire, then the living entity would be a dead stone. Śrīla Narottama dāsa Ṭhākura, therefore, advises that one turn his desire towards serving the Supreme Personality of Godhead. Then desire becomes purified. And when one's desires are purified, one becomes liberated from all material contamination. The conclusion is that the different philosophers' theories to explain the varieties of life and their pleasure and pain are all imperfect. The real explanation is that we are eternal servants of God and that as soon as we forget this relationship we are thrown into the material world, where we create our different activities and suffer or enjoy the result. We are drawn into this material world by desire, but the same desire must be purified and employed in the devotional service of the Lord. Then our disease of wandering in the universe under different forms and conditions will end.

TEXT 23

अव्यक्तस्याप्रमेयस्य नानाशक्त्युदयस्य च ।
न वै चिकीर्षितं तात को वेदाथ स्वसम्भवम् ॥२३॥

avyaktasyāprameyasya
nānā-śakty-udayasya ca
na vai cikīrṣitaṁ tāta
ko vedātha sva-sambhavam

avyaktasya—of the unmanifested; *aprameyasya*—of the Transcendence; *nānā*—various; *śakti*—energies; *udayasya*—of Him who gives rise to; *ca*—also; *na*—never; *vai*—certainly; *cikīrṣitam*—the plan; *tāta*—my dear boy; *kaḥ*—who; *veda*—can know; *atha*—therefore; *sva*—own; *sambhavam*—origin.

TRANSLATION

The Absolute Truth, Transcendence, is never subject to the understanding of imperfect sensory endeavor, nor is He subject to direct experience. He is the master of varieties of energies, like the full material energy, and no one can understand His plans or actions; therefore it should be concluded that although He is the original cause of all causes, no one can know Him by mental speculation.

PURPORT

The question may be raised, "Since there are so many varieties of philosophers theorizing in different ways, which of them is correct?" The answer is that the Absolute Truth, Transcendence, is never subject to direct experience or mental speculation. The mental speculator may be called Dr. Frog. The story is that a frog in a three-foot well wanted to calculate the length and breadth of the Atlantic Ocean on the basis of his knowledge of his own well. But it was an impossible task for Dr. Frog. A person may be a great academician, scholar or professor, but he cannot speculate and expect to understand the Absolute Truth, for his senses are limited. The cause of all causes, the Absolute Truth, can be known from the Absolute Truth Himself, and not by our ascending process to reach Him. When the sun is not visible at night or when it is covered by a cloud in the day, it is not possible to uncover it, either by bodily or mental strength or by scientific instruments, although the sun is there in the sky. No one can say that he has discovered a torchlight so powerful that if one goes on a roof and focuses the torchlight on the night sky, the sun will then be seen. There is no such torchlight, nor is it possible.

The word *avyakta*, "unmanifested," in this verse indicates that the Absolute Truth cannot be manifested by any strain of so-called scientific advancement of knowledge. Transcendence is not the subject matter of direct experience. The Absolute Truth may be known in the same way as the sun covered by a cloud or covered by night, for when the sun rises in the morning, in its own way, then everyone can see the sun, everyone can see the world, and everyone can see himself. This understanding of self-realization is called *ātma-tattva*. Unless, however, one comes to this point of understanding *ātma-tattva*, one remains in the darkness in which he was born. Under the circumstances, no one can understand the plan of the Supreme Personality of Godhead. The Lord is equipped with varieties of energies, as stated in the Vedic literature (*parāsya śaktir vividhaiva śrūyate*). He is equipped with the energy of eternal time. Not only does He have the material energy which we see and experience, but He has also many reserve energies that He can manifest in due course of time when necessary. The material scientist can simply study the partial understanding of the varieties of energies; he can take up one of the energies and try to understand it with limited knowledge, but still it is not possible to understand the Absolute Truth in full by dint of material science. No material scientist can foretell what is going to happen in the future. The *bhakti-yoga* process, however, is completely different from so-called scientific advancement of knowledge. A devotee completely surrenders unto the Supreme, who reveals Himself by His causeless mercy. As stated in *Bhagavad-gītā, dadāmi buddhi-yogaṁ tam.* The Lord says, "I give him intelligence." What is that intelligence? *Yena mām upayānti te.* The Lord gives one the intelligence to cross over the ocean of nescience and come back home, back to Godhead. In conclusion, the cause of all causes, the Absolute Truth, or Supreme Brahman, cannot be understood by philosophical speculation, but He reveals Himself to His devotee because the devotee fully surrenders unto His lotus feet. *Bhagavad-gītā* is therefore to be accepted as a revealed scripture spoken by the Absolute Truth Himself when He descended to this planet. If any intelligent man wants to know what God is, he should study this transcendental literature under the guidance of a bona fide spiritual master. Then it is very easy to understand Kṛṣṇa as He is.

TEXT 24

न चैते पुत्रक भ्रातुर्हन्तारो धनदानुगाः ।
विसर्गादानयोस्तात पुंसो दैवं हि कारणम् ॥२४॥

na caite putraka bhrātur
hantāro dhanadānugāḥ

visargādānayos tāta
puṁso daivaṁ hi kāraṇam

na—never; *ca*—also; *ete*—all these; *putraka*—my dear son; *bhrātuḥ*—of your brother; *hantāraḥ*—killers; *dhanada*—of Kuvera; *anugāḥ*—followers; *visarga*—of birth; *ādānayoḥ*—of death; *tāta*—my dear son; *puṁsaḥ*—of a living entity; *daivam*—the Supreme; *hi*—certainly; *kāraṇam*—the cause.

TRANSLATION

My dear son, those Yakṣas, who are descendants of Kuvera, are not actually the killers of your brother; the birth and death of every living entity are caused by the Supreme, who is certainly the cause of all causes.

TEXT 25

स एव विश्वं सृजति स एवावति हन्ति च ।
अथापि ह्यनहंकारान्नाज्यते गुणकर्मभिः ॥२५॥

sa eva viśvaṁ sṛjati
sa evāvati hanti ca
athāpi hy anahaṅkārān
nājyate guṇa-karmabhiḥ

saḥ—He; *eva*—certainly; *viśvam*—the universe; *sṛjati*—creates; *saḥ*—He; *eva*—certainly; *avati*—maintains; *hanti*—annihilates; *ca*—also; *atha api*—moreover; *hi*—certainly; *anahaṅkārāt*—from being without ego; *na*—not; *ajyate*—becomes entangled; *guṇa*—by the modes of material nature; *karmabhiḥ*—by activities.

TRANSLATION

The Supreme Personality of Godhead creates this material world, maintains it, and annihilates it in due course of time, but because He is transcendental to such activities, He is never affected by ego in such action or by the modes of material nature.

PURPORT

In this verse the word *anahaṅkāra* means "without ego." The conditioned soul has a false ego, and as a result of his *karma* he gets different types of bodies in this material world. Sometimes he gets the body of a demigod, and he thinks that body to be his identity. Similarly, when he gets the body of a dog he identifies his self with that body. But for the Supreme Personality of Godhead there is no such distinction between the body and the soul. *Bhagavad-gītā*, therefore, certifies that anyone who thinks of Kṛṣṇa as an ordinary human being is without knowledge of His transcendental nature and is a great fool. The Lord says, *na māṁ karmāṇi limpanti:* He is not affected by anything He does, because He is never contaminated by the material modes of nature. That we have a material body proves that we are infected by the three material modes of nature. The Lord says to Arjuna, "You and I had many, many births previously, but I remember everything, whereas you do not." That is the difference between the living entity, or conditioned soul, and the Supreme Soul. The Supersoul, the Supreme Personality of Godhead, has no material body, and because He has no material body, He is not affected by any work He executes. There are many Māyāvādī philosophers who consider that Kṛṣṇa's body is the effect of a concentration of the material mode of goodness, and they distinguish Kṛṣṇa's soul from Kṛṣṇa's body. The real situation, however, is that the body of the conditioned soul, even if he has a large accumulation of material goodness, is material, whereas Kṛṣṇa's body is never material; it is transcendental. Kṛṣṇa has no false ego, for He does not identify Himself with the false and temporary body. His body is always eternal; He descends to this world in His own original, spiritual body. This is explained in *Bhagavad-gītā* as *paraṁ bhāvam.* The words *paraṁ bhāvaṁ* and *divyam* are especially significant in understanding Kṛṣṇa's personality.

TEXT 26

एष भूतानि भूतात्मा भूतेशो भूतभावनः ।
स्वशक्त्या मायया युक्तः सृजत्यत्ति च पाति च॥२६॥

eṣa bhūtāni bhūtātmā
bhūteśo bhūta-bhāvanaḥ

sva-śaktyā māyayā yuktaḥ
sṛjaty atti ca pāti ca

eṣaḥ—this; *bhūtāni*—all created beings; *bhūta-ātmā*—the Supersoul of all living entities; *bhūta-īśaḥ*—the controller of everyone; *bhūta-bhāvanaḥ*—the maintainer of everyone; *sva-śaktyā*—through His energy; *māyayā*—the external energy; *yuktaḥ*—through such agency; *sṛjati*—creates; *atti*—annihilates; *ca*—and; *pāti*—maintains; *ca*—and.

TRANSLATION

The Supreme Personality of Godhead is the Supersoul of all living entities. He is the controller and maintainer of everyone; through the agency of His external energy, He creates, maintains and annihilates everyone.

PURPORT

There are two kinds of energies in the matter of creation. The Lord creates this material world through His external, material energy, whereas the spiritual world is a manifestation of His internal energy. He is always associated with the internal energy, but He is always aloof from the material energy. Therefore in *Bhagavad-gītā* (9.4) the Lord says, *mat-sthāni sarva-bhūtāni na cāhaṁ teṣv avasthitaḥ:* "All living entities are living on Me or on My energy, but I am not everywhere." He is personally always situated in the spiritual world. In the material world also, wherever the Supreme Lord is personally present is to be understood as being the spiritual world. For example, the Lord is worshiped in the temple by pure devotees. The temple is therefore to be understood as being the spiritual world.

TEXT 27

तमेव मृत्युममृतं तात दैवं
सर्वात्मनोपेहि जगत्परायणम् ।
यस्मै बलिं विश्वसृजो हरन्ति
गावो यथा वै नसि दामयन्त्रिताः ॥२७॥

tam eva mṛtyum amṛtaṁ tāta daivaṁ
sarvātmanopehi jagat-parāyaṇam
yasmai baliṁ viśva-sṛjo haranti
gāvo yathā vai nasi dāma-yantritāḥ

tam—unto Him; *eva*—certainly; *mṛtyum*—death; *amṛtam*—immortality; *tāta*—my dear son; *daivam*—the Supreme; *sarva-ātmanā*—in all respects; *upehi*—surrender; *jagat*—of the world; *parāyaṇam*—ultimate goal; *yasmai*—unto whom; *balim*—offerings; *viśva-sṛjaḥ*—all the demigods like Brahmā; *haranti*—bear; *gāvaḥ*—bulls; *yathā*—as; *vai*—without fail; *nasi*—in the nose; *dāma*—by a rope; *yantritāḥ*—controlled.

TRANSLATION

My dear boy Dhruva, please surrender unto the Supreme Personality of Godhead, who is the ultimate goal of the progress of the world. Everyone, including the demigods headed by Lord Brahmā, is working under His control, just as a bull, prompted by a rope in its nose, is controlled by its owner.

PURPORT

The material disease is to declare independence from the supreme controller. Factually, our material existence begins when we forget the supreme controller and wish to lord it over material nature. Everyone in the material world is trying his best to become the supreme controller—individually, nationally, socially and in many other ways. Dhruva Mahārāja was advised to stop fighting by his grandfather, who was concerned that Dhruva was adhering to a personal ambition to fight to annihilate the whole race of Yakṣas. In this verse, therefore, Svāyambhuva Manu seeks to eradicate the last tinge of false ambition in Dhruva by explaining the position of the supreme controller. The words *mṛtyum amṛtam*, "death and immortality," are significant. In *Bhagavad-gītā* the Lord says, "I am ultimate death, who takes away everything from the demons." The demons' business is to continually struggle for existence as lords over material nature. The demons repeatedly meet death after death and create a network of involvement in the material world. The Lord is death for the demons, but for devotees He is *amṛta*, eternal life.

Devotees who render continuous service to the Lord have already attained immortality, for whatever they are doing in this life they will continue to do in the next. They will simply change their material bodies for spiritual bodies. Unlike the demons, they no longer have to change material bodies. The Lord, therefore, is simultaneously death and immortality. He is death for demons and immortality for devotees. He is the ultimate goal of everyone because He is the cause of all causes. Dhruva Mahārāja was advised to surrender unto Him in all respects, without keeping any personal ambition. One may put forward the argument, "Why are the demigods worshiped?" The answer is given here that demigods are worshiped by less intelligent men. The demigods themselves accept sacrifices for the ultimate satisfaction of the Supreme Personality of Godhead.

TEXT 28

यः पञ्चवर्षो जननीं त्वं विहाय
मातुः सपत्न्या वचसा भिन्नमर्मा ।
वनं गतस्तपसा प्रत्यगक्ष-
माराध्य लेभे मूर्ध्नि पदं त्रिलोक्याः ॥२८॥

yaḥ pañca-varṣo jananīṁ tvaṁ vihāya
mātuḥ sapatnyā vacasā bhinna-marmā
vanaṁ gatas tapasā pratyag-akṣam
ārādhya lebhe mūrdhni padaṁ tri-lokyāḥ

yaḥ—one who; *pañca-varṣaḥ*—five years old; *jananīm*—mother; *tvam*—you; *vihāya*—leaving aside; *mātuḥ*—of the mother; *sa-patnyāḥ*—of the co-wife; *vacasā*—by the words; *bhinna-marmā*—aggrieved at heart; *vanam*—to the forest; *gataḥ*—went; *tapasā*—by austerity; *pratyak-akṣam*—the Supreme Lord; *ārādhya*—worshiping; *lebhe*—achieved; *mūrdhni*—on the top; *padam*—the position; *tri-lokyāḥ*—of the three worlds.

TRANSLATION

My dear Dhruva, at the age of only five years you were very grievously afflicted by the words of your mother's co-wife, and

you very boldly gave up the protection of your mother and went to the forest to engage in the yogic process for realization of the Supreme Personality of Godhead. As a result of this you have already achieved the topmost position in all the three worlds.

PURPORT

Manu was very proud that Dhruva Mahārāja was one of the descendants in his family because at the age of only five years Dhruva began meditating upon the Supreme Personality of Godhead and within six months he was able to see the Supreme Lord face to face. Factually, Dhruva Mahārāja is the glory of the Manu dynasty, or the human family. The human family begins from Manu. The Sanskrit word for man is *manuṣya*, which means "descendant of Manu." Not only is Dhruva Mahārāja the glory of the family of Svāyambhuva Manu, but he is the glory of the entire human society. Because Dhruva Mahārāja had already surrendered to the Supreme Godhead, he was especially requested not to do anything unbefitting a surrendered soul.

TEXT 29

तमेनमङ्गात्मनि मुक्तविग्रहे
व्यपाश्रितं निर्गुणमेकमक्षरम् ।
आत्मानमन्विच्छ विमुक्तमात्मदृग्
यस्मिन्निदं भेदमसत्प्रतीयते ॥२९॥

tam enam aṅgātmani mukta-vigrahe
vyapāśritaṁ nirguṇam ekam akṣaram
ātmānam anviccha vimuktam ātma-dṛg
yasminn idaṁ bhedam asat pratīyate

tam—Him; *enam*—that; *aṅga*—my dear Dhruva; *ātmani*—in the mind; *mukta-vigrahe*—free from anger; *vyapāśritam*—situated; *nirguṇam*—transcendental; *ekam*—one; *akṣaram*—the infallible Brahman; *ātmānam*—the self; *anviccha*—try to find out; *vimuktam*—uncontaminated; *ātma-dṛk*—facing towards the Supersoul; *yasmin*—in which; *idam*—this; *bhedam*—differentiation; *asat*—unreal; *pratīyate*—appears to be.

TRANSLATION

My dear Dhruva, please, therefore, turn your attention to the Supreme Person, who is the infallible Brahman. Face the Supreme Personality of Godhead in your original position, and thus, by self-realization, you will find this material differentiation to be merely flickering.

PURPORT

The living entities have three kinds of vision, according to their positions in self-realization. According to the bodily concept of life, one sees differentiation in terms of varieties of bodies. The living entity actually passes through many varieties of material forms, but despite all such changes of body, he is eternal. When living entities, therefore, are viewed in the bodily concept of life, one appears to be different from another. Lord Manu wanted to change the vision of Dhruva Mahārāja, who was looking upon the Yakṣas as different from him or as his enemies. Factually no one is an enemy or a friend. Everyone is passing through different types of bodies under the law of *karma*, but as soon as one is situated in his spiritual identity, he does not see differentiation in terms of this law. In other words, as stated in *Bhagavad-gītā* (18.54):

brahma-bhūtaḥ prasannātmā
na śocati na kāṅkṣati
samaḥ sarveṣu bhūteṣu
mad-bhaktiṁ labhate parām

A devotee, who is already liberated, does not see differentiation in terms of the outward body; he sees all living entities as spirit souls, eternal servants of the Lord. Dhruva Mahārāja was advised by Lord Manu to see with that vision. He was specifically advised to do so because he was a great devotee and should not have looked upon other living entities with ordinary vision. Indirectly Manu pointed out to Dhruva Mahārāja that out of material affection Dhruva thought of his brother as his kin and the Yakṣas as his enemies. Such observation of differentiation subsides as soon as one is situated in his original position as an eternal servant of the Lord.

TEXT 30

त्वं प्रत्यगात्मनि तदा भगवत्यनन्त
आनन्दमात्र उपपन्नसमस्तशक्तौ ।
भक्तिं विधाय परमां शनकैरविद्या-
ग्रन्थिं विभेत्स्यसि ममाहमिति प्ररूढम् ॥३०॥

tvaṁ pratyag-ātmani tadā bhagavaty ananta
ānanda-mātra upapanna-samasta-śaktau
bhaktiṁ vidhāya paramāṁ śanakair avidyā-
granthiṁ vibhetsyasi mamāham iti prarūḍham

tvam—you; *pratyak-ātmani*—unto the Supersoul; *tadā*—at that time; *bhagavati*—unto the Supreme Personality of Godhead; *anante*—who is unlimited; *ānanda-mātre*—the reservoir of all pleasure; *upapanna*—possessed of; *samasta*—all; *śaktau*—potencies; *bhaktim*—devotional service; *vidhāya*—by rendering; *paramām*—supreme; *śanakaiḥ*—very soon; *avidyā*—of illusion; *granthim*—the knot; *vibhetsyasi*—you will undo; *mama*—my; *aham*—I; *iti*—thus; *prarūḍham*—firmly fixed.

TRANSLATION

Thus regaining your natural position and rendering service unto the Supreme Lord, who is the all-powerful reservoir of all pleasure and who lives in all living entities as the Supersoul, you will very soon forget the illusory understanding of "I" and "my."

PURPORT

Dhruva Mahārāja was already a liberated person because at the age of five years he had seen the Supreme Personality of Godhead. But even though liberated, he was, for the time being, afflicted by the illusion of *māyā*, thinking himself the brother of Uttama in the bodily concept of life. The whole material world is working on the basis of "I" and "mine." This is the root of attraction to the material world. If one is attracted by this root of illusory conceptions—"I" and "mine"—he will have to remain within this material world in different exalted or nasty positions. By the grace of Lord Kṛṣṇa, the sages and Lord Manu reminded Dhruva Mahārāja that he should not continue this material conception of "I" and "mine." Simply by devotional service unto the Lord his illusion could be eradicated without difficulty.

TEXT 31

संयच्छ रोषं भद्रं ते प्रतीपं श्रेयसां परम् ।
श्रुतेन भूयसा राजन्नगदेन यथामयम् ॥३१॥

saṁyaccha roṣaṁ bhadraṁ te
pratīpaṁ śreyasāṁ param
śrutena bhūyasā rājann
agadena yathāmayam

saṁyaccha—just control; *roṣam*—anger; *bhadram*—all good fortune; *te*—to you; *pratīpam*—enemy; *śreyasām*—of all goodness; *param*—the foremost; *śrutena*—by hearing; *bhūyasā*—constantly; *rājan*—my dear King; *agadena*—by medicinal treatment; *yathā*—as; *āmayam*—disease.

TRANSLATION

My dear King, just consider what I have said to you, which will act as medicinal treatment upon disease. Control your anger, for anger is the foremost enemy on the path of spiritual realization. I wish all good fortune for you. Please follow my instructions.

PURPORT

Dhruva Mahārāja was a liberated soul, and actually he was not angry with anyone. But because he was the ruler, it was his duty to become angry for some time in order to keep law and order in the state. His brother, Uttama, was without fault, yet he was killed by one of the Yakṣas. It was the duty of Dhruva Mahārāja to kill the offender (life for life) because Dhruva was the king. When the challenge came, Dhruva Mahārāja fought vehemently and punished the Yakṣas sufficiently. But anger is such that if one increases it, it increases unlimitedly. In order that Dhruva Mahārāja's kingly anger not exceed the limit, Manu was kind enough to check his grandson. Dhruva Mahārāja could understand the purpose of his grandfather, and he immediately stopped the fighting. The words *śrutena bhūyasā*, "by constantly hearing," are very important in this verse. By constantly hearing about devotional service, one can check the force of anger, which is detrimental to the process of devotional service. Śrīla Parīkṣit Mahārāja said that the constant hearing of the pastimes of the Lord is the panacea for all material diseases. Everyone, therefore, should hear about the Supreme Personality of Godhead constantly. By hearing one can always remain in equilibrium, and thus his progress in spiritual life will not be hampered.

Dhruva Mahārāja's becoming angry with the miscreants was quite appropriate. There is a short story in this connection about a snake who became a devotee upon instruction by Nārada, who instructed him not to bite anymore. Since ordinarily a snake's business is to fatally bite other living entities, as a devotee he was forbidden to do so. Unfortunately, people took advantage of this nonviolence on the part of the snake, especially the children, who began to throw stones at him. He did not bite anyone, however, because it was the instruction of his spiritual master. After a while, when the snake met his spiritual master, Nārada, he complained, "I have given up the bad habit of biting innocent living entities, but they are mistreating me by throwing stones at me." Upon hearing this, Nārada Muni instructed him, "Don't bite, but do not forget to expand your hood as if you were going to bite. Then they will go away." Similarly, a devotee is always nonviolent; he is qualified with all good characteristics. But, in the common world, when there is mischief made by others, he should not forget to become angry, at least for the time being, in order to drive away the miscreants.

TEXT 32

येनोपसृष्टात्पुरुषाल्लोक उद्विजते भृशम् ।
न बुधस्तद्वशं गच्छेदिच्छन्नभयमात्मनः ॥३२॥

yenopasṛṣṭāt puruṣāl
loka udvijate bhṛśam
na budhas tad-vaśaṁ gacched
icchann abhayam ātmanaḥ

yena—by which; *upasṛṣṭāt*—being overwhelmed; *puruṣāt*—by the person; *lokaḥ*—everyone; *udvijate*—becomes terrified; *bhṛśam*—greatly; *na*—never; *budhaḥ*—a learned person; *tat*—of anger; *vaśam*—under the control; *gacchet*—should go; *icchan*—desiring; *abhayam*—fearlessness, liberation; *ātmanaḥ*—of the self.

TRANSLATION

A person who desires liberation from this material world should not fall under the control of anger because when bewildered by anger one becomes a source of dread for all others.

PURPORT

A devotee or saintly person should not be dreadful to others, nor should anyone be a source of dread to him. If one treats others with non-enmity, then no one will become his enemy. There is the example, however, of Jesus Christ, who had enemies, and they crucified him. The demonic are always present, and they find fault even in saintly persons. But a saintly person never becomes angry, even if there is very great provocation.

TEXT 33

हेलनं गिरिशभ्रातुर्धनदस्य त्वया कृतम् ।
यज्जघ्निवान् पुण्यजनान् भ्रातृघ्नानित्यमर्षितः ॥३३॥

helanaṁ giriśa-bhrātur
dhanadasya tvayā kṛtam
yaj jaghnivān puṇya-janān
bhrātṛ-ghnān ity amarṣitaḥ

helanam—disrespectful behavior; *giriśa*—of Lord Śiva; *bhrātuḥ*—the brother; *dhanadasya*—to Kuvera; *tvayā*—by you; *kṛtam*—was performed; *yat*—because; *jaghnivān*—you have killed; *puṇya-janān*—the Yakṣas; *bhrātṛ*—of your brother; *ghnān*—killers; *iti*—thus (thinking); *amarṣitaḥ*—angry.

TRANSLATION

My dear Dhruva, you thought that the Yakṣas killed your brother, and therefore you have killed great numbers of them. But by this action you have agitated the mind of Lord Śiva's brother Kuvera, who is the treasurer of the demigods. Please note that your actions have been very disrespectful to Kuvera and Lord Śiva.

PURPORT

Lord Manu stated that Dhruva Mahārāja had been offensive to Lord Śiva and his brother Kuvera because the Yakṣas belonged to Kuvera's family. They were not ordinary persons. As such, they have been described as *puṇya-janān*, pious men. Somehow or other the mind of Kuvera had been agitated, and Dhruva Mahārāja was advised to pacify him.

TEXT 34

तं प्रसादय वत्साशु संनत्या प्रश्रयोक्तिभिः ।
न यावन्महतां तेजः कुलं नोऽभिभविष्यति ॥३४॥

taṁ prasādaya vatsāśu
sannatyā praśrayoktibhiḥ
na yāvan mahatāṁ tejaḥ
kulaṁ no 'bhibhaviṣyati

tam—him; *prasādaya*—pacify; *vatsa*—my son; *āśu*—immediately; *sannatyā*—by offering obeisances; *praśrayā*—by respectful behavior; *uktibhiḥ*—by gentle words; *na yāvat*—before; *mahatām*—of great personalities; *tejaḥ*—wrath; *kulam*—family; *naḥ*—our; *abhibhaviṣyati*—will affect.

TRANSLATION

For this reason, my son, you should immediately pacify Kuvera with gentle words and prayers, and thus his wrath may not affect our family.

PURPORT

In our common dealings we should maintain friendship with everyone and certainly with such exalted demigods as Kuvera. Our behavior should be such that no one should become angry and thereby commit a wrong to individuals, families or society.

TEXT 35

एवं स्वायम्भुवः पौत्रमनुशास्य मनुर्ध्रुवम् ।
तेनाभिवन्दितः साकमृषिभिः स्वपुरं ययौ ॥३५॥

evaṁ svāyambhuvaḥ pautram
anuśāsya manur dhruvam
tenābhivanditaḥ sākam
ṛṣibhiḥ sva-puraṁ yayau

evam—thus; *svāyambhuvaḥ*—Lord Svāyambhuva Manu; *pautram*—to his grandson; *anuśāsya*—after giving instruction; *manuḥ*—Lord Manu; *dhruvam*—to Dhruva Mahārāja; *tena*—by him; *abhivanditaḥ*—being offered obeisances to; *sākam*—together; *ṛṣibhiḥ*—with the sages; *sva-puram*—to his own abode; *yayau*—went.

TRANSLATION

Thus Svāyambhuva Manu, after giving instruction to Dhruva Mahārāja, his grandson, received respectful obeisances from him. Then Lord Manu and the great sages went back to their respective homes.

Thus end the Bhaktivedanta purports of the Fourth Canto, Eleventh Chapter, of the Śrīmad-Bhāgavatam, *entitled "Svāyambhuva Manu Advises Dhruva Mahārāja to Stop Fighting."*

CHAPTER TWELVE

Dhruva Mahārāja Goes Back to Godhead

TEXT 1

मैत्रेय उवाच
ध्रुवं निवृत्तं प्रतिबुद्ध्य वैशसा-
दपेतमन्युं भगवान् धनेश्वरः ।
तत्रागतश्चारणयक्षकिन्नरैः
संस्तूयमानो न्यवदत्कृताञ्जलिम् ॥ १ ॥

maitreya uvāca
dhruvaṁ nivṛttaṁ pratibuddhya vaiśasād
apeta-manyuṁ bhagavān dhaneśvaraḥ
tatrāgataś cāraṇa-yakṣa-kinnaraiḥ
saṁstūyamāno nyavadat kṛtāñjalim

maitreyaḥ uvāca—Maitreya said; *dhruvam*—Dhruva Mahārāja; *nivṛttam*—ceased; *pratibuddhya*—having learned; *vaiśasāt*—from killing; *apeta*—subsided; *manyum*—anger; *bhagavān*—Kuvera; *dhana-īśvaraḥ*—master of the treasury; *tatra*—there; *āgataḥ*—appeared; *cāraṇa*—by the Cāraṇas; *yakṣa*—Yakṣas; *kinnaraiḥ*—and by the Kinnaras; *saṁstūyamānaḥ*—being worshiped; *nyavadat*—spoke; *kṛta-añjalim*—to Dhruva with folded hands.

TRANSLATION

The great sage Maitreya said: My dear Vidura, Dhruva Mahārāja's anger subsided, and he completely ceased killing Yakṣas. When Kuvera, the most blessed master of the treasury, learned this news, he appeared before Dhruva. While being worshiped by Yakṣas, Kinnaras and Cāraṇas, he spoke to Dhruva Mahārāja, who stood before him with folded hands.

TEXT 2

धनद उवाच
भो भोः क्षत्रियदायाद परितुष्टोऽस्मि तेऽनघ ।
यत्त्वं पितामहादेशाद्वैरं दुस्त्यजमत्यजः ॥ २ ॥

dhanada uvāca
bho bhoḥ kṣatriya-dāyāda
parituṣṭo 'smi te 'nagha
yat tvaṁ pitāmahādeśād
vairaṁ dustyajam atyajaḥ

dhana-daḥ uvāca—the master of the treasury (Kuvera) said; *bhoḥ bhoḥ*—O; *kṣatriya-dāyāda*—O son of a *kṣatriya; parituṣṭaḥ*—very glad; *asmi*—I am; *te*—with you; *anagha*—O sinless one; *yat*—because; *tvam*—you; *pitāmaha*—of your grandfather; *ādeśāt*—under the instruction; *vairam*—enmity; *dustyajam*—difficult to avoid; *atyajaḥ*—have given up.

TRANSLATION

The master of the treasury, Kuvera, said: O sinless son of a kṣatriya, I am very glad to know that under the instruction of your grandfather you have given up your enmity, although it is very difficult to avoid. I am very pleased with you.

TEXT 3

न भवानवधीद्यक्षान्न यक्षा भ्रातरं तव ।
काल एव हि भूतानां प्रभुरप्ययभावयोः ॥ ३ ॥

na bhavān avadhīd yakṣān
na yakṣā bhrātaraṁ tava
kāla eva hi bhūtānāṁ
prabhur apyaya-bhāvayoḥ

na—not; *bhavān*—you; *avadhīt*—killed; *yakṣān*—the Yakṣas; *na*—not; *yakṣāḥ*—the Yakṣas; *bhrātaram*—brother; *tava*—your; *kālaḥ*—

time; *eva*—certainly; *hi*—for; *bhūtānām*—of living entities; *prabhuḥ*—the Supreme Lord; *apyaya-bhāvayoḥ*—of annihilation and generation.

TRANSLATION

Actually, you have not killed the Yakṣas, nor have they killed your brother, for the ultimate cause of generation and annihilation is the eternal time feature of the Supreme Lord.

PURPORT

When the master of the treasury addressed him as sinless, Dhruva Mahārāja, considering himself responsible for killing so many Yakṣas, might have thought himself otherwise. Kuvera, however, assured him that factually he had not killed any of the Yakṣas; therefore, he was not at all sinful. He did his duty as a king, as it is ordered by the laws of nature. "Nor should you think that your brother was killed by the Yakṣas," said Kuvera. "He died or was killed in due course of time by the laws of nature. Eternal time, one of the features of the Lord, is ultimately responsible for annihilation and generation. You are not responsible for such actions."

TEXT 4

अहं त्वमित्यपार्था धीरज्ञानात्पुरुषस्य हि ।
स्वाप्नीवाभात्यतद्ध्यानाद्यया बन्धविपर्ययौ ॥ ४ ॥

ahaṁ tvam ity apārthā dhīr
ajñānāt puruṣasya hi
svāpnīvābhāty atad-dhyānād
yayā bandha-viparyayau

aham—I; *tvam*—you; *iti*—thus; *apārthā*—misconceived; *dhīḥ*—intelligence; *ajñānāt*—from ignorance; *puruṣasya*—of a person; *hi*—certainly; *svāpni*—a dream; *iva*—like; *ābhāti*—appears; *a-tat-dhyānāt*—from the bodily concept of life; *yayā*—by which; *bandha*—bondage; *viparyayau*—and misery.

TRANSLATION

Misidentification of oneself and others as "I" and "you" on the basis of the bodily concept of life is a product of ignorance. This bodily concept is the cause of repeated birth and death, and it makes us go on continuously in material existence.

PURPORT

The conception of "I" and "you," *ahaṁ tvam,* as separate from each other, is due to our forgetfulness of our eternal relationship with the Supreme Personality of Godhead. The Supreme Person, Kṛṣṇa, is the central point, and all of us are His parts and parcels, just as hands and legs are parts and parcels of the whole body. When we actually come to this understanding of being eternally related to the Supreme Lord, this distinction, which is based on the bodily concept of life, cannot exist. The same example can be cited herewith: the hand is the hand, and the leg is the leg, but when both of them engage in the service of the whole body, there is no such distinction as "hands" and "legs," for all of them belong to the whole body, and all the parts working together constitute the whole body. Similarly, when the living entities are in Kṛṣṇa consciousness, there is no such distinction as "I" and "you" because everyone is engaged in the service of the Lord. Since the Lord is absolute, the services are also absolute; even though the hand is working one way and the leg is working in another way, since the purpose is the Supreme Personality of Godhead, they are all one. This is not to be confused with the statement by the Māyāvādī philosopher that "everything is one." Real knowledge is that hand is hand, leg is leg, body is body, and yet all together they are one. As soon as the living entity thinks that he is independent, his conditional, material existence begins. The conception of independent existence is therefore like a dream. One has to be in Kṛṣṇa consciousness, his original position. Then he can be freed from material bondage.

TEXT 5

तद्गच्छ ध्रुव भद्रं ते भगवन्तमधोक्षजम् ।
सर्वभूतात्मभावेन सर्वभूतात्मविग्रहम् ॥ ५ ॥

tad gaccha dhruva bhadraṁ te
bhagavantam adhokṣajam
sarva-bhūtātma-bhāvena
sarva-bhūtātma-vigraham

tat—therefore; *gaccha*—come; *dhruva*—Dhruva; *bhadram*—good fortune; *te*—unto you; *bhagavantam*—unto the Supreme Personality of Godhead; *adhokṣajam*—who is beyond the concepts of material senses; *sarva-bhūta*—all living entities; *ātma-bhāvena*—by thinking of them as one; *sarva-bhūta*—in all living entities; *ātma*—the Supersoul; *vigraham*—having form.

TRANSLATION

My dear Dhruva, come forward. May the Lord always grace you with good fortune. The Supreme Personality of Godhead, who is beyond our sensory perception, is the Supersoul of all living entities, and thus all entities are one, without distinction. Begin, therefore, to render service unto the transcendental form of the Lord, who is the ultimate shelter of all living entities.

PURPORT

Here the word *vigraham*, "having specific form," is very significant, for it indicates that the Absolute Truth is ultimately the Supreme Personality of Godhead. That is explained in the *Brahma-saṁhitā. Sac-cid-ānanda-vigrahaḥ:* He has form, but His form is different from any kind of material form. The living entities are the marginal energy of the supreme form. As such, they are not different from the supreme form, but at the same time they are not equal to the supreme form. Dhruva Mahārāja is advised herewith to render service unto the supreme form. That will include service to other individual forms. For example, a tree has a form, and when water is poured on the root of the tree, the other forms—the leaves, twigs, flowers and fruits—are automatically watered. The Māyāvāda conception that because the Absolute Truth is everything He must be formless is rejected here. Rather, it is confirmed that the Absolute Truth has form, and yet He is all-pervading. Nothing is independent of Him.

TEXT 6

भजस्व भजनीयाङ्घ्रिमभवाय भवच्छिदम् ।
युक्तं विरहितं शक्त्या गुणमय्यात्ममायया ॥ ६ ॥

bhajasva bhajanīyāṅghrim
abhavāya bhava-cchidam
yuktaṁ virahitaṁ śaktyā
guṇa-mayyātma-māyayā

bhajasva—engage in devotional service; *bhajanīya*—worthy to be worshiped; *aṅghrim*—unto Him whose lotus feet; *abhavāya*—for deliverance from material existence; *bhava-chidam*—who cuts the knot of material entanglement; *yuktam*—attached; *virahitam*—aloof; *śaktyā*—to His potency; *guṇa-mayyā*—consisting of the modes of material nature; *ātma-māyayā*—by His inconceivable potency.

TRANSLATION

Engage yourself fully, therefore, in the devotional service of the Lord, for only He can deliver us from this entanglement of materialistic existence. Although the Lord is attached to His material potency, He is aloof from her activities. Everything in this material world is happening by the inconceivable potency of the Supreme Personality of Godhead.

PURPORT

In continuation of the previous verse, it is specifically mentioned here that Dhruva Mahārāja should engage himself in devotional service. Devotional service cannot be rendered to the impersonal Brahman feature of the Supreme Personality of Godhead. Whenever the word *bhajasva* appears, meaning "engage yourself in devotional service," there must be the servant, service and the served. The Supreme Personality of Godhead is served, the mode of activities to please Him is called service, and one who renders such service is called the servant. Another significant feature in this verse is that only the Lord, and no one else, is to be served. That is confirmed in the *Bhagavad-gītā* (*māṁ ekaṁ śaraṇaṁ vraja*). There is no need to serve the demigods, who are just like the hands and legs of the Supreme Lord. When the Supreme Lord is served, the hands and legs of the Supreme Lord are automatically served. There is no need of separate service. As stated in *Bhagavad-gītā* (12.7), *teṣām ahaṁ samuddhartā mṛtyu-saṁsāra-sāgarāt.* This means that the Lord, in order to show specific favor to the devotee, directs the devotee from within in such a way that ultimately he is delivered from the entanglement of material existence. No one but the Supreme Lord can help the living entity be delivered from the entanglement of this material world. The material energy is a manifestation of one of the Supreme Personality of Godhead's varieties of potencies (*parāsya śaktir vividhaiva śrūyate*). This material energy is one of the Lord's potencies, as much as heat and light are potencies of fire. The material energy is not different from the Supreme Godhead, but at the same time He has nothing to do with the material energy. The living entity, who is of the marginal energy, is entrapped by the material energy on the basis of his desire to lord it over the material world. The Lord is aloof from this, but when the same living entity engages himself in the devotional service of the Lord, then he becomes attached to this service. This situation is called *yuktam.* For devotees the Lord is present even in the material energy. This is the inconceivable potency of the Lord. Material energy acts in the three modes of material qualities, which produce the action and reaction of material existence. Those who are not devotees become involved in such activities, whereas devotees, who are dovetailed with the Supreme Personality of Godhead, are freed from such action and reaction of the material energy. The Lord is therefore described herewith as *bhavacchidam,* one who can give deliverance from the entanglement of material existence.

TEXT 7

वृणीहि कामं नृप यन्मनोगतं
मत्तस्त्वमौत्तानपदेऽविशङ्कितः ।
वरं वरार्होऽम्बुजनाभपादयो-
रनन्तरं त्वां वयमङ्ग शुश्रुम ॥७॥

vṛṇīhi kāmaṁ nṛpa yan mano-gataṁ
mattas tvam auttānapade 'viśaṅkitaḥ
varaṁ varārho 'mbuja-nābha-pādayor
anantaraṁ tvāṁ vayam aṅga śuśruma

vṛṇīhi—please ask; *kāmam*—desire; *nṛpa*—O King; *yat*—whatever; *manaḥ-gatam*—within your mind; *mattaḥ*—from me; *tvam*—you; *auttānapade*—O son of Mahārāja Uttānapāda; *aviśaṅkitaḥ*—without hesitation; *varam*—benediction; *vara-arhaḥ*—worthy to take benedictions; *ambuja*—lotus flower; *nābha*—whose navel; *pādayoḥ*—at His lotus feet; *anantaram*—constantly; *tvām*—about you; *vayam*—we; *aṅga*—dear Dhruva; *śuśruma*—have heard.

TRANSLATION

My dear Dhruva Mahārāja, son of Mahārāja Uttānapāda, we have heard that you are constantly engaged in transcendental loving service to the Supreme Personality of Godhead, who is known for His lotus navel. You are therefore worthy to take all benedictions from us. Please, therefore, ask without hesitation whatever benediction you want from me.

PURPORT

Dhruva Mahārāja, the son of King Uttānapāda, was already known throughout the universe as a great devotee of the Lord, constantly thinking of His lotus feet. Such a pure, uncontaminated devotee of the Lord is worthy to have all the benedictions that can be offered by the demigods. He does not have to worship the demigods separately for such benedictions. Kuvera is the treasurer of the demigods, and he is personally offering whatever benediction Dhruva Mahārāja would like to have from him. Śrīla Bilvamaṅgala Ṭhākura stated, therefore, that for persons who engage in the devotional service of the Lord, all material benedictions wait like maidservants. Mukti-devī is just waiting at the door of the devotee to offer liberation, or more than that, at any time. To be a devotee is therefore an exalted position. Simply by rendering transcendental loving service unto the Supreme Personality of Godhead, one can have all the benedictions of the world without separate endeavor. Lord Kuvera said to Dhruva Mahārāja that he had heard that Dhruva was always in *samādhi*, or thinking of the lotus feet of the Lord. In other words, he knew that for Dhruva Mahārāja there was nothing desirable within the three material worlds. He knew that Dhruva would ask for nothing but to remember the lotus feet of the Supreme Lord constantly.

TEXT 8

मैत्रेय उवाच
स राजराजेन वराय चोदितो
ध्रुवो महाभागवतो महामतिः ।
हरौ स वव्रेऽचलितां स्मृतिं यया
तरत्ययत्नेन दुरत्ययं तमः ॥ ८ ॥

maitreya uvāca
sa rāja-rājena varāya codito
dhruvo mahā-bhāgavato mahā-matiḥ
harau sa vavre 'calitāṁ smṛtiṁ yayā
taraty ayatnena duratyayaṁ tamaḥ

maitreyaḥ uvāca—the great sage Maitreya said; *saḥ*—he; *rāja-rājena*—by the king of kings (Kuvera); *varāya*—for a benediction; *coditaḥ*—being asked; *dhruvaḥ*—Dhruva Mahārāja; *mahā-bhāgavataḥ*—a first-class pure devotee; *mahā-matiḥ*—most intelligent or thoughtful; *harau*—unto the Supreme Personality of Godhead; *saḥ*—he; *vavre*—asked; *acalitām*—unflinching; *smṛtim*—remembrance; *yayā*—by which; *tarati*—crosses over; *ayatnena*—without difficulty; *duratyayam*—unsurpassable; *tamaḥ*—nescience.

TRANSLATION

The great sage Maitreya continued: My dear Vidura, when thus asked to accept a benediction from Kuvera the Yakṣarāja [King of the Yakṣas], Dhruva Mahārāja, that most elevated pure devotee, who was an intelligent and thoughtful king, begged that he might have unflinching faith in and remembrance of the Supreme Personality of Godhead, for thus a person can cross over the ocean of nescience very easily, although it is very difficult for others to cross.

PURPORT

According to the opinion of expert followers of Vedic rites, there are different types of benedictions in terms of religiosity, economic development, sense gratification and liberation. These four principles are known as *catur-vargas*. Of all the *catur-vargas*, the benediction of liberation is considered to be the highest in this material world. To be enabled to cross over material nescience is known as the highest *puruṣārtha*, or benediction for the human being. But Dhruva Mahārāja wanted a benediction which surpasses even the highest *puruṣārtha*, liberation. He wanted the benediction that he might constantly remember the lotus feet of the Lord. This stage of life is called *pañcama-puruṣārtha*. When a devotee comes to the platform of *pañcama-puruṣārtha*, simply engaging in devotional service to the Lord, the fourth *puruṣārtha*, liberation, becomes very insignificant in his eyes. Śrīla Prabodhānanda Sarasvatī has stated in this connection that for a devotee liberation is a hellish condition of life; as for sense gratification, which is available in the heavenly planets, the devotee considers it to be a will-o'-the-wisp, having no value in life. *Yogīs* endeavor to control the senses, but for a devotee controlling the senses is no difficulty at all. The senses are compared to serpents, but for a devotee the serpents' poison teeth are broken. Thus Śrīla Prabodhānanda Sarasvatī has analyzed all kinds of benedictions available in this world, and he has clearly declared that for a pure devotee they are all of no significance. Dhruva Mahārāja was also a *mahā-bhāgavata*, or a first-class pure devotee, and his intelligence was very great (*mahā-matiḥ*). Unless one is very intelligent, one cannot take to devotional service, or Kṛṣṇa consciousness. Naturally, anyone who is a first-class devotee must be a first-class intelligent person and therefore not interested in any kind of benediction within this material world. Dhruva Mahārāja was offered a benediction by the king of the kings. Kuvera, the treasurer of the demigods, whose only business is to supply immense riches to persons within this materialistic world, is described as the king of kings because unless one is blessed by Kuvera one cannot become a king. The king of kings personally offered Dhruva Mahārāja any amount of riches, but he declined to accept them. He is described, therefore, as *mahā-matiḥ*, very thoughtful, or highly intellectual.

TEXT 9

तस्य प्रीतेन मनसा तां दत्त्वैडविडस्ततः ।
पश्यतोऽन्तर्दधे सोऽपि स्वपुरं प्रत्यपद्यत ॥ ९ ॥

tasya prītena manasā
tāṁ dattvaiḍaviḍas tataḥ
paśyato 'ntardadhe so 'pi
sva-puraṁ pratyapadyata

tasya—with Dhruva; *prītena*—being very pleased; *manasā*—with such a mentality; *tām*—that remembrance; *dattvā*—having given; *aiḍaviḍaḥ*—Kuvera, son of Iḍaviḍā; *tataḥ*—thereafter; *paśyataḥ*—while Dhruva was looking on; *antardadhe*—disappeared; *saḥ*—he (Dhruva); *api*—also; *sva-puram*—to his city; *pratyapadyata*—returned.

TRANSLATION

The son of Iḍaviḍā, Lord Kuvera, was very pleased, and happily he gave Dhruva Mahārāja the benediction he wanted. Thereafter he disappeared from Dhruva's presence, and Dhruva Mahārāja returned to his capital city.

PURPORT

Kuvera, who is known as the son of Iḍaviḍā, was very pleased with Dhruva Mahārāja because he did not ask him for anything materially enjoyable. Kuvera is one of the demigods, so one may put forward the argument, "Why did Dhruva Mahārāja take a benediction from a demigod?" The answer is that for a Vaiṣṇava there is no objection to taking a benediction from a demigod if it is favorable for advancing Kṛṣṇa consciousness. The *gopīs*, for example, worshiped Kātyāyanī, a demigoddess, but the only benediction they wanted from the goddess was to have Kṛṣṇa as their husband. A Vaiṣṇava is not interested in asking any benediction from the demigods, nor is he interested in asking benedictions from the Supreme Personality of Godhead. It is said in the *Bhāgavatam* that liberation can be offered by the Supreme Person, but even if a pure devotee is offered liberation by the Supreme Lord, he refuses to accept it. Dhruva Mahārāja did not ask Kuvera for transference to the spiritual world, which is called liberation; he simply asked that wherever he would remain—whether in the spiritual or material world—he would always remember the Supreme Personality of

Godhead. A Vaiṣṇava is always respectful to everyone. So when Kuvera offered him a benediction, he did not refuse it. But he wanted something which would be favorable to his advancement in Kṛṣṇa consciousness.

TEXT 10

अथायजत यज्ञेशं क्रतुभिर्भूरिदक्षिणैः ।
द्रव्यक्रियादेवतानां कर्म कर्मफलप्रदम् ॥१०॥

athāyajata yajñeśaṁ
kratubhir bhūri-dakṣiṇaiḥ
dravya-kriyā-devatānāṁ
karma karma-phala-pradam

atha—thereafter; *ayajata*—he worshiped; *yajña-īśam*—the master of sacrifices; *kratubhiḥ*—by sacrificial ceremonies; *bhūri*—great; *dakṣiṇaiḥ*—by charities; *dravya-kriyā-devatānām*—of (sacrifices including various) paraphernalia, activities and demigods; *karma*—the objective; *karma-phala*—the result of activities; *pradam*—who awards.

TRANSLATION

As long as he remained at home, Dhruva Mahārāja performed many great ceremonial sacrifices in order to please the enjoyer of all sacrifices, the Supreme Personality of Godhead. Prescribed ceremonial sacrifices are especially meant to please Lord Viṣṇu, who is the objective of all such sacrifices and who awards the resultant benedictions.

PURPORT

In *Bhagavad-gītā* (3.9) it is said, *yajñārthāt karmaṇo 'nyatra loko 'yaṁ karma-bandhanaḥ:* one should act or work only in order to please the Supreme Lord, otherwise one becomes entangled in the resultant reactions. According to the four divisions of *varṇa* and *āśrama, kṣatriyas* and *vaiśyas* are especially advised to perform great ceremonial sacrifices and to distribute their accumulated money very liberally. Dhruva Mahārāja, as a king and ideal *kṣatriya,* performed many such sacrifices, giving very liberally in charity. *Kṣatriyas* and *vaiśyas* are supposed to earn their money and accumulate great riches. Sometimes they do it by acting sinfully. *Kṣatriyas* are meant to rule over a country; Dhruva Mahārāja, for example, in the course of ruling, had to fight and kill many Yakṣas. Such action is necessary for *kṣatriyas*. A *kṣatriya* should not be a coward, and he should not be nonviolent; to rule over the country he has to act violently.

Kṣatriyas and *vaiśyas* are therefore especially advised to give in charity at least fifty percent of their accumulated wealth. In *Bhagavad-gītā* it is recommended that even though one enters the renounced order of life, he still cannot give up the performance of *yajña*, *dāna* and *tapasya*. They are never to be given up. *Tapasya* is meant for the renounced order of life; those who are retired from worldly activities should perform *tapasya*, penances and austerities. Those who are in the material world, the *kṣatriyas* and *vaiśyas*, must give charity. *Brahmacārīs*, in the beginning of their lives, should perform different kinds of *yajñas*.

Dhruva Mahārāja, as an ideal king, practically emptied his treasury by giving charity. A king is not meant simply to realize taxes from the citizens and accumulate wealth to spend in sense gratification. World monarchy has failed ever since kings began to satisfy their personal senses with the taxes accumulated from the citizens. Of course, whether the system is monarchy or democracy, the same corruption is still going on. At the present moment there are different parties in the democratic government, but everyone is busy trying to keep his post or trying to keep his political party in power. The politicians have very little time to think of the welfare of the citizens, whom they oppress with heavy taxes in the form of income tax, sales tax and many other taxes—people sometimes have eighty to ninety percent of their income taken away, and these taxes are lavishly spent for the high salaries drawn by the officers and rulers. Formerly, the taxes accumulated from the citizens were spent for performing great sacrifices as enjoined in the Vedic literature. At the present moment, however, almost all forms of sacrifice are not at all possible; therefore, it is recommended in the *śāstras* that people should perform *saṅkīrtana-yajña*. Any householder, regardless of his position, can perform this *saṅkīrtana-yajña* without expenditure. All the family members can sit down together and simply clap their hands and chant the Hare Kṛṣṇa *mahā-mantra*. Somehow or other, everyone can manage to perform such a *yajña* and distribute *prasāda* to the people in general. That is quite sufficient for this age of Kali. The Kṛṣṇa consciousness movement is based on this principle: chant the Hare Kṛṣṇa *mantra* at every moment, as much as possible, both inside and outside of the temples, and, as far as possible, distribute *prasāda.* This process can be accelerated with the cooperation of state administrators and those who are producing the country's wealth. Simply by liberal distribution of *prasāda* and *saṅkīrtana,* the whole world can become peaceful and prosperous.

Generally in all the material sacrifices recommended in the Vedic literature there are offerings to the demigods. This demigod worship is especially meant for less intelligent men. Actually, the result of such sacrifice goes to the Supreme Personality of Godhead, Nārāyaṇa. Lord Kṛṣṇa says in *Bhagavad-gītā* (5.29), *bhoktāraṁ yajña-tapasām:* He is actually the enjoyer of all sacrifices. His name, therefore, is Yajña-puruṣa.

Although Dhruva Mahārāja was a great devotee and had nothing to do with these sacrifices, to set an example to his people he performed many sacrifices and gave all his wealth in charity. For as long as he lived as a householder, he never spent a farthing for his sense gratification. In this verse the word *karma-phala-pradam* is very significant. The Lord awards everyone different kinds of *karma* as the individual living entities desire; He is the Supersoul present within the heart of everyone, and He is so kind and liberal that He gives everyone full facilities to perform whatever acts one wants. Then the result of the action is also enjoyed by the living entity. If anyone wants to enjoy or lord it over material nature, the Lord gives him full facilities, but he becomes entangled in the resultant reactions. Similarly, if anyone wants to engage himself fully in devotional service, the Lord gives him full facilities, and the devotee enjoys the results. The Lord is therefore known as *karma-phala-prada.*

TEXT 11

सर्वात्मन्यच्युतेऽसर्वे तीव्रौघां भक्तिमुद्वहन् ।
ददर्शात्मनि भूतेषु तमेवावस्थितं विभुम् ॥११॥

sarvātmany acyute 'sarve
tīvraughāṁ bhaktim udvahan

dadarśātmani bhūteṣu
tam evāvasthitaṁ vibhum

sarva-ātmani—unto the Supersoul; *acyute*—infallible; *asarve*—without any limit; *tīvra-oghām*—with unrelenting force; *bhaktim*—devotional service; *udvahan*—rendering; *dadarśa*—he saw; *ātmani*—in the Supreme Spirit; *bhūteṣu*—in all living entities; *tam*—Him; *eva*—only; *avasthitam*—situated; *vibhum*—all-powerful.

TRANSLATION

Dhruva Mahārāja rendered devotional service unto the Supreme, the reservoir of everything, with unrelenting force. While carrying out his devotional service to the Lord, he could see that everything is situated in Him only and that He is situated in all living entities. The Lord is called Acyuta because He never fails in His prime duty, to give protection to His devotees.

PURPORT

Not only did Dhruva Mahārāja perform many sacrifices, but he carried on his transcendental occupation of engagement in the devotional service of the Lord. The ordinary *karmīs*, who want to enjoy the results of fruitive activities, are concerned only with sacrifices and ritualistic ceremonies as enjoined in the Vedic *śāstras*. Although Dhruva Mahārāja performed many sacrifices in order to be an exemplary king, he was constantly engaged in devotional service. The Lord always protects His surrendered devotee. A devotee can see that the Lord is situated in everyone's heart, as stated in the *Bhagavad-gītā* (*īśvaraḥ sarva-bhūtānāṁ hṛd-deśe 'rjuna tiṣṭhati*). Ordinary persons cannot understand how the Supreme Lord is situated in everyone's heart, but a devotee can actually see Him. Not only can the devotee see Him outwardly, but he can see, with spiritual vision, that everything is resting in the Supreme Personality of Godhead, as described in *Bhagavad-gītā* (*mat-sthāni sarva-bhūtāni*). That is the vision of a *mahā-bhāgavata*. He sees everything others see, but instead of seeing merely the trees, the mountains, the cities or the sky, he sees only his worshipable Supreme Personality of Godhead in everything because everything is resting in Him only. This is the vision of the *mahā-bhāgavata.* In summary, a *mahā-bhāgavata,* a highly elevated pure devotee, sees the Lord everywhere, as well as within the heart of everyone. This is possible for devotees who have developed elevated devotional service to the Lord. As stated in the *Brahma-saṁhitā* (5.38), *premāñjana-cchurita-bhakti-vilocanena:* only those who have smeared their eyes with the ointment of love of Godhead can see everywhere the Supreme Lord face to face; it is not possible by imagination or so-called meditation.

TEXT 12

तमेवं शीलसम्पन्नं ब्रह्मण्यं दीनवत्सलम् ।
गोप्तारं धर्मसेतूनां मेनिरे पितरं प्रजाः ॥१२॥

tam evaṁ śīla-sampannaṁ
brahmaṇyaṁ dīna-vatsalam
goptāraṁ dharma-setūnāṁ
menire pitaraṁ prajāḥ

tam—him; *evam*—thus; *śīla*—with godly qualities; *sampannam*—endowed; *brahmaṇyam*—respectful to the *brāhmaṇas; dīna*—to the poor; *vatsalam*—kind; *goptāram*—protector; *dharma-setūnām*—of religious principles; *menire*—thought; *pitaram*—father; *prajāḥ*—the citizens.

TRANSLATION

Dhruva Mahārāja was endowed with all godly qualities; he was very respectful to the devotees of the Supreme Lord and very kind to the poor and innocent, and he protected religious principles. With all these qualifications, he was considered to be the direct father of all the citizens.

PURPORT

The personal qualities of Dhruva Mahārāja described herein are the exemplary qualities of a saintly king. Not only a king but also the leaders of a modern democratic or impersonal government must be qualified with all these godly characteristics. Then the citizens of the state can be happy. It is clearly stated here that the citizens thought of Dhruva Mahārāja as their father; as a child, depending on the able father, is completely satisfied, so the citizens of the state, being protected by the state or the king, should remain satisfied in every respect. At the present moment, however, there is no guarantee by the government of even the primary necessities of life in the state, namely, the protection of the lives and property of the citizens.

One word is very significant in this connection: *brahmaṇyam.* Dhruva Mahārāja was very devoted to the *brāhmaṇas,* who engage in the study of the *Vedas* and thereby know the Supreme Personality of Godhead. They are always busy propagating Kṛṣṇa consciousness. The state should be very respectful to societies that distribute God consciousness all over the world, but, unfortunately, at the present moment there is no state or government support given to such movements. As for good qualities, it is very difficult to find anyone in state administration with any good qualities. The administrators simply sit in their administrative posts and say no to every request, as if they were paid to say no to the citizens. Another word, *dīna-vatsalam,* is very significant also. The state head should be very kind to the innocent. Unfortunately, in this age the state agents and the presidents draw good salaries from the state, and they pose themselves as very pious, but they allow the running of slaughterhouses, where innocent animals are killed. If we try to compare the godly qualities of Dhruva Mahārāja to the qualities of modern statesmen, we can see that there is no actual comparison. Dhruva Mahārāja was present in the Satya-yuga, as will be clear from the next verses. He was the ideal king in Satya-yuga. The government administration in the present age (Kali-yuga) is bereft of all godly qualities. Considering all these points, the people today have no alternative but to take to Kṛṣṇa consciousness for protection of religion, life and property.

TEXT 13

षट्त्रिंशद्वर्षसाहस्रं शशास क्षितिमण्डलम् ।
भोगैः पुण्यक्षयं कुर्वन्नभोगैरशुभक्षयम् ॥१३॥

ṣaṭ-triṁśad-varṣa-sāhasraṁ
śaśāsa kṣiti-maṇḍalam

bhogaiḥ puṇya-kṣayaṁ kurvann
abhogair aśubha-kṣayam

ṣaṭ-triṁśat—thirty-six; *varṣa*—years; *sāhasram*—thousand; *śaśāsa*—ruled; *kṣiti-maṇḍalam*—the earth planet; *bhogaiḥ*—by enjoyment; *puṇya*—of reactions of pious activities; *kṣayam*—diminution; *kurvan*—doing; *abhogaiḥ*—by austerities; *aśubha*—of inauspicious reactions; *kṣayam*—diminution.

TRANSLATION

Dhruva Mahārāja ruled over this planet for thirty-six thousand years; he diminished the reactions of pious activities by enjoyment, and by practicing austerities he diminished inauspicious reactions.

PURPORT

That Dhruva Mahārāja ruled over the planet for thirty-six thousand years means that he was present in the Satya-yuga because in the Satya-yuga people used to live for one hundred thousand years. In the next *yuga*, Tretā, people used to live for ten thousand years, and in the next *yuga*, Dvāpara, for one thousand years. In the present age, the Kali-yuga, the maximum duration of life is one hundred years. With the change of the *yugas*, the duration of life and memory, the quality of kindness and all other good qualities diminish. There are two kinds of activities, namely pious and impious. By executing pious activities one can gain facilities for higher material enjoyment, but due to impious activities one has to undergo severe distress. A devotee, however, is not interested in enjoyment or affected by distress. When he is prosperous he knows, "I am diminishing the results of my pious activities," and when he is in distress he knows, "I am diminishing the reactions of my impious activities." A devotee is not concerned with enjoyment or distress; he simply desires to execute devotional service. It is said in the *Śrīmad-Bhāgavatam* that devotional service should be *apratihatā*, unchecked by the material conditions of happiness or distress. The devotee undergoes processes of austerity such as observing Ekādaśī and similar other fasting days and refraining from illicit sex life, intoxication, gambling and meat-eating. Thus he becomes purified from the reactions of his past impious life, and because he engages in devotional service, which is the most pious activity, he enjoys life without separate endeavor.

TEXT 14

एवं बहुसवं कालं महात्माविचलेन्द्रियः ।
त्रिवर्गौपयिकं नीत्वा पुत्रायादान्नृपासनम् ॥१४॥

evaṁ bahu-savaṁ kālaṁ
mahātmāvicalendriyaḥ
tri-vargaupayikaṁ nītvā
putrāyādān nṛpāsanam

evam—thus; *bahu*—many; *savam*—years; *kālam*—time; *mahā-ātmā*—great soul; *avicala-indriyaḥ*—without being disturbed by sense agitation; *tri-varga*—three kinds of worldly activities; *aupayikam*—favorable for executing; *nītvā*—having passed; *putrāya*—to his son; *adāt*—he handed over; *nṛpa-āsanam*—the royal throne.

TRANSLATION

The self-controlled great soul Dhruva Mahārāja thus passed many, many years favorably executing three kinds of worldly activities, namely religiosity, economic development and satisfaction of all material desires. Thereafter he handed over the charge of the royal throne to his son.

PURPORT

Perfection of materialistic life is suitably attained by the process of observing religious principles. This leads automatically to successful economic development, and thus there is no difficulty in satisfying all material desires. Since Dhruva Mahārāja, as a king, had to keep up his status quo or it would not have been possible to rule over the people in general, he did it perfectly. But as soon as he saw that his son was grown up and could take charge of the royal throne, he immediately handed over the charge and retired from all material engagements.

One word used here is very significant—*avicalendriyaḥ*, which means that he was not disturbed by the agitation of the senses nor was his sensory power diminished, although in years he was a very old man. Since he ruled over the world for thirty-six thousand years, naturally one may conclude that he became very, very old, but factually his senses were very young—and yet he was not interested in sense gratification. In other words, he remained self-controlled. He performed his duties perfectly according to the materialistic way. That is the way of behavior of great devotees. Śrīla Raghunātha dāsa Gosvāmī, one of the direct disciples of Lord Caitanya, was the son of a very rich man. Although he had no interest in enjoying material happiness, when he was entrusted with doing something in managing the state, he did it perfectly. Śrīla Gaurasundara advised him, "From within, keep yourself and your mind completely aloof, but externally execute the material duties just as they need to be done." This transcendental position can be achieved by devotees only, as described in the *Bhagavad-gītā:* while others, such as *yogīs*, try to control their senses by force, devotees, even though possessing full sensory powers, do not use them because they engage in higher, transcendental activities.

TEXT 15

मन्यमान इदं विश्वं मायारचितमात्मनि ।
अविद्यारचितस्वप्नगन्धर्वनगरोपमम् ॥१५॥

manyamāna idaṁ viśvaṁ
māyā-racitam ātmani
avidyā-racita-svapna-
gandharva-nagaropamam

manyamānaḥ—realizing; *idam*—this; *viśvam*—universe; *māyā*—by the external energy; *racitam*—manufactured; *ātmani*—unto the living entity; *avidyā*—by illusion; *racita*—manufactured; *svapna*—a dream; *gandharva-nagara*—phantasmagoria; *upamam*—like.

TRANSLATION

Śrīla Dhruva Mahārāja realized that this cosmic manifestation bewilders living entities like a dream or phantasmagoria because it is a creation of the illusory, external energy of the Supreme Lord.

PURPORT

In the deep forest it sometimes appears that there are big palaces and nice cities. That is technically called *gandharva-nagara.* Similarly, in dreams also we create many false things out of imagination. A self-realized person, or a devotee, knows well that this material cosmic manifestation is a temporary, illusory representation appearing to be truth. It is like a phantasmagoria. But behind this shadow creation there is reality—the spiritual world. A devotee is interested in the spiritual world, not its shadow. Since he has realization of the supreme truth, a devotee is not interested in this temporary shadow of truth. This is confirmed in the *Bhagavad-gītā* (*paraṁ dṛṣṭvā nivartate*).

TEXT 16

आत्मस्त्र्यपत्यसुहृदो बलमृद्धकोश-
मन्तःपुरं परिविहारभुवश्च रम्याः ।
भूमण्डलं जलधिमेखलमाकलय्य
कालोपसृष्टमिति स प्रययौ विशालाम् ॥१६॥

ātma-stry-apatya-suhṛdo balam ṛddha-kośam
antaḥ-puraṁ parivihāra-bhuvaś ca ramyāḥ
bhū-maṇḍalaṁ jaladhi-mekhalam ākalayya
kālopasṛṣṭam iti sa prayayau viśālām

ātma—body; *strī*—wives; *apatya*—children; *suhṛdaḥ*—friends; *balam*—influence, army; *ṛddha-kośam*—rich treasury; *antaḥ-puram*—female residential quarters; *parivihāra-bhuvaḥ*—pleasure-grounds; *ca*—and; *ramyāḥ*—beautiful; *bhū-maṇḍalam*—the complete earth; *jala-dhi*—by oceans; *mekhalam*—bound; *ākalayya*—considering; *kāla*—by time; *upasṛṣṭam*—created; *iti*—thus; *saḥ*—he; *prayayau*—went; *viśālām*—to Badarikāśrama.

TRANSLATION

Thus Dhruva Mahārāja, at the end, left his kingdom, which extended all over the earth and was bounded by the great oceans. He considered his body, his wives, his children, his friends, his army, his rich treasury, his very comfortable palaces and his many

enjoyable pleasure-grounds to be creations of the illusory energy. Thus in due course of time he retired to the forest in the Himalayas known as Badarikāśrama.

PURPORT

In the beginning of his life, when he went to the forest in search of the Supreme Personality of Godhead, Dhruva Mahārāja realized that all bodily conceptions of pleasure are products of the illusory energy. In the very beginning, of course, he was after the kingdom of his father, and in order to get it he went to search for the Supreme Lord. But he later realized that everything is the creation of the illusory energy. From the acts of Śrīla Dhruva Mahārāja we can understand that somehow or other if one becomes Kṛṣṇa conscious—it does not matter what his motivation is in the beginning—he will eventually realize the real truth by the grace of the Lord. In the beginning, Dhruva Mahārāja was interested in the kingdom of his father, but later he became a great devotee, *mahā-bhāgavata*, and had no interest in material enjoyment. The perfection of life can be achieved only by devotees. Even if one completes only a minute percentage of devotional service and then falls down from his immature position, he is better than a person who fully engages in the fruitive activities of this material world.

TEXT 17

तस्यां विशुद्धकरणः शिववार्विगाह्य
बद्ध्वासनं जितमरुन्मनसाहृताक्षः ।
स्थूले दधार भगवत्प्रतिरूप एतद्
ध्यायंस्तदव्यवहितो व्यसृजत्समाधौ ॥१७॥

tasyāṁ viśuddha-karaṇaḥ śiva-vār vigāhya
baddhvāsanaṁ jita-marun manasāhṛtākṣaḥ
sthūle dadhāra bhagavat-pratirūpa etad
dhyāyaṁs tad avyavahito vyasṛjat samādhau

tasyām—in Badarikāśrama; *viśuddha*—purified; *karaṇaḥ*—his senses; *śiva*—pure; *vāḥ*—water; *vigāhya*—bathing in; *baddhvā*—having fixed; *āsanam*—sitting position; *jita*—controlled; *marut*—breathing process; *manasā*—by the mind; *āhṛta*—withdrawn; *akṣaḥ*—his senses; *sthūle*—physical; *dadhāra*—he concentrated; *bhagavat-pratirūpe*—on the exact form of the Lord; *etat*—the mind; *dhyāyan*—meditating upon; *tat*—that; *avyavahitaḥ*—without stopping; *vyasṛjat*—he entered; *samādhau*—into trance.

TRANSLATION

In Badarikāśrama Dhruva Mahārāja's senses became completely purified because he bathed regularly in the crystal-clear purified water. He fixed his sitting position and by yogic practice controlled the breathing process and the air of life; in this way his senses were completely withdrawn. Then he concentrated his mind on the arcā-vigraha form of the Lord, which is the exact replica of the Lord and, thus meditating upon Him, entered into complete trance.

PURPORT

Here is a description of the *aṣṭāṅga-yoga* system, to which Dhruva Mahārāja was already accustomed. *Aṣṭāṅga-yoga* was never meant to be practiced in a fashionable city. Dhruva Mahārāja went to Badarikāśrama, and in a solitary place, alone, he practiced *yoga.* He concentrated his mind on the *arcā-vigraha,* the worshipable Deity of the Lord, which exactly represents the Supreme Lord, and thus thinking constantly of that Deity, he became absorbed in trance. Worship of the *arcā-vigraha* is not idol worship. The *arcā-vigraha* is an incarnation of the Lord in a form appreciable by a devotee. Therefore devotees engage in the temple in the service of the Lord as *arcā-vigraha,* a form made of *sthūla* (material) objects such as stone, metal, wood, jewels or paint. All of these are called *sthūla,* or physical representations. Since the devotees follow the regulative principles of worship, even though the Lord is there in His physical form, He is nondifferent from His original, spiritual form. Thus the devotee gets the benefit of achieving the ultimate goal of life, that is to say, becoming always absorbed in thought of the Lord. This incessant thought of the Lord, as prescribed in the *Bhagavad-gītā,* makes one the topmost *yogī.*

TEXT 18

भक्तिं हरौ भगवति प्रवहन्नजस्र-
मानन्दबाष्पकलया मुहुरर्द्यमानः ।
विक्लिद्यमानहृदयः पुलकाचिताङ्गो
नात्मानमस्मरदसाविति मुक्तलिङ्गः ॥१८॥

bhaktiṁ harau bhagavati pravahann ajasram
ānanda-bāṣpa-kalayā muhur ardyamānaḥ
viklidyamāna-hṛdayaḥ pulakācitāṅgo
nātmānam asmarad asāv iti mukta-liṅgaḥ

bhaktim—devotional service; *harau*—unto Hari; *bhagavati*—the Supreme Personality of Godhead; *pravahan*—constantly engaging in; *ajasram*—always; *ānanda*—blissful; *bāṣpa-kalayā*—by a stream of tears; *muhuḥ*—again and again; *ardyamānaḥ*—being overcome; *viklidyamāna*—melting; *hṛdayaḥ*—his heart; *pulaka*—standing of hairs; *ācita*—covered; *aṅgaḥ*—his body; *na*—not; *ātmānam*—body; *asmarat*—he remembered; *asau*—he; *iti*—thus; *mukta-liṅgaḥ*—free from the subtle body.

TRANSLATION

Because of his transcendental bliss, incessant tears flowed from his eyes, his heart melted, and there was shivering and standing of the hairs all over his body. Thus transformed, in a trance of devotional service, Dhruva Mahārāja completely forgot his bodily existence, and thus he immediately became liberated from material bondage.

PURPORT

Due to constant engagement in devotional service—hearing, chanting, remembering, worshiping the Deity, etc., as prescribed in nine varieties—there are different symptoms which appear in the body of a devotee. These eight bodily transformations, which indicate that a devotee is already liberated within himself, are called *aṣṭa-sāttvika-vikāra.* When a devotee completely forgets his bodily existence, he should be understood to be liberated. He is no longer encaged in the body. The example is given that when a coconut becomes completely dry, the coconut pulp within the coconut shell separates from the bondage of the shell and the outer covering. By moving the dry coconut, one can hear that the pulp within is no longer attached to the shell or to the covering. Similarly, when one is fully absorbed in devotional service, he is completely disconnected from the two material coverings, the subtle and gross bodies. Dhruva Mahārāja actually attained this stage of life by constantly discharging devotional service. He has already been described as a *mahā-bhāgavata*, for unless one becomes a *mahā-bhāgavata*, or a first-class pure devotee, these symptoms are not visible. Lord Caitanya exhibited all these symptoms. Ṭhākura Haridāsa also exhibited them, and there are many pure devotees who manifested such bodily symptoms. They are not to be imitated, but when one is actually advanced, these symptoms are exhibited. At that time it is to be understood that a devotee is materially free. Of course, from the beginning of devotional service the path of liberation immediately opens, just as the coconut taken from the tree immediately begins to dry; it simply takes some time for the shell and pulp to separate from one another.

An important word in this verse is *mukta-liṅgaḥ. Mukta* means "liberated," and *liṅga* means "the subtle body." When a man dies, he quits the gross body, but the subtle body of mind, intelligence and ego carries him to a new body. While existing in the present body, the same subtle body carries him from one stage of life to another (for example, from childhood to boyhood) by mental development. The mental condition of a baby is different from that of a boy, the mental condition of a boy is different from that of a young man, and the mental condition of a young man is different from that of an old man. So at death the process of changing bodies takes place due to the subtle body; the mind, intelligence and ego carry the soul from one gross body to another. This is called transmigration of the soul. But there is another stage, when one becomes liberated even from the subtle body; at that time the living entity is competent and fully prepared to be transferred to the transcendental or spiritual world.

The description of the bodily symptoms of Śrī Dhruva Mahārāja makes it apparent that he became perfectly fit to be transferred to the spiritual world. One can experience the distinction between the subtle and gross bodies even daily; in a dream, one's gross body is lying on the bed while the subtle body carries the soul, the living entity, to another atmosphere. But because the gross body has to be continued, the subtle body comes back and settles in the present gross body. Therefore one has to become free from the subtle body also. This freedom is known as *mukta-liṅga.*

TEXT 19

स ददर्श विमानाग्र्यं नभसोऽवतरद् ध्रुवः ।
विभ्राजयद्दश दिशो राकापतिमिवोदितम् ॥१९॥

sa dadarśa vimānāgryaṁ
nabhaso 'vatarad dhruvaḥ
vibhrājayad daśa diśo
rākāpatim ivoditam

saḥ—he; *dadarśa*—saw; *vimāna*—an airplane; *agryam*—very beautiful; *nabhasaḥ*—from the sky; *avatarat*—descending; *dhruvaḥ*—Dhruva Mahārāja; *vibhrājayat*—illuminating; *daśa*—ten; *diśaḥ*—directions; *rākā-patim*—the full moon; *iva*—like; *uditam*—visible.

TRANSLATION

As soon as the symptoms of his liberation were manifest, he saw a very beautiful airplane coming down from the sky, as if the brilliant full moon were coming down, illuminating all the ten directions.

PURPORT

There are different levels of acquired knowledge—direct knowledge, knowledge received from authorities, transcendental knowledge, knowledge beyond the senses, and finally spiritual knowledge. When one surpasses the stage of acquiring knowledge by the descending process, he is immediately situated on the transcendental platform. Dhruva Mahārāja, being liberated from the material concept of life, was situated in transcendental knowledge and could perceive the presence of a transcendental airplane which was as brilliant as the full moonlight. This is not possible in the stages of direct or indirect perception of knowledge. Such knowledge is a special favor of the Supreme Personality of Godhead. One can, however, rise to this platform of knowledge by the gradual process of advancing in devotional service, or Kṛṣṇa consciousness.

TEXT 20

तत्रानु देवप्रवरौ चतुर्भुजौ
श्यामौ किशोरावरुणाम्बुजेक्षणौ ।
स्थिताववष्टभ्य गदां सुवाससौ
किरीटहाराङ्गदचारुकुण्डलौ ॥२०॥

tatrānu deva-pravarau catur-bhujau
śyāmau kiśorāv aruṇāmbujekṣaṇau
sthitāv avaṣṭabhya gadāṁ suvāsasau
kirīṭa-hārāṅgada-cāru-kuṇḍalau

tatra—there; *anu*—then; *deva-pravarau*—two very beautiful demigods; *catuḥ-bhujau*—with four arms; *śyāmau*—blackish; *kiśorau*—quite young; *aruṇa*—reddish; *ambuja*—lotus flower; *īkṣaṇau*—with eyes; *sthitau*—situated; *avaṣṭabhya*—holding; *gadām*—clubs; *suvāsasau*—with nice garments; *kirīṭa*—helmets; *hāra*—necklaces; *aṅgada*—bracelets; *cāru*—beautiful; *kuṇḍalau*—with earrings.

TRANSLATION

Dhruva Mahārāja saw two very beautiful associates of Lord Viṣṇu in the plane. They had four hands and a blackish bodily luster, they were very youthful, and their eyes were just like reddish lotus flowers. They held clubs in their hands, and they were dressed in very attractive garments with helmets and were decorated with necklaces, bracelets and earrings.

PURPORT

The inhabitants of Viṣṇuloka are of the same bodily feature as Lord Viṣṇu, and they also hold club, conchshell, lotus flower and disc. In this verse it is distinctly stated that they had four hands and were nicely dressed; the description of their bodily decorations corresponds exactly to that of Viṣṇu. So the two uncommon personalities who descended from the airplane came directly from Viṣṇuloka, or the planet where Lord Viṣṇu lives.

TEXT 21

विज्ञाय तावुत्तमगायकिङ्करा-
वभ्युत्थितः साध्वसविस्मृतक्रमः ।
ननाम नामानि गृणन्मधुद्विषः
पार्षत्प्रधानाविति संहताञ्जलिः ॥२१॥

vijñāya tāv uttamagāya-kiṅkarāv
abhyutthitaḥ sādhvasa-vismṛta-kramaḥ
nanāma nāmāni gṛṇan madhudviṣaḥ
pārṣat-pradhānāv iti saṁhatāñjaliḥ

vijñāya—after understanding; *tau*—them; *uttama-gāya*—of Lord Viṣṇu (of excellent renown); *kiṅkarau*—two servants; *abhyutthitaḥ*—stood up; *sādhvasa*—by being puzzled; *vismṛta*—forgot; *kramaḥ*—proper behavior; *nanāma*—offered obeisances; *nāmāni*—names; *gṛṇan*—chanting; *madhu-dviṣaḥ*—of the Lord (the enemy of Madhu); *pārṣat*—associates; *pradhānau*—chief; *iti*—thus; *saṁhata*—respectfully joined; *añjaliḥ*—with folded hands.

TRANSLATION

Dhruva Mahārāja, seeing that these uncommon personalities were direct servants of the Supreme Personality of Godhead, immediately stood up. But, being puzzled, in hastiness he forgot how to receive them in the proper way. Therefore he simply offered obeisances with folded hands and chanted and glorified the holy names of the Lord.

PURPORT

Chanting of the holy names of the Lord is perfect in every way. When Dhruva Mahārāja saw the Viṣṇudūtas, the direct associates of Lord Viṣṇu, four-handed and nicely decorated, he could understand who they were, but for the time being he was puzzled. But simply by chanting the holy name of the Lord, the Hare Kṛṣṇa *mantra*, he could satisfy the uncommon guests who had all of a sudden arrived before him. The chanting of the holy name of the Lord is perfect; even though one does not know how to please Lord Viṣṇu or His associates, simply by sincerely chanting the holy name of the Lord, everything becomes perfect. A devotee, therefore, either in danger or in happiness, constantly chants the Hare Kṛṣṇa *mantra.* When he is in danger he is immediately relieved, and when he is in a position to see Lord Viṣṇu or His associates directly, by chanting this *mahā-mantra* he can please the Lord. This is the absolute nature of the *mahā-mantra.* Either in danger or in happiness, it can be chanted without limitation.

TEXT 22

तं कृष्णपादाभिनिविष्टचेतसं
बद्धाञ्जलिं प्रश्रयनम्रकन्धरम् ।
सुनन्दनन्दावुपसृत्य सस्मितं
प्रत्यूचतुः पुष्करनाभसम्मतौ ॥२२॥

taṁ kṛṣṇa-pādābhiniviṣṭa-cetasaṁ
baddhāñjaliṁ praśraya-namra-kandharam
sunanda-nandāv upasṛtya sasmitaṁ
pratyūcatuḥ puṣkaranābha-sammatau

tam—him; *kṛṣṇa*—of Lord Kṛṣṇa; *pāda*—of the lotus feet; *abhiniviṣṭa*—absorbed in thought; *cetasam*—whose heart; *baddha-añjalim*—with folded hands; *praśraya*—very humbly; *namra*—bowed; *kandharam*—whose neck; *sunanda*—Sunanda; *nandau*—and Nanda; *upasṛtya*—approaching; *sa-smitam*—smilingly; *pratyūcatuḥ*—addressed; *puṣkara-nābha*—of Lord Viṣṇu, who has a lotus navel; *sammatau*—confidential servants.

TRANSLATION

Dhruva Mahārāja was always absorbed in thinking of the lotus feet of Lord Kṛṣṇa. His heart was full with Kṛṣṇa. When the two confidential servants of the Supreme Lord, who were named

Nanda and Sunanda, approached him, smiling happily, Dhruva stood with folded hands, bowing humbly. They then addressed him as follows.

PURPORT

In this verse the word *puṣkaranābha-sammatau* is significant. Kṛṣṇa, or Lord Viṣṇu, is known for His lotus eyes, lotus navel, lotus feet and lotus palms. Here He is called *puṣkara-nābha,* which means "the Supreme Personality of Godhead, who has a lotus navel," and *sammatau* means "two confidential or very obedient servants." The materialistic way of life differs from the spiritual way of life in that one is disobedience and the other is obedience to the will of the Supreme Lord. All living entities are part and parcel of the Supreme Lord, and they are supposed to be always agreeable to the order of the Supreme Person; that is perfect oneness.

In the Vaikuṇṭha world all the living entities are in oneness with the Supreme Godhead because they never defy His orders. Here in the material world, however, they are not *sammata,* agreeable, but always *asammata,* disagreeable. This human form of life is a chance to be trained to be agreeable to the orders of the Supreme Lord. To bring about this training in society is the mission of the Kṛṣṇa consciousness movement. As stated in the *Bhagavad-gītā,* the laws of material nature are very strict; no one can overcome the stringent laws of material nature. But one who becomes a surrendered soul and agrees to the order of the Supreme Lord can easily overcome those stringent laws. The example of Dhruva Mahārāja is very fitting. Simply by becoming agreeable to the orders of the Supreme Personality of Godhead and by developing love of Godhead, Dhruva got the chance to personally meet the confidential servants of Lord Viṣṇu face to face. What was possible for Dhruva Mahārāja is possible for everyone. Anyone who very seriously engages in devotional service can obtain, in due course of time, the same perfection of the human form of life.

TEXT 23

सुनन्दनन्दावूचतुः

भो भो राजन् सुभद्रं ते वाचं नोऽवहितः शृणु ।
यः पञ्चवर्षस्तपसा भवान्देवमतीतृपत् ॥२३॥

sunanda-nandāv ūcatuḥ
bho bho rājan subhadraṁ te
vācaṁ no 'vahitaḥ śṛṇu
yaḥ pañca-varṣas tapasā
bhavān devam atītṛpat

sunanda-nandau ūcatuḥ—Sunanda and Nanda said; *bhoḥ bhoḥ rājan*—O dear King; *su-bhadram*—good fortune; *te*—unto you; *vācam*—words; *naḥ*—our; *avahitaḥ*—attentively; *śṛṇu*—hear; *yaḥ*—who; *pañca-varṣaḥ*—five years old; *tapasā*—by austerity; *bhavān*—you; *devam*—the Supreme Personality of Godhead; *atītṛpat*—greatly satisfied.

TRANSLATION

Nanda and Sunanda, the two confidential associates of Lord Viṣṇu, said: Dear King, let there be all good fortune unto you. Please attentively hear what we shall say. When you were only five years old, you underwent severe austerities, and you thereby greatly satisfied the Supreme Personality of Godhead.

PURPORT

What was possible for Dhruva Mahārāja is possible for anyone. Any five-year-old child can be trained, and within a very short time his life will become successful by realization of Kṛṣṇa consciousness. Unfortunately, this training is lacking all over the world. It is necessary for the leaders of the Kṛṣṇa consciousness movement to start educational institutions in different parts of the world to train children, starting at the age of five years. Thus such children will not become hippies or spoiled children of society; rather, they can all become devotees of the Lord. The face of the world will then change automatically.

TEXT 24

तस्याखिलजगद्धातुरावां देवस्य शार्ङ्गिणः ।
पार्षदाविह सम्प्राप्तौ नेतुं त्वां भगवत्पदम् ॥२४॥

tasyākhila-jagad-dhātur
āvāṁ devasya śārṅgiṇaḥ

pārṣadāv iha samprāptau
netuṁ tvāṁ bhagavat-padam

tasya—His; *akhila*—entire; *jagat*—universe; *dhātuḥ*—creator; *āvām*—we; *devasya*—of the Supreme Personality of Godhead; *śārṅgiṇaḥ*—who has the bow named Śārṅga; *pārṣadau*—associates; *iha*—now; *samprāptau*—approached; *netum*—to take; *tvām*—you; *bhagavat-padam*—to the position of the Supreme Personality of Godhead.

TRANSLATION

We are representatives of the Supreme Personality of Godhead, the creator of the whole universe, who carries in His hand the bow named Śārṅga. We have been specifically deputed to take you to the spiritual world.

PURPORT

In *Bhagavad-gītā* the Lord says that simply by knowing His transcendental pastimes (whether within this material world or in the spiritual world), anyone who understands factually who He is, how He appears and how He acts can be immediately fit for transfer to the spiritual world. This principle stated in the *Bhagavad-gītā* operated in the case of King Dhruva. Throughout his life he tried to understand the Supreme Personality of Godhead by austerity and penances. Now, the mature result was that Dhruva Mahārāja became fit to be carried to the spiritual world, accompanied by the confidential associates of the Lord.

TEXT 25

सुदुर्जयं विष्णुपदं जितं त्वया
यत्सूरयोऽप्राप्य विचक्षते परम् ।
आतिष्ठ तच्चन्द्रदिवाकरादयो
ग्रहर्क्षताराः परियन्ति दक्षिणम् ॥२५॥

sudurjayaṁ viṣṇu-padaṁ jitaṁ tvayā
yat sūrayo 'prāpya vicakṣate param
ātiṣṭha tac candra-divākarādayo
graharkṣa-tārāḥ pariyanti dakṣiṇam

sudurjayam—very difficult to achieve; *viṣṇu-padam*—planet known as Vaikuṇṭhaloka or Viṣṇuloka; *jitam*—conquered; *tvayā*—by you; *yat*—which; *sūrayaḥ*—great demigods; *aprāpya*—without achieving; *vicakṣate*—simply see; *param*—supreme; *ātiṣṭha*—please come; *tat*—that; *candra*—the moon; *diva-ākara*—sun; *ādayaḥ*—and others; *graha*—the nine planets (Mercury, Venus, Earth, Mars, Jupiter, Saturn, Uranus, Neptune and Pluto); *ṛkṣa-tārāḥ*—stars; *pariyanti*—circumambulate; *dakṣiṇam*—to the right.

TRANSLATION

To achieve Viṣṇuloka is very difficult, but by your austerity you have conquered. Even the great ṛṣis and demigods cannot achieve this position. Simply to see the supreme abode [the Viṣṇu planet], the sun and moon and all the other planets, stars, lunar mansions and solar systems are circumambulating it. Now please come; you are welcome to go there.

PURPORT

Even in this material world the so-called scientists, philosophers and mental speculators strive to merge into the spiritual sky, but they can never go there. But a devotee, by executing devotional service, not only realizes what the spiritual world actually is, but factually goes there to live an eternal life of bliss and knowledge. The Kṛṣṇa consciousness movement is so potent that by adopting these principles of life and developing love of God one can very easily go back home, back to Godhead. Here the practical example is the case of Dhruva Mahārāja. While the scientist and philosopher go to the moon but are disappointed in their attempts to stay there and live, the devotee makes an easy journey to other planets and ultimately goes back to Godhead. Devotees have no interest in seeing other planets, but while going back to Godhead, they see all of them as passing phases, just as one who is going to a distant place passes through many small stations.

TEXT 26

अनास्थितं ते पितृभिरन्यैरप्यङ्ग कर्हिचित् ।
आतिष्ठ जगतां वन्द्यं तद्विष्णोः परमं पदम् ॥२६॥

anāsthitaṁ te pitṛbhir
anyair apy aṅga karhicit
ātiṣṭha jagatāṁ vandyaṁ
tad viṣṇoḥ paramaṁ padam

anāsthitam—never achieved; *te*—your; *pitṛbhiḥ*—by forefathers; *anyaiḥ*—by others; *api*—even; *aṅga*—O Dhruva; *karhicit*—at any time; *ātiṣṭha*—please come and live there; *jagatām*—by the inhabitants of the universe; *vandyam*—worshipable; *tat*—that; *viṣṇoḥ*—of Lord Viṣṇu; *paramam*—supreme; *padam*—situation.

TRANSLATION

Dear King Dhruva, neither your forefathers nor anyone else before you ever achieved such a transcendental planet. The planet known as Viṣṇuloka, where Lord Viṣṇu personally resides, is the highest of all. It is worshipable by the inhabitants of all other planets within the universe. Please come with us and live there eternally.

PURPORT

When Dhruva Mahārāja went to perform austerities, he was very determined to achieve a post never dreamed of by his forefathers. His father was Uttānapāda, his grandfather was Manu, and his great-grandfather was Lord Brahmā. So Dhruva wanted a kingdom even greater than Lord Brahmā could achieve, and he requested Nārada Muni to give him facility for achieving it. The associates of Lord Viṣṇu reminded him that not only his forefathers but everyone else before him was unable to attain Viṣṇuloka, the planet where Lord Viṣṇu resides. This is because everyone within this material world is either a *karmī*, a *jñānī* or a *yogī*, but there are hardly any pure devotees. The transcendental planet known as Viṣṇuloka is especially meant for devotees, not for *karmīs*, *jñānīs* or *yogīs*. Great *ṛṣis* or demigods can hardly approach Brahmaloka, and as stated in *Bhagavad-gītā*, Brahmaloka is not a permanent residence. Lord Brahmā's duration of life is so long that it is difficult to estimate even the duration of one day in his life, and yet Lord Brahmā also dies, as do the residents of his planet. *Bhagavad-gītā* (8.16) says, *ābrahma-bhuvanāl lokāḥ punar āvartino 'rjuna:* except for those who go to Viṣṇuloka, everyone is subjected to the four principles of material life, namely birth, death, old age and disease. The Lord says, *yad gatvā na nivartante tad dhāma paramaṁ mama:* "The planet from which, once going, no one returns, is My supreme abode." (Bg. 15.6) Dhruva Mahārāja was reminded, "You are going in our company to that planet from which no one returns to this material world." Material scientists are attempting to go to the moon and other planets, but they cannot imagine going to the topmost planet, Brahmaloka, for it is beyond their imagination. By material calculation, traveling at the speed of light it would take forty thousand light-years to reach the topmost planet. By mechanical processes we are unable to reach the topmost planet of this universe, but the process called *bhakti-yoga,* as executed by Mahārāja Dhruva, can give one the facility not only to reach other planets within this universe, but also to reach beyond this universe to the Viṣṇuloka planets. We have outlined this in our small booklet *Easy Journey to Other Planets.*

TEXT 27

एतद्विमानप्रवरमुत्तमश्लोकमौलिना ।
उपस्थापितमायुष्मन्नधिरोढुं त्वमर्हसि ॥२७॥

etad vimāna-pravaram
uttamaśloka-maulinā
upasthāpitam āyuṣmann
adhiroḍhuṁ tvam arhasi

etat—this; *vimāna*—airplane; *pravaram*—unique; *uttamaśloka*—the Supreme Personality of Godhead; *maulinā*—by the head of all living entities; *upasthāpitam*—sent; *āyuṣman*—O immortal one; *adhiroḍhum*—to board; *tvam*—you; *arhasi*—are worthy.

TRANSLATION

O immortal one, this unique airplane has been sent by the Supreme Personality of Godhead, who is worshiped by selected

prayers and who is the chief of all living entities. You are quite worthy to board such a plane.

PURPORT

According to astronomical calculation, along with the polestar there is another star, which is called Śiśumāra, where Lord Viṣṇu, who is in charge of the maintenance of this material world, resides. Śiśumāra or Dhruvaloka can never be reached by anyone but the Vaiṣṇavas, as will be described by the following *ślokas.* The associates of Lord Viṣṇu brought the special airplane for Dhruva Mahārāja and then informed him that Lord Viṣṇu had especially sent this airplane.

The Vaikuṇṭha airplane does not move by mechanical arrangement. There are three processes for moving in outer space. One of the processes is known to the modern scientist. It is called *ka-pota-vāyu. Ka* means "outer space," and *pota* means "ship." There is a second process also called *kapota-vāyu. Kapota* means "pigeon." One can train pigeons to carry one into outer space. The third process is very subtle. It is called *ākāśa-patana.* This *ākāśa-patana* system is also material. Just as the mind can fly anywhere one likes without mechanical arrangement, so the *ākāśa-patana* airplane can fly at the speed of mind. Beyond this *ākāśa-patana* system is the Vaikuṇṭha process, which is completely spiritual. The airplane sent by Lord Viṣṇu to carry Dhruva Mahārāja to Śiśumāra was a completely spiritual, transcendental airplane. Material scientists can neither see such vehicles nor imagine how they fly in the air. The material scientist has no information about the spiritual sky, although it is mentioned in the *Bhagavad-gītā* (*paras tasmāt tu bhāvo 'nyaḥ*).

TEXT 28

मैत्रेय उवाच
निशम्य वैकुण्ठनियोज्यमुख्ययो-
र्मधुच्युतं वाचमुरुक्रमप्रियः ।
कृताभिषेकः कृतनित्यमङ्गलो
मुनीन् प्रणम्याशिषमभ्यवादयत् ॥२८॥

maitreya uvāca
niśamya vaikuṇṭha-niyojya-mukhyayor
madhu-cyutaṁ vācam urukrama-priyaḥ
kṛtābhiṣekaḥ kṛta-nitya-maṅgalo
munīn praṇamyāśiṣam abhyavādayat

maitreyaḥ uvāca—the great sage Maitreya said; *niśamya*—after hearing; *vaikuṇṭha*—of the Lord; *niyojya*—associates; *mukhyayoḥ*—of the chief; *madhu-cyutam*—like pouring honey; *vācam*—speeches; *urukrama-priyaḥ*—Dhruva Mahārāja, who was very dear to the Lord; *kṛta-abhiṣekaḥ*—took his sacred bath; *kṛta*—performed; *nitya-maṅgalaḥ*—his daily spiritual duties; *munīn*—to the sages; *praṇamya*—having offered obeisances; *āśiṣam*—blessings; *abhyavādayat*—accepted.

TRANSLATION

The great sage Maitreya continued: Mahārāja Dhruva was very dear to the Supreme Personality of Godhead. When he heard the sweet speeches of the Lord's chief associates in the Vaikuṇṭha planet, he immediately took his sacred bath, dressed himself with suitable ornaments, and performed his daily spiritual duties. Thereafter he offered his respectful obeisances to the great sages present there and accepted their blessings.

PURPORT

We should mark how dutiful Dhruva Mahārāja was in his devotional service, even at the time he left this material world. He was constantly alert in the performance of devotional duties. Every devotee should take his bath early in the morning and decorate his body with *tilaka*. In Kali-yuga one can hardly acquire gold or jeweled ornaments, but the twelve *tilaka* marks on the body are sufficient as auspicious decorations to purify the body. Since Dhruva Mahārāja was living at that time at Badarikāśrama, there were other great sages there. He did not become puffed up because the airplane sent by Lord Viṣṇu was waiting for him; as a humble Vaiṣṇava, he accepted blessings from all the sages before riding on the plane brought by the chief of the Vaikuṇṭha associates.

TEXT 29

परीत्याभ्यर्च्य धिष्ण्याग्र्यं पार्षदावभिवन्द्य च ।
इयेष तदधिष्ठातुं बिभ्रद्रूपं हिरण्मयम् ॥२९॥

parītyābhyarcya dhiṣṇyāgryaṁ
pārṣadāv abhivandya ca
iyeṣa tad adhiṣṭhātuṁ
bibhrad rūpaṁ hiraṇmayam

parītya—having circumambulated; *abhyarcya*—having worshiped; *dhiṣṇya-agryam*—the transcendental airplane; *pārṣadau*—unto the two associates; *abhivandya*—having offered obeisances; *ca*—also; *iyeṣa*—he attempted; *tat*—that plane; *adhiṣṭhātum*—to board; *bibhrat*—illuminating; *rūpam*—his form; *hiraṇmayam*—golden.

TRANSLATION

Before getting aboard, Dhruva Mahārāja worshiped the airplane, circumambulated it, and also offered obeisances to the associates of Viṣṇu. In the meantime he became as brilliant and illuminating as molten gold. He was thus completely prepared to board the transcendental plane.

PURPORT

In the absolute world, the plane, the associates of Lord Viṣṇu and Lord Viṣṇu Himself are all spiritual. There is no material contamination. In quality, everything there is one. As Lord Viṣṇu is worshipable, so also are His associates, His paraphernalia, His airplane and His abode, for everything of Viṣṇu's is as good as Lord Viṣṇu. Dhruva Mahārāja knew all this very well, as a pure Vaiṣṇava, and he offered his respects to the associates and to the plane before riding in it. But in the meantime, his body changed into spiritual existence, and therefore it was illuminating like molten gold. In this way he also became one with the other paraphernalia of Viṣṇuloka.

Māyāvādī philosophers cannot imagine how this oneness can be achieved even in different varieties. Their idea of oneness is that there is no variety. Therefore they have become impersonalists. As Śiśumāra, Viṣṇuloka or Dhruvaloka are completely different from this material world, so a Viṣṇu temple within this world is also completely different from this material world. As soon as we are in a temple we should know very well that we are situated differently from the material world. In the temple, Lord Viṣṇu, His throne, His room and all other things associated with the temple are transcendental. The three modes, *sattva-guṇa*, *rajo-guṇa* and *tamo-guṇa*, have no entrance into the temple. It is said, therefore, that to live in the forest is in the mode of goodness, to live in the city is in the mode of passion, and to live in a brothel, liquor shop or slaughterhouse is in the mode of ignorance. But to live in the temple means to live in Vaikuṇṭhaloka. Everything in the temple is as worshipable as Lord Viṣṇu, or Kṛṣṇa.

TEXT 30

तदोत्तानपदः पुत्रो ददर्शान्तकमागतम् ।
मृत्योर्मूर्ध्नि पदं दत्त्वा आरुरोहाद्भुतं गृहम् ॥३०॥

tadottānapadaḥ putro
dadarśāntakam āgatam
mṛtyor mūrdhni padaṁ dattvā
ārurohādbhutaṁ gṛham

tadā—then; *uttānapadaḥ*—of King Uttānapāda; *putraḥ*—son; *dadarśa*—could see; *antakam*—death personified; *āgatam*—approached him; *mṛtyoḥ mūrdhni*—on the head of death; *padam*—feet; *dattvā*—placing; *āruroha*—got up; *adbhutam*—wonderful; *gṛham*—on the airplane which resembled a big house.

TRANSLATION

When Dhruva Mahārāja was attempting to get on the transcendental plane, he saw death personified approach him. Not caring for death, however, he took advantage of the opportunity to put his feet on the head of death, and thus he got up on the airplane, which was as big as a house.

PURPORT

To take the passing away of a devotee and the passing away of a nondevotee as one and the same is completely misleading. While ascending the transcendental airplane, Dhruva Mahārāja suddenly saw death personified before him, but he was not afraid. Instead of death's giving him trouble, Dhruva Mahārāja took advantage of death's presence and put his feet on the head of death. People with a poor fund of knowledge do not know the difference between the death of a devotee and the death of a nondevotee. In this connection, an example can be given: a cat carries its kittens in its mouth, and it also catches a rat in its mouth. Superficially, the catching of the rat and the kitten appear to be one and the same, but actually they are not. When the cat catches the rat in its mouth it means death for the rat, whereas when the cat catches the kitten, the kitten enjoys it. When Dhruva Mahārāja boarded the airplane, he took advantage of the arrival of death personified, who came to offer him obeisances; putting his feet on the head of death, he got up on the unique airplane, which is described here to be as big as a house (*gṛham*).

There are many other similar instances in *Bhāgavata* literature. It is stated that when Kardama Muni created an airplane to carry his wife, Devahūti, all over the universe, the airplane was like a big city, carrying many houses, lakes and gardens. Modern scientists have manufactured big airplanes, but they are packed with passengers, who experience all sorts of discomforts while riding in them.

Material scientists are not even perfect in manufacturing a material airplane. In order to compare to the plane used by Kardama or the plane sent from Viṣṇuloka, they must manufacture an airplane equipped like a big city, with all the comforts of life—lakes, gardens, parks, etc. Their plane must be able to fly in outer space and hover, and visit all other planets. If they invent such a plane, they will not have to make different space stations for fuel to travel into outer space. Such a plane would have an unlimited supply of fuel, or, like the plane from Viṣṇuloka, would fly without it.

TEXT 31

तदा दुन्दुभयो नेदुर्मृदङ्गपणवादयः ।
गन्धर्वमुख्याः प्रजगुः पेतुः कुसुमवृष्टयः ॥३१॥

tadā dundubhayo nedur
mṛdaṅga-paṇavādayaḥ

gandharva-mukhyāḥ prajaguḥ
petuḥ kusuma-vṛṣṭayaḥ

tadā—at that time; *dundubhayaḥ*—kettledrums; *neduḥ*—resounded; *mṛdaṅga*—drums; *paṇava*—small drums; *ādayaḥ*—etc.; *gandharva-mukhyāḥ*—the chief residents of Gandharvaloka; *prajaguḥ*—sang; *petuḥ*—showered; *kusuma*—flowers; *vṛṣṭayaḥ*—like rains.

TRANSLATION

At that time drums and kettledrums resounded from the sky, the chief Gandharvas began to sing, and other demigods showered flowers like torrents of rain upon Dhruva Mahārāja.

TEXT 32

स च स्वर्लोकमारोक्ष्यन् सुनीतिं जननीं ध्रुवः ।
अन्वस्मरदगं हित्वा दीनां यास्ये त्रिविष्टपम् ॥३२॥

sa ca svarlokam ārokṣyan
sunītiṁ jananīṁ dhruvaḥ
anvasmarad agaṁ hitvā
dīnāṁ yāsye tri-viṣṭapam

saḥ—he; *ca*—also; *svaḥ-lokam*—to the celestial planet; *ārokṣyan*—about to ascend; *sunītim*—Sunīti; *jananīm*—mother; *dhruvaḥ*—Dhruva Mahārāja; *anvasmarat*—immediately remembered; *agam*—difficult to attain; *hitvā*—leaving behind; *dīnām*—poor; *yāsye*—I shall go; *tri-viṣṭapam*—to the Vaikuṇṭha planet.

TRANSLATION

Dhruva was seated in the transcendental airplane, which was just about to start, when he remembered his poor mother, Sunīti. He thought to himself, "How shall I go alone to the Vaikuṇṭha planet and leave behind my poor mother?"

PURPORT

Dhruva had a feeling of obligation to his mother, Sunīti. It was Sunīti who had given him the clue which had now enabled him to be personally carried to the Vaikuṇṭha planet by the associates of Lord Viṣṇu. He now remembered her and wanted to take her with him. Actually, Dhruva Mahārāja's mother, Sunīti, was his *patha-pradarśaka-guru. Patha-pradarśaka-guru* means "the *guru,* or the spiritual master, who shows the way." Such a *guru* is sometimes called *śikṣā-guru.* Although Nārada Muni was his *dīkṣā-guru* (initiating spiritual master), Sunīti, his mother, was the first who gave him instruction on how to achieve the favor of the Supreme Personality of Godhead. It is the duty of the *śikṣā-guru* or *dīkṣā-guru* to instruct the disciple in the right way, and it depends on the disciple to execute the process. According to śāstric injunctions, there is no difference between *śikṣā-guru* and *dīkṣā-guru,* and generally the *śikṣā-guru* later on becomes the *dīkṣā-guru.* Sunīti, however, being a woman, and specifically his mother, could not become Dhruva Mahārāja's *dīkṣā-guru.* Still, he was not less obliged to Sunīti. There was no question of carrying Nārada Muni to Vaikuṇṭhaloka, but Dhruva Mahārāja thought of his mother.

Whatever plan the Supreme Personality of Godhead contemplates immediately fructifies. Similarly, a devotee who is completely dependent on the Supreme Lord can also fulfill his wishes by the grace of the Lord. The Lord fulfills His wishes independently, but a devotee fulfills his wishes simply by being dependent on the Supreme Personality of Godhead. Therefore as soon as Dhruva Mahārāja thought of his poor mother, he was assured by the associates of Viṣṇu that Sunīti was also going to Vaikuṇṭhaloka, in another plane. Dhruva Mahārāja had thought that he was going alone to Vaikuṇṭhaloka, leaving behind his mother, which was not very auspicious because people would criticize him for going alone to Vaikuṇṭhaloka and not carrying with him Sunīti, who had given him so much. But Dhruva also considered that he was not personally the Supreme. Therefore, if Kṛṣṇa fulfilled his desires, only then would it be possible. Kṛṣṇa could immediately understand his mind, and He told Dhruva that his mother was also going with him. This incident proves that a pure devotee like Dhruva Mahārāja can fulfill all his desires; by the grace of the Lord, he becomes exactly like the Lord, and thus whenever he thinks of anything, his wish is immediately fulfilled.

TEXT 33

इति व्यवसितं तस्य व्यवसाय सुरोत्तमौ ।
दर्शयामासतुर्देवीं पुरो यानेन गच्छतीम् ॥३३॥

iti vyavasitaṁ tasya
vyavasāya surottamau
darśayām āsatur devīṁ
puro yānena gacchatīm

iti—thus; *vyavasitam*—contemplation; *tasya*—of Dhruva; *vyavasāya*—understanding; *sura-uttamau*—the two chief associates; *darśayām āsatuḥ*—showed (to him); *devīm*—exalted Sunīti; *puraḥ*—before; *yānena*—by airplane; *gacchatīm*—going forward.

TRANSLATION

The great associates of Vaikuṇṭhaloka, Nanda and Sunanda, could understand the mind of Dhruva Mahārāja, and thus they showed him that his mother, Sunīti, was going forward in another plane.

PURPORT

This incident proves that the *śikṣā-* or *dīkṣā-guru* who has a disciple who strongly executes devotional service like Dhruva Mahārāja can be carried by the disciple even though the instructor is not as advanced. Although Sunīti was an instructor to Dhruva Mahārāja, she could not go to the forest because she was a woman, nor could she execute austerities and penances as Dhruva Mahārāja did. Still, Dhruva Mahārāja was able to take his mother with him. Similarly, Prahlāda Mahārāja also delivered his atheistic father, Hiraṇyakaśipu. The conclusion is that a disciple or an offspring who is a very strong devotee can carry with him to Vaikuṇṭhaloka either his father, mother or *śikṣā-* or *dīkṣā-guru.* Śrīla Bhaktisiddhānta Sarasvatī Ṭhākura used to say, "If I could perfectly deliver even one soul back home, back to Godhead, I would think my mission—propagating Kṛṣṇa consciousness—to be successful." The Kṛṣṇa consciousness movement is spreading now all over the world, and sometimes I think that even though I am crippled in many ways, if one of my disciples becomes as strong as Dhruva Mahārāja, then he will be able to carry me with him to Vaikuṇṭhaloka.

TEXT 34

तत्र तत्र प्रशंसद्भिः पथि वैमानिकैः सुरैः ।
अवकीर्यमाणो ददृशे कुसुमैः क्रमशो ग्रहान् ॥३४॥

tatra tatra praśaṁsadbhiḥ
pathi vaimānikaiḥ suraiḥ
avakīryamāṇo dadṛśe
kusumaiḥ kramaśo grahān

tatra tatra—here and there; *praśaṁsadbhiḥ*—by persons engaged in the praise of Dhruva Mahārāja; *pathi*—on the path; *vaimānikaiḥ*—carried by different types of airplanes; *suraiḥ*—by the demigods; *avakīryamāṇaḥ*—being covered; *dadṛśe*—could see; *kusumaiḥ*—by flowers; *kramaśaḥ*—one after another; *grahān*—all the planets of the solar system.

TRANSLATION

While Dhruva Mahārāja was passing through space, he gradually saw all the planets of the solar system, and on the path he saw all the demigods in their airplanes showering flowers upon him like rain.

PURPORT

There is a Vedic version, *yasmin vijñāte sarvam evaṁ vijñātaṁ bhavati*, which means that by knowing the Supreme Personality of Godhead, everything becomes known to the devotee. Similarly, by going to the planet of the Supreme Personality of Godhead, one can know all the other planetary systems on the path to Vaikuṇṭha. We should remember that Dhruva Mahārāja's body was different from our bodies. While boarding the Vaikuṇṭha airplane, his body changed to a completely spiritual golden hue. No one can surpass the higher planets in a material body, but when one gets a spiritual body he can travel not only to the higher planetary system of this material world, but even to the still higher planetary system known as Vaikuṇṭhaloka. It is well known that

Nārada Muni travels everywhere, both in the spiritual and material worlds.

It should be noted also that while Sunīti was going to Vaikuṇṭhaloka she also changed her body into spiritual form. Like Śrī Sunīti, every mother should train her child to become a devotee like Dhruva Mahārāja. Sunīti instructed her son, even at the age of five years, to be unattached to worldly affairs and to go to the forest to search out the Supreme Lord. She never desired that her son remain at home comfortably without ever undertaking austerities and penances to achieve the favor of the Supreme Personality of Godhead. Every mother, like Sunīti, must take care of her son and train him to become a *brahmacārī* from the age of five years and to undergo austerities and penances for spiritual realization. The benefit will be that if her son becomes a strong devotee like Dhruva, certainly not only will he be transferred back home, back to Godhead, but she will also be transferred with him to the spiritual world, even though she may be unable to undergo austerities and penances in executing devotional service.

TEXT 35

त्रिलोकीं देवयानेन सोऽतिव्रज्य मुनीनपि ।
परस्ताद्यद् ध्रुवगतिर्विष्णोः पदमथाभ्यगात् ॥३५॥

tri-lokīṁ deva-yānena
so 'tivrajya munīn api
parastād yad dhruva-gatir
viṣṇoḥ padam athābhyagāt

tri-lokīm—the three planetary systems; *deva-yānena*—by the transcendental airplane; *saḥ*—Dhruva; *ativrajya*—having surpassed; *munīn*—great sages; *api*—even; *parastāt*—beyond; *yat*—which; *dhruva-gatiḥ*—Dhruva, who attained permanent life; *viṣṇoḥ*—of Lord Viṣṇu; *padam*—abode; *atha*—then; *abhyagāt*—achieved.

TRANSLATION

Dhruva Mahārāja thus surpassed the seven planetary systems of the great sages who are known as saptarṣi. Beyond that region, he

achieved the transcendental situation of permanent life in the planet where Lord Viṣṇu lives.

PURPORT

The airplane was piloted by the two chief associates of Lord Viṣṇu, namely Sunanda and Nanda. Only such spiritual astronauts can pilot their airplane beyond the seven planets and arrive in the region of eternal blissful life. It is confirmed in the *Bhagavad-gītā* also (*paras tasmāt tu bhāvo 'nyaḥ*) that beyond this planetary system begins the spiritual sky, where everything is permanent and blissful. The planets there are known as Viṣṇuloka or Vaikuṇṭhaloka. Only there can one get an eternal blissful life of knowledge. Below Vaikuṇṭhaloka is the material universe, where Lord Brahmā and others in Brahmaloka can live until the annihilation of this universe; but that life is not permanent. That is also confirmed in the *Bhagavad-gītā* (*ābrahma-bhuvanāl lokāḥ*). Even if one goes to the topmost planet, one cannot achieve eternal life. Only by arriving in Vaikuṇṭhaloka can one live an eternally blissful life.

TEXT 36

यद् भ्राजमानं स्वरुचैव सर्वतो
लोकास्त्रयो ह्यनु विभ्राजन्त एते ।
यन्नाव्रजञ्जन्तुषु येऽननुग्रहा
व्रजन्ति भद्राणि चरन्ति येऽनिशम् ॥३६॥

yad bhrājamānaṁ sva-rucaiva sarvato
lokās trayo hy anu vibhrājanta ete
yan nāvrajañ jantuṣu ye 'nanugrahā
vrajanti bhadrāṇi caranti ye 'niśam

yat—which planet; *bhrājamānam*—illuminating; *sva-rucā*—by self-effulgence; *eva*—only; *sarvataḥ*—everywhere; *lokāḥ*—planetary systems; *trayaḥ*—three; *hi*—certainly; *anu*—thereupon; *vibhrājante*—give off light; *ete*—these; *yat*—which planet; *na*—not; *avrajan*—have reached; *jantuṣu*—to living entities; *ye*—those who; *ananugrahāḥ*—not merciful; *vrajanti*—reach; *bhadrāṇi*—welfare activities; *caranti*—engage in; *ye*—those who; *aniśam*—constantly.

TRANSLATION

The self-effulgent Vaikuṇṭha planets, by whose illumination alone all the illuminating planets within this material world give off reflected light, cannot be reached by those who are not merciful to other living entities. Only persons who constantly engage in welfare activities for other living entities can reach the Vaikuṇṭha planets.

PURPORT

Here is a description of two aspects of the Vaikuṇṭha planets. The first is that in the Vaikuṇṭha sky there is no need of the sun and moon. This is confirmed by the *Upaniṣads* as well as *Bhagavad-gītā* (*na tad bhāsayate sūryo na śaśāṅko na pāvakaḥ*). In the spiritual world the Vaikuṇṭhalokas are themselves illuminated; there is therefore no need of sun, moon or electric light. It is in fact the illumination of the Vaikuṇṭhalokas which is reflected in the material sky. Only by this reflection are the suns in the material universes illuminated; after the illumination of the sun, all the stars and moons are illuminated. In other words, all the luminaries in the material sky borrow illumination from Vaikuṇṭhaloka. From this material world, however, people can be transferred to the Vaikuṇṭhaloka, if they incessantly engage in welfare activities for all other living entities. Such incessant welfare activities can really be performed only in Kṛṣṇa consciousness. There is no philanthropic work within this material world but Kṛṣṇa consciousness that can engage a person twenty-four hours a day.

A Kṛṣṇa conscious being is always engaged in planning how to take all of suffering humanity back home, back to Godhead. Even if one is not successful in reclaiming all the fallen souls back to Godhead, still, because he is Kṛṣṇa conscious, his path to Vaikuṇṭhaloka is open. He personally becomes qualified to enter the Vaikuṇṭhalokas, and if anyone follows such a devotee, he also enters into Vaikuṇṭhaloka. Others, who engage in envious activities, are known as *karmīs*. *Karmīs* are envious of one another. Simply for sense gratification, they can kill thousands of innocent animals. *Jñānīs* are not as sinful as *karmīs*, but they do not try to reclaim others back to Godhead. They perform austerities for their own liberation. *Yogīs* are also engaged in self-aggrandizement by trying to attain mystic powers. But devotees, Vaiṣṇavas, who are servants of the Lord, come forward in the actual field of work in Kṛṣṇa consciousness to reclaim fallen souls. Only Kṛṣṇa conscious persons are eligible to enter into the spiritual world. That is clearly stated in this verse and is confirmed in *Bhagavad-gītā*, wherein the Lord says that there is no one dearer to Him than those who preach the gospel of *Bhagavad-gītā* to the world.

TEXT 37

शान्ताः समदृशः शुद्धाः सर्वभूतानुरञ्जनाः ।
यान्त्यञ्जसाच्युतपदमच्युतप्रियबान्धवाः ॥३७॥

śāntāḥ sama-dṛśaḥ śuddhāḥ
sarva-bhūtānurañjanāḥ
yānty añjasācyuta-padam
acyuta-priya-bāndhavāḥ

śāntāḥ—peaceful; *sama-dṛśaḥ*—equipoised; *śuddhāḥ*—cleansed, purified; *sarva*—all; *bhūta*—living entities; *anurañjanāḥ*—pleasing; *yānti*—go; *añjasā*—easily; *acyuta*—of the Lord; *padam*—to the abode; *acyuta-priya*—with devotees of the Lord; *bāndhavāḥ*—friends.

TRANSLATION

Persons who are peaceful, equipoised, cleansed and purified, and who know the art of pleasing all other living entities, keep friendship only with devotees of the Lord; they alone can very easily achieve the perfection of going back home, back to Godhead.

PURPORT

The description of this verse fully indicates that only devotees are eligible to enter into the kingdom of Godhead. The first point stated is that devotees are peaceful, for they have no demands for their personal sense gratification. They are simply dedicated to the service of the Lord. *Karmīs* cannot be peaceful because they have immense demands for sense gratification. As for *jñānīs*, they cannot be peaceful because they are too busy trying to attain liberation or merge into the existence of the Supreme. Similarly, *yogīs* are also restless to get mystic power. But a devotee is peaceful because he is fully surrendered to the Supreme Personality of Godhead and thinks of himself as completely helpless; just as a child feels complete peace in depending on the parent, so a devotee is completely peaceful, for he depends on the mercy of the Supreme Personality of Godhead.

A devotee is equipoised. He sees everyone on the same transcendental platform. A devotee knows that although a conditioned soul has a particular type of body according to his past fruitive activities, factually everyone is part of the Supreme Lord. A devotee sees all living entities with spiritual vision and does not discriminate on the platform of the bodily concept of life. Such qualities develop only in the association of devotees. Without the association of devotees, one cannot advance in Kṛṣṇa consciousness. Therefore, we have established the International Society for Krishna Consciousness. Factually, whoever lives in this society automatically develops Kṛṣṇa consciousness. Devotees are dear to the Supreme Personality of Godhead, and the Supreme Personality of Godhead is only dear to devotees. On this platform only can one make progress in Kṛṣṇa consciousness. Persons in Kṛṣṇa consciousness, or devotees of the Lord, can please everyone, as is evident in the Kṛṣṇa consciousness movement. We invite everyone, without discrimination; we request everyone to sit down and chant the Hare Kṛṣṇa *mantra* and take as much *prasāda* as we can supply, and thus everyone is pleased with us. This is the qualification. *Sarva-bhūtānurañjanāḥ.* As for purification, no one can be more pure than devotees. Anyone who once utters the name of Viṣṇu immediately becomes purified, inside and outside (*yaḥ smaret puṇḍarīkākṣam*). Since a devotee constantly chants the Hare Kṛṣṇa *mantra*, no contamination of the material world can touch him. He is, therefore, actually purified. *Muci haya śuci haya yadi kṛṣṇa bhaje.* It is said that even a cobbler or person born in the family of a cobbler can be elevated to the position of a *brāhmaṇa* (*śuci*) if he takes to Kṛṣṇa consciousness. Any person who is purely Kṛṣṇa conscious and who engages in chanting the Hare Kṛṣṇa *mantra* is the purest in the whole universe.

TEXT 38

इत्युत्तानपदः पुत्रो ध्रुवः कृष्णपरायणः ।
अभूत्त्रयाणां लोकानां चूडामणिरिवामलः ॥३८॥

ity uttānapadaḥ putro
dhruvaḥ kṛṣṇa-parāyaṇaḥ
abhūt trayāṇāṁ lokānāṁ
cūḍā-maṇir ivāmalaḥ

iti—thus; *uttānapadaḥ*—of Mahārāja Uttānapāda; *putraḥ*—the son; *dhruvaḥ*—Dhruva Mahārāja; *kṛṣṇa-parāyaṇaḥ*—fully Kṛṣṇa conscious; *abhūt*—became; *trayāṇām*—of the three; *lokānām*—worlds; *cūḍā-maṇiḥ*—the summit jewel; *iva*—like; *amalaḥ*—purified.

TRANSLATION

In this way, the fully Kṛṣṇa conscious Dhruva Mahārāja, the exalted son of Mahārāja Uttānapāda, attained the summit of the three statuses of planetary systems.

PURPORT

The exact Sanskrit terminology for Kṛṣṇa consciousness is here mentioned: *kṛṣṇa-parāyaṇaḥ. Parāyaṇa* means "going forward." Anyone who is going forward to the goal of Kṛṣṇa is called *kṛṣṇa-parāyaṇa*, or fully Kṛṣṇa conscious. The example of Dhruva Mahārāja indicates that every Kṛṣṇa conscious person can expect to reach the topmost summit of all three planetary systems within the universe. A Kṛṣṇa conscious person can occupy an exalted position beyond the imagination of any ambitious materialist.

TEXT 39

गम्भीरवेगोऽनिमिषं ज्योतिषां चक्रमाहितम् ।
यस्मिन् भ्रमति कौरव्य मेढ्यामिव गवां गणः ॥३९॥

gambhīra-vego 'nimiṣaṁ
jyotiṣāṁ cakram āhitam

yasmin bhramati kauravya
meḍhyām iva gavāṁ gaṇaḥ

gambhīra-vegaḥ—with great force and speed; *animiṣam*—unceasingly; *jyotiṣām*—of luminaries; *cakram*—sphere; *āhitam*—connected; *yasmin*—around which; *bhramati*—encircles; *kauravya*—O Vidura; *meḍhyām*—a central pole; *iva*—as; *gavām*—of bulls; *gaṇaḥ*—a herd.

TRANSLATION

Saint Maitreya continued: My dear Vidura, descendant of Kuru, as a herd of bulls circumambulates a central pole on their right side, all the luminaries within the universal sky unceasingly circumambulate the abode of Dhruva Mahārāja with great force and speed.

PURPORT

Each and every planet within the universe travels at a very high speed. From a statement in *Śrīmad-Bhāgavatam* it is understood that even the sun travels sixteen thousand miles in a second, and from *Brahma-saṁhitā* we understand from the *śloka, yac-cakṣur eṣa savitā sakala-grahāṇām* that the sun is considered to be the eye of the Supreme Personality of Godhead, Govinda, and it also has a specific orbit within which it circles. Similarly, all other planets have their specific orbits. But together all of them encircle the polestar, or Dhruvaloka, where Dhruva Mahārāja is situated at the summit of the three worlds. We can only imagine how highly exalted the actual position of a devotee is, and certainly we cannot even conceive how exalted is the position of the Supreme Personality of Godhead.

TEXT 40

महिमानं विलोक्यास्य नारदो भगवानृषिः ।
आतोद्यं वितुदञ् श्लोकान् सत्रेऽगायत्प्रचेतसाम् ॥४०॥

mahimānaṁ vilokyāsya
nārado bhagavān ṛṣiḥ

ātodyaṁ vitudañ ślokān
satre 'gāyat pracetasām

mahimānam—glories; *vilokya*—observing; *asya*—of Dhruva Mahārāja; *nāradaḥ*—the great sage Nārada; *bhagavān*—equally as exalted as the Supreme Personality of Godhead; *ṛṣiḥ*—the saint; *ātodyam*—the stringed instrument, *vīṇā; vitudan*—playing on; *ślokān*—verses; *satre*—in the sacrificial arena; *agāyat*—chanted; *pracetasām*—of the Pracetās.

TRANSLATION

After observing the glories of Dhruva Mahārāja, the great sage Nārada, playing his vīṇā, went to the sacrificial arena of the Pracetās and very happily chanted the following three verses.

PURPORT

The great sage Nārada was the spiritual master of Dhruva Mahārāja. Certainly he was very glad to see Dhruva's glories. As a father is very happy to see the son's advancement in every respect, so the spiritual master is very happy to observe the ascendancy of his disciple.

TEXT 41

नारद उवाच
नूनं सुनीतेः पतिदेवताया-
स्तपःप्रभावस्य सुतस्य तां गतिम् ।
दृष्ट्वाभ्युपायानपि वेदवादिनो
नैवाधिगन्तुं प्रभवन्ति किं नृपाः ॥४१॥

nārada uvāca
nūnaṁ sunīteḥ pati-devatāyās
tapaḥ-prabhāvasya sutasya tāṁ gatim
dṛṣṭvābhyupāyān api veda-vādino
naivādhigantuṁ prabhavanti kiṁ nṛpāḥ

nāradaḥ uvāca—Nārada said; *nūnam*—certainly; *sunīteḥ*—of Sunīti; *pati-devatāyāḥ*—very much attached to her husband; *tapaḥ-prabhā-*

vasya—by the influence of austerity; *sutasya*—of the son; *tām*—that; *gatim*—position; *dṛṣṭvā*—observing; *abhyupāyān*—the means; *api*—although; *veda-vādinaḥ*—strict followers of the Vedic principles, or the so-called Vedāntists; *na*—never; *eva*—certainly; *adhigantum*—to attain; *prabhavanti*—are eligible; *kim*—what to speak of; *nṛpāḥ*—ordinary kings.

TRANSLATION

The great sage Nārada said: Simply by the influence of his spiritual advancement and powerful austerity, Dhruva Mahārāja, the son of Sunīti, who was devoted to her husband, acquired an exalted position not possible to attain even for the so-called Vedāntists or strict followers of the Vedic principles, not to speak of ordinary human beings.

PURPORT

In this verse the word *veda-vādinaḥ* is very significant. Generally, a person who strictly follows the Vedic principles is called *veda-vādī.* There are also so-called Vedāntists who advertise themselves as followers of Vedānta philosophy but who misinterpret *Vedānta.* The expression *veda-vāda-ratāḥ* is also found in the *Bhagavad-gītā*, referring to persons who are attached to the *Vedas* without understanding the purport of the *Vedas.* Such persons may go on talking about the *Vedas* or may execute austerities in their own way, but it is not possible for them to attain to such an exalted position as Dhruva Mahārāja. As far as ordinary kings are concerned, it is not at all possible. The specific mention of kings is significant because formerly kings were also *rājarṣis*, for the kings were as good as great sages. Dhruva Mahārāja was a king, and at the same time he was as learned as a great sage. But without devotional service, neither a great king, a *kṣatriya*, nor a great *brāhmaṇa* strictly adhering to the Vedic principles can be elevated to the exalted position attained by Dhruva Mahārāja.

TEXT 42

यः पञ्चवर्षो गुरुदारवाक्शरै-
र्भिन्नेन यातो हृदयेन दूयता ।

वनं मदादेशकरोऽजितं प्रभुं
जिगाय तद्भक्तगुणैः पराजितम् ॥४२॥

yaḥ pañca-varṣo guru-dāra-vāk-śarair
bhinnena yāto hṛdayena dūyatā
vanaṁ mad-ādeśa-karo 'jitaṁ prabhuṁ
jigāya tad-bhakta-guṇaiḥ parājitam

yaḥ—he who; *pañca-varṣaḥ*—at the age of five years; *guru-dāra*—of the wife of his father; *vāk-śaraiḥ*—by the harsh words; *bhinnena*—being very much aggrieved; *yātaḥ*—went; *hṛdayena*—because his heart; *dūyatā*—very much pained; *vanam*—to the forest; *mat-ādeśa*—according to my instruction; *karaḥ*—acting; *ajitam*—unconquerable; *prabhum*—the Supreme Personality of Godhead; *jigāya*—he defeated; *tat*—His; *bhakta*—of devotees; *guṇaiḥ*—with the qualities; *parājitam*—conquered.

TRANSLATION

The great sage Nārada continued: Just see how Dhruva Mahārāja, aggrieved at the harsh words of his stepmother, went to the forest at the age of only five years and under my direction underwent austerity. Although the Supreme Personality of Godhead is unconquerable, Dhruva Mahārāja defeated Him with the specific qualifications possessed by the Lord's devotees.

PURPORT

The Supreme Godhead is unconquerable; no one can conquer the Lord. But He voluntarily accepts subordination to the devotional qualities of His devotees. For example, Lord Kṛṣṇa accepted subordination to the control of mother Yaśodā because she was a great devotee. The Lord likes to be under the control of His devotees. In the *Caitanya-caritāmṛta* it is said that everyone comes before the Lord and offers Him exalted prayers, but the Lord does not feel as pleased when offered such prayers as He does when a devotee, out of pure love, chastises Him as a subordinate. The Lord forgets His exalted position and willingly submits to His pure devotee. Dhruva Mahārāja conquered the Supreme Lord because at a very tender age, only five years old, he underwent all the austerities of devotional service. This devotional service was of course executed under the direction of a great sage, Nārada. This is the first principle of devotional service—*ādau gurv-āśrayam.* In the beginning one must accept a bona fide spiritual master, and if a devotee follows strictly the direction of the spiritual master, as Dhruva Mahārāja followed the instruction of Nārada Muni, then it is not difficult for him to achieve the favor of the Lord.

The sum total of devotional qualities is development of unalloyed love for Kṛṣṇa. This unalloyed love for Kṛṣṇa can be achieved simply by hearing about Kṛṣṇa. Lord Caitanya accepted this principle—that if one in any position submissively hears the transcendental message spoken by Kṛṣṇa or about Kṛṣṇa, then gradually he develops the quality of unalloyed love, and by that love only he can conquer the unconquerable. The Māyāvādī philosophers aspire to become one with the Supreme Lord, but a devotee surpasses that position. Not only does a devotee become one in quality with the Supreme Lord, but he sometimes becomes the father, mother or master of the Lord. Arjuna also, by his devotional service, made Lord Kṛṣṇa his chariot driver; he ordered the Lord, "Put my chariot here," and the Lord executed his order. These are some examples of how a devotee can acquire the exalted position of conquering the unconquerable.

TEXT 43

यः क्षत्रबन्धुर्भुवि तस्याधिरूढ-
मन्वारुरुक्षेदपि वर्षपूगैः ।
षट्पञ्चवर्षो यदहोभिरल्पैः
प्रसाद्य वैकुण्ठमवाप तत्पदम् ॥४३॥

yaḥ kṣatra-bandhur bhuvi tasyādhirūḍham
anv āruruksed api varṣa-pūgaiḥ
ṣaṭ-pañca-varṣo yad ahobhir alpaiḥ
prasādya vaikuṇṭham avāpa tat-padam

yaḥ—one who; *kṣatra-bandhuḥ*—the son of a *kṣatriya; bhuvi*—on the earth; *tasya*—of Dhruva; *adhirūḍham*—the exalted position; *anu*—after; *āarurukṣet*—can aspire to attain; *api*—even; *varṣa-pūgaiḥ*—after many years; *ṣaṭ-pañca-varṣaḥ*—five or six years old; *yat*—which; *ahobhiḥ alpaiḥ*—after a few days; *prasādya*—after pleasing; *vaikuṇṭham*—the Lord; *avāpa*—attained; *tat-padam*—His abode.

TRANSLATION

Dhruva Mahārāja attained an exalted position at the age of only five or six years, after undergoing austerity for six months. Alas, a great kṣatriya cannot achieve such a position even after undergoing austerities for many, many years.

PURPORT

Dhruva Mahārāja is described herein as *kṣatra-bandhuḥ,* which indicates that he was not fully trained as a *kṣatriya* because he was only five years old; he was not a mature *kṣatriya.* A *kṣatriya* or *brāhmaṇa* has to take training. A boy born in the family of a *brāhmaṇa* is not immediately a *brāhmaṇa;* he has to take up the training and the purificatory process.

The great sage Nārada Muni was very proud of having a devotee-disciple like Dhruva Mahārāja. He had many other disciples, but he was very pleased with Dhruva Mahārāja because in one lifetime, by dint of his severe penances and austerities, he had achieved Vaikuṇṭha, which was never achieved by any other king's son or *rājarṣi* throughout the whole universe. There is the instance of the great King Bharata, who was also a great devotee, but he attained Vaikuṇṭhaloka in three lives. In the first life, although he executed austerities in the forest, he became a victim of too much affection for a small deer, and in his next life he had to take birth as a deer. Although he had a deer's body, he remembered his spiritual position, but he still had to wait until the next life for perfection. In the next life he took birth as Jaḍa Bharata. Of course, in that life he was completely freed from all material entanglement, and he attained perfection and was elevated to Vaikuṇṭhaloka. The lesson from the life of Dhruva Mahārāja is that if one likes, one can attain Vaikuṇṭhaloka in one life, without waiting for many other lives. My Guru Mahārāja, Śrī Śrīmad Bhaktisiddhānta Sarasvatī Gosvāmī Prabhupāda, used to say that every one of his disciples could attain Vaikuṇṭhaloka in this life, without waiting for another life to execute devotional service. One simply has to become as serious and sincere as Dhruva Mahārāja; then it is quite possible to attain Vaikuṇṭhaloka and go back home, back to Godhead, in one life.

TEXT 44

मैत्रेय उवाच
एतत्तेऽभिहितं सर्वं यत्पृष्टोऽहमिह त्वया ।
ध्रुवस्योद्दामयशसश्चरितं सम्मतं सताम् ॥४४॥

maitreya uvāca
etat te 'bhihitaṁ sarvaṁ
yat pṛṣṭo 'ham iha tvayā
dhruvasyoddāma-yaśasaś
caritaṁ sammataṁ satām

maitreyaḥ uvāca—the great sage Maitreya said; *etat*—this; *te*—unto you; *abhihitam*—described; *sarvam*—everything; *yat*—what; *pṛṣṭaḥ aham*—I was asked; *iha*—here; *tvayā*—by you; *dhruvasya*—of Dhruva Mahārāja; *uddāma*—greatly uplifting; *yaśasaḥ*—whose reputation; *caritam*—character; *sammatam*—approved; *satām*—by great devotees.

TRANSLATION

The great sage Maitreya continued: My dear Vidura, whatever you have asked from me about the great reputation and character of Dhruva Mahārāja I have explained to you in all detail. Great saintly persons and devotees very much like to hear about Dhruva Mahārāja.

PURPORT

Śrīmad-Bhāgavatam means everything in relationship with the Supreme Personality of Godhead. Whether we hear the pastimes and activities of the Supreme Lord or we hear about the character, reputation and activities of His devotees, they are all one and the same. Neophyte devotees simply try to understand the pastimes of the Lord and are not very interested in hearing about the activities of His devotees, but such discrimination should not be indulged in by any real devotee. Sometimes less intelligent men try to hear about the *rāsa* dance of Kṛṣṇa and do not take care to hear about other portions of *Śrīmad-Bhāgavatam,* which they completely avoid. There are professional *Bhāgavata* reciters who abruptly go to the *rāsa-līlā* chapters of *Śrīmad-Bhāgavatam,* as if other portions of *Śrīmad-Bhāgavatam* were useless. This kind of discrimination and abrupt adoption of the *rāsa-līlā* pastimes of the Lord is not approved by the *ācāryas.* A sincere devotee should read every chapter and every word of *Śrīmad-Bhāgavatam,* for the beginning verses describe that it is the ripened fruit of all Vedic literature. Devotees should not try to avoid even a word of *Śrīmad-Bhāgavatam.* The great sage Maitreya therefore affirmed herein that the *Bhāgavatam* is *sammataṁ satām,* approved by great devotees.

TEXT 45

धन्यं यशस्यमायुष्यं पुण्यं स्वस्त्ययनं महत् ।
स्वर्ग्यं ध्रौव्यं सौमनस्यं प्रशस्यमघमर्षणम् ॥४५॥

dhanyaṁ yaśasyam āyuṣyaṁ
puṇyaṁ svasty-ayanaṁ mahat
svargyaṁ dhrauvyaṁ saumanasyaṁ
praśasyam agha-marṣaṇam

dhanyam—bestowing wealth; *yaśasyam*—bestowing reputation; *āyuṣyam*—increasing the duration of life; *puṇyam*—sacred; *svasti-ayanam*—creating auspiciousness; *mahat*—great; *svargyam*—bestowing achievement of heavenly planets; *dhrauvyam*—or Dhruvaloka; *saumanasyam*—pleasing to the mind; *praśasyam*—glorious; *agha-marṣaṇam*—counteracting all kinds of sinful activities.

TRANSLATION

By hearing the narration of Dhruva Mahārāja one can fulfill desires for wealth, reputation and increased duration of life. It is so auspicious that one can even go to a heavenly planet or attain Dhruvaloka, which was achieved by Dhruva Mahārāja, just by hearing about him. The demigods also become pleased because

this narration is so glorious, and it is so powerful that it can counteract all the results of one's sinful actions.

PURPORT

There are different types of men in this world, not all of them pure devotees. Some are *karmīs*, desiring to acquire vast wealth. There are also persons who are only after reputation. Some desire to be elevated to the heavenly planets or to go to Dhruvaloka, and others want to please the demigods to get material profits. Herein it is recommended by Maitreya that every one of them can hear the narration about Dhruva Mahārāja and thus get their desired goal. It is recommended that the devotees (*akāma*), the *karmīs* (*sarva-kāma*) and the *jñānīs*, who desire to be liberated (*mokṣa-kāma*), should all worship the Supreme Personality of Godhead to acquire their desired goals of life. Similarly, if anyone hears about the activities of the Lord's devotee, he can achieve the same result. There is no difference between the activities and character of the Supreme Personality of Godhead and those of His pure devotees.

TEXT 46

श्रुत्वैतच्छ्रद्धयाभीक्ष्णमच्युतप्रियचेष्टितम् ।
भवेद्भक्तिर्भगवति यया स्यात्क्लेशसंक्षयः ॥४६॥

śrutvaitac chraddhayābhīkṣṇam
acyuta-priya-ceṣṭitam
bhaved bhaktir bhagavati
yayā syāt kleśa-saṅkṣayaḥ

śrutvā—by hearing; *etat*—this; *śraddhayā*—with faith; *abhīkṣṇam*—repeatedly; *acyuta*—to the Supreme Personality of Godhead; *priya*—dear; *ceṣṭitam*—activities; *bhavet*—develops; *bhaktiḥ*—devotion; *bhagavati*—unto the Supreme Personality of Godhead; *yayā*—by which; *syāt*—must be; *kleśa*—of miseries; *saṅkṣayaḥ*—complete diminution.

TRANSLATION

Anyone who hears the narration of Dhruva Mahārāja, and who repeatedly tries with faith and devotion to understand his pure

character, attains the pure devotional platform and executes pure devotional service. By such activities one can diminish the threefold miserable conditions of material life.

PURPORT

Here the word *acyuta-priya* is very significant. Dhruva Mahārāja's character and reputation are great because he is very dear to Acyuta, the Supreme Personality of Godhead. As the pastimes and activities of the Supreme Lord are pleasing to hear, hearing about His devotees, who are very dear to the Supreme Person, is also pleasing and potent. If one simply reads over and over again about Dhruva Mahārāja by hearing and reading this chapter, one can attain the highest perfection of life in any way he desires; most importantly, he gets the chance to become a great devotee. To become a great devotee means to finish all miserable conditions of materialistic life.

TEXT 47

महत्त्वमिच्छतां तीर्थं श्रोतुः शीलादयो गुणाः ।
यत्र तेजस्तदिच्छूनां मानो यत्र मनस्विनाम् ॥४७॥

mahattvam icchatāṁ tīrthaṁ
śrotuḥ śīlādayo guṇāḥ
yatra tejas tad icchūnāṁ
māno yatra manasvinām

mahattvam—greatness; *icchatām*—for those desiring; *tīrtham*—the process; *śrotuḥ*—of the hearer; *śīla-ādayaḥ*—high character, etc.; *guṇāḥ*—qualities; *yatra*—in which; *tejaḥ*—prowess; *tat*—that; *icchūnām*—for those who desire; *mānaḥ*—adoration; *yatra*—in which; *manasvinām*—for thoughtful men.

TRANSLATION

Anyone who hears this narration of Dhruva Mahārāja acquires exalted qualities like him. For anyone who desires greatness, prowess or influence, here is the process by which to acquire them, and for thoughtful men who want adoration, here is the proper means.

PURPORT

In the material world everyone is after profit, respectability and reputation, everyone wants the supreme exalted position, and everyone wants to hear about the great qualities of exalted persons. All ambitions which are desirable for great persons can be fulfilled simply by reading and understanding the narration of Dhruva Mahārāja's activities.

TEXT 48

प्रयतः कीर्तयेत्प्रातः समवाये द्विजन्मनाम् ।
सायं च पुण्यश्लोकस्य ध्रुवस्य चरितं महत् ॥४८॥

prayataḥ kīrtayet prātaḥ
samavāye dvi-janmanām
sāyaṁ ca puṇya-ślokasya
dhruvasya caritaṁ mahat

prayataḥ—with great care; *kīrtayet*—one should chant; *prātaḥ*—in the morning; *samavāye*—in the association; *dvi-janmanām*—of the twice-born; *sāyam*—in the evening; *ca*—also; *puṇya-ślokasya*—of sacred renown; *dhruvasya*—of Dhruva; *caritam*—character; *mahat*—great.

TRANSLATION

The great sage Maitreya recommended: One should chant of the character and activities of Dhruva Mahārāja both in the morning and in the evening, with great attention and care, in a society of brāhmaṇas or other twice-born persons.

PURPORT

It is said that only in the association of devotees can one understand the importance of the character and pastimes of the Supreme Personality of Godhead or His devotees. In this verse it is especially recommended that Dhruva Mahārāja's character be discussed in a society of the twice-born, which refers to the qualified *brāhmaṇas*, *kṣatriyas* and *vaiśyas*. One should especially seek the society of *brāhmaṇas* who are elevated to the position of Vaiṣṇavas. Thus discussion of *Śrīmad-Bhāgavatam*, which describes the character and pastimes of devotees and the Lord, is very quickly effective. The International Society for Krishna Consciousness has been organized for this purpose. In every center of this Society—not only in the morning, evening or noon, but practically twenty-four hours a day—there is continuous devotional service going on. Anyone who comes in contact with the Society automatically becomes a devotee. We have actual experience that many *karmīs* and others come to the Society and find a very pleasing and peaceful atmosphere in the temples of ISKCON. In this verse the word *dvi-janmanām* means "of the twice-born." Anyone can join the International Society for Krishna Consciousness and be initiated to become twice-born. As recommended by Sanātana Gosvāmī, by the process of initiation and authorized training, any man can become twice-born. The first birth is made possible by the parents, and the second birth is made possible by the spiritual father and Vedic knowledge. Unless one is twice-born one cannot understand the transcendental characteristics of the Lord and His devotees. Study of the *Vedas* is therefore forbidden for *śūdras.* Simply by academic qualifications a *śūdra* cannot understand the transcendental science. At the present moment, throughout the entire world the educational system is geared to produce *śūdras.* A big technologist is no more than a big *śūdra. Kalau śūdra-sambhavaḥ:* in the age of Kali, everyone is a *śūdra.* Because the whole population of the world consists only of *śūdras*, there is a decline of spiritual knowledge, and people are unhappy. The Kṛṣṇa consciousness movement has been started especially to create qualified *brāhmaṇas* to broadcast spiritual knowledge all over the world, for thus people may become very happy.

TEXTS 49–50

पौर्णमास्यां सिनीवाल्यां द्वादश्यां श्रवणेऽथवा ।
दिनक्षये व्यतीपाते सङ्क्रमेऽर्कदिनेऽपि वा ॥४९॥
श्रावयेच्छ्रद्दधानानां तीर्थपादपदाश्रयः ।
नेच्छंस्तत्रात्मनात्मानं सन्तुष्ट इति सिध्यति॥५०॥

paurṇamāsyāṁ sinīvālyāṁ
dvādaśyāṁ śravaṇe 'thavā

dina-kṣaye vyatīpāte
saṅkrame 'rkadine 'pi vā
śrāvayec chraddadhānānāṁ
tīrtha-pāda-padāśrayaḥ
necchaṁs tatrātmanātmānaṁ
santuṣṭa iti sidhyati

paurṇamāsyām—on the full moon; *sinīvālyām*—on the dark moon; *dvādaśyām*—on the day after Ekādaśī; *śravaṇe*—during the Śravaṇa star's appearance; *athavā*—or; *dina-kṣaye*—at the end of the *tithi; vyatīpāte*—a particular day of the name; *saṅkrame*—at the end of the month; *arkadine*—on Sunday; *api*—also; *vā*—or; *śrāvayet*—one should recite; *śraddadhānānām*—to a receptive audience; *tīrtha-pāda*—of the Supreme Personality of Godhead; *pada-āśrayaḥ*—taken shelter of the lotus feet; *na icchan*—without desiring remuneration; *tatra*—there; *ātmanā*—by the self; *ātmānam*—the mind; *santuṣṭaḥ*—pacified; *iti*—thus; *sidhyati*—becomes perfect.

TRANSLATION

Persons who have completely taken shelter of the lotus feet of the Lord should recite this narration of Dhruva Mahārāja without taking remuneration. Specifically, recitation is recommended on the full moon or dark moon day, on the day after Ekādaśī, on the appearance of the Śravaṇa star, at the end of a particular tithi, or the occasion of Vyatīpāta, at the end of the month, or on Sunday. Such recitation should of course be performed before a favorable audience. When recitation is performed this way, without professional motive, the reciter and audience become perfect.

PURPORT

Professional reciters may ask money to extinguish the blazing fire within their bellies, but they cannot make any spiritual improvement or become perfect. It is therefore strictly forbidden to recite *Śrīmad-Bhāgavatam* as a profession to earn a livelihood. Only one who is completely surrendered at the lotus feet of the Supreme Personality of

Godhead, depending fully on Him for personal maintenance or even for maintenance of his family, can attain perfection by recitation of *Śrīmad-Bhāgavatam*, which is full of narrations of the pastimes of the Lord and His devotees. The process can be summarized as follows: the audience must be faithfully receptive to the *Bhāgavata* message, and the reciter should completely depend on the Supreme Personality of Godhead. *Bhāgavata* recitation must not be a business. If done in the right way, not only does the reciter achieve perfect satisfaction, but the Lord also is very satisfied with the reciter and the audience, and thus both are liberated from material bondage simply by the process of hearing.

TEXT 51

ज्ञानमज्ञाततत्त्वाय यो दद्यात्सत्पथेऽमृतम् ।
कृपालोर्दीननाथस्य देवास्तस्यानुगृह्णते ॥५१॥

jñānam ajñāta-tattvāya
yo dadyāt sat-pathe 'mṛtam
kṛpālor dīna-nāthasya
devās tasyānugṛhṇate

jñānam—knowledge; *ajñāta-tattvāya*—to those who are unaware of the truth; *yaḥ*—one who; *dadyāt*—imparts; *sat-pathe*—on the path of truth; *amṛtam*—immortality; *kṛpāloḥ*—kind; *dīna-nāthasya*—protector of the poor; *devāḥ*—the demigods; *tasya*—to him; *anugṛhṇate*—give blessings.

TRANSLATION

The narration of Dhruva Mahārāja is sublime knowledge for the attainment of immortality. Persons unaware of the Absolute Truth can be led to the path of truth. Those who out of transcendental kindness take on the responsibility of becoming master-protectors of the poor living entities automatically gain the interest and blessings of the demigods.

PURPORT

Jñānam ajñāta means knowledge which is unknown almost throughout the entire world. No one knows actually what is the Absolute Truth.

Materialists are very proud of their advancement in education, in philosophical speculation and in scientific knowledge, but no one actually knows what the Absolute Truth is. The great sage Maitreya, therefore, recommends that to enlighten people about the Absolute Truth (*tattva*), devotees should preach the teachings of *Śrīmad-Bhāgavatam* throughout the entire world. Śrīla Vyāsadeva especially compiled this great literature of scientific knowledge because people are completely unaware of the Absolute Truth. In the beginning of *Śrīmad-Bhāgavatam*, First Canto, it is said that Vyāsadeva, the learned sage, compiled this great *Bhāgavata Purāṇa* just to stop the ignorance of the mass of people. Because people do not know the Absolute Truth, this *Śrīmad-Bhāgavatam* was specifically compiled by Vyāsadeva under the instruction of Nārada. Generally, even though people are interested in understanding the truth, they take to speculation and reach at most the conception of impersonal Brahman. But very few men actually know the Personality of Godhead.

Recitation of *Śrīmad-Bhāgavatam* is specifically meant to enlighten people about the Absolute Truth, the Supreme Personality of Godhead. Although there is no fundamental difference between impersonal Brahman, localized Paramātmā and the Supreme Person, factual immortality cannot be obtained unless and until one attains the stage of associating with the Supreme Person. Devotional service, which leads to the association of the Supreme Lord, is actual immortality. Pure devotees, out of compassion for the fallen souls, are *kṛpālu*, very kind to people in general; they distribute this *Bhāgavata* knowledge all over the world. A kindhearted devotee is called *dīna-nātha*, protector of the poor, ignorant mass of people. Lord Kṛṣṇa is also known as *dīna-nātha* or *dīna-bandhu*, the master or actual friend of the poor living entities, and His pure devotee also takes the same position of *dīna-nātha*. The *dīna-nāthas*, or devotees of Lord Kṛṣṇa, who preach the path of devotional service, become the favorites of the demigods. Generally people are interested in worshiping the demigods, especially Lord Śiva, in order to obtain material benefits, but a pure devotee, who engages in preaching the principles of devotional service, as prescribed in the *Śrīmad-Bhāgavatam*, does not need to separately worship the demigods; the demigods are automatically pleased with him and offer all the blessings within their capacity. As by watering the root of a tree the leaves and branches are automatically watered, so, by executing pure devotional service to the

Lord, the branches, twigs and leaves of the Lord, known as demigods, are automatically pleased with the devotee, and they offer all benedictions.

TEXT 52

इदं मया तेऽभिहितं कुरूद्वह
ध्रुवस्य विख्यातविशुद्धकर्मणः ।
हित्वार्भकः क्रीडनकानि मातु-
र्गृहं च विष्णुं शरणं यो जगाम ॥५२॥

idaṁ mayā te 'bhihitaṁ kurūdvaha
dhruvasya vikhyāta-viśuddha-karmaṇaḥ
hitvārbhakaḥ krīḍanakāni mātur
gṛhaṁ ca viṣṇuṁ śaraṇaṁ yo jagāma

idam—this; *mayā*—by me; *te*—unto you; *abhihitam*—described; *kuru-udvaha*—O great one among the Kurus; *dhruvasya*—of Dhruva; *vikhyāta*—very famous; *viśuddha*—very pure; *karmaṇaḥ*—whose activities; *hitvā*—giving up; *arbhakaḥ*—child; *krīḍanakāni*—toys and playthings; *mātuḥ*—of his mother; *gṛham*—home; *ca*—also; *viṣṇum*—to Lord Viṣṇu; *śaraṇam*—shelter; *yaḥ*—one who; *jagāma*—went.

TRANSLATION

The transcendental activities of Dhruva Mahārāja are well known all over the world, and they are very pure. In childhood Dhruva Mahārāja rejected all kinds of toys and playthings, left the protection of his mother and seriously took shelter of the Supreme Personality of Godhead, Viṣṇu. My dear Vidura, I therefore conclude this narration, for I have described to you all its details.

PURPORT

It is said by Cāṇakya Paṇḍita that life is certainly short for everyone, but if one acts properly, his reputation will remain for a generation. As the Supreme Personality of Godhead, Kṛṣṇa, is everlastingly famous, so the reputation of Lord Kṛṣṇa's devotee is also everlasting. Therefore in describing Dhruva Mahārāja's activities two specific words have been used—*vikhyāta*, very famous, and *viśuddha*, transcendental. Dhruva Mahārāja's leaving home at a tender age and taking shelter of the Supreme Personality of Godhead in the forest is a unique example in this world.

Thus end the Bhaktivedanta purports of the Fourth Canto, Twelfth Chapter, of the Śrīmad-Bhāgavatam, *entitled "Dhruva Mahārāja Goes Back to Godhead."*

CHAPTER THIRTEEN

Description of the Descendants of Dhruva Mahārāja

TEXT 1

सूत उवाच
निशम्य कौषारविणोपवर्णितं
ध्रुवस्य वैकुण्ठपदाधिरोहणम् ।
प्ररूढभावो भगवत्यधोक्षजे
प्रष्टुं पुनस्तं विदुरः प्रचक्रमे ॥ १ ॥

sūta uvāca
niśamya kauṣāraviṇopavarṇitaṁ
dhruvasya vaikuṇṭha-padādhirohaṇam
prarūḍha-bhāvo bhagavaty adhokṣaje
praṣṭuṁ punas taṁ viduraḥ pracakrame

sūtaḥ uvāca—Sūta Gosvāmī said; *niśamya*—after hearing; *kauṣāraviṇā*—by the sage Maitreya; *upavarṇitam*—described; *dhruvasya*—of Mahārāja Dhruva; *vaikuṇṭha-pada*—to the abode of Viṣṇu; *adhirohaṇam*—ascent; *prarūḍha*—increased; *bhāvaḥ*—devotional emotion; *bhagavati*—unto the Supreme Personality of Godhead; *adhokṣaje*—who is beyond the reach of direct perception; *praṣṭum*—to inquire; *punaḥ*—again; *tam*—unto Maitreya; *viduraḥ*—Vidura; *pracakrame*—attempted.

TRANSLATION

Sūta Gosvāmī, continuing to speak to all the ṛṣis, headed by Śaunaka, said: After hearing Maitreya Ṛṣi describe Dhruva

Mahārāja's ascent to Lord Viṣṇu's abode, Vidura became very much enlightened in devotional emotion, and he inquired from Maitreya as follows.

PURPORT

As evidenced in the topics between Vidura and Maitreya, the activities of the Supreme Personality of Godhead and the devotees are so fascinating that neither the devotee who is describing them nor the devotee who is hearing is at all fatigued by the inquiries and answers. Transcendental subject matter is so nice that no one becomes tired of hearing or speaking. Others, who are not devotees, may think, "How can people devote so much time simply to talks of God?" But devotees are never satisfied or satiated in hearing and speaking about the Supreme Personality of Godhead or about His devotees. The more they hear and talk, the more they become enthusiastic to hear. The chanting of the Hare Kṛṣṇa *mantra* is simply the repetition of three words, *Hare*, *Kṛṣṇa* and *Rāma*, but still devotees can go on chanting this Hare Kṛṣṇa *mantra* twenty-four hours a day without feeling fatigued.

TEXT 2

विदुर उवाच

के ते प्रचेतसो नाम कस्यापत्यानि सुव्रत ।
कस्यान्ववाये प्रख्याताः कुत्र वा सत्रमासत ॥ २ ॥

vidura uvāca
ke te pracetaso nāma
kasyāpatyāni suvrata
kasyānvavāye prakhyātāḥ
kutra vā satram āsata

viduraḥ uvāca—Vidura inquired; *ke*—who were; *te*—they; *pracetasaḥ*—the Pracetās; *nāma*—of the name; *kasya*—whose; *apatyāni*—sons; *su-vrata*—O Maitreya, who have taken an auspicious vow; *kasya*—whose; *anvavāye*—in the family; *prakhyātāḥ*—famous; *kutra*—where; *vā*—also; *satram*—the sacrifice; *āsata*—was performed.

TRANSLATION

Vidura inquired from Maitreya: O greatly advanced devotee, who were the Pracetās? To which family did they belong? Whose sons were they, and where did they perform the great sacrifices?

PURPORT

The great Nārada's singing, in the previous chapter, of three verses in the sacrificial arena of the Pracetās gave another impetus to Vidura to ask further questions.

TEXT 3

मन्ये महाभागवतं नारदं देवदर्शनम् ।
येन प्रोक्तः क्रियायोगः परिचर्याविधिर्हरेः ॥ ३ ॥

manye mahā-bhāgavataṁ
nāradaṁ deva-darśanam
yena proktaḥ kriyā-yogaḥ
paricaryā-vidhir hareḥ

manye—I think; *mahā-bhāgavatam*—the greatest of all devotees; *nāradam*—the sage Nārada; *deva*—the Supreme Personality of Godhead; *darśanam*—who met; *yena*—by whom; *proktah*—spoken; *kriyā-yogaḥ*—devotional service; *paricaryā*—for rendering service; *vidhih*—the procedure; *hareḥ*—to the Supreme Personality of Godhead.

TRANSLATION

Vidura continued: I know that the great sage Nārada is the greatest of all devotees. He has compiled the pāñcarātrika procedure of devotional service and has directly met the Supreme Personality of Godhead.

PURPORT

There are two different ways of approaching the Supreme Lord. One is called *bhāgavata-mārga*, or the way of *Śrīmad-Bhāgavatam*, and the other is called *pāñcarātrika-vidhi. Pāñcarātrika-vidhi* is the method of temple worship, and *bhāgavata-vidhi* is the system of nine processes which begin with hearing and chanting. The Kṛṣṇa conscious movement accepts both processes simultaneously and thus enables one to make steady progress on the path of realization of the Supreme Personality of Godhead. This *pāñcarātrika* procedure was first introduced by the great sage Nārada, as referred to here by Vidura.

TEXT 4

स्वधर्मशीलैः पुरुषैर्भगवान् यज्ञपूरुषः ।
इज्यमानो भक्तिमता नारदेनेरितः किल ॥ ४ ॥

sva-dharma-śīlaiḥ puruṣair
bhagavān yajña-pūruṣaḥ
ijyamāno bhaktimatā
nāradeneritaḥ kila

sva-dharma-śīlaiḥ—executing sacrificial duties; *puruṣaiḥ*—by the men; *bhagavān*—the Supreme Personality of Godhead; *yajña-pūruṣaḥ*—the enjoyer of all sacrifices; *ijyamānaḥ*—being worshiped; *bhaktimatā*—by the devotee; *nāradena*—by Nārada; *īritaḥ*—described; *kila*—indeed.

TRANSLATION

While all the Pracetās were executing religious rituals and sacrificial ceremonies and thus worshiping the Supreme Personality of Godhead for His satisfaction, the great sage Nārada described the transcendental qualities of Dhruva Mahārāja.

PURPORT

Nārada Muni is always glorifying the pastimes of the Lord. In this verse we see that not only does he glorify the Lord, but he also likes to glorify the devotees of the Lord. The great sage Nārada's mission is to broadcast the devotional service of the Lord. For this purpose he has compiled the *Nārada-pañcarātra*, a directory of devotional service, so that devotees can always take information about how to execute devotional service and thus engage twenty-four hours a day in performing sacrifices for the pleasure of the Supreme Personality of Godhead. As stated in the *Bhagavad-gītā*, the Lord has created four orders of social life, namely *brāhmaṇa*, *kṣatriya*, *vaiśya* and *śūdra*. In the *Nārada-*

pañcarātra it is very clearly described how each of the social orders can please the Supreme Lord. In the *Bhagavad-gītā* (18.45) it is stated, *sve sve karmaṇy abhirataḥ saṁsiddhiṁ labhate naraḥ:* by executing one's prescribed duties one can please the Supreme Lord. In the *Śrīmad-Bhāgavatam* (1.2.13) also it is stated, *svanuṣṭhitasya dharmasya saṁsiddhir hari-toṣaṇam:* the perfection of duty is to see that by discharging one's specific duties one satisfies the Supreme Personality of Godhead. When the Pracetās were performing sacrifices according to this direction, Nārada Muni was satisfied to see these activities, and he also wanted to glorify Dhruva Mahārāja in that sacrificial arena.

TEXT 5

यास्ता देवर्षिणा तत्र वर्णिता भगवत्कथाः ।
मह्यं शुश्रूषवे ब्रह्मन् कार्त्स्न्येनाचष्टुमर्हसि ॥ ५ ॥

yās tā devarṣiṇā tatra
varṇitā bhagavat-kathāḥ
mahyaṁ śuśrūṣave brahman
kārtsnyenācaṣṭum arhasi

yāḥ—which; *tāḥ*—all those; *devarṣiṇā*—by the great sage Nārada; *tatra*—there; *varṇitāḥ*—narrated; *bhagavat-kathāḥ*—preachings pertaining to the activities of the Lord; *mahyam*—unto me; *śuśrūṣave*—very eager to hear; *brahman*—my dear *brāhmaṇa; kārtsnyena*—fully; *ācaṣṭum arhasi*—kindly explain.

TRANSLATION

My dear brāhmaṇa, how did Nārada Muni glorify the Supreme Personality of Godhead, and what pastimes were described in that meeting? I am very eager to hear of them. Kindly explain fully about that glorification of the Lord.

PURPORT

Śrīmad-Bhāgavatam is the record of *bhagavat-kathā*, topics about the pastimes of the Lord. What Vidura was anxious to hear from Maitreya we can also hear five thousand years later, provided we are very eager.

TEXT 6

मैत्रेय उवाच
ध्रुवस्य चोत्कलः पुत्रः पितरि प्रस्थिते वनम् ।
सार्वभौमश्रियं नैच्छदधिराजासनं पितुः ॥ ६ ॥

maitreya uvāca
dhruvasya cotkalaḥ putraḥ
pitari prasthite vanam
sārvabhauma-śriyaṁ naicchad
adhirājāsanaṁ pituḥ

maitreyaḥ uvāca—the great sage Maitreya said; *dhruvasya*—of Dhruva Mahārāja; *ca*—also; *utkalaḥ*—Utkala; *putraḥ*—son; *pitari*—after the father; *prasthite*—departed; *vanam*—for the forest; *sārva-bhauma*—including all lands; *śriyam*—opulence; *na aicchat*—did not desire; *adhirāja*—royal; *āsanam*—throne; *pituḥ*—of the father.

TRANSLATION

The great sage Maitreya replied: My dear Vidura, when Mahārāja Dhruva departed for the forest, his son, Utkala, did not desire to accept the opulent throne of his father, which was meant for the ruler of all the lands of this planet.

TEXT 7

स जन्मनोपशान्तात्मा निःसङ्गः समदर्शनः ।
ददर्श लोके विततमात्मानं लोकमात्मनि ॥ ७ ॥

sa janmanopaśāntātmā
niḥsaṅgaḥ sama-darśanaḥ
dadarśa loke vitatam
ātmānaṁ lokam ātmani

saḥ—his son Utkala; *janmanā*—from the very beginning of his birth; *upaśānta*—very well satisfied; *ātmā*—soul; *niḥsaṅgaḥ*—without attachment; *sama-darśanaḥ*—equipoised; *dadarśa*—saw; *loke*—in the world;

vitatam—spread; *ātmānam*—the Supersoul; *lokam*—all the world; *ātmani*—in the Supersoul.

TRANSLATION

From his very birth, Utkala was fully satisfied and unattached to the world. He was equipoised, for he could see everything resting in the Supersoul and the Supersoul present in everyone's heart.

PURPORT

The symptoms and characteristics of Utkala, the son of Mahārāja Dhruva, are those of a *mahā-bhāgavata.* As stated in the *Bhagavad-gītā* (6.30), *yo māṁ paśyati sarvatra sarvaṁ ca mayi paśyati:* a highly advanced devotee sees the Supreme Personality of Godhead everywhere, and he also sees everything resting in the Supreme. It is also confirmed in the *Bhagavad-gītā* (9.4), *mayā tatam idaṁ sarvaṁ jagad avyakta-mūrtinā:* Lord Kṛṣṇa is spread all over the universe in His impersonal feature. Everything is resting on Him, but that does not mean that everything is He Himself. A highly advanced *mahā-bhāgavata* devotee sees in this spirit: he sees the same Supersoul, Paramātmā, existing within everyone's heart, regardless of discrimination based on the different material forms of the living entities. He sees everyone as part and parcel of the Supreme Personality of Godhead. The *mahā-bhāgavata,* who experiences the Supreme Godhead's presence everywhere, is never missing from the sight of the Supreme Lord, nor is the Supreme Lord ever lost from his sight. This is possible only when one is advanced in love of Godhead.

TEXTS 8–9

आत्मानं ब्रह्म निर्वाणं प्रत्यस्तमितविग्रहम् ।
अवबोधरसैकात्म्यमानन्दमनुसन्ततम् ॥ ८ ॥
अव्यवच्छिन्नयोगाग्निदग्धकर्ममलाशयः ।
स्वरूपमवरुन्धानो नात्मनोऽन्यं तदैक्षत ॥ ९ ॥

ātmānaṁ brahma nirvāṇaṁ
pratyastamita-vigraham

avabodha-rasaikātmyam
ānandam anusantatam

avyavacchinna-yogāgni-
dagdha-karma-malāśayaḥ
svarūpam avarundhāno
nātmano 'nyaṁ tadaikṣata

ātmānam—self; *brahma*—spirit; *nirvāṇam*—extinction of material existence; *pratyastamita*—ceased; *vigraham*—separation; *avabodha-rasa*—by the mellow of knowledge; *eka-ātmyam*—oneness; *ānandam*—bliss; *anusantatam*—expanded; *avyavacchinna*—continuous; *yoga*—by practice of *yoga; agni*—by the fire; *dagdha*—burned; *karma*—fruitive desires; *mala*—dirty; *āśayaḥ*—in his mind; *svarūpam*—constitutional position; *avarundhānaḥ*—realizing; *na*—not; *ātmanaḥ*—than the Supreme Soul; *anyam*—anything else; *tadā*—then; *aikṣata*—saw.

TRANSLATION

By expansion of his knowledge of the Supreme Brahman, he had already attained liberation from the bondage of the body. This liberation is known as nirvāṇa. He was situated in transcendental bliss, and he continued always in that blissful existence, which expanded more and more. This was possible for him by continual practice of bhakti-yoga, which is compared to fire because it burns away all dirty, material things. He was always situated in his constitutional position of self-realization, and he could not see anything else but the Supreme Lord and himself engaged in discharging devotional service.

PURPORT

These two verses explain the verse in the *Bhagavad-gītā* (18.54):

brahma-bhūtaḥ prasannātmā
na śocati na kāṅkṣati
samaḥ sarveṣu bhūteṣu
mad-bhaktiṁ labhate parām

"One who is transcendentally situated at once realizes the Supreme Brahman and becomes fully joyful. He never laments nor desires to have anything. He is equally disposed towards every living entity. In that state he achieves pure devotional service unto Me." This is also explained by Lord Caitanya in His *Śikṣāṣṭaka* in the beginning of the first verse:

ceto-darpaṇa-mārjanaṁ bhava-mahā-dāvāgni-nirvāpaṇaṁ
śreyaḥ-kairava-candrikā-vitaraṇaṁ vidyā-vadhū-jīvanam

The *bhakti-yoga* system is the topmost *yoga* system, and in this system the chanting of the holy name of the Lord is the foremost performance of devotional service. By chanting the holy name one can attain the perfection of *nirvāṇa,* or liberation from material existence, and so increase one's blissful life of spiritual existence as described by Lord Caitanya (*ānandāmbudhi-vardhanam*). When one is situated in that position, he no longer has any interest in material opulence or even a royal throne and sovereignty over the whole planet. This situation is called *viraktir anyatra syāt.* It is the result of devotional service.

The more one makes advancement in devotional service, the more one becomes detached from material opulence and material activity. This is the spiritual nature, full of bliss. This is also described in *Bhagavad-gītā* (2.59). *Paraṁ dṛṣṭvā nivartate:* one ceases to take part in material enjoyment upon tasting superior, blissful life in spiritual existence. By advancement in spiritual knowledge, which is considered to be like blazing fire, all material desires are burned to ashes. The perfection of mystic *yoga* is possible when one is continuously in connection with the Supreme Personality of Godhead by discharging devotional service. A devotee is always thinking of the Supreme Person at every step of his life. Every conditioned soul is full of the reactions of his past life, but all dirty things are immediately burned to ashes if one simply executes devotional service. This is described in the *Nārada-pañcarātra: sarvopādhi-vinirmuktaṁ tat-paratvena nirmalam.*

TEXT 10

जडान्धबधिरोन्मत्तमूकाकृतिरतन्मतिः ।
लक्षितः पथि बालानां प्रशान्तार्चिरिवानलः ॥१०॥

jaḍāndha-badhironmatta-
mūkākṛtir atan-matiḥ
lakṣitaḥ pathi bālānāṁ
praśāntārcir ivānalaḥ

jaḍa—foolish; *andha*—blind; *badhira*—deaf; *unmatta*—mad; *mūka*—dumb; *ākṛtiḥ*—appearance; *a-tat*—not like that; *matiḥ*—his intelligence; *lakṣitaḥ*—he was seen; *pathi*—on the road; *bālānām*—by the less intelligent; *praśānta*—calmed; *arciḥ*—with flames; *iva*—like; *analaḥ*—fire.

TRANSLATION

Utkala appeared to the less intelligent persons on the road to be foolish, blind, dumb, deaf and mad, although actually he was not so. He remained like fire covered with ashes, without blazing flames.

PURPORT

In order to avoid contradiction, botheration and unfavorable situations created by materialistic persons, a great saintly person like Jaḍa Bharata or Utkala remains silent. The less intelligent consider such saintly persons to be mad, deaf or dumb. Factually, an advanced devotee avoids speaking with persons who are not in devotional life, but to those who are in devotional life he speaks in friendship, and he speaks to the innocent for their enlightenment. For all practical purposes, the whole world is full of nondevotees, and so one kind of very advanced devotee is called *bhajanānandī.* Those who are *goṣṭhy-ānandī,* however, preach to increase the number of devotees. But even such preachers also avoid opposing elements who are unfavorably disposed towards spiritual life.

TEXT 11

मत्वा तं जडमुन्मत्तं कुलवृद्धाः समन्त्रिणः ।
वत्सरं भूपतिं चक्रुर्यवीयांसं भ्रमेः सुतम् ॥११॥

matvā taṁ jaḍam unmattaṁ
kula-vṛddhāḥ samantriṇaḥ

vatsaraṁ bhūpatiṁ cakrur
yavīyāṁsaṁ bhrameḥ sutam

matvā—thinking; *tam*—Utkala; *jaḍam*—without intelligence; *unmattam*—mad; *kula-vṛddhāḥ*—the elderly members of the family; *samantriṇaḥ*—with the ministers; *vatsaram*—Vatsara; *bhū-patim*—ruler of the world; *cakruḥ*—they made; *yavīyāṁsam*—younger; *bhrameḥ*—of Bhrami; *sutam*—son.

TRANSLATION

For this reason the ministers and all the elderly members of the family thought Utkala to be without intelligence and, in fact, mad. Thus his younger brother, named Vatsara, the son of Bhrami, was elevated to the royal throne, and he became king of the world.

PURPORT

It appears that although there was monarchy, it was not at all an autocracy. There were senior family members and ministers who could make changes and elect the proper person to the throne, although the throne could be occupied only by the royal family. In modern days also, wherever there is monarchy, sometimes the ministers and elderly members of the family select one member from the royal family to occupy the throne in preference to another.

TEXT 12

स्वर्वीथिर्वत्सरस्येष्टा भार्यासूत षडात्मजान् ।
पुष्पार्णं तिग्मकेतुं च इषमूर्जं वसुं जयम् ॥१२॥

svarvīthir vatsarasyeṣṭā
bhāryāsūta ṣaḍ-ātmajān
puṣpārṇaṁ tigmaketuṁ ca
iṣam ūrjaṁ vasuṁ jayam

svarvīthiḥ—Svarvīthi; *vatsarasya*—of King Vatsara; *iṣṭā*—very dear; *bhāryā*—wife; *asūta*—gave birth to; *ṣaṭ*—six; *ātmajān*—sons; *puṣpārṇam*—Puṣpārṇa; *tigmaketum*—Tigmaketu; *ca*—also; *iṣam*—Iṣa; *ūrjam*—Ūrja; *vasum*—Vasu; *jayam*—Jaya.

TRANSLATION

King Vatsara had a very dear wife whose name was Svarvīthi, and she gave birth to six sons, named Puṣpārṇa, Tigmaketu, Iṣa, Ūrja, Vasu and Jaya.

PURPORT

Vatsara's wife is mentioned here as *iṣṭā*, which means "worshipable." In other words, it appears that Vatsara's wife had all good qualities; for example, she was always very faithful and obedient and affectionate to her husband. She had all good qualities for managing household affairs. If both the husband and wife are endowed with good qualities and live peacefully, then nice children take birth, and thus the whole family is happy and prosperous.

TEXT 13

पुष्पार्णस्य प्रभा भार्या दोषा च द्वे बभूवतुः ।
प्रातर्मध्यन्दिनं सायमिति ह्यासन् प्रभासुताः ॥१३॥

puṣpārṇasya prabhā bhāryā
doṣā ca dve babhūvatuḥ
prātar madhyandinaṁ sāyam
iti hy āsan prabhā-sutāḥ

puṣpārṇasya—of Puṣpārṇa; *prabhā*—Prabhā; *bhāryā*—wife; *doṣā*—Doṣā; *ca*—also; *dve*—two; *babhūvatuḥ*—were; *prātaḥ*—Prātar; *madhyandinam*—Madhyandinam; *sāyam*—Sāyam; *iti*—thus; *hi*—certainly; *āsan*—were; *prabhā-sutāḥ*—sons of Prabhā.

TRANSLATION

Puṣpārṇa had two wives, named Prabhā and Doṣā. Prabhā had three sons, named Prātar, Madhyandinam and Sāyam.

TEXT 14

प्रदोषो निशिथो व्युष्ट इति दोषासुतास्त्रयः ।
व्युष्टः सुतं पुष्करिण्यां सर्वतेजसमादधे ॥१४॥

pradoṣo niśitho vyuṣṭa
iti doṣā-sutās trayaḥ
vyuṣṭaḥ sutaṁ puṣkariṇyāṁ
sarvatejasam ādadhe

pradoṣaḥ—Pradoṣa; *niśithaḥ*—Niśitha; *vyuṣṭaḥ*—Vyuṣṭa; *iti*—thus; *doṣā*—of Doṣā; *sutāḥ*—sons; *trayaḥ*—three; *vyuṣṭaḥ*—Vyuṣṭa; *sutam*—son; *puṣkariṇyām*—in Puṣkariṇī; *sarva-tejasam*—named Sarvatejā (all-powerful); *ādadhe*—begot.

TRANSLATION

Doṣā had three sons—Pradoṣa, Niśitha and Vyuṣṭa. Vyuṣṭa's wife was named Puṣkariṇī, and she gave birth to a very powerful son named Sarvatejā.

TEXTS 15–16

स चक्षुः सुतमाकूत्यां पत्न्यां मनुमवाप ह ।
मनोरसूत महिषी विरजान्नड्वला सुतान् ॥१५॥
पुरुं कुत्सं त्रितं द्युम्नं सत्यवन्तमृतं व्रतम् ।
अग्निष्टोममतीरात्रं प्रद्युम्नं शिबिमुल्मुकम् ॥१६॥

sa cakṣuḥ sutam ākūtyāṁ
patnyāṁ manum avāpa ha
manor asūta mahiṣī
virajān naḍvalā sutān

puruṁ kutsaṁ tritaṁ dyumnaṁ
satyavantam ṛtaṁ vratam
agniṣṭomam atīrātraṁ
pradyumnaṁ śibim ulmukam

saḥ—he (Sarvatejā); *cakṣuḥ*—named Cakṣuḥ; *sutam*—son; *ākūtyām*—in Ākūti; *patnyām*—wife; *manum*—Cākṣuṣa Manu; *avāpa*—obtained; *ha*—indeed; *manoḥ*—of Manu; *asūta*—gave birth to; *mahiṣī*—queen; *virajān*—without passion; *naḍvalā*—Naḍvalā; *sutān*—

sons; *purum*—Puru; *kutsam*—Kutsa; *tritam*—Trita; *dyumnam*—Dyumna; *satyavantam*—Satyavān; *ṛtam*—Ṛta; *vratam*—Vrata; *agniṣṭomam*—Agniṣṭoma; *atīrātram*—Atīrātra; *pradyumnam*—Pradyumna; *śibim*—Śibi; *ulmukam*—Ulmuka.

TRANSLATION

Sarvatejā's wife, Ākūti, gave birth to a son named Cākṣuṣa, who became the sixth Manu at the end of the Manu millennium. Naḍvalā, the wife of Cākṣuṣa Manu, gave birth to the following faultless sons: Puru, Kutsa, Trita, Dyumna, Satyavān, Ṛta, Vrata, Agniṣṭoma, Atīrātra, Pradyumna, Śibi and Ulmuka.

TEXT 17

उल्मुकोऽजनयत्पुत्रान्पुष्करिण्यां षडुत्तमान् ।
अङ्गं सुमनसं ख्यातिं क्रतुमङ्गिरसं गयम् ॥१७॥

ulmuko 'janayat putrān
puṣkariṇyāṁ ṣaḍ uttamān
aṅgaṁ sumanasaṁ khyātiṁ
kratum aṅgirasaṁ gayam

ulmukaḥ—Ulmuka; *ajanayat*—begot; *putrān*—sons; *puṣkariṇyām*—in Puṣkariṇī, his wife; *ṣaṭ*—six; *uttamān*—very good; *aṅgam*—Aṅga; *sumanasam*—Sumanā; *khyātim*—Khyāti; *kratum*—Kratu; *aṅgirasam*—Aṅgirā; *gayam*—Gaya.

TRANSLATION

Of the twelve sons, Ulmuka begot six sons in his wife Puṣkariṇī. They were all very good sons, and their names were Aṅga, Sumanā, Khyāti, Kratu, Aṅgirā and Gaya.

TEXT 18

सुनीथाङ्गस्य या पत्नी सुषुवे वेनमुल्बणम् ।
यद्दौःशील्यात्स राजर्षिर्निर्विण्णो निरगात्पुरात् ॥१८॥

sunīthāṅgasya yā patnī
suṣuve venam ulbaṇam
yad-dauḥśīlyāt sa rājarṣir
nirviṇṇo niragāt purāt

sunīthā—Sunīthā; *aṅgasya*—of Aṅga; *yā*—she who; *patnī*—the wife; *suṣuve*—gave birth to; *venam*—Vena; *ulbaṇam*—very crooked; *yat*—whose; *dauḥśīlyāt*—on account of bad character; *saḥ*—he; *rāja-ṛṣiḥ*—the saintly King Aṅga; *nirviṇṇaḥ*—very disappointed; *niragāt*—went out; *purāt*—from home.

TRANSLATION

The wife of Aṅga, Sunīthā, gave birth to a son named Vena, who was very crooked. The saintly King Aṅga was very disappointed with Vena's bad character, and he left home and kingdom and went out to the forest.

TEXTS 19–20

यमङ्ग शेपुः कुपिता वाग्वज्रा मुनयः किल ।
गतासोस्तस्य भूयस्ते ममन्थुर्दक्षिणं करम् ॥१९॥
अराजके तदा लोके दस्युभिः पीडिताः प्रजाः ।
जातो नारायणांशेन पृथुराद्यः क्षितीश्वरः ॥२०॥

yam aṅga śepuḥ kupitā
vāg-vajrā munayaḥ kila
gatāsos tasya bhūyas te
mamanthur dakṣiṇaṁ karam

arājake tadā loke
dasyubhiḥ pīḍitāḥ prajāḥ
jāto nārāyaṇāṁśena
pṛthur ādyaḥ kṣitīśvaraḥ

yam—him (Vena) whom; *aṅga*—my dear Vidura; *śepuḥ*—they cursed; *kupitāḥ*—being angry; *vāk-vajrāḥ*—whose words are as strong as a thunderbolt; *munayaḥ*—great sages; *kila*—indeed; *gata-asoḥ tasya*—after he died; *bhūyaḥ*—moreover; *te*—they; *mamanthuḥ*—churned; *dakṣiṇam*—right; *karam*—hand; *arājake*—being without a king; *tadā*—then; *loke*—the world; *dasyubhiḥ*—by rogues and thieves; *pīḍitāḥ*—suffering; *prajāḥ*—all the citizens; *jātaḥ*—advented; *nārāyaṇa*—of the Supreme Personality of Godhead; *aṁśena*—by a partial representation; *pṛthuḥ*—Pṛthu; *ādyaḥ*—original; *kṣiti-īśvaraḥ*—ruler of the world.

TRANSLATION

My dear Vidura, when great sages curse, their words are as invincible as a thunderbolt. Thus when they cursed King Vena out of anger, he died. After his death, since there was no king, all the rogues and thieves flourished, the kingdom became unregulated, and all the citizens suffered greatly. On seeing this, the great sages took the right hand of Vena as a churning rod, and as a result of their churning, Lord Viṣṇu in His partial representation made His advent as King Pṛthu, the original emperor of the world.

PURPORT

Monarchy is better than democracy because if the monarchy is very strong the regulative principles within the kingdom are upheld very nicely. Even one hundred years ago in the state of Kashmir in India, the king was so strong that if a thief were arrested in his kingdom and brought before him, the king would immediately chop off the hands of the thief. As a result of this severe punishment there were practically no theft cases within the kingdom. Even if someone left something on the street, no one would touch it. The rule was that the things could be taken away only by the proprietor and that no one else would touch them. In the so-called democracy, wherever there is a theft case the police come and take note of the case, but generally the thief is never caught, nor is any punishment offered to him. As a result of incapable government, at the present moment thieves, rogues and cheaters are very prominent all over the world.

TEXT 21

विदुर उवाच

तस्य शीलनिधेः साधोर्ब्रह्मण्यस्य महात्मनः ।
राज्ञः कथमभूद्दुष्टा प्रजा यद्विमना ययौ ॥२१॥

vidura uvāca
tasya śīla-nidheḥ sādhor
brahmaṇyasya mahātmanaḥ
rājñaḥ katham abhūd duṣṭā
prajā yad vimanā yayau

viduraḥ uvāca—Vidura said; *tasya*—of him (Aṅga); *śīla-nidheḥ*—reservoir of good characteristics; *sādhoḥ*—saintly person; *brahmaṇyasya*—lover of brahminical culture; *mahātmanaḥ*—great soul; *rājñaḥ*—of the king; *katham*—how; *abhūt*—it was; *duṣṭā*—bad; *prajā*—son; *yat*—by which; *vimanāḥ*—being indifferent; *yayau*—he left.

TRANSLATION

Vidura inquired from the sage Maitreya: My dear brāhmaṇa, King Aṅga was very gentle. He had high character and was a saintly personality and lover of brahminical culture. How is it that such a great soul got a bad son like Vena, because of whom he became indifferent to his kingdom and left it?

PURPORT

In family life a man is supposed to live happily with father, mother, wife and children, but sometimes, under certain conditions, a father, mother, child or wife becomes an enemy. It is said by Cāṇakya Paṇḍita that a father is an enemy when he is too much in debt, a mother is an enemy if she marries for a second time, a wife is an enemy when she is very beautiful, and a son is an enemy when he is a foolish rascal. In this way, when a family member becomes an enemy it is very difficult to live in family life or remain a householder. Generally such situations occur in the material world. Therefore according to Vedic culture one has to take leave of his family members just after his fiftieth year so that the balance of his life may be completely devoted in search of Kṛṣṇa consciousness.

TEXT 22

किं वांहो वेन उद्दिश्य ब्रह्मदण्डमयूयुजन् ।
दण्डव्रतधरे राज्ञि मुनयो धर्मकोविदाः ॥२२॥

kiṁ vāṁho vena uddiśya
brahma-daṇḍam ayūyujan
daṇḍa-vrata-dhare rājñi
munayo dharma-kovidāḥ

kim—why; *vā*—also; *aṁhaḥ*—sinful activities; *vene*—unto Vena; *uddiśya*—seeing; *brahma-daṇḍam*—the curse of a *brāhmaṇa; ayūyujan*—they desired to award; *daṇḍa-vrata-dhare*—who carries the rod of punishment; *rājñi*—unto the king; *munayaḥ*—the great sages; *dharma-kovidāḥ*—completely conversant with religious principles.

TRANSLATION

Vidura also inquired: How is it that the great sages, who were completely conversant with religious principles, desired to curse King Vena, who himself carried the rod of punishment, and thus awarded him the greatest punishment [brahma-śāpa]?

PURPORT

It is understood that the king is able to give punishment to everyone, but in this case it appears that the great sages punished him. The king must have done something very serious, otherwise how could the great sages, who were supposed to be the greatest and most tolerant, still punish him in spite of their elevated religious consciousness? It appears also that the king was not independent of the brahminical culture. Above the king was the control of the *brāhmaṇas,* and if needed the *brāhmaṇas* would dethrone the king or kill him, not with any weapon, but with the *mantra* of a *brahma-śāpa.* The *brāhmaṇas* were so powerful that simply by their cursing one would immediately die.

TEXT 23

नावध्येयः प्रजापालः प्रजाभिरघवानपि ।
यदसौ लोकपालानां बिभर्त्योजः स्वतेजसा ॥२३॥

nāvadhyeyaḥ prajā-pālaḥ
prajābhir aghavān api

yad asau loka-pālānāṁ
bibharty ojaḥ sva-tejasā

na—never; *avadhyeyaḥ*—to be insulted; *prajā-pālaḥ*—the king; *prajābhiḥ*—by the citizens; *aghavān*—ever sinful; *api*—even though; *yat*—because; *asau*—he; *loka-pālānām*—of many kings; *bibharti*—maintains; *ojaḥ*—prowess; *sva-tejasā*—by personal influence.

TRANSLATION

It is the duty of all citizens in a state never to insult the king, even though he sometimes appears to have done something very sinful. Because of his prowess, the king is always more influential than all other ruling chiefs.

PURPORT

According to Vedic civilization the king is supposed to be the representative of the Supreme Personality of Godhead. He is called *nara-nārāyaṇa*, indicating that Nārāyaṇa, the Supreme Personality of Godhead, appears in human society as the king. It is etiquette that neither a *brāhmaṇa* nor a *kṣatriya* king is ever insulted by the citizens; even though a king appears to be sinful, the citizens should not insult him. But in the case of Vena it appears that he was cursed by the *nara-devatās;* therefore, it was concluded that his sinful activities were very grievous.

TEXT 24

एतदाख्याहि मे ब्रह्मन् सुनीथात्मजचेष्टितम् ।
श्रद्दधानाय भक्ताय त्वं परावरवित्तमः ॥२४॥

etad ākhyāhi me brahman
sunīthātmaja-ceṣṭitam
śraddadhānāya bhaktāya
tvaṁ parāvara-vittamaḥ

etat—all these; *ākhyāhi*—please describe; *me*—unto me; *brahman*—O great *brāhmaṇa; sunīthā-ātmaja*—of the son of Sunīthā, Vena;

ceṣṭitam—activities; *śraddadhānāya*—faithful; *bhaktāya*—unto your devotee; *tvam*—you; *para-avara*—with past and future; *vit-tamaḥ*—well conversant.

TRANSLATION

Vidura requested Maitreya: My dear brāhmaṇa, you are well conversant with all subjects, both past and future. Therefore I wish to hear from you all the activities of King Vena. I am your faithful devotee, so please explain this.

PURPORT

Vidura accepted Maitreya as his spiritual master. A disciple always inquires from the spiritual master, and the spiritual master answers the question, provided the disciple is very gentle and devoted. Śrīla Viśvanātha Cakravartī Ṭhākura said that by the mercy of the spiritual master one is blessed with the mercy of the Supreme Lord. The spiritual master is not inclined to disclose all the secrets of transcendental science unless the disciple is very submissive and devoted. As stated in the *Bhagavad-gītā*, the process of receiving knowledge from the spiritual master entails submission, inquiry and service.

TEXT 25

मैत्रेय उवाच

अङ्गोऽश्वमेधं राजर्षिराजहार महाक्रतुम् ।
नाजग्मुर्देवतास्तस्मिन्नाहूता ब्रह्मवादिभिः ॥२५॥

maitreya uvāca
aṅgo 'śvamedhaṁ rājarṣir
ājahāra mahā-kratum
nājagmur devatās tasminn
āhūtā brahma-vādibhiḥ

maitreyaḥ uvāca—Maitreya answered; *aṅgaḥ*—King Aṅga; *aśvamedham*—*aśvamedha* sacrifice; *rāja-ṛṣiḥ*—the saintly king; *ājahāra*—executed; *mahā-kratum*—great sacrifice; *na*—not; *ājagmuḥ*—came; *devatāḥ*—the demigods; *tasmin*—in that sacrifice; *āhūtāḥ*—being invited; *brahma-vādibhiḥ*—by the *brāhmaṇas* expert in executing sacrifices.

TRANSLATION

Śrī Maitreya replied: My dear Vidura, once the great King Aṅga arranged to perform the great sacrifice known as aśvamedha. All the expert brāhmaṇas present knew how to invite the demigods, but in spite of their efforts, no demigods participated or appeared in that sacrifice.

PURPORT

A Vedic sacrifice is not an ordinary performance. The demigods used to participate in such sacrifices, and the animals sacrificed in such performances were reincarnated with new life. In this age of Kali there are no powerful *brāhmaṇas* who can invite the demigods or give renewed life to animals. Formerly, the *brāhmaṇas* well conversant in Vedic *mantras* could show the potency of the *mantras*, but in this age, because there are no such *brāhmaṇas*, all such sacrifices are forbidden. The sacrifice in which horses were offered was called *aśvamedha*. Sometimes cows were sacrificed (*gavālambha*), not for eating purposes, but to give them new life in order to show the potency of the *mantra*. In this age, therefore, the only practical *yajña* is *saṅkīrtana-yajña*, or chanting of the Hare Kṛṣṇa *mantra* twenty-four hours a day.

TEXT 26

तमूचुर्विस्मितास्तत्र यजमानमथर्त्विजः ।
हवींषि हूयमानानि न ते गृह्णन्ति देवताः ॥२६॥

tam ūcur vismitās tatra
yajamānam athartvijaḥ
havīṁṣi hūyamānāni
na te gṛhṇanti devatāḥ

tam—unto King Aṅga; *ūcuḥ*—said; *vismitāḥ*—in wonder; *tatra*—there; *yajamānam*—to the institutor of the sacrifice; *atha*—then; *ṛtvijaḥ*—the priests; *havīṁṣi*—offerings of clarified butter; *hūyamānāni*—being offered; *na*—not; *te*—they; *gṛhṇanti*—accept; *devatāḥ*—the demigods.

TRANSLATION

The priests engaged in the sacrifice then informed King Aṅga: O King, we are properly offering the clarified butter in the sacrifice, but despite all our efforts the demigods do not accept it.

TEXT 27

राजन् हवींष्यदुष्टानि श्रद्धयासादितानि ते ।
छन्दांस्ययातयामानि योजितानि धृतव्रतैः ॥२७॥

rājan havīṁṣy aduṣṭāni
śraddhayāsāditāni te
chandāṁsy ayāta-yāmāni
yojitāni dhṛta-vrataiḥ

rājan—O King; *havīṁṣi*—sacrificial offerings; *aduṣṭāni*—not polluted; *śraddhayā*—with great faith and care; *āsāditāni*—collected; *te*—your; *chandāṁsi*—the *mantras; ayāta-yāmāni*—not deficient; *yojitāni*—properly executed; *dhṛta-vrataiḥ*—by qualified *brāhmaṇas.*

TRANSLATION

O King, we know that the paraphernalia to perform the sacrifice is well collected by you with great faith and care and is not polluted. Our chanting of the Vedic hymns is also not deficient in any way, for all the brāhmaṇas and priests present here are expert and are executing the performances properly.

PURPORT

It is the practice of the *brāhmaṇas* conversant with the science to pronounce a Vedic *mantra* in the right accent. The combination of the *mantra* and Sanskrit words must be chanted with the right pronunciation, otherwise it will not be successful. In this age the *brāhmaṇas* are neither well versed in the Sanskrit language nor very pure in practical life. But by chanting the Hare Kṛṣṇa *mantra* one can attain the highest benefit of sacrificial performances. Even if the Hare Kṛṣṇa *mantra* is not chanted properly, it still has so much potency that the chanter gains the effect.

TEXT 28

न विदामेह देवानां हेलनं वयमण्वपि ।
यन्न गृह्णन्ति भागान् स्वान् ये देवाः कर्मसाक्षिणः ॥२८॥

na vidāmeha devānāṁ
helanaṁ vayam aṇv api
yan na gṛhṇanti bhāgān svān
ye devāḥ karma-sākṣiṇaḥ

na—not; *vidāma*—can find; *iha*—in this connection; *devānām*—of the demigods; *helanam*—insult, neglect; *vayam*—we; *aṇu*—minute; *api*—even; *yat*—because of which; *na*—not; *gṛhṇanti*—accept; *bhāgān*—shares; *svān*—own; *ye*—who; *devāḥ*—the demigods; *karma-sākṣiṇaḥ*—witnesses for the sacrifice.

TRANSLATION

Dear King, we do not find any reason that the demigods should feel insulted or neglected in any way, but still the demigods who are witnesses for the sacrifice do not accept their shares. We do not know why this is so.

PURPORT

It is indicated herein that if there is negligence on the part of the priest, the demigods do not accept their share in sacrifices. Similarly, in devotional service there are offenses known as *sevā-aparādha.* Those who are engaged in worshiping the Deity, Rādhā and Kṛṣṇa, in the temple, should avoid such offenses in service. The offenses in service are described in *The Nectar of Devotion.* If we simply make a show of offering services to the Deity but do not care for the *sevā-aparādha*, certainly the Rādhā-Kṛṣṇa Deity will not accept offerings from such nondevotees. Devotees engaged in temple worship should not, therefore, manufacture their own methods, but should strictly follow the regulative principles of cleanliness, and then offerings will be accepted.

TEXT 29

मैत्रेय उवाच
अङ्गो द्विजवचः श्रुत्वा यजमानः सुदुर्मनाः ।
तत्प्रष्टुं व्यसृजद्वाचं सदस्यांस्तदनुज्ञया ॥२९॥

maitreya uvāca
aṅgo dvija-vacaḥ śrutvā
yajamānaḥ sudurmanāḥ
tat praṣṭuṁ vyasṛjad vācaṁ
sadasyāṁs tad-anujñayā

maitreyaḥ uvāca—the great sage Maitreya answered; *aṅgaḥ*—King Aṅga; *dvija-vacaḥ*—the *brāhmaṇas'* words; *śrutvā*—after hearing; *yajamānaḥ*—the performer of the sacrifice; *sudurmanāḥ*—very much aggrieved in mind; *tat*—about that; *praṣṭum*—in order to inquire; *vyasṛjat vācam*—he spoke; *sadasyān*—to the priests; *tat*—their; *anujñayā*—taking permission.

TRANSLATION

Maitreya explained that King Aṅga, after hearing the statements of the priests, was greatly aggrieved. At that time he took permission from the priests to break his silence and inquired from all the priests who were present in the sacrificial arena.

TEXT 30

नागच्छन्त्याहुता देवा न गृह्णन्ति ग्रहानिह ।
सदसस्पतयो ब्रूत किमवद्यं मया कृतम् ॥३०॥

nāgacchanty āhutā devā
na gṛhṇanti grahān iha
sadasas-patayo brūta
kim avadyaṁ mayā kṛtam

na—not; *āgacchanti*—are coming; *āhutāḥ*—being invited; *devāḥ*—the demigods; *na*—not; *gṛhṇanti*—are accepting; *grahān*—shares;

iha—in the sacrifice; *sadasaḥ-patayaḥ*—my dear priests; *brūta*—kindly tell me; *kim*—what; *avadyam*—offense; *mayā*—by me; *kṛtam*—was committed.

TRANSLATION

King Aṅga addressed the priestly order: My dear priests, kindly tell me what offense I have committed. Although invited, the demigods are neither taking part in the sacrifice nor accepting their shares.

TEXT 31

सदसस्पतय ऊचुः

नरदेवेह भवतो नाघं तावन्मनाक् स्थितम् ।
अस्त्येकं प्राक्तनमघं यदिहेदृक् त्वमप्रजः ॥३१॥

sadasas-pataya ūcuḥ
nara-deveha bhavato
nāghaṁ tāvan manāk sthitam
asty ekaṁ prāktanam aghaṁ
yad ihedṛk tvam aprajaḥ

sadasaḥ-patayaḥ ūcuḥ—the head priests said; *nara-deva*—O King; *iha*—in this life; *bhavataḥ*—of you; *na*—not; *agham*—sinful activity; *tāvat manāk*—even very slight; *sthitam*—situated; *asti*—there is; *ekam*—one; *prāktanam*—in the previous birth; *agham*—sinful activity; *yat*—by which; *iha*—in this life; *īdṛk*—like this; *tvam*—you; *aprajaḥ*—without any son.

TRANSLATION

The head priests said: O King, in this life we do not find any sinful activity, even within your mind, so you are not in the least offensive. But we can see that in your previous life you performed sinful activities due to which, in spite of your having all qualifications, you have no son.

PURPORT

The purpose of marrying is to beget a son, because a son is necessary to deliver his father and forefathers from any hellish conditional life in which they may be. Cāṇakya Paṇḍita therefore says, *putra-hīnaṁ gṛhaṁ śūnyam:* without a son, married life is simply abominable. King Aṅga was a very pious king in this life, but because of his previous sinful activity he could not get a son. It is concluded, therefore, that if a person does not get a son it is due to his past sinful life.

TEXT 32

तथा साधय भद्रं ते आत्मानं सुप्रजं नृप ।
इष्टस्ते पुत्रकामस्य पुत्रं दास्यति यज्ञभुक् ॥३२॥

tathā sādhaya bhadraṁ te
ātmānaṁ suprajaṁ nṛpa
iṣṭas te putra-kāmasya
putraṁ dāsyati yajña-bhuk

tathā—therefore; *sādhaya*—execute the sacrifice to get; *bhadram*—good fortune; *te*—to you; *ātmānam*—your own; *su-prajam*—good son; *nṛpa*—O King; *iṣṭaḥ*—being worshiped; *te*—by you; *putra-kāmasya*—desiring to have a son; *putram*—a son; *dāsyati*—He will deliver; *yajña-bhuk*—the Lord, the enjoyer of the sacrifice.

TRANSLATION

O King, we wish all good fortune for you. You have no son, but if you pray at once to the Supreme Lord and ask for a son, and if you execute the sacrifice for that purpose, the enjoyer of the sacrifice, the Supreme Personality of Godhead, will fulfill your desire.

TEXT 33

तथा स्वभागधेयानि ग्रहीष्यन्ति दिवौकसः ।
यद्यज्ञपुरुषः साक्षादपत्याय हरिर्वृतः ॥३३॥

tathā sva-bhāgadheyāni
grahīṣyanti divaukasaḥ
yad yajña-puruṣaḥ sākṣād
apatyāya harir vṛtaḥ

tathā—thereupon; *sva-bhāga-dheyāni*—their shares in the sacrifice; *grahīṣyanti*—will accept; *diva-okasaḥ*—all the demigods; *yat*—because; *yajña-puruṣaḥ*—the enjoyer of all sacrifices; *sākṣāt*—directly; *apatyāya*—for the purpose of a son; *hariḥ*—the Supreme Personality of Godhead; *vṛtaḥ*—is invited.

TRANSLATION

When Hari, the supreme enjoyer of all sacrifices, is invited to fulfill your desire for a son, all the demigods will come with Him and take their shares in the sacrifice.

PURPORT

Whenever a sacrifice is performed, it is meant for satisfying Lord Viṣṇu, the enjoyer of the fruits of all sacrifices; and when Lord Viṣṇu agrees to come to a sacrificial arena, all the demigods naturally follow their master, and their shares are offered in such sacrifices. The conclusion is that the sacrifices performed are meant for Lord Viṣṇu, not for the demigods.

TEXT 34

तांस्तान् कामान् हरिर्दद्याद्यान् यान् कामयते जनः ।
आराधितो यथैवैष तथा पुंसां फलोदयः ॥३४॥

tāṁs tān kāmān harir dadyād
yān yān kāmayate janaḥ
ārādhito yathaivaiṣa
tathā puṁsāṁ phalodayaḥ

tān tān—those; *kāmān*—desired objects; *hariḥ*—the Lord; *dadyāt*—will award; *yān yān*—whatsoever; *kāmayate*—desires; *janaḥ*—the person; *ārādhitaḥ*—being worshiped; *yathā*—as; *eva*—certainly; *eṣaḥ*—the Lord; *tathā*—similarly; *puṁsām*—of men; *phala-udayaḥ*—the result.

TRANSLATION

The performer of the sacrifices [under karma-kāṇḍa activities] achieves the fulfillment of the desire for which he worships the Lord.

PURPORT

In the *Bhagavad-gītā* the Lord says that He awards benedictions to the worshiper according to his desire. The Supreme Personality of Godhead gives all living entities conditioned within this material world full freedom to act in their own way. But to His devotee He says that instead of working in that way, it is better to surrender unto Him, for He will take charge of the devotee. That is the difference between a devotee and a fruitive actor. The fruitive actor enjoys only the fruits of his own activities, but a devotee, being under the guidance of the Supreme Lord, simply advances in devotional service to achieve the ultimate goal of life—to go back home, back to Godhead. The significant word in this verse is *kāmān*, which means "sense gratificatory desires." A devotee is devoid of all *kāmān.* He is *anyābhilāṣitā-śūnya:* a devotee is always devoid of all desires for sense gratification. His only aim is to satisfy or gratify the senses of the Lord. That is the difference between a *karmī* and a devotee.

TEXT 35

इति व्यवसिता विप्रास्तस्य राज्ञः प्रजातये ।
पुरोडाशं निरवपन् शिपिविष्टाय विष्णवे ॥३५॥

iti vyavasitā viprās
tasya rājñaḥ prajātaye
puroḍāśaṁ niravapan
śipi-viṣṭāya viṣṇave

iti—thus; *vyavasitāḥ*—having decided; *viprāḥ*—the *brāhmaṇas; tasya*—his; *rājñaḥ*—of the king; *prajātaye*—for the purpose of getting a son; *puroḍāśam*—the paraphernalia of sacrifice; *niravapan*—offered; *śipi-viṣṭāya*—to the Lord, who is situated in the sacrificial fire; *viṣṇave*—to Lord Viṣṇu.

TRANSLATION

Thus for the sake of a son for King Aṅga, they decided to offer oblations to Lord Viṣṇu, who is situated in the hearts of all living entities.

PURPORT

According to sacrificial rituals, animals are sometimes sacrificed in the *yajña* arena. Such animals are sacrificed not to kill them but to give them new life. Such action was an experiment to observe whether the Vedic *mantras* were being properly pronounced. Sometimes small animals are killed in a medical laboratory to investigate therapeutic effects. In a medical clinic, the animals are not revived, but in the *yajña* arena, when animals were sacrificed, they were again given life by the potency of Vedic *mantras*. The word *śipi-viṣṭāya* appears in this verse. *Śipi* means "the flames of the sacrifice." In the sacrificial fire if the oblations are offered into the flames, then Lord Viṣṇu is situated there in the form of the flames. Therefore Lord Viṣṇu is known as Śipiviṣṭa.

TEXT 36

तस्मात्पुरुष उत्तस्थौ हेममाल्यमलाम्बरः ।
हिरण्मयेन पात्रेण सिद्धमादाय पायसम् ॥३६॥

tasmāt puruṣa uttasthau
hema-māly amalāmbaraḥ
hiraṇmayena pātreṇa
siddham ādāya pāyasam

tasmāt—from that fire; *puruṣaḥ*—a person; *uttasthau*—appeared; *hema-mālī*—with a golden garland; *amala-ambaraḥ*—in white garments; *hiraṇmayena*—golden; *pātreṇa*—with a pot; *siddham*—cooked; *ādāya*—carrying; *pāyasam*—rice boiled in milk.

TRANSLATION

As soon as the oblation was offered in the fire, a person appeared from the fire altar wearing a golden garland and a white dress. He was carrying a golden pot filled with rice boiled in milk.

TEXT 37

स विप्रानुमतो राजा गृहीत्वाञ्जलिनौदनम् ।
अवघ्राय मुदा युक्तः प्रादात्पत्न्या उदारधीः ॥३७॥

sa viprānumato rājā
gṛhītvāñjalinaudanam
avaghrāya mudā yuktaḥ
prādāt patnyā udāra-dhīḥ

saḥ—he; *vipra*—of the *brāhmaṇas; anumataḥ*—taking permission; *rājā*—the King; *gṛhītvā*—taking; *añjalinā*—in his joined palms; *odanam*—rice boiled in milk; *avaghrāya*—after smelling; *mudā*—with great delight; *yuktaḥ*—fixed; *prādāt*—offered; *patnyai*—to his wife; *udāra-dhīḥ*—liberal-minded.

TRANSLATION

The King was very liberal, and after taking permission from the priests, he took the preparation in his joined palms, and after smelling it he offered a portion to his wife.

PURPORT

The word *udāra-dhīḥ* is significant in this connection. The wife of the King, Sunīthā, was not fit to accept this benediction, yet the King was so liberal that without hesitation he offered to his wife the boiled rice in milk *prasāda* received from the *yajña-puruṣa*. Of course, everything is designed by the Supreme Personality of Godhead. As will be explained in later verses, this incident was not very favorable for the King. Since the King was very liberal, the Supreme Personality of Godhead, in order to increase his detachment from this material world, willed that a cruel son be born of the Queen so that the King would have to leave home. As stated above, Lord Viṣṇu fulfills the desires of the *karmīs* as they desire, but the Lord fulfills the desire of a devotee in a different way so that the devotee may gradually come to Him. This is confirmed in the *Bhagavad-gītā* (*dadāmi buddhi-yogaṁ taṁ yena mām upayānti te*). The Lord gives the devotee the opportunity to make progress further and further so that he may come back home, back to Godhead.

TEXT 38

सा तत्पुंसवनं राज्ञी प्राश्य वै पत्युरादधे ।
गर्भं काल उपावृत्ते कुमारं सुषुवेऽप्रजा ॥३८॥

sā tat puṁ-savanaṁ rājñī
prāśya vai patyur ādadhe
garbhaṁ kāla upāvṛtte
kumāraṁ suṣuve 'prajā

sā—she; *tat*—that food; *pum-savanam*—which produces a male child; *rājñī*—the Queen; *prāśya*—eating; *vai*—indeed; *patyuḥ*—from the husband; *ādadhe*—conceived; *garbham*—pregnancy; *kāle*—when the due time; *upāvṛtte*—appeared; *kumāram*—a son; *suṣuve*—gave birth to; *aprajā*—having no son.

TRANSLATION

Although the Queen had no son, after eating that food, which had the power to produce a male child, she became pregnant by her husband, and in due course of time she gave birth to a son.

PURPORT

Among the ten kinds of purificatory processes, one is *puṁ-savanam*, in which the wife is offered some *prasāda*, or remnants of foodstuff offered to Lord Viṣṇu, so that after sexual intercourse with her husband she may conceive a child.

TEXT 39

स बाल एव पुरुषो मातामहमनुव्रतः ।
अधर्मांशोद्भवं मृत्युं तेनाभवदधार्मिकः ॥३९॥

sa bāla eva puruṣo
mātāmaham anuvrataḥ
adharmāṁśodbhavaṁ mṛtyuṁ
tenābhavad adhārmikaḥ

saḥ—that; *bālaḥ*—child; *eva*—certainly; *puruṣaḥ*—male; *mātāmaham*—maternal grandfather; *anuvrataḥ*—a follower of; *adharma*—of irreligion; *aṁśa*—from a portion; *udbhavam*—who appeared; *mṛtyum*—death; *tena*—by this; *abhavat*—he became; *adhārmikaḥ*—irreligious.

TRANSLATION

That boy was born partially in the dynasty of irreligion. His grandfather was death personified, and the boy grew up as his follower; he became a greatly irreligious person.

PURPORT

The child's mother, Sunīthā, was the daughter of death personified. Generally the daughter receives the qualifications of her father, and the son acquires those of the mother. So, according to the axiomatic truth that things equal to the same thing are equal to one another, the child born of King Aṅga became the follower of his maternal grandfather. According to *smṛti-śāstra,* a child generally follows the principles of his maternal uncle's house. *Narāṇāṁ mātula-karma* means that a child generally follows the qualities of his maternal family. If the maternal family is very corrupt or sinful, the child, even though born of a good father, becomes a victim of the maternal family. According to Vedic civilization, therefore, before the marriage takes place an account is taken of both the boy's and girl's families. If according to astrological calculation the combination is perfect, then marriage takes place. Sometimes, however, there is a mistake, and family life becomes frustrating.

It appears that King Aṅga did not get a very good wife in Sunīthā because she was the daughter of death personified. Sometimes the Lord arranges an unfortunate wife for His devotee so that gradually, due to family circumstances, the devotee becomes detached from his wife and home and makes progress in devotional life. It appears that by the arrangement of the Supreme Personality of Godhead, King Aṅga, although a pious devotee, got an unfortunate wife like Sunīthā and later on a bad child like Vena. But the result was that he got complete freedom from the entanglement of family life and left home to go back to Godhead.

TEXT 40

स शरासनमुद्यम्य मृगयुर्वनगोचरः ।
हन्त्यसाधुर्मृगान् दीनान् वेनोऽसावित्यरौज्जनः ॥४०॥

sa śarāsanam udyamya
mṛgayur vana-gocaraḥ

hanty asādhur mṛgān dīnān
veno 'sāv ity arauj janaḥ

saḥ—that boy of the name Vena; *śarāsanam*—his bow; *udyamya*—taking up; *mṛgayuḥ*—the hunter; *vana-gocaraḥ*—going into the forest; *hanti*—used to kill; *asādhuḥ*—being very cruel; *mṛgān*—deer; *dīnān*—poor; *venaḥ*—Vena; *asau*—there he is; *iti*—thus; *araut*—would cry; *janaḥ*—all the people.

TRANSLATION

After fixing his bow and arrow, the cruel boy used to go to the forest and unnecessarily kill innocent deer, and as soon as he came all the people would cry, "Here comes cruel Vena! Here comes cruel Vena!"

PURPORT

Kṣatriyas are allowed to hunt in the forest for the purpose of learning the killing art, not to kill animals for eating or for any other purpose. The *kṣatriya* kings were sometimes expected to cut off the head of a culprit in the state. For this reason the *kṣatriyas* were allowed to hunt in the forest. Because this son of King Aṅga, Vena, was born of a bad mother, he was very cruel, and he used to go to the forest and unnecessarily kill the animals. All the neighboring inhabitants would be frightened by his presence, and they would call, "Here comes Vena! Here comes Vena!" So from the beginning of his life he was fearful to the citizens.

TEXT 41

आक्रीडे क्रीडतो बालान् वयस्यानतिदारुणः ।
प्रसह्य निरनुक्रोशः पशुमारममारयत् ॥४१॥

ākrīḍe krīḍato bālān
vayasyān atidāruṇaḥ
prasahya niranukrośaḥ
paśu-māram amārayat

ākrīḍe—in the playground; *krīḍataḥ*—while playing; *bālān*—boys; *vayasyān*—of his age; *ati-dāruṇaḥ*—very cruel; *prasahya*—by force;

niranukrośaḥ—merciless; *paśu-māram*—as if slaughtering animals; *amārayat*—killed.

TRANSLATION

The boy was so cruel that while playing with young boys of his age he would kill them very mercilessly, as if they were animals meant for slaughter.

TEXT 42

तं विचक्ष्य खलं पुत्रं शासनैर्विविधैर्नृपः ।
यदा न शासितुं कल्पो भृशमासीत्सुदुर्मनाः ॥४२॥

taṁ vicakṣya khalaṁ putraṁ
śāsanair vividhair nṛpaḥ
yadā na śāsituṁ kalpo
bhṛśam āsīt sudurmanāḥ

tam—him; *vicakṣya*—observing; *khalam*—cruel; *putram*—son; *śāsanaiḥ*—by punishments; *vividhaiḥ*—different kinds of; *nṛpaḥ*—the King; *yadā*—when; *na*—not; *śāsitum*—to bring under control; *kalpaḥ*—was able; *bhṛśam*—greatly; *āsīt*—became; *su-durmanāḥ*—aggrieved.

TRANSLATION

After seeing the cruel and merciless behavior of his son, Vena, King Aṅga punished him in different ways to reform him, but was unable to bring him to the path of gentleness. He thus became greatly aggrieved.

TEXT 43

प्रायेणाभ्यर्चितो देवो येऽप्रजा गृहमेधिनः ।
कदपत्यभृतं दुःखं ये न विन्दन्ति दुर्भरम् ॥४३॥

prāyeṇābhyarcito devo
ye 'prajā gṛha-medhinaḥ
kad-apatya-bhṛtaṁ duḥkhaṁ
ye na vindanti durbharam

prāyeṇa—probably; *abhyarcitaḥ*—was worshiped; *devaḥ*—the Lord; *ye*—they who; *aprajāḥ*—without a son; *gṛha-medhinaḥ*—persons living at home; *kad-apatya*—by a bad son; *bhṛtam*—caused; *duḥkham*—unhappiness; *ye*—they who; *na*—not; *vindanti*—suffer; *durbharam*—unbearable.

TRANSLATION

The King thought to himself: Persons who have no son are certainly fortunate. They must have worshiped the Lord in their previous lives so that they would not have to suffer the unbearable unhappiness caused by a bad son.

TEXT 44

यतः पापीयसी कीर्तिरधर्मश्च महान्नृणाम् ।
यतो विरोधः सर्वेषां यत आधिरनन्तकः ॥४४॥

yataḥ pāpīyasī kīrtir
adharmaś ca mahān nṛṇām
yato virodhaḥ sarveṣāṁ
yata ādhir anantakaḥ

yataḥ—on account of a bad son; *pāpīyasī*—sinful; *kīrtiḥ*—reputation; *adharmaḥ*—irreligion; *ca*—also; *mahān*—great; *nṛṇām*—of men; *yataḥ*—from which; *virodhaḥ*—quarrel; *sarveṣām*—of all people; *yataḥ*—from which; *ādhiḥ*—anxiety; *anantakaḥ*—endless.

TRANSLATION

A sinful son causes a person's reputation to vanish. His irreligious activities at home cause irreligion and quarrel among everyone, and this creates only endless anxiety.

PURPORT

It is said that a married couple must have a son, otherwise their family life is void. But a son born without good qualities is as good as a blind eye. A blind eye has no use for seeing, but it is simply unbearably painful. The King therefore thought himself very unfortunate to have such a bad son.

TEXT 45

कस्तं प्रजापदेशं वै मोहबन्धनमात्मनः ।
पण्डितो बहु मन्येत यदर्थाः क्लेशदा गृहाः ॥४५॥

kas taṁ prajāpadeśaṁ vai
moha-bandhanam ātmanaḥ
paṇḍito bahu manyeta
yad-arthāḥ kleśadā gṛhāḥ

kaḥ—who; *tam*—him; *prajā-apadeśam*—son in name only; *vai*—certainly; *moha*—of illusion; *bandhanam*—bondage; *ātmanaḥ*—for the soul; *paṇḍitaḥ*—intelligent man; *bahu manyeta*—would value; *yat-arthāḥ*—because of whom; *kleśa-dāḥ*—painful; *gṛhāḥ*—home.

TRANSLATION

Who, if he is considerate and intelligent, would desire such a worthless son? Such a son is nothing but a bond of illusion for the living entity, and he makes one's home miserable.

TEXT 46

कदपत्यं वरं मन्ये सदपत्याच्छुचां पदात् ।
निर्विद्येत गृहान्मर्त्यो यत्क्लेशनिवहा गृहाः ॥४६॥

kad-apatyaṁ varaṁ manye
sad-apatyāc chucāṁ padāt
nirvidyeta gṛhān martyo
yat-kleśa-nivahā gṛhāḥ

kad-apatyam—bad son; *varam*—better; *manye*—I think; *sat-apatyāt*—than a good son; *śucām*—of grief; *padāt*—the source; *nirvidyeta*—becomes detached; *gṛhāt*—from home; *martyaḥ*—a mortal man; *yat*—because of whom; *kleśa-nivahāḥ*—hellish; *gṛhāḥ*—home.

TRANSLATION

Then the King thought: A bad son is better than a good son because a good son creates an attachment for home, whereas a bad

son does not. A bad son creates a hellish home from which an intelligent man naturally becomes very easily detached.

PURPORT

The King began to think in terms of attachment and detachment from one's material home. According to Prahlāda Mahārāja, the material home is compared to a blind well. If a man falls down into a blind well, it is very difficult to get out of it and begin life again. Prahlāda Mahārāja has advised that one give up this blind well of home life as soon as possible and go to the forest to take shelter of the Supreme Personality of Godhead. According to Vedic civilization, this giving up of home by *vānaprastha* and *sannyāsa* is compulsory. But people are so attached to their homes that even up to the point of death they do not like to retire from home life. King Aṅga, therefore, thinking in terms of detachment, accepted his bad son as a good impetus for detachment from home life. He therefore considered his bad son his friend since he was helping him become detached from his home. Ultimately one has to learn how to detach oneself from attachment to material life; therefore, if a bad son, by his bad behavior, helps a householder to go away from home, it is a boon.

TEXT 47

एवं स निर्विण्णमना नृपो गृहा-
न्निशीथ उत्थाय महोदयोदयात् ।
अलब्धनिद्रोऽनुपलक्षितो नृभि-
र्हित्वा गतो वेनसुवं प्रसुप्ताम् ।।४७।।

evaṁ sa nirviṇṇa-manā nṛpo gṛhān
niśītha utthāya mahodayodayāt
alabdha-nidro 'nupalakṣito nṛbhir
hitvā gato vena-suvaṁ prasuptām

evam—thus; *saḥ*—he; *nirviṇṇa-manāḥ*—being indifferent in mind; *nṛpaḥ*—King Aṅga; *gṛhāt*—from home; *niśīthe*—in the dead of night; *utthāya*—getting up; *mahā-udaya-udayāt*—opulent by the blessings of great souls; *alabdha-nidraḥ*—being without sleep; *anupalakṣitaḥ*—without being seen; *nṛbhiḥ*—by people in general; *hitvā*—giving up; *gataḥ*—went off; *vena-suvam*—the mother of Vena; *prasuptām*—sleeping deeply.

TRANSLATION

Thinking like that, King Aṅga could not sleep at night. He became completely indifferent to household life. Once, therefore, in the dead of night, he got up from bed and left Vena's mother [his wife], who was sleeping deeply. He gave up all attraction for his greatly opulent kingdom, and, unseen by anyone, he very silently gave up his home and opulence and proceeded towards the forest.

PURPORT

In this verse the word *mahodayodayāt* indicates that by the blessings of a great soul one becomes materially opulent, but when one gives up attachment to material wealth, that should be considered an even greater blessing from the great souls. It was not a very easy task for the King to give up his opulent kingdom and young, faithful wife, but it was certainly a great blessing of the Supreme Personality of Godhead that he could give up the attachment and go out to the forest without being seen by anyone. There are many instances of great souls' leaving home in this way in the dead of night, giving up attachment for home, wife and money.

TEXT 48

विज्ञाय निर्विद्य गतं पतिं प्रजाः
पुरोहितामात्यसुहृद्गणादयः ।
विचिक्युरुर्व्यामतिशोककातरा
यथा निगूढं पुरुषं कुयोगिनः ॥४८॥

vijñāya nirvidya gataṁ patiṁ prajāḥ
purohitāmātya-suhṛd-gaṇādayaḥ
vicikyur urvyām atiśoka-kātarā
yathā nigūḍhaṁ puruṣaṁ kuyoginaḥ

vijñāya—after understanding; *nirvidya*—being indifferent; *gatam*—had left; *patim*—the King; *prajāḥ*—all the citizens; *purohita*—priests; *āmātya*—ministers; *suhṛt*—friends; *gaṇa-ādayaḥ*—and people in general; *vicikyuḥ*—searched; *urvyām*—on the earth; *ati-śoka-kātarāḥ*—being greatly aggrieved; *yathā*—just as; *nigūḍham*—concealed; *puruṣam*—the Supersoul; *ku-yoginaḥ*—inexperienced mystics.

TRANSLATION

When it was understood that the King had indifferently left home, all the citizens, priests, ministers, friends, and people in general were greatly aggrieved. They began to search for him all over the world, just as a less experienced mystic searches out the Supersoul within himself.

PURPORT

The example of searching for the Supersoul within the heart by the less intelligent mystics is very instructive. The Absolute Truth is understood in three different features, namely impersonal Brahman, localized Paramātmā, and the Supreme Personality of Godhead. Such *kuyoginaḥ*, or less intelligent mystics, can by mental speculation reach the point of the impersonal Brahman, but they cannot find the Supersoul, who is sitting within each living entity. When the King left, it was certain that he was staying somewhere else, but because the citizens did not know how to find him they were frustrated like the less intelligent mystics.

TEXT 49

अलक्षयन्तः पदवीं प्रजापते-
हतोद्यमाः प्रत्युपसृत्य ते पुरीम् ।
ऋषीन् समेतानभिवन्द्य साश्रवो
न्यवेदयन् पौरव भर्तृविप्लवम् ॥४९॥

alakṣayantaḥ padavīṁ prajāpater
hatodyamāḥ pratyupasṛtya te purīm
ṛṣīn sametān abhivandya sāśravo
nyavedayan paurava bhartṛ-viplavam

alakṣayantaḥ—not finding; *padavīm*—any trace; *prajāpateḥ*—of King Aṅga; *hata-udyamāḥ*—having become disappointed; *pratyupasṛtya*—after returning; *te*—those citizens; *purīm*—to the city; *ṛṣīn*—the great sages; *sametān*—assembled; *abhivandya*—after making respectful obeisances; *sa-aśravaḥ*—with tears in their eyes; *nyavedayan*—informed; *paurava*—O Vidura; *bhartṛ*—of the King; *viplavam*—the absence.

TRANSLATION

When the citizens could not find any trace of the King after searching for him everywhere, they were very disappointed, and they returned to the city, where all the great sages of the country assembled because of the King's absence. With tears in their eyes the citizens offered respectful obeisances and informed the sages in full detail that they were unable to find the King anywhere.

Thus end the Bhaktivedanta purports of the Fourth Canto, Thirteenth Chapter, of the Śrīmad-Bhāgavatam, *entitled "Description of the Descendants of Dhruva Mahārāja."*

CHAPTER FOURTEEN

The Story of King Vena

TEXT 1

मैत्रेय उवाच
भृग्वादयस्ते मुनयो लोकानां क्षेमदर्शिनः ।
गोप्तर्यसति वै नृणां पश्यन्तः पशुसाम्यताम् ॥ १ ॥

maitreya uvāca
bhṛgv-ādayas te munayo
lokānāṁ kṣema-darśinaḥ
goptary asati vai nṛṇāṁ
paśyantaḥ paśu-sāmyatām

maitreyaḥ uvāca—the great sage Maitreya continued; *bhṛgu-ādayaḥ*—headed by Bhṛgu; *te*—all of them; *munayaḥ*—the great sages; *lokānām*—of the people; *kṣema-darśinaḥ*—who always aspire for the welfare; *goptari*—the King; *asati*—being absent; *vai*—certainly; *nṛṇām*—of all the citizens; *paśyantah*—having understood; *paśu-sāmyatām*—existence on the level of the animals.

TRANSLATION

The great sage Maitreya continued: O great hero Vidura, the great sages, headed by Bhṛgu, were always thinking of the welfare of the people in general. When they saw that in the absence of King Aṅga there was no one to protect the interests of the people, they understood that without a ruler the people would become independent and nonregulated.

PURPORT

In this verse the significant word is *kṣema-darśinaḥ*, which refers to those who are always looking after the welfare of the people in general.

All the great sages headed by Bhṛgu were always thinking of how to elevate all the people of the universe to the spiritual platform. Indeed, they advised the kings of every planet to rule the people with that ultimate goal of life in mind. The great sages used to advise the head of the state, or the king, and he used to rule the populace in accordance with their instruction. After the disappearance of King Aṅga, there was no one to follow the instructions of the great sages. Consequently all the citizens became unruly, so much so that they could be compared to animals. As described in *Bhagavad-gītā* (4.13), human society must be divided into four orders according to quality and work. In every society there must be an intelligent class, administrative class, productive class and worker class. In modern democracy these scientific divisions are turned topsy-turvy, and by vote *śūdras*, or workers, are chosen for administrative posts. Having no knowledge of the ultimate goal of life, such persons whimsically enact laws without knowledge of life's purpose. The result is that no one is happy.

TEXT 2

वीरमातरमाहूय सुनीथां ब्रह्मवादिनः ।
प्रकृत्यसम्मतं वेनमभ्यषिञ्चन् पतिं भुवः ॥ २ ॥

vīra-mātaram āhūya
sunīthāṁ brahma-vādinaḥ
prakṛty-asammatam venam
abhyaṣiñcan patiṁ bhuvaḥ

vīra—of Vena; *mātaram*—mother; *āhūya*—calling; *sunīthām*—of the name Sunīthā; *brahma-vādinaḥ*—the great sages learned in the *Vedas; prakṛti*—by the ministers; *asammatam*—not approved of; *venam*—Vena; *abhyaṣiñcan*—enthroned; *patim*—the master; *bhuvaḥ*—of the world.

TRANSLATION

The great sages then called for the Queen Mother, Sunīthā, and with her permission they installed Vena on the throne as master of the world. All the ministers, however, disagreed with this.

TEXT 3

श्रुत्वा नृपासनगतं वेनमत्युग्रशासनम् ।
निलिल्युर्दस्यवः सद्यः सर्पत्रस्ता इवाखवः ॥ ३ ॥

śrutvā nṛpāsana-gataṁ
venam atyugra-śāsanam
nililyur dasyavaḥ sadyaḥ
sarpa-trastā ivākhavaḥ

śrutvā—after hearing; *nṛpa*—of the King; *āsana-gatam*—ascended to the throne; *venam*—Vena; *ati*—very; *ugra*—severe; *śāsanam*—punisher; *nililyuḥ*—hid themselves; *dasyavaḥ*—all the thieves; *sadyaḥ*—immediately; *sarpa*—from snakes; *trastāḥ*—being afraid; *iva*—like; *ākhavaḥ*—rats.

TRANSLATION

It was already known that Vena was very severe and cruel; therefore, as soon as all the thieves and rogues in the state heard of his ascendance to the royal throne, they became very much afraid of him. Indeed, they hid themselves here and there as rats hide themselves from snakes.

PURPORT

When the government is very weak, rogues and thieves flourish. Similarly, when the government is very strong, all the thieves and rogues disappear or hide themselves. Of course Vena was not a very good king, but he was known to be cruel and severe. Thus the state at least became freed from thieves and rogues.

TEXT 4

स आरूढनृपस्थान उन्नद्धोऽष्टविभूतिभिः ।
अवमेने महाभागान् स्तब्धः सम्भावितः स्वतः॥ ४ ॥

sa ārūḍha-nṛpa-sthāna
unnaddho 'ṣṭa-vibhūtibhiḥ

avamene mahā-bhāgān
stabdhaḥ sambhāvitaḥ svataḥ

saḥ—King Vena; *ārūḍha*—ascended to; *nṛpa-sthānaḥ*—the seat of the king; *unnaddhaḥ*—very proud; *aṣṭa*—eight; *vibhūtibhiḥ*—by opulences; *avamene*—began to insult; *mahā-bhāgān*—great personalities; *stabdhaḥ*—inconsiderate; *sambhāvitaḥ*—considered great; *svataḥ*—by himself.

TRANSLATION

When the King ascended to the throne, he became all-powerful with eight kinds of opulences. Consequently he became too proud. By virtue of his false prestige, he considered himself to be greater than anyone. Thus he began to insult great personalities.

PURPORT

In this verse the word *aṣṭa-vibhūtibhiḥ*, meaning "by eight opulences," is very important. The king is supposed to possess eight kinds of opulences. By dint of mystic *yoga* practice, kings generally acquired these eight opulences. These kings were called *rājarṣis*, kings who were also great sages. By practicing mystic *yoga*, a *rājarṣi* could become smaller than the smallest, greater than the greatest, and could get whatever he desired. A *rājarṣi* could also create a kingdom, bring everyone under his control and rule everyone. These were some of the opulences of a king. King Vena, however, was not practiced in *yoga*, but he became very proud of his royal position nonetheless. Because he was not very considerate, he began to misuse his power and insult great personalities.

TEXT 5

एवं मदान्ध उत्सिक्तो निरङ्कुश इव द्विपः ।
पर्यटन् रथमास्थाय कम्पयन्निव रोदसी ॥ ५ ॥

evaṁ madāndha utsikto
niraṅkuśa iva dvipaḥ
paryaṭan ratham āsthāya
kampayann iva rodasī

evam—thus; *mada-andhaḥ*—being blind with power; *utsiktaḥ*—proud; *niraṅkuśaḥ*—uncontrolled; *iva*—like; *dvipaḥ*—an elephant; *paryaṭan*—traveling; *ratham*—a chariot; *āsthāya*—having mounted; *kampayan*—causing to tremble; *iva*—indeed; *rodasī*—the sky and earth.

TRANSLATION

When he became overly blind due to his opulences, King Vena mounted a chariot and, like an uncontrolled elephant, began to travel through the kingdom, causing the sky and earth to tremble wherever he went.

TEXT 6

न यष्टव्यं न दातव्यं न होतव्यं द्विजाः क्वचित् ।
इति न्यवारयद्धर्मं भेरीघोषेण सर्वशः ॥ ६ ॥

na yaṣṭavyaṁ na dātavyaṁ
na hotavyaṁ dvijāḥ kvacit
iti nyavārayad dharmaṁ
bherī-ghoṣeṇa sarvaśaḥ

na—not; *yaṣṭavyam*—any sacrifices can be performed; *na*—not; *dātavyam*—any charity can be given; *na*—not; *hotavyam*—any clarified butter can be offered; *dvijāḥ*—O twice-born; *kvacit*—at any time; *iti*—thus; *nyavārayat*—he stopped; *dharmam*—the procedures of religious principles; *bherī*—of kettledrums; *ghoṣeṇa*—with the sound; *sarvaśaḥ*—everywhere.

TRANSLATION

All the twice-born [brāhmaṇas] were forbidden henceforward to perform any sacrifice, and they were also forbidden to give charity or offer clarified butter. Thus King Vena sounded kettledrums throughout the countryside. In other words, he stopped all kinds of religious rituals.

PURPORT

What was committed by King Vena many years ago is at present being carried out by atheistic governments all over the world. The world situation is so tense that at any moment governments may issue declarations to stop religious rituals. Eventually the world situation will become so degraded that it will be impossible for pious men to live on the planet. Therefore sane people should execute Kṛṣṇa consciousness very seriously, so that they can go back home, back to Godhead, without having to further suffer the miserable conditions predominant in this universe.

TEXT 7

वेनस्यावेक्ष्य मुनयो दुर्वृत्तस्य विचेष्टितम् ।
विमृश्य लोकव्यसनं कृपयोचुः स्म सत्रिणः ॥ ७ ॥

venasyāvekṣya munayo
durvṛttasya viceṣṭitam
vimṛśya loka-vyasanaṁ
kṛpayocuḥ sma satriṇaḥ

venasya—of King Vena; *āvekṣya*—after observing; *munayaḥ*—all the great sages; *durvṛttasya*—of the great rogue; *viceṣṭitam*—activities; *vimṛśya*—considering; *loka-vyasanam*—danger to the people in general; *kṛpayā*—out of compassion; *ūcuḥ*—talked; *sma*—in the past; *satriṇaḥ*—the performers of sacrifices.

TRANSLATION

Therefore all the great sages assembled together and, after observing cruel Vena's atrocities, concluded that a great danger and catastrophe was approaching the people of the world. Thus out of compassion they began to talk amongst themselves, for they themselves were the performers of the sacrifices.

PURPORT

Before King Vena was enthroned, all the great sages were very much anxious to see to the welfare of society. When they saw that King Vena was most irresponsible, cruel and atrocious, they again began to think of the welfare of the people. It should be understood that sages, saintly persons and devotees are not unconcerned with the people's welfare.

Ordinary *karmīs* are busy acquiring money for sense gratification, and ordinary *jñānīs* are socially aloof when they speculate on liberation, but actual devotees and saintly persons are always anxious to see how the people can be made happy both materially and spiritually. Therefore the great sages began to consult one another on how to get out of the dangerous atmosphere created by King Vena.

TEXT 8

अहो उभयतः प्राप्तं लोकस्य व्यसनं महत् ।
दारुण्युभयतो दीप्ते इव तस्करपालयोः ॥ ८ ॥

aho ubhayataḥ prāptaṁ
lokasya vyasanaṁ mahat
dāruṇy ubhayato dīpte
iva taskara-pālayoḥ

aho—alas; *ubhayataḥ*—from both directions; *prāptam*—received; *lokasya*—of the people in general; *vyasanam*—danger; *mahat*—great; *dāruṇi*—a log; *ubhayataḥ*—from both sides; *dīpte*—burning; *iva*—like; *taskara*—from thieves and rogues; *pālayoḥ*—and from the king.

TRANSLATION

When the great sages consulted one another, they saw that the people were in a dangerous position from both directions. When a fire blazes on both ends of a log, the ants in the middle are in a very dangerous situation. Similarly, at that time the people in general were in a dangerous position due to an irresponsible king on one side and thieves and rogues on the other.

TEXT 9

अराजकभयादेष कृतो राजातदर्हणः ।
ततोऽप्यासीद्भयं त्वद्य कथं स्यात्स्वस्ति देहिनाम् ॥ ९ ॥

arājaka-bhayād eṣa
kṛto rājātad-arhaṇaḥ

tato 'py āsīd bhayaṁ tv adya
kathaṁ syāt svasti dehinām

arājaka—being without a king; *bhayāt*—out of fear; *eṣaḥ*—this Vena; *kṛtaḥ*—was made; *rājā*—the king; *a-tat-arhaṇaḥ*—though not qualified for it; *tataḥ*—from him; *api*—also; *āsīt*—there was; *bhayam*—danger; *tu*—then; *adya*—now; *katham*—how; *syāt*—can there be; *svasti*—happiness; *dehinām*—of the people in general.

TRANSLATION

Thinking to save the state from irregularity, the sages began to consider that it was due to a political crisis that they made Vena king although he was not qualified. But alas, now the people were being disturbed by the king himself. Under such circumstances, how could the people be happy?

PURPORT

In *Bhagavad-gītā* (18.5) it is stated that even in the renounced order one should not give up sacrifice, charity and penance. The *brahmacārīs* must perform sacrifices, the *gṛhasthas* must give in charity, and those in the renounced order of life (the *vānaprasthas* and *sannyāsīs*) must practice penance and austerities. These are the procedures by which everyone can be elevated to the spiritual platform. When the sages and saintly persons saw that King Vena had stopped all these functions, they became concerned about the people's progress. Saintly people preach God consciousness, or Kṛṣṇa consciousness, because they are anxious to save the general populace from the dangers of animalistic life. There must be a good government to see that the citizens are actually executing their religious rituals, and thieves and rogues must be curbed. When this is done, the people can advance peacefully in spiritual consciousness and make their lives successful.

TEXT 10

अहेरिव पयःपोषः पोषकस्याप्यनर्थभृत् ।
वेनः प्रकृत्यैव खलः सुनीथागर्भसम्भवः ॥१०॥

aher iva payaḥ-poṣaḥ
poṣakasyāpy anartha-bhṛt
venaḥ prakṛtyaiva khalaḥ
sunīthā-garbha-sambhavaḥ

aheḥ—of a snake; *iva*—like; *payaḥ*—with milk; *poṣaḥ*—the maintaining; *poṣakasya*—of the maintainer; *api*—even; *anartha*—against the interest; *bhṛt*—becomes; *venaḥ*—King Vena; *prakṛtyā*—by nature; *eva*—certainly; *khalaḥ*—mischievous; *sunīthā*—of Sunīthā, Vena's mother; *garbha*—the womb; *sambhavaḥ*—born of.

TRANSLATION

The sages began to think within themselves: Because he was born from the womb of Sunīthā, King Vena is by nature very mischievous. Supporting this mischievous king is exactly like maintaining a snake with milk. Now he has become a source of all difficulties.

PURPORT

Saintly persons are generally aloof from social activities and the materialistic way of life. King Vena was supported by the saintly persons just to protect the citizens from the hands of rogues and thieves, but after his ascendance to the throne, he became a source of trouble to the sages. Saintly people are especially interested in performing sacrifices and austerities for the advancement of spiritual life, but Vena, instead of being obliged because of the saints' mercy, turned out to be their enemy because he prohibited them from executing their ordinary duties. A serpent who is maintained with milk and bananas simply stores poison in his teeth and awaits the day to bite his master.

TEXT 11

निरूपितः प्रजापालः स जिघांसति वै प्रजाः ।
तथापि सान्त्वयेमामुं नास्मांस्तत्पातकं स्पृशेत् ॥११॥

nirūpitaḥ prajā-pālaḥ
sa jighāṁsati vai prajāḥ

tathāpi sāntvayemāmuṁ
nāsmāṁs tat-pātakaṁ spṛśet

nirūpitaḥ—appointed; *prajā-pālaḥ*—the king; *saḥ*—he; *jighāṁsati*—desires to harm; *vai*—certainly; *prajāḥ*—the citizens; *tathā āpi*—nevertheless; *sāntvayema*—we should pacify; *amum*—him; *na*—not; *asmān*—us; *tat*—his; *pātakam*—sinful result; *spṛśet*—may touch.

TRANSLATION

We appointed this Vena king of the state in order to give protection to the citizens, but now he has become the enemy of the citizens. Despite all these discrepancies, we should at once try to pacify him. By doing so, we may not be touched by the sinful results caused by him.

PURPORT

The saintly sages elected King Vena to become king, but he proved to be mischievous; therefore the sages were very much afraid of incurring sinful reaction. The law of *karma* prohibits a person even to associate with a mischievous individual. By electing Vena to the throne, the saintly sages certainly associated with him. Ultimately King Vena became so mischievous that the saintly sages actually became afraid of becoming contaminated by his activities. Thus before taking any action against him, the sages tried to pacify and correct him so that he might turn from his mischief.

TEXT 12

तद्विद्वद्भिरसद्वृत्तो वेनोऽस्माभिः कृतो नृपः ।
सान्त्वितो यदि नो वाचं न ग्रहीष्यत्यधर्मकृत् ।
लोकधिक्कारसन्दग्धं दहिष्यामः स्वतेजसा ॥१२॥

tad-vidvadbhir asad-vṛtto
veno 'smābhiḥ kṛto nṛpaḥ
sāntvito yadi no vācaṁ
na grahīṣyaty adharma-kṛt
loka-dhikkāra-sandagdhaṁ
dahiṣyāmaḥ sva-tejasā

tat—his mischievous nature; *vidvadbhiḥ*—aware of; *asat-vṛttaḥ*—impious; *venaḥ*—Vena; *asmābhiḥ*—by us; *kṛtaḥ*—was made; *nṛpaḥ*—king; *sāntvitaḥ*—(in spite of) being pacified; *yadi*—if; *naḥ*—our; *vācam*—words; *na*—not; *grahīṣyati*—he will accept; *adharma-kṛt*—the most mischievous; *loka-dhik-kāra*—by public condemnation; *san-dagdham*—burned; *dahiṣyāmaḥ*—we shall burn; *sva-tejasā*—by our prowess.

TRANSLATION

The saintly sages continued thinking: Of course we are completely aware of his mischievous nature. Yet nevertheless we enthroned Vena. If we cannot persuade King Vena to accept our advice, he will be condemned by the public, and we will join them. Thus by our prowess we shall burn him to ashes.

PURPORT

Saintly persons are not interested in political matters, yet they are always thinking of the welfare of the people in general. Consequently they sometimes have to come down to the political field and take steps to correct the misguided government or royalty. However, in Kali-yuga, saintly persons are not as powerful as they previously were. They used to be able to burn any sinful man to ashes by virtue of their spiritual prowess. Now saintly persons have no such power due to the influence of the age of Kali. Indeed, the *brāhmaṇas* do not even have the power to perform sacrifices in which animals are put into a fire to attain a new life. Under these circumstances, instead of actively taking part in politics, saintly persons should engage in chanting the *mahā-mantra*, Hare Kṛṣṇa. By the grace of Lord Caitanya, by simply chanting this Hare Kṛṣṇa *mahā-mantra*, the general populace can derive all benefits without political implications.

TEXT 13

एवमध्यवसायैनं मुनयो गूढमन्यवः ।
उपव्रज्याब्रुवन् वेनं सान्त्वयित्वा च सामभिः ॥१३॥

evam adhyavasāyainaṁ
munayo gūḍha-manyavaḥ

upavrajyābruvan venaṁ
sāntvayitvā ca sāmabhiḥ

evam—thus; *adhyavasāya*—having decided; *enam*—him; *munayaḥ*—the great sages; *gūḍha-manyavaḥ*—concealing their anger; *upavrajya*—having approached; *abruvan*—spoke; *venam*—to King Vena; *sāntvayitvā*—after pacifying; *ca*—also; *sāmabhiḥ*—with sweet words.

TRANSLATION

The great sages, having thus decided, approached King Vena. Concealing their real anger, they pacified him with sweet words and then spoke as follows.

TEXT 14

मुनय ऊचुः
नृपवर्य निबोधैतद्यत्ते विज्ञापयाम भोः ।
आयुःश्रीबलकीर्तीनां तव तात विवर्धनम् ॥१४॥

munaya ūcuḥ
nṛpa-varya nibodhaitad
yat te vijñāpayāma bhoḥ
āyuḥ-śrī-bala-kīrtīnāṁ
tava tāta vivardhanam

munayaḥ ūcuḥ—the great sages said; *nṛpa-varya*—O best of the kings; *nibodha*—kindly try to understand; *etat*—this; *yat*—which; *te*—to you; *vijñāpayāma*—we shall instruct; *bhoḥ*—O King; *āyuḥ*—duration of life; *śrī*—opulences; *bala*—strength; *kīrtīnām*—good reputation; *tava*—your; *tāta*—dear son; *vivardhanam*—which will increase.

TRANSLATION

The great sages said: Dear King, we have come to give you good advice. Kindly hear us with great attention. By doing so, your duration of life and your opulence, strength and reputation will increase.

PURPORT

According to Vedic civilization, in a monarchy the king is advised by saintly persons and sages. By taking their advice, he can become the greatest executive power, and everyone in his kingdom will be happy, peaceful and prosperous. The great kings were very responsible in taking the instructions given by great saintly personalities. The kings used to accept the instructions given by great sages like Parāśara, Vyāsadeva, Nārada, Devala and Asita. In other words, they would first accept the authority of saintly persons and then execute their monarchical power. Unfortunately, in the present age of Kali, the head of government does not follow the instructions given by the saintly persons; therefore neither the citizens nor the men of government are very happy. Their duration of life is shortened, and almost everyone is wretched and bereft of bodily strength and spiritual power. If citizens want to be happy and prosperous in this democratic age, they should not elect rascals and fools who have no respect for saintly persons.

TEXT 15

धर्म आचरितः पुंसां वाङ्मनःकायबुद्धिभिः ।
लोकान् विशोकान् वितरत्यथानन्त्यमसङ्गिनाम् ॥१५॥

dharma ācaritaḥ puṁsāṁ
vāṅ-manaḥ-kāya-buddhibhiḥ
lokān viśokān vitaraty
athānantyam asaṅginām

dharmaḥ—religious principles; *ācaritaḥ*—executed; *puṁsām*—to persons; *vāk*—by words; *manaḥ*—mind; *kāya*—body; *buddhibhiḥ*—and by intelligence; *lokān*—the planets; *viśokān*—without misery; *vitarati*—bestow; *atha*—certainly; *ānantyam*—unlimited happiness, liberation; *asaṅginām*—to those free from material influence.

TRANSLATION

Those who live according to religious principles and who follow them by words, mind, body and intelligence are elevated to the

heavenly kingdom, which is devoid of all miseries. Being thus rid of the material influence, they achieve unlimited happiness in life.

PURPORT

The saintly sages herein instruct that the king or head of government should set an example by living a religious life. As stated in *Bhagavad-gītā*, religion means worshiping the Supreme Personality of Godhead. One should not simply make a show of religious life, but should perform devotional service perfectly with words, mind, body and good intelligence. By doing so, not only will the king or government head rid himself of the contamination of the material modes of nature, but the general public will also, and they will all become gradually elevated to the kingdom of God and go back home, back to Godhead. The instructions given herein serve as a summary of how the head of government should execute his ruling power and thus attain happiness not only in this life but also in the life after death.

TEXT 16

स ते मा विनशेद्वीर प्रजानां क्षेमलक्षणः ।
यस्मिन् विनष्टे नृपतिरैश्वर्यादवरोहति ॥१६॥

sa te mā vinaśed vīra
prajānāṁ kṣema-lakṣaṇaḥ
yasmin vinaṣṭe nṛpatir
aiśvaryād avarohati

saḥ—that spiritual life; *te*—by you; *mā*—do not; *vinaśet*—let it be spoiled; *vīra*—O hero; *prajānām*—of the people; *kṣema-lakṣaṇaḥ*—the cause of prosperity; *yasmin*—which; *vinaṣṭe*—being spoiled; *nṛpatiḥ*—the king; *aiśvaryāt*—from opulence; *avarohati*—falls down.

TRANSLATION

The sages continued: O great hero, for this reason you should not be the cause of spoiling the spiritual life of the general populace. If their spiritual life is spoiled because of your activities, you will certainly fall down from your opulent and royal position.

PURPORT

Formerly, in practically all parts of the world, there were monarchies, but gradually as monarchy declined from the ideal life of religion to the godless life of sense gratification, monarchies all over the world were abolished. However, simply abolishing monarchy and replacing it with democracy is not sufficient unless the government men are religious and follow in the footsteps of great religious personalities.

TEXT 17

राजन्नसाध्वमात्येभ्यश्चोरादिभ्यः प्रजा नृपः ।
रक्षन् यथा बलिं गृह्णन्निह प्रेत्य च मोदते ॥१७॥

rājann asādhv-amātyebhyaś
corādibhyaḥ prajā nṛpaḥ
rakṣan yathā baliṁ gṛhṇann
iha pretya ca modate

rājan—O King; *asādhu*—mischievous; *amātyebhyaḥ*—from ministers; *cora-ādibhyaḥ*—from thieves and rogues; *prajāḥ*—the citizens; *nṛpaḥ*—the king; *rakṣan*—protecting; *yathā*—accordingly as; *balim*—taxes; *gṛhṇan*—accepting; *iha*—in this world; *pretya*—after death; *ca*—also; *modate*—enjoys.

TRANSLATION

The saintly persons continued: When the king protects the citizens from the disturbances of mischievous ministers as well as from thieves and rogues, he can, by virtue of such pious activities, accept taxes given by his subjects. Thus a pious king can certainly enjoy himself in this world as well as in the life after death.

PURPORT

The duty of a pious king is described very nicely in this verse. His first and foremost duty is to give protection to the citizens from thieves and rogues as well as from ministers who are no better than thieves and rogues. Formerly, ministers were appointed by the king and were not elected. Consequently, if the king was not very pious or strict, the ministers would become thieves and rogues and exploit the innocent citizens. It is the king's duty to see that there is no increase of thieves and rogues either in the government secretariat or in the departments of public affairs. If a king cannot give protection to citizens from thieves and rogues both in the government service and in public affairs, he has no right to exact taxes from them. In other words, the king or the government that taxes can levy taxes from the citizens only if the king or government is able to give protection to the citizens from thieves and rogues.

In the Twelfth Canto of *Śrīmad-Bhāgavatam* (12.1.42) there is a description of these thieves and rogues in government service. As stated, *prajās te bhakṣayiṣyanti mlecchā rājanya-rūpiṇaḥ:* "These proud *mlecchas* [persons who are less than *śūdras*], representing themselves as kings, will tyrannize their subjects, and their subjects, on the other hand, will cultivate the most vicious practices. Thus practicing evil habits and behaving foolishly, the subjects will be like their rulers." The idea is that in the democratic days of Kali-yuga, the general population will fall down to the standard of *śūdras.* As stated (*kalau śūdra-sambhavaḥ*), practically the whole population of the world will be *śūdra.* A *śūdra* is a fourth-class man who is only fit to work for the three higher social castes. Being fourth-class men, *śūdras* are not very intelligent. Since the population is fallen in these democratic days, they can only elect a person in their category, but a government cannot run very well when it is run by *śūdras.* The second class of men, known as *kṣatriyas,* are especially meant for governing a country under the direction of saintly persons (*brāhmaṇas*) who are supposed to be very intelligent. In other ages—in Satya-yuga, Tretā-yuga and Dvāpara-yuga—the general populace was not so degraded, and the head of government was never elected. The king was the supreme executive personality, and if he caught any ministers stealing like thieves and rogues, he would at once have them killed or dismissed from service. As it was the duty of the king to kill thieves and rogues, it was similarly his duty to immediately kill dishonest ministers in government service. By such strict vigilance, the king could run the government very well, and the citizens would be happy to have such a king. The conclusion is that unless the king is perfectly able to give protection to the citizens from rogues and thieves, he has no right to levy taxes from the citizens for his own sense gratification. However, if he gives all protection to the citizens and levies taxes on them, he can live very happily and peacefully in this life, and at the end of this life be elevated to the heavenly kingdom or even to the Vaikuṇṭhas, where he will be happy in all respects.

TEXT 18

यस्य राष्ट्रे पुरे चैव भगवान् यज्ञपूरुषः ।
इज्यते स्वेन धर्मेण जनैर्वर्णाश्रमान्वितैः ॥१८॥

yasya rāṣṭre pure caiva
bhagavān yajña-pūruṣaḥ
ijyate svena dharmeṇa
janair varṇāśramānvitaiḥ

yasya—whose; *rāṣṭre*—in the state or kingdom; *pure*—in the cities; *ca*—also; *eva*—certainly; *bhagavān*—the Supreme Personality of Godhead; *yajña-pūruṣaḥ*—who is the enjoyer of all sacrifices; *ijyate*—is worshiped; *svena*—their own; *dharmeṇa*—by occupation; *janaiḥ*—by the people; *varṇa-āśrama*—the system of eight social orders; *anvitaiḥ*—who follow.

TRANSLATION

The king is supposed to be pious in whose state and cities the general populace strictly observes the system of eight social orders of varṇa and āśrama, and where all citizens engage in worshiping the Supreme Personality of Godhead by their particular occupations.

PURPORT

The state's duty and the citizen's duty are very nicely explained in this verse. The activities of the government head, or king, as well as the activities of the citizens, should be so directed that ultimately everyone engages in devotional service to the Supreme Personality of Godhead. The king, or government head, is supposed to be the representative of the Supreme Personality of Godhead and is therefore supposed to see that things go on nicely and that the citizens are situated in the scientific social order comprised of four *varṇas* and four *āśramas*. In the *Viṣṇu Purāṇa* it is stated that unless people are educated or situated in the scientific social order comprised of four *varṇas* (*brāhmaṇa, kṣatriya, vaiśya* and *śūdra*) and four *āśramas* (*brahmacarya, gṛhastha, vāna-prastha* and *sannyāsa*), society can never be considered real human society, nor can it make any advancement towards the ultimate goal of human life. It is the duty of the government to see that things go on in terms of *varṇa* and *āśrama*. As stated herein, *bhagavān yajña-pūruṣaḥ*—the Supreme Personality of Godhead, Kṛṣṇa, is the *yajña-pūruṣa*. As stated in *Bhagavad-gītā* (5.29): *bhoktāraṁ yajña-tapasām*. Kṛṣṇa is the ultimate purpose of all sacrifice. He is also the enjoyer of all sacrifices; therefore He is known as *yajña-pūruṣa*. The word *yajña-pūruṣa* indicates Lord Viṣṇu or Lord Kṛṣṇa, or any Personality of Godhead in the category of *viṣṇu-tattva*. In perfect human society, people are situated in the orders of *varṇa* and *āśrama* and are engaged in worshiping Lord Viṣṇu by their respective activities. Every citizen engaged in an occupation renders service by the resultant actions of his activities. That is the perfection of life. As stated in *Bhagavad-gītā* (18.46):

yataḥ pravṛttir bhūtānāṁ
yena sarvam idaṁ tatam
sva-karmaṇā tam abhyarcya
siddhiṁ vindati mānavaḥ

"By worship of the Lord, who is the source of all beings and who is all-pervading, man can, in the performance of his own duty, attain perfection."

Thus the *brāhmaṇas, kṣatriyas, śūdras* and *vaiśyas* must execute their prescribed duties as these duties are stated in the *śāstras*. In this way everyone can satisfy the Supreme Personality of Godhead, Viṣṇu. The king, or government head, has to see that the citizens are thus engaged. In other words, the state or the government must not deviate from its duty by declaring that the state is a secular one, which has no interest in whether or not the people advance in *varṇāśrama-dharma*. Today people engaged in government service and people who rule over the citizens have no respect for the *varṇāśrama-dharma*. They complacently feel that the state is secular. In such a government, no one can be happy. The people must follow the *varṇāśrama-dharma*, and the king must see that they are following it nicely.

TEXT 19

तस्य राज्ञो महाभाग भगवान् भूतभावनः ।
परितुष्यति विश्वात्मा तिष्ठतो निजशासने ॥१९॥

tasya rājño mahā-bhāga
bhagavān bhūta-bhāvanaḥ
paritusyati viśvātmā
tiṣṭhato nija-śāsane

tasya—with him; *rājñaḥ*—the king; *mahā-bhāga*—O noble one; *bhagavān*—the Supreme Personality of Godhead; *bhūta-bhāvanaḥ*—who is the original cause of the cosmic manifestation; *paritusyati*—becomes satisfied; *viśva-ātmā*—the Supersoul of the entire universe; *tiṣṭhataḥ*—being situated; *nija-śāsane*—in his own governing situation.

TRANSLATION

O noble one, if the king sees that the Supreme Personality of Godhead, the original cause of the cosmic manifestation and the Supersoul within everyone, is worshiped, the Lord will be satisfied.

PURPORT

It is a fact that the government's duty is to see that the Supreme Personality of Godhead is satisfied by the activities of the people as well as by the activities of the government. There is no possibility of happiness if the government or citizenry have no idea of Bhagavān, the Supreme Personality of Godhead, who is the original cause of the cosmic manifestation, or if they have no knowledge of *bhūta-bhāvana*, who is *viśvātmā*, or the Supersoul, the soul of everyone's soul. The conclusion is that without engaging in devotional service, neither the citizens nor the government can be happy in any way. At the present moment neither the king nor the governing body is interested in seeing that the people are engaged in the devotional service of the Supreme Personality of Godhead. Rather, they are more interested in advancing the machinery of sense gratification. Consequently they are becoming more and more implicated in the complex machinery of the stringent laws of nature. People should be freed from the entanglement of the three modes of material nature, and the only process by which this is possible is surrender unto the Supreme Personality of Godhead. This is advised in *Bhagavad-gītā*. Unfortunately neither the government nor the people in general have any idea of this; they are simply interested in sense gratification and in being happy in this life. The word *nija-śāsane* ("in his own governmental duty") indicates that both the government and the citizens are responsible for the execution of *varṇāśrama-dharma*. Once the populace is situated in the *varṇāśrama-dharma*, there is every possibility of real life and prosperity both in this world and in the next.

TEXT 20

तस्मिंस्तुष्टे किमप्राप्यं जगतामीश्वरेश्वरे ।
लोकाः सपाला ह्येतस्मै हरन्ति बलिमादृताः ॥२०॥

tasmiṁs tuṣṭe kim aprāpyaṁ
jagatām īśvareśvare
lokāḥ sapālā hy etasmai
haranti balim ādṛtāḥ

tasmin—when He; *tuṣṭe*—is satisfied; *kim*—what; *aprāpyam*—impossible to achieve; *jagatām*—of the universe; *īśvara-īśvare*—the controller of the controllers; *lokāḥ*—the inhabitants of the planets; *sapālāḥ*—with their presiding deities; *hi*—for this reason; *etasmai*—unto Him; *haranti*—offer; *balim*—paraphernalia for worship; *ādṛtāḥ*—with great pleasure.

TRANSLATION

The Supreme Personality of Godhead is worshiped by the great demigods, controllers of universal affairs. When He is satisfied, nothing is impossible to achieve. For this reason all the demigods, presiding deities of different planets, as well as the inhabitants of their planets, take great pleasure in offering all kinds of paraphernalia for His worship.

PURPORT

All Vedic civilization is summarized in this verse: all living entities, either on this planet or on other planets, have to satisfy the Supreme Personality of Godhead by their respective duties. When He is satisfied, all necessities of life are automatically supplied. In the *Vedas* it is also stated: *eko bahūnāṁ yo vidadhāti kāmān* (*Kaṭha Upaniṣad* 2.2.13). From the *Vedas* we understand that He is supplying everyone's necessities, and we can actually see that the lower animals, the birds and the bees, have no business or profession, yet they are not dying for want of food. They are all living in nature's way, and they all have the necessities of life provided—namely eating, sleeping, mating and defending.

Human society, however, has artificially created a type of civilization which makes one forgetful of his relationship with the Supreme Personality of Godhead. Modern society even enables one to forget the Supreme Personality of Godhead's grace and mercy. Consequently modern civilized man is always unhappy and in need of things. People do not know that the ultimate goal of life is to approach Lord Viṣṇu and satisfy Him. They have taken this materialistic way of life as everything and have become captivated by materialistic activities. Indeed, their leaders are always encouraging them to follow this path, and the general populace, being ignorant of the laws of God, are following their blind leaders down the path of unhappiness. In order to rectify this world situation, all people should be trained in Kṛṣṇa consciousness and act in accordance with the *varṇāśrama* system. The state should also see that the people are engaged in satisfying the Supreme Personality of Godhead. This is the primary duty of the state. The Kṛṣṇa consciousness movement was started to convince the general populace to adopt the best process by which to satisfy the Supreme Personality of Godhead and thus solve all problems.

TEXT 21

तं सर्वलोकामरयज्ञसंग्रहं
त्रयीमयं द्रव्यमयं तपोमयम् ।
यज्ञैर्विचित्रैर्यजतो भवाय ते
राजन् स्वदेशाननुरोद्धुमर्हसि ॥२१॥

taṁ sarva-lokāmara-yajña-saṅgrahaṁ
trayīmayaṁ dravyamayaṁ tapomayam
yajñair vicitrair yajato bhavāya te
rājan sva-deśān anuroddhum arhasi

tam—Him; *sarva-loka*—in all planets; *amara*—with the predominating deities; *yajña*—sacrifices; *saṅgraham*—who accepts; *trayī-mayam*—the sum total of the three *Vedas; dravya-mayam*—the owner of all paraphernalia; *tapaḥ-mayam*—the goal of all austerity; *yajñaiḥ*—by sacrifices; *vicitraiḥ*—various; *yajataḥ*—worshiping; *bhavāya*—for elevation; *te*—your; *rājan*—O King; *sva-deśān*—your countrymen; *anuroddhum*—to direct; *arhasi*—you ought.

TRANSLATION

Dear King, the Supreme Personality of Godhead, along with the predominating deities, is the enjoyer of the results of all sacrifices in all planets. The Supreme Lord is the sum total of the three Vedas, the owner of everything, and the ultimate goal of all austerity. Therefore your countrymen should engage in performing various sacrifices for your elevation. Indeed, you should always direct them towards the offering of sacrifices.

TEXT 22

यज्ञेन युष्मद्विषये द्विजातिभि-
र्वितायमानेन सुराः कला हरेः ।
स्विष्टाः सुतुष्टाः प्रदिशन्ति वाञ्छितं
तद्धेलनं नार्हसि वीर चेष्टितुम् ॥२२॥

yajñena yuṣmad-viṣaye dvijātibhir
vitāyamānena surāḥ kalā hareḥ
sviṣṭāḥ sutuṣṭāḥ pradiśanti vāñchitaṁ
tad-dhelanaṁ nārhasi vīra ceṣṭitum

yajñena—by sacrifice; *yuṣmat*—your; *viṣaye*—in the kingdom; *dvi-jātibhiḥ*—by the *brāhmaṇas; vitāyamānena*—being performed; *su-*

rāḥ—all the demigods; *kalāḥ*—expansions; *hareḥ*—of the Personality of Godhead; *su-iṣṭāḥ*—being properly worshiped; *su-tuṣṭāḥ*—very much satisfied; *pradiśanti*—will give; *vāñchitam*—desired result; *tat-helanam*—disrespect to them; *na*—not; *arhasi*—you ought; *vīra*—O hero; *ceṣṭitum*—to do.

TRANSLATION

When all the brāhmaṇas engage in performing sacrifices in your kingdom, all the demigods, who are plenary expansions of the Lord, will be very much satisfied by their activities and will give you your desired result. Therefore, O hero, do not stop the sacrificial performances. If you stop them, you will disrespect the demigods.

TEXT 23

वेन उवाच
बालिशा बत यूयं वा अधर्मे धर्ममानिनः ।
ये वृत्तिदं पतिं हित्वा जारं पतिमुपासते ॥२३॥

vena uvāca
bāliśā bata yūyaṁ vā
adharme dharma-māninaḥ
ye vṛttidaṁ patiṁ hitvā
jāraṁ patim upāsate

venaḥ—King Vena; *uvāca*—replied; *bāliśāḥ*—childish; *bata*—oh; *yūyam*—all of you; *vā*—indeed; *adharme*—in irreligious principles; *dharma-māninaḥ*—accepting as religious; *ye*—all of you who; *vṛttidam*—providing maintenance; *patim*—husband; *hitvā*—giving up; *jāram*—paramour; *patim*—husband; *upāsate*—worship.

TRANSLATION

King Vena replied: You are not at all experienced. It is very much regrettable that you are maintaining something which is not religious and are accepting it as religious. Indeed, I think you are giving up your real husband, who maintains you, and are searching after some paramour to worship.

PURPORT

King Vena was so foolish that he accused the saintly sages of being inexperienced like small children. In other words, he was accusing them of not having perfect knowledge. In this way he could reject their advice and make accusations against them, comparing them to a woman who does not care for her husband who maintains her but goes to satisfy a paramour who does not maintain her. The purpose of this simile is apparent. It is the duty of the *kṣatriyas* to engage the *brāhmaṇas* in different types of religious activities, and the king is supposed to be the maintainer of the *brāhmaṇas.* If the *brāhmaṇas* do not worship the king but instead go to the demigods, they are as polluted as unchaste women.

TEXT 24

अवजानन्त्यमी मूढा नृपरूपिणमीश्वरम् ।
नानुविन्दन्ति ते भद्रमिह लोके परत्र च ॥२४॥

avajānanty amī mūḍhā
nṛpa-rūpiṇam īśvaram
nānuvindanti te bhadram
iha loke paratra ca

avajānanti—disrespect; *amī*—those (who); *mūḍhāḥ*—being ignorant; *nṛpa-rūpiṇam*—in the form of the king; *īśvaram*—the Personality of Godhead; *na*—not; *anuvindanti*—experience; *te*—they; *bhadram*—happiness; *iha*—in this; *loke*—world; *paratra*—after death; *ca*—also.

TRANSLATION

Those who, out of gross ignorance, do not worship the king, who is actually the Supreme Personality of Godhead, experience happiness neither in this world nor in the world after death.

TEXT 25

को यज्ञपुरुषो नाम यत्र वो भक्तिरीदृशी ।
भर्तृस्नेहविदूराणां यथा जारे कुयोषिताम् ॥२५॥

ko yajña-puruṣo nāma
yatra vo bhaktir īdṛśī
bhartṛ-sneha-vidūrāṇāṁ
yathā jāre kuyoṣitām

kaḥ—who (is); *yajña-puruṣaḥ*—the enjoyer of all sacrifices; *nāma*—by name; *yatra*—unto whom; *vaḥ*—your; *bhaktiḥ*—devotional service; *īdṛśī*—so great; *bhartṛ*—for the husband; *sneha*—affection; *vidūrāṇām*—bereft of; *yathā*—like; *jāre*—unto the paramour; *ku-yoṣitām*—of unchaste women.

TRANSLATION

You are so much devoted to the demigods, but who are they? Indeed, your affection for these demigods is exactly like the affection of an unchaste woman who neglects her married life and gives all attention to her paramour.

TEXTS 26–27

विष्णुर्विरिञ्चो गिरिश इन्द्रो वायुर्यमो रविः ।
पर्जन्यो धनदः सोमः क्षितिरग्निरपाम्पतिः ॥२६॥
एते चान्ये च विबुधाः प्रभवो वरशापयोः ।
देहे भवन्ति नृपतेः सर्वदेवमयो नृपः ॥२७॥

viṣṇur viriñco giriśa
indro vāyur yamo raviḥ
parjanyo dhanadaḥ somaḥ
kṣitir agnir apāmpatiḥ

ete cānye ca vibudhāḥ
prabhavo vara-śāpayoḥ
dehe bhavanti nṛpateḥ
sarva-devamayo nṛpaḥ

viṣṇuḥ—Lord Viṣṇu; *viriñcaḥ*—Lord Brahmā; *giriśaḥ*—Lord Śiva; *indraḥ*—Lord Indra; *vāyuḥ*—Vāyu, the director of the air; *yamaḥ*—Yama, the superintendent of death; *raviḥ*—the sun-god; *parjanyaḥ*—

the director of rainfall; *dhana-daḥ*—Kuvera, the treasurer; *somaḥ*—the moon-god; *kṣitiḥ*—the predominating deity of the earth; *agniḥ*—the fire-god; *apām-patiḥ*—Varuṇa, the lord of waters; *ete*—all these; *ca*—and; *anye*—others; *ca*—also; *vibudhāḥ*—demigods; *prabhavaḥ*—competent; *vara-śāpayoḥ*—in both benediction and curse; *dehe*—in the body; *bhavanti*—abide; *nṛpateḥ*—of the king; *sarva-devamayaḥ*—comprising all demigods; *nṛpaḥ*—the king.

TRANSLATION

Lord Viṣṇu; Lord Brahmā; Lord Śiva; Lord Indra; Vāyu, the master of air; Yama, the superintendent of death; the sun-god; the director of rainfall; Kuvera, the treasurer; the moon-god; the predominating deity of the earth; Agni, the fire-god; Varuṇa, the lord of waters, and all others who are great and competent to bestow benedictions or to curse, all abide in the body of the king. For this reason the king is known as the reservoir of all demigods, who are simply parts and parcels of the king's body.

PURPORT

There are many demons who think of themselves as the Supreme and present themselves as the directors of the sun, moon and other planets. This is all due to false pride. Similarly, King Vena developed the demonic mentality and presented himself as the Supreme Personality of Godhead. Such demons are numerous in this age of Kali, and all of them are condemned by great sages and saintly persons.

TEXT 28

तस्मान्मां कर्मभिर्विप्रा यजध्वं गतमत्सराः ।
बलिं च मह्यं हरत मत्तोऽन्यः कोऽग्रभुक् पुमान् ॥२८॥

tasmān māṁ karmabhir viprā
yajadhvaṁ gata-matsarāḥ
baliṁ ca mahyaṁ harata
matto 'nyaḥ ko 'gra-bhuk pumān

tasmāt—for this reason; *mām*—me; *karmabhiḥ*—by ritualistic activities; *viprāḥ*—O *brāhmaṇas; yajadhvam*—worship; *gata*—without; *matsarāḥ*—being envious; *balim*—paraphernalia for worship; *ca*—also; *mahyam*—unto me; *harata*—bring; *mattaḥ*—than me; *anyaḥ*—other; *kaḥ*—who (is); *agra-bhuk*—the enjoyer of the first oblations; *pumān*—personality.

TRANSLATION

King Vena continued: For this reason, O brāhmaṇas, you should abandon your envy of me, and, by your ritualistic activities, you should worship me and offer me all paraphernalia. If you are intelligent, you should know that there is no personality superior to me, who can accept the first oblations of all sacrifices.

PURPORT

As stated by Kṛṣṇa Himself throughout *Bhagavad-gītā*, there is no truth superior to Him. King Vena was imitating the Supreme Personality of Godhead and was also speaking out of false pride, presenting himself as the Supreme Lord. These are all characteristics of a demonic person.

TEXT 29

मैत्रेय उवाच
इत्थं विपर्ययमतिः पापीयानुत्पथं गतः।
अनुनीयमानस्तद्याच्ञां न चक्रे भ्रष्टमङ्गलः ॥२९॥

maitreya uvāca
ittham viparyaya-matiḥ
pāpīyān utpatham gataḥ
anunīyamānas tad-yācñām
na cakre bhraṣṭa-maṅgalaḥ

maitreyaḥ uvāca—Maitreya said; *ittham*—thus; *viparyaya-matiḥ*—one who has developed perverse intelligence; *pāpīyān*—most sinful; *utpatham*—from the right path; *gataḥ*—having gone; *anunīyamānaḥ*—

being offered all respect; *tat-yācñām*—the request of the sages; *na*—not; *cakre*—accepted; *bhraṣṭa*—bereft of; *maṅgalaḥ*—all good fortune.

TRANSLATION

The great sage Maitreya continued: Thus the King, who became unintelligent due to his sinful life and deviation from the right path, became actually bereft of all good fortune. He could not accept the requests of the great sages, which the sages put before him with great respect, and therefore he was condemned.

PURPORT

The demons certainly cannot have any faith in the words of authorities. In fact, they are always disrespectful to authorities. They manufacture their own religious principles and disobey great personalities like Vyāsa, Nārada, and even the Supreme Personality of Godhead, Kṛṣṇa. As soon as one disobeys authority, he immediately becomes very sinful and loses his good fortune. The King was so puffed up and impudent that he dared disrespect the great saintly personalities, and this brought him ruination.

TEXT 30

इति तेऽसत्कृतास्तेन द्विजाः पण्डितमानिना ।
भग्नायां भव्ययाच्ञायां तस्मै विदुर चुक्रुधुः ॥३०॥

iti te 'sat-kṛtās tena
dvijāḥ paṇḍita-māninā
bhagnāyāṁ bhavya-yācñāyāṁ
tasmai vidura cukrudhuḥ

iti—thus; *te*—all the great sages; *asat-kṛtāḥ*—being insulted; *tena*—by the King; *dvijāḥ*—the *brāhmaṇas; paṇḍita-māninā*—thinking himself to be very learned; *bhagnāyām*—being broken; *bhavya*—auspicious; *yācñāyām*—their request; *tasmai*—at him; *vidura*—O Vidura; *cukrudhuḥ*—became very angry.

TRANSLATION

My dear Vidura, all good fortune unto you. The foolish King, who thought himself very learned, thus insulted the great sages, and the sages, being brokenhearted by the King's words, became very angry at him.

TEXT 31

हन्यतां हन्यतामेष पापः प्रकृतिदारुणः ।
जीवञ्जगदसावाशु कुरुते भस्मसाद् ध्रुवम् ॥३१॥

hanyatāṁ hanyatām eṣa
pāpaḥ prakṛti-dāruṇaḥ
jīvañ jagad asāv āśu
kurute bhasmasād dhruvam

hanyatām—kill him; *hanyatām*—kill him; *eṣaḥ*—this king; *pāpaḥ*—representative of sin; *prakṛti*—by nature; *dāruṇaḥ*—most dreadful; *jīvan*—while living; *jagat*—the whole world; *asau*—he; *āśu*—very soon; *kurute*—will make; *bhasmasāt*—into ashes; *dhruvam*—certainly.

TRANSLATION

All the great saintly sages immediately cried: Kill him! Kill him! He is the most dreadful, sinful person. If he lives, he will certainly turn the whole world into ashes in no time.

PURPORT

Saintly persons are generally very kind to all kinds of living entities, but they are not unhappy when a serpent or a scorpion is killed. It is not good for saintly persons to kill, but they are encouraged to kill demons, who are exactly like serpents and scorpions. Therefore all the saintly sages decided to kill King Vena, who was so dreadful and dangerous to all human society. We can appreciate the extent to which the saintly sages actually controlled the king. If the king or government becomes demonic, it is the duty of a saintly person to upset the government and replace it with deserving persons who follow the orders and instructions of saintly persons.

TEXT 32

नायमर्हत्यसद्वृत्तो नरदेववरासनम् ।
योऽधियज्ञपतिं विष्णुं विनिन्दत्यनपत्रपः ॥३२॥

nāyam arhaty asad-vṛtto
naradeva-varāsanam
yo 'dhiyajña-patiṁ viṣṇuṁ
vinindaty anapatrapaḥ

na—never; *ayam*—this man; *arhati*—deserves; *asat-vṛttaḥ*—full of impious activities; *nara-deva*—of the worldly king or worldly god; *vara-āsanam*—the exalted throne; *yaḥ*—he who; *adhiyajña-patim*—the master of all sacrifices; *viṣṇum*—Lord Viṣṇu; *vinindati*—insults; *anapatrapaḥ*—shameless.

TRANSLATION

The saintly sages continued: This impious, impudent man does not deserve to sit on the throne at all. He is so shameless that he even dared insult the Supreme Personality of Godhead, Lord Viṣṇu.

PURPORT

One should not at any time tolerate blasphemy and insults against Lord Viṣṇu or His devotees. A devotee is generally very humble and meek, and he is reluctant to pick a quarrel with anyone. Nor does he envy anyone. However, a pure devotee immediately becomes fiery with anger when he sees that Lord Viṣṇu or His devotee is insulted. This is the duty of a devotee. Although a devotee maintains an attitude of meekness and gentleness, it is a great fault on his part if he remains silent when the Lord or His devotee is blasphemed.

TEXT 33

को वैनं परिचक्षीत वेनमेकमृतेऽशुभम् ।
प्राप्त ईदृशमैश्वर्यं यदनुग्रहभाजनः ॥३३॥

ko vainaṁ paricakṣīta
venam ekam ṛte 'śubham
prāpta īdṛśam aiśvaryaṁ
yad-anugraha-bhājanaḥ

kaḥ—who; *vā*—indeed; *enam*—the Lord; *paricakṣīta*—would blaspheme; *venam*—King Vena; *ekam*—alone; *ṛte*—but for; *aśubham*—inauspicious; *prāptaḥ*—having obtained; *īdṛśam*—like this; *aiśvaryam*—opulence; *yat*—whose; *anugraha*—mercy; *bhājanaḥ*—receiving.

TRANSLATION

But for King Vena, who is simply inauspicious, who would blaspheme the Supreme Personality of Godhead, by whose mercy one is awarded all kinds of fortune and opulence?

PURPORT

When human society individually or collectively becomes godless and blasphemes the authority of the Supreme Personality of Godhead, it is certainly destined for ruination. Such a civilization invites all kinds of bad fortune due to not appreciating the mercy of the Lord.

TEXT 34

इत्थं व्यवसिता हन्तुमृषयो रूढमन्यवः ।
निजघ्नुर्हुङ्कृतैर्वेनं हतमच्युतनिन्दया ॥३४॥

itthaṁ vyavasitā hantum
ṛṣayo rūḍha-manyavaḥ
nijaghnur huṅkṛtair venaṁ
hatam acyuta-nindayā

ittham—thus; *vyavasitāḥ*—decided; *hantum*—to kill; *ṛṣayaḥ*—the sages; *rūḍha*—manifested; *manyavaḥ*—their anger; *nijaghnuḥ*—they killed; *hum-kṛtaiḥ*—by angry words or by sounds of *hum; venam*—King Vena; *hatam*—dead; *acyuta*—against the Supreme Personality of Godhead; *nindayā*—by blasphemy.

TRANSLATION

The great sages, thus manifesting their covert anger, immediately decided to kill the King. King Vena was already as good as dead due to his blasphemy against the Supreme Personality of Godhead. Thus without using any weapons, the sages killed King Vena simply by high-sounding words.

TEXT 35

ऋषिभिः स्वाश्रमपदं गते पुत्रकलेवरम् ।
सुनीथा पालयामास विद्यायोगेन शोचती ॥३५॥

ṛṣibhiḥ svāśrama-padaṁ
gate putra-kalevaram
sunīthā pālayām āsa
vidyā-yogena śocatī

ṛṣibhiḥ—by the sages; *sva-āśrama-padam*—to their own respective hermitages; *gate*—having returned; *putra*—of her son; *kalevaram*—the body; *sunīthā*—Sunīthā, the mother of King Vena; *pālayām āsa*—preserved; *vidyā-yogena*—by *mantra* and ingredients; *śocatī*—while lamenting.

TRANSLATION

After all the sages returned to their respective hermitages, the mother of King Vena, Sunīthā, became very much aggrieved because of her son's death. She decided to preserve the dead body of her son by the application of certain ingredients and by chanting mantras [mantra-yogena].

TEXT 36

एकदा मुनयस्ते तु सरस्वत्सलिलाप्लुताः ।
हुत्वाग्नीन् सत्कथाश्चक्रुरुपविष्टाः सरित्तटे ॥३६॥

ekadā munayas te tu
sarasvat-salilāplutāḥ

hutvāgnīn sat-kathāś cakrur
upaviṣṭāḥ sarit-taṭe

ekadā—once upon a time; *munayaḥ*—all those great saintly persons; *te*—they; *tu*—then; *sarasvat*—of the River Sarasvatī; *salila*—in the water; *āplutāḥ*—bathed; *hutvā*—offering oblations; *agnīn*—into the fires; *sat-kathāḥ*—discussions about transcendental subject matters; *cakruḥ*—began to do; *upaviṣṭāḥ*—sitting; *sarit-taṭe*—by the side of the river.

TRANSLATION

Once upon a time, the same saintly persons, after taking their bath in the River Sarasvatī, began to perform their daily duties by offering oblations into the sacrificial fires. After this, sitting on the bank of the river, they began to talk about the transcendental person and His pastimes.

TEXT 37

वीक्ष्योत्थितांस्तदोत्पातानाहुर्लोकभयङ्करान् ।
अप्यभद्रमनाथाया दस्युभ्यो न भवेद्भुवः ॥३७॥

vīkṣyotthitāṁs tadotpātān
āhur loka-bhayaṅkarān
apy abhadram anāthāyā
dasyubhyo na bhaved bhuvaḥ

vīkṣya—having seen; *utthitān*—developed; *tadā*—then; *utpātān*—disturbances; *āhuḥ*—they began to say; *loka*—in society; *bhayam-karān*—causing panic; *api*—whether; *abhadram*—misfortune; *anāthā-yāḥ*—having no ruler; *dasyubhyaḥ*—from thieves and rogues; *na*—not; *bhavet*—may happen; *bhuvaḥ*—of the world.

TRANSLATION

In those days there were various disturbances in the country that were creating a panic in society. Therefore all the sages began to talk amongst themselves: Since the King is dead and there is no

protector in the world, misfortune may befall the people in general on account of rogues and thieves.

PURPORT

Whenever there is a disturbance in the state, or a panic situation, the property and lives of the citizens become unsafe. This is caused by the uprising of various thieves and rogues. At such a time it is to be understood that the ruler, or the government, is dead. All of these misfortunes happened due to the death of King Vena. Thus the saintly persons became very anxious for the safety of the people in general. The conclusion is that even though saintly persons have no business in political affairs, they are always compassionate upon the people in general. Thus even though they are always aloof from society, out of mercy and compassion they consider how the citizens can peacefully execute their rituals and follow the rules and regulations of *varṇāśrama-dharma.* That was the concern of these sages. In this age of Kali, everything is disturbed. Therefore saintly persons should take to the chanting of the Hare Kṛṣṇa *mantra,* as recommended in the *śāstras:*

harer nāma harer nāma
harer nāmaiva kevalaṁ
kalau nāsty eva nāsty eva
nāsty eva gatir anyathā

Both for spiritual and material prosperity, everyone should devotedly chant the Hare Kṛṣṇa *mantra.*

TEXT 38

एवं मृशन्त ऋषयो धावतां सर्वतोदिशम् ।
पांसुः समुत्थितो भूरिश्चोराणामभिलुम्पताम् ॥३८॥

evaṁ mṛśanta ṛṣayo
dhāvatāṁ sarvato-diśam
pāṁsuḥ samutthito bhūriś
corāṇām abhilumpatām

evam—thus; *mṛśantaḥ*—while considering; *ṛṣayaḥ*—the great saintly persons; *dhāvatām*—running; *sarvataḥ-diśam*—from all directions; *pāṁsuḥ*—dust; *samutthitaḥ*—arose; *bhūriḥ*—much; *corāṇām*—from thieves and rogues; *abhilumpatām*—engaged in plundering.

TRANSLATION

When the great sages were carrying on their discussion in this way, they saw a dust storm arising from all directions. This storm was caused by the running of thieves and rogues, who were engaged in plundering the citizens.

PURPORT

Thieves and rogues simply await some political upset in order to take the opportunity to plunder the people in general. To keep thieves and rogues inactive in their profession, a strong government is always required.

TEXTS 39–40

तदुपद्रवमाज्ञाय लोकस्य वसु लुम्पताम् ।
भर्तर्युपरते तस्मिन्नन्योन्यं च जिघांसताम् ॥३९॥
चोरप्रायं जनपदं हीनसत्त्वमराजकम् ।
लोकान्नावारयञ्छक्ता अपि तद्दोषदर्शिनः ॥४०॥

tad upadravam ājñāya
lokasya vasu lumpatām
bhartary uparate tasminn
anyonyaṁ ca jighāṁsatām

cora-prāyaṁ jana-padaṁ
hīna-sattvam arājakam
lokān nāvārayañ chaktā
api tad-doṣa-darśinaḥ

tat—at that time; *upadravam*—the disturbance; *ājñāya*—understanding; *lokasya*—of the people in general; *vasu*—riches; *lumpatām*—

by those who were plundering; *bhartari*—the protector; *uparate*—being dead; *tasmin*—King Vena; *anyonyam*—one another; *ca*—also; *jighāṁsatām*—desiring to kill; *cora-prāyam*—full of thieves; *jana-padam*—the state; *hīna*—bereft of; *sattvam*—regulation; *arājakam*—without a king; *lokān*—the thieves and rogues; *na*—not; *avārayan*—they subdued; *śaktāḥ*—able to do so; *api*—although; *tat-doṣa*—the fault of that; *darśinaḥ*—considering.

TRANSLATION

Upon seeing the dust storm, the saintly persons could understand that there were a great deal of irregularities due to the death of King Vena. Without government, the state was devoid of law and order, and consequently there was a great uprising of murderous thieves and rogues, who were plundering the riches of the people in general. Although the great sages could subdue the disturbance by their powers—just as they could kill the King—they considered it improper on their part to do so. Thus they did not attempt to stop the disturbance.

PURPORT

The saintly persons and great sages killed King Vena out of emergency, but they did not choose to take part in the government in order to subdue the uprising of thieves and rogues, which took place after the death of King Vena. It is not the duty of *brāhmaṇas* and saintly persons to kill, although they may sometimes do so in the case of an emergency. They could kill all the thieves and rogues by the prowess of their *mantras*, but they thought it the duty of *kṣatriya* kings to do so. Thus they reluctantly did not take part in the killing business.

TEXT 41

ब्राह्मणः समदृक् शान्तो दीनानां समुपेक्षकः ।
स्रवते ब्रह्म तस्यापि भिन्नभाण्डात्पयो यथा ॥४१॥

brāhmaṇaḥ sama-dṛk śānto
dīnānāṁ samupekṣakaḥ

sravate brahma tasyāpi
bhinna-bhāṇḍāt payo yathā

brāhmaṇaḥ—a *brāhmaṇa; sama-dṛk*—equipoised; *śāntaḥ*—peaceful; *dīnānām*—the poor; *samupekṣakaḥ*—grossly neglecting; *sravate*—diminishes; *brahma*—spiritual power; *tasya*—his; *api*—certainly; *bhinna-bhāṇḍāt*—from a cracked pot; *payaḥ*—water; *yathā*—just as.

TRANSLATION

The great sages began to think that although a brāhmaṇa is peaceful and impartial because he is equal to everyone, it is still not his duty to neglect poor humans. By such neglect, a brāhmaṇa's spiritual power diminishes, just as water kept in a cracked pot leaks out.

PURPORT

Brāhmaṇas, the topmost section of human society, are mostly devotees. They are generally unaware of the happenings within the material world because they are always busy in their activities for spiritual advancement. Nonetheless, when there is a calamity in human society, they cannot remain impartial. If they do not do something to relieve the distressed condition of human society, it is said that due to such neglect their spiritual knowledge diminishes. Almost all the sages go to the Himalayas for their personal benefit, but Prahlāda Mahārāja said that he did not want liberation alone. He decided to wait until he was able to deliver all the fallen souls of the world.

In their elevated condition, the *brāhmaṇas* are called Vaiṣṇavas. There are two types of *brāhmaṇas*—namely, *brāhmaṇa-paṇḍita* and *brāhmaṇa-vaiṣṇava.* A qualified *brāhmaṇa* is naturally very learned, but when his learning is advanced in understanding the Supreme Personality of Godhead, he becomes a *brāhmaṇa-vaiṣṇava.* Unless one becomes a Vaiṣṇava, one's perfection of brahminical culture is incomplete.

The saintly persons considered very wisely that although King Vena was very sinful, he was born in a family descending from Dhruva Mahārāja. Therefore the semen in the family must be protected by the Supreme Personality of Godhead, Keśava. As such, the sages wanted to take some steps to relieve the situation. For want of a king, everything was being disturbed and turned topsy-turvy.

TEXT 42

नाङ्गस्य वंशो राजर्षेरेष संस्थातुमर्हति ।
अमोघवीर्या हि नृपा वंशेऽस्मिन् केशवाश्रयाः ॥४२॥

nāṅgasya vaṁśo rājarṣer
eṣa saṁsthātum arhati
amogha-vīryā hi nṛpā
vaṁśe 'smin keśavāśrayāḥ

na—not; *aṅgasya*—of King Aṅga; *vaṁśaḥ*—family line; *rāja-ṛṣeḥ*—of the saintly King; *eṣaḥ*—this; *saṁsthātum*—to be stopped; *arhati*—ought; *amogha*—without sin, powerful; *vīryāḥ*—their semen; *hi*—because; *nṛpāḥ*—kings; *vaṁśe*—in the family; *asmin*—this; *keśava*—of the Supreme Personality of Godhead; *āśrayāḥ*—under the shelter.

TRANSLATION

The sages decided that the descendants of the family of the saintly King Aṅga should not be stopped, for in this family the semen was very powerful and the children were prone to become devotees of the Lord.

PURPORT

The purity of hereditary succession is called *amogha-vīrya.* The pious seminal succession in the twice-born families of the *brāhmaṇas* and *kṣatriyas* especially, as well as in the families of *vaiśyas* also, must be kept very pure by the observation of the purificatory processes beginning with *garbhādhāna-saṁskāra,* which is observed before conceiving a child. Unless this purificatory process is strictly observed, especially by the *brāhmaṇas,* the family descendants become impure, and gradually sinful activities become visible in the family. Mahārāja Aṅga was very pure because of the purification of semen in the family of Mahārāja Dhruva. However, his semen became contaminated in association with his wife, Sunīthā, who happened to be the daughter of death personified.

Because of this polluted semen, King Vena was produced. This was a catastrophe in the family of Dhruva Mahārāja. All the saintly persons and sages considered this point, and they decided to take action in this matter, as described in the following verses.

TEXT 43

विनिश्चित्यैवमृषयो विपन्नस्य महीपतेः ।
ममन्थुरूरुं तरसा तत्रासीद्बाहुको नरः ॥४३॥

viniścityaivam ṛṣayo
vipannasya mahīpateḥ
mamanthur ūruṁ tarasā
tatrāsīd bāhuko naraḥ

viniścitya—deciding; *evam*—thus; *ṛṣayaḥ*—the great sages; *vipannasya*—dead; *mahī-pateḥ*—of the King; *mamanthuḥ*—churned; *ūrum*—the thighs; *tarasā*—with specific power; *tatra*—thereupon; *āsīt*—was born; *bāhukaḥ*—of the name Bāhuka (dwarf); *naraḥ*—a person.

TRANSLATION

After making a decision, the saintly persons and sages churned the thighs of the dead body of King Vena with great force and according to a specific method. As a result of this churning, a dwarf-like person was born from King Vena's body.

PURPORT

That a person was born by the churning of the thighs of King Vena proves that the spirit soul is individual and separate from the body. The great sages and saintly persons could beget another person from the body of the dead King Vena, but it was not possible for them to bring King Vena back to life. King Vena was gone, and certainly he had taken another body. The saintly persons and sages were only concerned with the body of Vena because it was a result of the seminal succession in the family of Mahārāja Dhruva. Consequently, the ingredients by which another body could be produced were there in the body of King Vena. By a certain process, when the thighs of the dead body were churned, another body came out. Although dead, the body of King Vena was preserved by drugs, and *mantras* chanted by King Vena's mother. In this way the ingredients for the production of another body were there. When the body of the person named Bāhuka came out of the dead body of King Vena, it was really not very astonishing. It was simply a question of knowing how to do it. From the semen of one body, another body is produced, and the life symptoms are visible due to the soul's taking shelter of this body. One should not think that it was impossible for another body to come out of the dead body of Mahārāja Vena. This was performed by the skillful action of the sages.

TEXT 44

काककृष्णोऽतिह्रस्वाङ्गो ह्रस्वबाहुर्महाहनुः ।
ह्रस्वपान्निम्ननासाग्रो रक्ताक्षस्ताम्रमूर्धजः ॥४४॥

kāka-kṛṣṇo 'tihrasvāṅgo
hrasva-bāhur mahā-hanuḥ
hrasva-pān nimna-nāsāgro
raktākṣas tāmra-mūrdhajaḥ

kāka-kṛṣṇaḥ—as black as a crow; *ati-hrasva*—very short; *aṅgaḥ*—his limbs; *hrasva*—short; *bāhuḥ*—his arms; *mahā*—big; *hanuḥ*—his jaws; *hrasva*—short; *pāt*—his legs; *nimna*—flat; *nāsa-agraḥ*—the tip of his nose; *rakta*—reddish; *akṣaḥ*—his eyes; *tāmra*—copperlike; *mūrdha-jaḥ*—his hair.

TRANSLATION

This person born from King Vena's thighs was named Bāhuka, and his complexion was as black as a crow's. All the limbs of his body were very short, his arms and legs were short, and his jaws were large. His nose was flat, his eyes were reddish, and his hair copper-colored.

TEXT 45

तं तु तेऽवनतं दीनं किं करोमीति वादिनम् ।
निषीदेत्यब्रुवंस्तात स निषादस्ततोऽभवत् ॥४५॥

taṁ tu te 'vanataṁ dīnaṁ
kiṁ karomīti vādinam
niṣīdety abruvaṁs tāta
sa niṣādas tato 'bhavat

tam—unto him; *tu*—then; *te*—the sages; *avanatam*—bowed down; *dīnam*—meek; *kim*—what; *karomi*—shall I do; *iti*—thus; *vādinam*—inquiring; *niṣīda*—just sit down; *iti*—thus; *abruvan*—they replied; *tāta*—my dear Vidura; *saḥ*—he; *niṣādaḥ*—of the name Niṣāda; *tataḥ*—thereafter; *abhavat*—became.

TRANSLATION

He was very submissive and meek, and immediately after his birth he bowed down and inquired, "Sirs, what shall I do?" The great sages replied, "Please sit down [niṣīda]." Thus Niṣāda, the father of the Naiṣāda race, was born.

PURPORT

It is said in the *śāstras* that the head of the body represents the *brāhmaṇas*, the arms represent the *kṣatriyas*, the abdomen represents the *vaiśyas*, and the legs, beginning with the thighs, represent the *śūdras*. The *śūdras* are sometimes called black, or *kṛṣṇa*. The *brāhmaṇas* are called *śukla*, or white, and the *kṣatriyas* and the *vaiśyas* are a mixture of black and white. However, those who are extraordinarily white are said to have skin produced out of white leprosy. It may be concluded that white or a golden hue is the color of the higher caste, and black is the complexion of the *śūdras*.

TEXT 46

तस्य वंश्यास्तु नैषादा गिरिकाननगोचराः ।
येनाहरज्जायमानो वेनकल्मषमुल्बणम् ॥४६॥

tasya vaṁśyās tu naiṣādā
giri-kānana-gocarāḥ
yenāharaj jāyamāno
vena-kalmaṣam ulbaṇam

tasya—his (Niṣāda's); *vaṁśyāḥ*—descendants; *tu*—then; *naiṣādāḥ*—called Naiṣādas; *giri-kānana*—the hills and forests; *gocarāḥ*—inhabiting; *yena*—because; *aharat*—he took upon himself; *jāyamānaḥ*—being born; *vena*—of King Vena; *kalmaṣam*—all kinds of sin; *ulbaṇam*—very fearful.

TRANSLATION

After his [Niṣāda's] birth, he immediately took charge of all the resultant actions of King Vena's sinful activities. As such, this Naiṣāda class are always engaged in sinful activities like stealing, plundering and hunting. Consequently they are only allowed to live in the hills and forests.

PURPORT

The Naiṣādas are not allowed to live in cities and towns because they are sinful by nature. As such, their bodies are very ugly, and their occupations are also sinful. We should, however, know that even these sinful men (who are sometimes called Kirātas) can be delivered from their sinful condition to the topmost Vaiṣṇava platform by the mercy of a pure devotee. Engagement in the transcendental loving devotional service of the Lord can make anyone, however sinful he may be, fit to return home, back to Godhead. One has only to become free from all contamination by the process of devotional service. In this way everyone can become fit to return home, back to Godhead. This is confirmed by the Lord Himself in *Bhagavad-gītā* (9.32):

māṁ hi pārtha vyapāśritya
ye 'pi syuḥ pāpa-yonayaḥ
striyo vaiśyās tathā śūdrās
te 'pi yānti parāṁ gatim

"O son of Pṛthā, those who take shelter of Me, though they be of lower birth—women, *vaiśyas* [merchants], as well as *śūdras* [workers]—can approach the supreme destination."

Thus end the Bhaktivedanta purports of the Fourth Canto, Fourteenth Chapter, of the Śrīmad-Bhāgavatam, *entitled "The Story of King Vena."*

CHAPTER FIFTEEN

King Pṛthu's Appearance and Coronation

TEXT 1

मैत्रेय उवाच
अथ तस्य पुनर्विप्रैरपुत्रस्य महीपतेः ।
बाहुभ्यां मथ्यमानाभ्यां मिथुनं समपद्यत ॥ १ ॥

maitreya uvāca
atha tasya punar viprair
aputrasya mahīpateḥ
bāhubhyāṁ mathyamānābhyāṁ
mithunaṁ samapadyata

maitreyaḥ uvāca—Maitreya continued to speak; *atha*—thus; *tasya*—his; *punaḥ*—again; *vipraiḥ*—by the *brāhmaṇas; aputrasya*—without a son; *mahīpateḥ*—of the King; *bāhubhyām*—from the arms; *mathyamānābhyām*—being churned; *mithunam*—a couple; *samapadyata*—took birth.

TRANSLATION

The great sage Maitreya continued: My dear Vidura, thus the brāhmaṇas and the great sages again churned the two arms of King Vena's dead body. As a result a male and female couple came out of his arms.

TEXT 2

तद् दृष्ट्वा मिथुनं जातमृषयो ब्रह्मवादिनः ।
ऊचुः परमसन्तुष्टा विदित्वा भगवत्कलाम् ॥ २ ॥

tad dṛṣṭvā mithunaṁ jātam
ṛṣayo brahma-vādinaḥ

ūcuḥ parama-santuṣṭā
viditvā bhagavat-kalām

tat—that; *dṛṣṭvā*—seeing; *mithunam*—couple; *jātam*—born; *ṛṣayaḥ*—the great sages; *brahma-vādinaḥ*—very learned in Vedic knowledge; *ūcuḥ*—said; *parama*—very much; *santuṣṭāḥ*—being pleased; *viditvā*—knowing; *bhagavat*—of the Supreme Personality of Godhead; *kalām*—expansion.

TRANSLATION

The great sages were highly learned in Vedic knowledge. When they saw the male and female born of the arms of Vena's body, they were very pleased, for they could understand that the couple was an expansion of a plenary portion of Viṣṇu, the Supreme Personality of Godhead.

PURPORT

The method adopted by the great sages and scholars, who were learned in Vedic knowledge, was perfect. They removed all the reactions of King Vena's sinful activities by seeing that King Vena first gave birth to Bāhuka, described in the previous chapter. After King Vena's body was thus purified, a male and female came out of it, and the great sages could understand that this was an expansion of Lord Viṣṇu. This expansion, of course, was not *viṣṇu-tattva* but a specifically empowered expansion of Lord Viṣṇu known as *āveśa*.

TEXT 3

ऋषय ऊचुः
एष विष्णोर्भगवतः कला भुवनपालिनी ।
इयं च लक्ष्म्याः सम्भूतिः पुरुषस्यानपायिनी ॥ ३ ॥

ṛṣaya ūcuḥ
eṣa viṣṇor bhagavataḥ
kalā bhuvana-pālinī
iyaṁ ca lakṣmyāḥ sambhūtiḥ
puruṣasyānapāyinī

ṛṣayaḥ ūcuḥ—the sages said; *eṣaḥ*—this male; *viṣṇoḥ*—of Lord Viṣṇu; *bhagavataḥ*—of the Supreme Personality of Godhead; *kalā*—expansion; *bhuvana-pālinī*—who maintains the world; *iyam*—this female; *ca*—also; *lakṣmyāḥ*—of the goddess of fortune; *sambhūtiḥ*—expansion; *puruṣasya*—of the Lord; *anapāyinī*—inseparable.

TRANSLATION

The great sages said: The male is a plenary expansion of the power of Lord Viṣṇu, who maintains the entire universe, and the female is a plenary expansion of the goddess of fortune, who is never separated from the Lord.

PURPORT

The significance of the goddess of fortune's never being separated from the Lord is clearly mentioned herein. People in the material world are very fond of the goddess of fortune, and they want her favor in the form of riches. They should know, however, that the goddess of fortune is inseparable from Lord Viṣṇu. Materialists should understand that the goddess of fortune should be worshiped along with Lord Viṣṇu and should not be regarded separately. Materialists seeking the favor of the goddess of fortune must worship Lord Viṣṇu and Lakṣmī together to maintain material opulence. If a materialist follows the policy of Rāvaṇa, who wanted to separate Sītā from Lord Rāmacandra, the process of separation will vanquish him. Those who are very rich and have taken favor of the goddess of fortune in this world must engage their money in the service of the Lord. In this way they can continue in their opulent position without disturbance.

TEXT 4

अयं तु प्रथमो राज्ञां पुमान् प्रथयिता यशः ।
पृथुर्नाम महाराजो भविष्यति पृथुश्रवाः ॥ ४ ॥

ayaṁ tu prathamo rājñāṁ
pumān prathayitā yaśaḥ
pṛthur nāma mahārājo
bhaviṣyati pṛthu-śravāḥ

ayam—this; *tu*—then; *prathamaḥ*—the first; *rājñām*—of kings; *pumān*—the male; *prathayitā*—will expand; *yaśaḥ*—reputation; *pṛthuḥ*—Mahārāja Pṛthu; *nāma*—by name; *mahā-rājaḥ*—the great king; *bhaviṣyati*—will become; *pṛthu-śravāḥ*—of wide renown.

TRANSLATION

Of the two, the male will be able to expand his reputation throughout the world. His name will be Pṛthu. Indeed, he will be the first among kings.

PURPORT

There are different types of incarnations of the Supreme Personality of Godhead. In the *śāstras* it is said that Garuḍa (the carrier of Lord Viṣṇu) and Lord Śiva and Ananta are all very powerful incarnations of the Brahman feature of the Lord. Similarly, Śacīpati, or Indra, the King of heaven, is an incarnation of the lusty feature of the Lord. Aniruddha is an incarnation of the Lord's mind. Similarly, King Pṛthu is an incarnation of the ruling force of the Lord. Thus the saintly persons and great sages predicted the future activities of King Pṛthu, who was already explained as a partial incarnation of a plenary expansion of the Lord.

TEXT 5

इयं च सुदती देवी गुणभूषणभूषणा ।
अर्चिर्नाम वरारोहा पृथुमेवावरुन्धती ॥ ५ ॥

iyaṁ ca sudatī devī
guṇa-bhūṣaṇa-bhūṣaṇā
arcir nāma varārohā
pṛthum evāvarundhatī

iyam—this female child; *ca*—and; *su-datī*—who has very nice teeth; *devī*—the goddess of fortune; *guṇa*—by good qualities; *bhūṣaṇa*—ornaments; *bhūṣaṇā*—who beautifies; *arciḥ*—Arci; *nāma*—by name; *vara-ārohā*—very beautiful; *pṛthum*—unto King Pṛthu; *eva*—certainly; *avarundhatī*—being very much attached.

TRANSLATION

The female has such beautiful teeth and beautiful qualities that she will actually beautify the ornaments she wears. Her name will be Arci. In the future she will accept King Pṛthu as her husband.

TEXT 6

एष साक्षाद्धरेरंशो जातो लोकरिरक्षया ।
इयं च तत्परा हि श्रीरनुजज्ञेऽनपायिनी ॥ ६ ॥

eṣa sākṣād dharer aṁśo
jāto loka-rirakṣayā
iyaṁ ca tat-parā hi śrīr
anujajñe 'napāyinī

eṣaḥ—this male; *sākṣāt*—directly; *hareḥ*—of the Supreme Personality of Godhead; *aṁśaḥ*—partial representative; *jātaḥ*—born; *loka*—the entire world; *rirakṣayā*—with a desire to protect; *iyam*—this female; *ca*—also; *tat-parā*—very much attached to him; *hi*—certainly; *śrīḥ*—the goddess of fortune; *anujajñe*—took birth; *anapāyinī*—inseparable.

TRANSLATION

In the form of King Pṛthu, the Supreme Personality of Godhead has appeared through a part of His potency to protect the people of the world. The goddess of fortune is the constant companion of the Lord, and therefore she has incarnated partially as Arci to become King Pṛthu's queen.

PURPORT

In *Bhagavad-gītā* the Lord says that whenever one sees an extraordinary power, he should conclude that a specific partial representation of the Supreme Personality of Godhead is present. There are innumerable such personalities, but not all of them are direct *viṣṇu-tattva* plenary expansions of the Lord. Many living entities are classified among the *śakti-tattvas*. Such incarnations, empowered for specific purposes, are known as *śaktyāveśa-avatāras.* King Pṛthu was such a *śaktyāveśa-avatāra* of the Lord. Similarly, Arci, King Pṛthu's wife, was a *śaktyāveśa-avatāra* of the goddess of fortune.

TEXT 7

मैत्रेय उवाच

प्रशंसन्ति स्म तं विप्रा गन्धर्वप्रवरा जगुः ।
मुमुचुः सुमनोधाराः सिद्धा नृत्यन्ति स्वःस्त्रियः ॥ ७ ॥

maitreya uvāca
praśaṁsanti sma taṁ viprā
gandharva-pravarā jaguḥ
mumucuḥ sumano-dhārāḥ
siddhā nṛtyanti svaḥ-striyaḥ

maitreyaḥ uvāca—the great saint Maitreya said; *praśaṁsanti sma*—praised, glorified; *tam*—him (Pṛthu); *viprāḥ*—all the *brāhmaṇas; gandharva-pravarāḥ*—the best of the Gandharvas; *jaguḥ*—chanted; *mumucuḥ*—released; *sumanaḥ-dhārāḥ*—showers of flowers; *siddhāḥ*—the personalities from Siddhaloka; *nṛtyanti*—were dancing; *svaḥ*—of the heavenly planets; *striyaḥ*—women (the Apsarās).

TRANSLATION

The great sage Maitreya continued: My dear Vidurajī, at that time all the brāhmaṇas highly praised and glorified King Pṛthu, and the best singers of Gandharvaloka chanted his glories. The inhabitants of Siddhaloka showered flowers, and the beautiful women in the heavenly planets danced in ecstasy.

TEXT 8

शङ्खतूर्यमृदङ्गाद्या नेदुर्दुन्दुभयो दिवि ।
तत्र सर्वं उपाजग्मुर्देवर्षिपितृणां गणाः ॥ ८ ॥

śaṅkha-tūrya-mṛdaṅgādyā
nedur dundubhayo divi

tatra sarva upājagmur
devarṣi-pitṝṇāṁ gaṇāḥ

śaṅkha—conches; *tūrya*—bugles; *mṛdaṅga*—drums; *ādyāḥ*—and so on; *neduḥ*—vibrated; *dundubhayaḥ*—kettledrums; *divi*—in outer space; *tatra*—there; *sarve*—all; *upājagmuḥ*—came; *deva-ṛṣi*—demigods and sages; *pitṝṇām*—of forefathers; *gaṇāḥ*—groups.

TRANSLATION

Conchshells, bugles, drums and kettledrums vibrated in outer space. Great sages, forefathers and personalities from the heavenly planets all came to earth from various planetary systems.

TEXTS 9–10

ब्रह्मा जगद्गुरुर्देवैः सहासृत्य सुरेश्वरैः ।
वैन्यस्य दक्षिणे हस्ते दृष्ट्वा चिह्नं गदाभृतः ॥ ९ ॥
पादयोररविन्दं च तं वै मेने हरेः कलाम् ।
यस्याप्रतिहतं चक्रमंशः स परमेष्ठिनः ॥१०॥

brahmā jagad-gurur devaiḥ
sahāsṛtya sureśvaraiḥ
vainyasya dakṣiṇe haste
dṛṣṭvā cihnaṁ gadābhṛtaḥ

pādayor aravindaṁ ca
taṁ vai mene hareḥ kalām
yasyāpratihataṁ cakram
aṁśaḥ sa parameṣṭhinaḥ

brahmā—Lord Brahmā; *jagat-guruḥ*—the master of the universe; *devaiḥ*—by the demigods; *saha*—accompanied; *āsṛtya*—arriving; *sura-īśvaraiḥ*—with the chiefs of all the heavenly planets; *vainyasya*—of Mahārāja Pṛthu, the son of Vena; *dakṣiṇe*—right; *haste*—on the hand; *dṛṣṭvā*—seeing; *cihnam*—mark; *gadā-bhṛtaḥ*—of Lord Viṣṇu, who carries a club; *pādayoḥ*—on the two feet; *aravindam*—lotus flower; *ca*—also; *tam*—him; *vai*—certainly; *mene*—he understood; *hareḥ*—of the Supreme Personality of Godhead; *kalām*—part of a plenary expansion; *yasya*—whose; *apratihatam*—invincible; *cakram*—disc; *aṁśaḥ*—partial representation; *saḥ*—he; *parameṣṭhinaḥ*—of the Supreme Personality of Godhead.

TRANSLATION

Lord Brahmā, the master of the entire universe, arrived there accompanied by all the demigods and their chiefs. Seeing the lines of Lord Viṣṇu's palm on King Pṛthu's right hand and impressions of lotus flowers on the soles of his feet, Lord Brahmā could understand that King Pṛthu was a partial representation of the Supreme Personality of Godhead. One whose palm bears the sign of a disc, as well as other such lines, should be considered a partial representation or incarnation of the Supreme Lord.

PURPORT

There is a system by which one can detect an incarnation of the Supreme Personality of Godhead. Nowadays it has become a cheap fashion to accept any rascal as an incarnation of God, but from this incident we can see that Lord Brahmā personally examined the hands and feet of King Pṛthu for specific signs. In their prophecies the learned sages and *brāhmaṇas* accepted Pṛthu Mahārāja as a plenary partial expansion of the Lord. During the presence of Lord Kṛṣṇa, however, a king declared himself Vāsudeva, and Lord Kṛṣṇa killed him. Before accepting someone as an incarnation of God, one should verify his identity according to the symptoms mentioned in the *śāstras.* Without these symptoms the pretender is subject to be killed by the authorities for pretending to be an incarnation of God.

TEXT 11

तस्याभिषेक आरब्धो ब्राह्मणैर्ब्रह्मवादिभिः ।
आभिषेचनिकान्यस्मै आजह्रुः सर्वतो जनाः ॥११॥

tasyābhiṣeka ārabdho
brāhmaṇair brahma-vādibhiḥ

ābhiṣecanikāny asmai
ājahruḥ sarvato janāḥ

tasya—his; *abhiṣekaḥ*—coronation; *ārabdhaḥ*—was arranged; *brāhmaṇaiḥ*—by the learned *brāhmaṇas; brahma-vādibhiḥ*—attached to the Vedic rituals; *ābhiṣecanikāni*—various paraphernalia for performing the ceremony; *asmai*—unto him; *ājahruḥ*—collected; *sarvataḥ*—from all directions; *janāḥ*—people.

TRANSLATION

The learned brāhmaṇas, who were very attached to the Vedic ritualistic ceremonies, then arranged for the King's coronation. People from all directions collected all the different paraphernalia for the ceremony. Thus everything was complete.

TEXT 12

सरित्समुद्रा गिरयो नागा गावः खगा मृगाः ।
द्यौः क्षितिः सर्वभूतानि समाजह्रुरुपायनम् ॥१२॥

sarit-samudrā girayo
nāgā gāvaḥ khagā mṛgāḥ
dyauḥ kṣitiḥ sarva-bhūtāni
samājahrur upāyanam

sarit—the rivers; *samudrāḥ*—the seas; *girayaḥ*—the mountains; *nāgāḥ*—the serpents; *gāvaḥ*—the cows; *khagāḥ*—the birds; *mṛgāḥ*—the animals; *dyauḥ*—the sky; *kṣitiḥ*—the earth; *sarva-bhūtāni*—all living entities; *samājahruḥ*—collected; *upāyanam*—different kinds of presentations.

TRANSLATION

All the rivers, seas, hills, mountains, serpents, cows, birds, animals, heavenly planets, the earthly planet and all other living entities collected various presentations, according to their ability, to offer the King.

TEXT 13

सोऽभिषिक्तो महाराजः सुवासाः साध्वलङ्कृतः ।
पत्न्यार्चिषालङ्कृतया विरेजेऽग्निरिवापरः ॥१३॥

so 'bhiṣikto mahārājaḥ
suvāsāḥ sādhv-alaṅkṛtaḥ
patnyārciṣālaṅkṛtayā
vireje 'gnir ivāparaḥ

saḥ—the King; *abhiṣiktaḥ*—being coronated; *mahārājaḥ*—Mahārāja Pṛthu; *su-vāsāḥ*—exquisitely dressed; *sādhu-alaṅkṛtaḥ*—highly decorated with ornaments; *patnyā*—along with his wife; *arciṣā*—named Arci; *alaṅkṛtayā*—nicely ornamented; *vireje*—appeared; *agniḥ*—fire; *iva*—like; *aparaḥ*—another.

TRANSLATION

Thus the great King Pṛthu, exquisitely dressed with garments and ornaments, was coronated and placed on the throne. The King and his wife, Arci, who was also exquisitely ornamented, appeared exactly like fire.

TEXT 14

तस्मै जहार धनदो हैमं वीर वरासनम् ।
वरुणः सलिलस्रावमातपत्रं शशिप्रभम् ॥१४॥

tasmai jahāra dhanado
haimaṁ vīra varāsanam
varuṇaḥ salila-srāvam
ātapatraṁ śaśi-prabham

tasmai—unto him; *jahāra*—presented; *dhana-daḥ*—the treasurer of the demigods (Kuvera); *haimam*—made of gold; *vīra*—O Vidura; *vara-āsanam*—royal throne; *varuṇaḥ*—the demigod Varuṇa; *salila-srāvam*—dropping particles of water; *ātapatram*—umbrella; *śaśi-prabham*—as brilliant as the moon.

TRANSLATION

The great sage continued: My dear Vidura, Kuvera presented the great King Pṛthu with a golden throne. The demigod Varuṇa presented him with an umbrella that constantly sprayed fine particles of water and was as brilliant as the moon.

TEXT 15

वायुश्च वालव्यजने धर्मः कीर्तिमयीं स्रजम् ।
इन्द्रः किरीटमुत्कृष्टं दण्डं संयमनं यमः ॥१५॥

vāyuś ca vāla-vyajane
dharmaḥ kīrtimayīṁ srajam
indraḥ kirīṭam utkṛṣṭaṁ
daṇḍaṁ saṁyamanaṁ yamaḥ

vāyuḥ—the demigod of air; *ca*—also; *vāla-vyajane*—two *cāmaras* made of hair; *dharmaḥ*—the King of religion; *kīrti-mayīm*—expanding one's name and fame; *srajam*—garland; *indraḥ*—the King of heaven; *kirīṭam*—helmet; *utkṛṣṭam*—very valuable; *daṇḍam*—sceptor; *saṁyamanam*—for ruling the world; *yamaḥ*—the superintendent of death.

TRANSLATION

The demigod of air, Vāyu, presented King Pṛthu with two whisks [cāmaras] of hair; the King of religion, Dharma, presented him with a flower garland which would expand his fame; the King of heaven, Indra, presented him with a valuable helmet; and the superintendent of death, Yamarāja, presented him with a sceptor with which to rule the world.

TEXT 16

ब्रह्मा ब्रह्ममयं वर्म भारती हारमुत्तमम् ।
हरिः सुदर्शनं चक्रं तत्पत्न्यव्याहतां श्रियम् ॥१६॥

brahmā brahmamayaṁ varma
bhāratī hāram uttamam

hariḥ sudarśanaṁ cakraṁ
tat-patny avyāhatāṁ śriyam

brahmā—Lord Brahmā; *brahma-mayam*—made of spiritual knowledge; *varma*—armor; *bhāratī*—the goddess of learning; *hāram*—necklace; *uttamam*—transcendental; *hariḥ*—the Supreme Personality of Godhead; *sudarśanam cakram*—Sudarśana disc; *tat-patnī*—His wife (Lakṣmī); *avyāhatām*—imperishable; *śriyam*—beauty and opulence.

TRANSLATION

Lord Brahmā presented King Pṛthu with a protective garment made of spiritual knowledge. Bhāratī [Sarasvatī], the wife of Brahmā, gave him a transcendental necklace. Lord Viṣṇu presented him with a Sudarśana disc, and Lord Viṣṇu's wife, the goddess of fortune, gave him imperishable opulences.

PURPORT

All the demigods presented various gifts to King Pṛthu. Hari, an incarnation of the Supreme Personality of Godhead known as Upendra in the heavenly planet, presented the King with a Sudarśana disc. It should be understood that this Sudarśana disc is not exactly the same type of Sudarśana disc used by the Personality of Godhead, Kṛṣṇa, or Viṣṇu. Since Mahārāja Pṛthu was a partial representation of the Supreme Personality of Godhead's power, the Sudarśana disc given to him represented the partial power of the original Sudarśana disc.

TEXT 17

दशचन्द्रमसिं रुद्रः शतचन्द्रं तथाम्बिका ।
सोमोऽमृतमयानश्वांस्त्वष्टा रूपाश्रयं रथम् ॥१७॥

daśa-candram asiṁ rudraḥ
śata-candraṁ tathāmbikā
somo 'mṛtamayān aśvāṁs
tvaṣṭā rūpāśrayaṁ ratham

daśa-candram—decorated with ten moons; *asim*—sword; *rudraḥ*—Lord Śiva; *śata-candram*—decorated with one hundred moons; *tathā*—in that manner; *ambikā*—the goddess Durgā; *somaḥ*—the moon-demigod; *amṛta-mayān*—made of nectar; *aśvān*—horses; *tvaṣṭā*—the demigod Viśvakarmā; *rūpa-āśrayam*—very beautiful; *ratham*—a chariot.

TRANSLATION

Lord Śiva presented him with a sword within a sheath marked with ten moons, and his wife, the goddess Durgā, presented him with a shield marked with one hundred moons. The moon-demigod presented him with horses made of nectar, and the demigod Viśvakarmā presented him with a very beautiful chariot.

TEXT 18

अग्निराजगवं चापं सूर्यो रश्मिमयानिषून् ।
भूः पादुके योगमय्यौ द्यौः पुष्पावलिमन्वहम् ॥१८॥

agnir āja-gavaṁ cāpaṁ
sūryo raśmimayān iṣūn
bhūḥ pāduke yogamayyau
dyauḥ puṣpāvalim anvaham

agniḥ—the demigod of fire; *āja-gavam*—made of the horns of goats and cows; *cāpam*—a bow; *sūryaḥ*—the sun-god; *raśmi-mayān*—brilliant as sunshine; *iṣūn*—arrows; *bhūḥ*—Bhūmi, the predominating goddess of the earth; *pāduke*—two slippers; *yoga-mayyau*—full of mystic power; *dyauḥ*—the demigods in outer space; *puṣpa*—of flowers; *āvalim*—presentation; *anu-aham*—day after day.

TRANSLATION

The demigod of fire, Agni, presented him with a bow made of the horns of goats and cows. The sun-god presented him with arrows as brilliant as sunshine. The predominating deity of Bhūrloka presented him with slippers full of mystic power. The

demigods from outer space brought him presentations of flowers again and again.

PURPORT

This verse describes that the King's slippers were invested with mystic powers (*pāduke yogamayyau*). Thus as soon as the King placed his feet in the slippers they would immediately carry him wherever he desired. Mystic *yogīs* can transfer themselves from one place to another whenever they desire. A similar power was invested in the slippers of King Pṛthu.

TEXT 19

नाट्यं सुगीतं वादित्रमन्तर्धानं च खेचराः ।
ऋषयश्चाशिषः सत्याः समुद्रः शङ्खमात्मजम् ॥१९॥

nāṭyaṁ sugītaṁ vāditram
antardhānaṁ ca khecarāḥ
ṛṣayaś cāśiṣaḥ satyāḥ
samudraḥ śaṅkham ātmajam

nāṭyam—the art of drama; *su-gītam*—the art of singing sweet songs; *vāditram*—the art of playing musical instruments; *antardhānam*—the art of disappearing; *ca*—also; *khe-carāḥ*—demigods traveling in outer space; *ṛṣayaḥ*—the great sages; *ca*—also; *āśiṣaḥ*—blessings; *satyāḥ*—infallible; *samudraḥ*—the demigod of the ocean; *śaṅkham*—conchshell; *ātma-jam*—produced from himself.

TRANSLATION

The demigods who always travel in outer space gave King Pṛthu the arts to perform dramas, sing songs, play musical instruments and disappear at his will. The great sages also offered him infallible blessings. The ocean offered him a conchshell produced from the ocean.

TEXT 20

सिन्धवः पर्वता नद्यो रथवीथीर्महात्मनः ।
सूतोऽथ मागधो वन्दी तं स्तोतुमुपतस्थिरे ॥२०॥

sindhavaḥ parvatā nadyo
ratha-vīthīr mahātmanaḥ
sūto 'tha māgadho vandī
taṁ stotum upatasthire

sindhavaḥ—the seas; *parvatāḥ*—the mountains; *nadyaḥ*—the rivers; *ratha-vīthīḥ*—the paths for the chariot to pass; *mahā-ātmanaḥ*—of the great soul; *sūtaḥ*—a professional who offers praises; *atha*—then; *māgadhaḥ*—a professional bard; *vandī*—a professional who offers prayers; *tam*—him; *stotum*—to praise; *upatasthire*—presented themselves.

TRANSLATION

The seas, mountains and rivers gave him room to drive his chariot without impediments, and a sūta, a māgadha and a vandī offered prayers and praises. They all presented themselves before him to perform their respective duties.

TEXT 21

स्तावकांस्तानभिप्रेत्य पृथुर्वैन्यः प्रतापवान् ।
मेघनिर्ह्रादया वाचा प्रहसन्निदमब्रवीत् ॥२१॥

stāvakāṁs tān abhipretya
pṛthur vainyaḥ pratāpavān
megha-nirhrādayā vācā
prahasann idam abravīt

stāvakān—engaged in offering prayers; *tān*—those persons; *abhipretya*—seeing, understanding; *pṛthuḥ*—King Pṛthu; *vainyaḥ*—son of Vena; *pratāpa-vān*—greatly powerful; *megha-nirhrādayā*—as grave as the thundering of clouds; *vācā*—with a voice; *prahasan*—smiling; *idam*—this; *abravīt*—he spoke.

TRANSLATION

Thus when the greatly powerful King Pṛthu, the son of Vena, saw the professionals before him, to congratulate them he smiled,

and with the gravity of the vibrating sounds of clouds he spoke as follows.

TEXT 22

पृथुरुवाच
भोः सूत हे मागध सौम्य वन्दिँ-
ल्लोकेऽधुनास्पष्टगुणस्य मे स्यात् ।
किमाश्रयो मे स्तव एष योज्यतां
मा मय्यभूवन् वितथा गिरो वः ॥२२॥

pṛthur uvāca
bhoḥ sūta he māgadha saumya vandil̐
loke 'dhunāspaṣṭa-guṇasya me syāt
kim āśrayo me stava eṣa yojyatāṁ
mā mayy abhūvan vitathā giro vaḥ

pṛthuḥ uvāca—King Pṛthu said; *bhoḥ sūta*—O *sūta; he māgadha*—O *māgadha; saumya*—gentle; *vandin*—O devotee offering prayers; *loke*—in this world; *adhunā*—just now; *aspaṣṭa*—not distinct; *guṇasya*—whose qualities; *me*—of me; *syāt*—there may be; *kim*—why; *āśrayaḥ*—shelter; *me*—of me; *stavaḥ*—praise; *eṣaḥ*—this; *yojyatām*—may be applied; *mā*—never; *mayi*—unto me; *abhūvan*—were; *vitathāḥ*—in vain; *giraḥ*—words; *vaḥ*—your.

TRANSLATION

King Pṛthu said: O gentle sūta, māgadha and other devotee offering prayers, the qualities of which you have spoken are not distinct in me. Why then should you praise me for all these qualities when I do not shelter these features? I do not wish for these words meant for me to go in vain, but it is better that they be offered to someone else.

PURPORT

The prayers and praises by the *sūta*, *māgadha* and *vandī* all explained the godly qualities of Mahārāja Pṛthu, for he was a *śaktyāveśa* incarnation of the Supreme Personality of Godhead. Because the qualities were not yet manifest, however, King Pṛthu very humbly asked why the devotees should praise him with such exalted words. He did not want anyone to offer him prayers or glorify him unless he possessed the real qualities of which they spoke. The offering of prayers was certainly appropriate, for he was an incarnation of Godhead, but he warned that one should not be accepted as an incarnation of the Personality of Godhead without having the godly qualities. At the present moment there are many so-called incarnations of the Personality of Godhead, but these are merely fools and rascals whom people accept as incarnations of God although they have no godly qualities. King Pṛthu desired that his real characteristics in the future might justify such words of praise. Although there was no fault in the prayers offered, Pṛthu Mahārāja indicated that such prayers should not be offered to an unfit person who pretends to be an incarnation of the Supreme Personality of Godhead.

TEXT 23

तस्मात्परोक्षेऽस्मदुपश्रुतान्यलं-
करिष्यथ स्तोत्रमपीच्यवाचः ।
सत्युत्तमश्लोकगुणानुवादे
जुगुप्सितं न स्तवयन्ति सभ्याः ॥२३॥

tasmāt parokṣe 'smad-upaśrutāny alaṁ
kariṣyatha stotram apīcya-vācaḥ
saty uttamaśloka-guṇānuvāde
jugupsitaṁ na stavayanti sabhyāḥ

tasmāt—therefore; *parokṣe*—in some future time; *asmat*—my; *upaśrutāni*—about the qualities spoken of; *alam*—sufficiently; *kariṣyatha*—you will be able to offer; *stotram*—prayers; *apīcya-vācaḥ*—O gentle reciters; *sati*—being the proper engagement; *uttama-śloka*—of the Supreme Personality of Godhead; *guṇa*—of the qualities; *anuvāde*—discussion; *jugupsitam*—to an abominable person; *na*—never; *stavayanti*—offer prayers; *sabhyāḥ*—persons who are gentle.

TRANSLATION

O gentle reciters, offer such prayers in due course of time, when the qualities of which you have spoken actually manifest themselves in me. The gentle who offer prayers to the Supreme Personality of Godhead do not attribute such qualities to a human being, who does not actually have them.

PURPORT

Gentle devotees of the Supreme Personality of Godhead know perfectly well who is God and who is not. Nondevotee impersonalists, however, who have no idea what God is and who never offer prayers to the Supreme Personality of Godhead, are always interested in accepting a human being as God and offering such prayers to him. This is the difference between a devotee and a demon. Demons manufacture their own gods, or a demon himself claims to be God, following in the footsteps of Rāvaṇa and Hiraṇyakaśipu. Although Pṛthu Mahārāja was factually an incarnation of the Supreme Personality of Godhead, he rejected those praises because the qualities of the Supreme Person were not yet manifest in him. He wanted to stress that one who does not actually possess these qualities should not try to engage his followers and devotees in offering him glory for them, even though these qualities might be manifest in the future. If a man who does not factually possess the attributes of a great personality engages his followers in praising him with the expectation that such attributes will develop in the future, that sort of praise is actually an insult.

TEXT 24

महद्गुणानात्मनि कर्तुमीशः
कः स्तावकैः स्तावयतेऽसतोऽपि ।
तेऽस्याभविष्यन्निति विप्रलब्धो
जनावहासं कुमतिर्न वेद ॥२४॥

mahad-guṇān ātmani kartum īśaḥ
kaḥ stāvakaiḥ stāvayate 'sato 'pi

te 'syābhaviṣyann iti vipralabdho
janāvahāsaṁ kumatir na veda

mahat—exalted; *guṇān*—the qualities; *ātmani*—in himself; *kartum*—to manifest; *īśaḥ*—competent; *kaḥ*—who; *stāvakaiḥ*—by followers; *stāvayate*—causes to be praised; *asataḥ*—not existing; *api*—although; *te*—they; *asya*—of him; *abhaviṣyan*—might have been; *iti*—thus; *vipralabdhaḥ*—cheated; *jana*—of people; *avahāsam*—insult; *kumatiḥ*—a fool; *na*—does not; *veda*—know.

TRANSLATION

How could an intelligent man competent enough to possess such exalted qualities allow his followers to praise him if he did not actually have them? Praising a man by saying that if he were educated he might have become a great scholar or great personality is nothing but a process of cheating. A foolish person who agrees to accept such praise does not know that such words simply insult him.

PURPORT

Pṛthu Mahārāja was an incarnation of the Supreme Personality of Godhead, as Lord Brahmā and other demigods had already testified when they had presented the King with many heavenly gifts. Because he had just been coronated, however, he could not manifest his godly qualities in action. Therefore he was not willing to accept the praise of the devotees. So-called incarnations of Godhead should therefore take lessons from the behavior of King Pṛthu. Demons without godly qualities should not accept false praise from their followers.

TEXT 25

प्रभवो ह्यात्मनः स्तोत्रं जुगुप्सन्त्यपि विश्रुताः ।
ह्रीमन्तः परमोदाराः पौरुषं वा विगर्हितम् ॥२५॥

prabhavo hy ātmanaḥ stotram
jugupsanty api viśrutāḥ
hrīmantaḥ paramodārāḥ
pauruṣaṁ vā vigarhitam

prabhavaḥ—very powerful persons; *hi*—certainly; *ātmanaḥ*—of themselves; *stotram*—praise; *jugupsanti*—do not like; *api*—although; *viśrutāḥ*—very famous; *hrī-mantaḥ*—modest; *parama-udārāḥ*—very magnanimous persons; *pauruṣam*—powerful actions; *vā*—also; *vigarhitam*—abominable.

TRANSLATION

As a person with a sense of honor and magnanimity does not like to hear about his abominable actions, a person who is very famous and powerful does not like to hear himself praised.

TEXT 26

वयं त्वविदिता लोके सूताद्यापि वरीमभिः ।
कर्मभिः कथमात्मानं गापयिष्याम बालवत् ॥२६॥

vayaṁ tv aviditā loke
sūtādyāpi varīmabhiḥ
karmabhiḥ katham ātmānaṁ
gāpayiṣyāma bālavat

vayam—we; *tu*—then; *aviditāḥ*—not famous; *loke*—in the world; *sūta-ādya*—O persons headed by the *sūta; api*—just now; *varīmabhiḥ*—great, praiseworthy; *karmabhiḥ*—by actions; *katham*—how; *ātmānam*—unto myself; *gāpayiṣyāma*—I shall engage you in offering; *bālavat*—like children.

TRANSLATION

King Pṛthu continued: My dear devotees, headed by the sūta, just now I am not very famous for my personal activities because I have not done anything praiseworthy you could glorify. Therefore how could I engage you in praising my activities exactly like children?

Thus end the Bhaktivedanta purports of the Fourth Canto, Fifteenth Chapter, of the Śrīmad-Bhāgavatam, *entitled "King Pṛthu's Appearance and Coronation."*

CHAPTER SIXTEEN

Praise of King Pṛthu by the Professional Reciters

TEXT 1

मैत्रेय उवाच
इति ब्रुवाणं नृपतिं गायका मुनिचोदिताः ।
तुष्टुवुस्तुष्टमनसस्तद्वागमृतसेवया ॥ १ ॥

maitreya uvāca
iti bruvāṇaṁ nṛpatiṁ
gāyakā muni-coditāḥ
tuṣṭuvus tuṣṭa-manasas
tad-vāg-amṛta-sevayā

maitreyaḥ uvāca—the great sage Maitreya said; *iti*—thus; *bruvāṇam*—speaking; *nṛpatim*—the King; *gāyakāḥ*—the reciters; *muni*—by the sages; *coditāḥ*—having been instructed; *tuṣṭuvuḥ*—praised, satisfied; *tuṣṭa*—being pleased; *manasaḥ*—their minds; *tat*—his; *vāk*—words; *amṛta*—nectarean; *sevayā*—by hearing.

TRANSLATION

The great sage Maitreya continued: While King Pṛthu thus spoke, the humility of his nectarean speeches pleased the reciters very much. Then again they continued to praise the King highly with exalted prayers, as they had been instructed by the great sages.

PURPORT

Here the word *muni-coditāḥ* indicates instructions received from great sages and saintly persons. Although Mahārāja Pṛthu was simply enthroned on the royal seat and was not at that time exhibiting his godly powers, the reciters like the *sūta*, the *māgadha* and the *vandī* understood that King Pṛthu was an incarnation of God. They could understand this by the instructions given by the great sages and learned *brāhmaṇas*. We have to understand the incarnations of God by the instructions of authorized persons. We cannot manufacture a God by our own concoctions. As stated by Narottama dāsa Ṭhākura, *sādhu-śāstra-guru:* one has to test all spiritual matters according to the instructions of saintly persons, scriptures and the spiritual master. The spiritual master is one who follows the instructions of his predecessors, namely the *sādhus*, or saintly persons. A bona fide spiritual master does not mention anything not mentioned in the authorized scriptures. Ordinary people have to follow the instructions of *sādhu*, *śāstra* and *guru*. Those statements made in the *śāstras* and those made by the bona fide *sādhu* or *guru* cannot differ from one another.

Reciters like the *sūta* and the *māgadha* were confidentially aware that King Pṛthu was an incarnation of the Personality of Godhead. Although the King denied such praise because he was not at that time exhibiting his godly qualities, the reciters did not stop praising him. Rather, they were very pleased with the King, who, although actually an incarnation of God, was so humble and delightful in his dealings with devotees. In this connection we may note that previously (4.15.21) it was mentioned that King Pṛthu was smiling and was in a pleasant mood while speaking to the reciters. Thus we have to learn from the Lord or His incarnation how to become gentle and humble. The King's behavior was very pleasing to the reciters, and consequently the reciters continued their praise and even foretold the King's future activities, as they had been instructed by the *sādhus* and sages.

TEXT 2

नालं वयं ते महिमानुवर्णने
यो देववर्योऽवततार मायया ।
वेनाङ्गजातस्य च पौरुषाणि ते
वाचस्पतीनामपि बभ्रमुर्धियः ॥ २ ॥

nālaṁ vayaṁ te mahimānuvarṇane
yo deva-varyo 'vatatāra māyayā
venāṅga-jātasya ca pauruṣāṇi te
vācas-patīnām api babhramur dhiyaḥ

na alam—not able; *vayam*—we; *te*—your; *mahima*—glories; *anu-varṇane*—in describing; *yaḥ*—you who; *deva*—the Personality of Godhead; *varyaḥ*—foremost; *avatatāra*—descended; *māyayā*—by His internal potencies or causeless mercy; *vena-aṅga*—from the body of King Vena; *jātasya*—who have appeared; *ca*—and; *pauruṣāṇi*—glorious activities; *te*—of you; *vācaḥ-patīnām*—of great orators; *api*—although; *babhramuḥ*—became bewildered; *dhiyaḥ*—the minds.

TRANSLATION

The reciters continued: Dear King, you are a direct incarnation of the Supreme Personality of Godhead, Lord Viṣṇu, and by His causeless mercy you have descended on this earth. Therefore it is not possible for us to actually glorify your exalted activities. Although you have appeared through the body of King Vena, even great orators and speakers like Lord Brahmā and other demigods cannot exactly describe the glorious activities of Your Lordship.

PURPORT

In this verse the word *māyayā* means "by your causeless mercy." The Māyāvādī philosophers explain the word *māyā* as meaning "illusion" or "falseness." However, there is another meaning of *māyā*—that is, "causeless mercy." There are two kinds of *māyā*—*yogamāyā* and *mahāmāyā. Mahāmāyā* is an expansion of *yogamāyā*, and both these *māyās* are different expressions of the Lord's internal potencies. As stated in *Bhagavad-gītā*, the Lord appears through His internal potencies (*ātma-māyayā*). We should therefore reject the Māyāvāda explanation that the Lord appears in a body given by the external potency, the material energy. The Lord and His incarnation are fully independent and can appear anywhere and everywhere by virtue of the internal potency. Although born out of the so-called dead body of King Vena, King Pṛthu was still an incarnation of the Supreme Personality of Godhead by the

Lord's internal potency. The Lord can appear in any family. Sometimes He appears as a fish incarnation (*matsya-avatāra*) or a boar incarnation (*varāha-avatāra*). Thus the Lord is completely free and independent to appear anywhere and everywhere by His internal potency. It is stated that Ananta, an incarnation of the Lord who has unlimited mouths, cannot reach the end of His glorification of the Lord, although Ananta has been describing the Lord since time immemorial. So what to speak of demigods like Lord Brahmā, Lord Śiva and others? It is said that the Lord is *śiva-viriñci-nutam*—always worshiped by demigods like Lord Śiva and Lord Brahmā. If the demigods cannot find adequate language to express the glories of the Lord, then what to speak of others? Consequently reciters like the *sūta* and *māgadha* felt inadequate to speak about King Pṛthu.

By glorifying the Lord with exalted verses, one becomes purified. Although we are unable to offer prayers to the Lord in an adequate fashion, our duty is to make the attempt in order to purify ourselves. It is not that we should stop our glorification because demigods like Lord Brahmā and Lord Śiva cannot adequately glorify the Lord. Rather, as stated by Prahlāda Mahārāja, everyone should glorify the Lord according to his own ability. If we are serious and sincere devotees, the Lord will give us the intelligence to offer prayers properly.

TEXT 3

अथाप्युदारश्रवसः पृथोर्हरेः
कलावतारस्य कथामृतादृताः ।
यथोपदेशं मुनिभिः प्रचोदिताः
श्लाघ्यानि कर्माणि वयं वितन्महि ॥ ३ ॥

athāpy udāra-śravasaḥ pṛthor hareḥ
kalāvatārasya kathāmṛtādṛtāḥ
yathopadeśaṁ munibhiḥ pracoditāḥ
ślāghyāni karmāṇi vayaṁ vitanmahi

atha api—nevertheless; *udāra*—liberal; *śravasaḥ*—whose fame; *pṛthoḥ*—of King Pṛthu; *hareḥ*—of Lord Viṣṇu; *kalā*—part of a plenary expansion; *avatārasya*—incarnation; *kathā*—words; *amṛta*—nectarean; *ādṛtāḥ*—attentive to; *yathā*—according to; *upadeśam*—instruction; *munibhiḥ*—by the great sages; *pracoditāḥ*—being encouraged; *ślāghyāni*—laudable; *karmāṇi*—activities; *vayam*—we; *vitanmahi*—shall try to spread.

TRANSLATION

Although we are unable to glorify you adequately, we nonetheless have a transcendental taste for glorifying your activities. We shall try to glorify you according to the instructions received from authoritative sages and scholars. Whatever we speak, however, is always inadequate and very insignificant. Dear King, because you are a direct incarnation of the Supreme Personality of Godhead, all your activities are liberal and ever laudable.

PURPORT

However expert one may be, he can never describe the glories of the Lord adequately. Nonetheless, those engaged in glorifying the activities of the Lord should try to do so as far as possible. Such an attempt will please the Supreme Personality of Godhead. Lord Caitanya has advised all His followers to go everywhere and preach the message of Lord Kṛṣṇa. Since this message is essentially *Bhagavad-gītā*, the preacher's duty is to study *Bhagavad-gītā* as it is understood by disciplic succession and explained by great sages and learned devotees. One should speak to the general populace in accordance with one's predecessors—*sādhu*, *guru* and *śāstras*. This simple process is the easiest method by which one can glorify the Lord. Devotional service, however, is the real method, for by devotional service one can satisfy the Supreme Personality of Godhead with just a few words. Without devotional service, volumes of books cannot satisfy the Lord. Even though preachers of the Kṛṣṇa consciousness movement may be unable to describe the glories of the Lord, they can nonetheless go everywhere and request people to chant Hare Kṛṣṇa.

TEXT 4

एष धर्मभृतां श्रेष्ठो लोकं धर्मेऽनुवर्तयन् ।
गोप्ता च धर्मसेतूनां शास्ता तत्परिपन्थिनाम् ॥ ४ ॥

eṣa dharma-bhṛtāṁ śreṣṭho
lokaṁ dharme 'nuvartayan
goptā ca dharma-setūnāṁ
śāstā tat-paripanthinām

eṣaḥ—this King Pṛthu; *dharma-bhṛtām*—of persons executing religious activities; *śreṣṭhaḥ*—the best; *lokam*—the whole world; *dharme*—in religious activities; *anuvartayan*—engaging them properly; *goptā*—the protector; *ca*—also; *dharma-setūnām*—of the principles of religion; *śāstā*—the chastiser; *tat-paripanthinām*—of those who are against religious principles.

TRANSLATION

This King, Mahārāja Pṛthu, is the best amongst those who are following religious principles. As such, he will engage everyone in the pursuit of religious principles and give those principles all protection. He will also be a great chastiser to the irreligious and atheistic.

PURPORT

The duty of the king or the head of the government is described very nicely in this verse. It is the duty of the governmental head to see that people strictly follow a religious life. A king should also be strict in chastising the atheists. In other words, an atheistic or godless government should never be supported by a king or governmental chief. That is the test of good government. In the name of secular government, the king or governmental head remains neutral and allows people to engage in all sorts of irreligious activities. In such a state, people cannot be happy, despite all economic development. However, in this age of Kali there are no pious kings. Instead, rogues and thieves are elected to head the government. But how can the people be happy without religion and God consciousness? The rogues exact taxes from the citizens for their own sense enjoyment, and in the future the people will be so much harassed that according to *Śrīmad-Bhāgavatam* they will flee from their homes and country and take shelter in the forest. However, in Kali-yuga, democratic government can be captured by Kṛṣṇa conscious people. If this can be done, the general populace can be made very happy.

TEXT 5

एष वै लोकपालानां बिभर्त्येकस्तनौ तनूः ।
कालेकाले यथाभागं लोकयोरुभयोर्हितम् ॥ ५ ॥

eṣa vai loka-pālānāṁ
bibharty ekas tanau tanūḥ
kāle kāle yathā-bhāgaṁ
lokayor ubhayor hitam

eṣaḥ—this King; *vai*—certainly; *loka-pālānām*—of all the demigods; *bibharti*—bears; *ekaḥ*—alone; *tanau*—in his body; *tanūḥ*—the bodies; *kāle kāle*—in due course of time; *yathā*—according to; *bhāgam*—proper share; *lokayoḥ*—of planetary systems; *ubhayoḥ*—both; *hitam*—welfare.

TRANSLATION

This King alone, in his own body, will be able in due course of time to maintain all living entities and keep them in a pleasant condition by manifesting himself as different demigods to perform various departmental activities. Thus he will maintain the upper planetary system by inducing the populace to perform Vedic sacrifices. In due course of time he will also maintain this earthly planet by discharging proper rainfall.

PURPORT

The demigods in charge of the various departmental activities that maintain this world are but assistants to the Supreme Personality of Godhead. When an incarnation of Godhead descends on this planet, demigods like the sun-god, the moon-god or the King of heaven, Indra, all join Him. Consequently the incarnation of Godhead is able to act for the departmental demigods to keep the planetary systems in order. The protection of the earthly planet is dependent on proper rainfall, and as stated in *Bhagavad-gītā* and other scriptures, sacrifices are performed to please those demigods who are in charge of rainfall.

annād bhavanti bhūtāni
parjanyād anna-sambhavaḥ

yajñād bhavati parjanyo
yajñaḥ karma-samudbhavaḥ

"All living bodies subsist on food grains, which are produced from rains. Rains are produced by performance of *yajña* [sacrifice], and *yajña* is born of prescribed duties." (Bg. 3.14)

Thus the proper execution of *yajña*, sacrifice, is required. As indicated herein, King Pṛthu alone would induce all the citizens to engage in such sacrificial activities so that there would not be scarcity or distress. In Kali-yuga, however, in the so-called secular state, the executive branch of government is in the charge of so-called kings and presidents who are all fools and rascals, ignorant of the intricacies of nature's causes and ignorant of the principles of sacrifice. Such rascals simply make various plans, which always fail, and the people subsequently suffer disturbances. To counteract this situation, the *śāstras* advise:

harer nāma harer nāma
harer nāmaiva kevalam
kalau nāsty eva nāsty eva
nāsty eva gatir anyathā

Thus in order to counteract this unfortunate situation in government, the general populace is advised to chant the *mahā-mantra:* Hare Kṛṣṇa, Hare Kṛṣṇa, Kṛṣṇa Kṛṣṇa, Hare Hare/ Hare Rāma, Hare Rāma, Rāma Rāma, Hare Hare.

TEXT 6

वसु काल उपादत्ते काले चायं विमुञ्चति ।
समः सर्वेषु भूतेषु प्रतपन् सूर्यवद्विभुः ॥ ६ ॥

vasu kāla upādatte
kāle cāyaṁ vimuñcati
samaḥ sarveṣu bhūteṣu
pratapan sūryavad vibhuḥ

vasu—riches; *kāle*—in due course of time; *upādatte*—exacts; *kāle*—in due course of time; *ca*—also; *ayam*—this King Pṛthu; *vimuñcati*—returns; *samaḥ*—equal; *sarveṣu*—to all; *bhūteṣu*—living entities; *pratapan*—shining; *sūrya-vat*—like the sun-god; *vibhuḥ*—powerful.

TRANSLATION

This King Pṛthu will be as powerful as the sun-god, and just as the sun-god equally distributes his sunshine to everyone, King Pṛthu will distribute his mercy equally. Similarly, just as the sun-god evaporates water for eight months and, during the rainy season, returns it profusely, this King will also exact taxes from the citizens and return these monies in times of need.

PURPORT

The process of tax exaction is very nicely explained in this verse. Tax exaction is not meant for the sense gratification of the so-called administrative heads. Tax revenues should be distributed to the citizens in times of need, during emergencies such as famine or flood. Tax revenues should never be distributed amongst governmental servants in the form of high salaries and various other allowances. In Kali-yuga, however, the position of the citizens is very horrible because taxes are exacted in so many forms and are spent for the personal comforts of the administrators.

The example of the sun in this verse is very appropriate. The sun is many millions of miles away from the earth, and although the sun does not actually touch the earth, it manages to distribute land all over the planet by exacting water from the oceans and seas, and it also manages to make that land fertile by distributing water during the rainy season. As an ideal king, King Pṛthu would execute all this business in the village and state as expertly as the sun.

TEXT 7

तितिक्षत्यक्रमं वैन्य उपर्याक्रमतामपि ।
भूतानां करुणः शश्वदार्तानां क्षितिवृत्तिमान् ॥ ७ ॥

titikṣaty akramaṁ vainya
upary ākramatām api
bhūtānāṁ karuṇaḥ śaśvad
ārtānāṁ kṣiti-vṛttimān

titikṣati—tolerates; *akramam*—offense; *vainyaḥ*—the son of King Vena; *upari*—on his head; *ākramatām*—of those who are trampling;

api—also; *bhūtānām*—to all living entities; *karuṇaḥ*—very kind-hearted; *śaśvat*—always; *ārtānām*—to the aggrieved; *kṣiti-vṛtti-mān*—accepting the profession of the earth.

TRANSLATION

This King Pṛthu will be very, very kind to all citizens. Even though a poor person may trample over the King's head by violating the rules and regulations, the King, out of his causeless mercy, will be forgetful and forgiving. As a protector of the world, he will be as tolerant as the earth itself.

PURPORT

King Pṛthu is herein compared to the earthly planet as far as his tolerance is concerned. Although the earth is always trampled upon by men and animals, it still gives food to them by producing grains, fruits and vegetables. As an ideal king, Mahārāja Pṛthu is compared to the earthly planet, for even though some citizens might violate the rules and regulations of the state, he would still be tolerant and maintain them with fruits and grains. In other words, it is the duty of the king to look after the comforts of the citizens, even at the cost of his own personal convenience. This is not the case, however, in Kali-yuga, for in Kali-yuga the kings and heads of state enjoy life at the cost of taxes exacted from the citizens. Such unfair taxation makes the people dishonest, and the people try to hide their income in so many ways. Eventually the state will not be able to collect taxes and consequently will not be able to meet its huge military and administrative expenses. Everything will collapse, and there will be chaos and disturbance all over the state.

TEXT 8

देवेऽवर्षत्यसौ देवो नरदेववपुर्हरिः ।
कृच्छ्रप्राणाः प्रजा ह्येष रक्षिष्यत्यञ्जसेन्द्रवत् ॥ ८ ॥

dcvc 'varṣaty asau dcvo
naradeva-vapur hariḥ
kṛcchra-prāṇāḥ prajā hy eṣa
rakṣiṣyaty añjasendravat

deve—when the demigod (Indra); *avarṣati*—does not supply rains; *asau*—that; *devaḥ*—Mahārāja Pṛthu; *nara-deva*—of the king; *vapuḥ*—having the body; *hariḥ*—the Supreme Personality of Godhead; *kṛcchra-prāṇāḥ*—suffering living entities; *prajāḥ*—the citizens; *hi*—certainly; *eṣaḥ*—this; *rakṣiṣyati*—will protect; *añjasā*—very easily; *indra-vat*—like King Indra.

TRANSLATION

When there is no rainfall and the citizens are in great danger due to the scarcity of water, this royal Personality of Godhead will be able to supply rains exactly like the heavenly King Indra. Thus he will very easily be able to protect the citizens from drought.

PURPORT

King Pṛthu is very appropriately compared to the sun and the demigod Indra. King Indra of the heavenly planets is in charge of distributing water over the earth and other planetary systems. It is indicated that King Pṛthu would arrange for the distribution of rainfall personally if Indra failed to discharge his duty properly. Sometimes the King of heaven, Indra, would become angry at the inhabitants of the earth if they did not offer sacrifices to appease him. King Pṛthu, however, being an incarnation of the Supreme Personality of Godhead, did not depend on the mercy of the heavenly King. It is foretold herein that if there would be a scarcity of rain, King Pṛthu would manage to counteract the deficiency by virtue of his godly powers. Such powers were also exhibited by Lord Kṛṣṇa when He was present in Vṛndāvana. Indeed, when Indra poured incessant water on Vṛndāvana for seven days, the inhabitants were protected by Kṛṣṇa, who raised Govardhana Hill over their heads as a great umbrella. Thus Lord Kṛṣṇa is also known as Govardhana-dhārī.

TEXT 9

आप्याययत्यसौ लोकं वदनामृतमूर्तिना ।
सानुरागावलोकेन विशदस्मितचारुणा ॥ ९ ॥

āpyāyayaty asau lokaṁ
vadanāmṛta-mūrtinā

sānurāgāvalokena
viśada-smita-cāruṇā

āpyāyayati—enhances; *asau*—he; *lokam*—the whole world; *vadana*—by his face; *amṛta-mūrtinā*—moonlike; *sa-anurāga*—affectionate; *avalokena*—with glances; *viśada*—bright; *smita*—smiling; *cāruṇā*—beautiful.

TRANSLATION

This King, Pṛthu Mahārāja, by virtue of his affectionate glances and beautiful moonlike face, which is always smiling with great affection for the citizens, will enhance everyone's peaceful life.

TEXT 10

अव्यक्तवर्त्मैष निगूढकार्यो
गम्भीरवेधा उपगुप्तवित्तः ।
अनन्तमाहात्म्यगुणैकधामा
पृथुः प्रचेता इव संवृतात्मा ॥१०॥

avyakta-vartmaiṣa nigūḍha-kāryo
gambhīra-vedhā upagupta-vittaḥ
ananta-māhātmya-guṇaika-dhāmā
pṛthuḥ pracetā iva saṁvṛtātmā

avyakta—unmanifested; *vartmā*—his policies; *eṣaḥ*—this King; *nigūḍha*—confidential; *kāryaḥ*—his activities; *gambhīra*—grave, secret; *vedhāḥ*—his accomplishing; *upagupta*—secretly kept; *vittaḥ*—his treasury; *ananta*—unlimited; *māhātmya*—of glories; *guṇa*—of good qualities; *eka-dhāmā*—the only reservoir; *pṛthuḥ*—King Pṛthu; *pracetāḥ*—Varuṇa, the King of the seas; *iva*—like; *saṁvṛta*—covered; *ātmā*—self.

TRANSLATION

The reciters continued: No one will be able to understand the policies the King will follow. His activities will also be very confidential, and it will not be possible for anyone to know how he will make every activity successful. His treasury will always remain

unknown to everyone. He will be the reservoir of unlimited glories and good qualities, and his position will be maintained and covered just as Varuṇa, the deity of the seas, is covered all around by water.

PURPORT

There is a predominating deity for all the material elements, and Varuṇa, or Pracetā, is the predominating deity of the seas and the oceans. From outward appearances the seas and oceans are devoid of life, but a person acquainted with the sea knows that within the water exist many varieties of life. The king of that underwater kingdom is Varuṇa. Just as no one can understand what is going on beneath the sea, no one could understand what policy King Pṛthu was following to make everything successful. Indeed, King Pṛthu's path of diplomacy was very grave. His success was made possible because he was a reservoir of unlimited glorified qualities.

The word *upagupta-vittaḥ* is very significant in this verse. It indicates that no one would know the extent of the riches King Pṛthu would confidentially keep. The idea is that not only the king but everyone should keep his hard-earned money confidentially and secretly so that in due course of time the money can be spent for good, practical purposes. In Kali-yuga, however, the king or government has no well-protected treasury, and the only means of circulation is currency notes made of paper. Thus in times of distress the government artificially inflates the currency by simply printing papers, and this artificially raises the price of commodities, and the general condition of the citizens becomes very precarious. Thus keeping one's money very secretly is an old practice, for we find this practice present even during the reign of Mahārāja Pṛthu. Just as the king has the right to keep his treasury confidential and secret, the people should also keep their individual earnings a secret. There is no fault in such dealings. The main point is that everyone should be trained in the system of *varṇāśrama-dharma* so that the money is spent only for good causes and nothing else.

TEXT 11

दुरासदो दुर्विषह आसन्नोऽपि विदूरवत् ।
नैवाभिभवितुं शक्यो वेनारण्युत्थितोऽनलः ॥११॥

durāsado durviṣaha
āsanno 'pi vidūravat
naivābhibhavituṁ śakyo
venāraṇy-utthito 'nalaḥ

durāsadaḥ—unapproachable; *durviṣahaḥ*—unbearable; *āsannaḥ*—being approached; *api*—although; *vidūra-vat*—as if far away; *na*—never; *eva*—certainly; *abhibhavitum*—to be overcome; *śakyaḥ*—able; *vena*—King Vena; *araṇi*—the wood that produces fire; *utthitaḥ*—being born of; *analaḥ*—fire.

TRANSLATION

King Pṛthu was born of the dead body of King Vena as fire is produced from araṇi wood. Thus King Pṛthu will always remain just like fire, and his enemies will not be able to approach him. Indeed, he will be unbearable to his enemies, for although staying very near him, they will never be able to approach him but will have to remain as if far away. No one will be able to overcome the strength of King Pṛthu.

PURPORT

Araṇi wood is a kind of fuel used to ignite fire by friction. At the time of performing sacrifices, one can ignite a fire from *araṇi* wood. Although born of his dead father, King Pṛthu would still remain just like fire. Just as fire is not easily approached, King Pṛthu would be unapproachable by his enemies, even though they would appear to be very near him.

TEXT 12

अन्तर्बहिश्च भूतानां पश्यन् कर्माणि चारणैः ।
उदासीन इवाध्यक्षो वायुरात्मेव देहिनाम् ॥१२॥

antar bahiś ca bhūtānāṁ
paśyan karmāṇi cāraṇaiḥ
udāsīna ivādhyakṣo
vāyur ātmeva dehinām

antaḥ—internally; *bahiḥ*—externally; *ca*—and; *bhūtānām*—of living entities; *paśyan*—seeing; *karmāṇi*—activities; *cāraṇaiḥ*—by spies; *udāsīnaḥ*—neutral; *iva*—like; *adhyakṣaḥ*—the witness; *vāyuḥ*—the air of life; *ātmā*—the living force; *iva*—like; *dehinām*—of all the embodied.

TRANSLATION

King Pṛthu will be able to see all the internal and external activities of every one of his citizens. Still no one will be able to know his system of espionage, and he himself will remain neutral regarding all matters of glorification or vilification paid to him. He will be exactly like air, the life force within the body, which is exhibited internally and externally but is always neutral to all affairs.

TEXT 13

नादण्ड्यं दण्डयत्येष सुतमात्मद्विषामपि ।
दण्डयत्यात्मजमपि दण्ड्यं धर्मपथे स्थितः ॥१३॥

nādaṇḍyaṁ daṇḍayaty eṣa
sutam ātma-dviṣām api
daṇḍayaty ātmajam api
daṇḍyaṁ dharma-pathe sthitaḥ

na—not; *adaṇḍyam*—not punishable; *daṇḍayati*—punishes; *eṣaḥ*—this King; *sutam*—the son; *ātma-dviṣām*—of his enemies; *api*—even; *daṇḍayati*—he punishes; *ātma-jam*—his own son; *api*—even; *daṇḍyam*—punishable; *dharma-pathe*—on the path of piety; *sthitaḥ*—being situated.

TRANSLATION

Since this King will always remain on the path of piety, he will be neutral to both his son and the son of his enemy. If the son of his enemy is not punishable, he will not punish him, but if his own son is punishable, he will immediately punish him.

PURPORT

These are the characteristics of an impartial ruler. It is the duty of a ruler to punish the criminal and give protection to the innocent. King Pṛthu was so neutral that if his own son were punishable, he would not hesitate to punish him. On the other hand, if the son of his enemy were innocent, he would not engage in some intrigue in order to punish him.

TEXT 14

अस्याप्रतिहतं चक्रं पृथोरामानसाचलात् ।
वर्तते भगवानर्को यावत्तपति गोगणैः ॥१४॥

asyāpratihataṁ cakraṁ
pṛthor āmānasācalāt
vartate bhagavān arko
yāvat tapati go-gaṇaiḥ

asya—of this King; *apratihatam*—not being impeded; *cakram*—the circle of influence; *pṛthoḥ*—of King Pṛthu; *ā-mānasa-acalāt*—up to Mānasa Mountain; *vartate*—remains; *bhagavān*—the most powerful; *arkaḥ*—sun-god; *yāvat*—just as; *tapati*—shines; *go-gaṇaiḥ*—with rays of light.

TRANSLATION

Just as the sun-god expands his shining rays up to the Arctic region without impedance, the influence of King Pṛthu will cover all tracts of land up to the Arctic region and will remain undisturbed as long as he lives.

PURPORT

Although the Arctic region is not visible to ordinary persons, the sun shines there without impediment. Just as no one can check the sunshine from spreading all over the universe, no one could check the influence and reign of King Pṛthu, which would remain undisturbed as long as he lived. The conclusion is that the sunshine and the sun-god cannot be separated, nor could King Pṛthu and his ruling strength be separated.

His rule over everyone would continue without disturbance. Thus the King could not be separated from his ruling power.

TEXT 15

रञ्जयिष्यति यल्लोकमयमात्मविचेष्टितैः ।
अथामुमाहू राजानं मनोरञ्जनकैः प्रजाः ॥१५॥

rañjayiṣyati yal lokam
ayam ātma-viceṣṭitaiḥ
athāmum āhū rājānaṁ
mano-rañjanakaiḥ prajāḥ

rañjayiṣyati—will please; *yat*—because; *lokam*—the entire world; *ayam*—this King; *ātma*—personal; *viceṣṭitaiḥ*—by activities; *atha*—therefore; *amum*—him; *āhuḥ*—they call; *rājānam*—the King; *manaḥ-rañjanakaiḥ*—very pleasing to the mind; *prajāḥ*—the citizens.

TRANSLATION

This King will please everyone by his practical activities, and all of his citizens will remain very satisfied. Because of this the citizens will take great satisfaction in accepting him as their ruling king.

TEXT 16

दृढव्रतः सत्यसन्धो ब्रह्मण्यो वृद्धसेवकः ।
शरण्यः सर्वभूतानां मानदो दीनवत्सलः ॥१६॥

dṛḍha-vrataḥ satya-sandho
brahmaṇyo vṛddha-sevakaḥ
śaraṇyaḥ sarva-bhūtānāṁ
mānado dīna-vatsalaḥ

dṛḍha-vrataḥ—firmly determined; *satya-sandhaḥ*—always situated in truth; *brahmaṇyaḥ*—a lover of the brahminical culture; *vṛddha-sevakaḥ*—a servitor of the old men; *śaraṇyaḥ*—to be taken shelter of;

sarva-bhūtānām—of all living entities; *māna-daḥ*—one who gives respect to all; *dīna-vatsalaḥ*—very kind to the poor and helpless.

TRANSLATION

The King will be firmly determined and always situated in truth. He will be a lover of the brahminical culture and will render all service to old men and give shelter to all surrendered souls. Giving respect to all, he will always be merciful to the poor and innocent.

PURPORT

The word *vṛddha-sevakaḥ* is very significant. *Vṛddha* means "old men." There are two kinds of old men: one is old by age, and another is old by knowledge. This Sanskrit word indicates that one can be older by the advancement of knowledge. King Pṛthu was very respectful to the *brāhmaṇas*, and he protected them. He also protected persons advanced in age. Whatever the King would decide to do, no one would be able to stop. That is called *dṛḍha-saṅkalpa*, or *dṛḍha-vrata.*

TEXT 17

मातृभक्तिः परस्त्रीषु पत्न्यामर्ध इवात्मनः ।
प्रजासु पितृवत्स्निग्धः किङ्करो ब्रह्मवादिनाम् ॥१७॥

mātṛ-bhaktiḥ para-strīṣu
patnyām ardha ivātmanaḥ
prajāsu pitṛvat snigdhaḥ
kiṅkaro brahma-vādinām

mātṛ-bhaktiḥ—as respectful as one is to his mother; *para-strīṣu*—to other women; *patnyām*—to his own wife; *ardhaḥ*—half; *iva*—like; *ātmanaḥ*—of his body; *prajāsu*—unto the citizens; *pitṛ-vat*—like a father; *snigdhaḥ*—affectionate; *kiṅkaraḥ*—servant; *brahma-vādinām*—of the devotees who preach the glories of the Lord.

TRANSLATION

The King will respect all women as if they were his own mother, and he will treat his own wife as the other half of his body. He will

be just like an affectionate father to his citizens, and he will treat himself as the most obedient servant of the devotees, who always preach the glories of the Lord.

PURPORT

A learned man treats all women except his wife as his mother, looks on others' property as garbage in the street, and treats others as he would treat his own self. These are the symptoms of a learned person as described by Cāṇakya Paṇḍita. This should be the standard for education. Education does not mean having academic degrees only. One should execute what he has learned in his personal life. These learned characteristics were verily manifest in the life of King Pṛthu. Although he was the king, he treated himself as a servant of the Lord's devotees. According to Vedic etiquette, if a devotee came to a king's palace, the king would immediately offer his own seat to him. The word *brahma-vādinām* is very significant. *Brahma-vādī* refers to the devotees of the Lord. *Brahman*, *Paramātmā* and *Bhagavān* are different terms for the Supreme Brahman, and the Supreme Brahman is Lord Kṛṣṇa. This is accepted in *Bhagavad-gītā* (10.12) by Arjuna (*paraṁ brahma paraṁ dhāma*). Thus the word *brahma-vādinām* refers to the devotees of the Lord. The state should always serve the devotees of the Lord, and the ideal state should conduct itself according to the instructions of the devotee. Because King Pṛthu followed this principle, he is highly praised.

TEXT 18

देहिनामात्मवत्प्रेष्ठः सुहृदां नन्दिवर्धनः ।
मुक्तसङ्गप्रसङ्गोऽयं दण्डपाणिरसाधुषु ॥१८॥

dehināṁ ātmavat-preṣṭhaḥ
suhṛdāṁ nandi-vardhanaḥ
mukta-saṅga-prasaṅgo 'yaṁ
daṇḍa-pāṇir asādhuṣu

dehinām—to all living entities having a body; *ātma-vat*—as himself; *preṣṭhaḥ*—considering dear; *suhṛdām*—of his friends; *nandi-vardhanaḥ*—increasing pleasures; *mukta-saṅga*—with persons devoid of all material contamination; *prasaṅgaḥ*—intimately associated; *ayam*—this King; *daṇḍa-pāṇiḥ*—a chastising hand; *asādhuṣu*—to the criminals.

TRANSLATION

The King will consider all embodied living entities as dear as his own self, and he will always be increasing the pleasures of his friends. He will intimately associate with liberated persons, and he will be a chastising hand to all impious persons.

PURPORT

The word *dehinām* refers to those who are embodied. The living entities are embodied in different forms, which number 8,400,000 species. All of these were treated by the King in the same way he would treat himself. In this age, however, so-called kings and presidents do not treat all other living entities as their own self. Most of them are meat-eaters, and even though they may not be meat-eaters and may pose themselves to be very religious and pious, they still allow cow slaughter within their state. Such sinful heads of state cannot actually be popular at any time. Another significant word in this verse is *mukta-saṅga-prasaṅgaḥ*, which indicates that the King was always associating with liberated persons.

TEXT 19

अयं तु साक्षाद्भगवांस्त्र्यधीशः
कूटस्थ आत्मा कलयावतीर्णः ।
यस्मिन्नविद्यारचितं निरर्थकं
पश्यन्ति नानात्वमपि प्रतीतम् ॥१९॥

ayaṁ tu sākṣād bhagavāṁs try-adhīśaḥ
kūṭa-stha ātmā kalayāvatīrṇaḥ
yasminn avidyā-racitaṁ nirarthakaṁ
paśyanti nānātvam api pratītam

ayam—this King; *tu*—then; *sākṣāt*—directly; *bhagavān*—the Supreme Personality of Godhead; *tri-adhīśaḥ*—the master of the three planetary systems; *kūṭa-sthaḥ*—without any change; *ātmā*—the Supersoul; *kalayā*—by a partial plenary expansion; *avatīrṇaḥ*—descended; *yasmin*—in whom; *avidyā-racitam*—created by nescience; *nirarthakam*—without meaning; *paśyanti*—they see; *nānātvam*—material variegatedness; *api*—certainly; *pratītam*—understood.

TRANSLATION

This King is the master of the three worlds, and he is directly empowered by the Supreme Personality of Godhead. He is without change, and he is an incarnation of the Supreme known as a śaktyāveśa-avatāra. Being a liberated soul and completely learned, he sees all material varieties as meaningless because their basic principle is nescience.

PURPORT

The reciters of these prayers are describing the transcendental qualities of Pṛthu Mahārāja. These qualities are summarized in the words *sākṣād bhagavān.* This indicates that Mahārāja Pṛthu is directly the Supreme Personality of Godhead and therefore possesses unlimited good qualities. Being an incarnation of the Supreme Personality of Godhead, Mahārāja Pṛthu could not be equaled in his excellent qualities. The Supreme Personality of Godhead is fully equipped with six kinds of opulences, and King Pṛthu was also empowered in such a way that he could display these six opulences of the Supreme Personality of Godhead in full.

The word *kūṭa-stha*, meaning "without change," is also very significant. There are two kinds of living entities—*nitya-mukta* and *nitya-baddha.* A *nitya-mukta* never forgets his position as the eternal servant of the Supreme Personality of Godhead. One who does not forget this position and knows that he is part and parcel of the Supreme Lord is *nitya-mukta.* Such a *nitya-mukta* living entity represents the Supersoul as His expansion. As stated in the *Vedas, nityo nityānām.* Thus the *nitya-mukta* living entity knows that he is an expansion of the supreme *nitya*, or the eternal Supreme Personality of Godhead. Being in such a position, he sees the material world with a different vision. The living entity who is *nitya-baddha*, or eternally conditioned, sees the material varieties as being actually different from one another. In this connection we should remember that the embodiment of the conditioned soul is considered to be like a dress. One may dress in different ways, but a really learned man does not take dresses into consideration. As stated in *Bhagavad-gītā* (5.18):

vidyā-vinaya-sampanne
brāhmaṇe gavi hastini
śuni caiva śvapāke ca
paṇḍitāḥ sama-darśinaḥ

"The humble sage, by virtue of true knowledge, sees with equal vision a learned and gentle *brāhmaṇa*, a cow, an elephant, a dog and a dog-eater [outcaste]."

Thus a learned man does not look upon the dresses that externally cover the living entity, but sees the pure soul within the varieties of dress and knows very well that the varieties of dress are the creation of nescience (*avidyā-racitam*). Being a *śaktyāveśa-avatāra*, empowered by the Supreme Personality of Godhead, Pṛthu Mahārāja did not change his spiritual position, and consequently there was no possibility of his viewing the material world as reality.

TEXT 20

अयं भुवो मण्डलमोदयाद्रे-
गोप्तैकवीरो नरदेवनाथः ।
आस्थाय जैत्रं रथमात्तचापः
पर्यस्यते दक्षिणतो यथार्कः ॥२०॥

ayaṁ bhuvo maṇḍalam odayādrer
goptaika-vīro naradeva-nāthaḥ
āsthāya jaitraṁ ratham ātta-cāpaḥ
paryasyate dakṣiṇato yathārkaḥ

ayam—this King; *bhuvaḥ*—of the world; *maṇḍalam*—the globe; *ā-udaya-adreḥ*—from the mountain where the first appearance of the sun is visible; *goptā*—will protect; *eka*—uniquely; *vīraḥ*—powerful, heroic; *nara-deva*—of all kings, gods in human society; *nāthaḥ*—the master; *āsthāya*—being situated on; *jaitram*—victorious; *ratham*—his chariot; *ātta-cāpaḥ*—holding the bow; *paryasyate*—he will circumambulate; *dakṣiṇataḥ*—from the southern side; *yathā*—like; *arkaḥ*—the sun.

TRANSLATION

This King, being uniquely powerful and heroic, will have no competitor. He will travel around the globe on his victorious chariot, holding his invincible bow in his hand and appearing exactly like the sun, which rotates in its own orbit from the south.

PURPORT

In this verse the word *yathārkaḥ* indicates that the sun is not fixed but is rotating in its orbit, which is set by the Supreme Personality of Godhead. This is confirmed in the *Brahma-saṁhitā* and also in other parts of *Śrīmad-Bhāgavatam.* In the Fifth Canto of *Śrīmad-Bhāgavatam* it is stated that the sun rotates in its own orbit at the rate of sixteen thousand miles per second. Similarly, *Brahma-saṁhitā* states, *yasyājñayā bhramati sambhṛta-kāla-cakraḥ:* the sun rotates in its own orbit according to the order of the Supreme Personality of Godhead. The conclusion is that the sun is not fixed in one place. As far as Pṛthu Mahārāja is concerned, it is indicated that his ruling power would extend all over the world. The Himalaya Mountains, from which the sunrise is first seen, are called *udayācala* or *udayādri.* It is herein indicated that Pṛthu Mahārāja's reign over the world would cover even the Himalaya Mountains and extend to the borders of all oceans and seas. In other words, his reign would cover the entire planet.

Another significant word in this verse is *naradeva.* As described in previous verses, the qualified king—be he King Pṛthu or any other king who rules over the state as an ideal king—should be understood to be God in human form. According to Vedic culture, the king is honored as the Supreme Personality of Godhead because he represents Nārāyaṇa, who also gives protection to the citizens. He is therefore *nātha*, or the proprietor. Even Sanātana Gosvāmī gave respect to the Nawab Hussain Shah as *naradeva*, although the Nawab was Muhammadan. A king or governmental head must therefore be so competent to rule over the state that the citizens will worship him as God in human form. That is the perfectional stage for the head of any government or state.

TEXT 21

अस्मै नृपालाः किल तत्र तत्र
बलिं हरिष्यन्ति सलोकपालाः ।
मंस्यन्त एषां स्त्रिय आदिराजं
चक्रायुधं तद्यश उद्धरन्त्यः ॥२१॥

asmai nṛ-pālāḥ kila tatra tatra
baliṁ hariṣyanti saloka-pālāḥ
maṁsyanta eṣāṁ striya ādi-rājaṁ
cakrāyudhaṁ tad-yaśa uddharantyaḥ

asmai—unto him; *nṛ-pālāḥ*—all the kings; *kila*—certainly; *tatra tatra*—here and there; *balim*—presentations; *hariṣyanti*—will offer; *sa*—with; *loka-pālāḥ*—the demigods; *maṁsyante*—will consider; *eṣām*—of these kings; *striyaḥ*—wives; *ādi-rājam*—the original king; *cakra-āyudham*—bearing the disc weapon; *tat*—his; *yaśaḥ*—reputation; *uddharantyaḥ*—carrying on.

TRANSLATION

When the King travels all over the world, other kings, as well as the demigods, will offer him all kinds of presentations. Their queens will also consider him the original king, who carries in His hands the emblems of club and disc, and will sing of his fame, for he will be as reputable as the Supreme Personality of Godhead.

PURPORT

As far as reputation is concerned, King Pṛthu is already known as the incarnation of the Supreme Personality of Godhead. The word *ādi-rājam* means "the original king." The original king is Nārāyaṇa, or Lord Viṣṇu. People do not know that the original king, or Nārāyaṇa, is actually the protector of all living entities. As confirmed in the *Vedas: eko bahūnāṁ yo vidadhāti kāmān* (*Kaṭha Upaniṣad* 2.2.13). Actually the Supreme Personality of Godhead is maintaining all living entities. The king, or *naradeva*, is His representative. As such, the king's duty is to personally supervise the distribution of wealth for the maintenance of all living entities. If he does so, he will be as reputable as Nārāyaṇa. As mentioned in this verse (*tad-yaśaḥ*), Pṛthu Mahārāja was actually carrying with him the reputation of the Supreme Personality of Godhead because he was actually reigning over the world in that capacity.

TEXT 22

अयं महीं गां दुदुहेऽधिराजः
प्रजापतिर्वृत्तिकरः प्रजानाम् ।
यो लीलयाद्रीन् स्वशरासकोट्या
भिन्दन् समां गामकरोद्यथेन्द्रः ॥२२॥

ayaṁ mahīṁ gāṁ duduhe 'dhirājaḥ
prajāpatir vṛtti-karaḥ prajānām
yo līlayādrīn sva-śarāsa-koṭyā
bhindan samāṁ gām akarod yathendraḥ

ayam—this King; *mahīm*—the earth; *gām*—in the form of a cow; *duduhe*—will milk; *adhirājaḥ*—extraordinary king; *prajā-patiḥ*—progenitor of mankind; *vṛtti-karaḥ*—providing living facility; *prajānām*—of the citizens; *yaḥ*—one who; *līlayā*—simply by pastimes; *adrīn*—mountains and hills; *sva-śarāsa*—of his bow; *koṭyā*—by the pointed end; *bhindan*—breaking; *samām*—level; *gām*—the earth; *akarot*—will make; *yathā*—as; *indraḥ*—the King of heaven, Indra.

TRANSLATION

This King, this protector of the citizens, is an extraordinary king and is equal to the Prajāpati demigods. For the living facility of all citizens, he will milk the earth, which is like a cow. Not only that, but he will level the surface of the earth with the pointed ends of his bow, breaking all the hills exactly as King Indra, the heavenly King, breaks mountains with his powerful thunderbolt.

TEXT 23

विस्फूर्जयन्नाजगवं धनुः स्वयं
यदाचरत्क्ष्मामविषह्यमाजौ ।
तदा निलिल्युर्दिशि दिश्यसन्तो
लाङ्गूलमुद्यम्य यथा मृगेन्द्रः ॥२३॥

visphūrjayann āja-gavaṁ dhanuḥ svayaṁ
yadācarat kṣmām aviṣahyam ājau
tadā nililyur diśi diśy asanto
lāṅgūlam udyamya yathā mṛgendraḥ

visphūrjayan—vibrating; *āja-gavam*—made of the horns of goats and bulls; *dhanuḥ*—his bow; *svayam*—personally; *yadā*—when; *acarat*—will travel; *kṣmām*—on the earth; *aviṣahyam*—irresistible; *ājau*—in battle; *tadā*—at that time; *nililyuḥ*—will hide themselves; *diśi diśi*—in all directions; *asantaḥ*—demoniac men; *lāṅgūlam*—tail; *udyamya*—keeping high; *yathā*—as; *mṛgendraḥ*—the lion.

TRANSLATION

When the lion travels in the forest with its tail turned upward, all menial animals hide themselves. Similarly, when King Pṛthu will travel over his kingdom and vibrate the string of his bow, which is made of the horns of goats and bulls and is irresistible in battle, all demoniac rogues and thieves will hide themselves in all directions.

PURPORT

It is very appropriate to compare a powerful king like Pṛthu to a lion. In India, *kṣatriya* kings are still called *siṅgh,* which means "lion." Unless rogues, thieves and other demoniac people in a state are afraid of the executive head, who rules the kingdom with a strong hand, there cannot be peace or prosperity in the state. Thus it is most regrettable when a woman becomes the executive head instead of a lionlike king. In such a situation the people are considered very unfortunate.

TEXT 24

एषोऽश्वमेधाञ् शतमाजहार
सरस्वती प्रादुरभावि यत्र ।
अहार्षीद्यस्य हयं पुरन्दरः
शतक्रतुश्चरमे वर्तमाने ॥२४॥

eṣo 'śvamedhāñ śatam ājahāra
sarasvatī prādurabhāvi yatra
ahārṣīd yasya hayaṁ purandaraḥ
śata-kratuś carame vartamāne

eṣaḥ—this King; *aśvamedhān*—sacrifices known as *aśvamedha; śatam*—one hundred; *ājahāra*—will perform; *sarasvatī*—the river of the name Sarasvatī; *prādurabhāvi*—became manifest; *yatra*—where; *ahārṣīt*—will steal; *yasya*—whose; *hayam*—horse; *purandaraḥ*—the Lord Indra; *śata-kratuḥ*—who performed one hundred sacrifices; *carame*—while the last sacrifice; *vartamāne*—is occurring.

TRANSLATION

At the source of the River Sarasvatī, this King will perform one hundred sacrifices known as aśvamedha. In the course of the last sacrifice, the heavenly King Indra will steal the sacrificial horse.

TEXT 25

एष स्वसद्मोपवने समेत्य
सनत्कुमारं भगवन्तमेकम् ।
आराध्य भक्त्यालभतामलं तज्
ज्ञानं यतो ब्रह्म परं विदन्ति ॥२५॥

eṣa sva-sadmopavane sametya
sanat-kumāraṁ bhagavantam ekam
ārādhya bhaktyālabhatāmalaṁ taj
jñānaṁ yato brahma paraṁ vidanti

eṣaḥ—this King; *sva-sadma*—of his palace; *upavane*—in the garden; *sametya*—meeting; *sanat-kumāram*—Sanat-kumāra; *bhagavantam*—the worshipable; *ekam*—alone; *ārādhya*—worshiping; *bhaktyā*—with devotion; *alabhata*—he will achieve; *amalam*—without contamination; *tat*—that; *jñānam*—transcendental knowledge; *yataḥ*—by which; *brahma*—spirit; *param*—supreme, transcendental; *vidanti*—they enjoy, they know.

TRANSLATION

This King Pṛthu will meet Sanat-kumāra, one of the four Kumāras, in the garden of his palace compound. The King will worship him with devotion and will be fortunate to receive instructions by which one can enjoy transcendental bliss.

PURPORT

The word *vidanti* refers to one who knows something or enjoys something. When a person is properly instructed by a spiritual master and understands transcendental bliss, he enjoys life. As stated in *Bhagavad-gītā* (18.54), *brahma-bhūtaḥ prasannātmā na śocati na kāṅkṣati.* When one attains to the Brahman platform, he neither hankers nor laments. He actually partakes of transcendental, blissful enjoyment. Although King Pṛthu was an incarnation of Viṣṇu, he nonetheless taught the people in his kingdom to take instructions from a spiritual master who represents the disciplic succession. Thus one can become fortunate and enjoy a blissful life even within this material world. In this verse the verb *vidanti* is sometimes taken to mean "understanding." Thus when a person understands Brahman, or the supreme source of everything, he enjoys a blissful life.

TEXT 26

तत्र तत्र गिरस्तास्ता इति विश्रुतविक्रमः ।
श्रोष्यत्यात्माश्रिता गाथाः पृथुः पृथुपराक्रमः ॥२६॥

tatra tatra giras tās tā
iti viśruta-vikramaḥ
śroṣyaty ātmāśritā gāthāḥ
pṛthuḥ pṛthu-parākramaḥ

tatra tatra—here and there; *giraḥ*—words; *tāḥ tāḥ*—many, various; *iti*—thus; *viśruta-vikramaḥ*—he whose chivalrous activities are widely reputed; *śroṣyati*—will hear; *ātma-āśritāḥ*—about himself; *gāthāḥ*—songs, narrations; *pṛthuḥ*—King Pṛthu; *pṛthu-parākramaḥ*—distinctly powerful.

TRANSLATION

In this way when the chivalrous activities of King Pṛthu come to be known to the people in general, King Pṛthu will always hear about himself and his uniquely powerful activities.

PURPORT

To artificially advertise oneself and thus enjoy a so-called reputation is a kind of conceit. Pṛthu Mahārāja was famous amongst the people because of his chivalrous activities. He did not have to advertise himself artificially. One's factual reputation cannot be covered.

TEXT 27

दिशो विजित्याप्रतिरुद्धचक्रः
स्वतेजसोत्पाटितलोकशल्यः ।
सुरासुरेन्द्रैरुपगीयमान-
महानुभावो भविता पतिर्भुवः ॥२७॥

diśo vijityāpratiruddha-cakraḥ
sva-tejasotpāṭita-loka-śalyaḥ
surāsurendrair upagīyamāna-
mahānubhāvo bhavitā patir bhuvaḥ

diśaḥ—all directions; *vijitya*—conquering; *apratiruddha*—without check; *cakraḥ*—his influence or power; *sva-tejasā*—by his own prowess; *utpāṭita*—uprooted; *loka-śalyaḥ*—the miseries of the citizens; *sura*—of demigods; *asura*—of demons; *indraiḥ*—by the chiefs; *upagīyamāna*—being glorified; *mahā-anubhāvaḥ*—the great soul; *bhavitā*—he will become; *patiḥ*—the lord; *bhuvaḥ*—of the world.

TRANSLATION

No one will be able to disobey the orders of Pṛthu Mahārāja. After conquering the world, he will completely eradicate the threefold miseries of the citizens. Then he will be recognized all over the world. At that time both the suras and the asuras will undoubtedly glorify his magnanimous activities.

PURPORT

At the time of Mahārāja Pṛthu, the world was ruled by one emperor, although there were many subordinate states. Just as there are many united states in various parts of the world, in olden days the entire world was ruled through many states, but there was a supreme emperor who ruled over all subsidiary states. As soon as there were some discrepancies in the maintenance of the *varṇāśrama* system, the emperor would immediately take charge of the small states.

The word *utpāṭita-loka-śalyaḥ* indicates that Mahārāja Pṛthu completely uprooted all the miseries of his citizens. The word *śalya* means "piercing thorns." There are many kinds of miserable thorns that pierce the citizens of a state, but all competent rulers, even up to the reign of Mahārāja Yudhiṣṭhira, uprooted all the miserable conditions of the citizens. It is stated that during the reign of Mahārāja Yudhiṣṭhira there did not even exist severe cold or scorching heat, nor did the citizens suffer from any kind of mental anxiety. This is the standard of good government. Such a peaceful and prosperous government, devoid of anxiety, was established by Pṛthu Mahārāja. Thus the inhabitants of both saintly and demoniac planets were all engaged in glorifying the activities of Mahārāja Pṛthu. Persons or nations anxious to spread their influence all over the world should consider this point. If one is able to eradicate completely the threefold miseries of the citizens, he should aspire to rule the world. One should not aspire to rule for any political or diplomatic consideration.

Thus end the Bhaktivedanta purports of the Fourth Canto, Sixteenth Chapter, of the Śrīmad-Bhāgavatam, *entitled "Praise of King Pṛthu by the Professional Reciters."*

CHAPTER SEVENTEEN

Mahārāja Pṛthu Becomes Angry at the Earth

TEXT 1

मैत्रेय उवाच

एवं स भगवान् वैन्यः ख्यापितो गुणकर्मभिः ।
छन्दयामास तान् कामैः प्रतिपूज्याभिनन्द्य च॥ १ ॥

maitreya uvāca
evaṁ sa bhagavān vainyaḥ
khyāpito guṇa-karmabhiḥ
chandayām āsa tān kāmaiḥ
pratipūjyābhinandya ca

maitreyaḥ uvāca—the great sage Maitreya continued to speak; *evam*—thus; *saḥ*—he; *bhagavān*—the Personality of Godhead; *vainyaḥ*—in the form of the son of King Vena; *khyāpitaḥ*—being glorified; *guṇa-karmabhiḥ*—by qualities and factual activities; *chandayām āsa*—pacified; *tān*—those reciters; *kāmaiḥ*—by various presentations; *pratipūjya*—offering all respects; *abhinandya*—offering prayers; *ca*—also.

TRANSLATION

The great sage Maitreya continued: In this way the reciters who were glorifying Mahārāja Pṛthu readily described his qualities and chivalrous activities. At the end, Mahārāja Pṛthu offered them various presentations with all due respect and worshiped them adequately.

TEXT 2

ब्राह्मणप्रमुखान् वर्णान् भृत्यामात्यपुरोधसः ।
पौराञ्जानपदान् श्रेणीः प्रकृतीः समपूजयत् ॥ २ ॥

brāhmaṇa-pramukhān varṇān
bhṛtyāmātya-purodhasaḥ
paurāñ jāna-padān śreṇīḥ
prakṛtīḥ samapūjayat

brāhmaṇa-pramukhān—unto the leaders of the *brāhmaṇa* community; *varṇān*—to the other castes; *bhṛtya*—servants; *amātya*—ministers; *purodhasaḥ*—to the priests; *paurān*—to the citizens; *jāna-padān*—to his countrymen; *śreṇīḥ*—to different communities; *prakṛtīḥ*—to the admirers; *samapūjayat*—he gave proper respects.

TRANSLATION

King Pṛthu thus satisfied and offered all respect to all the leaders of the brāhmaṇas and other castes, to his servants, to his ministers and to the priests, citizens, general countrymen, people from other communities, admirers and others, and thus they all became happy.

TEXT 3

विदुर उवाच

कस्माद्दधार गोरूपं धरित्री बहुरूपिणी ।
यां दुदोह पृथुस्तत्र को वत्सो दोहनं च किम् ॥ ३ ॥

vidura uvāca
kasmād dadhāra go-rūpaṁ
dharitrī bahu-rūpiṇī
yāṁ dudoha pṛthus tatra
ko vatso dohanaṁ ca kim

viduraḥ uvāca—Vidura inquired; *kasmāt*—why; *dadhāra*—took; *go-rūpam*—the shape of a cow; *dharitrī*—the earth; *bahu-rūpiṇī*—who has many other forms; *yām*—whom; *dudoha*—milked; *pṛthuḥ*—King Pṛthu; *tatra*—there; *kaḥ*—who; *vatsaḥ*—the calf; *dohanam*—the milking pot; *ca*—also; *kim*—what.

TRANSLATION

Vidura inquired from the great sage Maitreya: My dear brāhmaṇa, since mother earth can appear in different shapes, why did

she take the shape of a cow? And when King Pṛthu milked her, who became the calf, and what was the milking pot?

TEXT 4

प्रकृत्या विषमा देवी कृता तेन समा कथम् ।
तस्य मेध्यं हयं देवः कस्य हेतोरपाहरत् ॥ ४ ॥

prakṛtyā viṣamā devī
kṛtā tena samā katham
tasya medhyaṁ hayaṁ devaḥ
kasya hetor apāharat

prakṛtyā—by nature; *viṣamā*—not level; *devī*—the earth; *kṛtā*—was made; *tena*—by him; *samā*—level; *katham*—how; *tasya*—his; *medhyam*—meant for offering in the sacrifice; *hayam*—horse; *devaḥ*—the demigod Indra; *kasya*—for what; *hetoḥ*—reason; *apāharat*—stole.

TRANSLATION

The surface of the earth is by nature low in some places and high in others. How did King Pṛthu level the surface of the earth, and why did the King of heaven, Indra, steal the horse meant for the sacrifice?

TEXT 5

सनत्कुमाराद्भगवतो ब्रह्मन् ब्रह्मविदुत्तमात् ।
लब्ध्वा ज्ञानं सविज्ञानं राजर्षिः कां गतिं गतः ॥ ५ ॥

sanat-kumārād bhagavato
brahman brahma-vid-uttamāt
labdhvā jñānaṁ sa-vijñānaṁ
rājarṣiḥ kāṁ gatiṁ gataḥ

sanat-kumārāt—from Sanat-kumāra; *bhagavataḥ*—the most powerful; *brahman*—my dear *brāhmaṇa; brahma-vit-uttamāt*—well versed in the Vedic knowledge; *labdhvā*—after achieving; *jñānam*—knowledge; *sa-vijñānam*—for practical application; *rāja-ṛṣiḥ*—the great saintly King; *kām*—which; *gatim*—destination; *gataḥ*—achieved.

TRANSLATION

The great saintly King, Mahārāja Pṛthu, received knowledge from Sanat-kumāra, who was the greatest Vedic scholar. After receiving knowledge to be applied practically in his life, how did the saintly King attain his desired destination?

PURPORT

There are four Vaiṣṇava *sampradāyas* (systems) of disciplic succession. One *sampradāya* comes from Lord Brahmā, one from the goddess of fortune, one from the Kumāras, headed by Sanat-kumāra, and one from Lord Śiva. These four systems of disciplic succession are still going on. As King Pṛthu has illustrated, one who is serious about receiving transcendental Vedic knowledge must accept a *guru,* or spiritual master, in one of these four disciplic successions. It is said that unless one accepts a *mantra* from one of these *sampradāyas,* the so-called *mantra* will not act in Kali-yuga. Many *sampradāyas* have sprung up without authority, and they are misleading the people by giving unauthorized *mantras.* The rascals of these so-called *sampradāyas* do not observe the Vedic rules and regulations. Although they are addicted to all kinds of sinful activities, they still offer the people *mantras* and thus mislead them. Intelligent persons, however, know that such *mantras* will never be successful, and as such they never patronize such upstart spiritual groups. People should be very careful of these nonsensical *sampradāyas.* To get some facility for sense gratification, unfortunate people in this age receive *mantras* from these so-called *sampradāyas.* Pṛthu Mahārāja, however, showed by his example that one should receive knowledge from a bona fide *sampradāya.* Therefore Mahārāja Pṛthu accepted Sanat-kumāra as his spiritual master.

TEXTS 6–7

यच्चान्यदपि कृष्णस्य भवान् भगवतः प्रभोः ।
श्रवः सुश्रवसः पुण्यं पूर्वदेहकथाश्रयम् ॥ ६ ॥
भक्ताय मेऽनुरक्ताय तव चाधोक्षजस्य च ।
वक्तुमर्हसि योऽदुह्यद्वैन्यरूपेण गामिमाम् ॥ ७ ॥

yac cānyad api kṛṣṇasya
bhavān bhagavataḥ prabhoḥ
śravaḥ suśravasaḥ puṇyaṁ
pūrva-deha-kathāśrayam

bhaktāya me 'nuraktāya
tava cādhokṣajasya ca
vaktum arhasi yo 'duhyad
vainya-rūpeṇa gām imām

yat—which; *ca*—and; *anyat*—other; *api*—certainly; *kṛṣṇasya*—of Kṛṣṇa; *bhavān*—your good self; *bhagavataḥ*—of the Supreme Personality of Godhead; *prabhoḥ*—powerful; *śravaḥ*—glorious activities; *su-śravasaḥ*—who is very pleasing to hear about; *puṇyam*—pious; *pūrva-deha*—of His previous incarnation; *kathā-āśrayam*—connected with the narration; *bhaktāya*—unto the devotee; *me*—to me; *anuraktāya*—very much attentive; *tava*—of you; *ca*—and; *adhokṣajasya*—of the Lord, who is known as Adhokṣaja; *ca*—also; *vaktum arhasi*—please narrate; *yaḥ*—one who; *aduhyat*—milked; *vainya-rūpeṇa*—in the form of the son of King Vena; *gām*—cow, earth; *imām*—this.

TRANSLATION

Pṛthu Mahārāja was a powerful incarnation of Lord Kṛṣṇa's potencies; consequently any narration concerning his activities is surely very pleasing to hear, and it produces all good fortune. As far as I am concerned, I am always your devotee as well as a devotee of the Lord, who is known as Adhokṣaja. Please therefore narrate all the stories of King Pṛthu, who, in the form of the son of King Vena, milked the cow-shaped earth.

PURPORT

Lord Kṛṣṇa is also known as *avatārī*, which means, "one from whom all the incarnations emanate." In *Bhagavad-gītā* (10.8) Lord Kṛṣṇa says, *ahaṁ sarvasya prabhavo mattaḥ sarvaṁ pravartate:* "I am the source of all spiritual and material worlds. Everything emanates from Me." Thus Lord Kṛṣṇa is the origin of everyone's appearance. As far as this material world is concerned, Lord Brahmā, Lord Viṣṇu and Lord Śiva are all emanations from Kṛṣṇa. These three incarnations of Kṛṣṇa are called *guṇa-avatāras.* The material world is governed by three material modes of nature, and Lord Viṣṇu, Lord Brahmā and Lord Śiva respectively take charge of the modes of goodness, passion and ignorance. Mahārāja Pṛthu is also an incarnation of those qualities of Lord Kṛṣṇa by which one rules over conditioned souls.

In this verse the word *adhokṣaja,* meaning "beyond the perception of the material senses," is very significant. No one can perceive the Supreme Personality of Godhead by mental speculation; therefore a person with a poor fund of knowledge cannot understand the Supreme Personality of Godhead. Since one can form only an impersonal idea on the strength of one's material senses, the Lord is known as Adhokṣaja.

TEXT 8

सूत उवाच
चोदितो विदुरेणैवं वासुदेवकथां प्रति ।
प्रशस्य तं प्रीतमना मैत्रेयः प्रत्यभाषत ॥ ८ ॥

sūta uvāca
codito vidureṇaivaṁ
vāsudeva-kathāṁ prati
praśasya taṁ prīta-manā
maitreyaḥ pratyabhāṣata

sūtaḥ uvāca—Sūta Gosvāmī said; *coditaḥ*—inspired; *vidureṇa*—by Vidura; *evam*—thus; *vāsudeva*—of Lord Kṛṣṇa; *kathām*—narration; *prati*—about; *praśasya*—praising; *tam*—him; *prīta-manāḥ*—being very pleased; *maitreyaḥ*—the saint Maitreya; *pratyabhāṣata*—replied.

TRANSLATION

Sūta Gosvāmī continued: When Vidura became inspired to hear of the activities of Lord Kṛṣṇa in His various incarnations, Maitreya, also being inspired and being very pleased with Vidura, began to praise him. Then Maitreya spoke as follows.

PURPORT

Talk of *kṛṣṇa-kathā*, or topics about Lord Kṛṣṇa or His incarnations, is spiritually so inspiring that the reciter and hearer are never exhausted. That is the nature of spiritual talks. We have actually seen that one can never become satiated by hearing the conversations between Vidura and Maitreya. Both of them are devotees, and the more Vidura inquires, the more Maitreya is encouraged to speak. A symptom of spiritual talks is that no one feels tired. Thus upon hearing the questions of Vidura, the great sage Maitreya did not feel disgusted but rather felt encouraged to speak at greater length.

TEXT 9

मैत्रेय उवाच
यदाभिषिक्तः पृथुरङ्ग विप्रै-
रामन्त्रितो जनतायाश्च पालः ।
प्रजा निरन्ने क्षितिपृष्ठ एत्य
क्षुत्क्षामदेहाः पतिमभ्यवोचन् ॥ ९ ॥

maitreya uvāca
yadābhiṣiktaḥ pṛthur aṅga viprair
āmantrito janatāyāś ca pālaḥ
prajā niranne kṣiti-pṛṣṭha etya
kṣut-kṣāma-dehāḥ patim abhyavocan

maitreyaḥ uvāca—the great sage Maitreya said; *yadā*—when; *abhiṣiktaḥ*—was enthroned; *pṛthuḥ*—King Pṛthu; *aṅga*—my dear Vidura; *upraiḥ*—by the *brāhmaṇas; āmantritaḥ*—was declared; *janatāyāḥ*—of the people; *ca*—also; *pālaḥ*—the protector; *prajāḥ*—the citizens; *niranne*—being without food grains; *kṣiti-pṛṣṭhe*—the surface of the globe; *etya*—coming near; *kṣut*—by hunger; *kṣāma*—skinny; *dehāḥ*—their bodies; *patim*—to the protector; *abhyavocan*—they said.

TRANSLATION

The great sage Maitreya continued: My dear Vidura, at the time King Pṛthu was enthroned by the great sages and brāhmaṇas and

declared to be the protector of the citizens, there was a scarcity of food grains. The citizens actually became skinny due to starvation. Therefore they came before the King and informed him of their real situation.

PURPORT

Information is given herein concerning the selection of the king by the *brāhmaṇas.* According to the *varṇāśrama* system, the *brāhmaṇas* are considered to be the heads of the society and therefore to be situated in the topmost social position. The *varṇāśrama-dharma,* the institution of four *varṇas* and four *āśramas,* is very scientifically designed. As stated in *Bhagavad-gītā, varṇāśrama-dharma* is not a man-made institution, but is God-made. In this narration it is clearly indicated that the *brāhmaṇas* used to control the royal power. When an evil king like Vena ruled, the *brāhmaṇas* would kill him through their brahminical powers and would select a proper ruler by testing his qualifications. In other words, the *brāhmaṇas,* the intelligent men or great sages, would control the monarchical powers. Here we have an indication of how the *brāhmaṇas* elected King Pṛthu to the throne as the protector of the citizens. The citizens, being skinny due to hunger, approached the King and informed him that necessary action should be taken. The structure of the *varṇāśrama-dharma* was so nice that the *brāhmaṇas* would guide the head of state. The head of state would then give protection to the citizens. The *kṣatriyas* would take charge of protecting the people in general, and under the protection of the *kṣatriyas,* the *vaiśyas* would protect the cows, produce food grains and distribute them. *Śūdras,* the working class, would help the higher three classes by manual labor. This is the perfect social system.

TEXTS 10–11

वयं राजञ्जाठरेणाभितप्ता
यथाग्निना कोटरस्थेन वृक्षाः ।
त्वामद्य याताः शरणं शरण्यं
यः साधितो वृत्तिकरः पतिर्नः ॥१०॥

तन्नो भवानीहतु रातवेऽन्नं
क्षुधार्दितानां नरदेवदेव ।
यावन्न नङ्क्ष्यामह उज्झितोर्जा
वार्तापतिस्त्वं किल लोकपालः ॥११॥

vayaṁ rājañ jāṭhareṇābhitaptā
yathāgninā koṭara-sthena vṛkṣāḥ
tvām adya yātāḥ śaraṇaṁ śaraṇyaṁ
yaḥ sādhito vṛtti-karaḥ patir naḥ

tan no bhavān īhatu rātave 'nnaṁ
kṣudhārditānāṁ naradeva-deva
yāvan na naṅkṣyāmaha ujjhitorjā
vārtā-patis tvaṁ kila loka-pālaḥ

vayam—we; *rājan*—O King; *jāṭhareṇa*—by the fire of hunger; *abhitaptāḥ*—very much aggrieved; *yathā*—just as; *agninā*—by the fire; *koṭara-sthena*—in the hollow of a tree; *vṛkṣāḥ*—trees; *tvām*—unto you; *adya*—today; *yātāḥ*—we have come; *śaraṇam*—shelter; *śaraṇyam*—worth taking shelter of; *yaḥ*—who; *sādhitaḥ*—appointed; *vṛtti-karaḥ*—one who gives employment; *patiḥ*—master; *naḥ*—our; *tat*—therefore; *naḥ*—to us; *bhavān*—Your Majesty; *īhatu*—please try; *rātave*—to give; *annam*—food grains; *kṣudhā*—with hunger; *arditānām*—suffering; *nara-deva-deva*—O supreme master of all kings; *yāvat na*—lest; *naṅkṣyāmahe*—we will perish; *ujjhita*—being bereft of; *ūrjāḥ*—food grains; *vārtā*—of occupational engagements; *patiḥ*—bestower; *tvam*—you; *kila*—indeed; *loka-pālaḥ*—the protector of the citizens.

TRANSLATION

Dear King, just as a tree with a fire burning in the hollow of the trunk gradually dries up, we are drying up due to the fire of hunger in our stomachs. You are the protector of surrendered souls, and you have been appointed to give employment to us. Therefore we have all come to you for protection. You are not only a king, but the incarnation of God as well. Indeed, you are the king

of all kings. You can give us all kinds of occupational engagements, for you are the master of our livelihood. Therefore, O king of all kings, please arrange to satisfy our hunger by the proper distribution of food grains. Please take care of us, lest we soon die for want of food.

PURPORT

It is the duty of the king to see that everyone in the social orders—*brāhmaṇa, kṣatriya, vaiśya* and *śūdra*—is fully employed in the state. Just as it is the duty of the *brāhmaṇas* to elect a proper king, it is the duty of the king to see that all the *varṇas*—*brāhmaṇa, kṣatriya, vaiśya* and *śūdra*—are fully engaged in their respective occupational duties. It is here indicated that although the people were allowed to perform their duties, they were still unemployed. Although they were not lazy, they still could not produce sufficient food to satisfy their hunger. When the people are perplexed in this way, they should approach the head of government, and the president or king should take immediate action to mitigate the distress of the people.

TEXT 12

मैत्रेय उवाच
पृथुः प्रजानां करुणं निशम्य परिदेवितम् ।
दीर्घं दध्यौ कुरुश्रेष्ठ निमित्तं सोऽन्वपद्यत ॥१२॥

maitreya uvāca
pṛthuḥ prajānāṁ karuṇaṁ
niśamya paridevitam
dīrghaṁ dadhyau kuruśreṣṭha
nimittaṁ so 'nvapadyata

maitreyaḥ uvāca—the great saint Maitreya said; *pṛthuḥ*—King Pṛthu; *prajānām*—of the citizens; *karuṇam*—pitiable condition; *niśamya*—hearing; *paridevitam*—lamentation; *dīrgham*—for a long time; *dadhyau*—contemplated; *kuru-śreṣṭha*—O Vidura; *nimittam*—the cause; *saḥ*—he; *anvapadyata*—found out.

TRANSLATION

After hearing this lamentation and seeing the pitiable condition of the citizens, King Pṛthu contemplated this matter for a long time to see if he could find out the underlying causes.

TEXT 13

इति व्यवसितो बुद्ध्या प्रगृहीतशरासनः ।
सन्दधे विशिखं भूमेः क्रुद्धस्त्रिपुरहा यथा ॥१३॥

iti vyavasito buddhyā
pragṛhīta-śarāsanaḥ
sandadhe viśikhaṁ bhūmeḥ
kruddhas tripura-hā yathā

iti—thus; *vyavasitaḥ*—having arrived at the conclusion; *buddhyā*—by intelligence; *pragṛhīta*—having taken up; *śarāsanaḥ*—the bow; *sandadhe*—fixed; *viśikham*—an arrow; *bhūmeḥ*—at the earth; *kruddhaḥ*—angry; *tri-pura-hā*—Lord Śiva; *yathā*—like.

TRANSLATION

Having arrived at a conclusion, the King took up his bow and arrow and aimed them at the earth, exactly like Lord Śiva, who destroys the whole world out of anger.

PURPORT

King Pṛthu found out the cause for the scarcity of food grains. He could understand that it was not the people's fault, for they were not lazy in executing their duties. Rather, the earth was not producing sufficient food grains. This indicates that the earth can produce sufficiently if everything is properly arranged, but sometimes the earth can refuse to produce food grains for various reasons. The theory that there is a scarcity of food grains due to an increase of population is not a very sound theory. There are other causes that enable the earth to produce profusely or to stop producing. King Pṛthu found out the proper causes and took the necessary steps immediately.

TEXT 14

प्रवेपमाना धरणी निशाम्योदायुधं च तम् ।
गौः सत्यपाद्रवद्भीता मृगीव मृगयुद्रुता ॥१४॥

pravepamānā dharaṇī
niśāmyodāyudhaṁ ca tam
gauḥ saty apādravad bhītā
mṛgīva mṛgayu-drutā

pravepamānā—trembling; *dharaṇī*—the earth; *niśāmya*—seeing; *udāyudham*—having taken his bow and arrow; *ca*—also; *tam*—the King; *gauḥ*—a cow; *satī*—becoming; *apādravat*—began to flee; *bhītā*—very much afraid; *mṛgī iva*—like a deer; *mṛgayu*—by a hunter; *drutā*—being followed.

TRANSLATION

When the earth saw that King Pṛthu was taking his bow and arrow to kill her, she became very much afraid and began to tremble. She then began to flee, exactly like a deer, which runs very swiftly when followed by a hunter. Being afraid of King Pṛthu, she took the shape of a cow and began to run.

PURPORT

Just as a mother produces various children, both male and female, the womb of mother earth produces all kinds of living entities in various shapes. Thus it is possible for mother earth to take on innumerable shapes. At this time, in order to avoid the wrath of King Pṛthu, she took the shape of a cow. Since a cow is never to be killed, mother earth thought it wise to take the shape of a cow in order to avoid King Pṛthu's arrows. King Pṛthu, however, could understand this fact, and therefore he did not stop chasing the cow-shaped earth.

TEXT 15

तामन्वधावत्तद्वैन्यः कुपितोऽत्यरुणेक्षणः ।
शरं धनुषि सन्धाय यत्र यत्र पलायते ॥१५॥

tām anvadhāvat tad vainyaḥ
kupito 'tyaruṇekṣaṇaḥ
śaraṁ dhanuṣi sandhāya
yatra yatra palāyate

tām—the cow-shaped earth; *anvadhāvat*—he chased; *tat*—then; *vainyaḥ*—the son of King Vena; *kupitaḥ*—being very much angry; *ati-aruṇa*—very red; *īkṣaṇaḥ*—his eyes; *śaram*—an arrow; *dhanuṣi*—on the bow; *sandhāya*—placing; *yatra yatra*—wherever; *palāyate*—she flees.

TRANSLATION

Seeing this, Mahārāja Pṛthu became very angry, and his eyes became as red as the early-morning sun. Placing an arrow on his bow, he chased the cow-shaped earth wherever she would run.

TEXT 16

सा दिशो विदिशो देवी रोदसी चान्तरं तयोः ।
धावन्ती तत्र तत्रैनं ददर्शानूद्यतायुधम् ॥१६॥

sā diśo vidiśo devī
rodasī cāntaraṁ tayoḥ
dhāvantī tatra tatrainaṁ
dadarśānūdyatāyudham

sā—the cow-shaped earth; *diśaḥ*—in the four directions; *vidiśaḥ*—randomly in other directions; *devī*—the goddess; *rodasī*—towards heaven and earth; *ca*—also; *antaram*—between; *tayoḥ*—them; *dhāvantī*—fleeing; *tatra tatra*—here and there; *enam*—the King; *dadarśa*—she saw; *anu*—behind; *udyata*—taken up; *āyudham*—his weapons.

TRANSLATION

The cow-shaped earth ran here and there in outer space between the heavenly planets and the earth, and wherever she ran, the King chased her with his bow and arrows.

TEXT 17

लोके नाविन्दत त्राणं वैन्यान्मृत्योरिव प्रजाः ।
त्रस्ता तदा निववृते हृदयेन विदूयता ॥१७॥

loke nāvindata trāṇaṁ
vainyān mṛtyor iva prajāḥ
trastā tadā nivavṛte
hṛdayena vidūyatā

loke—within the three worlds; *na*—not; *avindata*—could obtain; *trāṇam*—release; *vainyāt*—from the hand of the son of King Vena; *mṛtyoḥ*—from death; *iva*—like; *prajāḥ*—men; *trastā*—being very much afraid; *tadā*—at that time; *nivavṛte*—turned back; *hṛdayena*—within her heart; *vidūyatā*—very much aggrieved.

TRANSLATION

Just as a man cannot escape the cruel hands of death, the cow-shaped earth could not escape the hands of the son of Vena. At length the earth, fearful, her heart aggrieved, turned back in helplessness.

TEXT 18

उवाच च महाभागं धर्मज्ञापन्नवत्सल ।
त्राहि मामपि भूतानां पालनेऽवस्थितो भवान् ॥१८॥

uvāca ca mahā-bhāgaṁ
dharma-jñāpanna-vatsala
trāhi mām api bhūtānāṁ
pālane 'vasthito bhavān

uvāca—she said; *ca*—and; *mahā-bhāgam*—unto the great, fortunate King; *dharma-jña*—O knower of the principles of religion; *āpanna-vatsala*—O shelter of the surrendered; *trāhi*—save; *mām*—me; *api*—indeed; *bhūtānām*—of living entities; *pālane*—in protection; *avasthitaḥ*—situated; *bhavān*—Your Majesty.

TRANSLATION

Addressing the great, opulent King Pṛthu as the knower of religious principles and shelter of the surrendered, she said: Please save me. You are the protector of all living entities. Now you are situated as the King of this planet.

PURPORT

The cow-shaped earth addressed King Pṛthu as *dharma-jña*, which refers to one who knows the principles of religion. The principles of religion dictate that a woman, a cow, a child, a *brāhmaṇa* and an old man must be given all protection by the king or anyone else. Consequently mother earth took the shape of a cow. She was also a woman. Thus she appealed to the King as one who knows the principles of religion. Religious principles also dictate that one is not to be killed if he surrenders. She reminded King Pṛthu that not only was he an incarnation of God, but he was situated as the King of the earth as well. Therefore his duty was to excuse her.

TEXT 19

स त्वं जिघांससे कस्माद्दीनामकृतकिल्बिषाम् ।
अहनिष्यत्कथं योषां धर्मज्ञ इति यो मतः ॥१९॥

sa tvaṁ jighāṁsase kasmād
dīnām akṛta-kilbiṣām
ahaniṣyat kathaṁ yoṣāṁ
dharma-jña iti yo mataḥ

saḥ—that very person; *tvam*—you; *jighāṁsase*—want to kill; *kasmāt*—why; *dīnām*—poor; *akṛta*—without having done; *kilbiṣām*—any sinful activities; *ahaniṣyat*—would kill; *katham*—how; *yoṣām*—a woman; *dharma-jñaḥ*—the knower of religious principles; *iti*—thus; *yaḥ*—one who; *mataḥ*—is considered.

TRANSLATION

The cow-shaped earth continued to appeal to the King: I am very poor and have not committed any sinful activities. I do not

know why you want to kill me. Since you are supposed to be the knower of all religious principles, why are you so envious of me, and why are you so anxious to kill a woman?

PURPORT

The earth appealed to the King in two ways. A king who knows religious principles cannot kill anyone who has not committed sinful activities. Apart from this, a woman is not to be killed, even if she does commit some sinful activities. Since the earth was innocent and was also a woman, the King should not kill her.

TEXT 20

प्रहरन्ति न वै स्त्रीषु कृतागःस्वपि जन्तवः ।
किमुत त्वद्विधा राजन् करुणा दीनवत्सलाः ॥२०॥

praharanti na vai strīṣu
kṛtāgaḥsv api jantavaḥ
kim uta tvad-vidhā rājan
karuṇā dīna-vatsalāḥ

praharanti—strike; *na*—never; *vai*—certainly; *strīṣu*—women; *kṛta-āgaḥsu*—having committed sinful activities; *api*—although; *jantavaḥ*—human beings; *kim uta*—then what to speak of; *tvat-vidhāḥ*—personalities like you; *rājan*—O King; *karuṇāḥ*—merciful; *dīna-vatsalāḥ*—affectionate to the poor.

TRANSLATION

Even if a woman does commit some sinful activity, no one should place his hand upon her. And what to speak of you, dear King, who are so merciful. You are a protector, and you are affectionate to the poor.

TEXT 21

मां विपाट्याजरां नावं यत्र विश्वं प्रतिष्ठितम् ।
आत्मानं च प्रजाश्चेमाः कथमम्भसि धास्यसि ॥२१॥

māṁ vipāṭyājarāṁ nāvaṁ
yatra viśvaṁ pratiṣṭhitam
ātmānaṁ ca prajāś cemāḥ
katham ambhasi dhāsyasi

mām—me; *vipāṭya*—breaking to pieces; *ajarām*—very strong; *nāvam*—boat; *yatra*—where; *viśvam*—all worldly paraphernalia; *pratiṣṭhitam*—standing; *ātmānam*—yourself; *ca*—and; *prajāḥ*—your subjects; *ca*—also; *imāḥ*—all these; *katham*—how; *ambhasi*—in the water; *dhāsyasi*—you will hold.

TRANSLATION

The cow-shaped earth continued: My dear King, I am just like a strong boat, and all the paraphernalia of the world is standing upon me. If you break me to pieces, how can you protect yourself and your subjects from drowning?

PURPORT

Beneath the entire planetary system is the *garbha* water. Lord Viṣṇu lies on this *garbha* water, and from His abdomen a lotus stem grows, and all the planets within the universe are floating in the air, being supported by this lotus stem. If a planet is destroyed, it must fall into the water of *garbha*. The earth therefore warned King Pṛthu that he could gain nothing by destroying her. Indeed, how would he protect himself and his citizens from drowning in the *garbha* water? In other words, outer space may be compared to an ocean of air, and each and every planet is floating on it just as a boat or island floats on the ocean. Sometimes planets are called *dvīpa*, or islands, and sometimes they are called boats. Thus the cosmic manifestation is partially explained in this reference by the cow-shaped earth.

TEXT 22

पृथुरुवाच
वसुधे त्वां वधिष्यामि मच्छासनपराङ्मुखीम् ।
भागं बर्हिषि या वृङ्क्ते न तनोति च नो वसु ॥२२॥

pṛthur uvāca
vasudhe tvāṁ vadhiṣyāmi
mac-chāsana-parāṅ-mukhīm
bhāgaṁ barhiṣi yā vṛṅkte
na tanoti ca no vasu

pṛthuḥ uvāca—King Pṛthu replied; *vasu-dhe*—my dear earthly planet; *tvām*—you; *vadhiṣyāmi*—I shall kill; *mat*—my; *śāsana*—rulings; *parāk-mukhīm*—disobedient to; *bhāgam*—your share; *barhiṣi*—in the *yajña;* *yā*—who; *vṛṅkte*—accepts; *na*—not; *tanoti*—does deliver; *ca*—and; *naḥ*—to us; *vasu*—produce.

TRANSLATION

King Pṛthu replied to the earthly planet: My dear earth, you have disobeyed my orders and rulings. In the form of a demigod you accepted your share of the yajñas we performed, but in return you have not produced sufficient food grains. For this reason I must kill you.

PURPORT

The cow-shaped earthly planet submitted that she not only was a woman, but was innocent and sinless as well. Thus she argued that she should not be killed. Besides, she pointed out that being perfectly religious-minded, the King could not violate the religious principles that forbade killing a woman. In reply, Mahārāja Pṛthu informed her that first of all she had disobeyed his orders. This was her first sinful activity. Secondly he accused her of taking her share of the *yajñas* (sacrifices) but not producing sufficient food grains in return.

TEXT 23

यवसं जग्ध्यनुदिनं नैव दोग्ध्यौधसं पयः ।
तस्यामेवं हि दुष्टायां दण्डो नात्र न शस्यते ॥२३॥

yavasaṁ jagdhy anudinaṁ
naiva dogdhy audhasaṁ payaḥ
tasyām evaṁ hi duṣṭāyāṁ
daṇḍo nātra na śasyate

yavasam—green grass; *jagdhi*—you eat; *anudinam*—daily; *na*—never; *eva*—certainly; *dogdhi*—you yield; *audhasam*—in the milk bag; *payaḥ*—milk; *tasyām*—when a cow; *evam*—thus; *hi*—certainly; *duṣṭāyām*—being offensive; *daṇḍaḥ*—punishment; *na*—not; *atra*—here; *na*—not; *śasyate*—is advisable.

TRANSLATION

Although you are eating green grass every day, you are not filling your milk bag so we can utilize your milk. Since you are willfully committing offenses, it cannot be said that you are not punishable due to your assuming the form of a cow.

PURPORT

A cow eats green grasses in the pasture and fills her milk bag with sufficient milk so that the cowherdsmen can milk her. *Yajñas* (sacrifices) are performed to produce sufficient clouds that will pour water over the earth. The word *payaḥ* can refer both to milk and to water. As one of the demigods, the earthly planet was taking her share in the *yajñas*—that is, she was eating green grass—but in return she was not producing sufficient food grains—that is, she was not filling her milk bag. Pṛthu Mahārāja was therefore justified in threatening to punish her for her offense.

TEXT 24

त्वं खल्वोषधिबीजानि प्राक् सृष्टानि स्वयम्भुवा ।
न मुञ्चस्यात्मरुद्धानि मामवज्ञाय मन्दधीः ॥२४॥

tvaṁ khalv oṣadhi-bījāni
prāk sṛṣṭāni svayambhuvā
na muñcasy ātma-ruddhāni
mām avajñāya manda-dhīḥ

tvam—you; *khalu*—certainly; *oṣadhi*—of herbs, plants and grains; *bījāni*—the seeds; *prāk*—formerly; *sṛṣṭāni*—created; *svayambhuvā*—by Lord Brahmā; *na*—do not; *muñcasi*—deliver; *ātma-ruddhāni*—hidden within yourself; *mām*—me; *avajñāya*—disobeying; *manda-dhīḥ*—less intelligent.

TRANSLATION

You have so lost your intelligence that, despite my orders, you do not deliver the seeds of herbs and grains formerly created by Brahmā and now hidden within yourself.

PURPORT

While creating all the planets in the universe, Lord Brahmā also created the seeds of various grains, herbs, plants and trees. When sufficient water falls from the clouds, the seeds fructify and produce fruits, grains, vegetables, etc. By his example, Pṛthu Mahārāja indicates that whenever there is a scarcity in food production, the head of the government should take steps to see why production is being held up and what should be done to rectify the situation.

TEXT 25

अमूषां क्षुत्परीतानामार्तानां परिदेवितम् ।
शमयिष्यामि मद्बाणैर्भिन्नायास्तव मेदसा ॥२५॥

amūṣāṁ kṣut-parītānām
ārtānāṁ paridevitam
śamayiṣyāmi mad-bāṇair
bhinnāyās tava medasā

amūṣām—of all of them; *kṣut-parītānām*—suffering from hunger; *ārtānām*—of the distressed; *paridevitam*—the lamentation; *śamayiṣyāmi*—I shall pacify; *mat-bāṇaiḥ*—by my arrows; *bhinnāyāḥ*—being cut to pieces; *tava*—of you; *medasā*—by the flesh.

TRANSLATION

Now, with the help of my arrows, I shall cut you to pieces and with your flesh satisfy the hunger-stricken citizens, who are now crying for want of grains. Thus I shall satisfy the crying citizens of my kingdom.

PURPORT

Here we find some indication of how the government can arrange for the eating of cow flesh. It is here indicated that in a rare circumstance when there is no supply of grains, the government may sanction the eating of meat. However, when there is sufficient food, the government should not allow the eating of cow's flesh just to satisfy the fastidious tongue. In other words, in rare circumstances, when people are suffering for want of grains, meat-eating or flesh-eating can be allowed, but not otherwise. The maintenance of slaughterhouses for the satisfaction of the tongue and the killing of animals unnecessarily should never be sanctioned by a government.

As described in a previous verse, cows and other animals should be given sufficient grass to eat. If despite a sufficient supply of grass a cow does not supply milk, and if there is an acute shortage of food, the dried-up cow may be utilized to feed the hungry masses of people. According to the law of necessity, first of all human society must try to produce food grains and vegetables, but if they fail in this, they can indulge in flesh-eating. Otherwise not. As human society is presently structured, there is sufficient production of grains all over the world. Therefore the opening of slaughterhouses cannot be supported. In some nations there is so much surplus grain that sometimes extra grain is thrown into the sea, and sometimes the government forbids further production of grain. The conclusion is that the earth produces sufficient grain to feed the entire population, but the distribution of this grain is restricted due to trade regulations and a desire for profit. Consequently in some places there is scarcity of grain and in others profuse production. If there were one government on the surface of the earth to handle the distribution of grain, there would be no question of scarcity, no necessity to open slaughterhouses, and no need to present false theories about overpopulation.

TEXT 26

पुमान् योषिदुत क्लीब आत्मसम्भावनोऽधमः ।
भूतेषु निरनुक्रोशो नृपाणां तद्वधोऽवधः ॥२६॥

pumān yoṣid uta klība
ātma-sambhāvano 'dhamaḥ

bhūteṣu niranukrośo
nṛpāṇāṁ tad-vadho 'vadhaḥ

pumān—a man; *yoṣit*—a woman; *uta*—also; *klībaḥ*—a eunuch; *ātma-sambhāvanaḥ*—interested in self-maintenance; *adhamaḥ*—lowest of humankind; *bhūteṣu*—to other living entities; *niranukrośaḥ*—without compassion; *nṛpāṇām*—for the kings; *tat*—of him; *vadhaḥ*—killing; *avadhaḥ*—not killing.

TRANSLATION

Any cruel person—be he a man, woman or impotent eunuch—who is only interested in his personal maintenance and has no compassion for other living entities may be killed by the king. Such killing can never be considered actual killing.

PURPORT

The planet earth is actually a woman in her constitutional form, and as such she needs to be protected by the king. Pṛthu Mahārāja argues, however, that if a citizen within the state—be he man, woman or eunuch—is not compassionate upon his fellow men, he or she may be killed by the king, and such killing is never to be considered actual killing. As far as the field of spiritual activities is concerned, when a devotee is self-satisfied and does not preach the glories of Kṛṣṇa, he is not considered a first-class devotee. A devotee who tries to preach, who has compassion upon innocent persons who have no knowledge of Kṛṣṇa, is a superior devotee. In his prayer to the Lord, Prahlāda Mahārāja said that he was not personally interested in liberation from this material world; rather, he did not wish to be liberated from this material condition until all fallen souls were delivered. Even in the material field, if a person is not interested in others' welfare, he should be considered to be condemned by the Personality of Godhead or His incarnation like Pṛthu Mahārāja.

TEXT 27

त्वां स्तब्धां दुर्मदां नीत्वा मायागां तिलशः शरैः ।
आत्मयोगबलेनेमा धारयिष्याम्यहं प्रजाः ॥२७॥

tvāṁ stabdhāṁ durmadāṁ nītvā
māyā-gāṁ tilaśaḥ śaraiḥ
ātma-yoga-balenemā
dhārayiṣyāmy ahaṁ prajāḥ

tvām—you; *stabdhām*—very much puffed up; *durmadām*—mad; *nītvā*—bringing into such a condition; *māyā-gām*—false cow; *tilaśaḥ*—into small particles like grains; *śaraiḥ*—by my arrows; *ātma*—personal; *yoga-balena*—by mystic power; *imāḥ*—all these; *dhārayiṣyāmi*—shall uphold; *aham*—I; *prajāḥ*—all the citizens, or all the living entities.

TRANSLATION

You are very much puffed up with pride and have become almost insane. Presently you have assumed the form of a cow by your mystic powers. Nonetheless I shall cut you into small pieces like grain, and I will uphold the entire population by my personal mystic powers.

PURPORT

The earth informed King Pṛthu that if he destroyed her, he and his subjects would all fall down into the waters of the *garbha* ocean. King Pṛthu now replies to that point. Although the earth assumed the shape of a cow by her mystic powers in order to be saved from being killed by the King, the King was aware of this fact and would not hesitate to cut her to pieces, just like small bits of grain. As far as the destruction of the citizens is concerned, Mahārāja Pṛthu maintained that he could uphold everyone by his own mystic powers. He did not need the help of the earthly planet. Being the incarnation of Lord Viṣṇu, Pṛthu Mahārāja possessed the power of Saṅkarṣaṇa, which is explained by the scientists as the power of gravitation. The Supreme Personality of Godhead is holding millions of planets in space without any support; similarly, Pṛthu Mahārāja would not have had any difficulty supporting all his citizens and himself in space without the help of the planet earth. The Lord is known as Yogeśvara, master of all mystic powers. Consequently the planet earth was informed by the King that she need not worry about his standing without her help.

TEXT 28

एवं मन्युमयीं मूर्तिं कृतान्तमिव बिभ्रतम् ।
प्रणता प्राञ्जलिः प्राह मही सञ्जातवेपथुः ॥२८॥

evaṁ manyumayīṁ mūrtiṁ
kṛtāntam iva bibhratam
praṇatā prāñjaliḥ prāha
mahī sañjāta-vepathuḥ

evam—thus; *manyu-mayīm*—very much angry; *mūrtim*—form; *kṛta-antam*—death personified, Yamarāja; *iva*—like; *bibhratam*—possessing; *praṇatā*—surrendered; *prāñjaliḥ*—with folded hands; *prāha*—said; *mahī*—the planet earth; *sañjāta*—arisen; *vepathuḥ*—trembling in her body.

TRANSLATION

At this time Pṛthu Mahārāja became exactly like Yamarāja, and his whole body appeared very angry. In other words, he was anger personified. After hearing him, the planet earth began to tremble. She surrendered, and with folded hands began to speak as follows.

PURPORT

The Supreme Personality of Godhead is death personified to miscreants and the supreme beloved Lord to the devotees. In *Bhagavad-gītā* (10.34) the Lord says, *mṛtyuḥ sarva-haraś cāham:* "I am all-devouring death." Faithless unbelievers, who challenge the appearance of God, will be delivered by the Supreme Personality of Godhead when He appears before them as death. Hiraṇyakaśipu, for example, challenged the authority of the Supreme Personality of Godhead, and the Lord met him in the form of Nṛsiṁhadeva and killed him. Similarly, the planet earth saw Mahārāja Pṛthu as death personified, and she also saw him in the mood of anger personified. Therefore she began to tremble. One cannot challenge the authority of the Supreme Personality of Godhead in any circumstance. It is better to surrender unto Him and take His protection at all times.

TEXT 29

धरोवाच
नमः परस्मै पुरुषाय मायया
विन्यस्तनानातनवे गुणात्मने ।
नमः स्वरूपानुभवेन निर्धुत-
द्रव्यक्रियाकारकविभ्रमोर्मये ॥२९॥

dharovāca
namaḥ parasmai puruṣāya māyayā
vinyasta-nānā-tanave guṇātmane
namaḥ svarūpānubhavena nirdhuta-
dravya-kriyā-kāraka-vibhramormaye

dharā—the planet earth; *uvāca*—said; *namaḥ*—I offer my obeisances; *parasmai*—unto the Transcendence; *puruṣāya*—unto the person; *māyayā*—by the material energy; *vinyasta*—expanded; *nānā*—various; *tanave*—whose forms; *guṇa-ātmane*—unto the source of the three modes of material nature; *namaḥ*—I offer my obeisances; *svarūpa*—of the real form; *anubhavena*—by understanding; *nirdhuta*—not affected by; *dravya*—matter; *kriyā*—action; *kāraka*—doer; *vibhrama*—bewilderment; *ūrmaye*—the waves of material existence.

TRANSLATION

The planet earth spoke: My dear Lord, O Supreme Personality of Godhead, You are transcendental in Your position, and by Your material energy You have expanded Yourself in various forms and species of life through the interaction of the three modes of material nature. Unlike some other masters, You always remain in Your transcendental position and are not affected by the material creation, which is subject to different material interactions. Consequently You are not bewildered by material activities.

PURPORT

After King Pṛthu gave his royal command, the planet earth in the shape of a cow could understand that the King was a directly empowered incarnation of the Supreme Personality of Godhead. Consequently the King knew everything—past, present and future. Thus there was no possibility of the earth's cheating him. The earth was accused of hiding the seeds of all herbs and grains, and therefore she is preparing to explain how the seeds of these herbs and grains can be again exposed. The earth knew that the King was very angry with her, and she realized that unless she pacified his anger, there was no possibility of placing a positive program before him. Therefore in the beginning of her speech she very humbly presents herself as a part and parcel of the Supreme Personality of Godhead's body. She submits that the various bodily forms manifest in the physical world are but different parts and parcels of the supreme gigantic body. It is said that the lower planetary systems are parts and parcels of the legs of the Lord, whereas the upper planetary systems are parts and parcels of the Lord's head. The Lord creates this material world by His external energy, but this external energy is in one sense not different from Him. Yet at the same time the Lord is not directly manifest in the external energy but is always situated in the spiritual energy. As stated in *Bhagavad-gītā* (9.10), *mayādhyakṣeṇa prakṛtiḥ:* material nature is working under the direction of the Lord. Therefore the Lord is not unattached to the external energy, and He is addressed in this verse as *guṇa-ātmā,* the source of the three modes of material nature. As stated in *Bhagavad-gītā* (13.15), *nirguṇaṁ guṇa-bhoktṛ ca:* although the Lord is not attached to the external energy, He is nonetheless the master of it. The philosophy of Lord Caitanya, upholding that the Lord is simultaneously one with and different from His creation (*acintya-bhedābheda-tattva*), is very easily understandable in this connection. The planet earth explains that although the Lord is attached to the external energy, He is *nirdhuta;* He is completely free from the activities of the external energy. The Lord is always situated in His internal energy. Therefore in this verse it is stated: *svarūpa-anubhavena.* The Lord remains completely in His internal potency and yet has full knowledge of the external energy as well as the internal energy, just as His devotee remains always in a transcendental position, keeping himself in the service of the Lord without becoming attached to the material body. Śrīla Rūpa Gosvāmī says that the devotee who is always engaged in the devotional service of the Lord is always liberated, regardless of his material situation. If it is possible for a devotee to remain transcendental, it is certainly possible for the Supreme Personality of Godhead to remain in His internal potency without being attached to the external potency. There should be no difficulty in understanding this situation. Just as a devotee is never bewildered by his material body, the Lord is never bewildered by the external energy of this material world. A devotee is not hampered by the material body, although he is situated in a physical body that runs according to so many material conditions, just as there are five kinds of air functioning within the body, and so many organs—the hands, legs, tongue, genitals, rectum, etc.—all working differently. The spirit soul, the living entity, who is in full knowledge of his position is always engaged in chanting Hare Kṛṣṇa, Hare Kṛṣṇa, Kṛṣṇa Kṛṣṇa, Hare Hare/ Hare Rāma, Hare Rāma, Rāma Rāma, Hare Hare and is not concerned with the bodily functions. Although the Lord is connected with the material world, He is always situated in His spiritual energy and is always unattached to the functions of the material world. As far as the material body is concerned, there are six "waves," or symptomatic material conditions: hunger, thirst, lamentation, bewilderment, old age and death. The liberated soul is never concerned with these six physical interactions. The Supreme Personality of Godhead, being the all-powerful master of all energies, has some connection with the external energy, but He is always free from the interactions of the external energy in the material world.

TEXT 30

येनाहमात्मायतनं विनिर्मिता
धात्रा यतोऽयं गुणसर्गसङ्ग्रहः ।
स एव मां हन्तुमुदायुधः स्वरा-
डुपस्थितोऽन्यं शरणं कमाश्रये ॥३०॥

yenāham ātmāyatanaṁ vinirmitā
dhātrā yato 'yaṁ guṇa-sarga-saṅgrahaḥ
sa eva māṁ hantum udāyudhaḥ svarāḍ
upasthito 'nyaṁ śaraṇaṁ kam āśraye

yena—by whom; *aham*—I; *ātma-āyatanam*—resting place of all living entities; *vinirmitā*—was created; *dhātrā*—by the Supreme Lord;

yataḥ—on account of whom; *ayam*—this; *guṇa-sarga-saṅgrahaḥ*—combination of different material elements; *saḥ*—He; *eva*—certainly; *mām*—me; *hantum*—to kill; *udāyudhaḥ*—prepared with weapons; *sva-rāṭ*—completely independent; *upasthitaḥ*—now present before me; *anyam*—other; *śaraṇam*—shelter; *kam*—unto whom; *āśraye*—I shall resort to.

TRANSLATION

The planet earth continued: My dear Lord, You are the complete conductor of the material creation. You have created this cosmic manifestation and the three material qualities, and therefore You have created me, the planet earth, the resting place of all living entities. Yet You are always fully independent, my Lord. Now that You are present before me and ready to kill me with Your weapons, let me know where I should go to take shelter, and tell me who can give me protection.

PURPORT

The planet earth herein exhibits the symptoms of full surrender before the Lord. As stated, no one can protect the person whom Kṛṣṇa is prepared to kill, and no one can kill the person whom Kṛṣṇa protects. Because the Lord was prepared to kill the planet earth, there was no one to give protection to her. We are all receiving protection from the Lord, and it is therefore proper that every one of us surrender unto Him. In *Bhagavad-gītā* (18.66) the Lord instructs:

sarva-dharmān parityajya
māṁ ekaṁ śaraṇaṁ vraja
ahaṁ tvāṁ sarva-pāpebhyo
mokṣayiṣyāmi mā śucaḥ

"Abandon all varieties of religion and just surrender unto Me. I shall deliver you from all sinful reaction. Do not fear."

Śrīla Bhaktivinoda Ṭhākura sings: "My dear Lord, whatever I have—even my mind, the center of all material necessities, namely my home, my body and whatever I have in connection with this body—I now surrender unto You. You are now completely independent to act however You like. If You like, You can kill me, and if You like, You can save me. In any case, I am Your eternal servant, and You have every right to do whatever You like."

TEXT 31

य एतदादावसृजच्चराचरं
स्वमाययात्माश्रययावितर्क्यया ।
तयैव सोऽयं किल गोप्तुमुद्यतः
कथं नु मां धर्मपरो जिघांसति ॥३१॥

ya etad ādāv asṛjac carācaraṁ
sva-māyayātmāśrayayāvitarkyayā
tayaiva so 'yaṁ kila goptum udyataḥ
kathaṁ nu māṁ dharma-paro jighāṁsati

yaḥ—one who; *etat*—these; *ādau*—in the beginning of creation; *asṛjat*—created; *cara-acaram*—moving and nonmoving living entities; *sva-māyayā*—by His own potency; *ātma-āśrayayā*—sheltered under His own protection; *avitarkyayā*—inconceivable; *tayā*—by that same *māyā;* *eva*—certainly; *saḥ*—he; *ayam*—this King; *kila*—certainly; *goptum udyataḥ*—prepared to give protection; *katham*—how; *nu*—then; *mām*—me; *dharma-paraḥ*—one who is strictly following religious principles; *jighāṁsati*—desires to kill.

TRANSLATION

In the beginning of creation You created all these moving and nonmoving living entities by Your inconceivable energy. Through this very same energy You are now prepared to protect the living entities. Indeed, You are the supreme protector of religious principles. Why are You so anxious to kill me, even though I am in the form of a cow?

PURPORT

The planet earth argues that there is no doubt that one who creates can also annihilate by his sweet will. The planet earth questions why she should be killed when the Lord is prepared to give protection to everyone. After all, it is the earth that is the resting place for all other living entities, and it is the earth that produces grains for them.

TEXT 32

नूनं बतेशस्य समीहितं जनै-
स्तन्मायया दुर्जययाकृतात्मभिः ।
न लक्ष्यते यस्त्वकरोदकारयद्-
योऽनेक एकः परतश्च ईश्वरः ॥३२॥

nūnaṁ bateśasya samīhitaṁ janais
tan-māyayā durjayayākṛtātmabhiḥ
na lakṣyate yas tv akarod akārayad
yo 'neka ekaḥ parataś ca īśvaraḥ

nūnam—surely; *bata*—certainly; *īśasya*—of the Supreme Personality of Godhead; *samīhitam*—activities, plan; *janaiḥ*—by people; *tat-māyayā*—by His potency; *durjayayā*—which is unconquerable; *akṛta-ātmabhiḥ*—who are not sufficiently experienced; *na*—never; *lakṣyate*—are seen; *yaḥ*—he who; *tu*—then; *akarot*—created; *akārayat*—caused to create; *yaḥ*—one who; *anekaḥ*—many; *ekaḥ*—one; *parataḥ*—by His inconceivable potencies; *ca*—and; *īśvaraḥ*—controller.

TRANSLATION

My dear Lord, although You are one, by Your inconceivable potencies You have expanded Yourself in many forms. Through the agency of Brahmā, You have created this universe. You are therefore directly the Supreme Personality of Godhead. Those who are not sufficiently experienced cannot understand Your transcendental activities because these persons are covered by Your illusory energy.

PURPORT

God is one, but He expands Himself in a variety of energies—the material energy, the spiritual energy, the marginal energy and so forth.

Unless one is favored and especially endowed with grace, he cannot understand how the one Supreme Personality of Godhead acts through His different energies. The living entities are also the marginal energy of the Supreme Personality of Godhead. Brahmā is also one of these living entities, but he is especially empowered by the Supreme Personality of Godhead. Although Brahmā is supposed to be the creator of this universe, actually the Supreme Personality of Godhead is its ultimate creator. In this verse the word *māyayā* is significant. *Māyā* means "energy." Lord Brahmā is not the energetic but is one of the manifestations of the Lord's marginal energy. In other words, Lord Brahmā is only an instrument. Although sometimes plans appear contradictory, there is a definite plan behind all action. One who is experienced and is favored by the Lord can understand that everything is being done according to the Lord's supreme plan.

TEXT 33

सर्गादि योऽस्यानुरुणद्धि शक्तिभि-
र्द्रव्यक्रियाकारकचेतनात्मभिः ।
तस्मै समुन्नद्धनिरुद्धशक्तये
नमः परस्मै पुरुषाय वेधसे ॥३३॥

sargādi yo 'syānuruṇaddhi śaktibhir
dravya-kriyā-kāraka-cetanātmabhiḥ
tasmai samunnaddha-niruddha-śaktaye
namaḥ parasmai puruṣāya vedhase

sarga-ādi—creation, maintenance and dissolution; *yaḥ*—one who; *asya*—of this material world; *anuruṇaddhi*—causes; *śaktibhiḥ*—by His own potencies; *dravya*—physical elements; *kriyā*—senses; *kāraka*—controlling demigods; *cetanā*—intelligence; *ātmabhiḥ*—consisting of false ego; *tasmai*—unto Him; *samunnaddha*—manifest; *niruddha*—potential; *śaktaye*—one who possesses these energies; *namaḥ*—obeisances; *parasmai*—unto the transcendental; *puruṣāya*—Supreme Personality of Godhead; *vedhase*—unto the cause of all causes.

TRANSLATION

My dear Lord, by Your own potencies You are the original cause of the material elements, as well as the performing instruments (the senses), the workers of the senses (the controlling demigods), the intelligence and the ego, as well as everything else. By Your energy You manifest this entire cosmic creation, maintain it and dissolve it. Through Your energy alone everything is sometimes manifest and sometimes not manifest. You are therefore the Supreme Personality of Godhead, the cause of all causes. I offer my respectful obeisances unto You.

PURPORT

All activities begin with the creation of the total energy, the *mahat-tattva.* Then, by the agitation of the three *guṇas*, the physical elements are created, as well as the mind, ego and the controllers of the senses. All of these are created one after another by the inconceivable energy of the Lord. In modern electronics, a mechanic may, by pushing only one button, set off an electronic chain-reaction, by which so many actions are carried out one after another. Similarly, the Supreme Personality of Godhead pushes the button of creation, and different energies create the material elements and various controllers of the physical elements, and their subsequent interactions follow the inconceivable plan of the Supreme Personality of Godhead.

TEXT 34

स वै भवानात्मविनिर्मितं जगद्
भूतेन्द्रियान्तःकरणात्मकं विभो ।
संस्थापयिष्यन्नज मां रसातला-
दभ्युज्जहाराम्भस आदिसूकरः ॥३४॥

sa vai bhavān ātma-vinirmitaṁ jagad
bhūtendriyāntaḥ-karaṇātmakaṁ vibho
saṁsthāpayiṣyann aja māṁ rasātalād
abhyujjahārāmbhasa ādi-sūkaraḥ

saḥ—He; *vai*—certainly; *bhavān*—Yourself; *ātma*—by Yourself; *vinirmitam*—manufactured; *jagat*—this world; *bhūta*—the physical elements; *indriya*—senses; *antaḥ-karaṇa*—mind, heart; *ātmakam*—consisting of; *vibho*—O Lord; *saṁsthāpayiṣyan*—maintaining; *aja*—O unborn; *mām*—me; *rasātalāt*—from the plutonic region; *abhyujjahāra*—took out; *ambhasaḥ*—from the water; *ādi*—original; *sūkaraḥ*—the boar.

TRANSLATION

My dear Lord, You are always unborn. Once, in the form of the original boar, You rescued me from the waters in the bottom of the universe. Through Your own energy You created all the physical elements, the senses and the heart, for the maintenance of the world.

PURPORT

This refers to the time when Lord Kṛṣṇa appeared as the supreme boar, Varāha, and rescued the earth, which had been merged in water. The *asura* Hiraṇyākṣa had dislocated the earth from its orbit and thrown it beneath the waters of the Garbhodaka Ocean. Then the Lord, in the shape of the original boar, rescued the earth.

TEXT 35

अपामुपस्थे मयि नाव्यवस्थिताः
प्रजा भवानद्य रिरक्षिषुः किल ।
स वीरमूर्तिः समभूद्धराधरो
यो मां पयस्युग्रशरो जिघांससि ॥३५॥

apām upasthe mayi nāvy avasthitāḥ
prajā bhavān adya rirakṣiṣuḥ kila
sa vīra-mūrtiḥ samabhūd dharā-dharo
yo mām payasy ugra-śaro jighāṁsasi

apām—of the water; *upasthe*—situated on the surface; *mayi*—in me; *nāvi*—in a boat; *avasthitāḥ*—standing; *prajāḥ*—living entities; *bhavān*—Yourself; *adya*—now; *rirakṣiṣuḥ*—desiring to protect; *kila*—

indeed; *saḥ*—He; *vīra-mūrtiḥ*—in the form of a great hero; *samabhūt*—became; *dharā-dharaḥ*—the protector of the planet earth; *yaḥ*—one who; *mām*—me; *payasi*—for the sake of milk; *ugra-śaraḥ*—with sharpened arrows; *jighāṁsasi*—you desire to kill.

TRANSLATION

My dear Lord, in this way You once protected me by rescuing me from the water, and consequently Your name has been famous as Dharādhara—He who holds the planet earth. Yet at the present moment, in the form of a great hero, You are about to kill me with sharpened arrows. I am, however, just like a boat on the water, keeping everything afloat.

PURPORT

The Lord is known as Dharādhara, meaning, "He who keeps the planet earth on His tusks as the boar incarnation." Thus the planet earth in the shape of a cow is accounting the contradictory acts of the Lord. Although He once saved the earth, He now wants to upset the earth, which is like a boat on water. No one can understand the activities of the Lord. Due to a poor fund of knowledge, human beings sometimes think the Lord's activities contradictory.

TEXT 36

नूनं जनैरीहितमीश्वराणा-
मस्मद्विधैस्तद्गुणसर्गमायया ।
न ज्ञायते मोहितचित्तवर्त्मभि-
स्तेभ्यो नमो वीरयशस्करेभ्यः ॥३६॥

nūnaṁ janair īhitam īśvarāṇām
asmad-vidhais tad-guṇa-sarga-māyayā
na jñāyate mohita-citta-vartmabhis
tebhyo namo vīra-yaśas-karebhyaḥ

nūnam—surely; *janaiḥ*—by the people in general; *īhitam*—activities; *īśvarāṇām*—of the controllers; *asmat-vidhaiḥ*—like me; *tat*—

of the Personality of Godhead; *guṇa*—of the modes of material nature; *sarga*—which brings forth creation; *māyayā*—by Your energy; *na*—never; *jñāyate*—are understood; *mohita*—bewildered; *citta*—whose minds; *vartmabhiḥ*—way; *tebhyaḥ*—unto them; *namaḥ*—obeisances; *vīra-yaśaḥ-karebhyaḥ*—who bring renown to heroes themselves.

TRANSLATION

My dear Lord, I am also the creation of one of Your energies, composed of the three modes of material nature. Consequently I am bewildered by Your activities. Even the activities of Your devotees cannot be understood, and what to speak of Your pastimes. Thus everything appears to us to be contradictory and wonderful.

PURPORT

The activities of the Supreme Personality of Godhead in His various forms and incarnations are always uncommon and wonderful. It is not possible for a tiny human being to estimate the purpose and plans of such activities; therefore Śrīla Jīva Gosvāmī has said that unless the Lord's activities are accepted as inconceivable, they cannot be explained. The Lord is eternally existing as Kṛṣṇa, the Supreme Personality of Godhead, in Goloka Vṛndāvana. He has also simultaneously expanded Himself in innumerable forms, beginning with Lord Rāma, Lord Nṛsiṁha, Lord Varāha and all the incarnations coming directly from Saṅkarṣaṇa. Saṅkarṣaṇa is the expansion of Baladeva, and Baladeva is the first manifestation of Kṛṣṇa. Therefore all these incarnations are known as *kalā*.

The word *īśvarāṇām* refers to all the Personalities of Godhead. As stated in *Brahma-saṁhitā* (5.39): *rāmādi-mūrtiṣu kalā-niyamena tiṣṭhan.* In the *Śrīmad-Bhāgavatam* it is confirmed that all the incarnations are partial expansions, or *kalā*, of the Supreme Personality of Godhead. However, Kṛṣṇa is the original Supreme Personality of Godhead. One should not take the plural number of the word *īśvarāṇām* to mean that there are many Godheads. The fact is that God is one, but He exists eternally and expands Himself in innumerable forms and acts in various ways. Sometimes the common man is bewildered by all this and considers such activities contradictory, but they are not contradictory. There is a great plan behind all the Lord's activities.

For our understanding it is sometimes said that the Lord is situated in the heart of the thief as well as in the heart of the householder, but the Supersoul in the heart of the thief dictates, "Go and steal things from that particular house," and at the same time the Lord tells the householder, "Now be careful of thieves and burglars." These instructions to different persons appear contradictory, yet we should know that the Supersoul, the Supreme Personality of Godhead, has some plan, and we should not consider such activities contradictory. The best course is to surrender unto the Supreme Personality of Godhead wholeheartedly, and, being protected by Him, remain peaceful.

Thus end the Bhaktivedanta purports of the Fourth Canto, Seventeenth Chapter, of the Śrīmad-Bhāgavatam, *entitled "Mahārāja Pṛthu Becomes Angry at the Earth."*

CHAPTER EIGHTEEN

Pṛthu Mahārāja Milks the Earth Planet

TEXT 1

मैत्रेय उवाच
इत्थं पृथुमभिष्टूय रुषा प्रस्फुरिताधरम् ।
पुनराहावनिर्भीता संस्तभ्यात्मानमात्मना ॥ १ ॥

maitreya uvāca
ittham pṛthum abhiṣṭūya
ruṣā prasphuritādharam
punar āhāvanir bhītā
saṁstabhyātmānam ātmanā

maitreyaḥ uvāca—the great saint Maitreya continued to speak; *ittham*—thus; *pṛthum*—unto King Pṛthu; *abhiṣṭūya*—after offering prayers; *ruṣā*—in anger; *prasphurita*—trembling; *adharam*—his lips; *punaḥ*—again; *āha*—she said; *avaniḥ*—the planet earth; *bhītā*—in fear; *saṁstabhya*—after settling; *ātmānam*—the mind; *ātmanā*—by the intelligence.

TRANSLATION

The great saint Maitreya continued to address Vidura: My dear Vidura, at that time, after the planet earth finished her prayers, King Pṛthu was still not pacified, and his lips trembled in great anger. Although the planet earth was frightened, she made up her mind and began to speak as follows in order to convince the King.

TEXT 2

संनियच्छाभिभो मन्युं निबोध श्रावितं च मे ।
सर्वतः सारमादत्ते यथा मधुकरो बुधः ॥ २ ॥

sanniyacchābhibho manyuṁ
nibodha śrāvitaṁ ca me
sarvataḥ sāram ādatte
yathā madhu-karo budhaḥ

sanniyaccha—please pacify; *abhibho*—O King; *manyum*—anger; *nibodha*—try to understand; *śrāvitam*—what is said; *ca*—also; *me*—by me; *sarvataḥ*—from everywhere; *sāram*—the essence; *ādatte*—takes; *yathā*—as; *madhu-karaḥ*—the bumblebee; *budhaḥ*—an intelligent person.

TRANSLATION

My dear Lord, please pacify your anger completely and hear patiently whatever I submit before you. Please turn your kind attention to this. I may be very poor, but a learned man takes the essence of knowledge from all places, just as a bumblebee collects honey from each and every flower.

TEXT 3

अस्मिँल्लोकेऽथवामुष्मिन्मुनिभिस्तत्त्वदर्शिभिः ।
दृष्टा योगाः प्रयुक्ताश्च पुंसां श्रेयःप्रसिद्धये ॥ ३ ॥

asmil loke 'thavāmuṣmin
munibhis tattva-darśibhiḥ
dṛṣṭā yogāḥ prayuktāś ca
puṁsāṁ śreyaḥ-prasiddhaye

asmin—in this; *loke*—duration of life; *atha vā*—or; *amuṣmin*—in the next life; *munibhiḥ*—by the great sages; *tattva*—the truth; *darśibhiḥ*—by those who have seen it; *dṛṣṭāḥ*—prescribed; *yogāḥ*—methods; *prayuktāḥ*—applied; *ca*—also; *puṁsām*—of the people in general; *śreyaḥ*—benefit; *prasiddhaye*—in the matter of obtaining.

TRANSLATION

To benefit all human society, not only in this life but in the next, the great seers and sages have prescribed various methods conducive to the prosperity of the people in general.

PURPORT

Vedic civilization takes advantage of the perfect knowledge presented in the *Vedas* and presented by great sages and *brāhmaṇas* for the benefit of human society. Vedic injunctions are known as *śruti*, and the additional supplementary presentations of these principles, as given by the great sages, are known as *smṛti*. They follow the principles of Vedic instruction. Human society should take advantage of the instructions from both *śruti* and *smṛti*. If one wants to advance in spiritual life, he must take these instructions and follow the principles. In *Bhakti-rasāmṛta-sindhu*, Śrīla Rūpa Gosvāmī says that if one poses himself as advanced in spiritual life but does not refer to the *śrutis* and *smṛtis* he is simply a disturbance in society. One should follow the principles laid down in *śrutis* and *smṛtis* not only in one's spiritual life but in material life as well. As far as human society is concerned, it should follow the *Manu-smṛti* as well, for these laws are given by Manu, the father of mankind.

In the *Manu-smṛti* it is stated that a woman should not be given independence, but should be given protection by her father, husband and elderly sons. In all circumstances a woman should remain dependent upon some guardian. Presently women are given full independence like men, but actually we can see that such independent women are no happier than those women who are placed under guardians. If people follow the injunctions given by the great sages, *śrutis* and *smṛtis*, they can actually be happy in both this life and the next. Unfortunately rascals are manufacturing so many ways and means to be happy. Everyone is inventing so many methods. Consequently human society has lost the standard ways of life, both materially and spiritually, and as a result people are bewildered, and there is no peace or happiness in the world. Although they are trying to solve the problems of human society in the United Nations, they are still baffled. Because they do not follow the liberated instructions of the *Vedas*, they are unhappy.

Two significant words used in this verse are *asmin* and *amuṣmin*. *Asmin* means "in this life," and *amuṣmin* means "in the next life." Unfortunately in this age, even exalted professors and learned men believe that there is no next life and that everything is finished in this life. Since they are rascals and fools, what advice can they give? Still they are passing as learned scholars and professors. In this verse the word *amuṣmin* is very explicit. It is the duty of everyone to mold his life in such a way that he will have a profitable next life. Just as a boy is educated in order to become happy later, one should be educated in this life in order to attain an eternal and prosperous life after death. It is therefore essential that people follow what is given in the *śrutis* and *smṛtis* to make sure that the human mission is successful.

TEXT 4

तानातिष्ठति यः सम्यगुपायान् पूर्वदर्शितान् ।
अवरः श्रद्धयोपेत उपेयान् विन्दतेऽञ्जसा ॥ ४ ॥

tān ātiṣṭhati yaḥ samyag
upāyān pūrva-darśitān
avaraḥ śraddhayopeta
upeyān vindate 'ñjasā

tān—those; *ātiṣṭhati*—follows; *yaḥ*—anyone who; *samyak*—completely; *upāyān*—principles; *pūrva*—formerly; *darśitān*—instructed; *avaraḥ*—inexperienced; *śraddhayā*—with faith; *upetaḥ*—being situated; *upeyān*—the fruits of activities; *vindate*—enjoys; *añjasā*—very easily.

TRANSLATION

One who follows the principles and instructions enjoined by the great sages of the past can utilize these instructions for practical purposes. Such a person can very easily enjoy life and pleasures.

PURPORT

The Vedic principles (*mahājano yena gataḥ sa panthāḥ*) urge us to follow in the footsteps of great liberated souls. In this way we can receive benefit in both this life and the next, and we can also improve our material life. By following the principles laid down by great sages and saints of the past, we can very easily understand the aim of all life. The word *avaraḥ*, meaning "inexperienced," is very significant in this verse. Every conditioned soul is inexperienced. Everyone is *abodha-jāta*—born a fool and rascal. In democratic government at the present moment all kinds of fools and rascals are making decisions. But what can they do? What is the result of their legislation? They enact something today just to whimsically repeal it tomorrow. One political party utilizes a country for one purpose, and the next moment another political party forms a different type of government and nullifies all the laws and regulations. This process of chewing the chewed (*punaḥ punaś carvita-carvaṇānām*) will never make human society happy. In order to make all human society happy and prosperous, we should accept the standard methods given by liberated persons.

TEXT 5

ताननादृत्य योऽविद्वानर्थानारभते स्वयम् ।
तस्य व्यभिचरन्त्यर्था आरब्धाश्च पुनः पुनः ॥ ५ ॥

tān anādṛtya yo 'vidvān
arthān ārabhate svayam
tasya vyabhicaranty arthā
ārabdhāś ca punaḥ punaḥ

tān—those; *anādṛtya*—neglecting; *yaḥ*—anyone who; *avidvān*—rascal; *arthān*—schemes; *ārabhate*—begins; *svayam*—personally; *tasya*—his; *vyabhicaranti*—do not become successful; *arthāḥ*—purposes; *ārabdhāḥ*—attempted; *ca*—and; *punaḥ punaḥ*—again and again.

TRANSLATION

A foolish person who manufactures his own ways and means through mental speculation and does not recognize the authority of the sages who lay down unimpeachable directions is simply unsuccessful again and again in his attempts.

PURPORT

At the present moment it has become fashionable to disobey the unimpeachable directions given by the *ācāryas* and liberated souls of the past. Presently people are so fallen that they cannot distinguish between a liberated soul and a conditioned soul. A conditioned soul is hampered by four defects: he is sure to commit mistakes, he is sure to become illusioned, he has a tendency to cheat others, and his senses are imperfect. Consequently we have to take direction from liberated persons. This

Kṛṣṇa consciousness movement directly receives instructions from the Supreme Personality of Godhead via persons who are strictly following His instructions. Although a follower may not be a liberated person, if he follows the supreme, liberated Personality of Godhead, his actions are naturally liberated from the contamination of the material nature. Lord Caitanya therefore says: "By My order you may become a spiritual master." One can immediately become a spiritual master by having full faith in the transcendental words of the Supreme Personality of Godhead and by following His instructions. Materialistic men are not interested in taking directions from a liberated person, but they are very much interested in their own concocted ideas, which make them repeatedly fail in their attempts. Because the entire world is now following the imperfect directions of conditioned souls, humanity is completely bewildered.

TEXT 6

पुरा सृष्टा ह्योषधयो ब्रह्मणा या विशाम्पते ।
भुज्यमाना मया दृष्टा असद्भिरधृतव्रतैः ॥ ६ ॥

purā sṛṣṭā hy oṣadhayo
brahmaṇā yā viśāmpate
bhujyamānā mayā dṛṣṭā
asadbhir adhṛta-vrataiḥ

purā—in the past; *sṛṣṭāḥ*—created; *hi*—certainly; *oṣadhayaḥ*—herbs and food grains; *brahmaṇā*—by Lord Brahmā; *yāḥ*—all those which; *viśām-pate*—O King; *bhujyamānāḥ*—being enjoyed; *mayā*—by me; *dṛṣṭāḥ*—seen; *asadbhiḥ*—by nondevotees; *adhṛta-vrataiḥ*—devoid of all spiritual activities.

TRANSLATION

My dear King, the seeds, roots, herbs and grains, which were created by Lord Brahmā in the past, are now being used by nondevotees, who are devoid of all spiritual understanding.

PURPORT

Lord Brahmā created this material world for the use of the living entities, but it was created according to a plan that all living entities who might come into it to dominate it for sense gratification would be given directions by Lord Brahmā in the *Vedas* in order that they might ultimately leave it and return home, back to Godhead. All necessities grown on earth—namely fruits, flowers, trees, grains, animals and animal by-products—were created for use in sacrifice for the satisfaction of the Supreme Personality of Godhead, Viṣṇu. However, the planet earth in the shape of a cow herein submits that all these utilities are being used by nondevotees, who have no plans for spiritual understanding. Although there are immense potencies within the earth for the production of grains, fruits and flowers, this production is checked by the earth itself when it is misused by nondevotees, who have no spiritual goals. Everything belongs to the Supreme Personality of Godhead, and everything can be used for His satisfaction. Things should not be used for the sense gratification of the living entities. This is the whole plan of material nature according to the directions of this material nature.

In this verse the words *asadbhiḥ* and *adhṛta-vrataiḥ* are important. The word *asadbhiḥ* refers to the nondevotees. The nondevotees have been described in *Bhagavad-gītā* as *duṣkṛtinaḥ* (miscreants), *mūḍhāḥ* (asses or rascals), *narādhamāḥ* (lowest of mankind) and *māyayāpahṛta-jñānāḥ* (those who have lost their knowledge to the power of the illusory energy). All these persons are *asat*, nondevotees. Nondevotees are also called *gṛha-vrata*, whereas the devotee is called *dhṛta-vrata*. The whole Vedic plan is that the misguided conditioned souls who have come to lord it over material nature should be trained to become *dhṛta-vrata*. This means that they should take a vow to satisfy their senses or enjoy material life only by satisfying the senses of the Supreme Lord. Activities intended to satisfy the senses of the Supreme Lord, Kṛṣṇa, are called *kṛṣṇārthe 'khila-ceṣṭāḥ*. This indicates that one can attempt all kinds of work, but one should do so to satisfy Kṛṣṇa. This is described in *Bhagavad-gītā* as *yajñārthāt karma*. The word *yajña* indicates Lord Viṣṇu. We should work only for His satisfaction. In modern times (Kali-yuga), however, people have forgotten Viṣṇu altogether, and they conduct their activities for sense gratification. Such people will gradually become poverty-stricken, for they cannot use things which are to be enjoyed by the Supreme Lord for their own sense gratification. If they continue like this, there will ultimately be a state of poverty, and no grains, fruits or flowers will be produced. Indeed, it is stated in the Twelfth

Canto of *Bhāgavatam* that at the end of Kali-yuga people will be so polluted that there will no longer be any grains, wheat, sugarcane or milk.

TEXT 7

अपालितानादृता च भवद्भिर्लोकपालकैः ।
चोरीभूतेऽथ लोकेऽहं यज्ञार्थेऽग्रसमोषधीः ॥ ७ ॥

apālitānādṛtā ca
bhavadbhir loka-pālakaiḥ
corī-bhūte 'tha loke 'haṁ
yajñārthe 'grasam oṣadhīḥ

apālitā—without being taken care of; *anādṛtā*—being neglected; *ca*—also; *bhavadbhiḥ*—like your good self; *loka-pālakaiḥ*—by the governors or kings; *corī-bhūte*—being beset by thieves; *atha*—therefore; *loke*—this world; *aham*—I; *yajña-arthe*—for the purpose of performing sacrifices; *agrasam*—have hidden; *oṣadhīḥ*—all the herbs and grains.

TRANSLATION

My dear King, not only are grains and herbs being used by nondevotees, but, as far as I am concerned, I am not being properly maintained. Indeed, I am being neglected by kings who are not punishing these rascals who have turned into thieves by using grains for sense gratification. Consequently I have hidden all these seeds, which were meant for the performance of sacrifice.

PURPORT

That which happened during the time of Pṛthu Mahārāja and his father, King Vena, is also happening at this present moment. A huge arrangement exists for the production of large-scale industrial and agricultural products, but all these products are meant for sense gratification. Therefore despite such productive capacities there is scarcity because the world's population is full of thieves. The word *corī-bhūte* indicates that the population has turned to thievery. According to Vedic understanding, men are transformed into thieves when they plan economic development for sense gratification. It is also explained in *Bhagavad-gītā* that if one eats food grains without offering them to the Supreme Personality of Godhead, Yajña, he is a thief and liable to be punished. According to spiritual communism, all properties on the surface of the globe belong to the Supreme Personality of Godhead. The population has a right to use goods only after offering them to the Supreme Personality of Godhead. This is the process of accepting *prasāda.* Unless one eats *prasāda,* he is certainly a thief. It is the duty of governors and kings to punish such thieves and maintain the world nicely. If this is not done, grains will no longer be produced, and people will simply starve. Indeed, not only will people be obliged to eat less, but they will kill one another and eat each other's flesh. They are already killing animals for flesh, so when there will no longer be grains, vegetables and fruits, they will kill their own sons and fathers and eat their flesh for sustenance.

TEXT 8

नूनं ता वीरुधः क्षीणा मयि कालेन भूयसा ।
तत्र योगेन दृष्टेन भवानादातुमर्हति ॥ ८ ॥

nūnaṁ tā vīrudhaḥ kṣīṇā
mayi kālena bhūyasā
tatra yogena dṛṣṭena
bhavān ādātum arhati

nūnam—therefore; *tāḥ*—those; *vīrudhaḥ*—herbs and grains; *kṣīṇāḥ*—deteriorated; *mayi*—within me; *kālena*—in course of time; *bhūyasā*—very much; *tatra*—therefore; *yogena*—by proper means; *dṛṣṭena*—acknowledged; *bhavān*—Your Majesty; *ādātum*—to take; *arhati*—ought.

TRANSLATION

Due to being stocked for a very long time, all the grain seeds within me have certainly deteriorated. Therefore you should immediately arrange to take these seeds out by the standard process, which is recommended by the ācāryas or śāstras.

PURPORT

When there is a scarcity of grain, the government should follow the methods prescribed in the *śāstra* and approved by the *ācāryas;* thus there will be a sufficient production of grains, and food scarcity and famine can be checked. *Bhagavad-gītā* recommends that we perform *yajña*, sacrifices. By the performance of *yajña*, sufficient clouds gather in the sky, and when there are sufficient clouds, there is also sufficient rainfall. In this way agricultural matters are taken care of. When there is sufficient grain production, the general populace eats the grains, and animals like cows, goats and other domestic animals eat the grasses and grains also. According to this arrangement, human beings should perform the sacrifices recommended in the *śāstras*, and if they do so there will no longer be food scarcity. In Kali-yuga, the only sacrifice recommended is *saṅkīrtana-yajña.*

In this verse there are two significant words: *yogena*, "by the approved method," and *dṛṣṭena*, "as exemplified by the former *ācāryas.*" One is mistaken if he thinks that by applying modern machines such as tractors, grains can be produced. If one goes to a desert and uses a tractor, there is still no possibility of producing grains. We may adopt various means, but it is essential to know that the planet earth will stop producing grains if sacrifices are not performed. The earth has already explained that because nondevotees are enjoying the production of food, she has reserved food seeds for the performance of sacrifice. Now, of course, atheists will not believe in this spiritual method of producing grains, but whether they believe or not, the fact remains that we are not independent to produce grain by mechanical means. As far as the approved method is concerned, it is enjoined in the *śāstras* that intelligent men in this age will take to the *saṅkīrtana* movement, and by so doing they shall worship the Supreme Personality of Godhead Lord Caitanya, whose bodily complexion is golden and who is always accompanied by His confidential devotees to preach this Kṛṣṇa consciousness movement all over the world. In its present condition, the world can only be saved by introducing this *saṅkīrtana*, this Kṛṣṇa consciousness movement. As we have learned from the previous verse, one who is not in Kṛṣṇa consciousness is considered a thief. Even though he may be materially very advanced, a thief cannot be placed in a comfortable position. A thief is a thief, and he is punishable. Because people are without Kṛṣṇa consciousness, they have become thieves, and consequently they are being punished by the laws of material nature. No one can check this, not even by introducing so many relief funds and humanitarian institutions. Unless the people of the world take to Kṛṣṇa consciousness, there will be a scarcity of food and much suffering.

TEXTS 9–10

वत्सं कल्पय मे वीर येनाहं वत्सला तव ।
धोक्ष्ये क्षीरमयान् कामाननुरूपं च दोहनम् ॥ ९ ॥
दोग्धारं च महाबाहो भूतानां भूतभावन ।
अन्नमीप्सितमूर्जस्वद्भगवान् वाञ्छते यदि ॥१०॥

vatsaṁ kalpaya me vīra
yenāhaṁ vatsalā tava
dhokṣye kṣīramayān kāmān
anurūpaṁ ca dohanam

dogdhāraṁ ca mahā-bāho
bhūtānāṁ bhūta-bhāvana
annam īpsitam ūrjasvad
bhagavān vāñchate yadi

vatsam—a calf; *kalpaya*—arrange; *me*—for me; *vīra*—O hero; *yena*—by which; *aham*—I; *vatsalā*—affectionate; *tava*—your; *dhokṣye*—shall fulfill; *kṣīra-mayān*—in the form of milk; *kāmān*—desired necessities; *anurūpam*—according to different living entities; *ca*—also; *dohanam*—milking pot; *dogdhāram*—milkman; *ca*—also; *mahā-bāho*—O mighty-armed one; *bhūtānām*—of all living entities; *bhūta-bhāvana*—O protector of the living entities; *annam*—food grains; *īpsitam*—desired; *ūrjaḥ-vat*—nourishing; *bhagavān*—your worshipable self; *vāñchate*—desires; *yadi*—if.

TRANSLATION

O great hero, protector of living entities, if you desire to relieve the living entities by supplying them sufficient grain, and if you

desire to nourish them by taking milk from me, you should make arrangements to bring a calf suitable for this purpose and a pot in which the milk can be kept, as well as a milkman to do the work. Since I will be very much affectionate towards my calf, your desire to take milk from me will be fulfilled.

PURPORT

These are nice instructions for milking a cow. The cow must first have a calf so that out of affection for the calf she will voluntarily give sufficient milk. There must also be an expert milkman and a suitable pot in which to keep the milk. Just as a cow cannot deliver sufficient milk without being affectionate to her calf, the earth cannot produce sufficient necessities without feeling affection for those who are Kṛṣṇa conscious. Even though the earth's being in the shape of a cow may be taken figuratively, the meaning herein is very explicit. Just as a calf can derive milk from a cow, all living entities—including animals, birds, bees, reptiles and aquatics—can receive their respective foods from the planet earth, provided that human beings are not *asat*, or *adhṛta-vrata*, as we have previously discussed. When human society becomes *asat*, or ungodly, or devoid of Kṛṣṇa consciousness, the entire world suffers. If human beings are well-behaved, animals will also receive sufficient food and be happy. The ungodly human being, ignorant of his duty to give protection and food to the animals, kills them to compensate for the insufficient production of grains. Thus no one is satisfied, and that is the cause for the present condition in today's world.

TEXT 11

समां च कुरु मां राजन्देववृष्टं यथा पयः ।
अपर्तावपि भद्रं ते उपावर्तेत मे विभो ॥११॥

samāṁ ca kuru māṁ rājan
deva-vṛṣṭaṁ yathā payaḥ
apartāv api bhadraṁ te
upāvarteta me vibho

samām—equally level; *ca*—also; *kuru*—make; *mām*—me; *rājan*—O King; *deva-vṛṣṭam*—fallen as rain by the mercy of King Indra; *yathā*—

so that; *payaḥ*—water; *apa-ṛtau*—when the rainy season has ceased; *api*—even; *bhadram*—auspiciousness; *te*—unto you; *upāvarteta*—it can remain; *me*—on me; *vibho*—O Lord.

TRANSLATION

My dear King, may I inform you that you have to make the entire surface of the globe level. This will help me, even when the rainy season has ceased. Rainfall comes by the mercy of King Indra. Rainfall will remain on the surface of the globe, always keeping the earth moistened, and thus it will be auspicious for all kinds of production.

PURPORT

King Indra of the heavenly planets is in charge of throwing thunderbolts and giving rainfall. Generally thunderbolts are thrown on the tops of hills in order to break them to pieces. As these pieces are spread asunder in due course of time, the surface of the globe gradually becomes fit for agriculture. Level land is especially conducive to the production of grain. Thus the planet earth requested Mahārāja Pṛthu to level the surface of the earth, breaking up the high land and mountains.

TEXT 12

इति प्रियं हितं वाक्यं भुव आदाय भूपतिः ।
वत्सं कृत्वा मनुं पाणावदुहत्सकलौषधीः ॥१२॥

iti priyaṁ hitaṁ vākyaṁ
bhuva ādāya bhūpatiḥ
vatsaṁ kṛtvā manuṁ pāṇāv
aduhat sakalauṣadhīḥ

iti—thus; *priyam*—pleasing; *hitam*—beneficial; *vākyam*—words; *bhuvaḥ*—of the earth; *ādāya*—taking into consideration; *bhū-patiḥ*—the King; *vatsam*—calf; *kṛtvā*—making; *manum*—Svāyambhuva Manu; *pāṇau*—in his hands; *aduhat*—milked; *sakala*—all; *oṣadhīḥ*—herbs and grains.

TRANSLATION

After hearing the auspicious and pleasing words of the planet earth, the King accepted them. He then transformed Svāyambhuva Manu into a calf and milked all the herbs and grains from the earth in the form of a cow, keeping them in his cupped hands.

TEXT 13

तथापरे च सर्वत्र सारमाददते बुधाः ।
ततोऽन्ये च यथाकामं दुदुहुः पृथुभाविताम् ॥१३॥

tathāpare ca sarvatra
sāram ādadate budhāḥ
tato 'nye ca yathā-kāmaṁ
duduhuḥ pṛthu-bhāvitām

tathā—so; *apare*—others; *ca*—also; *sarvatra*—everywhere; *sāram*—the essence; *ādadate*—took; *budhāḥ*—the intelligent class of men; *tataḥ*—thereafter; *anye*—others; *ca*—also; *yathā-kāmam*—as much as they desired; *duduhuḥ*—milked; *pṛthu-bhāvitām*—the planet earth, controlled by Pṛthu Mahārāja.

TRANSLATION

Others, who were as intelligent as King Pṛthu, also took the essence out of the earthly planet. Indeed, everyone took this opportunity to follow in the footsteps of King Pṛthu and get whatever he desired from the planet earth.

PURPORT

The planet earth is also called *vasundharā*. The word *vasu* means "wealth," and *dharā* means "one who holds." All creatures within the earth fulfill the necessities required for human beings, and all living entities can be taken out of the earth by the proper means. As suggested by the planet earth, and accepted and initiated by King Pṛthu, whatever is taken from the earth—either from the mines, from the surface of the globe or from the atmosphere—should always be considered the property of the Supreme Personality of Godhead and should be used for Yajña, Lord Viṣṇu. As soon as the process of *yajña* is stopped, the earth will withhold all productions—vegetables, trees, plants, fruits, flowers, other agricultural products and minerals. As confirmed in *Bhagavad-gītā*, the process of *yajña* was instituted from the beginning of creation. By the regular performance of *yajña*, the equal distribution of wealth and the restriction of sense gratification, the entire world will be made peaceful and prosperous. As already mentioned, in this age of Kali the simple performance of *saṅkīrtana-yajña*—the holding of festivals as initiated by the International Society for Krishna Consciousness—should be introduced in every town and village. Intelligent men should encourage the performance of *saṅkīrtana-yajña* by their personal behavior. This means that they should follow the process of austerity by restricting themselves from illicit sex life, meat-eating, gambling and intoxication. If the intelligent men, or the *brāhmaṇas* of society, would follow the rules and regulations, certainly the entire face of this present world, which is in such chaotic condition, would change, and people would be happy and prosperous.

TEXT 14

ऋषयो दुदुहुर्देवीमिन्द्रियेष्वथ सत्तम ।
वत्सं बृहस्पतिं कृत्वा पयश्छन्दोमयं शुचि ॥१४॥

ṛṣayo duduhur devīm
indriyeṣv atha sattama
vatsaṁ bṛhaspatiṁ kṛtvā
payaś chandomayaṁ śuci

ṛṣayaḥ—the great sages; *duduhuḥ*—milked; *devīm*—the earth; *indriyeṣu*—in the senses; *atha*—then; *sattama*—O Vidura; *vatsam*—the calf; *bṛhaspatim*—the sage Bṛhaspati; *kṛtvā*—making; *payaḥ*—milk; *chandaḥ-mayam*—in the form of the Vedic hymns; *śuci*—pure.

TRANSLATION

All the great sages transformed Bṛhaspati into a calf, and making the senses into a pot, they milked all kinds of Vedic knowledge to purify words, mind and hearing.

PURPORT

Bṛhaspati is the priest of the heavenly planets. Vedic knowledge was received in logical order by the great sages through Bṛhaspati for the benefit of human society, not only on this planet, but throughout the universes. In other words, Vedic knowledge is considered one of the necessities for human society. If human society remains satisfied simply by taking grains from the planet earth as well as other necessities for maintaining the body, society will not be sufficiently prosperous. Humanity must have food for the mind and ear, as well as for the purpose of vibration. As far as transcendental vibrations are concerned, the essence of all Vedic knowledge is the *mahā-mantra*—Hare Kṛṣṇa, Hare Kṛṣṇa, Kṛṣṇa Kṛṣṇa, Hare Hare/ Hare Rāma, Hare Rāma, Rāma Rāma, Hare Hare. In Kali-yuga, if this Vedic *mahā-mantra* is chanted regularly and heard regularly by the devotional process of *śravaṇaṁ kīrtanam*, it will purify all societies, and thus humanity will be happy both materially and spiritually.

TEXT 15

कृत्वा वत्सं सुरगणा इन्द्रं सोममदूदुहन् ।
हिरण्मयेन पात्रेण वीर्यमोजो बलं पयः ॥१५॥

kṛtvā vatsaṁ sura-gaṇā
indraṁ somam adūduhan
hiraṇmayena pātreṇa
vīryam ojo balaṁ payaḥ

kṛtvā—making; *vatsam*—calf; *sura-gaṇāḥ*—the demigods; *indram*—Indra, King of heaven; *somam*—nectar; *adūduhan*—they milked out; *hiraṇmayena*—golden; *pātreṇa*—with a pot; *vīryam*—mental power; *ojaḥ*—strength of the senses; *balam*—strength of the body; *payaḥ*—milk.

TRANSLATION

All the demigods made Indra, the King of heaven, into a calf, and from the earth they milked the beverage soma, which is nectar. Thus they became very powerful in mental speculation and bodily and sensual strength.

PURPORT

In this verse the word *soma* means "nectar." *Soma* is a kind of beverage made in the heavenly planets from the moon to the kingdoms of the demigods in the various higher planetary systems. By drinking this *soma* beverage the demigods become more powerful mentally and increase their sensual power and bodily strength. The words *hiraṇmayena pātreṇa* indicate that this *soma* beverage is not an ordinary intoxicating liquor. The demigods would not touch any kind of liquor. Nor is *soma* a kind of drug. It is a different kind of beverage, available in the heavenly planets. *Soma* is far different from the liquors made for demoniac people, as explained in the next verse.

TEXT 16

दैतेया दानवा वत्सं प्रह्लादमसुरर्षभम् ।
विधायादूदुहन् क्षीरमयःपात्रे सुरासवम् ॥१६॥

daiteyā dānavā vatsaṁ
prahlādam asurarṣabham
vidhāyādūduhan kṣīram
ayaḥ-pātre surāsavam

daiteyāḥ—the sons of Diti; *dānavāḥ*—demons; *vatsam*—the calf; *prahlādam*—Prahlāda Mahārāja; *asura*—demon; *ṛṣabham*—the chief; *vidhāya*—making; *adūduhan*—they milked out; *kṣīram*—milk; *ayaḥ*—iron; *pātre*—in a pot; *surā*—liquor; *āsavam*—fermented liquids like beer.

TRANSLATION

The sons of Diti and the demons transformed Prahlāda Mahārāja, who was born in an asura family, into a calf, and they extracted various kinds of liquor and beer, which they put into a pot made of iron.

PURPORT

The demons also have their own types of beverages in the form of liquors and beers, just as the demigods use *soma-rasa* for their drinking purposes. The demons born of Diti take great pleasure in drinking wine and beer. Even today people of demoniac nature are very much addicted to liquor and beer. The name of Prahlāda Mahārāja is very significant in this connection. Because Prahlāda Mahārāja was born in a family of demons, as the son of Hiraṇyakaśipu, by his mercy the demons were and still are able to have their drinks in the form of wine and beer. The word *ayaḥ* (iron) is very significant. Whereas the nectarean *soma* was put in a golden pot, the liquors and beers were put in an iron pot. Because the liquor and beer are inferior, they are placed in an iron pot, and because *soma-rasa* is superior, it is placed in a golden pot.

TEXT 17

गन्धर्वाप्सरसोऽधुक्षन् पात्रे पद्ममये पयः ।
वत्सं विश्वावसुं कृत्वा गान्धर्वं मधु सौभगम् ॥१७॥

gandharvāpsaraso 'dhukṣan
pātre padmamaye payaḥ
vatsaṁ viśvāvasuṁ kṛtvā
gāndharvaṁ madhu saubhagam

gandharva—inhabitants of the Gandharva planet; *apsarasaḥ*—the inhabitants of the Apsarā planet; *adhukṣan*—milked out; *pātre*—in a pot; *padma-maye*—made of a lotus; *payaḥ*—milk; *vatsam*—calf; *viśvāvasum*—of the name Viśvāvasu; *kṛtvā*—making; *gāndharvam*—songs; *madhu*—sweet; *saubhagam*—beauty.

TRANSLATION

The inhabitants of Gandharvaloka and Apsaroloka made Viśvāvasu into a calf, and they drew the milk into a lotus flower pot. The milk took the shape of sweet musical art and beauty.

TEXT 18

वत्सेन पितरोऽर्यम्णा कव्यं क्षीरमधुक्षत ।
आमपात्रे महाभागाः श्रद्धया श्राद्धदेवताः ॥१८॥

vatsena pitaro 'ryamṇā
kavyaṁ kṣīram adhukṣata
āma-pātre mahā-bhāgāḥ
śraddhayā śrāddha-devatāḥ

vatsena—by the calf; *pitaraḥ*—the inhabitants of Pitṛloka; *aryamṇā*—by the god of Pitṛloka, Aryamā; *kavyam*—offerings of food to ancestors; *kṣīram*—milk; *adhukṣata*—took out; *āma-pātre*—into an unbaked earthen pot; *mahā-bhāgāḥ*—the greatly fortunate; *śraddhayā*—with great faith; *śrāddha-devatāḥ*—the demigods presiding over *śrāddha* ceremonies in honor of deceased relatives.

TRANSLATION

The fortunate inhabitants of Pitṛloka, who preside over the funeral ceremonies, made Aryamā into a calf. With great faith they milked kavya, food offered to the ancestors, into an unbaked earthen pot.

PURPORT

In *Bhagavad-gītā* (9.25) it is said, *pitṝn yānti pitṛ-vratāḥ.* Those who are interested in family welfare are called *pitṛ-vratāḥ.* There is a planet called Pitṛloka, and the predominating deity of that planet is called Aryamā. He is somewhat of a demigod, and by satisfying him one can help ghostly family members develop a gross body. Those who are very sinful and attached to their family, house, village or country do not receive a gross body made of material elements but remain in a subtle body, composed of mind, ego and intelligence. Those who live in such subtle bodies are called ghosts. This ghostly position is very painful because a ghost has intelligence, mind and ego and wants to enjoy material life, but because he doesn't have a gross material body, he can only create disturbances for want of material satisfaction. It is the duty of family members, especially the son, to offer oblations to the demigod Aryamā or to Lord Viṣṇu. From time immemorial in India the son of a dead man goes to Gayā and, at a Viṣṇu temple there, offers oblations for the benefit of his ghostly father. It is not that everyone's father becomes a ghost, but the oblations of *piṇḍa* are offered to the lotus feet of Lord Viṣṇu so that if a family member happens to become a ghost, he will be favored with a gross body. However, if one is habituated to taking the *prasāda* of Lord Viṣṇu, there is no chance of his becoming a ghost or anything lower than a human being. In Vedic civilization there is a performance called *śrāddha* by which food is offered with faith and devotion. If one offers oblations with faith and devotion—either to the lotus feet of Lord Viṣṇu or to His representative in Pitṛloka, Aryamā—one's forefathers will attain material bodies to enjoy whatever material enjoyment is due them. In other words, they do not have to become ghosts.

TEXT 19

प्रकल्प्य वत्सं कपिलं सिद्धाः सङ्कल्पनामयीम् ।
सिद्धिं नभसि विद्यां च ये च विद्याधरादयः ॥१९॥

prakalpya vatsaṁ kapilaṁ
siddhāḥ saṅkalpanāmayīm
siddhiṁ nabhasi vidyāṁ ca
ye ca vidyādharādayaḥ

prakalpya—appointing; *vatsam*—calf; *kapilam*—the great sage Kapila; *siddhāḥ*—the inhabitants of Siddhaloka; *saṅkalpanā-mayīm*—proceeding from will; *siddhim*—yogic perfection; *nabhasi*—in the sky; *vidyām*—knowledge; *ca*—also; *ye*—those who; *ca*—also; *vidyādhara-ādayaḥ*—the inhabitants of Vidyādhara-loka, and so on.

TRANSLATION

After this, the inhabitants of Siddhaloka, as well as the inhabitants of Vidyādhara-loka, transformed the great sage Kapila into a calf, and making the whole sky into a pot, they milked out specific yogic mystic powers, beginning with aṇimā. Indeed, the inhabitants of Vidyādhara-loka acquired the art of flying in the sky.

PURPORT

The inhabitants of both Siddhaloka and Vidyādhara-loka are naturally endowed with mystic yogic powers by which they not only can fly in outer space without a vehicle but can also fly from one planet to another simply by exerting their will. Just as fish can swim within water, the residents of Vidyādhara-loka can swim in the ocean of air. As far as the inhabitants of Siddhaloka are concerned, they are endowed with all mystic powers. The *yogīs* in this planet practice the eightfold yogic mysticism—namely *yama, niyama, āsana, prāṇāyāma, pratyāhāra, dhāraṇā, dhyāna* and *samādhi.* By regularly practicing the yogic processes one after another, the *yogīs* attain various perfections; they can become smaller than the smallest, heavier than the heaviest, etc. They can even manufacture a planet, get whatever they like and control whatever man they want. All the residents of Siddhaloka are naturally endowed with these mystic yogic powers. It is certainly a very wonderful thing if we see a person on this planet flying in the sky without a vehicle, but in Vidyādhara-loka such flying is as commonplace as a bird's flying in the sky. Similarly, in Siddhaloka all the inhabitants are great *yogīs*, perfect in mystic powers.

The name of Kapila Muni is significant in this verse because He was the expounder of the Sāṅkhya philosophical system, and His father, Kardama Muni, was a great *yogī* and mystic. Indeed, Kardama Muni prepared a great airplane, which was as large as a small town and had various gardens, palatial buildings, servants and maidservants. With all this paraphernalia, Kapiladeva's mother, Devahūti, and His father, Kardama Muni, traveled all over the universes and visited different planets.

TEXT 20

अन्ये च मायिनो मायामन्तर्धानाद्भुतात्मनाम् ।
मयं प्रकल्प्य वत्सं ते दुदुहुर्धारणामयीम् ॥२०॥

anye ca māyino māyām
antardhānādbhutātmanām
mayaṁ prakalpya vatsaṁ te
duduhur dhāraṇāmayīm

anye—others; *ca*—also; *māyinaḥ*—mystic magicians; *māyām*—mystic powers; *antardhāna*—disappearing; *adbhuta*—wonderful; *ātmanām*—of the body; *mayam*—the demon named Maya; *prakalpya*—making; *vatsam*—the calf; *te*—they; *duduhuḥ*—milked out; *dhāraṇāmayīm*—proceeding from will.

TRANSLATION

Others also, the inhabitants of planets known as Kimpuruṣa-loka, made the demon Maya into a calf, and they milked out mystic powers by which one can disappear immediately from another's vision and appear again in a different form.

PURPORT

It is said that the inhabitants of Kimpuruṣa-loka can perform many wonderful mystic demonstrations. In other words, they can exhibit as many wonderful things as one can imagine. The inhabitants of this planet can do whatever they like, or whatever they imagine. Such powers are also mystic powers. The possession of such mystic power is called *īśitā.* The demons generally learn such mystic powers by the practice of *yoga.* In the *Daśama-skandha,* the Tenth Canto, of *Śrīmad-Bhāgavatam,* there is a vivid description of how the demons appear before Kṛṣṇa in various wonderful forms. For instance, Bakāsura appeared before Kṛṣṇa and His cowherd boyfriends as a gigantic crane. While present on this planet, Lord Kṛṣṇa had to fight with many demons who could exhibit the wonderful mystic powers of Kimpuruṣa-loka. Although the inhabitants of Kimpuruṣa-loka are naturally endowed with such powers, one can attain these powers on this planet by performing different yogic practices.

TEXT 21

यक्षरक्षांसि भूतानि पिशाचाः पिशिताशनाः ।
भूतेशवत्सा दुदुहुः कपाले क्षतजासवम् ॥२१॥

yakṣa-rakṣāṁsi bhūtāni
piśācāḥ piśitāśanāḥ
bhūteśa-vatsā duduhuḥ
kapāle kṣatajāsavam

yakṣa—the Yakṣas (the descendants of Kuvera); *rakṣāṁsi*—the Rākṣasas (meat-eaters); *bhūtāni*—ghosts; *piśācāḥ*—witches; *piśita-aśanāḥ*—who are all habituated to eating flesh; *bhūteśa*—Lord Śiva's incarnation Rudra; *vatsāḥ*—whose calf; *duduhuḥ*—milked out; *kapāle*—in a pot of skulls; *kṣata-ja*—blood; *āsavam*—a fermented beverage.

TRANSLATION

Then the Yakṣas, Rākṣasas, ghosts and witches, who are habituated to eating flesh, transformed Lord Śiva's incarnation Rudra [Bhūtanātha] into a calf and milked out beverages made of blood and put them in a pot made of skulls.

PURPORT

There are some types of living entities in the form of human beings whose living conditions and eatables are most abominable. Generally they eat flesh and fermented blood, which is mentioned in this verse as *kṣatajāsavam.* The leaders of such degraded men known as Yakṣas, Rākṣasas, *bhūtas* and *piśācas,* are all in the mode of ignorance. They have been placed under the control of Rudra. Rudra is the incarnation of Lord Śiva and is in charge of the mode of ignorance in material nature. Another name of Lord Śiva is Bhūtanātha, meaning "master of ghosts." Rudra was born from between Brahmā's eyes when Brahmā was very angry at the four Kumāras.

TEXT 22

तथाहयो दन्दशूकाः सर्पा नागाश्च तक्षकम् ।
विधाय वत्सं दुदुहुर्बिलपात्रे विषं पयः ॥२२॥

tathāhayo dandaśūkāḥ
sarpā nāgāś ca takṣakam
vidhāya vatsaṁ duduhur
bila-pātre viṣaṁ payaḥ

tathā—similarly; *ahayaḥ*—snakes without hoods; *dandaśūkāḥ*—scorpions; *sarpāḥ*—cobras; *nāgāḥ*—big snakes; *ca*—and; *takṣakam*—Takṣaka, chief of the snakes; *vidhāya*—making; *vatsam*—calf; *duduhuḥ*—milked out; *bila-pātre*—in the pot of snake holes; *viṣam*—poison; *payaḥ*—as milk.

TRANSLATION

Thereafter cobras and snakes without hoods, large snakes, scorpions and many other poisonous animals took poison out of the

planet earth as their milk and kept this poison in snake holes. They made a calf out of Takṣaka.

PURPORT

Within this material world there are various types of living entities, and the different types of reptiles and scorpions mentioned in this verse are also provided with their sustenance by the arrangement of the Supreme Personality of Godhead. The point is that everyone is taking his eatables from the planet earth. According to one's association with the material qualities, one develops a certain type of character. *Payaḥ-pānaṁ bhujaṅgānām:* if one feeds a serpent milk, the snake will simply increase his venom. However, if one supplies milk to a talented sage or saint, the sage will develop finer brain tissues by which he can contemplate higher, spiritual life. Thus the Lord is supplying everyone food, but according to the living entity's association with the modes of material nature, the living entity develops his specific character.

TEXTS 23–24

पशवो यवसं क्षीरं वत्सं कृत्वा च गोवृषम् ।
अरण्यपात्रे चाधुक्षन्मृगेन्द्रेण च दंष्ट्रिणः ॥२३॥
क्रव्यादाः प्राणिनः क्रव्यं दुदुहुः स्वे कलेवरे ।
सुपर्णवत्सा विहगाश्चरं चाचरमेव च ॥२४॥

paśavo yavasaṁ kṣīraṁ
vatsaṁ kṛtvā ca go-vṛṣam
araṇya-pātre cādhukṣan
mṛgendreṇa ca daṁṣṭriṇaḥ

kravyādāḥ prāṇinaḥ kravyaṁ
duduhuḥ sve kalevare
suparṇa-vatsā vihagāś
caraṁ cācaram eva ca

paśavaḥ—cattle; *yavasam*—green grasses; *kṣīram*—milk; *vatsam*—the calf; *kṛtvā*—making; *ca*—also; *go-vṛṣam*—the bull carrier of Lord

Śiva; *araṇya-pātre*—in the pot of the forest; *ca*—also; *adhukṣan*—milked out; *mṛga-indreṇa*—by the lion; *ca*—and; *daṁṣṭriṇaḥ*—animals with sharp teeth; *kravya-adāḥ*—animals who eat raw flesh; *prāṇinaḥ*—living entities; *kravyam*—flesh; *duduhuḥ*—took out; *sve*—own; *kale-vare*—in the pot of their body; *suparṇa*—Garuḍa; *vatsāḥ*—whose calf; *vihagāḥ*—the birds; *caram*—moving living entities; *ca*—also; *aca-ram*—nonmoving living entities; *eva*—certainly; *ca*—also.

TRANSLATION

The four-legged animals like the cows made a calf out of the bull who carries Lord Śiva and made a milking pot out of the forest. Thus they got fresh green grasses to eat. Ferocious animals like tigers transformed a lion into a calf, and thus they were able to get flesh for milk. The birds made a calf out of Garuḍa and took milk from the planet earth in the form of moving insects and nonmoving plants and grasses.

PURPORT

There are many carnivorous birds descended from Garuḍa, the winged carrier of Lord Viṣṇu. Indeed, there is a particular type of bird that is very fond of eating monkeys. Eagles are fond of eating goats, and of course many birds eat only fruits and berries. Therefore the words *caram*, referring to moving animals, and *acaram*, referring to grasses, fruits and vegetables, are mentioned in this verse.

TEXT 25

वटवत्सा वनस्पतयः पृथग्रसमयं पयः ।
गिरयो हिमवद्वत्सा नानाधातून् स्वसानुषु ॥२५॥

vaṭa-vatsā vanaspatayaḥ
pṛthag rasamayaṁ payaḥ
girayo himavad-vatsā
nānā-dhātūn sva-sānuṣu

vaṭa-vatsāḥ—making the banyan tree a calf; *vanaḥ-patayaḥ*—the trees; *pṛthak*—different; *rasa-mayam*—in the form of juices; *payaḥ*—

milk; *girayaḥ*—the hills and mountains; *himavat-vatsāḥ*—making the Himalayas the calf; *nānā*—various; *dhātūn*—minerals; *sva*—own; *sānuṣu*—on their peaks.

TRANSLATION

The trees made a calf out of the banyan tree, and thus they derived milk in the form of many delicious juices. The mountains transformed the Himalayas into a calf, and they milked a variety of minerals into a pot made of the peaks of hills.

TEXT 26

सर्वे स्वमुख्यवत्सेन स्वे स्वे पात्रे पृथक् पयः ।
सर्वकामदुघां पृथ्वीं दुदुहुः पृथुभाविताम् ॥२६॥

sarve sva-mukhya-vatsena
sve sve pātre pṛthak payaḥ
sarva-kāma-dughāṁ pṛthvīṁ
duduhuḥ pṛthu-bhāvitām

sarve—all; *sva-mukhya*—by their own chiefs; *vatsena*—as the calf; *sve sve*—in their own; *pātre*—pots; *pṛthak*—different; *payaḥ*—milk; *sarva-kāma*—all desirables; *dughām*—supplying as milk; *pṛthvīm*—the planet earth; *duduhuḥ*—milked out; *pṛthu-bhāvitām*—controlled by King Pṛthu.

TRANSLATION

The planet earth supplied everyone his respective food. During the time of King Pṛthu, the earth was fully under the control of the King. Thus all the inhabitants of the earth could get their food supply by creating various types of calves and putting their particular types of milk in various pots.

PURPORT

This is evidence that the Lord supplies food to everyone. As confirmed in the *Vedas: eko bahūnāṁ yo vidadhāti kāmān.* Although the Lord is one, He is supplying all necessities to everyone through the medium of the planet earth. There are different varieties of living entities on different planets, and they all derive their eatables from their planets in different forms. On the basis of these descriptions, how can one assume that there is no living entity on the moon? Every moon is earthly, being composed of the five elements. Every planet produces different types of food according to the needs of its residents. According to the Vedic *śāstras*, it is not true that the moon does not produce food or that no living entity is living there.

TEXT 27

एवं पृथ्वादयः पृथ्वीमन्नादाः स्वन्नमात्मनः ।
दोहवत्सादिभेदेन क्षीरभेदं कुरूद्वह ॥२७॥

evaṁ pṛthv-ādayaḥ pṛthvīm
annādāḥ svannam ātmanaḥ
doha-vatsādi-bhedena
kṣīra-bhedaṁ kurūdvaha

evam—thus; *pṛthu-ādayaḥ*—King Pṛthu and others; *pṛthvīm*—the earth; *anna-adāḥ*—all living entities desiring food; *su-annam*—their desired foodstuff; *ātmanaḥ*—for self-preservation; *doha*—for milking; *vatsa-ādi*—by calves, pots and milkers; *bhedena*—different; *kṣīra*—milk; *bhedam*—different; *kuru-udvaha*—O chief of the Kurus.

TRANSLATION

My dear Vidura, chief of the Kurus, in this way King Pṛthu and all the others who subsist on food created different types of calves and milked out their respective eatables. Thus they received their various foodstuffs, which were symbolized as milk.

TEXT 28

ततो महीपतिः प्रीतः सर्वकामदुघां पृथुः ।
दुहितृत्वे चकारेमां प्रेम्णा दुहितृवत्सलः ॥२८॥

tato mahīpatiḥ prītaḥ
sarva-kāma-dughāṁ pṛthuḥ
duhitṛtve cakāremāṁ
premṇā duhitṛ-vatsalaḥ

tataḥ—thereafter; *mahī-patiḥ*—the King; *prītaḥ*—being pleased; *sarva-kāma*—all desirables; *dughām*—producing as milk; *pṛthuḥ*—King Pṛthu; *duhitṛtve*—treating as his daughter; *cakāra*—did; *imām*—unto the planet earth; *premṇā*—out of affection; *duhitṛ-vatsalaḥ*—affectionate to his daughter.

TRANSLATION

Thereafter King Pṛthu was very satisfied with the planet earth, for she sufficiently supplied all food to various living entities. Thus he developed an affection for the planet earth, just as if she were his own daughter.

TEXT 29

चूर्णयन् स्वधनुष्कोट्या गिरिकूटानि राजराट् ।
भूमण्डलमिदं वैन्यः प्रायश्चक्रे समं विभुः ॥२९॥

cūrṇayan sva-dhanuṣ-koṭyā
giri-kūṭāni rāja-rāṭ
bhū-maṇḍalam idaṁ vainyaḥ
prāyaś cakre samaṁ vibhuḥ

cūrṇayan—making into pieces; *sva*—his own; *dhanuḥ-koṭyā*—by the power of his bow; *giri*—of the hills; *kūṭāni*—the tops; *rāja-rāṭ*—the emperor; *bhū-maṇḍalam*—the whole earth; *idam*—this; *vainyaḥ*—the son of Vena; *prāyaḥ*—almost; *cakre*—made; *samam*—level; *vibhuḥ*—the powerful.

TRANSLATION

After this, the king of all kings, Mahārāja Pṛthu, leveled all rough places on the surface of the globe by breaking up the hills with the strength of his bow. By his grace the surface of the globe almost became flat.

PURPORT

Generally the mountainous and hilly portions of the earth are made flat by the striking of thunderbolts. Generally this is the business of King Indra of the heavenly planets, but King Pṛthu, an incarnation of the Supreme Personality of Godhead, did not wait for King Indra to break up the hills and mountains but did so himself by using his strong bow.

TEXT 30

अथास्मिन् भगवान् वैन्यः प्रजानां वृत्तिदः पिता ।
निवासान् कल्पयाञ्चक्रे तत्र तत्र यथार्हतः ॥३०॥

athāsmin bhagavān vainyaḥ
prajānāṁ vṛttidaḥ pitā
nivāsān kalpayāṁ cakre
tatra tatra yathārhataḥ

atha—thus; *asmin*—on this planet earth; *bhagavān*—the Personality of Godhead; *vainyaḥ*—son of Vena; *prajānām*—of the citizens; *vṛttidaḥ*—who supplies employment; *pitā*—a father; *nivāsān*—residences; *kalpayām*—suitable; *cakre*—make; *tatra tatra*—here and there; *yathā*—as; *arhataḥ*—desirable, suitable.

TRANSLATION

To all the citizens of the state, King Pṛthu was as good as a father. Thus he was visibly engaged in giving them proper subsistence and proper employment for subsistence. After leveling the surface of the globe, he earmarked different places for residential quarters, inasmuch as they were desirable.

TEXT 31

ग्रामान् पुरः पत्तनानि दुर्गाणि विविधानि च ।
घोषान् व्रजान् सशिबिरानाकरान् खेटखर्वटान्॥३१॥

grāmān puraḥ pattanāni
durgāṇi vividhāni ca

ghoṣān vrajān sa-śibirān
ākarān kheṭa-kharvaṭān

grāmān—villages; *puraḥ*—cities; *pattanāni*—settlements; *durgāṇi*—forts; *vividhāni*—of different varieties; *ca*—also; *ghoṣān*—habitations for the milkmen; *vrajān*—pens for cattle; *sa-śibirān*—with camps; *ākarān*—mines; *kheṭa*—agricultural towns; *kharvaṭān*—mountain villages.

TRANSLATION

In this way the King founded many types of villages, settlements and towns and built forts, residences for cowherdsmen, stables for the animals, and places for the royal camps, mining places, agricultural towns and mountain villages.

TEXT 32

प्राक्पृथोरिह नैवैषा पुरग्रामादिकल्पना ।
यथासुखं वसन्ति स्म तत्र तत्राकुतोभयाः ॥३२॥

prāk pṛthor iha naivaiṣā
pura-grāmādi-kalpanā
yathā-sukhaṁ vasanti sma
tatra tatrākutobhayāḥ

prāk—before; *pṛthoḥ*—King Pṛthu; *iha*—on this planet; *na*—never; *eva*—certainly; *eṣā*—this; *pura*—of towns; *grāma-ādi*—of villages, etc.; *kalpanā*—planned arrangement; *yathā*—as; *sukham*—convenient; *vasanti sma*—lived; *tatra tatra*—here and there; *akutaḥ-bhayāḥ*—without hesitation.

TRANSLATION

Before the reign of King Pṛthu there was no planned arrangement for different cities, villages, pasturing grounds, etc. Every thing was scattered, and everyone constructed his residential quarters according to his own convenience. However, since King Pṛthu plans were made for towns and villages.

PURPORT

From this statement it appears that town and city planning is not new but has been coming down since the time of King Pṛthu. In India we can see regular planning methods evident in very old cities. In *Śrīmad-Bhāgavatam* there are many descriptions of such ancient cities. Even five thousand years ago, Lord Kṛṣṇa's capital, Dvārakā, was well planned, and similar other cities—Mathurā and Hastināpura (now New Delhi)—were also well planned. Thus the planning of cities and towns is not a modern innovation but was existing in bygone ages.

Thus end the Bhaktivedanta purports of the Fourth Canto, Eighteenth Chapter, of the Śrīmad-Bhāgavatam, *entitled "Pṛthu Mahārāja Milks the Earth Planet."*

CHAPTER NINETEEN

King Pṛthu's One Hundred Horse Sacrifices

TEXT 1

मैत्रेय उवाच
अथादीक्षत राजा तु हयमेधशतेन सः ।
ब्रह्मावर्ते मनोः क्षेत्रे यत्र प्राची सरस्वती ॥ १ ॥

maitreya uvāca
athādīkṣata rājā tu
hayamedha-śatena saḥ
brahmāvarte manoḥ kṣetre
yatra prācī sarasvatī

maitreyaḥ uvāca—the sage Maitreya said; *atha*—thereafter; *adīkṣata*—took initiation; *rājā*—the King; *tu*—then; *haya*—horse; *medha*—sacrifices; *śatena*—to perform one hundred; *saḥ*—he; *brahmāvarte*—known as Brahmāvarta; *manoḥ*—of Svāyambhuva Manu; *kṣetre*—in the land; *yatra*—where; *prācī*—eastern; *sarasvatī*—the river named Sarasvatī.

TRANSLATION

The great sage Maitreya continued: My dear Vidura, King Pṛthu initiated the performance of one hundred horse sacrifices at the spot where the River Sarasvatī flows towards the east. This piece of land is known as Brahmāvarta, and it was controlled by Svāyambhuva Manu.

TEXT 2

तदभिप्रेत्य भगवान् कर्मातिशयमात्मनः ।
शतक्रतुर्न ममृषे पृथोर्यज्ञमहोत्सवम् ॥ २ ॥

tad abhipretya bhagavān
karmātiśayam ātmanaḥ
śata-kratur na mamṛṣe
pṛthor yajña-mahotsavam

tat abhipretya—considering this matter; *bhagavān*—the most powerful; *karma-atiśayam*—excelling in fruitive activities; *ātmanaḥ*—of himself; *śata-kratuḥ*—King Indra, who had performed a hundred sacrifices; *na*—not; *mamṛṣe*—did tolerate; *pṛthoḥ*—of King Pṛthu; *yajña*—sacrificial; *mahā-utsavam*—great ceremonies.

TRANSLATION

When the most powerful Indra, the King of heaven, saw this, he considered the fact that King Pṛthu was going to exceed him in fruitive activities. Thus Indra could not tolerate the great sacrificial ceremonies performed by King Pṛthu.

PURPORT

In the material world everyone who comes to enjoy himself or lord it over material nature is envious of others. This envy is also found in the personality of the King of heaven, Indra. As evident from revealed scriptures, Indra was several times envious of many persons. He was especially envious of great fruitive activities and the execution of *yoga* practices, or *siddhis.* Indeed, he could not tolerate them, and he desired to break them up. He was envious due to fear that those who performed great sacrifices for the execution of mystic *yoga* might occupy his seat. Since no one in this material world can tolerate another's advancement, everyone in the material world is called *matsara,* envious. In the beginning of *Śrīmad-Bhāgavatam* it is therefore said that *Śrīmad-Bhāgavatam* is meant for those who are completely *nirmatsara* (nonenvious). In other words, one who is not free from the contamination of envy cannot advance in Kṛṣṇa consciousness. In Kṛṣṇa consciousness, however, if someone excels another person, the devotee who is excelled thinks how fortunate the other person is to be advancing in devotional service. Such nonenvy is typical of Vaikuṇṭha. However, when one is envious of his competitor, that is material. The demigods posted in the material world are not exempt from envy.

TEXT 3

यत्र यज्ञपतिः साक्षाद्भगवान् हरिरीश्वरः ।
अन्वभूयत सर्वात्मा सर्वलोकगुरुः प्रभुः ॥ ३ ॥

yatra yajña-patiḥ sākṣād
bhagavān harir īśvaraḥ
anvabhūyata sarvātmā
sarva-loka-guruḥ prabhuḥ

yatra—where; *yajña-patiḥ*—the enjoyer of all sacrifices; *sākṣāt*—directly; *bhagavān*—the Supreme Personality of Godhead; *hariḥ*—Lord Viṣṇu; *īśvaraḥ*—the supreme controller; *anvabhūyata*—became visible; *sarva-ātmā*—the Supersoul of everyone; *sarva-loka-guruḥ*—the master of all planets, or the teacher of everyone; *prabhuḥ*—the proprietor.

TRANSLATION

The Supreme Personality of Godhead, Lord Viṣṇu, is present in everyone's heart as the Supersoul, and He is the proprietor of all planets and the enjoyer of the results of all sacrifices. He was personally present at the sacrifices made by King Pṛthu.

PURPORT

In this verse the word *sākṣāt* is significant. Pṛthu Mahārāja was a *śaktyāveśa-avatāra* incarnation of Lord Viṣṇu. Actually Pṛthu Mahārāja was a living entity, but he acquired specific powers from Lord Viṣṇu. Lord Viṣṇu, however, is directly the Supreme Personality of Godhead, and thus belongs to the category of *viṣṇu-tattva.* Mahārāja Pṛthu belonged to the *jīva-tattva.* The *viṣṇu-tattva* indicates God, whereas the *jīva-tattva* indicates the part and parcel of God. When God's part and parcel is especially empowered, he is called *śaktyāveśa-avatāra.* Lord Viṣṇu is herein described as *harir īśvaraḥ.* The Lord is so kind that He takes all miserable conditions away from His devotees. Consequently He is called

Hari. He is described as *īśvara* because He can do whatever He likes. He is the supreme controller. The supreme *īśvara puruṣottama* is Lord Kṛṣṇa. He exhibits His powers as *īśvara*, or the supreme controller, when He assures His devotee in *Bhagavad-gītā* (18.66): "Abandon all varieties of religion and just surrender unto Me. I shall deliver you from all sinful reaction. Do not fear." He can immediately make His devotee immune from all the reactions caused by sinful life if the devotee simply surrenders unto Him. He is described herein as *sarvātmā*, meaning that He is present in everyone's heart as the Supersoul, and as such He is the supreme teacher of everyone. If we are fortunate enough to take the lessons given by Lord Kṛṣṇa in *Bhagavad-gītā*, our lives immediately become successful. No one can give better instructions to human society than Lord Kṛṣṇa.

TEXT 4

अन्वितो ब्रह्मशर्वाभ्यां लोकपालैः सहानुगैः ।
उपगीयमानो गन्धर्वैर्मुनिभिश्चाप्सरोगणैः ॥ ४ ॥

anvito brahma-śarvābhyāṁ
loka-pālaiḥ sahānugaiḥ
upagīyamāno gandharvair
munibhiś cāpsaro-gaṇaiḥ

anvitaḥ—being accompanied; *brahma*—by Lord Brahmā; *śarvābhyām*—and by Lord Śiva; *loka-pālaiḥ*—by the predominating chiefs of all different planets; *saha anugaiḥ*—along with their followers; *upagīyamānaḥ*—being praised; *gandharvaiḥ*—by the residents of Gandharvaloka; *munibhiḥ*—by great sages; *ca*—also; *apsaraḥ-gaṇaiḥ*—by the residents of Apsaroloka.

TRANSLATION

When Lord Viṣṇu appeared in the sacrificial arena, Lord Brahmā, Lord Śiva and all the chief predominating personalities of every planet, as well as their followers, came with Him. When He appeared on the scene, the residents of Gandharvaloka, the great sages, and the residents of Apsaroloka all praised Him.

TEXT 5

सिद्धा विद्याधरा दैत्या दानवा गुह्यकादयः ।
सुनन्दनन्दप्रमुखाः पार्षदप्रवरा हरेः ॥ ५ ॥

siddhā vidyādharā daityā
dānavā guhyakādayaḥ
sunanda-nanda-pramukhāḥ
pārṣada-pravarā hareḥ

siddhāḥ—the residents of Siddhaloka; *vidyādharāḥ*—the residents of Vidyādhara-loka; *daityāḥ*—the demoniac descendants of Diti; *dānavāḥ*—the *asuras; guhyaka-ādayaḥ*—the Yakṣas, etc.; *sunanda-nanda-pramukhāḥ*—headed by Sunanda and Nanda, the chief of Lord Viṣṇu's associates from Vaikuṇṭha; *pārṣada*—associates; *pravarāḥ*—most respectful; *hareḥ*—of the Supreme Personality of Godhead.

TRANSLATION

The Lord was accompanied by the residents of Siddhaloka and Vidyādhara-loka, all the descendants of Diti, and the demons and the Yakṣas. He was also accompanied by His chief associates, headed by Sunanda and Nanda.

TEXT 6

कपिलो नारदो दत्तो योगेशाः सनकादयः ।
तमन्वीयुर्भागवता ये च तत्सेवनोत्सुकाः ॥ ६ ॥

kapilo nārado datto
yogeśāḥ sanakādayaḥ
tam anvīyur bhāgavatā
ye ca tat-sevanotsukāḥ

kapilaḥ—Kapila Muni; *nāradaḥ*—the great sage Nārada; *dattaḥ*—Dattātreya; *yoga-īśāḥ*—the masters of mystic power; *sanaka-ādayaḥ*—headed by Sanaka; *tam*—Lord Viṣṇu; *anvīyuḥ*—followed;

bhāgavatāḥ—great devotees; *ye*—all those who; *ca*—also; *tat-sevana-utsukāḥ*—always eager to serve the Lord.

TRANSLATION

Great devotees, who were always engaged in the service of the Supreme Personality of Godhead, as well as the great sages named Kapila, Nārada and Dattātreya, and masters of mystic powers, headed by Sanaka Kumāra, all attended the great sacrifice with Lord Viṣṇu.

TEXT 7

यत्र धर्मदुघा भूमिः सर्वकामदुघा सती ।
दोग्धि स्माभीप्सितानर्थान् यजमानस्य भारत ॥ ७ ॥

yatra dharma-dughā bhūmiḥ
sarva-kāma-dughā satī
dogdhi smābhīpsitān arthān
yajamānasya bhārata

yatra—where; *dharma-dughā*—producing sufficient milk for religiosity; *bhūmiḥ*—the land; *sarva-kāma*—all desires; *dughā*—yielding as milk; *satī*—the cow; *dogdhi sma*—fulfilled; *abhīpsitān*—desirable; *arthān*—objects; *yajamānasya*—of the sacrificer; *bhārata*—my dear Vidura.

TRANSLATION

My dear Vidura, in that great sacrifice the entire land came to be like the milk-producing kāma-dhenu, and thus, by the performance of yajña, all daily necessities for life were supplied.

PURPORT

In this verse the word *dharma-dughā* is significant, for it indicates *kāma-dhenu. Kāma-dhenu* is also known as *surabhi. Surabhi* cows inhabit the spiritual world, and, as stated in *Brahma-saṁhitā*, Lord Kṛṣṇa is engaged in tending these cows: *surabhīr abhipālayantam.* One can milk a *surabhi* cow as often as one likes, and the cow will deliver as much milk as one requires. Milk, of course, is necessary for the production of so many milk products, especially clarified butter, which is required for the performance of great sacrifices. Unless we are prepared to perform the prescribed sacrifices, our supply of the necessities of life will be checked. *Bhagavad-gītā* confirms that Lord Brahmā created human society along with *yajña*, the performance of sacrifice. *Yajña* means Lord Viṣṇu, the Supreme Personality of Godhead, and sacrifice means working for the satisfaction of the Supreme Personality of Godhead. In this age, however, it is very difficult to find qualified *brāhmaṇas* who can perform sacrifices as prescribed in the *Vedas*. Therefore it is recommended in *Śrīmad-Bhāgavatam* (*yajñaiḥ saṅkīrtana-prāyaiḥ*) that by performing *saṅkīrtana-yajña* and by satisfying the *yajña-puruṣa*, Lord Caitanya, one can derive all the results derived by great sacrifices in the past. King Pṛthu and others derived all the necessities of life from the earthly planet by performing great sacrifices. Now this *saṅkīrtana* movement has already been started by the International Society for Krishna Consciousness. People should take advantage of this great sacrifice and join in the Society's activities; then there will be no scarcity. If *saṅkīrtana-yajña* is performed, there will be no difficulty, not even in industrial enterprises. Therefore this system should be introduced in all spheres of life—social, political, industrial, commercial, etc. Then everything will run very peacefully and smoothly.

TEXT 8

ऊहुः सर्वरसान्नद्यः क्षीरदध्यन्नगोरसान् ।
तरवो भूरिवर्ष्माणः प्रासूयन्त मधुच्युतः ॥ ८ ॥

ūhuḥ sarva-rasān nadyaḥ
kṣīra-dadhy-anna-go-rasān
taravo bhūri-varṣmāṇaḥ
prāsūyanta madhu-cyutaḥ

ūhuḥ—bore; *sarva-rasān*—all kinds of tastes; *nadyaḥ*—the rivers; *kṣīra*—milk; *dadhi*—curd; *anna*—different kinds of food; *go-rasān*—other milk products; *taravaḥ*—trees; *bhūri*—great; *varṣmāṇaḥ*—having bodies; *prāsūyanta*—bore fruit; *madhu-cyutaḥ*—dropping honey.

TRANSLATION

The flowing rivers supplied all kinds of tastes—sweet, pungent, sour, etc.—and very big trees supplied fruit and honey in abundance. The cows, having eaten sufficient green grass, supplied profuse quantities of milk, curd, clarified butter and similar other necessities.

PURPORT

If rivers are not polluted and are allowed to flow in their own way, or sometimes allowed to flood the land, the land will become very fertile and able to produce all kinds of vegetables, trees and plants. The word *rasa* means "taste." Actually all *rasas* are tastes within the earth, and as soon as seeds are sown in the ground, various trees sprout up to satisfy our different tastes. For instance, sugarcane provides its juices to satisfy our taste for sweetness, and oranges provide their juices to satisfy our taste for a mixture of the sour and the sweet. Similarly, there are pineapples and other fruits. At the same time, there are chilies to satisfy our taste for pungency. Although the earth's ground is the same, different tastes arise due to different kinds of seeds. As Kṛṣṇa says in *Bhagavad-gītā* (7.10), *bījaṁ māṁ sarva-bhūtānām:* "I am the original seed of all existences." Therefore all arrangements are there. And as stated in *Īśopaniṣad: pūrṇam idam.* Complete arrangements for the production of all the necessities of life are made by the Supreme Personality of Godhead. People should therefore learn how to satisfy the *yajña-puruṣa,* Lord Viṣṇu. Indeed, the living entity's prime business is to satisfy the Lord because the living entity is part and parcel of the Lord. Thus the whole system is so arranged that the living entity must do his duty as he is constitutionally made. Without doing so, all living entities must suffer. That is the law of nature.

The words *taravo bhūri-varṣmāṇaḥ* indicate very luxuriantly grown, big-bodied trees. The purpose of these trees was to produce honey and varieties of fruit. In other words, the forest also has its purpose in supplying honey, fruits and flowers. Unfortunately in Kali-yuga, due to an absence of *yajña,* there are many big trees in the forests, but they do not supply sufficient fruits and honey. Thus everything is dependent on the performance of *yajña.* The best way to perform *yajña* in this age is to spread the *saṅkīrtana* movement all over the world.

TEXT 9

सिन्धवो रत्ननिकरान् गिरयोऽन्नं चतुर्विधम् ।
उपायनमुपाजह्रुः सर्वे लोकाः सपालकाः ॥ ९ ॥

sindhavo ratna-nikarān
girayo 'nnaṁ catur-vidham
upāyanam upājahruḥ
sarve lokāḥ sa-pālakāḥ

sindhavaḥ—the oceans; *ratna-nikarān*—heaps of jewels; *girayaḥ*—the hills; *annam*—eatables; *catuḥ-vidham*—four kinds of; *upāyanam*—presentations; *upājahruḥ*—brought forward; *sarve*—all; *lokāḥ*—the people in general of all planets; *sa-pālakāḥ*—along with the governors.

TRANSLATION

King Pṛthu was presented with various gifts from the general populace and predominating deities of all planets. The oceans and seas were full of valuable jewels and pearls, and the hills were full of chemicals and fertilizers. Four kinds of edibles were produced profusely.

PURPORT

As stated in *Īśopaniṣad*, this material creation is supplied with all the potencies for the production of all necessities required by the living entities—not only human beings, but animals, reptiles, aquatics and trees. The oceans and seas produce pearls, coral and valuable jewels so that fortunate law-abiding people can utilize them. Similarly, the hills are full of chemicals so that when rivers flow down from them the chemicals spread over the fields to fertilize the four kinds of foodstuffs. These are technically known as *carvya* (those edibles which are chewed), *lehya* (those which are licked up), *cūṣya* (those which are swallowed) and *peya* (those which are drunk).

Pṛthu Mahārāja was greeted by the residents of other planets and their presiding deities. They presented various gifts to the King and acknowledged him as the proper type of king by whose planning and activities everyone throughout the universe could be happy and prosperous. It is clearly indicated in this verse that the oceans and seas are meant for producing jewels, but in Kali-yuga the oceans are mainly being utilized for fishing. *Śūdras* and poor men were allowed to fish, but the higher classes like the *kṣatriyas* and *vaiśyas* would gather pearls, jewels and coral. Although poor men would catch tons of fish, they would not be equal in value to one piece of coral or pearl. In this age so many factories for the manufacture of fertilizers have been opened, but when the Personality of Godhead is pleased by the performance of *yajñas*, the hills automatically produce fertilizing chemicals, which help produce edibles in the fields. Everything is dependent on the people's acceptance of the Vedic principles of sacrifice.

TEXT 10

इति चाधोक्षजेशस्य पृथोस्तु परमोदयम् ।
असूयन् भगवानिन्द्रः प्रतिघातमचीकरत् ॥१०॥

iti cādhokṣajeśasya
pṛthos tu paramodayam
asūyan bhagavān indraḥ
pratighātam acīkarat

iti—thus; *ca*—also; *adhokṣaja-īśasya*—who accepted Adhokṣaja as his worshipable Lord; *pṛthoḥ*—of King Pṛthu; *tu*—then; *parama*—the topmost; *udayam*—opulence; *asūyan*—being envious of; *bhagavān*—the most powerful; *indraḥ*—the King of heaven; *pratighātam*—impediments; *acīkarat*—made.

TRANSLATION

King Pṛthu was dependent on the Supreme Personality of Godhead, who is known as Adhokṣaja. Because King Pṛthu performed so many sacrifices, he was superhumanly enhanced by the mercy of the Supreme Lord. King Pṛthu's opulence, however, could not be tolerated by the King of heaven, Indra, who tried to impede the progress of his opulence.

PURPORT

In this verse there are three significant purposes expressed in the words *adhokṣaja, bhagavān indraḥ* and *pṛthoḥ.* Mahārāja Pṛthu is an incarnation of Viṣṇu, yet he is a great devotee of Lord Viṣṇu. Although an empowered incarnation of Lord Viṣṇu, he is nonetheless a living entity. As such, he must be a devotee of the Supreme Personality of Godhead. Although one is empowered by the Supreme Personality of Godhead and is an incarnation, he should not forget his eternal relationship with the Supreme Personality of Godhead. In Kali-yuga there are many self-made incarnations, rascals, who declare themselves to be the Supreme Personality of Godhead. The words *bhagavān indraḥ* indicate that a living entity can even be as exalted and powerful as King Indra, for even King Indra is an ordinary living entity in the material world and possesses the four defects of the conditioned soul. King Indra is described herein as *bhagavān,* which is generally used in reference to the Supreme Personality of Godhead. In this case, however, King Indra is addressed as *bhagavān* because he has so much power in his hands. Despite his becoming *bhagavān,* he is envious of the incarnation of God, Pṛthu Mahārāja. The defects of material life are so strong that due to contamination King Indra becomes envious of an incarnation of God.

We should try to understand, therefore, how a conditioned soul becomes fallen. The opulence of King Pṛthu was not dependent on material conditions. As described in this verse, he was a great devotee of Adhokṣaja. The word *adhokṣaja* indicates the Personality of Godhead, who is beyond the expression of mind and words. However, the Supreme Personality of Godhead appears before the devotee in His original form of eternal bliss and knowledge. The devotee is allowed to see the Supreme Lord face to face, although the Lord is beyond the expression of our senses and beyond our direct perception.

TEXT 11

चरमेणाश्वमेधेन यजमाने यजुष्पतिम् ।
वैन्ये यज्ञपशुं स्पर्धन्नपोवाह तिरोहितः ॥११॥

carameṇāśvamedhena
yajamāne yajuṣ-patim

vainye yajña-paśuṁ spardhann
apovāha tirohitaḥ

carameṇa—by the last one; *aśva-medhena*—by the *aśvamedha* sacrifice; *yajamāne*—when he was performing the sacrifice; *yajuḥ-patim*—for satisfaction of the Lord of *yajña*, Viṣṇu; *vainye*—the son of King Vena; *yajña-paśum*—the animal meant to be sacrificed in the *yajña; spardhan*—being envious; *apovāha*—stole; *tirohitaḥ*—being invisible.

TRANSLATION

When Pṛthu Mahārāja was performing the last horse sacrifice [aśvamedha-yajña], King Indra, invisible to everyone, stole the horse intended for sacrifice. He did this because of his great envy of King Pṛthu.

PURPORT

King Indra is known as *śata-kratu*, which indicates that he has performed one hundred horse sacrifices (*aśvamedha-yajña*). We should know, however, that the animals sacrificed in the *yajña* were not killed. If the Vedic *mantras* were properly pronounced during the sacrifice, the animal sacrificed would come out again with a new life. That is the test for a successful *yajña*. When King Pṛthu was performing one hundred *yajñas*, Indra became very envious because he did not want anyone to excel him. Being an ordinary living entity, he became envious of King Pṛthu, and, making himself invisible, he stole the horse and thus impeded the *yajña* performance.

TEXT 12

तमत्रिर्भगवानैक्षत्त्वरमाणं विहायसा ।
आमुक्तमिव पाखण्डं योऽधर्मे धर्मविभ्रमः ॥१२॥

tam atrir bhagavān aikṣat
tvaramāṇaṁ vihāyasā
āmuktam iva pākhaṇḍaṁ
yo 'dharme dharma-vibhramaḥ

tam—King Indra; *atriḥ*—the sage Atri; *bhagavān*—most powerful; *aikṣat*—could see; *tvaramāṇam*—moving very hastily; *vihāyasā*—in outer space; *āmuktam iva*—like a liberated person; *pākhaṇḍam*—imposter; *yaḥ*—one who; *adharme*—in irreligion; *dharma*—religion; *vibhramaḥ*—mistaking.

TRANSLATION

When King Indra was taking away the horse, he dressed himself to appear as a liberated person. Actually this dress was a form of cheating, for it falsely created an impression of religion. When Indra went into outer space in this way, the great sage Atri saw him and understood the whole situation.

PURPORT

The word *pākhaṇḍa* used in this verse is sometimes pronounced *pāṣaṇḍa*. Both of these words indicate an imposter who presents himself as a very religious person but in actuality is sinful. Indra took up the saffron-colored dress as a way of cheating others. This saffron dress has been misused by many imposters who present themselves as liberated persons or incarnations of God. In this way people are cheated. As we have mentioned many times, the conditioned soul has a tendency to cheat; therefore this quality is also visible in a person like King Indra. It is understood that even King Indra is not liberated from the clutches of material contamination. Thus the words *āmuktam iva*, meaning "as if he were liberated," are used. The saffron dress worn by a *sannyāsī* announces to the world that he has renounced all worldly affairs and is simply engaged in the service of the Lord. Such a devotee is actually a *sannyāsī*, or liberated person. In *Bhagavad-gītā* (6.1) it is said:

anāśritaḥ karma-phalaṁ
kāryaṁ karma karoti yaḥ
sa sannyāsī ca yogī ca
na niragnir na cākriyaḥ

"One who is unattached to the fruits of his work and who works as he is obligated is in the renounced order of life, and he is the true mystic, not he who lights no fire and performs no work."

In other words, one who offers the results of his activities to the Supreme Personality of Godhead is actually a *sannyāsī* and *yogī*. Cheating *sannyāsīs* and *yogīs* have existed since the time of Pṛthu Mahārāja's sacrifice. This cheating was very foolishly introduced by King Indra. In some ages such cheating is very prominent, and in other ages not so prominent. It is the duty of a *sannyāsī* to be very cautious because, as stated by Lord Caitanya, *sannyāsīra alpa chidra sarva-loke gāya:* a little spot in a *sannyāsī*'s character will be magnified by the public (Cc. *Madhya* 12.51). Therefore, unless one is very sincere and serious, he should not take up the order of *sannyāsa*. One should not use this order as a means to cheat the public. It is better not to take up *sannyāsa* in this age of Kali because provocations are very strong in this age. Only a very exalted person advanced in spiritual understanding should attempt to take up *sannyāsa*. One should not adopt this order as a means of livelihood or for some material purpose.

TEXT 13

अत्रिणा चोदितो हन्तुं पृथुपुत्रो महारथः ।
अन्वधावत संक्रुद्धस्तिष्ठ तिष्ठेति चाब्रवीत् ॥१३॥

atriṇā codito hantuṁ
pṛthu-putro mahā-rathaḥ
anvadhāvata saṅkruddhas
tiṣṭha tiṣṭheti cābravīt

atriṇā—by the great sage Atri; *coditaḥ*—being encouraged; *hantum*—to kill; *pṛthu-putraḥ*—the son of King Pṛthu; *mahā-rathaḥ*—a great hero; *anvadhāvata*—followed; *saṅkruddhaḥ*—being very angry; *tiṣṭha tiṣṭha*—just wait, just wait; *iti*—thus; *ca*—also; *abravīt*—he said.

TRANSLATION

When the son of King Pṛthu was informed by Atri of King Indra's trick, he immediately became very angry and followed Indra to kill him, calling, "Wait! Wait!"

PURPORT

The words *tiṣṭha tiṣṭha* are used by a *kṣatriya* when he challenges his enemy. When fighting, a *kṣatriya* cannot flee from the battlefield. However, when a *kṣatriya* out of cowardice flees from the battlefield, showing his back to his enemy, he is challenged with the words *tiṣṭha tiṣṭha.* A real *kṣatriya* does not kill his enemy from behind, nor does a real *kṣatriya* turn his back on the battlefield. According to *kṣatriya* principle and spirit, one either attains victory or dies on the battlefield. Although King Indra was very exalted, being the King of heaven, he became degraded due to his stealing the horse intended for sacrifice. Therefore he fled without observing the *kṣatriya* principles, and the son of Pṛthu had to challenge him with the words *tiṣṭha tiṣṭha.*

TEXT 14

तं तादृशाकृतिं वीक्ष्य मेने धर्मं शरीरिणम् ।
जटिलं भस्मनाच्छन्नं तस्मै बाणं न मुञ्चति ॥१४॥

taṁ tādṛśākṛtiṁ vīkṣya
mene dharmaṁ śarīriṇam
jaṭilaṁ bhasmanācchannaṁ
tasmai bāṇaṁ na muñcati

tam—him; *tādṛśa-ākṛtim*—in such dress; *vīkṣya*—after seeing; *mene*—considered; *dharmam*—pious or religious; *śarīriṇam*—having a body; *jaṭilam*—having knotted hair; *bhasmanā*—by ashes; *ācchannam*—smeared all over the body; *tasmai*—unto him; *bāṇam*—arrow; *na;*—not; *muñcati*—he did release.

TRANSLATION

King Indra was fraudulently dressed as a sannyāsī, having knotted his hair on his head and smeared ashes all over his body. Upon seeing such dress, the son of King Pṛthu considered Indra a religious man and pious sannyāsī. Therefore he did not release his arrows.

TEXT 15

वधान्निवृत्तं तं भूयो हन्तवेऽत्रिरचोदयत् ।
जहि यज्ञहनं तात महेन्द्रं विबुधाधमम् ॥१५॥

vadhān nivṛttaṁ taṁ bhūyo
hantave 'trir acodayat
jahi yajña-hanaṁ tāta
mahendraṁ vibudhādhamam

vadhāt—from killing; *nivṛttam*—stopped; *tam*—the son of Pṛthu; *bhūyaḥ*—again; *hantave*—for the purpose of killing; *atriḥ*—the great sage Atri; *acodayat*—encouraged; *jahi*—kill; *yajña-hanam*—one who impeded the performance of a *yajña; tāta*—my dear son; *mahā-indram*—the great heavenly King Indra; *vibudha-adhamam*—the lowest of all demigods.

TRANSLATION

When Atri Muni saw that the son of King Pṛthu did not kill Indra but returned deceived by him, Atri Muni again instructed him to kill the heavenly King because he thought that Indra had become the lowliest of all demigods due to his impeding the execution of King Pṛthu's sacrifice.

TEXT 16

एवं वैन्यसुतः प्रोक्तस्त्वरमाणं विहायसा ।
अन्वद्रवदभिक्रुद्धो रावणं गृध्रराडिव ॥१६॥

evaṁ vainya-sutaḥ proktas
tvaramāṇaṁ vihāyasā
anvadravad abhikruddho
rāvaṇaṁ gṛdhra-rāḍ iva

evam—thus; *vainya-sutaḥ*—the son of King Pṛthu; *proktaḥ*—being ordered; *tvaramāṇam*—Indra, who was moving hastily; *vihāyasā*—in the sky; *anvadravat*—began to chase; *abhikruddhaḥ*—being very angry; *rāvaṇam*—Rāvaṇa; *gṛdhra-rāṭ*—the king of vultures; *iva*—like.

TRANSLATION

Being thus informed, the grandson of King Vena immediately began to follow Indra, who was fleeing through the sky in great haste. He was very angry with him, and he chased him just as the king of the vultures chased Rāvaṇa.

TEXT 17

सोऽश्वं रूपं च तद्धित्वा तस्मा अन्तर्हितः स्वराट् ।
वीरः स्वपशुमादाय पितुर्यज्ञमुपेयिवान् ॥१७॥

so 'śvaṁ rūpaṁ ca tad dhitvā
tasmā antarhitaḥ svarāṭ
vīraḥ sva-paśum ādāya
pitur yajñam upeyivān

saḥ—King Indra; *aśvam*—the horse; *rūpam*—the false dress of a saintly person; *ca*—also; *tat*—that; *hitvā*—giving up; *tasmai*—for him; *antarhitaḥ*—disappeared; *sva-rāṭ*—Indra; *vīraḥ*—the great hero; *sva-paśum*—his animal; *ādāya*—having taken; *pituḥ*—of his father; *yajñam*—to the sacrifice; *upeyivān*—he came back.

TRANSLATION

When Indra saw that the son of Pṛthu was chasing him, he immediately abandoned his false dress and left the horse. Indeed, he disappeared from that very spot, and the great hero, the son of Mahārāja Pṛthu, returned the horse to his father's sacrificial arena.

TEXT 18

तत्तस्य चाद्भुतं कर्म विचक्ष्य परमर्षयः ।
नामधेयं ददुस्तस्मै विजिताश्व इति प्रभो ॥१८॥

tat tasya cādbhutaṁ karma
vicakṣya paramarṣayaḥ
nāmadheyaṁ dadus tasmai
vijitāśva iti prabho

tat—that; *tasya*—his; *ca*—also; *adbhutam*—wonderful; *karma*—activity; *vicakṣya*—after observing; *parama-ṛṣayaḥ*—the great sages; *nāmadheyam*—the name; *daduḥ*—they offered; *tasmai*—to him; *vijita-aśvaḥ*—Vijitāśva (he who has won the horse); *iti*—thus; *prabho*—my dear Lord Vidura.

TRANSLATION

My dear Lord Vidura, when the great sages observed the wonderful prowess of the son of King Pṛthu, they all agreed to give him the name Vijitāśva.

TEXT 19

उपसृज्य तमस्तीव्रं जहाराश्वं पुनर्हरिः ।
चषालयूपतश्छन्नो हिरण्यरशनं विभुः ॥१९॥

upasṛjya tamas tīvraṁ
jahārāśvaṁ punar hariḥ
caṣāla-yūpataś channo
hiraṇya-raśanaṁ vibhuḥ

upasṛjya—creating; *tamaḥ*—darkness; *tīvram*—dense; *jahāra*—took away; *aśvam*—the horse; *punaḥ*—again; *hariḥ*—King Indra; *caṣāla-yūpataḥ*—from the wooden instrument where the animals were sacrificed; *channaḥ*—being covered; *hiraṇya-raśanam*—tied with a gold chain; *vibhuḥ*—very powerful.

TRANSLATION

My dear Vidura, Indra, being the King of heaven and very powerful, immediately brought a dense darkness upon the sacrificial arena. Covering the whole scene in this way, he again took away the horse, which was chained with golden shackles near the wooden instrument where animals were sacrificed.

TEXT 20

अत्रिः सन्दर्शयामास त्वरमाणं विहायसा ।
कपालखट्वाङ्गधरं वीरो नैनमबाधत ॥२०॥

atriḥ sandarśayām āsa
tvaramāṇaṁ vihāyasā
kapāla-khaṭvāṅga-dharaṁ
vīro nainam abādhata

atriḥ—the great sage Atri; *sandarśayām āsa*—caused to see; *tvaramāṇam*—going very hastily; *vihāyasā*—in the sky; *kapāla-khaṭvāṅga*—a staff with a skull at the top; *dharam*—who carried; *vīraḥ*—the hero (King Pṛthu's son); *na*—not; *enam*—the King of heaven, Indra; *abādhata*—killed.

TRANSLATION

The great sage Atri again pointed out to the son of King Pṛthu that Indra was fleeing through the sky. The great hero, the son of Pṛthu, chased him again. But when he saw that Indra was carrying in his hand a staff with a skull at the top and was again wearing the dress of a sannyāsī, he still chose not to kill him.

TEXT 21

अत्रिणा चोदितस्तस्मै सन्दधे विशिखं रुषा ।
सोऽश्वं रूपं च तद्धित्वा तस्थावन्तर्हितः स्वराट्॥ २१॥

atriṇā coditas tasmai
sandadhe viśikhaṁ ruṣā
so 'śvaṁ rūpaṁ ca tad dhitvā
tasthāv antarhitaḥ svarāṭ

atriṇā—by the great sage Atri; *coditaḥ*—inspired; *tasmai*—for Lord Indra; *sandadhe*—fixed; *viśikham*—his arrow; *ruṣā*—out of great anger; *saḥ*—King Indra; *aśvam*—horse; *rūpam*—the dress of a *sannyāsī; ca*—also; *tat*—that; *hitvā*—giving up; *tasthau*—he remained there; *antarhitaḥ*—invisible; *sva-rāṭ*—the independent Indra.

TRANSLATION

When the great sage Atri again gave directions, the son of King Pṛthu became very angry and placed an arrow on his bow. Upon

seeing this, King Indra immediately abandoned the false dress of a sannyāsī and, giving up the horse, made himself invisible.

TEXT 22

वीरश्चाश्वमुपादाय पितृयज्ञमथाव्रजत् ।
तदवद्यं हरे रूपं जगृहुर्ज्ञानदुर्बलाः ॥२२॥

vīraś cāśvam upādāya
pitṛ-yajñam athāvrajat
tad avadyaṁ hare rūpaṁ
jagṛhur jñāna-durbalāḥ

vīraḥ—the son of King Pṛthu; *ca*—also; *aśvam*—the horse; *upādāya*—taking; *pitṛ-yajñam*—to the sacrificial arena of his father; *atha*—thereafter; *avrajat*—went; *tat*—that; *avadyam*—abominable; *hareḥ*—of Indra; *rūpam*—dress; *jagṛhuḥ*—adopted; *jñāna-durbalāḥ*—those with a poor fund of knowledge.

TRANSLATION

Then the great hero, Vijitāśva, the son of King Pṛthu, again took the horse and returned to his father's sacrificial arena. Since that time, certain men with a poor fund of knowledge have adopted the dress of a false sannyāsī. It was King Indra who introduced this.

PURPORT

Since time immemorial, the *sannyāsa* order has carried the *tridaṇḍa.* Later Śaṅkarācārya introduced the *ekadaṇḍi-sannyāsa.* A *tridaṇḍi-sannyāsī* is a Vaiṣṇava *sannyāsī,* and an *ekadaṇḍi-sannyāsī* is a Māyāvādī *sannyāsī.* There are many other types of *sannyāsīs,* who are not approved by Vedic rituals. A type of pseudo-*sannyāsa* was introduced by Indra when he tried to hide himself from the attack of Vijitāśva, the great son of King Pṛthu. Now there are many different types of *sannyāsīs.* Some of them go naked, and some of them carry a skull and trident, generally known as *kāpālika.* All of them were introduced under some meaningless circumstances, and those who have a poor fund of knowledge accept these false *sannyāsīs* and their pretenses, although they are not bona fide guides to spiritual advancement. At the present moment some missionary institutions, without referring to the Vedic rituals, have introduced some *sannyāsīs* who engage in sinful activities. The sinful activities forbidden by the *śāstras* are illicit sex, intoxication, meat-eating and gambling. These so-called *sannyāsīs* indulge in all these activities. They eat meat and flesh, fish, eggs and just about everything. They sometimes drink with the excuse that without alcohol, fish and meat, it is impossible to remain in the cold countries near the Arctic zone. These *sannyāsīs* introduce all these sinful activities in the name of serving the poor, and consequently poor animals are cut to pieces and go into the bellies of these *sannyāsīs.* As described in the following verses, such *sannyāsīs* are *pākhaṇḍīs.* Vedic literature states that a person who puts Lord Nārāyaṇa on the level with Lord Śiva or Lord Brahmā immediately becomes a *pākhaṇḍī.* As stated in the *Purāṇas:*

yas tu nārāyaṇaṁ devaṁ
brahma-rudrādi-daivataiḥ
samatvenaiva vīkṣeta
sa pāṣaṇḍī bhaved dhruvam

In Kali-yuga the *pākhaṇḍīs* are very prominent. However, Lord Śrī Caitanya Mahāprabhu has tried to kill all these *pākhaṇḍīs* by introducing His *saṅkīrtana* movement. Those who take advantage of this *saṅkīrtana* movement of the International Society for Krishna Consciousness will be able to save themselves from the influence of these *pākhaṇḍīs.*

TEXT 23

यानि रूपाणि जगृहे इन्द्रो हयजिहीर्षया ।
तानि पापस्य खण्डानि लिङ्गं खण्डमिहोच्यते ॥२३॥

yāni rūpāṇi jagṛhe
indro haya-jihīrṣayā
tāni pāpasya khaṇḍāni
liṅgaṁ khaṇḍam ihocyate

yāni—all those which; *rūpāṇi*—forms; *jagṛhe*—accepted; *indraḥ*—the King of heaven; *haya*—the horse; *jihīrṣayā*—with a desire to steal; *tāni*—all those; *pāpasya*—of sinful activities; *khaṇḍāni*—signs; *liṅgam*—the symbol; *khaṇḍam*—the word *khaṇḍa; iha*—here; *ucyate*—is said.

TRANSLATION

Whatever different forms Indra assumed as a mendicant because of his desire to seize the horse were symbols of atheistic philosophy.

PURPORT

According to Vedic civilization, *sannyāsa* is one of the essential items in the program of the *varṇa-āśrama* institution. One should accept *sannyāsa* according to the *paramparā* system of the *ācāryas.* At the present moment, however, many so-called *sannyāsīs* or mendicants have no understanding of God consciousness. Such *sannyāsa* was introduced by Indra because of his jealousy of Mahārāja Pṛthu, and what he introduced is again appearing in the age of Kali. Practically none of the *sannyāsīs* in this age are bona fide. No one can introduce any new system into the Vedic way of life; if one does so out of malice, he is to be known as a *pāṣaṇḍī*, or atheist. In the Vaiṣṇava *Tantra* it is said:

yas tu nārāyaṇaṁ devaṁ
brahma-rudrādi-daivataiḥ
samatvenaiva vīkṣeta
sa pāṣaṇḍī bhaved dhruvam

Although it is forbidden, there are many *pāṣaṇḍīs* who coin terms like *daridra-nārāyaṇa* and *svāmi-nārāyaṇa*, although not even such demigods as Brahmā and Śiva can be equal to Nārāyaṇa.

TEXTS 24–25

एवमिन्द्रे हरत्यश्वं वैन्ययज्ञजिघांसया ।
तद्गृहीतविसृष्टेषु पाखण्डेषु मतिर्नृणाम् ॥२४॥
धर्म इत्युपधर्मेषु नग्नरक्तपटादिषु ।
प्रायेण सज्जते भ्रान्त्या पेशलेषु च वाग्मिषु ॥२५॥

evam indre haraty aśvaṁ
vainya-yajña-jighāṁsayā
tad-gṛhīta-visṛṣṭeṣu
pākhaṇḍeṣu matir nṛṇām

dharma ity upadharmeṣu
nagna-rakta-paṭādiṣu
prāyeṇa sajjate bhrāntyā
peśaleṣu ca vāgmiṣu

evam—thus; *indre*—when the King of heaven; *harati*—stole; *aśvam*—the horse; *vainya*—of the son of King Vena; *yajña*—the sacrifice; *jighāṁsayā*—with a desire to stop; *tat*—by him; *gṛhīta*—accepted; *visṛṣṭeṣu*—abandoned; *pākhaṇḍeṣu*—towards the sinful dress; *matiḥ*—attraction; *nṛṇām*—of the people in general; *dharmaḥ*—system of religion; *iti*—thus; *upadharmeṣu*—towards false religious systems; *nagna*—naked; *rakta-paṭa*—red-robed; *ādiṣu*—etc.; *prāyeṇa*—generally; *sajjate*—is attracted; *bhrāntyā*—foolishly; *peśaleṣu*—expert; *ca*—and; *vāgmiṣu*—eloquent.

TRANSLATION

In this way, King Indra, in order to steal the horse from King Pṛthu's sacrifice, adopted several orders of sannyāsa. Some sannyāsīs go naked, and sometimes they wear red garments and pass under the name of kāpālika. These are simply symbolic representations of their sinful activities. These so-called sannyāsīs are very much appreciated by sinful men because they are all godless atheists and very expert in putting forward arguments and reasons to support their case. We must know, however, that they are only passing as adherents of religion and are not so in fact. Unfortunately, bewildered persons accept them as religious, and being attracted to them, they spoil their life.

PURPORT

As stated in *Śrīmad-Bhāgavatam*, men in this age of Kali are short-lived, devoid of spiritual knowledge, and susceptible to accept false religious systems due to their unfortunate condition. Thus they always remain mentally disturbed. The Vedic *śāstras* practically prohibit the adoption of *sannyāsa* in the age of Kali because less intelligent men may accept the *sannyāsa* order for cheating purposes. Actually the only religion is the religion of surrender unto the Supreme Personality of Godhead. We must serve the Lord in Kṛṣṇa consciousness. All other systems of *sannyāsa* and religion are actually not bona fide. In this age they are simply passing for religious systems. This is most regrettable.

TEXT 26

तदभिज्ञाय भगवान् पृथुः पृथुपराक्रमः ।
इन्द्राय कुपितो बाणमादत्तोद्यतकार्मुकः ॥२६॥

tad abhijñāya bhagavān
pṛthuḥ pṛthu-parākramaḥ
indrāya kupito bāṇam
ādattodyata-kārmukaḥ

tat—that; *abhijñāya*—understanding; *bhagavān*—the incarnation of Godhead; *pṛthuḥ*—King Pṛthu; *pṛthu-parākramaḥ*—celebrated as very powerful; *indrāya*—upon Indra; *kupitaḥ*—being very angry; *bāṇam*—an arrow; *ādatta*—took up; *udyata*—having taken up; *kārmukaḥ*—the bow.

TRANSLATION

Mahārāja Pṛthu, who was celebrated as very powerful, immediately took up his bow and arrows and prepared to kill Indra himself, because Indra had introduced such irregular sannyāsa orders.

PURPORT

It is the duty of the king not to tolerate the introduction of any irreligious systems. Since King Pṛthu was an incarnation of the Supreme Personality of Godhead, certainly his duty was to cut down all kinds of irreligious systems. Following in his footsteps, all heads of state should themselves be bona fide representatives of God and should cut down all irreligious systems. Unfortunately they are cowards who declare a secular state. Such a mentality is a way of compromising religious and irreligious systems, but because of this citizens are generally becoming uninterested in spiritual advancement. Thus the situation deteriorates to such an extent that human society becomes hellish.

TEXT 27

तमृत्विजः शक्रवधाभिसन्धितं
विचक्ष्य दुष्प्रेक्ष्यमसह्यरंहसम् ।
निवारयामासुरहो महामते
न युज्यतेऽत्रान्यवधः प्रचोदितात् ॥२७॥

tam ṛtvijaḥ śakra-vadhābhisandhitaṁ
vicakṣya duṣprekṣyam asahya-raṁhasam
nivārayām āsur aho mahā-mate
na yujyate 'trānya-vadhaḥ pracoditāt

tam—King Pṛthu; *ṛtvijaḥ*—the priests; *śakra-vadha*—killing the King of heaven; *abhisandhitam*—thus preparing himself; *vicaksya*—having observed; *duṣprekṣyam*—terrible to look at; *asahya*—unbearable; *raṁhasam*—whose velocity; *nivārayām āsuḥ*—they forbade; *aho*—oh; *mahā-mate*—O great soul; *na*—not; *yujyate*—is worthy for you; *atra*—in this sacrificial arena; *anya*—others; *vadhaḥ*—killing; *pracoditāt*—from being so directed in the scriptures.

TRANSLATION

When the priests and all the others saw Mahārāja Pṛthu very angry and prepared to kill Indra, they requested him: O great soul, do not kill him, for only sacrificial animals can be killed in a sacrifice. Such are the directions given by śāstra.

PURPORT

Animal killing is intended for different purposes. It tests the proper pronunciation of Vedic *mantras*, and an animal being put into the sacrificial fire should come out with a new life. No one should ever be killed in a sacrifice meant for the satisfaction of Lord Viṣṇu. How then could Indra be killed when he is actually worshiped in the *yajña* and accepted as part and parcel of the Supreme Personality of Godhead? Therefore the priests requested King Pṛthu not to kill him.

TEXT 28

वयं मरुत्वन्तमिहार्थनाशनं
ह्वयामहे त्वच्छ्रवसा हतत्विषम् ।
अयातयामोपहवैरनन्तरं
प्रसह्य राजन् जुहवाम तेऽहितम् ॥२८॥

vayaṁ marutvantam ihārtha-nāśanaṁ
hvayāmahe tvac-chravasā hata-tviṣam
ayātayāmopahavair anantaraṁ
prasahya rājan juhavāma te 'hitam

vayam—we; *marut-vantam*—King Indra; *iha*—here; *artha*—of your interest; *nāśanam*—the destroyer; *hvayāmahe*—we shall call; *tvat-śravasā*—by your glory; *hata-tviṣam*—already bereft of his power; *ayātayāma*—never before used; *upahavaiḥ*—by *mantras* of invocation; *anantaram*—without delay; *prasahya*—by force; *rājan*—O King; *juhavāma*—we shall sacrifice in the fire; *te*—your; *ahitam*—enemy.

TRANSLATION

Dear King, Indra's powers are already reduced due to his attempt to impede the execution of your sacrifice. We shall call him by Vedic mantras which were never before used, and certainly he will come. Thus by the power of our mantra, we shall cast him into the fire because he is your enemy.

PURPORT

By chanting the Vedic *mantras* properly in a sacrifice, one can perform many wonderful things. In Kali-yuga, however, there are no qualified *brāhmaṇas* who can chant the *mantras* properly. Consequently no attempt should be made to perform such big sacrifices. In this age the only sacrifice recommended is the *saṅkīrtana* movement.

TEXT 29

इत्यामन्त्र्य क्रतुपतिं विदुरास्यर्त्विजो रुषा ।
स्रुग्घस्तान्जुह्वतोऽभ्येत्य स्वयम्भूः प्रत्यषेधत ॥२९॥

ity āmantrya kratu-patiṁ
vidurāsyartvijo ruṣā
srug-ghastāñ juhvato 'bhyetya
svayambhūḥ pratyaṣedhata

iti—thus; *āmantrya*—after informing; *kratu-patim*—King Pṛthu, the master of the sacrifice; *vidura*—O Vidura; *asya*—of Pṛthu; *ṛtvijaḥ*—the priests; *ruṣā*—in great anger; *sruk-hastān*—with the sacrificial ladle in hand; *juhvataḥ*—performing the fire sacrifice; *abhyetya*—having begun; *svayambhūḥ*—Lord Brahmā; *pratyaṣedhata*—asked them to stop.

TRANSLATION

My dear Vidura, after giving the King this advice, the priests who had been engaged in performing the sacrifice called for Indra, the King of heaven, in a mood of great anger. When they were just ready to put the oblation in the fire, Lord Brahmā appeared on the scene and forbade them to start the sacrifice.

TEXT 30

न वध्यो भवतामिन्द्रो यद्यज्ञो भगवत्तनुः ।
यं जिघांसथ यज्ञेन यस्येष्टास्तनवः सुराः ॥३०॥

na vadhyo bhavatām indro
yad yajño bhagavat-tanuḥ
yaṁ jighāṁsatha yajñena
yasyeṣṭās tanavaḥ surāḥ

na—not; *vadhyaḥ*—ought to be killed; *bhavatām*—by all of you; *indraḥ*—the King of heaven; *yat*—because; *yajñaḥ*—a name of Indra;

bhagavat-tanuḥ—part of the body of the Supreme Personality of Godhead; *yam*—whom; *jighāṁsatha*—you wish to kill; *yajñena*—by performing sacrifice; *yasya*—of Indra; *iṣṭāḥ*—being worshiped; *tanavaḥ*—parts of the body; *surāḥ*—the demigods.

TRANSLATION

Lord Brahmā addressed them thus: My dear sacrificial performers, you cannot kill Indra, the King of heaven. It is not your duty. You should know that Indra is as good as the Supreme Personality of Godhead. Indeed, he is one of the most powerful assistants of the Personality of Godhead. You are trying to satisfy all the demigods by the performance of this yajña, but you should know that all these demigods are but parts and parcels of Indra, the King of heaven. How, then, can you kill him in this great sacrifice?

TEXT 31

तदिदं पश्यत महद्धर्मव्यतिकरं द्विजाः ।
इन्द्रेणानुष्ठितं राज्ञः कर्मैतद्विजिघांसता ॥३१॥

tad idaṁ paśyata mahad-
dharma-vyatikaraṁ dvijāḥ
indreṇānuṣṭhitaṁ rājñaḥ
karmaitad vijighāṁsatā

tat—then; *idam*—this; *paśyata*—just see; *mahat*—great; *dharma*—of religious life; *vyatikaram*—violation; *dvijāḥ*—O great *brāhmaṇas;* *indreṇa*—by Indra; *anuṣṭhitam*—performed; *rājñaḥ*—of the King; *karma*—activity; *etat*—this sacrifice; *vijighāṁsatā*—desiring to impede.

TRANSLATION

In order to make trouble and impede the performance of King Pṛthu's great sacrifice, King Indra has adopted some means that in the future will destroy the clear path of religious life. I draw your attention to this fact. If you oppose him any further, he will

further misuse his power and introduce many other irreligious systems.

TEXT 32

पृथुकीर्तेः पृथोर्भूयात्तर्ह्येकोनशतक्रतुः ।
अलं ते क्रतुभिः स्विष्टैर्यद्भवान्मोक्षधर्मवित् ॥३२॥

pṛthu-kīrteḥ pṛthor bhūyāt
tarhy ekona-śata-kratuḥ
alaṁ te kratubhiḥ sviṣṭair
yad bhavān mokṣa-dharma-vit

pṛthu-kīrteḥ—of wide renown; *pṛthoḥ*—of King Pṛthu; *bhūyāt*—let it be; *tarhi*—therefore; *eka-ūna-śata-kratuḥ*—he who performed ninety-nine *yajñas; alam*—there is nothing to be gained; *te*—of you; *kratubhiḥ*—by performing sacrifices; *su-iṣṭaiḥ*—well performed; *yat*—because; *bhavān*—yourself; *mokṣa-dharma-vit*—the knower of the path of liberation.

TRANSLATION

"Let there be only ninety-nine sacrificial performances for Mahārāja Pṛthu," Lord Brahmā concluded. Lord Brahmā then turned towards Mahārāja Pṛthu and informed him that since he was thoroughly aware of the path of liberation, what was the use in performing more sacrifices?

PURPORT

Lord Brahmā came down to pacify King Pṛthu regarding his continual performance of one hundred sacrifices. King Pṛthu was determined to perform one hundred sacrifices, and King Indra took this very seriously because Indra himself was known as the performer of one hundred sacrifices. Just as it is the nature of all living entities within this material world to become envious of their competitors, King Indra, although King of heaven, was also envious of King Pṛthu and therefore wanted to stop him from performing one hundred sacrifices. Actually there was great competition, and King Indra, to satisfy his senses, began to invent so many irreligious systems to obstruct King Pṛthu. To stop these irreligious inventions, Lord Brahmā personally appeared in the sacrificial arena. As far as Mahārāja Pṛthu was concerned, he was a great devotee of the Supreme Personality of Godhead; therefore it was not necessary for him to perform the prescribed Vedic ritualistic ceremonies. Such ceremonies are known as *karma*, and there is no need for a devotee in the transcendental position to execute them. As the ideal king, however, it was King Pṛthu's duty to perform sacrifices. A compromise was therefore to be worked out. By the blessings of Lord Brahmā, King Pṛthu would become more famous than King Indra. Thus Pṛthu's determination to perform one hundred sacrifices was indirectly fulfilled by the blessings of Lord Brahmā.

TEXT 33

नैवात्मने महेन्द्राय रोषमाहर्तुमर्हसि ।
उभावपि हि भद्रं ते उत्तमश्लोकविग्रहौ ॥३३॥

naivātmane mahendrāya
roṣam āhartum arhasi
ubhāv api hi bhadraṁ te
uttamaśloka-vigrahau

na—not; *eva*—certainly; *ātmane*—nondifferent from you; *mahā-indrāya*—upon the King of heaven, Indra; *roṣam*—anger; *āhartum*—to apply; *arhasi*—you ought; *ubhau*—both of you; *api*—certainly; *hi*—also; *bhadram*—good fortune; *te*—unto you; *uttama-śloka-vigrahau*—incarnations of the Supreme Personality of Godhead.

TRANSLATION

Lord Brahmā continued: Let there be good fortune to both of you, for you and King Indra are both part and parcel of the Supreme Personality of Godhead. Therefore you should not be angry with King Indra, who is nondifferent from you.

TEXT 34

मास्मिन्महाराज कृथाः स्म चिन्तां
निशामयास्मद्वच आदृतात्मा ।
यद्ध्यायतो दैवहतं नु कर्तुं
मनोऽतिरुष्टं विशते तमोऽन्धम् ॥३४॥

māsmin mahārāja kṛthāḥ sma cintāṁ
niśāmayāsmad-vaca ādṛtātmā
yad dhyāyato daiva-hataṁ nu kartuṁ
mano 'tiruṣṭaṁ viśate tamo 'ndham

mā—do not; *asmin*—in this; *mahā-rāja*—O King; *kṛthāḥ*—do; *sma*—as done in the past; *cintām*—agitation of the mind; *niśāmaya*—please consider; *asmat*—my; *vacaḥ*—words; *ādṛta-ātmā*—being very respectful; *yat*—because; *dhyāyataḥ*—of him who is contemplating; *daiva-hatam*—that which is thwarted by providence; *nu*—certainly; *kartum*—to do; *manaḥ*—the mind; *ati-ruṣṭam*—very angry; *viśate*—enters; *tamaḥ*—darkness; *andham*—dense.

TRANSLATION

My dear King, do not be agitated and anxious because your sacrifices have not been properly executed due to providential impediments. Kindly take my words with great respect. We should always remember that if something happens by providential arrangement, we should not be very sorry. The more we try to rectify such reversals, the more we enter into the darkest region of materialistic thought.

PURPORT

Sometimes the saintly or very religious person also has to meet with reversals in life. Such incidents should be taken as providential. Although there may be sufficient cause for being unhappy, one should avoid counteracting such reversals, for the more we become implicated in rectifying such reversals, the more we enter into the darkest regions of material anxiety. Lord Kṛṣṇa has also advised us in this connection. We should tolerate things instead of becoming agitated.

TEXT 35

क्रतुर्विरमतामेष देवेषु दुरवग्रहः ।
धर्मव्यतिकरो यत्र पाखण्डैरिन्द्रनिर्मितैः ॥३५॥

kratur viramatām eṣa
deveṣu duravagrahaḥ
dharma-vyatikaro yatra
pākhaṇḍair indra-nirmitaiḥ

kratuḥ—the sacrifice; *viramatām*—let it stop; *eṣaḥ*—this; *deveṣu*—amongst the demigods; *duravagrahaḥ*—addiction to unwanted things; *dharma-vyatikaraḥ*—violation of religious principles; *yatra*—where; *pākhaṇḍaiḥ*—by sinful activities; *indra*—by the King of heaven; *nirmitaiḥ*—manufactured.

TRANSLATION

Lord Brahmā continued: Stop the performance of these sacrifices, for they have induced Indra to introduce so many irreligious aspects. You should know very well that even amongst the demigods there are many unwanted desires.

PURPORT

There are many competitors in ordinary business affairs, and the *karma-kāṇḍa* chapters of the *Vedas* sometimes cause competition and envy amongst *karmīs.* A *karmī* must be envious because he wishes to enjoy material pleasures to their fullest extent. That is the material disease. Consequently there is always competition amongst *karmīs*, either in ordinary business affairs or in the performance of *yajña.* Lord Brahmā's purpose was to end the competition between Lord Indra and Mahārāja Pṛthu. Because Mahārāja Pṛthu was a great devotee and incarnation of God, he was requested to stop the sacrifices so that Indra might not further introduce irreligious systems, which are always followed by criminal-minded people.

TEXT 36

एभिरिन्द्रोपसंसृष्टैः पाखण्डैर्हारिभिर्जनम् ।
ह्रियमाणं विचक्ष्वैनं यस्ते यज्ञध्रुगश्वमुट् ॥३६॥

ebhir indropasaṁsṛṣṭaiḥ
pākhaṇḍair hāribhir janam
hriyamāṇaṁ vicakṣvainaṁ
yas te yajña-dhrug aśva-muṭ

ebhiḥ—by these; *indra-upasaṁsṛṣṭaiḥ*—created by the King of heaven, Indra; *pākhaṇḍaiḥ*—sinful activities; *hāribhiḥ*—very attractive to the heart; *janam*—the people in general; *hriyamāṇam*—being carried away; *vicakṣva*—just see; *enam*—these; *yaḥ*—one who; *te*—your; *yajña-dhruk*—creating a disturbance in the performance of the sacrifice; *aśva-muṭ*—who stole the horse.

TRANSLATION

Just see how Indra, the King of heaven, was creating a disturbance in the midst of the sacrifice by stealing the sacrificial horse. These attractive sinful activities he has introduced will be carried out by the people in general.

PURPORT

As stated in *Bhagavad-gītā* (3.21):

yad yad ācarati śreṣṭhas
tad tad evetaro janaḥ
sa yat pramāṇaṁ kurute
lokas tad anuvartate

"Whatever action is performed by a great man, common men follow in his footsteps. And whatever standards he sets by exemplary acts, all the world pursues."

For his own sense gratification, King Indra thought to defeat Mahārāja Pṛthu in the performance of one hundred horse sacrifices. Consequently he stole the horse and hid himself amid so many irreligious personalities, taking on the false guise of a *sannyāsī*. Such activities are attractive to the people in general; therefore they are dangerous. Lord Brahmā thought that instead of allowing Indra to further introduce such irreligious systems, it would be better to stop the sacrifice. A similar stance was taken by Lord Buddha when people were overly engrossed in the animal sacrifices recommended by Vedic instructions. Lord Buddha had to introduce the religion of nonviolence by contradicting the Vedic sacrificial instructions. Actually, in the sacrifices the slaughtered animals were given a new life, but people without such powers were taking advantage of such Vedic rituals and unnecessarily killing poor animals. Therefore Lord Buddha had to deny the authority of the *Vedas* for the time being. One should not perform sacrifices that will induce reversed orders. It is better to stop such sacrifices.

As we have repeatedly explained, due to a lack of qualified brahminical priests in Kali-yuga, it is not possible to perform the ritualistic ceremonies recommended in the *Vedas*. Consequently the *śāstras* instruct us to perform the *saṅkīrtana-yajña*. By the *saṅkīrtana* sacrifice, the Supreme Personality of Godhead, in His form of Lord Caitanya, will be satisfied and worshiped. The entire purpose of performing sacrifices is to worship the Supreme Personality of Godhead, Viṣṇu. Lord Viṣṇu, or Lord Kṛṣṇa, is present in His form of Lord Caitanya; therefore people who are intelligent should try to satisfy Him by performing *saṅkīrtana-yajña*. This is the easiest way to satisfy Lord Viṣṇu in this age. People should take advantage of the injunctions in different *śāstras* concerning sacrifices in this age and not create unnecessary disturbances during the sinful age of Kali. In Kali-yuga men all over the world are very expert in opening slaughterhouses for killing animals, which they eat. If the old ritualistic ceremonies were observed, people would be encouraged to kill more and more animals. In Calcutta there are many butcher shops which keep a deity of the goddess Kālī, and animal-eaters think it proper to purchase animal flesh from such shops in hope that they are eating the remnants of food offered to goddess Kālī. They do not know that goddess Kālī never accepts nonvegetarian food because she is the chaste wife of Lord Śiva. Lord Śiva is also a great Vaiṣṇava and never eats nonvegetarian food, and the goddess Kālī accepts the remnants of food left by Lord Śiva. Therefore there is no possibility of her eating flesh or fish. Such offerings are accepted by the associates of goddess Kālī known as *bhūtas, piśācas* and Rākṣasas, and those who take the *prasāda* of goddess Kālī in the shape of flesh or fish are not actually taking the *prasāda* left by goddess Kālī, but the food left by the *bhūtas* and *piśācas.*

TEXT 37

भवान् परित्रातुमिहावतीर्णो
धर्मं जनानां समयानुरूपम् ।
वेनापचारादवलुप्तमद्य
तद्देहतो विष्णुकलासि वैन्य ॥३७॥

bhavān paritrātum ihāvatīrṇo
dharmaṁ janānāṁ samayānurūpam
venāpacārād avaluptam adya
tad-dehato viṣṇu-kalāsi vainya

bhavān—Your Majesty; *paritrātum*—just to deliver; *iha*—in this world; *avatīrṇaḥ*—incarnated; *dharmam*—religious system; *janānām*—of the people in general; *samaya-anurūpam*—according to the time and circumstances; *vena-apacārāt*—by the misdeeds of King Vena; *avaluptam*—almost vanished; *adya*—at the present moment; *tat*—his; *dehataḥ*—from the body; *viṣṇu*—of Lord Viṣṇu; *kalā*—part of a plenary portion; *asi*—you are; *vainya*—O son of King Vena.

TRANSLATION

O King Pṛthu, son of Vena, you are the part-and-parcel expansion of Lord Viṣṇu. Due to the mischievous activities of King Vena, religious principles were almost lost. At that opportune moment you descended as the incarnation of Lord Viṣṇu. Indeed, for the protection of religious principles you have appeared from the body of King Vena.

PURPORT

The way in which Lord Viṣṇu kills the demons and protects the faithful is mentioned in *Bhagavad-gītā* (4.8):

paritrāṇāya sādhūnāṁ
vināśāya ca duṣkṛtām
dharma-saṁsthāpanārthāya
sambhavāmi yuge yuge

"In order to deliver the pious and to annihilate the miscreants, as well as to reestablish the principles of religion, I advent Myself millennium after millennium."

In two hands Lord Viṣṇu always carries a club and a *cakra* to kill demons, and in His other two hands He holds a conchshell and a lotus to give protection to His devotees. When His incarnation is present on this planet or in this universe, the Lord kills the demons and protects His devotees simultaneously. Sometimes Lord Viṣṇu appears in His person as Lord Kṛṣṇa or Lord Rāma. All of these appearances are mentioned in the *śāstras.* Sometimes He appears as a *śaktyāveśa-avatāra* like Lord Buddha. As explained before, these *śaktyāveśa-avatāras* are incarnations of Viṣṇu's power invested in a living entity. Living entities are also part and parcel of Lord Viṣṇu, but they are not as powerful; therefore when a living entity descends as an incarnation of Viṣṇu, he is especially empowered by the Lord.

When King Pṛthu is described as an incarnation of Lord Viṣṇu, it should be understood that he is a *śaktyāveśa-avatāra,* part and parcel of Lord Viṣṇu, and is specifically empowered by Him. Any living being acting as the incarnation of Lord Viṣṇu is thus empowered by Lord Viṣṇu to preach the *bhakti* cult. Such a person can act like Lord Viṣṇu and defeat demons by arguments and preach the *bhakti* cult exactly according to the principles of *śāstra.* As indicated in *Bhagavad-gītā,* whenever we find someone extraordinary preaching the *bhakti* cult, we should know that he is especially empowered by Lord Viṣṇu, or Lord Kṛṣṇa. As confirmed in *Caitanya-caritāmṛta* (*Antya* 7.11), *kṛṣṇa-śakti vinā nahe tāra pravartana:* one cannot explain the glories of the holy name of the Lord without being specifically empowered by Him. If one criticizes or finds fault with such an empowered personality, one is to be considered an offender against Lord Viṣṇu and is punishable. Even though such offenders may dress as Vaiṣṇavas with false *tilaka* and *mālā,* they are never forgiven by the Lord if they offend a pure Vaiṣṇava. There are many instances of this in the *śāstras.*

TEXT 38

स त्वं विमृश्यास्य भवं प्रजापते
सङ्कल्पनं विश्वसृजां पिपीपृहि ।
ऐन्द्रीं च मायामुपधर्ममातरं
प्रचण्डपाखण्डपथं प्रभो जहि ॥३८॥

sa tvaṁ vimṛśyāsya bhavaṁ prajāpate
saṅkalpanaṁ viśva-sṛjāṁ pipīpṛhi
aindrīṁ ca māyām upadharma-mātaraṁ
pracaṇḍa-pākhaṇḍa-pathaṁ prabho jahi

saḥ—the aforesaid; *tvam*—you; *vimṛśya*—considering; *asya*—of the world; *bhavam*—existence; *prajā-pate*—O protector of the people; *saṅkalpanam*—the determination; *viśva-sṛjām*—of the progenitors of the world; *pipīpṛhi*—just fulfill; *aindrīm*—created by the King of heaven; *ca*—also; *māyām*—illusion; *upadharma*—of the irreligious system of so-called *sannyāsa; mātaram*—the mother; *pracaṇḍa*—furious, dangerous; *pākhaṇḍa-patham*—the path of sinful activities; *prabho*—O Lord; *jahi*—please conquer.

TRANSLATION

O protector of the people in general, please consider the purpose of your being incarnated by Lord Viṣṇu. The irreligious principles created by Indra are but mothers of so many unwanted religions. Please therefore stop these imitations immediately.

PURPORT

Lord Brahmā addresses King Pṛthu as *prajāpate* just to remind him of his great responsibility in maintaining the peace and prosperity of the citizens. Mahārāja Pṛthu was empowered by the Supreme Personality of Godhead for this purpose only. It is the duty of the ideal king to see that people are properly executing religious principles. Lord Brahmā especially requested King Pṛthu to conquer the pseudoreligious principles produced by King Indra. In other words, it is the duty of the state or king to put a stop to pseudoreligious systems produced by unscrupulous persons. Originally a religious principle is one, given by the Supreme Personality of Godhead, and it comes through the channel of disciplic succession in two forms. Lord Brahmā requested Pṛthu Mahārāja to desist from his unnecessary competition with Indra, who was determined to stop Pṛthu Mahārāja from completing one hundred *yajñas*. Instead of creating adverse reactions, it was better for Mahārāja Pṛthu to stop the *yajñas* in the interest of his original purpose as an incarnation. This purpose was to establish good government and set things in the right order.

TEXT 39

मैत्रेय उवाच

इत्थं स लोकगुरुणा समादिष्टो विशाम्पतिः ।
तथा च कृत्वा वात्सल्यं मघोनापि च सन्दधे ॥३९॥

maitreya uvāca
itthaṁ sa loka-guruṇā
samādiṣṭo viśāmpatiḥ
tathā ca kṛtvā vātsalyaṁ
maghonāpi ca sandadhe

maitreyaḥ uvāca—the great sage Maitreya continued to speak; *ittham*—thus; *saḥ*—King Pṛthu; *loka-guruṇā*—by the original teacher of all people, Lord Brahmā; *samādiṣṭaḥ*—being advised; *viśām-patiḥ*—the king, master of the people; *tathā*—in that way; *ca*—also; *kṛtvā*—having done; *vātsalyam*—affection; *maghonā*—with Indra; *api*—even; *ca*—also; *sandadhe*—concluded peace.

TRANSLATION

The great sage Maitreya continued: When King Pṛthu was thus advised by the supreme teacher, Lord Brahmā, he abandoned his eagerness to perform yajñas and with great affection concluded a peace with King Indra.

TEXT 40

कृतावभृथस्नानाय पृथवे भूरिकर्मणे ।
वरान्ददुस्ते वरदा ये तद्बर्हिषि तर्पिताः ॥४०॥

kṛtāvabhṛtha-snānāya
pṛthave bhūri-karmaṇe
varān dadus te varadā
ye tad-barhiṣi tarpitāḥ

kṛta—having performed; *avabhṛtha-snānāya*—taking a bath after the sacrifice; *pṛthave*—unto King Pṛthu; *bhūri-karmaṇe*—famous for performing many virtuous acts; *varān*—benedictions; *daduḥ*—gave; *te*—all of them; *vara-dāḥ*—the demigods, bestowers of benedictions; *ye*—who; *tat-barhiṣi*—in the performance of such a *yajña; tarpitāḥ*—became pleased.

TRANSLATION

After this, Pṛthu Mahārāja took his bath, which is customarily taken after the performance of a yajña, and received the benedictions and due blessings of the demigods, who were very pleased by his glorious activities.

PURPORT

Yajña means Lord Viṣṇu, for all *yajña* is meant to please the Supreme Personality of Godhead, Lord Viṣṇu. Since the demigods automatically become very pleased with the performance of sacrifice, they bestow benediction upon the executors of *yajñas.* When one pours water on the root of a tree, the branches, trunk, twigs, flowers and leaves are all satisfied. Similarly, when one gives food to the stomach, all parts of the body are rejuvenated. In the same way, if one simply satisfies Lord Viṣṇu by the performance of *yajña,* one satisfies all the demigods automatically. In turn, the demigods offer their benedictions to such a devotee. A pure devotee therefore does not ask benedictions directly from the demigods. His only business is to serve the Supreme Personality of Godhead. Thus he is never in need of those things supplied by the demigods.

TEXT 41

विप्राः सत्याशिषस्तुष्टाः श्रद्धया लब्धदक्षिणाः ।
आशिषो युयुजुः क्षत्तरादिराजाय सत्कृताः ॥४१॥

viprāḥ satyāśiṣas tuṣṭāḥ
śraddhayā labdha-dakṣiṇāḥ
āśiṣo yuyujuḥ kṣattar
ādi-rājāya sat-kṛtāḥ

viprāḥ—all the *brāhmaṇas; satya*—true; *āśiṣaḥ*—whose benedictions; *tuṣṭāḥ*—being very satisfied; *śraddhayā*—with great respect; *labdha-dakṣiṇāḥ*—who obtained rewards; *āśiṣaḥ*—benedictions; *yuyujuḥ*—offered; *kṣattaḥ*—O Vidura; *ādi-rājāya*—upon the original king; *sat-kṛtāḥ*—being honored.

TRANSLATION

With great respect, the original king, Pṛthu, offered all kinds of rewards to the brāhmaṇas present at the sacrifice. Since all these brāhmaṇas were very much satisfied, they gave their heartfelt blessings to the King.

TEXT 42

त्वयाहूता महाबाहो सर्व एव समागताः ।
पूजिता दानमानाभ्यां पितृदेवर्षिमानवाः ॥४२॥

tvayāhūtā mahā-bāho
sarva eva samāgatāḥ
pūjitā dāna-mānābhyāṁ
pitṛ-devarṣi-mānavāḥ

tvayā—by you; *āhūtāḥ*—were invited; *mahā-bāho*—O great mighty-armed one; *sarve*—all; *eva*—certainly; *samāgatāḥ*—assembled; *pūjitāḥ*—were honored; *dāna*—by charity; *mānābhyām*—and by respect; *pitṛ*—the inhabitants of Pitṛloka; *deva*—demigods; *ṛṣi*—great sages; *mānavāḥ*—as well as common men.

TRANSLATION

All the great sages and brāhmaṇas said: O mighty King, by your invitation all classes of living entities have attended this assembly. They have come from Pitṛloka and the heavenly planets, and great sages as well as common men have attended this meeting. Now all of them are very much satisfied by your dealings and your charity towards them.

Thus end the Bhaktivedanta purports of the Fourth Canto, Nineteenth Chapter, of the Śrīmad-Bhāgavatam, *entitled "King Pṛthu's One Hundred Horse Sacrifices."*

Appendixes

About the Author

His Divine Grace A.C. Bhaktivedanta Swami Prabhupāda appeared in this world in 1896 in Calcutta, India. He first met his spiritual master, Śrīla Bhaktisiddhānta Sarasvatī Gosvāmī, in Calcutta in 1922. Bhaktisiddhānta Sarasvatī, a prominent religious scholar and the founder of sixty-four Gauḍīya Maṭhas (Vedic institutes), liked this educated young man and convinced him to dedicate his life to teaching Vedic knowledge. Śrīla Prabhupāda became his student, and eleven years later (1933) at Allahabad he became his formally initiated disciple.

At their first meeting, in 1922, Śrīla Bhaktisiddhānta Sarasvatī Ṭhākura requested Śrīla Prabhupāda to broadcast Vedic knowledge through the English language. In the years that followed, Śrīla Prabhupāda wrote a commentary on the *Bhagavad-gītā*, assisted the Gauḍīya Maṭha in its work and, in 1944, started *Back to Godhead*, an English fortnightly magazine. Maintaining the publication was a struggle. Singlehandedly, Śrīla Prabhupāda edited it, typed the manuscripts, checked the galley proofs, and even distributed the individual copies. Once begun, the magazine never stopped; it is now being continued by his disciples in the West and is published in over thirty languages.

Recognizing Śrīla Prabhupāda's philosophical learning and devotion, the Gauḍīya Vaiṣṇava Society honored him in 1947 with the title "Bhaktivedanta." In 1950, at the age of fifty-four, Śrīla Prabhupāda retired from married life, adopting the *vānaprastha* (retired) order to devote more time to his studies and writing. Śrīla Prabhupāda traveled to the holy city of Vṛndāvana, where he lived in very humble circumstances in the historic medieval temple of Rādhā-Dāmodara. There he engaged for several years in deep study and writing. He accepted the renounced order of life (*sannyāsa*) in 1959. At Rādhā-Dāmodara, Śrīla Prabhupāda began work on his life's masterpiece: a multivolume annotated translation of the eighteen-thousand-verse *Śrīmad-Bhāgavatam* (*Bhāgavata Purāṇa*). He also wrote *Easy Journey to Other Planets.*

After publishing three volumes of the *Bhāgavatam*, Śrīla Prabhupāda came to the United States, in September 1965, to fulfill the mission of his spiritual master. Subsequently, His Divine Grace wrote more than sixty volumes of authoritative annotated translations and summary studies of the philosophical and religious classics of India.

When he first arrived by freighter in New York City, Śrīla Prabhupāda was practically penniless. Only after almost a year of great difficulty did he establish the International Society for Krishna Consciousness, in July of 1966. Before his passing away on November 14, 1977, he guided the Society and saw it grow to a worldwide confederation of more than one hundred *āśramas,* schools, temples, institutes and farm communities.

In 1968, Śrīla Prabhupāda created New Vrindaban, an experimental Vedic community in the hills of West Virginia. Inspired by the success of New Vrindaban, now a thriving farm community of more than two thousand acres, his students have since founded several similar communities in the United States and abroad.

In 1972, His Divine Grace introduced the Vedic system of primary and secondary education in the West by founding the Gurukula school in Dallas, Texas. Since then, under his supervision, his disciples have established children's schools throughout the United States and the rest of the world, with the principal educational center now located in Vṛndāvana, India.

Śrīla Prabhupāda also inspired the construction of several large international cultural centers in India. The center at Śrīdhāma Māyāpur in West Bengal is the site for a planned spiritual city, an ambitious project for which construction will extend over many years to come. In Vṛndāvana, India, are the magnificent Kṛṣṇa-Balarāma Temple and International Guesthouse, and Śrīla Prabhupāda Memorial and Museum. There is also a major cultural and educational center in Bombay. Other centers are planned in a dozen important locations on the Indian subcontinent.

Śrīla Prabhupāda's most significant contribution, however, is his books. Highly respected by the academic community for their authority, depth and clarity, they are used as standard textbooks in numerous college courses. His writings have been translated into over fifty languages. The Bhaktivedanta Book Trust, established in 1972 to publish the works of His Divine Grace, has thus become the world's largest publisher of books in the field of Indian religion and philosophy.

In just twelve years, in spite of his advanced age, Śrīla Prabhupāda circled the globe fourteen times on lecture tours that took him to six continents. In spite of such a vigorous schedule, Śrīla Prabhupāda continued to write prolifically. His writings constitute a veritable library of Vedic philosophy, religion, literature and culture.

References

The purports of *Śrīmad-Bhāgavatam* are all confirmed by standard Vedic authorities. The following authentic scriptures are cited in this volume. For specific page references, consult the general index.

Bhagavad-gītā

Bhakti-rasāmṛta-sindhu

Bhāgavata Purāṇa. See: Śrīmad-Bhāgavatam

Brahma-saṁhitā

Caitanya-candrāmṛta

Caitanya-caritāmṛta

Hari-bhakti-sudhodaya

Hari-bhakti-vilāsa

Īśopaniṣad

Kaṭha Upaniṣad

Mukunda-mālā-stotra

Nārada-pañcarātra

Śikṣāṣṭaka

Śiva Purāṇa

Śrīmad-Bhāgavatam

Taittirīya Upaniṣad

Vedānta-sūtra

GENEALOGICAL TABLE

The Descendants of the Daughters of Svāyambhuva Manu

The Manus are administrators of universal affairs, and all the members of human society descend from the original Manu. (The word "man"—or, in Sanskrit, *manuṣya*—comes from the name *Manu.*) The Vedic literatures explain that during one day in the life of the demigod Brahmā (4,320,000,000 years), fourteen Manus come and go. Svāyambhuva Manu, the first of the fourteen, is Brahmā's son, and he in turn had two sons and three daughters. This chart delineates the offspring of Svāyambhuva Manu's daughters.

+indicates marriage ties

- Svāyambhuva Manu (+ Śatarūpā)
  - Uttānapāda
    - (+ Suruci) — Uttama
    - (+ Sunīti) — Dhruva — (*For the descendants of Dhruva, see the following genealogical table.*)
  - Priyavrata — (*For the descendants of Priyavrata, see* Śrīmad-Bhāgavatam, *Canto Five.*)
  - Ākūti (+ Ruci)
    - YAJÑA + Dakṣiṇā
      - Toṣa
      - Pratoṣa
      - Santoṣa
      - Bhadra
      - Śānti
      - Iḍaspati
      - Idhma
      - Kavi
      - Vibhu
      - Svahna
      - Sudeva
      - Rocana
  - Kalā (+ Marīci)
    - Kaśyapa — (*For the descendants of Kaśyapa, see the table in* Śrīmad-Bhāgavatam, *Canto Six.*)
    - Pūrṇimā
      - Viraja
      - Viśvaga
      - Devakulyā
  - Anasūyā (+ Atri)
    - Soma
    - Dattātreya
    - Durvāsā
  - Śraddhā (+ Aṅgirā)
    - (daughters)
      - Sinīvālī
      - Kuhū
      - Rākā
      - Anumati
    - (sons)
      - Utathya
      - Bṛhaspati

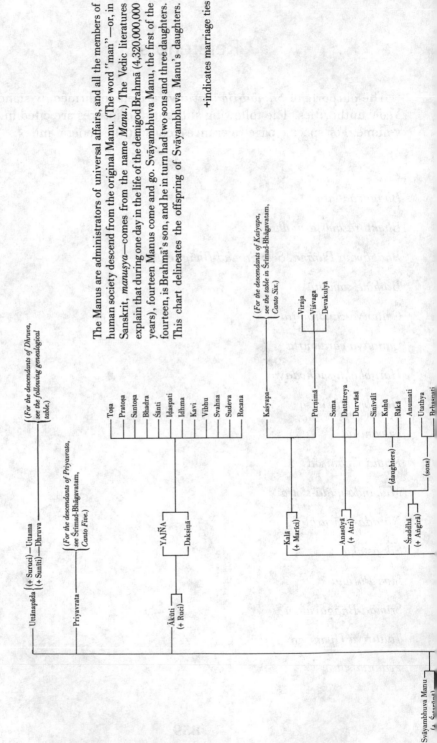

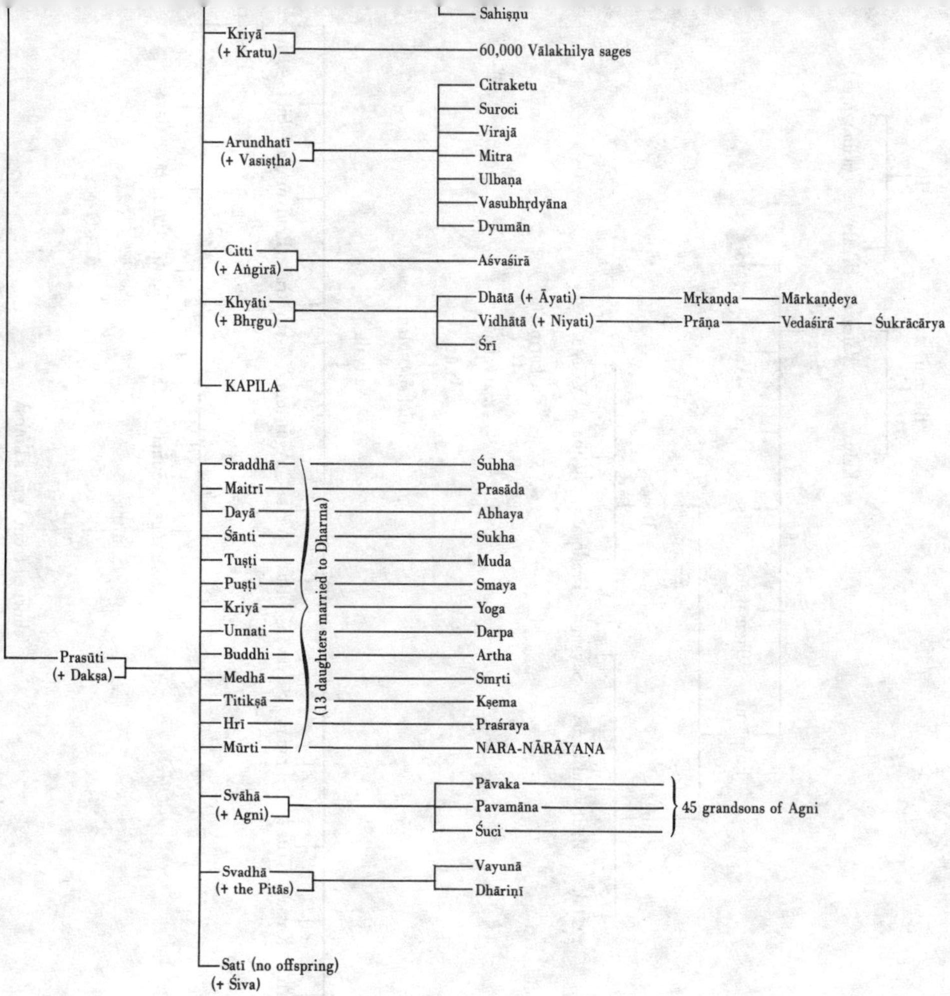
Sahiṣṇu
Kriyā (+ Kratu)
60,000 Vālakhilya sages
Arundhatī (+ Vasiṣṭha)
Citraketu
Suroci
Virajā
Mitra
Ulbaṇa
Vasubhṛdyāna
Dyumān
Citti (+ Aṅgirā)
Aśvaśirā
Khyāti (+ Bhṛgu)
Dhātā (+ Āyati)
Mṛkaṇḍa
Mārkaṇḍeya
Vidhātā (+ Niyati)
Prāṇa
Vedaśirā
Śukrācārya
Śrī
KAPILA
Prasūti (+ Dakṣa)
Sraddhā
Śubha
Maitrī
Prasāda
Dayā
Abhaya
Śānti
Sukha
Tuṣṭi
Muda
Puṣṭi
Smaya
Kriyā
Yoga
Unnati
Darpa
Buddhi
Artha
Medhā
Smṛti
Titikṣā
Kṣema
Hrī
Praśraya
Mūrti
NARA-NĀRĀYAṆA
(13 daughters married to Dharma)
Svāhā (+ Agni)
Pāvaka
Pavamāna
Śuci
45 grandsons of Agni
Svadhā (+ the Pitās)
Vayunā
Dhāriṇī
Satī (no offspring) (+ Śiva)

GENEALOGICAL TABLE

The Descendants of Dhruva Mahārāja

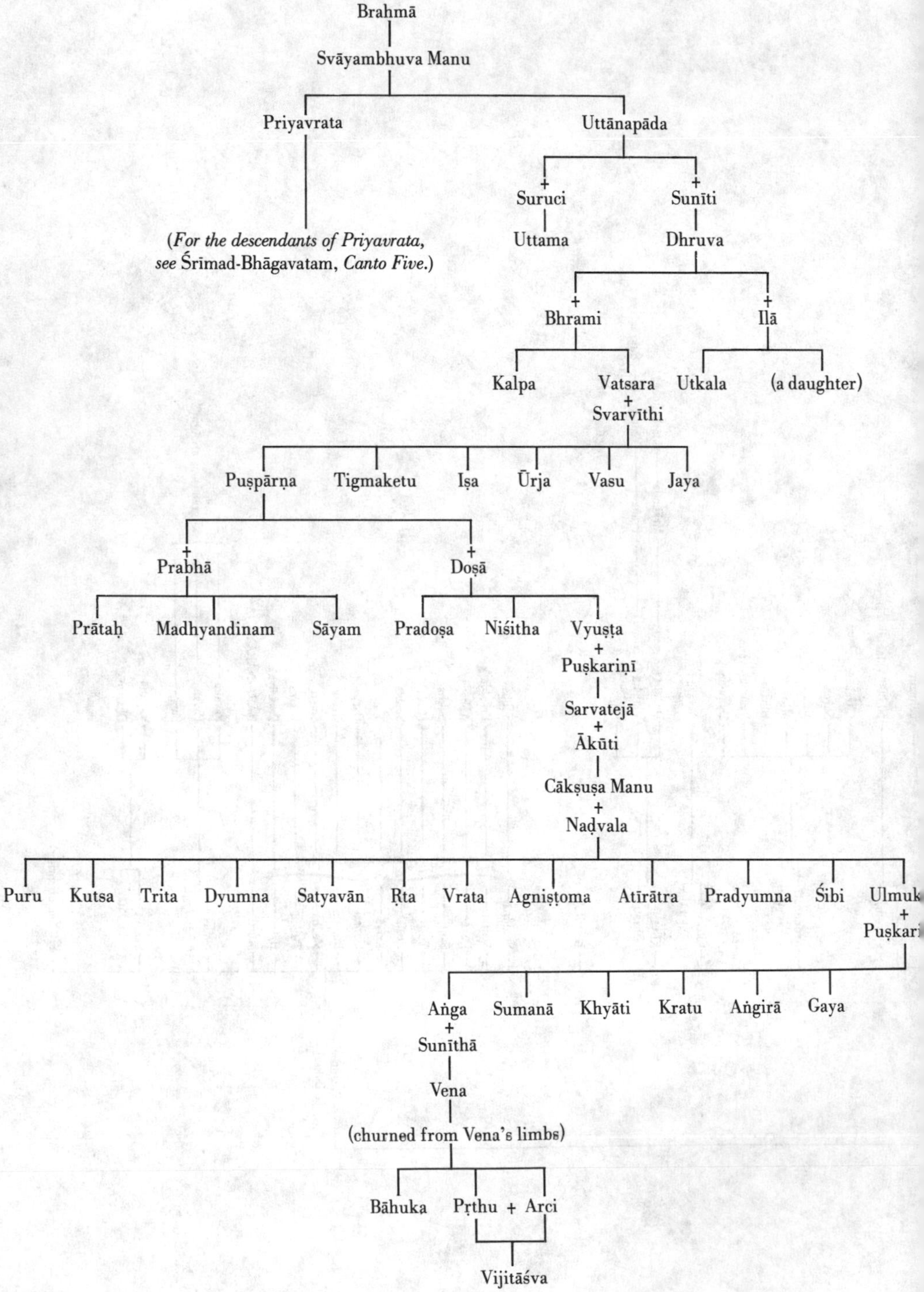

(*For other descendants of Pṛthu, see the following volume of* Śrīmad-Bhāgavatam.)

GLOSSARY

A

Ācamana—purification by sipping water and chanting names of the Lord, especially before a sacrifice.

Ācārya—an ideal teacher, who teaches by his personal example; a spiritual master.

Adhokṣaja—the Supreme Lord, who is beyond material sense perception.

Advaita Prabhu—an incarnation of Viṣṇu who appeared as a principal associate of Lord Caitanya Mahāprabhu.

Agni—the demigod in charge of fire.

Ajāmila—a fallen *brāhmaṇa* who was saved from hell by chanting the name of Lord Nārāyaṇa at the time of death.

Ākūti—one of Svāyambhuva Manu's three daughters and the wife of Ruci.

Ananta—the Lord's thousand-headed serpent incarnation, who serves as the bed of Viṣṇu and sustains the planets on His hoods.

Aṅga Mahārāja—the father of King Vena.

Aṇimā—the mystic power to become as small as an atom.

Aniruddha—one of the four original expansions of Lord Kṛṣṇa in the spiritual world; also, a grandson of Lord Kṛṣṇa.

Ārati—a ceremony for greeting the Lord with chanting and offerings of food, lamps, fans, flowers and incense.

Arcanā—the devotional process of Deity worship.

Arci—the wife of King Pṛthu.

Arjuna—one of the five Pāṇḍava brothers; Kṛṣṇa became his chariot driver and spoke the *Bhagavad-gītā* to him.

Aryamā—the demigod in charge of Pitṛloka, the planet where qualified departed ancestors reside.

Asita—an ancient authority on the *Vedas.*

Āśrama—one of four spiritual orders of life. *See also: Brahmacarya; Gṛhastha; Vānaprastha; Sannyāsa*

Aṣṭāṅga-yoga—the mystic *yoga* system propounded by Patañjali.

Asura—an atheistic demon; a gross materialist.

Aśvatthāmā—the nefarious son of the great military teacher Droṇācārya; he murdered the children of the Pāṇḍavas.

Atri—one of the seven great sages born directly from Brahmā; the father of the Lord's incarnation Dattātreya.

Avatāra—a descent, or incarnation, of the Supreme Lord.

Āveśa—*See: Śakty-āveśa*

B

Bāhuka—the personified sins of King Vena.

Balarāma (Baladeva)—a plenary expansion of the Supreme Personality of Godhead appearing as the son of Rohiṇī and elder brother of Lord Kṛṣṇa.

Bhagavad-gītā—the discourse between the Supreme Lord, Kṛṣṇa, and His devotee Arjuna expounding devotional service as both the principal means and the ultimate end of spiritual perfection.

Bhāgavata—anything related to Bhagavān, the Supreme Lord, especially the devotee of the Lord and the scripture *Śrīmad-Bhāgavatam*.

Bhajanānandī—a devotee who performs his devotional activities in seclusion, not attempting to preach.

Bhakta—a devotee of the Supreme Lord.

Bhaktisiddhānta Sarasvatī Ṭhākura—(1874-1937) the spiritual master of the author, His Divine Grace A. C. Bhaktivedanta Swami Prabhupāda, and thus the spiritual grandfather of the present-day Kṛṣṇa consciousness movement. A powerful preacher, he founded sixty-four missions in India.

Bhaktivinoda Ṭhākura—(1838-1915) the great-grandfather of the present-day Kṛṣṇa consciousness movement, the spiritual master of Śrīla Gaurakiśora dāsa Bābājī and the father of Śrīla Bhaktisiddhānta Sarasvatī.

Bhakti-yoga—linking with the Supreme Lord by devotional service.

Bharata Mahārāja—a great devotee of the Lord who developed an attachment causing him to take birth as a deer. In his next life, as the *brāhmaṇa* Jaḍa Bharata, he attained spiritual perfection.

Bhāratī—*See:* Sarasvatī

Bhṛgu—the most powerful of the sages born directly from Brahmā.

Bilvamaṅgala Ṭhākura—a great devotee-author, whose works include the *Kṛṣṇa-karṇāmṛta*.

Brahmā—the first created living being and secondary creator of the material universe.
Brahma-śāpa—a *brāhmaṇa's* curse.
Brahmacarya—celibate student life; the first order of Vedic spiritual life.
Brahmaloka—the highest planet of the universe, that of the demigod Brahmā.
Brahman—the Absolute Truth; especially the impersonal aspect of the Absolute.
Brāhmaṇa—a member of the intellectual, priestly class; the first Vedic social order.
Bṛhaspati—the spiritual master of King Indra and chief priest for the demigods.

C

Caitanya Mahāprabhu—(1486-1534) the Supreme Lord appearing as His own greatest devotee to teach love of God, especially through the process of *saṅkīrtana.*
Cakra (Sudarśana)—the disc weapon of the Supreme Lord.
Cāmara—a yak-tail fan used in Deity worship.
Cāṇakya Paṇḍita—the *brāhmaṇa* advisor to King Candragupta responsible for checking Alexander the Great's invasion of India. He is a famous author of books on politics and morality.
Caṇḍāla—an outcaste or untouchable; a dog-eater.
Candana—a cosmetic paste made from sandalwood; used in Deity worship.
Cāturmāsya—the four months of the rainy season in India. Devotees take special vows of austerity during this time.

D

Daivī-māyā—the Lord's divine deluding potency, the material energy.
Dakṣa—one of the sons of Brahmā and a chief progenitor of universal population.
Dākṣāyaṇī—Satī, daughter of Dakṣa and wife of Lord Śiva.
Daridra-nārāyaṇa—"poor Nārāyaṇa," an offensive term used by Māyāvādīs to equate poor men with the Supreme Lord.

Dattātreya—an incarnation of the Supreme Lord who appeared as the son of Atri Muni to teach the path of mystic *yoga.*

Devahūti—the daughter of Svāyambhuva Manu who was the wife of Kardama Muni and the mother of Lord Kapila.

Devala—an ancient authority on the *Vedas.*

Dharma—religion; duty, especially everyone's eternal service nature.

Dhruva Mahārāja—a great devotee who as a child performed severe austerities to meet the Lord and get the kingdom denied him. He thus received an entire planet and God realization as well.

Droṇācārya—the military teacher of the Pāṇḍavas. He was obliged to fight against them in the Battle of Kurukṣetra.

Durgā—the personified material energy and the wife of Lord Śiva.

Durvāsā Muni—a powerful mystic *yogī,* famous for his fearful curses.

E

Ekādaśī—a special day for increased remembrance of Kṛṣṇa, which comes on the eleventh day after both the full and new moon. Abstinence from grains and beans is prescribed.

G

Gadādhara—an intimate associate of Lord Śrī Caitanya Mahāprabhu.

Gāñjā—marijuana.

Garbhādhāna-saṁskāra—the Vedic ceremony of purification to be performed by parents before conceiving a child.

Garuḍa—Lord Viṣṇu's eternal carrier, a great devotee in a birdlike form.

Gauḍīya Vaiṣṇava sampradāya—the authorized Vaiṣṇava disciplic succession of bona fide spiritual masters coming through Lord Śrī Caitanya Mahāprabhu; also, the followers in that tradition.

Gaurakiśora dāsa Bābājī—the disciple of Śrīla Bhaktivinoda Ṭhākura who was the spiritual master of Śrīla Bhaktisiddhānta Sarasvatī Ṭhākura.

Gaurasundara—the beautiful, golden-complexioned Lord, Śrī Caitanya Mahāprabhu.

Goloka Vṛndāvana (Kṛṣṇaloka)—the highest spiritual planet, Lord Kṛṣṇa's personal abode.

Gopīs—Kṛṣṇa's cowherd girl friends, who are His most surrendered and confidential devotees.

Govinda—the Supreme Lord, Kṛṣṇa, who gives pleasure to the land, the cows and the senses.

Gṛha-vrata—one attached to the material duties of family life.

Gṛhastha—regulated householder life; the second order of Vedic spiritual life.

Guru—a spiritual master.

H

Hare (Harā)—*See:* Rādhārāṇī

Hare Kṛṣṇa mantra—*See: Mahā-mantra*

Hari—the Supreme Lord, who removes all obstacles to spiritual progress.

Haridāsa Ṭhākura—a great devotee and associate of Lord Śrī Caitanya Mahāprabhu who chanted three hundred thousand names of God a day.

Hiraṇyakaśipu—a demoniac king killed by the Lord's incarnation Nṛsiṁhadeva.

I

Indra—the chief of the administrative demigods and king of the heavenly planets.

ISKCON—the International Society for Krishna Consciousness.

J

Jaḍa Bharata—Bharata Mahārāja in his final birth as a renounced *brāhmaṇa.* He gave wonderful spiritual instruction to Mahārāja Rahūgaṇa.

Jagannātha—the Supreme Lord, who is Lord of the universe, and the particular Deity form of that Lord.

Jīva Gosvāmī—one of the six Vaiṣṇava spiritual masters who directly followed Lord Śrī Caitanya Mahāprabhu and systematically presented His teachings.

Jīva-tattva—the living entities, atomic parts of the Supreme Lord.

Jñānī—one who cultivates knowledge by empirical speculation.

K

Kalā—a form of the Lord that is an expansion of the Lord's original form.

Kali-yuga (Age of Kali)—the present age, characterized by quarrel; it is last in the cycle of four and began five thousand years ago.

Kāma—lust.

Kapila—the incarnation of the Supreme Lord who appeared as the son of Kardama Muni and Devahūti and taught the Kṛṣṇa conscious Sāṅkhya philosophy.

Kāraṇodakaśāyī Viṣṇu—Mahā-Viṣṇu, the expansion of the Supreme Lord from whom all material universes emanate.

Karatālas—hand cymbals used in *kīrtana.*

Kardama Muni—the father of Lord Kapila and one of the chief forefathers of the population of the universe.

Karma—material, fruitive activity and its reactions.

Karma-kāṇḍa—the portions of the *Vedas* describing rituals to be performed for material benefit.

Karmī—one engaged in *karma* (fruitive activity); a materialist.

Kārttikeya—the younger son of Lord Śiva and Pārvatī. He is the presiding deity of warfare.

Kaśyapa—a great saint who was the father of many demigods and also of the Supreme Lord's incarnation Vāmanadeva.

Keśava—the Supreme Lord, Kṛṣṇa, who has fine, black hair.

Kīrtana—the devotional process of chanting the names and glories of the Supreme Lord.

Kṛṣṇa—the Supreme Personality of Godhead appearing in His original, two-armed form.

Kṛṣṇadāsa Kavirāja—the great Vaiṣṇava spiritual master who recorded the biography and teachings of Lord Śrī Caitanya Mahāprabhu in the *Caitanya-caritāmṛta.*

Kṛṣṇaloka—*See:* Goloka Vṛndāvana

Kṣatriya—a warrior or administrator; the second Vedic social order.

Kṣattā—*See:* Vidura.

Kuntī—the aunt of Lord Kṛṣṇa and mother of the Pāṇḍavas.

Kuru—the founder of the dynasty in which the Pāṇḍavas, as well as their archrivals, the sons of Dhṛtarāṣṭra, took birth.

Kuvera—the treasurer of the demigods; father of Nalakūvara and Maṇigrīva.

L

Lakṣmī—the goddess of fortune and eternal consort of the Supreme Lord as Nārāyaṇa.

Loka—a planet.

M

Madhvācārya—a great thirteenth-century Vaiṣṇava spiritual master who preached the theistic philosophy of dualism.

Mahā-mantra—the great chant for deliverance:
Hare Kṛṣṇa, Hare Kṛṣṇa, Kṛṣṇa Kṛṣṇa, Hare Hare
Hare Rāma, Hare Rāma, Rāma Rāma, Hare Hare.

Mahā-Viṣṇu—the expansion of the Supreme Lord from whom all material universes emanate.

Mahābhārata—Vyāsadeva's epic history of greater India, which includes the events of the Kurukṣetra war and the narration of *Bhagavad-gītā*.

Mahāmāyā—the illusory, material energy of the Supreme Lord.

Maheśvara—*See:* Śiva

Maitreya Muni—the great sage who spoke *Śrīmad-Bhāgavatam* to Vidura.

Mantra—a transcendental sound or Vedic hymn, which can deliver the mind from illusion.

Manu, Svāyambhuva—*See:* Svāyambhuva Manu

Mathurā—Lord Kṛṣṇa's abode, surrounding Vṛndāvana, where He took birth and to which He later returned after performing His childhood Vṛndāvana pastimes.

Māyā—the inferior, illusory energy of the Supreme Lord, which rules over this material creation; forgetfulness of one's relationship with Kṛṣṇa.

Maya Dānava—the architect of the demons.

Māyāvādī—an impersonalist philosopher who conceives of the Absolute as ultimately formless and the living entity as equal to God.

Mīmāṁsakas—atheistic philosophers who say that even if God exists, He is obliged to reward us the fruits of our work.

Mṛdaṅga—a clay drum used for congregational chanting.

Mukti-devī—the demigoddess who is the personification of liberation.

N

Nanda—one of the chief personal servants of Lord Nārāyaṇa in His spiritual abode, Vaikuṇṭha.

Nara-Nārāyaṇa—an incarnation of the Supreme Lord appearing as two sages to teach by example the practice of austerities.

Nārada Muni—a pure devotee of the Lord who travels throughout the universes in his eternal body, glorifying devotional service. He is the spiritual master of Vyāsadeva and of many other great devotees.

Nārāyaṇa—Lord Kṛṣṇa's expansion as the Supreme Lord, the resting place of all living entities, in His majestic four-armed form; Lord Viṣṇu.

Narottama dāsa Ṭhākura—a Vaiṣṇava spiritual master in the disciplic succession from Lord Śrī Caitanya Mahāprabhu. A disciple of Lokanātha dāsa Gosvāmī, he wrote many Bengali songs glorifying Lord Kṛṣṇa.

Nityānanda Prabhu—the incarnation of Lord Balarāma who appeared as the principal associate of Lord Śrī Caitanya Mahāprabhu.

P

Pañcarātra—Vedic literature describing the process of Deity worship for devotees in the present age.

Pāṇḍavas—Yudhiṣṭhira, Bhīma, Arjuna, Nakula and Sahadeva, the five warrior-brothers who were intimate friends and devotees of Lord Kṛṣṇa.

Paramparā—a disciplic succession of bona fide spiritual masters.

Parāśara—a great sage and the father of Śrīla Vyāsadeva.

Parīkṣit Mahārāja—the emperor of the world who heard *Śrīmad-Bhāgavatam* from Śukadeva Gosvāmī and thus attained perfection.

Pārvatī—Satī, Lord Śiva's consort, reborn as the daughter of the king of the Himalaya Mountains.

Piṇḍa—an offering made to departed ancestors.

Prabodhānanda Sarasvatī—a great Vaiṣṇava poet-philosopher and devotee of Lord Śrī Caitanya Mahāprabhu; the uncle of Gopāla Bhaṭṭa Gosvāmī.

Prahlāda Mahārāja—a devotee persecuted by his demoniac father but protected and saved by the Lord in the form of Nṛsiṁhadeva.

Prajāpatis—the demigods in charge of populating the universe.
Prasādam—the Lord's mercy; food or other items spiritualized by being first offered to the Supreme Lord.
Prasūti—a daughter of Svāyambhuva Manu who was the wife of Dakṣa.
Priyavrata—the son of Svāyambhuva Manu and brother of Uttānapāda who once ruled the universe.
Pṛthu Mahārāja—an empowered incarnation of Lord Kṛṣṇa who demonstrated how to be an ideal ruler.
Purāṇas—the eighteen Vedic supplementary literatures; historical scriptures.

R

Rādhārāṇī—Lord Kṛṣṇa's most intimate consort, the personification of His internal, spiritual potency.
Raghunātha dāsa Gosvāmī—one of the six Vaiṣṇava spiritual masters who directly followed Lord Śrī Caitanya Mahāprabhu and systematically presented His teachings.
Rājarṣi—a great saintly king.
Rāmacandra—an incarnation of the Supreme Lord as the perfect king.
Rāmānanda Rāya—an intimate associate of Lord Śrī Caitanya Mahāprabhu in His later pastimes.
Rāmānujācārya—a great eleventh-century Vaiṣṇava spiritual master of the Śrī-sampradāya.
Rāsa-līlā—the pure exchange of spiritual love between Kṛṣṇa and His most advanced, confidential servitors, the cowherd damsels of Vrajabhūmi.
Rāvaṇa—a demoniac ruler who was killed by Lord Rāmacandra.
Ṛṣi—a sage.
Rudra—*See:* Śiva
Rūpa Gosvāmī—the chief of the six Vaiṣṇava spiritual masters who directly followed Lord Śrī Caitanya Mahāprabhu and systematically presented His teachings.

S

Sac-cid-ānanda-vigraha—the Lord's transcendental form, which is eternal and full of knowledge and bliss.

Śacīpati—*See:* Indra
Sahasra-śīrṣā—*See:* Ananta
Śaivites—devotees of Lord Śiva.
Śakty-āveśa—empowered by the Supreme Lord with one or more of the Lord's opulences.
Sālokya—the liberation of residing on the same planet as the Supreme Lord.
Sāmīpya—the liberation of becoming a personal associate of the Supreme Lord.
Sampradāya—a disciplic succession of spiritual masters; also, the followers in that tradition.
Sanātana Gosvāmī—one of the six Vaiṣṇava spiritual masters who directly followed Lord Śrī Caitanya Mahāprabhu and systematically presented His teachings.
Śaṅkara—*See:* Śiva
Śaṅkarācārya—the incarnation of Lord Śiva as the great philosopher who, on the order of the Supreme Lord, preached impersonalism based on the *Vedas*.
Saṅkarṣaṇa—one of the four original expansions of Lord Kṛṣṇa in the spiritual world; also, another name of Balarāma, given by Garga Muni.
Saṅkīrtana—congregational or public glorification of the Supreme Lord, Kṛṣṇa, especially through chanting of the Lord's holy names.
Sannyāsa—renounced life; the fourth order of Vedic spiritual life.
Sarasvatī—the goddess of learning and the wife of Lord Brahmā.
Sārṣṭi—the liberation of achieving equal opulence with the Lord.
Sārūpya—the liberation of attaining a spiritual form like that of the Supreme Lord.
Śāstra—revealed scripture, such as the Vedic literature.
Satī—the wife of Lord Śiva and the daughter of Dakṣa.
Satyabhāmā—one of the principal queens of Lord Kṛṣṇa during His pastimes in the city of Dvārakā.
Śeṣa Nāga—*See:* Ananta
Siddhi—mystic power or perfection acquired by *yoga* practice, natural to residents of Siddhaloka.
Sītā—the eternal consort of Lord Rāmacandra.

Śiva—the special incarnation of the Lord as the demigod in charge of the mode of ignorance and the destruction of the material manifestation.

Smṛti—revealed scriptures supplementary to the *śruti,* or original Vedic scriptures, which are the *Vedas* and *Upaniṣads.*

Somarāja—Candra, the demigod in charge of the moon.

Śravaṇaṁ kīrtanaṁ viṣṇoḥ—the devotional process of hearing and chanting about Lord Viṣṇu, or Kṛṣṇa.

Śrīdhara Svāmī—a Vaiṣṇava spiritual master in the line of Śrī Viṣṇusvāmi who was an early commentator on *Bhagavad-gītā* and *Śrīmad-Bhāgavatam.*

Śrīvāsa Ṭhākura—an intimate associate of Lord Caitanya.

Śruti—knowledge via hearing; the original Vedic scriptures (the *Vedas* and *Upaniṣads*), given directly by the Supreme Lord.

Śūdra—a laborer; the fourth of the Vedic social orders.

Śukadeva Gosvāmī—the great devotee sage who originally spoke *Śrīmad-Bhāgavatam* to King Parīkṣit just prior to the king's death.

Śukra—*See:* Śukrācārya

Śukrācārya—the spiritual master of the demons.

Sunanda—one of the chief personal servants of Lord Nārāyaṇa in His spiritual abode, Vaikuṇṭha.

Sunīthā—the wife of King Aṅga and mother of Vena.

Sunīti—the mother of Dhruva Mahārāja.

Suruci—the stepmother of Dhruva Mahārāja.

Svāmī—a controller of the mind and senses; the title of one in the renounced, or *sannyāsa,* order.

Svāmi-nārāyaṇa—the impersonalist misconception that one can become God simply by adopting the dress of a *sannyāsī.*

Svāyambhuva Manu—the Manu who appears first in Brahmā's day and who was the grandfather of Dhruva Mahārāja.

Śyāmasundara—the Supreme Personality of Godhead, Kṛṣṇa, who is blackish and very beautiful.

T

Takṣaka—the king of the snakes.

Tapasya—austerity; accepting some voluntary inconvenience for a higher purpose.

Ṭhākura Haridāsa—*See:* Haridāsa Ṭhākura

Tilaka—auspicious clay markings placed by devotees on the forehead and other parts of the body.

Tithis—days of the Vedic calendar measured according to the phases of the moon.

U

Uddhava—a confidential friend of Lord Kṛṣṇa's in Vṛndāvana.

Upendra—Vāmanadeva, who sometimes appears as the younger brother of Indra.

Utkala—the eldest son of Dhruva Mahārāja.

Uttama—the brother of Dhruva Mahāraja.

Uttānapāda—the king who was a son of Svāyambhuva Manu and father of Dhruva Mahārāja.

V

Vaikuṇṭha—the spiritual world, where there is no anxiety.

Vaiṣṇava—a devotee of the Supreme Lord, Viṣṇu, or Kṛṣṇa.

Vaiśyas—farmers and merchants; the third Vedic social order.

Vāmana—the incarnation of the Supreme Lord as a dwarf *brāhmaṇa*, to whom Bali Mahārāja surrendered.

Vānaprastha—one who has retired from family life; the third order of Vedic spiritual life.

Varāha—the incarnation of the Supreme Lord as a boar.

Varṇa—one of the four Vedic social-occupational divisions of society, distinguished by quality of work and situation with regard to the modes of nature (*guṇas*). *See also: Brāhmaṇa; Kṣatriya; Vaiśya; Śūdra*

Varṇāśrama-dharma—the Vedic social system of four social and four spiritual orders. *See also: Varṇa; Āśrama*

Varuṇa—the demigod in charge of the oceans.

Vedas—the original revealed scriptures, first spoken by Lord Kṛṣṇa.

Vena—the demoniac son of King Aṅga and father of King Pṛthu.

Vidura—a great devotee who heard *Śrīmad-Bhāgavatam* from Maitreya Muni.

Vijitāśva—the eldest son of King Pṛthu (also known as Antardhāna).

Vīṇā—a stringed musical instrument.

Vīrarāghava Ācārya—a Vaiṣṇava spiritual master in the line of Rāmānujācārya, and commentator on *Śrīmad-Bhāgavatam*.

Virāṭ-rūpa—the conception likening the physical form of the universe to the Lord's bodily form.

Viṣṇu—the Supreme Lord; Lord Kṛṣṇa's expansion in Vaikuṇṭha and for the creation and maintenance of the material universes.

Viṣṇu-tattva—the status or category of Godhead. The term applies to primary expansions of the Supreme Lord.

Viṣṇudūtas—the messengers of Lord Viṣṇu who come to take perfected devotees back to the spiritual world at the time of death.

Viṣṇuloka—the abode of Lord Viṣṇu, the Supreme Personality of Godhead.

Viśvakarmā—the architect of the demigods.

Viśvanātha Cakravartī Ṭhākura—a great Vaiṣṇava spiritual master in the line of Lord Śrī Caitanya Mahāprabhu. He was a commentator on *Śrīmad-Bhāgavatam.*

Viśvāvasu—a leader of the Gandharvas, singers in the heavenly planets.

Vrajabhūmi—*See:* Vṛndāvana

Vṛndāvana—Kṛṣṇa's eternal abode, where He fully manifests His quality of sweetness; the village on this earth in which He enacted His childhood pastimes five thousand years ago.

Vyāsadeva—the incarnation of Lord Kṛṣṇa who gave the *Vedas, Purāṇas, Vedānta-sūtra* and *Mahābhārata* to mankind.

Y

Yajña—a Vedic sacrifice; also, the Supreme Lord, the goal and enjoyer of all sacrifices.

Yajña-puruṣa—the supreme enjoyer of all sacrifices.

Yakṣas—ghostly followers of the demigod Kuvera.

Yamarāja—the demigod in charge of death and of punishing the sinful.

Yaśodā—the foster mother of Kṛṣṇa; the Queen of Vraja and wife of Mahārāja Nanda.

Yogamāyā—the internal, spiritual energy of the Supreme Lord; also, its personification as Kṛṣṇa's younger sister.

Yogī—a transcendentalist who, in one way or another, is striving for union with the Supreme.

Yudhiṣṭhira—one of the five Pāṇḍava brothers. He ruled the earth after the Kurukṣetra war.

Yugas—ages in the life of a universe, recurring in cycles of four.

Sanskrit Pronunciation Guide

Throughout the centuries, the Sanskrit language has been written in a variety of alphabets. The mode of writing most widely used throughout India, however, is called *devanāgarī*, which means, literally, the writing used in "the cities of the demigods." The *devanāgarī* alphabet consists of forty-eight characters: thirteen vowels and thirty-five consonants. Ancient Sanskrit grammarians arranged this alphabet according to practical linguistic principles, and this order has been accepted by all Western scholars. The system of transliteration used in this book conforms to a system that scholars in the last fifty years have accepted to indicate the pronunciation of each Sanskrit sound.

Vowels

अ a आ ā इ i ई ī उ u ऊ ū ऋ ṛ

ॠ ṝ ऌ ḷ ए e ऐ ai ओ o औ au

Consonants

Gutturals:	क ka	ख kha	ग ga	घ gha	ङ ṅa
Palatals:	च ca	छ cha	ज ja	झ jha	ञ ña
Cerebrals:	ट ṭa	ठ ṭha	ड ḍa	ढ ḍha	ण ṇa
Dentals:	त ta	थ tha	द da	ध dha	न na
Labials:	प pa	फ pha	ब ba	भ bha	म ma
Semivowels:	य ya	र ra	ल la	व va	
Sibilants:	श śa	ष ṣa	स sa		
Aspirate:	ह ha	Anusvāra: ं ṁ	Visarga: ः ḥ		

Numerals

०-0 १-1 २-2 ३-3 ४-4 ५-5 ६-6 ७-7 ८-8 ९-9

The vowels are written as follows after a consonant:

ा ā ि i ी ī ु u ू ū ृ ṛ ॄ ṝ े e ै ai ो o ौ au

For example: क ka का kā कि ki की kī कु ku कू kū

कृ kṛ कॄ kṝ के ke कै kai को ko कौ kau

Generally two or more consonants in conjunction are written together in a special form, as for example: क्ष kṣa त्र tra

The vowel "a" is implied after a consonant with no vowel symbol.

The symbol virāma (्) indicates that there is no final vowel: क्

The vowels are pronounced as follows:

a — as in but

ā — as in far but held twice as long as a

ai — as in aisle

au — as in how

e — as in they

i — as in pin

ī — as in pique but held twice as long as i

ḷ — as in lree

o — as in go

ṛ — as in rim

ṝ — as in reed but held twice as long as ṛ

u — as in push

ū — as in rule but held twice as long as u

The consonants are pronounced as follows:

Gutturals
(pronounced from the throat)

k — as in kite

kh — as in Eckhart

g — as in give

gh — as in dig-hard

ṅ — as in sing

Labials
(pronounced with the lips)

p — as in pine

ph — as in up-hill (not f)

b — as in bird

bh — as in rub-hard

m — as in mother

Cerebrals
(pronounced with tip of tongue against roof of mouth)
ṭ — as in tub
ṭh — as in light-heart
ḍ — as in dove
ḍh — as in red-hot
ṇ — as in sing

Dentals
(pronounced as cerebrals but with tongue against teeth)
t — as in tub
th — as in light-heart
d — as in dove
dh — as in red-hot
n — as in nut

Aspirate
h — as in home

Anusvāra
ṁ — a resonant nasal sound like in the French word *bon*

Palatals
(pronounced with middle of tongue against palate)
c — as in chair
ch — as in staunch-heart
j — as in joy
jh — as in hedgehog
ñ — as in canyon

Semivowels
y — as in yes
r — as in run
l — as in light
v — as in vine, except when preceded in the same syllable by a consonant, then like in swan

Sibilants
ś — as in the German word s*prechen*
ṣ — as in shine
s — as in sun

Visarga
ḥ — a final **h**-sound: **aḥ** is pronounced like **aha**; **iḥ** like **ihi**

There is no strong accentuation of syllables in Sanskrit, or pausing between words in a line, only a flowing of short and long (twice as long as the short) syllables. A long syllable is one whose vowel is long (**ā, ai, au, e, ī, o, ṝ, ū**) or whose short vowel is followed by more than one consonant (including **ḥ** and **ṁ**). Aspirated consonants (consonants followed by an **h**) count as single consonants.

Index of Sanskrit Verses

This index constitutes a complete listing of the first and third lines of each of the Sanskrit poetry verses of this volume of *Śrīmad-Bhāgavatam,* arranged in English alphabetical order. The first column gives the Sanskrit transliteration; the second, the chapter-verse reference. Apostrophes are alphabetized as *a*'s.

A

abādhanta munīn anye 5.16
ab-bhakṣa uttamaślokam 8.74
ābhiṣecanikāny asmai 15.11
abhivandya pituḥ pādāv 9.45
ābhṛtātmā muniḥ śānto 8.56

abhūt trayāṇāṁ lokānāṁ 12.38
abhyadhāvan gajā mattāḥ 10.26
abhyadhāyi mahā-bāho 7.1
abhyarcitas tvayā nūnaṁ 9.52
abhyavarṣan prakupitāḥ 10.12

ābrahma-ghoṣorjita-yajña-vaiśasaṁ 4.6
ādhāraṁ mahad-ādīnāṁ 8.78
adharmāṁśodbhavaṁ mṛtyuṁ 13.39
adhi puṇyajana-strīṇāṁ 6.30
adhvaryuṇā hūyamāne 4.33

adhvaryuṇātta-haviṣā 7.18
āgneyya iṣṭayo yajñe 1.62
agnir āja-gavaṁ cāpaṁ 15.18
agniṣṭomam atīrātraṁ 13.16
agniṣvāttā barhiṣadaḥ 1.63

ahaṁ brahmā ca śarvaś ca 7.50
ahaṁ ca tasmin bhavatābhikāmaye 3.9
ahaṁ tvam ity apārthā dhīr 12.4
ahaniṣyat kathaṁ yoṣāṁ 17.19
ahārṣīd yasya hayaṁ purandaraḥ 16.24

ahayo 'śani-niḥśvāsā 10.26
aher iva payaḥ-poṣaḥ 14.10
aho anātmyaṁ mahad asya paśyata 4.29

aho bata mamānātmyaṁ 9.31
aho me bata daurātmyaṁ 8.67

aho tejaḥ kṣatriyāṇāṁ 8.26
aho ubhyataḥ prāptaṁ 14.8
āhvayantam ivoddhastair 6.13
aindrīṁ ca māyām upadharma- 19.38
aiṣyaty acirato rājan 8.69

ajaṁ loka-guruṁ natvā 2.7
ājñapta evaṁ kupitena manyunā 5.5
ajo 'dhyatiṣṭhat khalu pārameṣṭhyaṁ 8.20
akalpa eṣām adhiroḍhum añjasā 3.21
ākarṇyātmajam āyāntam 9.37

ākramyorasi dakṣasya 5.22
ākrīḍe krīḍato bālān 13.41
ākūtiṁ rucaye prādād 1.2
ākūtir devahūtiś ca 1.1
alabdha-nidro 'nupalakṣito nṛbhir 13.47

alakṣayantaḥ padavīṁ prajāpater 13.49
alaṁ te kratubhiḥ sviṣṭair 19.32
alaṁ vatsātiroṣeṇa 11.7
amaṅgalānāṁ ca tamisram ulbaṇaṁ 6.45
āma-pātre mahā-bhāgāḥ 18.18

amarṣayitvā tam asahya-tejasaṁ 5.11
amogha-vīryā hi nṛpā 14.42
aṁśāṁśās te deva marīcy-ādaya ete 7.43
āmuktam iva pākhaṇḍaṁ 19.12
amūṣāṁ kṣut-parītānām 17.25

anādṛtā yajña-sadasy adhīśvarī 4.9
anāhutā apy abhiyanti sauhṛdaṁ 3.13
ananta-māhātmya-guṇaika-dhāmā 16.10
ananvitaṁ te bhagavan viceṣṭitaṁ 7.34
ananya-bhāvaika-gatiṁ 7.59

ananya-bhāve nija-dharma-bhāvite 8.22
anāsthitaṁ te pitṛbhir 12.26

aṅgaṁ sumanasaṁ khyātiṁ 13.17
aṅga-saṅgād utpulakāv 9.48
aṅgena sandhyābhra-rucā 6.36

aṅgo 'śvamedhaṁ rājarṣir 13.25
aṅgo dvija-vacaḥ śrutvā 13.29
anicchann apy adām bālām 2.13
āninye sva-gṛhaṁ putryāḥ 1.5
annam īpsitam ūrjasvad 18.10

antar bahiś ca bhūtānāṁ 16.12
anunīyamānas tad-yācñāṁ 14.29
anurakta-prajaṁ rājā 9.66
anvabhūyata sarvātmā 19.3
anvadhāvata saṅkruddhas 19.13

anvadravad abhikruddho 19.16
anvasmarad agaṁ hitvā 12.32
anveṣantī vanaṁ mātā 9.23
anvito brahma-śarvābhyāṁ 19.4
anvīyamānaḥ sa tu rudra-pārṣadair 5.6

anyāṁś ca hasta-caraṇa-śravaṇa- 9.6
anye ca māyino māyām 18.20
apālitānādṛtā ca 18.7
apām upasthe mayi nāvy avasthitāḥ 17.35
apare jagṛhur devān 5.16

apartāv api bhadraṁ te 18.11
apaśyamānaḥ sa tadātatāyinaṁ 10.21
āplutyāvabhṛthaṁ yatra 2.35
aprauḍhaivātmanātmānam 1.66
apsaro-muni-gandharva- 1.22

apy abhadram anāthāyā 14.37
apy anāthaṁ vane brahman 8.66
apy arvāg-vṛttayo yasya 7.24
āpyāyayaty asau lokaṁ 16.9
apy evam arya bhagavān 9.17

ārādhayādhokṣaja-pāda-padmaṁ 8.19
ārādhito yathaivaiṣa 13.34
ārādhya bhuktyālabhatāmalaṁ taj 16.25

ārādhyāpa durārādhyaṁ 11.11
arājaka-bhayād eṣa 14.9
arājake tadā loke 13.20

araṇya-pātre cādhukṣan 18.23
arcanti kalpaka-taruṁ 9.9
arcir nāma varārohā 15.5
arcitvā kratunā svena 7.55

arhitārhaṇako rājñā 8.63
āropya kariṇīṁ hṛṣṭaḥ 9.53
arudra-bhāgaṁ tam avekṣya 4.9
āruhya śibikāṁ sārdham 9.41
arvāk patantam arhattama-nindayāpād 7.15

asahantas tan-ninādam 10.7
āsanāni mahārhāṇi 9.61
āsan kṛta-svastyayanās 3.4
āsasāda mahā-krādaḥ 10.27
āśāsānā jīvitam adhvarasya 6.6

āśiṣo yuyujuḥ kṣattar 19.41
asmai nṛ-pālāḥ kila tatra tatra 16.21
asmil loke 'thavāmuṣmin 18.3
āsthāya jaitraṁ ratham ātta-cāpaḥ 16.20
astraughaṁ vyadhamad bāṇair 10.16

āstṛtās tā raṇa-bhuvo 10.19
asty ekaṁ prāktanam aghaṁ 13.31
asūta mithunaṁ tat tu 8.2
asūyan bhagavān indraḥ 19.10
asyāpratihataṁ cakraṁ 16.14

atas tavotpannam idaṁ kalevaraṁ 4.18
aṭaty unmattavan nagno 2.14
athābhiṣṭuta evaṁ vai 9.18
atha deva-gaṇāḥ sarve 6.1
athādīkṣata rājā tu 19.1

athājighran muhur mūrdhni 9.44
atha mātropadiṣṭena 8.30
athāmum āhū rājānaṁ 16.15
athāpi bhaktyeśa tayopadhāvatām 7.38
athāpi hy anahaṅkārān 11.25

athāpi me 'vinītasya 8.36
athāpi yūyaṁ kṛta-kilbiṣā bhavaṁ 6.5
athāpy udāra-śravasaḥ pṛthor hareḥ 16.3

athartvijo yajamānaḥ sadasyāḥ 5.7
athāsmad-aṁśa-bhūtās te 1.31

athāsmin bhagavān vainyaḥ 18.30
athātaḥ kīrtaye vaṁśaṁ 8.6
atha tasya punar viprair 15.1
athāyajata yajñeśaṁ 12.10
atiṣṭhad eka-pādena 1.19

ātiṣṭha jagatāṁ vandyaṁ 12.26
ātiṣṭha tac candra-divākarādayo 12.25
ātiṣṭha tat tāta vimatsaras tvam 8.19
ātma-māyāṁ samāviśya 7.51
ātmanaḥ sadṛśaṁ putraṁ 1.65

ātmānam anviccha vimuktam ātma-dṛg 11.29
ātmānaṁ brahma nirvāṇaṁ 13.8
ātmānaṁ ca prajāś cemāḥ 17.21
ātmānaṁ ca pravayasam 9.67
ātmānaṁ toṣayan dehī 8.33

ātmārāmaṁ kathaṁ dveṣṭi 2.2
ātma-stry-apatya-suhṛdo balam 12.16
ātma-vṛtty-anusāreṇa 8.72
ātma-yoga-balenemā 17.27
ātmeśvara upadraṣṭā 7.50

ātodyaṁ vitudañ ślokān 12.40
ato nivartatām eṣa 8.32
atrāgatās tanu-bhṛtāṁ manaso 'pi 1.28
atreḥ patny anasūyā trīñ 1.15
atrer gṛhe sura-śreṣṭhāḥ 1.16

atriḥ sandarśayām āsa 19.20
atriṇā coditas tasmai 19.21
atriṇā codito hantuṁ 19.13
autkaṇṭhyād bāṣpa-kalayā 7.11
auttānapāda bhagavāṁs tava 10.30

auttānapādiḥ sa tadā 10.13
auttānapādiṁ kṛpayā pitāmaho 11.6
avabodha-rasaikātmyam 13.8
avaghrāya mudā yuktaḥ 13.37
avajānanty amī mūḍhā 14.24

avakīryamāṇo dadṛśe 12.34
avamene mahā-bhāgān 14.4
avaraḥ śraddhayopeta 18.4
avaruhya nṛpas tūrṇam 9.42
avidyā-racita-svapna- 12.15

avyaktasyāprameyasya 11.23
avyakta-vartmaiṣa nigūḍha-kāryo 16.10
avyavacchinna-yogāgni- 13.9
ayaṁ bhuvo maṇḍalam odayādrer 16.20
ayaṁ mahīṁ gāṁ duduhe 'dhirājaḥ 16.22

ayaṁ tu deva-yajana 2.18
ayaṁ tu loka-pālānāṁ 2.10
ayaṁ tu prathamo rājñāṁ 15.4
ayaṁ tu sākṣād bhagavāṁs 16.19
ayaṁ tvat-kathā-mṛṣṭa-pīyūṣa-nadyāṁ 7.35

ayātayāmopahavair anantaraṁ 19.28
āyatiṁ niyatiṁ caiva 1.44
āyuḥ-śrī-bala-kīrtīnāṁ 14.14
āyuṣo 'pacayaṁ jantos 11.21

B

bāhubhyām aśvinoḥ pūṣṇo 7.5
bāhubhyāṁ mathyamānābhyāṁ 15.1
bāhuṁ prakoṣṭhe 'kṣa-mālām 6.38
bahv evam udvigna-dṛśocyamāne 5.12
bālasya paśyato dhāma 9.26

baliṁ ca mahyaṁ harata 14.28
bāliśā bata yūyaṁ vā 14.23
bālo 'py ayaṁ hṛdā dhatte 8.26
bālo 'si bata nātmānam 8.12
bhāgaṁ barhiṣi yā vṛṅkte 17.22

bhagasya netre bhagavān 5.20
bhagavān svena bhāgena 7.49
bhagavān vāsudevas taṁ 8.40
bhagnāyāṁ bhavya-yācñāyāṁ 14.30
bhajasva bhajanīyāṅghrim 12.6

bhaktāya me 'nuraktāya 17.7
bhaktiṁ harau bhagavati pravahann 12.18
bhaktiṁ muhuḥ pravahatāṁ tvayi 9.11
bhaktiṁ vidhāya paramāṁ śanakair 11.30
bhallaiḥ sañchidyamānānāṁ 10.18

bhāra-vyayāya ca bhuvaḥ 1.59
bhartary uparate tasminn 14.39
bhartṛ-sneha-vidūrāṇāṁ 14.25

bhava-cchidaḥ pāda-mūlaṁ 9.31
bhava-cchidam ayāce 'haṁ 9.34

bhavaṁ bhavāny apratipūruṣaṁ ruṣā 4.2
bhavāṁs tu puṁsaḥ paramasya 6.49
bhavān paritrātum ihāvatīrṇo 19.37
bhavantv adhvaryavaś cānye 7.5
bhava-stavāya kṛta-dhīr 7.11

bhavasya patnī tu satī 1.65
bhavatānugṛhītānām 6.52
bhava-vrata-dharā ye ca 2.28
bhaved bhaktir bhagavati 12.46
bhave śīlavatāṁ śreṣṭhe 2.1

bhavitāro 'ṅga bhadraṁ te 1.31
bhavo bhavānyā nidhanaṁ prajāpater 5.1
bho bhoḥ kṣatriya-dāyāda 12.2
bho bho rājan subhadraṁ te 12.23
bhogaiḥ puṇya-kṣayaṁ kurvann 12.13

bhoḥ sūta he māgadha saumya 15.22
bhrājamānaṁ vitimiraṁ 2.5
bhrātur vadhābhitaptena 11.9
bhṛgoḥ śmaśrūṇi rohantu 6.51
bhṛgor luluñce sadasi 5.19

bhṛguḥ khyātyāṁ mahā-bhāgaḥ 1.43
bhṛguḥ pratyasṛjac chāpaṁ 2.27
bhṛguṁ babandha maṇimān 5.17
bhṛgv-ādayas te munayo 14.1
bhṛtyānurakto bhagavān 9.18

bhūḥ pāduke yogamayyau 15.18
bhujyamānā mayā dṛṣṭā 18.6
bhuktvā cehāśiṣaḥ satyā 9.24
bhū-maṇḍalam idaṁ vainyaḥ 18.29
bhū-maṇḍalaṁ jaladhi-mekhalam 12.16

bhūrjair oṣadhihiḥ pūgai 6.17
bhūtaiḥ pañcabhir ārabdhair 11.15
bhūtānāṁ karuṇaḥ śaśvad 16.7
bhūtāni cātmany apṛthag-didṛkṣatāṁ 6.46
bhūta-preta-piśācānāṁ 5.25

bhūteśa-vatsā duduhuḥ 18.21
bhūteṣu niranukrośo 17.26

bhūyān anugraha aho bhavatā kṛto me 7.13
bhūyas tad deva-yajanaṁ 7.7
brahmā brahmamayaṁ varma 15.16

brahma ca brāhmaṇāṁś caiva 2.30
brahma dhārayamāṇasya 8.78
brahmā jagad-gurur devaiḥ 15.9
brahmaṇā coditaḥ sṛṣṭāv 1.17
brāhmaṇaḥ sama-dṛk śānto 14.41

brāhmaṇaiḥ kula-vṛddhaiś ca 9.39
brāhmaṇa-pramukhān varṇān 17.2
brahma-rudrau ca bhūtāni 7.52
brahmāvarte manoḥ kṣetre 19.1
bṛhaspati-savaṁ nāma 3.3

brūhy asmat-pitṛbhir brahmann 8.37
buddhir medhā titikṣā hrīr 1.50
buddhyā parābhidyāyinyā 2.23

C

caṇḍeśaḥ pūṣaṇaṁ devaṁ 5.17
carameṇāśvamedhena 19.11
carantaṁ viśva-suhṛdaṁ 6.35
caranti dakṣiṇī-kṛtya 9.21
caṣāla-yūpataś channo 19.19

caturtham api vai māsaṁ 8.75
cetas tat-pravaṇaṁ yuñjann 1.26
chandāṁsy ayāta-yāmāni 13.27
chandayām āsa tān kāmaiḥ 17.1
chindann api tad uddhartuṁ 5.22

chindyāt prasahya ruśatīm asatīṁ 4.17
citā-bhasma-kṛta-snānaḥ 2.15
citraketuḥ surociś ca 1.41
citraketu-pradhānās te 1.40
cittis tv atharvaṇaḥ patnī 1.42

codito vidureṇaivaṁ 17.8
cora-prāyaṁ jana-padaṁ 14.40
corī-bhūte 'tha loke 'haṁ 18.7
cūrṇayan sva-dhanuṣ-koṭyā 18.29
cūtaiḥ kadambair nīpaiś ca 6.15
cūta-pallava-vāsaḥ-sraṅ- 9.55

D

dadarśa deho hata-kalmaṣaḥ satī 4.27
dadarśa himavad-droṇyāṁ 10.5
dadarśa loke vitatam 13.7
dadarśātmani bhūteṣu 12.11
dadhmau śaṅkhaṁ bṛhad-bāhuḥ 10.6

dadhyañcam aśvaśirasaṁ 1.42
dadṛśuḥ śivam āsīnaṁ 6.33
dadṛśus tatra te ramyām 6.23
daiteyā dānavā vatsaṁ 18.16
daivīṁ māyām upāśritya 9.33

daivopasāditam yāvad 8.29
dakṣaṁ babhāṣa ābhāṣya 7.49
dakṣaṁ sa-yajñaṁ jahi mad-bhaṭānāṁ 5.4
dakṣāya brahma-putrāya 1.11
dakṣāya śāpaṁ visasarja dāruṇaṁ 2.20

dakṣo 'thāpa upaspṛśya 2.17
dakṣo gṛhītārhaṇa-sādanottamaṁ 7.25
daṇḍa-vrata-dhare rājñi 13.22
daṇḍayaty ātmajam api 16.13
darśanīyatamaṁ śāntaṁ 8.49

darśayām āsatur devīṁ 12.33
darśitaḥ kṛpayā puṁsāṁ 8.35
dāruṇy ubhayato dīpte 14.8
daśa-candram asiṁ rudraḥ 15.17
dattā bata mayā sādhvī 2.16

dattaṁ durvāsasaṁ somam 1.15
dattāṁ saparyāṁ varam āsanaṁ ca sā 4.8
dehe bhavanti nṛpateḥ 14.27
dehinām ātmavat-preṣṭhaḥ 16.18
devā brahmādayaḥ sarve 1.55

devāḥ prakṛta-sarvāṅgā 7.4
devahūtim adāt tāta 1.10

devakulyāṁ hareḥ pāda- 1.14
deva-māyābhibhūtānāṁ 7.2
devānāṁ bhagna-gātrāṇām 6.52

deve 'varṣaty asau devo 16.8
dhanur visphūrjayan divyaṁ 10.16

dhanyaṁ yaśasyam āyuṣyaṁ 12.45
dharma ācaritaḥ puṁsāṁ 14.15
dharma eva matiṁ dattvā 7.57

dharma ity upadharmeṣu 19.25
dharmārtha-kāma-mokṣākhyaṁ 8.41
dharma-vyatikaro yatra 19.35

dharmo 'gniḥ kaśyapaḥ śukro 9.21
dharmopalakṣaṇam idaṁ trivṛd 7.27

dhātāraṁ ca vidhātāraṁ 1.43
dhāvantī tatra tatrainaṁ 17.16
dhiyā viśuddhayā dadhyau 7.18
dhokṣye kṣīramayān kāmān 18.9
dhruvam nivṛttaṁ pratibuddhya 12.1
dhruvasya cotkalaḥ putraḥ 13.6

dhruvasyoddātma-yaśasaś 12.44
dhruvāya pathi dṛṣṭāya 9.58
dhruve prayuktām asurais 10.29
dhruvo bhrātṛ-vadhaṁ śrutvā 10.4

dhyāyan bhagavato rūpaṁ 8.77
dhyāyan brahma padaikena 8.76
dina-kṣaye vyatīpate 12.49
dīrghaṁ dadhyau kuruśreṣṭha 17.12
dīrghaṁ śvasantī vṛjinasya pāram 8.17

diśo vijityāpratiruddha-cakraḥ 16.27
divy avādyanta tūryāṇi 1.54
dogdhāraṁ ca mahā-bāho 18.10
dogdhi smābhīpsitān arthān 19.7
doha-vatsādi-bhedena 18.27

doṣān pareṣāṁ hi guṇeṣu sādhavo 4.12
drakṣye cirotkaṇṭha-manā maharṣibhir 3.10
dravya-kriyā-devatānāṁ 12.10
dṛḍha-vrataḥ satya-sandho 16.16
dṛgbhyāṁ prapaśyan prapibann 9.3

dṛṣṭaḥ kiṁ no dṛgbhir asad-grahais 7.37
dṛṣṭā yogāḥ prayuktāś ca 18.3
dṛṣṭvābhyupāyān api veda-vādino 12.41
dṛṣṭvā saṁjñapanaṁ yogaṁ 5.24
dṛṣṭvā sva-nilayābhyāśe 3.7
dṛśyād adabhra-karuṇena vilokanena 1.57

druhyaty ajñaḥ pṛthag-dṛṣṭis 2.21
drumaiḥ kāma-dughair hṛdyaṁ 6.28
druma-jātibhir anyaiś ca 6.18
duhitṛtve cakāremāṁ 18.28

durāsado durviṣaha 16.11
duruktau kalir ādhatta 8.4
durvāsāḥ śaṅkarasyāṁśo 1.33
dvandva-śvabhre khala-mṛga-bhaye 7.28
dvitīyaṁ ca tathā māsaṁ 8.73
dyauḥ kṣitiḥ sarva-bhūtāni 15.12

E

ebhir indropasaṁsṛṣṭaiḥ 19.36
ekadā munayas te tu 14.36
ekadā suruceḥ putram 8.9
ekaikaṁ yugapat sarvān 10.8
ekaṁ hy eva hares tatra 8.41

ekas tvam eva bhagavann idam 9.7
eke kālaṁ pare daivaṁ 11.22
eko mayeha bhagavān vividha- 1.28
eṣa bhūtāni bhūtātmā 11.26
eṣa dharma-bhṛtāṁ śreṣṭho 16.4

eṣa eva hi lokānāṁ 2.31
eṣa kardama-dauhitra- 1.46
eṣa me śiṣyatāṁ prāpto 2.11
eṣa sākṣād dharer aṁśo 15.6
eṣa sva-sadmopavane sametya 16.25

eṣa te rudra bhāgo 'stu 6.53
eṣa vai loka-pālānāṁ 16.5
eṣa viṣṇor bhagavataḥ 15.3
eṣo 'śvamedhāñ śatam ājahāra 16.24
etad ākhyāhi me brahman 2.3

etad ākhyāhi me brahman 13.24
etad bhagavataḥ śambhoḥ 7.60
etad vimāna-pravaram 12.27
etat te 'bhihitaṁ sarvaṁ 12.44
etāvad uktvā virarāma śaṅkaraḥ 4.1

ete cānye ca vibudhāḥ 14.27
etena dharma-sadane ṛṣi-mūrtinādya 1.56

evam adhyavasāyainaṁ 14.13
evaṁ bahu-savaṁ kālaṁ 12.14
evaṁ bhagavatādiṣṭaḥ 7.55

evaṁ bhagavato rūpaṁ 8.52
evaṁ dākṣāyaṇī hitvā 7.58
evaṁ giritraḥ priyayābhibhāṣitaḥ 3.15
evam indre haraty aśvaṁ 19.24
evaṁ kāma-varaṁ dattvā 1.32

evaṁ kāyena manasā 8.59
evaṁ madāndha utsikto 14.5
evaṁ manyumayīṁ mūrtiṁ 17.28
evaṁ mṛśanta ṛṣayo 14.38
evaṁ pravartate sargaḥ 11.16

evaṁ pṛthv-ādayaḥ pṛthvīṁ 18.27
evaṁ sa bhagavān vainyaḥ 17.1
evaṁ sa nirviṇṇa-manā nṛpo gṛhān 13.47
evaṁ sañjalpitaṁ mātur 8.24
evaṁ sura-gaṇais tāta 1.58

evaṁ sva-dehaṁ mahatāṁ mahīyasā 4.26
evaṁ svāyambhuvaḥ pautram 11.35
evaṁ vainya-sutaḥ proktas 19.16
evaṁ-vidhāny anekāni 10.28

G

gadā-parigha-nistriṁśa- 10.25
gambhīra-vego 'nimiṣaṁ 12.39
gandharva-mukhyāḥ prajaguḥ 12.31
gandharvāpsaraso 'dhukṣan 18.17
garbhaṁ kāla upāvṛtte 13.38

garbhe tvaṁ sādhayātmānaṁ 8.13
gatāsos tasya bhūyas te 13.19
gatvodīcīṁ diśaṁ rājā 10.5
gauḥ saty apādravad bhītā 17.14
gavayaiḥ śarabhair vyāghrai 6.20

gāvo na kālyanta idaṁ kuto rajo 5.8
ghoṣān vrajān sa-śibirān 18.31
giraḥ śrutāyāḥ puṣpiṇyā 2.25
girayo himavad-vatsā 18.25
gītāyanair dundubhi-śaṅkha-veṇubhir 4.5

goptā ca dharma-setūnāṁ 16.4
goptāraṁ dharma-setūnāṁ 12.12
goptary asati vai nṛṇāṁ 14.1
gotraṁ tvadīyaṁ bhagavān vṛṣadhvajo 4.23
grāmān puraḥ pattanāni 18.30

gṛheṣu kūṭa-dharmeṣu 2.22
gṛhītvā mṛga-śāvākṣyāḥ 2.12
guṇādhikān mudaṁ lipsed 8.34
guṇāṁś ca phalgūn bahulī-kariṣṇavo 4.12
guṇa-vyatikarād rājan 11.16

H

hāhā-kāras tadaivāsīt 10.14
haṁsa-kāraṇḍava-kulair 9.64
hanta priyā daivatamasya devī 4.28
hanty asādhur mṛgān dīnān 13.40
hanyamānā diśo bhejur 4.34

hāra-keyūra-mukuṭair 10.19
harau sa vavre 'calitāṁ smṛtiṁ yayā 12.8
hariḥ sudarśanaṁ cakraṁ 15.16
hataḥ puṇya-janenādrau 10.3
hatāvaśiṣṭā itare raṇājirād 10.10

hato 'yaṁ mānavaḥ sūryo 10.14
havīṁṣi hūyamānāni 13.26
helanaṁ giriśa-bhrātur 11.33
hiraṇmayena pātreṇa 13.36
hiraṇmayena pātreṇa 18.15

hitvā miṣantaṁ pitaraṁ sanna-vācaṁ 8.14
hitvārbhakaḥ krīḍanakāni mātur 12.52
hitvā yakṣeśvara-purīṁ 6.28
hrasva-pān nimna-nāsāgro 14.44
hrīmantaḥ paramodārāḥ 15.25

hriyamāṇaṁ vicakṣvainaṁ 19.36
hṛt-padma-karṇikā-dhiṣṇyam 8.50
hutvāgnīn sat-kathāś cakrur 14.36

I

icchantas tat pratīkartum 10.12
idam apy acyuta viśva-bhāvanaṁ 7.32
idaṁ mayā te 'bhihitaṁ kurūdvaha 12.52
idaṁ pavitraṁ param īśa-ceṣṭitaṁ 7.61
idhmaḥ kavir vibhuḥ svahnaḥ 1.7

ijyamāno bhaktimatā 13.4
ijyate svena dharmeṇa 14.18
ilāyām api bhāryāyāṁ 10.2
indraḥ kirīṭam utkṛṣṭaṁ 15.15
indrāya kupito bāṇam 19.26

indreṇānuṣṭhitaṁ rājñaḥ 19.31
iṣṭas te putra-kāmasya 13.32
iṣṭvābhipede duravāpam anyato 8.21
iṣṭvā māṁ yajña-hṛdayaṁ 9.24
iṣṭvā sa vājapeyena 3.3

īśvarāt kṣīṇa-puṇyena 9.35
iti bruvaṁś citra-rathaḥ sva-sārathiṁ 10.22
iti bruvāṇaṁ nṛpatiṁ 16.1
iti cādhokṣajeśasya 19.10
iti dakṣaḥ kavir yajñaṁ 7.48

iti devarṣiṇā proktaṁ 8.70
iti nyavārayad dharmaṁ 14.6
iti priyaṁ hitaṁ vākyaṁ 18.12
iti tasya vacaḥ śrutvā 1.29
iti te 'sat-kṛtās tena 14.30

iti vyavasitaṁ tasya 12.33
iti vyavasitā viprās 13.35
iti vyavasito buddhyā 17.13
itthaṁ pṛthum abhiṣṭūya 18.1
itthaṁ sa loka-guruṇā 19.39

itthaṁ viparyaya-matiḥ 14.29
itthaṁ vyavasitā hantum 14.34
ity adhvare dakṣam anūdya śatru-han 4.24
ity ajenānunītena 7.1
ity āmantrya kratu-patiṁ 19.29

ity arcitaḥ sa bhagavān 9.26
ity udāhṛtam ākarṇya 8.39
ity uktas taṁ parikramya 8.62

ity uttānapadaḥ putro 12.38
iyaṁ ca lakṣmyāḥ sambhūtiḥ 15.3
iyaṁ ca sudatī devī 15.5

iyaṁ ca tat-parā hi śrīr 15.6
iyeṣa tad adhiṣṭhātuṁ 12.29

J

jaḍāndha-badhironmatta- 13.10
jagad-udbhava-sthiti-layeṣu daivato 7.39
jagarha sāmarṣa-vipannayā girā 4.10
jagāv asūn yad-vimatātmajā satī 4.29
jagdhasya mohād dhi viśuddhim andhaso 4.18

jahi yajña-hanaṁ tāta 19.15
jaitraṁ syandanam āsthāya 10.4
jajñe himavataḥ kṣetre 7.58
jāmātuḥ śvaśurasyāpi 3.1
janaṁ janena janayan 11.19

jananyābhihitaḥ panthāḥ 8.40
jāne tvām īśaṁ viśvasya 6.42
janmauṣadhi-tapo-mantra- 6.9
japaś ca paramo guhyaḥ 8.53
jaṭilaṁ bhasmanācchannaṁ 19.14

jāto nārāyaṇāṁśena 13.20
jāye uttānapādasya 8.8
jihāsatī dakṣa-ruṣā manasvinī 4.26
jīvañ jagad asāv āśu 14.31
jīvatād yajamāno 'yaṁ 6.51

jñānam ajñāta-tattvāya 12.51
jñānasya cārthasya guṇasya cāśrayo 7.31
juhāvaitac chiras tasmin 5.26
juhvataḥ sruva-hastasya 5.19
juṣṭaṁ kinnara-gandharvair 6.9

juṣṭāṁ puṇyajana-strībhir 6.27

K

kadalī-khaṇḍa-saṁruddha- 6.21
kad-apatya-bhṛtaṁ duḥkhaṁ 13.43
kad-apatyaṁ varaṁ manye 13.46
kāka-kṛṣṇo 'tihrasvāṅgo 14.44
kāla eva hi bhūtānāṁ 12.3

kalahaṁsa-kula-preṣṭhaṁ 6.29
kāle kāle yathā-bhāgaṁ 16.5

kalpānta etad akhilaṁ jaṭhareṇa 9.14
kāñcī-kalāpa-paryastaṁ 8.49
kapāla-khaṭvāṅga-dharaṁ 19.20

kapilo nārado datto 19.6
karāla-daṁṣṭrābhir udasta-bhāgaṇaṁ 5.11
karāla-daṁṣṭro jvalad-agni-mūrdhajaḥ 5.3
kariṣyaty uttamaślokas 8.57
karmabhiḥ katham ātmānaṁ 15.26

karmaṇodavasānena 7.56
karma pravṛttaṁ ca nivṛttam apy ṛtaṁ 4.20
karma santānayām āsa 7.16
karmaśreṣṭhaṁ varīyāṁsaṁ 1.38
karma-tantraṁ vitanute 2.22

karṇāntraikapadāśvāsyair 6.21
karṇau pidhāya nirayād yad akalpa īśe 4.17
karoty akartaiva nihanty ahantā 11.18
kasmād dadhāra go-rūpam 17.3
kas taṁ carācara-guruṁ 2.2

kas taṁ prajāpadeśaṁ vai 13.45
kasyānvavāye prakhyātāḥ 13.2
kaśyapaṁ pūrṇimānaṁ ca 1.13
kathaṁ sutāyāḥ pitṛ-geha-kautukaṁ 3.13
kathaṁ tv avadyaṁ kṛtavān 11.12

kaustubhābharaṇa-grīvaṁ 8.48
kaviś ca bhārgavo yasya 1.45
kāyān āviviśus tigmā 10.17
kecid babhañjuḥ prāg-vaṁśaṁ 5.14
kecit karma vadantya enaṁ 11.22

ke te pracetaso nāma 13.2
kharjūrāmrātakāmrādyaiḥ 6.18
kim āśrayo me stava eṣa yojyatāṁ 15.22
kim uta tvad-vidhā rājan 17.20
kiṁ vāṁho vena uddiśya 13.22

kiṁ vā na riṣyate kāmo 8.64
kiṁ vā śivākhyam aśivaṁ na vidus 4.16
kiñcic cikīrṣavo jātā 1.16
kirīṭinaṁ kuṇḍalinaṁ 8.48

kīrtyamāne hṛṣīkeśe 7.48
kīrtyamāne nṛbhir nāmni yajñeśa te 7.47

ko vainaṁ paricakṣīta 14.33
ko yajña-puruṣo nāma 14.25
krator api kriyā bhāryā 1.39
kratur viramatām eṣa 19.35

kravyādāḥ prāṇinaḥ kravyaṁ 18.24
kṛcchra-prāṇaḥ prajā hy eṣa 16.8
kṛcchrāt saṁstabhya ca manaḥ 7.12
krīḍā-bhāṇḍaṁ viśvam idaṁ yasya 7.43
krīḍanti puṁsaḥ siñcantyo 6.25

kṛpālor dīna-nāthasya 12.51
kṛpāvalokena hasad- 1.25
kṛtābhiṣekaḥ kṛta-nitya-maṅgalo 12.28
kṛtāñjaliṁ brahmamayena kambunā 9.4
kṛtāvabhṛtha-snānāya 19.40

kṛtvā samānāv anilau jitāsanā 4.25
kṛtvā vatsaṁ sura-gaṇā 18.15
kṛtvocitāni nivasann 8.43
kṛtvorau dakṣiṇe savyaṁ 6.38
kruddhaḥ sudaṣṭauṣṭha-puṭaḥ sa 5.2

kṣamāpyaivaṁ sa mīḍhvāṁsaṁ 7.16
kṣaṇenācchāditaṁ vyoma 10.23
kṣemāya tatra sā bhūyān 6.4
kṣipraṁ vineśur vidura 11.2
kṣipto 'py asad-viṣaya-lālasa ātma- 7.44

kubjakair mallikābhiś ca 6.16
kūja-dvihaṅga-mithunair 9.63
kumudotpala-kahlāra- 6.19
kuṇḍeṣv amūtrayan kecid 5.15
kurv adhvarasyoddharaṇaṁ hatasya 6.48

L

labdhāvalokair yayatur 1.58
labdhvā dravyamayīm arcāṁ 8.56
labdhvā jñānaṁ sa-vijñānaṁ 17.5
labdhvāpy asiddhārtham ivaika- 9.28
lājākṣataiḥ puṣpa-phalais 9.57

lakṣayāmaḥ kumārasya 8.27
lakṣitaḥ pathi bālānāṁ 13.10
lālito nitarāṁ pitrā 9.60
lālyamānaṁ janair evaṁ 9.53
liṅgaṁ ca tāpasābhīṣṭaṁ 6.36

loka-dhikkāra-sandagdham 14.12
lokāḥ sapālā hy etasmai 14.20
lokā nirucchvāsa-nipīḍitā bhṛśaṁ 8.80
lokān nāvārayañ chaktā 14.40
lokān viśokān vitaraty 14.15

lokasya yad varṣati cāśiṣo 'rthinas 4.15
loke nāvindata trāṇaṁ 17.17
lupta-kriyāyāśucaye 2.13

M

mā bhaiṣṭa bālaṁ tapaso duratyayān 8.82
mahad-guṇān ātmani kartum īśaḥ 15.24
mahāmaṇi-vrātamaye 9.60
mahattvam icchatāṁ tīrthaṁ 12.47
mahimānaṁ vilokyāsya 12.40

mahyaṁ śuśrūṣave brahman 13.5
maitrīṁ samānād anvicchen 8.34
māmaṅgalaṁ tāta pareṣu maṁsthā 8.17
mamanthur ūruṁ tarasā 14.43
mā mā śucaḥ sva-tanayaṁ 8.68

maṁsyanta eṣāṁ striya ādi-rājaṁ 16.21
māṁ vipāṭyājarāṁ nāvaṁ 17.21
manāṁsi kakubho vātāḥ 1.53
mandāraiḥ pārijātaiś ca 6.14
maṇi-pradīpā ābhānti 9.62
manor asūta mahiṣī 13.15

manos tu śatarūpāyāṁ 1.1
mantreṇānena devasya 8.54
manyamāna idaṁ viśvaṁ 12.15
manye mahā-bhāgavataṁ 13.3
marīci-miśrā ṛṣayo 1.8

mārkaṇḍeyo mṛkaṇḍasya 1.45
māsair ahaṁ ṣaḍbhir amuṣya pādayoś 9.30
māsmin mahārāja kṛthāḥ sma cintāṁ 19.34
mathnā conmathitātmānaḥ 2.25
matir vidūṣitā devaiḥ 9.32
mātṛ-bhaktiḥ para-strīṣu 16.17
mātuḥ sapatnyāḥ sa durukti-viddhaḥ 8.14

mātuḥ sapatnyā vāg-bāṇair 9.29
matvā nirastam ātmānam 10.9
matvā taṁ jaḍam unmattaṁ 13.11

mā vaḥ padavyaḥ pitar asmad-āsthitā 4.21
māyā hy eṣā bhavadīyā hi bhūman 7.37
mayaitat prārthitaṁ vyarthaṁ 9.34
mayaṁ prakalpya vatsaṁ te 18.20
mayūra-kekābhirutaṁ 6.12

medhā smṛtiṁ titikṣā tu 1.52
meḍhyāṁ go-cakravat sthāsnu 9.21
megha-nirhrādayā vācā 15.21
mene tadātmānam asaṅga-raṁhasā 5.5
mithunaṁ brahma-varcasvī 1.3

mitrasya cakṣuṣekṣeta 7.3
mṛd-dārv-ayaḥ-kāñcana-darbha- 4.6
mṛgaiḥ śākhāmṛgaiḥ kroḍair 6.20
mṛṣādharmasya bhāryāsīd 8.2
mṛṣṭa-catvara-rathyāṭṭa- 9.57

mṛtyor mūrdhni padaṁ dattvā 12.30
mukta-saṅga-prasaṅgo 'yaṁ 16.18
mumucuḥ sumano-dhārāḥ 15.7
munayaḥ padavīṁ yasya 8.31
munayas tuṣṭuvus tuṣṭā 1.54

mūrdhnā dhṛtāñjali-puṭā 7.23
mūrtiḥ sarva-guṇotpattir 1.52
muṣṇaṁs teja upānītas 7.19

N

na bhavān avadhīd yakṣān 12.3
na brahma-bandhuṣu ca vāṁ 7.13
na budhas tad-vaśaṁ gacched 11.32
na caite putraka bhrātur 11.24
nādaṇḍyaṁ daṇḍayaty eṣa 16.13

nadatsu yātudhāneṣu 10.15
nādhunāpy avamānaṁ te 8.27
na evādṛśyatācchanna 10.13
nāgacchanty āhutā devā 13.30
nāghaṁ prajeśa bālānāṁ 7.2

na gṛhīto mayā yat tvaṁ 8.11
nāhaṁ na yajño na ca yūyam anye 6.7

naicchan mukti-pater muktiṁ 9.29
naitādṛśānāṁ sva-jana-vyapekṣayā 3.18
naitat svarūpaṁ bhavato 'sau padārtha- 7.31

naite gṛhān brahma-sutā 8.1
naitena dehena hare kṛtāgaso 4.22
naivābhibhavituṁ śakyo 16.11
naivaṁ vidāmo bhagavan prāṇa-rodhaṁ 8.81
naivātmane mahendrāya 19.33

nājagmur devatās tasminn 13.25
na jñāyate mohita-citta-vartmabhis 17.36
na lakṣyate yas tv akarod akārayad 17.32
nālaṁ vayaṁ te mahimānuvarṇane 16.2
nalinīṣu kalaṁ kūjat- 6.19

nāmadheyaṁ dadus tasmai 19.18
namaḥ parasmai puruṣāya māyayā 17.29
namaḥ svarūpānubhavena nirdhuta- 17.29
namaskṛtaḥ prāha śaśāṅka-śekharaṁ 6.41
namas te śrita-sattvāya 7.40

na muñcasy ātma-ruddhāni 17.24
nānā-druma-latā-gulmair 6.10
nānāmala-prasravaṇair 6.11
nanāma mātarau śīrṣṇā 9.45
nanāma nāmāni gṛṇan madhudviṣaḥ 12.21

nānā-maṇimayaiḥ śṛṅgair 6.10
nanāma tatrārdham ibhendra-dhiṣṭhitā 8.79
nandā cālakanandā ca 6.24
nāṅgasya vaṁśo rājarṣer 14.42
nānuvindanti te bhadram 14.24

nanv ekasyāparādhena 11.9
nānyair adhiṣṭhitaṁ bhadra 9.20
nānyaṁ tataḥ padma-palāśa-locanād 8.23
nāradas tad upākarṇya 8.25
nāradāya pravocantaṁ 6.37

nara-deveha bhavato 13.31
nārāyaṇaś ca viśvātmā 6.3
nāścaryam etad yad asatsu sarvadā 4.13
nāsmat-kulocitaṁ tāta 10.8
naṣṭa-śaucā mūḍha-dhiyo 2.29

nātman śritaṁ tava vidanty adhunāpi 7.30
nāṭyaṁ sugītaṁ vāditram 15.19

nāvadhyeyaḥ prajā-pālaḥ 13.23
na vadhyo bhavatām indro 19.30
na vai cikīrṣitaṁ tāta 11.23

na vai mukundasya padāravindayo 9.36
na vai satāṁ tvac-caraṇārpitātmanāṁ 6.46
na vai sva-pakṣo 'sya vipakṣa eva vā 11.20
na vatsa nṛpater dhiṣṇyaṁ 8.11
na veda-vādān anuvartate matiḥ 4.19

na vidāmeha devānāṁ 13.28
na vidur mṛgayanto 'pi 8.31
nāyam arhaty asad-vṛtto 14.32
nāyaṁ mārgo hi sādhūnāṁ 11.10
na yaṣṭavyaṁ na dātavyaṁ 14.6

na yasya loke 'sty atiśāyanaḥ priyas 4.11
na yatra bhāgaṁ tava bhāgino daduḥ 6.50
na yāvan mahatāṁ tejaḥ 11.34
necchaṁs tatrātmanātmānaṁ 12.50
nijaghnur huṅkṛtair venaṁ 14.34

nililyur dasyavaḥ sadyaḥ 14.3
nimitta-mātraṁ tatrāsīn 11.17
nināya lokaṁ param arka-maṇḍalaṁ 11.5
nipetur gaganād asya 10.24
nirgatena muner mūrdhnaḥ 1.21

nirguṇāya ca yat-kāṣṭhāṁ 7.40
nirūpitaḥ prajā-pālaḥ 14.11
nirvāsitaḥ pañca-varṣaḥ 8.65
nirvidyeta gṛhān martyo 13.46
nirvṛtyā parayā tūrṇaṁ 8.52

niśamya gadatām evam 11.1
niśamya kauṣāraviṇopavarṇitaṁ 13.1
niśamya tasya munayaḥ 10.29
niśamya tat-paura-mukhān nitāntaṁ 8.15
niśamya vaikuṇṭha-niyojya- 12.28
niścakrāma purāt tūrṇam 9.40

niścakrāma tataḥ kiñcid 2.33
niṣīdety abruvaṁs tāta 14.46
niṣidhyamānaḥ sa sadasya-mukhyair 2.19

nivārayām āsur aho mahā-mate 19.27
nivāsān kalpayāṁ cakre 18.30
niyatenaika-bhūtena 8.51

nṛpa-varya nibodhaitad 14.14
nṛtyanti sma striyo devya 1.55
nūnaṁ bateśasya samīhitaṁ janais 17.32
nūnaṁ bhavān bhagavato 8.38

nūnaṁ janair īhitam īśvarāṇām 17.36
nūnaṁ sunīteḥ pati-devatāyās 12.41
nūnaṁ tā vīrudhaḥ kṣīṇā 18.8
nūnaṁ veda bhavān yasya 8.12
nūnaṁ vimuṣṭa-matayas tava 9.9

O

oṁ namo bhagavate vāsudevāya 8.54

P

padaṁ tri-bhuvanotkṛṣṭaṁ 8.37
pādayor aravindaṁ ca 15.10
padbhyāṁ nakha-maṇi-śreṇyā 8.50
pāṁsuḥ samutthito bhūriś 14.38
panasodumbarāśvattha- 6.17

pañcame māsy anuprāpte 8.76
paṇḍito bahu manyeta 13.45
pāṇiṁ viprāgni-mukhataḥ 2.11
pāpacyamānena hṛdāturendriyaḥ 3.21
pārakya-buddhiṁ kurute 7.53

parān duruktair vitundanty aruntudās 6.47
parastād yad dhruva-gatir 12.35
paricaryā bhagavato 8.58
paricaryamāṇo bhagavān 8.59
parirebhe 'ṅgajaṁ dorbhyāṁ 9.43

pariṣvajyāha jīveti 9.46
parituṣṭātmabhis tāta 7.6
parituṣyati viśvātmā 14.19
parituṣyet tatas tāta 8.29
parītyābhyarcya dhiṣṇyāgryaṁ 12.29

parjanyo dhanadaḥ somaḥ 14.26
pārṣadāv iha samprāptau 12.24
pārśva-bhramad-vyajana-cāmara-rāja- 7.21
paryak-kṛtācala-cchāyo 6.32
paryastaṁ nandayā satyāḥ 6.22

paryaṭan ratham āsthāya 14.5
pāṣaṇḍinas te bhavantu 2.28
paśavo yavasaṁ kṣīraṁ 18.23
paśya prayāntīr abhavānya-yoṣito 3.12
paśyato 'ntardadhe so 'pi 12.9

pāṭalāśoka-bakulaiḥ 6.15
patiḥ pramatha-nāthānāṁ 2.15
patiṁ bhūta-patiṁ devam 3.7
patnī marīces tu kalā 1.13
patnyārciṣālaṅkṛtayā 15.13

paurān jāna-padān śreṇīḥ 17.2
paurṇamāsyāṁ sinīvālyāṁ 12.49
pāvakaṁ pavamānaṁ ca 1.60
pavitra-kīrtiṁ tam alaṅghya-śāsanaṁ 4.14
payaḥ-phena-nibhāḥ śayyā 9.61

payaḥ stanābhyāṁ susrāva 9.50
piṅgaiḥ piśaṅgair makarodarānanaiḥ 5.13
pitary apratirūpe sve 1.66
pitṛbhya ekāṁ yuktebhyo 1.49
pitror agāt straiṇa-vimūḍha-dhīr gṛhān 4.3

plāvitai rakta-kaṇṭhānāṁ 6.12
prabhavo hy ātmanaḥ stotram 15.25
pradoṣo niśitho vyuṣṭa 13.14
praharanti na vai strīṣu 17.20
prajām ātma-samāṁ mahyaṁ 1.20

prajā niranne kṣiti-pṛṣṭha etya 17.9
prajāpater dagdha-śīrṣṇo 7.3
prajāpater duhitaraṁ 10.1
prajāpates te śvaśurasya sāmprataṁ 3.8
prajāpatiḥ sa bhagavān 1.3

prajāpatīnāṁ sarveṣāṁ 3.2
prajāsu pitṛvat snigdhaḥ 16.17
prājñaiḥ parasmai puruṣāya cetasā 3.22
prakalpya vatsaṁ kapilaṁ 18.19
prākārair gopurāgāraiḥ 9.56

prāk pṛthor iha naivaiṣā 18.32
prakṛty-asammataṁ venam 14.2
prakṛtyā viṣamā devī 17.4
praṇamya daṇḍavad bhūmāv 1.24
praṇatā prāñjaliḥ prāha 17.28

praṇatāśrayaṇaṁ nṛmṇaṁ 8.46
prāṇāyāmena saṁyamya 1.19
prāṇāyāmena tri-vṛtā 8.44
praṇemuḥ sahasotthāya 7.22
prāṅ-niṣaṇṇaṁ mṛḍaṁ dṛṣṭvā 2.8

prāpta īdṛśam aiśvaryaṁ 14.33
prāptaṁ kimpuruṣair dṛṣṭvā 6.31
prāpya saṅkalpa-nirvāṇaṁ 9.27
prarūḍha-bhāvo bhagavaty adhokaṣaje 13.1
prasādābhimukhaṁ śaśvat 8.45

prasādayadhvaṁ pariśuddha-cetasā 6.5
prasādya jagad-ātmānaṁ 9.34
prasahya niranukrośaḥ 13.41
praśaṁsanti sma taṁ viprā 15.7
praśasya taṁ prīta-manā 17.8

prasthite tu vanaṁ pitrā 9.22
prasūti-miśrāḥ striya udvigna-cittā 5.9
prasūtiṁ mānavīṁ dakṣa 1.47
prātar madhyandinaṁ sāyam 13.13
pratilabdhaś ciraṁ naṣṭo 9.51

pratyāhuḥ ślakṣṇayā vācā 1.29
pratyudgama-praśrayaṇābhivādanaṁ 3.22
pratyutthānābhivādārhe 2.12
pravepamānā dharaṇī 17.14
prāyacchad yat-kṛtaḥ sargas 1.11

prayataḥ kīrtayet prātaḥ 12.48
prāyeṇābhyarcito devo 13.43
prāyeṇa sajjate bhrāntyā 19.25
prāyo vivṛkṇāvayavā vidudruvur 10.20
pretāvāseṣu ghoreṣu 2.14

preyān na te 'nyo 'sty amutas tvayi 7.38
prītaḥ pratyāha taṁ bālaṁ 8.39
priyavratottānapādau 1.9
priyavratottānapādau 8.7
pṛthag-dhiyaḥ karma-dṛśo durāśayāḥ 6.47

pṛthuḥ prajānāṁ karuṇaṁ 17.12
pṛthu-kīrteḥ pṛthor bhūyāt 19.32
pṛthur nāma mahārājo 15.4
pūjitā dāna-mānābhyāṁ 19.42
pulahasya gatir bhāryā 1.38

pulastyo 'janayat patnyām 1.36
pumān śeṣe siddhair hṛdi 7.42
pumān yoṣid uta klība 17.26
puṁsām amāyināṁ samyag 8.60
puṁso moham ṛte bhinnā 8.28

punar āhāvanir bhītā 18.1
puṇyaṁ madhuvanaṁ yatra 8.42
purā kalpāpāye sva-kṛtam udarī-kṛtya 7.42
purā sṛṣṭā hy oṣadhayo 18.6
purā viśva-sṛjāṁ satre 2.4

purīṁ didṛkṣann api nāviśad dviṣāṁ 10.21
pūrṇimāsūta virajaṁ 1.14
puroḍāśaṁ niravapan 7.17
puroḍāśam niravapan 13.35
puruṁ kutsaṁ tritaṁ dyumnaṁ 13.16

pūṣā tu yajamānasya 7.4
pūṣṇo hy apātayad dantān 5.21
puṣpārṇaṁ tigmaketuṁ ca 13.12

puṣpārṇasya prabhā bhāryā 13.13
putram utkala-nāmānaṁ 10.2
putrikā-dharmam āśritya 1.2

R

racitātma-bheda-mataye sva-saṁsthayā 7.39
rāja-lakṣmīm anādṛtya 8.70
rājā na śraddadhe bhadram 9.37
rājan havīṁṣy aduṣṭāni 13.27
rājan kiṁ dhyāyase dīrghaṁ 8.64

rājann asādhv-amātyebhyaś 14.17
rājñaḥ katham abhūd duṣṭā 13.21
rakṣan yathā baliṁ gṛhṇann 14.17
rakta-kaṇṭha-khagānīka- 6.29
ramaṇaṁ viharantīnām 6.11

rañjayiṣyati yal lokam 16.15
rāvaṇaḥ kumbhakarṇaś ca 1.37
ṛbhavo nāma tapasā 4.33
ṛṣayaś cāśiṣaḥ satyāḥ 15.19
ṛṣayo duduhur devīm 18.14

ṛṣibhiḥ svāśrama-padaṁ 14.35
ṛṣīn sametān abhivandya sāśravo 13.49
ṛṣīn ṣaṣṭi-sahasrāṇi 1.39
ṛte svasṝr vai jananīṁ ca sādarāḥ 4.7
ṛte viriñcāṁ śarvaṁ ca 2.6

rudraṁ ca svena bhāgena 7.56
rūpaṁ sthaviṣṭham aja te mahad- 9.13
rurujur yajña-pātrāni 5.15

S

sa ārūḍha-nṛpa-sthāna 14.4
sa bāla eva puruṣo 13.39
sabhājitās tayoḥ samyag 1.32
sā brahmaṇi sva-mahimany api 9.10
sa cakṣuḥ sutam ākūtyāṁ 13.15

sa ca svarlokam ārokṣyan 12.32
sada āgnīdhra-śālāṁ ca 5.14
sa dadarśa vimānāgryaṁ 12.19
sadasas-patayo būta 13.30
sadasas-patibhir dakṣo 2.7

sad-aśvaṁ ratham āruhya 9.39
sadā vidviṣator evaṁ 3.1
sadbhir ācaritaḥ panthā 2.10
sādhūnāṁ bruvato vṛttaṁ 2.9
sādhu-vādas tadā teṣāṁ 5.25

sā diśo vidiśo devī 17.16
sadyaḥ supta ivottasthau 7.9
sa eva māṁ hantum udāyudhaḥ 17.30
sa eva viśvaṁ sṛjati 11.25
sāgnayo 'nagnayas teṣāṁ 1.63

saha bhāgaṁ na labhatāṁ 2.18
saha patnyā yayāv ṛkṣaṁ 1.17
sahasraśīrṣāpi tato garutmatā 9.1
sa ittham ādiśya surān ajas tu taiḥ 6.8
sa janmanopaśāntātmā 13.7

sa khalv idaṁ bhagavān kāla-śaktyā 11.18
śakteḥ śivasya ca paraṁ 6.42
śakty-ṛṣṭibhir bhuśuṇḍībhiś 10.11
salilaiḥ śucibhir mālyair 8.55
sa-loka-pālā munayo manūnām 6.39

samādhinā naika-bhavena yat padaṁ 9.30
samāhitaḥ paryacarad 8.71
samaḥ sarveṣu bhūteṣu 16.6
samāṁ ca kuru māṁ rājan 18.11
samatvena ca sarvātmā 11.13

śamayiṣyāmi mad-bāṇair 17.25
sambhāvitasya sva-janāt parābhavo 3.25
samprasanne bhagavati 11.14
saṁsarantv iha ye cāmum 2.24
saṁsmārito marma-bhidaḥ kuvāg-iṣūn 3.15

saṁsthāpayiṣyann aja māṁ rasātalād 17.34
samudra ūrmibhir bhīmaḥ 10.27
saṁvidhāya maheṣvāsa 2.34
saṁyaccha roṣaṁ bhadraṁ te 11.31
śanair hṛdi sthāpya dhiyorasi sthitaṁ 4.25

śanair vyudasyābhidhyāyen 8.44
sanakādyā nāradaś ca 8.1
sanandanādyair mahā-siddhaiḥ 6.34
sanat-kumārād bhagavato 17.5
sañchinna-bhinna-sarvāṅgāḥ 6.2

sandadhe 'stram upaspṛśya 11.1
sandadhe viśikhaṁ bhūmeḥ 17.13
sandadhuḥ kasya kāyena 7.8
sandhīyamāna etasmin 11.2
sandhīyamāne śirasi 7.9

saṅgraheṇa mayākhyātaḥ 8.5
śaṅkhābja-cakra-śara-cāpa-padmair 7.20
śaṅkha-cakra-gadā-padmair 8.47
śaṅkha-dundubhi-nādena 9.40
śaṅkha-tūrya-mṛdaṅgādyā 15.8
sanniyacchābhibho manyuṁ 18.2
sanniyamyātmanātmānaṁ 8.24

śāntāḥ sama-dṛśaḥ śuddhāḥ 12.37
śāntiḥ sukhaṁ mudaṁ tuṣṭiḥ 1.51
sāntvito yadi no vācaṁ 14.12
sānurāgāvalokena 16.9
sa-pārṣada-yakṣā maṇiman-madādayaḥ 4.4

saparyāṁ vividhair dravyair 8.54
sa prasīda tvam asmākam ākāṅkṣatāṁ 7.47
śapyamāne garimaṇi 5.21

śarair avidhyan yugapad 10.10
sa rāja-rājena varāya codito 12.8
śaraṁ dhanuṣi sandhāya 17.15
śaraṇaṁ taṁ prapadye 'haṁ 1.20
śaraṇyaḥ sarva-bhūtānāṁ 16.16
sargādi yo 'syānuruṇaddhi śaktibhir 17.33
sarit-samudrā girayo 15.12
sarva-bhakṣā dvijā vṛttyai 2.26
sārvabhauma-śriyaṁ naicchad 13.6
sarva-bhūtātma-bhāvena 11.11
sarva-bhūtātma-bhāvena 12.5
sarva-bhūtātmanāṁ brahman 7.54

sarva evartvijo dṛṣṭvā 5.18
sarva-kāma-dughāṁ pṛthvīṁ 18.26
sarvataḥ sāram ādatte 18.2
sarvātmany acyute 'sarve 12.11
sarvato 'laṅkṛtaṁ śrīmad- 9.56

sarvato mana ākṛṣya 8.77
sarve sva-mukhya-vatsena 18.26
śaśaṁsa nirvyalīkena 7.12
sa śarāsanam udyamya 13.40
sasṛjus tigma-gataya 10.28

śastāṅkurāṁśukaiś cārcet 8.55
śastrair astrānvitair evam 5.23
śata-kratur na mamṛṣe 19.2
sa taṁ vivakṣantam atad-vidaṁ harir 9.4
sa tān āpatato vīra 10.8

sa tān pṛṣatkair abhidhāvato mṛdhe 11.5
sā tat puṁ-savanaṁ rājñī 13.38
sa te mā vinaśed vīra 14.16
satī dākṣāyaṇī devī 3.5
ṣaṭ-pañca-varṣo yad ahobhir alpaiḥ 12.43

sat-saṅkalpasya te brahman 1.30
ṣaṭ-triṁśad-varṣa-sāhasraṁ 9.22
ṣaṭ-triṁśad-varṣa-sāhasraṁ 12.13
sattvaṁ viśuddhaṁ vasudeva-śabditaṁ 3.23
sattve ca tasmin bhagavān vāsudevo 3.23

sa tūpalabhyāgatam ātma-yoniṁ 6.40
sa tvaṁ harer anudhyātas 11.12

sa tvaṁ jighāṁsase kasmād 17.19
sa tvaṁ vimṛśyāsya bhavaṁ prajāpate 19.38
satyaṁ surucyābhihitaṁ bhavān me 8.18

satyāśiṣo hi bhagavaṁs tava pāda- 9.17
saty uttamaśloka-guṇānuvāde 15.23
saudarya-sampraśna-samartha-vārtayā 4.8
sa vai bhavān ātma-vinirmitaṁ jagad 17.34
sa vai dhiyā yoga-vipāka-tīvrayā 9.2

sa vai tadaiva pratipāditāṁ giraṁ 9.5
sa viprānumato rājā 13.37
sa vīra-mūrtiḥ samabhūd dharā-dharo 17.35
savṛndaiḥ kadalī-stambhaiḥ 9.54
sāyaṁ ca puṇya-ślokasya 12.48

sa yojana-śatotsedhaḥ 6.32
serṣyaṁ mahāpūruṣa-pāda-pāṁsubhir 4.13
setuṁ vidhāraṇaṁ puṁsām 2.30
siddhārthākṣata-dadhy-ambu- 9.58
siddhā vidyādharā daityā 19.5

siddhiṁ nabhasi vidyāṁ ca 18.19
sindhavaḥ parvatā nadyo 15.20
sindhavo ratna-nikarān 19.9
sinīvālī kuhū rākā 1.34
śivāpadeśo hy aśivo 2.15

śivāvalokād abhavac 7.10
ślakṣṇayā sūktayā vācā 1.26
smayamānam abhidhyāyet 8.51
smṛtau hatāyāṁ bhṛta-māna-durdṛśaḥ 3.17
snāpayām āsa tanayaṁ 9.44

snātvānusavanaṁ tasmin 8.43
so 'bhiṣikto mahārājaḥ 15.13
so 'nanta 'nta-karaḥ kālo 11.19
so 'nya-janmani dahrāgnir 1.36
so 'pi saṅkalpajaṁ viṣṇoḥ 9.27

so 'śvaṁ rūpaṁ ca tad dhitvā 19.17
so 'śvaṁ rūpaṁ ca tad dhitvā 19.21
so 'yaṁ durmarṣa-hṛdayo brahma- 4.30
so 'yaṁ śamo bhagavatā 8.35
so 'yam sthiti-vyatikaropaśamāya sṛṣṭān 1.57
somo 'bhūd brahmaṇo 'ṁśena 1.33
somo 'mṛta-mayān aśvāṁs 15.17

sotsṛjya dhairyaṁ vilalāpa śoka- 8.16
spṛṣṭvā jalaṁ pīta-dukūla-saṁvṛtā 4.24
spṛṣṭvā mūrdhany agha-ghnena 8.25

śraddadhānāya bhaktāya 13.24
śraddhā maitrī dayā śāntis 1.49
śraddhāsūta śubhaṁ maitrī 1.50
śraddhā tv aṅgirasaḥ patnī 1.34
śraddhāya vākyaṁ devarṣer 9.38

śrāntaṁ śayānaṁ kṣudhitaṁ 8.66
śravaḥ suśravasaḥ puṇyaṁ 17.6
sravate brahma tasyāpi 14.41
śrāvayec chraddadhānānāṁ 12.50
śreyo diśaty abhimataṁ 8.60

śrīvatsāṅkaṁ ghana-śyāmaṁ 8.47
sṛjan rakṣan haran viśvaṁ 7.51
śṛṇvaṁs tad-valgu-gītāni 9.59
śṛṇvataḥ śraddadhānasya 1.47
śroṣyaty ātmāśritā gāthāḥ 16.26

sṛṣṭvānuviśya puruṣas tad-asad- 9.7
srug-ghastāñ juhvato 'bhyetya 19.29
śrutaṁ bhāgavatāc chiṣyād 7.60
śrutena bhūyasā rājann 11.31
śrutvā dṛṣṭvādbhutatamaṁ 9.65

śrutvaitac chraddhayābhīkṣṇam 12.46
śrutvā nṛpāsana-gataṁ 14.3
śruyatāṁ brahmarṣayo me 2.9
stanyena vṛddhaś ca vilajjate yāṁ 8.18
stāvakāṁs tān abhipretya 15.21

sthitāv avaṣṭabhya gadāṁ suvāsasau 12.20
sthūle dadhāra bhagavat-pratirūpa 12.17
strī-kāmaḥ so 'stv atitarāṁ 2.23
stūyamāno nadal līlayā yogibhir 7.46
śuddhaṁ sva-dhāmny uparatākhila- 7.26

sudurjayaṁ viṣṇu-padaṁ jitaṁ tvayā 12.25
sudurlabhaṁ yat paramaṁ padaṁ 9.28
suduṣkaraṁ karma kṛtvā 8.69

suhṛd-didṛkṣā-pratighāta-durmanāḥ 4.2
suhṛd-didṛkṣuḥ pariśaṅkitā bhavān 4.1
śūla-paṭṭiśa-nistriṁśa- 6.1

sunanda-nandādy-anugair vṛtaṁ mudā 7.25
sunanda-nanda-pramukhāḥ 19.5
sunanda-nandāv upasṛtya sasmitaṁ 12.22
sunāsaṁ subhruvaṁ cāru- 8.45

sunīthāṅgasya yā patnī 13.18
sunīthā pālayām āsa 14.35
sunītiḥ suruciś cāsya 9.41
sunītir asya jananī 9.49
suparṇa-vatsā vihagāś 18.24

surāsurendrair upagīyamāna- 16.27
sura-vidviṭ-kṣapaṇair udāyudhair 7.32
suruciḥ preyasī patyur 8.8
suruciḥ śṛṇvato rājñaḥ 8.10
surucis taṁ samutthāpya 9.46

surucyā durvaco-bāṇair 8.36
śuśrāva śabdaṁ jaladher iveritaṁ 10.22
sūto 'tha māgadho vandī 15.20
suto me bālako brahman 8.65
sva-dharma-śīlaiḥ puruṣair 13.4

svāgataṁ te prasīdeśa tubhyaṁ namaḥ 7.36
svāhābhimāninaś cāgner 1.60
svānāṁ yathā vakra-dhiyāṁ 3.19
sva-pārṣada-sainyaṁ ca tad- 5.1
svāpnīvābhāty atad-dhyānād 12.4

svārājyaṁ yacchato mauḍhyān 9.35
svargyaṁ dhrauvyaṁ saumanasyaṁ 12.45

svarṇārṇa-śata-patraiś ca 6.16
svarūpam avarundhāno 13.9
svarvīthir vatsarasyeṣṭā 13.12

sva-śaktyā māyayā yuktaḥ 11.26
sva-tejasā bhūta-gaṇān samutthitān 4.10
svāyambhuvasyāpi manor 8.6

svayambhuve namaskṛtya 6.2
svāyambhuvo mudā yukto 1.5

svecchāvatāra-caritair 8.57
sviṣṭaḥ sutuṣṭāḥ pradiśanti vāñchitaṁ 14.22
śyāmo hiraṇya-raśano 'rka-kirīṭa-juṣṭo 7.20

T

tābhyāṁ krodhaś ca hiṁsā ca 8.3
tābhyāṁ tayor abhavatāṁ 1.44
tad abhijñāya bhagavān 19.26
tad abhipretya bhagavān 19.2
tadābhiṣicyamānābhyāṁ 9.50

tadā dundubhayo nedur 12.31
tad ākarṇya vibhuḥ prāha 6.4
tadā nililyur diśi diśy asanto 16.23
tad-anna-tṛptair asu-bhṛdbhir īḍitā 4.21
tadā sarvāṇi bhūtāni 7.6

tadā sva-prabhayā teṣāṁ 7.19
tad avadyaṁ hare rūpaṁ 19.22
tadā vṛṣadhvaja-dveṣa- 7.10
tad brāhmaṇān parama sarva-vipatsu 7.14
tad brahma paramaṁ śuddhaṁ 2.32

tad brahma viśva-bhavam ekam 9.16
tad-darśanenāgata-sādhvasaḥ kṣitāv 9.3
tad-deva-yajanaṁ dagdhvā 5.26
tad dṛṣṭvā mithunaṁ jātam 15.2
tad gaccha dhruva bhadraṁ te 12.5

tad-gṛhīta-visṛṣṭeṣu 19.24
tad idaṁ paśyata mahad- 19.31
tadottānapadaḥ putro 12.30
tad-rociṣā pratihate 1.25
tad upadravam ājñāya 14.39

tad upaśrutya nabhasi 3.5
tad-vidvadbhir asad-vṛtto 14.12
ta ete munayaḥ kṣattar 1.46
ta evaikonapañcāśat 1.61
ta evam utsanna-bhayā urukrame 9.1

tair alātāyudhaiḥ sarve 4.34
tair ardyamānāḥ subhṛśaṁ 5.18
tais tigma-dhāraiḥ pradhane śilī- 11.4
tam abhyadhāvan kupitā udāyudhāḥ 11.4
tām āgatāṁ tatra na kaścanādriyad 4.7

tamaḥ kim etat kuta etad rajo 'bhūd 5.7
tamālaiḥ śāla-tālaiś ca 6.14

tā mantra-hṛdayenaiva 8.58
tām anvadhāvat tad vainyaḥ 17.15
tām anvagacchan druta-vikramāṁ satīm 4.4

tam anvīyur bhāgavatā 19.6
tam āśu devaṁ priyayā vihīnaṁ 6.6
tam atrir bhagavān aikṣat 19.12
taṁ bhakti-bhāvo 'bhyagṛṇād asatvaraṁ 9.5
taṁ brahma-nirvāṇa-samādhim āśritaṁ 6.39

taṁ dhāvamānam anudhāvanty anīśā 11.20
taṁ dṛṣṭvopavanābhyāsa 9.42
tam enam aṅgātmani mukta-vigrahe 11.29
tam eva dayitaṁ bhūyo 7.59
tam eva mṛtyum amṛtaṁ tāta daivaṁ 11.27

tam evaṁ śīla-sampannaṁ 12.12
tam eva vatsāśraya bhṛtya-vatsalaṁ 8.22
tāṁ kāma-yānāṁ bhagavān 1.6
taṁ kiṁ karomīti gṛṇantam āha 5.4
taṁ kṛṣṇa-pādābhiniviṣṭa-cetasaṁ 12.22

taṁ nas tvaṁ śava-śayanābha-śānta- 7.33
taṁ niḥśvasantaṁ sphuritādharoṣṭhaṁ 8.15
taṁ nirantara-bhāvena 8.61
taṁ prasādaya vatsāśu 11.34
tam ṛtvijaḥ śakra-vadhābhisandhitaṁ 19.27

tāṁ sārikā-kanduka-darpaṇāmbuja- 4.5
taṁ sarva-lokāmara-yajña- 14.21
tāṁ śaśaṁsur janā rājñīṁ 9.51
tāṁs tān kāmān harir dadyād 13.34
taṁ tādṛśākṛtiṁ vīkṣya 19.14

taṁ tu te 'vanataṁ dīnaṁ 14.45
tam ūcur vismitās tatra 13.26
tam upāgatam ālakṣya 7.22
taṁ vicakṣya khalaṁ putraṁ 13.42
taṁ yajñiyaṁ pañca-vidhaṁ ca 7.41

tān anādṛtya yo 'vidvān 18.5
tān ātiṣṭhati yaḥ samyag 18.4
tān hanyamānān abhivīkṣya guhyakān 11.6

tāni pāpasya khaṇḍāni 19.23
taṅ-mālya-bhasma-nṛkapāly avasat 4.16

tan me prasīdedam amartya vāñchitaṁ 3.14
tan no bhavān īhatu rātave 'nnaṁ 17.11
tapasārādhya puruṣaṁ 8.13
tapo-vanaṁ gate tasmin 8.63
tapyamānaṁ tri-bhuvanaṁ 1.21

tapye dvitīye 'py asati 9.33
tāra-hema-mahāratna- 6.27
taravo bhūri-varṣmāṇaḥ 19.8
taruṇaṁ ramaṇīyāṅgam 8.46
tāsāṁ prasūti-prasavaṁ 1.12

tasmā apy anubhāvena 7.57
tasmād viniṣkramya vivṛddha-manyur 2.19
tasmai jahāra dhanado 15.14
tasmai namanti bhūtāni 9.47
tasmai samunnaddha-niruddha- 17.33

tasmān māṁ karmabhir viprā 14.28
tasmāt parokṣe 'smad-upaśrutāny 15.23
tasmāt puruṣa uttasthau 13.36
tasmā unmāda-nāthāya 2.16
tasmiṁs tuṣṭe kim aprāpyaṁ 14.20

tasmin bhaginyo mama bhartṛbhiḥ 3.9
tasmin brahmaṇy advitīye 7.52
tasmin brahmarṣayaḥ sarve 3.4
tasmin mahā-yogamaye 6.33
tasminn abhidhyāyati viśvam ātmano 8.80

tasmin prasūna-stabaka- 1.18
tasmin samastātmani mukta-vairake 4.11
tasyābhiṣeka ārabdho 15.11
tasyaivaṁ vadataḥ śāpaṁ 2.27
tasyaivaṁ vadataḥ śāpaṁ 2.33

tasyākhila-jagad-dhātur 12.24
tasya medhyaṁ hayaṁ devaḥ 17.4
tasyām evaṁ hi duṣṭāyāṁ 17.23

tasyāṁ sasarja duhitṝḥ 1.48
tasyāṁ viśuddha-karaṇaḥ śiva-vār 12.17

tasyāpavargya-śaraṇaṁ tava pāda- 9.8
tasya prītena manasā 12.9
tasya rājño mahā-bhāga 14.19

tasyārṣāstraṁ dhanuṣi prayuñjataḥ 11.3
tasya śīla-nidheḥ sādhor 13.21

tasya te cāpa-nirmuktā 10.17
tasya vaṁśyās tu naiṣādā 14.46
tasya vyabhicaranty arthā 18.5
tasya yakṣa-patir devaḥ 1.37
tataḥ khe 'dṛśyata girir 10.25

tataḥ parigha-nistriṁśaiḥ 10.11
tataḥ sva-bhartuś caraṇāmbujāsavaṁ 4.27
tathā ca kṛtvā vātsalyaṁ 19.39
tathā cikīrṣamāṇaṁ taṁ 8.10
tathāhayo dandaśūkāḥ 18.22

tathā manur vo bhagavān pitāmaho 8.21
tathāmara-gaṇāḥ sarve 2.4
tathāpare ca sarvatra 18.13
tathāpare siddha-gaṇā maharṣibhir 6.41
tathāpi mānaṁ na pituḥ prapatsyase 3.20

tathāpi sāntvayemāmuṁ 14.11
tathāpy ahaṁ yoṣid atattva-vic ca te 3.11
tathāribhir na vyathate śilīmukhaiḥ 3.19
tathā sādhaya bhadraṁ te 13.32
tathā sva-bhāgadheyāni 13.33

tato 'nye ca yathā-kāmaṁ 18.13
tato 'py āsīd bhayaṁ tv adya 14.9
tato 'tikāyas tanuvā spṛśan divaṁ 5.3
tato gantāsi mat-sthānaṁ 9.25
tato mahīpatiḥ prītaḥ 18.28

tato mīḍhvāṁsam āmantrya 7.7
tato niṣkramya balina 10.7
tato viniḥśvasya satī vihāya taṁ 4.3
tat paśyatāṁ khe bhuvi cādbhutaṁ 4.28
tat-prabhāvam avijñāya 8.68

tat-prādurbhāva-saṁyoga- 1.23
tat praṣṭuṁ vyasṛjad vācaṁ 13.29
tat prayacchāmi bhadraṁ te 9.19
tat-putra-pautra-naptṝṇām 1.9
tat-putrāv aparāv āstāṁ 1.35

tatrābhiṣiktaḥ prayatas 8.71
tatrāgataś cāraṇa-yakṣa-kinnaraiḥ 12.1

tatrānu deva-pravarau catur-bhujau 12.20
tatra praviṣṭam ṛṣayo 2.5
tatra sarva upājagmur 15.8

tatra svasṝr me nanu bhartṛ-sammitā 3.10
tatra tatra giras tās tā 16.26
tatra tatra praśaṁsadbhiḥ 12.34
tatra tatropasaṅkḷptair 9.54
tatra yogena dṛṣṭena 18.8

tat-sambandhi śruta-prāyaṁ 1.10
tat tasya cādbhutaṁ karma 19.18
tat tāto gaccha bhadraṁ te 8.42
tat-tejasā hata-rucaḥ 7.23
tat te nirīkṣyo na pitāpi deha-kṛd 3.24

tattvaṁ na te vayam anañjana rudra- 7.27
tāvat sa rudrānucarair mahā-makho 5.13
tava varada varāṅghrāv 7.29
tāv imau vai bhagavato 1.59
tayā hatātmasv anukarma-cetaḥsv 6.49

tayaiva so 'yaṁ kila goptum udyataḥ 17.31
tayoḥ samabhaval lobho 8.3
tayor vyavāyāt sambhūtir 11.15
tayoś ca mithunaṁ jajñe 8.4
te 'pi cāmum amṛṣyantaḥ 10.10

te 'pi viśva-sṛjaḥ satraṁ 2.34
te 'syābhaviṣyann iti vipralabdho 15.24
tebhyo 'gnayaḥ samabhavan 1.61
tebhyo dadhāra kanye dve 1.64
te brahma-viṣṇu-giriśāḥ praṇato 'smy 1.27

te na smaranty atitarāṁ priyam īśa 9.12
teṣām āpatatāṁ vegaṁ 4.32
te vai lalāṭa-lagnais tair 10.9
te yady anutpādita-doṣa-dṛṣṭayo 3.16
tirohitaṁ sahasaivopalakṣya 9.2

tīrthapāda-padāmbhoja- 6.24
tiryaṅ-naga-dvija sarīsṛpa-deva- 9.13
tiṣṭhaṁs tayaiva puruṣatvam upetya 7.26
titikṣaty akramaṁ vainya 16.7
titikṣayā karuṇayā 11.13

toṣaḥ pratoṣaḥ santoṣo 1.7

trāhi mām api bhūtānāṁ 17.18
trastā tadā nivavṛte 17.17
trayāṇām eka-bhāvānāṁ 7.54
trayodaśādād dharmāya 1.48

triḥ śrutvaitat pumān puṇyaṁ 8.5
tri-lokīṁ deva-yānena 12.35
tri-rātrānte tri-rātrānte 8.72
tri-vargaupayikaṁ nītvā 12.14
tṛṇa-parṇādibhiḥ śīrṇaiḥ 8.73

tṛṣārto 'vagāḍho na sasmāra dāvaṁ 7.35
tṛtīyaṁ cānayan māsaṁ 8.74
tuṣitā nāma te devā 1.8
tuṣṭāyāṁ toṣam āpanno 1.6
tuṣṭuvus tuṣṭa-manasas 16.1

tvad-bhrātary uttame naṣṭe 9.23
tvad-dattayā vayunayedam acaṣṭa 9.8
tvām adya yātāḥ śaraṇaṁ śaraṇyaṁ 17.10
tvam eva bhagavann etac 6.43
tvam eva dharmārtha-dughābhipattaye 6.44

tvaṁ karmaṇāṁ maṅgala maṅgalānāṁ 6.45
tvaṁ khalv oṣadhi-bījāni 17.24
tvaṁ kratus tvaṁ havis tvaṁ hutāśaḥ 7.45
tvaṁ nitya-mukta-pariśuddha- 9.15
tvaṁ pratyag-ātmani tadā bhagavaty 11.30

tvaṁ purā gāṁ rasāyā mahā-sūkaro 7.46
tvām ṛte 'dhīśa nāṅgair makhaḥ 7.36
tvaṁ sadasya-rtvijo dampatī devatā 7.45
tvāṁ stabdhāṁ durmadāṁ nītvā 17.27
tvan-māyayārtham abhipadya kalevare 7.44

tvayāhūtā mahā-bāho 19.42
tvayaiva loke 'vasitaś ca setavo 6.44
tvayātmano 'rdhe 'ham adabhra- 3.14
tvayoditaṁ śobhanam eva śobhane 3.16
tvayy etad āścaryam ajātma-māyayā 3.11

U

ubhābhyāṁ rahitaḥ sva-stho 11.21
ubhāv api hi bhadraṁ te 19.33
ubhe te brahma-vādinyau 1.64

ūcuḥ parama-santuṣṭā 15.2
udāsīna ivādhyakṣo 16.12

udatiṣṭhad rathas tasya 10.15
udatiṣṭhan sadasyās te 2.6
udavasya sahartvigbhiḥ 7.56
udyamya śūlaṁ jagad-antakāntakaṁ 5.6
udyānāni ca ramyāṇi 9.63

ūhuḥ sarva-rasān nadyaḥ 19.8
ujjahāra sada-stho 'kṣṇā 5.20
ulbaṇo vasubhṛdyāno 1.41
ulmuko 'janayat putrān 13.17
upagīyamāno gandharvair 19.4

upaguhya jahāv ādhiṁ 9.49
upajahruḥ prayuñjānā 9.59
upalabhya puraivaitad 6.3
upariṣṭād ṛṣibhyas tvaṁ 9.25
upaskṛtaṁ prati-dvāram 9.55

upasṛjya tamas tīvraṁ 19.19
upasthāpitam āyuṣmann 12.27
upāsyamānaṁ sakhyā ca 6.34
upaviṣṭaṁ darbhamayyāṁ 6.37
upavrajyābruvan venaṁ 14.13

upāyanam upājahruḥ 19.9
upayeme bhramiṁ nāma 10.1
ūrjāyāṁ jajñire putrā 1.40
ūrubhir hema-tālābhair 10.18
utatthyo bhagavān sākṣād 1.35

utkṛtya rudraḥ sahasotthito hasan 5.2
utpatty-adhvany aśaraṇa uru-kleśa- 7.28
utpetur utpātatamāḥ sahasraśo 5.12

uttamaṁ nārurukṣantaṁ 8.9
uttamaś ca dhruvaś cobhāv 9.48

uttamas tv akṛtodvāho 10.3
uttānapādo rājarṣiḥ 9.65

utthāya cakre śirasābhivandanam 6.40
uttiṣṭhann eka-pādena 1.23
uvāca ca mahā-bhāgaṁ 17.18
uvāca vāmaṁ cakṣurbhyāṁ 2.8

V

vadhān nivṛttaṁ taṁ bhūyo 19.15
vadho yad upadevānām 11.8
vaidūrya-kṛta-sopānā 6.31
vainyasya dakṣiṇe haste 15.9
vainye yajña-paśuṁ spardhann 19.11

vaiṣṇavaṁ yajña-santatyai 7.17
vaitānike karmaṇi yan- 1.62
vakṣasy adhiśrita-vadhūr vana-māly 7.21
vaktum arhasi yo 'duhyad 17.7
vākyaṁ sapatnyāḥ smaratī saroja- 8.16

vana-kuñjara-saṅghṛṣṭa- 6.30
vanaṁ gatas tapasā pratyag-akṣam 11.28
vanaṁ mad-ādeśa-karo 'jitaṁ 12.42
vanaṁ saugandhikaṁ cāpi 6.23
vanaṁ viraktaḥ prātiṣṭhad 9.67

vāñchanti tad-dāsyam ṛte 'rtham 9.36
vāpyo vaidūrya-sopānāḥ 9.64
varaṁ varārho 'mbuja-nābha-pādayor 12.7
varān dadus te varadā 19.40
vārbhiḥ sravadbhir udghuṣṭe 1.18

vārtā-hartur atiprīto 9.38
vartate bhagavān arko 16.14
varuṇaḥ salila-srāvam 15.14
vāsudevasya kalayā 8.7
vasudhe tvāṁ vadhiṣyāmi 17.22

vasu kāla upādatte 16.6
vātā na vānti na hi santi dasyavaḥ 5.8
vaṭa-vatsā vanaspatayaḥ 18.25
vatsaṁ bṛhaspatiṁ kṛtvā 18.14
vatsaṁ kalpaya me vīra 18.9

vatsaṁ kṛtvā manuṁ pāṇāv 18.12
vatsaṁ viśvāvasuṁ kṛtvā 18.17
vatsaraṁ bhūpatiṁ cakrur 13.11
vatsena pitaro 'ryamṇā 18.18
vavṛṣū rudhiraughāsṛk- 10.24

vayaṁ ca tatrābhisarāma vāma te 3.8
vayaṁ marutvantam ihārtha-nāśanaṁ 19.28
vayaṁ rājañ jāṭhareṇābhitaptā 17.10

vayaṁ tv aviditā loke 15.26
vāyu-bhakṣo jita-śvāso 8.75

vāyuś ca vāla-vyajane 15.15
vedāhaṁ te vyavasitaṁ 9.19
venaḥ prakṛtyaiva khalaḥ 14.10
venāṅga-jātasya ca pauruṣāṇi te 16.2
venāpacārād avaluptam adya 19.37

venasyāvekṣya munayo 14.7
vibhrājayad daśa diśo 12.19
vicikyur urvyām atiśoka-kātarā 13.48
vidhāyādūduhan kṣīram 18.16
vidhāya kārtsnyena ca tad 7.8

vidhāya vatsaṁ duduhur 18.22
vidhehi tan no vrjinād vimokṣaṁ 8.81
viduḥ pramāṇaṁ bala-vīryayor vā 6.7
vidveṣam akarot kasmād 2.1
vidveṣas tu yataḥ prāṇāṁs 2.3

vidyā-buddhir avidyāyāṁ 2.24
vidyā-tapo-vitta-vapur-vayaḥ-kulaiḥ 3.17
vidyā-tapo-vrata-dharān mukhataḥ sma 7.14
vidyā-tapo-yoga-patham 6.35
vigarhya yāta pāṣaṇḍaṁ 2.84

vijñāya nirvidya gataṁ patiṁ prajāḥ 13.48
vijñāya śāpaṁ giriśānugāgraṇīr 2.20
vijñāya tāv uttamagāya-kiṅkarāv 12.21
vikalpe vidyamāne 'pi 8.28

viklidyamāna-hṛdayaḥ pulakācitāṅgo 12.18
vīkṣyoḍha-vayasaṁ taṁ ca 9.66
vīkṣyotthitāṁs tadotpātān 14.37
vilokya bhūteśa-giriṁ 6.22
vimāna-yānāḥ sa-preṣṭhā 3.6

vimṛśya loka-vyasanaṁ 14.7
vimukto jīva-nirmukto 11.14
viniḥsṛtā āviviśur dviṣad-balaṁ 11.3
vinindyaivaṁ sa giriśam 2.17
viniścityaivam ṛṣayo 14.43

viprāḥ satyāśiṣas tuṣṭāḥ 19.41
vīraḥ sva-paśum ādāya 19.17
virajenātmanā sarve 2.35

viraktaś cendriya-ratau 8.61
vīra-mātaram āhūya 14.2

vīraś cāśvam upādāya 19.22
virodhi tad yaugapadaika-kartari 4.20
viśantu śiva-dīkṣāyāṁ 2.29
visargādānayos tāta 11.24
vismayaṁ param āpanno 5.23

viṣṇur viriñco giriśa 14.26
visphurat-taḍitā dikṣu 10.23
visphūrjayann āja-gavaṁ dhanuḥ 16.23
viṣvaksenāṅghri-saṁsparśa- 9.43
viśvaṁ sṛjasi pāsy atsi 6.43

viśvodbhava-sthiti-layeṣu 1.27
vitatya nṛtyaty uditāstra-dor-dhvajān 5.10
vitāyamāna-yaśasas 1.22
vitṛṣo 'pi pibanty ambhaḥ 6.26
vitta-dehendriyārāmā 2.26

vitudann aṭate vīṇāṁ 8.38
vrajantam iva mātaṅgair 6.13
vrajantīḥ sarvato digbhya 3.6
vrīḍā mamābhūt kujana-prasaṅgatas 4.22
vṛṇīhi kāmaṁ nṛpa yan mano-gataṁ 12.7

vṛṣa-haṁsa-suparṇa-sthān 1.24
vyaktaṁ tvam utkṛṣṭa-gateḥ prajāpateḥ 3.20
vyaktāvyaktam idaṁ viśvaṁ 11.17
vyapeta-narma-smitam āśu tadā 'haṁ 4.23
vyuṣṭaḥ sutaṁ puṣkariṇyāṁ 13.14

Y

yac cānyad api kṛṣṇasya 17.6
yadābhiṣiktaḥ pṛthur aṅga viprair 17.9
yadābhiṣikto dakṣas tu 3.2
yadaika-pādena sa pārthivārbhakas 8.79
yadā na śāsituṁ kalpo 13.42

yad-aṅgajāṁ svāṁ puruṣa-dviḍ 4.30
yad-anudhyāyino dhīrā 9.52
yad asau loka-pālānāṁ 13.23
yad ātmānaṁ parāg gṛhya 11.10
yad bhrājamānaṁ sva-rucaiva sarvato 12.36

yad-buddhy-avasthitim akhaṇḍitayā 9.15
yad-dauḥśīlyāt sa rājarṣir 13.18
yad dhyāyato daiva-hataṁ nu kartuṁ 19.34
yad dvy-akṣaraṁ nāma gireritaṁ nṛṇāṁ 4.14
yadi racita-dhiyaṁ māvidya-loko 7.29

yadi vrajiṣyasy atihāya mad-vaco 3.25
yad yajña-puruṣaḥ sākṣād 13.33
ya etad ādāv asṛjac carācaraṁ 17.31
ya etan martyam uddiśya 2.21
yāḥ kardama-sutāḥ proktā 1.12

yaḥ kṣatra-bandhur bhuvi 12.43
yaḥ pañca-varṣas tapasā 12.23
yaḥ pañca-varṣo guru-dāra-vāk-śarair 12.42
yaḥ pañca-varṣo jananīṁ tvam vihāya 11.28
yajamāna-paśoḥ kasya 5.24

yaj jaghnivān puṇya-janān 11.33
yajña-ghna-ghnena yajuṣā 4.32
yajñair vicitrair yajato bhavāya te 14.21
yajñas te rudra bhāgena 6.53
yajñena yuṣmad-viṣaye dvijātibhir 14.22

yajño 'yaṁ tava yajanāya kena sṛṣṭo 7.33
yakṣa-rakṣāṁsi bhūtāni 18.21
yam aṅga śepuḥ kupitā 13.19
yāṁ dudoha pṛthus tatra 17.3
yaṁ jighāṁsatha yajñena 19.30

yaṁ pūrve cānusantasthur 2.31
yaṁ sapta-rātraṁ prapaṭhan 8.53
yāni rūpāṇi jagṛhe 19.23
yā nirvṛtis tanu-bhṛtāṁ tava pāda- 9.10
yan-māyayā gahanayāpahṛtātma- 7.30

yan-nābhi-sindhu-ruha-kāñcana- 9.14
yan na gṛhṇanti bhāgān svān 13.28
yan-nāmadheyam abhidhāya 10.30
yan nāvrajañ jantuṣu ye 'nugrahā 12.36
yānty añjasācyuta-padam 12.37

yāsāṁ vrajadbhiḥ śiti-kaṇṭha maṇḍitaṁ 3.12
yasmai baliṁ viśva-sṛjo haranti 11.27
yasmin bhramati kauravya 12.39
yasminn avidyā-racitaṁ nirarthakaṁ 16.19
yasmin vinaṣṭe nṛpatir 14.16

yasmin viruddha-gatayo hy aniśaṁ 9.16
yasmin yadā puṣkara-nābha-māyayā 6.48
yās tā devarṣiṇā tatra 13.5
yas tayoḥ puruṣaḥ sākṣād 1.4
yā strī sā dakṣiṇā bhūter 1.4

yas tv anta-kāle vyupta-jaṭā-kalāpaḥ 5.10
yasyāṅghri-padmaṁ paricarya viśva- 8.20
yasya prasanno bhagavān 9.47
yasyāpratihataṁ cakram 15.10
yasya rāṣṭre pure caiva 14.18

yasya yad daiva-vihitaṁ 8.33
yataḥ pāpīyasī kīrtir 13.44
yathā gatir deva-manuṣyayoḥ pṛthak 4.19
yathā kṛtas te saṅkalpo 1.30
yathā-mati gṛṇanti sma 7.24

yathā pumān na svāṅgeṣu 7.53
yathā-sukhaṁ vasanti sma 18.32
yathopadeśaṁ munibhiḥ pracoditāḥ 16.3
yatiṣyati bhavān kāle 8.32
yato hi vaḥ prāṇa-nirodha āsīd 8.82

yato virodhaḥ sarveṣāṁ 13.44
yat-pāda-padmaṁ mahatāṁ mano 4.15
yat paśyantīnāṁ duhitṝṇāṁ prajeśaḥ 5.9
yat-prasādaṁ sa vai puṁsāṁ 8.30
yatra dharma-dughā bhūmiḥ 19.7

yatra graharkṣa-tārāṇāṁ 9.20
yatra sphaṭika-kuḍyeṣu 9.62
yatra tejas tad icchūnāṁ 12.47
yatra yajña-patiḥ sākṣād 19.3
yat-tejasāhaṁ susamiddha-tejā 7.41

yat tvaṁ pitāmahādeśād 12.2
yāvan na naṅkṣyāmaha ujjhitorjā 17.11
yavasaṁ jagdhy anudinaṁ 17.23
yayau madhuvanaṁ puṇyaṁ 8.62
yayau sva-dhiṣṇyān nilayaṁ pura- 6.8

yayoḥ sura-striyaḥ kṣattar 6.25
yayor janmany ado viśvam 1.53
yayos tat-snāna-vibhraṣṭa- 6.26
ye 'bhyāgatān vakra-dhiyābhicakṣate 3.18
yenāhaṁ ātmāyatanaṁ vinirmitā 17.30

yenāharaj jāyamāno 14.46
yenāñjasolbaṇam uru-vyasanaṁ 9.11
yena proktaḥ kriyā-yogaḥ 13.3
yena puṇya-janān etān 11.7
yenodvigna-dṛśaḥ kṣattar 10.6

yenopasṛṣṭāt puruṣāl 11.32
ye tv abja-nābha bhavadīya- 9.12
ye vṛttidaṁ patiṁ hitvā 14.23
yo 'dhiyajña-patiṁ viṣṇuṁ 14.32
yo 'ṅkaṁ premṇāruruksantaṁ 8.67

yo 'ntaḥ praviśya mama vācam 9.6
yo 'sau mayāvidita-tattva-dṛśā 7.15
yogaṁ kriyonnatir darpam 1.51
yo līlayādrīn sva-śarāsa-koṭyā 16.22
yo māyayā viracitaṁ nijayātmanīdaṁ 1.56

yo mṛgyate hasta-gṛhīta-padmayā 8.23
yo nārada-vacas tathyaṁ 9.32
yo nityadākarṇya naro 'nukīrtayed 7.61
yo viśvasṛg-yajña-gataṁ varoru mām 3.24
yuktaṁ virahitaṁ śaktyā 12.6

Index of Verses Quoted

This index lists the verses quoted in the purports and footnotes of this volume of *Śrīmad-Bhāgavatam*. Numerals in boldface type refer to the first or third lines of verses quoted in full; numerals in roman type refer to partially quoted verses.

abhyāsa-yoga yuktena, 115
ābrahma-bhuvanāl lokāḥ, 506, 577, 588
aham ādir hi devānām, 297
ahaṁ sa ca mama priyaḥ, 279
ahaṁ sarvasya prabhavaḥ, 82, 298, 747
ahaṁ tvāṁ sarva-pāpebhyo, **770**
amāninā mānadena, 227
anādir ādir govindaḥ, **519**
ānanda-cinmaya-rasa, 371
anāśritaḥ karma-phalaṁ, **823**
aṇḍāntarastha-paramāṇu, 390
annād bhavanti bhūtāni, **719–20**
ante nārāyaṇa-smṛtiḥ, 433
anyābhilāṣitā-śūnyam, 375
aprāṇasyaiva dehasya, 276
asaṅgo hy ayaṁ puruṣaḥ, 113
āśrāvayeti catur-akṣaraṁ, 284
athāto brahma-jijñāsā, 75

bhagavad-bhakti-hīnasya, 276
bhaktyā mām abhijānāti, 269, 417
bhogaiśvarya-prasaktānām, 428
bhoktāraṁ yajña-tapasām, 86, 130, 296, 556, 668
bhuñjāna evātma-kṛtaṁ vipākam, 224
bījaṁ māṁ sarva-bhūtānām, 818
brahma-bhūtaḥ prasannātmā, 335, **536**, **618–19**, 740

cetasā nānya-gāminā, 115
ceto-darpaṇa-mārjanaṁ, 619

dadāmi buddhi-yogaṁ tam, 529, 640
daivī hy eṣa guṇamayī, 229, 421
daivīṁ prakṛtim āśritāḥ, 176
dharma-saṁsthāpanārthāya, **846**
dhyānāvasthita-tad-gatena, 257

ekale īśvara kṛṣṇa, 288
eko bahūnāṁ yo vidadhāti kāmān, 671, 736–37, 804

guru-kṛṣṇa-prasāde pāya, 333

hare kṛṣṇa, hare kṛṣṇa, **499, 769, 794**
harer nāma harer nāma, **684, 720**
hariṁ vinā na sṛtiṁ taranti, 445, 506
hṛṣīkeṇa hṛṣīkeśa-sevanaṁ, 115, 510

īśvaraḥ paramaḥ kṛṣṇaḥ, **519**
īśvaraḥ sarva-bhūtānāṁ, 557

janmādy asya yataḥ, 298, 422
jīva-bhūtāṁ mahā-bāho, 299
jīveta yo mukti-pade sa, 224
jñānaṁ sāttvikaṁ kaivalyam, 115

kalau nāsty eva nāsty eva, **684, 720**
kalau śūdra-sambhavaḥ, 604, 666

kāmais tais tair hṛta-jñānāḥ, 87
krodha bhakta-dveṣi jane, 130
kṛṣṇa-śakti vinā nahe tāra pravartana, 846
kṛṣṇas tu bhagavān svayam, 288
kṣīne puṇye martya-lokaṁ viśanti, 412, 447

loko 'yaṁ karma-bandhanaḥ, 233

mad-bhakta-pūjābhyadhikā, 91
mahājano yena gataḥ sa panthāḥ, 782
mahātmānas tu māṁ pārtha, 176
mahīyasāṁ pāda-rajo-, 134
mama māyā duratyayā, 229
māṁ ca yo 'vyabhicāreṇa, 114
mām ekaṁ śaraṇaṁ vraja, 548
mām eva ye prapadyante, 77, 229, 502
māṁ hi pārtha vyapāśritya, **692**
man-manā bhava mad-bhakto, 111
mat-sthāni sarva-bhūtāni, 532, 557
mattaḥ sarvam pravartate, 82
mayādhyakṣeṇa prakṛtiḥ, 768
māyām etāṁ taranti te, 77, 229, 503
mayā tatam idaṁ sarvaṁ, 617
māyāvādam asac-chāstram, 78
mṛtyuḥ sarva-haraś cāham, 766
muci haya śuci haya yadi kṛṣṇa bhaje, 591

na māṁ karmāṇi limpanti, 273, 531
narāṇāṁ mātula-karma, 642
nārāyaṇaḥ paro 'vyaktāt, 268, 297
na tad bhāsayate sūryo, 589
nirguṇaṁ guṇa-bhoktṛ ca, 768
nityo nityānāṁ cetanaś cetanānām, 422

oṁ namo bhagavate vāsudevāya, 446
oṁ tad viṣṇoḥ paramaṁ padaṁ, 430

paṇḍitāḥ sama-darśinaḥ, 85, 301
paraṁ brahma paraṁ dhāma, 731
paraṁ dṛṣṭvā nivartate, 208, 563, 619
paras tasmāt tu bhāvo 'nyaḥ, 578, 588
parāsya śaktir vividhaiva, 306, 529, 549
paritrāṇāya sādhūnām, 255, **846**
patitānāṁ pāvanebhyo, 230
patraṁ puṣpaṁ phalaṁ toyaṁ, 296
payaḥ-pānaṁ bhujaṅgānām, 802
pitṝn yānti pitṛ-vratāḥ, 797
prajās te bhakṣayiṣyanti, 666
prakṛteḥ kriyamāṇāni, 516
premāñjana-cchurita-bhakti-vilocanena, 399, 558
priyo hi jñānino 'tyartham, 279
punaḥ punaś carvita-carvaṇānām, 783
putra-hīnaṁ gṛhaṁ śūnyam, 636

rāmādi-mūrtiṣu kalā-niyamena tiṣṭhan, 777

sac-cid-ānanda-vigrahaḥ, 547
sadā paśyanti sūrayaḥ, 257
sa guṇān samatītyaitān, 114
samaḥ sarveṣu bhūteṣu, **536, 618–19**
samatvenaiva vīkṣeta, **831, 832**
sambhavāmy ātma-māyayā, 116
samo 'haṁ sarva-bhūteṣu, 131
sannyāsīra alpa chidra sarva-loke gāya, 824
sarva-dharmān parityajya, **770**
sarvaṁ khalv idaṁ brahma, 298
sarvopādhi-vinirmuktaṁ, 619
sa sannyāsī ca yogī ca, **823**
satāṁ prasaṅgān mama vīrya-saṁvido, 414
sattvaṁ viśuddhaṁ vasudeva-, 135–36
sa vai puṁsāṁ paro dharmaḥ, 157
sa yat pramāṇaṁ kurute, **843**
sevonmukhe hi, 259
śiva-hīna-yajña, 241
striyo vaiśyās tathā śudrāḥ, 141, **692**
śuni caiva śvapāke ca, **734**
sva-karmaṇā tam abhyarcya, **668**
svanuṣṭhitasya dharmasya, 615
sve sve karmaṇy abhirataḥ, 615

tad viṣṇoḥ paramaṁ padaṁ, 257
tasmin tuṣṭe jagat tuṣṭaḥ, 88
tena tyaktena bhuñjīthāḥ, 453
tene brahma hṛdā, 82, 297
teṣām ahaṁ samuddhartā, 549

tīrthī-kurvanti tīrthāni, 204
tṛṇād api sunīcena, 227

ūrdhvaṁ gacchanti sattva-sthāḥ, 517

vaiṣṇavānāṁ yathā śambhuḥ, 55, 130, 148, 213
vāñchā-kalpatarubhyaś ca, 230
vartamānāni cārjuna, 188
vāsudevaḥ sarvam iti, 20, 115
vedāhaṁ samatītāni, 188, 421, 443
vedaiś ca sarvair aham eva, 82, 293
veda-vāda-ratāḥ pārtha, 263
vidyā-vinaya-sampanne, **734**
viṣṇur mahān sa iha yasya kalā-viśeṣo, 419
viṣṇu-śaktiḥ parā proktā, 408
viṣṭabhyāham idaṁ kṛtsnam, 390
viśvaṁ pūrṇa-sukhāyate, 395, 414

yac-cakṣur eṣa savitā sakala-grahāṇām, 593
yad gatvā na nivartante, 436, 577
yad yad ācarati śreṣthas, **843**
yaḥ smaret puṇḍarīkākṣam, 591
yajante śraddhayānvitāḥ, 87
yajanti hi sumedhasaḥ, 88, 125, 233
yajñād bhavati parjanyo, **719–20**
yajñaiḥ saṅkīrtana-prāyaiḥ, 88, 125, 233, 284, 817
yajñārthāt karmaṇo 'nyatra, 7, 233, 525, 554
yaṁ brahmā varuṇendra-rudra, 257
yām imāṁ puṣpitāṁ vācaṁ, 262
yānti deva-vratā devān, 38, 139, 412, 525
yasmin vijñāte sarvam evaṁ vijñātaṁ bhavati, 419, 586
yas tu nārāyaṇaṁ devaṁ, **831**
yasyaika-niśvasita-kālam athāvalambya, **419**
yasyājñayā bhramati sambhṛta-kāla-cakraḥ, 735
yasya prasādād bhagavat-prasādaḥ, 433
yataḥ pravṛttir bhūtānāṁ, **668**
yat-kīrtanaṁ yat-smaraṇaṁ, 156
yato bhaktir adhokṣaje, 157
yato vā imāni bhūtāni, 19, 298
yayātmā suprasīdati, 157
yena māṁ upayānti te, 529
ye 'py anya-devatā-bhaktā, 87
yogināṁ api sarveṣāṁ, 390
yo māṁ paśyati sarvatra, 617
yo me bhaktyā prayacchati, 296

General Index

Numerals in boldface type indicate references to translations of the verses of *Śrīmad-Bhāgavatam.*

A

Abhaya (son of Dharma), **40**
Abhiṣeka ceremony, 463
Abhodha-jāta defined, 782
Absolute pleasure & pain, 103-4
Absolute Truth, 75
  beyond atheists, 419-20
  beyond mental speculation, **528,** 529
  compared to sun, 528
  ignorance of, 606-7
  knowledge of, 528, 529
  Lord as, 547
  personal & impersonal views of, 407, 424
  three features of, 649
  See also: Kṛṣṇa; Supreme Brahman; Supreme Lord; Truth
Ācārya(s). See: Spiritual master(s)
Acintya-bhedābheda-tattva
  defined, 302
  philosophy, 521, 768
Activities
  divisions of, **144**-45
  of Lord. *See:* Supreme Lord, activities of; Supreme Lord, pastimes of
  material & spiritual, 405-6
  of materialists & renunciants, **144**-45
  pious. *See:* Pious activities
  sinful. *See:* Sinful activities
  See also: Duty; *Karma;* Pious activities; Work
Adharma (irreligion), **311,** 313
Adhokṣaja defined, 116, 157
Ādi-puruṣa defined, 422
Ādi-rājam defined, 736
Administrators. *See:* King(s); *Kṣatriya(s);* Government(s), leader(s); Politician(s)
Advaita Prabhu, 217
Advancement, spiritual
  via associating with devotees, 591
  envy blocks, 812
  śruti & *smṛti* for, 781
  See also: Devotional service
Agastya (son of Pulastya), **32**
Age (time of life) for retiring from family, 627
Age, present. *See:* Kali-yuga
Agni (sage), **430, 705**
Agni, Lord, 705
  descendants of, **46-48**
    accept oblations, **46**-47
    impersonalists worship, **48**
  discusses sacrifice, **283-84**
  family of, **46-48**
  impersonalists worship, **48**
  prayers to Viṣṇu, **283-84**
Agniṣṭoma, **624**
Agniṣvāttas (Pitās), **49**
Agriculture. *See:* Food; *Vaiśyas*
Ahaitukī defined, 426
Ahaṁ brahmāsmi defined, 80, 135
Air of life
  controlled by *yoga,* 152
  See also: Breathing; *Prāṇāyāma*
Airplane(s)
  of demigods, **94, 100, 205**-6
  in Dhruva's day, 468
  of Kardama Muni, 582, 799
  modern, 468, 582
  persons on, as unit energies, 393
  spiritual
    Dhruva boarded, **581,** 582, 586
    Dhruva circumambulated, **580**
    Dhruva saw, **568**
    Lord sent, **577-78**
    Nanda & Sunanda piloted, 588
Ajāmila, 224

Ājyapas (Pirās), **49**
Ākāśa-patana defined, 578
Ākūti (Sarvatejā's wife), **624**
Ākūti (Svāyambhuva's daughter)
children of, **4, 5, 6**
daughter of Manu, **1, 2**
given to Ruci conditionally, **3**
Alakanandā Lake, **200–201**
Alakanandā River, **202**
Alakāpurī, 201-2
Dhruva attacked, **482, 483, 493,** 507
Alcohol, "*sannyāsīs*" drink, 831
See also: Liquor
Allahabad, 352
Amaraloka, 473
Ambikā. *See:* Satī
Americans, 344
Amogha-vīrya defined, 688
Amuṣmin defined, 781
Anahaṅkāra defined, 531
Analogies
airplane & total energy, 393
approaching city & realizing Absolute Truth, 424
astronauts & demigod worshipers, 412
autumn rains & purification, 244
bees & highly qualified men, 132
blind well & family life, 647
boat & Earth, **776**
boats & planets, 759
bodily parts & social orders, 691
body & society, 276, 345
body & unified existence, **300–301**
body parts & souls, **300–301**
brāhmaṇa & law student, 63
building constructor & Lord, 25
bulls circling & planets orbiting, **430, 593**
calf & devotee, **425,** 426
cat's kitten & Lord's devotee, 582
child & devotee, 591
coconut drying & devotee serving, 567
cow & Earth, 790
cow & Lord, **425,** 426
cowherd boy & Śiva, **248**
Analogies (*continued*)
criminal department & ignorance mode, 221
crows & ritual performers, 147
curd & Śiva, 139
darkness & *māyā,* 502
demigods & transcendentalists, **143**
Dhruva & elephant, **391,** 392
Dhruva & snake, **321**
diseased body-parts & conditioned souls, **300–301**
dream & material world, 448-49, **562–**63
dress & body, 734
Earth & mother, 754
electrical powerhouse & Lord, 521, 774
electrified copper & devotional service, 114
father & Śiva, 250
father's son & spiritual master's disciple, 594
feeding stomach & satisfying Lord, 849
fire & Lord, 291, 521
fire & material existence, **413,** 414
fire & Pṛthu, **726**
fire in wood & Lord's energy in nature, **407,** 408
government servants & demigods, 87-90
heat & earthen pot, 343-44
heated iron & devotional service, 114
hot iron rod & Deity form, 365
insect & Brahmā, 442
islands & planets, 759
jewel on snake & material assets, 106
law enforcement & Lord's mercy, 520
limbs serving body & living entities serving Lord, 546, 548-49
lion & Pṛthu, **738**
mad elephant & offender to devotee, 69
mango & devotional service, 415
milk and yogurt & Lord and living beings, 302
mountain & Dhruva, **487**
ocean & material existence, **413,** 414
ocean & outer space, 759
one with zeros & devotional service, 107
passengers & unit energies, 393
pleasing master & pleasing Lord, 232

Analogies (*continued*)
poisoned milk & possessions of bad men, 106
poor man's request & Dhruva's desire, **451**
potter & Lord, 518-19
river's waves & devotional service, **413,** 414
root & Lord, 88
serpents & senses, 552
snake & Dhruva, **321**
snake & malicious persons, 106
snake & Vena, **659**
stomach & Lord, 88
sun & Absolute Truth, 528
sun & Dhruva, **488, 489**
sun & Kṛṣṇa, 502
sun & Lord, 44
sun & Nārada, 347
sun & powerful beings, 143
sun-god & Pṛthu, **721, 728**
swan & *paramahaṁsa,* 438
tigers & malicious persons, 108
touchstone & Lord, 522
transforming bell metal & initiation, 367
vomiting & suicide, **142**
watering tree's root & serving Lord, 288, 396, 547, 607-8, 849
wind blowing dust & *karma* impelling living entities, **524**
woman with paramour & *brāhmaṇas* worshiping demigods, **673,** 674, **675**
Ananta, Lord, 259, 696, 716
Anasūyā (daughter of Kardama), **14**
Anātmya defined, 445
Ancestry (parentage), 106-7
Aṅga, King
bad son begotten by, 642
demigods refused sacrifice by, **631-33**
kingdom renounced by, **625, 627, 648-50**
parents of, **624**
purity of, 688
quoted on bad son, **645-47**
son lacking by, **635, 636**
Sunīthā given sacrificial *prasāda* by, **640, 641**
Aṅga (*continued*)
Sunīthā polluted semen of, 688
as Sunīthā's husband, **625,** 642
Angels, **193-94**
Anger
bad effect of, 66, 68-70
at blasphemy, 130
of Dakṣa at Śiva, **59,** 105, 111
Dakṣa bewildered by, 66, 68-69
Dakṣa's, foreseen by Śiva, **105, 107-109**
detrimental vs. devotional, 539
in devotee, 482
of Dhruva at insult, **321-22**
effect of, 66, 68-70
in hosts, **105, 107**
at insults to Lord or devotee, 130
need to avoid, 69
personified in Vīrabhadra, **169**
proper use of, 130
in Pṛthu, **766,** 768, **779**
in saintly persons absent, 540
of Satī at Dakṣa, **128-**29
of Satī at Śiva, **120-21**
of Śiva on Satī's death, **165-67**
Anger (descendant of Brahmā), **312**
Aṅgirā, **624**
descendants of, **31**
Animal(s)
in bodily concept of life, **510**
dead due to Śiva, **271-72**
devotees compared with, 510
fresh flesh for, **803**
humans compared with, 510
in Kailāsa, **199, 200**
killing of
as wrong, 272
See also: Animal slaughter
Lord supplies needs of, 671
maintain offspring, 517
mantras tested on, 125, 272
in medical experiment, 639
punishment of, need for, 249
rejuvenated by *mantras,* 125, 184, 272
sacrifice of, 631, 639, 822, 835, 844
device for, **184**
not for eating, 184

Animal(s)
sacrifice of (*continued*)
new life given at, 125, **184,** 272
See also: Aśvamedha sacrifices
Vena killed, **643**
See also: Cow(s); *specific animals*
Animal slaughter
Buddha stopped, 844
condemned, 763
for godless food production, 790
in Kali-yuga, 844
modern leaders allow, 559, 732
"*sannyāsīs*" implicated in, 831
sinful reaction to, 508
See also: Hunting; Meat-eating
Aniruddha (grandson of Kṛṣṇa), **181,** 182
Aniruddha, Lord, 696
Anīśāḥ defined, 524
Annihilation of universe(s)
Lord during, 286
in lower planets, **285**
Śiva at, 174
at sleep of Brahmā, 286
Anucarāḥ defined, 123
Anumati (daughter of Aṅgirā), **31**
Anxiety
envy causes, 226
freedom from, **274–**75, 384
See also: Suffering
Anyābhilāṣitā-śūnya defined, 446
Apauruṣeya, Vedas as, 81-82
Apavarga (liberation), 374, 375
See also: Liberation
Appearance of Lord. *See: Avatāras;* Incarnations; Supreme Lord, advent(s) of
Approaching city compared to realizing Absolute Truth, 424
Apratihatā defined, 560
Apsarās, **194, 796,** 814
Araṇi wood, **726**
Arcanā. See: Deity worship
Arcā-vigraha. See: Deity forms
Arci
identity of, **694, 695, 697,** 698
at Pṛthu's coronation, **702**
Arctic region, Pṛthu's power extended to, **728**
Arjuna
Aśvatthāmā excused by, 246-47
Kṛṣṇa drove chariot of, 597
as Kṛṣṇa's disciple, 349
as Nara of Nara-Nārāyaṇa, **46**
quoted on Kṛṣṇa as Supreme Brahman, 731
Arrows of Dhruva, **501–5**
Ārta-bandhu defined, 409
Artha (son of Dharma), **40**
Arthadam defined, 289
Artha-vit defined, 438
Arundhatī (wife of Kratu), **34,** 35
Aruṇi (son of Brahmā), **309**
Aryamā, **797,** 798
Asadbhiḥ defined, 785
Āsana (sitting place), 354
Āsanas (sitting postures), 152, **215**
yoga-kakṣām, 217
Asat-śāstra defined, 78
Asita, 663
Asmin defined, 781
Āśrama & varṇa system. *See: Varṇāśrama-dharma*
Association
of devotees, **413,** 414-15, **416,** 420, **590,** 591, 603-4
of Lord, 607
sinful reaction via, 660
for spiritual or material life, 153-54
See also: Devotee(s), associating with; Materialist(s), associating with
Aṣṭāṅga-yoga
bath purifies one for, 354
breathing exercise for, **354–**55
goal of, 355
instructed to Dhruva, 353, 354
for meditating on Viṣṇu, 354
purpose of, 354
sitting postures for, 215
Aṣṭa-sāttvika-vikāra defined, 566
Aṣṭa-vibhūtibhiḥ defined, 654
Aṣṭottara-śata defined, 114
Astrology & marriage, 642
Astronauts compared to demigod worshipers, 412

Asura(s)
envy of Lord in, 215
See also: Atheist(s); Demon(s)
Āśutoṣa defined, 190
Aśvamedha (horse) sacrifices
by Aṅga, **631**
by Indra, 822
by Pṛthu, **739, 811–22, 827, 828, 830, 833, 839, 841–43**
Aśvatthāmā, 246-47
Aśvini-kumāra, **238**
Atharvā, **35**
Atheism, 86
Atheist(s)
associating with, 154
deny *Vedas,* 80, 82-83
envy Lord, 111
government should chastise, 718
Lord
as death to, 766
& living entity as considered by, 421
not understood by, 419-20
material creation not understood by, 518
Śiva's followers as, **77**, 78, **80**
spiritual solution to food shortage rejected by, 788
See also: Demon(s); Materialist(s); Nondevotee(s); *Pāṣaṇḍī*
Atirātra, **624**
Atlantic Ocean, Dr. Frog couldn't calculate, 528
Ātmā
defined, 14, 445
See also: Soul(s)
Ātma-māyā defined, 116, 422
Ātma-tattva defined, 529
Atoms, Lord enters, 390
Atri Muni
addressed by deities, **27, 29**
asks about Lord, **24–26**
austerities of, **18, 20**
called for *jagad-īśvara,* 25
concentrated on Supersoul, 20
dazzled by deities, **23**
deities welcomed by, **22–26**
desire of, 19
desire of fulfilled, 28, **29**
Atri Muni (*continued*)
didn't know God, 19, 25, 28
fire from, **20**
Indra's trick seen by, **823, 824**
prays to deities, **24–26**
Pṛthu's son advised by, **824, 826, 829**
not pure devotee, 19
sons of, **14**
Attachment
for women, 378
See also: Bodily concept of life; Desire, material
Auspiciousness, knowledge as, 135
Austerities
of Atri Muni, **18, 20**
demigods fear, by others, 447
by devotee, 560
in devotional service, 384-85
by Dhruva, **384, 386–88**, 475, **573,** 574, **575**, 576, **596–97, 598**
elevation via, to serve Lord, 213
four listed, 793
human life for, 478
in Kṛṣṇa consciousness movement, 478
needed for success, 326
by renunciants, 555, 658
in Śiva, 212, **213**
Authorities, spiritual
demons disrespect, 678
See also: Brāhmaṇa(s); Devotee(s); Spiritual master(s)
Avatāra(s)
guṇa-, 748
Matsya, 716
śaktyāveśa-, 697-98, 813, 846
Varāha, 716
See also: Incarnations; Supreme Lord, advent(s) of
Avidyā defined, 424
Avyakta defined, 528

B

Bad & good as mental concoction, 448
See also: Bodily concept of life; Duality, material
Badarikāśrama, Dhruva retired to, **564, 565**

Badarī-nārāyaṇa, 352
Bāhuka (Niṣāda)
born from Vena's body, **689, 690,** 694
Naiṣāda race from, **691, 692**
Bakāsura demon, 800
Balarāma (Baladeva), 777
at Aniruddha's marriage, **181,** 182
Banyan tree in calf form, **804**
Banyan tree of Kailāsa, **209, 210**
Barhi, King, 172
Barhiṣadas (Pitās), **49**
Bathing
in *aṣṭāṅga-yoga,* 354
avabhṛtha-snāna, **87**
by demigod women, **203, 204–5**
as devotee's duty, 579
neglected by ignorant beings, 65
persons neglecting, 252
after sacrifice, **87**
sites for, in Vṛndāvana, 352-53
See also: Cleanliness; Purification
Battlefield
soldiers decorated on, 492
See also: War
Beads of Śiva, **215**
Beauty, pride in, **106**
Beer, demons drink, 795-96
See also: Alcohol
Bees compared to best men, 132
Behavior, etiquette &, **341**
Beings, living. *See:* Animal(s); Human being(s); Living entities
Benediction(s)
on *brāhmaṇa* by Sanātana, 240-41
by demigods, 330, 553, 849
Lord sanctions, 350
devotee's desire for, as honest, 344
devotional service excels material, 550, 552
in devotional service to Lord, **373**
Dhruva asks, from Nārada, **345, 347**
easy from Śiva, 240
Hare Kṛṣṇa *mantra* as, 240-41
for hearing causes of devastation, **313**
for hearing of Dakṣa's *yajña,* **308**
for hearing of Kardama's descendants, **38**
Benedictions (*continued*)
from Lord, 343, 350-51
as beyond expectation, 349
compared with demigods', 330
worship for, 330
Lord sanctions, 350
spiritual, from Śiva, 240
Bhadra (son of Yajña), **9**
Bhaga
arrested by Śiva's men, **179, 181**
Brahmā's request for, **231**
vision restored to, **237**
Bhagālin, deity of, 303
Bhagavad-gītā
See also: Bhagavad-gītā cited; *Bhagavad-gītā* quoted
accepted by *ācāryas,* 82
as *apauruṣeya,* 82
defects absent in, 82
duty to study, 717
envious commentators on, 111
God known via, 529
misinterpretation of, 111
preachers of, 590
preaching about, liberation via, 289
as principal book on Kṛṣṇa, 289
Bhagavad-gītā cited
See also: Bhagavad-gītā quoted
on anger, lust, & passion, 69
on *aṣṭāṅga-yoga,* 353
on Brahmaloka, 576
on Brahmā's day, 472
on continuing duty, 328
on demigods' falling back to earth, 447
on demigod worship, 87, 286
on demoniac nature, 439
on devotee as *mukta* (liberated soul), 441
on devotees, 281
on devotees & *yogīs,* 562
on eating, 385, 787
on energies of Lord, 279, 298
on equilibrium of liberated soul, 103
on following in great man's footsteps, 843
on fool misunderstanding Kṛṣṇa, 421, 531
on knowing Lord's appearance & activities, 574
on Kṛṣṇa as supreme truth, 677

Bhagavad-gītā cited (*continued*)
on learned person's vision, 513
on Lord
advent of, via internal potency, 715
directing nature, 519
as enjoyer, proprietor, & friend, 452-53
fulfilling desire, 638
guiding devotee, 401, 409, 426
mission of, 255
as within & without, 417
on men who approach God, 19
on *mūḍhas,* 269
on nondevotees, 785
on power as Lord's representation, 697
on preachers, 590, 846
on rain by sacrifice, 788
on religion, 664
on renounced order of life, 555
on sacrifice, charity, & penance, 658
on sacrifice for satisfying Lord, 785
on saintly kings in disciplic succession, 475-76
on social orders, 222, 614
on spiritual vision, 449
on submission to spiritual master, 630
on surrender after many births, 409
on surrendered soul surpassing nature's laws, 572
on topmost *yogī,* 565
on transcendental position, 145, 335
on *varṇāśrama-dharma,* 750
on Vāsudeva, 20
on *Vedas* & materialists, 72
on work for Viṣṇu, 7
Bhagavad-gītā quoted
See also: Bhagavad-gītā cited
on approaching Supreme as open to all, 692
on being Kṛṣṇa's devotee, 111
on Brahmaloka & down again, 506, 588
on dearness of knowledgeable, 279-90
on demigod worship, 87
on demigod worshipers, 412, 525
on devotional service & transcendence, 514, 618-19, 740
on devotional service, 114, 269
on enjoyer of sacrifice, 296
Bhagavad-gītā quoted (*continued*)
on equal view of all, 85, 301
on falling from heavenly planets, 412
on *karma,* 525
on knowing Lord, 269
on Kṛṣṇa
as enjoyer of sacrifices, 556, 668
as original seed, 818
as Supreme Brahman, 731
on Kṛṣṇa's transcendental nature, 531
on Lord
in all, 390
as all-pervading & aloof, 532, 617
as Brahman, 389
as death, 522, 533, 766
delivering devotee from material existence, 549
directing nature, 516, 768
as equal-minded, 131
as goal of *Vedas,* 293
guiding devotee, 529, 640
in heart, 557
killing demons & protecting devotees, 845-46
knowledge possessed by, 188, 421
known via devotional service, 417
as origin of all, 82
& sacrifices, 130
as source, 297, 298, 299
as source of demigods, 297-98
as source of everything, 747
within everything, 557
on *mahātmās,* 176
on material desire blocking devotional service, 428
on material life, 576-77
on modes of nature, 421, 516
on oblations to family members, 797
on offerings to Lord, 296
on overcoming illusory energy, 501-2
on overcoming nature, 229
on rain by sacrifice, 719-20
on rascals & Kṛṣṇa, 269
on real renunciant, 823
on results of worship, 28
on sacrifice for Lord, 86
on social orders, 652

Bhagavad-gītā quoted (*continued*)
on spiritual sky, 578, 588
on spiritual vision, 536, 617, 734
on spiritual world, 208
on Supersoul, 768
on supreme abode, 436, 577, 589
on surrender to Lord, 77, 111, 229, 548, 770, 814
on tasting spiritual life, 563, 619
on topmost *yogī*, 390
on Vāsudeva, 115
on *Vedas'* followers, 262-63
on *Vedas'* foolish followers, 595
on women & *śūdras*, 141
on work & worship, 554, 615, 668
on *yajña* (work for Lord), 233
Bhagavān. *See:* Kṛṣṇa; Supreme Lord
Bhagavata-kathā defined, 615
Bhāgavata Purāṇa. See: Śrīmad-Bhāgavatam
Bhāgavata-vidhi defined, 613
Bhaktas. See: Devotee(s)
Bhakta-vatsala, Lord as, 279-80
Bhakti
defined, 406, 510
preacher of, 846
See also: Devotional service; Kṛṣṇa consciousness; Love, for Lord
Bhakti-bhāva defined, 403
See also: Devotional service
Bhakti-rasāmṛta-sindhu cited
on *brāhmaṇa* meditator, 372
on Deity worship, 252
on desirelessness, 375
on spiritual life without *śruti* & *smṛti*, 781
Bhaktisiddhānta Sarasvatī, 1-2, 67-68
quoted
on attaining Vaikuṇṭha in this life, 598
on saving even one soul, 585
Bhaktivedanta Swami
lacked *tulasī* leaves, 368
obeisances by, 1-2
Bhaktivinoda Ṭhākura quoted
on living entity drowning in material nature, 526
on surrender to Lord, 770-71
Bhaktivinoda Ṭhākura quoted (*continued*)
on waking up to self-realization, 405
Bhakti-yoga. See: Devotional service
Bharata Mahārāja, 243
three lives of, 598
Bhāratī, **704**
Bhavāpyaya defined, 412
Bhīti (Fear), **312**
Bhrami, **621**
Bhṛgu Muni, **651**-52
arrested by Śiva's men, **179, 180**
asks forgiveness from Lord, **267**
Brahmā's request for, **231**
brings demigods to fight, **162**
curses followers of Śiva, **76-84**
descendants of, **36, 37**
discusses illusion of all, **266-67**
goat's beard for, **238**
invites Śiva, **241**
power of, in *mantra* chanting, **161**, 162
power of, vs. Śiva's, 168-69
prays to Viṣṇu, **266-67**
Bhūrloka, goddess of, 705
Bhūta(s), 844-45
defined, 84
See also: Ghost(s)
Bhuvaneśvara, worship in, 303
Bilvamaṅgala Ṭhākura cited on devotional service & liberation, 550
Bird(s)
carnivorous, 803
in Kailāsa, **195, 199, 207**
at Uttānapāda's palace, **474**
Birth
forced via nature, 371
via *karma,* 311
pride in status by, 106
spiritual, 604
See also: Transmigration of souls(s)
Birth-death cycle
bodily concept causes, **546**
Lord stops, 412, **445**
See also: Birth; Bondage, material; Death; Transmigration of soul(s)
Blasphemy
anger at, 130

Blasphemy (*continued*)
dealing with, process for, **140,** 141
death for, **140,** 141
devotee doesn't tolerate, 227
discussed by Satī, **140**
duty &, **143**
happiness impossible via, **189**
of *Vedas,* 80, 82-83, **84**
See also: Offenses
Blessing(s). *See:* Benediction(s)
Bliss, transcendental
on Brahman platform, 740
in hearing Lord's pastimes, **274–**75
via knowing Lord's pastimes, 424
personal, compared with impersonal, **411,** 412
by pleasing Lord, 514, 515
spiritual life as, 619
spiritual pain as, 103-4
Utkala in, **618**
See also: Ecstasy; Enjoyment; Happiness
Boar incarnation of Lord, **293,** 371, **775, 776**
Boat(s)
Earth compared to, **776**
planets compared to, 759
Bodily concept of life
animals in, **510**
in *brāhmaṇas* now, 75-76
conditioned soul in, 531
as contamination, 155, 156
in Dakṣa, 105
in Dakṣa & followers, 71
devotee free from, 416
everyone in, **266–67**
in followers of *Vedas,* 72
forgotten in Lord's service, 155-56
as illusion, 290, 564
Kṛṣṇa dispels, 546
Lord not understood in, **267**
offenses to great souls by, **134–**35
purification beyond, 155-56
relationships in, break, 127-28
in Satī, 96, **98–99**
Śiva removes, 135-36
transcending it, 155-56

Bodily concept of life (*continued*)
in *Vedas,* **72**
vision according to, 536
yogīs in, 416
See also: Duality, material; Ego, false; Illusion; "I-&-mine" conception; Materialism; *Māyā*
Body, material
attained by Satī, 156
change of. *See:* Death; Transmigration
compared to dress, 734
for conditioned soul, 531
consciousness apart from, 243
dead
decoration of, **276**
society compared to, **276**
demigods control, 447
devotee undisturbed by, 416, 769
during dream, 568
eating to maintain, 384-85
elements create, **515,** 516
fit in spiritual life, 152
forced on living beings, 371
given via *karma,* 371
human
as chance for liberation, 289, 290
illusory attraction in, **289,** 290
See also: Human being(s)
identifying with. *See:* Bodily concept of life
karma determines, 371, 536
obeisances to Lord in, 100-113
oblations award, to ghostly family members, 797-98
parts of, living entities compared to, 546
parts of, social orders compared to, 691
Satī ashamed of, **148, 149**
semen produces, 690
soul
in, 690, 734, 769
keeps fresh, 152
& Supersoul in, 511
survives, 516
spiritual energy enlivens, 407-8
subtle
during dream, 568

Body, material
subtle (*continued*)
of ghosts, 797
transmigration via, 567
See also: Ego, false; Intelligence
symptoms of, 769
as temple of Lord, 111, 112, 113
temporary, 289-90
tilaka purifies, 579
yoga for health of, 152
See also: Bodily concept of life; Senses
Body, spiritual
of Kṛṣṇa, 531
Vaikuṇṭha via, 586-87
Bondage, material
to bodily concept of life, **546**
Lord can deliver us from, **548,** 549
via work, 233
See also: Life, material; *Māyā;* Modes of nature; Suffering
Boys, training of, 344
Brahmā, Lord
addressed by Śiva, **236-38**
addressed Atri Muni, **27, 29**
addressed Śiva, **220-32**
advised marriage of Śiva & Satī, **65**
advised demigods, **189-92**
afraid of Śiva, 219
angered by Kumāras, 211-12
asked Dakṣa to stay, 68
Atri as noticed by, 20, 21
avoided Dakṣa's sacrifice, **188**
behavior of, as scandalous, 267
in bodily illusion, **266,** 267
born from Viṣṇu, 100, 297-98
cause of, Viṣṇu as, 297-98
celibate sons of, **309-**10
in charge of materialists, 65
compared to insect, 442
cosmic dissolutions during life of, 430
as created being, 81-82
created good & bad, 311
as creator, 521, 522, **762,** 773, 784-85, 817
as creator secondarily, 2
criticized by Dakṣa, 66
day of, 472
Brahmā (*continued*)
devastation at sleep of, 286
as Dhruva's great-grandfather, 440
Dhruva wanted to excel, 428, 442
dies also, 576, 588
directed by Vāsudeva (Supersoul), 20, 21
disciplic succession from, 746
discusses
bewildered materialists, 226, 228
blasphemy, **189**
injured parties, **231, 232**
Śiva, **190-92, 222, 223**
Śiva & sacrifice, **230-31, 232**
Śiva's status, **220, 221, 229**
empowered by Lord, 314
exalted by Lord's mercy, **325-26**
Hiraṇyakaśipu &, 445
as incarnation of Viṣṇu, 299
independent of Lord never, **300**
inferior to Śiva, 139, 220
instructed by Lord, 82
Kṛṣṇa as origin of, 748
kuśa grass symbol of, **22,** 23
Lord
enlightened, **408-9**
glorified by, **715,** 716
may play part of, 139, 314
Lord of, Viṣṇu as, 257
as lord of universe, 28
as Lord's instrument, **772,** 773
on lotus flower, **419**
Nārāyaṇa above, 831
neglected by Dakṣa, 91
as nondifferent from Lord, **297-**98, **300, 301-2**
offers Viṣṇu obeisances, 257
one with & different from Viṣṇu, 302-3
passion mode controlled by, 748
planet of. *See:* Brahmaloka
as plenary expansion of Lord, 314
prays to Viṣṇu, **268**
present for Pṛthu from, **704**
Pṛthu advised by, about Indra & horse sacrifices, **839-43, 845, 847**
at Pṛthu's horse sacrifices, **814**
Pṛthu's identity understood by, **700**

Brahmā (*continued*)
Pṛthu's priests advised by, **838, 839**
as qualitative incarnation of Viṣṇu, 299
quoted on Kṛṣṇa as cause of all causes, 519
respects Śiva, **138,** 139
Śiva born from, 212, 801
Śiva's obeisances to, **218**
smiling at Śiva, **219**
son(s) of
bad group of, **311, 312,** 313
celibate group of, **309–10**
Svāyambhuva Manu as, **314**
as *svayambhū,* 100
swan carrier of, **22,** 23
Vedas not authored by, 81-82
Viṣṇu Lord of, 257
Viṣṇu may be, 139
Brahma-bandhu(s)
Dakṣa as, 247
defined, 159, 247
less intelligent, 4-5
Vedas inaccessible to, 4-5
Brahmacārī(s), 309-10
duty of, 658
from five years old, 587
sacrifices for, 555
Satyaloka attainable by, 505
Brahmacarya system
benefit in, 309-10
as division of life, 339
See also: Brahmacārī(s)
Brahmajyoti. See: Brahman effulgence
Brahmaloka (Satyaloka)
elevation to, 505
temporary, 576, 588
travel to, calculated, 577
Brahma-maya defined, 402
Brahman (impersonal Absolute)
basis of, Lord as, 389-90
brāhmaṇas should know, 75
defined, 389
devotees realize, 265
devotional service on level of, 114
energies of, **423,** 424
everything as, 298
as expanding unlimitedly, 389
Brahman (*continued*)
gradations of, among beings, 15-16
humans should know, 75
impersonalists rise to & fall from, 441
knowledge about
as incomplete, 135-36
Śiva gives, 135-36
Lord as source of, **423,** 607
material world caused by, **423**
meditation on
compared with meditation on Lord, 356
as difficult, 356
via mental speculation, 649
taught by *Vedas,* 80
See also: Brahman effulgence
Brahman, Supreme. *See:* Supreme Brahman
Brāhmaṇa(s)
abandon duty now, 75-76
absent nowadays, 163
afraid of Dakṣa, 126-27
alone hear *Vedas,* 63
Americans trained as, 344
animals sacrificed by, 125
argue scripture, 125
bad food eaten by, 75-76
birth doesn't qualify, 4-5, 75, 76
blasphemy heard by, **140,** 141
blasphemy toward, 80
blessed by Sanātana, 240-41
bodily concept of, 75-76
born from Lord's mouth, 248
brahma-bandhus &, 4-5, 159, 247
Brahman known by, 75
Caitanya's principle on, 76
caste *brāhmaṇas,* 365
chanting of *mantras* by, 125, 161, 365
charity & preaching for, 248
citizens should respect, 629
cobblers can become, 591
contrasted to *kṣatriyas,* 344
creation of, in present age, 163, 344-45
criticize
brahminical candidates, 75, 76, 365
chanting of *praṇava,* 365
Śiva's followers, 294
cursed by Nandīśvara, **75**

Brāhmaṇa(s) (continued)
curses by, 76-77, 628
at Dakṣa's sacrifice, **124**-25, 128-29
describe Viṣṇu as sacrifice, **291**
as devotees, 687
duty of, 752
as *dvija* (twice-born), 132
elevation to status of, 75, 76
falsity of, 75-76
family spirit kept by, 334
follow *varṇa* & *āśrama* system, **222**
forbearing, 159
function of, in Lord's body, 248
as "head" of society, 345
not heavily punished, 246-47
if ignorant of Śiva, 70
ignored Sati, 126-27
impersonalist, worship fire-gods, **48**
in Kali-yuga, 661, 817, 836, 844
know Brahman, 75
Kṛṣṇa consciousness spread by, 559
Kṛṣṇa consciousness movement creates, 604
kṣatriya kings guided by, 628, 666, 750
mantra-chanting by, 125, 161-63 365
meditation by one, 372
modern, 75-76, 344, 365, 631, 632
needed in society, 344-45
not neglected by Śiva or Viṣṇu, **246**, 247
Parikṣit tolerated, 228
part of Lord's cosmic form, 222, 248
permanent class of, 83
power of, in *mantra*-chanting, 161-63
power of, vs. Śiva's, 168-69
pray to Viṣṇu, **291**, **293-94**
priests pray to Viṣṇu, **262**
protected by Viṣṇu, 294
Pṛthu praised by, 698
Pṛthu satisfied, **850**
qualification vs. birthright for, 4-5, 75, 76
Ruci as, **4**, 5
rules & regulations for, 793
sacrifice by, of animals, 125
Śiva protector of, **248**
social status of, 687, 691
spirit in, not in *kṣatriyas*, 344
training required for, 598

Brāhmaṇa(s) (continued)
two types of, 687
unqualified, 4-5
Vedic, compared with modern, 631, 632
Vena stopped sacrifices by, **655**
worship in meditation by, 372
See also: Sage(s); Saintly person(s); *specific brāhmaṇas*
Brahmānanda (*brahma-nirvāṇa*) defined, 137, 217, **411**, 412, 423
Brahman effulgence. *See:* Brahman (impersonal Absolute)
Brahman platform, 740
Brahma-saṁhitā cited
See also: Brahma-saṁhitā quoted
on Brahman effulgence, 423
on desire trees, 206
on Govinda, 422
on Satī's power, 166
on seeing Lord, 253, 278
on Śiva, 139
on Śiva & Viṣṇu, 220
on unity in diversity, 302
Brahma-saṁhitā quoted
See also: Brahma-saṁhitā cited
on Kṛṣṇa & *surabhi* cows, 816
on Kṛṣṇa as cause of all causes, 519
on Lord as seen by love, 399, 558
on Lord dispelling devotee's *karma*, 525
on Lord in atoms, 390
on Lord's expansions, 777
on Lord's form, 547
on Lord's incarnation, 371
on Mahā-Viṣṇu, 419
on sun's orbit, 735
Brahma-śāpa mantra, 628
Brahma-tejas
in chanting *mantras*, 163
vs. *śiva-tejas*, 168-69
Brahma-vādī defined, 731
Brahmāvarta, **811**
Brahmi, **479**
Brahmins. *See: Brāhmaṇa(s)*
Brain, intelligence not in, 238-39
Breathing
exercise for *yoga* (*prāṇāyāma*)
of Atri Muni, **20**

Breathing
exercise for *yoga* (*prāṇāyāma*) (*contd.*)
for controlling mind, **354–55**
by Dhruva, **387, 388, 392–93,** 394
of spiritual compared with material beings, 394
stopped by Dhruva, **392–94**
Bṛhaspati, **31, 793,** 794
Bṛhaspati-sava sacrifice, **91, 92**
British Museum, Red Fort's jewels in, 472
Buddha, Lord, 78, 80
animal slaughter stopped by, 844
as *śaktyāveśa-avatāra*, 846
Buddhi (daughter of Dakṣa), **40**
Buddhists, 80
Buddhi-yoga defined, 145
Bull carrier of Śiva, **22,** 23, **803**
Bulls circling compared to planets orbiting, **430, 593**

C

Caitanya, Lord, 567, 567, 661, 661
angry at offenders, 130
asked Indians to preach, 366
author's obeisances to, 2
brāhmaṇa status ignored by, 76
cited. *See:* Caitanya cited
condemned impersonalists, 371
devotees in footsteps of, 217, 264
famous-man inquiry of, 463
gift of, in this age, 163
Hare Kṛṣṇa *mantra* given by, 502
invited by Advaita, 217
made easy devotional life, 385
need for following, 385
philosophy of, 521, 768
pure devotional service taught by, 426
quoted. *See:* Caitanya quoted
Raghunātha dāsa advised by, 562
recommended chanting, 125
sacrifice (*yajña*) for, 125, 284
saṅkīrtana satisfies, 788, 817, 844
saṅkīrtana started by, 831
as Viṣṇu, 284
as worshiped in this age, 125, 284
Caitanya-caritāmṛta cited
on curses & benedictions, 77
on Lord & pure devotees, 596
Caitanya-caritāmṛta quoted
on *guru* & Kṛṣṇa, 333
on Kṛṣṇa as master, 288
on Lord empowering us to glorify Him, 846
Caitanya cited
See also: Caitanya quoted
on Buddhists, 80
on cleansing mind, 115, 116
on humility, 459
on living entity as Lord's servant, 441
on love for Kṛṣṇa, 597
on offending devotee, 69
on preaching Kṛṣṇa's message, 717
Caitanya quoted
See also: Caitanya cited
on becoming a spiritual master, 784
on desiring devotional service, 439-40
on hearing of Kṛṣṇa, 290
on *sannyāsī*, 824
on tolerance, 227
on transcendence, 619
Caitya-guru, Lord as, 355
Cākṣuṣa Manu, **624**
Calcutta, Kālī butcher shops in, 844
Calf
Aryamā in form of, **797**
banyan tree in form of, **804**
Bṛhaspati in form of, **793**
in cow-Earth analogy, 790
devotee compared to, **425,** 426
Garuḍa in form of, **803**
Himalayas in form of, **804**
Indra in form of, **794**
Kapila in form of, **798**
lion in form of, **803**
Maya demon in form of, **800**
Prahlāda in form of, **795**
Śiva (Rudra) in form of, **801**
Śiva's bull in form of, **803**
Svāyambhuva Manu in form of, **792**
Takṣaka in form of, **802**
Viśvāvasu in form of, **796**
See also: Cow(s)

Cānakya Paṇḍita
cited
on enemies in family, 627
on envy, 106
on learned person, 731
on married life, 8
on short life & lasting reputation, 608
quoted on son & marriage, 636
Caṇḍalas, 366
Caṇḍeśa, **179**
Candle power compared to consciousness, 15-16
Cāraṇas, **543**
Carvya defined, 819
Caste division(s)
boys trained by, 344
as eternal, 83
maintenance of, 334
in modern society, 344-45
spirit in, four kinds of, 344
See also: Varṇāśrama systems; Vedic culture
"Caste system." *See: Varṇāśrama-dharma*
Cat's kitten compared to Lord's devotee, 582
Caturmāsya months, 284
Cāturmāsya vow, 72
Catur-vargas defined, 551-52
Cause, ultimate
Lord as, 423, **518,** 519, **520,** 524, **530**
time as, **545**
Cause & effect, Lord as, 298
Celibacy, 309-10
See also: Brahmacarya system
Celibates. *See: Brahmacārī(s); Sannyāsī(s)*
Ceremonies. *See:* Ritualistic ceremonies; Sacrifices
Chaitanya. *See:* Caitanya, Lord
Chanting
accompanies Deity worship, **364-**65, 369
of Ajāmila, 224
ancient & modern, 125
animals rejuvenated by, 125, 184, 272
by Bhṛgu, **161,** 162
brāhmaṇas' power in, 161-**63**
before Caitanya's form, 284
Chanting (*continued*)
by caste *brāhmaṇas*, 365
Hare Kṛṣṇa, 227
as best benediction, 240-41
brāhmaṇa gets, from Sanātana, 240-41
before Caitanya's form, 284
as Caitanya's gift, 163
Caitanya worshiped by, 125
compared with other sacrifices, 291-92
controls mind, 355
death surpassed via, **499**
in devotional service, 619
equals all sacrifices, 291-92
in Kṛṣṇa consciousness movement, 385
liberation via, 289
Lord manifest in, 364
meaning of, 291
as meditation on Lord, 355, 363-64, 371
perfection via, 163, 290, 570-71
proper way of, 364
recommended for present age, 88, 125, 161, 162, 163, 233-34, 284, 291-92, 294, 371
tolerance in, 227
as transcendental vibration, 125
without changing life-style, 290
See also: Hare Kṛṣṇa *mantra*
in Kṛṣṇa consciousness movement, 385
of Kṛṣṇa's name overcomes obstacles, 294
about Lord
Kṛṣṇa consciousness movement for, 290
liberation via, **289,** 289-90
name of, 252, 294
overcomes obstacles, 294
perfection via, 289-90, 389
purification via, 115-16, 156, **251-52,** 252
recommended now, 233-34, 284, 291-92
in spiritual world, 208
tolerance in, 227
tongue's use in, 259
without changing life-style, 290
as *yajña* (sacrifice), 284, 291-92
See also: Chanting, of Hare Kṛṣṇa; Chanting, in *saṅkīrtana;* Hare Kṛṣṇa *mantra*
of Lord's name by Ajāmila, 224

Chanting (*continued*)
- of *mantras*
  - airplanes run by, 205
  - animals used to test, 125, 184, 272
  - Bhṛgu's use of, **161,** 162
  - for *brāhmaṇas* only, 365
  - *brāhmaṇas'* power in, 161-63
  - at Dakṣa's sacrifice, **124–**25
  - in Deity worship, 369
  - devotees eligible for, 365
  - disciplic succession needed for, 363, 365
  - given by spiritual master, 363, 365
  - impossible now, 161, 162-63
  - meant to please Viṣṇu, 284
  - for offering oblations, 128-29
  - *praṇava* (*oṁ*), **364–**65
  - for protecting sacrifices, 161
  - qualifications for, 363, 365
  - rules for, 365
  - for sacrifices, 284
  - for seeing flying beings, **363**
  - to Śiva, 128-29
  - *svāhā,* 128-29
  - tested on animals, 125, 184, 272
  - worked wonders, 161, 162
  - worship of Lord by, 372
- for offering oblations, 128-29
- of *oṁ namo bhagavate vāsudevāya,* **364–**65, 372
- for present age, 88, 125, 161, 162, 163, 233-34, 284, 291-92, 294, 371
- purification via, 252
- recommended now, 88, 125, 161, 162, 233-284, 291-92, 371
- in *saṅkīrtana*
  - before Caitanya's form, 284
  - as recommended now, 88, 125, 233-34, 281, 291-92
  - as *yajña* (sacrifice), 161, 284, 291-92
- in spiritual world, 208
- of *svāhā,* 128-29
- tested via animal sacrifice, 125, 184, 272
- tolerance in, 227
- of Vedic *mantras,* 632, 639

Charity
- *gṛhasthas* give, 658

Charity (*continued*)
- *kṣatriyas* & *vaiśyas* give, 554, 555
- at sacrifices, 434

Chastity, Satī example of, 55

Cheating tendency, 823, 824

Chemical(s)
- fertile, from hills, 819, 820
- life not from, 518
- *See also:* Elements, material

Child (Children)
- behavior of, 335
- devotee compared to, 591
- in happy family, 622
- Kṛṣṇa conscious training for, 573
- maintenance of, 517
- maternal relatives influence, 642
- training of, 344

Cities
- ancient, 809
- of Uttānapāda received Dhruva, **466–69**
- of Yakṣas attacked by Dhruva, **482, 483, 493,** 507
- *See also: names of specific cities*

Citizen(s)
- duty of, 667-70
- good government helps, 742, 752
- happiness of, 663, 669, 670
- king protects, 665-67, 735-36
- king to be respected by, **629**
- pleaded with Pṛthu, **749–52**
- in Pṛthu's kingdom, **807, 808**
- saintly king satisfies, 476, 477, 558-59
- *See also:* Population

Citraketu (son of Vasiṣṭha), **34, 35**

Citti (wife of Atharvā), **35**

City-example of realizing Absolute Truth, 424

Civilization
- based on *Vedas,* 80, 83
- modern
  - ancient civilization compared with, 472
  - animal slaughter in, 508
  - godless & unhappy, 671
- *See also:* Society; Vedic culture

Cleanliness
- in Deity worship, 633
- in worship, 252
- *See also:* Bathing; Purification

Cobbler can become *brāhmaṇa*, 591
Coconut drying & devotee serving, analogy of, 567
Colors of social orders, 691
Communism, spiritual, 787
Comparisons. *See:* Analogies
Compassion
for inferiors, **341**
in Lord's devotees, 226, 228, 301
of Nārada for Dhruva, **348**
Competition
among *karmīs*, 842
material vs. spiritual, 812-13
Concentration of mind. *See:* Meditation
Conchshell-touch of Lord inspired Dhruva, **401-3**, 418
Conditioned soul(s)
body obtained by, 531
can't imitate transcendentalists, 143
cheating by, 823
compared with
Lord, 371
spiritual beings, 394
defects in, 783
degraded by tongue, 259
delivered by devotees, 229
devotee's compassion for, 301
as diseased parts of Lord, 301
as embodied, 734
forced by nature, 371
independence misunderstood by, 451
Indra as, 821, 823
jīvas, 15
Lord gives free will to, 638
nature exploited by, 442
part of Lord but diseased, 301
protection for, by surrender to Lord, 267
as *puruṣa*, 390
Śiva concerned with, 217
suffer in material modes, 15
training for, 785
See also: Animal(s); Human being(s); Living entities; *Nitya-baddha*
Consciousness
apart from brain, 238-39
compared to candle power, 15-16
compared to light, 15-16
Consciousness (*continued*)
of devotee in rebirth, 243
gradations in living beings, 15-16
independent of body, 238-39, 243
individual & unchanging, 238-39, 243
in Lord & living beings, 15-16
material, giving up, 355
"percentages" of, in beings, 15-16
pure
as *kaivalya*, 115
Kṛṣṇa consciousness as, **113**-14
Lord revealed to, **113**, 114, 115
See also: Knowledge; Soul(s)
Copper charged by electricity, analogy of, 114
Cosmic form of God. *See:* Universal form
Cosmic manifestation. *See:* Creation (act of); Creation, material; Material nature; Material world; Universe(s)
Cow(s)
Earth in shape of, **744-45**, **754-57**, **759-61**, **765**, 767, 790, **792**
eaten in emergency only, 763
fresh grasses for, **803**
killing of. *See:* Animal slaughter
Lord compared to, **425**, 426
milk from, 761, 790, **792**
protection of, 750
in sacrifice, 631
surabhi, 816-17
Creation (act of)
by Brahmā, **762**
by five elements, **515**, 516, 517
karma continues in, 311
by Lord's energy, **518**, 519, **520**, 521, **774**, **775**
of material & spiritual worlds, 532
in two stages, 2
Creation, material
Lord one with & different from, 768
Lord's existence precedes, 25
in two stages, 2
See also: Creation (act of); Material world; Material nature; Universe(s)
Criminal department & ignorance mode, analogy of, 221
Criticism. *See:* Blasphemy; Insults

Cruelty condemned, 764
Crying
two types of, 458
woman &, 121
Culture. *See:* Civilization, modern; Society, human; *Varṇāśrama-dharma;* Vedic culture
Cunning (grandson of Brahmā), **312**
Curses
by Bhṛgu on Śiva's followers, **76–84**
by *brāhmaṇas,* 76-77, 628
on *brāhmaṇas* by Nandīśvara, **75–76**
countercursing at sacrifice, 70
on Dakṣa by Nandīśvara, 73
by Dakṣa on Śiva, **67**
on Dakṣa's followers, **71**
on followers of Śiva, **76–84**
on intoxication, 78
to lose knowledge, **71**
by Nandīśvara
effects of, **73–76**
on materialists & *brāhmaṇas,* **70–75**
on Parīkṣit by *brāhmaṇa* boy, 228
by sages, **626**
transcending them, 76-77
Cūṣya defined, 819
Cycle, *yuga. See: Yuga(s),* four
Cycle of birth & death. *See:* Birth & death, repeated; Transmigration of soul(s)

D

Dahrāgni, **32**
Dakṣa
accused by Satī, **131–49**
addressed by Viṣṇu, **297**
anger bewildered, 66, 68-69
angered by Śiva's neglect, 59, 110-11
argument defending, 141
as asked to stay for sacrifice, 68-69
attacked by Vīrabhadra, **179, 181, 182, 183, 184**
blessed by demigods, **305**
bodily concept in, 71, 105, 134
bodily luster of, **57, 58**
as *brāhmaṇa* unqualified, 159, 247
Dakṣa (*continued*)
Brahmā's request for, **231**
as chief Prajāpati, **90**
compared with Śiva's power, 174
consciousness unchanged in, 238-39, **243**
considered obeisances to body, 111
considered Śiva poor, 146
couldn't understand Śiva, **146,** 147
criticized Brahmā, 66
criticized/praised Śiva, 61
criticized Śiva, **60–65**
cursed by Nandīśvara, **73**
curses Śiva, **67**
danger to, due to offenses, **173,** 174
daughter(s) of, **39, 40**
descendants of, **40, 46–50**
See also: Satī
dead though living, 158
death of, **184–85**
Dakṣa revived from, **243**
as merciful act, 247, 248-49, 250
need for, 189, 248-49
defense of position of, 141
didn't invite Śiva, 89-90, 91, 92
discussed by Śiva, **105–13, 117–18**
dissatisfied with Satī, 50-51
dowry of, for Satī, 50-51
as *durātmā,* 176
duty of, to all, 158
embodied envy & offense, 149
envy of Śiva in
basis of, **110–11**
as basis of anger, 110-11
Dakṣa tried to hide, 60
in him alone, **131,** 133
as long-standing, 60, 111
as offense to great soul, **134, 135**
polluted his good qualities, 106
questioned by Vidura, **53, 54, 55**
as fault finder, **131–33**
followers of
curse on, 71
feared him, 126-27
as ignorant, 71
polluted sacrifice, **251–52**
goat's head for
consciousness unchanged in, 138-39, **143**

Dakṣa
goat's head for (*continued*)
didn't hamper him, 238-39
joined to him, **242**
greatness of, 55, 141
as hardhearted, 158, **159,** 173, 176
hell awaited, 250
ill fame of, **159**
knew Śiva's pure character, 60
as *mahātmā,* 176
as materialistic, 71, 105, 134, 146
name of, defined, 159
narration about
hearing of, **308**
Uddhava spoke, **307**
neglected Satī, **159,** 173
neglected Śiva in sacrifice, 89-90, 91, 92, **128-**29
as offender of great soul, **134, 135, 148**
as Prajāpati, 141, 158
prays to Śiva, **246, 248, 249-50**
prays to Viṣṇu, **260, 261**
pride in, **90,** 91, 106
punishment for, purpose in, 189, 247, 248-49, 250
purified seeing Śiva, **244**
regrets Śiva's marrying Satī, **63, 65**
revived by Śiva, **243**
as ritual performer, **146**
sacrifice of
animals dead at, **271-72**
attacked by Śiva's men, **177-80**
avoided by Brahmā & Viṣṇu, **188**
begun again, **251-53, 295**
brāhmaṇas at, 125, 126-27
chanting of *mantras* at, 125
conclusion of, **304-5**
darkness threatens, **171, 172**
demigods defend, **161-63**
demigods travel to, 92, **94-95**
fighting spirit at, 182
hearing about, **308**
members of, approach Brahmā, **188**
narration about, Uddhava spoke, **307**
neglected demigods, 91
neglected Śiva, 89-90, 91, 92, **128-**29, 233

Dakṣa
sacrifice of (*continued*)
polluted by Śiva's men, **251-52**
prayers to Viṣṇu at, **260-94**
purification for, **251-52**
remnants of, denied Śiva, 233
as useless, 130
Viṣṇu appeared at, **253-55**
Viṣṇu takes share of, **296**
Satī accuses, **131-49**
Satī tried to convince, 139-40
not self-realized, 111
sexually able, 159
Śiva's respect to, 112-13
Śiva warns about, **105, 107, 117-18**
wife of
asked favor of Lord, 277
as aunt of Viṣṇu, 276-77
knew danger to him, **173,** 174
knew Śiva's power, **174**
prays to Viṣṇu, **276**
worships Śiva, **302-3, 304**
Dākṣāyaṇī. *See:* Sati
Dakṣiṇā
as goddess of fortune, **6**
Manu glad because of, **6**
married Yajña, 6, **8**
Ḍamaru drum of Śiva, 23
Dambha (Bluffing), **311, 312**
Damsels of heaven, **203**
Dance of Śiva, **174**
Daṇḍavat defined, 22
Dangers of material life, **263-64**
Dantavakra, **181,** 182
Darkness, *māyā* compared to, 502
See also: Ignorance
Darpa (son of Dharma), **40**
Darwin's theory of evolution, 519
Dattātreya, **816**
born to Atri, **30**
as incarnation of God, **14, 30**
Daughter receives father's qualities, 642
Dayā (daughter of Dakṣa), **40**
Death
chanting Lord's name as protection from, **499**
of devotee & nondevotee contrasted, 582

Death (*continued*)
Dhruva surpassed, **581–**82
for envious men, **226**
everyone subject to, 577
good for offenders, 189
insults compared to, **118**
Lord as, 522, 533, 766
politicians don't quit till, 478
remembering Lord at, 433
suicide for hearing blasphemy, **140,** 141
suicide of Satī, **150, 151–53, 155**
Sunīthā's father as personification of, 642
yogīs control, 150-51
See also: Birth-death cycle; Transmigration of soul(s)
Death (descendant of Brahmā), **31**
Decoration(s)
on soldiers, 492
of *tilaka,* 579
in Uttānapāda's palace, **470, 471, 473, 474**
at Uttānapāda's reception for Dhruva, **466–68**
Deer
Bharata as, 598
in Kailāsa, **199, 200**
Defects, four, 783
Deficiencies in living beings, 82
Dehinam defined, 732
Deity form of Supreme Lord
as actually Lord, 365
bathing ceremony for, 463
compared to hot iron rod, 365
devotees worship, 565
of earth & water, **369**
meditation on
by *brāhmaṇas,* 372
as necessary, 369
worship by, 372
offerings to, 633
as *Vedas,* 293
Deity worship
according to time & place, **364–**66, 369
authority followed in, 368
by *brāhmaṇa* who meditated, 372
chanting accompanies, **364–**65, 369
cleanliness in, 252
Deity worship (*continued*)
criticized by some, 366
equals study of *Vedas,* 293
flowers offered in, 364, **367,** 368
food offered in, **364,** 365, **367,** 368, 369
Ganges or Yamunā water in, 368
in Kṛṣṇa consciousness movement, 365-66
mantra-chanting accompanies, **364,** 365
by meditation, 372
as necessary, 369
offenses in, 252
paraphernalia for, 372
as *samādhi* (trance), 362
tulasī leaves for, **367–**68
as *Vedas,* **293**
water for, 368
Delhi, Red Fort in, 472
Demigod(s)
advised by Brahmā, **189–92**
advised by Lord about Dhruva, **396**
afraid of Dakṣa, 126-27
airplanes of, **94, 100, 205–**6
all present in sacrifices, 89-90, 234
Aṅga's sacrifice refused by, 631-33
appeal to Lord about Dhruva, **394**
appearing "greater" than God, 139
approach Brahmā, **188**
approach Śiva, **210–16**
attend Dakṣa's sacrifice, **92, 94–96**
benedictions from, 330, 553
bless Dakṣa, 305
body controlled by, 447
Brahmā's request for, **232**
can't check Kṛṣṇa's will, 294
can't harm Lord's devotee, 294
as "childish," **236**
compared to government servants, 87-88
compared to Lord's limbs, 548-49
at cosmic-crisis time, 440
couldn't satisfy Dhruva, 349
descendants from, six kinds of, 9-10
devotees please, 607-8
devotees uninterested in benediction of, 849
Dhruva accused, of polluting his intelligence, **446–47**

Demigod(s) (*continued*)
Dhruva honored by, 468, **583, 586**
discussed by Śiva, **236-38**
envy in, 813
fame of, "ruined" by Śiva, **60-61**
fire-gods, **46-48**
forgiven by Śiva, **236**
as gods under Kṛṣṇa, 287-88
ignored Satī, 126-27
included in Viṣṇu, 91
invite Śiva to sacrifice, **241**
of Kailāsa, **193-94**
leader of, Yajña as, **9,** 10
life spans of, 473
Lord above, 445, **533,** 534, 637
Lord &. *See:* Supreme Lord, demigods &...
Lord of, Viṣṇu as, 257
as Lord's assistants, 719
as Lord's servants, **285,** 286, 287-88
manifested by external energy, 281
as materialistic, 67-68
in material modes, 281
must all be satisfied, 89-90, 234
neglected by Dakṣa, 91
oblations to
fire-gods accept, **46**-47
in sacrifices, 128
offer Śiva obeisances, **216, 218**
offer Viṣṇu obeisances, **257**
pleased with Lord's devotees, 296
pleasing them, as necessary, 89-90, 234
positions of, impermanent, 447
prasāda of Viṣṇu for, 303-4
pray to Nara-Nārāyaṇa Ṛṣi, **43, 44**
pray to Viṣṇu, **285**
presents for Pṛthu from, 704, **705-6**
as progenitors. *See:* Prajāpatis
Pṛthu glorified by, **698, 699**
Pṛthu pleased, **849**
pure devotee's consideration of, 442
Ṛbhu, **162**
react to Satī's death, **157,** 158
respected by Lord's devotees, 296
respect for, 87-88
restored by Śiva, **237-38**
at sacrifices, 631, 633

Demigod(s) (*continued*)
sacrifices need presence of, 89-90, 234
sacrifices satisfy, 234, **673,** 849
sacrificial oblations to, 128
sacrificial remnants to, 233
satisfied via worship to Lord, 88
seen by Satī, **94**
as servants of Lord, **285,** 286, 288
Śiva "ruined" fame of, **60-61**
Śiva's abode viewed by, **193-209**
soma drunk by, 795, 796
source of, Lord as, 297-98
subdemigods (*upadevas*), 94
subordinate to Kṛṣṇa, 287-88
suffocated by Dhruva, **393-94**
Tuṣitas, **9**-10
Vena's opinion of, **676**
Viṣṇu Lord of, 257
wives of
bathe in Kailāsa, 203, **204-5**
decorations of, **92, 94**
go to sacrifice, **92, 94**
sex by, **203**
worshipers of, 412, 525, 556, 607
worship goddess of fortune, **329,** 330
worship Lord, **670,** 716
worship to. *See:* Worship, to demigod(s)
See also: specific demigods
Democracy
administrators in, 652
corruption in, 555
foolish decision-makers in, 782-83
Kṛṣṇa conscious, 477, 718
monarchy compared with, 626
Demon(s)
authorities disrespected by, 678
Brahmaloka attainable by, 505
created by Brahmā, 311
created by Śiva, **167-68, 169**
devotee compared with, 710
as division of men, 255
envy of Lord in, 111
false God accepted by, 710
in Kali-yuga, 676
Kṛṣṇa fought, 800
liquor drunk by, 795, 796
Lord kills, 533, 534, 845-46

Demon(s) (*continued*)
Lord's killing of, 225, 255
as material world majority, 255
mystic powers of, 800
at Pṛthu's horse sacrifices, **815**
saintly persons kill, 679
Śiva spiritual master of, 54
Śiva tries to deliver, 217
See also: Atheist(s); Impersonalist(s); Materialist(s); Nondevotee(s); *specific demons*
Desire(s)
as life's symptom, 453, 527
material
absent in devotional service, 374-75
absent in liberation, 374-75, 377
as demoniac, 439
devotee free of, 638
in devotees, Lord fulfills, 343, 350-51, 373
devotee should reject, 426, 428, 446, 453
in Dhruva, 343
Lord fulfills, **637-**38
lust as, 69, 208
vs. spiritual, 342
pure devotee free of, 439-40
purified via worshiping Lord, 330
results according to, 28
Śiva satisfies, **136-37**
species according to, 519, 527
worship for fulfilling, 286
worship to Lord with, 343, 350-51, **373**
See also: Sense gratification; Sex life
Desire tree(s), **206**
Lord compared to, **410**
Destinations via Lord's will, **223-**24
Destiny
enjoyment or suffering via, **335, 336**
See also: Karma
Detachment
developed via *Vedas,* 144
via devotional service, 619
from family life, 647, 648
inspired by Dhruva, 316
in liberated souls, 103
Lord arranges, for devotee, 642
of Lord in His activities, **273**
Detachment (*continued*)
opulence in, **146**
See also: Retirement; *Sannyāsīs; Vānaprasthas*
Determination
in devotional service, 382, 385
results according to, 28
to satisfy Lord, 382
Devahūti, **1, 11,** 582, 799
Devakulyā (son of Pūrṇimā), **13**
Devala, 663
Devas. See: Demigod(s)
Devastation, causes of, 313
Deva-yajña, 88
Devotee(s) of Supreme Lord
accept difficulty as mercy, 224, 250, 336-37
accept gain from Lord, 346
not affected by material modes, 265
all as pleasing to, 395
alone know Lord, 282-83
amaze world, 390, 391-92
anger used by, 482, 539
animals contrasted to, 510
as *apārakya-buddhi,* 301
associating with, 153-54, **413,** 414-15, **416,** 420, **590,** 591, 603-4
austerity by, 560
bathing as duty of, 579
to become one, as not easy, 385
to become one, Caitanya enables, 385
to become one, possible for everyone, 366-67
as best friends to all, 264
bewildered by *māyā* never, 229
beyond
brāhmaṇa status, 76
enjoying or renouncing, 145
material qualities, 265, 281
pious or impious acts, 275
sacrifices, 275
Vedas, 145
blaspheming them, 130
in bliss, 514, 515
body doesn't disturb, 416, 769
as *brāhmaṇas,* 163
brāhmaṇas as, 687

Devotee(s) of Lord (*continued*)
as Brahman-realized, 265
Caitanya's advice to, 459
in Caitanya's footsteps, 264
as candidates for spiritual world, 224
can influence world, 393
can't imitate Dhruva, 385
chant Hare Kṛṣṇa, 571, 591, 612
chant *praṇava* (*oṁ*) *mantras,* 365
compared to
calf, **425,** 426
child, 591
coconut drying, 567
kitten in cat's mouth, 582
compared with
impersonalists, 269
jñānīs, 279-80
as compassionate, 764
compassion in, 226, 228, 230, 301
for inferiors, **341**
consider incarnations special, 371
create pilgrimage sites, 203-4
curse no one, 77
dear to all, 488-89
dear to Lord, 279-80
death of, 582
Deity worship by, 362, 565
Deity worship necessary for, 369
deliver envious men, 226
deliver fallen souls, 226, 229
demigods' benedictions disinterest, 849
demigods pleased with, 296, 607-8
demigods respected by, 87-88, 296
demon contrasted to, 710
depend on Lord, 267
depends on Lord's mercy, 591
desire honest gain, 346
desires in, as spiritual, 343
desires in, Lord fulfills, 343, 350-51, **373**
determination for, 382, 385
in devotional service, 406, 408, 409, 453, 560-61
distressed to see distress, 226
as division of men, 255
don't order Lord, 116
duty of, 680
eating by, 369-70, 384-85

Devotee(s) of Lord (*continued*)
envious never, 396
equal toward everyone, 591
equal vision in, 85, 225, 301
everyone can become, 366-67
false, 846
forgive offenders, 226, 227, 228
friendship for equals among, **341**
Gauḍīya Vaiṣṇavas, Vṛndāvana for, 332
go back to Godhead, 590
government should be instructed by, 731
greatness of, 463, 550, 608
hearing about, 599-602, 612
hears about Lord, 414, 612
as highest in ecstasy, **374**
immortality achieved by, 533-34
impersonalists contrasted to, 597
impersonalist's question to, 414
included in Lord, 91-92
indifferent to honor & dishonor, 459
inferior, compared with superior, 764
initiation of, as open to all, 366-67
inspired by Dhruva, 316
jñānīs contrasted to, 412, 453, 515, 576, 590, 591, 601, 657
karmīs contrasted to, 412, 453, 515, 576, 589-91, 601, 638, 640, 657
killing by, 505
kill no one, 226
as kind, 607
king served, 731
knowledge may lack in, 279-80
know Lord by service, 269
know Lord's qualities, 282-83
in Kṛṣṇa consciousness, 553
as liberated, 351, 441, 566-67, 768-69
liberation as viewed by, 441, 552
Lord
absolves sins of, 814
arranging detachment of, 642
compared to, 769
"conquered" by, 596, 597
dispels *karma* of, 525
favors, 440, 445
fulfills desires of, 584, 640
giving bad wife to, 642
glorified by, 401

Devotee(s) of Lord
Lord (*continued*)
guides, 401, 409, 426, 640
known by, 419, 420, 424, 529, 586, 710
loved by, 400, 766
never forgotten by, 409
protects, 255, 286, 294, 381, **425,** 426, 465, **498–**99, **557,** 845-46
relieves distress of, 813-14
reveals knowledge to, 448
sanctifies, 203, 204
satisfied by, 514, 515, 638
saves, 549
seen by, 399, 557-58, 821
Lord's benedictions declined by, 553
Lord's kindness to, 328
at Lord's lotus feet, 203, 204, **452,** 453
Lord's mercy on, 529
in Lord's spiritual energy, 407, 408
material desires absent in, 638
material desires should be rejected by, 426, 428, 446, 453
materialistic, 450
material world disinterests, 563
māyā bewilders never, 130
may be poor, 147
meditate on Lord's feet, 155
meditation by, pleasure in, 155
meetings among, etiquette for, **341**
mercy of, as necessary, 229
in mixed knowledge, 423-24
mundane history disinterests, 523
neophyte, 599-600
neophyte, vs. Śaivites, 70
nondevotees contrasted to, 407, 408, 582, 612, 710
obeisances as offered by, 112-13, 116-17
obeisances to, 112-13
offenses to, by materialistic men, **134–**35
offenses to, effect of, 69
offense to, 432, 680, 846
offers Lord things, 296
oneness in outlook of, 301
as *para-duḥkha-duḥkhī*, 226
as peaceful, 590-91
perfection achieved by, 564
perfectional stage of, 374
Devotee(s) of Lord (*continued*)
places of pilgrimages for, 352-53
please everyone, 591
prayers by, 716
as preacher(s)
as best well-wishers, 264
books (two) for, 289-90
Caitanya's advice to, 290
criticized by some, 366
deliver materialists, 226, 229
everyone should be, 290
Indians should be, 366
must go everywhere, 366
Nārada as, 347
problems don't exist for, 395
protected by Lord, 255, 286, 294, 381
protected from sin, 386
prowess not shown by, **228**
pure. *See:* Pure devotee(s)
purified by Lord, 203, 204
purified of bodily life, 155, 156
purity of, 591
qualities of, **513**
regulated eating for, 369
remain so in rebirth, 243
respect all, 303
respect demigods, 87-88, 296
respected by all, 461
respect for, importance of, 112-13
ritualistic ceremonies unnecessary for, 840
sacrifice (*yajña*) by, 284
sacrifices don't concern, 286
sanctified by Lord, 203, 204
sanctifying effect of, 203, 204
in *sannyāsa*, 830
satisfaction attained by, 157
satisfaction of, as first importance, 91
satisfied by available food, 369-70
see
Lord always good, 225
Lord by love, 253
in relation to Lord, 303
sense gratification as viewed by, 552
senses controlled by, 552
senses purified by, 115-16
service to, 432

Devotee(s) of Lord (*continued*)
Siddhas as, 274, 275
sincerity essential for, 426
Śiva greatest of, 55, 85, 130, 137, 213
Śiva worshiped by, 137
as spiritual masters, 76
spiritual vision in, 536, 557-58, 591
spiritual world achieved by, 575, 589, 590
Śrīmad-Bhāgavatam for, 600
Śrīmad-Bhāgavatam should be preached by, 607
surpass *yogīs,* 390
surrenders to Lord, 529
take responsibility for own sins, 224
temple-worship instruction to, 633
three types of, 513
tilaka purifies, 579
as *tīrtha-pāda,* 204
tolerance in, 226-27, 228
tolerate no blasphemy, 227
as transcendental, 562, 768-69
transcendental status of, 145, 255, 265
welfare work by, 656-57
wife of, 642
world as viewed by, 414
yogīs compared with, 412, 416, 453, 515, 562, 576, 590, 591
See also: Sage(s); Saintly person(s); Transcendentalist(s); *specific devotee(s)*
Devotees of Śiva. *See:* Śiva, followers of
Devotional service to Supreme Lord
activities of, listed, 370
for all beings, 288, 366-67
anger hampers, 539
associating with devotees in, **413,** 414-15
begin right away, 339
beings with tongue, 259
beyond enjoyment & renunciation, 145
bliss of, 412
as Brahman platform, 114
as Brahman realization, 265
Caitanya enables, 385
as changeless, 415
chanting Lord's name in, 619
chanting process in. *See:* Chanting
child may perform, 329

Devotional service to Lord (*continued*)
compared
to electricity, 114
to fire, 114
to heated iron, 114
with *karma-kāṇḍa,* 327-29
to mango, 415
to river's waves, **413,** 414
with selfish work, 233
to watering tree's root, 547, 607-8
defined, 548
demigods satisfied by, 88
desire absent in, 374-75
desire for, as spiritual, 343
desires fulfilled in, 343, 350-51, **373**
despite material desires, 343
detachment by, 619
determination in, 382, 385
devotee in, 406, 408, 409, **452,** 453, 560-61
Dhruva in, 403, **557,** 579
Dhruva inspires, 316, 385
diet in, *prasāda* as, 259
as difficult, 382
difficult & easy, 337
duty continues in, 328
as duty of living beings, 306
as easy, 329
easy via Caitanya's grace, 385
at end of life, 339
for everyone, 288, 366-67
finish it this life, 382, 385
freedom from bondage by, 233
as freedom from material modes, 265-66
gain via, beyond expectation, 349
by goddess of fortune, **329,** 330
Goloka Vṛndāvana via, 415
as greatest *yoga,* 152-53
hearing process in. *See:* Supreme Lord, hearing about
as highest Vedic knowledge, 214
ideal in, Śiva as, 213
immortality by, 607
independence as, 451
influences world, 393
instructed by Śiva, **214**
intelligence required for, 552

Devotional service to Lord (*continued*)
in internal energy of Lord, 115
in *kaivalya* stage, 115
knowledge basis of, 212-13
in Kṛṣṇa consciousness movement, 414, 604
for liberated persons, 374-75
liberation surpassed via, 375, 550, 552
liberation via, 441, 506, 527, 566-67
Lord known via, 268-69, 282-83, 417
Lord's abode via, 526
Lord satisfied by, 717
Lord seen via, 253, 399
at Lord's lotus feet, 203-4
material assets used in, 106-7
material desire blocks, 428
via meditational worship, 372
mind purified in, 115-16
mixed with material knowledge, 423-24
Nārada-pañcarātra as directory of, 614
offenses in, 633
offerings to Lord in, 296
as one in front of zeros, 107
perfection via, 572
permanent value of, 564
pilgrimage places for, 352-53
prayers in, 259, 260
problems absent in, 395
protection by Lord in, 381
as protection from sin, 286
pure devotional service, 425-26, 619, 740
pure stage of. *See:* Pure devotional service
purified senses for, 213
purifying effect of, 115-16, **203-4**
reaction absent in, 7
regulative principles for, 385
remembrance process in, 210-11
saintly persons in, **510**
samādhi in, 145
sanctifying effect of, 203-4
satisfaction attained in, 157
sense gratification absent in, 374-75
senses in, 406
sinners saved by, 692
Śiva exemplary in, 213
smaraṇam process in, 210-11
space travel by, 577

Devotional service to Lord (*continued*)
spiritualizing effect of, 203-4
spiritual master motivates, 349
spiritual master required for, 597
spiritual master tests, 337, 339
as *śuddha-sattva*, 114
tongue's use in, 259
as topmost *yoga*, 619
transcendence by, 514, 515
transforms material consciousness, 114
universal propagation of, 366-67
as *vimukti*, 375
without knowing God's name, 19
See also: Devotees; Kṛṣṇa consciousness; Supreme Lord, worship of; Worship, to Lord
Dhāma defined, 352
Dhāriṇī (daughter of Pitās), **49**
Dharma, **430, 703**
Nara-Nārāyaṇa Ṛṣi sons of, **40-43**
sons & wives of, **40**
Dharma-jña defined, 757
Dhātā (son of Bhṛgu), **36, 37**
Dhṛta-vrata defined, 785
Dhruvaloka
cosmic dissolution survived by, 403-4, **430,** 435
Lord awarded, to Dhruva, **429-30**
Lord created, 398, 403
as polestar, 403, 430, 435, 593
as Śiśumāra, 578
stars & planets circle, **430, 593**
as Viṣṇu's abode, 435, 436, 578
Dhruva Mahārāja
as *ācārya,* 382, 385
acted according to Nārada, **383**
addresses Nārada, **342-47**
airplane arrived for, **568**
airplane boarded by, **581,** 582, 586
airplane circumambulated by, **580**
allowed to chant *praṇava,* 365
anger of, **507**-8, 538, 539
angry at insult, **321-22**
arrows of, **484, 490-92, 501-5**
asks greatest kingdom, **345, 347**
asks Nārada's help, **345, 347**
attacking Alakāpurī, **482, 483, 493,** 507

Dhruva (*continued*)
austerities by, **384, 386-88**, 475, **573,** 574, **575,** 576, **596-97, 598**
in Badarikāśrama, **564, 565**
begged to remember Lord, **551,** 552-54
body of, spiritualized, 580, 586
Brahmā forefather of, **325-26**, 440
Brahmā's position envied by, 442
breathing control of, **387, 388, 393,** 394
broken heart of, **343-44**
can't be imitated, 385
captured Lord (Brahman), **389**
as child, **333-34,** 335, 348
in childhood, **608,** 609
compared
to heavy elephant, **391-93**
to mountain in rain, **487**
to snake, **321**
to sun emerging from fog, **489**
to sun setting in ocean, **488,** 489
death surpassed by, **581-82**
demigods
accused by, of polluting his intelligence, **446-47**
honored, 468, **583, 586**
describes Nārada, 347
desired
devotee's association, **413,** 414
gain honestly, 346
greatest kingdom, 344, **345-46,** 349
kingdom, 428, 437
Nārada's blessing, 346
desire of
demigods couldn't grant, 349
as material, 343
Nārada could fulfill, 346, 347, 349
determination in, 382
as devotional inspiration, 316
devotional service by, 403, **557,** 579
didn't know distinction between mothers, **319**
discouraged by Nārada, **337-39**
discussed by Lord, **396**
discussed by Nārada, **380-82**
in ecstatic love of God, **400**
eternal abode achieved by, **587-88**

Dhruva (*continued*)
exemplary
in devotional life, 385
in pious acts, 316
fame of, **608,** 609
father of. *See:* Uttānapāda
father's fears for, **379,** 381
fixed mind on Lord, **388, 389,** 396
following in footsteps of, 385
forest diet of, **384, 386-87**
ghāṭa named for, 352-53
glad to meet Nārada, 346, 347
goes to Madhuvana forest, **376**
goes to mother, **321-22**
greatness of, 428, **595, 596, 598**
hearing about, **600-603, 605**
benefit in, 316
heaviness of
amazed stepmother, 392
false argument against, 392
in meditation, **389,** 390, **391-93**
as hero, 463
identified with total energy, 393
instructed by mother, **323-29**
instructed by Nārada, **334-41, 349-74**
insulted by Suruci, **318-20**
insult to, as benediction, 325
intelligent, 552
kingdom renounced by, **561, 563-64**
knew Nārada's power, 346
as *kṣatriya*, 333-34, 344, 511, 598
Kuvera
advised, **545-48, 550**
offended by, **541**
offered benediction to, **550, 551**
pleased with, **544, 553**
lamented his material desires, **410,** 428, **436,** 437, **438, 439,** 442, **444-48, 450-51**
leaves home, **331**
as liberated, 537, 538, **566**
Lord
"conquered" by, **596**
enlightened, **401, 402,** 403, **404-5,** 418
fulfilled desire of, **428,** 437, 443
known by, 419, 420
& living entities as considered by, 421

Dhruva
Lord (*continued*)
pleased by, 396
protected, 381
seen by, **398–400,** 403, 404
Lord's benediction on, **429–36**
Lord's shelter sought by, **608,** 609
in *māyā,* 537
meditates on Lord, **388, 389, 396**
meditation site of, **351,** 352-53
not merging with Lord, 396
mother of. *See:* Sunīti
mystic storm engulfed, **494–97**
Nanda & Sunanda assured, about Sunīti, 584, **585**
Nanda & Sunanda invited, to Viṣṇuloka, **573–78**
Nārada
could satisfy, 344, 347, 349
glorified, **614,** 615
instructs, **334–41, 349–74**
sent to, 333
spiritual master of, 403, 446, 447, 576, 598
tests, 337, 339
neglected by father, **316,** 317, **378–**79
as noble, **459**
planet of. *See:* Dhruvaloka
as *prabhu,* 382
prayer(s) by
on association with pure devotees, **573–78**
on devotional service & Lord, **425**
on Garbhodakaśāyī Viṣṇu, **419**
on impersonal Brahman, **423**
on Lord & living entities, **417, 420–21**
on Lord & surrendered souls, **408–9**
on Lord as all-powerful, **404–5**
on Lord as one & different, **407**
on Lord as worshiped by sense enjoyers, **410**
on transcendental bliss, **411**
presses down Earth, **391–**92
pride in, **333–34,** 344
as pure devotee, **512,** 550, **551,** 552, 564, 567
qualities of, **558,** 559

Dhruva (*continued*)
quoted. *See:* Dhruva Mahārāja, prayer(s) by
receives *praṇava* (*oṁ*) *mantra,* **364**
refuses Nārada's instructions, **342–47**
reign of, **431,** 443, 471, **558,** 559, **560, 561**
respected stepmother, 459
sacrifices by, **554,** 556
sages' blessings accepted by, **579**
sages encouraged, **498–99**
as saintly king, **558,** 559
in Satya-yuga, 471, 472, 559, 560
seminal succession from, 687-89
senses of, 562
space travel by, **586–88**
suffocating all, **393–94**
at summit of universe, **592,** 593
Sunīti
accompanied, to spiritual world, 584, **585,** 587
reunited with, **462–64**
as Sunīti's son, 463, 465, **583–**84, **585,** 587
Suruci blessed, **460,** 461
Svāyambhuva Manu
advised, **507–41**
grandfather of, **327**
proud of, 535
tested by Nārada, 337, 339
Utkala uninterested in kingship of, **616**
Uttama reunited with, **462**
Uttānapāda
enthroned, **476**
reunited with, **454–56,** 457, **458, 459**
satisfied by, **475**
Uttānapāda's reception for, **465–69**
Vena as descendant of, 687-89
Viṣṇu's associates received respects from, **570–72, 580**
wives of, **479, 480**
worshiped Lord, 465
Yakṣas vs., **482–99, 501–7**
in yogic trance, **565, 566**
Difficulties, 395
Dīkṣā-vidhāna defined, 367

Disciple(s)
of Śiva. *See:* Śiva, followers of
spiritual master engages, 349
tested by spiritual master, 337, 339
See also: specific disciples
Disciple & spiritual master, 584, 585, 594, 630
Disciplic succession(s)
bogus compared with bona fide, 746
Lord understood via, 357-58
needed to receive *mantras,* 363, 365
religious principles via, 848
of Śiva, 55, 217
See also: Spiritual master(s)
Disc of Viṣṇu, **22,** 23
Disease, material, 539, 842
Distress
acceptance of, as Lord's mercy, **336**–37
material vs. spiritual, 103-4
See also: Suffering
Diti, descendants of, **795–96, 815**
Divorce, 122
Doṣā, **622, 623**
Downfall. *See:* Falldown
Dowry in Vedic system, 97
Dr. Frog, 528
Dṛḍha-vrata defined, 730
Dream
body & soul during, 568
living entity's independence compared to, 546
material world compared to, 448-49, **562**–63
Dress, body compared to, 734
Drinking & drugs. *See:* Intoxication
Drum symbol of Śiva, **22,** 23
Duality, material, animosity creates, 459
See also: Bodily concept of life; Good & bad; "I-&-mine" conception
Durātmā defined, 176
Durgā, goddess, 306, **705**
See also: Satī
Durukti (Harsh Speech), **312**
Durvāsā
born to Atri, **30**
as incarnation of Śiva, **14,** 16, **30**
Durvibhāvyā defined, 520
Duṣkṛtinaḥ defined, 785
Dust storm, **171, 172**
Dust storm after Vena's death, **685, 686**
Duty
of all to serve Lord, 306
of *brāhmaṇas,* 752
brāhmaṇas now abandon, 75-76
of citizens, 667-70
continues in Lord's service, 328
& criticizing others, **143**
of devotee, 680
of family members, 797
of father to maintain family, 378
of government leaders, 667-71, 728
of king, 665-66, 718, 722, 737, 752, 787, 834, 847
of Kṛṣṇa conscious preachers, 717
of living entity, 818
next-life preparation as, 781-82
for pleasing Lord, 7, 232-33
pleasing Lord as, 615
of Prajāpati, **158**
to protect master, 160
of saintly persons, 679
of *sannyāsī,* 823-24
of Satī's attendants, 160
in social orders, 658
of spiritual master to disciple, 349
Dvāpara-yuga, life span in, 471, 560
Dvārakā, 352, 430, 809
Dvija defined, 132
Dvīpa defined, 759
Dyumān (son of Kratu), **35**
Dyumna, **624**

E

Earth planet
compared to boat, **776**
compared to cow, 790
compared to mother, 754
in cow form, **744–45, 754–57, 759–61, 765,** 767, 790, **792**
demigods fall to, 447
food produced or withheld by, 753, 788, 790, 793

Earth planet (*continued*)
- Kṛṣṇa consciousness movement as hope of, 788
- life's necessities from, 802, 805, 817
- nondevotees misuse products of, **784,** 785
- pleaded with Pṛthu, **757–59, 767, 770–77, 780, 782–84, 786, 787, 789–91**
- Pṛthu
  - attacked, **753–56**
  - compared to, **722**
  - leveled, **745, 806**
  - milked, **744–45, 792**
  - pleased, **792, 806**
  - threatened, **760–62, 764–66**
- in Pṛthu's time, **804**
- quoted on
  - Lord, **767, 772, 774**
  - Pṛthu & herself, **757–59, 770, 771, 775–77**
- rain for, 719-20
- saintly king ruled, 475, 742
- surrendered to Lord, 770
- tastes produced from, 818
- Varāha rescued, **775,** 776
- as *vasundharā,* 792
- as woman, 764

Easy Journey to Other Planets, 577

Eating
- by *brāhmaṇas,* 75-76
- degradation or elevation via, 259
- by devotees, 369-70, 384-85
- by Dhruva in forest, **384, 386–87**
- to maintain body, 384-85
- *See also:* Food; Meat-eating; *Prasāda*

Economic development
- via religious principles, 561
- *See also:* Materialism; Wealth

Ecstasy
- devotee highest in, **374**
- in meditating on Lord, 155
- purification via, 155, 156
- transcendental, Dhruva in, **400**
- *See also:* Bliss, transcendental; Happiness; Love, for Lord

Education
- of boys, 344

Education (*continued*)
- of *brāhmaṇas,* need for, 344–45
- compared to jewel on snake, 106
- material, as nescience, **73**
- pride in, **106**
- in service to Lord, 106-7
- spiritual
  - as beyond academic degrees, 731
  - decline of, 604
  - eternal life by, 781-82
  - Kṛṣṇa conscious, for children, 573
  - *See also:* Knowledge

Ego, false, 531
- envy due to, **110–11**
- *See also:* Bodily concept of life; Duality, material; "I-&-mine" conception; Illusion; Pride, false

Ekadaṇḍi-sannyāsī defined, 830

Ekādaśī, devotee observes, 560

Electrical powerhouse & Lord, analogy of, 521, 774

Electricity in copper, analogy of, 114

Elements, material
- creation by, **515,** 516, 517
- creation of, 774, **775**
- Deity incarnates in, 565
- *See also:* Chemicals; Energies, material; Nature, material; *specific elements*

Elephants in Kailāsa, **196**

Empiric philosophers. *See: Jñānīs;* Philosophers, speculative

Empiric philosophy. *See:* Philosophy

Enemies
- as bodily concept, 536
- in family, 627
- material consciousness imagines, 448
- Pṛthu impartial to, **727–**28
- Pṛthu overcame, **726**

Energy (energies) of Supreme Lord
- as basis of all, 297-98
- of Brahman, **423,** 424
- compared to fire in wood, **407,** 408
- as energy & energetic, 46
- as everything, **291,** 292
- external, 518, **532,** 768, 769
- as "female," 306
- illusory, **517**

Energy (energies) of Lord (*continued*)
inconceivable, **520,** 521, 522, 549
inferior & superior, 299
internal, 532, 768, 769
living entity as, 299
Lord acts via, **407,** 518, 519, **520,** 521, **532**
Lord controls, 281
marginal, 448-49, 547
material, 406, 449, 502, 549, **563-64, 767,** 768, 769
compared with spiritual, 407, 408
creation, maintenance, & annihilation in, 281
demigods manifest by, 281
devotees beyond, 281
Durgā as, 306
Lord beyond, **280-**81
personified by Sati, 166
Satī as, 166
spiritual bliss surpasses, 619
spiritual world beyond, 281
universe as, **43**
variety in, 43
Nara as, 46
as nondifferent from Him, 279, **291,** 298-99
spiritual, 405-6, 769
devotional service in, 115
as direct will of Lord, 116
free from covering, 115
living entities as, 279
Lord appears by, 281, 370-71
Lord revealed in, 116
mahātmās in, 176
samādhi under, 116
variety of, 529, 773
See also: Elements, material; Material nature; *Māyā;* Supreme Lord, potency of
Energy, unit & total identification of, 393
Enjoyment (sense gratification)
absent in devotional service, 374-75
absent in liberation, 374-75
desired by Satī, 96, 99
as destined, **335, 336**
diminishes results of piety, 339
Enjoyment (sense gratification) (*contd.*)
eating for, devotee avoids, 384-85
merging with Lord as, 375
need to transcend, **340**
soul beyond, 335
women expand, 96
See also: Happiness
Enlightenment via Lord's spiritual energy, 405-6
See also: Education, spiritual; God consciousness; Knowledge; Kṛṣṇa consciousness; Self-realization
Entities, individual. *See:* Living entities
Envy
anxiety by, 226
in atheists & demons, 111
in Dakṣa. *See:* Dakṣa, envy of Śiva in
death caused by, **226**
faultfinding, **131-**33
to great souls, **134-**35
not in Lord's devotee, 396
in *karmī,* 842
Kṛṣṇa consciousness movement vs., 226
Kṛṣṇa consciousness blocked by, 812
of Kṛṣṇa in scholars, 111
to Lord or devotee, 130
in materialistic men, 111, **134, 226**
in material opulence, 106
in material world, 812-13
offenses to great souls by, **134-**35
in people & snakes, 106
of self-realized by others, **110,** 111
See also: Anger
Envy (descendant of Brahmā), **312**
Equals, meeting with, **341**
Equilibrium in liberated souls, 103
Eternal life
as human mission, 781-82
in Vaikuṇṭha, 588
See also: Immortality
Etiquette
for friends visiting friends, **101-2, 105, 107,** 108
in respecting devotees, 112-13
in social system, 83
to superior, equal, or inferior, **341**
Evolution concepts, material vs. spiritual, 519

Excessive Pain (descendant of Brahmā), **312**
Existence. *See:* Living entities; Material world; Soul
External energy of Supreme Lord. *See:* Energies of Supreme Lord, material
Eyes for seeing God, 253, 278

F

Faith as inspired by Dhruva, 316
Falldown
from Brahman effulgence, 441
from heavenly planets, **412**
of monarchy, 555
See also: Offenses
False ego. *See:* Ego, false
Falsity (daughter of Brahmā), **311**
Fame, Śiva kills, 61
Family life
abandoning of, for Lord, 332
detachment from, 627, 647, 648
disobedience in, 379
divorce in, 122
enemies in, 627
father's duty to maintain, 378
ghosts in, oblations for, 797-98
happy, 622
home of, compared to blind well, 647
insults from relatives, **108-**9, 118
materialistic, ignorance in, 72
materialistic, in *Vedas,* **72**
monarchy controlled by, 621
parents' duty to daughters, 66
purification of, 688
respect for parents in, 218
satisfaction in, 8
wife as meaning of, 310
woman's weakness in, 122
See also: Gṛhastha(s); Marriage
Farmers. *See: Vaiśyas*
Fasting, 385
by devotee, 560
Father(s)
daughter &, 642
as enemy, 627
maintains family, 378
Father(s) (*continued*)
son &, 594
See also: Family life; *Gṛhastha(s); specific fathers*
Faultfinding, **131-**33
Fear
of Dakṣa in men, 126-27
envy causes, 226
freedom from, **274-75**
as needless under spiritual master, 384
Fear (descendant of Brahmā), **312**
Feeding stomach & satisfying Lord, analogy of, 849
Fertilizers, 820
Finger position for speaking, **215**
Fire
analogy of fire & devotional service, 114
from Atri Muni, **20**
Lord compared to, 521
material existence compared to, **413,** 414
oblations offered in, 128
Pṛthu compared to, **726**
sacrificial, 639
Suruci died in, **432**
in wood compared to Lord's energy in nature, **407,** 408
Fire-god. *See:* Agni
Fishing as poor man's occupation, 820
Flesh-eating. *See:* Meat-eating
Flower(s)
kapittha, 384
offered in Deity worship, 365, 372
Flower shower by demigods for Dhruva, **583, 586**
Flying by yogic power, 363
Food
abominable, 259
devotee's eating of, **384-85**
Earth produces or withholds, 753, 788, 790, 793
not for sense gratification, 384-85
four kinds of, 819
as government's responsibility, 762, 763
in Kali-yuga decreases, 785-86
Lord supplies, 802, 804-5
for maintaining body, 384-85

Food (*continued*)
offered
in Deity worship, 365, **367**, 368, **369**, 372, 385
to forefathers, 797-98
in sacrifice, two kinds of, 146-47
planets produce, 805
rain produces, 762, **791**
shortage of, solution to, 788, 789
vaiśyas produce, 750
Forbearance. *See:* Tolerance
Force, unit & total identification of, 393
Forefathers. *See:* Pitā(s)
Forest(s)
on bank of Yamunā, **351**, 352
on Kailāsa (Saugandhika), **201-2**, **206**, **207**
Lord's protection in, 381
Madhuvana, as auspicious, **376**
mirage in, 563
Suruci died in fire in, **432**
taking shelter of Lord in, 332
of Vṛndāvana, listed, 352
Vṛndāvana as, 332
Forgiveness
in Lord's devotees, 226-27, 228
See also: Tolerance
Form of Lord. *See:* Supreme Lord, form(s) of
Fortune, goddess of. *See:* Goddess of fortune
Freedom from material world, 514
See also: Independence; Liberation
Freedom from matter. *See:* Liberation
Freedom from reactions, 7
Friends (relatives), etiquette for visiting, **101-2, 105, 107, 108**
"Frog, Dr.," 528
Fruit
Dhruva ate, **384**
offered in Deity worship, **367**, 368, 369
Fruitive activity
by followers of *Vedas*, **72, 74**
See also: Karma; Pious activities; Work
Fruitive workers. *See: Karmīs;* Materialists
Future, people fleeing to forest in, 718

G

Gadādhara, 502
Gandharva(s), **21, 41, 42, 583**
discuss demigods, **287**
in Kailāsa, **193-94**
music milked by, **796**
pray to Viṣṇu, **287**
Pṛthu glorified by, **698**
at Pṛthu's horse sacrifices, **814**
as subdemigods, 94
Gandharva-nagara defined, 563
Ganges River
Devakulyā deity of, **13**
in Kailāsa, 201
from Lord's feet, **13, 202**, 203
Lord's feet &, **202**, 203
Satī's lake as, 201
on Śiva's head, 201
water of, in Deity worship, 368
Gāñjā (marijuana), 78, 79, 97
Garbhādhāna-saṁskāra purification, 688
Garbhodaka Ocean
planets above, 759
Varāha rescued Earth from, 775
Garbhodakaśāyī Viṣṇu, 28, 398, **419**, 521
Garuḍa, **22**, 23, 254, **398, 436**
as Brahman incarnation, 696
in calf form, **803**
carnivorous descendants of, 803
Gati (wife of Pulaha), **33**
Gauḍīya Vaiṣṇavas, 332
See also: Devotee(s)
Gaurakiśora dāsa Bābājī, 67
Gaya, **624**
Gayā, oblations for forefathers in, 797
Gāyatrī *mantra*, 162
Ghāṭas of Vṛndāvana, listed, 352-53
Ghost(s)
in family, oblations for, 797-98
as flesh-eaters, **801**
Śiva lord of, 54, 84
See also: Śiva, followers of
Glorification to Lord
by devotee, 401
via Lord empowering us, 846

Glorification to Lord (*continued*)
Lord pleased by, 717
via Lord's mercy, 404
via Lord's spiritual energy, 406
purifying power of, 716
See also: Chanting of Supreme Lord's holy names; *Saṅkīrtana-yajña*
Goal of life
Lord as, 426, **533**
satisfying Lord as, 671
thinking of Lord as, 565
Vaikuṇṭha as, 598
See also: Perfection
Goat's head for Dakṣa, **238,** 239, **242–43**
God. *See:* Kṛṣṇa; Supersoul; Supreme Lord; Viṣṇu
God consciousness
for happiness, 718
modern government neglects, 559
saintly persons preach, 658
See also: Kṛṣṇa consciousness
Goddess of fortune
always serves Lord, **329,** 330
always with Lord, 6, 277
Arci as partial incarnation of, **697**
born with Yajña, **5**
demigods worship, **329,** 330
disciplic succession from, 746
incarnation of, as Dakṣiṇā, **5–**6, 7
inseparable from Lord, **695**
Lord not attached to, **273**
on Lord's chest, 256
as Lord's feminine feature, 359
materialists seek, 695
present for Pṛthu from, **704**
as worshiped for opulence, 330
Godhead, returning to
for devotees, 575, 590
via devotional service, 692
via Kṛṣṇa consciousness, 656
in one life, 598-99
via *Vedas,* 785
See also: Kṛṣṇa; Spiritual world; Supreme Lord; Vṛndāvana
"Gods." *See:* Demigods
Gold
demigods' airplanes made of, 468
in Uttānapāda's palace, **471**
Golden pot, *soma* in, 796
Goloka Vṛndāvana, 415, 451, 777
beyond material qualities, 280-81
desire trees in, 206
quality in, 281
See also: Spiritual world; Vṛndāvana
Good & bad as mental concoction, 448
See also: Bodily concept of life; Duality, material; "I-&-mine" conception
Good in all, 132-33
Goodness
creation based on, 313
mode of. *See:* Goodness, mode of
pure, as absent, 168–69
See also: Suddha-sattva
Goodness, mode of
controlled by Viṣṇu, **282,** 299
elevation via, 517
vs. ignorance, 168–69
Kṛṣṇa's body beyond, 531
maintenance via, 517
need to transcend, 283
as source of religion, knowledge, etc., 282
Viṣṇu governs, 748
Good works. *See:* Pious activities
Gopīs worshiped Kātyāyanī, 553
Goṣṭhy-ānandī defined, 620
Gosvāmīs, six, 76, 461
author's obeisances to, 2
See also: Jīva Gosvāmī; Raghunātha dāsa Gosvāmī; Rūpa Gosvāmī; Sanātana Gosvāmī
Govardhana Hill, 270-71, 723
Government(s)
departments compared to material modes, 221
devotee should instruct, 731
duty of, 667-71, 728
food responsibility of, 762, 763
leader(s)
as blind, 671
citizen's relationship to, 735-36, 742, 752
in democracy, 652

Government(s)
leader(s) (*continued*)
in Dhruva's day vs. nowadays, 477, 555, 558-59
economy inflated by, 725
happiness for, 664, 669, 670
in Kali-yuga, 663, 718, 720-22, 725, 732
misery should be dispelled by, 742
religious duty of, 658, 664, 665
sense gratification pursued by, 669-70
taxation by, 721, 722
in *yugas*, 666
See also: King(s); *Kṣatriya(s);* Politician(s)
politics upsets, 783
religion threatened by, 655-56
secular, 668-69, 718, 720, 834-35
strong vs. weak, 653, 738
thieves &, 665-66, **683-86,** 738
See also: Civilization, modern; Kings; *Kṣatriya(s); specific forms of government*
Governors of planets, **278**
Govinda, 203
See also: Kṛṣṇa
Govinda dāsī, *tulasī* grown by, 368
Grains, food. *See:* Food
Grass, *kuśa*, **22,** 23
Gravitation, power of, 765
Greatness in seeing good, 132-33
Great personalities, offenses to, **134-**35
Great souls, associating with, 154
Greed (son of Brahmā), **312**
Gṛhastha(s)
chanting Hare Kṛṣṇa, 555
distinct from *sannyāsīs,* 145
duty of, 658
sex life for, 505
thief &, 777
See also: Family life; Father; Husband; Marriage; Mother; Wife
Grief
effect of, 322
Lord mitigates, 328, 331
as useless, 332
by words of relative, 108-9
Guṇa-avatāras, 221, 748
Brahmā & Śiva as, 299
Guṇas. See Modes of nature
Guru. See: Spiritual master(s)

H

Hair (on Śiva's followers), 79
Haṁsa (son of Brahmā), **309**
Hand position for speaking, **215**
Happiness
in abominable life, 290
by accepting difficulty, **336-**37
of citizens, 663, 669, 670
by depending on Lord, **336-**37
for devotees of Lord, 155
diminishes results of piety, 339
for family, 622
fire of, in Atri Muni, **20**
God consciousness for, 718
in goodness mode, 282
for government leaders, 664, **665,** 667, 669, 670
in happiness or distress, **340**
by hearing Lord's pastimes, **274-**75
illusory, in abominable life, 290
illusory, misleads us, **289-**90
of *karmīs, jñānīs, yogīs,* & devotees, 412
by Lord's grace, 327
from Lord's lotus feet, 155
in married life, 8
material
ignorance in, 72
as impossible, 156, 157
soul beyond, 335
women expand, 96
in material world compared with spiritual worlds, 103-4
by meditating on Lord, 155
need to transcend, **340**
by right treatment of others, **341**
via saintly king, 476, 477
sensuous, 411
by serving Lord, 157
for society, 793, 794
Vedic instructions for, 781, 783
See also: Bliss; Ecstasy; Enjoyment, material

Hardwar, 352
Hare Kṛṣṇa *mantra*
absolute nature of, 571
addresses Lord's spiritual energy, 405
benefits everyone, 661, 684
devotee chants, 571, 591, 612
for good government, 720
for Kali-yuga, 684
māyā dispelled by, 502, 503
nonmaterial, 402
as practical sacrifice, 555-56, 631-33
preachers propagate, 717
salvation via, 478
for society, 794
See also: Chanting, Hare Kṛṣṇa; *Saṅkīrtana-yajña*
Hare Kṛṣṇa movement. *See:* Kṛṣṇa consciousness movement
Hari-bhakti-vilāsa cited on becoming Vaiṣṇava, 366-67
Haridāsa Ṭhākura, 76, 567
exemplary in tolerance, 227
Harsh Speech (descendant of Brahmā), **312**
Hastināpura, 809
Hatred as cause of devastation, 313
Havirbhū (wife of Pulastya), **32**
Health, *yoga* for, 152
Hearing about Supreme Lord
bliss in, **274-**75
bogus vs. bona fide, 599-600
books (two) for, 289-90
Caitanya recommended, 290
devotee addicted to, 414
in devotee's association, 414, 603-4
ever fresh, 612
for everyone, 290
Kṛṣṇa consciousness movement for, 290
liberation via, **289-**90
love of God by, 597
perfection via, 289-90
as pleasing, 602
purification by, 115-16
by Siddhas, **274,** 275
value of, 539
See also: Kṛṣṇa-kathā
Heart
broken, 343
cleansing of, 313
compared to earthen pot, 312, 343
meditation on Lord in, 355-62
See also: Mind
Heavenly planet(s)
airplanes of, **205-**6
attained by *yogīs,* 152-53
attained via pious activities, **223-**24
attract materialist, 72
Bṛhaspati as priest of, 794
elevation to, 517
falling from, **412,** 447
karmīs seek, 412
king of. *See:* Indra, King
Kṛṣṇa took *pārijāta* tree from, 473
residents of. *See:* Demigods
soma beverage in, 795
survive destruction, 285
time on, vs. Earth time, 473
trees in, 473-74
See also: Spiritual world; Universe(s)
Hell (descendant of Brahmā), **312**
Hellish planets, Nārada visits, 352
Hell via sinful killing, **507-**8
Higher planets. *See:* Heavenly planets
Himalayas
in calf form, **804**
Dhruva retired to, **564**
Pṛthu's reign extended to, 735
sages go to, 687
Satī daughter of, 306
Uttama killed by Yakṣa in, **481, 482**
Yakṣas from, 483
Hiṁsā (Envy), **312**
Hindus follow Manu's laws, 488
Hiraṇyakaśipu, 294, 710
Brahmā &, 445
Nṛsiṁhadeva killed, 766
Prahlāda &, 585, 796
Hiraṇyākṣa, 775
History (mundane) & devotees, 523
Hitler, 522-23
Holy men. *See:* Devotee(s); Sage(s); Saintly person(s); Spiritual master(s)

Holy names. *See:* Chanting, Hare Kṛṣṇa; Hare Kṛṣṇa *mantra*
Home life
meaning of, 310
See also: Family life
Honor
as destined, 336
as illusory, **335**
Horse sacrifices. *See:* Aśvamedha sacrifices
Householders. *See: Gṛhasthas*
Human being(s)
accepting good in, 132-33
accepting Lord's will for, 340
all can be Vaiṣṇavas (devotees), 366-67
animalistic
defy *Vedas,* 83
punishment for, 249
ritual performers as, 249
animals compared with, 510
anxiety in, 226
austerity for, 478
benefit by Śiva, 64-65, **136-37**
best relief work for, 264
in bodily concept, 99
as boys, training for, 344
can't imitate Śiva, 143
can't imitate transcendentalists, 143
classes of
according to desire, 342
demons & devotees as, 255
materialists & salvationists as, 137
compared to ass or cow, 99
control of senses for, 248
dangerous position of, **263-64**
degraded by tongue, 259
delivered by devotees, 226, 229
demoniac. *See:* Demon(s)
in different modes, 65
don't accept Lord's acts, 270
envy in, 111, 226
etiquette in meetings among, **341**
four kinds of activity for, 377
four kinds of spirit in, 344
four principles of life for, 137
frustrated, attempt liberation, 137
godless, 790
Human being(s) (*continued*)
greatness in, as finding good, 132-33
in ignorance, Śiva benefits, 65, 137
illusory attraction in, **289,** 290
interpret *Śrīmad-Bhāgavatam,* 270
life
as *arthadam,* 289
as chance for liberation, 289, 290
general conception of, 339
perfection via, 289, 290
principles for, four given, 137
spirituality at end of, 339
Lord's plan inconceivable to, 777
malicious kind of, 107-8
as Manu's descendants, 488, 535
materialistic. *See:* Materialists
meant to know Brahman, 75
meetings among, etiquette for, **341**
mission of, 781-82
offenses to great souls by, **134-**35
protection for, by surrender to Lord, 267
sacrifice for, 788
sacrifices necessary for, 232-34
self-realization for, 405
spirit in, four kinds of, 344
spiritual training for, 572
surrender by, 357
twice-born, defined, 132
See also: Society, human; Soul(s), conditioned
Hunting, by *kṣatriyas,* 643
See also: Animal slaughter; Killing; Meat-eating
Husband
good, 622
See also: Family life; Father; *Gṛhastha(s);* Marriage; *specific husbands*
Hymns. *See: Mantra(s)*

I

"I-&-mine" conception, 537-38
See also: Bodily concept of life; Duality, material; Good & bad; *Māyā*
Iḍaspati (son of Yajña), **9**
Iḍaviḍā (wife of Viśravā), **32, 553**

Identity. *See:* Self-realization; Soul(s)
Idhma (son of Yajña), **9**
Ignorance
  of Absolute Truth, 606-7
  bodily concept caused by, **546**
  in Brahman, **423,** 424
  in everyone, **266-67**
  of God's name, 19
  living entity in, 421
  material education as, **73**
  in material happiness, 72
  mode of. *See:* Ignorance, mode of
  in ritual performers, **262-**63
  Ṛṣabhadeva cited on, 445
  Śiva removes, 135-36
  of Vedic followers, **72**
  See also: Bodily concept; Ignorance, mode of; Illusion; *Māyā*
Ignorance, mode of
  annihilation by, 517
  as auspicious, 221
  compared to criminal department, 221
  vs. goodness, 168-69
  persons in, Śiva benefits, 64-65
  Śiva incarnation of, 221
  Śiva in charge of, 103, 748, 801
Ilā, **480**
Illusion
  of accepting world as real, 99
  dissatisfaction as, **335**
  everyone in, **266-67**
  happiness in, as abominable life, 290
  material world as, 99
  by *māyā's* influence, 290
  as neglect of spiritual identity, 289, 290
  See also: Bodily concept; Ignorance; *Māyā*
Immortality
  via devotional service, 533-34, 607
  Lord gives, 445
  See also: Eternal life
Impersonalism
  Śiva taught, 78
  See also: Oneness
Impersonalist(s)
  in Brahman effulgence temporarily, 441
  can't know Lord, 269
  compared with personalists, 269
Impersonalist(s) (*continued*)
  consider
    Dhruva merged in Lord, 396
    Lord mundane, 269, 370, 371
    Lord's acts unbelievable, 270
    Lord woman, 359
  curse regarding, **78**
  devotee contrasted to, 597
  devotee questioned by, 414
  followers of Śiva as, 78
  impersonal thinking of, 407
  knowledge lacking in, 409
  "liberation" of, 506
  Lord's body misunderstood by, 531, 715
  māyā as explained by, 715
  meditation by, 369
  monist's vision, 279
  offensive to Lord, 371
  oneness concept of, 546, 547, 580
  opposed to scripture, 78
  in *sannyāsa*, 830
  Supreme Brahman misunderstood by, 519
  "unification of soul" idea of, 396
  worship Agni, **48**
Impious activities, 339
  See also: Sinful activities
Incarnation(s) of Supreme Lord
  advents of, 715-16
  as auspicious, 221
  as boar. *See:* Varāha
  Brahmā as, 299
  for creation, maintenance, & annihilation, 521
  Dattātreya as, **30**
  Deity. *See:* Deity form(s)
  demigods accompany, 719
  devotee's view of, 371
  as fish, 716
  not forced to appear, 370-71
  as free & transcendental, 370-71
  via internal potency, 370-71
  Kṛṣṇa origin of, 747-48
  living entities empowered as, 846
  as Lord's expansions, 777
  for material modes, 221
  as Nara-Nārāyaṇa, **40-43**
  Pṛśnigarbha as, 398

Incarnation(s) of Lord (*continued*)
qualitative (*guṇa-avatāras*), 299
Sahasraśīrṣā as, **398**
Śiva as, 131, 299
true & false, 700, 709-11, 714, 821
types of, 696
Vāmanadeva as, **218**
Yajña as, **5-6**
See also: Avatāra(s); Supreme Lord, advent(s) of; Supreme Lord, expansion(s) of
Independence
devotional service as, 451
of living entities false, 524, 533, 546
See also: Freedom; Liberation
India
ancient cities in, 809
ceremonial decorations in, 466
Manu's laws followed in, 488
oblations for forefathers in, 797
politicians in, 478
punishment of thieves in, 626
Indian people, 366
Indra, Lord
in calf form, **794**
as conditioned soul, 821, 823
describes Lord's form, **270**
envy in, 812
horse sacrifices by, 822
irreligion introduced by, **838-39**, 840, **842, 847**
as lusty incarnation, 696
prays to Viṣṇu, **270**
present for Pṛthu from, **703**
Pṛthu
compared to, **723, 737**
envied by, **812, 820,** 821, 822, 839-40
made peace with, **848**
threatened, **834, 835**
at Pṛthu's horse sacrifices, **739, 745**
rain supplied by, **723, 791**
sacrificial priests advised Pṛthu about, **835, 836**
as sham *sannyāsī,* 823, 824, **825, 829-30, 832, 833**
stole Pṛthu's sacrificial horse, **822, 823,** 825, **828, 833, 843**
Indra (*continued*)
Vṛndāvana flooded by, 723
Yajña as, **9**
Industry, big, 786
Inferiors, meeting with, **341**
Initiation, spiritual, as second birth, 604
Insect & Brahmā, analogy of, 442
Insult(s)
children ignore, 335
to Dhruva by stepmother, **318-20**
as illusory, **335**
by relatives, **108-**9, 118
Intellectual(s). *See: Brāhmaṇa(s); Jñānī(s);* Sage(s)
Intelligence
brain &, 238-39
devotional service requires, 552
of one meditating on Lord, 111
as worshiping Lord, 243
Internal energy of Supreme Lord. *See:* Energies of Supreme Lord, spiritual
International Society for Krishna Consciousness, 290
See also: Kṛṣṇa consciousness movement
Intoxication
curse pertaining to, 78
of demigods & demons contrasted, 795, 796
by followers of Śiva, 78, 79, 83, 214
of "*sannyāsīs,*" 831
in Śiva worship, 79
wives' property sold for, 97
Invitations, etiquette regarding, **101-2, 105, 107,** 108
Iron in fire, analogy of, 114
Iron pot, liquor & beer in, **795,** 796
Irreligion
as cause of devastation, 313
descendants of, **311-**13
Indra introduced, **838-39**, 840, **842, 847**
leaders should dispel, 834
See also: Atheists; Demons
Irreligion (son of Brahmā), **311,** 313
Iṣa, **622**
Īśa, Śiva as, 14
Īśitā defined, 800

ISKCON. *See:* Kṛṣṇa consciousness movement
Islands & plants, analogy of, 759
Īśopaniṣad
cited
on knowledge & nescience, 424
on Lord as uncontaminated, 421
on Lord's arrangement for producing necessities, 818
on satisfaction with one's quota from Lord, 453
quoted on Lord's arrangement for producing necessities, 819
Īśvarāṇām defined, 777

J

Jaḍa Bharata, 598, 620
Jagadīśvara, status of, 25
Jagāi & Mādhāi, 130
Jagannātha Purī
as pilgrimage site, 352
temple *prasāda* from, 303
Jaya, **622**
Jealousy. *See:* Envy
Jesus Christ, 227, 540
Jewels
oceans produce, 819, 820
in Uttānapāda's palace, **470, 471, 474**
Jews, Hitler killed, 523
Jīva(s), 15
See also: Living entities; Soul(s)
Jīva Gosvāmī cited
on Atri Muni, 20
on Dhruva, 389, 390
on giving daughter away, 3
on Lord as Brahman, 389, 390
on Lord's activities, 777
on Satī, 156
on *śuddha-sattva,* 114
Jīva-tattva defined, **813**
See also: Living entities; Soul(s)
Jñāna. See: Knowledge
Jñānam ajñāta defined, 606
Jñāna-miśra-bhaktas defined, 423-24
Jñānī(s), 374
attain Brahmaloka, 505
devotees compared with, 412, 453, 515, 576, 590, 591, 601, 657
See also: Impersonalist(s); Philosopher(s), speculative
Jungle(s). *See:* Forest(s)

K

Kailāsa (abode of Śiva)
Alakā area of, 200-201
almost like Kṛṣṇa's abode, 206-7
animals in, **199, 200**
banyan tree of, **209, 210**
beauty & opulence of, **193-209**
birds in, **195, 199, 207**
deer in, **199, 200**
desire trees in, **206**
forest in, **206**
Ganges in, 201
lotus flowers in, **201,** 202, **207**
near Kuvera's abode, **206**
residents of, **193-94**
rivers in, **203**
trees in, **196-98**
Kaivalya defined, 115
Kalā (daughter of Kardama), **13**
Kali (descendant of Brahmā), **313**
Kālī, goddess, 844
Kali-yuga (present Age of quarrel)
all *śūdras* in, 163
animal slaughter in, 844
brāhmaṇas absent in, 162-63
brāhmaṇas in, 75-76, 661, 817, 836, 844
chanting of *mantras* in, as impossible, 161, 162-63
chanting recommended in, 125, 233-34, 284, 291-92, 371
"classless" society in, 222
demons in, 676
food supply decreases in, 785-86
government leaders in, 559, 663, 666, 718, 720-22, 725, 732
Hare Kṛṣṇa *mantra* for, 684
imitation incarnations in, 821

Kali-yuga (*continued*)
life span in, 471-72, 560
mantras in, 746
oceans in, 820
pākhaṇḍīs (fake *sannyāsīs*) in, 831, 832
people disturbed in, 833-34
perfection of life in, 163
population as *śūdra* in, 604, 666
sacrifice difficult in, 125, 161, 233, 234, 291-92
sacrifice for, 125, 233-34, 284, 291-92
saintly persons in, 661
saṅkīrtana chanting for, 233-34, 284, 291-92, 434, 555-56, 631, 788, 793, 818, 836, 844
sannyāsa in, 824, 834
taxation in, 721, 722
trees in, 818
varṇa & *āśrama* neglected in, 222
See also: Society
Kalpa, **479**
Kāma defined, 527
Kāma-dhenu cows, **816**-17
Kāmān defined, 638
Kāpālika sannyāsī, 830
Kapila Muni
aunt of, 276-77
in calf form, **798**
parents of, 799
at Pṛthu's horse sacrifices, **816**
Kapittha flower, 384
Kapota-vāyu defined, 578
Kāraṇodakaśāyī Viṣṇu. *See:* Mahā-Viṣṇu; Viṣṇu
Kardama Muni, **11**
airplane of, 582, 799
descendants of, **12-14**, **30-37**
Kapila son of, 277, 799
Karma
via bad association, 660
birth after birth, 311
bodies according to, 536
bondage via, 233
forces living beings, 371
living entities under, 524, 525, 531
Lord awards, **525,** 556
Karma (continued)
ritualistic ceremonies as, 840
See also: Pious activities; Sinful activity; Work
Karma-kāṇḍa process, 329
Karmaśreṣtha (son of Pulaha), **33**
Karmī(s), 374
competition among, 842
devotees compared with, 412, 453, 515, 576, 589-91, 601, 638, 640, 657
as envious, 842
as fruitive ritualists, 557
heavenly planets sought by, 412
in ISKCON temples, 604
See also: Materialists; Nondevotees; Soul, conditioned
Kārttikeya, Lord, 306
Kashmir state, king punishing thief in, 626
Kaśyapa, **13, 430**
Kaṭha Upaniṣad quoted on Lord maintaining living entities, 422, 671, 736-37
Kātyāyanī, goddess, *gopīs* worshiped, 553
Kavi (son of Prāṇa), **37**
Kavi (son of Yajña), **9**
Kavya defined, **797**
Kesava-śruti cited on *yoga,* 152
Keśinī (wife of Viśravā), **32**
Khyāti, **624**
Khyāti (wife of Bhṛgu), **36, 37**
Killing
of animals. *See:* Animal(s), sacrifice of; Animal slaughter; Hunting; Meat-eating
beneficial, 505
of blasphemers, **140,** 141
devotees avoid, 226, 227
of fake incarnation, 700
by king, 764
by Lord, **522,** 770-71
of demons, 225
necessary & unnecessary, 508, 511
by providence of envious, 226
religious principles on, 757, 758
by saintly persons, 679, 686
Kimpuruṣas, **800**

Kindness of Kṛṣṇa to devotee, 328
King(s)
  brāhmaṇas above, 628, 750
  citizens should respect, **629**
  devotees served by, 731
  duty of, 665-66, 718, 722, 737, 752, 787, 834, 847
  happiness for, **665,** 667
  of heavenly planets. *See:* Indra
  irreligion dispelled by, 834
  in Kali-yuga, 666
  killing by, 505, 764
  as Lord's representative, 629, 667-68, 735-37
  mystic *yoga* practiced by, 654
  opulences of, 654
  pious, **665-**66, **667**
  protects citizens, 665-67
  punishing thieves, 626, 666, 787
  punishment by, 189
  religious, 664
  sages above, 652, 663, 679
  as saintly sages, 475-76, 595, 654
  strong or weak, 172
  taxation by, **665,** 666, 667
  See also: Leaders, government; *Kṣatriyas;* Monarchy; Politicians; *specific kings*
Kingdom of God. *See:* Godhead, returning to; Spiritual world; Vṛndāvana
Kinnara(s), **41, 42, 543**
  in Kailāsa, **193-94**
  as subdemigods, 94
Kirātas, 692
Kīrtana. See: Chanting; *Saṅkīrtana*
Knowledge
  of Absolute Truth, 528, 529
  bogus, compared with bona fide, 746
  of Brahman for humans, 75
  compared to jewel on snake, 106
  in devotional service, 212-13
  about God. *See:* Supreme Lord, knowledge about
  of impersonal Absolute, 424
  by Kṛṣṇa consciousness, 568-69
  lacking in followers of *Vedas,* **72**
  levels of, 568-69
Knowledge (*continued*)
  about Lord
    all may have, 270-71
    beyond goodness mode, 283
    beyond material qualities, 283
    in devotee, 269
    in devotee alone, 282-83
    devotee may lack, 279-80
    by devotional service only, 268-69
    by direct acceptance, 270-71
    as energetic & energies, 279
    of His oneness with beings, 279
    of His pastimes, 270-71
    of His qualities, 282-83
    not in followers of *Vedas,* **262-**63,
    in *kaivalya* stage, 115
    in nonmaterialistic men, 278
    persons having, 279
    in *śuddha-sattva,* 114
    in *vasudeva* stage, 114-15
    via Vedic literature, **44**
  of Lord & living entity compared, 421
  Lord reveals, to devotee, 419, 420, 448
  material, Lord beyond, **268-**69
  of material world as illusion, 99
  of modes of work, 212-13
  pride in, 106
  spiritual
    complete scope of, 135-36
    Śiva gives, 135-36
    See also: Kṛṣṇa consciousness
  Supersoul prompts, 297
  as surrender to Lord, 409
  Vedas as source of, 80
  Vedic, 781, 794
  See also: Education; Philosophy; *Vedas*
Kratu, **624**
  sons of, **33-**34
Krishna. *See:* Kṛṣṇa
Kriyā (daughter of Dakṣa), **40**
Kriyā (Kratu's wife), **33,** 34
Krodha (Anger), **312**
Kṛṣṇa, Lord
  abode(s) of
    as beyond material qualities, 280-81
    desire trees in, 206
    See also: Spiritual world; *specific abodes*

Kṛṣṇa (*continued*)
accepted by *ācāryas*, 82
not accepted by some, 270
accepting Him directly, 270-71
activities (pastimes) of, 270-71
advent(s) of
devotee's view of, 370-71
as free & transcendental, 370-71
by His internal energy, 370-71
to relieve world, 46
as *akiñcana-gocara*, 106
above all, 287-88
as all & yet apart, 291, 298, 302
as all-pervading, 390
alone God, 287-88
approached by depleted men, 106
as Arjuna's chariot driver, 597
author of *Vedas*, 81-82
author's obeisances to, 2
as *avatārī*, 747
as basis of everything, 82, 297, 298
benedictions from, 349
beyond material creation, 82
body of, 531
books (two) about, 289-90
Brahmā instructed by, 82
as *caitya-guru*, 355
as cause of all causes, 519
chanting about
Kṛṣṇa consciousness movement for, 290
liberation via, **289**, 290
overcomes obstacles, 294
perfection via, **289**, 290
purification via, 156
as recommended now, 233-34
See also: Chanting; Hare Kṛṣṇa *mantra*; *Saṅkīrtana*
checked by none, 294
compared to
one with zeros, 107
sun, 502
considered ordinary by rascals, 269
controls & enters all, 390
controls *pradhāna* & *prakṛti*, 390
creator of *varṇa* & *āśrama*, 222
Deity form of. *See:* Deity form of Supreme Lord

Kṛṣṇa (*continued*)
demigods servants of, 287-88
as demigods' source, 297-98
demons fought, 800
desires fulfilled by, 343
devotees of. *See:* Devotees of Supreme Lord
direct acceptance of, 270-71
distress of, as bliss, 104
energy of, Lord appears by, 370-71
engaged disciple (Arjuna), 349
enters & controls all, 390
envy of Him in scholars, 111
as everything, 291-92
expansions of, all beings as, 287-88
expansions of, as *svāṁśa* & *vibhinnāṁśa*, 288
as father of all, 81
feet of. *See:* Kṛṣṇa, lotus feet of
not forced to appear, 370-71
form(s) of
as knowable, 270-71
manifests in Hare Kṛṣṇa *mantra*, 364
meditation on, 390
as God, 287-88
gopīs wanted to marry, 553
Govardhana Hill raised by, 723
hearing about. *See:* Hearing about Supreme Lord
incarnation(s) of. *See:* Incarnation(s) of Supreme Lord
incarnations originate from, 747-48
instructed Brahmā, 82
killed fake Vāsudeva, 700
killing by, can't be checked, 294
kindness of, to devotees, 328
knowable by all, 270-71
knowledge about. *See:* Knowledge, about Lord
lifted Govardhana Hill, 270-71
lotus feet of
devotees think of, 155
meditation on, 355
pilgrimage sites compared with, 203-4
pleasure from, 155
sanctifying effect of, 203-4

Kṛṣṇa
lotus feet of (*continued*)
shelter saintly persons, 203-4
as *tīrtha-pāda*, 203
love for, 597
manifests in Hare Kṛṣṇa *mantra*, 364
master of *pradhāna* & *puruṣa*, 390
meditation on. *See:* Meditation, on Lord
mercy of, on devotee, 328
as Nārāyaṇa, 359
of Nara-Nārāyaṇa, **46**
as Nārāyaṇa's basis, 359
one with & different from all, 291, 292, 298-99, 302
as original seed, 818
as origin of all, 82, 297, 298
pārijāta pastime of, 473-74
pastimes of, 270-71
"percentage" of, in beings, 15
pleasing Him pleases demigods, 234
praying to, purification by, 156
protection by, as best, 294
protects devotee, 294
quoted on worship to devotees, 91
relieves distress, 328, 331
remembering Him, purification by, 156
respected superiors, 218
revealed to pure consciousness, **113,** 114, 115
sanctifying effect of, 203-4
satisfied by *varṇa* & *āśrama*, 222
seen by purified senses, 115-16
service to. *See:* Devotional service
social orders part of, 222
society instructed by, 814
as source of all, 82, 297, 298
as source of demigods, 297-98
as Supreme Brahman, 731
as Supreme Lord, 677, 777, 814
as supreme spiritual master, 355
surabhi cows tended by, 816
surrender to
protection by, 286
transcends curses, 76-77
taught respect, 218
topics of, 749
transcendental status of, 82

Kṛṣṇa (*continued*)
as Vāsudeva, 114
above Viṣṇu, 287-88
as Viṣṇu, 356
Viṣṇu part of, 287-88
worship to. *See:* Worship, to Lord
as *yogeśvara*, 215
See also: Supreme Lord
Kṛṣṇa consciousness
advancing in, 553, 591
for all people, 366-67
Americans in, 344
begin right away, 339
beyond pious or impious acts, 275
beyond sacrifices, 275
bodily concept dispelled by, 546
brāhmaṇas spread, 559
brahminical training in, 344
in Caitanya's footsteps, 264
children should be trained in, 573
compared
to electrified copper, 114
to heated iron, 114
to one in front of zeros, 107
criticized by Indians, 366
dangers without, **263-64**
Deity worship in, 365-66
to deliver envious, 226
despite material desires, 343
duty continues in, 328
enables wonderful deeds, 390, 391-92
envy blocks, 812
for everyone, 366-67
exalted status of, 592
as freedom from material modes, 265-66
Godhead via, 656
in government, 477, 718
as greatest relief work, 264
by hating causes of devastation, 313
influences world, 393
in *kaivalya* stage, 115
knowing Lord via, 268-69
knowledge by, 568-69
Lord revealed in, **113,** 114, 115
material assets check, 106
material assets used in, 106-7
material desires rejected in, 446

Kṛṣṇa consciousness (*continued*)
material exhaustion helps, 106
māyā contrasted to, 502
movement for. *See:* Kṛṣṇa consciousness movement
necessity of, 559
with ordinary consciousness, 391-92
persons in. *See:* Devotee(s)
preachers of. *See:* Preacher(s)
as pure condition, **113,** 114
pure stage of, attainment of, 114
pure stage of, Lord revealed in, **113,** 114, 115
purifies consciousness, 239
purifying power of, 591
purpose of, 290
reaction absent in, 7
regulative principles in, 385
remains after rebirth, 243
retiring from family life for, 627
with rituals of *Vedas,* 248
sacrifice (*yajña*) in, 284
Śiva in, **113**
society dead without, 276
society needs, 790
as *śuddha-sattva,* 114
test for, by spiritual master, 337, 339
transforms material consciousness, 114
truth realized by, 564
universal propagation of, 366-67
universal work of, 366
welfare work in, 589
See also: Devotional service; Kṛṣṇa consciousness movement
Kṛṣṇa consciousness movement
associating with devotees in, 414, 591
austerities in, 478
basis of, 556
devotional service in, 414
disciples in, message to, 585-86
festivals in, 793
Godhead in, 575
instructions received by, 784
invitation from, 591
leaders in, instruction to, 573
parallel processes in, 613-14
purpose of, 523, 572, 604, 671
Kṛṣṇa consciousness movement (*contd.*)
saṅkīrtana-yajña by, 434, 817
temples of, 604
as world's hope, 788
See also: Saṅkīrtana-yajña
Kṛṣṇadāsa Kavirāja Gosvāmī cited on material consciousness, 448
Kṛṣṇa defined, 691
Kṛṣṇa-kathā (topics of Kṛṣṇa), 749
defined, 274, 366
Kṛṣṇaloka (Goloka)
beyond material qualities, 280-81
desire trees in, 206
Kṛṣṇa-parāyaṇaḥ defined, 592
Kṛṣṇa-prasāda. See: Prasāda
Kṣatriya(s)
Americans not, 344
as "arms" of society, 345
blasphemy if heard by, 141
boys trained as, 344
brāhmaṇas guide, 666
contrasted to *brāhmaṇas,* 344
defined, 83
Dhruva as, **333-34,** 511, 598
discussed by Nārada, **333-34**
duty of, 554-55
family spirit kept by, 334
fight at marriages, 182
fighting principles of, 825
hunting allowed for, 643
jewels gathered by, 820
killing by, 508
lionlike, 738
ornaments decorating, 492
as part of Lord's cosmic form, 222
permanent class of, 83
pride in, **333-34**
protected people, 750
qualifications for, two given, 334
in social body, 691
spirit in, vs. *brāhmaṇas,* 344
sporting spirit of, 485
training required for, 598
See also: King(s); Government(s), leader(s); Politician(s); *specific* kṣatriyas
Kṣema (son of Dharma), **40**
Kṣema-darśinaḥ defined, 651

Kṣirodakaśāyī Viṣṇu, 28, 398, 440
  See also: Supersoul
Kuhū (daughter of Aṅgirā), **31**
Kulaśekhara, King, quoted on desiring devotional service, 439
Kumāras, four
  angered Brahmā, 211-12
  Brahmā angry at, 801
  as *brahmacārīs* (celibate), **309,** 310
  disciplic succession from, 746
  refused to marry, 211-12
  Sanaka, **285, 293**
  saw Lord, 444
  sitting with Śiva, **211-**12
  See also: Sanaka-kumāra; Sanandana-kumāra; Sanātana-kumāra; Sanat-kumāra
Kumbhakarṇa, **32**
Kuṅkuma, **204-5**
Kuntīdevī, 106
Kuśa grass of Brahmā, **22,** 23
Kutsa, **624**
Kuvera, Lord
  abode of, **206**
  benediction to Dhruva offered by, **550, 551**
  Dhruva
    advised by, **545-48, 550**
    offended, **541**
    pleased, **544, 553**
  parents of, **32**
  present for Pṛthu from, **703**
  quoted. *See:* Kuvera quoted
  sitting with Śiva, **211,** 212
  as treasurer of demigods, 552
Kuvera quoted
  on bodily concept of life, **546**
  on Supreme Lord, **547, 548**
  on time, **545**
Kuyoginaḥ defined, 649

L

Laborer class. *See: Śūdras*
Laghimā-siddhi defined, 363
Lake of Satī (Alakanandā), **200-201**
Lakṣmī (goddess of fortune)
  always serves Lord, **329,** 330
  always with Lord, 6, 277
  born with Yajña, **5-**7
  demigods worship, **329,** 330
  incarnation of, as Dakṣiṇā, 6, 8
  Lord not attached to, **273**
  on Lord's chest, 256
  as Lord's feminine feature, 359
  as Nārāyaṇa's wife, 8
  as worshiped for opulence, 330
Lakṣmī-Nārāyaṇa, 8
Lamentation
  soul beyond, 335
  as useless, 322, 336
Law(s)
  on giving daughter for son, 3
  of Manu, 488, 508, 781
    on punishment, 189
  of nature
    on animal slaughter, 508
    punishes thieves, 788-89
    on suffering, 818
    surrendered soul surpasses, 572
  of nature. *See:* Nature, law of
  punishment via, 189
  Vedic, transcendentalists surpass, **143, 144,** 145
Law & order
  execution of, Lord's mercy compared to, 520
  maintenance of, 508
Leaders, government. *See:* Government(s), leader(s)
Learned person
  spiritual vision in, 734
  symptoms of, 731
  See also: Sages
Learning (education)
  compared to jewel on snake, 106
  pride in, 106
  in service to Lord, 106-7
  See also: Knowledge
Lehya defined, 819
Liberated soul(s)
  beyond body's conditions, 669
  devotee as, 441, 768, 769

Liberated soul(s) (*continued*)
following in footsteps of, **782,** 783
materialists ignore, 783, 784
See also: Devotee(s); Pure devotee(s); *Nitya-mukta;* Spiritual master(s)
Liberation (*mukti*)
via associating with devotees, 154
beyond happiness & distress, **340**
beyond pain & pleasure, 335-36
via chanting about Lord, **289,** 290, 619
defined, 211
desire absent in, 374-75, 377
devotee gets, 223-24, 350-51
devotional service
from level of, 374-75
surpasses, 375, 550, 552
via devotional service, 441, 506, 527, 566-67
via devotion this life, 382, 385
of Dhruva, **566**
as freedom
from misery, 211
from reactions, 7
frustrated men attempt, 137
given by devotees, 226, 229-30
via hating causes of devastation, 313
via hearing about Lord, **289,** 290
human chance for, 289, 290
impersonal, as sense gratification, 375
Lord gives, 440-41
via Lord's will, **223-**24
via meditating on Lord, 211
merging with Lord as, 375
for preachers of Kṛṣṇa, 290
pure devotee rejects, 553
purification for, 313
via purifying desire, 527
via sacrifices, 284
via satisfying Lord, **514**
sense gratification absent in, 374-75
Śiva gives, 137
as surrender to Lord, 229
via tolerating happiness & distress, **340**
types of, 440-41
via *Vedas,* 80, 83
vimukti stage of, 375
via worship of Lord, 327
Liberation (*continued*)
via *yoga* process, 152-53
See also: Freedom; Independence; Purification; Salvation
Life
air
controlled via *yoga,* 152
See also: Breathing exercise
chemicals can't produce, 518
defeat in, 445
eternal. *See:* Eternal life
goal of. *See:* Goal of life
human. *See:* Human being(s)
of Lord & living entity contrasted, **525**
material. *See:* Material life
on moon & other planets, 805
span of
on earth & heavenly planets, 473
in goodness mode, 517
in *yugas,* 471-72, 560
species of
desires produce, 519, 527
number of, 417, 732
as spiritual energy, 407-8
See also: Living entities; Soul
Light
consciousness compared to, 15-16
in material & spiritual worlds, **589**
See also: Brahman (impersonal Absolute); Sun
Lion
in calf form, **803**
Pṛthu compared to, **738**
Liquor, demons like, 795, 796
See also: Intoxication
Living entity (entities)
beyond pain & pleasure, 335
born by *karma,* 311
compassion for, in devotee, 301
consciousness in, compared with Lord's, 15-16
consciousness varies in, 15-16
covered by material qualities, 298-99
deficiencies of, four given, 259
desire as symptom of, 453, 527
directed by Lord, 299-300
as diseased parts of Lord, 301

Living entity (entities) (*continued*)
duty of, to serve Lord, 306
as embodied, 732, 734
as empowered incarnations, 846
as energy of Lord, 279
father of, Kṛṣṇa as, 81
"female" in relation to Lord, 306
forced by nature, 371
generated to fill universe, 9-10
in goodness vs. other, 282
gradations among, 15
"independence" declared by, 524, 533, 546
independent of Lord never, **300**
as *jīvas,* 15
karma carried by, 311
karma controls, 524, 525, 531
kinds of, in time of Svāyambhuva, 9-10
as Kṛṣṇa's servants, 288
Lord
compared with, **420-21,** 422, 531, 547
feeds, 802, 804-5
saves, 549
as Lord's
dependents, 511
energy, 299
expansions, 287-88
marginal energy, 448-49, 773
parts & parcels, 15, 302, 399, 449, 451, 513, 525, 527, 546, 846
servants, 422, 441
sons, 81
in material & spiritual worlds, 572
in material modes, 282, 299
material vs. spiritual, 208, 394-95
in material world, 524, 527, 533
modes of nature control, 421, 802
nature exploited by, 527
nondifferent from Lord, **297-99, 300-2,** 379
"percentage" of Kṛṣṇa in, 15
pure constitutionally, 113-14
as *puruṣa,* 390
as servants, 418
should renounce sense gratification, 785
should satisfy Lord, 818
as spirit souls, 536

Living entity (entities) (*continued*)
surrender by, 357
two types of, 733
Vedas given to, 81
See also: Animal(s); Human being(s); Life; Soul(s)
Lobha (Greed), **312**
Logic of *nagna-mātṛkā,* 392
Lord Caitanya. *See:* Caitanya
Lotus feet of Lord. *See:* Kṛṣṇa, lotus feet of; Supreme Lord, lotus feet of
Lotus flower(s)
in Kailāsa, **201,** 202, **207**
of Lord & goddess of fortune, 331
Lord's face like, 331
Lotus stem
from Garbhodakaśāyi Viṣṇu, **419**
planets supported by, 759
Love
forgotten in material life, 127-28
for Lord
in devotee, 400, 428
by hearing about Lord, 597
Lord seen by, 399, 558, 617
in offerings to Lord, 296
See also: Devotional service; Kṛṣṇa consciousness
Lust
created via nice atmosphere, 208
need to avoid, 69
See also: Desire(s), material; Sense gratification; Sex life

M

Mada, 123
Madhuvana forest, **351,** 352, **398**
as auspicious, **376**
Madhvācārya, Śrīla, 82
Madhyandinam, **622**
Māgadha (poet)
praised Pṛthu, **707, 708**
Pṛthu's identity known to, 714
Magic powers. *See:* Mystic powers
Mahā-bhāgavata defined, 552
See also: Devotees, pure devotees
Mahābhārata, 4

Mahā defined, 211
Mahā-mantra. See: Hare Kṛṣṇa *mantra*
Mahāmāyā, 715
  See also: Māyā
Mahātmā
  Dakṣa as, 176
  defined, 176
Mahat-tattva
  defined, 390, 774
  includes all material entities, 390
Mahā-Viṣṇu, Lord, 28
  See also: Viṣṇu
Maintenance of offspring, 517
Maitreya Muni
  desired to describe piety, 316
  heard from Uddhava, **307**
  narrative arrangement by, 314
  Vidura inspired, **748,** 749
  as Vidura's spiritual master, **630**
Maitreya quoted
  on *brāhmaṇas* & demigods glorifying Pṛthu, **698, 699**
  on Dhruva, **599**
  on Dhruva & Kuvera, **543, 551**
  on Pṛthu
    Brahmā & Indra, **848**
    & citizenry, **749–50**
    & Earth planet, **779**
    & his praisers, **713**
    horse sacrifices by, **811**
  on sages' anxiety in Aṅga's absence, **651**
  on Vena, **678**
Maitrī (daughter of Dakṣa), **40**
Mālā of false devotee, 846
Malicious persons, **107–8**
Mānava defined, 488
Mango & devotional service, analogy of, 415
Maṇimān, **123, 179**
Mankind. *See:* Human being(s); Society, human
Mantra(s)
  airplanes run via, 205
  in animal sacrifice, 631, 639, 835
  animals rejuvenated by, 125, 272
  Bhṛgu's use of, **161,** 162
  bogus, compared with bona fide, 746
Mantra(s) (continued)
  for *brāhmaṇas* only, 365
  brāhmaṇas' power in, 161, 162
  brahma-śāpa, 628
  chanted at Dakṣa's sacrifice, **124,** 125
  chanting of, 632
    impossible now, 161, 162–63
    rules for, 365
  in Deity worship, 369
  devotees (Vaiṣṇavas) may chant, 365
  disciplic succession needed for, 363, 365
  given by spiritual master, 363, 365
  Hare Kṛṣṇa *mantra. See:* Hare Kṛṣṇa *mantra*
  as meant to please Viṣṇu, 284
  must be via disciplic succession, 363, 365
  must be via spiritual master, 365
  for oblations to Śiva, 128–29
  for offering oblations, 128–29
  oṁ namo bhagavate vāsudevāya, worship of Lord by, 372
  praṇava (oṁ)
    for *brāhmaṇas* only, 365
    rules for chanting, 365
    for Vaiṣṇavas (devotees), 365
  for protecting sacrifices, **161**
  qualification for chanting, 365
  Ṛbhu demigods called by, **161,** 162
  requirement for receiving, 363, 365
  for sacrifices, 284, 836
  for seeing flying beings, **363**
  svāhā, 128–29
  tested on animals, 125, 184, 272
  Vena's body preserved by, **682,** 690
  viṣṇu-, 446
  worked wonders, 161, 162
  worship of Lord by, 372
  See also: Hare Kṛṣṇa *mantra;* Sound, transcendental
Manu(s)
  Cākṣuṣa, **624**
  humans as descendants of, 488, 535
  laws of, 488, 508, 781
  Svāyambhuva. *See:* Svāyambhuva Manu
Manu defined, 217
Manu-smṛti cited on family duty, 378–79
Manuṣya defined, 535

Marīci
  chief of sages, **9**
  descendants from, **9, 13, 14**
Marijuana (*gāñjā*), 78, 79, 97
Mārkaṇḍeya Muni, **37**
Marriage
  according to status, 66
  bodies shared in, 122
  decorated wives attend, **92, 94**
  of Dhruva, **479**
  divorce in, 122
  dowry system for, 97
  favored wife in, 317-18
  giving daughter in, for son, 3
  as "home" life, 310
  ideal life in, 8
  kṣatriya fighting at, 182
  Lakṣmī-Nārāyaṇa ideal in, 8
  parents' duty to arrange, 66
  pleasing wife in, 8
  for producing son, 635-36, 645
  satisfaction in, 8
  of Śiva & Satī
    Brahmā advised, **65**
    Dakṣa regrets, **63, 65**
  in Vedic culture, 642
  womanly weakness in, 122
  of Yajña & Dakṣiṇā, **8**
  See also: Family life; *Gṛhastha(s)*
Master, duty to protect, 160
Material assets, 106-7
Material body. *See:* Body, material
Material bondage, 233
  See also: Māyā
Material desire. *See:* Desire(s), material
Material elements. *See:* Elements, material
Material energy. *See:* Energies of Supreme Lord, material
Materialism
  based on woman, 96
  of Dakṣa, 105
  in followers of *Vedas,* **72, 74**
  pride in, **106**
Materialist(s)
  Absolute Truth unknown to, 607
  avoid them, 68, 153-54
  benefit by Śiva, **136-37**
Materialist(s) (*continued*)
  Brahmā discusses, **226, 228, 229**
  can't know Lord, **268-**69, 278
  compared to snakes, 106
  consider God dead, 216-17
  cursed by Nandīśvara, **71-75**
  degraded via offenses, **134-**35
  demigods as, 67
  demigod worship by, 87
  don't accept Lord's acts, 270
  envy in, 106, 111, **226**
  fall down by offenses, 134-35
  frustrated, attempt liberation, 137
  goddess of fortune sought by, 695
  interpret *Śrīmad-Bhāgavatam,* 270.
  as killed already, **226**
  liberated soul ignored by, 783, 784
  Lord as beyond, 216-17
  offend great souls, **134-35**
  pride in, 106
  purified by worshiping Lord, 330
  sacrifices
    necessary for, 232-34
    offered by, 130
    recommended for, 284
  saintly persons avoid, 620
  Śiva enlightens, 135
  Vedas followed by, **72, 74**
  worship demigods, 87
  worship goddess of fortune, 330
  See also: Atheist(s); Demon(s); *Karmī(s);* Nondevotee(s); Conditioned soul(s)
Material life
  compared to dreaming, 448-49
  as forgetting supreme controller, 533
  four principles of, 137
  modern man pursues, 671
  spiritual life compared with, 572
  See also: Materialism; Materialist(s)
Material nature
  "covers" Lord, 44
  fallen souls try to dominate, 442, 527
  forces birth, 371
  law of. *See:* Law(s), of nature
  Lord directs, 516, 517, 519, 768
  modes of. *See:* Modes of nature

Material possessions, 106-7
 See also: Wealth
Material world
 basis of, Lord as, **43,** 298, 299
 bondage in, by selfish work, 233
 Brahman causes, **423**
 cause of, Lord as, 44
 compared
  to dream, **562-**63
  to fire, **413,** 414
  to ocean, **413,** 414
  with spiritual world, 103-4, 394-95
 conserved in Lord, 286
 created by Brahmā secondarily, 2
 creation, maintenance, & destruction in, 281
 creation of
  karma continues in, 311
  in two stages, 2
 dangers in, **263-64**
 demons & devotees in, 255
 destruction of. *See:* Annihilation of universe(s)
 devotee's view of, 414
 devotee uninterested in, 563
 devotional service in, 415
 as energy of Lord, **43,** 299
 envy in, 812-13
 freedom from, 514
  See also: Liberation
 goodness not pure in, 169
 "I-&-mine" conception in, 537-38
 as illusion, 99
 living entities coming to, 524, 527, 533
 living entities in, 572
 Lord(s) of, 28
 Lord's existence precedes, 25
 Lord's presence in, 532
 as Lord's universal form, 43
 majority in, demons as, 255
 material perception of, compared with spiritual, 733-34
 motives in, 603
 Nārada's travels in, 347
 pleasing to devotee, 395
 pleasure & pain in, 103-4
 as problematic, 395
Material world (*continued*)
 protection in, by surrender to Lord, 267
 purpose of, 784-85
 reality in, 43
 as reflection of spiritual world, 99, 104
 satisfaction impossible in, 157
 sin inevitable in, 286
 situated in Lord, **43**
 spiritual world compared with, 459, 563, 588
 spiritual world illuminates, **589**
 suffocated by Dhruva, **393, 394**
 surrender in, 357
 as "unsteady field," 70
 variety in, 43
 women in, compared with spiritual world, 208
 See also: Creation (act of); Creation, the; Earth planet; Heavenly planet(s); Material nature
Mathurā, 352, 430, 809
Matsara defined, 812
Matter, subtle (*pradhāna*), 390
Māyā
 compared to darkness, 502
 conditioned soul struggles against, 451
 defined, 407, 773
 devotees save one from, 226, 229
 devotee surpasses, 463
 Dhruva &, 537
 false satisfaction in, 290
 Hare Kṛṣṇa *mantra* dispels, 502, 503
 human influenced by, **289,** 290
 Lord exists beyond, 25
 Lord's devotees surpass, 229
 two types of, 715
 See also: Bodily concept of life; Duality, material; Energies of Supreme Lord, material; Material nature
Māyā (Cheating), **311, 312**
Maya demon, **800**
Māyāvāda philosophy taught by Śiva, 78
Māyāvādīs. *See:* Impersonalist(s)
Māyayāpahṛta-jñānāḥ defined, 785
Meat-eating
 animal sacrifice compared with, 125
 by birds, 803

Meat-eating (*continued*)
cannibalistic, 787
in emergency only, 763
by followers of Śiva, 79
Medhā (daughter of Dakṣa), **40**
by "*sannyāsīs*," 831
by Yakṣas, Rākṣasas, ghosts, & witches, **801**
See also: Animal slaughter; Food; *Prasāda*
Medical experiments, animals in, 639
Meditation
in *aṣṭāṅga-yoga*, 354
banyan tree for, **210**
on Brahman, 356
brāhmaṇa who worshiped by, 372
chanting Hare Kṛṣṇa as, 355, 363-64, 371
on Deity form of Lord, 369, 372
by Dhruva on Lord, **388, 389, 396**
as difficult, **337-38**
easiest form of, 363-64
goal of, as thinking of Lord within, 355
impersonal
compared with meditation on Lord, 356
as difficult, 396
as invention, 356
as not recommended, 369
invented, compared with authorized, 361
liberation via, 210-11
on Lord
amazes world, 390, 391-92
in *aṣṭāṅga-yoga*, 354
brahmānanda in, 217
via chanting Hare Kṛṣṇa, 355, 363-64
compared with impersonal meditation, 356
at devastation, **285**
by Dhruva, **388, 389, 396**
fixing oneself in, **361**, 362
as goal of meditation, 355
as highest *yoga*, 390
on Him in heart, 355-62
on His form, worship by, 372
on His lotus feet, 155, 355
on His pastimes, 371
intelligence great in, 111
liberation by, 210-11
must follow authorities, 361
Meditation
on Lord (*continued*)
pleasure in, 155
purification via, 155, 156
as real meditation, 356, 389
via remembrance, 210-11
samādhi (trance) in, 217, 363
by Śiva, 116, **265**
worship via, 372
yoga as, 389
by *yogīs*, 210-11
must follow authorities, 361
mystic, **337, 338**
as recommended in Vedic literature, 356
as remembering Lord, 210-11
in *samādhi* (trance)
as absorption in thinking of Lord, 145
via chanting Hare Kṛṣṇa, 355
as controlled by Lord, 116
defined, 145, 217
Deity worship as, 362
in meditating on Lord, 217, 362
Śiva in, 116, **216**
by Satī on Śiva, **155**
by Śiva on Lord's lotus feet, **265**
on Supersoul
by Atri Muni, 20
by Śiva, 111, 116
on Viṣṇu
in *aṣṭāṅga-yoga*, 354
via remembrance, 210-11
by Śiva, **265**
by *yogīs*, 210-11
worship via, 372
yoga as, 210-11
by *yogīs* on Viṣṇu, 210-11
See also: Kṛṣṇa consciousness; Trance; *Yoga*
Meetings of superior, equal, or inferior, **341**
Memory benefit by celibacy, 309-10
Menakā (Menā), 156, **305**
Men as hardhearted, 126-27
Mental speculators. *See: Jñānī(s);* Philosopher(s), speculative
Merchants. *See: Vaiśyas*

Mercy of devotees on others, 226, 228, 230
Mercy of Lord. *See:* Supreme Lord, mercy of
Merging with Supreme
devotional service excels, 412
impersonalists fall down after, 441
Meru, daughters of, **37**
Metaphysics. *See:* Devotional service; Kṛṣṇa consciousness; Philosophy
Milk
cow makes, 761, 790
food symbolized as, **792–98, 800–805**
ocean of, 435, 440
poisoned, analogy of, 106
products from, 817
in snake-sage example, 802
of *surabhi* cow, 816-17
in swan-*paramahaṁsa* analogy, 438
Millenniums. *See: Yugas,* four
Mind
cleansing of, 313
compared to mirror, 115
concentrated on Lord, 327
disciplined via breathing exercise, 354–55
disciplined via chanting Hare Kṛṣṇa, 355
engaged in devotional service, 116
giving up material thoughts, 355
purified to know Lord, 115-16
See also: Meditation
Misery
Kṛṣṇa can mitigate, 328, 331
material, compared with spiritual, 103–4
See also: Suffering
Mitra (son of Kratu), **35, 237**
Modern Age. *See:* Kali-yuga; Society
Mode(s) of nature
all auspicious, 221
character according to, 802
compared to criminal department, 221
competition among, 168-69
controlling deities of, **24–25,** 65, 221, 299
control living beings, 299
cover living beings, 299
creation, maintenance, & annihilation by, 516, **517**
Mode(s) of nature (*continued*)
demigods manifest in, 281
devotees beyond, 281
elements created by, 774
freedom from, in Kṛṣṇa consciousness, 265-66
goodness. *See:* Goodness, mode of
ignorance. *See:* Ignorance, mode of
incarnations of, **24–25,** 65, 221, 299
living entities under, 421, 802
Lord beyond, 25, **280–**81, **282, 421, 518,** 519, **530,** 531, 768
passion. *See:* Passion, mode of
residences according to, 581
sufferings in, 15
surrender to Lord dispels, 670
temple above, 581
vasudeva platform above, 440
See also: Goodness; Ignorance; Passion
Mogul period, opulence in, 472
Mokṣa. See: Liberation
Monarchy
decline of, 555, 665
democracy compared with, 626
family power within, 621
true & false conception of, 476-77
See also: King(s)
Money
distribution of, impractical, 434
government inflates, 725
for Lord's service, 695
as secretly kept, 725
See also: Gold; Opulence(s); Wealth
Monism
true meaning of, 279
See also: Oneness
Monist(s)
followers of Śiva as, 78
vision of, 279
See also: Impersonalist(s)
Moon
in astronaut-demigod worshiper analogy, 412
life on, 805
travel to, 575
Moon-demigod, **705**
See also: Soma

Mother(s)
  Earth compared to, 754
  as enemy, 627
  son &, 587, 642
  See also: Family life; *Gṛhastha(s)*
Mountain(s)
  Kailāsa. *See:* Kailāsa
  minerals for, **804**
  in rain compared with Dhruva in battle, **487**
Ṛkṣa (of Atri Muni), **17, 18**
Mṛkaṇḍa (son of Dhātā), **37**
Mṛṣā (Falsity), **311**
Mṛtyu (Death), **312**
Mṛtyum amṛtam defined, 533
Muda (son of Dharma), **40**
Mūḍha defined, 269, 785
Mudrikāṣṭaka in Śiva worship, 79
Mukti
  as devotional service, 375
  See also: Liberation
Mukta. See: Liberated soul(s)
Mukta-liṅgaḥ defined, 567
Mukunda-mālā-stotra quoted on desiring devotional service, 439
Muni-coditāḥ defined, 713
Murder, punishment for, 189
Mūrti (daughter of Dakṣa), **40**
Music
  Gandharvas & Apsarās milked, **796**
  glorified Pṛthu, **699**
Mystic(s)
  oneness seen by, 279
  pray to Viṣṇu, **279, 280**
  See also: Yogī(s), mystic
Mystic meditation, **337, 338**
Mystic power(s)
  of demons, 800
  eight kinds of, 363
  of Kimpuruṣas, **800**
  of Pṛthu, **765**
  of Pṛthu's slippers, **705–6**
  of Siddhas, **798–99**
  of Vidyādharas, **798–99**
  of *yogīs*, 799
  See also: Yoga, mystic; *Yogī(s)*, mystic

N

Nāgas, **21**
Nagna-mātṛkā logic, 392
Naiṣāda race, **691, 692**
Namaḥ śivāya svāhā, chanting of, 128-29
Names differ but source is one, 299
Names of Lord. *See:* Chanting, Hare Kṛṣṇa; Hare Kṛṣṇa *mantra*
Nanda (Viṣṇu's servitor), **260**
Nanda & Sunanda (Viṣṇu's associates)
  bodily features of, **569–**70
  Dhruva
    assured by, about Sunīti, 584, **585**
    invited by, to Viṣṇuloka, **573–78**
    offered obeisances to, **570–72, 580**
  at Pṛthu's horse sacrifices, **815**
Nandā River, **203**
Nandī, **123**
Nandīśvara, **70, 179**
  curses of, **70–75**
    effects of, 73-74, 75-76
    as improper, 70
  follower of Śiva, **70**
Napoleon Bonaparte, 522-23
Nara (of Nara-Nārāyaṇa Ṛṣi), **46**
Nārada Muni, 663, 678
  addresses king, **377, 380–82**
  advises Dhruva, **334–41, 349–74**
  as all-knowing, 333
  as audience supreme, 214
  as authority on Lord, 357-58
  as Bhagavān, 349
  as *brahmacārī*, **309,** 310
  can bless like God, 349
  compared to sun, 347
  compassionate for Dhruva, **348**
  could fulfill Dhruva's desire, 346, 347, 349
  Dhruva glorified by, **614,** 615
  as Dhruva's spiritual master, 403, 446, 447, 576, 598
  discusses
    aṣṭāṅga-yoga, **353, 354**
    being satisfied, **336**
    Deity worship, **367, 369**
    Dhruva, **380–82**

Nārada Muni
discusses (*continued*)
difficulty for Dhruva, **337–39**
etiquette in meetings, **341**
fulfillment of devotee, **373**
insult, **333–35**
kṣatriyas, 333-35
mantra for Dhruva, **363, 364**
meditation on Lord's pastimes, **370**
praṇava (oṁ) mantra, **364**
protection by Lord, **380–81**
tolerance, **340**
Yamunā site, **351**
goes to king, **376**
good background of, 311
hell visited by, 352
instructed by Śiva, **214**
Lord glorified by, 614
news carried by, **165,** 166
pāñcarātrika process introduced by, **613,** 614
at Pṛthu's horse sacrifices, **816**
quoted on Dhruva, **595, 596, 598**
sent by Lord, 333
snake &, 539
as space traveler, 587
tests Dhruva, 337, 339
travels everywhere doing good, 347
as *tri-kāla-jña,* 333
Nārada-pañcarātra, 78
as directory of devotional service, 614
quoted on devotional service, 510, 619
Naradeva defined, 737
Narādhamāḥ defined, 785
Nara-nārāyaṇa, king as, 629
Nara-Nārāyaṇa Ṛṣi
appearance ("birth") of, **40–43**
as Arjuna & Kṛṣṇa, **46**
demigods pray to, **43, 44**
Dhruva's arrow from, **501**
as energy & energetic, **46**
parents of, **40**
Nārāyaṇa, Lord
appears in arena of sacrifice, **253–55**
avoided Dakṣa's sacrifice, 188
beauty of, **254, 255, 256**
Nārāyaṇa (*continued*)
beyond material knowledge, 268-69
bodily effulgence of, 254, 258
as cause supreme, 297
compared to sunrise, 255
demigods' obeisances to, **257**
in eight-armed form, **255**
as energy & energetic, 46
face & smile of, **256**
as husband of Lakṣmī, 8
Kṛṣṇa as, 359
Kṛṣṇa as basis of, 359
as Nara-Nārāyaṇa, 46
ornaments of, **255, 256**
as transcendental cause, 268
See also: Supreme Lord; Viṣṇu
Nārāyaṇa Ṛṣi. *See:* Nara-Nārāyaṇa Ṛṣi
Nārāyaṇa-śilā at sacrifices, 350
Nārāyaṇāstra defined, 502
Narottama dāsa Ṭhākura cited
on desiring to serve Lord, 527
on pilgrimages, 203-4
Narottama dāsa Ṭhākura quoted
on anger, 130
on saintly persons, spiritual master, & scriptures, 714
Nāstikas defined, 80
Nature, material. *See:* Material nature
Nawab Hussain Shah, 735
Nectar of Devotion, The, 633
See also: Bhakti-rasāmṛta-sindhu
Nescience. *See:* Ignorance
New Delhi, 809
Niḥspṛha defined, 453
Nikṛti (Cunning), **312**
Niraya (Hell), **312**
Nirguṇa, Lord as, 282
Nirṛti (demon), **311**
Nirvāṇa
defined, **618**
in Śiva worship, 79
Nirvindhyā River, **18**
Niṣāda (Bāhuka), **689–92**
Niśita, **623**
Niṣkāma defined, 453
Nitya-baddha defined, 733
See also: Conditioned soul(s)

Nitya-mukta defined, 733
See also: Liberated soul(s)
Nityānanda, Lord, 227, 502
Niyati (daughter of Meru), **37**
Nondevotee(s)
associating with, 153-54
Bhagavad-gītā cited on, 785
compared to rat in cat's mouth, 582
death of, 582
devotees contrasted to, 407, 408, 582, 612, 710
Earth's products misused by, **784,** 785
false God accepted by, 710
in Lord's external energy, 407, 408
world full of, 620
See also: Atheist(s); Demon(s); Impersonalist(s); Materialist(s)
Nonviolence, material, 505
Nṛsiṁhadeva, Lord, 766, 777

O

Obeisance(s)
by Atri Muni to deities, **22**
by author, 1-2
to body, 111-12
by Brahmā & Śiva to Lord's feet, 331
daṇḍavat (falling down), 22
by demigods to Śiva, **216, 218, 219**
by demigods to Viṣṇu, 257
by devotees, 112-13
to devotees, 230
by devotee to Lord, 116-17
if Lord reveals Himself, 116
to Lord
in body of all, 111-13
as person, 116-17
by Lord to superiors, 218
by self-realized souls, 111-13
by Śiva to Brahmā, **218**
by Śiva to Supersoul, 110-11, **113,** 116
by spiritual master to disciple, 112
to superiors, Lord taught, 218
by Vāmana to father, **218**
See also: Prayer(s)
Oblation(s)
accepted by fire-gods, **46-**47
Oblation(s) (*continued*)
by Bhṛgu save sacrifice, **161-62**
to fire-gods by impersonalists, **48**
for purification, **251-52**
at sacrifices, 128-29
to Śiva at sacrifices, 128-29
to Viṣṇu, accepted by Him, **260**
See also: Sacrifice(s)
Occupational duty. *See:* Duty; *Varṇāśrama-dharma*
Ocean
compared with Yakṣas, **488,** 489
"Dr. Frog" couldn't calculate, 528
jewels from, 819, 820
in Kali-yuga, 820
material existence compared to, **413,** 414
of milk, 435, 440
outer space compared to, 759
in Pṛthu's time, **706, 819**
as Varuṇa's kingdom, 725
Offenses
avoidance of, 542
of blasphemy, **140,** 141, 227
See also: Blasphemy
compared to mad elephant, 69
in Deity worship, 252, 633
to devotees (Vaiṣṇavas), 432, 680, 846
to devotees, effect of, 69, **134-**35
devotees tolerate, 226-27, 228, 229
to great souls, **134-**35
happiness impossible by, **189**
to Lord, 680, 681, 846
by materialistic men, **134-**35
punishment for, as good, 189
via thinking Lord mundane, 371
Offerings to Deity, 633
Old men, two types of, 730
Oṁ namo bhagavate vāsudevāya, chanting of
by *brāhmaṇas* & Vaiṣṇavas, 365
as confidential, 363
in Deity worship, **364,** 365
received in disciplic succession, 363
for seeing flying beings, **363**
worship to Lord by, 372
Oneness
devotee's compassion as, 300-301

Oneness (*continued*)
devotee's vision of, 302-3
impersonalists' concept of, 371, 580
of Lord & all, 279, 291, 292, **297**-98, 299-302, 521, 768
meaning of monism, 279
of merging with Lord, 375
perfection of, 572
as sense gratification, 375
of soul & Supersoul, Māyāvāda idea of, 396
true & false, 546
See also: Merging with Supreme
Opulence(s)
ancient, compared with modern, 472
bad effect of, 106
compared to jewel on snake, 106
controlled by Lord, 330
of Dhruva's era, 468
dissatisfaction in, 157
given by Satī, 147
material
detachment from, 648
pure devotee unchanged by, 428
by worshiping Lakṣmī & Viṣṇu, 695
See also: Gold; Money; Mystic powers; Wealth
obtained by Śiva worship, 147
obtained by worship of Lord, 330
pride in, **106**
of Pṛthu, **820,** 821
in renunciation, **146**
in service to Lord, 106-7
in Śiva, **146,** 212
Orders of life. *See: Varṇāśrama-dharma*
Ornaments
of demigod women, **92, 94**
of Satī from father, 97
sold for *gāñjā*, 97
on women at ceremonies, 92
women desire, 94, 96
Oversoul. *See:* Supersoul

P

Padma Purāṇa cited on liberation, 441
Pain
material compared with spiritual, 103-4
Pain (*continued*)
via words of relative, 108-9, 118
See also: Suffering
Pain (descendant of Brahmā), **312**
Paintings of Lord, 358
Pākhaṇḍī defined, 823, 831
Palace of Uttānapāda, **470, 471,** 472, **473, 474**
Palm of hand, divine lines on, **700**
Palm tree juice in Śiva worship, 79
Pañcama-puruṣārtha defined, 426, 552
Pāñcarātrika system, 163
Pāñcarātrika-vidhi defined, 613
Paramahaṁsa
defined, 438
Śiva as, 145
See also: Pure devotee(s); *specific paramahaṁsas*
Paramātmā. *See:* Supersoul
Paramparā system, 357-58
See also: Disciplic succession
Parāśara, 663
Para-upakāra, Kṛṣṇa consciousness as, 366
Parent(s)
duty of, to daughters, 66
respect for, Lord taught, 218
See also: Family life; *specific parents*
Parentage (ancestry)
pride in, 106
in service to Lord, 106-7
Pārijāta tree, Kṛṣṇa captured, 473-74
Parīkṣit Mahārāja, 228
Pārvatī. *See:* Sati
Pāṣaṇḍa defined, 86
Pāṣaṇḍī defined, 823, 832
Passion
need to avoid, 69
See also: Desire; Lust
Passion, mode of (*rajo-guṇa*)
Brahmā governs, 748
creation by, 517
Pastimes of Supreme Lord. *See:* Supreme Lord, pastimes of
Paśupati, Śiva as, 248
Patha-pradarśaka-guru defined, 584
Pāvaka (son of Agni), **46,** 47
Pavamāna (son of Agni), **46,** 47

Payaḥ defined, 761
Peace
via good marriage, 8
by goodness mode, 282
Lord creates, **44**
sacrifices needed for, 233-34
via *saṅkīrtana-yajña,* 556
via seeing all in Lord, **300**
Penance
needed for success, 326
See also: Austerities
Perfection
via chanting Lord's holy name, 163, 570-71
via devotional service, 564, 572
via following spiritual master, 383-84
via hearing about Dhruva, 602
stages of, according to goals, 374-75
of surrendering process, 357
See also: Life, goal of
Personalist(s). *See:* Devotee(s)
Persons. *See:* Human being(s); Living entities; Soul(s); Supreme Lord
Peya defined, 819
Phantasm. *See:* Dream
Philosopher(s)
as *manu* (thoughtful), 217
Māyāvādī. *See:* Impersonalist(s)
speculative, 281, 406, 526, 528
spiritual world beyond, 575
voidist, 407
See also: Devotee(s); Impersonalist(s); *Jñānī(s);* Scholar(s); Scientist(s)
Philosophy
of Caitanya, 521, 768
empiric, Lord as beyond, **268-**69
impersonalist, as taught by Śiva, 78
of oneness & difference, 301, 302
opposed to scripture, **77,** 78
Sāṅkhya, 799
speculative, Lord unknown by, **268-**69
Vaiṣṇava, 446
See also: Devotional service
See also: Absolute Truth; Knowledge; *specific philosophies*
Piety
defined, 303
See also: Pious activities
Pilgrimage, advice about, 203-4
Pilgrimage places
advantage in, 352
bank of Yamunā as, **351,** 352
best of, Vṛndāvana as, 352
created by devotees, 204
as *dhāmas,* 352
listed, 352-53
Lord easily approached in, 352
Lord's feet equal, 203-4
recommended living in, 352
Pious activities
destiny via, **223-**24
devotees beyond, 275
Dhruva exemplary in, 316
diminished via happiness, 340
via hearing causes of devastation, 313
heavenly elevation exhausts, 412
impious activities compared with, 560-61
Kṛṣṇa consciousness beyond, 275
Maitreya desired to describe, 316
of Manu's descendants, 314
need to transcend, 340
as worship to Lord for gain, 330
Piśācas, 844-45
Pitā(s), 28, 128
daughters of, **49**
divisions of, **49**
wife of, **40, 49**
worship, 525-26, **797**
Planet(s)
circle Dhruvaloka (polestar), 430, 593
compared to boats or islands, 759
created by Brahmā, 2
Earth. *See:* Earth planet
Garbha water under, 759
governors of, **278**
Heavenly. *See:* Heavenly planets
hellish, Nārada visits, 352
life on, 805
lower, destruction of, **284**
material
compared with spiritual, 588
devotees bypass, 575
See also: specific planets
as parts of universal body, 768
of seven sages, **587,** 588

Planet(s) (*continued*)
  Vaikuṇṭha, **589**
  of Viṣṇu, 435, **575**
  See also: Earth planet; Heavenly planet(s); Universe(s); *specific stars & planets*
Pleasure
  for devotees of Lord, 155
  diminishes results of piety, 340
  in goodness mode, 282
  by hearing Lord's pastimes, **274**–75
  in husband & wife, 8
  illusory, in abominable life, 290
  illusory, misleads us, **289**, 290
  by Lord's grace, 327
  from Lord's lotus feet, 155
  material
    ignorance in, 72
    as impossible, 156
    soul beyond, 335
    via *Vedas*, **72, 74**
    women &, 96
  in material worlds, 103-4
  in meditating on Lord, 155
  need to transcend, **340**
  via right treatment of others, **341**
  See also: Enjoyment
Poison
  milk, analogy of, 106
  Śiva drank, 101
  snakes extracting, **801-2**
Polestar
  as Dhruvaloka, 403, 430, 435, 593
  Śiśumāra near, 578
  stars & planets circle, **430,** 593
Politician(s)
  ancient, compared with modern, 478
  "independence" plans of, 451
  saintly persons shouldn't become, 661
  whimsical, 782-83
  See also: King(s); *Kṣatriya(s);* Government(s), leader(s)
Poor man's request compared to Dhruva's desire, **451**
Population
  in Kali-yuga, 604, 666, 785-86, 833-34
  "over-," 753, 763
  See also: Citizen(s)
Possession(s), material
  bad effect of, 106
  in service to Lord, 106-7
  See also: Wealth
Potency of Lord. *See:* Supreme Lord, potency of
Potter compared to Lord, 518-19
Poverty as spiritual advantage, 106
Power as Lord's representation, 697
  See also: Mystic power(s); Opulence(s)
Prabhā, **622**
Prabhu defined, 382
Prabhupāda defined, 382
Prabodhānanda Sarasvatī cited on devotee's attitude, 442, 552
Pracetās, **614,** 615
Pradhāna, 390
Pradoṣa, **623**
Pradyumna, **624**
Prahlāda Mahārāja
  in calf form, **795**
  demon's drinks by mercy of, 796
  Hiraṇyakaśipu saved by, 585
Prahlāda Mahārāja cited
  on *brahmānanda,* 216
  on glorifying Lord, 716
  on going to forest, 332
  on hearing Lord's pastimes, 275
  on home life as blind well, 647
  on liberating everyone before himself, 687, 764
  on perfection, 289
Praise, false, 710, **711**
Prajāpati Ruci. *See:* Ruci
Prajāpatis, **90**
Prakṛti
  defined, 390
  Lord master of, 390
  See also: Material nature
Pralaya dance of Śiva, **174**
Prāṇa (son of Vidhātā), **37**
Prāṇāyāma breathing exercise
  of Atri Muni, **20**
  See also: Breathing exercises of *yoga*
Prasāda
  from Aṅga's sacrifice, 640
  from Deity worship, 369-70

Prasāda (continued)
for demigods, 233, 303
denied Śiva, 233-34
devotee's eating of, 369-70, 384-85
devotees offer, **284**
distribution of, 434, 556
distribution of, now, 233
eating of, elevation by, 259
evolutionary value of, 798
food to be eaten as, 787
in Kṛṣṇa consciousness movement, 385
tongue should taste, 259
for wife before sexual intercourse, 641
Prasāda (son of Dharma), **40**
"*Prasāda*" of Goddess Kālī, 844-45
Praśraya (son of Dharma), **40**
Prasūti, **1, 11**
asked favor of Lord, 277
as aunt of Viṣṇu, 276-77
daughters of, **39, 40**
knew danger to Dakṣa, **173,** 174
knew Śiva's power, **174**
prays to Viṣṇu, **276**
as wife of Dakṣa, **38, 39**
Prātaḥ, **622**
Pratoṣa (son of Yajña), **9**
Pratyāhāra defined, 355
Prayāga, 352
Prayer(s)
by Atri Muni to deities, **24-26**
by Bhṛgu to Śiva, **266-67**
by *brāhmaṇas* to Viṣṇu, **291, 294**
by Brahmā to Viṣṇu, **268**
by Dakṣa's wife to Viṣṇu, **276**
by Dakṣa to Śiva, **246, 248, 249-50**
by demigods for Nara-Nārāyaṇa Ṛṣi, **43, 44**
by demigods to Viṣṇu, **285**
by Dhruva. *See:* Dhruva Mahārāja, prayers by
by fire-god to Viṣṇu, **283-84**
by Gandharvas to Viṣṇu, **287**
by governors of planets to Viṣṇu, **278**
by Indra to Viṣṇu, **270**
to Lord
by all at sacrifice, **260-94**
as always inadequate, 259, 260
Prayer(s)
to Lord (*continued*)
for gain, 243
by individual capacity, 259, 260
See also: Prayer(s), to Viṣṇu
by mystics to Viṣṇu, **276**
by priests' wives to Viṣṇu, **271-72**
purification via, 156
purifying power of, 716
by sages to Viṣṇu, **273**
by Siddhas to Viṣṇu, **274**
by Vidyādharas to Viṣṇu, **289**
to Viṣṇu
by all at sacrifice, **260-94**
by assembly members, **263-64**
by Bhṛgu, **266-67**
by *brāhmaṇas,* **291-94**
by Dakṣa, **260, 261**
by Dakṣa's wife, **276**
by fire-god, **283-84**
by Gandharvas, **287**
by governors of planets, **278**
by great mystics, **279, 280**
by Indra, **270**
by personified *Vedas,* **282**
by Prasūti, **276**
by priests at sacrifice, **262**
by sages, **273**
by Śiva, **265**
by Vidyādharas, **289**
by wives of sacrificial performers, **271-72**
See also: Worship
Preacher(s) of Kṛṣṇa consciousness
approach innocent & avoid inimical, 620
as best well-wishers, 264
books (two) for, 289-90
Caitanya accompanied by, 788
Caitanya's advice to, 290
criticized by some, 366
dear to Lord, 590
deliver materialists, 226-27, 229-30
devotees as, 607
duty of, 717
everyone should be, 290
Indians should be, 366
Lord empowers, 846

Preacher(s) (*continued*)
must go everywhere, 366
Nārada as, 347
save people, 658
as superior devotees, 764
See also: Saṅkīrtana-yajña; Sannyāsīs; Spiritual master(s)
Present Age of quarrel. *See:* Kali-yuga
Pride
in Dakṣa, **90,** 106
in Dhruva, 344
discussed by Śiva, **106**
effect of, 90, **106**
in *kṣatriyas,* **333–34**
for material assets, **106**
self-advertisement as, 741
of Vena, **654, 655,** 676-78
See also: Bodily concept of life; Ego, false; "I-&-mine" conception
Priest(s)
pray to Viṣṇu, **272**
Vedic. *See: Brāhmaṇas*
See also: Brāhmaṇa(s); Rituals, performer(s) of
Priyavrata, **10**
empowered by Lord, **315**
son of Manu, **315**
Problems, 394
Protection
of *brāhmaṇas* by Śiva, **248**
of citizens by king, 665-67
by Kṛṣṇa, as best, 294
by Lord
as best, 294
of *brāhmaṇas,* 294
of devotees, 255, 286, 294, **425,** 426, 465, **498–99, 557,** 845-46
for everyone, 772
in forest, 381, 381
from sin, 286
surrender brings, 770, 778
of surrendered souls, 267, 286, 381
of master, 160
religious principles on, 757
for woman, 781
Providence, envious killed by, **226**
Pṛśnigarbha, Lord, 398
Pṛthu Mahārāja
anger of, **766,** 768, **779**
born of Vena's body, **626, 726**
Brahmā advised, about Indra & horse sacrifices, **839–43, 845, 847**
brāhmaṇas satisfied by, **850**
citizens' plea to, **749–52**
citizens under, **729–31, 807, 808**
city planning by, **808**
compared to
earth planet, **722**
fire, **726**
Indra, **723, 737**
lion, **738**
sun-god, **721, 728**
Varuṇa, **725**
coronation of, **701, 702**
demigods pleased with, **849**
Earth
attacked by, **753–56**
during reign of, **804**
leveled by, **745, 806**
milked by, **744–45, 792**
pleased, **792, 806**
threatened by, **760–62, 764–66**
Earth's plea to, **757–59, 767,** 770-72, **780, 782–84,** 783-77, **786, 787, 789–91**
enemies overcome by, **726**
enemies treated equally by, **727–28**
glorification for, **698, 699, 713–42**
horse sacrifices by, **739, 811–22, 827, 828, 830, 833, 839, 841–43**
humility of, **713,** 714
identity of, **694–97, 700,** 708-9, 714, **715–**16, **733, 747,** 748, 767-68, 813, 821, **845,** 846
Indra
envied, **812, 820,** 821, 822, 839-40
pacified by, **848**
stole sacrificial horse of, **822, 823,** 825, **828, 833, 843**
threatened by, **834, 835**
as learned, 731, **733**
Lord attended horse sacrifices by, **813–16**
misery dispelled by, **742**

Pṛthu (*continued*)
mystic power of, **765**
mystic slippers of, **705–6**
as neutral, **727–**28
opulence of, **820,** 821
power of, **737, 738**
praise refused by, **708,** 709, **710–12,** 714
predictions about, **718–42**
presents offered to, **703–7**
qualities of, **733**
quoted on killing Earth, **760–62, 764, 765**
rain supplied by, **723**
reciprocal relationships with, **732**
reign of, **728–**29, **735, 808**
religious, **718, 757, 758**
reputation of, **736,** 737, **741, 742**
respected everyone, **730–31, 744**
sacrificial priests advised, about Indra, **835, 836**
sages satisfied by, **841**
Sanat-kumāra and, **740, 746**
satisfied sacrificial participants, **849–51**
secret style of, **724–25, 727**
son of, vs. Indra, **824–30**
taxation by, **721**
tolerant, **722**
Psychology for training boys, 344
Pulaha, sons of, **33**
Pulastya, sons of, **32**
Puṁ-savanam defined, 641
Punishment
for animalistic men, 249
of Aśvatthāmā by Arjuna, 246-47
benefit in, 189
for blasphemy, **140,** 141
for *brāhmaṇas,* 246-47
of Dakṣa, purpose in, 247, 248-49, 250
by king, 626, 728
by laws of nature, 788-89
of offenders of Śiva, **181–**82, **185, 237–23**
by Śiva, as fatherly, 250
two types of, 236
Purāṇas
quoted on Nārāyaṇa, Śiva, Brahmā, & *pākhaṇḍīs,* 831
Purāṇa(s) (continued)
unqualified commentaries on, 5
See also: Śrīmad-Bhāgavatam; specific purāṇas
Pure devotee(s)
amaze world, 390, 391-92
angry at blasphemy, 680
in bliss, 412
bodily symptoms of, 566, 567
can influence world, 393
create pilgrimage sites, 204
dear to Lord, 512
demigods as considered by, 442
in devotional service, **452**
as kind, 607
liberation rejected by, 553
Lord fulfills desires of, 584
in love of God, 428
material desires absent in, 439-40
as noble, 459
reciprocate according to one's position, 620
spiritual vision in, 557-58, 617
surpass *yogīs,* 390
as transcendental, **413**
two types of, 620
See also: Spiritual master(s); *specific pure devotees*
Pure devotional service
attainment of, 114
Lord revealed in, **113,** 114, 115
as unconditional, 114
Purification
of arena of sacrifice, **251–52**
for *aṣṭāṅga-yoga,* 354
bath & *tilaka* for, 579
via bathing in Yamunā, 354
from bodily relationships, 155-56
via chanting about Lord, 115-16, 156, 252
compared to autumn rain, 244
of consciousness, 239
of desire, 527
of devotees of Lord, 155-56, 560-61
via devotee's presence, 204
of Dhruva, **565**
via ecstasy for Lord, 155-56
of family, 688

Purification (*continued*)
via glorifying Lord, 716
via hearing about Lord, 115-16
via hearing causes of devastation, **313**
via hearing of Dakṣa *yajña,* **308**
of heart or mind, 115-16, 313
via Kṛṣṇa consciousness, 114, 239, 591
liberation by, 313
via Lord of worshiper, 330
Lord's lotus feet bring, 203-4
for maintaining status, 334
of materialistic worshiper, 330
via meditating on Lord, 155-56
of mind, 115-16, 313
oblations for, **251-52**
via praying to Lord, 156
puṁ-savanam ritual of, 641
saṁskāra rite for, 334
via seeing Śiva, 244
of senses, 115-16, 406
to see Lord, 115-16
to serve Lord, 213
via worshiping Lord, 330
via *yoga,* 155, 354
See also: Cleanliness; Hare Kṛṣṇa *mantra*
Purity, **113,** 114, 115
See also: Purification
Purṇimā (son of Marīci), **13**
Puru, **624**
Puruṣa
defined, 390
Lord as, 306
Lord master of, 390
Puruṣa incarnations. *See:* Garbhodakaśāyī Viṣṇu; Kṣīrodakaśāyī Viṣṇu; Mahā-Viṣṇu
Puruṣārtha defined, 426, 552
Pūṣā
arrested by Śiva's men, **179, 181**
Brahmā's request for, **231**
invalids to work through, **238**
as offender to Śiva, **181,** 238
restored by Śiva, **237-**38
teeth lost by, **181, 237-**38
Puṣkariṇī (wife of Ulmuka), **624**
Puṣkariṇī (wife of Vyuṣṭa), **623**
Puṣpārṇa, **622**
Puṣṭi (daughter of Dakṣa), **40**
Putrikā-dharma defined, 3

Q

Qualities
of devotees, **513**
material. *See:* Modes of nature

R

Rādhā-Kṛṣṇa Deity, offenses to, 633
Rādhārāṇī (Rādhā)
author's obeisances to, 2
as Lord's feminine feature, 359
taking shelter of, 332
Raghunātha dāsa Gosvāmī, Caitanya's advice to, 562
Rain
food produced via, 720, 762, 788
Indra supplies, **791**
on mountain compared to arrows on Dhruva, **487**
mystic, engulfed Dhruva, **494, 495**
Pṛthu would supply, if Indra failed, **723**
via sacrifice, 719-20, 761, 788
Rājarṣi defined, 475, 654
Rajo-guṇa. See: Passion, mode of
Rākā (daughter of Aṅgirā), **31**
Rākṣasa(s)
as flesh-eaters, **801**
as Kālī's associates, 844-45
See also: Demon(s)
Rāma(candra), Lord, 695, 777, 846
Rāmānanda Rāya, 76
cited on devotee as famous, 463
Rāmānujācārya, Śrīla, 82
Rāmeśvara, 352
Rasa (taste), 818
Rāsa dance, bogus hearing about, 600
Rascals (*mūḍhas*), 269
Rāvaṇa, 695, 710
couldn't be saved, 294
parents of, **32**
Ṛbhu (son of Brahmā), **309**
Ṛbhu demigods, **162-63**

Reactions
freedom from, 7
See also: Karma
Reality, spiritual world as, 99
Red Fort in Delhi, 472
Regulative principles
for devotional life, 385
four, 793
worship to Lord as, 87-88
Reincarnation. *See:* Birth-death cycle; Transmigration of soul(s)
Relationships
bodily
as contamination, 155, 156
transcending of, 155-56
broken easily, 127-28
Relatives/friends
etiquette for visiting, **101-2, 105, 107, 108**
unkind words from, **108**-9, 118
See also: Family life
Religion
government threatens, 655-56
money object of, 137
principles of. *See:* Religious principles
rituals not, 350
Śiva master of, **140,** 141
surrender to God as, 834
as surrender to Lord, 350
as worshiping Lord, 664
See also: Devotional service; Kṛṣṇa consciousness; Sacrifice(s); Worship
Religious principles
via disciplic succession, 848
economic development via, 561
government should enforce, 658
government should practice, 664, 665
on killing, 757, 758
on protection, 757
See also: Regulative principles; Religion; Vedic injunction(s)
Remembering Supreme Lord, **155,** 156-58, 210-11
at death, 433
Dhruva begged for, **551,** 552-54
Renounced order of life (*sannyāsa*)
as culmination of life, 339
Renounced order of life (*continued*)
distinct from family life, 145
one in, doesn't live at home, 310
See also: Brahmacārī(s); Sannyāsī(s); Vānaprastha(s)
Renunciation
developed via *Vedas,* 144
inspired by Dhruva, 316
in liberated souls, **146**
of Lord in His activities, **273**
opulence in, **146**
See also: Detachment; Retirement
Residences in modes of nature & beyond, 581
Respect
of devotee for all, 303
for superiors, 218
See also: Obeisances
Retirement
from family life, 647, 648
of Uttānapāda, **477**-78
See also: Detachment; *Sannyāsī(s); Vānaprastha(s)*
Ṛg-mantra, chanting of, 162
Rishis. See: Ṛṣi(s); Sage(s); Saintly person(s)
Ritualistic ceremonies
for bathing Deities, 463
decorations for, 466
devotees don't need, 840
as *karma,* 840
Vedic
as inadequate, 248
performers of, as animalistic, 249
performers of, don't know Lord, **262**-63
performers of, punishment for, 249
not real religion, 350
See also: Sacrifice(s)
See also: Sacrifice(s); Worship; *specific sacrifices & rituals*
River(s)
Alakanandā, **203**
Ganges. *See:* Ganges River
in Kailāsa, **203**
land fertilized by, 818
Nandā, **203**
Nirvindhyā, **18**

River(s) (*continued*)
water from, in Deity worship, 368
waves of, compared with devotional service, **413**, 414
Ṛkṣa mountain, **17, 18**
Rocana (son of Yajña), **9**
Ṛṣabha, King, 315
Ṛṣabhadeva cited on ignorance, 445
Ṛṣi(s)
as kind of progeny, 9-10
Marīci chief of, **9**
See also: Sages
Ṛta, **624**
Ruci
Ākūti given to, **3**
as *brāhmaṇa*, **4**, 5
children of, **4, 5, 6**
daughter of, **5, 6–**7
gives Manu son, 6-7
Rudra. *See:* Śiva
Rudra-sampradāya, 55, 217
Rulers. *See:* King(s); *Kṣatriya(s);* Government(s), leader(s)
Rūpa Gosvāmī cited
on devotee as liberated, 768
on devotee as protected, 488-89
on spiritual life without *śruti* & *smṛti*, 781

S

Sacrifice(s)
accepted by fire-gods, 46-47
for Age of present, **88**, 125, 161, 233-34, 284, 291-92
ancient & modern, 125
animals in, 631, 639, 822, 835, 844
See also: Animal(s), sacrifice of
arranged by leaders of creation, **56**
auspicious signs for, 92
for *brahmacārīs*, 555, 658
Bṛhaspati-sava, **91**, 92
to Caitanya Mahāprabhu, 284
chanting compared with other, 291-92
chanting Hare Kṛṣṇa as, 233-34, 291-92
charity at, 434
cleanliness in, 252
of Dakṣa. *See:* Dakṣa, sacrifice of

Sacrifice(s) (*continued*)
decorated women at, 92
defined, 233
to demigods, 87-88, 233, 234
demigods at, 631
demigods must all attend, 234
demigods satisfied by, 233, **673**, 939
by devotee, 284
devotee beyond, 275, 286
by Dhruva, **554**, 556
as difficult, 233, 234
economic importance of, **816**, 817, 820
fire-gods accept, 46-47
to fire-gods by impersonalists, **48**
food offered in, two kinds of, 146-47
freedom from bondage by, 233
goal of, Lord as, 7, 86, 91, 130, 233, 276, 284, 296
for humans, 788
by impersonalists to fire-gods, **48**
impossible now, 88, 125, 161, 233
as inadequate, 248
in Kali-yuga, 434, 631
liberation via, 284
Lord
accepts own share of, **296**
enjoyer of, **554**, 556, **637**, 668, **672**
not aimed at, 146-47
object of, 7, **283–84, 296**
of, 7
presence of, needed for, 176
sanctioned by, 350
satisfies, **86**
for satisfying, 785, 817, 844, 849
to Lord
compared with sacrifices to self, 86
remnants from, 147, 233
mantras in, 836
for material benefit, 130, 146-47
by materialists. *See:* Sacrifice(s), performers of
must satisfy all demigods, 234
necessary requisites for, 284
necessity for, 232-34, 284
for materialists, 130, 232-34
need demigods present, 234
need Śiva's presence, 241

Sacrifice(s) (*continued*)
oblations offered at, 128-29
oblations to Śiva at, 128-29
for peace & prosperity, 233-34
performers of
as animalistic, 249
don't know Lord, **262-63**
by Pracetās, **614,** 615
prasāda remnants of, 233, 303, 304
proper & improper, 130
rain via, 719-20, 761, 788
remnants of, denied Śiva, 233
ritualistic, as condemned, **146-47**
sanctions, 350
via *saṅkīrtana*, 88, 125, 233-34, 284, 291-92
for satisfying Lord, 785, 817, 844, 849
useless type of, 130, 144-47
vājapeya, 91
Vena stopped, **655**
Viṣṇu
goal of, 91, 130, 276, **283-84, 296**
necessary for, **276**
to Viṣṇu
cleanliness in, 252
remnants from, 147, 303, 304
for Viṣṇu vs. otherwise, 146-47
See also: Ritualistic ceremonies; Worship; *specific sacrifices*
Sadāśiva, 217
Sādhus. See: Devotee(s); *Ṛṣi(s);* Sage(s); Saintly person(s)
Saffron garments, significance of, 151
Sage(s)
Aṅga's absence concerned, **651**
Bṛhaspati as priest of, 794
curse by, **626**
describe Lord's detachment, **273**
Dhruva
accepted blessings of, **579**
encouraged by, **498-99**
Himalayas preferred by, 687
kinds of descendants from, 9-10
kings as, 595, 654
kings under, 652, 663, 679
pray to Viṣṇu, **273**
present for Pṛthu from, **706**
Sage(s) (*continued*)
protected by Lord, 381
Pṛthu satisfied, **851**
quoted
on pious king, **663-65, 667**
on sacrificial performances, **672, 673**
on Vena, **679-81**
on worshiping Lord, **669, 670**
seven planets of, **587,** 588
society after Vena's death as considered by, **683-84, 686**
society benefited by, **780-81, 782, 783**
sons of Kratu (Vālakhilyas), **33-**34
sons of Pulaha, **33**
sons of Vasiṣṭha, **34, 35**
Vena
advised by, **662-65, 667, 669, 670, 672, 673**
cursed by, **626, 628**
enthroned by, **652**
killed by, **682**
Vena's
position considered by, **656-61**
limbs churned by, **689-90, 693**
See also: Brāhmaṇa(s); Saintly person(s); Spiritual master(s)
Sahasraśirṣā incarnation, **398**
Sahiṣṇu (son of Pulaha), **32**
Saintly persons
anger absent in, 540
compassion of, 684
demons killed by, 679
in devotional service, **510**
duty of, 679
fools misunderstand, 620
forgiveness in, 226-27, 228
in Kali-yuga, 661
killing by, 679, 686
Lord seen by, 399
politics unsuitable for, 661
preach God consciousness, 658
reversals met by, 841
spiritual master follows, 714
See also: Brāhmaṇa(s); Devotee(s); Pure devotee(s); Sage(s); Spiritual master(s)

Śaivites. *See:* Śiva, follower(s) of
Śakti defined, 306
Śakti-tattvas defined, 697
Śaktyāveśa-avatāras defined, 697-98, 813, 846
Śālagrāma-śilā at sacrifices, 350
Salvation via Kṛṣṇa consciousness movement, 478
See also: Liberation
Śalya defined, 742
Samādhi
as absorption in Lord's thought, 145
via chanting Hare Kṛṣṇa, 355
controlled by Lord, 116
defined, 145, 217, 550
Deity worship as, 362
in meditating on Lord, 217, 362
Śiva in, 116, **216,** 217
See also: Meditation
Sampradāya(s). See: Disciplic succession(s)
Samprasanne defined, 514
Saṁsāra. See: Birth-death cycle; Transmigration of soul(s)
Saṁskāra rite, 334
Sanaka-kumāra, **285, 293,** 409, 444, **816**
Sanandana-kumāra, **444**
Sanātana-dharma system, 83
See also: Varṇāśrama system
Sanātana Gosvāmī
benedicts poor *brāhmaṇa,* 240-41
cited
on becoming Vaiṣṇava, 366-67
on Lord Pṛśnigarbha, 398
on twice-born process, 604
respected Nawab Hussian Shah, 735
Sanātana-kumāra, 409, 444
Sanat-kumāra, 444, **740, 746**
Śaṅkarācārya, 80
accepted Kṛṣṇa, 82
quoted on Nārāyaṇa's status, 268, 297
Saṅkarṣaṇa, Lord, 765, 777
See also: Balarāma
Sāṅkhya philosophy, 799
Saṅkīrtana-yajña
for Age of present, **88,** 125, 233-34, 284, 291-92
Saṅkīrtana-yajña (continued)
Caitanya satisfied via, 788, 817, 844
before Caitanya's form, 284
Caitanya started, 831
compared with other sacrifices, 291-92
for Kali-yuga, 788, 793, 818, 836, 844
by Kṛṣṇa consciousness movement, 434, 817
as practical sacrifice, 555-56, 631
society benefits by, 817
as *yajña* (sacrifice), 284, 291-92
See also: Chanting; Kṛṣṇa consciousness movement; Preachers, Kṛṣṇa conscious; Glorification of Supreme Lord
Sannyāsa (renounced order), 339
Sannyāsī(s)
bogus, compared with bona fide, 823-24, 830-32, **833,** 834
distinct from *gṛhasthas,* 145
don't live "at home," 310
duty of, 658, 823-24
impersonalist, 506, 830
in Kali-yuga, 824, 834
penances & austerities for, 555
Vaiṣṇava, 830
See also: Detachment; Preacher(s)
Sanskrit, chanting of, 632
Śānti (daughter of Dakṣa), **40**
Śānti (son of Yajña), **9**
Śānti (wife of Atharvā), 35
Santoṣa (son of Yajña), **9**
Śaraṇāgati defined, 381
Sarasvatī, goddess, **704**
Sarasvatī River, **683, 739, 811**
Śārṅga bow, **574**
Sarva-guṇa. See: Goodness, mode of
Sarvatejā, **623, 624**
Śāstra(s). See: Scripture(s)
Śatarūpā (wife of Manu)
daughters of, **1**
sons of, **315**
Ṣaṭ-cakra defined, 152
Satī (wife of Śiva)
accuses Dakṣa, **131-49**
addresses Śiva about sacrifice, **95-102**
advised by Śiva, **105-18**

Satī (*continued*)
angry
at Dakṣa, **128–**29, 130
at Śiva, **120–21**
appeals to Śiva, **102, 120–21**
argument against statements of, 141
ashamed of Dakṣa as father, **148–49**
attendants of
duty of, 160
fight demigods, **162–63**
bathing lake of, **200–201**
benefits Śiva worshipers, 147
body of, honored by Śiva, **153**
as chaste, 55
as childless, **50–**51
cleansed of contamination, 154, **155**
concentrated on Śiva, **155**
concerned for Śiva's honor, 129
considered as *śūdra,* 141
could destroy universe, 142
could kill Dakṣa, 166
cries before Śiva, **120,** 121
Dakṣa neglected, **127, 128, 159,** 173
Dakṣa questions marriage of, **63, 66**
as Dakṣa's pet daughter, 127, 165-66
as Dākṣāyaṇī (Dakṣa's daughter), 94, 149
as daughter of Himalayas, **305,** 306
death of, **155**
decided by her, 141, **142, 148–**50
demigods react to, **157,** 158
to purify herself, 154
by *yoga,* **150, 151–52, 153, 155**
decides on suicide, 141, **142, 148–**50
defended Śiva, 141
desired
to attend sacrifice, **95–102**
to convince Dakṣa, 139-40
to decorate herself, **96,** 97
to enjoy, 96, 99
didn't vilify Dakṣa, 141
discusses
blasphemy, **140,** 141
Śiva, **131–38**
Śiva's opulence, **146,** 147
dissatisfied ultimately, 157
distressed by Śiva, **120–21**
divided in decision, **119–**20

Satī (*continued*)
dowry of, from father, 97
eternally related to Śiva, 154, 306
as external (material) energy, 142, 166, 306
fearless, 123
forgot Dakṣa (by trance), 155, 156
gives opulence, 147
goes to Dakṣa's sacrifice, **123–34**
honored by Śiva, **153**
ill-received at sacrifice, **126–28**
knew *yoga,* 150
leaves Śiva, **121**
life air raised by, **151–52**
as marginal & external energy, 306
marriage of
Brahmā advised, 66
Dakṣa regrets, **63, 65**
material body attained by, 155, 156
as materialistic, 96, 99
meditated on Śiva, **155**
mother & sisters of, **126, 127**
motive of, 139-40
narration about, Uddhava spoke, **307**
neglected by Dakṣa, **127, 128,** 159, 173
next life of, 154, 156, **305–6**
ornaments of, from father, 97
as "poor woman," **98–99**
power of, 142, 166
purified of contamination, 154, **155**
sat on Śiva's lap, **153**
sees demigods' wives, **94**
warned by Śiva, **105, 107,** 108, **109–**10, **117–18**
weakness in, 122
welcomed by mother & sisters, **126, 127**
wife of Śiva eternally, 154, **306**
as woman or *śūdra,* 141
Satisfaction
in abominable life, 290
via accepting difficulty, **336–**37
via depending on Lord, **336–**37
fire of, in Atri Muni, **20**
in happiness or distress, **340**
impossible materially, 157
of *karmīs, jñānīs, yogīs,* & devotees, 515
in married life, 8

Satisfaction (*continued*)
via serving Lord, 157
See also: Enjoyment; Happiness
Satisfying Śiva
as easy, 190, 192
as unknown, 192
Sattva-guṇa. See: Goodness, mode of
Satyabhāmā, Queen, 473–74
Satyaloka. *See:* Brahmaloka
Satyavān, **624**
Satya-yuga
Dhruva lived in, 471, 472, 559, 560
life-span in, 431, 471, 560
Saugandhika forest, **201,** 202, **207**
Sāyam, **622**
Sāyujya-mukti defined, 441
See also: Liberation; Oneness
Scholars, modern
deny next life, 781
envious of Kṛṣṇa, 111
See also: Jñānīs; Philosophers, speculative; Scientists
Scientist(s), material
Absolute Truth beyond, 528, 529
airplanes made by, 582
nature exploited by, 442
space travel by, 575, 577
spiritual world beyond, 575, 578
See also: Philosopher(s), speculative; Scholar(s)
Scriptures, Vedic
Śiva's followers &, **78**
spiritual master follows, 714
See also: Bhagavad-gītā; Śāstra(s); Śrīmad-Bhāgavatam; specific Vedic literatures
Seeds
nondevotees misusing, **784, 786**
tastes arising from, 818
Self. *See:* Soul(s)
Self-realization, 480
complete scope of, 135-36
envy outside of, 110
Śiva gives, 135-36
See also: Absolute Truth; Devotional service; Kṛṣṇa consciousness; Knowledge; Spiritual life
Self-realized souls. *See:* Devotee(s); Pure devotees; Spiritual master(s)
Semen
body produced by, 690
conservation of, 309-10
in Dhruva's family, 687-89
meant for begetting, 310
value of withholding, 505-6
Sense gratification
absent
in devotional service, 374-75
in liberation, 374-75
conditioned souls compete for, 442
desired by Satī, 96-97
as destined, **335, 336**
devotee's view of, 552
diminishes results of piety, 340
eating for, devotee avoids, **384–85**
government leaders pursue, 669-70
living entities should renounce, 785
merging with Lord as, 375
need to transcend, **340**
soul beyond, 335
women expand, 96
world's production geared for, 786
worshiping Lord for, **410**
See also: Bodily concept of life; Desire(s), material; Enjoyment; Happiness; Sex life
Senses
Absolute Truth beyond range of, **528**
can't know Lord, 268
compared to serpents, 552
contaminated compared with purified, 213
controlled in humans, 248
devotee controls, 552, 562
of Dhruva, 562
Lord beyond, 115, 116, 216-17, **268–**69, 748, 821
material, compared with spiritual, 405–6
purification of, 406
purified
in devotional service, 115-16
to serve Lord, 213
See also: Body, material
Servants of God. *See:* Devotees

Service to God. *See:* Devotional service
Śeṣa (Ananta), **285,** 419
  See also: Balarāma
Sevā-aparādha defined, 633
Sevonmukha defined, 406
Sex life
  as basis of material life, 154
  of brother & sister, 311
  checks spiritual life, 154
  demigods morose after, 203
  of demigod women, **203**
  desire for, by nice atmosphere, **208**
  in material world compared with spiritual world, 208
  procreation via, 516
  suffering due to, 516
  Vedic culture restricts, 505
  wife takes *prasāda* before, 641
  See also: Desire(s), material; Sense gratification
Shower of flowers by demigods for Dhruva, **583, 586**
Śibi, **624**
Siddha(s), **21**
  as devotees of Lord, 274, 275
  discuss bliss of Lord's pastimes, **274**
  dismayed at Dhruva's battle plight, **488**
  fly without airships, 205, 363
  mystic powers of, **798**–99
  pray to Viṣṇu, **274**
  process for seeing, **363**
  Pṛthu glorified by, **698**
  at Pṛthu's horse sacrifices, **815**
  yogic perfection in, 363
Śikṣāṣṭaka quoted
  on desiring devotional service, 439-40
  on tolerance, 227
  on transcendence, 619
Simultaneous oneness & difference, 291, 292, 298, 301, 302
Sinful activities
  animal slaughter as, 508
  bad association as, 660
  devotional service dispels, 692
  four kinds of, 831
Sinful activities (*continued*)
  hearing about Dhruva counteracts, **600-601**
  as inevitable here, 286
  protection from, 286
  results of, diminished via suffering, 340
  by "*sannyāsīs,*" 831, **833**
  son-begetting prevented by, 636
  surrender absolves, 814
  by tongue, 259
Siṅgh defined, 738
Sinīvālī (daughter of Aṅgirā), **31**
Śipi defined, 639
Śiśumāra (*prajāpati*), **479**
Śiśumāra (star), 578
Sītā, 695
Sitting postures for *yoga*, 152, **215**
  of Śiva, 217
  yoga-kakṣām, 217
Śiva, Lord
  as *abhava*, 100
  abode of, **193-209**
    almost like Kṛṣṇa's, 206-7
    animals in, **199, 200**
    banyan tree in, **209, 210**
    birds in, **195, 199, 207**
    deer in, **199, 200**
    desire trees in, **206**
    forest in, **206**
    Ganges in, 201
    by Kuvera's abode, **206**
    lotus flowers in, **201,** 202, **207**
    residents of, **193-94**
    rivers in, **203**
    in space, 94
    trees in, **196-98**
  absorbed in trance, 116, **216**
  accepts good in all, 131-33
  addressed
    by Brahmā, **220-32**
    by Dakṣa, **246, 248, 249-50**
    by Satī, **95-102**
  addresses
    Brahmā, **236-38**
    Nārada, **214**
    Satī, **105-18**

Śiva (*continued*)
as *adhīśvara,* 213
as Advaita Prabhu, 217
advised *brāhmaṇa* to see Sanātana, 240
affected materially, 103, 104
as *aja,* 99
angry at Satī's death, **165–67**
animals dead due to, **271–72**
as annihilator, 521, 522
approached by demigods, **210–16**
as *īśa,* 14
associates sitting with, **211–**12
as Āśutoṣa, 61, 133, 190, 240
as *ātmā,* 121
as *ātmārāma,* 103
Atri Muni noticed by, **20**
attends sacrifice, **241**
as auspicious, 65, 135-36, **213**
avoided materialists, 67, 68
bad qualities not in, 132-33
banyan tree of, **209, 210**
beads of, **215**
behavior of, as scandalous, 267
benediction by, for beheading, 133
benediction from
as easy, 240
for spiritual life, 240
benefited by curse of Dakṣa, 67
benefits
everyone, **136–37, 212,** 213
ignorant beings, 54, 65
materialists, **136–37**
as best benediction-giver, 240
"best of the gentle," **53–**54
as best of Vaiṣṇava (devotees), 55, 130, 137, 148, 213
best of *yogīs,* 150
better seat for, than for Dakṣa, 110
beyond
illusion, 99
social orders, 145
Vedic rules, 143, 145
as Bhūtanātha, 54, **801**
as Bhūtarāṭ, 84
blasphemy of, dealing with, **140,** 141
as blue-throated, 101
bodily appearance of, **213–**14

Śiva (*continued*)
bodily decorations of, **64**
in bodily illusion, 267
born from Brahmā, 100, 211-12, 297, 801
brāhmaṇas not neglected by, **246,** 247
as Brahman incarnation, 696
bull of, **123**
in calf form, **803**
in calf form, **801**
can't check Kṛṣṇa's will, 294
can't harm Lord's devotee, 294
carrier of, **22,** 23
cause of, Viṣṇu as, 297
chastisement by, as fatherly, 236
chief of thinkers, 217
compared
to cowherd boy, **248**
to curd, 139
to father, 236, 250
to milk in yogurt, 220
to spider, **221**
to sun, 143
to Vāmanadeva, **218**
considers how to save souls, 217
as controller of religion, **140,** 141
controls his senses, **212,** 213
couldn't give Satī ornaments, 97
in crematoriums, **138**
criticized by Dakṣa, **60–65**
criticized/praised by Dakṣa, 61
cursed by Dakṣa, **66**
Dakṣa inferior to, 59
as Dakṣa's son-in-law, 59, **61–62**
dance of, at world's end, **174**
as demigod chief, 59
demigods restored by, **237–38**
demon created by, **167–68, 169**
denied sacrificial remnants, 233
described
by Dakṣa's wife, **174**
by Satī, **131–38**
at destruction of world, **174**
detached from material enjoyment, 96, 99
didn't get up for Dakṣa, **59**
didn't see Dakṣa enter, 111
directed by Vāsudeva (Supersoul), 20, 21
disciplic succession from, 217, 746

Śiva (*continued*)
discusses
Dakṣa, **105–**13, **117–18**
Dakṣa's envy, **117**
friends visiting friends, **105, 106, 107**
pride, **106**
Satī's reception by Dakṣa, **105, 107–**8, **109, 117–18**
visiting as guest, **105, 107**
drank poison, 101
drum symbol of, **22,** 23
Durvāsā incarnation of, **14,** 16, **30**
"duty" of, to respect Dakṣa, 112
easily pleased, 190, 192, 240
elevated status of, **138–**39
as enlightened, 99
enlightens devotees, 135-36
envy of, in Dakṣa alone, 131, 133
equally disposed to all, 85, 120-21, **131**
equal to Viṣṇu originally, 220
equating him with Viṣṇu, 136
eternally related to Satī, 306
exemplary in Lord's service, 213
"eyes" of, **62**
fame "ruined" by, **60–**61
as father to all, 236
feature of, for nondevotees, 214
finger position of, **215**
follower(s) of
as atheists, **78, 80**
attack sacrifice, **177–80**
bad habits of, 78, 79, 83, 252
bodies of, **177**
brāhmaṇa as, 240
compared with followers of *Vedas,* 84
couldn't harm sacrifice, 294
cursed by Bhṛgu, **76–84**
defeated by demigods, **162**
duty of, to Satī, 160
enlightened by him, 135-36
faithfulness of, 123
fight demigods on Satī's death, **162–63**
follow Satī, 123
imitate him, 214
as impersonalists (monists), 78
intoxication by, 78, 79, 214
knew Śiva's mind, 123

Śiva
followers of (*continued*)
Nandiśvara, **70, 179**
oppose scripture, 77, 78
opulence of, 147
Satī enriches, 147
should worship Viṣṇu, 135-36
as unclean, 252
following example of, 135-36
foresaw Dakṣa's behavior, 105
freed of demigods' association, 67
as friend of all, 137
Ganges from, 201
garlanded by skulls, **138**
as God & not God, 139, 220
honesty "lacking" in, **61–**62
husband of Satī eternally, 306
ignorance mode controlled by, 748
as illusioned, 267
imitating him, 143, 214
"inauspicious" qualities of, **138**
as incarnation
of Advaita, 217
of Durvāsā, **14,** 16
of ignorance, 221
of Lord, 131, 299
independent of Lord never, **300**
informed by Nārada, **165,** 166
instructing devotional service, **214**
instructing Nārada, **214**
as instructor supreme, 214
not invited by Dakṣa, 89-90
as invited to sacrifice, **241**
Kṛṣṇa as origin of, 748
Kṛṣṇa conscious, **113**
as Kuvera's brother, **541**
leaves assembly, **85**
liberation via, 137
as *loka-maṅgala,* 213
as lord
of low beings, 54-55, 65, 84, 249
of universe, 28
Lord glorified by, 716
Lord of, Viṣṇu as, 257
lotus feet of, Satī thinks of, **155**
as "mad" creature, **64–**65
as *maṅgala* (auspicious), 135-36

Śiva (*continued*)
materialists worship, 240
meditates on Supersoul (Vāsudeva), 110, 111, 116
meditating on Lord, **216**
as *mīḍhuṣṭama,* 240
name of, purifies, **135**
Nārāyaṇa above, 831
neglected in Dakṣa's sacrifice, 89-90, 91, 92
as "never-born," 100
as *nīlakaṇṭha,* 101
as *nirapatrapa,* 61
as nondifferent from Lord, **297-98, 299, 300,** 301
none know power of, **192**
none know to satisfy, 192
obeisances by
to Brahmā, **218**
to Supersoul, 112, **113**
to Viṣṇu, 257
oblations for, at sacrifices, 128-29
offenses overlooked by, 236
one with & different from Viṣṇu, 302
opulences(s) possessed by, **146,** 212
as *paramahaṁsa,* 145
as *paśupati,* 248
as peaceful, **53, 54**
"percentage" of Kṛṣṇa in, 15
possesses all opulences, 212
power of
vs. *brāhmaṇas',* 168
no one knew, **192**
prays to Viṣṇu, **265**
present for Pṛthu from, **705**
protects
animals & animallike, 248, 249
brāhmaṇas, **248**
religion, **140,** 141
at Pṛthu's horse sacrifices, **814**
punishment via, purpose in, 247, 248-49, 250
purification by seeing, 244
as qualitative incarnation of Viṣṇu, 299
regrets anger at Dakṣa, **265**
related to Kumāras, 212
in relation to universe, **220, 221**

Śiva (*continued*)
represents Supreme Person, 306
respected by great persons, **138-**39
respected Dakṣa's Supersoul, 112, 113
sacrifices need presence of, 241
Sadāśiva, 217
in *samādhi,* 116, **216,** 217
sees good in all, 131, **132-33**
sitting posture of, 215-17
sitting under tree, **210-16**
as spiritual master of all, **54-**55
story about, Uddhava spoke, **307**
superior status of, **138-**39, 220
as supreme instructor, 214
taught impersonalism, 78
as thoughtful, 217
as tolerant, 85, **265**
tolerated Dakṣa's curse, 70
unhappy remembering Dakṣa, **103,** 104
as Vaiṣṇava vegetarian, 844
Viṣṇu Lord of, 257
warns Satī, **105, 107-**8, **109, 117-18**
wife of. *See:* Satī
worshipers of, 607
See also: Śiva, follower(s) of
worship to. *See:* Worship, to Śiva
Yakṣas devoted to, 483
Śiva-āgama cited, 79
Śiva Purāṇa cited
on Śiva's teachings, 78
on Viṣṇu worship, 136
on worship of devotees, 91-92
Śiva-sakti defined, 221
Śiva-tejas vs. *brahma-tejas,* 168-69
Six Gosvāmīs, 461
See also: Jīva Gosvāmī; Raghunātha dāsa Gosvāmī; Rūpa Gosvāmī; Sanātana Gosvāmī
Slaughter. *See:* Animal slaughter; Killing
Sleep
material activities compared to, 405, 409
waking from, 243
See also: Dream
Smaraṇam defined, 210
Smaya (son of Dharma), **40**
Smṛti (son of Dharma), **40**
Smṛti defined, 781

Snake(s)
envy in, 106
with jewel, analogy of, 106
Nārada &, 539
poison extracted by, **801–2**
Vena compared to, **659**
Society, human
all *śūdras* now, 163
anxiety in, 226
best relief work in, 264
as bewildered, 784
as body of Lord, 248
brāhmaṇas absent in, 163
brāhmaṇa's duty in, 687
brāhmaṇas needed in, 344–45
chanting recommended for, 125
classless, as impossible, 222
compared to body, 345
dead without Kṛṣṇa consciousness, 276
as demons & devotees, 255
devotees can influence, 393
divisions of
based on *Vedas,* 80, 83
as body of Lord, 248
in castes, 80, 83, 344–45
as created by Lord, 222
distinctions in, 144–45
as part of Lord, 222
as permanent, 83
See also: Varṇāśrama-dharma
envy in, 226
food for, 763
four kinds of activity in, 377
four kinds of spirit in, 344
four principles in, 137
godless, 681, 790
happiness for, 793, 794
happy & unhappy, 781, 783
Hare Kṛṣṇa *mantra* for, 794
Kṛṣṇa consciousness movement in, 572
Kṛṣṇa instructs, 814
Manu's laws for, 781
meeting different statuses in, **341**
modern sacrifice for, 125
principles of life in, four given, 137
sacrifices necessary to, 232–34
sages benefit, **780–81, 782, 783**
Society (*continued*)
sanātana-dharma system of, 83
saṅkīrtana-yajña benefits, 817
scientific system of, 83
secular, as hellish, 834–35
social classes in, 652, 668
spirit in, four kinds of, 344
surrender in, 357
transcendentalists beyond, 145
varṇāśrama-dharma in. *See: Varṇāśrama-dharma*
Vedic knowledge for, 794
See also: Civilization, modern; Human beings; Kali-yuga; Population; *Varṇāśrama-dharma;* Vedic culture
Soldier(s). *See: Kṣatriya(s)*
Soma (moon-god), **162**
born to Atri, **30**
as incarnation of Brahmā, **14,** 16, **30**
Soma beverage, 284, **794,** 795, 796
Son(s)
Aṅga lacked, **635, 636**
bad, **645–47**
as enemy, 627
father &, 594
marriage for producing, 635-36, 645
mother &, 587, 642
See also: specific sons
Sorrow, material, compared with spiritual, 103–4
Soul(s)
beyond pain & pleasure, 335
in body, 690, 734, 769
body fresh due to, 152
body survived by, 516
brain unimportant for, 238-39
conditioned. *See:* Conditioned soul(s)
desires of, produce species, 519
during dream, 568
jīva, 15
knowledge in, as incomplete, 135
knowledge of self in. *See:* Self-realization
liberated. *See:* Liberated soul(s)
living entity as, 536
in material world, 394–95
See also: Conditioned soul(s)
as part of God, 15

Soul(s) (*continued*)
pure condition of, 113-14
as *puruṣa,* 390
suffers in material modes, 15
as Supersoul's dependent, 511
as Supersoul's servant, 403
transfer of, by *yoga,* 150-51, 152-53
transmigration of. *See:* Transmigration of soul(s)
"unification" of, with Supersoul, 396
Sound, transcendental
ancient & modern, 125
Lord inspires, 402
See also: Chanting Hare Kṛṣṇa; Hare Kṛṣṇa *mantra; Mantra(s)*
Space, outer, compared to ocean, 759
See also: Universe(s)
Space travel
by Dhruva, **586-88**
mechanical, compared with yogic, 577
by mystic airplane, 582
by Nārada Muni, 587
by scientist & devotee contrasted, 575
by Siddhas & Vidyādharas, 798-99
three types of, 578
Species of life
desires produce, 519, 527
number of, 417, 732
Speculation, mental
Absolute Truth beyond, **528,** 529
futility of, **783,** 784
impersonal Brahman by, 649
spiritual world beyond, 575
Speculation, philosophical, Lord unknown via, **268-**69
Speculative philosopher(s). *See: Jñānī(s);* Philosopher(s), speculative
Spirit. *See:* Body, spiritual; Brahman (impersonal Absolute); Soul(s); Spiritual world; Supreme Lord
Spiritualist(s). *See:* Devotee(s); Impersonalist(s); Sage(s); Transcendentalist(s); *Yogī(s)*
Spiritual knowledge. *See:* Knowledge, spiritual; Self-realization
Spiritual life
advancement in. *See:* Advancement, spiritual
Spiritual life (*continued*)
blissful, 619
life culminating in, 339
material life compared with, 572
women check, 99
See also: Devotional service; Kṛṣṇa consciousness; Self-realization; *Yoga*
Spiritual light. *See:* Brahman effulgence
Spiritual master(s)
accept Kṛṣṇa & *Gītā,* 82
accept Kṛṣṇa's deeds, 270-71
all people should accept, 367
all should become, 290
as *aṣṭottara-śata,* 114
birth status unimportant for, 76
bogus, compared with bona fide, 746
boys trained by, 344
caitya-guru, 355
devotee of Kṛṣṇa as, 76
devotional service requires, 597
dīkṣā & *śikṣā,* 584, 585
disciple &, 584, 585, 594, 630
disciplic line necessary for, 367
duty of, to engage disciple, 349
gives *mantra,* **363, 364**
instruction from, 740
as Lord in heart, 355
Lord sends, 333, 355
as Lord's representative, 382
obeisances by, to disciple, 112
perfection by following, 383-84
pleasing or displeasing Lord via, 432-33
as *prabhupāda,* 382
qualification for becoming, 784
sādhus & *śastras* followed by, 714
Śiva as, for all, **54-**55
in *śuddha-sattva* state, 114
tests disciple, 337, 339
Vedic knowledge via, 403
within & without, 355
See also: Authorities, spiritual; Devotees, pure
Spiritual world
absolute nature of, 580
attaining to. *See:* Liberation
beings in, 208, 394-95
beyond material qualities, **280-**81
chanting in, 208

Spiritual world (*continued*)
contrasted to material world, 103-4, 394-95
cows in, 816-17
demons absent in, 255
devotees attain, 223-24, 575, 589, 590
devotees candidates for, 223-24
eternal, 430
glorification of Lord in, 208
inhabitants of, 208, 394-95
by knowing Lord, 574
life meant for attaining, 598
living entities in, 572
Lord's presence as, 532
material world contrasted to, 459, 563, 588
material world reflection of, 99, 103-4
material world reflects light of, **589**
planets in, **589**
quality in, 281
as reality above illusion, 99
scientists unable to approach, 575, 578
sex in, 208
transcendentalists attain, 517
transfer, 567
women in, 208
See also: Godhead, returning to; Vṛndāvana
Śraddhā (wife of Aṅgirā), **31**
Śraddhā (wife of Dharma), **40**
Śrāddha ritual, 798
Śravaṇaṁ kīrtanam defined, 412
Śravaṇa star, **605**
Śrī (daughter of Bhṛgu), **36**
Śrī-bhāgavata-candra-candrikā cited on Satī's lake, 201
Śrīdhara Svāmī cited on *viṣṇu-prasāda*, 304
Śrīmad-Bhāgavatam
See also: Śrīmad-Bhāgavatam cited; *Śrīmad-Bhāgavatam* quoted
ancient cities in, 809
author's commentating on, 1-2
civilization-study in, 472
devotees should preach, 607
devotees should read, 600
discussing, among devotees, 603-4
Fourth Canto of, 2
Śrīmad-Bhāgavatam (continued)
hearing of, bogus & bona fide, 599-600, 605-6
Lord as approached via, 613
Lord's pastimes in, 615
materialist's view of, 270
as principal book on Kṛṣṇa, 289-90
professional reciters of, 600, 605
unqualified commentaries on, 5
Vyāsadeva compiled, 607
Śrīmad-Bhāgavatam cited
See also: Śrīmad-Bhāgavatam quoted
on devotional service, 560
on food supply decreasing in Kali-yuga, 785-86
on Kali-yuga men, 833-34
on Kṛṣṇa & mystic demons, 800
on Lord's incarnations, 777
on people fleeing to forest, 718
on pleasing Lord, 233
on pure devotee, Lord, & liberation, 553
on *saṅkīrtana* (chanting), 284
on Śiva's worshipers, 147
on *Śrīmad-Bhāgavatam* & nonenvious souls, 812
on sun's orbit, 735
on Vyāsadeva compiling *Bhāgavatam*, 607
Śrīmad-Bhāgavatam quoted
See also: Śrīmad-Bhāgavatam cited
on chanting in this age, 88
on decorating dead body, 276
on devotee's accepting difficulty, 224
on duty to satisfy Lord, 615
on falling from Brahman effulgence, 441
on hearing Kṛṣṇa's words from pure devotees, 414
on kings in Kali-yuga, 666
on Kṛṣṇa as God, 288
on Lord's inspiring Brahmā, 82
on Lord within, 297
on pilgrimage sites, 204
on purification via Lord, 156
on real satisfaction, 157
on *saṅkīrtana*, 125, 233, 284, 817
on weapon for this age, 502
Śrīnivāsa Ācārya cited on six Gosvāmīs, 461
Śrīvāsa Ṭhākura, 502

Śrīvatsa defined, 358
Śrutena bhūyasā defined, 539
Śruti defined, 781
Stars
circle Dhruvaloka, 430, **575**
See also: Planet(s); *specific stars & planets*
Sthūla defined, 565
Storm
dust, after Vena's death, **685, 686**
mystic, engulfed Dhruva, **494–97**
Straw mats, use of, 214
Strī defined, 96
Student(s). *See: Brahmacārī(s);* Disciple & spiritual master
Śubha (son of Dharma), **40**
Subtle body. *See:* Body, material
Success, **326**
Śuci (son of Agni), **46, 47**
Sudarśana disc, partial vs. plenary, 704
Śuddha-sattva
defined, 114-15
not in material world, 169
Lord revealed in, 114, 115
spiritual master in, 114
Sudeva (son of Yajña), **9**
Śūdra(s)
Americans as, 344
approaching supreme destination, 692
blasphemy if heard by, 141
as *brāhmaṇas,* 75, 76
defined, 83
fishing for, 820
Kali-yuga population as, 604, 666
as "legs" of society, 345
less intelligent, 4–5
part of Lord's cosmic form, 222
permanent class of, 83
social status of, 666, 691, 750
as spiritual masters, 75, 76
unfit to hear *Vedas,* 4–5, 63
Vedic study not for, 604
women as, 141
See also: Varṇāśrama-dharma
Suffering
acceptance of, as Lord's mercy, 336-37
counteracting measures complicate, 841-42
Suffering (*continued*)
as destined, **335, 336**
of devotees, Lord relieves, 813-14
diminishes results of impiety, 340
disregarding duty causes, 818
freedom from
by devotional service, 265-66, 286
by Kṛṣṇa's grace, 328, 331
from sin, 286
godlessness causes, 790
good government dispels, 742
by insults of relatives, 108-9, 118
Pṛthu dispelled, **742**
sex life causes, 505-6
soul beyond, 335
Yudhiṣṭhira dispelled, 742
Suffocation of universe by Dhruva, **393, 394**
Suicide
compared to vomiting, **142**
for hearing blasphemy, **140,** 141
of Satī by *yoga,* **150, 151–52, 153, 155**
Satī decides on, 141, **142, 148**–50
Sukha (son of Dharma), **40**
Śukla defined, 691
Śukra, **430**
Śukrācārya, **37**
Sumanā, **624**
Sun
Absolute Truth compared to, 528
Kṛṣṇa compared to, 502
light of, source of, 589
as Lord's eye, 593
Satyaloka above, 505
speed of, 593, 735
Sunanda (Viṣṇu's servitor), **260**
Sun emerging from fog & Dhruva emerging from Yakṣas, analogy of, **489**
Sun-god
Bhagavad-gītā spoken to, 476
present for Pṛthu from, **705**
Pṛthu compared to, **721, 728**
Sunīthā, Queen
Aṅga gave sacrificial *prasāda* to, **640, 641**
Aṅga's semen polluted by, 688
as Aṅga's wife, **625,** 642
as daughter of death personified, 642

Sunīthā (*continued*)
Vena's body preserved by, **682,** 690
as Vena's mother, **659**
Sunīti, Queen, **316**
body of, spiritualized, 587
compared to burnt leaf, **322**
Dhruva accompanied by, to spiritual world, 584, **585,** 587
Dhruva reunited with, **462–64**
as Dhruva's mother, 463, 465, **583–**84, **585,** 587
greatness of, 457
hears of insult, **322**
instructs Dhruva, **323, 329**
neglected by Uttānapāda, **324, 378–**79
worshiped Lord, 465
Sun setting compared to Dhruva fighting, **488,** 489
Superiors
meeting with, **341**
respect for, 218
Supersoul (Paramātmā)
as *ātmā,* 14
Atri meditated on, 20
as *caitya-guru* within, 355
Dattātreya incarnation of, **14,** 16
directs Brahmā & Śiva, 20, 21
directs everyone, 299-300
in heart, 617
in householder-thief example, 777-78
less intelligent mystics can't find, 649
Lord as, **407, 421, 532, 669,** 778, **813,** 814
obeisances to, 111-13
pleased by Dhruva, 396
prompts from within, 297
sends spiritual master, 333
Śiva meditates on, 110-11
Śiva's respects to, 112, **113**
soul
dependent on, 511
serves, 403
as supreme spiritual master, 355
as transcendental, 768
"unification" of, with soul, 396
Viṣṇu as, 297
See also: Supreme Lord; Viṣṇu
Supreme Brahman
impersonalists misunderstand, 519
Kṛṣṇa as, 731
realization of, 619, 740
See also: Supreme Lord
Supreme Lord
abode(s) of
beyond material qualities, 280-81
desire trees in, 206
quality in, 281
See also: Vṛndāvana; *specific abodes*
as absolute, 399
as Absolute Truth, 547
acceptance of, 270-71
accepted by *ācāryas,* 82
accepting will of, **340**
accepts offerings in love, 296
accepts own share, not others', 296
activities of
"contradictory," 776, **777–**78
His energies perform, **407,** 518, 519, **520,** 521, **532,** 773
See also: Supreme Lord, pastimes of
acts to show example, 273
as Acyuta, **557**
addressed by demigods about Dhruva, **394**
addresses
Atri Muni, **27, 29**
Dakṣa, **297**
demigods about Dhruva, **396**
as Adhokṣaja, 116, **747,** 748, **820,** 821
as *ādi-puruṣa,* 422
advent(s) of
beyond material qualities, 281
for devotee's deliverance & demon's demise, 845-46
devotees' view of, 371
as free & transcendental, 370-71
by His internal potency, 281, 715-16
living entity's appearance contrasted to, 422
for maintaining order, **44**
See also: Avatāras; Incarnations
as *akiñcana-gocara,* 106
as all-
knowing, 188

Supreme Lord
as all- (*continued*)
pervading, 390, 617
powerful, **404**
aloof from material creation, 291, 292, 297-98, 302, 519, 521, 532, **548,** 549, **767,** 768, 769
as *amṛta,* 277
anger & blessings of, as equal, 225
animals' needs supplied by, 671
as *antaḥ-praviṣṭaḥ śāstā,* 390
approached by depleted men, 106
approached in two ways, 613
in arena of sacrifice, **253-55**
asked to revive animals, **271-72**
associating with, 607
atheists can't understand, 419-20
atheists meet, as death, 766
as *ātmā,* 14
in atoms, 390
attached to nothing, **273**
attracted to Dhruva, 396
aunt of, Prasūti as, 276-77
author of *Vedas,* 81-82
author's obeisances to, 2
as basis
of Brahman, 389-90
of everything, 82, 297, 298
of universe, **43,** 44
of varieties, 43
beauty of, **254, 255, 256, 356-61**
inspires surrender, 357
behavior of, as good, 225
benedictions from
as beyond expectation, 349
compared with demigods', 330
benedictions sanctioned by, 350
beyond
attachment, **273**
contamination, 421
everyone's appreciation, **259,** 260
goodness mode, 283
impersonal Brahman, 607
materialists, 216-17
material knowledge, **268-**69
material qualities, 25, **280-**81, **282**
material senses, 115, 116, 216-17, **268-**69

Supreme Lord
beyond (*continued*)
material world, 82, 268-69
modes of nature, **518,** 519, **530,** 531
sense perception, 748, 821
Bhagavad-gītā reveals, 529
as *bhakta-vatsala,* 279-80
as *bhava-cchidam,* 549
as *bhṛtya-vatsala,* 328
as *bhūtāvāsa,* 511
birth-death cycle stopped by, **445**
birthless, 422
birth of. *See:* Supreme Lord, advent(s) of
blaspheming Him, 130
blissful always, 104
bodily effulgence of, **254, 258**
body, spiritual, of. *See:* Supreme Lord, form(s) of
body as temple of, 111
body of, 531
society as, 248
See also: Supreme Lord, form(s) of
books (two) about, 289-90
Brahmā
enlightened by, **408-9**
instructed by, 82
as instrument of, **772,** 773
& Śiva respect, 331
as Brahmā, 139, 314
brāhmaṇas not neglected by, **246,** 247
as Brahman's basis, **423**
Brahmā under, 831
Caitanya as, 284
as *caitya-guru,* 355
carrier of, **22,** 23
as cause
of all causes, 423, **518,** 519, **520,** 524, **530, 774**
of Brahmā & Śiva, 297-98
& effect, 297-98
of everything, 297-98
supreme, 297-98
transcendental, 268
of universe, 44
chanting about. *See:* Chanting, about Lord
checked by none, 294
cited. *See: Bhagavad-gītā* cited

Supreme Lord (*continued*)
commanding, as improper, 116
compared to
cow, **425,** 426
desire tree, **410**
devotee, 769
electric powerhouse, 521, 774
fire, 291, 521
one with zeros, 107
potter, 518-19
proprietor or master, 232
root, 88
stomach, 88
sun, 44
sunrise, 255
touchstone, 522
whole body, 546
compared with
conditioned souls, 15, 371
human beings, 273
consciousness in, vs. living beings, 15
conserves universe in Himself, **285**
considered ordinary by rascals, 269
as controller, **533,** 814
& enters all, 390
of everyone, 299-300
of goodness mode, **282,** 299
of internal energy, 116
of opulence, 330
of *pradhāna* & *prakṛti*, 390
"covered" by acts of nature, 44
as creator, **407, 518,** 519, **520,** 521, **522,** 523, **770-72,** 773
as creator, maintainer, & destroyer, **517,** 521, 522, **530, 532, 774**
at Dakṣa's sacrifice, 125
as death, 522, 533, 766
decorations on, **358, 359, 360**
in Deity. *See:* Deity forms
in Deity worship, **364,** 369
delivers us from material existence, **548,** 549
demigods
assist, 719
offer obeisances to, **257**
originate in, 397-98
sanctioned by, 350

Supreme Lord
demigods (*continued*)
servants of, **285,** 286, 287-88
under, 445, **533,** 534, 637
worship, **670,** 716
worship to, inspired by, 139
demons killed by, 225, 255, 845-46
dependence on protection by, 267
described by Ananta, 259
described in disciplic line, 357-58
desired to go to Dhruva, 396
desires fulfilled by, 343, 350-51, **373, 637-**38
at destruction of universe, **285**
determination to satisfy, 382
devotees of. *See:* Devotee(s)
devotional service to. *See:* Devotional service
as Dharādhara, **776**
Dhruva &. *See:* Dhruva, Lord & . . .
difficult to approach, 328
difficult to satisfy, 382
as *dīna-nātha*, 607
direct acceptance of, 270-71
directs everyone, 299, 300
direct will of, in spiritual energy, 116
discusses Dhruva, **395-96**
distress mitigated by, 328, 331
distress of, as bliss, 104
duty to please, 323-33, 554, 615, 671
in eight-armed form, 255, **270,** 271
energy of. *See:* Energies of Supreme Lord
engaged disciple (Arjuna), 349
enjoyer of sacrifices, 130
enters & controls all, 390
envy of Him in scholars, 111
equating Him with others, 136
equal toward everyone, 131, **523,** 524
eternally with Lakṣmī, 6, 277
as everything, 291-92
everything comes from, **557**
example set by, 273
existed before creation, 25, 277, 297, 299
expansions of, 694, 697, 733, **772,** 777
all beings as, 287-88
as *svāṁśa* & *vibhinnāṁśa*, 288
See also: Incarnation(s)

Supreme Lord (*continued*)
face & smile of, **256, 356**
fame of, 608
as father of all, 82
favors devotees, 279-80
feet of. *See:* Supreme Lord, lotus feet of
female never, 358-59
feminine feature of, 359
followers of. *See:* Devotee(s)
following instructions of, 784
food offered to. *See: Prasāda*
food supplied by, 802, 804-5
not forced to appear, 370-71
forgotten nowadays, 671
form(s) of
as basis of Brahman, 389-90
beauty of, **356-61**
as described in disciplic line, 357-58
devotional service reveals, 417
four- & eight-handed, **270,** 271
as four-handed Nārāyaṇa, **358,** 359
Indra describes, **270**
as knowable, 270-71
manifests in Hare Kṛṣṇa *mantra,* 364
meditation on, 217, **356-61,** 372, 390
as nondifferent, 399
as not imaginary, 357-58
paintings of, 358
as supreme, 547
form possessed by, 116
friendly attitude in, 296
as friend of distressed, **409**
as friend of poor, 607
fruitive results awarded by, **525**
fulfills devotee's desires, 343, 350-51, **373**
gain from, as beyond expectation, 349
Ganges from feet of, **13, 202,** 203
glance of, demigods pray for, **44**
glories of
Ananta describes, 259
as unlimited, 259, 260
glorification to. *See:* Glorification to Lord
as goal
of life, 426, **533**
of sacrifices, 130
of *Vedas,* 293

Supreme Lord (*continued*)
goddess of fortune always with, 6, 277, **695**
goodness controlled by, **282,** 299
as Govinda, 422, 423
as *guṇa-ātmā,* 768
as Hari, 813-14
hearing about. *See:* Hearing about Supreme Lord
in heart, **399, 401,** 557, 558, **813,** 814
in householder-thief example, 778
as ideal husband, 8
immortality given by, 445
incarnations of. *See:* Incarnation(s) of Supreme Lord
includes devotees, 91-92
independence from, in none, **300**
independent, 716, **770-71**
inspires demigod worship, 139
instructed Brahmā, 82
internal energy of. *See:* Supreme Lord, energy of, internal
as *īśvara,* 814
not *jñāni-vatsala,* 279-80
karma awarded by, 556
killing by, 294, 505, **522,** 770-71
of demons, 225, 255
kind to devotee, 328
king represents, 629, 667-68, 735-37
knowledgeable persons dear to, **279**
knowledge about. *See:* Knowledge, about Lord
knows everything, 421, 442-43
Kṛṣṇa as, 287-88, 777, 814
as liberated, **420-21,** 784
liberation via, 229, 440-41
living beings &. *See:* Living entities, Lord &...
lotus features of, **452,** 453, 572
lotus feet of
devotees think of, 155
Ganges from, **13, 202,** 203
Kailāsa rivers from, **202,** 203
meditation on, 155, 355
vs. pilgrimage sites, 203-4
pleasure from, 155
sanctifying effect of, 203-4

Supreme Lord
lotus feet of (*continued*)
Śiva meditates on, **265**
spiritualizing effect of, 203-4
as *tīrtha-pāda,* 203
love for. *See:* Love, for Lord
love for seeing, 253, 278
maintains everyone, **421,** 422, 671, 737
as male, 306, 358
manifests in Hare Kṛṣṇa *mantra,* 364
as master mystic, 765
master of *pradhāna* & *puruṣa,* 390
meditation on. *See:* Meditation, on Lord
mercy of
compared to law enforcement, 520
on devotee, 328, 409, **425,** 426, 445, 529, 591
devotee accepts, 224, 336-37
difficulty as, 336-37
enlightenment by, 405
glorifying Lord by, 404
knowledge by, 419, 420
liberation by, 506
needed for success, 326, **327**
punishment as, 250
via spiritual master, 630
merging with, as sense gratification, 375
mitigates distress, 328, 331
modes of nature under, **421,** 768
as *mukti-pati,* 440
as Mukunda, **452**
name of, if unknown, 19
Nārada glorifies, 614
Nara-Nārāyaṇa as, 46
nature directed by, 516, 517, 519, 768
as *nimitta-mātra,* 519, 521
as *nirguṇa,* 282
nondifferent from Brahmā & Śiva, **297-98, 300, 302**
obeisances to
by demigods, **257**
by devotee, 116-17
by Śiva, **113,** 116
oblations accepted by, **260**
offenses to, 680, 681, 846
as omniscient, 188

Supreme Lord (*continued*)
as one
with all beings, 279, **297-**98, 299-303
& different, **407,** 768
in many, 777
with His energies, 279, **291,** 299
as origin of all, 82, 297-98, 423, 747-48
ornaments of, **255-56**
paintings of, 258
parts of, types of, 15
pastime(s) of
not accepted by some, 270
as always good, 225
blissful always, 104
bliss via hearing of, **274-**75
direct acceptance of, 270-71
discussing, among devotees, 603-4
everyone may know, 270-71
hearing about, 539, 599-600, 602
Lord unattached to, **273**
meditation on, 371
in *Śrīmad-Bhāgavatam,* 615
See also: Supreme Lord, activities of
as person, 116-17, 405
plan of, 773, 774, 777, 778
pleasing
compared to watering root, 396
determination for, 382
via devotee's offering, 296
via Dhruva &, 396
as difficult, 382
as duty, 323-33
as necessary, 276
pleases all, 88, 396
pleases demigods, 234
via sacrifice, **86**
via share of sacrifice, **296**
via *varṇāśrama* society, 222
via work, 232-33
potency of
creation by, 516
internal, 715-16
See also: Energies of Supreme Lord
prasāda of, offered to demigods, 303, **304**
prayers to. *See:* Prayer(s), to Lord; Prayer(s), to Viṣṇu
presence of, as spiritual world, 532

Supreme Lord (*continued*)
presence of, for sacrifice, 276
as proprietor, 787, 792-93
protection by. *See:* Protection, by Lord
Pṛthu as partial expansion of, **697, 700**
at Pṛthu's horse sacrifices, **813-16**
punishment by, as mercy, 250
purifies materialistic worshiper, 330
as *puruṣa,* 258
as *puṣkara-nābha,* 572
qualities in, as transcendental, 282-83
qualities in, known to devotee, 282-83
quoted
on Dhruva's award, **429-35**
on hearing Kṛṣṇa's words from pure devotees, 414
See also: Bhagavad-gītā quoted
related to Lakṣmī eternally, 6, 277
relationship with, forgetfulness of, 546
relieves distress, 328, 331
remembrance about, **551,** 552-54, 606-7
See also: Remembering Supreme Lord
revealed
to devotees, 269
in Hare Kṛṣṇa *mantra,* 364
by His will, 116
in internal potency, 116
via love, 253, 255
to nonmaterialistic men, 278
to pure consciousness, **113,** 114, 115
to purified senses, 115-16
as sacrifice, **291**
sacrifice to. *See:* Sacrifice(s), to Lord
in sacrificial arena, **253-55**
saintly person sees, 399
sanctifying effect of, 203-4
sanctions demigods, 350
satisfying
determination for, 382
via devotee's qualities, 514, 515
as difficult, 382
via glorification, 717
via share of sacrifice, **296**
via *varṇāśrama* society, 222
via work, 232-33
seen
by devotee, 399

Supreme Lord
seen (*continued*)
after hard austerity, 444
via love, 253, 278, 558, 617
by nonmaterialistic men, 278
via purified senses, 115-16
on *vasudeva* platform, 440
sends representative (*guru*), 333
service to. *See:* Devotional service
as shelter
for one in forest, 332
for saintly persons, 203-4
from troubled life, **263-64**
as Śipiviṣṭa, 639
Śiva
& Brahmā respect, 331
equal to, originally, 220
under, 831
as *śiva-viriñci-nutam,* 331
social orders part of, 222
society as body of, 248
solves all problems, 394-95
as source
of all, 82, 297-98
of demigods, 297-98
spiritual energy of. *See:* Supreme Lord, internal energy of
spiritualizing effect of, 203-4
via spiritual master, 432-33
spiritual world by, 574
Śrīmad-Bhāgavatam as topics of, 615
success depends on, 326, **327**
sun as eye of, 593
as Supersoul, **407, 421, 532, 669,** 778, **813,** 814
See also: Supersoul
supreme above all, 287-88
as supreme spiritual master, 355
as supreme will, **223-**24
surrender to. *See:* Surrender, to Lord
as Śyāmasundara, 399
symbols of
four described, **358**
purpose of, 255
taking shelter of, in forest, 332
temple of. *See:* Temple(s)
thinking you are, 287

Supreme Lord (*continued*)
as time, **522, 523, 545**
topics of, 615, 749
as transcendental, 25, 82, **261,** 268, **280-81, 282,** 371, 421, **525, 530,** 531, **767,** 768, 769
as *try-adhīśa,* 421
universal form of, society in, 222
unlimited glories of, 259, 260
as Vāsudeva, 114-15
as *vatsala,* 279-80
Vena imitated, 676, 677
Viṣṇu as, 257
weapons of, 846
will of
spiritual energy under, 116
as supreme, **223-24**
as within & without, 417, **557**
work for
freedom via, 233
necessity of, 232-33
worshipable by all, 257
worshipers of. *See:* Devotee(s)
worship to. *See:* Worship, to Lord
as Yajñapuruṣa, 556, 668
as Yogeśvara, 765
See also: Absolute Truth; Brahman, Supreme; Kṛṣṇa; Nārāyaṇa; Viṣṇu
Surabhi cows, 816-17
Suras. See: Demigod(s); Devotee(s)
Suroci (son of Kratu), **35**
Surrender
imperfect & perfect, 357
to Lord
compared with surrender to others, 357
desires fulfilled in, 350-51
by devotee, 529
in forest, 332
as freedom from *māyā,* 229
as independence, 451
inspired by Lord's beauty, 357
meaning of, 381
nature's laws surpassed by, 572, 670
as person, 116-17
protection by, 267, 286, 381
as real religion, 834
Surrender
to Lord (*continued*)
recommended, 766, 770-71, 778
as religion, 350
revelation by, 405-6
sin absolved by, 814
by subordinates, 192
transcends curses, 76-77
as wisdom, 409
See also: Supreme Lord, surrender to
Suruci
advantage taken by, 317-18
amazed by Dhruva's acts, 392
Dhruva blessed by, **460,** 461
fate of, **432, 481**
favored by Uttānapāda, **316,** 317-18
insult by, as benediction, 325
insults Dhruva, **318-20**
Suniti's compassion on, 457
Sūta (a praiser)
praised Pṛthu, **707, 708**
Pṛthu's identity known to, 714
Sūta Gosvāmī quoted on Vidura & Maitreya, **748**
Svadhā (daughter of Dakṣa), **49**
Sva-dhāmnā defined, 405
Svāhā (daughter of Dakṣa), **46, 47**
Svāhā, chanting of, 128-29
Svahna (son of Yajña), **9**
Svāmī defined, 382
Svāṁśa expansions of Lord, 15, 287
See also: Viṣṇu-tattva
Svārājyam defined, 451
Svarvīthi, **622**
Svāyambhuva Manu
Brahmāvarta controlled by, **811**
in calf form, **792**
daughters of, **1, 11**
descendants of, **314, 315**
desired Lord as son, 3
Dhruva advised by, **507-41**
Dhruva as descendant of, 428, 535
as first mentioned in *Bhāgavatam,* 2
gave daughter for son, **3**
gets son of Ruci (Yajña), **6**
knew Lord would appear, 3
law of, cited on punishment, **314**

Svāyambhuva Manu (*continued*)
son of Brahmā, **314**
worship of Lord by, **327**
See also: Manu(s)
Svāyambhuva Manu quoted
on anger, **507, 538, 540**
on bodily concept of life, **510**
on creation & procreation, **515**
on devotee's good qualities, **513**
on liberation, **514**
on Lord as controller, **532, 533**
on Lord as creator, maintainer, & annihilator, **518, 530,** 532
on Lord as inconceivable, **528**
on Lord as ultimate cause, **518, 520, 530**
on Lord's transcendental nature, **522, 525, 530**
on philosophies of life, **526**
on time & *karma*, **523–24**
Śvetadvīpa, 430, 435
Swan & *paramahaṁsa,* analogy of, 438
Swan carrier of Brahmā, **22,** 23

T

Takṣaka, **802**
Tamo-guṇa. See: Ignorance, mode of
Tapasya
defined, 555
See also: Austerities
Tastes, Earth produces, 818
Taxation
by king, **665,** 666, 667
by modern leaders, 555, 721, 722
Teacher(s), spiritual. *See: Brāhmaṇa(s);* Spiritual master(s)
Tears, two types of, 458
Temple(s) of Supreme Lord
body as, 111
Deity in. *See:* Deity forms
ISKCON, 604
as spiritual world, 532
as transcendental, 581
See also: Prayers; Worship
Temple worship to Lord. *See:* Deity worship
Ṭhākura Haridāsa, 567
Thieves, 172
flourishing or fleeing, 653
government &, 665-66, **683–86,** 738
gṛhastha &, 778
kings punishing, 626, 666, 787
present population as, 786-89
punished & unpunished, 626
Thoughts of matter, giving up, 355
Thunderbolts, land leveled by, 791, 807
Tibetans, 483
Tigers & people, analogy of, 108
Tigmaketu, **622**
Tilaka
of false devotee, 846
purifies body, 579
Time
compared to snake, 264
heavenly happiness ended by, **412**
Lord as, **522, 523, 545**
present, calculated, 472
"*Tiṣṭha tiṣṭha*" challenge, 825
Titikṣā (daughter of Dakṣa), **40**
Tolerance
of all as Lord's will, **340**
in chanting Lord's name, 227
exemplary persons in, 227, 228
of happiness & distress, **340**
by Kṛṣṇa consciousness, 265
in Lord's devotees, 226-27, 228, 229
in Parīkṣit, 228
of relative's insults, 108-9
on transcendental platform, 335
Tongue, use of, 259
Toṣa (son of Yajña), **9**
Total & unit energy, identification of, 393
Touchstone
compared to Lord, 522
of Sanātana Gosvāmī, 240
Tractor in desert, example of, 788
Training for boys, 344
Trance
Dhruva in, **565, 566**
See also: Samādhi

Transcendence
via devotional service, 514, 515
hearing about, 612
See also: Liberation; Spiritual world
Transcendentalist(s)
beyond
social orders, 145
Vedic rules, **143, 144,** 145
compared to demigods in air, **143**
devotees as, 145
may seem mundane, 143
spiritual world attained by, 517
See also: Devotee(s); Sage(s); *Yogī(s); specific transcendentalists*
Transcendental sound, 125
See also: Chanting
Transmigration of soul(s)
to abominable forms, 290
complete change by, 289-90
consciousness carried in, 243
for devotees of Lord, 243
foods eaten in, 259
as forced, 371
freedom from. *See:* Liberation
via *karma,* 311, 371
via subtle body, 567
via *yoga* process, 150-51, 152-53
See also: Birth-death cycle
Travel, space. *See:* Space travel
Tree(s)
banyan tree of Śiva, **209, 210**
desire trees, **206**
on Earth & heavenly planets, 473-74
juices for, **804**
in Kailāsa, **196-98**
in Kali-yuga, 818
at Pṛthu's horse sacrifices, **818**
at Uttānapāda's reception for Dhruva, **466**
watering root of, serving Lord compared to, 547, 607-8, 849
Tretā-yuga, life span in, 471, 560
Tridaṇḍi-sannyāsī defined, 830
Trita, **624**
Truth
Kṛṣṇa consciousness reveals, 564
Truth *(continued)*
real & shadow, 563
See also: Absolute Truth; Knowledge
Try-adhīśa defined, 421
Tulasī plant, **367-68**
Tuṣitas (demigods), **9**
Tuṣṭi (daughter of Dakṣa), **40**
Twice-born persons, **603,** 604
defined, 132
See also: Brāhmaṇa(s); Kṣatriya(s); Vaiśya(s)

U

Uddhava, **307**
Ulbaṇa (son of Kratu), **35**
Ulmuka, **624**
Unhappiness (distress)
acceptance of, as Lord's mercy, 336-37
material vs. spiritual, 103-4
See also: Suffering
Unit & total energy, identification of, 393
United Nations, 781
United States of America, 344
Unity in diversity, 302
See also: Oneness
Universal form of Lord, 222
Universe(s)
basis of, Lord as, **43,** 297-98
cause of, Lord as, 44
conserved in Lord, 286
created by Brahmā secondarily, 2
creation of. *See:* Creation (act of)
at crisis time, 440
destruction of. *See:* Annihilation of universe(s)
dissolution of, **419, 430,** 435
as energy of Lord, 43, 299
as illusory, 99
light of, source of, 589
Lord(s) of, 28
Lord causes, **518**
Lord's existence precedes, 25
as Lord's universal form, 43
Nārada's travels in, 347

Universe(s) (*continued*)
reality in, 43
as reflection of spiritual world, 43, 99
situated in Lord, **43**
space travel in & beyond, 577
suffocated by Dhruva, **393–94**
variety in, 43
See also: Creation, the; Heavenly planet(s); Material world; Material nature; Planet(s)
Unkind words of relatives, **108–**9, 118
Unnati (daughter of Dakṣa), **40**
Upadeva-vara defined, 94
Upendra, Lord, 704
Uragas, 94
Ūrdhva-retāḥ defined, 309-10, 505
Ūrja, **622**
Ūrjā (wife of Vasiṣṭha), **34,** 35
Uśanā (son of Vedaśirā), **37**
Utathya (son of Aṅgirā), **31**
Utkala
Dhruva's kingdom didn't interest, **616**
family misunderstood, **621**
fools misunderstood, **620**
parents of, **480**
transcendental status of, **617, 618**
Uttama
death of, **432, 481**
Dhruva reunited with, **462**
Sunīti's kindness toward, 457
Yakṣa killed, 507
Uttānapāda, King, 428
addressed by Nārada, **377, 380–82**
afraid for Dhruva, **379,** 381
Dhruva
enthroned by, **476**
reunited with, **454–56,** 457, **458, 459**
satisfied, **475**
doubted Dhruva's survival, **454,** 465
empowered by Lord, **315**
explains to Nārada, **378–80**
favoritism in, 317, **324,** 378-79
meditated on Dhruva, **383**
neglected Dhruva, **316,** 317, **378–**79
neglected Sunīti, **378–**79
palace of, **470, 471,** 472, **473, 474**
queens of. *See:* Sunīti; Suruci
Uttānapāda (*continued*)
reception for Dhruva by, **465–69**
repents, **378–80**
retired to forest, **477–**78
as saintly king, 475, 476, 480
son of Manu, **10, 315**
sought self-realization, 480

V

Vagina in Śiva worship, 79
Vaikuṇṭha. *See:* Spiritual world
Vaiṣṇavas. *See:* Devotee(s)
Vaiṣṇavīya Purāṇa cited on God & demigods, 136
Vaiśya(s) (farmers & merchants)
approaching supreme destination, 692
as "belly" of society, 345
blasphemy if heard by, 141
charity distributed by, 554, 555
defined, 83
family spirit kept by, 334
jewels gathered by, 820
part of Lord's cosmic form, 222
permanent class of, 83
social role of, 691, 750
Vājapeya sacrifice of Dakṣa, **91**
Vālakhilyas, **33–**34
Vāmanadeva, **218**
Vānaprasthas, duty of, 658
See also: Retirement
Vandī
offered prayers for Pṛthu, **707,** 708
Pṛthu's identity known to, 714
Varāha, Lord (boar incarnation), **293,** 371, **775, 776**
Varāha Purāṇa cited on Lord's parts, 15
Variety in universe & Lord, 43
Varīyān (son of Pulaha), **33**
Varṇāśrama-dharma
always present, 83
as body of Lord, 248
brāhmaṇas follow, 222
created by Lord, 222
as etiquette standard, 83
Lord satisfied via, 222

Varṇāśrama-dharma (continued)
money in, 725
neglected now, 222
as permanent, 83
sannyāsa in, 832
social structure of, 750
social value of, 668, 670
worshiping Lord by, **667,** 668
See also: Brahmacārī(s); Brāhmaṇa(s); Gṛhastha(s); Kṣatriya(s); Sannyāsī(s); Society, human; *Śūdra(s); Vaiśya(s); Vānaprastha(s)*
Varuṇa, Lord
as ocean king, 725
present to Pṛthu from, **703**
Pṛthu compared to, **725**
Vasiṣṭha, sons of, **34, 35**
Vasu, **622**
Vasubhṛdyāna (son of Kratu), **35**
Vāsudeva, Lord
controls internal energy, 116
defined, 114-15
directs Brahmā & Śiva, 20, 21
has form, 116
Śiva meditates on, 116
See also: Supreme Lord
Vasudeva stage, 440
defined, 114-15
Lord revealed in, 114, 115
spiritual master in, 114
Vatsala, Lord as, 279-80
Vatsara, **479, 621, 622**
Vāyu, Lord, **480, 703**
Vayunā (daughter of Pitās), **49**
Vedānta quoted on source of everything, 422
Vedānta-sūtra
cited
on consciousness in beings, 15
on knowing Brahman, 75
quoted on source, 298
"Vedāntists," **595**
Vedas
activities in
design behind, 144-45
two kinds of, **144**
as *apauruṣeya,* 81-82
Vedas (continued)
authored by Kṛṣṇa, 81-82
authority of, as proved by deviants, 83
blasphemy to, 80, 82-83, **84**
Brahmā didn't author, 81-82
Brahman taught in, 80
brahminical qualification for hearing, 63
as bridge (*setu*), 83
Buddha rejected, 80, 844
civilization based on, 80, 83
compared to flowers, 74
Deity form as, 293
disbelievers in, 80
divisions of activities in, **144–**45
elevation via, 80, 83
as eternal, 81-82
etiquette established by, 83
follower(s) of
compared with Śiva's, 83, 84
curse on, **72, 74**
don't know Lord, **262–**63
Kṛṣṇa critical of, 262-63
as materialistic, **72, 74**
foolish followers of, 595
goal of
Lord as, 293
transcendence as, 145
going to Godhead via, 785
history of, as untraceable, 81-82
hymns of. *See: Mantras*
knowledge in, 781
known via Lord & spiritual master, 403
liberation via, 80, 83
Lord as beyond, 282
Lord's devotees beyond, 145
material happiness via, **72, 74**
as mother, 80
prayers by *Vedas* personified, **283–84**
qualification for knowing, 4-5, 63
rejected by animalistic persons, 83
rituals of, as inadequate, 248
sacrifices in. *See:* Sacrifice
as *setu* (bridge), 83
Śiva as beyond, 143, 145
society as divided by, 80, 83
śūdras can't understand, **63,** 604
supremacy of, as proved by deviants, 83

Vedas (continued)
as *traiguṇya-viṣayā,* 262
transcendentalists beyond, **143, 144,** 145
worship of Kṛṣṇa equals, 293
Yajur Veda, 7
See also: Vedic literature; *specific Vedic literatures*
Vedaśirā (son of Prāṇa), **37**
Veda Upaniṣad cited on sacrifices, 284
Veda-vāda-ratāḥ defined, 595
Veda-vādī defined, 595
Vedic culture
caste spirit in, 334
divisions of life in, 337, 339
divorce in, 122
dowry system in, 97
giving daughter for son in, 3
king in, 629, 663, 731, 735-36
knowledge in, 781
Manu's status in, 488
marriage in, 642
bodies shared in, 122
kṣatriya fighting at, 182
married life in, 8
retiring from family life in, 627, 647
saṁskāra system in, 334
sannyāsa in, 832
for satisfying Lord, 671
sex life in, 505
śrāddha ritual in, 798
See also: Society, human; *Varṇāśrama-dharma;* Vedic injunction(s)
Vedic injunction(s)
on following great souls, 782
as *śruti,* 781
on waking up to self-realization, 405
See also: Religious principles
Vedic literature
condemns bad association, 154
explains cause of universe, 44
Lord understood via, **44**
main books on Kṛṣṇa, 289-90
meditation as recommended in, 356
qualification for knowing, 4-5
unqualified commentaries on, 5
See also: Vedas
Vedic *mantras. See:* Hare Kṛṣṇa *mantra; Mantras; Vedas*
Vena, King
Aṅga disappointed with, **625, 627**
Bāhuka born from body of, **689, 690,** 694
compared to snake, **659**
cruelty of, **643, 644, 653**
demigods as considered by, **676**
as Dhruva's descendant, 687-89
false pride of, **654, 655,** 676-78
Lord imitated by, 676, 677
male & female born from body of, **693-97**
mischievous, **659,** 660, **661**
sacrifices stopped by, **655**
sages
advised, **662-65, 667, 670, 672, 673**
churned arms of, **693**
churned thighs of, **689-**90
considered position of, **656-61**
cursed, **626, 628**
enthroned, **652**
killed, **682**
scorned by, **673-79**
Sunīthā preserved body of, **682,** 690
as Sunīthā's son, **659**
thieves feared, **653**
Vibhakta-vīryaḥ defined, 520
Vibhinnāṁśa expansions of Lord, 15, 287-88
Vibhiṣaṇa (brother of Rāvaṇa), **32**
Vibhu (son of Yajña), **9**
Vidanti defined, 740
Vidhātā (son of Bhṛgu), **36, 37**
Vidura
asks about Atri's sons, **16**
asks about Dakṣa & Śiva, **53, 54, 55**
didn't offend demigods, 296
Maitreya inspired by, **748,** 749
as Maitreya's disciple, **630**
Vidura quoted
on Aṅga, **627**
on Nārada, **613**
on Pṛthu on Mother Earth, **744-45**
on sages cursing Vena, **628**
Vidyā. See: Knowledge

Vidyādhara(s), **21**
mystic powers of, **798–99**
at Pṛthu's horse sacrifices, **815**
Vijayadhvaja Tīrtha cited on demigods honoring Dhruva, 468
Violence. *See:* Killing
Vīrabhadra demon
as anger personified, 169
attacks Dakṣa, **179, 181, 182, 183, 184**
beheads Dakṣa, **184–85**
created by Śiva, **167–68**
described, **167–68, 175**
dust raised by, **171, 172**
pollution by, **251–52**
Virajā (son of Kratu), **35**
Viraja (son of Pūrṇimā), **13**
Vīrarāghava Ācārya cited
on *alakā*, 202
on Dakṣa, 176
on initiating *caṇḍālas*, 366
Vīrāsana sitting posture, **214**
Virāṭ-rūpa, society part of, 222
Vision
material, compared with spiritual, 536, 733-34
in pure devotee, 557-58
Visiting of friends (relatives), **101–2, 105, 107,** 108
Viṣṇu, Lord
abode of. *See:* Dhruvaloka; Viṣṇuloka
accepts offerings in love, 296
accepts own share, not others', 296
addresses Atri Muni, **27, 29**
addresses Dakṣa, **297**
as *amṛta*, 277
appears in arena of sacrifice, **253–55**
asked to make priests devotees, 278
asked to revive animals, **271–72**
associates of
bodily features of, **569–**70
as spiritual, 580
as *ātmā*, 14
aunt of, Prasūti as, 276-77
avoided Dakṣa's sacrifice, **188**
as basis of all, 297-98
beauty of, **254, 255, 256**
beyond material qualities, **282**
Viṣṇu (*continued*)
blaspheming Him, 130
bodily effulgence of, **254, 258**
as Brahmā, 139
brāhmaṇas not neglected by, **246,** 247
brāhmaṇas protected by, 294
Caitanya as, 284
carrier of, **22,** 23
as cause
of Brahmā & Śiva, 297
& effect, 297-98
supreme, 297-98
chanting about, purification by, 252
compared to
fire, 291
sunrise, 255
Dattātreya incarnation of, **14,** 16, **30**
defects absent in, 82
eight-handed form of, **255, 270,** 271
energy of
as basis of all, 297, 299
as cause & effect, 298
as everything, **291–**92
See also: Energies of Supreme Lord
equalizing Him with others, 136
existed before creation, 277, 297, 299
face & smile of, **256**
followers of, must be satisfied, 91-92
food offered to, 146-47, 303, 304
four- & eight-handed forms of, **270,** 271
friendly attitude in, 296
on Garbha water, 759
Garbhodakaśāyī Viṣṇu, 28
as goal of sacrifices, 7, 130, **283–84, 296**
as God above all, 257
goddess of fortune always with, 277
goodness mode controlled by, **282,** 289, 748
holds four items, 846
as incarnation (*guṇa-avatāra*), 299
incarnation(s) of
Brahmā & Śiva as, 299
qualitative (*guṇa-avatāras*), 299
See also: Incarnation(s) of Supreme Lord
includes devotees, 91-92
not known by followers of *Vedas*, **262–**63
Kṛṣṇa
above, 287-88

Viṣṇu
Kṛṣṇa (*continued*)
as, 356
as origin of, 287-88, 748
Kṣīrodakaśāyī Viṣṇu, 28
as Lord of universe, 28
lotus feet of, Śiva meditates on, **265**
Mahā-Viṣṇu, 25
as maintainer, 521, 522
meditation on. *See:* Meditation, on Viṣṇu
as *nirguṇa*, 282
obeisances to, by demigods, 257
oblations accepted by, **260**
as omniscient, 188
as one with & different from Brahmā & Śiva, 302
ornaments of, **255, 256**
"percentage" of Kṛṣṇa in, 15
planet of. *See:* Viṣṇuloka
pleased
via devotee's offering, 296
via share of sacrifice, **296**
pleasing
as necessary, 276
pleases all, 88
prasāda of, offered to demigods, 303, 304
prayers to. *See:* Prayers, to Viṣṇu
present for Pṛthu from, **704**
protected *brāhmaṇas*, 294
protection by, as best, 294
protects from sin, 286
qualities in, as transcendental, 282-83
sacrifice
not aimed at, 146-47
meant for, 7, 130, **283-84, 296**
needs presence of, 276
to, remnants of, 147, 233
as sacrifice, **291**
satisfied by share of sacrifice, **296**
seen via love, 253
service to. *See:* Devotional service to Supreme Lord
as shelter from troubled life, **263-64**
as source
of all, 297-98
of demigods, 297-98
as Supersoul within, 297

Viṣṇu (*continued*)
symbols of, purpose of, 255
transcendental status of, **261, 282**
worshipable by all, 257
worshipers of, may be poor, 147
worship to. *See:* Worship, to Viṣṇu
as Yajña, 7, 284
as Yajñeśa, 130
as Yajñeśvara, 276
See also: Garbhodakaśāyī Viṣṇu; Kṣīrodakaśāyi Viṣṇu; Nārāyaṇa; Supersoul; Supreme Lord
Viṣṇudūtas. *See* Viṣṇu, associates of
Viṣṇuloka
as achieved rarely, **575, 576**
inhabitants of, 569-70
stars circle, **575**
as transcendental planet, **576,** 577
Viṣṇu-mantra defined, 446
Viṣṇu Purāṇa cited
on living beings, 15
on Lord's energies, 291
on sacrifices, 284
on *varṇāśrama-dharma*, 668
Viṣṇu-tattva
defined, 813
"percentage" of Kṛṣṇa in, 15
See also: Svāṁśa expansions of Kṛṣṇa
Viśravā (son of Pulastya), **32**
Viśvaga (son of Pūrṇimā), **13**
Viśvakarmā, **705**
Viśvanātha Cakravartī Ṭhākura cited
on curse on Śiva, 67
on Dhruvaloka, 435
on Dhruva vs. Yakṣas, 487
on following spiritual master, 383-84
on impersonal Brahman, 423
on *mahātmā*, 176
on Manu, 3
on personal & impersonal realization, 424
on Satī, 156
on Śiva's unhappiness, 103
on spiritual master & Supreme Lord, 433, 630
Viśvanātha Cakravartī Ṭhākura criticizes ritual performers, 147
Viśvāvasu, **796**

Vow of *cāturmāsya*, 72
Vrata, **624**
Vṛndāvana
forests & *ghāṭas* of, 352-53
for Gauḍīya Vaiṣṇavas, 332
Goloka. *See:* Goloka Vṛndāvana
Kṛṣṇa protected, from Indra's flood, 723
as pilgrimage place, 352
taking shelter in, 332
See also: Spiritual world
Vyāsadeva, Śrīla, 607, 663, 678
Vyuṣṭa, **623**

W

War
Hitler & Napoleon waged, 522-23
modern, 507, 508
See also: Battlefield; *Kṣatriya(s)*
Warriors. *See: Kṣatriya(s)*
Water in Deity worship, **367,** 368
Watering tree's root, serving Lord compared to, 547, 607-8, 849
Water in swan-*paramahaṁsa* analogy, 438
Wealth
bad effect of, 106
for charity, 554, 555
compared to jewel on snake, 106
dissatisfaction in, 157
given by Sati, 147
obtained by Śiva worship, 147
obtained by worship of Lord, 330
pride in, **106**
in renunciation, 146
in service to Lord, 106-7
of Śiva, **146,** 212
See also: Gold; Money; Opulence, material
Weapon(s)
Hare Kṛṣṇa *mantra* as, 502
in Lord's hands, **255**
of Yakṣas, **486-87, 495**
Weeping. *See:* Crying
Welfare work
by devotees, 656-57
in Kṛṣṇa consciousness, 589
Well, blind, family life compared to, 647
Wife
of devotee, 642
as enemy, 627
good, 622
prasāda offered to, before sexual intercourse, 641
See also: Marriage; Mother
Wind blowing dust & *karma* impelling living entities, analogy of, **524**
Wine
demons &, 796
of Śiva's followers, 79, 83
See also: Intoxication
Wisdom. *See:* Knowledge
Witches, **801**
Woman (women)
addiction to, 378
approaching supreme destination, 692
as basis of material life, 96
check spiritual life, 99
of demigods, bathe in Kailāsa, **203, 204-5**
desire material enjoyment, 96, 99
desire to dress nicely, 94, 96, 98
Earth as, 764
father worshipable for, 117-18
as government leader, 738
husband worshipable for, 117-18
if favored by husband, 317-18
impunity for, **758**
learned man's view of, 731
less intelligent, 4-5
on level of *śūdras*, 141
in material vs. spiritual world, 208
with paramour compared to *brāhmaṇas* worshiping demigods, **673,** 674, **675**
protection for, 781
at sacrificial performances, 92
softhearted, 126-27
as *strī*, 96
Vedas inaccessible to, 4-5
weakness in, 122
weeping &, 121
as wife (wives)
abandoning of, 378-79
addiction to, 378
decorations of, 92

Woman (women)
as wife (wives) (*continued*)
husband pleases, 8
at sacrifices, **92, 94**
should obey husband, 122
See also: Marriage
as *yoṣit,* 99
See also: Gopīs; Mother; Wife
Work
bondage via, 233
continues in Lord's service, 328
knowledge of, in Lord's service, 212-13
for Lord
compared with other, 7, 233
reactionless, 7
See also: Duty; *Karma;* Pious activities
World. *See:* Earth planet; Material world
Worm, life as, 290
Worship
for Age of present, 125
cleanliness in, 252
by Dakṣa of Śiva, **302-3, 304**
Deity. *See:* Deity forms
to Deity form of Lord. *See:* Deity worship
to demigod(s), 412, 525-26, 556, 607
compared to bribery, 87-88
via fire-gods, **46-**47
by impersonalist, **48**
impossible now, 88
inspired by Lord, 139
as "irregular," 87-88
vs. worship to Lord, 87, 286, 327, 330
mantra for, 128
by materialists, 87
as not intelligent, 87, 286, 327, 330
at sacrifices, 128
as unnecessary, 87-88
Viṣṇu *prasāda* in, 303-4
as worship to Lord, 87-**88**
to devotees, 91-92
to goddess of fortune
by demigods, **329,** 330
for opulence, 330
& Viṣṇu, 330
highest form of, 91-92, 136
to Kṛṣṇa
equals study of *Vedas,* 293
Worship
to Kṛṣṇa (*continued*)
includes all, 288
See also: Worship, to Lord
to Lord
for age of present, 125
apart from demigods, 87-88
for benedictions, 330
by Brahmā, **325-26**
by *brāhmaṇa* who meditated, 372
as Caitanya, 788
via chanting *oṁ namo bhagavate vāsudevāya,* **364-**65
compared with demigod worship, 87-88, 286, 327, 330
by demigods, 698
demigods satisfied via, 88
desires fulfilled via, **373**
despite material desires, 343
by Dhruva & Suniti, 465
equals study of *Vedas,* 293
for gain, 349, 350
gain by, as beyond expectation, 349
& goddess of fortune, 330
happiness via, 327
includes all, 288
liberation via, 327
Lord reciprocates, **637-**38
by Manu, **327**
materialists purified by, 330
for material opulence, 695
via meditation, 372
via offerings, 296
opulence by, 330
pilgrimage places for, 352-53
prasāda from, 303, 304
for present age, 125
pure & impure, 426
religion as, 664
sacrifice meant for, 844
for sense gratification, **410**
for Śiva's followers, 135-36
undeviating practice of, 327
via *varṇāśrama-dharma,* **667,** 668
See also: Deity worship
to Pitās, 525-26
results according to, 28

Worship (*continued*)
to Śiva
by Dakṣa, **302-3, 304**
mantra for, 128-29
material benefit in, 137, 147, 240
by materialists, 240
opulence via, 147
process for, 79
at sacrifices, 128-29
Satī awards, 147
as Vaiṣṇava, 137
by Vaiṣṇavas, 137
viṣṇu-prasāda in, 303, 304
as *yaśoghna,* 61
to Viṣṇu
by all, 257
as best, 136
cleanliness in, 252
compared with demigod worship, 286
vs. demigods, 286
offenses in, 252
prasāda from, 303, 304
for Śiva's followers, 135-36
See also: Devotional service; Prayer(s); Ritualistic ceremonies; Sacrifice(s)

Y

Yajña(s). See: Sacrifice(s)
Yajña, Lord
born to Akūti, **5**
children of, **9, 10**
descendants from, kinds of, 9-10
given to Manu, **6**
as ideal husband, 8
as Indra, **9**
as leader of demigods, **9,** 10
married Dakṣiṇā, 6, **8**
name of, 7
Yajur Veda, Bhṛgu chants from, **161,** 162
Yakṣa(s), **123**
as demoniac, **497**
Dhruva vs., **482-99, 501-7**
as flesh-eaters, **801**
identity of, 483
Yakṣa(s) (*continued*)
military strength of, **486-87**
as pious, 541
at Pṛthu's horse sacrifices, **815**
Uttama killed by, **481, 482,** 507
Yakṣeśvara. *See:* Kuvera
Yamarāja, Lord, **703**
Yamunā River
bathing in, 354
pilgrimage sites on, **351,** 352-53
water of, in Deity worship, 368
Yaśodā, mother, 596
Yātanā (Excessive Pain), **312**
Yati (son of Brahmā), **309**
Yoga
āsanas in, 152, **215,** 217
aṣṭāṅga-, 565
bath in, 354
breathing exercise for, 355
instructed to Dhruva, **353, 354**
for meditating on Viṣṇu, 354
sitting postures for, 215
bhakti-
as greatest, 152-53
See also: Devotional service; Kṛṣṇa consciousness
bodily airs controlled by, 152
for bodily health, 152
breathing exercise for, **354-**55
buddhi-yoga, 145
control of mind in, 355
Dhruva executed, **565**
eightfold. *See: Yoga, aṣṭāṅga-yoga*
eight perfections of, 363
at end of life, 339
highest form of, 152-53, 390
impractical in this age, 152
liberation by, 152-53
mahā-yoga, 211
as meditation on Lord, 210-11, 389, 390
modern, compared with actual, 151, 152
mystic
king practiced, 654
processes of, 799
of Siddhas & Vidyādharas, **798-**99
See also: Mystic power(s)

Yoga (continued)
prāṇāyāma, of Atri Muni, 20
purification by, 155-56
remembering Lord in, 210-11
Satī's suicide by, **150, 151-52, 153, 155**
Siddhas perfect in, 274
sitting postures for, 152, **215,** 217
transfer of soul by, 150-51, 152-53
See also: Kṛṣṇa consciousness; Self-realization
Yoga (son of Dharma), **40**
Yoga-kakṣām sitting posture, 217
Yogamāyā potency, 715
See also: Energies of Supreme Lord, spiritual
Yogeśvara, Kṛṣṇa as, 215
Yogī(s)
in bodily concept of life, 416
bogus, compared with bona fide, 824
celibacy for, 309-10
choose death time, 150-51
devotees contrasted to, 412, 416, 453, 515, 562, 576, 590, 591
devotees surpass, 390
highest kind of, 390
liberation desired by, 211
meditate on Lord, 211, 355-62, 374
meditators on Lord as, 390
mystic
less intelligent, can't find Supersoul, 649
powers of, 799
travel by, 706
See also: Mystic power(s)
remember Viṣṇu for, 210-11
Śiva best of, 150
topmost, 565
transfer of soul by, 150-51, 152-53
See also: Devotee(s); Sage(s); Transcendentalist(s)
Yogīśvara, Śiva as, **215**
Yoṣit defined, 99
Yudhiṣṭhira Mahārāja, 742
Yugas, four
degradation during, 560
government leaders in, 666
Yugas, four (*continued*)
life spans in, 471-72
See also: Dvāpara-yuga; Kali-yuga; Satya-yuga; Tretā-yuga

KING ALFRED'S COLLEGE
LIBRARY